Lecture Notes in Artificial Intelligence 11907

Subseries of Lecture Notes in Computer Science

Series Editors

Randy Goebel
University of Alberta, Edmonton, Canada
Yuzuru Tanaka
Hokkaido University, Sapporo, Japan
Wolfgang Wahlster
DFKI and Saarland University, Saarbrücken, Germany

Founding Editor

Jörg Siekmann
DFKI and Saarland University, Saarbrücken, Germany

More information about this series at http://www.springer.com/series/1244

Ulf Brefeld · Elisa Fromont ·
Andreas Hotho · Arno Knobbe ·
Marloes Maathuis · Céline Robardet (Eds.)

Machine Learning and Knowledge Discovery in Databases

European Conference, ECML PKDD 2019
Würzburg, Germany, September 16–20, 2019
Proceedings, Part II

 Springer

Editors
Ulf Brefeld
Leuphana University
Lüneburg, Germany

Elisa Fromont ⓘ
IRISA/Inria
Rennes, France

Andreas Hotho ⓘ
University of Würzburg
Würzburg, Germany

Arno Knobbe ⓘ
Leiden University
Leiden, the Netherlands

Marloes Maathuis ⓘ
ETH Zurich
Zurich, Switzerland

Céline Robardet ⓘ
Institut National des Sciences Appliquées
Villeurbanne, France

ISSN 0302-9743   ISSN 1611-3349   (electronic)
Lecture Notes in Artificial Intelligence
ISBN 978-3-030-46146-1   ISBN 978-3-030-46147-8   (eBook)
https://doi.org/10.1007/978-3-030-46147-8

LNCS Sublibrary: SL7 – Artificial Intelligence

This Springer imprint is published by the registered company Springer Nature Switzerland AG
The registered company address is: Gewerbestrasse 11, 6330 Cham, Switzerland

Preface

We are delighted to introduce the proceedings of the 2019 edition of the European Conference on Machine Learning and Principles and Practice of Knowledge Discovery in Databases (ECML PKDD 2019). ECML PKDD is an annual conference that provides an international forum for the latest research in all areas related to machine learning and knowledge discovery in databases, including innovative applications. It is the premier European machine learning and data mining conference and builds upon a very successful series of ECML PKDD conferences.

ECML PKDD 2019 was held in Würzburg, Germany, during September 16–20, 2019. The conference attracted over 830 participants from 48 countries. It also received substantial attention from industry, both through sponsorship and participation at the conference.

The main conference program consisted of presentations and posters of 130 accepted papers and 5 keynote talks by the following distinguished speakers: Sumit Gulwani (Microsoft Research), Aude Billard (EPFL), Indrė Žliobaitė (University of Helsinki), Maria Florina Balcan (Carnegie Mellon University), and Tinne Tuytelaars (KU Leuven). In addition, there were 24 workshops, 8 tutorials, and 4 discovery challenges.

Papers were organized in three different tracks:

- Research Track: research or methodology papers from all areas in machine learning, knowledge discovery, and data mining
- Applied Data Science Track: papers on novel applications of machine learning, data mining, and knowledge discovery to solve real-world use cases, thereby bridging the gap between practice and current theory
- Journal Track: papers that were published in special issues of the journals *Machine Learning* and *Data Mining and Knowledge Discovery*

We received a record number of 733 submissions for the Research and Applied Data Science Tracks combined. We accepted 130 (18%) of these: 102 papers in the Research Track and 28 papers in the Applied Data Science Track. In addition, there were 32 papers from the Journal Track. All in all, the high-quality submissions allowed us to put together a very rich and exciting program.

For 60% of accepted Research Track and Applied Data Science Track papers, accompanying software and/or data were made available. These papers are flagged as Reproducible Research (RR) papers in the proceedings. RR flags, in use since 2016 in the ECML PKDD conference series, underline the importance given to RR in our community.

The Awards Committee selected research papers that were considered to be of exceptional quality and worthy of special recognition:

- Data Mining Best Student Paper Award: "FastPoint: Scalable Deep Point Processes" by Ali Caner Türkmen, Yuyang Wang, and Alexander J. Smola

- Machine Learning Best Student Paper Award: "Agnostic feature selection" by Guillaume Doquet and Michèle Sebag
- Test of Time Award for highest impact paper from ECML PKDD 2009: "Classifier Chains for Multi-label Classification" by Jesse Read, Bernhard Pfahringer, Geoff Holmes, and Eibe Frank

Besides the strong scientific program, ECML PKDD 2019 offered many opportunities to socialize and to get to know Würzburg. We mention the opening ceremony at the Neubau Church, the opening reception at the Residence Palace, the boat trip from Veitshöchheim to Würzburg, the gala dinner at the Congress Center, the poster session at the New University, and the poster session at the Residence Palace Wine Cellar. There were also social events for subgroups of participants, such as the PhD Forum, in which PhD students interacted with their peers and received constructive feedback on their research progress, and the Women in Science Lunch, in which junior and senior women met and discussed challenges and opportunities for women in science and technology.

We would like to thank all participants, authors, reviewers, area chairs, and organizers of workshops and tutorials for their contributions that helped make ECML PKDD 2019 a great success. Special thanks go to the University of Würzburg, especially to Lena Hettinger and the student volunteers, who did an amazing job. We would also like to thank the ECML PKDD Steering Committee and all sponsors. Finally, we thank Springer and Microsoft for their continuous support with the proceedings and the conference software.

February 2020

Ulf Brefeld
Elisa Fromont
Andreas Hotho
Arno Knobbe
Marloes Maathuis
Céline Robardet

Organization

General Chairs

Élisa Fromont	University of Rennes 1, France
Arno Knobbe	Leiden University, the Netherlands

Program Chairs

Ulf Brefeld	Leuphana University of Lüneburg, Germany
Andreas Hotho	University of Würzburg, Germany
Marloes Maathuis	ETH Zürich, Switzerland
Céline Robardet	INSA-Lyon, France

Journal Track Chairs

Karsten Borgwardt	ETH Zürich, Switzerland
Po-Ling Loh	University of Wisconsin, USA
Evimaria Terzi	Boston University, USA
Antti Ukkonen	University of Helsinki, Finland

Local Chairs

Lena Hettinger	University of Würzburg, Germany
Andreas Hotho	University of Würzburg, Germany
Kristof Korwisi	University of Würzburg, Germany
Marc Erich Latoschik	University of Würzburg, Germany

Proceedings Chairs

Xin Du	Technische Universiteit Eindhoven, the Netherlands
Wouter Duivesteijn	Technische Universiteit Eindhoven, the Netherlands
Sibylle Hess	Technische Universiteit Eindhoven, the Netherlands

Discovery Challenge Chairs

Sergio Escalera	University of Barcelona, Spain
Isabelle Guyon	Paris-Sud University, France

Workshop and Tutorial Chairs

Peggy Cellier	INSA Rennes, France
Kurt Driessens	Maastricht University, the Netherlands

Demonstration Chairs

Martin Atzmüller   Tilburg University, the Netherlands
Emilie Morvant   University of Saint-Etienne, France

PhD Forum Chairs

Tassadit Bouadi   University of Rennes 1, France
Tias Guns   Vrije Universiteit Bruxelles, Belgium

Production, Publicity and Public Relations Chairs

Parisa Kordjamshidi   Tulane University and Florida IHMC, USA
Albrecht Zimmermann   Université de Caen Normandie, France

Awards Committee

Katharina Morik   TU Dortmund, Germany
Geoff Webb   Monash University, Australia

Sponsorship Chairs

Albert Bifet   Télécom ParisTech, France
Heike Trautmann   University of Münster, Germany

Web Chairs

Florian Lautenschlager   University of Würzburg, Germany
Vanessa Breitenbach   University of Würzburg, Germany

ECML PKDD Steering Committee

Michele Berlingerio   IBM Research, Ireland
Albert Bifet   Télécom ParisTech, France
Hendrik Blockeel   KU Leuven, Belgium
Francesco Bonchi   ISI Foundation, Italy
Michelangelo Ceci   University of Bari Aldo Moro, Italy
Sašo Džeroski   Jožef Stefan Institute, Slovenia
Paolo Frasconi   University of Florence, Italy
Thomas Gärtner   University of Nottinghem, UK
Jaakko Hollmen   Aalto University, Finland
Neil Hurley   University College Dublin, Ireland
Georgiana Ifrim   University College Dublin, Ireland
Katharina Morik   TU Dortmund, Germany
Siegfried Nijssen   Université catholique de Louvain, Belgium
Andrea Passerini   University of Trento, Italy

Céline Robardet	INSA-Lyon, France
Michèle Sebag	Université Paris Sud, France
Arno Siebes	Utrecht University, the Netherlands
Myra Spiliopoulou	Magdeburg University, Germany
Jilles Vreeken	Saarland University, Germany

Program Committees

Guest Editorial Board, Journal Track

Annalisa Appice	University of Bari Aldo Moro, Italy
Marta Arias	Universitat Politècnica de Catalunya, Spain
Martin Atzmueller	Tilburg University, the Netherlands
Albert Bifet	Télécom ParisTech, France
Hendrik Blockeel	KU Leuven, Belgium
Toon Calders	University of Antwerp, Belgium
Michelangelo Ceci	University of Bari Aldo Moro, Italy
Loïc Cerf	Universidade Federal de Minas Gerais, Brazil
Nicolas Courty	Université Bretagne Sud, IRISA, France
Bruno Cremilleux	Université de Caen Normandie, France
Tijl De Bie	Ghent University, Belgium
Krzysztof Dembczyński	Poznan University of Technology, Poland
Yagoubi Djamel Edine	StarClay, France
Tapio Elomaa	Tampere University of Technology, Finland
Rémi Emonet	Université de Lyon à Saint Étienne, France
Stefano Ferilli	University of Bari, Italy
Joao Gama	University of Porto, Portugal
Tias Guns	VUB Brussels, Belgium
Amaury Habrard	Université Jean Monnet, France
Xiao He	NEC Laboratories Europe, Germany
Jaakko Hollmén	Aalto University, Finland
Szymon Jaroszewicz	Polish Academy of Sciences, Poland
Alipio Jorge	University of Porto, Portugal
Ajin Joseph	University of Alberta, Canada
Samuel Kaski	Aalto University, Finland
Kristian Kersting	TU Darmstadt, Germany
Dragi Kocev	Jožef Stefan Institute, Slovenia
Peer Kröger	Ludwig-Maximilians-Universität Munich, Germany
Ondrej Kuzelka	KU Leuven, Belgium
Mark Last	Ben-Gurion University of the Negev, Israel
Matthijs van Leeuwen	Leiden University, the Netherlands
Limin Li	Xi'an Jiaotong University, China
Jessica Lin	George Mason University, USA
Christoph Lippert	Hasso Plattner Institute, Germany
Brian Mac Namee	University College Dublin, Ireland

Area Chairs, Research and Applied Data Science Tracks

Fabrizio Angiulli	DIMES, University of Calabria, Italy
Roberto Bayardo	Google Research, USA
Michael Berthold	Universität Konstanz, Germany
Albert Bifet	Université Paris-Saclay, France
Hendrik Blockeel	KU Leuven, Belgium
Francesco Bonchi	ISI Foundation, Italy
Toon Calders	Universiteit Antwerpen, Belgium
Michelangelo Ceci	University of Bari, Italy
Nicolas Courty	IRISA, France
Bruno Crémilleux	Université de Caen Normandie, France
Philippe Cudre-Mauroux	Exascale Infolab, Switzerland
Jesse Davis	KU Leuven, Belgium
Tijl De Bie	Ghent University, Belgium
Tapio Elomaa	Tampere University, Finland
Amir-massoud Farahmand	Vector Institute, Canada
Paolo Frasconi	Università degli Studi di Firenze, Italy
Johannes Fürnkranz	TU Darmstadt, Germany
Patrick Gallinari	LIP6, France
Joao Gama	INESC TEC, LIAAD, Portugal
Aristides Gionis	Aalto University, Finland
Thomas Gärtner	University of Nottingham, UK
Allan Hanbury	Vienna University of Technology, Austria
Jaakko Hollmén	Aalto University, Finland
Eyke Hüllermeier	University of Paderborn, Germany
Alipio Jorge	INESC, Portugal
Marius Kloft	University of Southern California, USA
Nick Koudas	University of Toronto, Canada
Stefan Kramer	Johannes Gutenberg University Mainz, Germany
Sébastien Lefèvre	Université de Bretagne Sud, IRISA, France
Jörg Lücke	Universität Oldenburg, Germany
Giuseppe Manco	ICAR-CNR, Italy
Pauli Miettinen	Max-Planck Institute for Informatics, Germany
Anna Monreale	University of Pisa, Italy
Katharina Morik	TU Dortmund, Germany
Siegfried Nijssen	Université Catholique de Louvain, Belgium
Andrea Passerini	University of Trento, Italy
Mykola Pechenizkiy	TU Eindhoven, the Netherlands
Francois Petitjean	Monash University, Australia
Elmar Rueckert	University Luebeck, Germany
Tom Schaul	DeepMind, UK
Thomas Seidl	LMU Munich, Germany
Arno Siebes	Universiteit Utrecht, the Netherlands
Myra Spiliopoulou	Otto-von-Guericke-University Magdeburg, Germany
Einoshin Suzuki	Kyushu University, Japan

Marc Tommasi	Lille University, France
Celine Vens	KU Leuven, Belgium
Christel Vrain	University of Orleans, France
Jilles Vreeken	CISPA Helmholtz Center for Information Security, Germany
Min-Ling Zhang	Southeast University, Bangladesh
Herke van Hoof	University of Amsterdam, the Netherlands

Program Committee Members, Research and Applied Data Science Tracks

Ehsan Abbasnejad	The University of Adelaide, Australia
Leman Akoglu	CMU, USA
Tristan Allard	University of Rennes, France
Aijun An	York University, Canada
Ali Anaissi	The University of Sydney, Australia
Annalisa Appice	University of Bari, Italy
Paul Assendorp	Werum, Germany
Ira Assent	University of Aarhus, Denmark
Martin Atzmüller	Tilburg University, the Netherlands
Alexandre Aussem	Université Lyon 1, France
Suyash Awate	Indian Institute of Technology (IIT) Bombay, India
Antonio Bahamonde	Universidad de Oviedo, Spain
Jaume Baixeries	Universitat Politècnica de Catalunya, Spain
Vineeth N. Balasubramanian	Indian Institute of Technology, India
Jose Balcazar	Universitat Politecnica de Catalunya, Spain
Sambaran Bandyopadhyay	IBM Research, India
Zhifeng Bao	RMIT University, Australia
Mitra Baratchi	Leiden University, the Netherlands
Sylvio Barbon	Universidade Estadual de Londrina, Brazil
Gianni Barlacchi	FBK Trento, Italy
Martin Becker	Stanford University, USA
Srikanta Bedathur	IIT Delhi, India
Edward Beeching	Inria, France
Vaishak Belle	University of Edinburgh, UK
Andras Benczur	Hungarian Academy of Sciences, Hungary
Daniel Bengs	DIPF, Germany
Petr Berka	University of Economics, Prague, Czech Republic
Marenglen Biba	University of New York in Tirana, Albania
Chris Biemann	University of Hamburg, Germany
Battista Biggio	University of Cagliari, Italy
Thomas Bonald	Télécom ParisTech, France
Gianluca Bontempi	Université Libre de Bruxelles, Belgium
Henrik Bostrom	KTH Royal Institute of Technology, Sweden
Tassadit Bouadi	Université de Rennes 1, France
Ahcène Boubekki	Leuphana University of Lüneburg, Germany
Zied Bouraoui	Université d'Artois, France

Paula Branco	Dalhousie University, Canada
Pavel Brazdil	University of Porto, Portugal
Dariusz Brzezinski	Poznan University of Technology, Poland
Sebastian Buschjager	TU Dortmund, Germany
Ricardo Campello	University of Newcastle, Australia
Brais Cancela	University of A. Coruña, Spain
Francisco Casacuberta	Universidad Politecnica de Valencia, Spain
Remy Cazabet	University of Lyon, France
Peggy Cellier	IRISA, France
Loic Cerf	UFMG, Brazil
Tania Cerquitelli	Politecnico di Torino, Italy
Ricardo Cerri	Federal University of São Carlos, Brazil
Tanmoy Chakraborty	Indraprastha Institute of Information Technology Delhi (IIIT-D), India
Edward Chang	HTC Research & Healthcare, USA
Xiaojun Chang	Monash University, Australia
Jeremy Charlier	University of Luxembourg, Luxembourg
Abon Chaudhuri	Walmart Labs, USA
Keke Chen	Wright State University, USA
Giovanni Chierchia	ESIEE Paris, France
Silvia Chiusano	Politecnico di Torino, Italy
Sunav Choudhary	Adobe Research, India
Frans Coenen	The University of Liverpool, UK
Mario Cordeiro	Universidade do Porto, Portugal
Robson Cordeiro	University of São Paulo, Brazil
Roberto Corizzo	University of Bari, Italy
Fabrizio Costa	Exeter University, UK
Vitor Santos Costa	Universidade do Porto, Portugal
Adrien Coulet	Loria, France
Bertrand Cuissart	University of Caen, France
Boris Cule	Universiteit Antwerpen, Belgium
Alfredo Cuzzocrea	University of Trieste and ICAR-CNR, Italy
Alexander Dallmann	University of Würzburg, Germany
Claudia d'Amato	University of Bari, Italy
Maria Damiani	University of Milano, Italy
Martine De Cock	University of Washington Tacoma, USA
Tom Decroos	KU Leuven, Belgium
Juan Jose del Coz	University of Oviedo, Spain
Anne Denton	North Dakota State University, USA
Christian Desrosiers	ETS, Italy
Nicola Di Mauro	University of Bari, Italy
Claudia Diamantini	Università Politecnica delle Marche, Italy
Jilles Dibangoye	INSA-Lyon, France
Tom Diethe	University of Bristol, UK
Wei Ding	University of Massachusetts Boston, USA
Stephan Doerfel	Micromata GmbH, Germany

Carlotta Domeniconi	George Mason University, USA
Madalina Drugan	Eindhoven University of Technology, the Netherlands
Stefan Duffner	University of Lyon, France
Wouter Duivesteijn	TU Eindhoven, the Netherlands
Sebastijan Dumancic	KU Leuven, Belgium
Ines Dutra	INESC TEC, Portugal
Mireille El Gheche	EPFL, Switzerland
Jihane Elyahyioui	Monash University, Australia
Dora Erdos	Boston University, USA
Samuel Fadel	University of Campinas, Brazil
Ad Feelders	Universiteit Utrecht, the Netherlands
Jing Feng	TU Darmstadt, Germany
Stefano Ferilli	University of Bari, Italy
Carlos Ferreira	INESC TEC, Portugal
Cesar Ferri	Universitat Politecnica Valencia, Spain
Matthias Fey	TU Dortmund, Germany
Rémi Flamary	Université côte d'Azur, France
Razvan Florian	Romanian Institute of Science and Technology, Romania
Germain Forestier	University of Haute Alsace, France
Eibe Frank	University of Waikato, New Zealand
Fabio Fumarola	Universita degli Studi di Bari Aldo Moro, Italy
Paulo Gabriel	Universidade Federal de Uberlandia, Brazil
Amita Gajewar	Microsoft Corporation, USA
Esther Galbrun	Aalto University, Finland
Dragan Gamberger	Rudjer Boskovic Institute, Croatia
Byron Gao	Texas State University, USA
Junbin Gao	The University of Sydney, Australia
Paolo Garza	Politecnico di Torino, Italy
Konstantinos Georgatzis	QuantumBlack, Singapore
Pierre Geurts	Montefiore Institute, Belgium
Arnaud Giacometti	University of Tours, France
Rémi Gilleron	Lille University, France
Mike Gimelfarb	University of Toronto, Canada
Uwe Glasser	Simon Fraser University, Canada
Dorota Glowacka	University of Helsinki, Finland
Heitor Gomes	Télécom ParisTech, France
Rafael Gomes Mantovani	Federal Technology University of Parana, Brazil
Vicenç Gomez	Universitat Pompeu Fabra, Spain
Vanessa Gomez-Verdejo	Universidad Carlos III de Madrid, Spain
James Goulding	University of Nottingham, UK
Cédric Gouy-Pailler	CEA, France
Josif Grabocka	Universität Hildesheim, Germany
Michael Granitzer	University of Passau, Germany
Derek Greene	Data Analytics, Ireland
Quanquan Gu	University of California, Los Angeles, USA

Riccardo Guidotti	University of Pisa, Italy
Francesco Gullo	UniCredit R&D, Italy
Tias Guns	Vrije Universiteit Brussel, Belgium
Xueying Guo	University of California, Davis, USA
Deepak Gupta	University of Amsterdam, the Netherlands
Thomas Guyet	IRISA, France
Stephan Günnemann	Technical University of Munich, Germany
Maria Halkidi	University of Pireaus, Greece
Barbara Hammer	CITEC, Switzerland
Jiawei Han	UIUC, USA
Tom Hanika	University of Kassel, Germany
Mohammad Hasan	Indiana University and Purdue University Indianapolis, USA
Xiao He	Alibaba Group, China
Denis Helic	TU Graz, Austria
Andreas Henelius	University of Helsinki, Finland
Daniel Hernandez-Lobato	Universidad Autonoma de Madrid, Spain
Jose Hernandez-Orallo	Polytechnic University of Valencia, Spain
Sibylle Hess	TU Eindhoven, the Netherlands
Thanh Lam Hoang	IBM Research, Ireland
Frank Hoeppner	Ostfalia University of Applied Science, Germany
Arjen Hommersom	University of Nijmegen, the Netherlands
Tamas Horvath	University of Bonn and Fraunhofer IAIS, Germany
Homa Hosseinmardi	USC ISI, USA
Chao Huang	University of Notre Dame, USA
David Tse Jung Huang	The University of Auckland, New Zealand
Yuanhua Huang	European Bioinformatics Institute, UK
Neil Hurley	University College Dublin, Ireland
Dino Ienco	Irstea Institute, France
Angelo Impedovo	University of Bari Aldo Moro, Italy
Iñaki Inza	University of the Basque Country, Spain
Tomoki Ito	The University of Tokyo, Japan
Mahdi Jalili	RMIT University, Australia
Szymon Jaroszewicz	Polish Academy of Sciences, Poland
Giuseppe Jurman	Fondazione Bruno Kessler, Italy
Anup Kalia	IBM Research, USA
Toshihiro Kamishima	National Institute of Advanced Industrial Science and Technology, Japan
Michael Kamp	Fraunhofer IAIS, Germany
Bo Kang	Ghent University, Belgium
Pinar Karagoz	METU, Turkey
Konstantinos Karanasos	Microsoft, UK
Sarvnaz Karimi	DATA61, Australia
George Karypis	University of Minnesota, USA
Mehdi Kaytoue	Infologic, France
Mikaela Keller	University of Lille, France

Latifur Khan	The University of Texas at Dallas, USA
Beomjoon Kim	MIT, USA
Daiki Kimura	IBM Research AI, USA
Frank Klawonn	Helmholtz Centre for Infection Research, Germany
Jiri Klema	Czech Technical University, Czech Republic
Tomas Kliegr	University of Economics, Prague, Czech Republic
Dragi Kocev	Jozef Stefan Institute, Slovenia
Levente Kocsis	Hungarian Academy of Science, Hungary
Yun Sing Koh	The University of Auckland, New Zealand
Effrosyni Kokiopoulou	Google AI, Switzerland
Alek Kolcz	Twitter, USA
Wouter Kool	University of Amsterdam, the Netherlands
Irena Koprinska	The University of Sydney, Australia
Frederic Koriche	Université d'Artois, France
Lars Kotthoff	University of Wyoming, USA
Danai Koutra	University of Michigan, USA
Polychronis Koutsakis	Murdoch University, Australia
Tomas Krilavicius	Vytautas Magnus University, Lithuania
Yamuna Krishnamurthy	NYU, USA, and Royal Holloway University of London, UK
Narayanan C. Krishnan	IIT Ropar, India
Matjaz Kukar	University of Ljubljana, Slovenia
Meelis Kull	University of Tartu, Estonia
Gautam Kunapuli	UT Dallas, USA
Vinod Kurmi	IIT Kanpur, India
Ondrej Kuzelka	University of Leuven, Belgium
Nicolas Lachiche	University of Strasbourg, France
Sofiane Lagraa	University of Luxembourg, Luxembourg
Leo Lahti	University of Turku, Estonia
Christine Largeron	LabHC Lyon University, France
Christine Largouet	IRISA, France
Pedro Larranaga	Universidad Politécnica de Madrid, Spain
Niklas Lavesson	Jonkoping University, Sweden
Binh Le	University College Dublin, Ireland
Florian Lemmerich	RWTH Aachen University, Germany
Marie-Jeanne Lesot	LIP6, France
Dagang Li	Peking University, China
Jian Li	Tsinghua University, China
Jiuyong Li	University of South Australia, Australia
Limin Li	Xi'an Jiaotong University, China
Xiangru Lian	University of Rochester, USA
Jefrey Lijffijt	Ghent University, Belgium
Tony Lindgren	Stockholm University, Sweden
Marco Lippi	University of Modena and Reggio Emilia, Italy
Bing Liu	University of Illinois at Chicago, USA
Corrado Loglisci	Universita degli Studi di Bari Aldo Moro, Italy

Peter Lucas	Leiden University, the Netherlands
Sebastian Mair	Leuphana University, Germany
Arun Maiya	Institute for Defense Analyses, USA
Donato Malerba	University of Bari, Italy
Chaitanya Manapragada	Monash University, Australia
Luca Martino	University of Valencia, Spain
Elio Masciari	ICAR-CNR, Italy
Andres Masegosa	University of Almeria, Spain
Florent Masseglia	Inria, France
Antonis Matakos	Aalto University, Finland
Wannes Meert	KU Leuven, Belgium
Corrado Mencar	University of Bari Aldo Moro, Italy
Saayan Mitra	Adobe, USA
Atsushi Miyamoto	Hitachi America Ltd., USA
Dunja Mladenic	Jozef Stefan Institute, Slovenia
Sandy Moens	Universiteit Antwerpen, Belgium
Miguel Molina-Solana	Imperial College London, UK
Nuno Moniz	University of Porto, Portgual
Hankyu Moon	Samsung SDS Research, USA
Joao Moreira	INESC TEC, Portugal
Luis Moreira-Matias	Kreditech Holding SSL, Germany
Emilie Morvant	Université Jean Monnet, France
Andreas Mueller	Columbia Data Science Institute, USA
Asim Munawar	IBM Research, Japan
Pierre-Alexandre Murena	Télécom ParisTech, France
Mohamed Nadif	LIPADE, Université Paris Descartes, France
Jinseok Nam	Amazon, USA
Mirco Nanni	ISTI-CNR Pisa, Italy
Amedeo Napoli	LORIA, France
Sriraam Natarajan	UT Dallas, USA
Fateme Nateghi	KU Leuven, Belgium
Benjamin Negrevergne	Université Paris Dauphine, France
Benjamin Nguyen	INSA-CVL, France
Xia Ning	OSU, USA
Kjetil Norvag	NTNU, Norway
Eirini Ntoutsi	Leibniz Universität Hannover, Germany
Andreas Nurnberger	Magdeburg University, Germany
Luca Oneto	University of Pisa, Italy
Kok-Leong Ong	La Trobe University, Australia
Francesco Orsini	MDOTM S.r.l., Italy
Martijn van Otterlo	Tilburg University, the Netherlands
Nikunj Oza	NASA Ames, USA
Pance Panov	Jozef Stefan Institute, Slovenia
Apostolos Papadopoulos	Aristotle University of Thessaloniki, Greece
Panagiotis Papapetrou	Stockholm University, Sweden
Youngja Park	IBM, USA

Ioannis Partalas	Expedia Group, Switzerland
Charlotte Pelletier	Monash University, Australia
Jaakko Peltonen	University of Tampere, Finland
Lukas Pfahler	TU Dortmund, Germany
Nico Piatkowski	TU Dortmund, Germany
Andrea Pietracaprina	University of Padova, Italy
Gianvito Pio	University of Bari, Italy
Claudia Plant	University of Vienna, Austria
Marc Plantevit	Université de Lyon, France
Pascal Poncelet	Lirmm, France
Miguel Prada	Universidad de León, Spain
Paul Prasse	University of Potsdam, Germany
Philippe Preux	Inria, France
Buyue Qian	Xi'an Jiaotong University, China
Masoume Raeissi	CWI, the Netherlands
Dimitrios Rafailidis	Maastricht University, the Netherlands
Jorg Rahnenführer	TU Dortmund, Germany
Chedy Raissi	Inria, France
Sutharshan Rajasegarar	Deakin University, Australia
Jan Ramon	Inria, France
Santu Rana	Deakin University, Australia
Huzefa Rangwala	George Mason University, USA
Chotirat Ratanamahatana	Chulalongkorn University, Thailand
Jan Rauch	University of Economics, Prague, Czech Republic
Ievgen Redko	Laboratoire Hubert Curien, France
Chiara Renso	ISTI-CNR, Italy
Achim Rettinger	Trier University, Germany
Rita Ribeiro	University of Porto, Portugal
Fabrizio Riguzzi	Università di Ferrara, Italy
Jan van Rijn	Leiden University, the Netherlands
Matteo Riondato	Two Sigma Investments, USA
Pieter Robberechts	KU Leuven, Belgium
Juan Rodriguez	Universidad de Burgos, Spain
Fabrice Rossi	Université Paris 1 Pantheon-Sorbonne, France
Ryan Rossi	Adobe Research, USA
Celine Rouveirol	Université Paris-Nord, France
Yannick Rudolph	Leuphana University, Germany
Stefan Rueping	Fraunhofer IAIS, Germany
Anne Sabourin	Télécom ParisTech, France
Yvan Saeys	Ghent University, Belgium
Amrita Saha	IBM Research, India
Lorenza Saitta	Università del Piemonte Orientale, Italy
Tomoya Sakai	NEC, Japan
Tetsuya Sakurai	University of Tsukuba, Japan
Ansaf Salleb-Aouissi	Columbia University, USA
Somdeb Sarkhel	Adobe, USA

Claudio Sartori	University of Bologna, Italy
Luciano Sbaiz	Google AI, Switzerland
Pierre Schaus	UC Louvain, Belgium
Tobias Scheffer	University of Potsdam, Germany
Ute Schmid	University of Bamberg, Germany
Lars Schmidt-Thieme	University of Hildesheim, Germany
Christoph Schommer	University of Luxembourg, Luxembourg
Matthias Schubert	Ludwig-Maximilians-Universität München, Germany
Rajat Sen	UT Austin and Amazon, USA
Vinay Setty	University of Stavanger, Norway
Mattia Setzu	University of Pisa, Italy
Chao Shang	University of Connecticut, USA
Junming Shao	University of Electronic Science and Technology of China, China
Bernhard Sick	University of Kassel, Germany
Diego Silva	Universidade Federal de São Carlos, Brazil
Jonathan Silva	UFMS, Brazil
Nikola Simidjievski	University of Cambridge, UK
Andrzej Skowron	University of Warsaw, Poland
Dominik Slezak	University of Warsaw, Poland
Daniel V. Smith	DATA61, Australia
Gavin Smith	University of Nottingham, UK
Tomislav Smuc	Institute Ruđer Bošković, Croatia
Arnaud Soulet	University of Tours, France
Mauro Sozio	Institut Mines Télécom, France
Alessandro Sperduti	University of Padova, Italy
Jerzy Stefanowski	Poznan University of Technology, Poland
Bas van Stein	Leiden University, the Netherlands
Giovanni Stilo	University of L'Aquila, Italy
Mahito Sugiyama	National Institute of Informatics, Japan
Mika Sulkava	Natural Resources Institute Finland, Finland
Yizhou Sun	UCLA, USA
Viswanathan Swaminathan	Adobe, USA
Stephen Swift	Brunel University London, UK
Andrea Tagarelli	DIMES - UNICAL, Italy
Domenico Talia	University of Calabria, Italy
Letizia Tanca	Politecnico di Milano, Italy
Jovan Tanevski	Jozef Stefan Institute, Slovenia
Nikolaj Tatti	University of Helsinki, Finland
Maryam Tavakol	TU Dortmund, Germany
Maguelonne Teisseire	Irstea, France
Choon Hui Teo	Amazon, USA
Alexandre Termier	Université Rennes 1, France
Stefano Teso	KU Leuven, Belgium
Ljupco Todorovski	University of Ljubljana, Slovenia
Alexander Tornede	UPB, Germany

Ricardo Torres	IC-Unicamp, Brazil
Volker Tresp	Siemens AG and Ludwig Maximilian University of Munich, Germany
Isaac Triguero	University of Nottingham, UK
Ivor Tsang	University of Technology Sydney, Australia
Vincent Tseng	National Chiao Tung University, Taiwan
Charalampos Tsourakakis	Boston University, USA
Radu Tudoran	Huawei, Germany
Cigdem Turan	TU Darmstadt, Germany
Nikolaos Tziortziotis	Tradelab, France
Theodoros Tzouramanis	University of the Aegean, Greece
Antti Ukkonen	University of Helsinki, Finland
Elia Van Wolputte	KU Leuven, Belgium
Robin Vandaele	Ghent University, Belgium
Iraklis Varlamis	Harokopio University of Athens, Greece
Ranga Vatsavai	North Carolina State University, USA
Julien Velcin	University of Lyon, France
Bruno Veloso	University of Porto, Portugal
Shankar Vembu	University of Toronto, Canada
Deepak Venugopal	University of Memphis, USA
Ricardo Vigario	NOVA University of Lisbon, Portugal
Prashanth Vijayaraghavan	MIT, USA
Herna Viktor	University of Ottawa, Canada
Willem Waegeman	Universiteit Gent, Belgium
Di Wang	Microsoft, USA
Hao Wang	Leiden University, the Netherlands
Jianyong Wang	Tsinghua University, China
Yuyi Wang	ETH Zürich, Switzerland
Jeremy Weiss	Carnegie Mellon University, USA
Marcel Wever	Paderborn University, Germany
Joerg Wicker	The University of Auckland, New Zealand
Marco Wiering	University of Groningen, the Netherlands
Martin Wistuba	IBM Research, Ireland
Christian Wolf	INSA-Lyon, France
Christian Wressnegger	TU Braunschweig, Germany
Gang Wu	Adobe Research, USA
Lina Yao	UNSW, Australia
Philip Yu	University of Illinois at Chicago, USA
Bianca Zadrozny	IBM Research, USA
Gerson Zaverucha	Federal University of Rio de Janeiro, Brazil
Bernard Zenko	Jozef Stefan Institute, Slovenia
Chengkun Zhang	The University of Sydney, Australia
Jianpeng Zhang	TU Eindhoven, the Netherlands
Junping Zhang	Fudan University, China
Shichao Zhang	Guangxi Normal University, China
Yingqian Zhang	Eindhoven University of Technology, the Netherlands

Sichen Zhao	The University of Melbourne, Australia
Ying Zhao	Tsinghua University, China
Shuai Zheng	Hitachi America Ltd., USA
Arthur Zimek	University of Southern Denmark, Denmark
Albrecht Zimmermann	Université de Caen Normandie, France
Indre Zliobaite	University of Helsinki, Finland
Tanja Zseby	TU Wien, Austria

Sponsors

Contents – Part II

Supervised Learning

Exploiting the Earth's Spherical Geometry to Geolocate Images   3
  Mike Izbicki, Evangelos E. Papalexakis, and Vassilis J. Tsotras

Continual Rare-Class Recognition with Emerging Novel Subclasses   20
  Hung Nguyen, Xuejian Wang, and Leman Akoglu

Unjustified Classification Regions and Counterfactual Explanations
in Machine Learning   37
  Thibault Laugel, Marie-Jeanne Lesot, Christophe Marsala,
  Xavier Renard, and Marcin Detyniecki

Shift Happens: Adjusting Classifiers   55
  Theodore James Thibault Heiser, Mari-Liis Allikivi, and Meelis Kull

Beyond the Selected Completely at Random Assumption
for Learning from Positive and Unlabeled Data.   71
  Jessa Bekker, Pieter Robberechts, and Jesse Davis

Cost Sensitive Evaluation of Instance Hardness in Machine Learning   86
  Ricardo B. C. Prudêncio

Non-parametric Bayesian Isotonic Calibration: Fighting Over-Confidence
in Binary Classification 103
  Mari-Liis Allikivi and Meelis Kull

Multi-label Learning

PP-PLL: Probability Propagation for Partial Label Learning 123
  Kaiwei Sun, Zijian Min, and Jin Wang

Neural Message Passing for Multi-label Classification 138
  Jack Lanchantin, Arshdeep Sekhon, and Yanjun Qi

Assessing the Multi-labelness of Multi-label Data 164
  Laurence A. F. Park, Yi Guo, and Jesse Read

Synthetic Oversampling of Multi-label Data Based
on Local Label Distribution 180
  Bin Liu and Grigorios Tsoumakas

Large-Scale Learning

Distributed Learning of Non-convex Linear Models
with One Round of Communication   197
   Mike Izbicki and Christian R. Shelton

SLSGD: Secure and Efficient Distributed On-device Machine Learning   213
   Cong Xie, Oluwasanmi Koyejo, and Indranil Gupta

Trade-Offs in Large-Scale Distributed Tuplewise
Estimation And Learning   229
   Robin Vogel, Aurélien Bellet, Stephan Clémençon, Ons Jelassi,
   and Guillaume Papa

Deep Learning

Importance Weighted Generative Networks   249
   Maurice Diesendruck, Ethan R. Elenberg, Rajat Sen, Guy W. Cole,
   Sanjay Shakkottai, and Sinead A. Williamson

Linearly Constrained Weights: Reducing Activation Shift for Faster
Training of Neural Networks   266
   Takuro Kutsuna

LYRICS: A General Interface Layer to Integrate Logic Inference
and Deep Learning   283
   Giuseppe Marra, Francesco Giannini, Michelangelo Diligenti,
   and Marco Gori

Deep Eyedentification: Biometric Identification Using Micro-movements
of the Eye   299
   Lena A. Jäger, Silvia Makowski, Paul Prasse, Sascha Liehr,
   Maximilian Seidler, and Tobias Scheffer

Adversarial Invariant Feature Learning with Accuracy Constraint
for Domain Generalization   315
   Kei Akuzawa, Yusuke Iwasawa, and Yutaka Matsuo

Quantile Layers: Statistical Aggregation in Deep Neural Networks
for Eye Movement Biometrics   332
   Ahmed Abdelwahab and Niels Landwehr

Multitask Hopfield Networks   349
   Marco Frasca, Giuliano Grossi, and Giorgio Valentini

Meta-Learning for Black-Box Optimization   366
   Vishnu TV, Pankaj Malhotra, Jyoti Narwariya, Lovekesh Vig,
   and Gautam Shroff

Training Discrete-Valued Neural Networks with Sign Activations
Using Weight Distributions 382
  Wolfgang Roth, Günther Schindler, Holger Fröning,
  and Franz Pernkopf

Sobolev Training with Approximated Derivatives for Black-Box Function
Regression with Neural Networks.............................. 399
  Matthias Kissel and Klaus Diepold

Hyper-Parameter-Free Generative Modelling with Deep Boltzmann Trees ... 415
  Nico Piatkowski

L_0-ARM: Network Sparsification via Stochastic Binary Optimization....... 432
  Yang Li and Shihao Ji

Learning with Random Learning Rates 449
  Léonard Blier, Pierre Wolinski, and Yann Ollivier

FastPoint: Scalable Deep Point Processes........................ 465
  Ali Caner Türkmen, Yuyang Wang, and Alexander J. Smola

Single-Path NAS: Designing Hardware-Efficient ConvNets
in Less Than 4 Hours 481
  Dimitrios Stamoulis, Ruizhou Ding, Di Wang, Dimitrios Lymberopoulos,
  Bodhi Priyantha, Jie Liu, and Diana Marculescu

Probabilistic Models

Scalable Large Margin Gaussian Process Classification 501
  Martin Wistuba and Ambrish Rawat

Integrating Learning and Reasoning with Deep Logic Models............ 517
  Giuseppe Marra, Francesco Giannini, Michelangelo Diligenti,
  and Marco Gori

Neural Control Variates for Monte Carlo Variance Reduction........... 533
  Ruosi Wan, Mingjun Zhong, Haoyi Xiong, and Zhanxing Zhu

Data Association with Gaussian Processes 548
  Markus Kaiser, Clemens Otte, Thomas A. Runkler, and Carl Henrik Ek

Incorporating Dependencies in Spectral Kernels for Gaussian Processes..... 565
  Kai Chen, Twan van Laarhoven, Jinsong Chen, and Elena Marchiori

Deep Convolutional Gaussian Processes......................... 582
  Kenneth Blomqvist, Samuel Kaski, and Markus Heinonen

Bayesian Generalized Horseshoe Estimation of Generalized
Linear Models   598
   Daniel F. Schmidt and Enes Makalic

Fine-Grained Explanations Using Markov Logic   614
   Khan Mohammad Al Farabi, Somdeb Sarkhel, Sanorita Dey,
   and Deepak Venugopal

Natural Language Processing

Unsupervised Sentence Embedding Using Document
Structure-Based Context.   633
   Taesung Lee and Youngja Park

Copy Mechanism and Tailored Training for Character-Based
Data-to-Text Generation.   648
   Marco Roberti, Giovanni Bonetta, Rossella Cancelliere,
   and Patrick Gallinari

NSEEN: Neural Semantic Embedding for Entity Normalization   665
   Shobeir Fakhraei, Joel Mathew, and José Luis Ambite

Beyond Bag-of-Concepts: Vectors of Locally Aggregated Concepts.   681
   Maarten Grootendorst and Joaquin Vanschoren

A Semi-discriminative Approach for Sub-sentence Level Topic
Classification on a Small Dataset   697
   Cornelia Ferner and Stefan Wegenkittl

Generating Black-Box Adversarial Examples for Text Classifiers
Using a Deep Reinforced Model   711
   Prashanth Vijayaraghavan and Deb Roy

Author Index   727

Supervised Learning

Exploiting the Earth's Spherical Geometry to Geolocate Images

Mike Izbicki[1]([⊠]), Evangelos E. Papalexakis[2], and Vassilis J. Tsotras[2]

[1] Claremont McKenna College, Claremont, CA, USA
mike@izbicki.me
[2] University of California Riverside, Riverside, CA, USA
{epapalex,tsotras}@cs.ucr.edu

Abstract. Existing methods for geolocating images use standard classification or image retrieval techniques. These methods have poor theoretical properties because they do not take advantage of the earth's spherical geometry. In some cases, they require training data sets that grow exponentially with the number of feature dimensions. This paper introduces the *Mixture of von-Mises Fisher* (MvMF) loss function, which is the first loss function that exploits the earth's spherical geometry to improve geolocation accuracy. We prove that this loss requires only a dataset of size linear in the number of feature dimensions, and empirical results show that our method outperforms previous methods with orders of magnitude less training data and computation.

Keywords: Geolocation · Flickr · Deep learning · von Mises-Fisher

1 Introduction

Consider the two images below:

Most people recognize that the left image is of the Eiffel Tower, located in Paris, France. A trained expert can further recognize that the right image is a replica of the Eiffel Tower. The expert uses clues in the image's background (e.g. replicas of other famous landmarks, tall cement skyscrapers) to determine that this image was taken in Shenzhen, China. We call these images *strongly localizable* because

© Springer Nature Switzerland AG 2020
U. Brefeld et al. (Eds.): ECML PKDD 2019, LNAI 11907, pp. 3–19, 2020.
https://doi.org/10.1007/978-3-030-46147-8_1

the images contain all the information needed to exactly geolocate the images. Existing geolocation algorithms work well on strongly localizable images. These algorithms [e.g. 1,15,16,21,22] use deep neural networks to extract features, and can therefore detect the subtle clues needed to differentiate these images.

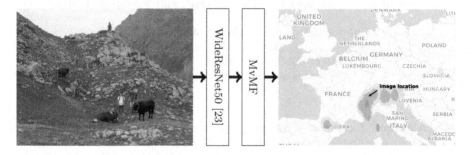

Fig. 1. To geolocate an image, we first generate features using the WideResNet50 [23], then pass these features to our novel *mixture of von Mises-Fisher* (MvMF) output layer. The MvMF outputs a probability distribution over the earth's surface, and is particularly well-suited for visualizing the output of hard-to-geolocate images.

Most images, however, are only *weakly localizable* because the image does not contain enough information to exactly geolocate it. Consider the image in Fig. 1 of two men hiking. An expert can use clues like the geology of the mountains, the breed of cattle, and the people's appearance to determine that this image was taken in the Alps. But the Alps are a large mountain range, and there is simply not enough information in the image to pinpoint exactly where in the Alps the image was taken. Existing geolocation algorithms are overconfident when predicting locations for these images. These algorithms use either image retrieval [1,7,8,21] or classification methods [15,16,22] to perform geolocation, and these procedures do not take advantage of the earth's spherical geometry. They therefore cannot properly represent the ambiguity of these weakly localizable images.

In this paper, we introduce the MvMF output layer for predicting GPS coordinates with deep neural networks. The MvMF has three advantages compared to previous methods:

1. The MvMF takes advantage of the earth's spherical geometry and so works with both strongly and weakly localizable images.
2. The MvMF has theoretical guarantees, whereas no previous method has a theoretical analysis.
3. The MvMF interpolates between the image retrieval and classification approaches to geolocation, retaining the benefits of both with the drawbacks of neither.

In our experiments, we use the WideResNet50 [23] convolutional neural network to generate features from images, but we emphasize that any deep neural network can be used with the MvMF layer. We provide TensorFlow code for the MvMF layer at https://github.com/mikeizbicki/geolocation.

In Sect. 2, we review prior work on the image geolocation problem. We focus our exposition on how previous methods ignore the earth's spherical geometry, and how this causes them to require more training data. Section 3 presents the MvMF output layer to fix these problems, while Sect. 4 provides the experimental results. Section 5 concludes the paper with a discussion on other possible application areas for the MvMF output layer.

2 Prior Work

Prior image geolocation methods use either image retrieval or classification techniques. This section describes the limitations of these techniques. We use standard theoretical results to show that these techniques require excessively large training datasets, and conduct novel experiments to verify that these theoretical flaws affect real world performance.

2.1 Image Retrieval

Im2GPS [7,8] was the first image geolocation system. The most important component of this system is a large database of images labelled with GPS coordinates and manually constructed features. To determine the location of a new image, Im2GPS performs a k-nearest neighbor query in the database, and outputs the average GPS coordinates of the returned images. Im2GPS-deep [21] significantly improved the results of the Im2GPS system by using deep neural networks to generate features.

These image retrieval systems have two basic disadvantages due to the curse of dimensionality. First, they have poor theoretical guarantees. Let d denote the dimensionality of the image feature vector ($d \approx 1 \times 10^5$ for Im2GPS and $d = 512$ for Im2GPS-deep). Then standard results for k-nearest neighbor queries show that in the worst case, a database with $\Omega(d^{d/2})$ images is needed for accurate queries (see Theorem 19.4 of [17]); that is, the amount of training data should grow exponentially with the number of feature dimensions. This is unrealistic for the feature dimensions used in practice. Second, image retrieval systems are slow. The nearest neighbor search is performed over millions of images, and because the dimensionality of the space is large, data structures like kd-trees do not speed up the search as much as we would like.

In Sect. 3.3 below, we show that the MvMF model this paper introduces can be interpreted as an image retrieval system. The MvMF, however, takes advantage of the earth's spherical geometry to avoid the curse of dimensionality.

2.2 Classification

Classification-based geolocation methods were introduced to overcome the performance limitations of image retrieval methods. The basic idea is as follows. First, the surface of the earth is partitioned into a series of classes. Then the standard cross entropy loss is used to classify images. The estimated position is

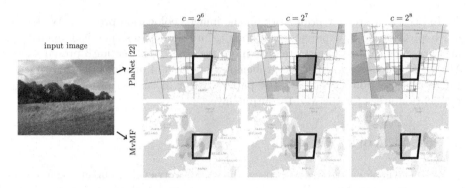

Fig. 2. The PlaNet [22] method's performance is highly sensative to the number of classes c. Consider the highlighted region. When $c = 2^6$, PlaNet assigns no probability to the region. (Brighter red indicates classes with higher probability.) When $c = 2^7$, PlaNet has split many other cells, causing the probability of the highlighted region to increase. When $c = 2^8$, PlaNet splits the highlighted region, causing the probability to drop again. This effect is exaggerated for weakly localizable images because many classes should be assigned high probability. In comparison, when the number of classes increases for the MvMF loss, the output smoothly takes on the shape of the underlying geography, which is the desired output for a weakly localizable image of grass. (Color figure online)

the center of the predicted class. These methods have better theoretical guarantees than the image retrieval methods and are faster because they avoid the expensive nearest neighbor queries. Unfortunately, these methods have two flaws: tuning the number of classes is difficult, and the cross entropy loss is not well correlated with geolocation performance.

We illustrate these flaws on the PlaNet algorithm [22], which is the earliest and most influential example of classification-based geolocation methods. The algorithm divides the world into a series of classes using an adaptive partitioning scheme based on Google's S2 geometry library. The classes are constructed according to the following recursive procedure: the world is initially divided into 6 classes; the class with the most images is then subdivided into smaller classes; and this procedure is repeated until the desired number of classes c is reached. Figure 2 shows an example class tiling generated using the PlaNet method for three different values of c.

The number of classes c is a hyperparameter that must be manually tuned,[1] and tuning this parameter is an instance of the classic bias-variance trade off. Recall that the *bias* of a model (also called the *approximation error*) is the error of the best possible model in a given class, and the *variance* (also called the *estimation error*) is the statistical error induced by the finite size of the training set. We make the following claim about PlaNet's geolocation method.

Claim 1. *Increasing the number of classes c reduces the model's bias but increases the model's variance.*

---

[1] The original PlaNet paper chose a value of $c \approx 2^{15}$.

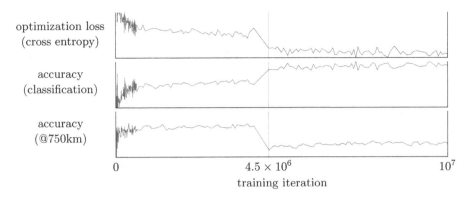

optimization loss
(cross entropy)

accuracy
(classification)

accuracy
(@750km)

0   4.5×10^6 10^7

training iteration

Fig. 3. Previous classification-based geolocation methods minimize the cross entropy loss [15,16,22], but these plots show that minimizing the cross entropy does not necessarily improve geolocation accuracy. (*Top*) Stochastic gradient descent directly minimizes the cross entropy loss, so the cross entropy decreases as training progresses. (*Middle*) The cross entropy loss is a convex surrogate for the classification accuracy, so classification accuracy increases as training progresses. (*Bottom*) The cross entropy is not a convex surrogate for the accuracy @750 km (which is the fraction of data points whose estimated location is within 750 km of their true location), so the geolocation accuracy does not necessarily increase as training progresses. In this particular run, the cross entropy loss at iteration 4.5×10^6 improves dramatically, but the geolocation accuracy worsens dramatically. This effect can be observed at all distance scales and for all hyperparameter values.

To understand this claim, observe that when c is small, the geographic area of each class is large, so fine-grained predictions are not possible, and the model has large bias. Increasing the number of classes c reduces the size of each class, allowing more fine-grained predictions, and reducing the model's bias. To see how c effects the model's variance, we appeal to Theorem 4 of Hazan et al. [9] that shows that the variance of a classifier using the cross entropy loss grows as $\Omega(cd)$. Therefore, as c increases, the variance must increase as well. Finding the optimal value of c is a difficult balancing act, as shown in Fig. 2.

In order to reduce the variance inherent in classification methods, the CPlaNet method [16] and the ISN method [15] use multiple cross entropy output layers to reduce the total number of classes needed. Both methods lack theoretical guarantees, and the optimal number of classes c still requires careful tuning.

A second problem with PlaNet, CPlaNet, and ISN is these methods all use the cross entropy loss for training. The cross entropy is closely associated with classification accuracy, but as we show in Fig. 3, is not necessarily correlated with geolocation performance. The fundamental problem is that the cross entropy loss does not incorporate knowledge about the earth's spherical geometry.

In Sect. 3.2 below, we show that our MvMF method has an interpretation as a classification-based geolocation method. In contrast to all previous methods, however, the MvMF uses a loss function that exploits the earth's spherical geometry and so is highly correlated with geolocation performance. We also show that the variance of the MvMF grows as $O(d)$, and so increasing the number of classes c reduces the model's bias without increasing the variance.

3   Geolocation via the MvMF

The MvMF is the first geolocation method that exploits the earth's spherical geometry, and it is specifically designed to overcome the disadvantages of the image retrieval and classification methods for geolocation. In this section, we first introduce the MvMF as a probabilistic model, then describe two alternative interpretations of the MvMF as a classification model with a non-standard loss or as an image retrieval model using non-standard features. A powerful property of the MvMF model is that it can interpolate between the classification and image retrieval approaches to geolocation, getting the best of both techniques while avoiding the limitations of both. We prove that when the MvMF's parameters are properly initialized, only $O(d)$ training data points are needed.

3.1   The Probabilistic Interpretation

This subsection formally introduces the MvMF output layer as a mixture of von Mises-Fisher distributions. Then we describe the training and inference procedures.

The *von Mises-Fisher* (vMF) distribution is one of the standard distributions in the field of directional statistics, which is the study of distributions on spheres. The vMF can be considered the spherical analogue of the Gaussian distribution [e.g. 13] and enjoys many of the Gaussian's nice properties. Thus, the *mixture of vMF* (MvMF) distribution can be seen as the spherical analogue of the commonly used Gaussian mixture model (GMM). While the MvMF model has previously been combined with deep learning for clustering [5] and facial recognition [6], we are the first to combine the MvMF and deep learning to predict GPS coordinates.

Formally, the vMF distribution is parameterized by the *mean direction* $\mu \in \mathbb{S}^2$, and the *concentration parameter* $\kappa \in \mathbb{R}^+$. The density is defined for all points $\mathbf{y} \in \mathbb{S}^2$ as

$$\text{vMF}(\mathbf{y}; \mu, \kappa) = \frac{\kappa}{\sinh \kappa} \exp(\kappa_i \mu^\top \mathbf{y}). \tag{1}$$

An important property of the vMF distribution is that it is symmetric about μ for all $\mu \in \mathbb{S}^2$. As shown in Fig. 4, a gaussian distribution over GPS coordinates does not account for the earth's spherical geometry, and is therefore not symmetrical when projected onto the sphere.

The *mixture of vMF* (MvMF) distribution is a convex combination of vMF distributions. If the mixture contains c component vMF distributions, then it is parameterized by a collection of mean directions $M = (\mu_1, ..., \mu_c)$, a collection of concentration parameters $K = (\kappa_1, ..., \kappa_c)$, and a vector of mixing weights $\Gamma \in \mathbb{R}^c$ satisfying $\sum_{i=1}^c \Gamma_i = 1$. Notice that we use capital Greek letters for

high variance		low variance	
vMF	Gaussian	vMF	Gaussian

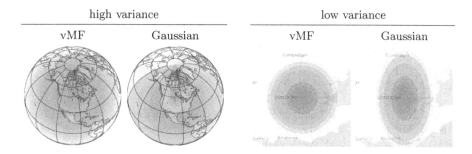

Fig. 4. The vMF distribution takes into account the curvature of the earth's surface, and so contour lines are equidistant from the center at all scales and locations. The Gaussian distribution over GPS coordinates, in contrast, becomes elongated far from the equator, and has discontinuities at the poles and at longitude $\pm 180°$.

the parameters of the mixture distribution and lowercase Greek letters for the parameters of the corresponding component distributions. The density is given by

$$\text{MvMF}(\mathbf{y}; M, K, \Gamma) = \sum_{i=1}^{c} \Gamma_i \, \text{vMF}(\mathbf{y}, M_i, K_i). \tag{2}$$

To construct the MvMF loss function from this density, we assume that the mean direction and concentration parameters do not depend on the input features. The mixing weights are parameterized using the standard softmax function as

$$\Gamma_i(\mathbf{x}; W) = \frac{\exp(-\mathbf{x}^\top \mathbf{w}_i)}{\sum_{j=1}^{c} \exp(-\mathbf{x}^\top \mathbf{w}_j)}. \tag{3}$$

where $W = (\mathbf{w}_1, ..., \mathbf{w}_c)$ and each $\mathbf{w}_i \in \mathbb{R}^d$. Taking the negative log of Eq. (2) and substituting Γ_i gives us the final MvMF loss:

$$\ell_{\text{MvMF}}(\mathbf{x}, \mathbf{y}; M, K, W) = -\log \sum_{i=1}^{c} \left(\Gamma_i(\mathbf{x}; W) \, \text{vMF}(\mathbf{y}, M_i, K_i) \right). \tag{4}$$

When training a model with the MvMF loss, our goal is to find the best values for M, K, and W for a given dataset. Given a training dataset $(\mathbf{x}_1, \mathbf{y}_1), ..., (\mathbf{x}_n, \mathbf{y}_n)$ the training procedure solves the optimization

$$\hat{M}, \hat{K}, \hat{W} = \underset{M, K, W}{\arg\min} \frac{1}{n} \sum_{i=1}^{n} \ell_{\text{MvMF}}(\mathbf{x}_i, \mathbf{y}_i; M, K, W). \tag{5}$$

Training mixture models is difficult due to their non-convex loss functions, and good initial conditions are required to ensure convergence to a good local minimum. We use the following initialization in our experiments: initialize the W randomly using the Glorot method [4]; initialize μ_i to the center of the ith class used by the PlaNet method; and initialize all κ_i to the same initial value κ^0. We suggest using $\kappa^0 = \exp(16)$ based on experiments in Sect. 4.

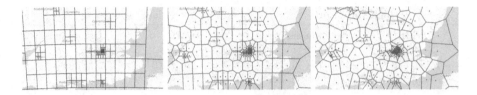

Fig. 5. (*Left*) Classes near London created using the PlaNet method. (*Middle*) Classes of the MvMF method with the μ_i initialized from the centers of the PlaNet classes. (*Right*) After training with the MvMF loss, the μ_i have shifted slightly to better fit the data, resulting in a new class partition.

The estimated GPS coordinate $\hat{\mathbf{y}}$ of a feature vector $\mathbf{x}$ is the coordinate with minimum loss. That is,

$$\hat{\mathbf{y}} = \underset{\mathbf{y}\in\mathbb{S}^2}{\arg\min}\, \ell_{\mathrm{MvMF}}(\mathbf{x}, \mathbf{y}; M, K, W). \tag{6}$$

Notice that this optimization is distinct from (5). This optimization does not get evaluated during model training, but only during inference. This optimization is non-convex, and may have up to c distinct local minima. Algorithms exist for finding the minima of mixture models [3], but these algorithms require significant computation. Calculating $\hat{\mathbf{y}}$ for a single image may be feasible, but calculating $\hat{\mathbf{y}}$ for an entire test set is prohibitive. The classification interpretation of the MvMF loss presents an easy to interpret, computationally more efficient method for inference.

3.2   Interpretation as a Classifier

The MvMF model can be interpreted as a classification model where each component represents a class. The mixture weights $\Gamma_i(\mathbf{x}, W)$ then become the probability associated with each class. The estimated location $\tilde{\mathbf{y}}$ is then the mean direction of the class with largest weight. Formally,

$$\tilde{\mathbf{y}} = \mu_{\tilde{i}}, \quad \text{where} \quad \tilde{i} = \underset{i\in\{1,\dots,c\}}{\arg\max}\, \Gamma_i(\mathbf{x}, W). \tag{7}$$

Because this optimization is over a discrete space, it is extremely fast. When the mean directions M are initialized using the centers of the PlaNet classes, then there is a one-to-one correspondence between the MvMF classes and the PlaNet classes, albeit with the class shapes differing slightly (see Fig. 5). In our experiments in Sect. 4, we use $\tilde{\mathbf{y}}$ as the estimated position.

Another advantage of the MvMF classes over the PlaNet classes is that the MvMF classes are fully parameterized by M. This means by jointly optimizing both W and M, we can learn not only which classes go with which images, but where on the earth the classes should be located.

3.3   Interpretation as an Image Retrieval Method

We now describe how the MvMF model interpolates between classification models and image retrieval models. Recall that

$$\Gamma_i(\mathbf{x}, W) = \frac{\exp(-\mathbf{x}^\top \mathbf{w}_i)}{\sum_{j=1}^c \exp(-\mathbf{x}^\top \mathbf{w}_j)} \propto \exp(-\mathbf{x}^\top \mathbf{w}_i). \tag{8}$$

Solving for the $\tilde{i}$ in Eq. (7) that maximizes Γ_i is therefore equivalent to finding the $\mathbf{w}_i$ that minimizes the inner product with $\mathbf{x}$. Minimum inner product search is a well studied problem, and in particular, it can be reduced to nearest neighbor search [2]. Therefore, when the number of classes equals the number of data points (i.e. $c = n$), and for each i we have $\mu_i = \mathbf{y}_i$ and $\mathbf{w}_i = \dot{\mathbf{x}}_i$, then solving Eq. (7) to find the output class is equivalent to solving a nearest neighbor problem.

3.4   Analysis

Our analysis states that the MvMF's estimation error converges to zero at a rate of $O(\sqrt{d/n})$, where d is the number of feature dimensions and n the number of data points. This is in contrast to nearest neighbor methods (which converge at the exponential rate $\Omega(dn^{1/d})$ [Theorem 19.4 of 17]), and the cross entropy loss (which converges at a rate of $\Omega(\sqrt{cd/n})$ [Theorem 4 of 9]). Because c and d are both large in the geolocation setting, the MvMF loss requires significantly less training data to converge.

We use three assumptions to simplify our analysis. The first assumption states that our analysis only applies to the convergence of the W parameter. We argue that this is a mild assumption because W is the most important parameter to learn. The second assumption states that our features have bounded size, which is true of all image deep neural networks. The final assumption states that our analysis requires a good initial parameter guess. This is unsurprising as mixture models are known to be highly sensitive to their initial conditions. We now state these assumptions formally and describe their implications in more detail.

Assumption 1. *We optimize only W using stochastic gradient descent (SGD). In particular, we do not optimize M, K, or the deep network generating features.*

SGD is an iterative algorithm, where each iteration t considers only a single data point $(\mathbf{x}_t, \mathbf{y}_t)$ sampled uniformly at random from the underlying data distribution. On each iteration t, the model weights are denoted by W_t. These weights are updated according to the rule

$$W_{t+1} = W_t - \eta_t \frac{d}{dW_t} \ell_{\mathrm{MvMF}}(\mathbf{x}_t, \mathbf{y}_t; M, K, W_t)$$

starting from some initial W_0. The variable η_t is called the step size.

SGD is the most common algorithm for optimizing deep neural networks, and in practice it is common to train all parameters of a network at the same time. Analyzing such training procedures, however, is a difficult open problem due to the highly non-convex nature of neural networks. To better understand these systems, it is common to analyze the convergence of a single parameter while holding all others fixed, and that is our strategy.

The W parameter is the most important to analyze because it determines which class an image will be assigned to. The M and K parameters determine properties of the classes, and their convergence does not significantly effect geolocation. The M parameter is initialized to the classes of the PlaNet method, so improvements in M can only make it better than the PlaNet method. And the K value does not affect the classification-based inference in Eq. (7).

Assumption 2. *For all* $\mathbf{x}$, *we have* $\|\mathbf{x}\| \leq \sqrt{d}$.

This is a standard assumption for the analysis of SGD algorithms, and it is equivalent to assuming that the individual features are bounded. Let $\mathbf{x}_i$ denote the ith feature in $\mathbf{x}$, and assume that each feature $\mathbf{x}_i \in [-1, 1]$. Then,

$$\|\mathbf{x}\|^2 = \sum_{i=1}^{d} \mathbf{x}_i^2 \leq \sum_{i=1}^{d} 1 = d.$$

It is common to scale images so that each pixel value is in the range $[-1, 1]$, and all deep neural networks are designed to keep their output features bounded.

Assumption 3. *Let* W^* *be a (possibly local) minimizer of* ℓ_{MvMF}. *Let* $\mathcal{W}$ *be a convex subset of* $\mathbb{R}^{d \times c}$ *containing* W^* *such that* ℓ_{MvMF} *is convex in* $\mathcal{W}$. *Finally, for all time steps* t, *we assume that* $W_t \in \mathcal{W}$.

This is our most complicated assumption. Informally, it states that we limit our analysis of ℓ_{MvMF} to a convex region around a possibly local minimum W^*. We must limit our analysis to this convex region because existing analyses of SGD work only for convex losses and the ℓ_{MvMF} is non-convex.

We argue this is not a limiting assumption for two reasons. First, SGD will eventually converge to a region satisfying the properties of $\mathcal{W}$. To see this, observe that SGD will converge to a local minimum with probability 1, and (due to the smoothness of ℓ_{MvMF}) every local minimum of ℓ_{MvMF} is contained in a convex set $\mathcal{W}$ over which ℓ_{MvMF} is convex. Second, if SGD does not converge to a sufficiently good local minimum, the procedure can be repeated from a different random initialization until a good local minimum is reached. In our experiments, however, we found that it was never necessary to rerun SGD from a different initialization.

Theorem 1. *Under Assumptions 1–3, at each iteration* t, *the MvMF's estimation error is bounded by*

$$\mathbb{E}\left(\ell_{MvMF}(\mathbf{x}, \mathbf{y}; M, K, W_t) - \ell_{MvMF}(\mathbf{x}, \mathbf{y}; M, K, W^*)\right) \leq 2\sqrt{\frac{d}{n}}. \qquad (9)$$

Table 1. Details of the training environment for previous work on image geolocation.

Method	Training		
	Images	Features	Output method
Im2GPS [7,8]	6×10^6	Custom	Retrieval
Im2GPS-deep [21]	28×10^6	VGG [18]	Retrieval
PlaNet [22]	126×10^6	InceptionV1 [19]	Classification
CPlaNet [16]	30×10^6	InceptionV3 [20]	Classification (modified)
ISN [15]	16×10^6	ResNet [10] + custom	Classification (modified)

We sketch the proof of Theorem 1 here and defer a full proof to the Appendix for space reasons. Standard results show that the estimation error of SGD is bounded by $\rho/\sqrt{n}$, where ρ is an upper bound on the gradient of the loss function. We show that for the MvMF loss, the gradient is bounded by $\rho \leq \sqrt{d}$. The cross entropy loss used by other classification-based geolocation methods has worse performance guarantees because its gradient is bounded by $\rho \leq \sqrt{cd}$. The $\sqrt{cd/n}$ convergence rate for the cross entropy loss is known to be tight [9], and so the MvMF loss has strictly better convergence.

4 Experiments

The empirical performance of an image geolocation system is determined by three factors: the training data, the feature generation method, and the output method. Prior work on image geolocation introduced improvements in all three areas, making it difficult to determine exactly which improvement was responsible for better performance (see Table 1 for a summary). In particular, no prior work attempts to isolate the effects of the output method, and no prior work compares different output methods side by side.

In our experiments, we follow a careful procedure to generate a standard training dataset with standard features so that we can isolate the effects of the output method. Because prior work does not follow this procedure, an exhaustive empirical comparison would require reimplementing all previous methods from scratch. This is infeasible from both a manpower and computational perspective, so we focus our comparison on the PlaNet method, since it is representative of classification methods using the cross entropy loss. We show that the cross entropy-based methods require careful tuning of the hyperparameter c, but that our MvMF's performance always improves when increasing the number of classes c (as our theory predicts). This leads to significantly better performance of the MvMF method.

4.1 Procedure

We now describe our standardized training procedure. We pay special attention to how it improves upon previous training procedures for comparing output methods.

Training Data. The previous methods' training datasets are not only of different sizes, but also sampled from entirely different distributions. The Im2GPS [7,8] and Im2GPS-deep [21] methods download data from Flickr, then filter the images using user specified tags to remove weakly localizable images. For example, it is assumed that images with the tag #birthday are likely to be of indoor scenes with few geographic clues, and so images with this tag are removed from the dataset. The CPlaNet [16] and ISN [15] datasets are also acquired from Flickr, and they introduce other criteria for filtering the data to ensure only high quality images are included. The PlaNet [22] dataset uses geotagged images crawled from all over the web with no filtering. The dataset is much larger, but is significantly harder to train from, because the data is noisier with more weakly localizable images. Most of these datasets are proprietary and not publicly available.

For our training data, we use a previously existing publicly available dataset of geotagged images from Mousselly et al. [14]. This dataset contains about 6 million images crawled from Flickr,[2] and the crawl was designed to be as representative as possible of Flickr's image database. The only filtering the dataset performed was to remove low resolution images. This dataset therefore comes from a distribution more similar to the PlaNet dataset than the other datasets.

Features. Even if all previous models had been trained on the same data, it would still be impossible to directly compare the efficacy of output methods because each model uses different features. We use the WideResnet50 model [23] to generate a standard set of features in our experiments. WideResnet50 was originally trained on the ImageNet dataset for image classification, so we "fine-tune" the model's parameters to the geolocation problem. We chose the WideResnet50 model because empirical results show that fine-tuning works particularly well on resnet models [12], and the WideResnet50 is the best performing resnet model.

Fine-tuning a model is computationally cheaper than training from scratch, but it is still expensive. We therefore fine-tune the model only once, and use the resulting features in all experiments. To ensure that our fine-tuned features do not favor the MvMF method, we create a simple classification problem to fine-tune the features on. We associate each image with the country the image was taken in or "no country" for images from Antarctica or international waters. In total, this gives us a classification problem with 194 classes. We then fine-tune

---

[2] The dataset originally contained about 14 million images, but many of them have since been deleted from Flickr and so were unavailable to us.

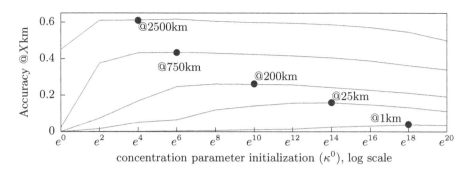

Fig. 6. Higher values of κ^0 result in better performance at fine grained prediction, and lower values of κ^0 result in better performance for course-grained prediction.

the WideResnet50 model for 20 epochs using the cross entropy loss, WideResnet50's standard feature augmentation, and the Adam [11] variant of SGD with a learning rate of 1×10^{-5}. This took about 2 months on a 4 CPU system with a Tesla K80 GPU and 64 GB of memory. Because this fine-tuning procedure uses a cross entropy loss, the resulting features should perform especially well with cross entropy geolocation methods. Nonetheless, we shall see that the MvMF loss still outperforms cross entropy methods.

4.2 Results

We perform 3 experiments using the standardized training data and features described above.

Tuning the MvMF's Hyperparameters. In this experiment, we set $c = 2^{15}$ and train MvMF models with $\kappa^0 = 0...20$. The results are shown in Fig. 6. Accuracy @Xkm is a standard method for evaluating the performance of a geolocation system, and is equal to the fraction of data points whose estimated location is within Xkm of the true location. (Higher values are better.) For small X, Accuracy @Xkm measures the ability to geolocate strongly localizable images, and for large X, Accuracy @Xkm measures the ability to geolocate weakly localizable images.

We see that large values of κ^0 cause better geolocation for strongly localizable images, and small values of κ^0 cause better geolocation for weakly localizable images. This behavior has an intuitive explanation. When κ^0 is small, the variance of each component vMF distribution is large. So on each SGD step, weights from vMF components that are far away from the training data point will be updated. If the image is weakly localizable, then there are many locations where it might be placed, so many component weights should be updated. Conversely, when κ^0 is large, the component variances are small, and so only a small number of components get updated with each SGD step. Strongly localizable images can

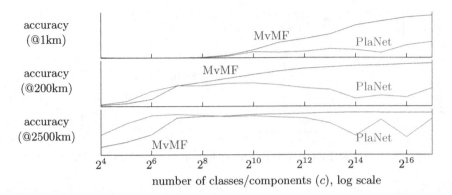

Fig. 7. The performance of the MvMF output layer increases monotonically as we increase the number of mixture components c, whereas the perfomance of PlaNet depends unpredictably on c.

be exactly located to a small number of components, and so only a few components should be updated. We suggest using a value of $\kappa^0 = 16$ as a good balance, and use this value in all other experiments.

Tuning the Number of Classes c. This experiment demonstrates that c must be carefully tuned in the PlaNet method, but that increasing c always increases performance of the MvMF method. We emphasize that the original PlaNet paper [22] does not report results on the tuning of c, and so observing these limitations of the PlaNet method is one of the contributions of our work.

We train a series of models using the MvMF loss and PlaNet loss, varying c from 2^4 to 2^{17}. Theoretically, both methods support class sizes larger than $c = 2^{17}$, but our GPU hardware only had enough memory for 2^{17} classes. Figure 7 shows the results. For all X, we observe that PlaNet's performance is highly unpredictable as c varies, but the MvMF method always has improved accuracy as c increases.

Note that Fig. 2 shows qualitatively why the PlaNet method is more sensitive to c than the MvMF. In that figure, as c increases and classes get split, the probability that was previously assigned to those classes gets completely reallocated. Similarly, Fig. 3 illustrates a single training run of the PlaNet method. Because the cross entropy loss does not directly optimize the desired outcome (geolocation), improvements to the cross entropy loss sometimes result in worse geolocation performance.

Fine-Tuned Performance. In this experiment, we select several cross entropy and MvMF models and perform a second round of fine-tuning, this time with their true loss functions. We fine-tune with the Adam optimizer running for 5 epochs with learning rate 1×10^{-5}, which takes approximately 2 weeks per model on a single GPU. We evaluate the resulting model against the standard

Table 2. Results on the Im2GPS test set [7]. The MvMF loss significantly outperforms the cross entropy loss at all distances when using standardized data and features. The MvMF loss trained on the standardized features even outperforms the PlaNet method, which was trained on a much larger dataset and required significantly more computation.

Loss	Data/features	c	Accuracy @				
			1 km	25 km	200 km	750 km	250 km
Cross entropy	PlaNet [22]	$\approx 2^{15}$	**8.4**	24.5	37.6	53.6	71.3
Cross entropy	Standardized	2^{13}	1.0	4.1	10.1	24.8	44.8
Cross entropy	Standardized	2^{15}	0.6	2.0	7.3	26.1	49.9
Cross entropy	Standardized	2^{17}	1.8	6.0	11.8	27.9	51.3
MvMF	Standardized	2^{13}	4.6	28.0	35.4	50.5	73.4
MvMF	Standardized	2^{15}	6.0	31.2	41.1	58.0	75.7
MvMF	Standardized	2^{17}	**8.4**	**32.6**	**39.4**	**57.2**	**80.2**

Im2GPS test set introduced by [7]. The results are shown in Table 2. When using the standardized training data and features, the MvMF loss significantly outperforms the cross entropy loss.

In Table 2, we also include results reported in the original PlaNet paper [22]. These results use a training data set that is 2 orders of magnitude larger than the standardized training set, and so have significantly better performance than the cross entropy loss on the standard training set. This illustrates that the training data has a huge impact on the final model's performance. Surprisingly, the MvMF loss trained on standardized training set with only 6 million data points outperforms the PlaNet method trained on 126 million images. Other models have been evaluated on the Im2GPS test set as well [e.g. 7,8,15,16,21,22], but we do not report their performance here because we could not do a fair comparison where all models were trained using the same training data and features.

5   Conclusion

The MvMF is the first method for image geolocation that takes advantage of the earth's geometry. The MvMF has better theoretical guarantees than previous image retrieval and classification methods, and these guarantees translate into better real world performance. We emphasize that the MvMF layer can be applied to any geolocation problem, not just image geolocation.

Acknowledgments. We thank an anonymous reviewer for identifying a mistake in the first version of our proof. E. Papalexakis was supported by the Department of the Navy, Naval Engineering Education Consortium under award no. N00174-17-1-0005 and the National Science Foundation CDS&E Grant no. OAC-1808591. V. Tsotras was supported by National Science Foundation grants IIS-1527984 and SES-1831615.

References

1. Arandjelovic, R., Gronat, P., Torii, A., Pajdla, T., Sivic, J.: NetVLAD: CNN architecture for weakly supervised place recognition. In: CVPR, June 2016
2. Bachrach, Y., et al.: Speeding up the Xbox recommender system using a Euclidean transformation for inner-product spaces. In: Proceedings of the 8th ACM Conference on Recommender Systems, pp. 257–264. ACM (2014)
3. Carreira-Perpinan, M.A.: Mode-finding for mixtures of gaussian distributions. TPAMI **22**(11), 1318–1323 (2000)
4. Glorot, X., Bengio, Y.: Understanding the difficulty of training deep feedforward neural networks. In: AIStats, pp. 249–256 (2010)
5. Gopal, S., Yang, Y.: Von Mises-Fisher clustering models. In: ICML, pp. 154–162 (2014)
6. Hasnat, M., Bohné, J., Milgram, J., Gentric, S., Chen, L., et al.: von Mises-Fisher mixture model-based deep learning: application to face verification. arXiv preprint arXiv:1706.04264 (2017)
7. Hays, J., Efros, A.A.: IM2GPS: estimating geographic information from a single image. In: CVPR. IEEE (2008)
8. Hays, J., Efros, A.A.: Large-scale image geolocalization. In: Choi, J., Friedland, G. (eds.) Multimodal Location Estimation of Videos and Images, pp. 41–62. Springer, Cham (2015). https://doi.org/10.1007/978-3-319-09861-6_3
9. Hazan, E., Koren, T., Levy, K.Y.: Logistic regression: tight bounds for stochastic and online optimization. In: COLT (2014)
10. He, K., Zhang, X., Ren, S., Sun, J.: Identity mappings in deep residual networks. In: Leibe, B., Matas, J., Sebe, N., Welling, M. (eds.) ECCV 2016. LNCS, vol. 9908, pp. 630–645. Springer, Cham (2016). https://doi.org/10.1007/978-3-319-46493-0_38
11. Kingma, D.P., Adam, J.B.: A method for stochastic optimization. arXiv preprint arXiv:1412.6980 (2014)
12. Kornblith, S., Shlens, J., Le, Q.V.: Do better ImageNet models transfer better? arXiv preprint arXiv:1805.08974 (2018)
13. Mardia, K.V., Jupp, P.E.: Directional Statistics. Wiley, Hoboken (2009)
14. Mousselly-Sergieh, H., Watzinger, D., Huber, B., Döller, M., Egyed-Zsigmond, E., Kosch, H.: World-wide scale geotagged image dataset for automatic image annotation and reverse geotagging. In: MMSys, 2014
15. Muller-Budack, E., Pustu-Iren, K., Ewerth, R.: Geolocation estimation of photos using a hierarchical model and scene classification. In: ECCV (2018)
16. Seo, P.H., Weyand, T., Sim, J., Han, B.: CPlaNet: enhancing image geolocalization by combinatorial partitioning of maps. arXiv preprint arXiv:1808.02130 (2018)
17. Shalev-Shwartz, S., Ben-David, S.: Understanding Machine Learning: From Theory to Algorithms. Cambridge University Press, Cambridge (2014)
18. Simonyan, K., Zisserman, A.: Very deep convolutional networks for large-scale image recognition. arXiv preprint arXiv:1409.1556 (2014)
19. Szegedy, C., et al.: Going deeper with convolutions. In: CVPR (2015)

20. Szegedy, C., Vanhoucke, V., Ioffe, S., Shlens, J., Wojna, Z.: Rethinking the inception architecture for computer vision. In: CVPR (2016)
21. Vo, N., Jacobs, N., Hays, J.: Revisiting IM2GPS in the deep learning era. In: ICCV, pp. 2640–2649. IEEE (2017)
22. Weyand, T., Kostrikov, I., Philbin, J.: PlaNet - Photo Geolocation with Convolutional Neural Networks. In: Leibe, B., Matas, J., Sebe, N., Welling, M. (eds.) ECCV 2016. LNCS, vol. 9912, pp. 37–55. Springer, Cham (2016). https://doi.org/10.1007/978-3-319-46484-8_3
23. Zagoruyko, S., Komodakis, N.: Wide residual networks. arXiv preprint arXiv:1605.07146 (2016)

Continual Rare-Class Recognition
with Emerging Novel Subclasses

Hung Nguyen$^{(\boxtimes)}$, Xuejian Wang, and Leman Akoglu

Heinz College of Information Systems and Public Policy,
Carnegie Mellon University, Pittsburgh, USA
{hungnguy,xuejianw,lakoglu}@andrew.cmu.edu

Abstract. Given a labeled dataset that contains a rare (or minority) class of *of-interest* instances, as well as a large class of instances that are *not* of interest, how can we learn to recognize future *of-interest* instances over a continuous stream? We introduce RARECOGNIZE, which (i) estimates a *general* decision boundary between the rare and the majority class, (ii) learns to recognize individual rare subclasses that exist within the training data, as well as (iii) flags instances from previously unseen rare subclasses as newly emerging. The learner in (i) is general in the sense that by construction it is dissimilar to the *specialized* learners in (ii), thus distinguishes minority from the majority without overly tuning to what is seen in the training data. Thanks to this generality, RARECOGNIZE ignores all future instances that it labels as majority and recognizes the recurrent as well as emerging *rare* subclasses only. This saves effort at test time as well as ensures that the model size grows moderately over time as it only maintains specialized minority learners. Through extensive experiments, we show that RARECOGNIZE outperforms state-of-the-art baselines on three real-world datasets that contain corporate-risk and disaster documents as rare classes.

1 Introduction

Given a labeled dataset containing (1) a rare (or minority) class of *of-interest* documents, and (2) a large set of *not-of-interest* documents, how can we learn a model that can effectively identify future *of-interest* documents over a continuous stream? Different from the traditional classification setup, the stream might contain *of-interest* (as well as *not-of-interest*) documents from *novel subclasses that were not seen in the training data*. Therefore, the model is required to continually recognize both the recurring as well as the emerging instances from the underlying rare class distribution.

    Let us motivate this setting with a couple of real-world examples. Suppose we are given a large collection of social media documents (e.g. Twitter posts). A subset of the collection is labeled as *risky*, indicating posts that constitute (financial, reputational, etc.) risk to a corporation. The rest (majority) of the collection is *not-risky*. The goal is then to learn a model that can continually identify future posts that are *risky* over the social-media stream. Here, the rare class

© Springer Nature Switzerland AG 2020
U. Brefeld et al. (Eds.): ECML PKDD 2019, LNAI 11907, pp. 20–36, 2020.
https://doi.org/10.1007/978-3-030-46147-8_2

contains *risky* documents of a few known types, such as bankruptcy, corruption, and spying. However, it is unrealistic to assume that it contains examples from all possible risk types—given the large spectrum, labeling effort, and potentially evolving nature of risk.

Consider another case where the training set consists of news articles. A subset of the articles belongs to the rare class of *disasters*, indicating news about natural or man-made disasters. The rest are *not-disaster* articles. Similar to the first case, the rare class might contain articles about floods, earthquakes, etc. however it is hard to imagine it would contain instances from all possible types of disasters. The goal is to learn to continually recognize future articles on disasters.

In both examples above, the model needs to learn from and generalize beyond the labeled data so as to recognize future rare-class instances, both from *recurring* (i.e., seen in the training data) as well as from *novel subclasses*; for instance sexual assault, cyber attack, etc. in risk domain and explosions, landslides, etc. in disasters domain. In machine learning terms, this is a very challenging setup in which the learner needs to generalize not only to unseen instances but also to *unseen distributions*. In other words, this setting involves test data that has a related yet different distribution than the data the model was trained on.

The stream classification problem under emerging novel classes has been studied by both machine learning and data mining communities. The area is referred to under various names including open-world classification [13,14], life-long learning [1], and continual learning [12]. In principle, these build a "never-ending learner" that can (1) assign those recurring instances from known old classes to their respective class, (2) recognize emerging classes, and (3) grow/extend the current learner to incorporate the new class(es). The existing methods differ in terms of accuracy-efficiency trade-offs and various assumptions that they make. (See Sect. 5 for detailed related work.) A common challenge that all of them face is what is known as *catastrophic forgetting*, mainly due to model growth. In a nutshell, the issue is the challenge of maintaining performance on old classes as the model is constantly grown to accommodate the new ones.

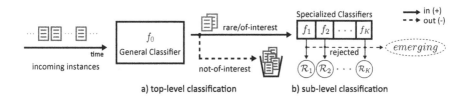

Fig. 1. An illustration of the recognition flow in our proposed model.

Our work is different from all prior work in one key aspect: our goal is not to recognize *any and every* newly emerging class—but only those (sub)classes related to the rare class *of-interest*. That is, our primary goal is to recognize rare-class instances. *Not-of-interest* instances, as long as they are filtered out accurately, are ignored—*no matter they are recurrent or novel*, as depicted in

Fig. 1. This way, we carefully avoid the aforementioned issue that current models face. Our model grows slowly, only when novel *rare* subclasses are recognized. Thanks to a moderate model size (by definition, rare subclasses are far fewer), our model is not only less prone to catastrophic forgetting but also (a) is faster at test time, and (b) requires much less memory.

We summarize the main contributions of this work as follows.

- **Problem and Formulation:** We address the problem of recognizing instances from a rare, *of-interest* class over a stream continually. The setting differs from traditional (binary) classification in that the data distribution (for both rare and majority class) might change over time, where novel subclasses emerge. We formulate a new model called RARECOGNIZE that *simultaneously* learns (*i*) a separate specialized classifier (SC) that recognizes an individual rare subclass, as well as (*ii*) a general classifier (GC) that separates rare instances from the majority. While being discriminative, GC is constructed to be dissimilar to the individual SCs such that it can generalize without overly tuning to seen rare subclasses in the training data.
- **Efficient Algorithm:** Our proposed solution exhibits two key properties: runtime and memory efficiency; both essential for the stream setting. Given a new instance that GC labels as belonging to the majority class, we simply do nothing—no matter it is recurrent or emerging. By not processing the majority of the incoming instances, we achieve *fast response time*. Moreover RARECOGNIZE remains compact, i.e. *memory-efficient*, as it requires space linear in the number of *rare* subclasses which only grows slowly.
- **Applications:** Recognizing recurrent as well as novel instances that belong to a certain class *of-interest* is a broad problem that finds numerous applications, e.g. in monitoring and surveillance. For example, such instances could be production-line items with the goal to continually recognize faulty ones where novel fault types might emerge over time. They could also be public documents, such as social media posts, where the goal is to recognize public posts *of-interest* such as bullying, shaming, disasters, threat, etc.

Reproducibility: We share the source code for RARECOGNIZE and our public-domain datasets at https://github.com/hungnt55/RaRecognize.

2   Problem Setup and Preliminary Data Analysis

Problem Setup and Overview. We start by introducing the problem statement more formally with proper notation. As input, a labeled training dataset $\mathcal{D} = \mathcal{R} \cup \mathcal{N} \in \mathbb{R}^{n \times d}$ containing n d-dimensional instances is provided. The set $\mathcal{R} = \{(\mathbf{x}_1, y_1), (\mathbf{x}_2, y_2), \ldots, (\mathbf{x}_{n_0}, y_{n_0})\}$ consists of $|\mathcal{R}| = n_0$ instances belonging to the *of-interest* rare class where $y_i = +1$ for $i = 1, \ldots, n_0$ and the set $\mathcal{N} = \{(\mathbf{x}_{n_0+1}, y_{n_0+1}), \ldots, (\mathbf{x}_n, y_n)\}$ consists of $|\mathcal{N}| = (n - n_0)$ instances from the *not-of-interest* class where $y_i = -1$ for $i = (n_0 + 1), \ldots, n$. Without loss of generality, we will refer to the data instances as documents and to the rare class as the *risk* class in the rest of this section to present our ideas more concretely.

Given $\mathcal{D}$, the goal is to recognize future *risk* documents, *either recurring or newly emerging*, over a stream (or set) of new documents $\mathbf{x}_{n+1}, \mathbf{x}_{n+2}, \ldots$ (here, each document has a vector representation denoted by $\mathbf{x}$ such as bag-of-words, embedding, etc.). The new documents may associate with recurring risk, i.e., belong to known/seen risk subclasses $1, \ldots, K$ in $\mathcal{R}$. They may also be emerging, i.e., from previously unknown/unseen new risk subclasses $(K + 1), (K + 2), \ldots$; which differentiates our setup from the traditional classification problem.

Therefore, we start by decomposing $\mathcal{R}$ into known risk subclasses, $\mathcal{R} = \bigcup_{k=1}^{K} \mathcal{R}_k$, where $\mathcal{R}_k$ contains the documents that belong to the kth risk subclass. Given $\{\{\mathcal{R}_1, \ldots, \mathcal{R}_K\}, \mathcal{N}\}$ our approach involves simultaneously training the following two types of classifiers:

1. A *general* classifier (GC) f_0 to separate $\mathcal{R}$ and $\mathcal{N}$ that can generalize to unseen subclasses of $\mathcal{R}$,
2. A *specialized* classifier (SC) f_k, $k = 1 \ldots K$, to separate $\mathcal{R}_k$ and $\mathcal{R} \backslash \mathcal{R}_k$.

At test time, we first employ f_0. Our goal is not to recognize every emerging novel class, but only the novel risk subclasses (in addition to recurring ones), thus our first step is to recognize risk. If f_0 labels an incoming document $\mathbf{x}$ as -1 (i.e., not-risk), we discard it. Otherwise, the incoming document is flagged as risky. For only those labeled as $+1$, we employ f_k's to further identify the type of risk. Among the f_k's that accept $\mathbf{x}$ as belonging to the kth risk subclass, we assign it to the subclass that is $\arg\max_k f_k(\mathbf{x})$. If all f_k's reject, then $\mathbf{x}$ is considered to be associated with a new type of emerging risk. (See Fig. 1.)

The Classifier Models. Our risk detector is f_0 which we learn using the entire labeled dataset $\mathcal{D}$. As such, it is trained on a few known risk subclasses in $\mathcal{R}$ but is desired to be *general* enough to recognize other types of future risk.

To achieve this generality, our main idea is to avoid building f_0 on factors that are too specific to any known risk subclass (such that f_0 is not overly fit to existing or known risk types) but rather, to identify broad factors about risk that are *common* to all risk subclasses (such that f_0 can employ this broader view to spot risk at large).

In fact, factors specific to the known risk subclasses are to be captured by the corresponding f_k's. Then, f_0 is to identify discriminative signals of risk that are sufficiently different from those used by all f_k's. Moreover, each f_k should differ from other $f_{k'}$'s, $k' \neq k$, to ensure that they are as *specialized* as possible to their respective risk types. Such dependence among the models is exactly why we train all these $(K + 1)$ classifiers *simultaneously*, to enforce the aforementioned constraints conjointly. We present our specific model formulation and optimization in Sect. 3.

Preliminary Data Analysis. Before model formulation, we perform an exploratory analysis on one of our real-world datasets containing documents labeled as risky and not-risky. The goal of the analysis is to see if our hypothesized ideas get realized in the data.

In particular, we aim to find out if there exists (1) factors that are specific to each risk subclass, as well as (2) factors beyond those specific ones that are still discriminative of risk. For simplicity and interpretability, we use the bag-of-words representation of the data in this section, thus factors correspond to individual words. However, our proposed model can handle other document vector representations in general.

To this end, we formulate a constrained optimization problem to find word sets that cover or characterize different document sets. Here, we define a word to *cover* a document if the word appears in it at least once. Given the set of unique words $\mathcal{V}$, $|\mathcal{V}| = d$, we look for a set of words $\mathcal{V}_k \subset \mathcal{V}$ that covers all the documents in $\mathcal{R}_k$ but as few as those in $\mathcal{R} \backslash \mathcal{R}_k$ for all $k = 1 \ldots K$ (i.e., specific words for each risk subclass), and another set of words $\mathcal{V}_0 \subset \mathcal{V}$ that covers all risk documents in $\mathcal{R}$ but as few as those in $\mathcal{N}$. We restrict the word sets to be *non-overlapping*, i.e., $\mathcal{V}_k \cap \mathcal{V}_{k'} = \emptyset$ $\forall k, k' \in \{0, \ldots, K\}$, such that each word can only characterize either one of $\mathcal{R}_1, \ldots, \mathcal{R}_K$ or $\mathcal{R}$ at large. Under these conditions, if we could find a set $\mathcal{V}_0$ that shares no words with any $\mathcal{V}_k$'s while still being able to cover the risky documents but only a few (if at all) not-risky ones, then we can conclude that broad risk terms exist and a *general* f_0 can be trained.

Our setup is a constrained mixed-integer linear program (MILP) as follows:

$$\min_{\Phi} \quad |\mathbf{v}_0| + \sum_{k=1}^{K} |\mathbf{v}_k| + o + \alpha + \beta$$

$$\text{s.t.} \quad \mathbf{z}_k + \mathbf{R}_k \cdot \mathbf{v}_k \geq 1 \quad \forall k = 1 \ldots K \qquad \triangleright \text{ risk subclass coverage with exoneration}$$

$$\mathbf{z}_0 + \sum_{k=1}^{K} \mathbf{R}_k \cdot \mathbf{v}_0 \geq 1 \qquad \triangleright \text{ risk coverage with exoneration}$$

$$|\mathbf{z}_0| + \sum_{k=1}^{K} |\mathbf{z}_k| \leq o \qquad \triangleright \text{ \# unexplained documents less than } o$$

$$\mathbf{v}_0 + \sum_{k=1}^{K} \mathbf{v}_k \leq 1 \qquad \triangleright \text{ each word used for at most 1 set}$$

$$\sum_{i \in \mathcal{N}} \mathbf{N}_i \cdot \mathbf{v}_0 \leq \alpha \qquad \triangleright \text{ cap on cross-coverage of not-risk}$$

$$\sum_{k=1}^{K} \sum_{i \in \mathbf{R}_k} \sum_{k' \neq k} \mathbf{R}_{k,i} \cdot \mathbf{v}_{k'} \leq \beta \qquad \triangleright \text{ cap on cross-coverage among risk subclasses}$$

The program is parameterized by $\Phi = \{\{\mathbf{v}_k\}_{k=0}^{K}, \{\mathbf{z}_k\}_{k=0}^{K}, o, \alpha, \beta\}$. $\mathbf{R}_k \in \mathbb{R}^{n_k \times d}$ denotes the data matrix encoding the word occurrences for n_k documents in risk subclass $k = 1 \ldots K$, and $\mathbf{N} \in \mathbb{R}^{(n-n_0) \times d}$ is the corresponding data matrix for the not-risk documents. $\mathbf{v}_0 \in \mathbb{R}^d$ and $\mathbf{v}_k \in \mathbb{R}^d$'s depict (binary) variables to be estimated that capture the word assignments to the sets $\mathcal{V}_0$ and $\mathcal{V}_k$'s respectively. (e.g., jth entry of $\mathbf{v}_0$ is set to 1 if word j is assigned to $\mathcal{V}_0$ and to 0 otherwise.)

Ideally all of o, α, and β are zero; that is, all documents are covered without any exoneration and no cross-coverage exists. However, that yields no feasible solution. Instead, we define them as scalar upper-bound variables added

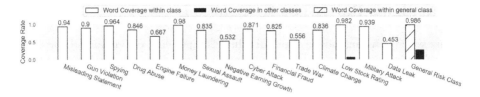

Fig. 2. Within- and cross-coverage rates of $\mathcal{V}_k$'s and $\mathcal{V}_0$ (resp.) for $\mathcal{R}_k$'s and $\mathcal{R}$.

Fig. 3. Wordclouds representing 3 example risk subclasses and the overall risk class. Notice that the former are quite specific, and the latter are broader.

to our minimization objective toward setting them to as small values as possible. Finally, our objective aims to find the smallest-size possible word sets. This ensures that the most important words are selected which also facilitates interpretability.

We provide an exploratory analysis on a dataset containing corporate risk documents as the *of-interest* class. It contains 15 risk subclasses as outlined by Fig. 2. (See Sec. 4.1 for details.) First the quantitative measures: as shown in the figure, the MILP finds word sets $\mathcal{V}_k$'s with at least 82.5% up to 98.2% coverage for 11/15 of the subclasses with an overall coverage of 96.7% (rest are the exonerated ones). Moreover, cross-coverage is either zero or very low for all the subclasses. These suggest that accurate SCs can be learned. Importantly, there exist words $\mathcal{V}_0$ that are *distinct* from all $\mathcal{V}_k$'s and yet able to cover 98.6% of the overall risk documents, promising that a broad GC can be learned.

To equip the reader with intuition, we present the selected words for 3 example risk subclasses along with the general risk class words in Fig. 3 (word size is proportional to the within vs. cross-coverage ratio). It is easy to see that very specific words are selected for subclasses; such as `password`, `cyberattack`, `malware` for Cyber attack, and `cosby`, `weinstein`, `fondle` for Sexual assault. On the other hand, in the general risk class, a set of broader corporate risk words appear such as `fraud`, `stock`, `breach` and `sentence`.

These preliminary results show promise for the feasibility of our hypothesized models and demonstrate the rationale behind our proposed RARECOGNIZE, which we formally introduce next.

3   Continual Rare-Class Recognition

In this section, we introduce the individual components of our model, present the underlying reasoning for our formulation, show convexity and present the optimization steps, and conclude with space and time-complexity analysis.

3.1   Model Formulation

As discussed in the previous section, our goal is to learn (1) specialized classifiers f_k's and (2) a general classifier f_0.

The **specialized classifier** f_k, $k = 1 \dots K$, is to learn a decision boundary that separates the kth rare subclass instances $\mathcal{R}_k$ from the remainder of rare instances $\mathcal{R} \backslash \mathcal{R}_k$. Let us write down the regularized loss function for each f_k as

$$\mathcal{L}(f_k; \mathbf{w}_k, b_k) = \sum_{i=1}^{n_0} \underbrace{\max\left(0, \left[1 - y_i(\mathbf{w}_k^T \mathbf{x}_i + b_k)\right]\right)}_{\ell(\mathbf{x}_i, y_i; \mathbf{w}_k, b_k)} + \frac{\lambda_k}{2}\|\mathbf{w}_k\|^2 \tag{1}$$

where $y_i = +1$ for $\mathbf{x}_i \in \mathcal{R}_k$ and $y_i = -1$ otherwise. We adopt the hinge loss and the ridge regularization as in Eq. (1), however, one could instead use other loss functions, such as the logistic, exponential or cross-entropy losses, as well as other norms for regularization.

The **general classifier** f_0 is to separate rare class instances $\mathcal{R}$ from the majority instances $\mathcal{N}$, without relying on factors specific to known rare subclasses. One way to achieve this *de-correlation* is to enforce f_0 to learn coefficients $\mathbf{w}_0$ that are different from all $\mathbf{w}_k$'s. The loss function can be written as

$$\mathcal{L}(f_0; \mathbf{w}_0, b_0) = \sum_{i=1}^{n} \ell(\mathbf{x}_i, y_i; \mathbf{w}_0, b_0) + \frac{\lambda_0}{2}\|\mathbf{w}_0\|^2 + \frac{\mu}{2}\sum_{k=1}^{K} \mathbf{w}_0^T \mathbf{w}_k, \tag{2}$$

where $y_i = +1$ for $\mathbf{x}_i \in \mathcal{R} = \{\mathcal{R}_1 \cup \dots \cup \mathcal{R}_K\}$ and $y_i = -1$ otherwise. As required, the third term in Eq. (2) penalizes $\mathbf{w}_0$ being correlated with any $\mathbf{w}_k$, enforcing it to be as orthogonal to $\mathbf{w}_k$'s as possible. However, it does not prevent $\mathbf{w}_0$ from capturing *different yet correlated features* to those captured by $\mathbf{w}_k$'s. This issue can arise when features exhibit multi-collinearity.

For example, in a document dataset the words `earthquake`, `shockwave`, and `aftershock` could be collinear. In this case it is possible that f_k estimates large coefficients on a strict subset of these words (e.g., `shockwave` and `aftershock`) as they are redundant. This leaves room for f_0 to capitalize on the remaining words (e.g., `earthquake`), which is undesirable since we aim f_0 to learn about the rare class boundaries beyond the specifics of the known subclasses.

Therefore, we reformulate the model correlation penalty as follows.

$$\frac{\mu}{2}\sum_{k=1}^{K}\sum_{p,q} \left(w_{0,p}w_{k,q}\,\mathbf{x}_{[p]}^T\mathbf{x}_{[q]}\right)^2 = \frac{\mu}{2}\left\|(\mathbf{X}^T\mathbf{X}) \odot (\mathbf{w}_0\mathbf{w}_k^T)\right\|_F^2, \tag{3}$$

where $w_{0,p}$ and $w_{k,q}$ denote the pth and qth entries of $\mathbf{w}_0$ and $\mathbf{w}_k$ respectively, $\mathbf{X} \in \mathbb{R}^{n \times d}$ denotes the input data matrix, $\mathbf{x}_{[p]}, \mathbf{x}_{[q]}$ respectively denote the pth and qth columns of $\mathbf{X}$, and $\odot$ depicts the element-wise multiplication.

We call Eq. (3) the cross-correlation penalty. Similarly, we introduce self-correlation penalty to each model $k = 0, \dots, K$ by adding to the respective loss the term $\sum_{p,q} \left(w_{k,p} w_{k,q} \, \mathbf{x}_{[p]}^T \mathbf{x}_{[q]} \right)^2$. Self-correlation prevents each model from estimating large coefficients on higly correlated (near-redundant) features, which improves sparsity and interpretability, and as we show also ensures convexity.

Then, the overall loss function incorporating the cross- and self-correlation penalty terms for all models $f_0, f_1, \dots, f_K$ is given as follows.

$$
\begin{aligned}
\mathcal{L} = &\sum_{i=1}^{n} \ell(\mathbf{x}_i, y_i; \mathbf{w}_0, b_0) + \frac{\lambda_0}{2} \|\mathbf{w}_0\|^2 + \sum_{k=1}^{K} \left[\sum_{i=1}^{n_0} \ell(\mathbf{x}_i, y_i; \mathbf{w}_k, b_k) + \frac{\lambda_k}{2} \|\mathbf{w}_k\|^2 \right] \\
&+ \frac{\mu}{2} \sum_{p,q} \left\{ \underbrace{\frac{1}{2}(w_{0,p}^2 w_{0,q}^2) + \frac{1}{2} \sum_{k=1}^{K} (w_{k,p}^2 w_{k,q}^2)}_{\text{self-correlation}} + \underbrace{w_{0,p}^2 (\sum_{k=1}^{K} w_{k,q}^2)}_{\text{cross-correlation}} \right\} (\mathbf{x}_{[p]}^T \mathbf{x}_{[q]})^2 \quad (4)
\end{aligned}
$$

3.2   Convexity and Optimization

We train all the models $f_0, f_1, \dots, f_K$ *simultaneously* by minimizing the total overall loss $\mathcal{L}$. A conjoint optimization is performed because the cross-correlation penalty terms between $\mathbf{w}_0$ and $\mathbf{w}_k$'s induce dependence between the models.

For optimization we employ the accelerated subgradient descent algorithm which is guaranteed to find the global optimum solution because, as we show next, our loss function $\mathcal{L}$ is convex.

Theorem 1. *The joint loss function $\mathcal{L}$ involving the cross- and self-correlation penalty terms among $\mathbf{w}_0, \mathbf{w}_1, \dots, \mathbf{w}_K$ remains convex.*

Proof. The non-negative sum of convex functions is also convex. The first line of $\mathcal{L}$ as given above is known to be convex since $\ell(\cdot)$ (hinge loss) and L-p norms for $p \geq 1$ are both convex. The proof is then by showing that the overall correlation penalty term in the second line of $\mathcal{L}$ is also convex by showing that its Hessian matrix is positive semi-definite (PSD). See extended version [10] for details. □

Since our total loss is a convex function, we can use gradient-based optimization to solve it to optimality. To this end, we provide the gradient updates for both $\mathbf{w}_0$ and $\mathbf{w}_k$'s in closed form as follows.

Partial Derivative of $\mathcal{L}$ w.r.t. $\mathbf{w}_0$:

$$
\frac{\partial \mathcal{L}}{\partial w_{0,p}} = \sum_{i=1}^{n} \frac{\partial \left[1 - y_i(\mathbf{w}_0^T \mathbf{x}_i + b_0) \right]_+}{\partial w_{0,p}} + \lambda_0 w_{0,p} + \mu w_{0,p} \sum_{q=1}^{d} \left(\sum_{k=1}^{K} w_{k,q}^2 + w_{0,q}^2 \right) \left(\mathbf{x}_{[p]}^T \mathbf{x}_{[q]} \right)^2
$$

where

$$\frac{\partial \left[1 - y_i(\mathbf{w}_0^T \mathbf{x}_i + b_0)\right]_+}{\partial w_{0,p}} = \begin{cases} 0 & \text{if } y_i(\mathbf{w}_0^T \mathbf{x}_i + b_0) \geq 1 \\ -y_i x_{i,p} & \text{otherwise.} \end{cases} \tag{5}$$

The vector-update $\frac{\partial \mathcal{L}}{\partial \mathbf{w}_0}$ can be given in matrix-vector form using the above gradients as

$$\frac{\partial \mathcal{L}}{\partial \mathbf{w}_0} = \left[\mathbf{X}^T(-\mathbf{y} \odot \mathbb{I}(1 - \mathbf{y} \odot (\mathbf{X}\mathbf{w}_0 + b_0) > 0)) + \mathbf{w}_0 \odot \left(\lambda_0 \mathbf{1} + \mu(\mathbf{X}^T \mathbf{X})^2 (\sum_k \mathbf{w}_k^2 + \mathbf{w}_0^2))\right]\right. \tag{6}$$

where $\mathbb{I}(\cdot)$ is the indicator function, $\mathbf{1}$ is a length-n all-ones vector, and $(\mathbf{A})^2 = \mathbf{A} \odot \mathbf{A}$, i.e., element-wise product, for both matrix $\mathbf{A}$ as well as for vector $\mathbf{a}$.

Partial Derivative of $\mathcal{L}$ w.r.t. $\mathbf{w}_k$: The steps for each $\mathbf{w}_k$ is similar, we directly provide the vector-update below.

$$\frac{\partial \mathcal{L}}{\partial \mathbf{w}_k} = \left[\mathbf{R}^T(-\mathbf{y}_0 \odot \mathbb{I}(1 - \mathbf{y}_0 \odot (\mathbf{R}\mathbf{w}_k + b_k) > 0)) + \mathbf{w}_k \odot \left(\lambda_k \mathbf{1} + \mu(\mathbf{X}^T \mathbf{X})^2 (\mathbf{w}_k^2 + \mathbf{w}_0^2))\right)\right] \tag{7}$$

where $\mathbf{R} \in \mathbb{R}^{n_0 \times d}$ and $\mathbf{y}_0 \in \mathbb{R}^{n_0}$ consist of only the rare-class instances.

3.3 Time and Space-Complexity Analysis

Time Complexity. The (first) gradient term in Eq. (6) that is related to the hinge-loss is $\mathcal{O}(nd)$. The (second) term related to the correlation-based regularization requires $\mathbf{X}^T \mathbf{X}$ which can be computed in $\mathcal{O}(nd^2)$ apriori and *reused* over the gradient iterations. The term $(\sum_k \mathbf{w}_k^2 + \mathbf{w}_0^2)$ takes $\mathcal{O}(Kd)$, and its following multiplication with $(\mathbf{X}^T \mathbf{X})^2$ takes an additional $\mathcal{O}(d^2)$. The remaning operations (summation with $\lambda_0 \mathbf{1}$ and element-wise product with $\mathbf{w}_0$) are only $\mathcal{O}(d)$. As such, the overall computational complexity for subgradient descent for $\mathbf{w}_0$ is $\mathcal{O}(nd^2 + t[nd + Kd + d^2])$, where t is the number of gradient iterations.

The time complexity for updating the $\mathbf{w}_k$'s can be derived similarly as Eq. (7) consists of similar terms, which can be written as $\mathcal{O}(t[n_0 d + d^2])$. Note that we omit the $\mathcal{O}(nd^2)$ this time as $\mathbf{X}^T \mathbf{X}$ needs to be computed only once and can be shared across all update rules. Moreover, the number of iterations t is the same as before since the parameter estimation is conjoint.

Space Complexity. We require $\mathcal{O}(d^2)$ storage for keeping $(\mathbf{X}^T \mathbf{X})^2$, $\mathcal{O}(Kd)$ for all the parameter vectors $\mathbf{w}_0, \ldots, \mathbf{w}_K$, and $\mathcal{O}(nd)$ for storing $\mathbf{X}$, for an overall $\mathcal{O}(d^2 + Kd + nd)$ space complexity.

Remarks on Massive and/or High-Dimensional Datasets: Note that both time and space complexity of our RARECOGNIZE is quadratic in d and linear in n. We conclude with parting remarks on cases with large d and huge n.

First, high-dimensional data with large d: In this case, we propose two possible directions to make the problem tractable. Of course, the first one is dimensionality reduction or representation learning. When the data lies on a relatively low-d manifold, one could instead use compound features. We apply our RAREC-OGNIZE to document datasets, where compound features are not only fewer but also sufficiently expressive of the data. The second direction is to get rid of feature correlations, for instance via factor analysis. This would drop the term $\left(\mathbf{x}_{[p]}^T \mathbf{x}_{[q]}\right)^2$ from $\mathcal{L}$ (See (4)) and lead to updates that are only *linear* in d.

Next, massive data with huge n: We presented our optimization using batch subgradient descent. When n is very, very large then storing the original data in memory may not be feasible. We remark that one could directly employ mini-batch or even stochastic gradient descent in such cases, dropping the space requirement to $O(d^2 + Kd)$.

4 Evaluation

We design experiments to evaluate our proposed method with respect to the following questions:

- **(RQ1) Top-level classification (via GC f_0):** How does RARECOGNIZE perform in differentiating rare-class instances from the majority compared with the state-of-the-art?
- **(RQ2) Sub-level classification (via SCs f_k's):** How does RARECOGNIZE perform in recognizing recurrent and emerging rare subclasses among the compared methods?
- **(RQ3) Interpretability:** Can we interpret RARECOGNIZE as a model as to what it has learned and what insights can we draw?
- **(RQ4) Efficiency:** What is the scalability of RARECOGNIZE? How does it compare to the baselines w.r.t. the running time-vs-performance trade-off?

4.1 Experiment Setup

Dataset Description. In this study, we use 3 different datasets with characteristics summarized in Table 1. The first two datasets are obtained from our industry collaborator (proprietary) and a third public one which we put together.

Table 1. Summary of datasets.

Name	$|\mathcal{R}|$	$|\mathcal{N}|$	K	Avg. $|\mathcal{R}_k|$
RISK-DOC	2948	2777	15	196.5
RISK-SEN	1551	7755	8	193.9
NYT-DSTR	2127	10560	13	163.6

RISK-DOC: This dataset contains online documents, e.g. news articles, social network posts, which are labeled risky or non-risky to the corporate entities mentioned. If a document is risky, it is further assigned to one of the 15 risk subclasses: {Climate change, Cyber attack, Data leak, Drug abuse, Engine failure, Fraud, Gun violation, Low stock, Military attack, Misleading statement, Money laundering, Negative growth, Sexual assault, Spying, Trade war}.

RISK-SEN: This contains labeled sentences attracted from news articles and categorized into 8 different subclasses: {Bankruptcy, Bribery corruption, Counterfeiting, Cyber privacy, Environment, Fraud false claims, Labor, Money laundering}. The majority class consists of non-risky sentences. Note that this dataset comes from a set of articles different from RISK-DOC.

NYT-DSTR: Extracted from the New York Times, this dataset is comprised of articles on the topics of disasters, i.e. both natural and human-instigated. These topics cover 13 disasters from {Drought, Earthquakes, Explosions, Floods, Forest and bush fire, Hazardous and toxic substance, Landslides, Lighting, Snowstorms, Tornado, Tropical storm, Volcanoes, Water pollution}. It also includes a class of random non-disaster news articles from New York Times.

Document Representations. In this study we apply our work to document datasets, for which we need to define a feature representation. There are numerous options. We report results with tfidf with top 1 K words based on frequency, as well as PCA- and ICA-projected data. Linear embedding techniques reduce dimensionality while preserving interpretability. We omit results using non-linear feature representations (e.g., doc2vec [6]) as they did not provide any significant performance gain despite computational overhead.

Train/Test Splits. For each dataset, we randomly partition 2/3 of rare subclasses as seen and 1/3 of them as unseen. For training, we use 80% of the seen subclass instances at random and the rest 20% forms a seen subclass test set, denoted by $\mathcal{R}_s$. The set of unseen subclass instances, denoted by $\mathcal{R}_u$, goes into the test as well. Thus, the rare subclass test consists of 2 parts, i.e. $\mathcal{R}_{test} = \mathcal{R}_s \cup \mathcal{R}_u$. In addition, we also reserve a random 80% of the majority class for training and the rest 20% for testing, denoted by $\mathcal{N}_{test}$. Further, to obtain stable results, we repeat our experiment on 5 different random train/test constructions and report averaged outcomes.

Performance Metrics. (1) For measuring top-level classification performance, we use 3 common metrics [8,16]: *Precision, Recall, F1* formally defined in our context as:

$$Precision = \frac{|\mathcal{R}_{test} \cap \hat{\mathcal{R}}_{test}|}{|\hat{\mathcal{R}}_{test}|}, Recall = \frac{|\mathcal{R}_{test} \cap \hat{\mathcal{R}}_{test}|}{|\mathcal{R}_{test}|}, F1 = \frac{2 * Precision * Recall}{Precision + Recall},$$

where $\hat{\mathcal{R}}_{test}$ is the set of examples predicted as rare subclass. To identify which part of the test (seen or unseen subclasses) the model makes mistakes, we also measure *Precision (seen), Recall (seen)* and *Recall (unseen)* defined as follows:

$$Precision(seen) = \frac{|\mathcal{R}_s \cap \hat{\mathcal{R}}_{test}|}{|\hat{\mathcal{R}}_{test}|}, Recall(seen) = \frac{|\mathcal{R}_s \cap \hat{\mathcal{R}}_{test}|}{|\mathcal{R}_s|}, Recall(unseen) = \frac{|\mathcal{R}_u \cap \hat{\mathcal{R}}_{test}|}{|\mathcal{R}_u|}.$$

(2) For sub-level classification test, to quantify the fraction of seen subclass test instances correctly classified and unseen subclass test instances as emerging, we use the following metric:

$$acc(rare) = \frac{\overbrace{|\mathcal{R}_u \cap \hat{\mathcal{R}}_u|}^{acc(emerging)} + \overbrace{\sum_{k=1}^{K} |\mathcal{R}_{ks} \cap \hat{\mathcal{R}}_{ks}|}^{acc(recurrent)}}{|\mathcal{R}_{test}|},$$

where $\mathcal{R}_{ks}$ is the set of test examples in subclass k and $\hat{\mathcal{R}}_{ks}$ is the set of examples assigned to that subclass. Here *acc(rare)* = 1 if both seen subclass test instances are perfectly classified to their respective subclasses and unseen subclass instances as emerging. For all of the above metrics, the higher is better.

Compared Methods. We compare RARECOGNIZE with 2 state-of-the-art methods and 2 simple baselines:

- RARECOGNIZE-1K, RARECOGNIZE-PCA, RARECOGNIZE-ICA: 3 versions of RARECOGNIZE when tfidf with 1K word dictionary, PCA and ICA representations are used. In RARECOGNIZE-PCA, we drop the feature correlation terms $\left(\mathbf{x}_{[p]}^T \mathbf{x}_{[q]}\right)^2$ since features are orthogonal. For the sub-level classification, RARECOGNIZE learns a rejection threshold for each specialized classifier based on extreme value theory [15].
- L2AC [16]: the most recent method (2019) in open-world classification setting that is based on deep neural networks. We use the recommended parameters $k = 5, n = 9$ (in their notation) from the paper.
- SENCFOREST [8]: another state-of-the-art ensemble method (2017) using random decision trees for classification under emerging classes. We run SENCFOREST with 100 trees and subsample size 100 as suggested in their paper.
- BASELINE: a baseline of RARECOGNIZE when both cross- and self-correlation terms in Eq. 4 are removed, via setting $\mu = 0$. Basically, BASELINE is independently trained $f_0, \ldots, f_K$.
- BASELINE-r: a variant of BASELINE when classification threshold (0.5 by default) is chosen so that the *Recall* matches that of RARECOGNIZE.

Note that SENCFOREST and L2AC aim to detect *any* emerging class without categorizing into rare or majority. For fair comparison, we only inlcude new *rare* subclasses in our test data and consider their rejected instances as belonging to those. In reality, however, emerging classes need to be categorized as rare or not, which these existing methods did not address.

Table 2. Performance of methods on the three datasets.

Methods	Precision			Recall			F1		
	RISK-DOC	RISK-SEN	NYT-DSTR	RISK-DOC	RISK-SEN	NYT-DSTR	RISK-DOC	RISK-SEN	NYT-DSTR
SENCFOREST	0.46±0.12	0.14±0.03	0.36±0.09	0.59±0.09	0.41±0.08	0.39±0.10	0.52±0.11	0.21±0.04	0.37±0.06
L2AC	0.79±0.08	0.47±0.06	0.31±0.07	0.57±0.29	0.85±0.05	0.76±0.07	0.63±0.24	0.60±0.04	0.44±0.07
BASELINE	0.89±0.04	0.79±0.05	0.86±0.03	0.52±0.06	0.55±0.04	0.63±0.03	0.65±0.05	0.65±0.03	0.73±0.03
BASELINE-r	0.76±0.10	0.56±0.07	0.71±0.07	0.58±0.13	0.57±0.14	0.79±0.04	0.65±0.10	0.55±0.06	0.75±0.04
RARECOGNIZE-1K	0.89±0.02	0.83±0.09	0.84±0.03	0.58±0.13	0.57±0.14	0.79±0.04	0.70±0.09	0.66±0.08	**0.81±0.02**
RARECOGNIZE-PCA	0.85±0.06	0.79±0.10	0.84±0.10	0.58±0.17	0.71±0.17	0.80±0.07	0.68±0.14	0.73±0.09	**0.81±0.01**
RARECOGNIZE-ICA	0.74±0.07	0.72±0.11	0.84±0.12	0.73±0.24	0.85±0.18	0.82±0.08	**0.71±0.09**	**0.78±0.07**	**0.81±0.04**

4.2 Experiment Results

In the following, we sequentially answer the questions by analyzing our experimental results and comparing between methods.

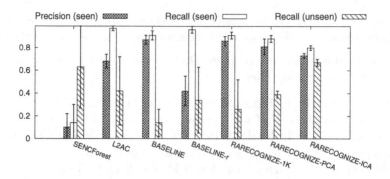

Fig. 4. *Precision (seen)*, *Recall (seen)* and *Recall (unseen)* of methods on RISK-DOC (RARECOGNIZE-ICA achieves the best balance between *Precision* and *Recall* on both seen and unseen test instances).

(RQ1) Top-level Classification into Rare vs. Majority Class. We report the *Precision*, *Recall* and *F1* of all methods on three datasets in Table 2. For SENCFOREST, L2AC, BASELINE and BASELINE-r, we report results for the representation (tfidf top-1K, PCA, ICA) that yielded the highest *F1* value.

From Table 2, we see that RARECOGNIZE-1K, RARECOGNIZE-PCA and RARECOGNIZE-ICA outperform other methods in terms of *F1* score in all cases and *Precision*, *Recall* in most cases. Compared to BASELINE and BASELINE-r, *F1* score of RARECOGNIZE-ICA is 6–13% higher than the best result among the two. This demonstrates that cross- and self-correlations are crucial in RARECOGNIZE. Surprisingly, the gap to SENCFOREST and L2AC is even larger in terms of *F1*, between 8–37% higher. This shows that previous methods on detecting any new emerging classes do not work well when we only target rare subclasses.

Among the three versions of RARECOGNIZE, RARECOGNIZE-ICA gives the highest *F1*. RARECOGNIZE-ICA achieves the best balance between precision and recall while RARECOGNIZE-1K and RARECOGNIZE-PCA seem to have very high *Precision* but much lower *Recall*. That means that RARECOGNIZE-1K and RARECOGNIZE-PCA are better than RARECOGNIZE-ICA at discarding majority samples and worse at recognizing rare subclasses.

In Fig. 4, we have the *Precision (seen)*, *Recall (seen)* and *Recall (unseen)* measures of all the methods on RISK-DOC (Figures for other datasets are similar, see [10]). This figure shows that RARECOGNIZE-ICA also achieves a good balance between seen and unseen subclass classification, i.e., it recognizes both these subclasses equally well. On the other hand, most of other methods achieve high *Precision (seen)* and *Recall (seen)* but much lower *Recall (unseen)*, except SENCFOREST which only has high *Recall (unseen)*. This is because SENCFOREST rejects most instances as unseen which however hurts *Precision* drastically.

(RQ2) Sub-level Classification into Recurrent and Emerging Rare Subclasses. We report the *acc(rare)* of all the methods in Table 3 (Breakdown of errors in confusion tables are given in the extended version of this article [10]).

Table 3. *acc(rare)* of methods on the three datasets.

Methods	RISK-DOC	RISK-SEN	NYT-DSTR
SENCFOREST	0.37 ± 0.09	0.41 ± 0.08	0.34 ± 0.04
L2AC	0.22 ± 0.17	0.20 ± 0.20	0.08 ± 0.12
BASELINE	0.41 ± 0.07	0.37 ± 0.04	0.41 ± 0.04
BASELINE-r	0.43 ± 0.16	0.38 ± 0.03	0.42 ± 0.04
RARECOGNIZE-1K	0.45 ± 0.08	0.38 ± 0.12	0.46 ± 0.12
RARECOGNIZE-PCA	0.50 ± 0.14	0.59 ± 0.14	0.65 ± 0.15
RARECOGNIZE-ICA	$\mathbf{0.63 \pm 0.14}$	$\mathbf{0.62 \pm 0.09}$	$\mathbf{0.64 \pm 0.15}$

Tables 2 and 3 reflect that all three versions of RARECOGNIZE are always better or comparable to the others in terms of *acc(rare)* and RARECOGNIZE-ICA achieves the highest value. RARECOGNIZE-ICA achieves significantly higher *acc(rare)* than all the baselines. SENCFOREST seems to perform the next best due to the fact that it classifies most of the instances as emerging which results in high classification performance on unseen subclasses.

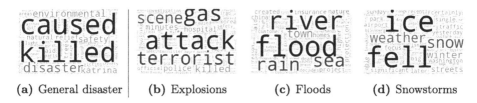

(a) General disaster   (b) Explosions   (c) Floods   (d) Snowstorms

Fig. 5. Word clouds for the weights of general and 3 specialized classifiers in RARECOGNIZE-1K on NYT-DSTR (See [10] for other subclasses).

(RQ3) Model Interpretation. In Fig. 5, we plot the wordclouds representing the general and 3 specialized classifiers for 3 disaster subclasses (sizes of the words proportional to their weights learned by RARECOGNIZE-1K). Existing methods, SENCFOREST and L2AC, are not interpretable due to respective ensemble and deep neural network-based models they employ.

From Fig. 5, specialized disaster classifiers are clearly characterized by specific words closely related to the respective disasters, whereas the general classifier is heavily weighted by common words to every disaster. Specifically, Explosions classifier picks up `attack, gas, terrorist, scene` as most weighted keywords, and Snowstorms classifier puts heavy weights on words `ice, fell, snow, weather`. The general classifier is highlighted by the words `caused, killed, disaster` which describe consequences of most disasters. Wordclouds on other disaster subclasses, along with those for other datasets can be found in [10].

Thanks to the interpretability that RARECOGNIZE offers, we can look deeper into the significance of individual words in classifying documents. Besides its promising quantitative performance, these qualitative results confirm that our method has learned what agrees with human intuition.

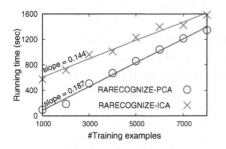
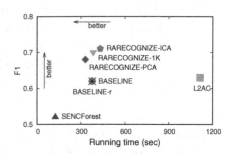

Fig. 6. RARECOGNIZE scales linearly in number of training examples.

Fig. 7. Time-Performance trade-off of all compared methods.

(RQ4) Scalability and Time-Performance Trade-off. Besides our formal complexity analysis, we demonstrate the scalability of RARECOGNIZE empirically. Figure 6 shows the running time of RARECOGNIZE-PCA and RARECOGNIZE-ICA when varying the amount of training data. The running time increases linearly with the data size. RARECOGNIZE with PCA is faster than that with ICA thanks to no feature correlations (i.e. $\left(\mathbf{x}_{[p]}^{T}\mathbf{x}_{[q]}\right)^{2}$ dropped).

In Fig. 7, we show the time-performance trade-off among all compared methods. We conclude that RARECOGNIZE with three representations run relatively fast, only slower than SENCFOREST, and returns the highest performance in terms of *F1*. L2AC consumes a huge amount of time for training a neural network, with subpar performance.

5   Related Work

Our work is closely related with two fields, namely open-world classification and continual learning. Both belong to the category of lifelong machine learning [1].

Open-World Classification. Traditional close-world classification assumes that all test classes are known and seen in training data [4,17]. However, such assumption could be violated in reality. Open-world classification, in contrast, assumes unseen and novel classes could emerge during test time, and addresses the classification problem by recognizing unseen classes. Previous works [8,9,13,14,16] propose different approaches under this setting.

Specifically, DOC [13] leverages convolutional neural nets (CNNs) with multiple sigmoid functions to classify examples as seen or emerging. [14] follows the same DOC module and performs hierarchical clustering to all rejected samples.

Later, L2AC [16] proposes to use a meta-classifier and a ranker to add or delete a class without re-training. However, it requires a large amount of computation in both training and testing due to the top-k search over all training data.

SENCForest [8] is a randomized ensemble method. It grows multiple random forests and rejects examples when all random forests yield "new class". Under the same setting, SENC-MaS [9] maintains matrix sketchings to decide whether an example belongs to a seen class or emerging.

In the emerging rare subclass setting, the previous approaches aim at recognizing *any and every* classes and are not able to ignore the *not-of-interest* classes while recognizing emerging ones, thus consume much more memory and time.

Continual Learning. There are recent works investigating continual learning or incremental learning [11,12]. They aim at solving the issue of catastrophic forgetting [2] in connectionist networks. In this field, models are proposed to continually learn new classes without losing performance on old seen classes.

Previous works [3,5,7,11] show promising results. However, the number of documents in rare subclasses *of-interest* in our setting is usually not large enough for neural networks to be sufficiently trained. Consequently, the neural network approach does not perform well in rare-class classification and recognition.

6 Conclusion

We proposed RARECOGNIZE for rare-class recognition over a continuous stream, in which new subclasses may emerge. RARECOGNIZE employs a general classifier to filter out not-rare class instances (top-level) and a set of specialized classifiers that recognize known rare subclasses or otherwise reject as emerging (sub-level). Since majority of incoming instances are filtered out and new rare subclasses are a few, RARECOGNIZE processes incoming data fast and grows in size slowly. Extensive experiments show that it outperforms two most recent state of the art as well as two simple baselines significantly in both top- and sub-level tasks, while achieving the best efficiency-performance balance and offering interpretability. Future work will extend RARECOGNIZE to an end-to-end system that clusters emerging instances and trains all the relevant models incrementally.

Acknowledgments. This research is sponsored by NSF CAREER 1452425 and IIS1408287. In addition, the researchers gratefully acknowledge the support of the Risk and Regulatory Services Innovation Center at Carnegie Mellon University sponsored by PwC. Conclusions in this material are those of the authors and do not necessarily reflect the views, expressed or implied, of the funding parties.

References

1. Chen, Z., Liu, B.: Lifelong machine learning. Synth. Lect. Artif. Intell. Mach. Learn. **10**(3), 1–145 (2016)
2. French, R.: Catastrophic forgetting in connectionist networks. Trends Cogn. Sci. **3**, 128–135 (1999)

3. Kemker, R., Kanan, C.: Fearnet: brain-inspired model for incremental learning. In ICLR (2018)
4. Kim, Y.: Convolutional neural networks for sentence classification. In: EMNLP (2014)
5. Kirkpatrick, J., et al.: Overcoming catastrophic forgetting in neural networks. PNAS **114**(13), 3521–3526 (2017)
6. Le, Q.V., Mikolov, T.: Distributed representations of sentences and documents. ICML **14**, 1188–1196 (2014)
7. Lee, S.-W., Kim, J.-H., Jun, J., Ha, J.-W., Zhang, B.-T.: Overcoming catastrophic forgetting by incremental moment matching. In NeurIPS, pp. 4652–4662 (2017)
8. Mu, X., Ting, K.M., Zhou, Z.-H.: Classification under streaming emerging new classes: a solution using completely-random trees. IEEE TKDE **29**(8), 1605–1618 (2017)
9. Mu, X., Zhu, F., Du, J., Lim, E.-P., Zhou, Z.-H.: Streaming classification with emerging new class by class matrix sketching. In: AAAI (2017)
10. Nguyen, H., Wang, X., Akoglu, L.: Continual rare-class recognition with emerging novel subclasses. arXiv preprint (2019)
11. Rebuffi, S.-A., Kolesnikov, A., Sperl, G., Lampert, C.H.: ICARL: Incremental classifier and representation learning. In: CVPR, pp. 2001–2010 (2017)
12. Shin, H., Lee, J.K., Kim, J., Kim, J.: Continual learning with deep generative replay. In: NeurIPS, pp. 2990–2999 (2017)
13. Shu, L., Xu, H., Liu, B.: Doc: deep open classification of text documents. In: EMNLP (2017)
14. Shu, L., Xu, H., Liu, B.: Unseen class discovery in open-world classification. arXiv preprint arXiv:1801.05609 (2018)
15. Siffer, A., Fouque, P.-A., Termier, A., Largouet, C.: Anomaly detection in streams with extreme value theory. In: KDD, pp. 1067–1075. ACM (2017)
16. Xu, H., Liu, B., Shu, L., Yu, P.: Open-world learning and application to product classification. In: WWW (2019)
17. Zhang, X., Zhao, J., LeCun, Y.: Character-level convolutional networks for text classification. In: NeurIPS, pp. 649–657 (2015)

Unjustified Classification Regions and Counterfactual Explanations in Machine Learning

Thibault Laugel[1(✉)], Marie-Jeanne Lesot[1], Christophe Marsala[1], Xavier Renard[2], and Marcin Detyniecki[1,2,3]

[1] Sorbonne Université, CNRS, LIP6, 75005 Paris, France
thibault.laugel@lip6.fr
[2] AXA, Paris, France
[3] Polish Academy of Science, IBS PAN, Warsaw, Poland

Abstract. Post-hoc interpretability approaches, although powerful tools to generate explanations for predictions made by a trained black-box model, have been shown to be vulnerable to issues caused by lack of robustness of the classifier. In particular, this paper focuses on the notion of explanation justification, defined as connectedness to ground-truth data, in the context of counterfactuals. In this work, we explore the extent of the risk of generating unjustified explanations. We propose an empirical study to assess the vulnerability of classifiers and show that the chosen learning algorithm heavily impacts the vulnerability of the model. Additionally, we show that state-of-the-art post-hoc counterfactual approaches can minimize the impact of this risk by generating less local explanations (Source code available at: https://github.com/thibaultlaugel/truce).

Keywords: Machine learning interpretability · Counterfactual explanations

1 Introduction

The soaring number of machine learning applications has been fueling the need for reliant interpretability tools to explain the predictions of models without sacrificing their predictive accuracy. Among these, post-hoc interpretability approaches [12] are popular as they can be used for any classifier regardless of its training data (i.e. *blackbox* assumption). However, this has also been a common criticism for such approaches, as it also implies that there is no guarantee that the built explanations are faithful to ground-truth data.

A specific type of interpretability approach generate counterfactual explanations (e.g. [11,25,28,30]), inspired from counterfactual reasoning (e.g. [5]) which aims at answering the question: *What will be the consequence of performing this action?* Adapted to the context of machine learning classification, counterfactual

© Springer Nature Switzerland AG 2020
U. Brefeld et al. (Eds.): ECML PKDD 2019, LNAI 11907, pp. 37–54, 2020.
https://doi.org/10.1007/978-3-030-46147-8_3

explanations try to identify how altering an input observation can influence its prediction, and in particular change its predicted class. These approaches have been recently under the spotlight as they provide a user with directly actionable explanations that can be easily understood [30].

However, used in a post-hoc context, counterfactual explanation approaches are vulnerable to aforementioned issues, leading to explanations that may not be linked to any ground-truth data and therefore not satisfying in the context of interpretability. In particular, [21] argues that an important criterion for interpretability is that counterfactual explanations should be *justified*, meaning continuously connected to ground-truth instances from the same class. However, they show that this connectedness criterion is not guaranteed in the post-hoc context, leading to unconnected classification regions and hence potential issues interpretability-wise. This paper is an extension of this previous work, proposing to further study the apparition of these unconnected regions and analyze how existing counterfactual approaches can avoid generating unjustified explanations.

This paper proposes the following contributions:

- We pursue the analysis of [21] about the unconnectedness of classification regions and analyze the vulnerability of various classifiers. We show that classifiers are not equally vulnerable.
- We study the link between unconnectedness and overfitting and show that controlling overfitting helps reducing unconnectedness.
- We show that state-of-the-art post-hoc counterfactual approaches may generate justified explanations but at the expense of counterfactual proximity.

Section 2 is devoted to presenting the state-of-the-art of post-hoc interpretability and counterfactual explanations, as well as highlighting studies that are similar to this work. Section 3 recalls the motivations and definition and for ground-truth backed counterfactual explanations, while Sect. 4 describes the algorithms used for this analysis. The study itself, as well as the obtained results, are presented in Sect. 5.

2   Background

2.1   Post-hoc Interpretability

In order to build explanations for predictions made by a trained black-box model, post-hoc interpretability approaches generally rely on sampling instances and labelling them with the model to gather information about its behavior, either locally around a prediction [26] or globally [6]. These instances are then used to approximate the decision function of the black-box and build understandable explanations, using for instance a surrogate model (e.g. a linear model in [26] or a decision tree in [13]), or by computing meaningful coefficients (e.g. Shapeley values [24] or decision rules [29]). Other methods rely on specific instances to build explanations using comparison to relevant neighbors, such as case-based reasoning approaches [17] and counterfactual explanation approaches.

Instead of simply identifying important features, the latter aim at finding the minimal perturbation required to alter a given prediction. A counterfactual explanation is thus a specific data instance, close to the observation whose prediction is being explained, but predicted to belong to a different class. This form of explanation provides a user with tangible explanations that are directly understandable and actionable; this can be opposed to other types of explanations using feature importance vectors, which are arguably harder to use and to understand for a non-expert user [30]. Several formalizations of the counterfactual problem can be found in the literature, depending on the formulation of the minimization problem and on the used distance metric. For instance, [20] looks uniformly for the L_2-closest instance of an other class, while [11] uses a local decision tree trained on instances sampled with a genetic algorithm to find the local L_0-closest instance. Another formulation of the counterfactual problem can be found in [19], which uses search algorithms to find the instance that has the highest probability of belonging to another class within a certain maximum distance. Finally, the problem in [30], formulated as a tradeoff between the L_1 closest instance and a specific classification score target, is another way to tackle the counterfactual problem.

2.2 Studies of Post-hoc Interpretability Approaches

The post-hoc paradigm, and in particular the need for post-hoc approaches to use instances that were not used to train the model to build their explanations, raises questions about their relevance and usefulness. Troublesome issues have been identified: for instance, it has been noticed [2] that modeling the decision function of a black-box classifier with a surrogate model trained on generated instances can result in explanation vectors that point in the wrong directions in some areas of the feature space in trivial problems. The stability of post-hoc explainer systems has been criticized as well, showing that because of this sampling, some approaches are locally not stable enough [1] or on the contrary too stable and thus not locally accurate enough [22].

Recently, a few works [23,27] have started questioning the post-hoc paradigm itself and criticizing the risk of generating explanations that are disconnected from the ground truth, which is the main topic of this work. Identifying relevant ground-truth instances for a specific prediction has also been studied before (e.g. [16]), but generally require retraining the classifier, which is not possible in the context of a black-box. In a similar fashion, [15] try to identify which predictions can be trusted in regard to ground-truth instances based on their distance to training data in the context of new predictions.

2.3 Adversarial Examples

Although not sharing the same purpose, both counterfactual explanations and adversarial examples [3] are similar in the way they are generated, i.e. by trying to perturb an instance to alter its prediction. Studies in the context of image classification using deep neural networks [9] have shown that the connectedness

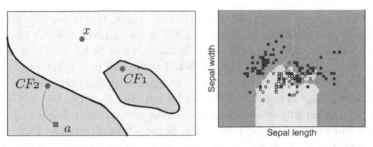

(a) Illustration of the idea behind con- (b) Decision boundary of a RF
nectedness   classifier

Fig. 1. Left picture: illustration of the connectedness notion. The decision boundary learned by a classifier (illustrated by the yellow and green regions) has created two green regions. $CF1$ and $CF2$ are two candidate counterfactual explanations for x. $CF1$ can be connected to the training instance a by a continuous path that do not cross the decision boundary of f, while $CF1$ can not. Right picture: a random forest classifier with 200 trees has been trained on 80% of the dataset (a 2D version of the iris dataset) with 0.79 ± 0.01 accuracy over the test set. Because of its low robustness, unconnected classification regions can be observed (e.g. small red square in the light blue region). (Color figure online)

notion studied in this paper was not enough for adversarial examples detection. However, since adversarial examples have been generally studied in the context of high-dimensional unstructured data, (i.e. images, text and sound for instance), as shown exhaustively in existing surveys (e.g. [4]), they remain out of the scope of this study.

The goal of this work is to study a desideratum for counterfactual explanations in the context of interpretability in structured data; it is not to detect a classification error nor an adversarial example.

3   Justification Using Ground-Truth Data

This section recalls the definitions and intuitions behind the notion of *justification*, which is the main topic of this work.

3.1   Intuition and Definitions

The notion of ground-truth justification proposed in [21] aims at making a distinction between an explanation that has been generated because of some previous knowledge (such as training data) and one that would be a consequence of an artifact of the classifier. While generalization is a desirable property for a classifier for prediction, it is different in the context of interpretability, since an explanation that a user can not understand is useless.

For this purpose, an intuitive desideratum for counterfactual explanations can be formulated based on the distance between the explanation and ground-truth observations, defining a plausibility notion that is similar to the trust score proposed in [15]): to guarantee useful (plausible) explanations, a counterfactual example could be thus required to be close to existing instances from the same class. Detecting whether an explanation satisfies this criterion thus becomes similar to an outlier detection problem, where the goal is to have counterfactual explanations that do not lie out of the distribution of ground-truth instances.

However, discriminating counterfactual explanations based on their distance to ground-truth data does not seem to be good enough, as issues created by classification artifacts can arise in dense training regions as well. Such artifacts can be caused by a lack of robustness of the classifier (e.g. overfitting), or simply because it is forced to make a prediction in an area he does not have much information about. These issues may lead to classification regions that are close to but not supported by any ground-truth data, which is problematic in the context of interpretability.

In this context, a requirement for counterfactual explanations is proposed, where the relation expected between an explanation and ground-truth data is defined using the topological notion of path connectedness. In order to be more easily understood and employed by a user, it is argued that the counterfactual instance should be continuously connected to an observation from the training dataset. The idea of this *justification* is not to identify the instances from the training data that are *responsible* for the prediction of the counterfactual (such as in the aforementioned work of [16]), but the ones that are correctly being predicted to belong to the same class for similar reasons.

The following definition is thus introduced:

Definition 1 (Justification [21]). *Given a classifier $f : \mathcal{X} \to \mathcal{Y}$ trained on a dataset X, a counterfactual example $e \in \mathcal{X}$ is* justified *by an instance $a \in X$ correctly predicted if $f(e) = f(a)$ and if there exists a continuous path h between e and a such that no decision boundary of f is met.*

Formally, e is justified by $a \in X$ if: $\exists h : [0,1] \to \mathcal{X}$ such that: (i) h is continuous, (ii) $h(0) = a$, (iii) $h(1) = e$ and (iv) $\forall t \in [0,1], f(h(t)) = f(e)$.

This notion can be adapted to datasets by approximating the function h with a high-density path, defining ϵ-*chainability*, with $\epsilon \in \mathbb{R}^+$: an ϵ-*chain* between e and a is a finite sequence $e_0, e_1, \ldots e_N \in \mathcal{X}$ such that $e_0 = e$, $e_N = a$ and $\forall i < N, d(e_i, e_{i+1}) < \epsilon$, with d a distance metric.

Definition 2 (ϵ-justification [21]). *Given a classifier $f : \mathcal{X} \to \mathcal{Y}$ trained on a dataset X, a counterfactual example $e \in \mathcal{X}$ is ϵ-justified by an instance $a \in X$ accurately predicted if $f(e) = f(a)$ and if there exists an ϵ-chain $\{e_i\}_{i \leq N} \in \mathcal{X}^N$ between e and a such that $\forall i \leq N, f(e_i) = f(e)$.*

Consequently, a justified (resp. unjustified) counterfactual explanation (written JCF, resp. UCF) is a counterfactual example that does (resp. does not) satisfy Definition 2. Setting the value of ϵ, ideally as small as possible to guarantee a good approximation by the ϵ-chain of function h of Definition 1, depends on the considered problem (dataset and classifier) and can heavily influence the obtained results. A discussion about this problem is proposed in Sect. 5.

Since connectedness in unordered categorical data can not be properly defined, the notion of justification can not be directly applied to these domains. Hence, we restrict the analysis of this paper to numerical data.

Figure 1 illustrates both the idea behind the notion of connectedness and the issue it tries to tackle. The left picture illustrates an instance x whose prediction by a binary classifier is to be interpreted, as well as two potential counterfactual explanations, $CF1$ and $CF2$. $CF2$ can be connected to a ground-truth instance a without crossing the decision boundary of f and is therefore justified. On the contrary, $CF1$ is not since it lies in a classification region that does not contain any ground-truth instance from the same class (green "pocket"). In the right picture, a classifier with low robustness creates classification regions that can not be connected to any instance from the training data.

3.2   Implementation

For an efficiency purpose, it is possible to draw a link between connectedness and density-based clustering. In particular, the well-known DBSCAN [8] approach uses the distance between observations to evaluate and detect variations in the density of the data. Two parameters ϵ and $minPts$ control the resulting clusters (resp. outliers), built from the core points, which are instances that have at least (resp. less than) $minPts$ neighbors in an ϵ-ball. Thus, having an instance being ϵ-justified by another is equivalent to having them both belong to the same DBSCAN cluster when setting the parameters $minPts = 2$ and same ϵ.

4   Procedures for Assessing the Risk of Unconnectedness

In this section, the two algorithms proposed by [21] and used in the experiments and discussion are described: LRA (*Local Risk Assessment*) is a diagnostic tool assessing the presence of unjustified regions in the neighborhood of an instance whose prediction is to be interpreted; VE (*Vulnerability Evaluation*) assesses whether or not a given counterfactual explanation is connected to ground-truth data.

4.1   LRA Procedure

This section recalls the *LRA* procedure, used to detect unjustified classification regions. Given a black-box classifier $f : \mathcal{X} \rightarrow \mathcal{Y}$ trained on the dataset X of instances of $\mathcal{X}$ and an instance $x \in \mathcal{X}$ whose prediction $f(x)$ is to be explained, the aim is to assess the risk of generating unjustified counterfactual examples in a local neighborhood of x. To do this, a generative approach is proposed that aims at finding which regions of this neighborhood are ϵ-connected to instances of X (i.e. verify Definition 2). The three main steps of the LRA procedure, described below, are written down in Algorithm 1.

Definition Step. A local neighborhood of the instance x being examined is defined as the ball of center x and radius the distance between x and the closest ground-truth instance a_0 correctly predicted to belong to another class.

Initial Assessment Step. A high number n of instances are generated in the defined area and labelled using f. The instances predicted to belong to the class $f(a_0)$, as well as a_0, are clustered using DBSCAN (with parameters $minPts = 2$ and ϵ). The instances belonging to the same cluster as a_0 are identified as JCF.

Iteration Step. If some instances do not belong to the same cluster as a_0, new instances are generated in the spherical layer between a_0 and a_1, the second closest ground-truth instance correctly predicted to belong to the same class. Along with the previously generated instances, a_0 and a_1, the subset of the new instances that are predicted to belong to the same class as a_0 and a_1 are clustered. Again, new JCF can be identified. If a cluster detected at a previous step remains the same (i.e. does not increase in size), it means that the procedure has detected an enclosed unconnected region (pocket) and the cluster is therefore labelled as UCF. This step is repeated when all instances of the initial assessment step are identified either as JCF or UCF.

In the end, the LRA procedure returns n_J (resp. n_U) the number of JCF (resp. UCF) originally generated in the local neighborhood defined in the Definition Step. If $n_U > 0$, there exists a risk of generating unjustified counterfactual examples in the studied area.

In particular, the following criteria are calculated:

$$S_x = \mathbb{1}_{n_U > 0} \quad \text{and} \quad R_x = \frac{n_U}{n_U + n_J}.$$

S_x labels the studied instance x as being vulnerable to the risk of having UCF in the area (i.e. having a non-null risk). The risk itself, measured by R_x, describes the likelihood of having an unjustified counterfactual example in the studied area when looking for counterfactual examples. As these scores are calculated for a specific instance x with a random generation component, their average values $\bar{S}$ and $\bar{R}$ for 10 runs of the procedure for each x and over multiple instances are calulated.

4.2 VE Procedure

A variation of the LRA procedure, *Vulnerability Evaluation* (VE), is proposed to analyze how troublesome unjustified regions are for counterfactual approaches.

The goal of the VE procedure is to assess the risk for state-of-the-art methods to generate UCF in regions where there is a risk. Given an instance $x \in X$, the LRA procedure is first used to calculate the risk R_x and focus on the instances where this risk is "significant" (i.e. for instance where $R_x > 0.25$). Using a state-of-the-art method, a counterfactual explanation $E(x) \in \mathcal{X}$ is then generated. To check whether $E(x)$ is justified or not, a similar procedure as LRA is used: instances are generated uniformly in the local hyperball with center $E(x)$ and

---

Algorithm 1: LRA [21]

Require: x, f, X

1: Generate n instances in the ball $\mathcal{B}(x, d(x, a_0))$
2: Label these instances using f, keep the subset D of instances classified similarly as a_0
3: Perform DBSCAN over $D \cup \{a_0\}$
4: Identify the instances of D that belong to the same cluster as a_0 as JCF. Calculate current n_J
5: **while** Some instances are neither JCF nor UCF **do**
6:     Generate new instances in the spherical layer defined by the next closest ground-truth instance
7:     Label these instances using f
8:     Apply DBSCAN to the subset of these instances classified as $f(a_0)$, along with previously generated instances and relevant ground-truth instances
9:     Update n_J and n_U
10: **end while**
11: **return** n_J, n_U ;

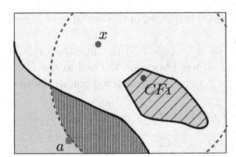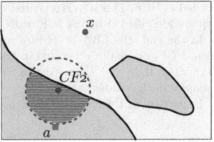

Fig. 2. Illustration of the VE procedure for two counterfactual explanation candidates. Left: CF1, which is not justified. Right: CF2, justified (Color figure online)

radius the distance between $E(x)$ and the closest ground-truth instance b_0 correctly predicted to belong to the same class as $E(x)$. The DBSCAN algorithm is then used with parameters $minPts = 2$ and same ϵ on the generated instances that are predicted to belong to $f(E(x))$. $E(x)$ is identified as a JCF if it belongs to the same DBCSCAN cluster as b_0 (cf. Definition 2).

If not, like with LRA, iteration steps are performed as many times as necessary by expanding the exploration area to b_1, the second closest ground-truth instance predicted to belong to $f(E(x))$.

An illustration of the procedure in a 2-dimensional binary classification setting is shown in Fig. 2 for two counterfactual explanations $CF1$ and $CF2$ (blue dots), generated for the observation x (red dot). In the left picture, two clusters (hatched areas) are identified by DBSCAN in the explored area (blue dashed circle): $CF1$ and a, the closest training instance, do not belong to the same cluster, defining $CF1$ as unjustified. In the right picture, $CF2$ belongs to the same cluster as a and is therefore defined as justified.

In the end, the VE procedure returns a binary value indicating whether or not the analyzed counterfactual explanation $E(x)$ is justified, written $J_{E(x)}$ ($J_{E(x)} = 1$ if $E(x)$ is justified). Again, we also measure the average value $\bar{J}$ of $J_{E(x)}$ for multiple runs of the procedure for the instance x and over multiple instances.

5   Experimental Study: Assessing the Risk of Unjustified Regions

The two presented procedures LRA and VE can be used to analyze the unconnectedness of classification regions. As explained earlier, setting the values of n and ϵ is crucial for the experiments, as these parameters are central to the definition and procedures used. Therefore, a first experiment and discussion (cf. Sect. 5.2) are conducted on this problem. Once adequate values are found, a second experiment (see Sect. 5.3) is performed, where we discuss how exposed different classifiers are to the threat unjustified classification regions. The link between this notion and overfitting is also studied. Finally, in a third experiment (cf. Sect. 5.4), the vulnerability of state-of-the-art post-hoc counterfactual approaches is analyzed, and we look into how they can minimize the problem of unjustified counterfactual explanations.

5.1   Experimental Protocol

In this section, we present the experimental protocol considered for our study.

Datasets. The datasets considered for these experiments include 2 low-dimensional datasets (half-moons and wine) as well as 4 real datasets (Boston Housing [14], German Credit [7], Online News Popularity [10]. Propublica Recidivism [18]). These structured datasets present the advantage of naturally understandable features and are commonly used in the interpretability (and fairness) literature. All include less than 70 numerical attributes. As mentioned earlier, categorical features are excluded from the scope of the study.

Classifiers. For each considered dataset, the data is rescaled and a train-test split of the data is performed with 70%–30% proportion. Several binary classifiers are trained on each dataset: a random forest classifier, a support vector classifier with Gaussian kernel, an XGboost classifier, a Naive Bayes classifier and a k-nearest-neighbors classifier. Unless specified, the associated hyperparameters are chosen using a 5-fold cross validation to optimize accuracy. The AUC score values obtained on the test set with these classifiers are shown in Table 1. Several variations of the same classifier are also considered for one of the experiments (Sect. 5.3), with changes in the values of one of the associated hyperparameters: the maximum depth allowed for each tree of the random forest algorithm, and the γ coefficient of the Gaussian kernel of the support vector classifier.

Protocol. The test set is also used to run the experiments, as described earlier. In Sect. 5.3, the LRA procedure is applied to each instance of the considered test sets, and the scores $\bar{S}$ and $\bar{R}$ are calculated and analyzed for each dataset and classifier. In Sect. 5.4, three post-hoc counterfactual approaches from the state-of-the-art (HCLS [19], GS [20] and LORE [11]) are used to generate explanations $E(x)$ for each instance of the considered test sets, and the VE procedure is applied to the obtained counterfactuals to calculate the scores $\bar{J}$, as well as the distance $d(x, E(x))$.

Table 1. AUC scores obtained on the test sets for a random forest (RF), support vector classifier (SVM), XGBoost (XGB), naive Bayes classifier (NB) k-nearest neighbors (KNN) and nearest neighbor (1-NN)

Dataset	RF	SVM	XGB	NB	KNN	1-NN
Half-moons	0.98 ± 0.01	0.99 ± 0.00	0.99 ± 0.00	0.95 ± 0.01	0.99 ± 0.00	0.95 ± 0.01
Wine	0.98 ± 0.01	0.99 ± 0.00	0.99 ± 0.00	0.95 ± 0.01	0.99 ± 0.00	0.95 ± 0.01
Boston	0.96 ± 0.02	0.97 ± 0.04	0.97 ± 0.03	0.87 ± 0.08	0.93 ± 0.06	0.85 ± 0.04
Credit	0.75 ± 0.05	0.64 ± 0.04	0.70 ± 0.08	0.66 ± 0.04	0.66 ± 0.02	0.55 ± 0.05
News	0.68 ± 0.02	0.68 ± 0.01	0.70 ± 0.02	0.65 ± 0.02	0.65 ± 0.02	0.55 ± 0.01
Recidivism	0.81 ± 0.01	0.82 ± 0.01	0.84 ± 0.01	0.78 ± 0.02	0.81 ± 0.02	0.68 ± 0.02

5.2   Defining the Problem Granularity: Choosing n and ϵ

As presented in [21] and mentioned above, the values of n and ϵ are crucial since they define the notion of ϵ-justification and impact the average distance between the generated instances. Choosing inadequate values for n and ϵ may lead to having some unconnected regions not being detected as such and vice versa.

These two values are obviously linked, as n defines, for a given $x \in X$, the density of the sampling in the initial assessment step of the LRA procedure, hence the average pairwise distance between the generated observations, and therefore the value ϵ should be taking. Identifying an adequate value for ϵ depends on the local topology of the decision boundary of the classifier, as well as the radius of the hyperball defined in LRA (cf. Sect. 4.1). In practice, because the instances B_x are generated in the initial assessment step before running DBSCAN, it is easier to set the value of ϵ to the maximum value of the distances of B to their closest neighbors: $\epsilon = \max_{x_i \in B_x} \min_{x_j \in B_x \setminus \{x_i\}} d(x_i, x_j)$. Using this value, the training instance a_0 is guaranteed to be in an actual cluster (i.e. not detected as an outlier), which is a desirable property of the approach: it is expected that since is a_0 correctly predicted, it should be possible to generate a close neighbor classified similarly (in the same "pocket"). The problem thus becomes of setting the value of n alone.

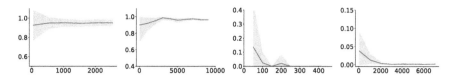

Fig. 3. Average R_x score for several instances of the half-moons dataset depending on the value of n. The first two instances are selected to verify $S_x = 1$, while the last two verify $S_x = 0$. After n reaches a certain value, R_x hardly changes anymore

In order to have the best performance, n should have the highest value as possible. However, this also increases dramatically the running time of the algorithm. Besides the complexity of the classifier's decision boundary, the value of n required to saturate the local space increases exponentially with the dimension of the problem. Furthermore, as the radius of generation increases during the iteration steps, the number of instances should also increase to guarantee constant space saturation across various steps. Instead, we choose to set a high initial value of n at the first step, leading to an even higher complexity.

In this context, we are interested in identifying a value for n that properly captures the complexity of the local decision boundary of the classifier without generating an unrequired amount of instances. We thus look at the value of R_x for several instances and several values of n to detect the threshold above which generating more instances does not change the output of the LRA procedure. Figure 3 illustrates this result for several instances of the half-moond dataset (two with $S_x = 1$ and two with $S_x = 0$: the R_x score reaches a plateau after a certain value of n. Using this assumption, the LRA procedure can be tested with various values of n to ensure a reasonable value is chosen for the results of the other experiments presented in the next section.

5.3 Detecting Unjustified Regions

While the existence and dangers of unjustified regions has been shown in [21], the extent to which classifiers are vulnerable to this issue remains unclear.

Comparing the Vulnerability of Classifiers. In Table 2 are shown the proportion $\bar{S}$ of the studied instance that have unjustified classification regions in their neighborhood (LRA returning $S_x = 1$). Every classifier seems to be generating unjustified regions in the neighborhoods of test instances: in some cases, as much as 93% of the tested instances are concerned (XGB classifier trained on the German Credit dataset).

However, the extent to which each classifier is vulnerable greatly varies. For instance, among the considered classifiers, the random forest and XGBoost algorithms seem to be more exposed than other classifiers (average $\bar{S}$ value across dataset resp. 0.63 and 0.54, vs. 0.39 for the SVM for instance). The learning algorithm, and thus the associated complexity of the learned decision boundary,

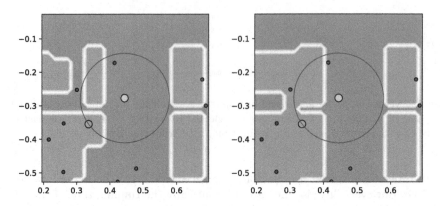

Fig. 4. Illustration of the LRA procedure applied to an instance of the half-moons dataset. Left: RF with no maximum depth precised. Right: maximum depth allowed is 10 (Color figure online)

heavily influences the creation of classification regions. A link with predictive accuracy can thus be expected. This can be also observed in the results of the Naive Bayes classifier: while this classifier seems to be the more robust to the studied problem (average value of $\bar{S}$ across all datasets equals 0.29), it should be noted that it is also the classifier that performs the worst in terms of prediction (besides 1-NN, cf. Table 1).

These results are further confirmed by the values of $\bar{R}$ shown in Table 4, which also give an indication of the relative size of these unjustified classification regions: for instance, despite having similar values for $\bar{S}$ on the German Credit dataset, RF and XGboost have a higher $\bar{R}$ values than KNN, indicating that the formed unconnected regions are wider in average.

Differences in results can also be observed between datasets, since more complex datasets (e.g. less separable classes, higher dimension...) may also lead to classifiers learning more complex decision boundaries (when possible), and maybe favoring overfitting. This phenomenon is further studied in the next experiment.

Link Between Justification and Overfitting. To further study the relation between the creation of unjustified regions and the learning algorithm of the classifier, we analyze the influence of overfitting over the considered metrics. For this purpose, we attempt to control overfitting by changing the values of the hyperparameters of two classifiers: the maximum depth allowed for a tree for RF, and the γ parameter of the Gaussian kernel for SVM. For illustration purposes, we apply the LRA procedure in a two-dimensional setting (half-moons) to a classifier deliberately chosen for its low robustness (a random forest with only 3 trees). Figure 4 shows a zoomed in area of the decision boundary of the classifier (colored areas, the green and purple dots represent training instances), as well as the result of LRA for a specific instance x (yellow instance). In the

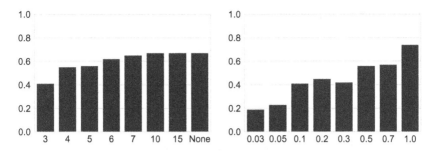

Fig. 5. $\bar{R}$ scores for RF (left) and SVM (right) classifiers on the Boston dataset for various values of hyperparameters (resp. maximum number of trees and γ parameter of the Gaussian kernel). "None" (left) means no maximum tree depth restriction is set

left figure, the considered classifier has no limitation on the depth of the trees it can use, wereas in the right one this parameter is set to 10. As explained earlier, LRA explores the local neighborhood of x (blue circle), delimited by its closest neighbor from the training set correctly classified a_0 (orange instance). In the left figure, within this neighborhood, a green square region is detected as an unjustified region (top left from x): there is no green instance in this region, hence $S_x = 1$. However, in the right picture, this region is connected to green instances: $S_x = 0$.

Quantitative results of this phenomenon are shown in Fig. 5, which illustrates the evolution of $\bar{S}$ and $\bar{R}$ scores for the two mentioned classifiers (left: RF; right: SVM). As expected, the more overfitting is allowed (i.e. when the maximum tree depth of RF and when the γ parameter of the RBF kernel of SVM increase), and the more prone to generate unjustified regions these two classifiers seem.

However, it should be noted that models such as logistic regression or 1-nearest neighbor (not appearing in Tables 2 and 3) have, by construction, no UCF ($\bar{S} = 0.0$): a logistic regression creates only two connected classification regions, and the predictions of a 1-NN classifier are by construction connected to their closest neighbor from the training data, despite this classifier being frequently referred to as an example of overfitting. Therefore, the notion of overfitting is not sufficient to describe the phenomenon of unconnectedness.

The tradeoff there seems to be between justification and accuracy (cf. Tables 1 and 2) seems to indicate that a lower complexity of the decision border favors better justification scores for at the cost of predictive performance (cf. Table 1 for the comparatively lower predictive performance of the 1-NN classifier).

Table 2. Proportion of instances being at risk of generating a UCF ($\bar{S}$ score) over the test sets for 6 datasets

Dataset	RF	SVM	XGB	NB	KNN
Half-moons	0.37	0.00	0.05	0.00	0.02
Wine	0.21	0.08	0.15	0.08	0.15
Boston	0.63	0.29	0.62	0.44	0.25
Credit	0.93	0.76	0.93	0.27	0.92
News	0.85	0.72	0.86	0.57	0.68
Recidivism	0.81	0.50	0.61	0.36	0.73

Table 3. Average risk of generating an UCF ($\bar{R}$) and standard deviations for 6 datasets

Dataset	RF	SVM	XGB	NB	KNN
Half-moons	0.07(0.17)	0.00(0.00)	0.01(0.02)	0.0(0.0)	0.00(0.00)
Wine	0.01(0.02)	0.02(0.07)	0.00(0.01)	0.01(0.02)	0.01(0.01)
Boston	0.16(0.25)	0.06(0.13)	0.14(0.24)	0.07(0.14)	0.03(0.05)
Credit	0.44(0.37)	0.10(0.14)	0.45(0.37)	0.06(0.17)	0.31(0.27)
News	0.35 (0.28)	0.18(0.28)	0.33(0.30)	0.12(0.24)	0.37(0.38)
Recidivism	0.26(0.30)	0.14(0.21)	0.21(0.28)	0.08(0.20)	0.20(0.30)

5.4   Vulnerability of Post-hoc Counterfactual Approaches

In the post-hoc context, because no assumption is made about the classifier nor any training data, counterfactual approaches have been shown to be subject to generating unjustified explanations [21]. The state-of-the-art approaches mentioned in Sect. 5.1 are applied to the considered datasets in order to assess the extent of this risk.

The VE procedure is applied to the counterfactual explanations generated using state-of-the-art approaches for instances facing a significant justification risk (constraint arbitrarily set to $R_x \geq 0.25$) of the previously considered datasets, on which a random forest classifier was trained. The results ($\bar{J}$ score) are shown in Table 4. In addition to J_x, the distance between each tested instance and its generated counterfactual explanations are calculated, and represented in the table by their average value $\bar{d}$.

As expected, every considered counterfactual approach seems to be generating to some extent unjustified explanations: the Justification scores of the tested approaches can even fall as low as 30% (GS on the Online News Popularity dataset). However, some differences can be observed between the approaches: for instance, HCLS and LORE seem to achieve better performance than GS in terms of justification across all datsets (average $\bar{J}$ across datasets equals resp. 0.74 and 0.91 for HCLS and LORE, against only 0.62 for GS). However, we observe that the average distance $\bar{d}$ is also higher (resp. 1.38 and 1.46 for HCLS and LORE, against 0.90 for GS). This can be explained by the fact that GS directly minimizes a L_2 distance (the considered d distance), while LORE minimizes a L_0 distance in a local neighborhood. By looking for counterfactuals in the direct proximity of x, GS thus tend to find unjustified regions more easily than the other approaches, whereas looking further away from the decision boundary probably enables LORE to favor explanations located closer to ground-truth instances, therefore more frequently justified.

Another observation is that despite achieving better performance than GS by trying to maximize the classification probability of the generated counterfactual, HCLS still comes short in terms of justification. This tend to illustrate that classification confidence, when available, is not a good way to detect unconnected classification regions and guarantee justified explanations, some unconnected regions probably having high classification confidence.

These results highlight that while classification confidence, when available, does not seem to help in generating justified explanations, there seems to be a tradeoff with the counterfactual distance, as LORE achieves in some cases perfect justification scores (e.g. Boston and Credit datasets).

Table 4. Proportion of generated counterfactuals that are justified ($\bar{J}$) for vulnerable instances ($R_x \geq 0.25$)

Dataset	HCLS		GS		LORE	
	$\bar{J}$	$\bar{d}$	$\bar{J}$	$\bar{d}$	$\bar{J}$	$\bar{d}$
Half-moons	0.83	0.45 (0.27)	0.67	0.48 (0.26)	0.83	1.19 (0.18)
Boston	0.86	1.99 (0.88)	0.84	0.84 (1.03)	1.0	1.58 (0.98)
Credit	0.65	1.78 (0.94)	0.59	0.82 (0.71)	1.0	1.57 (1.11)
News	0.46	1.81 (0.75)	0.30	1.68 (0.99)	0.77	1.74 (0.83)
Recidivism	0.91	0.89 (1.08)	0.70	0.70 (1.09)	0.98	1.23 (0.90)

6   Conclusion

The justification constraint that is studied in this work comes from an intuitive requirement explanations for machine learning predictions should satisfy, as well as from the assumption that post-hoc counterfactual explanations are not able to distinguish UCF from JCF. Results highlight that this vulnerability greatly depends on the nature of the classifier, and that all learning algorithms are not equally likely to form unconnected classification regions. In particular, controlling overfitting seems to be very important for some of the studied classifiers. In light of this study, generating justified counterfactual explanations in the post-hoc context seems complicated and using the training instances, when available, is necessary. To reduce the impact of these issues, state-of-the-art approaches may look for explanations located further away from the decision boundary. However, this raises the question of explanation locality, as explanations located far away from the decision boundary may be less tailored for each instance, and thus less useful in the case of counterfactuals.

Despite the importance of justification, the question of whether this requirement is sufficient to guarantee useful explanations remains. In particular, questions arise when a counterfactual explanation lies in a justified region where the associated ground-truth instances are far away (e.g. out of distribution). In this context, adding a distance constraint (as discussed in Sect. 3) to ensure plausible justified explanations may constitute an interesting lead for future works.

Extending these notions to high-dimensional data (e.g. images) however needs further research, as neither connectedness nor distance helps in guaranteeing useful explanations. A good example of this is adversarial examples, which are defined as being close to original observations and have been proven to be connected to ground-truth instances in the case of deep neural networks but do not constitute satisfying counterfactual explanations.

Finally, results about the link between justification and overfitting raise the question of the accuracy of the classifier in these unconnected regions. In this regard, future works include analyzing the connectedness of classification errors.

Acknowledgements. This work has been done as part of the Joint Research Initiative (JRI) project "Interpretability for human-friendly machine learning models" funded by the AXA Research Fund.

References

1. Alvarez Melis, D., Jaakkola, T.: Towards robust interpretability with self-explaining neural networks. In: Advances in Neural Information Processing Systems, vol. 31, pp. 7786–7795 (2018)
2. Baehrens, D., Schroeter, T., Harmeling, S., Hansen, K., Muller, K.R.: How to explain individual classification decisions Motoaki Kawanabe. J. Mach. Learn. Res. **11**, 1803–1831 (2010)
3. Biggio, B., et al.: Evasion attacks against machine learning at test time. In: Blockeel, H., Kersting, K., Nijssen, S., Železný, F. (eds.) ECML PKDD 2013. LNCS (LNAI), vol. 8190, pp. 387–402. Springer, Heidelberg (2013). https://doi.org/10.1007/978-3-642-40994-3_25
4. Biggio, B., Roli, F.: Wild patterns: ten years after the rise of adversarial machine learning. Pattern Recogn. **84**, 317–331 (2018)
5. Bottou, L., et al.: Counterfactual reasoning and learning systems: the example of computational advertising. J. Mach. Learn. Res. **14**, 3207–3260 (2013)
6. Craven, M.W., Shavlik, J.W.: Extracting tree-structured representations of trained neural networks. In: Advances in Neural Information Processing Systems, vol. 8, pp. 24–30 (1996)
7. Dua, D., Graff, C.: UCI machine learning repository (2017)
8. Ester, M., Kriegel, H.P., Sander, J., Xu, X.: A density-based algorithm for discovering clusters in large spatial databases with noise. In: Proceedings of the 2nd International Conference on Knowledge Discovery and Data Mining (KDD 1996), pp. 226–231 (1996)
9. Fawzi, A., Moosavi-Dezfooli, S.M., Frossard, P., Soatto, S.: Empirical study of the topology and geometry of deep networks. In: The IEEE Conference on Computer Vision and Pattern Recognition (CVPR), June 2018

10. Fernandes, K., Vinagre, P., Cortez, P.: A proactive intelligent decision support system for predicting the popularity of online news. In: Pereira, F., Machado, P., Costa, E., Cardoso, A. (eds.) EPIA 2015. LNCS (LNAI), vol. 9273, pp. 535–546. Springer, Cham (2015). https://doi.org/10.1007/978-3-319-23485-4_53

11. Guidotti, R., Monreale, A., Ruggieri, S., Pedreschi, D., Turini, F., Giannotti, F.: Local rule-based explanations of black box decision systems. arXiv preprint arXiv:1805.10820 (2018)

12. Guidotti, R., Monreale, A., Ruggieri, S., Turini, F., Giannotti, F., Pedreschi, D.: A survey of methods for explaining black box models. ACM Comput. Surv. (CSUR) **51**(5), 93 (2018)

13. Hara, S., Hayashi, K.: Making tree ensembles interpretable. In: ICML Workshop on Human Interpretability in Machine Learning (WHI 2016) (2016)

14. Harrison, D., Rubinfeld, D.: Hedonic prices and the demand for clean air. Environ. Econ. Manag. **5**, 81–102 (1978)

15. Jiang, H., Kim, B., Guan, M., Gupta, M.: To trust or not to trust a classifier. In: Advances in Neural Information Processing Systems, vol. 31, pp. 5541–5552 (2018)

16. Kabra, M., Robie, A., Branson, K.: Understanding classifier errors by examining influential neighbors. In: 2015 IEEE Conference on Computer Vision and Pattern Recognition (CVPR), pp. 3917–3925 (2015)

17. Kim, B., Rudin, C., Shah, J.A.: The Bayesian case model: a generative approach for case-based reasoning and prototype classification. In: Advances in Neural Information Processing Systems, pp. 1952–1960 (2014)

18. Larson, J., Mattu, S., Kirchner, L., Angwin, J.: How We Analyzed the COMPAS Recidivism Algorithm. ProPublica, Manhattan (2016)

19. Lash, M., Lin, Q., Street, N., Robinson, J., Ohlmann, J.: Generalized inverse classification. In: Proceedings of the 2017 SIAM International Conference on Data Mining, pp. 162–170 (2017)

20. Laugel, T., Lesot, M.-J., Marsala, C., Renard, X., Detyniecki, M.: Comparison-based inverse classification for interpretability in machine learning. In: Medina, J., et al. (eds.) IPMU 2018. CCIS, vol. 853, pp. 100–111. Springer, Cham (2018). https://doi.org/10.1007/978-3-319-91473-2_9

21. Laugel, T., Lesot, M.J., Marsala, C., Renard, X., Detyniecki, M.: The dangers of post-hoc interpretability: Unjustified counterfactual explanations. In: Proceedings of the 28th International Joint Conference on Artificial Intelligence IJCAI 2019 (2019, to appear)

22. Laugel, T., Renard, X., Lesot, M.J., Marsala, C., Detyniecki, M.: Defining locality for surrogates in post-hoc interpretablity. In: ICML Workshop on Human Interpretability in Machine Learning (WHI 2018) (2018)

23. Lipton, Z.C.: The mythos of model interpretability. In: ICML Workshop on Human Interpretability in Machine Learning (WHI 2017) (2017)

24. Lundberg, S.M., Lee, S.I.: A unified approach to interpreting model predictions. In: Advances in Neural Information Processing Systems, vol. 30, pp. 4765–4774 (2017)

25. Martens, D., Provost, F.: Explaining data-driven document classifications. MIS Q. **38**(1), 73–100 (2014)

26. Ribeiro, M.T., Singh, S., Guestrin, C.: "Why should I trust you?": explaining the predictions of any classifier. In: Proceedings of the 22nd ACM SIGKDD International Conference on Knowledge Discovery and Data Mining, KDD 2016, pp. 1135–1144 (2016)

27. Rudin, C.: Please stop explaining black box models for high stakes decisions. In: NeurIPS Workshop on Critiquing and Correcting Trends in Machine Learning (2018)

28. Russell, C.: Efficient search for diverse coherent explanations. In: Proceedings of the Conference on Fairness, Accountability, and Transparency, (FAT* 2019), pp. 20–28 (2019)

29. Turner, R.: A model explanation system. In: NIPS Workshop on Black Box Learning and Inference (2015)

30. Wachter, S., Mittelstadt, B., Russell, C.: Counterfactual explanations without opening the black box; automated decisions and the GDPR. Harv. J. Law Technol. **31**(2), 841–887 (2018)

Shift Happens: Adjusting Classifiers

Theodore James Thibault Heiser[ORCID], Mari-Liis Allikivi[ORCID], and Meelis Kull[(✉)][ORCID]

Institute of Computer Science, University of Tartu, Tartu, Estonia
{mari-liis.allikivi,meelis.kull}@ut.ee

Abstract. Minimizing expected loss measured by a proper scoring rule, such as Brier score or log-loss (cross-entropy), is a common objective while training a probabilistic classifier. If the data have experienced dataset shift where the class distributions change post-training, then often the model's performance will decrease, over-estimating the probabilities of some classes while under-estimating the others on average. We propose unbounded and bounded general adjustment (UGA and BGA) methods that transform all predictions to (re-)equalize the average prediction and the class distribution. These methods act differently depending on which proper scoring rule is to be minimized, and we have a theoretical guarantee of reducing loss on test data, if the exact class distribution is known. We also demonstrate experimentally that, when in practice the class distribution is known only approximately, there is often still a reduction in loss depending on the amount of shift and the precision to which the class distribution is known.

Keywords: Multi-class classification · Proper scoring rule · Dataset shift · Classifier calibration · Classifier adjustment

1 Introduction

Classical supervised machine learning is built on the assumption that the joint probability distribution that features and labels are sourced from does not change during the life cycle of the predictive model: from training to testing and deployment. However, in reality this assumption is broken more often than not: medical diagnostic classifiers are often trained with an oversampling of disease-positive instances, surveyors are often biased to collecting labelled samples from certain segments of a population, user demographics and preferences change over time on social media and e-commerce sites, etc.

While these are all examples of dataset shift, the nature of these shifts can be quite different. There have been several efforts to create taxonomies of dataset shift [11,14]. The field of *transfer learning* offers many methods of learning models for scenarios with awareness of the shift during training. However, often the shift is not yet known during training and it is either too expensive or even impossible to retrain once the shift happens. There are several reasons for it: original training data or training infrastructure might not be available; shift

© Springer Nature Switzerland AG 2020
U. Brefeld et al. (Eds.): ECML PKDD 2019, LNAI 11907, pp. 55–70, 2020.
https://doi.org/10.1007/978-3-030-46147-8_4

happens so frequently that there is no time to retrain; the kind of shift is such that without having labels in the shifted context there is no hope of learning a better model than the original.

In this work we address multi-class classification scenarios where training a classifier for the shifted deployment context is not possible (due to any of the above reasons), and the only possibility is to post-process the outputs from an existing classifier that was trained before the shift happened. To succeed, such post-processing must be guided by some information about the shifted deployment context. In the following, we will assume that we know the overall expected class distribution in the shifted context, at least approximately. For example, consider a medical diagnostic classifier of disease sub-types, which has been trained on the cases of country A, and gets deployed to a different country B. It is common that the distribution of sub-types can vary between countries, but in many cases such information is available. So here many labels are available but not the feature values (country B has data about sub-types in past cases, but no diagnostic markers were measured back then), making training of a new model impossible. Still, the model *adjustment* methods proposed in this paper can be used to adjust the existing model to match the class distribution in the deployment context. As another example, consider a bank's fraud detection classifier trained on one type of credit cards and deployed to a new type of credit cards. For new cards there might not yet be enough cases of fraud to train a new classifier, but there might be enough data to estimate the class distribution, that is the prevalence of fraud. The old classifier might predict too few or too many positives on the new data, so it must be adjusted to the new class distribution.

In many application domains, including the above examples of medical diagnostics and fraud detection, it is required that the classifiers would output confidence information in addition to the predicted class. This is supported by most classifiers, as they can be requested to provide for each instance the class probabilities instead of a single label. For example, the feed-forward neural networks for classification typically produce class probabilities using the final soft-max layer. Such confidence information can then be interpreted by a human expert to choose the action based on the prediction, or feeded into an automatic cost-sensitive decision-making system, which would use the class probability estimates and the mis-classification cost information to make cost-optimal decisions. Probabilistic classifiers are typically evaluated using *Brier score* or *log-loss* (also known as *squared error* and *cross-entropy*, respectively). Both measures belong to the family of proper scoring rules: measures which are minimized by the true posterior class probabilities produced by the Bayes-optimal model. Proper losses also encourage the model to produce calibrated probabilities, as every proper loss decomposes into *calibration loss* and *refinement loss* [9].

Our goal is to improve the predictions of a given model in a shifted deployment context, using the information about the expected class distribution in this context, without making any additional assumptions about the type of dataset shift. The idea proposed by Kull et al. [9] is to take advantage of a property that many dataset shift cases share: a difference in the classifier's average prediction and the expected class distribution of the data. They proposed two different *adjustment procedures* which transform the predictions to re-equalise the average prediction with the expected class distribution, resulting in a theoretically guaranteed reduction of Brier score or log-loss. Interestingly, it turned out that different loss measures require different adjustment procedures. They proved that their proposed *additive adjustment* (additively shifting all predictions, see Sect. 2 for the definitions) is guaranteed to reduce Brier score, while it can increase log-loss in some circumstances. They also proposed *multiplicative adjustment* (multiplicatively shifting and renormalising all predictions) which is guaranteed to reduce log-loss, while it can sometimes increase Brier score. It was proved that if the adjustment procedure is *coherent* with the proper loss (see Sect. 2), then the reduction of loss is guaranteed, assuming that the class distribution is known exactly. They introduced the term *adjustment loss* to refer to the part of calibration loss which can be eliminated by adjustment. Hence, adjustment can be viewed as a weak form of calibration. In the end, it remained open: (1) whether for every proper scoring rule there exists an adjustment procedure that is guaranteed to reduce loss; (2) is there a general way of finding an adjustment procedure to reduce a given proper loss; (3) whether this reduction of loss from adjustment materializes in practice where the new class distribution is only known approximately; (4) how to solve algorithm convergence issues of the multiplicative adjustment method; (5) how to solve the problem of additive adjustment sometimes producing predictions with negative 'probabilities'.

The contributions of our work are the following: (1) we construct a family called BGA (Bounded General Adjustment) of adjustment procedures, with one procedure for each proper loss, and prove that each BGA procedure is guaranteed to reduce the respective proper loss, if the class distribution of the dataset is known; (2) we show that each BGA procedure can be represented as a convex optimization task, leading to a practical and tractable algorithm; (3) we demonstrate experimentally that even if the new class distribution is only known approximately, the proposed BGA methods still usually improve over the unadjusted model; (4) we prove that the BGA procedure of log-loss is the same as multiplicative adjustment, thus solving the convergence problems of multiplicative adjustment; (5) we construct another family called UGA (Unbounded General Adjustment) with adjustment procedures that are dominated by the respective BGA methods according to the loss, but are theoretically interesting by being coherent to the respective proper loss in the sense of Kull et al. [9], and by containing the additive adjustment procedure as the UGA for Brier score.

Section 2 of this paper provides the background for this work, covering the specific types of dataset shift and reviewing some popular methods of adapting to them. We also review the family of proper losses, i.e. the loss functions that adjustment is designed for. Section 3 introduces the UGA and BGA families of adjustment procedures and provides the theoretical results of the paper. Section 4 provides experimental evidence for the effectiveness of BGA adjustment in practical settings. Section 5 concludes the paper, reviewing its contributions and proposing open questions.

2   Background and Related Work

2.1   Dataset Shift and Prior Probability Adjustment

In supervised learning, dataset shift can be defined as any change in the joint probability distribution of the feature vector X and label Y between two data generating processes, that is $\mathbb{P}_{old}(X, Y) \neq \mathbb{P}_{new}(X, Y)$, where $\mathbb{P}_{old}$ and $\mathbb{P}_{new}$ are the probability distributions before and after the shift, respectively. While the proposed adjustment methods are in principle applicable for any kind of dataset shift, there are differences in performance across different types of shift. According to Moreno-Torres et al. [11] there are 4 main kinds of shift: covariate shift, prior probability shift, concept shift and other types of shift. *Covariate shift* is when the distribution $\mathbb{P}(X)$ of the covariates/features changes, but the posterior class probabilities $P(Y|X)$ do not. At first, this may not seem to be of much interest since the classifiers output estimates of posterior class probabilities and these remain unshifted. However, unless the classifier is Bayes-optimal, then covariate shift can still result in a classifier under-performing [14]. Many cases of covariate shift can be modelled as sample selection bias [8], often addressed by retraining the model on a reweighted training set [7,13,15].

Prior probability shift is when the prior class probabilities $\mathbb{P}(Y)$ change, but the likelihoods $\mathbb{P}(X|Y)$ do not. An example of this is down- or up-sampling of the instances based on their class in the training or testing phase. Given the new class distribution, the posterior class probability predictions can be modified according to Bayes' theorem to take into account the new prior class probabilities, as shown in [12]. We will refer to this procedure as the *Prior Probability Adjuster* (PPA) and the formal definition is as follows:

$$\text{PPA:} \qquad \mathbb{P}_{new}(Y=y|X) = \frac{\mathbb{P}_{old}(Y=y|X)\mathbb{P}_{new}(Y=y)/\mathbb{P}_{old}(Y=y)}{\sum_{y'} \mathbb{P}_{old}(Y=y'|X)\mathbb{P}_{new}(Y=y')/\mathbb{P}_{old}(Y=y')}$$

In *other types of shift* both conditional probability distributions $\mathbb{P}(X|Y)$ and $\mathbb{P}(Y|X)$ change. The special case where $\mathbb{P}(Y)$ or $\mathbb{P}(X)$ remains unchanged is called *concept shift*. Concept shift and other types of shift are in general hard to adapt to, as the relationship between X and Y has changed in an unknown way.

2.2   Proper Scoring Rules and Bregman Divergences

The best possible probabilistic classifier is the Bayes-optimal classifier which for any instance X outputs its true posterior class probabilities $\mathbb{P}(Y|X)$. When choosing a loss function for evaluating probabilistic classifiers, it is then natural to require that the loss would be minimized when the predictions match the correct posterior probabilities. Loss functions with this property are called proper scoring rules [5,9,10]. Note that throughout the paper we consider multi-class classification with k classes and represent class labels as one-hot vectors, i.e. the label of class i is a vector of $k - 1$ zeros and a single 1 at position i.

Definition 1 (Proper Scoring Rule (or Proper Loss)). *In a k-class clas-sification task a loss function* $f : [0,1]^k \times \{0,1\}^k \to \mathbb{R}$ *is called a* proper scoring rule *(or* proper loss*), if for any probability vectors* $p, q \in [0,1]^k$ *with* $\sum_{i=1} p_i = 1$ *and* $\sum_{i=1} q_i = 1$ *the following inequality holds:*

$$\mathbb{E}_{Y \sim q}[f(q, Y)] \leq \mathbb{E}_{Y \sim q}[f(p, Y)]$$

where Y is a one-hot encoded label randomly drawn from the categorical distri-bution over k classes with class probabilities represented by vector q. The loss function f is called strictly proper *if the inequality is strict for all* $p \neq q$.

This is a useful definition, but it does not give a very clear idea of what the geometry of these functions looks like. Bregman divergences [4] were developed independently of proper scoring rules and have a constructive definition (note that many authors have the arguments p and q the other way around, but we use this order to match proper losses).

Definition 2 (Bregman Divergence). *Let* $\phi : \Omega \to \mathbb{R}$ *be a strictly convex function defined on a convex set* $\Omega \subseteq \mathbb{R}^k$ *such that* ϕ *is differentiable on the relative interior of* Ω, $ri(\Omega)$. *Denoting the dot product by* $\langle \cdot, \cdot \rangle$, *the Bregman divergence* $d_\phi : ri(\Omega) \times \Omega \to [0, \infty)$ *is defined as*

$$d_\phi(p, q) = \phi(q) - \phi(p) - \langle q - p, \nabla\phi(p) \rangle$$

Previous works [1] have shown that the two concepts are closely related. Every Bregman divergence is a strictly proper scoring rule and every strictly proper scoring rule (within an additive constant) is a Bregman divergence. Best known functions in these families are *squared Euclidean distance* defined as $d_{SED}(\mathbf{p}, \mathbf{q}) = \sum_{j=1}^d (p_j - q_j)^2$ and *Kullback-Leibler-divergence* $d_{KL}(\mathbf{p}, \mathbf{q}) = \sum_{j=1}^d q_j \log \frac{q_j}{p_j}$. When used as a scoring rule to measure loss of a prediction against labels, they are typically referred to as *Brier Score* d_{BS}, and *log-loss* d_{LL}, respectively.

2.3   Adjusted Predictions and Adjustment Procedures

Let us now come to the main scenario of this work, where dataset shift of unknown type occurs after a probabilistic k-class classifier has been trained. Suppose that we have a test dataset with n instances from the post-shift dis-tribution. We denote the predictions of the existing probabilistic classifier on these data by $p \in [0,1]^{n \times k}$, where p_{ij} is the predicted class j probability on the i-th instance, and hence $\sum_{j=1}^k p_{ij} = 1$. We further denote the hidden actual labels in the one-hot encoded form by $y \in \{0,1\}^{n \times k}$, where $y_{ij} = 1$ if the i-th instance belongs to class j, and otherwise $y_{ij} = 0$. While the actual labels are hidden, we assume that the overall class distribution $\pi \in [0,1]^k$ is known, where $\pi_j = \frac{1}{n} \sum_{i=1}^n y_{ij}$. The following theoretical results require π to be known exactly, but in the experiments we demonstrate benefits from the proposed adjustment methods also in the case where π is known approximately. As discussed in the introduction, examples of such scenarios include medical diagnostics and fraud detection. Before introducing the adjustment procedures we define what we mean by *adjusted predictions*.

Definition 3 (Adjusted Predictions). *Let $p \in [0,1]^{n \times k}$ be the predictions of a probabilistic k-class classifier on n instances and let $\pi \in [0,1]^k$ be the actual class distribution on these instances. We say that* predictions p are adjusted on this dataset, *if the average prediction is equal to the class proportion for every class j, that is $\frac{1}{n}\sum_{i=1}^{n} p_{ij} = \pi_j$.*

Essentially, the model provides adjusted predictions on a dataset, if for each class its predicted probabilities on the given data are on average neither under- nor over-estimated. Note that this definition was presented in [9] using random variables and expected values, and our definition can be viewed as a finite case where a random instance is drawn from the given dataset.

Consider now the case where the predictions are not adjusted on the given test dataset, and so the estimated class probabilities are on average too large for some class(es) and too small for some other class(es). This raises a question of whether the overall loss (as measured with some proper loss) could be reduced by shifting all predictions by a bit, for example with additive shifting by adding the same constant vector ε to each prediction vector $p_i.$. The answer is not obvious as in this process some predictions would also be moved further away from their true class. This is in some sense analogous to the case where a regression model is on average over- or under-estimating its target, as there also for some instances the predictions would become worse after shifting. However, additive shifting still pays off, if the regression results are evaluated by mean squared error. This is well known from the theory of linear models where mean squared error fitting leads to an intercept value such that the average predicted target value on the training set is equal to the actual mean target value (unless regularisation is applied). Since Brier score is essentially the same as mean squared error, it is natural to expect reduction of Brier score after additive shifting of predictions towards the actual class distribution. This is indeed so, and [9] proved that *additive adjustment* guarantees a reduction of Brier score. Additive adjustment is a method which adds the same constant vector to all prediction vectors to achieve equality between average prediction vector and actual class distribution.

Definition 4 (Additive Adjustment). Additive adjustment *is the function $\alpha_+ : [0,1]^{n \times k} \times [0,1]^k \rightarrow [0,1]^{n \times k}$ which takes in the predictions of a probabilistic k-class classifier on n instances and the actual class distribution π on these instances, and outputs adjusted predictions $a = \alpha_+(p, \pi)$ defined as $a_i. = p_i. + (\varepsilon_1, \ldots, \varepsilon_k)$ where $a_i. = (a_{i1}, \ldots, a_{ik})$, $p_i. = (p_{i1}, \ldots, p_{ik})$, and $\varepsilon_j = \pi_j - \frac{1}{n}\sum_{i=1}^{n} p_{ij}$ for each class $j \in \{1, \ldots, k\}$.*

It is easy to see that additive adjustment procedure indeed results in adjusted predictions, as $\frac{1}{n}\sum_{i=1}^{n} a_{ij} = \frac{1}{n}\sum_{i=1}^{n} p_{ij} + \varepsilon_j = \pi_j$. Note that even if the original predictions p are probabilities between 0 and 1, the additively adjusted predictions a can sometimes go out from that range and be negative or larger than 1. For example, if an instance i is predicted to have probability $p_{ij} = 0$ to be in class j and at the same time on average the overall proportion of class j is over-estimated, then $\varepsilon_j < 0$ and the adjusted prediction $a_{ij} = \varepsilon_j$ is negative. While such predictions are no longer probabilities in the standard sense, these can still be evaluated with Brier score. So it is always true that the overall Brier score on adjusted predictions is lower than on the original predictions, $\frac{1}{n} d_{BS}(a_{i\cdot}, y_{i\cdot}) \leq \frac{1}{n} d_{BS}(p_{i\cdot}, y_{i\cdot})$, with equality only when the original predictions are already adjusted, $a = p$. Note that whenever we mention the guaranteed reduction of loss, it always means that there is no reduction in the special case where the predictions are already adjusted, since then adjustment has no effect.

Additive adjustment is just one possible transformation of unadjusted predictions into adjusted predictions, and there are infinitely many other such transformations. We will refer to these as *adjustment procedures*. If we have explicitly required the output values to be in the range $[0, 1]$ then we use the term *bounded adjustment procedure*, otherwise we use the term *unbounded adjustment procedure*, even if actually the values do not go out from that range.

Definition 5 (Adjustment Procedure). Adjustment procedure *is any function* $\alpha : [0,1]^{n \times k} \times [0,1]^k \to [0,1]^{n \times k}$ *which takes as arguments the predictions* p *of a probabilistic k-class classifier on n instances and the actual class distribution* π *on these instances, such that for any p and π the output predictions* $a = \alpha(p, \pi)$ *are adjusted, that is* $\frac{1}{n} \sum_{i=1}^{n} a_{ij} = \pi_j$ *for each class* $j \in \{1, \ldots, k\}$.

In this definition and also in the rest of the paper we assume silently, that p contains valid predictions of a probabilistic classifier, and so for each instance i the predicted class probabilities add up to 1, that is $\sum_{j=1}^{k} p_{ij} = 1$. Similarly, we assume that π contains a valid class distribution, with $\sum_{j=1}^{k} \pi_j = 1$.

Definition 6 (Bounded Adjustment Procedure). *An adjustment procedure* $\alpha : [0,1]^{n \times k} \times [0,1]^k \to [0,1]^{n \times k}$ *is bounded, if for any p and π the output predictions* $a = \alpha(p, \pi)$ *are in the range $[0, 1]$, that is* $a_{ij} \in [0, 1]$ *for all i, j.*

An example of a bounded adjustment procedure is the *multiplicative adjustment* method proposed in [9], which multiplies the prediction vector componentwise with a constant weight vector and renormalizes the result to add up to 1.

Definition 7 (Multiplicative Adjustment). Multiplicative adjustment *is the function* $\alpha_* : [0,1]^{n \times k} \times [0,1]^k \to [0,1]^{n \times k}$ *which takes in the predictions of a probabilistic k-class classifier on n instances and the actual class distribution* π *on these instances, and outputs adjusted predictions* $a = \alpha_*(p, \pi)$ *defined as* $a_{ij} = \frac{w_j p_{ij}}{z_i}$, *where* $w_1, \ldots, w_k \geq 0$ *are real-valued weights chosen based on p and π such that the predictions* $\alpha_*(p, \pi)$ *would be adjusted, and z_i are the renormalisation factors defined as* $z_i = \sum_{j=1}^{k} w_j p_{ij}$.

As proved in [9], the suitable class weights $w_1, \ldots, w_k$ are guaranteed to exist, but finding these weights is a non-trivial task and the algorithm based on coordinate descent proposed in [9] can sometimes fail to converge. In the next Sect. 3 we will propose a more reliable algorithm for multiplicative adjustment.

It turns out that the adjustment procedure should be selected depending on which proper scoring rule is aimed to be minimised. It was proved in [9] that Brier score is guaranteed to be reduced with additive adjustment and log-loss with multiplicative adjustment. It was shown that when the 'wrong' adjustment method is used, then the loss can actually increase. In particular, additive adjustment can increase log-loss and multiplicative adjustment can increase Brier score. A sufficient condition for a guaranteed reduction of loss is *coherence* between the adjustment procedure and the proper loss corresponding to a Bregman divergence. Intuitively, coherence means that the effect of adjustment is the same across instances, where the effect is measured as the difference of divergences of this instance from any fixed class labels j and j'. The definition is the following:

Definition 8 (Coherence of Adjustment Procedure and Bregman Divergence [9]**).** *Let $\alpha : [0,1]^{n \times k} \times [0,1]^k \to [0,1]^{n \times k}$ be an adjustment procedure and d_ϕ be a Bregman divergence. Then α is called to be coherent with d_ϕ if and only if for any predictions p and class distribution π the following holds for all $i = 1, \ldots, n$ and $j, j' = 1, \ldots, k$:*

$$(d_\phi(a_{i\cdot}, c_j) - d_\phi(p_{i\cdot}, c_j)) - (d_\phi(a_{i\cdot}, c_{j'}) - d_\phi(p_{i\cdot}, c_{j'})) = const_{j,j'}$$

where $const_{j,j'}$ is a quantity not depending on i, and where $a = \alpha(p, \pi)$ and c_j is a one-hot vector corresponding to class j (with 1 at position j and 0 elsewhere).

The following result can be seen as a direct corollary of Theorem 4 in [9].

Theorem 9 (Decomposition of Bregman Divergences [9]**).** *Let d_ϕ be a Bregman divergence and let $\alpha : [0,1]^{n \times k} \times [0,1]^k \to [0,1]^{n \times k}$ be an adjustment procedure coherent with d_ϕ. Then for any predictions p, one-hot encoded true labels $y \in \{0,1\}^{n \times k}$ and class distribution π (with $\pi_j = \frac{1}{n} \sum_{i=1}^n y_{ij}$) the following decomposition holds:*

$$\frac{1}{n} \sum_{i=1}^n d_\phi(p_{i\cdot}, y_{i\cdot}) = \frac{1}{n} \sum_{i=1}^n d_\phi(p_{i\cdot}, a_{i\cdot}) + \frac{1}{n} \sum_{i=1}^n d_\phi(a_{i\cdot}, y_{i\cdot}) \tag{1}$$

Proof. The proofs and source code are in the Online Supplementary[1].

Due to non-negativity of d_ϕ this theorem gives a guaranteed reduction of loss, that is the loss on the adjusted probabilities a (average divergence between a and y) is less than the loss on the original unadjusted probabilities (average divergence between p and y), unless the probabilities are already adjusted ($p = a$). As additive adjustment can be shown to be coherent with the squared Euclidean distance and multiplicative adjustment with KL-divergence [9], the respective guarantees of loss reduction follow from Theorem 9.

---

[1] Proofs, code: https://github.com/teddyheiser/Shift_Happens_ECML_PKDD_2019.

3   General Adjustment

Our main contribution is a family of adjustment procedures called BGA (Bounded General Adjustment). We use the term 'general' to emphasise that it is not a single method, but a family with exactly one adjustment procedure for each proper loss. We will prove that every adjustment procedure of this family is guaranteed to reduce the respective proper loss, assuming that the true class distribution is known exactly. To obtain more theoretical insights and answer the open questions regarding coherence of adjustment procedures with Bregman divergences and proper losses, we define a weaker variant of BGA called UGA (Unbounded General Adjustment). As the name says, these methods can sometimes output predictions that are not in the range $[0, 1]$. On the other hand, the UGA procedures turn out to be coherent with their corresponding divergence measure, and hence have the decomposition stated in Theorem 9 and also guarantee reduced loss. However, UGA procedures have less practical value, as each UGA procedure is dominated by the respective BGA in terms of reductions in loss. We start by defining the UGA procedures, as these are mathematically simpler.

3.1   Unbounded General Adjustment (UGA)

We work here with the same notations as introduced earlier, with p denoting the $n \times k$ matrix with the outputs of a k-class probabilistic classifier on a test dataset with n instances, and y denoting the matrix with the same shape containing one-hot encoded actual labels. We denote the unknown true posterior class probabilities $\mathbb{P}(Y|X)$ on these instances by q, again a matrix with the same shape as p and y.

Our goal is to reduce the loss $\frac{1}{n} \sum_{i=1}^{n} d_\phi(p_{i\cdot}, y_{i\cdot})$ knowing the overall class distribution π, while not having any other information about labels y. Due to the defining property of any proper loss, the expected value of this quantity is minimised at $p = q$. As we know neither y nor q, we consider instead the set of all possible predictions Q_π that are adjusted to π, that is $Q_\pi = \left\{ a \in \mathbb{R}^{n \times k} \mid \frac{1}{n} \sum_{i=1}^{n} a_{i,j} = \pi_j, \ \sum_{j=1}^{k} a_{i,j} = 1 \right\}$. Note that here we do not require $a_{ij} \geq 0$, as in this subsection we are working to derive unbounded adjustment methods which allow predictions to go out from the range $[0, 1]$.

The question is now whether there exists a prediction matrix $a \in Q_\pi$ that is better than p (i.e. has lower divergence from y) regardless of what the actual labels y are (as a sidenote, y also belongs to Q_π). It is not obvious that such a exists, as one could suspect that for any a there exists some bad y such that the original p would be closer to y than the 'adjusted' a is.

Now we will define UGA and prove that it outputs adjusted predictions $a^\star$ that are indeed better than p, regardless of what the actual labels y are.

Definition 10 (Unbounded General Adjuster (UGA)). *Consider a k-class classification task with a test dataset of n instances, and let d_ϕ be a Bregman diver-*

gence. Then the unbounded general adjuster corresponding to d_ϕ *is the function* $\alpha^\star : \mathbb{R}^{n \times k} \times \mathbb{R}^k \to \mathbb{R}^{n \times k}$ *defined as follows:*

$$\alpha^\star(p, \pi) = \arg\min_{a \in Q_\pi} \frac{1}{n} \sum_{i=1}^{n} d_\phi(p_{i\cdot}, a_{i\cdot})$$

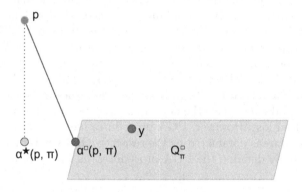

Fig. 1. A schematic explanation with $\alpha^\star(p, \pi)$ of UGA and $\alpha^\square(p, \pi)$ of BGA.

The definition of UGA is correct in the sense that the optimisation task used to define it has a unique optimum. This is because it is a convex optimisation task, as will be explained in Sect. 3.3. Intuitively, Q_π can be thought of as an infinite hyperplane of adjusted predictions, also containing the unknown y. The original prediction p is presumably not adjusted, so it does not belong to Q_π. UGA essentially 'projects' p to the hyperplane Q_π, in the sense of finding a in the hyperplane which is closest from p according to d_ϕ, see the diagram in Fig. 1.

The following theorem guarantees that the loss is reduced after applying UGA by showing that UGA is coherent with its Bregman divergence.

Theorem 11. *Let $\alpha^\star$ be the unbounded general adjuster corresponding to the Bregman divergence d_ϕ. Then $\alpha^\star$ is coherent with d_ϕ.*

The next theorem proves that UGA is actually the one and only adjustment procedure that decomposes in the sense of Theorem 9. Therefore, UGA coincides with additive and multiplicative adjustment on Brier score and log-loss, respectively.

Theorem 12. *Let d_ϕ be a Bregman divergence, let p be a set of predictions, and π be a class distribution over k classes. Suppose $a \in Q_\pi$ is such that for any $y \in Q_\pi$ the decomposition of Eq. (1) holds. Then $a = \alpha^\star(p, \pi)$.*

As explained in the example of additive adjustment (which is UGA for Brier score), some adjusted predictions can get out from the range $[0, 1]$. It is clear that a prediction involving negative probabilities cannot be optimal. In the following section we propose the Bounded General Adjuster (BGA) which does not satisfy the decomposition property but is guaranteed to be at least as good as UGA.

3.2 Bounded General Adjustment

For a given class distribution π, let us constrain the set of all possible adjusted predictions Q_π further, by requiring that all probabilities are non-negative:

$$Q_\pi^\square = \{a \in Q_\pi \mid a_{i,j} \geq 0 \text{ for } i = 1, \ldots, n \text{ and } j = 1, \ldots, k\}$$

We now propose our bounded general adjuster (BGA), which outputs predictions within $Q_\pi^\square$.

Definition 13 (Bounded General Adjuster (BGA)). *Consider a k-class classification task with a test dataset of n instances, and let d_ϕ be a Bregman divergence. Then the* bounded general adjuster *corresponding to d_ϕ is the function $\alpha^\square : [0,1]^{n \times k} \times [0,1]^k \to [0,1]^{n \times k}$ defined as follows:*

$$\alpha^\square(p, \pi) = \underset{a \in Q_\pi^\square}{\arg\min} \frac{1}{n} \sum_{i=1}^n d_\phi(p_i, a_i.)$$

Similarly as for UGA, the correctness of BGA is guaranteed by the convexity of the optimisation task, as shown in Sect. 3.3. BGA solves almost the same optimisation task as UGA, except that instead of considering the whole hyperplane Q_π it finds the closest a within a bounded subset $Q_\pi^\square$ within the hyperplane. Multiplicative adjustment is the BGA for log-loss, because log-loss is not defined at all outside the $[0, 1]$ bounds, and hence the UGA for log-loss is the same as the BGA for log-loss. The following theorem shows that there is a guaranteed reduction of loss after BGA, and the reduction is at least as big as after UGA.

Theorem 14. *Let d_ϕ be a Bregman divergence, let p be a set of predictions, and π be a class distribution over k classes. Then for any $y \in Q_\pi^\square$ the following holds:*

$$\sum_{i=1}^n (d_\phi(p_i., y_i.) - d_\phi(a_i^\square, y_i.))$$

$$\geq \sum_{i=1}^n d_\phi(p_i., a_i^\square) \geq \sum_{i=1}^n d_\phi(p_i., a_i^\star.) = \sum_{i=1}^n (d_\phi(p_i., y_i.) - d_\phi(a_i^\star., y_i.))$$

Note that the theorem is even more general than we need and holds for all $y \in Q_\pi^\square$, not only those y which represent label matrices. A corollary of this theorem is that the BGA for Brier score is a new adjustment method dominating over additive adjustment in reducing Brier score. In practice, all practitioners should prefer BGA over UGA when looking to adjust their classifiers. Coherence and decomposition are interesting from a theoretical perspective but from a loss reduction standpoint, BGA is superior to UGA.

3.3   Implementation

Both UGA and BGA are defined through optimisation tasks, which can be shown to be convex. First, the objective function is convex as a sum of convex functions (Bregman divergences are convex in their second argument [2]). Second, the equality constraints that define Q_π are linear, making up a convex set. Finally, the inequality constraints of $Q_\pi^\square$ make up a convex set, which after intersecting with Q_π remains convex. These properties are sufficient [3] to prove that both the UGA and BGA optimisation tasks are convex.

UGA has only equality constraints, so Newton's method works fine with it. For Brier score there is a closed form solution [9] of simply adding the difference between the new distribution and the old distribution for every set of k probabilities. BGA computations are a little more difficult due to inequality constraints, therefore requiring interior point methods [3]. While multiplicative adjustment is for log-loss both BGA and UGA at the same time, it is easier to calculate it as a UGA, due to not having inequality constraints.

4   Experiments

4.1   Experimental Setup

While our theorems provide loss reduction guarantees when the exact class distribution is known, this is rarely something to be expected in practice. Therefore, the goal of our experiments was to evaluate the proposed adjustment methods in the setting where the class distribution is known approximately. For loss measures we selected Brier score and log-loss, which are the two most well known proper losses. As UGA is dominated by BGA, we decided to evaluate only BGA, across a wide range of different types of dataset shift, across different classifier learning algorithms, and across many datasets. We compare the results of BGA with the prior probability adjuster (PPA) introduced in Sect. 2, as this is to our knowledge the only existing method that inputs nothing else than the predictions of the model and the shifted class distribution. As reviewed in [17], other existing transfer learning methods need either the information about the features or a limited set of labelled data from the shifted context.

To cover a wide range of classifiers and datasets, we opted for using OpenML [16], which contains many datasets, and for each dataset many runs of different learning algorithms. For each run OpenML provides the predicted class probabilities in 10-fold cross-validation. As the predictions in 10-fold cross-validation are obtained with 10 different models trained on different subsets of folds, we compiled the prediction matrix p from one fold at a time. From OpenML we downloaded all user-submitted sets of predictions for both binary and multiclass (up to eight classes) classification tasks, restricting ourselves to tasks with the number of instances in the interval of $[2000, 1000000]$. Then we discarded every dataset that included a predicted score outside the range $(0, 1)$. To emphasize, we did not include runs which contain a 0 or a 1 anywhere in the predictions, since log-loss becomes infinite in case of errors with full confidence. We discarded datasets with less than 500 instances and sampled datasets with more than 1000 instances down to 1000 instances. This left us with 590 sets of predictions, each from a different model. These 590 sets of predictions come from 59 different runs from 56 different classification tasks. The list of used datasets and the source code for running the experiments is available in the Online Supplementary at https://github.com/teddyheiser/Shift_Happens_ECML_PKDD_2019.

Shifting. For each dataset we first identified the majority class(es). After sorting the classes by size decreasingly, the class(es) $1, \ldots, m$ were considered as majority class(es), where j was the smallest possible integer such that $\pi_1 + \cdots + \pi_m > 0.5$. We refer to other class(es) as minority class(es). We then created 4 variants of each dataset by artificially inducing shift in four ways. Each of those shifts has a parameter $\varepsilon \in [0.1, 0.5]$ quantifying the amount of shift, and ε was chosen uniformly randomly and independently for each adjustment task.

The first method induces prior probability shift by undersampling the majority class(es), reducing their total proportion from $\pi_1 + \cdots + \pi_m$ to $\pi_1 + \cdots + \pi_m - \varepsilon$. The second method induces a variety of concept shift by selecting randomly a proportion ε of instances from majority class(es) and changing their labels into uniformly random minority class labels. The third method induces covariate shift by deleting within class m the proportion ε of the instances with the lowest values of the numeric feature which correlates best with this class label. The fourth method was simply running the other three methods all one after another, which produces an other type of shift.

Approximating the New Class Distribution. It is unlikely that a practitioner of adjustment would know the exact class distribution of a shifted dataset. To investigate this, we ran our adjustment algorithms on our shifted datasets with not only the exact class distribution, but also eight 'estimations' of the class distribution obtained by artificially modifying the correct class distribution $(\pi_1, \ldots, \pi_k)$ into $(\pi_1 + \delta, \ldots, \pi_m + \delta, \pi_{m+1} - \delta', \ldots, \pi_k - \delta'$, where δ was one of eight values $+0.01, -0.01, +0.02, -0.02, +0.04, -0.04, +0.08, -0.08$, and δ' was chosen to ensure that the sum of class proportions adds up to 1. If any resulting class proportion left the [0,1] bounds, then the respective adjustment task was skipped. In total, we recorded results for 17527 adjustment tasks resulting from combinations of dataset fold, shift amount, shift method, and estimated class distribution.

Adjustment. For every combination of shift and for the corresponding nine different class distribution estimations, we adjusted the datasets/predictions using the three above-mentioned adjusters: Brier-score-minimizing-BGA, log-loss-minimizing-BGA, and PPA. PPA has a simple implementation, but for the general adjusters we used the CVXPY library [6] to perform convex optimization. For Brier-score-minimizing-BGA, the selected method of optimization was OSQP (as part of the CVXPY library). For log-loss-minimizing-BGA, we used the ECOS optimizer with the SCS optimizer as backup (under rare conditions the optimizers could numerically fail, occurred 30 times out of 17527). For both

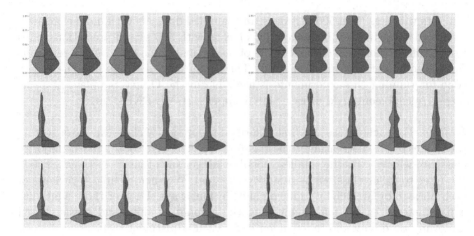

Fig. 2. The reduction in Brier score (left figure) and log-loss (right figure) after BGA adjustment (left side of the violin) and after PPA adjustment (right side of the violin). The rows correspond to different amounts of shift (with high shift at the top and low at the bottom). The columns correspond to amount of induced error in class distribution estimation, starting from left: 0.00, 0.01, 0.02, 0.04 and 0.08.

Brier score and log loss, we measured the unadjusted loss and the loss after running the dataset through the aforementioned three adjusters.

4.2 Results

On different datasets the effects of our shifting procedures vary and thus we have categorized the shifted datasets into 3 equal-sized groups by the amount of squared Euclidean distance between the original and new class distributions (high, medium and low shift). Note that these are correlated to the shift amount parameter ε, but not determined by it. Figures 2 and 3 both visualise the loss reduction after adjustment in proportion to the loss before adjustment. In these violin plots the part of distributions above 0 stands for reduction of loss and below 0 for increased loss after adjustment. For example, proportional reduction value 0.2 means that 20% of the loss was eliminated by adjustment. The left side of the left-most violins in Fig. 2 show the case where BGA for Brier score is evaluated on Brier score (with high shift at the top row and low at the bottom). Due to guaranteed reduction in loss the left sides of violins are all above 0. In contrast, the right side of the same violins shows the effect of PPA adjustment, and PPA can be seen to sometimes increase the loss, while also having lower average reduction of loss (the horizontal black line marking the mean is lower). When the injected estimation error in the class distribution increases (next 4 columns of violins), BGA adjustment can sometimes increase the loss as well, but is on average still reducing loss more than PPA in all of the violin plots. Similar patterns of results can be seen in the right subfigure of Fig. 2, where BGA for log-loss is compared with PPA, both evaluated on log-loss. The mean

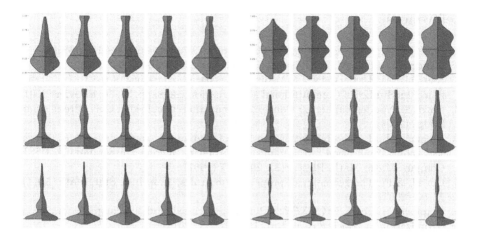

Fig. 3. The reduction in Brier score (left figure) and log-loss (right figure) after BGA adjustment to reduce Brier score (left side of the violin) and after BGA to reduce log-loss (right side of the violin). The rows correspond to different amounts of shift (high at the top and low at the bottom). The columns correspond to amount of induced error in class distribution estimation, starting from left: 0.00, 0.01, 0.02, 0.04 and 0.08.

proportional reduction of loss by BGA is higher than by PPA in 13 out of 15 cases. The bumps in some violins are due to using 4 different types of shift.

Figure 3 demonstrates the differences between BGA aiming to reduce Brier score (left side of each violin) and BGA to reduce log loss (right side of each violin), evaluated on Brier score (left subfigure) and log-loss (right subfigure). As seen from the right side of the leftmost violins, BGA aiming to reduce the wrong loss (log-loss) can actually increase loss (Brier score), even if the class distribution is known exactly. Therefore, as expected, it is important to adjust by minimising the same divergence that is going to be used to test the method.

5   Conclusion

In this paper we have constructed a family BGA of adjustment procedures aiming to reduce any proper loss of probabilistic classifiers after experiencing dataset shift, using knowledge about the class distribution. We have proved that the loss is guaranteed to reduce, if the class distribution is known exactly. According to our experiments, BGA adjustment to an approximated class distribution often still reduces loss more than prior probability adjustment.

Acknowledgments. This work was supported by the Estonian Research Council under grant PUT1458.

References

1. Banerjee, A., Guo, X., Wang, H.: On the optimality of conditional expectation as a Bregman predictor. IEEE Trans. Inf. Theory **51**(7), 2664–2669 (2005)
2. Bauschke, H.H., Borwein, J.M.: Joint and separate convexity of the Bregman distance. In: Studies in Computational Mathematics, vol. 8, pp. 23–36. Elsevier (2001)
3. Boyd, S., Vandenberghe, L.: Convex Optimization. Cambridge Univ. Press, Cambridge (2004)
4. Bregman, L.M.: The relaxation method of finding the common point of convex sets and its application to the solution of problems in convex programming. USSR Comput. Math. Math. Phys. **7**(3), 200–217 (1967)
5. Dawid, A.P.: The geometry of proper scoring rules. Ann. Inst. Stat. Math. **59**(1), 77–93 (2007)
6. Diamond, S., Boyd, S.: CVXPY: a Python-embedded modeling language for convex optimization. J. Mach. Learn. Res. **17**(83), 1–5 (2016)
7. Gretton, A., Smola, A.J., Huang, J., Schmittfull, M., Borgwardt, K.M., Schölkopf, B.: Covariate shift by kernel mean matching. In: Dataset shift in machine learning, pp. 131–160 (2009)
8. Hein, M.: Binary classification under sample selection bias. In: Candela, J., Sugiyama, M., Schwaighofer, A., Lawrence, N. (eds.) Dataset Shift in Machine Learning. MIT Press, Cambridge, pp. 41–64 (2009)
9. Kull, M., Flach, P.: Novel decompositions of proper scoring rules for classification: score adjustment as precursor to calibration. In: Appice, A., Rodrigues, P.P., Santos Costa, V., Soares, C., Gama, J., Jorge, A. (eds.) ECML PKDD 2015. LNCS (LNAI), vol. 9284, pp. 68–85. Springer, Cham (2015). https://doi.org/10.1007/978-3-319-23528-8_5
10. Merkle, E.C., Steyvers, M.: Choosing a strictly proper scoring rule. Decis. Anal. **10**(4), 292–304 (2013)
11. Moreno-Torres, J.G., Raeder, T., Alaiz-Rodríguez, R., Chawla, N.V., Herrera, F.: A unifying view on dataset shift in classification. Pattern Recogn. **45**(1), 521–530 (2012)
12. Saerens, M., Latinne, P., Decaestecker, C.: Adjusting the outputs of a classifier to new a priori probabilities: a simple procedure. Neural Comp. **14**(1), 21–41 (2002)
13. Shimodaira, H.: Improving predictive inference under covariate shift by weighting the log-likelihood function. J. Stat. Plan. Infer. **90**(2), 227–244 (2000)
14. Storkey, A.: When training and test sets are different: characterizing learning transfer. Dataset shift in machine learning, pp. 3–28 (2009)
15. Sugiyama, M., Krauledat, M., Müller, K.R.: Covariate shift adaptation by importance weighted cross validation. J. Mach. Learn. Res. **8**(May), 985–1005 (2007)
16. Vanschoren, J., van Rijn, J.N., Bischl, B., Torgo, L.: OpenML: networked science in machine learning. SIGKDD Explor. **15**(2), 49–60 (2013)
17. Weiss, K., Khoshgoftaar, T.M., Wang, D.D.: A survey of transfer learning. J. Big Data **3**(1), 1–40 (2016). https://doi.org/10.1186/s40537-016-0043-6

Beyond the Selected Completely at Random Assumption for Learning from Positive and Unlabeled Data

Jessa Bekker$^{(\boxtimes)}$ ⓘ, Pieter Robberechts ⓘ, and Jesse Davis ⓘ

Department of Computer Science, KU Leuven, Leuven, Belgium
{jessa.bekker,pieter.robberechts,jesse.davis}@kuleuven.be

Abstract. Most positive and unlabeled data is subject to selection biases. The labeled examples can, for example, be selected from the positive set because they are easier to obtain or more obviously positive. This paper investigates how learning can be enabled in this setting. We propose and theoretically analyze an empirical-risk-based method for incorporating the labeling mechanism. Additionally, we investigate under which assumptions learning is possible when the labeling mechanism is not fully understood and propose a practical method to enable this. Our empirical analysis supports the theoretical results and shows that taking into account the possibility of a selection bias, even when the labeling mechanism is unknown, improves the trained classifiers.

Keywords: PU learning · Unlabeled data · Classification

1 Introduction

Positive and unlabeled learning focuses on the setting where the training data contains some labeled positive examples and unlabeled examples, which could belong to either the positive or negative class. This contrasts to supervised learning, where a learner has a fully labeled training set and to semi-supervised learning, where a learner (usually) observes some labeled examples from each class. Positive and unlabeled (PU) data naturally arises in many applications. Electronic medical records (EMR) list diseases that a patient has been diagnosed with, however, many diseases are undiagnosed. Therefore, the absence of a diagnosis does not imply that a patient does not have the disease. Similarly, automatically constructed knowledge bases (KBs) are incomplete, and hence any absent tuple may be either true (i.e., belong in the knowledge base) or false [37].

Elkan and Noto [12] formalized one of the most commonly made assumptions in PU learning: the observed positive examples were selected completely at random from the set of all positive examples. This assumption means that the probability of observing the label of a positive example is constant (i.e., the same for all positive examples), which facilitates and simplifies both theoretical analysis and algorithmic design. This setting has been extensively explored in the literature [4,5,7,9,10,15,16,21,22,24,26,27].

© Springer Nature Switzerland AG 2020
U. Brefeld et al. (Eds.): ECML PKDD 2019, LNAI 11907, pp. 71–85, 2020.
https://doi.org/10.1007/978-3-030-46147-8_5

Unfortunately, the "selected completely at random" assumption is often violated in real-world data sets. For example, a patient's EMR will only contain a diagnosis if she visits a doctor, which will be influenced by factors such as the severity of the symptoms and her socio-economic status. The problem of biases in the observed labels has been recognized in the recommender systems and retrieval literature [19,25,32]. However, these works differ from PU learning in that the labels for some examples from each "class" are observed. Still, within the context of PU learning, there has been little (or no) work that focuses on coping with biases in the observed positive labels.

The contribution of this paper is to take a step towards filling that gap by proposing and analyzing a new, less restrictive assumption for PU learning: the *Selected At Random (SAR)* assumption. Instead of assuming a constant probability for all positive examples to be labeled, it assumes that the probability is a function of a subset of an example's attributes. To help analyze this new setting, we leverage the idea of a propensity score, which is a term originating from the causal inference literature [17]. Intuitively, the propensity score can be thought of as an instance-specific probability that an example was selected to be labeled. We show theoretically how using propensity scores in a SAR setting provides benefits. Then, we discuss a practical approach for learning the propensity scores from the data and using them to learn a model. Empirically, we show that for SAR PU data, our approach results in improved performance over making the standard selected completely at random assumption.

2   Preliminaries

PU learning entails learning a binary classifier only given access to positive examples and unlabeled data. This paper considers the single-training set scenario, where the data can be viewed as a set of triples (x, y, s) with x a vector of the attributes, y the class and s a binary variable representing whether the tuple was selected to be labeled. While y is always missing, information about it can be derived from the value of s. If $s = 1$, then the example belongs to the positive class as $\Pr(y = 1|s = 1) = 1$. If $s = 0$, the instance can belong to either class.

In PU learning, it is common to make the *Selected Completely at Random (SCAR)* assumption, which assumes that the observed positive examples are a random subset of the complete set of positive examples. Selecting a positive example is therefore independent of the example's attributes $\Pr(s = 1|y = 1, x) = \Pr(s = 1|y = 1)$. The probability for selecting a positive example to be labeled is known as the label frequency $c = \Pr(s = 1|y = 1)$. A neat advantage of the SCAR assumption is that, using the label frequency, a model that predicts the probability of an example being labeled can be transformed to the classifier: $\Pr(y = 1|x) = \Pr(s = 1|x)/c$.

Knowing the label frequency is equivalent to knowing the class prior $\alpha = \Pr(y = 1)$ as one can be derived from the other: $c = \Pr(s = 1)/\alpha$. Under the SCAR assumption, PU learning can therefore be reduced to estimating the class prior or label frequency and training a model to predict the observed labels.

Estimating the label frequency is an ill-defined problem because it is not identifiable: the absence of a label can be explained by either a small prior probability for the positive class or a low label frequency [33]. For the class prior to be identifiable, additional assumptions are necessary. Different assumptions have been proposed, but they are all based on attributing as many missing classes as possible to a lower label frequency as opposed to a lower positive class probability. The following assumptions are listed from strongest to strictly weaker. The strongest assumption is that the classes are non-overlapping, which makes the class prior and the labeled distribution match the unlabeled one as closely as possible [12,29]. Others make the assumption that there exists a positive subdomain of the instance space, but the classes can overlap elsewhere [1,28,33]. Ramaswamy et al. [30] assumes that a function exists which only selects positive instances. Finally, the irreducibility assumption states that the negative distribution cannot be a mixture that contains the positive distribution [3,18].

3   Labeling Mechanisms for PU Learning

The labeling mechanism determines which positive examples are labeled. To date, PU learning has largely focused on the SCAR setting. However, labels are not missing completely at random in most real-world problems. For example, facts in automatically constructed KBs are biased in several ways. One, they are learned from Web data, and only certain types of information appear on the Web (e.g., there is more text about high-level professional sports teams than low-level ones). Two, the algorithms that extract information from the Web employ heuristics to ensure that only information that is likely to be accurate (e.g., redundancy) is included in the KB. Similarly, biases arise when people decide to like items online, bookmark web pages, or subscribe to mail lists. Therefore, we believe it is important to consider and study other labeling mechanisms.

When Elkan and Noto [12] first formalized the SCAR assumption, they noted the similarity of the PU setting to the general problem of learning in the presence of missing data. Specifically, they noted that the SCAR assumption is somewhat analogous with the missing data mechanism called *Missing Completely At Random (MCAR)* [31]. Apart from MCAR, the two other classes of missing data mechanisms are *Missing At Random (MAR)* and *Missing Not At Random (MNAR)*. To complete this analogy, we propose the following corresponding classes of PU labeling mechanisms:

SCAR *Selected Completely At Random*: The labeling mechanism does not depend on the attributes of the example, nor on the probability of the example being positive: each positive example has the same probability to be labeled.

SAR *Selected At Random*: The labeling mechanism depends on the values of the attributes of the example, but given the attribute values it does not depend on the probability of the example being positive.

SNAR *Selected Not At Random*: All other cases: The labeling mechanism depends on the real probability of this example being positive, even given the attribute values.

There is one very important difference between PU labeling mechanisms and missingness mechanisms in that the labeling always depends on the class value: only positive examples can be selected to be labeled. According to the missingness taxonomy, all PU labeling mechanisms are therefore MNAR. SNAR is a peculiar class because it depends on the real class probability, while the class needs to be positive by definition. The class probability refers to the probability of an identical instance to this one being positive. Consider, for example, the problem of classifying pages as interesting. If a page is moderately interesting to you, some days you might like it while other days you might not. The labeling mechanism in this case could depend on how much you like them and therefore on the instance's class probability.

4   Learning with SAR Labeling Mechanisms

In this paper, we focus on SAR labeling mechanisms, where the key question is how we can enable learning from SAR PU data. Our key insight is that the labeling mechanism is also related to the notion of a propensity score from causal inference [17]. In causal inference, the propensity score is the probability that an instance is assigned to the treatment or control group. This probability is instance-specific and based on a set of the instance's attributes. We use an analogous idea and define the propensity score as the labeling probability for positive examples:

Definition 1 (Propensity Score). *The propensity score for x, denoted $e(x)$, is the label assignment probability for positive instances with attributes x,*

$$e(x) = \Pr(s = 1 | y = 1, x).$$

A crucial difference with the propensity score from causal inference is that our score is conditioned on the class being positive.

We incorporate the propensity score when learning in a PU setting by using the propensity scores to reweight the data. Our scheme generalizes an approach taken for SCAR data [11,21,34] to the SAR setting. In causal inference, inverse-propensity-scoring is a standard method where the examples are weighted with the inverse of their propensity score [17,23,32]. This cannot be applied when working with positive and unlabeled data, because we have zero probability for labeling negative examples. But we can do a different kind of weighting. The insight is that for each labeled example $(x_i, s = 1)$ that has a propensity score e_i, there are expected to be $\frac{1}{e_i}$ positive examples, of which $\frac{1}{e_i} - 1$ did not get selected to be labeled. This insight can be used in algorithms that use counts, to estimate the correct count from the observed positives and their respective propensity scores. In general, this can be formulated as learning with negative weights: every labeled example gets a weight $\frac{1}{e_i}$ and for every labeled example a negative example is added to the dataset that gets a negative weight $1 - \frac{1}{e_i}$.

We now provide a theoretical analysis of the propensity-weighted method, to characterize its appropriateness. We consider two cases: (1) when we know the true propensity scores and (2) when we must estimate them from data. All the proofs are deferred to the appendix (https://dtai.cs.kuleuven.be/software/sar).

4.1   Case 1: True Propensity Scores Known

Standard evaluation measures, such as Mean Absolute Error (MAE), Mean Square Error (MSE) and log loss, can be formulated as follows:[1]

$$R(\hat{\mathbf{y}}|\mathbf{y}) = \frac{1}{n} \sum_{i=1}^{n} y_i \delta_1(\hat{y}_i) + (1 - y_i)\delta_0(\hat{y}_i),$$

where $\mathbf{y}$ and $\hat{\mathbf{y}}$ are vectors of size n containing, respectively, the true labels and predicted labels. The function $\delta_y(\hat{y})$ represents the cost for predicting $\hat{y}$ when the class is y, for example:

$$\text{MAE} : \delta_y(\hat{y}) = |y - \hat{y}|,$$
$$\text{MSE} : \delta_y(\hat{y}) = (y - \hat{y})^2,$$
$$\text{Log Loss} : \delta_1(\hat{y}) = -\ln\hat{y} , \ \ \delta_0(\hat{y}) = -\ln(1 - \hat{y}).$$

We can formulate propensity-weighted variants of these cost functions as:

Definition 2 (Propensity-Weighted Estimator). *Given the propensity scores* $\mathbf{e}$ *and PU labels* $\mathbf{s}$, *the propensity weighted estimator of* $R(\hat{\mathbf{y}}|\mathbf{y})$ *is*

$$\hat{R}(\hat{\mathbf{y}}|\mathbf{e}, \mathbf{s}) = \frac{1}{n} \sum_{i=1}^{n} s_i \left(\frac{1}{e_i}\delta_1(\hat{y}_i) + (1 - \frac{1}{e_i})\delta_0(\hat{y}_i) \right) + (1 - s_i)\delta_0(\hat{y}_i),$$

where $\mathbf{y}$ *and* $\hat{\mathbf{y}}$ *are vectors of size* n *containing, respectively, the true labels and predicted labels. The function* $\delta_y(\hat{y})$ *represents the cost for predicting* $\hat{y}$ *when the class is* y.

This estimator is unbiased:

$$\mathbb{E}[\hat{R}(\hat{\mathbf{y}}|\mathbf{e}, \mathbf{s})])$$
$$= \frac{1}{n} \sum_{i=1}^{n} y_i e_i \left(\frac{1}{e_i}\delta_1(\hat{y}_i) + (1 - \frac{1}{e_i})\delta_0(\hat{y}_i) \right) + (1 - y_i e_i)\delta_0(\hat{y}_i)$$
$$= \frac{1}{n} \sum_{i=1}^{n} y_i\delta_1(\hat{y}_i) + (1 - y_i)\delta_0(\hat{y}_i)$$
$$= R(\hat{\mathbf{y}}|\mathbf{y}).$$

To characterize how much the estimator can vary from the expected value, we provide the following bound:

Proposition 1 (Propensity-Weighted Estimator Bound). *For any predicted classes* $\hat{\mathbf{y}}$ *and real classes* $\mathbf{y}$ *of size* n, *with probability* $1 - \eta$, *the propensity-weighted estimator* $\hat{R}(\hat{\mathbf{y}}|\mathbf{e}, \mathbf{s})$ *does not differ from the true evaluation measure* $R(\hat{\mathbf{y}}|\mathbf{y})$ *more than*

$$|\hat{R}(\hat{\mathbf{y}}|\mathbf{e}, \mathbf{s}) - R(\hat{\mathbf{y}}|\mathbf{y})| \leq \sqrt{\frac{\delta_{max}^2 \ln\frac{2}{\eta}}{2n}},$$

with δ_{max} *the maximum absolute value of cost function* δ_y.

---

[1] We assume that $0 < \hat{y} < 1$.

The propensity-weighted estimator can be used as the risk for Empirical Risk Minimization (ERM), which searches for a model in the hypothesis space $\mathcal{H}$ by minimizing the risk:

$$\hat{\mathbf{y}}_{\hat{R}} = \underset{\hat{\mathbf{y}} \in \mathcal{H}}{\operatorname{argmin}} \hat{R}(\hat{\mathbf{y}}|\mathbf{e}, \mathbf{s}).$$

The following proposition characterizes how much the estimated risk for hypothesis $\hat{\mathbf{y}}_{\hat{R}}$ can deviate from its true risk.

Proposition 2 (Propensity-Weighted ERM Generalization Error Bound). *For a finite hypothesis space $\mathcal{H}$, the difference between the propensity-weighted risk of the empirical risk minimizer $\hat{\mathbf{y}}_{\hat{R}}$ and its true risk is bounded, with probability $1 - \eta$, by:*

$$R(\hat{\mathbf{y}}_{\hat{R}}|\mathbf{y}) \leq \hat{R}(\hat{\mathbf{y}}_{\hat{R}}|\mathbf{e}, \mathbf{s}) + \sqrt{\frac{\delta_{max}^2 \ln \frac{|\mathcal{H}|}{\eta}}{2n}}.$$

4.2   Case 2: Propensity Scores Estimated from Data

Often the exact propensity score is unknown, but we have an estimate $\hat{e}$ of it. In this case, the bias of the propensity-weighted estimator is:

Proposition 3 (Propensity-Weighted Estimator Bias).

$$bias(\hat{R}(\hat{\mathbf{y}}|\hat{\mathbf{e}}, \mathbf{s})) = \frac{1}{n} \sum_{i=1}^{n} y_i (1 - \frac{e_i}{\hat{e}_i}) (\delta_1(\hat{y}_i) - \delta_0(\hat{y}_i)).$$

From the bias, it follows that the propensity scores only need to be accurate for positive examples. An incorrect propensity score has a larger impact when the predicted classes have more extreme values (i.e., tend towards zero or one). Underestimated propensity scores are expected to result in a model with a higher bias. Lower propensity scores result in learning models that estimate the positive class to be more prevalent than it is, which results in a larger $(\delta_1(\hat{y}_i) - \delta_0(\hat{y}_i))$ for positive examples.

Side Note on Sub-optimality of Expected Risk. Another method that one might be inclined to use when incorporating the propensity score is to minimize the expected risk[2]:

$$\hat{R}_{\exp}(\hat{\mathbf{y}}|\mathbf{e}, \mathbf{s}) = \mathbb{E}_{\mathbf{y}|\mathbf{e}, \mathbf{s}, \hat{\mathbf{y}}} [R(\hat{\mathbf{y}}|\mathbf{y})]$$

$$= \frac{1}{n} \sum_{i=1}^{n} \left(s_i + (1 - s_i) \frac{\hat{y}_i(1 - e_i)}{1 - \hat{y}_i e_i} \right) \delta_1(\hat{y}_i) + (1 - s_i) \frac{1 - \hat{y}_i}{1 - \hat{y}_i e_i} \delta_0(\hat{y}_i).$$

---

[2] Derivation in appendix, available on https://dtai.cs.kuleuven.be/software/sar.

However, the expected risk is not an unbiased estimator of the true risk and as a result, $\hat{\mathbf{y}}_{\hat{R}_{\mathrm{exp}}} = \mathrm{argmin}_{\hat{\mathbf{y}} \in \mathcal{H}} \hat{R}_{\mathrm{exp}}(\hat{\mathbf{y}}|\mathbf{e}, \mathbf{s})$ is not expected to be the best hypothesis. In fact, the hypothesis of always predicting the positive class $\forall_i : \hat{y}_i = 1$ always has an expected risk $\hat{R}_{\mathrm{exp}}(\hat{\mathbf{y}}|\mathbf{e}, \mathbf{s}) = 0$.

5   Learning Under the SAR Assumption

If the propensity scores for all examples are known (i.e., the exact labeling mechanism is known), they can be directly incorporated into the learning algorithm. However, it is more likely that they are unknown. Therefore, this section investigates how to permit learning in the SAR setting when the exact propensity scores are unknown. We discuss two such settings. The first is interesting from a theoretical perspective and the second from a practical perspective.

5.1   Reducing SAR to SCAR

Learning the propensity scores from positive and unlabeled data requires making additional assumptions: if any arbitrary instance can have any propensity score, then it is impossible to know if an instance did not get labeled because of a low propensity score or a low class probability. Therefore, the propensity score needs to depend on fewer attributes than the final classifier [17]. A simple way to accomplish this is to assume that the propensity function only depends on a subset of the attributes x_e called the *propensity attributes*:

$$\mathrm{Pr}(s = 1|y = 1, x) = \mathrm{Pr}(s = 1|y = 1, x_e)$$
$$e(x) = e(x_e).$$

Often, this a realistic assumption. It is trivially true if the labeling mechanism does not have access to all attributes (e.g., because some were collected later). It may also arise if a labeler cannot interpret some attributes (e.g., raw sensor values) or only uses the attributes that are known to be highly correlated with the class.

To see why this can be a sufficient assumption for learning in a SAR setting, consider the case where the propensity attributes x_e have a finite number of configurations, which is true if these attributes are all discrete. In this case, it is possible to partition the data into strata, with one stratum for each configuration of x_e. Within a stratum, the propensity score is a constant (i.e., all positive examples have the same propensity score) and can thus be determined using standard SCAR PU learning techniques. Note that, as previously discussed, the SCAR assumption alone is not enough to enable learning from PU data, and hence one of the additional assumptions [1,3,28,30,33] must be made.

Reducing SAR to SCAR is interesting because it demonstrates that learning in the SAR setting is possible. However, it is suboptimal in practice as it does not work if x_e contains a continuous variable. Even for the discrete case, the number of configurations grows exponentially as the size of x_e increases. Furthermore, information is lost by partitioning the data. Some smoothness of the classifier over the propensity attributes is expected, but this is not encouraged when learning different classifiers for each configuration. Similarly, the propensity score itself is expected to be a smooth function over the propensity variables.

5.2   EM for Propensity Estimation

The problems with reducing the SAR to the SCAR case motivate the need to jointly search for a classifier and lower dimensional propensity score function that best explain the observed data. This approach also offers the advantage that it relaxes the additional assumptions: if they hold in the majority of the propensity attributes' configurations, the models' smoothness helps to overcome potential issues arising in the configurations where the assumptions are violated. This subsection presents a simple expectation-maximization method for simultaneously training the classification and the propensity score model. It aims to maximize the expected log likelihood of the combination of models.

Expectation. Given the expected classification model $\hat{f}$ and propensity score model $\hat{e}$, the expected probability of the positive class $\hat{y}_i$ of instance x_i with label s_i is:[3]

$$\hat{y}_i = \Pr(y_i = 1|s_i, x_i, \hat{f}, \hat{e})$$

$$= s_i + (1 - s_i) \frac{\hat{f}(x_i)(1 - \hat{e}(x_i))}{1 - \hat{f}(x_i)\hat{e}(x_i)}.$$

Maximization. Given the expected probabilities of the positive class $\hat{y}_i$, the models f and e are trained to optimize the expected log likelihood:

$$\operatorname{argmax}_{f,e} \sum_{i=1}^{n} \mathbb{E}_{y_i|x_i,s_i,\hat{f},\hat{e}} \ln \Pr(x_i, s_i, y_i|f, e)$$

$$= \operatorname{argmax}_{f} \sum_{i=1}^{n} \left[\hat{y}_i \ln f(x_i) + (1 - \hat{y}_i) \ln(1 - f(x_i)) \right],$$

$$\operatorname{argmax}_{e} \sum_{i=1}^{n} \hat{y}_i \left[s_i \cdot \ln e(x_i) + (1 - s_i) \cdot \ln(1 - e(x_i)) \right]$$

From the maximization formula, it can be seen that to optimize the log likelihood, both models need to optimize the log loss of a weighted dataset. The

---

[3] All derivations for this section are in the appendix, available on https://dtai.cs. kuleuven.be/software/sar.

classification model f receives each example i twice, once as positive, weighted by the expected probability of it being positive $\hat{y}_i$ and once as negative, weighted by the expected probability of it being negative $(1 - \hat{y}_i)$. The propensity score model e receives each example once, positive if the observed label is positive and negative otherwise, weighted by the expected probability of it being positive $\hat{y}_i$.

Because this approach minimizes log loss, it will work best if the classes are separable. If the classes are not separable, then the trained classification model is not expected to be the optimal one for the trained propensity model (see previous section). In that case, it is advisable to retrain the classifier with the obtained propensity score, using the propensity-weighted risk estimation method.

The classification model is initialized by fitting a balanced model which considers the unlabeled examples as negative. The propensity score model is initialized by using the classification model to estimate the probabilities of each unlabeled example being positive.

Classic EM converges when the log likelihood stops improving. However, the likelihood could stop improving before the propensity score model has converged. Convergence is therefore formulated as convergence of both the log likelihood and the propensity model. We measure the change in the propensity score model by the average slope of the minimum square error line through the propensity score prediction of the last n iterations.

6   Empirical Evaluation

This section illustrates empirically that the SAR assumption facilitates better learning from SAR PU data. We compare both SAR and SCAR methods, so that the gain of using an instance-dependent propensity score over a constant label frequency can be observed. More specifically, we address the following questions:

Q1. Does propensity score weighting (SAR) improve classification performance over assuming that data is SCAR and using class prior weighting?

Q2. Can the propensity score function be recovered?

Q3. Does the number of propensity attributes affect the performance?

6.1   Data

We use eight real-world datasets which cover a range of application domains such as text, images and tabular data. These datasets are summarized in Table 1. Since the 20 News Groups, Cover Type, Diabetes and Image Segmentation datasets are originally multi-class datasets, we first transformed them by either grouping or ignoring classes. For 20 News Groups,[4] we distinguish between computer (pos) and recreational (neg) documents. After removing their headers, footers, quotes, and English stop words, the documents were transformed to 200 word occurrence attributes using the Scikit-Learn[5] count vectorizer. For Cover Type (see footnote

---

[4] http://archive.ics.uci.edu/ml/.

[5] http://scikit-learn.org.

4), we distinguish the Lodgepole Pine (pos) from all other cover types (neg). The Diabetes (see footnote 4) data was preprocessed in a similar manner to Strack et al. [35]. Additionally, we dropped attributes with the same value in 95% of the examples, and replaced uncommon attribute values by "other". The positive class is patients being readmitted within 30 days. Image Segmentation (see footnote 4) was used to distinguish between nature (sky, grass or foliage) and other scenes (brickface, cement, window, path). Adult (see footnote 4), Breast Cancer (see footnote 4), Mushroom (see footnote 4), and Splice[6] were used as is. To enable using logistic regression, all the datasets were further preprocessed to have exclusively continuous attributes, scaled between -1 and 1. Multivalued attributes were binarized.

Table 1. Datasets

Dataset	# Instances	# Attrib	$\Pr(y = 1)$
20 Newsgroups	3,979	200	0.55
Adult	48,842	14	0.24
Breast cancer	683	9	0.35
Cover type	581,0124	54	0.49
Diabetes	99,492	127	0.11
Image Segm.	2,310	18	0.43
Mushroom	8,124	111	0.48
Splice	3,175	60	0.52

6.2   Methodology and Approaches

Constructing Datasets. First, we extended each dataset with four artificial binary propensity attributes $x_e^{(i)} \in \{0, 1\}$. Therefore, we clustered each dataset into five groups (based on the attribute values) and generated for each group a random distribution between propensity attribute values $\{0, 1\}$. Intuitively, this corresponds to a scenario where examples that are in the same cluster have the same prior probability of belonging to the positive class. However, which examples are labeled depend on the propensity attributes.

Next, the datasets were randomly partitioned into train (80%) and test (20%) sets five times. For each of the five train-test splits, we transformed the data into positive and unlabeled datasets by sampling the examples to be labeled according to the following propensity score:

$$e(x_e) = \prod_{i=1}^{k} \left(p_{\text{low}}^{1-x_e^{(i)}} \cdot p_{\text{high}}^{x_e^{(i)}} \right)^{\frac{1}{k}}$$

---

[6] Available on LIBSVM Data repository https://www.csie.ntu.edu.tw/~cjlin/libsvmtools/datasets/.

This gives propensity scores between p_{low} and p_{high}, with all artificial propensity attributes x_e attributing equally to it. In our experiments the propensity scores were between 0.2 and 0.8. We generated five of such labelings for each of the five train-test splits and report the average performance over these 25 experiments.

Approach. We compare the classification performance of our EM method under the SAR assumption[7] against four baselines. First, we assume the data is SCAR and compare against two state-of-the art methods to estimate the class prior: KM2 from Ramaswamy et al. [30][8] and TIcE from Bekker and Davis [1][9] with standard settings. Second, we use the naive baseline which assumes that all unlabeled examples belong to the negative class (denoted Naive). Finally, as an illustrative upper bound on performance, we show results when given fully super-vised data (denoted Sup.). All approaches use logistic regression with default parameters from Scikit-Learn[10] as the base classifier for the classification model and also for the propensity score model in the SAR setting.

6.3   Results

Q1. Figure 1 compares SAR-EM to all baselines. Because we are considering models that predict probabilities for binary classification problems, we report two standard metrics. First, we report MSE which measures the quality of the model's probability estimates [13]. Second, we report ROC-AUC, which measures predictive performance. When the propensity attributes are known, learning both the propensity score and the classification model from the data outperforms assuming the data is SCAR and learning under that assumption. Based on each method's average ROC-AUC ranks over all eight benchmark datasets, the Friedman test [8] rejects the null-hypothesis that all methods perform the same ($p < 0.001$), regardless of the number of propensity attributes used. Moreover, using the Nemenyi post-hoc test on the ranks, the performance of our SAR-EM method is significantly better ($p < 0.01$) than the naive approach, KM2 and TIcE. Note that the naive approach sometimes outperforms the SCAR approaches. This can be explained by the SCAR methods' goal of predicting the correct ratio of the instance space as positive. When it picks the wrong subspace to get to this ratio, it results in both false positives and false negatives, where the more conservative naive approach would only give the false negatives.

Q2. To evaluate the quality of the learned propensity scores for each example, we report the MSE [13]. Except for the mushroom dataset, the EM method always obtains very accurate propensity score estimates with MSEs below 0.1 (Fig. 2). Furthermore, the MSEs are often very close to zero.

---

[7] Implementation available on https://dtai.cs.kuleuven.be/software/sar.

[8] http://web.eecs.umich.edu/~cscott/code/kernel_MPE.zip.

[9] https://dtai.cs.kuleuven.be/software/tice/.

[10] https://scikit-learn.org/stable/.

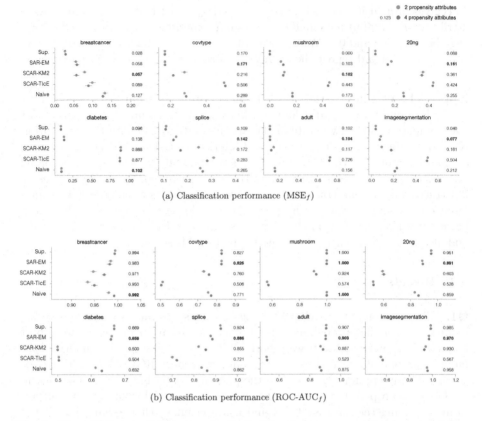

(a) Classification performance (MSE$_f$)

(b) Classification performance (ROC-AUC$_f$)

Fig. 1. Given SAR data, jointly learning both the unknown propensity scores and the classification model almost always outperforms learning under the SCAR assumption. The dots correspond to the mean performance for respectively two (grey) and four (blue) propensity attributes. The error bars represent a 95% confidence interval around the mean. The exact performance metric value is given on the right for the setting with four propensity attributes, with the best performing algorithm highlighted in bold (ignoring Supervised). (Color figure online)

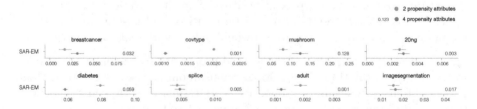

Fig. 2. Accuracy of the propensity score estimates (MSE$_e$). The dots correspond to the mean performance for respectively two (grey) and four (blue) propensity attributes. The error bars represent a 95% confidence interval around the mean. The exact performance metric value is given on the right for the setting with four propensity attributes. (Color figure online)

Q3. Finally, we observe no correlation between the number of propensity attributes and the MSE and ROC-AUC of the classification model, nor the MSE of the propensity score estimates (Fig. 1a).

7   Related Work

PU learning is an active area and for a broad overview see [2]. This work focuses on approaches that modify learning methods by exploiting the assumptions about the labeling mechanism (e.g., [9,12,16,22,27,36]) for the single training set scenario. The key difference is that this paper generalizes past work, which has focused on the SCAR assumption, to the less restrictive SAR setting. The weighting scheme used in this paper has been used under the SCAR assumption [11,21,34]. Furthermore, a special case of this method has been applied matrix completion [16].

Almost all PU learning work that we are aware of focuses on the SCAR setting. One recent exception assumes that the probability of observing a label for a positive example depends on how difficult the example is to label [14]. That is, the more similar a positive example is to a negative one, the less likely it is to be labeled. The difficulty of labeling is defined by the *probabilistic gap* $\Delta \Pr(x) = \Pr(y = 1|x) - \Pr(y = 0|x)$ [14]. Based on properties of the probabilistic gap, it is possible to identify reliable positive and negative examples [14]. Because the probabilistic gap labeling mechanism depends on the attribute values x, it is a specific case of SAR. Concretely, it assumes a propensity score that is a non-negative, monotonically decreasing function of the probabilistic gap $\Delta \Pr(x)$.

PU learning is a special case of semi-supervised learning [6]. It is also related to one-class learning [20]. The work on dealing with biases in the observed ratings for recommender systems [32] and implicit feedback [19] is closely related to ours. They also make use of propensity scores to cope with the biases. However, there is a crucial difference: they perform inverse propensity weighting, which is not possible in our setting. In those works, the propensity score for each example is non-zero. In contrast, in PU learning, the propensity score for any negative example is zero: you never observe these labels. Moreover, they assume that examples for the full label space are available (e.g., observe at least one rating of each category for recommender systems) to learn the propensity model, which is not the case for PU learning because we have no known negative examples. This necessitates different ways to learn the propensity scores and weigh the data in our setting.

8   Conclusions

We investigated learning from SAR PU data: positive and unlabeled data with non-uniform labeling mechanisms. We proposed and theoretically analyzed an empirical-risk-minimization based method for weighting PU datasets with the propensity scores to achieve unbiased learning. We explored which assumptions are necessary to learn from SAR PU data generated by an unknown labeling mechanism and proposed a practical EM-based method for this setting. Empirically, for SAR PU data, our proposed propensity weighted method offers superior predictive performance over making the SCAR assumption. Moreover, we are able to accurately estimate each example's propensity score.

Acknowledgments. JB is supported by IWT(SB/141744). PR is supported by by Nano4Sports and Research Foundation - Flanders (G0D8819N). JD is partially supported by KU Leuven Research Fund (C14/17/07, C32/17/036), Research Foundation - Flanders (EOS No. 30992574, G0D8819N) and VLAIO-SBO grant HYMOP (150033).

References

1. Bekker, J., Davis, J.: Estimating the class prior in positive and unlabeled data through decision tree induction. In: Proceedings of the 32th AAAI Conference on Artificial Intelligence (2018)
2. Bekker, J., Davis, J.: Learning from positive and unlabeled data: a survey. In: Machine Learning (2020)
3. Blanchard, G., Lee, G., Scott, C.: Semi-supervised novelty detection. J. Mach. Learn. Res. **11**, 2973–3009 (2010)
4. Blockeel, H.: PU-learning disjunctive concepts in ILP. In: ILP 2017 Late Breaking Papers (2017)
5. Chang, S., et al.: Positive-unlabeled learning in streaming networks. In: Proceedings of the 22nd ACM Conference on Knowledge Discovery and Data Mining, pp. 755–764 (2016)
6. Chapelle, O., Scholkopf, B., Zien, A.: Semi-supervised learning. IEEE Trans. Neural Networks **20**(3), 542 (2009)
7. Claesen, M., De Smet, F., Suykens, J.A.K., De Moor, B.: A robust ensemble approach to learn from positive and unlabeled data using SVM base models. Neurocomputing **160**, 73–84 (2015)
8. Demšar, J.: Statistical comparisons of classifiers over multiple data sets. J. Mach. Learn. Res. **7**(Jan), 1–30 (2006)
9. Denis, F., Gilleron, R., Letouzey, F.: Learning from positive and unlabeled examples. Theoret. Comput. Sci. **348**(1), 70–83 (2005)
10. Denis, F.Ç.: PAC learning from positive statistical queries. In: Richter, M.M., Smith, C.H., Wiehagen, R., Zeugmann, T. (eds.) ALT 1998. LNCS (LNAI), vol. 1501, pp. 112–126. Springer, Heidelberg (1998). https://doi.org/10.1007/3-540-49730-7_9
11. Du Plessis, M., Niu, G., Sugiyama, M.: Convex formulation for learning from positive and unlabeled data. In: International Conference on Machine Learning, pp. 1386–1394 (2015)
12. Elkan, C., Noto, K.: Learning classifiers from only positive and unlabeled data. In: KDD (2008)
13. Flach, P.: Performance evaluation in machine learning: the good, the bad, the ugly and the way forward. In: Proceedings of the 33th AAAI Conference on Artificial Intelligence (2019)
14. He, F., Liu, T., Webb, G.I., Tao, D.: Instance-dependent PU learning by Bayesian optimal relabeling. arXiv preprint arXiv:1808.02180 (2018)
15. Hou, M., Chaib-draa, B., Li, C., Zhao, Q.: Generative adversarial positive-unlabelled learning. In: Proceedings of the Twenty-Seventh International Joint Conference on Artificial Intelligence, IJCAI 2018, pp. 2255–2261, July 2018

16. Hsieh, C.J., Natarajan, N., Dhillon, I.: PU learning for matrix completion. In: International Conference on Machine Learning, pp. 2445–2453 (2015)
17. Imbens, G.W., Rubin, D.B.: Causal Inference in Statistics, Social, and Biomedical Sciences. Cambridge University Press, Cambridge (2015)
18. Jain, S., White, M., Radivojac, P.: Estimating the class prior and posterior from noisy positives and unlabeled data. In: NIPS (2016)
19. Joachims, T., Swaminathan, A., Schnabel, T.: Unbiased learning-to-rank with biased feedback. In: Proceedings of the Tenth ACM International Conference on Web Search and Data Mining, pp. 781–789 (2017)
20. Khan, S., Madden, M.: One-class classification: taxonomy of study and review of techniques. Knowl. Eng. Rev. **29**, 345–374 (2014)
21. Kiryo, R., Niu, G., du Plessis, M.C., Sugiyama, M.: Positive-unlabeled learning with non-negative risk estimator. In: Advances in Neural Information Processing Systems, pp. 1675–1685 (2017)
22. Lee, W.S., Liu, B.: Learning with positive and unlabeled examples using weighted logistic regression. In: ICML, pp. 448–455 (2003)
23. Little, R., Rubin, D.: Statistical Analysis with Missing Data. Wiley, Hoboken (2002)
24. Liu, B., Dai, Y., Li, X.L., Lee, W., Yu, P.: Building text classifiers using positive and unlabeled examples. In: ICDM, pp. 179–186 (2003)
25. Marlin, B.M., Zemel, R.S.: Collaborative prediction and ranking with non-random missing data. In: Proceedings of the 2009 ACM Conference on Recommender Systems, pp. 5–12 (2009)
26. Mordelet, F., Vert, J.P.: A bagging SVM to learn from positive and unlabeled examples. Pattern Recogn. Lett. **37**, 201–209 (2014)
27. Northcutt, C.G., Wu, T., Chuang, I.L.: Learning with confident examples: rank pruning for robust classification with noisy labels. In: Proceedings of the Thirty-Third Conference on Uncertainty in Artificial Intelligence (2017)
28. du Plessis, M.C., Niu, G., Sugiyama, M.: Class-prior estimation for learning from positive and unlabeled data. Mach. Learn. **106**(4), 463–492 (2016). https://doi.org/10.1007/s10994-016-5604-6
29. du Plessis, M.C., Sugiyama, M.: Class prior estimation from positive and unlabeled data. IEICE Trans. **97**–D, 1358–1362 (2014)
30. Ramaswamy, H., Scott, C., Tewari, A.: Mixture proportion estimation via kernel embedding of distributions. In: ICML (2016)
31. Rubin, D.: Inference and missing data. Biometrika **63**, 581–592 (1976)
32. Schnabel, T., Swaminathan, A., Singh, A., Chandak, N., Joachims, T.: Recommendations as treatments: debiasing learning and evaluation. In: ICML (2016)
33. Scott, C.: A rate of convergence for mixture proportion estimation, with application to learning from noisy labels. In: AISTATS (2015)
34. Steinberg, D., Cardell, N.S.: Estimating logistic regression models when the dependent variable has no variance. Commun. Stat. Theory Methods **21**(2), 423–450 (1992)
35. Strack, B., et al.: Impact of HbA1c measurement on hospital readmission rates: analysis of 70,000 clinical database patient records. BioMed Res. Int. **2014**, 11 (2014)
36. Ward, G., Hastie, T., Barry, S., Elith, J., Leathwick, J.R.: Presence-only data and the EM algorithm. Biometrics **65**(2), 554–563 (2009)
37. Zupanc, K., Davis, J.: Estimating rule quality for knowledge base completion with the relationship between coverage assumption. In: Proceedings of the Web Conference (2018)

Cost Sensitive Evaluation of Instance Hardness in Machine Learning

Ricardo B. C. Prudêncio[✉]

Centro de Informática, Universidade Federal de Pernambuco, Recife, Brazil
rbcp@cin.ufpe.br

Abstract. Measuring hardness of individual instances in machine learning contributes to a deeper analysis of learning performance. This work proposes instance hardness measures for binary classification in cost-sensitive scenarios. Here cost curves are generated for each instance, defined as the loss observed for a pool of learning models for that instance along the range of cost proportions. Instance hardness is defined as the area under the cost curves and can be seen as an expected loss of difficulty along cost proportions. Different cost curves were proposed by considering common decision threshold choice methods in literature, thus providing alternative views of instance hardness.

1 Introduction

Measuring difficulty in machine learning (ML) strongly contributes to understanding the potential advantages and limitations of the learning algorithms. Previous work has mainly focused on deriving complexity measures for datasets [1,7,14]. Alternatively, the current work follows the instance-level approach, focused on measuring hardness for individual instances. Instance hardness measures can be useful to a deeper analysis of algorithm performance and to investigate specific causes of bad learning behavior [12,17]. Distinct areas of ML have developed methods which somehow rely on measuring difficulty of instances (e.g., dynamic classifier selection [4,19,20], noise detection [3,16,18] and active learning [13]).

In [11,16,17], instance hardness is defined based on the learning behavior of a pool of algorithms (e.g., the proportion of algorithms that misclassified the instance). In [15], the authors addressed instance difficulty by proposing four types of examples: safe (easy instances), borderline, rare and outliers (difficult instances). Each instance is categorized into a difficulty type by considering the distribution of classes in the neighborhood of the instance. However, these straightforward ideas do not consider an important practical issue, which is the cost associated to the classifier errors [5]. The costs of false positives and false negatives may vary at deployment time. In this sense, misclassification in specific areas of the instance space may have more significance. Instance hardness measures should identify such areas by defining difficulty not only in terms of observed errors, but also in terms of expected costs.

© Springer Nature Switzerland AG 2020
U. Brefeld et al. (Eds.): ECML PKDD 2019, LNAI 11907, pp. 86–102, 2020.
https://doi.org/10.1007/978-3-030-46147-8_6

Additionally, in cost-sensitive scenarios, when a model returns scores (e.g., class probabilities), decision thresholds can be adapted according to the error costs. For instance, when the cost of false negatives is higher than false positives, the threshold can be set to increase the number of positive predictions. In [9], the loss of a model depends on the *threshold choice method* (TCM) adopted. Yet, model performance for instances may vary too, requiring new hardness measures.

This work proposes a new framework to measure instance hardness for binary classification problems in cost-sensitive scenarios. Initially, the concept of *instance cost curve* is proposed, which plots the loss produced by a model for that instance along the cost proportions. A different instance cost curve is produced for each different TCM. This is a new concept which extends previous work on cost curves, now aiming to evaluate and inspect loss for individual instances. Instance cost curves were derived for five different TCMs: score-fixed, score-driven, rate-driven, score-uniform and rate-uniform methods [9].

By plotting an instance cost curve, one can visualize how difficult the instance is for each cost proportion. A global instance hardness measure can be defined as the area under the cost curve (i.e., the expected loss obtained for a learned model for an instance along the range of cost proportions). In order to avoid defining instance hardness based upon a single model, the ensemble strategy proposed in [17] was adopted here. More specifically, a set of instance cost curves is generated using a pool of learned models and the average instance hardness is computed.

The proposed framework addresses different issues. First, it is possible to identify the hard instances in a problem and under which operation conditions (cost proportions) they are difficult. The use of different TCMs provides new perspectives for measuring hardness, including misclassification evaluation, probability estimation and ranking performance. Yet, for some TCMs, hardness can be measured under cost proportion uncertainty. The instance-level approach also supports the development of hardness measures for groups of instances and particularly class hardness measures. Different ML areas which already use instance hardness measures can benefit from the proposed framework. The adequate hardness measure must be chosen depending on the application objectives. For instance, if one wants to improve class probability estimation, a hardness measure based on scores should be adopted. We believe that such areas can be extended more adequately to cost-sensitive scenarios by adopting the proposed measures.

2   Notation and Basic Definitions

The basic notation adopted in this work is based on [9]. Instances are classified into one of the classes $Y = \{0, 1\}$, in which 0 is the positive class and 1 is the negative class. A model m is a scoring function that receives an instance x as input and returns a score $s = m(x)$ indicating the chance of a negative class prediction. A model is transformed into a classifier assuming a decision threshold t. If $s \leq t$ then x is classified as positive and classified as negative otherwise.

The classifier errors can be associated to different costs. The cost of a *false negative* is c_0, while the cost of a *false positive* is c_1. As in [9], the costs are normalized by setting $c_0 + c_1 = b$ and the *cost proportion* $c = c_0/b$ represents the operating condition faced by a model when it is deployed. For simplicity, this work adopted $b = 2$ and hence $c \in [0,1]$, $c_0 = 2c$ and $c_1 = 2(1 - c)$.

Let $f_0(s)$ and $f_1(s)$ be the score density functions respectively for the positive and negative classes. The *true positive* rate obtained by setting a threshold t is defined as $F_0(t) = \int_{-\infty}^{t} f_0(s)ds$. The *true positive* rate, in turn, is defined as $F_1(t) = \int_{-\infty}^{t} f_1(s)ds$. The positive rate $R(t)$ (i.e., the proportion of instances predicted as positive) is $R(t) = \pi_0 F_0(t) + \pi_1 F_1(t)$, in which π_0 and π_1 are the proportions of positive and negative examples. The loss for a threshold t and a cost proportion c is defined as:

$$
\begin{aligned}
Q(t,c) &= c_0\pi_0\left(1 - F_0(t)\right) + c_1\pi_1 F_1(t) \\
&= 2\{c\pi_0\left(1 - F_0(t)\right) + (1 - c)\pi_1 F_1(t)\}
\end{aligned}
\tag{1}
$$

A *threshold choice method* (TCM) is a function $T(c)$ which defines the decision threshold according to the operation condition. The expected loss of a model can be expressed as Eq. 2, in which $w_c(c)$ is the distribution of cost proportions:

$$
L = \int_0^1 Q(T(c), c)w_c(c)dc
\tag{2}
$$

3   Instance Hardness and Cost Curves

By assuming uniform distribution of operation conditions, in [9] it is proved that the loss L is directly related to different performance measures depending on the TCM. If the threshold is fixed (e.g., 0.5) regardless c, L is the error rate at that threshold. Under the score-driven TCM (i.e., $T(c) = c$), in turn, the loss is equal to the Brier score of the model. Under the rate-driven method, when a threshold is set to obtain a desired positive prediction rate, the loss is linearly related to AUC. The appropriate measure depends on the cost-sensitive scenario.

Similarly, instance hardness may depend on the TCM. For instance, consider three positive instances with scores 0.2, 0.6 and 0.8. The 1st instance is correctly classified if a fixed $t = 0.5$ is adopted, while the 2nd and 3rd instances are false negatives. In this case, instance hardness depends solely on the threshold and the score. In case $T(c) = c$ is adopted, the 1st instance is very easy since it is correctly classified in a wide range of operation conditions. Yet, the 3rd instance is harder than the 2nd one. Here, hardness also depends on the operation condition.

This paper proposes a new framework for instance hardness evaluation which takes the above nuances into account. The expected model loss expressed in Eq. 2 is an aggregation over the operation conditions. The main idea is to transform the loss function to be expressed as an aggregation over scores (instead of costs) and then to define the contribution of each instance in the model loss. Initially, $Q(t,c)$ (Eq. 1) is decomposed into two functions respectively for false negatives and false positives. For false negatives: $Q_0(t,c) = 2c\pi_0(1 - F_0(t))$. After some algebraic operations, this term is defined as an integral over scores:

$$
\begin{aligned}
Q_0(t, c) &= 2c\pi_0(1 - F_0(t)) \\
&= 2c\pi_0\left(1 - \int_{-\infty}^{t} f_0(s)ds\right) \\
&= 2c\pi_0\left(\int_s f_0(s)ds - \int_s \delta(s,t)f_0(s)ds\right) \\
&= 2c\pi_0\left(\int_s (1 - \delta(s,t))f_0(s)ds\right) \\
&= \int_s 2c\pi_0(1 - \delta(s,t))f_0(s)ds
\end{aligned}
\tag{3}
$$

where $\delta(s, t) = 1$ if $s \le t$ and $= 0$ otherwise. Notice that a false negative occurs when the instance is positive and $1 - \delta(s,t) = 1$, i.e., $s > t$. The expected loss of the positive class over the operation conditions can be expressed as:

$$
\begin{aligned}
L_0 &= \int_c Q_0(t, c)dc \\
&= \int_c \int_s 2c\pi_0(1 - \delta(s,t))f_0(s)dsdc \\
&= \int_s \int_c \pi_0 f_0(s)2c(1 - \delta(\mathbf{s}, \mathbf{t}))dcds
\end{aligned}
\tag{4}
$$

In Eq. 4, a positive instance is associated to a loss $2c$ when it is incorrectly classified, i.e., when $1 - \delta(s,t) = 1$. Otherwise, the loss is zero. Then, the *instance cost curve* for a positive instance with score s is defined as:

$$
QI_0(s, t, c) = 2c(1 - \delta(s, t))
\tag{5}
$$

Depending on the TCM, different curves can be produced along c. *Instance hardness* is then defined as the area under the instance cost curve (the expected loss for the range of operation conditions). In general, given a TCM $T(c)$, the hardness of a positive instance with score s is:

$$
IH_0^T(s) = \int_c QI_0(s, T(c), c)dc
\tag{6}
$$

By replacing the instance hardness Eq. 6 in Eq. 4, the expected loss for the positive class is alternatively defined as an aggregation of hardness over the distribution of scores:

$$
L_0 = \pi_0 \int_s IH_0^T(s)f_0(s)ds
\tag{7}
$$

A similar derivation can be performed in order to define instance cost curves and hardness values for negative instances. An error for a negative instance occurs when $\delta(s,t) = 1$ and the associated loss is $2(1 - c)$. The instance cost curve for a negative instance with score s is defined as:

$$
QI_1(s, t, c) = 2(1 - c)\delta(s, t)
\tag{8}
$$

Instance hardness assuming a function $T(c)$ and the loss relative to the negative class is defined as:

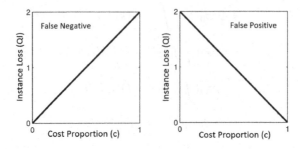

Fig. 1. Instance cost curves assuming the SF method.

$$IH_1^T(s) = \int_c QI_1(s, T(c), c)dc \qquad (9)$$

$$L_1 = \pi_1 \int_s IH_1^T(s)f_1(s)ds \qquad (10)$$

In this work, the hardness measures for five TCMs [10] were derived. For robustness, as in [17], a set of models can be used to compute the average hardness across models. All implementations are provided in an online material[1].

3.1   Score-Fixed Instance Hardness

The *score-fixed* (SF) method assumes a fixed threshold regardless the condition c. Typically, t is set to 0.5. Consider a positive instance with score $s > t$. This instance is always a false negative regardless c, as the threshold is fixed. In this case, $\delta(s, t) = 0$. By replacing it in Eq. 5, the instance cost curve is defined as:

$$QI_0(s, t, c) = 2c \qquad (11)$$

In turn, the cost curve for a false positive instance is:

$$QI_1(s, t, c) = 2(1 - c) \qquad (12)$$

Figure 1 illustrates the SF instance cost curves for false negatives and false positives. For correctly classified instances, the cost curve is just a constant line $QI(s, t, c) = 0$. By integrating QI, the instance hardness values respectively for false negatives and false positives are derived as follows:

$$IH_0^{sf}(x) = \int_0^1 2c\,dc = \left[c^2\right]_0^1 = 1 \qquad (13)$$

---

[1] https://tinyurl.com/y3cthlv8.

$$IH_1^{sf}(x) = \int_0^1 2(1-c)\,dc = \left[2c - c^2\right]_0^1 = 1 \tag{14}$$

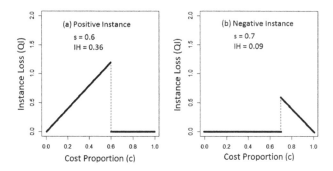

Fig. 2. Instance cost curves assuming the SD method.

For correctly classified instances (either positive or negative), $IH^{sf}(x) = 0$. The SF hardness is simply the 0|1 loss. By adopting a pool of models, instance hardness is the proportion of incorrect classifications provided by the pool.

3.2   Score-Driven Instance Hardness

Although SF is frequently used, when the classifier errors have different costs, it is sound to assign thresholds accordingly [6]. In the *score-driven* (SD) TCM [8], the threshold is set to c (i.e., $T(c) = c$). For instance, if $c = 0.7$, the cost of false negatives is high. By setting $t = 0.7$, the classifier predicts more instances as positive, minimizing the number of false negatives. In the SD method, a positive instance is predicted as negative when $s > c$ and correctly predicted otherwise. Then $\delta(s,t) = 0$ if $s > c$, which results in the following instance cost curve (Eq. 15) by replacing $\delta(s,t)$ in Eq. 5. The area under the curve is defined in Eq. 16. Figure 2(a) illustrates the SD cost curve for a positive instance with $s = 0.6$.

$$QI_0(s,t,c) = \begin{cases} 2c, & \text{if } s > c \\ 0, & \text{otherwise} \end{cases} \tag{15}$$

$$IH^{sd}(x) = \int_0^s 2c\,dc = \left[c^2\right]_0^s = s^2 \tag{16}$$

Since $y = 0$ for positive instances, the above measure can be replaced by $(y-s)^2$, which is the squared-error of the model. For negative instances, Eq. 17 and 18 define the cost curve and hardness measure. Figure 2(b) illustrates the curve for a negative instance with $s = 0.7$. For negative instances, $y = 1$. Again hardness corresponds to $(y - s)^2$, the squared-error. When the ensemble is adopted, the hardness of an instance is the average squared-error obtained by the pool.

$$QI_1(s, t, c) = \begin{cases} 2(1 - c), & \text{if } s \leq c \\ 0, & \text{otherwise} \end{cases} \tag{17}$$

$$IH^{sd}(x) = \int_s^1 2(1 - c)\, dc = \left[2c - c^2\right]_s^1 = (1 - s)^2 \tag{18}$$

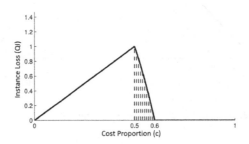

Fig. 3. Instance cost curve for a positive instance - RD method.

3.3   Rate-Driven Instance Hardness

The SD method is a natural choice when the model is assumed to be a class probability estimator. However, SD is sensitive to the score estimation [9]. If scores are highly concentrated, a small change in operating condition (and in the threshold) may drastically affect performance. As an alternative, the positive rate $R(t)$ can be used to define thresholds [10]. In the *rate-driven* (RD) method, the threshold is set to achieve a desired positive rate, i.e., $T^{rd}(c) = R^{-1}(c)$. For instance, if $c = 0.7$ the threshold t is set in such a way that 70% of the instances are classified as positive. The operating condition c is then expressed as the desired positive rate: $c = R(t)$. Scores can be seen as rank indicators instead of probabilities. The RD cost curve for a positive instance is defined as:

$$QI_0(s, t, c) = \begin{cases} 2c, & \text{if } s > R^{-1}(c) \\ 0, & \text{otherwise} \end{cases} \tag{19}$$

For $R(s) \leq c$ (equivalent to $s \leq R^{-1}(c)$) loss is zero. When $R(s) > c$, the loss varies linearly. The RD hardness is defined in Eq. 20, which is related to the position of the instance in the ranking produced by the model (i.e., $R(s)$). Different from SD, which measures error, RD measures ranking performance. A hard instance for SD may be easy for RD depending on the score distribution.

$$IH^{rd}(x) = \int_0^{R(s)} 2c\, dc = \left[c^2\right]_0^{R(s)} = R(s)^2 \tag{20}$$

An adjustment is necessary when the cost curve is built for real datasets. In such case, the range of desired positive rates is continuous, whereas the number of observed rates is limited by the dataset size. Figure 3 shows the cost curve for x_6 and model m_1 in Table 1. The positive rate of x_6 is 0.6, i.e., $R(0.75) = 0.6$. The previous observed positive rate is 0.5 assuming the previous score 0.7 as threshold ($R(0.7) = 0.5$). Instance x_6 is correctly classified if the desired positive rate is equal or higher than 0.6, (loss is zero for $c \in [0.6; 1]$). For $c < 0.5$, the instance is classified as negative and its loss varies linearly. Positive rates between 0.5 and 0.6 can not be produced using m_1. In such cases, the loss is estimated from stochastic interpolation between 0.5 and 0.6 (dashed area in Fig. 3).

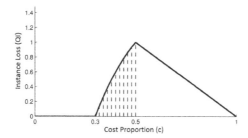

Fig. 4. Instance cost curve for a negative instance - RD method.

Table 1. Example of instances and scores provided by four models.

Instance	Label	m_1	m_2	m_3	m_4
x_1	1	0.70	0.60	0.00	0.65
x_2	1	0.80	1.00	1.00	0.90
x_3	1	0.80	0.95	0.93	0.88
x_4	1	0.70	0.25	0.91	0.48
x_5	0	0.80	0.68	0.78	0.74
x_6	0	0.75	0.64	0.83	0.70
x_7	0	0.10	0.37	0.78	0.24
x_8	0	0.55	0.30	0.95	0.43
x_9	0	0.80	0.72	1.00	0.76
x_{10}	0	0.15	0.25	0.87	0.20

In the general case, the loss is zero for $c \geq R(s)$. If there are l instances with score s, the previous observed positive rate is $R(s) - l/n$. For the interval $[0; R(s) - l/n]$, the loss is $Q(s, T^{rd}(c), c) = 2c$. For the interval $[R(s) - l/n; R(s)]$, the loss is derived from interpolation of the rates $R(s) - l/n$ and $R(s)$ as follows:

$$Q_0(s, T^{rd}(c), c) = 2c \left(\frac{R(s) - c}{R(s) - (R(s) - l/n)} \right) = 2c \left(\frac{R(s) - c}{l/n} \right) \qquad (21)$$

When a positive rate c is desired, the instance is incorrectly classified with the frequency $\left(\frac{R(s)-c}{l/n}\right)$. The hardness of positive instances can be derived as:

$$
\begin{aligned}
IH_0^{rd}(s) &= \int_0^{R(s)-l/n} 2c\,dc + \int_{R(s)-l/n}^{R(s)} 2c\left(\frac{R(s)-c}{l/n}\right)dc \\
&= \left[c^2\right]_0^{R(s)-l/n} + \frac{2n}{l}\left[\frac{R(s)c^2}{2} - \frac{c^3}{3}\right]_{R(s)-l/n}^{R(s)} \\
&= (R(s)-l/n)^2\frac{lR(s)}{n} - \frac{2l^2}{3n^2} = R(s)^2 + \frac{l}{n}\left(\frac{l}{3n} - R(s)\right)
\end{aligned}
\tag{22}
$$

For large values of n, the expression approaches $R(s)^2$, which is equivalent to the continuous case (Eq. 20). In turn, Eq. 23 defines the RD cost curve for negative instances with score s and Eq. 34 the corresponding hardness measure.

$$
QI_1(s,t,c) = \begin{cases} 2(1-c), & \text{if } s \le R^{-1}(c) \\ 0, & \text{otherwise} \end{cases}
\tag{23}
$$

$$
IH^{rd}(x) = \int_{R(s)}^1 2(1-c)\,dc = \left[2c - c^2\right]_{R(s)}^1 = (1-R(s))^2
\tag{24}
$$

Hardness is given by the square of the negative rate $(1 - R(s))$. It assesses the ranking quality of the negative instances. For real datasets, the cost curve is derived by interpolating the points $R(s) - l/n$ and $R(s)$:

$$
Q_1(s, T^{rd}(c), c) = 2(1-c)\left(\frac{c-R(s)}{l/n}\right)
\tag{25}
$$

Instance hardness is derived by Eq. 26. For large n, $IH_1^{rd}(x)$ approaches $(1 - R(s)^2)$. Figure 4 presents the RD curve for instance x_4 using m_1. The positive rate of x_4 is $R(0.7) = 0.5$. As there are two negative instances with score 0.7, the previous rate is 0.3. The dashed area represents the interpolated loss in $[0.3; 0.5]$.

$$
\begin{aligned}
IH_1^{rd}(x) &= \int_{R(s)}^1 2(1-c)\,dc + \int_{R(s)-l/n}^{R(s)} 2(1-c)\left(\frac{c-R(s)}{l/n)}\right)dc \\
&= (1-R(s))^2 + \frac{l}{n}\left(\frac{l}{3n} + (1-R(s))\right)
\end{aligned}
\tag{26}
$$

3.4   Score-Uniform Instance Hardness

The SD method assumes that c is known at deployment and then adequate thresholds can be chosen. However, in some situations the operating condition is poorly assessed. In the worst case, a random selection is performed using the *score-uniform* (SU) method [10]: $T^{su}(c) = U[0, 1]$. The instance cost curve and hardness for a positive instance can be derived as follows:

$$QI_0(s, T^{su}(c), c) = \int_0^1 QI_0(s, t, c)dt$$
$$= \int_0^1 2c(1 - \delta(s, t))dt \quad (27)$$
$$= \int_0^s 2cdt = 2cs$$

$$IH_0^{su}(s) = \int_0^1 2csdc = s\left[c^2\right]_0^1 = s \quad (28)$$

The slope of the curve depends on s and ranges from 0 to $2c$ (i.e., from always correctly predicted to always incorrectly predicted). For a positive instance, $y = 0$ and then $IH_0^{su}(x) = s = |y - s|$, which is the absolute error of the model for that instance. Similarly for a negative instance, $IH_0^{su}(x) = (1 - s) = |y - s|$, again the absolute error of the model as derived below.

$$QI_1(s, T^{su}(c), c) = \int_0^1 QI_1(s, t, c)dt$$
$$= \int_0^1 2(1 - c)\delta(s, t)dt \quad (29)$$
$$= \int_s^1 2(1 - c)dt$$
$$= 2(1 - c)(1 - s)$$

$$IH_1^{su}(s) = \int_0^1 2(1 - c)(1 - s)dc$$
$$= (1 - s)\left[2c - c^2\right]_0^1 = (1 - s) \quad (30)$$

3.5   Rate-Uniform Instance Hardness

Similar to SU, uncertain operation conditions can also be defined in terms of rates. By adopting uniform distribution of positive rates, the following cost curve is derived for positive instances, with instance hardness defined in Eq. 32.

$$QI_0(s, T^{ru}(c), c) = \int_0^1 QI_0(s, R^{-1}(r), c)dr$$
$$= \int_0^1 2c(1 - \delta(s, R^{-1}(r)))dr \quad (31)$$
$$= \int_0^{R(s)} 2cdr = 2cR(s)$$

$$IH_0^{ru}(x) = \int_0^1 2cR(s)dc = R(s)\left[c^2\right]_0^1 = R(s) \tag{32}$$

While hardness for RD is the square positive rate, for RU it is the absolute positive rate. Poorly ranked instances will be more penalized, which is reasonable since the operation condition is uncertain. For a negative instance, hardness is its negative rate, as derived in the following equations.

$$
\begin{aligned}
QI_1(s, T^{ru}(c), c) &= \int_0^1 QI_1(s, R^{-1}(r), c)dr \\
&= \int_0^1 2(1-c)\delta(s, R^{-1}(r))dr \\
&= \int_{R(s)}^1 2(1-c)dr = 2(1-c)(1-R(s))
\end{aligned}
\tag{33}
$$

$$
\begin{aligned}
IH_1^{su}(s) &= \int_0^1 2(1-c)(1-R(s))dc \\
&= (1-R(s))\left[2c - c^2\right]_0^1 = (1-R(s))
\end{aligned}
\tag{34}
$$

4 Experiments

This section provides examples of the proposed cost curves and hardness measures. Figure 5 and 6 present the cost curves respectively for the negative and positive instances in Table 1 using SF, SD and RD. The hardest negative instances are x_1 and x_4. In particular, x_1 is even harder to rank, given the RD hardness. Considering the positive class, x_5, x_6 and x_9 have the highest hardness values. However, for higher costs, they are easy for RD and SD. Different from SF, the RD and SD methods can take advantage on the operation condition known in deployment. Figure 7 in turn presents the *class cost curves* produced by averaging the instance cost curves for each class. Class hardness (CH) is defined as the average instance hardness in a given class. It is an estimation of the class loss defined in Eq. 7 and 10. By assuming SF and SD, the positive class is relatively more difficult than the negative class. A more balanced difficulty is observed by assuming the RD method. Although the scores of the positive instances are not well calibrated, they can produce a good ranking of instances.

Following, the framework was applied to a real dataset (German Credit, in Fig. 8). The negative class is the majority (700 instances), while the positive class has 300 instances. Both classes are largely spread, although the negative class seems to be more compact. There is a class boundary in which the classes are highly mixed. Five models were learned in this dataset using diverse algorithms

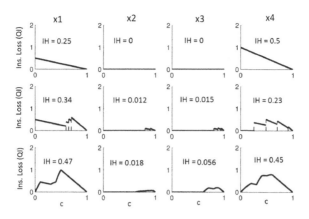

Fig. 5. Instance cost curves for negative instances considering the TCMs: SF (1st row), SD (2nd row) and RD (3rd row).

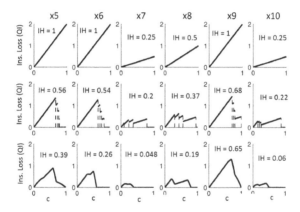

Fig. 6. Instance cost curves for positive instances considering the TCMs: SF (1st row), SD (2nd row) and RD (3rd row).

in Weka[2], with scores computed by 10-fold cross validation. Scores were more concentrated towards 1, as negative is the majority class. By considering a fixed threshold 0.5, many errors were observed for the positive class, particularly in the class boundary (see Fig. 9(d)). The negative class is much easier (class hardness is 0.12 against 0.56 for the positive class). By considering SD, as thresholds are adapted, instances are in general easier, compared to SF (see Fig. 9(b) and (e)). In fact, positive class hardness is 0.37 for SD. As there are still some hard positive instances in the boundary, this class is still much harder than the negative one (whose hardness is 0.10). For RD, hardness is more balanced among classes.

---

[2] J48, IBk, Logistic Regression, Naive Bayes and Random Forest were adopted. IBK adopted $k = 5$. The other algorithms were applied using default parameter values.

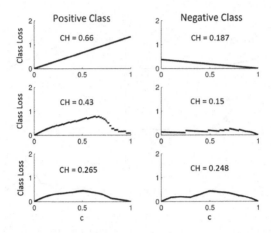

Fig. 7. Class cost curves and hardness under different TCMs.

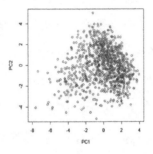

Fig. 8. German dataset visualized using PCA.

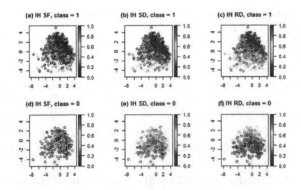

Fig. 9. Hardness of instances for the German-credit dataset.

Some negative instances are poorly ranked (see Fig. 9(c)). On the other hand, some positive instances in the boundary, which are difficult for SF and SD, are easier to rank (see Fig. 9(f)). For RD, class hardness is respectively 0.25 and 0.17 for negatives and positives. The negative class becomes harder than the positive. Although with good absolute scores, the negative instances are harder to rank.

Differences in difficulty can also be analyzed at specific operation conditions. For the negative class, higher losses tend to be observed for higher values of c, as expected. However different patterns are seen depending on the TCM (see Fig. 10). For $c = 0.8$, the number of hard instances for RD is high, but extremely hard instances are not observed. Notice that false positives are penalized by a low cost in this case $(1 - c) = 0.2$. For $c = 0.5$, in turn, some very hard instances in the class boundary are observed for RD. Distinct patterns can also be observed for the positive class, which is difficult for SD (see Fig. 11). For $c = 0.2$ in SD, most instances are hard, but not extremely hard as for $c = 0.5$. In this case, the higher cost impacts instance hardness.

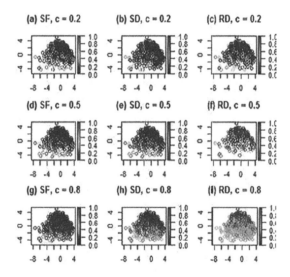

Fig. 10. Instance hardness for different c - Class 1.

Figure 12 presents the instance hardness for SU and RU, in which c is uncertain. In these cases, hardness is more distributed and more difficult instances are found beyond class boundary. Class hardness for SU is 0.22 and 0.54 respectively for classes 1 and 0, which represents a harder scenario compared to SD. Similarly for RU, class hardness is 0.39 and 0.35, which is greater than class hardness for RD. The increase in hardness reflects the uncertainty in the cost proportions.

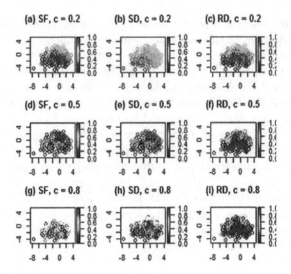

Fig. 11. Instance hardness for different c - Class 0.

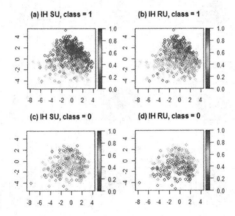

Fig. 12. Instance hardness under the SU and RU methods.

5   Conclusion

This paper proposes a new framework for measuring instance hardness in binary classification. This work addresses different perspectives of evaluation by considering different TCMs in the definition of instance hardness. Future works point at three directions: (1) derive new measures within the framework by adopting other TCMs and distributions of operating condition; (2) perform more extensive experiments on a large set of real problems using the proposed measures - such studies would reveal advantages, limitations and relationships between algorithms in different scenarios, which is relevant for understanding learning behavior [2]; and (3) develop applications in different contexts. In *dynamic algorithm selection*, for example, instance cost curves can be adopted to select algorithms for specific regions in the instance space given the operation condition. In *active learning*, expected hardness can be used for selecting unlabeled instances for label acquisition. In *noise filtering* and *acquisition of missing values*, the effect of data preprocessing in the instance hardness can be analyzed.

References

1. Basu, M., Ho, T. (eds.): Data Complexity in Pattern Recognition. Springer, London (2006). https://doi.org/10.1007/978-1-84628-172-3
2. Brazdil, P., Giraud-Carrier, C.: Metalearning and algorithm selection: progress, state of the art and introduction to the 2018 special issue. Mach. Learn. **107**(1), 1–14 (2017). https://doi.org/10.1007/s10994-017-5692-y
3. Brodley, C.E., Friedl, M.A.: Identifying mislabeled training data. J. Artif. Intell. Res. **11**, 131–167 (1999)
4. Cruz, R.M.O., Sabourin, R., Cavalcanti, G.D.C.: Prototype selection for dynamic classifier and ensemble selection. Neural Comput. Appl. **29**(2), 447–457 (2016). https://doi.org/10.1007/s00521-016-2458-6
5. Drummond, C., Holte, R.C.: Cost curves: an improved method for visualizing classifier performance. Mach. Learn. **65**(1), 95–130 (2006). https://doi.org/10.1007/s10994-006-8199-5
6. Flach, P., Matsubara, E.T.: A simple lexicographic ranker and probability estimator. In: Kok, J.N., Koronacki, J., Mantaras, R.L., Matwin, S., Mladenič, D., Skowron, A. (eds.) ECML 2007. LNCS (LNAI), vol. 4701, pp. 575–582. Springer, Heidelberg (2007). https://doi.org/10.1007/978-3-540-74958-5_55
7. Garcia, L.P., Carvalho, A.C., Lorena, A.C.: Effect of label noise in the complexity of classification problems. Neurocomputing **160**, 108–119 (2015)
8. Hernández-Orallo, J., Flach, P., Ferri, C.: Brier curves: a new cost-based visualisation of classifier performance. In: 28th International Conference on Machine Learning (2011)
9. Hernández-Orallo, J., Flach, P., Ferri, C.: A unified view of performance metrics: translating threshold choice into expected classification loss. J. Mach. Learn. Res. **13**(1), 2813–2869 (2012)
10. Hernández-Orallo, J., Flach, P., Ferri, C.: ROC curves in cost space. Mach. Learn. **93**(1), 71–91 (2013). https://doi.org/10.1007/s10994-013-5328-9
11. Luengo, J., Shim, S.O., Alshomrani, S., Altalhi, A., Herrera, F.: CNC-NOS: class noise cleaning by ensemble filtering and noise scoring. Knowl.-Based Syst. **140**, 27–49 (2018)
12. Martınez-Plumed, F., Prudêncio, R.B., Martınez-Usó, A., Hernández-Orallo, J.: Making sense of item response theory in machine learning. In: European Conference on Artificial Intelligence, ECAI, pp. 1140–1148 (2016)
13. Melville, P., Mooney, R.J.: Diverse ensembles for active learning. In: Proceedings of the 21st International Conference on Machine Learning, p. 74 (2004)
14. Morán-Fernández, L., Bolón-Canedo, V., Alonso-Betanzos, A.: Can classification performance be predicted by complexity measures? A study using microarray data. Knowl. Inf. Syst. **51**(3), 1067–1090 (2016). https://doi.org/10.1007/s10115-016-1003-3

15. Napierala, K., Stefanowski, J.: Types of minority class examples and their influence on learning classifiers from imbalanced data. J. Intell. Inf. Syst. **46**(3), 563–597 (2015). https://doi.org/10.1007/s10844-015-0368-1
16. Sluban, B., Lavrac, N.: Relating ensemble diversity and performance: a study in class noise detection. Neurocomputing **160**, 120–131 (2015)
17. Smith, M.R., Martinez, T., Giraud-Carrier, C.: An instance level analysis of data complexity. Mach. Learn. **95**(2), 225–256 (2013). https://doi.org/10.1007/s10994-013-5422-z
18. Verbaeten, S., Van Assche, A.: Ensemble methods for noise elimination in classification problems. In: Windeatt, T., Roli, F. (eds.) MCS 2003. LNCS, vol. 2709, pp. 317–325. Springer, Heidelberg (2003). https://doi.org/10.1007/3-540-44938-8_32
19. Woloszynski, T., Kurzynski, M., Podsiadlo, P., Stachowiak, G.W.: A measure of competence based on random classification for dynamic ensemble selection. Inf. Fusion **13**(3), 207–213 (2012)
20. Woods, K., Kegelmeyer, W., Bowyer, K.: Combination of multiple classifiers using local accuracy estimates. IEEE Trans. Pattern Anal. Mach. Intell. **19**, 405–410 (1997)

Non-parametric Bayesian Isotonic Calibration: Fighting Over-Confidence in Binary Classification

Mari-Liis Allikivi[(✉)] and Meelis Kull

Institute of Computer Science, University of Tartu, Tartu, Estonia
{mari-liis.allikivi,meelis.kull}@ut.ee

Abstract. Classifiers can often output a score or a probability indicating how sure they are about the predicted class. Classifier calibration methods can map these into *calibrated* class probabilities, supporting cost-optimal decision making. Isotonic calibration is the standard non-parametric calibration method for binary classifiers, and it can be shown to yield the most likely monotonic calibration map on the given data, where monotonicity means that instances with higher predicted scores are more likely to be positive. Another non-parametric method is ENIR (ensemble of near-isotonic regression models) which allows for some non-monotonicity, but adds a penalty for it. We first demonstrate that these two methods tend to be over-confident and show that applying label smoothing improves calibration of both methods in more than 90% of studied cases. Unfortunately, label smoothing reduces confidence on the under-confident predictions also, and it does not reduce the raggedness of isotonic calibration. As the main contribution we propose a non-parametric Bayesian isotonic calibration method which has the flexibility of isotonic calibration to fit maps of all monotonic shapes but it adds smoothness and reduces over-confidence without requiring label smoothing. The method introduces a prior over piecewise linear monotonic calibration maps and uses a simple Monte Carlo sampling based approach to approximate the posterior mean calibration map. Our experiments demonstrate that on average the proposed method results in better calibrated probabilities than the state-of-the-art calibration methods, including isotonic calibration and ENIR.

Keywords: Binary classification · Classifier calibration · Non-parametric Bayesian

1 Introduction

With the advances in artificial intelligence, classifiers are being incorporated into more and more decision-making processes. Sometimes it is enough to base the decisions only on the classifier's predicted labels. However, more often decision making benefits from knowing about how confident the classifier is in its prediction. For instance, in a medical diagnostic setting a high-confidence predicted

© Springer Nature Switzerland AG 2020
U. Brefeld et al. (Eds.): ECML PKDD 2019, LNAI 11907, pp. 103–120, 2020.
https://doi.org/10.1007/978-3-030-46147-8_7

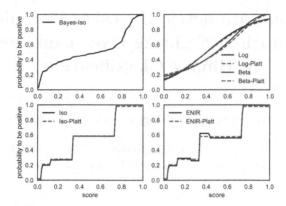

Fig. 1. Examples of calibration curves of the state-of-the-art calibration methods with and without Platt correction.

positive might be fully trusted by the doctor, whereas for low-confidence predicted positives the doctor might conduct additional tests. This usage requires the diagnostic classifier to be well-calibrated and not over-confident, since errors at high confidence levels are very costly. Most algorithms for learning binary classifiers can provide some kind of scores interpretable as confidence levels. For instance, in margin-based classifiers the distance from the decision boundary reflects confidence. For decision-maker's benefit it is useful if the confidence scores can be related to the expected probability of error. This is achieved, if the classifier outputs *calibrated class probabilities* [20]. The class probabilities in binary classification are calibrated, if among all instances predicted to be positive with probability p, the proportion of actual positives is also approximately p, for any $p \in [0, 1]$. Such interpretability of predicted probabilities combined with information about how much a false positive or a false negative would cost, allows decision-makers to estimate the expected cost for each possible decision and to follow the least costly option [5].

If the classifier outputs non-calibrated probabilities or confidence scores that are not probabilities at all, then one can apply classifier calibration methods to transform these outputs into the scale of calibrated probabilities. In case of binary classification this transformation can be represented as a mapping from real-valued output scores into probabilities to be positive, known as the *calibration map*, see examples in Fig. 1. There are two approaches to finding these mappings: parametric and non-parametric. The best known parametric and non-parametric calibration methods are logistic calibration (also known as Platt scaling) [16] and isotonic calibration [21], respectively. Both methods model calibration maps as non-strictly monotonically increasing, also called *isotonic*. The reasoning behind this assumption is that if the classifier's confidence in the positive prediction increases then the probability to be positive should also increase.

Logistic calibration (also known as Platt scaling) fits a logistic sigmoid on the training data [16]. This method has two parameters, one determining its centre and another determining its slope at the centre. It can be implemented by applying univariate logistic regression to predict the binary label (1 for positive and 0 for negative) from the model output score. To reduce overfitting, Platt proposed a correction to the procedure and instead of 1 and 0 use labels $1 - \frac{1}{N_+ + 2}$ and $0 + \frac{1}{N_- + 2}$ in fitting logistic regression [16], where N_+ and N_- are the numbers of positives and negatives in the training data. This correction procedure is essentially label smoothing [6] but with a particular fixed amount of smoothing. We use notation 'Log' and 'Log-Platt' to refer to the uncorrected and corrected method, respectively.

Logistic calibration can be derived from first principles if assuming that the model output scores on the positives and negatives are both Gaussian distributed, with the same variance but different means. If the model outputs scores that are already probabilities but still require calibration, then it is more natural to use beta distributions instead of Gaussians, because beta distributions have support over the range $[0, 1]$. Following this reasoning, the paper [8] derived the Beta calibration method [8]. Beta calibration is a parametric family with 3 parameters, allowing a larger variety of shapes for the calibration map than logistic calibration. The family contains reverse sigmoidal functions and also the identity map, allowing the method to return the probabilities unchanged if the model is already calibrated, a property that logistic calibration does not have.

Isotonic calibration is a non-parametric method, not constrained by the shapes within a particular parametric family. It uses PAV (pool adjacent violators) algorithm to learn a calibration map which is optimal on the training data, in the sense that no other monotonic calibration map yields a lower squared error between the resulting calibrated probabilities and actual binary labels [21]. As optimality is determined on the scores present in the training instances, the values of the calibration map on other scores are not determined: these gaps are filled in by linear interpolation or by extension into a piecewise constant function.

Ensemble of near isotonic regression (ENIR), is a calibration method that is based on and is shown to improve isotonic calibration [10]. It drops the monotonicity constraint, which makes sense in cases where the ROC curve of the classifier is non-convex. ENIR makes multiple calls to the near isotonic regression algorithm [18] which introduces a penalty for non-monotonicity into the loss measure. Each call is with a different value for penalty and the results are averaged with weights to obtain the final calibration function.

Finally, there are several non-parametric methods using binning, either by fixed width, fixed size, or more advanced methods, such as BBQ [12] and ABB [11]. However, these methods have been shown in [10] to be inferior to ENIR, so we will not consider them further in this paper.

It has been shown in [14] that logistic calibration outperforms isotonic calibration on smaller datasets and vice versa on larger datasets. This is because non-parametric methods overfit on smaller data whereas parametric methods have less tendency to overfit. At the same time, when enough data is provided for calibration, non-parametric methods can learn many different shapes while parametric methods are restricted to their parametric families. These statements will become one of the basis for constructing our experiments and interpreting the results.

In the following Sect. 2 we introduce proper losses as evaluation measures for calibration. In Sect. 3 we demonstrate that the existing non-parametric calibration methods are over-confident and propose to use Platt's correction, reducing log-loss and squared error in more than 90% of our studied cases. In Sect. 4 we propose our main contribution, a new non-parametric Bayesian isotonic calibration method. In Sect. 5 we perform experiments on synthetic and real data to demonstrate that on average, the new method performs either best or tied with best for all considered calibration set sizes and loss measures. Finally, Sect. 6 concludes and discusses future work.

2   Evaluation of Calibration

Following the definition of calibrated probabilities one needs to check whether among all instances with the same predicted probability p the actual proportion of positives is also close to p. However, for methods outputting a continuous scale of probabilities in $[0, 1]$ there is hardly any hope to find multiple instances with exactly the same predicted probability p. One way to evaluate calibration methods is to introduce bins around p and compare p to the empirical proportion of positives in the bins, as done by measures such as ECE (expected calibration error) [7]. Such methods ignore the differences of predictions within each bin, and therefore measure calibration to a limited granularity.

However, there is an alternative to this: *proper losses* (also called *proper scoring rules*). Proper losses are minimized if the calibration method achieves perfectly calibrated probabilities, due to the decomposition into *calibration loss* and *refinement loss* [3,9]. Since refinement loss cannot decrease during calibration, any reduction in overall loss must be due to the reduction in calibration loss.

The best known proper losses are log-loss (a.k.a. cross-entropy) and Brier score (a.k.a. squared error), which are standard evaluation measures of class probability estimators [14]. If the instance is positive and the model predicts it to be positive with probability $\hat{p}$, then log-loss (LL) penalizes it with loss $-\ln \hat{p}$ and Brier score (BS) with loss $(1 - \hat{p})^2$. If the instance is negative, then the losses are $-\ln(1 - \hat{p})$ and $\hat{p}^2$, respectively. Both these losses are non-negative and minimized if the prediction is correct and with full confidence, i.e., $\hat{p} = 1$ for positives and $\hat{p} = 0$ for negatives. However, these measures behave differently with respect to over- and under-confidence. Brier score is symmetric in the sense that over- and under-estimating the calibrated probability to be positive by the same amount results in the same loss according to Brier score. In contrast, log-loss is highly sensitive to over-confidence, particularly at the high confidence cases. As an extreme case, full confidence in the wrong prediction yields infinite

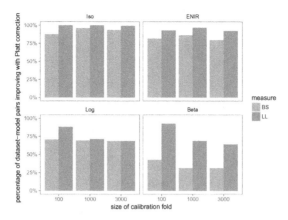

Fig. 2. Percentage of 153 dataset-model pairs where Platt correction improves over the uncorrected calibration method for Brier score (BS) and log-loss (LL).

log-loss. Even if this happens only with one instance in the test set, the overall loss on the whole test set is still infinite due to averaging. Exactly this can happen often with isotonic calibration and ENIR, whenever the lowest score in the training set has a negative class and/or highest score has positive class. While penalized infinitely by log-loss, any other proper loss would also penalize this.

3   Simple Improvement of Existing Methods

This motivates our first contribution: a simple improvement of isotonic calibration and ENIR. On these calibration methods we propose to use the same correction procedure as Platt used for logistic calibration. This means that isotonic calibration and ENIR should also be applied after replacing the class labels 1 and 0 by $1 - \frac{1}{N_+ + 2}$ and $0 + \frac{1}{N_- + 2}$, respectively, where N_+ and N_- are the numbers of positives and negatives in the training data.

We have evaluated this simple modification on $459 = 9 \times 17 \times 3$ calibration tasks, obtained by training 9 different models on 17 datasets and in each using either 100, 1000 or 3000 instances for learning the calibration map (see details about the experimental setup in Sect. 5.2). In 458 cases out of 459 log-loss was reduced when starting to use Platt's correction on isotonic calibration (Fig. 2 top left, where the 459 cases are split between calibration sizes 100, 300, and 1000). The benefit is also obvious for Brier score, with improvement in 92% of the cases (424 out of 459). For reference, Fig. 2 also shows the impact of Platt's correction on logistic and beta calibration methods. For logistic calibration the results confirm the benefit of Platt's correction, as expected. For beta calibration the correction turns out to be useful only for log-loss, and not for Brier score (improvement in <50% of cases).

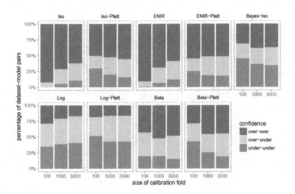

Fig. 3. Proportion of under- and over-confidence for 9 calibration methods on 153 data-model pairs over 3 different calibration data sizes.

Isotonic calibration can suffer infinite log-loss due to over-confidence on instances at either end of the ranking by score. To understand the effect of Platt's correction on over- and under-confidence a bit better, we performed the following analysis. We considered the first and last 2.5% of the instances according to the ranking by score. We say that a calibration method is over-confident on the last 2.5% instances, if the average calibrated probability on these instances is closer to 1 than the actual proportion of positives. Otherwise, we call it under-confident. Note that here we do not have a zone of being calibrated between over- and under-confidence, because we are interested in seeing the changes in over- and under-confidence after Platt correction. Similarly, we say that a calibration method is over-confident on the first 2.5% instances, if the average calibrated probability according to this method on these instances is closer to 0 than the actual proportion of positives (because here the model is over-confident in predicting the negative class).

Figure 3 shows the proportions of cases where the calibration method is over-confident at both ends (over-over), under-confident at both ends (under-under) or over-confident at one end and under-confident at the other (over-under). As expected, Platt correction reduces the proportion of over-over and increases the proportion of under-under. Overall, the balance between over- and under-confidence varies significantly across different methods. Interestingly, the most equal proportions of over- and under-confidence are shown by Bayes-Iso (non-parametric Bayesian isotonic calibration), which we will next motivate and present.

4   Proposed Method

Even though Platt correction helps to overcome some issues regarding over-confidence, there is no clear justification behind it. In case of fully separable training data where all negative instances have lower scores than positives it can be thought of as performing Laplace smoothing, which is a standard method to estimating class proportions, e.g. within a leaf of a decision tree. Laplace smoothing has a Bayesian interpretation, but this interpretation does not seem to apply to the Platt correction method. Our goal is to propose a fully Bayesian non-parametric calibration method which would perform well on both smaller and larger datasets, as opposed to current non-parametric methods which are outperformed by parametric methods on smaller datasets.

Suppose we have a fixed scoring classifier and we need to learn a calibration map $\widehat{cal}$ from N training instances, given the (uncalibrated) scores $\mathbf{s}^{tr} = (s_1, \ldots, s_N)$ predicted by the classifier and the actual labels $\mathbf{y}^{tr} = (y_1, \ldots, y_N)$. The calibration map would be evaluated by drawing a random test instance X, applying the classifier to obtain its score $\mathsf{S} = classifier(\mathsf{X})$, and then testing the calibrated probability $\mathsf{C} = \widehat{cal}(\mathsf{S})$ against the actual class Y with respect to a loss measure l by calculating $l(\mathsf{C}, \mathsf{Y})$. If the loss measure is a proper loss, then the expected loss would be minimized by the perfect calibration map cal defined as $cal(\mathsf{S}) = \mathbb{E}[\mathsf{Y}|\mathsf{S}]$. This result follows from the fact that Bregman divergences are minimized at the conditional expectation [1] and the proper losses are Bregman divergences where one of the inputs has been restricted to be binary [17]. Note that the perfectly calibrated probabilities $cal(S)$ are different from the Bayes-optimal probability estimator $\mathbb{E}[\mathsf{Y}|\mathsf{X}]$.

Isotonic calibration aims to find calibrated probability estimates $\hat{\mathbf{c}} = (\hat{c}_1, \ldots, \hat{c}_N)$ at the sorted scores $s_1 \leq \cdots \leq s_N$ present in the training data, where $\hat{\mathbf{c}}$ must belong to the space $\mathcal{I}^N$ of all real-valued vectors of length N constrained with isotonicity $0 \leq \hat{c}_1 \leq \cdots \leq \hat{c}_N \leq 1$. This discrete calibration map can then be extended to $\widehat{cal}$ as a piecewise constant calibration map, or linear interpolation could be used to fill in the gaps between training scores. Since proper losses are minimized at the conditional expectation [1,17], it is easy to show that due to pooling the isotonic calibration $\widehat{cal}_{iso}$ is minimizing any proper loss l on the training data. This means that $\hat{\mathbf{c}}^{iso} = \arg\min_{\hat{\mathbf{c}} \in \mathcal{I}^N} L(\hat{\mathbf{c}}, \mathbf{y}^{tr})$ where $L(\hat{\mathbf{c}}, \mathbf{y}^{tr}) = \sum_{i=1}^{N} l(\hat{c}_i, y_i^{tr})$.

4.1   Non-parametric Bayesian Isotonic Calibration

Inspired by isotonic calibration, we aim to estimate the calibration map on the predicted scores present in the training data, and elsewhere we would use linear interpolation. While standard isotonic finds the monotonic calibration map which minimises the loss on the training data (in the spirit of maximum likelihood), we aim to minimise the expected loss on future test data (in the spirit of maximum a posteriori). However, to avoid having to define a prior over all possible isotonic calibration maps from $\mathbb{R}$ to $[0, 1]$, we narrow the aim to minimise the expected loss on only those future test data which contain the same scores as our training data. Due to this we only need to define the prior over the N scores present in the training data. As actual test labels are not available during training, then the expected loss on future test data can never be known in practice, but can still be estimated based on the training data. To derive such an estimator, we will reason about the test labels and introduce notation for them. To avoid confusion with the actual test labels, we will be using the term *hypothetical labels* from now on. These hypothetical labels will only be used notationally, for deriving the methods, and these are not needed for running the proposed calibration algorithm.

Following the Bayesian paradigm we assume that the perfect calibration map $\mathbf{C} = (\mathsf{C}_1, \ldots, \mathsf{C}_N)$ was drawn from $\mathcal{I}^N$ according to some prior distribution that we will specify in Sect. 4.2. We assume that both the training labels $\mathbf{Y}^{tr} = (\mathsf{Y}_1^{tr}, \ldots, \mathsf{Y}_N^{tr})$ and hypothetical labels $\mathbf{Y}^{hyp} = (\mathsf{Y}_1^{hyp}, \ldots, \mathsf{Y}_N^{hyp})$ were drawn independently according to the probabilities $\mathbf{C}$, that is $\mathsf{Y}_i^{tr}, \mathsf{Y}_i^{hyp} \sim Bernoulli(\mathsf{C}_i)$ for $i = 1, \ldots, N$. We define non-parametric Bayesian isotonic calibration as follows:

$$\hat{\mathbf{c}}^{Bayes-iso} = \arg\min_{\hat{\mathbf{c}} \in \mathcal{I}^N} \mathbb{E}\left[L(\hat{\mathbf{c}}, \mathbf{Y}^{hyp}) \mid \mathbf{Y}^{tr} = \mathbf{y}^{tr}\right] \tag{1}$$

where $L(\hat{\mathbf{c}}, \mathbf{y}) = \sum_{i=1}^N l(\hat{c}_i, y_i)$.

The following Theorem 1 will form the basis for calculating this conditional expectation numerically. It proves that the conditional expectation of Eq. (1) can be calculated as a ratio of two unconditional expectations involving the calibration map $\mathbf{C}$ and its likelihood under the observed training data, $\mathbb{P}(\mathbf{Y}^{tr} = \mathbf{y}^{tr} \mid \mathbf{C})$. This result can be thought of as Bayesian model averaging: models are sampled from the model prior and averaged weighting by their likelihoods.

Theorem 1. *Let $\mathbf{C}$, $\mathbf{Y}^{tr}$ and $\mathbf{Y}^{hyp}$ be random vectors of length N as defined above. Suppose we observe $\mathbf{Y}^{tr} = \mathbf{y}^{tr}$, then for $\hat{\mathbf{c}}^{Bayes-iso}$ as defined in Eq. (1) the following holds:*

$$\hat{\mathbf{c}}^{Bayes-iso} = \frac{\mathbb{E}\left[\mathbf{C} \cdot \mathbb{P}(\mathbf{Y}^{tr} = \mathbf{y}^{tr} \mid \mathbf{C})\right]}{\mathbb{E}\left[\mathbb{P}(\mathbf{Y}^{tr} = \mathbf{y}^{tr} \mid \mathbf{C})\right]} \tag{2}$$

$$where \quad \mathbb{P}(\mathbf{Y}^{tr} = \mathbf{y}^{tr} \mid \mathbf{C}) = \prod_{\substack{i=1 \\ y_i^{tr}=1}}^N \mathsf{C}_i \prod_{\substack{i=1 \\ y_i^{tr}=0}}^N (1 - \mathsf{C}_i) \tag{3}$$

Proof. Since proper losses are minimized at the conditional expectation [1,17], we have $\hat{\mathbf{c}}^{Bayes-iso} = \mathbb{E}\left[\mathbf{Y}^{hyp} \mid \mathbf{Y}^{tr} = \mathbf{y}^{tr}\right]$. According to the law of iterated expectations this is equal to $\mathbb{E}\left[\mathbb{E}\left[\mathbf{Y}^{hyp} \mid \mathbf{C}\right] \mid \mathbf{Y}^{tr} = \mathbf{y}^{tr}\right]$ which simplifies into $\mathbb{E}\left[\mathbf{C} \mid \mathbf{Y}^{tr} = \mathbf{y}^{tr}\right]$ as the components in random binary vector $\mathbf{Y}^{hyp}$ have been drawn according to probabilities in random vector $\mathbf{C}$. From the definition of conditional expectation and Bayes formula we get:

$$\mathbb{E}\left[\mathbf{C} \mid \mathbf{Y}^{tr} = \mathbf{y}^{tr}\right] = \int \mathbf{C}\, f_{\mathbf{C}|\mathbf{Y}^{tr}}(\mathbf{C}, \mathbf{y}^{tr})\, d\mathbf{C} =$$

$$\int \mathbf{C}\, \frac{\mathbb{P}(\mathbf{Y}^{tr} = \mathbf{y}^{tr} | \mathbf{C}) f_{\mathbf{C}}(\mathbf{C})}{\mathbb{P}(\mathbf{Y}^{tr} = \mathbf{y}^{tr})}\, d\mathbf{C} = \frac{\mathbb{E}\left[\mathbf{C}\, \mathbb{P}(\mathbf{Y}^{tr} = \mathbf{y}^{tr} | \mathbf{C})\right]}{\mathbb{P}(\mathbf{Y}^{tr} = \mathbf{y}^{tr})}$$

Eq. (2) follows from this using the law of iterated expectations and the fact that for binary variables the expectations are probabilities. Finally, the calculation of likelihood in Eq. (3) is straightforward, due to independence of the components within the binary vector.

Our proposed non-parametric Bayesian isotonic calibration maps can be calculated by drawing many isotonic calibration maps from the prior distribution, calculating their likelihoods according to the training labels, and using these as weights in averaging all the sampled maps into one final result as is described in Algorithm 1. The algorithm returns a calibration map that is constructed from pairs of scores and calibrated probabilities, which are joined by linear interpolation as in isotonic calibration, to make predictions over all possible scores. Algorithm description mentions bounds which will be explained in Sect. 4.3. The time complexity of this algorithm is $\mathbb{O}(sn)$ where n is the size of calibration data and s is the number of candidate maps to be sampled from the prior.

Data: scores, labels, nrSamples
Result: calibration map
1. Calculate lower and upper bounds from labels
2. Generate nrSamples sample maps from prior with bounds
3. Evaluate the likelihood of each sample according to labels as shown in Eq. (3)
4. Calculate weighted average of sampled maps using likelihoods as weights
5. Compose the calibration map by joining the scores and the weighted average of the sample maps by linear interpolation

Algorithm 1: Bayes-Iso algorithm.

4.2 Selecting the Prior over Isotonic Maps

To fully specify our calibration method we must specify the prior distribution over the calibration maps in space $\mathcal{I}^N$. It is crucial to choose a prior which assigns a reasonably high probability density to all calibration maps that we deem reasonable, otherwise the method would never output such maps, even if made likely by the data.

One possible simple prior can be defined as sampling N independent values uniformly from $[0, 1]$ and sorting them to obtain an isotonic calibration map belonging to $\mathcal{I}^N$. However, this prior is highly concentrated around the calibration map where the values $C_1, \ldots, C_N$ are equally spaced, represented as the diagonal in Fig. 4A. Note that in this figure the X-axis represents relative ranks of scores rather than absolute scores coming out from the classifier. Concentration of probability mass around the diagonal implies that any calibration map that is not around the diagonal would be almost impossible to learn. However, in practice the true calibration map can be far from the diagonal, particularly if the classes are imbalanced.

Therefore, we need a prior that covers the space of all isotonic calibration maps more broadly. We have considered the existing priors on Bayesian isotonic regression (not restricted to output in the range $[0, 1]$) [13] but these do not adapt easily to our situation or do not provide broad coverage of the space of all isotonic calibration maps. Our proposed solution to achieve broad coverage is straightforward - while drawing a calibration map from our prior we first pick uniformly randomly a point in the 2-dimensional space of Fig. 4 and then start to construct a map that goes through this chosen point. Note that we use the discrete uniform distribution for X-axis (because these are ranks $1, \ldots, N$) and continuous uniform distribution for Y-axis (because these are probabilities). In the next steps we apply the same procedure recursively, while ensuring isotonicity. This means that we next choose the second point uniformly randomly to the left and below from the first point and the third point uniformly randomly to the right and above from the first point. For example, if the first point is (x_1, y_1), then the second point (x_2, y_2) is chosen by sampling x_2 uniformly from $\{1, 2, \ldots, x_1 - 1\}$, and y_2 uniformly from $[0, y_1]$. Similarly, (x_3, y_3) is chosen by sampling x_3 uniformly from $\{x_1 + 1, x_1 + 2, \ldots, N\}$, and y_3 uniformly from $[y_1, 1]$. This procedure recursively delves into all ranges between existing points, until all points $1, \ldots, N$ on the X-axis have been chosen. Figure 4B shows a random sample of 200 calibration maps drawn from this prior for $N = 100$. Note that we have renormalised the X-axis to be from 0 to 1 instead of from 1 to 100.

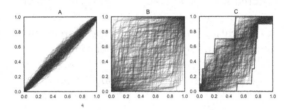

Fig. 4. Examples of 200 sampled curves of size 100. (A) Samples from a bad prior. (B) Samples from our defined prior. (C) Samples from our defined prior using bounds.

4.3   Practically Efficient Sampling from Prior

Having defined the prior we have fully specified our non-parametric Bayesian isotonic calibration method. However, straightforward implementation of this would result in poor performance. The reason is that the space of isotonic calibration maps $\mathcal{I}^N$ is vast and maps with the highest likelihoods are hardly ever found when randomly sampling from the prior. As a result, the estimation of $\mathbb{E}\left[\mathbf{C} \cdot \mathbb{P}(\mathbf{Y}^{tr} = \mathbf{y}^{tr} \mid \mathbf{C})\right]$ would mostly be based on maps C with low likelihood and numerically dominated by very few maps with higher likelihood, resulting in a high variance estimate that would not be precise enough. If we can avoid sampling maps that have near-zero likelihoods, then the estimate stabilises, while still being a good approximation of the true posterior mean map. Therefore, we propose a method to use training data to obtain a lower and upper bound and to sample only those calibration maps that are fully between them. This does change our prior and in this sense is not purely Bayesian, but in practice it provides a reasonably good estimate of the posterior mean with the original prior.

Our algorithm is inspired by calibration methods that use binning. Let us consider a bin of B consecutive instances with labels $y_{j+1}, y_{j+2}, \ldots, y_{j+B}$ within a full ranked list of N training instances. If the proportion of positives in this bin is p, then this can be used as an estimate for the average calibrated probability within this bin, that is $\overline{C} = \frac{1}{B} \sum_{i=1}^{B} C_{j+i} \approx p$. However, since the calibration is isotonic, we know that $C_{j+1} \leq \overline{C} \leq C_{j+B}$. Hence, we can use p as an approximate upper bound for C_{j+1} and an approximate lower bound for C_{j+B}. Taking into account that the estimation of the proportion of positives has variance in the order of $1/\sqrt{B}$, we use in practice the bounds $C_{j+1} \leq p + 1/\sqrt{B}$ and $C_{j+B} \geq p - 1/\sqrt{B}$.

The above shows how a bin can be used to set bounds for the lower and upper end of the bin. In order to obtain bounds for the calibrated probability at a given test instance we apply the above reasoning on the bins of size B to the left and to the right of this instance within the ranking. If the considered instance is close to one end of the full ranking, then of course the size of the bin towards that end would necessarily be smaller. In the experiments we used the bin size $B = N/10$. The advantage of a larger bin is that p can be approximated more precisely, but at the same time the average is taken over a region where the calibrated probability within the ranking is varying more, so there is a tradeoff in selecting the size of B.

This method results in non-monotonic bounds: for $s_i < s_{i+1}$ the lower bound at s_i could be higher than at s_{i+1}. In such cases we extended the lower bound to monotonicity, that is s_i would adopt the lower bound from s_{i+1}. Symmetrically, the same can happen with upper bounds: for $s_i < s_{i+1}$ the upper bound at s_i could be higher than at s_{i+1}. In this case we raise the upper bound of s_{i+1} to match the upper bound of s_i. By ensuring monotonicity this way the bounds can only become wider, lower bounds can only be lowered and upper bounds raised.

One possibility to apply the bounds on the sampling is to perform rejection sampling - the drawn calibration maps which fall out of bounds would be discarded. However, this can make the sampling very slow, as with tight bounds most of the maps would be discarded. Fortunately, it is easy to modify our prior slightly to be easily directly sampled from between the bounds. After drawing the X-axis value from the discrete uniform distribution we draw the Y-axis value from the uniform distribution between the bounds, rather than between 0 and 1. Similarly, we can at each step sample along the X-axis first, and then sample along the Y-axis uniformly, constrained between the bounds. An example of sampling from between bounds can be seen in Fig. 4C. Note that the bounds shown are learned from the actual training labels in an example dataset, which is why they are not symmetric. They are shown to illustrate the idea, in reality the bounds will be always different for different datasets.

5   Experiments

We start the experiments with a case study on a synthetic dataset, in order to demonstrate empirically how our proposed Bayesian isotonic calibration converges to the true perfect calibration map as the dataset size increases, outperforming all state-of-the-art calibration methods. More precisely, we will demonstrate how Bayes-Iso works in the setting that it is designed for. This is followed by a large-scale study on real datasets, illustrating which calibration methods work well when calibration data size is changed. We will see that based on average ranks over all dataset-model pairs Bayes-Iso performs either best or tied with best for all considered training set sizes and loss measures.

5.1   Experiments on Synthetic Data

Bayes-Iso is designed to be better whenever the true calibration function is not in the families of parametric methods. In such cases parametric methods perform poorly due to model mismatch and the existing non-parametric methods due to over-confidence. We will demonstrate this effect on a synthetic dataset. We have generated a dataset where the calibration map does not belong to the logistic and beta calibration map families, because in case of parametric shapes it would be clear that parametric methods would be the best choice. According to our generative model the classes are balanced, and a hypothetical scoring classifier is generating scores that are on actual negatives distributed as $Beta(1, 3)$, and on positives as a balanced mixture of $Beta(1.5, 3)$ and $Beta(30, 3)$. The perfect calibration map is shown in Fig. 5 with a red dashed line and on our generated test data with 100000 instances results with ideal log-loss of 0.1620 and Brier score of 0.4741. Table 1 shows how close to the ideal each of the calibration methods reaches on training set sizes 100 and 3000 (on size 1000 methods ranked identically to 3000, not shown). Results were averaged over 10 replicate experiments. Note that according to the results in Sect. 3, we applied Platt correction on all reference methods, except for beta calibration with Brier score. Bayes-Iso algorithm used 10000 samples to estimate the calibration map.

Results in Table 1 show that Bayes-Iso gets very close to the ideal, winning over all other methods. Even though the true calibration map is not in the parametric family, Beta calibration gets close enough shape to be the second best on the smallest dataset. This example demonstrates that existing parametric methods are often better than non-parametric ones on smaller datasets, because they don't overfit to small data as easily. Bayes-Iso on the other hand is less-confident than other non-parametric methods and works well also on small datasets. On bigger datasets non-parametric methods dominate over parametric ones as expected, and Bayes-Iso shows the best results. Figure 5 demonstrates the variance of all considered calibration methods across the 10 replicate experiments on training set size 1000. We can see that for size 1000 parametric methods clearly cannot learn the true calibration function whereas non-parametric methods can.

Table 1. Average Brier score and log-loss on synthetic datasets of sizes 100 and 3000. Beta calibration is used for Brier score and Beta-Platt for log-loss. Numbers in subscript show the ranking of the scores.

Method	BS100	LL100	BS3000	LL3000
Ideal	.1621	.4741	.1621	.4741
Bayes-Iso	$.1655_1$	$.4878_1$	$.1625_1$	$.4753_1$
ENIR-Platt	$.1683_3$	$.5029_3$	$.1627_2$	$.4778_2$
Iso-Platt	$.1685_4$	$.5036_4$	$.1627_3$	$.4779_3$
Beta(-Platt)	$.1672_2$	$.4895_2$	$.1660_4$	$.4862_4$
Log-Platt	$.1720_5$	$.5112_5$	$.1721_5$	$.5097_5$

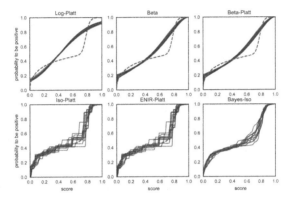

Fig. 5. 10 calibration maps learned on 10 replicate synthetic datasets of size 1000 for six different calibration methods (blue). True underlying calibration map (red). (Color figure online)

Since Bayes-Iso is a non-deterministic method its results can vary on the same dataset across different runs. Figure 6 shows results on 10 runs on exactly the same dataset on each of the 3 data sizes, complemented with bounds as learned within the Bayes-Iso method. The figure demonstrates that each of the runs results in a high-quality calibration map with very low variance across runs. But we can also notice that the larger the calibration data, the more differences the learned maps start to have. This is expected as we need more and more sampling to converge with Bayes-Iso in case of larger data.

5.2   Experimental Setup on Real Data

The methods are evaluated on the following 17 datasets from OpenML [19]: SEA(50), BNG(breast-w), BNG(sonar), BNG(heart-statlog), 2dplanes, house_16H, cal_housing, houses, house_8L, fried, letter, BNG(spectf_test), BNG(Australian), BNG(SPECTF), skin-segmentation, creditcard, numerai28.6. These were selected as datasets with a binary target variable, no missing values,

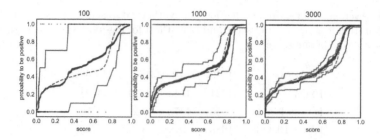

Fig. 6. 10 calibration maps for different sized data learned with Bayes-Iso on the same dataset (blue). Green lines show the lower and upper bounds for sampling, red line shows the true underlying calibration map. (Color figure online)

at most 100 numerical features, and the number of instances between 20000 and 1 million.

Performance of calibration methods is known to vary with dataset size [14]. We decided that we can see size-related effects best if we fix particular sizes (100, 1000 and 3000) for the fold on which we apply the calibration method. To make the losses on different sizes directly comparable we further chose to keep the classifier and the test set constant. We achieved all this by first randomly downsampling all datasets to the same size of 20000 instances, and then running 5-fold nested cross validation. In the internal 5-fold cross-validation we use 4 folds to train the model and 1 fold to calibrate. This 1 internal fold was big enough (3200) to allow randomly sampling calibration datasets of required 3 sizes. The goodness of the calibration maps are evaluated on the outer fold, that we call the test fold, which is of size 4000. To make experiments run faster we have trained the classification models on 3000 out of the 12800 instances of the 4 internal folds. This choice certainly makes the models weaker but still allows to achieve our objective of comparing calibration methods. The classification models were trained with 9 different learning algorithms, selected from among the same as used in the large-scale comparisons in [14] and [2]: decision tree (DT), naive bayes (NB), support vector machine (SVM), random forest (RF), logistic regression (LR), K-nearest neighbors (KNN), boosted trees (ADA), bagged trees (BAG-DT) and artificial neural networks (ANN). The implementations for these algorithms were taken from the scikit-learn package [15] using the default parameters, except for the decision tree, for which we used minimum leaf size of 10.

Overall, we trained a classifier for each of the $17 \times 9 \times 5 \times 5 = 3825$ combinations of 17 datasets, 9 classifier learning algorithms, 5 external and 5 internal cross-validation folds. For each trained classifier we learned $3 \times 9 = 27$ calibration maps resulting from 3 dataset sizes and 9 calibration algorithms (logistic, beta, isotonic calibration and ENIR with and without Platt correction, and Bayes-Iso).

We used existing packages for Beta calibration and ENIR, and modified scikit-learn implementation for logistic calibration (to switch off Platt correction). Other methods were implemented from scratch.[1]

---

[1] Code with implementations of the algorithms and experiments on real data is available at https://github.com/mlkruup/bayesiso.

5.3   Experiment Results on Real Data

First, we evaluated Bayes-Iso against other non-parametric methods (that are Platt corrected). Table 2 shows the percentage of dataset-model pairs where Bayes-Iso outperformed both Iso-Platt and ENIR-Platt, across different sizes of calibration datasets. Bayes-Iso was the best non-parametric method on the majority of cases, in particular on smaller sizes. This is expected as isotonic calibration and ENIR are known to be overfitting on smaller datasets but more suitable on larger ones, where they become more competitive to Bayes-Iso.

Increase in dataset size leads to Bayes-Iso sampling the space of isotonic maps more sparsely, and more often a single map dominates all others within the sample, in the sense that its likelihood is higher than all others summed up. This can be used as an indicator flag of potential poor performance. The column 3000 LH in Table 2 shows results where the flagged cases (27% of all cases) have been eliminated. The improvement from 56% and 59% in column 3000 to 71% and 73% in column 3000 LH means that there is a big potential in improving our method further by more efficient bounds and more sampling. It is also comforting that Bayes-Iso can *itself* flag cases of potential instability.

Secondly, we wanted to compare all state-of-the-art calibration methods, including the parametric ones, to Bayes-Iso. We have an initial hypothesis that Bayes-Iso should perform well both on larger and smaller datasets whereas parametric methods work better on smaller and other non-parametric methods on larger datasets. We demonstrate this in a large-scale comparison against all considered calibration methods. We performed Friedman test with post hoc analysis on average ranks [4] of models ordered by log-loss and Brier score. The results are illustrated as critical difference diagrams in Fig. 7. We can see that Bayes-Iso performs either best or tied with the best, based on the average ranks across all dataset-model pairs. This holds true for all sizes of the calibration set (100, 1000, 3000) and both loss measures (BS, LL). This supports our hypothesis about the behaviour of the methods with respect to the calibration set sizes.

It is not easy to give recommendations for the most suitable calibration method for different models since good performance for a calibration method is more dependent on the dataset size and how a particular model is performing on a dataset. Factors like calibration data size, goodness of the model, distribution of scores in the classes, class distribution, shape of the true calibration map are probably more important factors and most likely have joint effects when deciding on the best method to use. We have found some examples about how these factors affect the performance of Bayes-Iso. One discovered case is when

Table 2. Percentage of improved dataset-model pairs where Bayes-Iso improved on other non-parametric methods.

Size	100	1000	3000	3000 LH
BS	86%	79%	56%	71%
LL	92%	84%	59%	73%

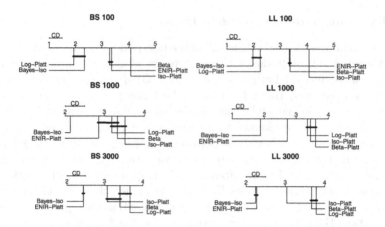

Fig. 7. Critical difference diagrams based on ranks of methods over 153 dataset-model pairs over different calibration dataset sizes and losses.

we have a small dataset and a model with very high accuracy. In this case Bayes-Iso is too under-confident when compared to ENIR-Platt and Iso-Platt. The reason could be that since the model is very good then even with small dataset for calibration it is beneficial to have high confidence predictions. Because of the joint effects of the formerly mentioned factors, these patterns are difficult to identify and interpret. Extensive experiments left for future work could give us more insight into these effects and help us identify situations where one or another calibration method is the most suitable.

6   Conclusions

For decision-making purposes it is important that the classifiers were well-calibrated. Parametric calibration methods work well on small datasets, but on bigger datasets the parametric assumption often does not hold and non-parametric methods perform better. In this work we have first demonstrated that existing non-parametric calibration methods produce over-confident predictions. We have discovered that the same correction method that was used in logistic calibration by Platt can be used for reducing over-confidence in isotonic calibration and ENIR, reducing log-loss and Brier score in more than 90% of our studied cases. Our main contribution is a novel non-parametric Bayesian isotonic calibration (Bayes-Iso). Bayes-Iso has the flexibility of isotonic calibration to fit maps of all monotonic shapes but it additionally provides smoothness and reduces over-confidence without requiring a separate correction procedure. When comparing against the state-of-the-art methods on 153 calibration tasks Bayes-Iso works either best or tied with the best depending on the size of the calibration dataset. The current version of Bayes-Iso experiences instability when scaling up to learn a calibration map from many more than 3000 instances. As future work we envision ways to make Bayes-Iso scale up to much larger sizes, as the calibration map could easily be learned in bins of 1000 consecutively ranked instances and later merged into a single calibration map.

Acknowledgments. This work was supported by the Estonian Research Council under grant PUT1458.

References

1. Banerjee, A., Guo, X., Wang, H.: On the optimality of conditional expectation as a Bregman predictor. IEEE Trans. Inf. Theory **51**(7), 2664–2669 (2005)
2. Caruana, R., Niculescu-Mizil, A.: An empirical comparison of supervised learning algorithms. In: Proceedings of the 23rd International Conference on Machine Learning, pp. 161–168. ACM (2006)
3. DeGroot, M.H., Fienberg, S.E.: The comparison and evaluation of forecasters. Statistician **32**, 12–22 (1983)
4. Demšar, J.: Statistical comparisons of classifiers over multiple data sets. J. Mach. Learn. Res. **7**(Jan), 1–30 (2006)
5. Elkan, C.: The foundations of cost-sensitive learning. In: International Joint Conference on Artificial Intelligence, vol. 17, pp. 973–978. Lawrence Erlbaum Associates Ltd (2001)
6. Goodfellow, I., Bengio, Y., Courville, A.: Deep Learning. MIT Press, Cambridge (2016)
7. Guo, C., Pleiss, G., Sun, Y., Weinberger, K.Q.: On calibration of modern neural networks. In: Proceedings of the 34th International Conference on Machine Learning, vol. 70, pp. 1321–1330. JMLR (2017)
8. Kull, M., De Menezes E Silva Filho, T., Flach, P.: Beta calibration: a well-founded and easily implemented improvement on logistic calibration for binary classifiers, pp. 623–631. JMLR (2017)
9. Kull, M., Flach, P.: Novel decompositions of proper scoring rules for classification: score adjustment as precursor to calibration. In: Appice, A., Rodrigues, P.P., Santos Costa, V., Soares, C., Gama, J., Jorge, A. (eds.) ECML PKDD 2015. LNCS (LNAI), vol. 9284, pp. 68–85. Springer, Cham (2015). https://doi.org/10.1007/978-3-319-23528-8_5
10. Naeini, M.P., Cooper, G.F.: Binary classifier calibration using an ensemble of near isotonic regression models. In: IEEE 16th International Conference on Data Mining, pp. 360–369. IEEE (2016)
11. Naeini, M.P., Cooper, G.F., Hauskrecht, M.: Binary classifier calibration using a Bayesian non-parametric approach. In: Proceedings of the 2015 SIAM International Conference on Data Mining, pp. 208–216. SIAM (2015)
12. Naeini, M.P., Cooper, G.F., Hauskrecht, M.: Obtaining well calibrated probabilities using Bayesian binning. In: Proceedings of the 29th AAAI Conference on Artificial Intelligence, pp. 2901–2907. AAAI Press (2015)
13. Neelon, B., Dunson, D.B.: Bayesian isotonic regression and trend analysis. Biometrics **60**(2), 398–406 (2004)
14. Niculescu-Mizil, A., Caruana, R.: Predicting good probabilities with supervised learning. In: Proceedings of the 22nd International Conference on Machine Learning, ICML 2005, pp. 625–632. ACM (2005)
15. Pedregosa, F., et al.: Scikit-learn: machine learning in Python. JMLR **12**, 2825–2830 (2011)

16. Platt, J., et al.: Probabilistic outputs for support vector machines and comparisons to regularized likelihood methods. Adv. Large Margin Classif. **10**(3), 61–74 (1999)
17. Reid, M.D., Williamson, R.C.: Information, divergence and risk for binary experiments. J. Mach. Learn. Res. **12**(Mar), 731–817 (2011)
18. Tibshirani, R.J., Hoefling, H., Tibshirani, R.: Nearly-isotonic regression. Technometrics **53**(1), 54–61 (2011)
19. Vanschoren, J., Van Rijn, J.N., Bischl, B., Torgo, L.: OpenML: networked science in machine learning. ACM SIGKDD Explor. Newslett. **15**(2), 49–60 (2014)
20. Zadrozny, B., Elkan, C.: Obtaining calibrated probability estimates from decision trees and Naive Bayesian classifiers. In: ICML, vol. 1, pp. 609–616. Citeseer (2001)
21. Zadrozny, B., Elkan, C.: Transforming classifier scores into accurate multiclass probability estimates. In: Proceedings of the 8th ACM SIGKDD International Conference on Knowledge Discovery and Data Mining, pp. 694–699. ACM (2002)

Multi-label Learning

PP-PLL: Probability Propagation for Partial Label Learning

Kaiwei Sun, Zijian Min, and Jin Wang$^{(\boxtimes)}$

Key Laboratory of Data Engineering and Visual Computing,
Chongqing University of Posts and Telecommunications, Chongqing 400065, China
{sunkw,wangjin}@cqupt.edu.cn, s170201098@stu.cqupt.edu.cn

Abstract. Partial label learning (PLL) is a weakly supervised learning framework which learns from the data where each example is associated with a set of candidate labels, among which only one is correct. Most existing approaches are based on the disambiguation strategy, which either identifies the valid label iteratively or treats each candidate label equally based on the averaging strategy. In both cases, the disambiguation strategy shares a common shortcoming that the ground-truth label may be overwhelmed by the false positive candidate labels, especially when the number of candidate labels becomes large. In this paper, a probability propagation method for partial label learning (PP-PLL) is proposed. Specifically, based on the manifold assumption, a biconvex regular function is proposed to model the linear mapping relationships between input features and output true labels. In PP-PLL, the topological relations among training samples are used as additional information to strengthen the mutual exclusiveness among candidate labels, which helps to prevent the ground-truth label from being overwhelmed by a large number of candidate labels. Experimental studies on both artificial and real-world data sets demonstrate that the proposed PP-PLL method can achieve superior or comparable performance against the state-of-the-art methods.

Keywords: Partial label learning · Disambiguation strategy · Manifold assumption · Biconvex regular function

1 Introduction

In many real-world scenarios, data with explicit label information is hard to obtain. Thus, we have to face with the problem of learning from ambiguous data. Recently, partial label learning (PLL) provides an effective solution to cope with this problem and has been widely used in many real-world applications such as automatic image annotation [3], web mining [13], ecoinformatics [12], etc. Partial label learning is regarded as a weakly-supervised learning where each sample is associated with a set of candidate labels, among which only one is correct [2]. During the training process, the correct label of each training sample is concealed in its candidate label set and not directly accessible to the learning algorithm.

© Springer Nature Switzerland AG 2020
U. Brefeld et al. (Eds.): ECML PKDD 2019, LNAI 11907, pp. 123–137, 2020.
https://doi.org/10.1007/978-3-030-46147-8_8

Since the exact labeling information is concealed in the candidate label set, the key to partial label learning is to disambiguate labels in candidate label set. To this end, many disambiguation methods have been proposed to extract the ground-truth label from the ambiguously labeled data. These methods can be categorized into two groups, i.e. identification based disambiguation strategies (IDS) and averaging based disambiguation strategies (ADS). The IDS methods regard the ground-truth label as a latent variable which is identified via iterative refining procedure [10,12,15,17,19]. The ADS methods treat each candidate label equally and make the final prediction by averaging the modeling outputs [2,21]. Although IDS and ADS methods have yielded relatively good performance for partial label learning, they still suffer from some defects. Due to some misleading information in the candidate label set, both IDS and ADS methods have the risk that the ground-truth label may be overwhelmed by false positive labels, especially when the number of partially labeled training samples or the size of candidate label set becomes large [19].

To extract as much useful information about the ground-truth label as possible from the partially labeled data, many weakly-supervised learning algorithms assume that there exists a potential structure in the feature space of data, which helps to reveal the mapping from input features to ground-truth labels. Clustering based assumption and manifold based assumption are among the most common ones of them [24]. In the clustering based assumption, data samples are clustered into several clusters based on some similarity criterion such as Euclidean distance, and samples within the same cluster are assumed to belong to the same label. The manifold based assumption can be viewed as the extension of clustering based assumption. It assumes that the feature space of data follows a manifold structure, and the output of each sample is similar to its neighbors. Furthermore, manifold assumption based disambiguation strategies (MADS) have also been proposed to alleviate the negative impact of false positive labels [5,14,19,21]. However, the existing MADS methods ignore the mapping relationships from input features to ground-truth label and excessively rely on the potential topological structure of feature space, which makes the prediction trend to be the frequent labels.

In this paper, a probability propagation method for partial label learning (PP-PLL) is proposed. In PP-PLL, based on the manifold assumption we further assume that neighboring samples have similar label distribution, and we utilize the maximum entropy model to form a biconvex objective function. The objective function is then optimized by the alternating method, which can be regarded as a process of probability propagation. Different from the strategies mentioned above, our proposed PP-PLL method utilizes the potential topological structure of feature space as additional information, which strengthens the exclusiveness among labels and mitigates the risk of the ground-truth label being overwhelmed by candidate labels. Furthermore, in the process of probability propagation the mapping from input features to the ground-truth labels is modeled, which makes it less dependent on the intrinsic topological, and more accurately distinguishes the ground-truth label from false positive labels in the candidate label set. Compared with many state-of-the-art partial label learning methods, our proposed method can achieve better generalization performance and superior prediction performance.

The rest of this paper is organized as follows. In Sect. 2, we briefly introduce related works. The concrete formulation of our proposed PP-PLL method is presented in Sect. 3. In Sect. 4, the optimization of our model is presented. Section 5 provides experimental studies on various data sets, followed by the conclusions and future works in Sect. 6.

2   Related Work

In partial label learning framework, the label information is no longer unique and explicit. Real semantic information is concealed in the candidate label set, making the learning from data extremely difficult. Existing methods for partial label learning can be roughly grouped into three categories: ADS (Averaging-based Disambiguation Strategies), IDS (Identification-based Disambiguation Strategies) and MADS (Manifold Assumption-based Disambiguation Strategies).

ADS methods identify the ground-truth label via giving the label in candidate label set the same weight for each sample, and then obtain prediction by averaging the outputs from all candidate labels or the candidate labels in its neighbors. Following such strategy, ADS methods can be further divided into discrimination-based learning and instance-based learning. For the discrimination-based learning, Cour et al. [2,3] suppose that a parametric model $F(\mathbf{x}_i, y; \theta)$ discriminates the average modeling output of candidate labels from non-candidate labels as much as possible. For the instance-based learning, Hüllermeier and Beringer [9] suppose that the model predicts unseen instance by aggregating the weight of its neighbors' candidate labels. Although ADS methods are intuitive with strong explanatory, the critical defect is that the false positive labels in each set of candidate labels have greater advantages in weight assignment, especially when the size of each candidate label set becomes large.

Different from ADS, existing IDS approaches consider the ground-truth label as a latent variable, determined directly as $\hat{y}_i = \arg\max_{y \in S_i} F(\boldsymbol{x}_i, y; \boldsymbol{\theta})$. Furthermore, the objective function is defined according to the maximum likelihood criterion [7,10,12,23]: $\sum_{i=1}^{m} \log \left(\sum_{y \in S_i} F(\boldsymbol{x}_i, y; \boldsymbol{\theta}) \right)$ which is generally refined iteratively via utilizing Expectation-Maximization (EM) procedure [4], or the maximum margin criterion [15,18]: $\sum_{i=1}^{m} \left(\max_{y \in S_i} F(\boldsymbol{x}_i, y; \boldsymbol{\theta}) - \max_{y \notin S_i} F(\boldsymbol{x}_i, y; \boldsymbol{\theta}) \right)$ which is optimized via the Pegasos method that alternately performs sub-gradient descent and projection operations to update the model iteratively. Experimental results demonstrate that IDS have achieved more desirable performance than ADS. Nonetheless, the information from the false positive labels in all sets of candidate labels would mislead the model into updating towards the wrong direction, especially when the number of partially labeled training samples become large.

The strategies mentioned above utilize the set of candidate labels to construct partial label learning algorithms. However, their performance improvements are usually limited by false positive labels. To break through this limitation, manifold assumption-based disambiguation strategies (MADS) are proposed to extract as much useful labeling information as possible from the ambiguously labeled data through manifold assumption. To the best of our knowledge, the concept of neighbor samples in partial label learning was first proposed by Hüllermeier and Beringer [9]. However, it is unable to guarantee that the prediction of each sample is similar to its neighbors. This is why we generalize it into ADS. Following manifold assumption, existing MADS can be divided into nonparametric and parametric model. Regardless of the model proposed, a weighted graph of k-nearest neighbors should be constructed at first stage. At second stage, the prediction is obtained directly by label propagation [5,19] for nonparametric, and by a feature-aware disambiguation for parametric model [21]. Different from IDS and ADS, MADS can extract additional information from the ambiguously labeled data, however, existing MADS excessively relies on the potential topological structure of feature space.

In the next section, a novel partial label learning approach named PP-PLL will be introduced. To address the problem mentioned above, PP-PLL utilizes the character of the optimizing a biconvex formulation presented in this paper to achieve probability propagation.

3   The PP-PLL Method

Let $\mathcal{X} = \mathbb{R}^d$ denote the d-dimensional feature space, and $\mathcal{Y} = \{1, 2, \ldots, q\}$ be a label set with q class labels. Partial label learning is aimed at learning a classifier $f : \mathcal{X} \to \mathcal{Y}$ from training data $\mathcal{D} = \{(\boldsymbol{x}_i, S_i) \,|\, 1 \leq i \leq m\}$ to predict the ground-truth label of the unseen samples, where $\boldsymbol{x}_i \in \mathcal{X}$ is a d-dimensional feature vector $(x_{i1}, x_{i2}, \ldots, x_{id})^\top$, and $S_i \subseteq \mathcal{Y}$ is the candidate label set associated with $\boldsymbol{x}_i$. The ground-truth label y_i for $\boldsymbol{x}_i$ is concealed in S_i, i.e. $y_i \in S_i$, and is not directly accessible to the learning algorithm.

Let $\mathcal{F}$ denote the set of $m \times q$ matrices with nonnegative entries. A matrix $\boldsymbol{F} = \left[F_1^\top, \ldots, F_m^\top\right]^\top \in \mathcal{F}$ corresponds to ultimate label probability distribution of m partial label samples, and each sample $\boldsymbol{x}$ is labeled as $\hat{y}_i = \arg\max_{j \leq q} F_{ij}$. Therefore, one of the main goals is to obtain the ultimate label distribution matrix $\boldsymbol{F}$. To this end, some existing partial label learning approaches [7,10,12] regard the ground-truth label as a latent variable and estimate the ground-truth label by an iterative procedure. Although this kind of strategies have the capability of mapping from input features to ground-truth label, they are failed to correct the wrong updating direction caused by false positive labels during the iterative learning process.

Accordingly, we proposed PP-PLL under the assumption that the probability distribution of candidate labels for each sample is similar to its neighbors. At first stage, we construct a weighted graph $G = (V, E)$ over the ambiguously labeled data, where each sample is considered as a node of the graph. In order to characterize the manifold structure of feature space via conducting some affinity relationship, $E = \{(\boldsymbol{x}_i, \boldsymbol{x}_j) \,|\, \boldsymbol{x}_i \in k\mathrm{NN}(\boldsymbol{x}_j), i \neq j\}$ is denoted as the set of directed edges from $\boldsymbol{x}_i$ to $\boldsymbol{x}_j$ in graph G if $\boldsymbol{x}_i$ belongs to the k-nearest neighbors of $\boldsymbol{x}_j$. Furthermore, $\mathbf{W} = [w_{ij}]_{m \times m}$ is denoted as the non-negative weight matrix where $w_{ij} = 0$ if $(\boldsymbol{x}_i, \boldsymbol{x}_j) \notin E$. Otherwise, the j-th weight column $\mathbf{w}_{\cdot j} = (w_{i_1 j}, w_{i_2 j}, \ldots, w_{i_k j})^\top$ is denoted as the k-nearest neighbors' optimal weight column corresponding to the j-th sample via optimizing the following linear least square problem:

$$\min_{\mathbf{w}_{\cdot j}} \left\| \boldsymbol{x}_j - \sum_{(\boldsymbol{x}_i, \boldsymbol{x}_j) \in E} w_{ij} \cdot \boldsymbol{x}_i \right\|_2^2 \tag{1}$$

$$\text{s.t.} \quad w_{ij} \geq 0 \quad (\forall (\boldsymbol{x}_i, \boldsymbol{x}_j) \in E, 0 \leq i, j \leq m)$$

The OP(1) can be re-written as

$$\min_{\mathbf{w}_{\cdot j}} \left(\boldsymbol{x}_j - \boldsymbol{X}_j^\top \cdot \mathbf{w}_{\cdot j} \right)^\top \cdot \left(\boldsymbol{x}_j - \boldsymbol{X}_j^\top \cdot \mathbf{w}_{\cdot j} \right) \tag{2}$$

As shown in OP(2), the $k \times d$ matrix $\boldsymbol{X}_j = (\boldsymbol{x}_{i_1}, \boldsymbol{x}_{i_2}, \ldots, \boldsymbol{x}_{i_k})^\top$ denotes the k-nearest neighbors of $\boldsymbol{x}_j$. We further convert OP(2) into a standard quadratic programming (QP) problem:

$$\min_{\mathbf{w}_{\cdot j}} \frac{1}{2} \mathbf{w}_{\cdot j}^\top \left(2 \boldsymbol{X}_j \boldsymbol{X}_j^\top \right) \mathbf{w}_{\cdot j} - 2 \boldsymbol{x}_j^\top \boldsymbol{X}_j^\top \mathbf{w}_{\cdot j} \tag{3}$$

$$\text{s.t.} \quad w_{ij} \geq 0 \quad (\forall (\boldsymbol{x}_i, \boldsymbol{x}_j) \in E, 0 \leq i, j \leq m)$$

Therefore, the optimized weight of OP(3) can be obtained through any off-the-shelf QP method. Although the restriction $\sum_{(\boldsymbol{x}_i, \boldsymbol{x}_j) \in E} w_{ij} = 1$ is to avoid probability divergence during subsequent iterative probability propagation procedure, it would cause some linear combinations of k-nearest neighbors far away from the center sample. As a consequence, we would rather apply the normalization of each weight column than embed restriction $\sum_{(\boldsymbol{x}_i, \boldsymbol{x}_j) \in E} w_{ij} = 1$ for the j-th sample. In other words, for each weight column, we utilize the following normalized column vector to replace primary weight column vector:

$$\mathbf{h}_{\cdot j} = \mathbf{w}_{\cdot j} / \sum_{(\boldsymbol{x}_i, \boldsymbol{x}_j) \in E} w_{ij} \quad (0 \leq j \leq m) \tag{4}$$

At second stage, we develop a novel regularization framework that incorporates probabilistic propagation with the maximum entropy model:

$$\mathcal{J}(\mathcal{D}, \boldsymbol{\theta}, \boldsymbol{F}) = \mathcal{L}(\mathcal{D}, \boldsymbol{F}, \boldsymbol{\theta}) + \lambda \Omega(\boldsymbol{\theta}) + \mu \mathcal{Q}(\boldsymbol{F}) \tag{5}$$

As shown in Eq. (5), the first term $\mathcal{L}$ in the object function $\mathcal{J}$ is denoted as fidelity term with a definition of the conditional probability matrix of the ground-truth labels $\mathcal{C} = [p(y_i = j|\boldsymbol{x}_i, \boldsymbol{\theta})]_{m \times q}$. The definition of $\mathcal{C}$ is shown as:

$$P(y_i = j|\boldsymbol{x}_i, \boldsymbol{\theta}) = \begin{cases} \exp\left(\boldsymbol{\theta}_j^{\top} \boldsymbol{x}\right) / \sum_{j' \in S_i} \exp\left(\boldsymbol{\theta}_{j'}^{\top} \boldsymbol{x}\right), & \text{if } j \in S_i \\ 0, & \text{otherwise} \end{cases} \tag{6}$$

where $\boldsymbol{\theta} \in \mathbb{R}^{d \times q}$ is a parameter matrix learned from the object function $\mathcal{J}$. This term suggests that the finally obtained label distribution matrix $\boldsymbol{F}$ is closed to the maximum entropy model which builds a linear discriminative mapping from input features to ground-truth labels smoothly. Meanwhile, we choose to apply the Kullback-Leibler divergence of $\boldsymbol{F}$ relative to $\mathcal{C}$ rather than the quadratic form to preserve the convex properties of the object function $\mathcal{J}$ with respect to $\boldsymbol{\theta}$. Therefore $\mathcal{L}$ is formalized as:

$$\mathcal{L}(\mathcal{D}, \boldsymbol{F}, \boldsymbol{\theta}) = \sum_{i=1}^{m} \sum_{j \in S_i} \boldsymbol{F}_{ij} \log \frac{\boldsymbol{F}_{ij}}{\mathcal{C}_{ij}} \tag{7}$$

The second term Ω in the object function $\mathcal{J}$ is aimed at avoiding parameter redundancy caused by conditional probability matrix, which is defined as an Frobenius norm:

$$\Omega(\boldsymbol{\theta}) = \frac{1}{2} \|\boldsymbol{\theta}\|_F^2 \tag{8}$$

The third term $\mathcal{Q}(\boldsymbol{F})$ in the object function $\mathcal{J}$ is formalized a smoothness constraint which is to ensure the probability distribution candidate labels of each sample not to vary too much from its k-nearest neighbors to satisfy the realization of the manifold assumption. Based on the above description, $\mathcal{Q}$ can be defined as:

$$\mathcal{Q}(\boldsymbol{F}) = \frac{1}{2} \sum_{i,j=1}^{n} w_{ij} \left\| \frac{1}{\sqrt{D_{ii}}} \boldsymbol{F}_i - \frac{1}{\sqrt{D_{jj}}} \boldsymbol{F}_j \right\|_2^2 \tag{9}$$

where w_{ij} is the similarity weight between the i-th sample and the j-th sample in graph G, and D_{ll} is the l-th diagonal element in diagonal matrix $\boldsymbol{D} = \text{diag}\left[\sum_{i=1}^{m} w_{i,1}, \sum_{i=1}^{m} w_{i,2}, \ldots, \sum_{i=1}^{m} w_{i,m}\right]$. As shown in Eq. (9), minimizing $\mathcal{Q}$ will force $\boldsymbol{F}_i$ $(i = 1, 2, \ldots, m)$ to get closer to $\boldsymbol{F}_j$ (if $\boldsymbol{x}_j \in k\text{NN}(\boldsymbol{x}_i)$) when w_{ij} is larger.

Finally, a novel regularization framework that incorporates probabilistic label propagation with maximum likelihood criterion is presented as a constrained optimization problem:

$$\min_{\boldsymbol{\theta}, \boldsymbol{F}} \sum_{i=1}^{m} \sum_{j \in S_i} \boldsymbol{F}_{ij} \log \frac{\boldsymbol{F}_{ij}}{\mathcal{C}_{ij}} + \frac{\lambda}{2} \|\boldsymbol{\theta}\|_F^2 + \frac{\mu}{2} \sum_{i,j=1}^{n} w_{ij} \left\| \frac{\boldsymbol{F}_i}{\sqrt{D_{ii}}} - \frac{\boldsymbol{F}_j}{\sqrt{D_{jj}}} \right\|_2^2 \tag{10}$$

$$\text{s.t.} \quad \sum_{j=1}^{q} \boldsymbol{F}_{ij} = 1, \boldsymbol{F}_{ij} \geq 0, \quad \forall i = 1, 2, \ldots, m$$

4 Optimization

Apparently, OP(10) is convex with respect to $\boldsymbol{\theta}$ when $\boldsymbol{F}$ is fixed, and it is also convex with respect to $\boldsymbol{F}$ when $\boldsymbol{\theta}$ is fixed. Therefore, OP(10) is regarded as a biconvex problem which can be solved in an alternating way [6]. Specifically, we first optimize OP(10) regarding $\boldsymbol{F}$ when $\boldsymbol{\theta}$ is treated as a constant, and then optimize OP(10) regarding $\boldsymbol{\theta}$ when $\boldsymbol{F}$ is substituted by $\boldsymbol{F}^*$ which is the optimized value of $\boldsymbol{F}$ in previous step.

4.1 Updating F

When $\boldsymbol{\theta}$ is assumed as a constant, the conditional probability matrix $\mathcal{C} \in \mathbb{R}^{m \times q}$ corresponding to $\boldsymbol{\theta}$ is also considered as a constant.Therefore the optimization of OP(10) can be simplified to

$$\min_{F} \quad \sum_{i=1}^{m} \sum_{j \in S_i} F_{ij} \log \frac{F_{ij}}{\mathcal{C}_{ij}} + \frac{\mu}{2} \sum_{i,j=1}^{n} w_{ij} \left\| \frac{1}{\sqrt{D_{ii}}} F_i - \frac{1}{\sqrt{D_{jj}}} F_j \right\|_2^2 \tag{11}$$

$$\text{s.t.} \quad \sum_{j=1}^{q} \mathbf{F}_{ij} = 1, \mathbf{F}_{ij} \geq 0, \quad \forall i = 1, 2, \ldots, m$$

which is similar to a label propagation problem [22]. The first term of the OP(11) guarantees that the ultimate label distribution $\boldsymbol{F}$ should be close to constant matrix $\mathcal{C}$, which is denoted as the mapping relationship from input features to the ground-truth label. The second term guarantees that the ultimate label distribution $\boldsymbol{F}$ of each sample should be close to its k-nearest neighbors, which satisfies manifold assumption. In this paper, we present another convex function with respect to $\boldsymbol{F}$:

$$\mathcal{OB} = \frac{1}{2} \left\| \boldsymbol{F} - \mathcal{C} \right\|_F^2 + \frac{\mu}{2} \sum_{i,j=1}^{n} w_{ij} \left\| \frac{1}{\sqrt{D_{ii}}} F_i - \frac{1}{\sqrt{D_{jj}}} F_j \right\|_2^2 \tag{12}$$

As shown in $\mathcal{OB}$, the first term in OP(11) is replaced by the quadratic form, which is convex regarding $\boldsymbol{F}$, and the optimal solution of $\mathcal{OB}$ can be obtained directly via derivation rather than traditional Lagrangian method which is time-consuming. Through label propagation method, the obtained optimal solution of $\mathcal{OB}$ is the approximation of the solution of OP(11). Differentiating the $\mathcal{OB}$ below with respect to $\boldsymbol{F}$, we have

$$\left. \frac{\partial \mathcal{OB}}{\partial F} \right|_{F = \tilde{F}^*} = \tilde{F}^* - \mathcal{C} + \mu \left(\tilde{F}^* - H\tilde{F}^* \right) = 0 \tag{13}$$

where $\boldsymbol{H}$ is equal to the $m \times m$ matrix $(\mathbf{h}_{.1}, \mathbf{h}_{.2}, \cdots, \mathbf{h}_{.m})$. Since $\boldsymbol{I} - \frac{\mu}{1+\mu} \boldsymbol{H}$ is invertible, we have

$$\tilde{F}^* = \frac{1}{1 + \mu} \left(\boldsymbol{I} - \frac{\mu}{1 + \mu} \boldsymbol{H} \right)^{-1} \mathcal{C} \tag{14}$$

In order to satisfy the constraints in OP(11), $\tilde{F}^*$ is re-scaled into F^* via consulting the sample in the ambiguously labeled data, which is similar to the E-step in PL-EM [10]:

$$\forall 1 \leq i \leq m: \quad F^*_{i,j} = \begin{cases} \tilde{F}^*_{i,j} / \sum_{j' \in S_i} \tilde{F}^*_{i,j'}, & \text{if } j \in S_i \\ 0, & \text{otherwise} \end{cases} \tag{15}$$

4.2 Updating θ

When $F \in \mathbb{R}^{m \times q}$ is replaced by F^*, we have

$$\min_{\theta} \quad \sum_{i=1}^{m} \sum_{j \in S_i} F^*_{ij} \log \frac{F^*_{ij}}{C_{ij}} + \frac{\lambda}{2} \|\theta\|^2_F \tag{16}$$

which is optimized via L-BFGS [11]. Apparently, the process of optimizing OP(16) is similar to M-step in PL-EM, which models the mapping relationship from input features to the ground-truth label.

At the beginning of optimization, it is necessary to initialize the conditional probability matrix $C = [p(y_i = j | x_i, \theta)]_{m \times q}$ as follows:

$$p(y_i = j | x_i, \theta) = \begin{cases} \frac{1}{|S_i|} & \text{if } j \in S_i \\ 0, & \text{otherwise} \end{cases} \tag{17}$$

Then we iteratively update the parameter θ by combining label propagation with PL-EM algorithm, which is collectively called probability propagation procedure. During the testing phase, the conditional probability matrix C' of each unseen sample x' is calculated as:

$$C' = \left[\exp\left(\theta_k^\top x'\right) \Big/ \sum_{j' \in \mathcal{Y}} \exp\left(\theta_{j'}^\top x'\right) \right]_{1 \times q} \tag{18}$$

And then, the ultimate label distribution F' of each unseen sample x' can be calculated according to Eq. (14) and Eq. (15). Finally, the predicted label y' of each unseen sample x' is given as follows:

$$y' = \arg\max_{k \in \mathcal{Y}} \left[F'_{1,k} \right]_{1 \times q} \tag{19}$$

The complete procedure of PP-PLL is presented in Algorithm 1, where we creatively embed alternating optimization method into PL-EM algorithm to update parameter θ. At first, given a partial label training dataset, a weighted graph is constructed via asymmetric k-NN graph (Steps 1–9). And then, an probability propagation procedure based on EM procedure with alternating optimization is implemented to calculate the optimal parameters (Step 10–15). Finally, the predicted label of the unseen data is obtained according to the optimal parameters (Step 16).

Algorithm 1. PP-PLL

Input:

$\mathcal{D}$: the PL training set $\{(\boldsymbol{x}_i, S_i) \,|\, 1 \le i \le m\}$

k: the number of nearest neighbors used for the similarity matrix

λ, μ: the parameters trading off each term in the object function

T: the number of iterations

$\boldsymbol{x}'$: the unseen data

Output:

y': the predicted label for $\boldsymbol{x}'$

Process:

1: Construct weight graph $G = (V, E)$ by the asymmetric k-NN graph with $V = \{\boldsymbol{x}_i | 1 \le i \le m\}$ and $E = \{(\boldsymbol{x}_i, \boldsymbol{x}_j) \,|\, \boldsymbol{x}_i \in k\mathrm{NN}\,(\boldsymbol{x}_j)\,, i \ne j\}$;

2: Initialize weight matrix $\mathbf{W} = [w_{ij}]_{m \times m}$ with $w_{ij} = 0$;

3: **for** $j = 1$ **to** m **do**

4: Determine the j-th weight column corresponding to the j-th sample $\hat{\mathbf{w}}_{\cdot j} = (\hat{w}_{i_1 j}, \hat{w}_{i_2 j}, \ldots, \hat{w}_{i_k j})^\top$ via solving OP(3);

5: Normalize the $\hat{\mathbf{w}}_{\cdot j}$ to $\hat{\mathbf{h}}_{\cdot j} = \hat{\mathbf{w}}_{\cdot j} / \sum_{a=1}^{k} \hat{w}_{i_a j} = \left(\hat{h}_{i_1 j}, \hat{h}_{i_2 j}, \ldots, \hat{h}_{i_k j} \right)^\top$

6: **for** $\boldsymbol{x}_{i_a} \in k\mathrm{NN}\,(\boldsymbol{x}_j)$ **do**

7:    Set $w_{i_a j} = \hat{h}_{i_a j}$;

8: **end for**

9: **end for**

10: Initial $\mathcal{C} \in \mathbb{R}^{m \times q}$ according to Eq. (17);

11: **for** $t = 1$ **to** T **do**

12: Update $\boldsymbol{F}$ according to Eq. (15);

13: Caculate $\boldsymbol{\theta}$ by solving OP(16);

14: Update $\mathcal{C}$ by updated $\boldsymbol{\theta} \in \mathbb{R}^{d \times q}$;

15: **end for**

16: Return the predicted label y' according to Eq. (18) and Eq. (19).

5   Experiments

5.1   Experimental Setup

To verify the performance of the proposed PP-PLL method, we conduct extensive experiments on four controlled UCI datasets and five real-world datasets. Characteristics of the experimental datasets are summarized in Table 1.

Controlled UCI Datasets. To generate artificial PL datasets, controlled UCI datasets are controlled by two parameters p and r, where p controls the proportion of partially labeled samples, and r controls the size of distracting labels set in the candidate label set.

Real-World Datasets. In addition, we have also collected five real-world datasets which are partially labeled. The real-world datasets can be summarized into four task domains:

– **Bird Song Classification**: Spectrogram of the birds are considered as instances while candidate labels is composed of bird species jointly singing [1].
– **Automatic Face Naming**: Each face recognized from images or a videos are considered as instances and the names extracted from the corresponding image captions or video subtitles are regarded as candidate labels, such as Yahoo! News [8] and Lost [2];
– **Facial Age Estimation**: Human faces constitute the instance space and candidate labels is composed of the ages annotated by ten crowd-sourced labels and the ground-truth ages, such as FG-NET [16];
– **Objective Classification**: Image segmentations are considered as instances and the objects appearing within the same image are represented as the candidate labels, such as MSRCv2 [12].

The average number of the candidate labels (Avg. CLs) for each real-world dataset is also recorded in Table 1.

Table 1. Characteristics of the experimental datasets

	Controlled UCI datasets				Real-world datasets				
Dataset	Glass	Ecoli	Segment	Letter	Lost	FG-NET	MSRCv2	BirdSong	Yahoo! News
Examples	214	336	2310	20000	1122	1002	1758	4,998	22991
Features	10	7	18	16	108	262	48	38	163
Classes	7	8	7	26	16	78	32	13	219
Avg. CLs	-	-	-	-	2.23	7.48	3.16	2.18	1.91

Comparing Algorithms. In this paper, the effectiveness of PP-PLL is evaluated against five state-of-the-art partial label learning algorithms, and the recommended parameters for each comparing algorithm in corresponding literature are used in our experiments:

– **PL-KNN** [9]: An k-nearest neighbor approach based on ADS averages the output of respective neighbors to disambiguate the set of candidate labels [Recommended configuration: $k = 10$]
– **PL-SVM** [15]: A maximum margin approach based on IDS incorporates maximum margin to disambiguate the set of candidate labels [Recommended configuration: regularization parameter pool with $\{10^{-3}, \cdots, 10^3\}$]
– **PL-LEAF** [21]: A partial-label learning method disambiguate the set of candidate labels via postulating that the potentially useful information from feature space [Recommended configuration: $k = 10$, $C_1 = 10$, $C_2 = 1$];
– **PL-ECOC** [20]: It learns from partial-label training instances via adapting error-correcting output codes [Recommended configuration: the codeword length $L = \lceil \log_2(q) \rceil \rceil$];
– **GM-PLL** [14]: A partial-label learning method disambiguate the set of candidate labels via incorporating the instance relationship and the co-occurrence possibility of varying label based on Graph Matching (GM) scheme [Recommended configuration:set β among $\{0.3, 0.4, \ldots, 0.8\}$].

The parameters employed by PP-PLL are set as $T = 60$, $k = 10$, $\mu = 1$ and $\lambda = 0.005$, which the analysis of parameter configuration is conducted in Subsect. 5.3. In this paper, we perform ten runs of 50%/50% random train/test on four controlled UCI datasets as well as five real-world partial label datasets, and we evaluate comparing algorithms by the mean predictive accuracies (with standard deviation). Furthermore, we adopt pairwise t-test at 0.05 significance level to investigate whether PP-PLL is significantly superior/inferior to the comparing algorithms.

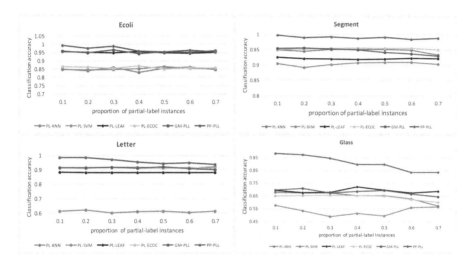

Fig. 1. The classification accuracy of each comparing method on four controlled UCI datasets with stochastic r.

5.2 Experimental Results

Since four controlled UCI datasets are generated manually via two parameters while five real-world datasets are generated via real world scenarios, we perform two series of experiments to evaluate the performance of the proposed method. Meanwhile, the following two subsections exhibit the experimental results separately.

Controlled UCI Datasets. In Fig. 1, the classification accuracy of each comparing algorithm is illustrated where the probability of generating partial labeled data p varies from 0.1 to 0.7 with step-size 0.1, while the size of distracting labels set r is randomly selected among $\{1, 2, 3\}$.

From Fig. 1, we can see that PP-PLL achieves better classification accuracy than the comparing algorithms in most cases. Table 2 reports the experimental results with fixed value of r, along with the win/tie/loss counts between PP-PLL and other comparing algorithms. The result of statistical comparisons in Table 2 shows that PP-PLL achieves competitive classification performance against other state-of-the-art partial label learning algorithms on most controlled UCI datasets.

Table 2. Win/tie/loss counts (pairwise t-test at 0.05 significance level) on the controlled UCI datasets between PP-PLL and the comparing algorithms with classification accuracy.

	PP-LEAF	PL-KNN	PL-SVM	PL-ECOC	GM-PLL
vary $p(r = 1)$	26/1/1	28/0/0	28/0/0	28/0/0	19/7/2
vary $p(r = 2)$	26/2/1	26/2/0	28/0/0	26/2/0	14/9/5
vary $p(r = 3)$	26/2/0	26/1/1	28/0/0	25/2/1	16/8/4
In Total	**79/3/2**	**80/3/1**	**84/0/0**	**79/4/1**	**49/24/11**

Real-World Datasets. We compare the PP-PLL with all above comparing algorithms on the real-world datasets from four task domains mentioned above. The classification performance of each algorithm in terms of accuracy is reported in Table 3. As shown in Table 3, which is classification accuracy of each algorithm on the real-world datasets, it is obvious that PP-PLL achieves superior classification accuracy comparing with all the counterpart algorithms on these real-world datasets except for GM-PLL, PL-SVM and PL-ECOC on Yahoo! News.

Table 3. Classification accuracy (mean $\pm$ standard deviation) of each algorithm on the real-world datasets. Furthermore, • or ∘ is denoted as whether PP-PLL is statistically superior or inferior to the comparing algorithm (pairwise t-test at 0.05 significance level).

	Lost	MSRCv2	Yahoo!News	BirdSong	FG-NET
PP-PLL	0.748 ± 0.031	0.546 ± 0.045	0.554 ± 0.004	0.850 ± 0.24	0.128 ± 0.007
GM-PLL	0.737 ± 0.043 •	0.530 ± 0.019 •	0.629 ± 0.007 ∘	0.663 ± 0.010 •	0.065 ± 0.021 •
PL-KNN	0.332 ± 0.030 •	0.417 ± 0.012 •	0.457 ± 0.009 •	0.614 ± 0.024 •	0.037 ± 0.008 •
PL-SVM	0.639 ± 0.056 •	0.417 ± 0.027 •	0.636 ± 0.018 ∘	0.662 ± 0.032 •	0.058 ± 0.010 •
PL-ECOC	0.703 ± 0.052 •	0.505 ± 0.027 •	0.662 ± 0.010 ∘	0.740 ± 0.016 •	0.040 ± 0.018 •

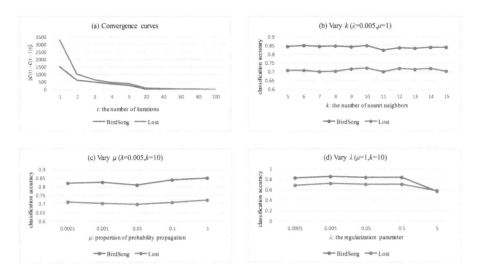

Fig. 2. Parameter sensitivity analysis of PP-PLL on the real-world datasets BirdSong and Lost.

5.3 Sensitivity Analysis

Figure 2 shows the performance of PP-PLL under different parameter configurations, and the convergence of PP-PLL on BirdSong and Lost. As shown in (a), $\|\mathcal{C}(t) - \mathcal{C}(t-1)\|_F^2$ which is the square of Frobenius norm about difference in the conditional probability matrix $\mathcal{C}$ between two continuous iterations gradually approaches 0 as t tends to be infinite. Especially when the number of iterations reaches 20–40 loops, PP-PLL becomes convergent. Therefore, the convergence of PP-PLL is demonstrated, and PP-PLL shows relative stability with the varying of parameters (k, μ, λ) in (b)–(d). In addition, Fig. 2 also reports that the parameter configuration specified for Subsect. 5.1 $(T = 60, k = 10, \mu = 1, \lambda = 0.005)$ naturally follows from the analysis mentioned above, and makes PP-PLL obtain relatively superior performance compared with other parameter combinations.

6 Conclusion

In this paper, we present a biconvex formulation containing a mapping relationships from input features to the ground-truth label based on manifold assumption, which is optimized by the alternating optimization method, to deal with partial label learning via probability propagation procedure. Extensive experimental results on controlled UCI datasets as well as real-world datasets demonstrate that our proposed method can achieve superior classification performance than the state-of-the-art partial label learning algorithms. However, In terms of weighted graph, how to create a more meaningful weight matrix will be one of the future directions of partial label learning. It would help all MADS (Manifold

Assumption based Disambiguation Strategies) extend to the more special situations, especially when the size of each candidate label set is too large, which causes the information of the ground-truth label in each candidate label set to disappear. For PP-PLL, an important future work is to combine weighted graph with probability distribution of candidate label sets, to improve the availability of candidate label sets.

Acknowledgments. This study was supported by National Natural Science Foundation of China (Grant No. 61806033).

References

1. Briggs, F., Fern, X.Z., Raich, R.: Rank-loss support instance machines for MIML instance annotation. In: Proceedings of the 18th ACM SIGKDD International Conference on Knowledge Discovery and Data Mining, pp. 534–542. ACM (2012)
2. Cour, T., Sapp, B., Taskar, B.: Learning from partial labels. J. Mach. Learn. Res. **12**(May), 1501–1536 (2011)
3. Cour, T., Sapp, B., Jordan, C., Taskar, B.: Learning from ambiguously labeled images. In: 2009 IEEE Conference on Computer Vision and Pattern Recognition, pp. 919–926. IEEE (2009)
4. Dempster, A.P., Laird, N.M., Rubin, D.B.: Maximum likelihood from incomplete data via the EM algorithm. J. Roy. Stat. Soc. Ser. B (Methodological) **39**(1), 1–22 (1977)
5. Gong, C., Liu, T., Tang, Y., Yang, J., Yang, J., Tao, D.: A regularization approach for instance-based superset label learning. IEEE Trans. Cybern. **48**(3), 967–978 (2018)
6. Gorski, J., Pfeuffer, F., Klamroth, K.: Biconvex sets and optimization with biconvex functions: a survey and extensions. Math. Methods Oper. Res. **66**(3), 373–407 (2007)
7. Grandvalet, Y., Bengio, Y.: Learning from partial labels with minimum entropy (2004)
8. Guillaumin, M., Verbeek, J., Schmid, C.: Multiple instance metric learning from automatically labeled bags of faces. In: Daniilidis, K., Maragos, P., Paragios, N. (eds.) ECCV 2010. LNCS, vol. 6311, pp. 634–647. Springer, Heidelberg (2010). https://doi.org/10.1007/978-3-642-15549-9_46
9. Hüllermeier, E., Beringer, J.: Learning from ambiguously labeled examples. Intell. Data Anal. **10**(5), 419–439 (2006)
10. Jin, R., Ghahramani, Z.: Learning with multiple labels. Adv. Neural Inf. Process. Syst. 921–928 (2003)
11. Liu, D.C., Nocedal, J.: On the limited memory BFGS method for large scale optimization. Math. Program. **45**(1–3), 503–528 (1989)
12. Liu, L., Dietterich, T.G.: A conditional multinomial mixture model for superset label learning. Adv. Neural Inf. Process. Syst. 548–556 (2012)
13. Luo, J., Orabona, F.: Learning from candidate labeling sets. Adv. Neural Inf. Process. Syst. 1504–1512 (2010)
14. Lyu, G., Feng, S., Wang, T., Lang, C., Li, Y.: GM-Pll: Graph matching based partial label learning. arXiv preprint arXiv:1901.03073 (2019)

15. Nguyen, N., Caruana, R.: Classification with partial labels. In: Proceedings of the 14th ACM SIGKDD International Conference on Knowledge Discovery and Data Mining, pp. 551–559. ACM (2008)
16. Panis, G., Lanitis, A., Tsapatsoulis, N., Cootes, T.F.: Overview of research on facial ageing using the FG-net ageing database. IET Biometrics 5(2), 37–46 (2016)
17. Yi-Chen, C., Patel, V.M., Chellappa, R., Phillips, P.J.: Ambiguously labeled learning using dictionaries. IEEE Trans. Inf. Foren. Secur. 9(12), 2076–2088 (2014)
18. Yu, F., Zhang, M.L.: Maximum margin partial label learning. In: Asian Conference on Machine Learning, pp. 96–111 (2016)
19. Zhang, M.L., Yu, F.: Solving the partial label learning problem: an instance-based approach. In: Twenty-Fourth International Joint Conference on Artificial Intelligence (2015)
20. Zhang, M.L., Yu, F., Tang, C.Z.: Disambiguation-free partial label learning. IEEE Trans. Knowl. Data Eng. 29(10), 2155–2167 (2017)
21. Zhang, M.L., Zhou, B.B., Liu, X.Y.: Partial label learning via feature-aware disambiguation. In: Proceedings of the 22nd ACM SIGKDD International Conference on Knowledge Discovery and Data Mining, pp. 1335–1344. ACM (2016)
22. Zhou, D., Bousquet, O., Lal, T.N., Weston, J., Schölkopf, B.: Learning with local and global consistency. Adv. Neural Inf. Process. syst. 16, 321–328 (2004)
23. Zhou, Y., He, J., Gu, H.: Partial label learning via gaussian processes. IEEE Trans. Cybern. 47(12), 4443–4450 (2017)
24. Zhu, X., Goldberg, A.B.: Introduction to semi-supervised learning. Synthesis Lect. Artif. Intell. Mach. Learn. 3(1), 1–130 (2009)

Neural Message Passing for Multi-label Classification

Jack Lanchantin$^{(\boxtimes)}$, Arshdeep Sekhon, and Yanjun Qi

Department of Computer Science, University of Virginia,
Charlottesville, VA 22903, USA
{jjl5sw,as5cu,yq2h}@virginia.edu

Abstract. Multi-label classification (MLC) is the task of assigning a set of target labels for a given sample. Modeling the combinatorial label interactions in MLC has been a long-haul challenge. We propose Label Message Passing (LaMP) Neural Networks to efficiently model the joint prediction of multiple labels. LaMP treats labels as nodes on a label-interaction graph and computes the hidden representation of each label node conditioned on the input using attention-based neural message passing. Attention enables LaMP to assign different importances to neighbor nodes per label, learning how labels interact (implicitly). The proposed models are simple, accurate, interpretable, structure-agnostic, and applicable for predicting dense labels since LaMP is incredibly parallelizable. We validate the benefits of LaMP on seven real-world MLC datasets, covering a broad spectrum of input/output types and outperforming the state-of-the-art results. Notably, LaMP enables intuitive interpretation of how classifying each label depends on the elements of a sample and at the same time rely on its interaction with other labels (We provide our code and datasets at https://github.com/QData/LaMP.).

1 Introduction

Multi-label classification (MLC) is receiving increasing attention in areas such as natural language processing, computational biology, and image recognition. Accurate and scalable MLC methods are in urgent need for applications like assigning topics to web articles, or identifying binding proteins on DNA. The most common and straightforward MLC method is the binary relevance (BR) approach that considers multiple target labels independently [46]. However, in many MLC tasks there is a clear dependency structure among labels, which BR methods ignore.

Unfortunately, accurately modelling all combinatorial label interactions is an NP-hard problem. Many types of models, including a few deep neural network (DNN) based, have been introduced to approximately model such interactions, thus boosting classification accuracy.

Our main concern of this paper is how to represent multiple labels jointly (and conditioned on the input features) in order to make accurate predictions.

© Springer Nature Switzerland AG 2020
U. Brefeld et al. (Eds.): ECML PKDD 2019, LNAI 11907, pp. 138–163, 2020.
https://doi.org/10.1007/978-3-030-46147-8_9

The most relevant literature addressing this concern falls roughly into three groups.

The first group, probabilistic classifier chain (PCC) models, formulate the joint label dependencies using the chain rule and perform MLC in a sequential prediction manner [36,39,55]. Notably, [36] used a recurrent neural network (RNN) sequence to sequence (Seq2Seq) architecture [17] for MLC and achieved the state-of-the-art performance on multiple text-based datasets. However, these methods are inherently unfit for MLC tasks due to their incapacity to be parallelized, and inability to perform well in dense label settings, or when there are a large number of positive labels (since errors propagate in the sequential prediction). We refer the reader to the supplementary material for a full background and analysis of PCC methods (Appendix A). The second group learns a shared latent space representing both input features and output labels, and then upsamples from the space to reconstruct the target labels [6,57]. The main drawback of this group is the interpretability issue with a learned low dimensional latent space, as many real-world applications prefer interpretable predictors. The third group models conditional label dependencies using a structured output or graphical model representation [29,45]. However, these methods are often limited to only considering pair-wise dependencies due to computational constraints, or are forced to use some variation of approximate inference which has no clear representation of conditional dependencies.

Thus our main question is: *is it possible to have accurate, flexible and explainable MLC methods that are applicable to many dense labels?* This paper provides empirical results showing that this is possible through extending attention based Message Passing Neural Networks (MPNNs) to learn the joint representation of multiple labels conditioned on input features.

MPNNs [15] are a class of methods that efficiently learn the joint representations of variables using neural message passing strategies. They provide a flexible framework for modeling multiple variables jointly which have no explicit ordering.

The key idea of our method is to rely on attention-based neural message passing entirely to draw global dependencies from labels to input features, and from labels to labels. To the best of our knowledge, this is the first extension of MPNNs to model a conditional joint representation of output labels, and additionally the first extension of MPNNs to model the interactions of variables where the exact structure is unknown. We name the proposed method Label Message Passing (LaMP) Networks since it performs neural message passing on an unknown, fully-connected label-to-label graph. Through intra-attention (aka self-attention), LaMP assigns different importance to different neighbor nodes per label, dynamically learning how labels interact conditioned on a specific input. We further extend LaMP to cases when a known label interaction graph is provided by modifying the intra-attention to only attend over a node's known neighbors. LaMP networks allow for parallelization in training and testing and can work with dense labels, overcoming the drawbacks of PCC methods.

LaMP most closely belongs to the third MLC category we mentioned above, however it trains a unified model to classify each label *and* model the label to label dependencies at the same time, in an end-to-end fashion. The important aspect is that LaMP networks automatically learn the output label dependency structure conditioned on a specific input using neural message passing. This in turn can easily be interpreted to understand the conditional structure.

The main contributions of this paper include: (1) **Accurate MLC**: Our model achieves similar, or better performance compared to the previous state of the art across five MLC metrics. We validate our model on eight MLC datasets which cover a wide spectrum of input data structure: sequences (English text, DNA), tabular (binary word vectors), graph (drug molecules), and images, as well as output label structure: unknown and graph. (2) **Interpretable**: Although deep-learning based systems have widely been viewed as "black boxes", our attention based LaMP models allow for a straightforward way to extract three different types of model visualization: intermediate network predictions, label to feature dependencies, and label to label dependencies.

2   Method: LaMP Networks

Notations. We define the following notations, used throughout the paper. Let $\mathcal{D} = \{(\boldsymbol{x}_n, \boldsymbol{y}_n)\}_{n=1}^N$ be the set of data samples with inputs $\boldsymbol{x} \in X$ and outputs $\boldsymbol{y} \in Y$. Inputs $\boldsymbol{x}$ are a (possibly ordered) set of S components $\{x_1, x_2, ..., x_S\}$, and outputs $\boldsymbol{y}$ are a set of L labels $\{y_1, y_2, ..., y_L\}$. MLC involves predicting the set of binary labels $\{y_1, y_2, ..., y_L\}, y_i \in \{0, 1\}$ given input $\boldsymbol{x}$.

In general we can assume to represent the input feature components as embedded vectors $\{\boldsymbol{z}_1, \boldsymbol{z}_2, ..., \boldsymbol{z}_S\}$, $\boldsymbol{z}_i \in \mathbb{R}^d$, using some learned embedding matrix $\mathbf{W}^x \in \mathbb{R}^{\delta \times d}$. Here d is the embedding size and, δ is the size of x_i. x_i can be any component of a particular input (for example, words in a sentence, patches of an image, nodes of a known graph, or one of the tabular features).

Similarly, labels can be first represented as embedded vectors $\{\boldsymbol{u}_1^{t=0}, \boldsymbol{u}_2^{t=0}, ..., \boldsymbol{u}_L^{t=0}\}$, $\boldsymbol{u}_i^t \in \mathbb{R}^d$, through a learned embedding matrix $\mathbf{W}^y \in \mathbb{R}^{L \times d}$, where L denotes the number of labels. Here we use t to represent the 'state' of the embedding after the tth update step. This is because in LaMP networks, each label embedding is updated for t steps before the predictions are made. The key idea of LaMP networks is that labels are represented as nodes in a label-interaction graph G_{yy} denoting nodes as embedding vectors $\{\boldsymbol{u}_{1:L}^t\}$. LaMP networks use MPNN modules with attention to pass messages from input embeddings $\{\boldsymbol{z}_{1:S}\}$ to G_{yy}, and then within G_{yy} to model the joint prediction of labels.

2.1   Background: Message Passing Neural Networks

Message Passing Neural Networks (MPNNs) [15] are a generalization of graph neural networks (GNNs) [41]. MPNNs model variables as nodes on a graph G. Here $G = (V, E)$, where V describes the set of nodes (variables) and E denotes the set of edges (about how variables interact with other variables). In MPNNs, joint representations of nodes and edges are modelled using message passing rather than explicit probabilistic formulations, allowing for efficient inference. MPNNs model the joint dependencies using message function M^t and node update function U^t for T time steps, where t is the current time step. The hidden state $\boldsymbol{v}_i^t \in \mathbb{R}^d$ of node $i \in G$ is updated based on messages $\boldsymbol{m}_i^t$ from its neighboring nodes $\{\boldsymbol{v}_{j\in\mathcal{N}(i)}^t\}$ defined by neighborhood $\mathcal{N}(i)$:

$$\boldsymbol{m}_i^t = \sum_{j\in\mathcal{N}(i)} M^t(\boldsymbol{v}_i^t, \boldsymbol{v}_j^t), \tag{1}$$

$$\boldsymbol{v}_i^{t+1} = U^t(\boldsymbol{m}_i^t). \tag{2}$$

After T rounds of iterative updates to spread information to distant nodes, a readout function R is used on the updated node embeddings to make predictions like classifying nodes or classifying properties about the graph.

Many possibilities exist for functions M^t and U^t. We specifically choose to pass messages using intra-attention (also called as self-attention) neural message passing which enable nodes to attend over their neighborhoods differentially. This allows for the network to learn different importances for different nodes in a neighborhood, without depending on knowing the graph structure upfront (essentially learning the unknown graph structure) [53]. In this formulation, messages for node $\boldsymbol{v}_i^t$ are obtained by a weighted sum of all its neighboring nodes $\{\boldsymbol{v}_{j\in\mathcal{N}(i)}^t\}$ where the weights are calculated by attention representing the importance of each neighbor for a specific node [2]. In the rest of the paper, we use "graph attention" and "neural message passing" interchangeably.

Intra-attention neural message passing works as follows. We first calculate attention weights α_{ij}^t for pair of nodes $(\boldsymbol{v}_i^t, \boldsymbol{v}_j^t)$ using attention function $a(\cdot)$:

$$\alpha_{ij}^t = \text{softmax}_j(e_{ij}^t) = \frac{\exp(e_{ij}^t)}{\sum_{k\in\mathcal{N}(i)} \exp(e_{ik}^t)} \tag{3}$$

$$e_{ij}^t = a(\boldsymbol{v}_i^t, \boldsymbol{v}_j^t) \tag{4}$$

$$a(\boldsymbol{v}_i^t, \boldsymbol{v}_j^t) = \frac{(\mathbf{W}^q \boldsymbol{v}_i^t)^\top (\mathbf{W}^u \boldsymbol{v}_j^t)}{\sqrt{d}} \tag{5}$$

where e_{ij}^t represents the importance of node j for node i, however un-normalized. e_{ij}^t are normalized across all neighboring nodes of node i using a softmax function (Eq. 3) to get α_{ij}^t. For the attention function $a(\cdot)$, we used a scaled dot product with node-wise linear transformations $\mathbf{W}^q \in \mathbb{R}^{d\times d}$ on node $\boldsymbol{v}_i^t$ and $\mathbf{W}^u \in \mathbb{R}^{d\times d}$ on node $\boldsymbol{v}_j^t$. Scaling by $\sqrt{d}$ is used to mitigate training issues [52].

Then we use a so called attention message function M_{atn}^t to produce the message from node j to node i using the learned attention weights α_{ij}^t and another transformation matrix $\mathbf{W}^v \in \mathbb{R}^{d\times d}$:

$$M_{\text{atn}}(\boldsymbol{v}_i^t, \boldsymbol{v}_j^t; \boldsymbol{W}) = \alpha_{ij}^t \mathbf{W}^v \boldsymbol{v}_j^t, \tag{6}$$

$$\boldsymbol{m}_i^t = \boldsymbol{v}_i^t + \sum_{j\in\mathcal{N}(i)} M_{\text{atn}}(\boldsymbol{v}_i^t, \boldsymbol{v}_j^t; \boldsymbol{W}). \tag{7}$$

Equation 7 computes the full message m_i^t for node v_i^t by linearly combining messages from all neighbor nodes $j \in \mathcal{N}(i)$ with a residual connection on the current v_i^t.

Lastly, node v_i^t is updated to next state v_i^{t+1} using message m_i^t by a multi-layer perceptron (MLP) update function U_{mlp}, plus a m_i^t residual connection:

$$U_{\mathrm{mlp}}(m_i^t; W) = \mathrm{ReLU}(W^r m_i^t + b_1)^\top W^b + b_2 \tag{8}$$

$$v_i^{t+1} = m_i^t + U_{\mathrm{mlp}}(m_i^t; W). \tag{9}$$

Function U_{mlp} is parameterized with matrices $\{W^r \in \mathbb{R}^{d \times d}, W^b \in \mathbb{R}^{d \times d}\}$. It is important to note that W in Eq. 9 are shared (i.e., separately applied) across all nodes. This can be viewed as 1-dimensional convolution operation with kernel and stride sizes of 1. Weight sharing across nodes is a key aspect of MPNNs, where node dependencies are learned in an order-invariant manner.

2.2   LaMP: Label Message Passing

Given the input embeddings $\{z_1, z_2, ..., z_S\}$, the goal of Label Message Passing is to model the conditional dependencies between label embeddings $\{u_1^t, u_2^t, ..., u_L^t\}$ using Message Passing Neural Networks. We assume that the label embeddings are nodes on a label-interaction graph called G_{yy}, where the initial state of the embeddings $\{u_{1:L}^0\}$ at $t = 0$ are obtained using label embedding matrix W^y.

Each step t in Label Message Passing consists of two parts in order to update the label embeddings: (a) Feature-to-Label Message Passing, where messages are passed from the input embeddings to the label embeddings, and (b) Label-to-Label Message Passing, where messages are passed between labels. An overview of our model is shown in Fig. 1. We explain these two parts in detail in the following subsections. LaMP Networks use T steps of attention-based neural message passing to update the label nodes before a readout function makes a prediction for each label i on its final state u_i^T.

Updating Label Embeddings via Feature-to-Label Message Passing

Given a particular input x with embedded feature components $\{z_1, z_2, ..., z_S\}$, the first step in LaMP is to update the label embeddings by passing messages from the input embeddings to the label embeddings, as shown in the "Feature-to-Label MP" block of Fig. 1. To do this, LaMP uses neural message passing module MPNN_{xy} to update the ith label node's embedding u_i^t using the embeddings of all the components of an input.

That is, we update each u_i^t by using a weighted sum of all input embeddings $\{z_{1:S}\}$, in which the weights represent how important an input component is to the ith label node. The weights for the message are learned via Label-to-Feature attention (i.e., each label attends to each input embedding differently to compute the weights).

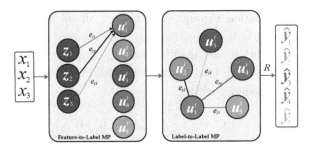

Fig. 1. LaMP Networks. Given input $\mathbf{x}$, we encode its components $\{x_1, x_2, x_3\}$ as embedded input nodes $\{z_1, z_2, z_3\}$. We encode labels $\{y_1, y_2, ..., y_5\}$ as embedded label nodes $\{u_1^t, u_2^t, ..., u_5^t\}$ of label-interaction graph G_{yy}. First, MPNN_{xy} is used to pass messages from the input nodes to the labels nodes and update the label nodes. Then, MPNN_{yy} is used to pass messages between the label nodes and update label nodes. Finally, readout function R performs node-level classification on label nodes to make binary label predictions $\{\hat{y}_1, \hat{y}_2, ..., \hat{y}_5\}$.

In this step, messages are only passed from the input nodes to the label nodes, and not vice versa (i.e. Feature-to-Label message passing is directed).

More specifically, to update label embedding u_i^t, MPNN_{xy} uses attention message function M_{atn}^t on all embeddings of the input $\{z_{1:S}\}$ to produce messages m_i^t, and MLP update function U_{mlp} to produce the updated intermediate embedding state $u_i^{t'}$:

$$m_i^t = u_i^t + \sum_{j=1}^{S} M_{\text{atn}}(u_i^t, z_j; \boldsymbol{W}_{\text{xy}}), \tag{10}$$

$$u_i^{t'} = m_i^t + U_{\text{mlp}}(m_i^t; \boldsymbol{W}_{\text{xy}}). \tag{11}$$

The key advantage of Feature-to-Label message passing with attention is that each label node can attend differently on input elements (e.g. different words in an input sentence).

Updating Label Embeddings via Label-to-Label Message Passing

At this point, an independent prediction can be made for each label conditioned on $\mathbf{x}$ using $\{u_{1:L}^{t'}\}$. However, in order to consider label dependencies, we model interactions between the label nodes $\{u_{1:L}^{t'}\}$ using Label-to-Label message passing and update them accordingly, as shown in the "Label-to-Label MP" block of Fig. 1. Given the exponentially large number of possible conditional dependencies, we use neural message passing as an efficient way to much such interactions, which has been shown to work well in practice for other tasks.

We assume there exist a label interaction graph $G_{yy} = (V_{yy}, E_{yy})$, $V_{yy} = \{y_{1:L}\}$, and E_{yy} includes all undirected pairwise edges connecting node y_i and node y_j. At this stage, we use another message passing module, MPNN_{yy} to pass messages between labels and update them. The label embedding $u_i^{t'}$ is updated by a weighted combination through attention of all its neighbor label nodes $\{u_{j\in\mathcal{N}(i)}^{t'}\}$.

MPNN$_{yy}$ uses attention message function $M_{atn}^{t'}$ on all neighbor label embeddings $\{u_{j\in\mathcal{N}(i)}^{t'}\}$ to produce message m_i^t, and MLP update function $U_{mlp}^{t'}$ to compute updated embedding u_i^{t+1}:

$$m_i^{t'} = u_i^{t'} + \sum_{j\in\mathcal{N}(i)} M_{atn}(u_i^{t'}, u_j^{t'}; \boldsymbol{W}_{yy}), \tag{12}$$

$$u_i^{t+1} = m_i^{t'} + U_{mlp}(u_i^{t'}, m_i^{t'}; \boldsymbol{W}_{yy}). \tag{13}$$

If there exists a known label interaction graph G_{yy}, message m_i^t for node i is computed using its neighboring nodes $j \in \mathcal{N}(i)$, where the neighbors $\mathcal{N}(i)$ are defined by the graph. If there is no known G_{yy} graph, we assume a fully connected graph, which means $\mathcal{N}(i) = \{j \in V_{yy}\}$ (including i).

Message Passing for Multiple Time Steps

To learn more complex relations among nodes, we compute a total of T time steps of updates. This is essentially a stack of T MPNN layers. In our implementation, the label embeddings are updated by MPNN$_{xy}$ and MPNN$_{yy}$ for T time steps to produce $\{u_1^T, u_2^T, ..., u_L^T\}$.

2.3   Readout Layer (MLC Predictions from the Label Embeddings)

After T updates to the label embeddings, the last module predicts each label $\{\hat{y}_1, ...\hat{y}_L\}$. A readout function R projects each of the L label embeddings u_i^T using projection matrix $\mathbf{W}^o \in \mathbb{R}^{L\times d}$, where row $\mathbf{W}_i^o \in \mathbb{R}^d$ is the learned output vector for label i. The calculated vector of size $L \times 1$ is then fed through an element-wise sigmoid function to produce probabilities of each label being positive:

$$\hat{y}_i = R(u_i^T; \mathbf{W}^o) = \text{sigmoid}(\mathbf{W}_i^o u_i^T). \tag{14}$$

2.4   Model Details

Multi-head Attention. In order to allow a particular node to attend to multiple other nodes (or multiple groups of nodes) at once, LaMP uses multiple attention heads. Inspired by [52], we use K independent attention heads for each $\mathbf{W}^{\cdot}$ matrix during the message computation, where each matrix column $\mathbf{W}_j^{\cdot,k}$ is of dimension d/K. The generated representations are concatenated (denoted by $\|$) and linearly transformed by matrix $\mathbf{W}^z \in \mathbb{R}^{d\times d}$. Multi-head attention changes message passing function M_{atn}, but update function U_{mlp} stays the same.

$$e_{ij}^{t,k} = (\mathbf{W}^{q,k} v_i^t)^\top (\mathbf{W}^{u,k} v_j^t)/\sqrt{d} \tag{15}$$

$$\alpha_{ij}^{t,k} = \frac{\exp(e_{ij}^{t,k})}{\sum_{j \in \mathcal{N}(i)} \exp(e_{ij}^{t,k})} \tag{16}$$

$$M_{\text{atn}}^k(\boldsymbol{v}_i^t, \boldsymbol{v}_j^t; \boldsymbol{W}) = \alpha_{ij}^{t,k} \mathbf{W}^{v,k} \boldsymbol{v}_j^t, \tag{17}$$

$$\boldsymbol{m}_i^t = \boldsymbol{v}_i^t + \left(\left\| \prod_{k=1}^{K} \left[\sum_{j \in \mathcal{N}(i)} M_{\text{atn}}^k(\boldsymbol{v}_i^t, \boldsymbol{v}_j^t; \boldsymbol{W}) \right] \right) \mathbf{W}^c \tag{18}$$

Matrices $\mathbf{W}^q, \mathbf{W}^u, \mathbf{W}^v, \mathbf{W}^r, \mathbf{W}^b, \mathbf{W}^c$, are not shared across time steps (but are shared across nodes).

Label Embedding Weight Sharing. To enforce each label's input embedding to correspond to that particular label, the label embedding matrix weights $\mathbf{W}^y$ are shared with the readout projection matrix $\mathbf{W}^o$. In other words, $\mathbf{W}^y$ is used to produce the initial node vectors for G_{yy}, and then is used again to calculate the pre-sigmoid output values for each label, so $\mathbf{W}^o \equiv \mathbf{W}^y$. This was shown beneficial in Seq2Seq models for machine translation [38].

2.5 Loss Function

The final output of LaMP networks $\hat{\boldsymbol{y}}$ are trained using the mean binary cross entropy (BCE) over all outputs y_i. For one sample, given true binary label vector $\boldsymbol{y}$ and predicted labels $\hat{\boldsymbol{y}}$, the output loss $\mathcal{L}_{out}$ is:

$$\mathcal{L}_{out}(\boldsymbol{y}, \hat{\boldsymbol{y}}) = \frac{1}{L} \sum_{i=1}^{L} -(y_i \log(\hat{y}_i) + (1 - y_i) \log(1 - \hat{y}_i)) \tag{19}$$

The final outputs $\hat{y}_i$ are computed from the final label node states $\boldsymbol{u}_i^T$ (Eq. 14). However, since LaMP networks iteratively update the label nodes from $t = 0$ to T, we can "probe" the label nodes at each intermediate state from $t = 1$ to $T-1$ and enforce an auxilary loss on those states. To do this, we use the same matrix W^o to extract the intermediate prediction $\hat{y}_i^t$ at state t: $\hat{y}_i^t = R(\boldsymbol{u}_i^t; \mathbf{W}^o)$. We use the same BCE loss on the these predictions to compute intermediate loss $\mathcal{L}_{int}$:

$$\mathcal{L}_{int}(\boldsymbol{y}, \hat{\boldsymbol{y}}^t) = \frac{1}{L} \sum_{i=1}^{L} -(y_i \log(\hat{y}_i^t) + (1 - y_i) \log(1 - \hat{y}_i^t)). \tag{20}$$

We note that the intermediate predictions $\hat{y}_i^t$ are computed for both $\boldsymbol{u}_i^t$ (after Label-to-Label message passing), as well as $\boldsymbol{u}_i^{t'}$ (after Feature-to-Label message passing). The final loss is a combination of both the original and intermediate, where the intermediate loss is weighted by λ:

$$\mathcal{L}_{LaMP} = \mathcal{L}_{out}(\boldsymbol{y}, \hat{\boldsymbol{y}}) + \lambda \sum_{t=1}^{T-1} \mathcal{L}_{int}(\boldsymbol{y}, \hat{\boldsymbol{y}}^t) \tag{21}$$

In LaMP networks, $p(y_i|\{y_{j\neq i}\}, \boldsymbol{z}_{1:S}; \boldsymbol{W})$ is approximated by jointly representing $\{y_{1:L}\}$ using message passing from $\{\boldsymbol{z}_{1:S}\}$ and from the embeddings of all neighboring labels $\{y_{j\in\mathcal{N}(i)}\}$.

2.6 LaMP Variation: Input Encoding with Feature Message Passing (FMP)

Thus far, we have assumed that we use the raw feature embeddings $\{\boldsymbol{z}_1, \boldsymbol{z}_2, ..., \boldsymbol{z}_S\}$ to pass messages to the labels. However, we could also update the feature embeddings before they are passed to the label nodes by modelling the interactions between features.

For a particular input $\boldsymbol{x}$, we first assume that the input features $\{x_{1:S}\}$ are nodes on a graph, G_{xx}. $G_{xx} = (V_{xx}, E_{xx})$, $V_{xx} = \{x_{1:S}\}$, and E includes all undirected pairwise edges connecting node $\boldsymbol{x}_i$ and node $\boldsymbol{x}_j$. MPNN$_{xx}$, parameterized by $\boldsymbol{W}_{xx}$, is used to pass messages between the input embeddings in order to update their states. Nodes on G_{xx} are represented as embedding vectors $\{\boldsymbol{z}_1^t, \boldsymbol{z}_2^t, ..., \boldsymbol{z}_S^t\}$, where the initial states $\{\boldsymbol{z}_{1:S}^0\}$ are obtained using embedding matrix $\boldsymbol{W}^x$ on input components $\{x_1, x_2, ..., x_S\}$. The embeddings are then updated by MPNN$_{xx}$ using message passing for T time steps to produce $\{\boldsymbol{z}_1^T, \boldsymbol{z}_2^T, ..., \boldsymbol{z}_S^T\}$.

To update input embedding $\boldsymbol{z}_i^t$, MPNN$_{xx}$ uses attention message function M_{atn}^t (Eq. 6) on all neighboring input embeddings $\{\boldsymbol{z}_{j\in\mathcal{N}(i)}^t\}$ to produce messages $\boldsymbol{m}_i^t$, and MLP update function U_{mlp} (Eq. 9) to produce updated embedding $\boldsymbol{z}_i^{t+1}$:

$$\boldsymbol{m}_i^t = \boldsymbol{z}_i^t + \sum_{j\in\mathcal{N}(i)} M_{\text{atn}}(\boldsymbol{z}_i^t, \boldsymbol{z}_j^t; \boldsymbol{W}_{xx}), \tag{22}$$

$$\boldsymbol{z}_i^{t+1} = \boldsymbol{m}_i^t + U_{\text{mlp}}(\boldsymbol{m}_i^t; \boldsymbol{W}_{xx}). \tag{23}$$

If there exists a known G_{xx} graph, message $\boldsymbol{m}_i^t$ for node i is computed using its neighboring nodes $j \in \mathcal{N}(i)$, where the neighbors $\mathcal{N}(i)$ are defined by the graph. If there is no known graph, we assume a fully connected G_{xx} graph, which means $\mathcal{N}(i) = \{j \in V_{xx}\}$. Inputs with a sequential ordering can be modelled as a fully connected graph using positional embeddings [4].

In summary, MPNN$_{xx}$ is used to update input feature nodes $\{\boldsymbol{z}_{1:S}^t\}$ by passing messages within the feature-interaction graph. MPNN$_{xy}$, is used to update output label nodes $\{\boldsymbol{u}_{1:L}^t\}$ by passing messages from the features to labels (from input nodes $\{\boldsymbol{z}_{1:S}^t\}$ to output nodes $\{\boldsymbol{u}_{1:L}^t\}$). MPNN$_{yy}$, is used to update output label nodes $\{\boldsymbol{u}_{1:L}^t\}$ by passing messages within the label-interaction graph (between label nodes). Once messages have been passed to update the feature and label nodes for T integrative updates, a readout function R is then used on the label nodes to make a binary classification prediction on each label, $\{\hat{y}_1, \hat{y}_2, ..., \hat{y}_L\}$. Figure 1 shows the LaMP network without the feature-interaction graph.

2.7   Advantages of LaMP Models

Efficiently Handling Dense Label Predictions. It is known that autoregressive models such as RNN Seq2Seq suffer from the propagation of errors over the sequential positive label predictions. This makes it difficult for these models to handle dense, or many positive label, samples. In addition, autoregressive models require a time consuming post-processing step such as beam search to obtain the optimal label set. Lastly, autoregressive models require a predefined label ordering for training the sequential prediction, which can lead to instabilities at testing time [54].

Motivated by the drawbacks of autoregressive models for MLC, the proposed LaMP model removes the reliance on sequential predictions, beam search, and a chosen label ordering, while still modelling the label dependencies. This is particularly beneficial when the number of positive output labels is large (i.e. dense). LaMP networks predict the output *set* of labels all at once, which is made possible by the fact that inference doesn't use a probabilistic chain, but there is still a representation of label dependencies via label to label attention. As an additional benefit, as noted by [5], it may be useful to maintain 'soft' predictions for each label in MLC. This is a major drawback of the PCC models which make 'hard' predictions of the positive labels, defaulting all other labels to 0.

Structure Agnostic. Many input or output types are instances where the relational structure is not made explicit, and must be inferred or assumed [4]. LaMP networks allow for greater flexibility of both input structures (known structure such as sequence or graph, or unknown such as tabular), as well as output structures (e.g., known graph vs unknown structure). To the best of our knowledge, this is the first work to use MPNNs to *infer* the relational structure of the data by using attention mechanisms.

Interpretability. Our formulation of LaMP allows us to visualize predictions in several different ways. First, since predictions are made in an iterative manner via graph update steps, we can "probe" each label's state at each step to get intermediate predictions. Second, we can visualize the attention weights which automatically learn the relational structure. Combining these two visualization methods allows us to see how the predictions change from the initial predictions given only the input sequence to the final state where messages have been passed from other labels, leading us to better insights for specific MLC samples.

2.8   Connecting to Related Topics

Structured Output Predictions. The use of graph attention in LaMP models is closely connected to the literature of structured output prediction for MLC. [14] used conditional random fields (CRFs) [29] to model dependencies among labels and features for MLC by learning a distribution over pairs of labels to input features, but these are limited to pairwise dependencies.

Table 1. ebF1 Scores across all 8 datasets

	Reuters	Bibtex	Bookmarks	Delicious	RCV1	TFBS	SIDER	NUSWIDE
FastXML [37]	–	–	–	–	0.841	–	–	–
Madjarov [32]	–	0.434	0.257	0.343	–	–	–	–
SPEN [5]	–	0.422	0.344	0.375	–	–	–	–
RNN Seq2Seq [36]	0.894	0.393	0.362	0.320	**0.890**	0.249	0.356	0.329
Emb + MLP	0.854	0.363	0.368	0.371	0.865	0.167	**0.766**	0.371
Emb + LaMP$_{el}$	0.859	0.379	0.351	0.358	0.868	0.289	0.767	**0.376**
Emb + LaMP$_{fc}$	0.896	0.427	0.376	0.368	0.871	0.319	0.763	**0.376**
Emb + LaMP$_{pr}$	0.895	0.424	0.373	0.366	0.870	0.317	0.765	0.372
FMP + LaMP$_{el}$	0.883	0.435	0.375	0.369	0.887	0.310	**0.766**	–
FMP + LaMP$_{fc}$	**0.906**	0.445	**0.389**	**0.372**	0.889	**0.321**	0.764	–
FMP + LaMP$_{pr}$	0.902	**0.447**	0.386	**0.372**	0.887	0.321	**0.766**	–

To overcome the naive pairwise dependency constraint of CRFs, structured prediction energy networks (SPENS) [5] and related methods [20,50] locally optimize an unconstrained structured output. In contrast to SPENs which use an iterative refinement of the output label predictions, our method is a simpler feed forward block to make predictions in one step, yet still models dependencies through attention mechanisms on embeddings, which gives the added interpretability benefit.

Multi-label Classification By Modeling Label Interaction Graphs. [19] formulate MLC using a label graph and they introduced a conditional dependency SVM where they first trained separate classifiers for each label given the input and all other true labels and used Gibbs sampling to find the optimal label set. The main drawback is that this method does not scale to a large number of labels. [42] proposes a method to label the pairwise edges of randomly generated label graphs, and requires some chosen aggregation method over all random graphs. The authors introduce the idea that variation in the graph structure shifts the inductive bias of the base learners. Our fully connected label graph with attention on the neighboring nodes can be regarded as a form of graph ensemble learning [22]. [11] use graph neural networks for MLC, but focus on graph inputs. They do not explicitly model label the label-to-label dependencies, thus resulting in a worse performance than LaMP.

Graph Neural Networks (GNNs). Passing embedding messages from node to neighbor nodes connects to a large body of literature on graph neural networks [4] and embedding models for structures [8].

The key idea is that instead of conducting probabilistic operations (e.g., product or re-normalization), the proposed models perform nonlinear function mappings in each step to learn feature representations of structured components. [3,15,53] all follow similar ideas to pass the embedding from node to neighbor nodes or neighbor edges.

There have been many recent works extending the basic GNN framework to update nodes using various message passing, update, and readout functions

$[3, 12, 15, 21, 24, 26, 31, 59]$. We refer the readers to [4] for a survey. However, none of these have used GNNs for MLC. In addition, none of these have attempted to learn the graph structure by using neural attention on fully connected graphs.

3 Experiments

We validate our model on eight real world MLC datasets. These datasets vary in the number of samples, number of labels, input type (sequential, tabular, graph, vector), and output type (unknown, known label graph). They also cover a wide spectrum of input data types, including: raw English text (sequential form), binary word vector (tabular form), drug molecules (graph form), and images (vector form). Data statistics are in Table 6 and Appendix D.1. Due to the space limit, we move the details of evaluation metrics to Appendix D.2 and the hyperparameters to Appendix D.3. Details of previous results from the state-of-the-art baselines are in Appendix D.4.

3.1 LaMP Variations

For LaMP models, we use two variations of input features, and three variations of Label-to-Label Message Passing. For input features, we use (1) **Emb**, which is the raw learned feature embeddings of dimension d, and (2) **FMP**[1] which is the updated state of each feature embedding after 2 layers of Feature Message Passing, as explained in Sect. 2.6. For each of the two input feature variations, we use three variations of the label graph which Label-to-Label Message Passing uses to update the labels given the input features, explained as follows.

Table 2. miF1 Scores across all 8 datasets

	Reuters	Bibtex	Bookmarks	Delicious	RCV1	TFBS	SIDER	NUSWIDE
FastXML [37]	–	–	–	–	0.847	–	–	–
SVM [9]	0.787	–	–	–	–	–	–	–
GAML [11]	–	–	0.333	–	–	–	–	0.398
Madjarov [32]	–	0.462	0.268	0.339	–	–	–	–
RNN Seq2Seq [36]	0.858	0.384	0.329	0.329	**0.884**	0.311	0.389	0.418
Emb + MLP	0.835	0.389	0.349	0.385	0.855	0.218	0.795	0.465
Emb + LaMP$_{el}$	0.842	0.413	0.334	0.372	0.858	0.401	0.797	**0.472**
Emb + LaMP$_{fc}$	0.871	0.458	0.363	0.379	0.859	0.449	0.797	0.470
Emb + LaMP$_{pr}$	0.877	0.462	0.363	0.380	0.859	0.448	**0.798**	0.468
FMP + LaMP$_{el}$	0.870	0.455	0.355	0.381	0.877	0.445	0.795	–
FMP + LaMP$_{fc}$	0.886	0.465	**0.373**	0.384	0.877	**0.450**	0.795	–
FMP + LaMP$_{pr}$	**0.889**	**0.473**	0.371	**0.386**	0.877	0.449	0.797	–

---

[1] For NUS-WIDE, since we use the 128-dimensional cVLAD features as input to compare to [11], we cannot use the **FMP** method.

LaMP$_{el}$ uses an edgeless label graph and messages are not passed between labels, assuming no label dependencies.

LaMP$_{fc}$ uses a fully connected label graph where each label is able to attend to all other labels (including itself) in order to compute the messages.

LaMP$_{pr}$ uses a prior label graph where each label is able to attend to only other labels from the known label graph (including itself) in order to compute the messages. For RCV1, we use the known tree label structure, and for TFBS we use known protein-protein interactions (PPI) from [44]. For all other datasets, we create a graph where we place an edge on the adjacency matrix for all labels that co-occur in any sample for the training set. This is summarized in the last column of Appendix Table 5.

3.2   Performance Evaluation

ebF1. Table 1 shows the most commonly used evaluation, example-based F1 (ebF1) scores, for the seven datasets. LaMP outperforms the baseline MLP models which assume no label dependencies, as well as RNN Seq2Seq, which models label dependencies using a classifier chain. More importantly, we compare using an output graph with no edges (LaMP$_{el}$), which assumes no label dependencies vs. an output graph with edges (LaMP$_{fc}$). The two models have the same architecture and number of parameters, with the only thing varying being the message passing between label nodes. We can see that for most datasets, modelling label dependencies using LaMP$_{fc}$ does in fact help. We found that using a known prior label structure (LaMP$_{pr}$) did not improve the results significantly. LaMP$_{fc}$ predictions produced an average 1.8% ebF1 score increase over the independent LaMP$_{el}$ predictions. LaMP$_{pr}$ resulted in an average 1.7% ebF1 score increase over LaMP$_{el}$. When comparing to the MLP baseline, LaMP$_{fc}$ and LaMP$_{pr}$ produced an average 18.5% and 18.4% increase, respectively.

miF1. While high ebF1 scores indicate strong average F1 scores over all samples, the label-based Micro-averaged F1 (miF1) scores indicate strong results on the most frequent labels. Table 2 shows the miF1 scores, for the all datasets. LaMP$_{fc}$ produced an average 1.6% miF1 score increase over the independent LaMP$_{el}$. LaMP$_{pr}$ produced an average 1.8% miF1 score increase over LaMP$_{el}$. When comparing to the MLP baseline, LaMP$_{fc}$ and LaMP$_{pr}$ resulted in an average 20.2% and 20.5% increase, respectively.

maF1. Contrarily, high label-based Macro-averaged F1 (maF1) scores indicate strong results on less frequent labels. Table 2 shows maF1 scores, which show the strongest improvement of LaMP$_{fc}$ and LaMP$_{pr}$ variation over independent predictions. LaMP$_{fc}$ resulted in an average 2.4% maF1 score increase over the independent LaMP$_{el}$. LaMP$_{pr}$ produced an average 2.1% maF1 score increase over LaMP$_{el}$. This indicates that Label-to-Label message passing can help boost the accuracy of rare label predictions. When comparing to Emb + MLP, LaMP$_{fc}$ and LaMP$_{pr}$ produced an average 57.0% and 56.7% increase, respectively (Table 3).

Table 3. maF1 Scores across all 8 datasets

	Reuters	Bibtex	Bookmarks	Delicious	RCV1	TFBS	SIDER	NUSWIDE
SVM [9]	0.468	–	–	–	–	–	–	–
FastXML [37]	–	–	–	–	0.592	–	–	–
GAML [11]	–	–	0.217	–	–	–	–	0.114
Madjarov [32]	–	0.316	0.119	0.142	–	–	–	–
RNN Seq2Seq [36]	0.457	0.282	0.237	0.166	0.741	0.210	0.207	0.143
Emb + MLP	0.366	0.275	0.248	0.180	0.667	0.094	0.665	0.173
Emb + LaMP$_{el}$	0.476	0.308	0.229	0.176	0.680	0.326	0.666	0.198
Emb + LaMP$_{fc}$	0.547	0.366	0.271	0.192	0.691	0.362	0.663	**0.203**
Emb + LaMP$_{pr}$	**0.560**	0.372	0.267	0.192	0.698	0.365	0.663	0.196
FMP + LaMP$_{el}$	0.508	0.353	0.266	0.192	0.742	**0.368**	0.664	–
FMP + LaMP$_{fc}$	0.520	0.371	**0.286**	0.195	**0.743**	0.364	**0.668**	–
FMP + LaMP$_{pr}$	0.517	**0.376**	0.280	**0.196**	0.740	0.364	0.664	–

Other Metrics. Due to space constraints, we report subset accuracy in Appendix (supplementary) Table 7. RNN Seq2Seq models mostly perform all other models for this metric since they are trained to maximize it [36]. However, for all other metrics, RNN Seq2Seq does not perform as well, concluding that for most applications, PCC models aren't necessary. We also report Hamming Accuracy in Appendix Table 8, and we note that LaMP networks outperform or perform similarly to baseline methods, but we observe that this metric is mostly unhelpful.

Metrics Performance Summary. While LaMP does not explicitly model label dependencies as autoregressive or structured prediction models do, the attention weights do learn some dependencies among labels (Sect. 3.3). This is indicated by the fact that LaMP, which uses Label-to-Label attention, mostly outperforms the ones which don't, indicating that it is learning label dependencies.

Speed. LaMP results in a mean of 1.7x and 5.0x training and testing speedups, respectively, over the previous state-of-the-art probabilistic MLC method, RNN Seq2Seq. Speedups over RNN Seq2Seq model are shown in Table 4.

3.3   Interpretability Evaluation

The structure of LaMP networks allows for three different types of visualization methods to understand how the network predicts each label. We explain the three types here and show the results for a sample from the Bookmarks dataset using the FMP + LaMP$_{fc}$ model.

Intermediate Output Prediction. One advantage of the multi step formulation of label embedding updates is that it gives us the ability to probe the state of each label at intermediate steps and view the model's predictions at those steps. To do this, we use the readout function R on each intermediate label embeddings state u_i^t to find the probability that the label embedding would predict a positive label. In other words, this is the post-sigmoid output of the readout function of each embedding $R(\boldsymbol{u}_i^t; \mathbf{W}^o)$ at each step $t = 1, ..., T$. We note that each step contains two stages: $t.1$ is the output after the Feature-to-Label message passing, and $t.2$ is output after the Label-to-Label message passing. The output after the second stage of the final step (i.e. $T.2$) is the model's final output.

Figure 2(a) shows the intermediate prediction outputs from the $T = 2$ step model. On the horizontal axis are a selected subset of all possible labels, with the red colored axis labels being all true positive labels. On the vertical axis, each row represents one of the label embedding states in the $T = 2$ step model. Each cell represents the readout function's prediction for each label embedding's state. The brighter the grid cell, the more likely that label is positive at the current stage. Starting from the bottom, the first row (1.1) shows the prediction of each label after the first Feature-to-Label message passing. The second row (1.2) shows the prediction of each label after the first Label-to-Label message passing. This is then repeated once more in (2.1) and (2.2) for the second layer's output states, where the final output, 2.2 is the network's final output predictions. The most important aspect of this figure is that we can see the labels "design", "html", and "web design", all change from weakly positive to strongly positive after the first Label-to-Label message passing step (row 1.2). In other words, this indicates that these labels change to a strongly positive prediction by passing messages between each other.

Label-to-Feature Attention. While the iterative prediction visualization shows how the model updates its prediction of each label, it doesn't explicitly show how or why. To understand why each label changes its predictions, we first look at the Feature-to-Label attention, which tells us the input nodes that each label node attends to in order to update its state (and thus producing the predictions in Fig. 2(a)). Figure 2(b) shows us which input nodes (i.e. features) each of the positive label attends to in order to make its first update step 1.1. The colors represent

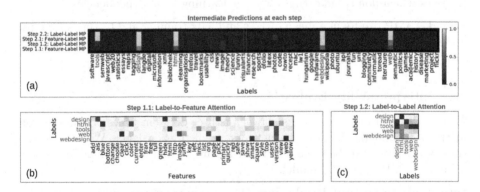

Fig. 2. (a) Visualization of Model Predictions and Attention Weights Intermediate Predictions: this shows the readout function predictions for each intermediate state in the two update steps. **(b) Label-to-Feature Attention Weights** for the first step of Feature-to-Label message passing (1.1). **(c) Label-to-Label Attention Weights** for the first step of Label-to-Label message passing (1.2).

Table 4. Speed. Each column shows training or testing speed for LaMP in minutes per epoch. Speedups over RNN Seq2Seq are in parentheses. Since LaMP does not depend on sequential prediction, we see a drastic speedup, especially during testing where RNN Seq2Seq requires beam search.

Dataset	Training	Testing
Reuters	0.788 (1.5x)	0.116 (2.1x)
Bibtex	0.376 (2.1x)	0.080 (2.1x)
Delicious	3.172 (1.1x)	0.473 (3.2x)
Bookmarks	9.664 (1.2x)	1.849 (1.3x)
RCV1	98.346 (1.2x)	1.003 (1.7x)
TFBS	187.14 (2.5x)	13.04 (4.2x)
NUS-WIDE	3.201 (1.2x)	0.921 (8.0x)
SIDER	0.027 (2.5x)	0.003 (21x)

the post-softmax attention weight (summed over the 4 attention heads), with the darker cells representing high attention. In this example, we can see that the "web design" label attends to the "pick", "smart", and "version" features, but as we can see from the first row of Fig. 2(a), prediction for the current state of the "web design" label isn't very strong yet.

Label-to-Label Attention. Label-to-Feature attention shows us the input nodes that each label node attends to in order to make its first update, but the second step of the label graph update is the Label-to-Label message passing step where labels are updated according to the states of all other nodes after the first Feature-to-Label message passing. Figure 2(c) shows us the first Label-to-Label attention stage 1.2 where each label node can attend to the other label nodes in order to update its state. Here we show only the Label-to-Label attention for the positive labels in this example. We then look at the second row of Fig. 2(a) which shows the model's prediction of each label node after the Label-to-Label attention. The interesting thing to note here is we can see many of the true positive labels change their state to positive after the positive labels attend to each other during the Label-to-Label attention step, indicating that dependencies are learned.

Attention weights for the second step $t = 2$ are not as interpretable since they model higher order interactions. We have added these plots in Appendix Fig. 3.

4 Conclusion

In this work we present Label Message Passing (LaMP) Networks which achieve better than, or close to the same accuracy as previous methods across five metrics and seven datasets. In addition, the iterative label embedding updates with attention of LaMP provide a straightforward way to shed light on the model's predictions and allow us to extract three forms of visualizations, including conditional label dependencies which influence MLC classifications.

A   Appendix: MLC Background

A.1   Background of Multi-label Classification

MLC has a rich history in text [33,51], images [13,46], bioinformatics [13,46], and many other domains. MLC methods can roughly be broken into several groups, which are explained as follows.

Label powerset models (LP) [40,49], classify each input into one label combination from the set of all possible combinations $\mathcal{Y} = \{\{1\}, \{2\}, ..., \{1,2,...,L\}\}$. LP explicitly models the joint distribution by predicting the one subset of all positive labels. Since the label set Y grows exponentially in the number of total labels (2^L), classifying each possible label set is intractable for a modest L. In addition, even in small L tasks, LP suffers from the "subset scarcity problem" where only a small amount of the label subsets are seen during training, leading to bad generalization.

Binary relevance (BR) methods predict each label separately as a logistic regression classifier for each label [16,58]. The naïve approach to BR prediction is to predict all labels independently of one another, assuming no dependencies among labels. That is, BR uses the following conditional probability parameterized by learned weights W:

$$P_{BR}(Y|X;W) = \prod_{i=1}^{L} p(Y_i|X_{1:S};W) \tag{24}$$

Probabilistic classifier chain (PCC) methods [10,39] are autoregressive models that estimate the true joint probability of output labels given the input by using the chain rule, predicting one label at a time:

$$P_{PCC}(Y|X;W) = \prod_{i=1}^{L} p(Y_i|Y_{1:i-1}, X_{1:S};W) \tag{25}$$

Two issues with PCC models are that inference is very slow if L is large, and the errors propagate as L increases [34]. To mitigate the problems with both LP and PCC methods, one solution is to only predict the true labels in the LP subset. In other words, only predicting the positive labels (total of ρ for a particular sample) and ignoring all other labels, which we call PCC+. Similar to PCC, the joint probability of PCC+ can be computed as product of conditional probabilities, but unlike PCC, only $\rho < L$ terms are predicted as positive:

$$P_{PCC+}(Y|X;W) = \prod_{i=1}^{\rho} p(Y_{p_i}|Y_{p_{1:i-1}}, x_{1:S};W) \tag{26}$$

This can be beneficial when the number of possible labels L is large, reducing the total number of prediction steps. However, in both PCC and PCC+, inference is done using beam search, which is a costly dynamic programming step to find the optimal prediction.

Recently, Recurrent neural network (RNN) based encoder-decoder models following PCC and PCC+ have shown state-of-the-art performance for solving MLC. However, the sequential nature of modeling label dependencies through an RNN limits its ability in parallel computation, predicting dense labels, and providing interpretable results.

The main drawback of classifier chain models is that their inherently sequential nature precludes parallelization during training and inference. This can be detrimental when there are a large number of positive labels as the classifier chain has to sequentially predict each label, and often requires beam search to obtain the optimal set. Aside from time-cost disadvantages, PCC methods have several other drawbacks. First, PCC methods require a defined ordering of labels for the sequential prediction, but MLC output labels are an unordered set, and the chosen order can lead to prediction instability [36]. Secondly, even if the optimal ordering is known, PCC methods struggle to accurately capture long-range dependencies among labels in cases where the number of positive labels is large (i.e., dense labels). For example, the Delicious dataset we used in the experiment has a median of 19 positive labels per sample, so it can be difficult to correctly predict the labels at the end of the prediction chain. Lastly, many real-world applications prefer interpretable predictors. For instance, in the task of predicting which proteins (labels) will bind to a DNA sequence based binding site, users care about how a prediction is made and how the interactions among labels (proteins) influence the binding predictions. An important task is modelling what is known as "co-binding" effects, where one protein will *only* bind if there is another specific protein already binding, or similarly will not bind if there is another already binding.

LaMP methods approximate the following factored formulation, where $\mathcal{N}(Y_i)$ denotes the neighboring nodes of Y_i.

$$P_{G2G}(Y|X;W) = \prod_{i=1}^{L} p(Y_i|\{Y_{\mathcal{N}(Y_i)}\}, X_{1:S}; W). \tag{27}$$

A.2   Seq2Seq Models

In machine translation (MT), sequence-to-sequence (Seq2Seq) models have proven to be the superior method, where an encoder RNN reads the source language sentence into an encoder hidden state, and a decoder RNN translates the hidden state into a target sentence, predicting each word autoregressively [43]. [2] improved this model by introducing "neural attention" which allows the decoder RNN to "attend" to every encoder word at each step of the autoregressive translation.

Recently, [36] showed that, across several metrics, state-of-the-art MLC results could be achieved by using a recurrent neural network (RNN) based encoder-to-decoder framework for Eq. 26 (PCC+). They use a Seq2Seq RNN model (Seq2Seq Autoregressive) which uses one RNN to encode x, and a second RNN to predict each positive label sequentially, until it predicts a 'stop' signal.

This type of model seeks to maximize the 'subset accuracy', or correctly predict every label as its exact 0/1 value.

[52] eliminated the need for the recurrent network in MT by introducing the Transformer. Instead of using an RNN to model dependencies, the Transformer explicitly models pairwise dependencies among all of the features by using attention [2, 56] between signals. This speeds up training time because RNNs can't be fully parallelized but, the transformer still uses an autoregressive decoder.

A.3   Drawbacks of Autoregressive Models

Seq2Seq MLC [36] uses an encoder RNN encoding elements of an input sequence, a decoder RNN predicting output labels one after another, and beam search that computes the probability of the next T predictions of labels and then chooses the solution with the max combined probability.

Autoregressive models have been proven effective for machine translation and MLC [2, 36, 43]. However, predictions must be made sequentially, eliminating parallelization. Also, beam search is typically used at test time to find optimal predictions. But beam search is limited by the time cost of large beams sizes, making it difficult to optimally predict many output labels [27].

In addition to speed constraints, beam search for autoregressive inference introduces a second drawback: initial wrong predictions will propagate when using a modest beam size (e.g. most models use a beam size of 5). This can lead to significant decreases in performance when the number of positive labels is large. For example, the Delicious dataset has a median of 19 positive labels per sample, and it can be very difficult to correctly predict the labels at the end of the prediction chain.

Autoregressive models are well suited for machine translation because these models mimic the sequential decoding process of real translation. However, for MLC, the output labels have no intrinsic ordering. While the joint probability of the output labels is independent of the label ordering via autoregressive based inference, the chosen ordering can make a difference in practice [36, 54]. Some ordering of labels must be used during training, and this chosen ordering can lead to unstable predictions at test time.

Our LaMP connects to [18] who removed the autoregressive decoder in MT with the Non-Autoregressive Transformer. In this model, the encoder makes a proxy prediction, called "fertilities", which are used by the decoder to predict all translated words at once. The difference between their model and ours is that we have a constant label at each position, so we don't need to marginalize over all possible labels at each position.

B Appendix: Dataset Details

Table 5. Dataset Statistics. We use 7 well studied MLC datasets, plus our own TFBS protein binding dataset. Each dataset varies in the input type, number of samples, number of labels, and number of input features. The last column shows the prior graph structure type we explore for the LaMP$_{pr}$ model.

Dataset	Input Type	Domain	#Train	#Val	#Test	Labels (L)	Features	Prior graph structure
Reuters-21578	Sequential	Text	6,993	777	3,019	90	23,662	Co-occur
RCV1-V2	Sequential	Text	703,135	78,126	23,149	103	368,998	Tree
TFBS	Sequential	Biology	1,671,873	301,823	323,796	179	4	PPI
BibTex	Binary Vector	Text	4,377	487	2,515	159	1,836	Co-occur
Delicious	Binary Vector	Text	11,597	1,289	3,185	983	500	Co-occur
Bookmarks	Binary Vector	Text	48,000	12,000	27,856	208	368,998	Co-occur
NUS-WIDE	Vector	Image	129,431	32,358	107,859	85	128	Co-occur
SIDER	Graph	Drug	1,141	143	143	27	37	Co-occur

Table 6. Additional Dataset Statistics. Here we show additional statistics of datasets with respect to the specific number of labels for each dataset. This shows how each dataset has a varying degree of MLC difficulty regarding the number of labels which need to be predicted.

Dataset	Mean labels /sample	Median labels /sample	Max labels /sample	Mean samples /label	Median samples /label	Max samples /label
Reuters-21578	1.23	1	15	106.50	18	2,877
RCV1-V2	3.21	3	17	24,362	7,250	363,991
TFBS	7.62	2	178	84,047	45,389	466,876
BibTex	2.38	2	28	72.79	54	689
Delicious	19.06	20	25	250.15	85	5,189
Bookmarks	2.03	1	44	584.67	381	4,642
NUS-WIDE	1.86	1	12	3721.7	1104	44255
SIDER	15.3	16	26	731.07	851	1185

C Appendix: Extra Metrics

Here we provide the results from an extra two metrics: subset accuracy and hamming accuracy.

Table 7. Subset Accuracy Scores across all 7 datasets

	Reuters	Bibtex	Bookmarks	Delicious	RCV1	TFBS	SIDER	NUSWIDE
Madjarov	-	**0.202**	0.209	**0.018**	–	–	–	–
RNN Seq2Seq	**0.837**	0.195	**0.273**	0.016	**0.6798**	**0.114**	0.000	0.252
Emb + MLP	0.774	0.151	0.234	0.180	0.620	0.040	0.014	0.263
Emb + LaMP$_{el}$	0.757	0.141	0.214	0.176	0.619	0.077	0.014	0.268
Emb + LaMP$_{fc}$	0.813	0.171	0.234	0.192	0.630	0.086	0.007	**0.269**
Emb + LaMP$_{pr}$	0.813	0.169	0.232	0.192	0.621	0.087	0.007	0.267
FMP + LaMP$_{el}$	0.808	0.158	0.231	0.192	0.656	0.084	0.007	–
FMP + LaMP$_{fc}$	0.835	0.182	0.242	0.195	0.660	0.090	0.014	–
FMP + LaMP$_{pr}$	0.828	0.185	0.241	0.196	0.659	0.090	0.007	–

Table 8. Hamming Accuracy across all 7 datasets

	Reuters	Bibtex	Bookmarks	Delicious	RCV1	TFBS	SIDER	NUSWIDE
Madjarov	–	0.988	0.991	0.982	–	–	–	–
RNN Seq2Seq	0.996	0.985	0.990	0.980	0.9925	0.961	0.593	0.980
Emb + MLP	0.996	0.987	0.991	0.982	0.992	0.959	0.752	0.980
Emb + LaMP$_{el}$	0.996	0.987	0.991	0.982	0.992	0.963	0.750	0.980
Emb + LaMP$_{fc}$	0.997	0.988	0.992	0.982	0.992	0.964	0.752	0.980
Emb + LaMP$_{pr}$	0.997	0.988	0.991	0.982	0.992	0.964	0.751	0.980
FMP + LaMP$_{el}$	0.997	0.987	0.991	0.982	0.993	0.964	0.748	–
FMP + LaMP$_{fc}$	0.997	0.988	0.992	0.982	0.993	0.964	0.749	–
FMP + LaMP$_{pr}$	0.997	0.988	0.992	0.982	0.993	0.964	0.747	–

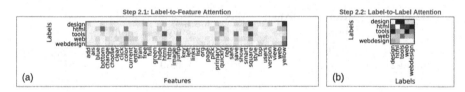

Fig. 3. This shows the step $t = 2$ visualization results from Fig. 2 (a). **2.1 Label-to-Feature Attention Weights (b)**. **2.2 Label-to-Label Attention Weights (c)**

D   Appendix: More About Experiments

D.1   Datasets

We test our method against baseline methods on seven different multi-label sequence classification datasets. The datasets are summarized in Table 6. We use Reuters-21578 [30], Bibtex [48], Delicious [47], Bookmarks [23], RCV1-V2 [30], our own DNA protein binding dataset (TFBS) from [7], and SIDER [28], which is side effects of drug molecules. As shown in the table, each dataset has a varying number of samples, number of labels, positive labels per sample, and samples per label. For BibTex and Delicious, we use 10% of the provided training set for validation. For the TFBS dataset, we use 1 layer of convolution at the first layer to extract "words" from the DNA characters (A, C, G, T), as commonly done in deep learning models for DNA.

For datasets which have sequential ordering of the input components (Reuters, RCV1), we add a positional encoding to the word embedding as used in [52] (sine and cosine functions of different frequencies) to encode the location of each word in the sentence. For datasets with no ordering or graph structure (Bibtex, Delicious, Bookmarks, which use bag-of-word input representations) we do not use positional encodings. For inputs with an explicit graph representation (SIDER), we use the known graph structure.

D.2   Evaluation Metrics

Multi-label classification methods can be evaluated with many different metrics which each evaluate different strengths or weaknesses. We use the same 5 evaluation metrics from [36].

All of our autoregressive models predict only the positive labels before outputting a stop signal. This is a special case of PCC models, which have been shown to outperform the binary prediction of each label in terms of performance and speed. These models use beam search at inference time with a beam size of 5. For the non-autoregressive models, to convert the labels to $\{0, 1\}$ we chose the best threshold on the validation set from the same set of thresholds used in [50].

Example-based measures are defined by comparing the target vector $\boldsymbol{y}$ to the prediction vector $\hat{\boldsymbol{y}}$. Subset Accuracy (ACC) requires an exact match of the predicted labels and the true labels: $\text{ACC}(\boldsymbol{y}, \hat{\boldsymbol{y}}) = \mathbb{I}[\boldsymbol{y} = \hat{\boldsymbol{y}}]$. Hamming Accuracy (HA) evaluates how many labels are correctly predicted in $\hat{y}$: $\text{HA}(\boldsymbol{y}, \hat{\boldsymbol{y}}) = \frac{1}{L} \sum_{j=1}^{L} \mathbb{I}[y_j = \hat{y}_j]$. Example-based F1 (ebF1) measures the ratio of correctly predicted labels to the sum of the total true and predicted labels: $\frac{2 \sum_{j=1}^{L} y_j \hat{y}_j}{\sum_{j=1}^{L} y_j + \sum_{j=1}^{L} \hat{y}_j}$.

Label-based measures treat each label y_j as a separate two-class prediction problem, and compute the number of true positives (tp_j), false positives (fp_j), and false negatives (fn_j) for a label. Macro-averaged F1 (maF1) measures the label-based F1 averaged over all labels: $\frac{1}{L} \sum_{j=1}^{L} \frac{2tp_j}{2tp_j + fp_j + fn_j}$. Micro-averaged F1 (miF1) measures the label-based F1 averaged over each sample: $\frac{\sum_{j=1}^{L} 2tp_j}{\sum_{j=1}^{L} 2tp_j + fp_j + fn_j}$. High maF1 scores usually indicate high performance on less frequent labels. High miF1 scores usually indicate high performance on more frequent labels.

D.3   Model Hyperparameter Tuning

For all 7 datasets (Table 6), we use the same LaMP model with $T = 2$ time steps, $d = 512$, and $K = 4$ attention heads. We trained our models on an

NVIDIA TITAN X Pascal with a batch size of 32. We used Adam [25] with betas $= (0.9, 0.999)$, eps $= 1e{-}08$, and a learning rate of 0.0002 for each dataset. We used dropout of $p = 0.2$ for the smaller datasets (Reuters, Bibtex, SIDER), and dropout of $p = 0.1$ for all other datasets. The LaMP models also use layer normalization [1] around each of the attention and feedforward layers. All LaMP models are trained with the LaMP loss (Eq. 21). The hyperparameter λ is selected from the best performing value in $\{0, 0.1, 0.2, 0.3\}$ for each model. MLP models are trained with regular binary cross entropy (Eq. 19), and RNN Seq2Seq model are trained with cross entropy across all possible labels at each position. To convert the soft predictions into $\{0, 1\}$ values, we use the same thresholds in [5] and select the best one for each metric on the validation set. For the TFBS dataset, which uses DNA input sequences, we use one layer of convolution to get 512 dimensional embeddings as commonly done for deep neural network prediction tasks on DNA sequences.

D.4 Baseline Comparisons

Briefly, we compare against the following methods for all reported datasets and metrics. For those results named as "Madjarov": we take the best method for each reported metric from [32] who compared 12 different types of models including SVMs, decision trees, boosting, classification rules, and neural networks. For results of "SPEN": Structured prediction energy networks from [5]. For results of "SVM": SVM method from the Reuters dataset authors [9]. For results of "FastXML": Fast random forest model [37]. For results of "GAML": graph attention for MLC from [11]. For "RNN Seq2Seq": RNN Sequence to Sequence model from [35] which is a PCC model that predicts only the positive labels. For "Emb + MLP": we use the mean embeddings of all input features as the input to a 4 layer multi-layer perceptron (MLP). This is a BR baseline which predicts all labels independently.

References

1. Ba, J.L., Kiros, J.R., Hinton, G.E.: Layer normalization. arXiv preprint arXiv:1607.06450 (2016)
2. Bahdanau, D., Cho, K., Bengio, Y.: Neural machine translation by jointly learning to align and translate. arXiv preprint arXiv:1409.0473 (2014)
3. Battaglia, P., Pascanu, R., Lai, M., Rezende, D.J., et al.: Interaction networks for learning about objects, relations and physics. In: Advances in Neural Information Processing Systems, pp. 4502–4510 (2016)
4. Battaglia, P.W., et al.: Relational inductive biases, deep learning, and graph networks. arXiv:1806.01261 (2018)
5. Belanger, D., McCallum, A.: Structured prediction energy networks. In: International Conference on Machine Learning, pp. 983–992 (2016)
6. Bhatia, K., Jain, H., Kar, P., Varma, M., Jain, P.: Sparse local embeddings for extreme multi-label classification. In: Neural Information Processing Systems, pp. 730–738 (2015)

7. The ENCODE Project Consortium, et al.: An integrated encyclopedia of DNA elements in the human genome. Nature **489**(7414), 57 (2012)
8. Dai, H., Dai, B., Song, L.: Discriminative embeddings of latent variable models for structured data. In: International Conference on Machine Learning, pp. 2702–2711 (2016)
9. Debole, F., Sebastiani, F.: An analysis of the relative hardness of Reuters-21578. Am. Soc. Inf. Sci. Technol. **56**(6), 584–596 (2005)
10. Dembczynski, K., Cheng, W., Hüllermeier, E.: Bayes optimal multilabel classification via probabilistic classifier chains (2010)
11. Do, K., Tran, T., Nguyen, T., Venkatesh, S.: Attentional multilabel learning over graphs-a message passing approach. arXiv preprint arXiv:1804.00293 (2018)
12. Duvenaud, D.K., et al.: Convolutional networks on graphs for learning molecular fingerprints. In: Advances in Neural Information Processing Systems, pp. 2224–2232 (2015)
13. Elisseeff, A., Weston, J.: A kernel method for multi-labelled classification. In: Advances in Neural Information Processing Systems, pp. 681–687 (2002)
14. Ghamrawi, N., McCallum, A.: Collective multi-label classification. In: 14th ACM International Conference on Information and Knowledge Management, pp. 195–200. ACM (2005)
15. Gilmer, J., Schoenholz, S.S., Riley, P.F., Vinyals, O., Dahl, G.E.: Neural message passing for quantum chemistry. arXiv preprint arXiv:1704.01212 (2017)
16. Godbole, S., Sarawagi, S.: Discriminative methods for multi-labeled classification. In: Dai, H., Srikant, R., Zhang, C. (eds.) PAKDD 2004. LNCS (LNAI), vol. 3056, pp. 22–30. Springer, Heidelberg (2004). https://doi.org/10.1007/978-3-540-24775-3_5
17. Graves, A.: Generating sequences with recurrent neural networks. arXiv preprint arXiv:1308.0850 (2013)
18. Gu, J., Bradbury, J., Xiong, C., Li, V.O., Socher, R.: Non-autoregressive neural machine translation. arXiv preprint arXiv:1711.02281 (2017)
19. Guo, Y., Gu, S.: Multi-label classification using conditional dependency networks. In: IJCAI Proceedings-International Joint Conference on Artificial Intelligence, vol. 22, p. 1300 (2011)
20. Gygli, M., Norouzi, M., Angelova, A.: Deep value networks learn to evaluate and iteratively refine structured outputs. arXiv preprint arXiv:1703.04363 (2017)
21. Hamilton, W.L., Ying, R., Leskovec, J.: Representation learning on graphs: methods and applications. arXiv preprint arXiv:1709.05584 (2017)
22. Hara, K., Saitoh, D., Shouno, H.: Analysis of dropout learning regarded as ensemble learning. In: Villa, A.E.P., Masulli, P., Pons Rivero, A.J. (eds.) ICANN 2016. LNCS, vol. 9887, pp. 72–79. Springer, Cham (2016). https://doi.org/10.1007/978-3-319-44781-0_9
23. Katakis, I., Tsoumakas, G., Vlahavas, I.: Multilabel text classification for automated tag suggestion
24. Kearnes, S., McCloskey, K., Berndl, M., Pande, V., Riley, P.: Molecular graph convolutions: moving beyond fingerprints. J. Comput. Aided Mol. Des. **30**(8), 595–608 (2016)
25. Kingma, D., Ba, J.: Adam: a method for stochastic optimization. arXiv preprint arXiv:1412.6980 (2014)
26. Kipf, T.N., Welling, M.: Semi-supervised classification with graph convolutional networks. arXiv preprint arXiv:1609.02907 (2016)
27. Koehn, P., Knowles, R.: Six challenges for neural machine translation. arXiv preprint arXiv:1706.03872 (2017)

28. Kuhn, M., Letunic, I., Jensen, L.J., Bork, P.: The sider database of drugs and side effects. Nucleic Acids Res. **44**(D1), D1075–D1079 (2015)

29. Lafferty, J., McCallum, A., Pereira, F.C.: Conditional random fields: probabilistic models for segmenting and labeling sequence data (2001)

30. Lewis, D.D., Yang, Y., Rose, T.G., Li, F.: RCV1: a new benchmark collection for text categorization research. J. Mach. Learn. Res. **5**(Apr), 361–397 (2004)

31. Li, Y., Tarlow, D., Brockschmidt, M., Zemel, R.: Gated graph sequence neural networks. arXiv preprint arXiv:1511.05493 (2015)

32. Madjarov, G., Kocev, D., Gjorgjevikj, D., Džeroski, S.: An extensive experimental comparison of methods for multi-label learning. Pattern Recogn. **45**(9), 3084–3104 (2012)

33. McCallum, A.: Multi-label text classification with a mixture model trained by EM

34. Montañes, E., Senge, R., Barranquero, J., Quevedo, J.R., del Coz, J.J., Hüllermeier, E.: Dependent binary relevance models for multi-label classification. Pattern Recogn. **47**(3), 1494–1508 (2014)

35. Nam, J., Kim, J., Loza Mencía, E., Gurevych, I., Fürnkranz, J.: Large-scale multi-label text classification—revisiting neural networks. In: Calders, T., Esposito, F., Hüllermeier, E., Meo, R. (eds.) ECML PKDD 2014. LNCS (LNAI), vol. 8725, pp. 437–452. Springer, Heidelberg (2014). https://doi.org/10.1007/978-3-662-44851-9_28

36. Nam, J., Mencía, E.L., Kim, H.J., Fürnkranz, J.: Maximizing subset accuracy with recurrent neural networks in multi-label classification. In: Advances in Neural Information Processing Systems, pp. 5419–5429 (2017)

37. Prabhu, Y., Varma, M.: FastXML: a fast, accurate and stable tree-classifier for extreme multi-label learning. In: Proceedings of the 20th ACM SIGKDD International Conference on Knowledge Discovery and Data Mining, pp. 263–272. ACM (2014)

38. Press, O., Wolf, L.: Using the output embedding to improve language models. arXiv preprint arXiv:1608.05859 (2016)

39. Read, J., Pfahringer, B., Holmes, G., Frank, E.: Classifier chains for multi-label classification. In: Buntine, W., Grobelnik, M., Mladenić, D., Shawe-Taylor, J. (eds.) ECML PKDD 2009. LNCS (LNAI), vol. 5782, pp. 254–269. Springer, Heidelberg (2009). https://doi.org/10.1007/978-3-642-04174-7_17

40. Read, J., Pfahringer, B., Holmes, G., Frank, E.: Classifier chains for multi-label classification. Mach. Learn. **85**(3), 333 (2011). https://doi.org/10.1007/s10994-011-5256-5

41. Scarselli, F., Gori, M., Tsoi, A.C., Hagenbuchner, M., Monfardini, G.: The graph neural network model. IEEE Trans. Neural Netw. **20**(1), 61–80 (2009)

42. Su, H., Rousu, J.: Multilabel classification through random graph ensembles. In: Asian Conference on Machine Learning, pp. 404–418 (2013)

43. Sutskever, I., Vinyals, O., Le, Q.V.: Sequence to sequence learning with neural networks. In: Advances in Neural Information Processing Systems, pp. 3104–3112 (2014)

44. Szklarczyk, D., et al.: The STRING database in 2017: quality-controlled protein-protein association networks, made broadly accessible. Nucleic Acids Res. **45**, D362–D368 (2016)

45. Tsochantaridis, I., Joachims, T., Hofmann, T., Altun, Y.: Large margin methods for structured and interdependent output variables. JMLR **6**(Sep), 1453–1484 (2005)

46. Tsoumakas, G., Katakis, I.: Multi-label classification: an overview. Int. J. Data Warehous. Min. **3**(3), 1–13 (2006)

47. Tsoumakas, G., Katakis, I., Vlahavas, I.: Effective and efficient multilabel classification in domains with large number of labels
48. Tsoumakas, G., Katakis, I., Vlahavas, I.: Mining multi-label data. In: Maimon, O., Rokach, L. (eds.) Data Mining and Knowledge Discovery Handbook, pp. 667–685. Springer, Boston (2009). https://doi.org/10.1007/978-0-387-09823-4_34
49. Tsoumakas, G., Vlahavas, I.: Random k-labelsets: an ensemble method for multilabel classification. In: Kok, J.N., Koronacki, J., Mantaras, R.L., Matwin, S., Mladenič, D., Skowron, A. (eds.) ECML 2007. LNCS (LNAI), vol. 4701, pp. 406–417. Springer, Heidelberg (2007). https://doi.org/10.1007/978-3-540-74958-5_38
50. Tu, L., Gimpel, K.: Learning approximate inference networks for structured prediction. arXiv preprint arXiv:1803.03376 (2018)
51. Ueda, N., Saito, K.: Parametric mixture models for multi-labeled text. In: Advances in Neural Information Processing Systems, pp. 737–744 (2003)
52. Vaswani, A., et al.: Attention is all you need. In: Advances in Neural Information Processing Systems, pp. 6000–6010 (2017)
53. Veličković, P., Cucurull, G., Casanova, A., Romero, A., Liò, P., Bengio, Y.: Graph attention networks. arXiv preprint arXiv:1710.10903 (2017)
54. Vinyals, O., Bengio, S., Kudlur, M.: Order matters: sequence to sequence for sets. arXiv preprint arXiv:1511.06391 (2015)
55. Wang, J., Yang, Y., Mao, J., Huang, Z., Huang, C., Xu, W.: CNN-RNN: a unified framework for multi-label image classification. In: Proceedings of the IEEE Conference on Computer Vision and Pattern Recognition, pp. 2285–2294 (2016)
56. Xu, K., et al.: Show, attend and tell: neural image caption generation with visual attention. In: International Conference on Machine Learning, pp. 2048–2057. http://www.jmlr.org/proceedings/papers/v37/xuc15.pdf
57. Yeh, C.K., Wu, W.C., Ko, W.J., Wang, Y.C.F.: Learning deep latent space for multi-label classification. In: AAAI, pp. 2838–2844 (2017)
58. Zhang, M.L., Zhou, Z.H.: A k-nearest neighbor based algorithm for multi-label classification. In: 2005 IEEE International Conference on Granular Computing, vol. 2, pp. 718–721. IEEE (2005)
59. Zheng, D., Luo, V., Wu, J., Tenenbaum, J.B.: Unsupervised learning of latent physical properties using perception-prediction networks. arXiv preprint arXiv:1807.09244 (2018)

Assessing the Multi-labelness
of Multi-label Data

Laurence A. F. Park[1(✉)], Yi Guo[1], and Jesse Read[2]

[1] Centre for Research in Mathematics, School of Computing,
Engineering and Mathematics, Western Sydney University, Sydney, Australia
{lapark,yi.guo}@westernsydney.edu.au
[2] DaSciM team, LIX Laboratory, École Polytechnique, 91120 Palaiseau, France
jesse.read@polytechnique.edu

Abstract. Before constructing a classifier, we should examine the data to gain an understanding of the relationships between the variables, to assist with the design of the classifier. Using multi-label data requires us to examine the association between labels: its multi-labelness. We cannot directly measure association between two labels, since the labels' relationships are confounded with the set of observation variables. A better approach is to fit an analytical model to a label with respect to the observations and remaining labels, but this might present false relationships due to the problem of multicollinearity between the observations and labels. In this article, we examine the utility of regularised logistic regression and a new form of split logistic regression for assessing the multi-labelness of data. We find that a split analytical model using regularisation is able to provide fewer label relationships when no relationships exist, or if the labels can be partitioned. We also find that if label relationships do exist, logistic regression with l_1 regularisation provides the better measurement of multi-labelness.

1 Introduction

Multi-label classification models allow the classification of a set of unknown binary labels conditioned on a set of known observations. A review of common multi-label classification algorithms is given in [7].

Before modelling any data, we should examine it to determine an appropriate form of model for the data. When faced with multi-label data, we must also examine the relationships between the labels to determine the *multi-labelness* of the data: if a multi-label model is appropriate and how the labels should be modelled. If we can detect that a given set of labels are independent from each other, we can include this knowledge in the model, making the fitting time faster, resulting in a less complex model.

Unfortunately, measuring high correlation between a pair of label variables does not imply that the multi-labelness of the data is high, since the correlation might be explained by a set of confounding observation variables. Therefore, to determine the set of relationships between labels, we must model each label,

© Springer Nature Switzerland AG 2020
U. Brefeld et al. (Eds.): ECML PKDD 2019, LNAI 11907, pp. 164–179, 2020.
https://doi.org/10.1007/978-3-030-46147-8_10

with respect to all other labels and all observation variables, and examine the coefficients of the model. The number of non-zero coefficients between labels of the model provide us with a measure of multi-labelness of the data.

When modelling the response of a label, with respect to the remaining labels and the observation variables, we introduce the problem of multicollinearity; there is likely to be correlation between the observation variables and the labels, so it is also likely that many subsets of observation variables and labels provide an equally good fit to the data, but our model will only provide one subset. This implies that even though a label is independent of other labels, the model may show association to other labels due to their multicollinearity with the set of observation variables, and suggest a false high multi-labelness of the data.

In this article, we investigate the use of logistic regression in a full and split form to measure the multi-labelness of the data. The contributions of this article are:

- Derivation of a split analytical model with regularisation (Sect. 3.2).
- Investigation of the utility of a full and split regularised model for measuring multi-labelness on synthetic data using various multi-label structures (Sect. 4).
- Verification of the analysis using real data (Sect. 5).

The article will proceed as follows: Sect. 2 introduces the problem and required background knowledge, Sect. 3 introduces measuring multi-labelness with full and split analytical models. Section 4 examines the utility of each analytical model for measuring multi-labelness on generated data. Finally, Sect. 5 verifies the findings using real data.

2 Background: Multi-label Data and Multicollinearity

The multi-label classification problem requires modelling L label set variables $y \in \{-1, +1\}^L$ conditioned on a set of M observation variables $x \in \mathbb{R}^M$. Typically, sample data is provided as a set of N label sets and associated observations (y, x), where the task is to construct a model f that provides good estimates of the label sets $\hat{y}$ conditioned on the observations, such that $\hat{y} = f(x)$, for a given metric [3,4].

A common technique for modelling multi-label relationships is to construct a set of models that predict only one label variable y_i or a subset of labels, based on the observations and a subset of the remaining labels. The coefficients of the models β provide us with insight of the level of association of the label y_i to each observation variable and remaining labels. For example, single label models can be chained [5,6], use a tree structure [2] or even retain cyclic dependencies in a network [1,8]. In each of these cases, higher level models predict the state of a label based on the predicted states of other labels. This implies that any error in label classification will be propagated through to other labels. Therefore, when constructing these models, if we can remove model dependencies between labels and maintain accuracy, then we should do so.

Before we fit a multi-label model to data, we should examine the data and determine if there is association between the labels; we call this measuring the *multi-labelness* of the data, where the measurement of multi-labelness is the number of inter-label relationships. Why is it important to examine the multi-labelness of the data?

- If no labels are associated to each other, then the multi-label problem reduces to a set of binary classification problems.
- If there are at least two sets of labels that have no association between them, then we can split the multi-label problems into a two or more multi-label classification problems, each independent of each other.

Also, knowing which labels are correlated will assist us in designing a suitable multi-label classifier.

Problem: Confounding Variables. When determining the dependence of one label variable y_i to another y_j, we must note that the set of observation variables are confounding variables. Both labels y_i and y_j are dependent on the observations x, so any association between the labels might actually be explained entirely by the observations x. Therefore, we must take our analysis a step further and model the variance of y_i with respect to each observation x and each other label variable y_{-i}. The fitted analytical model coefficients β will describe the level of association of y_i to x and y_{-i}.

Analytical models are fitted to data to provide us with deeper insight into the generating process behind the data. For example, when using simple linear regression, we can observe the fitted model coefficients β to identify how each of the observed variables effects the response variable. For our data we will model a given label y_i with respect to the observations x and the remaining labels y_{-i}. The coefficients of the analytical model β show which of the elements of x and y_{-i} are associated to y_i. If a coefficient β_i is found to be 0, we then assume that there is no association between the associated covariate and the response.

Problem: Multicollinearity. Unfortunately, the correlation between labels, that we use to improve the accuracy of predictions of a multi-label model, cause problems when analysing the coefficients of the analytical models. Multicollinearity occurs when two or more dependent variables are linearly related, and therefore, the analytical model can use different linear combinations of each variable to obtain the same model accuracy. In our case, we have the response label y_i in which we want to determine its relationship to the observed variables x and the remaining labels y_{-i}.

$$y_i = f(x, y_{-i}; \beta_i) \tag{1}$$

If we believe that another label y_j is also dependent on x, we get the relationships

$$y_i = f(x, y_j, y_{-(ij)}; \beta_i), \qquad y_j = f(x; \beta_j) \tag{2}$$

where $\boldsymbol{y}_{-(ij)}$ is the set of labels $\boldsymbol{y}$ excluding the labels y_i and y_j. If the above relationships hold, do we then conclude that the label y_i is dependent on y_j, or do we conclude that it is not dependent on y_j but dependent on $\boldsymbol{x}$, since y_j is dependent on $\boldsymbol{x}$? The former will suggest high multi-labelness, while the latter suggests low multi-labelness. Fitting a model to data containing the above relationships will provide a fit, but will not reveal the additional information that there may be another preferred fit that is just as suitable. In fact by definition, multi-label data must contain multicollinearity between the $\boldsymbol{x}$ and $\boldsymbol{y}$, otherwise we would not be able to obtain accurate label predictions (the set of labels must be associated to the set of observations).

If multicollinearity effects all multi-label models, we must ask how it effects the fit of analytical models and the measurement of multi-labelness, and what we can do to control it. In the next sections, we will investigate the effects of different forms of regularisation on multi-label analytical models.

3   Analytical Models for Measuring Multi-labelness

Analytical models can be used to gain insight into the associations between each label, which in turn allows us measure the multi-labelness of the data. But as we showed in the previous section, multi-label data suffers from multicollinearity, therefore, there may be many combinations of observation variables and label variables that can provide a good fit to a given label y_i.

Two well known forms of regularisation may be useful in reducing the effect of multicollinearity; the l_2 and l_1 norm. Analytical models provide a set of coefficients $\boldsymbol{\beta}$ that show how much of the variance of the response is explained by each covariate. Given the choice, we would rather the model to show most of the variance to be explained by the observations $\boldsymbol{x}$, but unfortunately regularisation does not take this into account.

In this section, we present two candidates for measuring the multi-labelness of data: an analytical model with regularisation, and we introduce a split model that models each label using the observations before modelling with respect to the other labels.

3.1   Regularisation of Analytical Models

Analytical models (as opposed to predictive models) are fit to data to provide insight into the associations between variables. A common form of analytical model for a binary response is logistic regression.

$$\log\left(\frac{p_i}{1 - p_i}\right) = \boldsymbol{\beta}_i \boldsymbol{x} \tag{3}$$

where $\boldsymbol{x}$ is the vector of observations, $\boldsymbol{\beta}_i$ is the vector of model coefficients and p_i is the probability of the response y_i being positive or negative. Once the model is fit to data, $\boldsymbol{\beta}_i$ is observed to determine which of the elements of $\boldsymbol{x}$ are associated to p_i.

A multi-label analytical model allows us to identify which of the elements of $\boldsymbol{x}$ and labels $\boldsymbol{y}_{-i}$ are associated to label y_i. Using logistic regression, we have:

$$\log\left(\frac{p_i}{1 - p_i}\right) = \boldsymbol{\beta}_{xi}\boldsymbol{x} + \boldsymbol{\beta}_{yi}\boldsymbol{y}_{-i} \tag{4}$$

where $\boldsymbol{\beta}_{xi}$ are the regression coefficients associated to the observations variables, and $\boldsymbol{\beta}_{yi}$ are the coefficients associated to the set of labels excluding the ith label.

Fitting the model to data consists of identifying the coefficients $\boldsymbol{\beta}_{xi}$ and $\boldsymbol{\beta}_{yi}$ that maximise the likelihood function, or equivalently minimise the negative log likelihood function. Regularisation is used to avoid overfitting the model, by penalising the likelihood, leading to lower model variance, but introducing a bias. Common forms of regularisation are l_1 and l_2 norm regularisation, giving the loss functions:

$$l_1 : \quad \lambda\|[\boldsymbol{\beta}_{xi} \ \boldsymbol{\beta}_{yi}]\|_1 - \mathcal{L}([\boldsymbol{\beta}_{xi} \ \boldsymbol{\beta}_{yi}]; [\boldsymbol{x} \ \boldsymbol{y}_{-i}], y_i)$$

$$l_2 : \quad \lambda\|[\boldsymbol{\beta}_{xi} \ \boldsymbol{\beta}_{yi}]\|_2 - \mathcal{L}([\boldsymbol{\beta}_{xi} \ \boldsymbol{\beta}_{yi}]; [\boldsymbol{x} \ \boldsymbol{y}_{-i}], y_i)$$

$$l_1 + l_2 : \quad \lambda(\|[\boldsymbol{\beta}_{xi} \ \boldsymbol{\beta}_{yi}]\|_1 + \|[\boldsymbol{\beta}_{xi} \ \boldsymbol{\beta}_{yi}]\|_2) - \mathcal{L}([\boldsymbol{\beta}_{xi} \ \boldsymbol{\beta}_{yi}]; [\boldsymbol{x} \ \boldsymbol{y}_{-i}], y_i)$$

where $\mathcal{L}([\boldsymbol{\beta}_{xi} \ \boldsymbol{\beta}_{yi}]; [\boldsymbol{x} \ \boldsymbol{y}_{-i}], y_i)$ is the log likelihood of the logistic regression model of label y_i with coefficients $\boldsymbol{\beta}_{xi}$ and $\boldsymbol{\beta}_{yi}$, $\|\boldsymbol{\beta}\|_1$ is the l_1 norm of $\boldsymbol{\beta}$, $\|\boldsymbol{\beta}\|_2$ is the l_2 norm, and λ is estimated using cross validation.

The l_2 norm induces bias in the coefficients $\boldsymbol{\beta}$ in an attempt to obtain a more robust set of coefficients that generalise to new data, but in the process, usually provides relationships between all variables. The l_1 norm induces bias in the coefficients to act as a variable selector, but is usually highly unstable when faced with multicollinearity. The combined $l_1 + l_2$ norm usually provides robustness and variable selection [9].

Multicollinearity in the data means that the l_1 regularisation might lead to different non-zero coefficients for a new sample. As a simple example, consider the case where all labels y_i are functions of $\boldsymbol{x}$, independent of the other y_j. Ideally, l_1 regularisation should provide zero to all coefficients of $\boldsymbol{\beta}_{yi}$, but the multicollinearity might lead to non-zero coefficient in $\boldsymbol{\beta}_{yi}$ in place of some from $\boldsymbol{\beta}_{xi}$.

3.2 Split Analytical Model

To measure the multi-labelness of data, a multi-label analytical model is used (such as logistic regression), and the label coefficients of the model are observed. We have stated that multi-label analytical models might provide superfluous inter-label relationships due to the multicollinearity of the multi-label data.

Rather than treating each observation $\boldsymbol{x}_j$ and labels $\boldsymbol{y}_{-ij}$ equally where j is the observation id, we propose that the model should first fit the variables $\boldsymbol{x}_j$ and then fit any residual variance to $\boldsymbol{y}_{-ij}$.

$$\text{logit}(p_{ij}) = \boldsymbol{\beta}_{xi}\boldsymbol{x}_j + \epsilon_{ij}$$

$$\epsilon_{ij} = \boldsymbol{\beta}_{yi}\boldsymbol{y}_{-ij} + \eta_{ij}$$

where p_{ij} is the probability of label i given $\boldsymbol{x}_j$, ϵ_{ij} is the residual of the ith label and jth observation after fitting the model using only the observations, and η_{ij} is the residual from fitting the labels to the residual from the previous model. This will force the multi-label model to not provide inter-label dependencies that could be explained with $\boldsymbol{x}_j$, due to the multicollinearity of the variables. We hypothesise that this split analytical model will provide a lower number of non-zero label coefficients $\boldsymbol{\beta}_{yi}$, since the model is forced to find associations between y_i and $\boldsymbol{x}$ first, hence providing a better measurement of multi-labelness.

The model residual cannot be measured from logistic regression in the model space, since the true label value of 0 or 1 is mapped to $-\infty$ or $+\infty$. Therefore we keep the model in the logistic space and instead supply an model offset z_{ij} for each label i and observation j.

$$\text{logit}(p_{ij}) = z_{ij} + \boldsymbol{\beta}_{yi}\boldsymbol{y}_{-ij} + \eta_{ij} \text{ where } z_{ij} = \boldsymbol{\beta}_{xi}\boldsymbol{x}_j$$

To generalise the model, we also add regularisation to each stage of the model, providing us with the fitting process:

$$\text{Stage 1: } \underset{\boldsymbol{\beta}_x}{\arg\min} \left(\lambda_x \|\boldsymbol{\beta}_x\|_m - \mathcal{L}(\boldsymbol{\beta}_x | \boldsymbol{x}, y_i) \right) \tag{5}$$

$$\text{Stage 2: } \underset{\boldsymbol{\beta}_y}{\arg\min} \left(\lambda_y \|\boldsymbol{\beta}_y\|_n - \mathcal{L}(\boldsymbol{\beta}_y | \boldsymbol{y}_{-i}, y_i, z_i) \right)$$

where m and n are either 1 or 2 (for l_1 or l_2 regularisation), $\mathcal{L}(\boldsymbol{\beta}_y | \boldsymbol{y}_{-i}, y_i, z_i)$ is the logistic regression log likelihood function using offset z_i for each observation, and λ_x and λ_y are estimated using cross validation.

4   Analysis of Full and Split Analytical Models

A full and split analytical model were presented in the previous section. In this section we devise an experiment to deduce where each form of model is most effective at measuring multi-labelness (identifying the number of inter-label relationships) of multi-label data, with minimum superfluous relationships.

4.1   Measuring Multi-labelness

Recall that multi-labelness is the number of inter-label relationships. The usual procedure for determining if an observation variable is associated to the response variable is to examine the standard error of the fitted regression coefficient, and assess if it provides evidence against the true coefficient being zero. Unfortunately, regularisation induces bias into the regression coefficient estimates $\boldsymbol{\beta}$, therefore the coefficient standard error is not as useful[1]. To determine significance we must compute the confidence interval for each coefficient. But, reporting

---

[1] Section 6 of https://cran.r-project.org/web/packages/penalized/vignettes/ penalized.pdf.

the interval of each coefficient would ignore any association between coefficients (treating them as independent), and be misleading.

We want to determine which form of regularisation provides an analytical model with a good fit to the data, and showing the least dependence between each label to the regression label. We are not concerned with the association between the observations x and the response label; our goal is to determine which form of regularisation provides the least label interdependence.

We are also not concerned with which labels are associated to the response. We stated that we cannot show causality, and that multicollinearity exists, so are unable to determine the true associations. The best we can do is to assess which form of regression provides the least inter-dependence between labels, while providing a good fit. Therefore, we measure multi-labelness as the *number of non-zero label coefficients* of the analytical model. The lower the number, the fewer relationships have been established between labels (meaning that more association has been found to the observations x) leading to lower complexity models.

4.2   Generating Multi-label Data

To assess the measurement of multi-labelness of different data structures from a given analytical model, we need to know the true underlying model form that generated the data. Unfortunately, we do not know the underlying model that was used to generate existing real multi-label data sets, therefore, if using them, we will not be able to determine what about the data is effecting the fit.

Therefore, we are required to simulate multi-label data using strategically designed multi-label data models, where the models exhibit the characteristics that we want to test, but remain simple in order to reduce the chance of other effects being introduced. We present ten multi-label data models, all using three observation variables and three label variables. Each data model consists of three observation variables $x_1, x_2, x_3 \in [-1, 1]$ which are independent, and all Bernoulli, with $p = 0.5$, and three response labels $y_1, y_2, y_3 \in [-1, 1]$. The models differ in the dependence of the response labels, and use the Model Factor a associated to the likelihood of the model (larger a leads to data that provides higher likelihood). The ten models are:

OneXOneY $\text{logit}(y_i) = ax_i \forall i$. All y_i depend on only one x_i. A multi-label model should find no interdependence between the labels. The non-zero label coefficient count should be 0.

ManyXOneY $\text{logit}(y_i) = ax_1/3 + ax_2/3 + ax_3/3 \forall i$. All y_i depend on every x_i. A multi-label model should find no interdependence between the labels. The non-zero label coefficient count should be 0.

OneXChainY $\text{logit}(y_1) = ax_1, \text{logit}(y_2) = ay_1, \text{logit}(y_3) = ay_2$. The first label y_1 depends on one observation variable x_1, the second label depends on the first and the third depends on the second. The non-zero label coefficient count should be 2.

ManyXChainY $\text{logit}(y_1) = ax_1/3 + ax_2/3 + ax_3/3, \text{logit}(y_2) = ay_1, \text{logit}(y_3) = ay_2$. The same as OneXChainY, but the first label depends on all observed variables x_i. The non-zero label coefficient count should be 2.

OneXPartitionY $\text{logit}(y_1) = ax_1, \text{logit}(y_2) = ay_1, \text{logit}(y_3) = ax_1$. The first and third labels depend on an observed variable x_1 and the second label depends on the first label. The non-zero label coefficient count should be 1.

ManyXPartitionY $\text{logit}(y_1) = ax_1/3 + ax_2/3 + ax_3/3, \text{logit}(y_2) = ay_1,$ $\text{logit}(y_3) = ax_1/3 + ax_2/3 + ax_3/3$. The same as OneXPartitionY, but the first and third labels depend on all observed variables x_i. The non-zero label coefficient count should be 1.

OneXTreeY $\text{logit}(y_1) = ax_1, \text{logit}(y_2) = ay_1, \text{logit}(y_3) = ay_1$. The first label depends on an observed variable, the second and third labels depend on the first label. The non-zero label coefficient count should be 2.

ManyXTreeY $\text{logit}(y_1) = ax_1/3 + ax_2/3 + ax_3/3, \text{logit}(y_2) = ay_1, \text{logit}(y_3) = ay_1$. The same as OneXTreeY, but the first label depends on all observed variables. The non-zero label coefficient count should be 2.

OneXFanY $\text{logit}(y_1) = ax_1, \text{logit}(y_2) = ay_1, \text{logit}(y_3) = ay_1/2 + ay_2/2$. The first label depends on an observed variable, the second label depend on the first label, and the third label depends on the second and first labels. The non-zero label coefficient count should be 3.

ManyXFanY $\text{logit}(y_1) = ax_1/3 + ax_2/3 + ax_3/3, \text{logit}(y_2) = ay_1, \text{logit}(y_3) = ay_1/2 + ay_2/2$. The same as OneXFanY, but the first label depends on all observed variables.

The dependencies of each model are shown in Fig. 1. These 10 data models contain a set of simple relationships that we would expect to find in multi-label data. We will generate data using these known models and examine how the analytical models measure their multi-labelness.

For this investigation, we generated 100 training and 100 testing data sets for each of the above ten data types using Model Factors $a = 0.1, 0.5, 1$ and 2, providing 4000 training and 4000 testing sets. The data was generated by sampling from the models using the model probabilities. We can see that as a increases, the probability of each label is likely to increase in magnitude, so the resulting data sample will have less variance.

In the following sections we will fit this generated data using logistic regression with regularisation, and examine how the regularisation effects the coefficients of the model.

4.3 Investigation: Full Model with l_1 and l_2 Regularisation

To begin our investigation, we examine the effect of l_1 (lasso regularisation), l_2 (ridge regularisation) and a combination of l_1 and l_2 (elastic net regularisation) regularisation.

To examine how well each analytical model is able to fit the data from each data model, we fitted the analytical model to the generated data and counted the number of non-zero coefficients associated to labels, from the fit. Since there

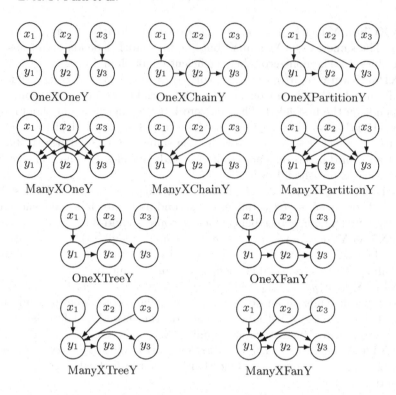

Fig. 1. Dependencies of the 10 data models used for simulation.

are three labels in each data set, each can have association to zero, one or two other labels, providing a range of zero to six non-zero coefficients for the three fitted labels. The results are shown in Fig. 2.

Figure 2 provides one plot for each data model type. Each plot contains sets of box plots for model factors 0.1, 0.5, 1 and 2, and each set of box plots contains three box plots of the non-zero label coefficient count for the three forms of regularisation over the 100 replications. As expected, l_2 regularisation provides all six of the label coefficients as non-zero. We can also see that l_1 provides either an equivalent or fewer number of non-zero label coefficients compared to $l_1 + l_2$. But we also find that each of these forms of regularisation provide non-zero label coefficients for the OneXOneY and ManyXOneY data, in which there is no interdependence on the labels. Therefore, using l_1, l_2 or a mixture will suggest that label dependencies exist, when in fact they do not.

4.4 Investigation: Split Model with l_1 and l_2 Regularisation

In this section, we will examine the effect of the two stage analytical model from Sect. 3.2 to try to force the dependence of y_i towards the observations x, and then fit the remaining label variance to the labels y_{-i}. The two stages of the split

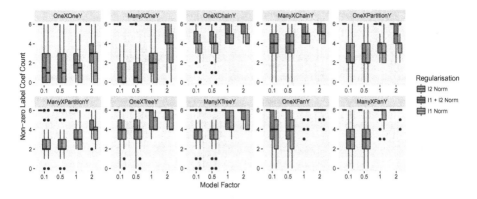

Fig. 2. The distribution of the number of non-zero label coefficients for $l_1, l_1 + l_2$ and l_2 regularisation, on each data type, using Model Factors 0.1, 0.5, 1, and 2.

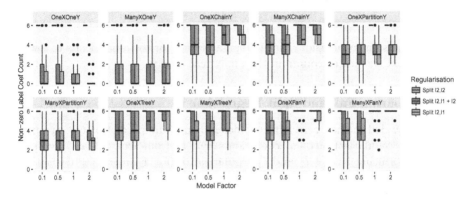

Fig. 3. The distribution of the number of non-zero label coefficients for split regularisation (l_2 for observed variables and $l_1, l_1 + l_2$ and l_2 for labels), on each data type, using Model Factors 0.1, 0.5, 1, and 2.

model from Eq. 5 require two norms to be set. We used the data from Sect. 4.2 to obtain results when each of m and n are 1 or 2. The results are shown in Figs. 3, 4 and 5.

Figure 3 provides box plots for the number of non-zero label coefficients using l_2 regularisation for the x variables and a selection of l_2, l_1 and $l_1 + l_2$ regularisation for the labels y_i. We find again that l_2 always provides 6 non-zero coefficients, and that l_1 provides either equivalent or fewer labels than $l_1 + l_2$. We also find that the median non-zero label coefficient count is 0 for l_1 and $l_1 + l_2$ regularisation for the OneXOneY and ManyXOneY data structures, showing that the split regularisation has had an impact in removing non-existent label inter-dependencies.

Figures 4 and 5 provide the non-zero label coefficient count when using the $l_1 + l_2$ regularisation for x and l_1 regularisation for x respectively. These results

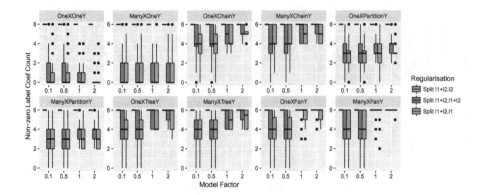

Fig. 4. The distribution of the number of non-zero label coefficients for split regularisation ($l + 1 + l_2$ for observed variables and $l_1, l_1 + l_2$ and l_2 for labels), on each data type, using Model Factors 0.1, 0.5, 1, and 2.

lead us to the same conclusion, that l_1 regularisation for the labels leads to lower non-zero label coefficient counts in the analytical models.

4.5 Comparing Full and Split Regression

We have provided the non-zero label coefficient count and prediction error results from using l_1 regularisation on all coefficients (Full l_1, from Sect. 4.3) and the split model results using $l_1, l_1 + l_2$ and l_2 regularisation for $\boldsymbol{x}$ and l_1 regularisation for $\boldsymbol{y}_{-i}$ in Figs. 6 and 7 (comparing the best forms of regularisation from the previous results).

Figure 6 shows that the split models provide a lower distribution (shifted towards zero) of non-zero label coefficients compared to the Full model for OneX-OneY, ManyXManyY, and for OneXPartitionY, ManyXPartitionY when the Model Factor (a) is high. For all other data models, the Full l_1 model provides an equivalent or fewer non-zero label coefficients.

The accuracy results in Fig. 7 provides the mean absolute error between the predicted label probability and the true label probability (from the model). We find that each analytical model provides equivalent accuracy, but there are a few occurrences (from the Fan, Tree and Chain data structures) of the Full l_1 model providing lower error when the Model factor (a) is 1 or 2.

The mean number of non-zero label coefficients for each regularisation method on each data type in Fig. 6 are shown in Table 1. We find that the split regularisation provided significantly fewer non-zero label coefficients for the data where there was no inter-label dependencies (OneXOneY and ManyXOneY) and the partitioned labels (OneXPartY and ManyXPartY), but provided more non-zero coefficients for the Chain, Tree and Fan data. This suggests that the Split models are useful when no label relationships exists, otherwise the Full model should be used for measuring multi-labelness.

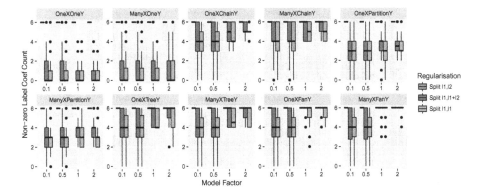

Fig. 5. The distribution of the number of non-zero label coefficients for split regularisation (l_1 for observed variables and $l_1, l_1 + l_2$ and l_2 for labels), on each data type, using Model Factors 0.1, 0.5, 1, and 2.

5   Full and Split Analytical Models on Real Data

In this section, we examine the effect of regularisation on the non-zero label coefficient proportion from five commonly used multi-label data sets. We assume that there is dependence amongst the labels in each of the data sets, due to their use in multi-label classification research.

We use the Emotions, Stare, Scene, Slashdot, and Enron multi-label data sets[2]. A 50/50 train/test split is used, and the regularisation parameters λ, λ_x and λ_y were fit using 10 fold cross validation on the training data. The models are then used to examine the effect of regularisation and the classification accuracy using the testing set. The mean non-zero label coefficient proportion for each label is reported, representing the detected number of relationships between labels. The accuracy is measured in terms of mean Hamming similarity (proportion of correctly predicted labels), Jaccard similarity (ratio of true positive count and 1 - true negative count) and Exact similarity (score 1 if all labels are correct, otherwise score 0) of the predicted label state compared to the true label state, computed over the set of test observations. Note that each model is a function of x and y_{-i}, therefore, we have provided two accuracy scores for each regularisation method for each metric, providing an evaluation interval. The lower score is computed using label estimates $\hat{y}_{-i}$ from an independent model (predicting each label based on the observations x alone, not using other label information). The upper score is computed using the true label values y_{-i}. The results are presented in Table 2.

---

[2] All available from http://mulan.sourceforge.net/datasets-mlc.html, https://sourceforge.net/projects/meka/files/Datasets/ (Slashdot), and http://cecas.clemson.edu/~ahoover/stare/ (Stare).

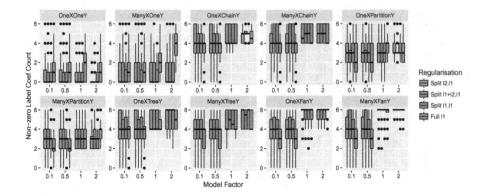

Fig. 6. The distribution of the number of non-zero label coefficients for split regularisation $(l_1, l_1 + l_2$ and l_2 for observed variables and l_1 for labels) and full l_1 regularisation, on each data type, using Model Factors 0.1, 0.5, 1, and 2.

5.1   Label Interdependence

We first examine the non-zero label coefficient proportion in Table 2 to determine which form of analytical model provides the most appropriate measure of multi-labelness. We find that using Full l_1 regularisation provides the lowest proportion over all but the Emotions data set, where it is close to the minimum. This is consistent with the simulated results, assuming that each of the multi-label data sets have no independent sets of labels. Calculating the maximum likelihood score for each data set also reveals that they all are most similar to the generated data where $a = 0.1$, further reinforcing the results from the generated data.

5.2   Effect of Label-Interdependence Reduction on Accuracy

We next assess the accuracy of the model to determine if the smaller number of label relationships is due to the model making better use of the observations $\boldsymbol{x}$ (meaning that the number of non-zero label coefficients is smaller, but the accuracy is not lower), or it is simply due to a poorer use of the label set $\boldsymbol{y}_{-i}$ (meaning that the number of non-zero label coefficients is smaller, and the accuracy is lower).

The accuracy of each regularised analytical model is provided as two scores; the first when using estimates of the label state (from an independent model), and the second when using the true labels. The second score provides us with a measure of the accuracy of the analytical model, the first score gives us an indication of the effect when using computed label relationships.

Most of the split models provide significantly greater upper scores. Examining the lower scores, we find that many of the Split score are significantly worse than the Full l_1 score. This suggests that the Full l_1 provides a good base set of label relationships and that further relationships can be found using Split regularisation, but they are only useful when obtaining accurate label estimates. These results align with those from the simulation; where the labels are

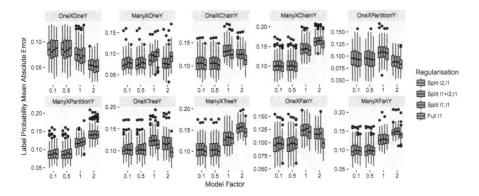

Fig. 7. The distribution of mean absolute error of the label probability and predicted probability for split regularisation ($l_1, l_1 + l_2$ and l_2 for observed variables and l_1 for labels) and full l_1 regularisation, on each data type, using Model Factors 0.1, 0.5, 1, and 2.

associated, Full l_1 provided the least number of non-zero label coefficients with equivalent accuracy to the other forms of regularisation.

These experiments conducted on both the generated and real data lead to the same conclusion, that a split analytical model provides a better measure of multi-labelness when the labels are all independent, or when they can be partitioned into models with high likelihood. Otherwise, using the full model with l_1 regularisation provides a better measure of multi-labelness. Analysing the results has shown that the regularisation has a major impact for the split model; it is shared for the observations and labels in the full model, but not for the split model. We will investigate this impact in future work.

Table 1. The mean number of non-zero label coefficients for each regularisation methods and each data type. A star (*) represents a significant difference to the Full l_1 regularisation using a paired Wilcoxon test.

Reg	OneXOneY	ManyXOneY	OneXChainY	ManyXChainY	OneXPartY
Full l_1	1.55	1.84	4.24	4.31	2.98
Split l_2,l_1	0.47*	0.82*	4.59*	4.55*	2.81*
Split $l_1 + l_2,l_1$	0.62*	0.80*	4.53*	4.51*	2.86*
Split l_1,l_1	0.59*	0.76*	4.55*	4.51*	2.77*

Reg	ManyXPartY	OneXTreeY	ManyXTreeY	OneXFanY	ManyXFanY
Full l_1	3.01	4.26	4.06	4.74	4.47
Split l_2,l_1	2.66*	4.62*	4.51*	4.78	4.67*
Split $l_1 + l_2,l_1$	2.69*	4.62*	4.53*	4.84*	4.74*
Split l_1,l_1	2.72*	4.62*	4.42*	4.83	4.67*

Table 2. Measurement of Hamming, Jaccard and Exact accuracy, and the average number of non-zero label coefficients for five commonly used multi-label data sets. Each cell contains the score when using label estimates $\hat{y}_i$ for prediction, and the true labels y_i for prediction. An asterisk (*) shows a significant difference of each Split method compared to Full l_1.

	Accuracy			Non-zero coefficients
	Hamming	Jaccard	Exact	
Emotions (5 labels)				
Full l_2	0.765, 0.822	0.508, 0.560	0.251, 0.309	1
Full $l_1 + l_2$	0.762, 0.828	0.533, 0.598	0.242, 0.358	0.866
Full l_1	0.746, 0.835	0.527, 0.622	0.222, 0.373	0.832
Split l_1, l_1	0.764*, 0.842	0.551*, 0.611	0.248, 0.349	0.8
Split l_2, l_1	0.748, 0.834	0.548*, 0.600	0.227, 0.344	0.832
Split $l_1 + l_2, l_1$	0.757, 0.838	0.551*, 0.608	0.239, 0.358	0.832
Stare (12 labels)				
Full l_2	0.920, 0.951	0.539, 0.596	0.410, 0.537	1
Full $l_1 + l_2$	0.907, 0.947	0.509, 0.577	0.364, 0.520	0.538
Full l_1	0.896, 0.945	0.495, 0.600	0.335, 0.531	0.461
Split l_1, l_1	0.864*, 0.954*	0.488*, 0.679*	0.335, 0.618*	0.872
Split l_2, l_1	0.860, 0.955*	0.471*, 0.676*	0.324, 0.624*	0.891
Split $l_1 + l_2, l_1$	0.874, 0.956*	0.497*, 0.684*	0.341, 0.635*	0.872
Scene (5 labels)				
Full l_2	0.894, 0.947	0.684, 0.789	0.579, 0.740	1
Full $l_1 + l_2$	0.834, 0.971	0.647, 0.904	0.528, 0.869	1
Full l_1	0.774, 0.976	0.616, 0.927	0.522, 0.903	1
Split l_1, l_1	0.749*, 0.975	0.613*, 0.926	0.523, 0.892*	1
Split l_2, l_1	0.746*, 0.976	0.611*, 0.928	0.523, 0.899	1
Split $l_1 + l_2, l_1$	0.745*, 0.976	0.613*, 0.927	0.525, 0.897	1
Slashdot (18 labels)				
Full l_2	0.956, 0.957	0.407, 0.403	0.367, 0.369	1
Full $l_1 + l_2$	0.947, 0.963	0.490, 0.523	0.397, 0.472	0.462
Full l_1	0.904, 0.969	0.463, 0.623	0.331, 0.570	0.424
Split l_1, l_1	0.857*, 0.976*	0.454, 0.736*	0.323*, 0.676*	0.886
Split l_2, l_1	0.907, 0.972*	0.483*, 0.652*	0.333, 0.612*	0.801
Split $l_1 + l_2, l_1$	0.835*, 0.976*	0.443*, 0.741*	0.324, 0.682*	0.848
Enron (47 labels)				
Full l_2	0.945, 0.948	0.200, 0.229	0.001, 0.001	1
Full $l_1 + l_2$	0.937, 0.957	0.318, 0.483	0.117, 0.195	0.210
Full l_1	0.929, 0.957	0.275, 0.482	0.013, 0.198	0.153
Split l_1, l_1	0.915*, 0.956	0.243*, 0.491	0.004, 0.200	0.315
Split l_2, l_1	0.898*, 0.963*	0.251*, 0.590*	0.001*, 0.289*	0.326
Split $l_1 + l_2, l_1$	0.917*, 0.957	0.247*, 0.502*	0.003*, 0.203	0.318

6   Conclusion

Examining the relationships between labels in multi-label data before constructing a multi-label classifier, provides us with insight as to how to design the classifier. Measuring the multi-labelness of the data (the number of relationships between labels) allows us to determine if a multi-label classifier is appropriate for the data.

Multi-labelness of data cannot simply be measured using the correlation between labels, since the label relationships are confounded by the data observations. Fitting an analytical model to a label with respect to the other labels and observations can also present false label relationships due to multicollinearity between the labels and observations.

We investigated the effect of using a full model and proposed a new split analytical model to minimise the number of spurious relationships and measure the multi-labelness of data. We examined l_1, l_2, and combined l_1 and l_2 regularisation with each of the full and split models. It was found that split analytical models using regularisation have a greater likelihood of detecting independence of labels. But if labels are not independent from each other, a full model using l_1 regularisation provides the fewest dependencies between labels making it more suitable for measuring the multi-labelness of data.

References

1. Guo, Y., Gu, S.: Multi-label classification using conditional dependency networks. In: IJCAI Proceedings-International Joint Conference on Artificial Intelligence, vol. 22, p. 1300 (2011)
2. Osojnik, A., Panov, P., Džeroski, S.: Multi-label classification via multi-target regression on data streams. Mach. Learn. **106**(6), 745–770 (2016). https://doi.org/10.1007/s10994-016-5613-5
3. Park, L.A.F., Read, J.: A blended metric for multi-label optimisation and evaluation. In: Berlingerio, M., Bonchi, F., Gärtner, T., Hurley, N., Ifrim, G. (eds.) ECML PKDD 2018. LNCS (LNAI), vol. 11051, pp. 719–734. Springer, Cham (2019). https://doi.org/10.1007/978-3-030-10925-7_44
4. Park, L.A.F., Simoff, S.: Using entropy as a measure of acceptance for multi-label classification. In: Fromont, E., De Bie, T., van Leeuwen, M. (eds.) IDA 2015. LNCS, vol. 9385, pp. 217–228. Springer, Cham (2015). https://doi.org/10.1007/978-3-319-24465-5_19
5. Read, J., Pfahringer, B., Holmes, G., Frank, E.: Classifier chains for multi-label classification. Mach. Learn. **85**(3), 333 (2011). https://doi.org/10.1007/s10994-011-5256-5
6. Sucar, L.E., Bielza, C., Morales, E.F., Hernandez-Leal, P., Zaragoza, J.H., Larrañaga, P.: Multi-label classification with Bayesian network-based chain classifiers. Pattern Recogn. Lett. **41**, 14–22 (2014)
7. Zhang, M.L., Zhou, Z.H.: A review on multi-label learning algorithms. IEEE Trans. Knowl. Data Eng. **26**(8), 1819–1837 (2014)
8. Zhang, M.-L., Zhang, K.: Multi-label learning by exploiting label dependency. In: Proceedings of the 16th ACM SIGKDD International Conference on Knowledge Discovery and Data Mining, pp. 999–1008. ACM (2010)
9. Zou, H., Hastie, T.: Regularization and variable selection via the elastic net. J. R. Stat. Soc.: Ser. B (Stat. Methodol.) **67**(2), 301–320 (2005)

Synthetic Oversampling of Multi-label Data Based on Local Label Distribution

Bin Liu[✉] and Grigorios Tsoumakas

School of Informatics, Aristotle University of Thessaloniki,
54124 Thessaloniki, Greece
{binliu,greg}@csd.auth.gr

Abstract. Class-imbalance is an inherent characteristic of multi-label data which affects the prediction accuracy of most multi-label learning methods. One efficient strategy to deal with this problem is to employ resampling techniques before training the classifier. Existing multi-label sampling methods alleviate the (global) imbalance of multi-label datasets. However, performance degradation is mainly due to rare sub-concepts and overlapping of classes that could be analysed by looking at the local characteristics of the minority examples, rather than the imbalance of the whole dataset. We propose a new method for synthetic oversampling of multi-label data that focuses on local label distribution to generate more diverse and better labeled instances. Experimental results on 13 multi-label datasets demonstrate the effectiveness of the proposed approach in a variety of evaluation measures, particularly in the case of an ensemble of classifiers trained on repeated samples of the original data.

Keywords: Multi-label learning · Class-imbalance · Synthetic oversampling · Local label distribution · Ensemble methods

1 Introduction

In multi-label data, each example is typically associated with a small number of labels, much smaller than the total number of labels. This results in a sparse label matrix, where a small total number of positive class values is shared by a much larger number of example-label pairs. From the viewpoint of each separate label, this gives rise to class imbalance, which has been recently recognized as a key challenge in multi-label learning [6,7,11,18,31].

Approaches for handling class imbalance in multi-label data can be divided into two categories: (a) reducing the imbalance level of multi-label data via resampling techniques, including synthetic data generation [5–8], and (b) making multi-label learning methods resilient to class imbalance [11,18,31]. This work focuses on the first category, whose approaches can be coupled with any multi-label learning method and are therefore more flexible.

Existing resampling approaches for multi-label data focus on class imbalance at the global scale of the whole dataset. However, previous studies of class

© Springer Nature Switzerland AG 2020
U. Brefeld et al. (Eds.): ECML PKDD 2019, LNAI 11907, pp. 180–193, 2020.
https://doi.org/10.1007/978-3-030-46147-8_11

imbalance in binary and multi-class classification [19,20] have found that the distribution of class values in the local neighbourhood of minority examples, rather than the global imbalance level, is the main reason for the difficulty of a classifier to recognize the minority class. We hypothesize that this finding is also true, and even more important to consider, in the more complex setting of multi-label data, where it has not been examined yet.

Consider for example the 2-dimensional multi-label datasets (a) and (b) in Fig. 1 concerning points in a plane. The points are characterized by three labels, concerning the shape of the points (triangles, circles), the border of the points (solid, none) and the color of the points (green, red). These datasets have the same level of label imbalance. Yet (b) appears much more challenging due to the presence of sub-concepts for the triangles and the points without border and the overlap of the green and red points as well as the points with solid and no border.

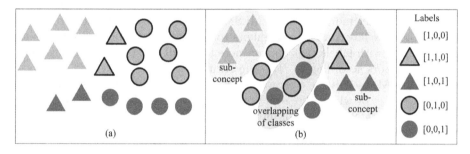

Fig. 1. Two 2-dimensional multi-label datasets (a) and (b) concerning points in a plane characterized by three labels. On the right we see the five different label combinations that exist in the datasets. (Color figure online)

This work proposes a novel multi-label synthetic oversampling method, named MLSOL, whose seed instance selection and synthetic instance generation processes depend on the local distribution of the labels. This allows MLSOL to create more diverse and better labelled synthetic instances. Furthermore, we consider the coupling of MLSOL and other resampling methods with a simple but flexible ensemble framework to further improve its performance and robustness. Experimental results on 13 multi-label datasets demonstrate the effectiveness of the proposed sampling approach, especially its ensemble version, for three different imbalance-aware evaluation metrics and six different multi-label methods.

The remainder of this paper is organized as follows. Section 2 offers a brief review of methods for addressing class imbalance in multi-label data. Then, our approach is introduced in Sect. 3. Section 4 presents and discusses the experimental results. Finally, Sect. 5 summarizes the main contributions of this work.

2   Related Work

A first approach to dealing with class imbalance in the context of multi-label data is to utilize the resampling technique, which is applied in a pre-processing step and is independent of the particular multi-label learning algorithm that will be subsequently applied to the data. LP-RUS and LP-ROS are two twin sampling methods, of which the former removes instances assigned with the most frequent labelset (i.e. particular combination of label values) and the latter replicates instances whose labelset appears the fewest times [4].

Instead of considering whole labelset, several sampling methods alleviate the imbalance of the dataset in the individual label aspect, i.e. increasing the frequency of minority labels and reducing the number of appearances of majority labels. ML-RUS and ML-ROS simply delete instances with majority labels and clone examples with minority labels, respectively [7]. MLeNN eliminates instances only with majority labels and similar labelset of its neighbors in a heuristic way based on the Edited Nearest Neighbor (ENN) rule [5]. To make a multi-label dataset more balanced, MLSMOTE randomly selects instance containing minority labels and its neighbors to generate synthetic instances which are associated with labels that appear more that half times of the seed instance and its neighbors according to *Ranking* strategy [6].

REMEDIAL tackles the concurrence of labels with different imbalance level in one instance, of which the level is assessed by *SCUMBLE*, by decomposing the sophisticated instance of into two simpler examples, but may introduce extra confusions into the learning task, i.e. there are several pairs of instances with same features and disparate labels [8]. The REMEDIAL could be either a standalone sampling method or the prior part of other sampling techniques, i.e. RHwRSMT combines REMEDIAL with MLSMOTE [9].

Apart from resampling methods, another group of approaches focuses on multi-label learning method handling the class-imbalance problem directly. Some methods deal with the imbalance issue of multi-label learning via transforming the multi-label dataset to several binary/multi-class classification problems. COCOA converts the original multi-label dataset to one binary dataset and several multi-class datasets for each label, and builds imbalance classifiers with the assistance of sampling for each dataset [31]. SOSHF transforms the multi-label learning task to an imbalanced single label classification assignment via cost-sensitive clustering, and the new task is addressed by oblique structured Hellinger decision trees [11]. Besides, many approaches aims to modify current multi-label learning methods to handle class-imbalance problem. ECCRU3 extends the ECC resilient to class imbalance by coupling undersampling and improving of the exploitation of majority examples [18]. Apart from ECCRU3, the modified models based on neural network [16,23,26], SVM [3], hypernetwork [24] and BR [10,12,25,28] have been proposed as well. Furthermore, other strategies, such as representation learning [17], constrained submodular minimization [29] and balanced pseudo-label [30], have been utilized to address the imbalance obstacle of multi-label learning as well.

3   Our Approach

We start by introducing our mathematical notation. Let $\mathcal{X} = \mathbb{R}^d$ be a d-dimensional input feature space, $L = \{l_1, l_2, ..., l_q\}$ a label set containing q labels and $\mathcal{Y} = \{0, 1\}^q$ a q-dimensional label space. $D = \{(\boldsymbol{x}_i, \boldsymbol{y}_i) | 1 \leqslant i \leqslant n\}$ is a multi-label training data set containing n instances. Each instance $(\boldsymbol{x}_i, \boldsymbol{y}_i)$ consists of a feature vector $\boldsymbol{x}_i \in \mathcal{X}$ and a label vector $\boldsymbol{y}_i \in \mathcal{Y}$, where y_{ij} is the j-th element of $\boldsymbol{y}_i$ and $y_{ij} = 1(0)$ denotes that l_j is (not) associated with i-th instance. A multi-label method learns the mapping function $h : \mathcal{X} \to \{0, 1\}^q$ and (or) $f : \mathcal{X} \to \mathbb{R}^q$ from D that given an unseen instance $\boldsymbol{x}$, outputs a label vector $\hat{\boldsymbol{y}}$ with the predicted labels of and (or) real-valued vector $\hat{\boldsymbol{f}}\boldsymbol{y}$ corresponding relevance degrees to $\boldsymbol{x}$ respectively.

We propose a novel Multi-Label Synthetic Oversampling approach based on the Local distribution of labels (MLSOL). The pseudo-code of MLSOL is shown in Algorithm 1. Firstly, some auxiliary variables, as the weight vector $\boldsymbol{w}$ and type matrix $\boldsymbol{T}$ used for seed instance selection and synthetic examples generation respectively, are calculated based on the local label distribution of instances (line 3–6 in Algorithm 1). Then in each iteration, the seed and reference instances are selected, upon which a synthetic example is generated and added into the dataset. The loop (line 7–12 in Algorithm 1) would terminate when expected number of new examples are created. The following subsections detail the definition of auxiliaries as well as strategies to pick seed instances and create synthetic examples.

Algorithm 1: MLSOL

---

input : multi-label data set: D, percentage of instances to generated: P,
         number of nearest neighbour: k
output: new data set D'

1 $GenNum \leftarrow |D| * P$;   /* number of instances to generate */
2 $D' \leftarrow D$;
3 Find the kNN of each instance ;
4 Calculate C according to Eq.(1) ;
5 Compute $\boldsymbol{w}$ according to Eq.(3) ;
6 $T \leftarrow \texttt{InitTypes}(C, k)$;   /* Initialize the type of instances */
7 **while** $GenNum > 0$ **do**
8   Select a seed instance $(\boldsymbol{x}_s, \boldsymbol{y}_s)$ from D based on the $\boldsymbol{w}$;
9   Randomly choose a reference instance $(\boldsymbol{x}_r, \boldsymbol{y}_r)$ from $kNN(\boldsymbol{x}_s)$;
10     $(\boldsymbol{x}_c, \boldsymbol{y}_c) \leftarrow \texttt{GenerateInstance}((\boldsymbol{x}_s, \boldsymbol{y}_s), T_s, (\boldsymbol{x}_r, \boldsymbol{y}_r), T_r)$;
11     $D' \leftarrow D' \cup (\boldsymbol{x}_c, \boldsymbol{y}_c)$;
12     $GenNum \leftarrow GenNum - 1$;

13 **return** D' ;

3.1   Selection of Seed Instances

We sample seed instances with replacement, with the probability of selection being proportional to the minority class values it is associated with, weighted by the difficulty of correctly classifying these values based on the proportion of opposite (majority) class values in the local neighborhood of the instance.

For each instance x_i we first retrieve its k nearest neighbours, $kNN(x_i)$. Then for each label l_j we compute the proportion of neighbours having opposite class with respect to the class of the instance and store the result in the matrix $C \in \mathbb{R}^{n \times q}$ according to the following equation, where $[\![\pi]\!]$ is the indicator function that returns 1 if π is true and 0 otherwise:

$$C_{ij} = \frac{1}{k} \sum_{x_m \in kNN(x_i)} [\![y_{mj} \neq y_{ij}]\!] \tag{1}$$

The values in C range from 0 to 1, with values close to 0 (1) indicating a safe (hostile) neighborhood of similarly (oppositely) labelled examples. A value of $C_{ij} = 1$ can further be viewed as a hint that x_i is an outlier in this neighborhood with respect to l_j.

The next step is to aggregate the values in C per training example, x_i, in order to arrive at a single sampling weight, w_i, characterizing the difficulty in correctly predicting the *minority* class values of this example. A straightforward way to do this is to simply sum these values for the labels where the instance contains the minority class. Assuming for simplicity of presentation that the value 1 corresponds to the minority class, we arrive at this aggregation as follows:

$$w_i = \sum_{j=1}^{q} C_{ij} [\![y_{ij} = 1]\!] \tag{2}$$

There are two issues with this. The first one is that we have also taken into account the outliers. We will omit them by adding a second indicator function requesting C_{ij} to be less than 1. The second issue is that this aggregation does not take into account the global level of class imbalance of each of the labels. The fewer the number of minority samples, the higher the difficulty of correctly classifying the corresponding minority class. In contrast, Eq. 2 treats all labels equally. To resolve this issue, we can normalize the values of the non-outlier minority examples in C so that they sum to 1 per label, by dividing with the sum of the values of all non-outlier minority examples of that label. This will increase the relative importance of the weights of labels with fewer samples. Addressing these two issues we arrive at the following proposed aggregation:

$$w_i = \sum_{j=1}^{q} \frac{C_{ij} [\![y_{ij} = 1]\!] [\![C_{ij} < 1]\!]}{\sum_{i=1}^{n} C_{ij} [\![y_{ij} = 1]\!] [\![C_{ij} < 1]\!]} \tag{3}$$

3.2 Synthetic Instance Generation

The definition of the type of each instance-label pair is indispensable for the assignment of appropriate labels to the new instances that we shall create. Inspired by [19], we distinguish minority class instances into four types, namely safe (SF), borderline (BD), rare (RR) and outlier (OT), according to the proportion of neighbours from the same (minority) class:

- SF: $0 \leqslant C_{ij} < 0.3$. The safe instance is located in the region overwhelmed by minority examples.
- BD: $0.3 \leqslant C_{ij} < 0.7$. The borderline instance is placed in the decision boundary between minority and majority classes.
- RR: $0.7 \leqslant C_{ij} < 1$, and only if the type of its neighbours from the minority class are RR or OT. Otherwise there are some SF or BD examples in the proximity, which suggests that it could be rather a BD. The rare instance, accompanied with isolated pairs or triples of minority class examples, is located in the majority class area and distant from the decision boundary.
- OT: $C_{ij} = 1$. The outlier is surrounded by majority examples.

For the sake of uniform representation, the type of majority class instance is defined as majority (MJ). Let $\boldsymbol{T} \in \{SF, BD, RR, OT, MJ\}^{n \times q}$ be the type matrix and T_{ij} be the type of y_{ij}. The detailed steps of obtaining $\boldsymbol{T}$ are illustrated in Algorithm 2.

Once the seed instance $(\boldsymbol{x}_s, \boldsymbol{y}_s)$ has been decided, the reference instance $(\boldsymbol{x}_r, \boldsymbol{y}_r)$ is randomly chosen from the k nearest neighbours of the seed instance. Using the selected seed and reference instance, a new synthetic instance is generated according to Algorithm 3. The feature values of the synthetic instance $(\boldsymbol{x}_c, \boldsymbol{y}_c)$ are interpolated along the line which connects the two input samples (line 1–2 in Algorithm 3). Once $\boldsymbol{x}_c$ is confirmed, we compute $cd \in [0, 1]$, which indicates whether the synthetic instance is closer to the seed $(cd < 0.5)$ or closer to the reference instance $(cd > 0.5)$ (line 3–4 in Algorithm 3).

With respect to label assignment, we employ a scheme considering the labels and types of the seed and reference instances as well as the location of the synthetic instance, which is able to create informative instances for difficult minority class labels without bringing in noise for majority labels. For each label l_j, y_{cj} is set as y_{sj} (line 6–7 in Algorithm 3) if y_{sj} and y_{rj} belong to the same class. In the case where y_{sj} is majority class, the seed instance and the reference example should be exchanged to guarantee that y_{sj} is always the minority class (line 9–11 in Algorithm 3). Then, θ, a threshold for cd is specified based on the type of the seed label, T_{sj} (line 12–16 in Algorithm 3), which is used to determine the instance (seed or reference) whose labels will be copied to the synthetic example. For SF, BD and RR, where the minority (seed) example is surrounded by several majority instances and suffers more risk to be classified wrongly, the cut-point of label assignment is closer to the majority (reference) instance. Specifically, $\theta = 0.5$ for SF represents that the frontier of label assignment is in the midpoint between seed and reference instance, $\theta = 0.75$ for BD denotes that the range of minority class extends as three times as large than the majority class, and $\theta > 1 \geqslant cd$ for RR ensures that the generated

---

Algorithm 2: InitTypes

---

    input : The matrix storing proportion of kNNs with opposite class for each
             instance and each label: C, number of nearest neighbour: k

    output: types of instances T

```
1  for i ← 1 to n do /* n is the number of instances        */
2  │  for j ← 1 to q do /* q is the number of labels         */
3  │  │  if y_ij = majority class then
4  │  │  │  T_ij ← MJ ;
5  │  │  else/* y_ij is the minority class                    */
6  │  │  │  if C_ij < 0.3 then T_ij ← SA ;
7  │  │  │  else if C_ij < 0.7 then T_ij ← BD ;
8  │  │  │  else if C_ij < 1 then T_ij ← RR ;
9  │  │  │  else T_ij ← OT ;
10 repeat /* re-examine RR type                              */
11 │  for i ← 1 to n do
12 │  │  for j ← 1 to q do
13 │  │  │  if T_ij = RR then
14 │  │  │  │  foreach x_m in kNN(x_i) do
15 │  │  │  │  │  if T_mj = SF or T_mj = BD then
16 │  │  │  │  │  │  T_ij ← BD;
17 │  │  │  │  │  │  break ;
18 until no change in T;
19 return T ;
```

---

instance is always set as minority class regardless of its location. With respect to OT as a singular point placed at majority class region, all possible synthetic instances are assigned the majority class due to the inability of an outlier to cover the input space. Finally, y_{cj} is set as y_{sj} if cd is not larger than θ, otherwise y_{cj} is equal to y_{rj} (line 17–20 in Algorithm 3).

Compared with MLSMOTE, MLSOL is able to generate more diverse and well-labeled synthetic instances. As the example in Fig. 2 shows, given a seed instance, the labels of the synthetic instance are fixed in MLSMOTE, while the labels of the new instance change according to its location in MLSOL, which avoids the introduction of noise as well.

3.3   Ensemble of Multi-Label Sampling (EMLS)

Ensemble is a effective strategy to increase overall accuracy and overcome overfitting problem, but has not been leveraged to multi-label sampling approaches. To improve the robustness of MLSOL and current multi-label sampling methods, we propose the ensemble framework called EMLS where any multi-label sampling approach and classifier could be embedded. In EMLS, M multi-label learning models are trained and each model is built upon a re-sampled dataset generated by a multi-label sampling method with various random seed. There are many

---

Algorithm 3: GenerateInstance

---

input : seed instance: $(\boldsymbol{x}_s, \boldsymbol{y}_s)$, types of seed instance: T_s, reference instance:
$(\boldsymbol{x}_r, \boldsymbol{y}_r)$, types of reference instance: T_r

output: synthetic instance: $(\boldsymbol{x}_c, \boldsymbol{y}_c)$

1 **for** $j \leftarrow 1$ **to** d **do**

2 $\quad\mid\quad x_{cj} \leftarrow x_{sj} + \texttt{Random}(0,1) * (x_{rj} - x_{sj})$;   /* Random(0,1) generates a
$\quad\quad\quad$ random value between 0 and 1 */

3 $d_s \leftarrow dist(x_c, x_s)$, $d_r \leftarrow dist(x_c, x_r)$; /* *dist* return the distance between 2
instances */

4 $cd \leftarrow d_s/(d_s + d_r)$;

5 **for** $j \leftarrow 1$ **to** q **do**

6 $\quad\mid\quad$ **if** $y_{sj} = y_{rj}$ **then**

7 $\quad\mid\quad\mid\quad y_{cj} \leftarrow y_{sj}$;

8 $\quad\mid\quad$ **else**

9 $\quad\mid\quad\mid\quad$ **if** $T_{sj} = MJ$ **then** /* ensure y_{sj} being minority class   */

10 $\quad\mid\quad\mid\quad\mid\quad s \longleftrightarrow r$; /* swap indices of seed and reference instance */

11 $\quad\mid\quad\mid\quad\mid\quad cd \leftarrow 1 - cd$;

12 $\quad\mid\quad\mid\quad$ **switch** T_{sj} **do**

13 $\quad\mid\quad\mid\quad\mid\quad$ **case** SF **do** $\theta \leftarrow 0.5$; break ;

14 $\quad\mid\quad\mid\quad\mid\quad$ **case** BD **do** $\theta \leftarrow 0.75$; break ;

15 $\quad\mid\quad\mid\quad\mid\quad$ **case** RR **do** $\theta \leftarrow 1 + 1e - 5$; break ;

16 $\quad\mid\quad\mid\quad\mid\quad$ **case** OL **do** $\theta \leftarrow 0 - 1e - 5$; break ;

17 $\quad\mid\quad\mid\quad$ **if** $cd \leqslant \theta$ **then**

18 $\quad\mid\quad\mid\quad\mid\quad y_{cj} \leftarrow y_{sj}$;

19 $\quad\mid\quad\mid\quad$ **else**

20 $\quad\mid\quad\mid\quad\mid\quad y_{cj} \leftarrow y_{rj}$;

21 **return** $(\boldsymbol{x}_t, \boldsymbol{y}_t)$;

---

random operations in existing and proposed multi-label learning sampling methods [6,7], which guarantees the diversity of training set for each model in the ensemble framework via employing different random seed. Then the bipartition threshold of each label is decided by maximizing F-measure on training set, as COCOA [31] and ECCRU3 [18] do. Given the test example, the predicting relevant scores is calculated as the average output relevant degrees obtained from M models, and the labels whose relevance degree is larger than the corresponding bipartition threshold are predicted as "1", and "0" otherwise.

3.4 Complexity Analysis

The complexity of searching kNN of input instances is $O(n^2d + n^2k)$. The complexity of computing C, $\boldsymbol{w}$ and T is $O(knq)$, $O(nq)$ and $O(nq)$, respectively. The complexity of creating instances is $O(nP(n + d))$ where nP is the number of generated examples. The overall complexity of MLSOL is $O(n^2d + n^2k + nkq)$, of which the kNN searching is the most time-consuming part.

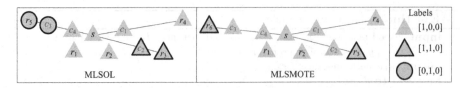

Fig. 2. An example of MLSOL excelling MLSMOTE. s is the seed instance, r_* are candidate reference instances (kNNs of s), and c_* are possible synthetic examples. The synthetic instances created by MLSMOTE are associated with unique label vector ([1,0,0]) decided by predominant kNNs, while MLSOL assigns labels to new examples according to its location. The two sampling approaches are identical if the synthetic instance (c_1 and c_4) is near the instance whose labels are same with majority kNNs or seed instance, otherwise (c_2 and c_3) the MLSMOTE introduces noise while MLSOL could tackle it by copying the labels of nearest instance to the new example.

Let's define $\Theta_t(n, d, q)$ and $\Theta_p(d, q)$ the complexity of training and prediction of multi-label learning method respectively, and $\Theta_s(n, d, q)$ the complexity of a multi-label sampling approach. The complexity of EMLS is $O(M\Theta_p(d, q))$ for prediction and $O\left(M\left(\Theta_s(n, d, q) + \Theta_t(n, d, q) + n\Theta_p(d, q)\right)\right)$ for training.

4   Empirical Analysis

4.1   Setup

Table 1 shows detailed information for the 13 benchmark multi-label datasets, obtained from Mulan's repository[1], that are used in this study. Besides, in textual data sets with more than 1000 features we applied a simple dimensionality reduction approach that retains the top 10% (bibtex, enron, medical) or top 1% (rcv1subset1, rcv1subset2, yahoo-Arts1, yahoo-Business1) of the features ordered by number of non-zero values (i.e. frequency of appearance). Besides, we remove labels only containing one minority class instance, because when splitting the dataset into training and test sets, there may be only majority class instances of those extremely imbalanced labels in training set.

Four multi-label sampling methods are used for comparison, namely the state-of-the-art MLSMOTE [6] and RHwRSMT [9] that integrates REMEDIAL [8] and MLSMOTE, as well as their ensemble versions, called EMLSMOTE and ERHwRSMT respectively. Furthermore, the base learning approach without employing any sampling approach, denoted as Default, is also used for comparing. For all sampling methods, the number of nearest neighbours is set to 5 and the Euclidean distance is used to measure the distance between the examples. In MLSOL, the sampling ratio is set to 0.3. In RHwRSMT, the threshold for decoupling instance is set to *SCUMBLE*. For MLSMOTE and RHwRSMT, the label generation strategy is *Ranking*. The ensemble size is set to 5 for all ensemble methods. In addition, six multi-label learning methods

---

[1] http://mulan.sourceforge.net/datasets-mlc.html.

Table 1. The 16 multi-label datasets used in this study. Columns n, d, q denote the number of instances, features and labels respectively, LC the label cardinality, $MeanImR$ the average imbalance ratio of labels, where imbalance ratio of a label is computed as the number of majority instances divided by the number of minority instance of the label.

Dataset	Domain	n	d	q	LC	$MeanImR$
bibtex	text	7395	183	159	2.402	87.7
cal500	music	502	68	174	26	22.3
corel5k	image	5000	499	347	3.517	522
enron	text	1702	100	52	3.378	107
flags	image	194	19	7	3.392	2.753
genbase	biology	662	1186	24	1.248	78.8
medical	text	978	144	35	1.245	143
rcv1subset1	text	6000	472	101	2.88	236
rcv1subset2	text	6000	472	101	2.634	191
scene	image	2407	294	6	1.074	4.662
yahoo-Arts1	text	7484	231	25	1.654	101
yahoo-Business1	text	11214	219	28	1.599	286
yeast	biology	2417	103	14	4.237	8.954

are employed as base learning methods, comprising four standard multi-label learning methods (BR [2], MLkNN [32], CLR [13], RAkEL [27]), as well as two state-of-the-art methods addressing the class imbalance problem (COCOA [31] and ECCRU3 [18]).

Three widely used imbalance aware evaluation metrics are leveraged to measure the performance of methods, namely macro-averaged F-measure, macro-averaged AUC-ROC (area under the receiver operating characteristic curve) and macro-averaged AUCPR (area under the precision recall curve). For simplicity, we omit the "macro-averaged" in further references to these metrics within the rest of this paper.

The experiments were conducted on a machine with 4×10-core CPUs running at 2.27 GHz. We apply 5×2-fold cross validation with multi-label stratification [22] to each dataset and the average results are reported. The implementation of our approach and the scripts of our experiments are publicly available at Mulan's GitHub repository[2]. The default parameters are used for base learners.

4.2   Results and Analysis

Detailed experimental results are listed in the supplementary material[3] of this paper. The statistical significance of the differences among the methods par-

---

[2] https://github.com/tsoumakas/mulan/tree/master/mulan.
[3] https://intelligence.csd.auth.gr/wp-content/uploads/2019/10/ecml-pkdd-2019-supplementary.pdf.

Table 2. Average rank of the compared methods using 6 base learners in terms of three evaluation metrics. A_1, A_2, EA_1 and, EA_2 stands for MLSMOTE, RHwRSMT, EMLSMOTE and ERHwRSMT, respectively. The parenthesis (n_1/n_2) indicates the corresponding method is significantly superior to n_1 methods and inferior to n_2 methods based on the Wilcoxon signed rank test with Bergman-Hommel's correction at the 5% level.

Base Method	Default	A_1	A_2	MLSOL	EA_1	EA_2	EMLSOL
F-measure							
BR	5.19(1/4)	3.73(2/2)	7.00(0/6)	4.23(2/2)	2.08(5/1)	4.38(1/2)	**1.38(6/0)**
MLkNN	5.81(1/5)	4.92(2/4)	7.00(0/6)	4.27(3/3)	**1.62(5/0)**	2.69(4/2)	1.69(5/0)
CLR	5.04(1/3)	4.5(1/3)	7.00(0/6)	4.15(1/3)	2.58(4/0)	2.62**(4/0)**	**2.12(4/0)**
RAkEL	5.04(1/4)	3.88(2/2)	7.00(0/6)	3.5(2/2)	2.46(5/1)	4.69(1/2)	**1.42(6/0)**
COCOA	3.58(1/0)	4.42(1/1)	6.35(0/5)	5.23(0/1)	3.27(1/0)	3.31(1/0)	**1.85(3/0)**
ECCRU3	3(2/0)	4.58(1/1)	6.31(0/5)	5.46(0/2)	3.35(1/0)	3.46(1/1)	**1.85(4/0)**
Total	7/16	9/13	0/34	8/13	21/2	12/7	**28/0**
AUC-ROC							
BR	5.23(1/3)	4.65(1/3)	6.27(0/6)	3.46(3/1)	2.81(4/1)	4.58(1/2)	**1.00(6/0)**
MLkNN	4.69(1/1)	3.73(2/2)	6.35(0/6)	4.23(2/1)	2.58(3/1)	5.35(1/4)	**1.08(6/0)**
CLR	4.35(0/1)	4.77(0/2)	5.58(0/3)	5.00(0/2)	2.85(4/1)	4.08(1/2)	**1.38(6/0)**
RAkEL	4.38(2/4)	3.73(3/2)	6.77(0/6)	3.54(3/2)	2.54(5/1)	6.00(1/5)	**1.04(6/0)**
COCOA	5.23(0/1)	4.73(0/1)	5.42(0/1)	4.54(0/1)	3.42(0/1)	3.65(0/1)	**1.00(6/0)**
ECCRU3	4.73(0/1)	4.23(0/2)	5.73(0/3)	5.46(0/1)	2.65(3/1)	4.12(1/2)	**1.08(6/0)**
Total	4/11	6/12	0/25	8/8	19/6	5/16	**36/0**
AUCPR							
BR	4.81(1/2)	3.85(1/2)	6.46(0/6)	4.15(1/2)	2.46(5/1)	5.19(1/2)	**1.08(6/0)**
MLkNN	5.04(0/2)	4.5(1/2)	5.92(0/5)	4.08(1/1)	3.04(4/1)	4.42(1/2)	**1.00(6/0)**
CLR	4.15(1/1)	4.88(0/2)	5.92(0/4)	5.00(0/3)	3.00(3/1)	3.81(2/1)	**1.23(6/0)**
RAkEL	4.42(1/2)	3.92(1/2)	6.77(0/6)	3.92(1/2)	2.5(5/1)	5.46(1/2)	**1.00(6/0)**
COCOA	5.31(0/1)	4.85(0/1)	5.31(0/1)	4.62(0/1)	3.15(0/1)	3.77(0/1)	**1.00(6/0)**
ECCRU3	4.96(0/2)	4.5(0/2)	5.50(0/3)	5.04(0/2)	2.88(5/1)	4.12(1/2)	**1.00(6/0)**
Total	3/10	3/11	0/25	3/11	22/6	6/10	**36/0**

ticipating in our empirical study is examined by employing the Friedman test, followed by the Wilcoxon signed rank test with Bergman-Hommel's correction at the 5% level, following literature guidelines [1,14]. Table 2 shows the average rank of each method as well as its significant wins/losses versus each one of the rest of the methods for each of the three evaluation metrics and each of the six base multi-label methods. The best results are highlighted with bold typeface.

We start our discussion by looking at the single model version of the three resampling methods. We first notice that RHwRSMT achieves the worst results and that it is even worse than no resampling at all (default), which is mainly due to the additional bewilderment yielded by REMEDIAL, i.e. there are several pairs of instances with same features and disparate labels. MLSOL and MLSMOTE exhibit similar total wins and losses, especially in AUCPR, which is considered as the most appropriate measure in the context of class imbalance [21]. Moreover, the wins and losses of MLSOL and MLSMOTE are not that different from no resampling at all. This is particularly true when using a multi-label learning method that already handles class imbalance, such as COCOA and ECCRU3, which is not surprising.

We then notice that the ensemble versions of the three multi-label resampling methods outperform their corresponding single model versions in all cases.

This verifies the known effectiveness of resampling approaches in reducing the error, in particular via reducing the variance component of the expected error [15]. Ensembling enables MLSMOTE and MLSOL to achieve much better results compared to no resampling and it even helps RHwRSMT to do slightly better than no resampling.

Focusing on the ensemble versions of the three resampling methods we notice that EMLSOL achieves the best average rank and the most significant wins without suffering any significant loss in all 18 different pairs of the 6 base multi-label methods and the 3 evaluation measures, with the exception that MLSMOTE with MLkNN as base learner achieves best average rank in terms of F-measure. EMLSMOTE comes second in total wins and losses in most cases, while ERHwRSMT does much worse than EMLSMOTE.

An interesting observation here is that while MLSOL and MLSMOTE have similar performance, MLSOL benefitted much more than MLSMOTE from the ensemble approach. This happens because randomization plays a more important role in MLSOL than in MLSMOTE. MLSOL uses weighted sampling for seed instance selection, while MLSMOTE takes all minority samples into account instead. This allows EMLSOL to create more diverse models, which achieve greater error correction when aggregated.

5   Conclusion

We proposed MLSOL, a new synthetic oversampling approach for tackling the class-imbalance problem in multi-label data. Based on the local distribution of labels, MLSOL selects more important and informative seed instances and generates more diverse and well-labeled synthetic instances. In addition, we employed MLSOL within a simple ensemble framework, which exploits the random aspects of our approach during sampling training examples to use as seeds and during the generation of synthetic training examples.

We experimentally compared the proposed approach against two state-of-the art resampling methods on 13 benchmark multi-label datasets. The results offer strong evidence on the superiority of MLSOL, especially of its ensemble version, in three different imbalance-aware evaluation measures using six different underlying base multi-label methods.

Acknowledgements. Bin Liu is supported from the China Scholarship Council (CSC) under the Grant CSC No. 201708500095.

References

1. Benavoli, A., Corani, G., Mangili, F.: Should we really use post-hoc tests based on mean-ranks? J. Mach. Learn. Res. **17**, 1–10 (2016)
2. Boutell, M.R., Luo, J., Shen, X., Brown, C.M.: Learning multi-label scene classification. Pattern Recogn. **37**(9), 1757–1771 (2004). https://doi.org/10.1016/j.patcog.2004.03.009

3. Cao, P., Liu, X., Zhao, D., Zaiane, O.: Cost sensitive ranking support vector machine for multi-label data learning. In: Abraham, A., Haqiq, A., Alimi, A.M., Mezzour, G., Rokbani, N., Muda, A.K. (eds.) HIS 2016. AISC, vol. 552, pp. 244–255. Springer, Cham (2017). https://doi.org/10.1007/978-3-319-52941-7_25

4. Charte, F., Rivera, A., del Jesus, M.J., Herrera, F.: A first approach to deal with imbalance in multi-label datasets. In: Pan, J.-S., Polycarpou, M.M., Woźniak, M., de Carvalho, A.C.P.L.F., Quintián, H., Corchado, E. (eds.) HAIS 2013. LNCS (LNAI), vol. 8073, pp. 150–160. Springer, Heidelberg (2013). https://doi.org/10.1007/978-3-642-40846-5_16

5. Charte, F., Rivera, A.J., del Jesus, M.J., Herrera, F.: MLeNN: a first approach to heuristic multilabel undersampling. In: Corchado, E., Lozano, J.A., Quintián, H., Yin, H. (eds.) IDEAL 2014. LNCS, vol. 8669, pp. 1–9. Springer, Cham (2014). https://doi.org/10.1007/978-3-319-10840-7_1

6. Charte, F., Rivera, A.J., Del Jesus, M.J., Herrera, F.: MLSMOTE: approaching imbalanced multilabel learning through synthetic instance generation. Knowl.-Based Syst. **89**, 385–397 (2015). https://doi.org/10.1016/j.knosys.2015.07.019

7. Charte, F., Rivera, A.J., del Jesus, M.J., Herrera, F.: Addressing imbalance in multilabel classification: measures and random resampling algorithms. Neurocomputing **163**, 3–16 (2015). https://doi.org/10.1016/j.neucom.2014.08.091

8. Charte, F., Rivera, A.J., del Jesus, M.J., Herrera, F.: Dealing with difficult minority labels in imbalanced mutilabel data sets. Neurocomputing **326–327**, 39–53 (2019). https://doi.org/10.1016/j.neucom.2016.08.158

9. Charte, F., Rivera, A.J., del Jesus, M.J., Herrera, F.: REMEDIAL-HwR: tackling multilabel imbalance through label decoupling and data resampling hybridization. Neurocomputing **326–327**, 110–122 (2019). https://doi.org/10.1016/j.neucom.2017.01.118

10. Chen, K., Lu, B.L., Kwok, J.T.: Efficient classification of multi-label and imbalanced data using min-max modular classifiers. In: Proceedings of the 2006 IEEE International Joint Conference on Neural Network, pp. 1770–1775. IEEE (2006). https://doi.org/10.1109/IJCNN.2006.246893

11. Daniels, Z.A., Metaxas, D.N.: Addressing imbalance in multi-label classification using structured hellinger forests. In: Proceedings of the 31st AAAI Conference on Artificial Intelligence, pp. 1826–1832 (2017)

12. Dendamrongvit, S., Kubat, M.: Undersampling approach for imbalanced training sets and induction from multi-label text-categorization domains. In: Theeramunkong, T., et al. (eds.) PAKDD 2009. LNCS (LNAI), vol. 5669, pp. 40–52. Springer, Heidelberg (2010). https://doi.org/10.1007/978-3-642-14640-4_4

13. Fürnkranz, J., Hüllermeier, E., Loza Mencía, E., Brinker, K.: Multilabel classification via calibrated label ranking. Mach. Learn. **73**(2), 133–153 (2008). https://doi.org/10.1007/s10994-008-5064-8

14. Garcia, S., Herrera, F.: An extension on "Statistical Comparisons of Classifiers over Multiple Data Sets" for all pairwise comparisons. J. Mach. Learn. Res. **9**, 2677–2694 (2008)

15. Hastie, T., Tibshirani, R., Friedman, J.: The Elements of Statistical Learning: Data Mining, Inference, and Prediction. Springer, New York (2016). https://doi.org/10.1007/978-0-387-21606-5

16. Li, C., Shi, G.: Improvement of learning algorithm for the multi-instance multi-label RBF neural networks trained with imbalanced samples. J. Inf. Sci. Eng. **29**(4), 765–776 (2013)

17. Li, L., Wang, H.: Towards label imbalance in multi-label classification with many labels. arXiv preprint arXiv:1604.01304 (2016)

18. Liu, B., Tsoumakas, G.: Making classifier chains resilient to class imbalance. In: 10th Asian Conference on Machine Learning (ACML 2018), Beijing, pp. 280–295 (2018)
19. Napierala, K., Stefanowski, J.: Types of minority class examples and their influence on learning classifiers from imbalanced data. J. Intell. Inf. Syst. **46**(3), 563–597 (2015)
20. Sáez, J.A., Krawczyk, B., Woźniak, M.: Analyzing the oversampling of different classes and types of examples in multi-class imbalanced datasets. Pattern Recogn. **57**, 164–178 (2016). https://doi.org/10.1016/j.patcog.2016.03.012
21. Saito, T., Rehmsmeier, M.: The precision-recall plot is more informative than the ROC plot when evaluating binary classifiers on imbalanced datasets. PLoS ONE (2015). https://doi.org/10.1371/journal.pone.0118432
22. Sechidis, K., Tsoumakas, G., Vlahavas, I.: On the stratification of multi-label data. In: Gunopulos, D., Hofmann, T., Malerba, D., Vazirgiannis, M. (eds.) ECML PKDD 2011. LNCS (LNAI), vol. 6913, pp. 145–158. Springer, Heidelberg (2011). https://doi.org/10.1007/978-3-642-23808-6_10
23. Sozykin, K., Khan, A.M., Protasov, S., Hussain, R.: Multi-label class-imbalanced action recognition in hockey videos via 3D convolutional neural networks. In: 19th IEEE/ACIS International Conference on Software Engineering, Artificial Intelligence, Networking and Parallel/Distributed Computing (SNPD), pp. 146–151 (2018)
24. Sun, K.W., Lee, C.H.: Addressing class-imbalance in multi-label learning via two-stage multi-label hypernetwork. Neurocomputing **266**, 375–389 (2017). https://doi.org/10.1016/j.neucom.2017.05.049
25. Tahir, M.A., Kittler, J., Yan, F.: Inverse random under sampling for class imbalance problem and its application to multi-label classification. Pattern Recogn. **45**(10), 3738–3750 (2012). https://doi.org/10.1016/j.patcog.2012.03.014
26. Tepvorachai, G., Papachristou, C.: Multi-label imbalanced data enrichment process in neural net classifier training. In: Proceedings of the International Joint Conference on Neural Networks, pp. 1301–1307 (2008). https://doi.org/10.1109/IJCNN.2008.4633966
27. Tsoumakas, G., Katakis, I., Vlahavas, I.: Random k-labelsets for multilabel classification. IEEE Trans. Knowl. Data Eng. **23**(7), 1079–1089 (2011)
28. Wan, S., Duan, Y., Zou, Q.: HPSLPred: an ensemble multi-label classifier for human protein subcellular location prediction with imbalanced source. Proteomics **17**(17–18), 1700262 (2017). https://doi.org/10.1002/pmic.201700262
29. Wu, B., Lyu, S., Ghanem, B.: Constrained submodular minimization for missing labels and class imbalance in multi-label learning. In: Proceedings of the Thirtieth AAAI Conference on Artificial Intelligence AAAI 2016, pp. 2229–2236. AAAI Press (2016)
30. Zeng, W., Chen, X., Cheng, H.: Pseudo labels for imbalanced multi-label learning. In: 2014 International Conference on Data Science and Advanced Analytics (DSAA), pp. 25–31, October 2014. https://doi.org/10.1109/DSAA.2014.7058047
31. Zhang, M.L., Li, Y.K., Liu, X.Y.: Towards class-imbalance aware multi-label learning. In: Proceedings of the 24th International Conference on Artificial Intelligence, pp. 4041–4047 (2015)
32. Zhang, M.L., Zhou, Z.H.: ML-KNN: a lazy learning approach to multi-label learning. Pattern Recogn. **40**(7), 2038–2048 (2007)

Large-Scale Learning

Distributed Learning of Non-convex Linear Models with One Round of Communication

Mike Izbicki[1(✉)] and Christian R. Shelton[2]

[1] Claremont McKenna College, Claremont, CA, USA
mike@izbicki.me
[2] UC Riverside, Riverside, CA, USA
cshelton@cs.ucr.edu

Abstract. We present the *optimal weighted average* (OWA) distributed learning algorithm for linear models. OWA achieves statistically optimal learning rates, uses only one round of communication, works on non-convex problems, and supports a fast cross validation procedure. The OWA algorithm first trains local models on each of the compute nodes; then a master machine merges the models using a second round of optimization. This second optimization uses only a small fraction of the data, and so has negligible computational cost. Compared with similar distributed estimators that merge locally trained models, OWA either has stronger statistical guarantees, is applicable to more models, or has a more computationally efficient merging procedure.

Keywords: Distributed machine learning · Linear models

1 Introduction

Many datasets are too large to fit in the memory of a single machine. To analyze them, we must partition the data onto many machines and use distributed algorithms. Existing distributed learning algorithms fall into one of two categories:

Interactive algorithms require many rounds of communication between machines. Representative examples include [4,8,14,16,23,27]. These algorithms resemble standard iterative algorithms where each iteration is followed by a communication step. The appeal of interactive algorithms is that they enjoy the same statistical performance as standard sequential algorithms. That is, given m machines each with n data points of dimension d, interactive algorithms have error that decays as $O(\sqrt{d/mn})$ for linear models. But, interactive algorithms have three main disadvantages. First, these algorithms are slow when communication latency is the bottleneck. An extreme example occurs in the *federated learning* environment proposed by McMahan et al. [18], which uses cell phones as the computational nodes. Recent work on interactive algorithms focuses on reducing this communication as much as possible [8,23,27]. Second, these algorithms require special implementations. They are not easy for non-experts to

© Springer Nature Switzerland AG 2020
U. Brefeld et al. (Eds.): ECML PKDD 2019, LNAI 11907, pp. 197–212, 2020.
https://doi.org/10.1007/978-3-030-46147-8_12

implement or use, and in particular they do not work with off-the-shelf statistics libraries provided by (for example) Python, R, and Matlab. Third, because of the many rounds of communication, any sensitive information in the data is likely to leak between machines.

Non-interactive algorithms require only a single round of communication. Each machine independently solves the learning problem on a small subset of data, then a master machine merges the solutions together. These algorithms solve all the problems of interactive ones: they are fast when communication is the main bottleneck; they are easy to implement with off-the-shelf statistics packages; and they are robust to privacy considerations. The downside is worse statistical performance. The popular naive averaging estimator has worst case performance $O(\sqrt{d/n})$ completely independent of the number of machines m. A growing body of work improves the analysis of the averaging estimator under special conditions [17,22,24–26], and develops more robust non-interactive estimators [2,6,9,12,15,28]. All of these estimators either work on only a limited class of models or have computationally intractable merge procedures.

In this paper, we propose a novel non-interactive estimator called the *optimal weighted average* (OWA). OWA's merge procedure uses a second round of optimization over the data. (All previous merge procedures do not depend on the data.) This data dependent merge procedure has four advantages: (i) OWA achieves the optimal error of $O(\sqrt{d/mn})$ in a general setting and with a simple analysis. In particular, we do not require a convex loss function. (ii) This second optimization uses a small number of data points projected onto a small dimensional space. It therefore has negligible computational and communication overhead. (iii) OWA is easily implemented on most distributed architectures with standard packages. Our implementation uses only a few dozen lines of Python and scikit-learn [21]. (iv) OWA is robust to the regularization strength used in the first round of optimization. In practice, this means that OWA does not require communication between nodes even in the model selection step of learning.

We also show a simple extension to the OWA algorithm that uses two rounds of communication to compute a cross validation estimate of the model's performance. The standard version of cross validation is too slow for large scale data, and therefore not widely used in the distributed setting. This procedure is the first fast cross validation method designed for the distributed setting, and is an additional advantage OWA has over interactive distributed learning algorithms.

Section 2 formally describes our problem setting, and Sect. 3 describes the OWA algorithm and its fast cross validation procedure. We take special care to show how OWA can be implemented with off-the-shelf optimizers. Section 4 provides a simple proof that OWA achieves the optimal $O(\sqrt{d/mn})$ error. Our main condition is that the single machine parameter vectors have a "sufficiently Gaussian" distribution. We show that this is a mild condition known to hold in many situations of interest. Section 5 compares OWA to existing distributed algorithms. We highlight how the analysis of existing algorithms requires more limiting assumptions than OWA's. Section 6 shows empirically that OWA performs well on synthetic and real world advertising data. We demonstrate that

OWA is robust to the strength of regularization, which is one of the reasons it performs well in practice.

2 Problem Setting

Let $\mathcal{Y} \subseteq \mathbb{R}$ be the space of response variables, $\mathcal{X} \subseteq \mathbb{R}^d$ be the space of covariates, and $\mathcal{W} \subseteq \mathbb{R}^d$ be the parameter space. We assume a linear model where the loss of data point $(\mathbf{x}, y) \in \mathcal{X} \times \mathcal{Y}$ given the parameter $\mathbf{w} \in \mathcal{W}$ is denoted by $\ell(y, \mathbf{x}^\mathsf{T}\mathbf{w})$. We define the true loss of parameter vector $\mathbf{w}$ to be $\mathcal{L}^*(\mathbf{w}) = \mathbb{E}\ell(y; \mathbf{x}^\mathsf{T}\mathbf{w})$, and the optimal parameter vector $\mathbf{w}^* = \arg\min_{\mathbf{w} \in \mathcal{W}} \mathcal{L}^*(\mathbf{w})$. We do not require that the model be correctly specified, nor do we require that ℓ be convex with respect to $\mathbf{w}$. Let $Z \subset \mathcal{X} \times \mathcal{Y}$ be a dataset of mn i.i.d. observations. Finally, let $r : \mathcal{W} \to \mathbb{R}$ be a regularization function (typically the L1 or L2 norm) and $\lambda \in \mathbb{R}$ be the regularization strength. Then the regularized empirical risk minimizer (ERM) is

$$\hat{\mathbf{w}}^{erm} = \arg\min_{\mathbf{w} \in \mathcal{W}} \sum_{(\mathbf{x},y) \in Z} \ell(y, \mathbf{x}^\mathsf{T}\mathbf{w}) + \lambda r(\mathbf{w}). \tag{1}$$

Assume that the dataset Z has been partitioned onto m machines so that each machine i has dataset Z_i of size n, and all the Z_i are disjoint. Then each machine calculates the local ERM

$$\hat{\mathbf{w}}_i^{erm} = \arg\min_{\mathbf{w} \in \mathcal{W}} \sum_{(\mathbf{x},y) \in Z_i} \ell(y, \mathbf{x}^\mathsf{T}\mathbf{w}) + \lambda r(\mathbf{w}). \tag{2}$$

Notice that computing $\hat{\mathbf{w}}_i^{erm}$ requires no communication with other machines. Our goal is to merge the $\hat{\mathbf{w}}_i^{erm}$s into a single improved estimate.

To motivate our OWA merge procedure, we briefly describe a baseline procedure called *naive averaging*:

$$\hat{\mathbf{w}}^{ave} = \frac{1}{m} \sum_{i=1}^{m} \hat{\mathbf{w}}_i^{erm}. \tag{3}$$

Naive averaging is simple to compute but has only limited theoretical guarantees. Recall that the quality of an estimator $\hat{\mathbf{w}}$ can be measured by the estimation error $\|\hat{\mathbf{w}} - \mathbf{w}^*\|$, and we can use the triangle inequality to decompose this error as

$$\|\hat{\mathbf{w}} - \mathbf{w}^*\| \leq \|\hat{\mathbf{w}} - \mathbb{E}\hat{\mathbf{w}}\| + \|\mathbb{E}\hat{\mathbf{w}} - \mathbf{w}^*\|. \tag{4}$$

We refer to $\|\hat{\mathbf{w}} - \mathbb{E}\hat{\mathbf{w}}\|$ as the variance of the estimator and $\|\mathbb{E}\hat{\mathbf{w}} - \mathbf{w}^*\|$ as the bias. McDonald et al. [17] show that the $\hat{\mathbf{w}}^{ave}$ estimator has lower variance than the estimator $\hat{\mathbf{w}}_i^{erm}$ trained on a single machine, but the same bias. Zhang et al. [25] extend this analysis to show that if $\hat{\mathbf{w}}_i^{erm}$ is a "nearly unbiased estimator," then naive averaging is optimal. But Rosenblatt and Nadler [22] show that in high dimensional regimes, all models are heavily biased, and so naive averaging is suboptimal. All three results require ℓ to be convex in addition to other technical assumptions. Our goal is to design a merging procedure that has good error bounds in a more general setting.

3   The OWA Estimator

The *optimal weighted average* (OWA) estimator uses a second round of optimization to calculate the optimal linear combination of the $\hat{\mathbf{w}}_i^{erm}$s. This second optimization reduces the bias at the optimal rate. Furthermore, this second optimization occurs over a small fraction of the dataset, so its computational and communication cost is negligible.

3.1   Warmup: The Full OWA

To motivate the OWA estimator, we first present a less efficient estimator that uses the full dataset for the second round of optimization. Define the matrix $\hat{W} : \mathbb{R}^{d \times m}$ to have its ith column equal to $\hat{\mathbf{w}}_i^{erm}$. Now consider the estimator

$$\hat{\mathbf{w}}^{owa,full} = \hat{W}\hat{\mathbf{v}}^{owa,full}, \tag{5}$$

where

$$\hat{\mathbf{v}}^{owa,full} = \arg\min_{\mathbf{v} \in \mathbb{R}^m} \sum_{(\mathbf{x},y) \in Z} \ell\left(y, \mathbf{x}^\mathsf{T}\hat{W}\mathbf{v}\right) + \lambda r(\hat{W}\mathbf{v}). \tag{6}$$

Notice that $\hat{\mathbf{w}}^{owa,full}$ is just the empirical risk minimizer when the parameter space $\mathcal{W}$ is restricted to the subspace $\hat{\mathcal{W}}^{owa} = \text{span}\{\hat{\mathbf{w}}_i^{erm}\}_{i=1}^m$. In other words, the $\hat{\mathbf{v}}^{owa,full}$ vector contains the optimal weights to apply to each $\hat{\mathbf{w}}_i^{erm}$ when averaging. Figure 1 shows graphically that no other estimator in $\hat{\mathcal{W}}^{owa}$ can have lower regularized empirical loss than $\hat{\mathbf{w}}^{owa,full}$.

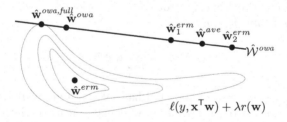

Fig. 1. $\hat{\mathbf{w}}^{owa,full}$ is the estimator with best loss in $\hat{\mathcal{W}}^{owa}$, and $\hat{\mathbf{w}}^{owa}$ is close with high probability.

3.2   The OWA Estimator

The OWA estimator uses fewer data points in the second round of optimization. Recall that in a linear model, the amount of data needed is proportional to the problem's dimension. Since the dimension of the second round is a fraction m/d smaller than the first round, only an m/d fraction of data is needed for the same accuracy. To simplify OWA's analysis in Sect. 4, we will assume here that this data is independent of the data used in the first round. This assumption,

---

Algorithm 1. Calculating $\hat{\mathbf{w}}^{owa}$ only

Preconditions:
    each machine i already has dataset Z_i
    the master machine additionally has dataset Z^{owa}
Each machine i independently:
    calculates $\hat{\mathbf{w}}_i^{erm}$ using Equation (2)
    transmits $\hat{\mathbf{w}}_i^{erm}$ to the master
The master calculates $\hat{\mathbf{w}}^{owa}$ using Equation (7)
    (optionally) master uses approximation Equation (9)

---

however, is an artifact of Sect. 4's simple analysis, and all our experiments in Sect. 6 reuse the same data for both optimizations.

Formally, let Z^{owa} be a set of $m^2 n/d$ additional data points sampled i.i.d. from the original data distribution. Thus the total amount of data the OWA estimator requires is $mn + m^2 n/d$. Whenever $m/d \leq 1$, this expression simplifies to $O(mn)$, which is the same order of magnitude of data in the original problem. The OWA estimator is then defined as

$$\hat{\mathbf{w}}^{owa} = \hat{W}\hat{\mathbf{v}}^{owa}, \tag{7}$$

where

$$\hat{\mathbf{v}}^{owa} = \arg\min_{\mathbf{v}\in\mathbb{R}^m} \sum_{(\mathbf{x},y)\in Z^{owa}} \ell\left(y, \mathbf{x}^\mathsf{T}\hat{W}\mathbf{v}\right) + \lambda r(\hat{W}\mathbf{v}). \tag{8}$$

Algorithm 1 shows the procedure for calculating $\hat{\mathbf{w}}^{owa}$ in a distributed setting. Notice that we assume that a predesignated master machine already has access to the full Z^{owa} dataset.[1] Because this data is pre-assigned to the master machine, each machine i only needs to transmit the local parameter vector $\hat{\mathbf{w}}_i^{erm}$ to the master. Thus, the total number of bits communicated is $O(dm)$, which is the same as the naive averaging estimator. OWA's merge procedure is more complicated than the naive averaging merge procedure, but still very fast. Notice that the projected data points $\mathbf{x}^\mathsf{T}\hat{W}$ have dimensionality $m \ll d$, and there are only $m^2 n/d$ of them. Because the optimization uses a smaller dimension and fewer data points, it takes a negligible amount of time. In Sect. 6, we show an experiment where the first round of optimizations takes about a day, and the second optimization takes about a minute.

3.3 Implementing OWA with Existing Optimizers

In theory, standard optimization algorithms can be used to directly solve the second round of optimization in Eq. (8). In practice, however, standard tools

---

[1] Other non-interactive estimators have made similar assumptions (e.g. [28]). If this assumption is too limiting, however, Appendix A shows how to transfer these data points to the master machine after optimizing the local models. The idea is to first project the data onto the subspace $\hat{W}^{owa}$ before transfer, reducing the dimensionality of the data. The communication complexity of this alternate procedure is $O(dm^2)$.

such as scikit-learn [21] do not support the regularization term $r(\hat{W}\mathbf{v})$, where the parameter vector is projected onto an alternative coordinate system before regularization. To make OWA easy to implement, we show in this section how to approximately solve (8) using these optimizers.

We suggest approximating the regularization term by L2 regularization directly on the $\mathbf{v}$ vector:

$$\lambda r(\hat{W}\mathbf{v}) \approx \lambda_2 \|\mathbf{v}\|^2, \tag{9}$$

where λ_2 is a new hyperparameter. We provide two justifications for this approximation:

1. When we want the parameter vector $\mathbf{w}$ to be sparse (and so the regularizer r is the L1 norm), we have no reason to believe that the $\mathbf{v}$ vector should be sparse. The desired sparsity is induced by the regularization when solving for $\hat{\mathbf{w}}_i^{erm}$s on the local machines, and it is maintained in any linear combination of the $\hat{\mathbf{w}}_i^{erm}$s.
2. As the size of the dataset increases, the importance of the regularizer decreases. In this second optimization, the dimensionality of the problem is small and the theory requires few data points, guaranteeing the optimization runs fast. If we can increase the number of data points by several orders of magnitude (say from m^2n/d to $100m^2n/d$), the optimization will remain fast in practice and the influence of the regularization term becomes negligible.

The new λ_2 regularization parameter should be set by cross validation. This is a fast procedure, however, because the second optimization has so little data. Furthermore, this cross validation can be computed locally on the master machine without any communication. We again emphasize that Sect. 6 contains experiments where the first round of optimization took about a day, and the second round (including the selection of λ_2) took only about a minute.

3.4   Fast Cross Validation for OWA

We now introduce a novel fast cross validation algorithm for estimating the predictive performance of OWA. The standard method for k-fold cross validation takes linear time in the number of folds k. For large scale problems, this is too computationally expensive, and so cross validation is typically not used in this regime. Our fast cross validation procedure can estimate the predictive performance of OWA in constant time (relative to k). This makes our procedure suitable for large scale problems. Our method has two restrictions. First, we require the number of folds k must be equal to the number of machines m. Second, we require each machine already have access to the full Z^{owa} dataset.

Our procedure uses two rounds of computation and is shown in Algorithm 2. The first round trains the local estimators $\hat{\mathbf{w}}_i^{erm}$ as in Algorithm 1, but then broadcasts these parameter vectors to all machines (rather than just the master). In the second round, each machine i calculates $\hat{\mathbf{w}}_{-i}^{owa}$, which is a version of the OWA estimator trained on the data from all the machines except machine i. More formally, we define the matrix $\hat{W}_{-i} : \mathbb{R}^{d \times (m-1)}$ to be the matrix $\hat{W}$ with

Algorithm 2. Calculating $\hat{\mathbf{w}}^{owa}$ with fast cross validation

Preconditions:
    each machine i already has dataset Z_i
    each machine (not just the master) also has dataset Z^{owa}
Each machine i independently:
    calculates $\hat{\mathbf{w}}_i^{erm}$ using Equation (2)
    broadcasts $\hat{\mathbf{w}}_i^{erm}$ to all other machines
Each machine i independently:
    calculates $\hat{\mathbf{w}}_{-i}^{owa}$ using Equation (10)
    (optionally) $\hat{\mathbf{w}}_{-i}^{owa}$ calculated with approx. Eq. (9)
    computes $\widehat{\mathrm{err}}_i$ using Equation (12)
    transmits $\widehat{\mathrm{err}}_i$ to the master
The master
    computes $\hat{\mathbf{w}}^{owa}$ using Equation (7)
    computes $\frac{1}{m} \sum_{i=1}^m \widehat{\mathrm{err}}_i$

ith column removed. That is, $\hat{W}_{-i}$ is the concatenation of the $\hat{\mathbf{w}}_j^{erm}$ vectors for all $j \neq i$. Then let $Z_{-i}^{owa} = \{Z_j\}_{j \neq i}$ be the data set used in the second round of optimization without the data points from machine i. Finally, define the estimator

$$\hat{\mathbf{w}}_{-i}^{owa} = \hat{W}_{-i} \hat{\mathbf{v}}_{-i}^{owa}, \tag{10}$$

where

$$\hat{\mathbf{v}}_{-i}^{owa} = \arg\min_{\mathbf{v} \in \mathbb{R}^{m-1}} \sum_{(\mathbf{x},y) \in Z_{-i}^{owa}} \ell\left(y, \mathbf{x}^\mathsf{T} \hat{W}_{-i} \mathbf{v}\right) + \lambda r(\hat{W}_{-i} \mathbf{v}). \tag{11}$$

Notice that $\hat{\mathbf{w}}_{-i}^{owa}$ does not depend on the local data set Z_i. So

$$\widehat{\mathrm{err}}_i = \frac{1}{n} \sum_{(\mathbf{x},y) \in Z_i} \ell(y, \mathbf{x}^\mathsf{T} \hat{\mathbf{w}}_{-i}^{owa}) \tag{12}$$

is an unbiased estimate of the true error $\mathcal{L}^*(\hat{\mathbf{w}}_{-i}^{owa})$. The algorithm then transmits the $\widehat{\mathrm{err}}_i$ values to the master machine, which computes $\hat{\mathbf{w}}^{owa}$ as normal and computes the average of the error estimates. In total, $O(dm^2)$ bits are transmitted in the first round, and $O(dm)$ bits in the second round. When compared with Algorithm 1, the fast cross validation method requires a factor of m times more communication, and approximately twice as much computation.

This fast cross validation procedure critically used the fact that the OWA estimator is non-interactive. Similar procedures can be developed for other non-interactive distributed learning algorithms, but this technique cannot be used to develop fast cross validation methods for interactive algorithms. OWA's fast cross validation procedure is closely related to the out-of-bag method [5], monoid fast cross validation [7], and incremental fast cross validation [10], but none of these previous methods was developed specifically for the distributed setting.

4   Analysis

A major advantage of OWA's analysis is that it requires only simple and general conditions. Essentially, we will prove that whenever ERM is an optimal estimator, then OWA is also optimal. In Sect. 5 below, we will see that previous methods require more complicated and less general conditions. In this section, we first describe our main condition in detail. Then we outline the argument that OWA's estimation error $\|\hat{\mathbf{w}}^{owa} - \mathbf{w}^*\|$ and generalization error $\mathcal{L}^*(\hat{\mathbf{w}}^{owa}) - \mathcal{L}^*(\mathbf{w}^*)$ both decay as $O(\sqrt{d/mn})$. Full proofs of all theorems are provided in Appendix B.

4.1   The Sub-Gaussian Tail (SGT) Condition

Recall that each estimator is a random vector that is a function of the data. Informally, our main condition is that these vectors follow an approximately Gaussian distribution. This is a mild condition that many statistical models are known to satisfy. For example, the estimated parameters for all generalized linear models (such as logistic regression and ordinary least squares regression) are known to be approximately Gaussian. We now formally define our criterion and describe in detail how to establish that it holds.

Definition 1. *We say that a statistical model satisfies the* sub-Gaussian tail (SGT) *condition if the empirical risk minimizer* $\hat{\mathbf{w}}$ *trained on* n *i.i.d. data points of dimension* d *has the sub-Gaussian estimation error*

$$\Pr\left[\|\hat{\mathbf{w}} - \mathbf{w}^*\| \le O(\sqrt{dt/n})\right] \ge 1 - \exp(-t). \tag{13}$$

Remark 1. Notice that if $\hat{\mathbf{w}}$ has a Gaussian distribution it will satisfy the SGT condition, even if $\hat{\mathbf{w}}$ has arbitrary non-zero mean. (This is a standard property of sub-Gaussian distributions.) Thus, the SGT condition makes no assumptions about the model's bias.

A large body of statistical literature establishes the SGT condition for many models. Chapter 7 of Lehmann [13] provides an elementary introduction to results in the asymptotic regime as $n \to \infty$. Lehman requires only that the loss ℓ be three times differentiable, that the data points be i.i.d., and that $\mathbf{w}^*$ be identifiable. For example, models using the non-convex sigmoid loss satisfy these conditions, and thus can be used with the OWA estimator. Lehmann [13] also contains references to stronger asymptotic results that relax these already mild conditions.

    Other work establishes the SGT condition in the non-asymptotic regime $n < \infty$. Panov et al. [20] provides a particularly strong example. Their only condition is that the empirical loss admit a local approximation via the so-called *bracketing device*, which can be thought of as a generalization of the Taylor expansion. The full explanation of this condition is rather technical, but we highlight that this result does not require a convex loss or even that the data be i.i.d.

    The proofs of theorems establishing the SGT condition are typically long and technical. In our view, a limitation of previous non-interactive estimators is that their analysis proves limited forms of the SGT condition from scratch. This makes their proofs long and technical as well. It also limits the applicability of their results, because they do not prove the more general versions of the SGT condition cited above. Our work improves on this practice by "factoring out" these technical details. By relying on this established body of literature to prove the SGT condition for us, we get simpler proofs that apply more generally. In particular, we essentially conclude that whenever the ERM estimator successfully learns on a single machine (i.e. the SGT condition holds), then the OWA estimator successfully learns in a distributed environment. No other distributed estimator (interactive or non-interactive) can make such a strong claim.

4.2 The Main Idea: $\hat{\mathcal{W}}^{owa}$ Contains Good Solutions

The most important idea of OWA's analysis is to show that when the local $\hat{\mathbf{w}}_i^{erm}$ estimators satisfy the SGT condition, then $\hat{\mathcal{W}}^{owa}$ is a good subspace to optimize over. In particular, if we let $\pi_{\hat{\mathcal{W}}^{owa}}\mathbf{w}^*$ denote the projection of $\mathbf{w}^*$ onto $\hat{\mathcal{W}}^{owa}$, then we have that $\pi_{\hat{\mathcal{W}}^{owa}}\mathbf{w}^* \approx \mathbf{w}^*$. This idea is formalized in the following lemma.

Lemma 2. *Assume the model satisfies the SGT condition. Let $t > 0$. Then with probability at least $1 - \exp(-t)$,*

$$\|\pi_{\hat{\mathcal{W}}^{owa}}\mathbf{w}^* - \mathbf{w}^*\| \leq O(\sqrt{dt/mn}). \tag{14}$$

The proof of Lemma 2 is a direct consequence of the SGT condition.

4.3 Bounding the Generalization Error

In order to connect the result of Lemma 1 to OWA's generalization error, we need to introduce a smoothness condition on the true loss function $\mathcal{L}^*$. Lipschitz continuity is a widely used technique in both convex and non-convex analysis.

Definition 2. *We say that $\mathcal{L}^*$ is β-Lipschitz continuous if for all $\mathbf{w}_1$ and $\mathbf{w}_2$,*

$$|\mathcal{L}^*(\mathbf{w}_1) - \mathcal{L}^*(\mathbf{w}_2)| \leq \beta\|\mathbf{w}_1 - \mathbf{w}_2\|. \tag{15}$$

We now state our first main result, which guarantees that OWA will generalize well.

Theorem 3. *Assume the model satisfies the SGT condition, and that $\mathcal{L}^*$ is β-Lipschitz continuous. Let $t > 0$. Then with probability at least $1 - \exp(-t)$,*

$$\mathcal{L}^*(\hat{\mathbf{w}}^{owa}) - \mathcal{L}^*(\mathbf{w}^*) \leq O(\beta\sqrt{dt/mn}). \tag{16}$$

4.4 Bounding the Estimation Error

To bound the estimation error, we introduce a quadratic restriction on the growth of the true loss $\mathcal{L}^*$.

Definition 3. *We say the true loss $\mathcal{L}^*$ satisfies the* lower *quadratic growth (lower QG) condition if for all points $\mathbf{w} \in \mathcal{W}$,*

$$\alpha_{lo}\|\mathbf{w} - \mathbf{w}^*\|^2 \leq \mathcal{L}^*(\mathbf{w}) - \mathcal{L}^*(\mathbf{w}^*). \tag{17}$$

We say that $\mathcal{L}^*$ satisfies the upper *quadratic growth (upper QG) condition if it satisfies*

$$\mathcal{L}^*(\mathbf{w}) - \mathcal{L}^*(\mathbf{w}^*) \leq \alpha_{hi}\|\mathbf{w} - \mathbf{w}^*\|^2. \tag{18}$$

The lower QG condition has previously been used to study the convergence of non-convex optimization (e.g. [1,3]). This condition is a generalization of strong convexity that needs to hold only at the optimum $\mathbf{w}^*$ rather than all points in the domain. In particular, functions satisfying the lower QG condition may have many local minima with different objective values. Karimi et al. [11] compares the lower QG condition to six related generalizations of convexity, and shows that the QG condition is the weakest of these conditions in the sense that it is implied by all other conditions.

The intuitive meaning of the lower and upper QG conditions is that a quadratic function can be used to lower and upper bound $\mathcal{L}^*$. As the domain $\mathcal{W}$ shrinks to include only the optimal point $\mathbf{w}^*$, these lower and upper bounds converge to the Taylor expansion of $\mathcal{L}^*$. In this limit, the constant α_{lo} is the minimum eigenvalue of the Hessian at $\mathbf{w}^*$, and α_{hi} is the maximum eigenvalue. The ratio α_{hi}/α_{lo} can then be thought of as a generalized condition number.

Our main result is:

Theorem 4. *Assume the SGT condition and that that $\mathcal{L}^*$ satisfies the lower and upper QG conditions. Let $t > 0$. Then with probability at least $1 - \exp(-t)$,*

$$\|\hat{\mathbf{w}}^{owa} - \mathbf{w}^*\| \leq O\left(\sqrt{(\alpha_{hi}/\alpha_{lo})(dt/mn)}\right). \tag{19}$$

Note that up to the constant factor $\sqrt{\alpha_{hi}/\alpha_{lo}}$, OWA's estimation error matches that of the oracle ERM.

5   Other Non-interactive Estimators

Compared with similar non-interactive distributed estimators, OWA either has stronger statistical guarantees, is applicable to more models, or has a more computationally efficient merging procedure.

Lee et al. [12] and Battey et al. [2] independently develop closed form formulas for debiasing L1 regularized least squares regressions. They combine these debiased estimators with the averaging estimator to create a non-interactive estimator that reduces both bias and variance at the optimal rate. OWA's advantage over these methods is that it is that it can be applied to a much larger class of problems.

Jordan et al. [9] develop a more general approach that uses a single approximate Newton step in the merge procedure. As long as the initial starting point (they suggest using $\hat{\mathbf{w}}^{ave}$) is within $O(\sqrt{1/n})$ of the true parameter vector, then this approach converges at the optimal rate. When implementing Jordan et al.'s approach, we found it suffered from two practical difficulties. First, Newton steps can diverge if the starting point is not close enough. We found in our experiments that $\hat{\mathbf{w}}^{ave}$ was not always close enough. Second, Newton steps require inverting a Hessian matrix. In Sect. 6, we consider a problem with dimension $d \approx 7 \times 10^5$; the corresponding Hessian is too large to practically invert. For these reasons, we do not compare against Jordan et al. [9] in our experiments.

Zhang et al. [25] provide a debiasing technique that works for any estimator. Let $s \in (0, 1)$, and Z_i^s be a bootstrap sample of Z_i of size sn. Then the bootstrap average estimator is

$$\hat{\mathbf{w}}^{boot} = \frac{\hat{\mathbf{w}}^{ave} - s\hat{\mathbf{w}}^{ave,s}}{1 - s}, \tag{20}$$

where

$$\hat{\mathbf{w}}^{ave,s} = \frac{1}{m} \sum_{i=1}^{m} \arg\min_{\mathbf{w}} \sum_{(\mathbf{x},y)\in Z_i^s} \ell(y, \mathbf{x}^T\mathbf{w}) + \lambda r(\mathbf{w}).$$

The intuition behind this estimator is to use the bootstrap sample to directly estimate and correct for the bias. When the loss function is convex, $\hat{\mathbf{w}}^{boot}$ enjoys a mean squared error (MSE) that decays as $O((mn)^{-1}+n^{-3})$. Theorem 2 directly implies that the MSE of $\hat{\mathbf{w}}^{owa}$ decays as $O((mn)^{-1})$ under more general conditions. There are two additional limitations to $\hat{\mathbf{w}}^{boot}$. First, the optimal value of s is not obvious and setting the parameter requires cross validation on the entire data set. Our proposed $\hat{\mathbf{w}}^{owa}$ estimator has a similar parameter λ_2 that needs tuning, but this tuning happens on a small fraction of the data and always with the L2 regularizer. So properly tuning λ_2 is more efficient than s. Second, performing a bootstrap on an unbiased estimator increases the variance. This means that $\hat{\mathbf{w}}^{boot}$ could perform worse than $\hat{\mathbf{w}}^{ave}$ on unbiased estimators. Our $\hat{\mathbf{w}}^{owa}$ estimator, in contrast, will perform at least as well as $\hat{\mathbf{w}}^{ave}$ with high probability even for highly biased estimators (see Fig. 1). The next section shows that $\hat{\mathbf{w}}^{owa}$ has better empirical performance than $\hat{\mathbf{w}}^{boot}$.

Liu and Ihler [15] propose a more Bayesian approach. Instead of averaging the model's parameters, they directly "average the models" with the following KL-average estimator:

$$\hat{\mathbf{w}}^{kl} = \arg\min_{\mathbf{w}\in\mathcal{W}} \sum_{i=1}^{m} \text{KL}(p(\cdot; \hat{\mathbf{w}}_i^{erm})\|p(\cdot; \mathbf{w})). \tag{21}$$

Liu and Ihler show theoretically that this is the best merge function in the class of functions that do not depend on the data. Since OWA's merge depends on the data, however, this bound does not apply. The main disadvantage of KL-averaging is computational. The minimization in (21) is performed via a bootstrap sample from the local models, which is computationally expensive. Let k be the size of the bootstrap sample. Then Liu and Ihler's method has MSE that shrinks as $O((mn)^{-1} + k^{-1})$. This implies that the bootstrap procedure requires as many samples as the original problem to get a MSE that shrinks at the same rate as the averaging estimator. Han and Liu [6] provide a method to reduce the MSE to $O((mn)^{-1} + (n^2 k)^{-1})$ using control variates, but the procedure remains prohibitively expensive. Their experiments show the procedure scaling only to datasets of size $mn \approx 10^4$, whereas our experiments involve a dataset of size $mn \approx 10^8$.

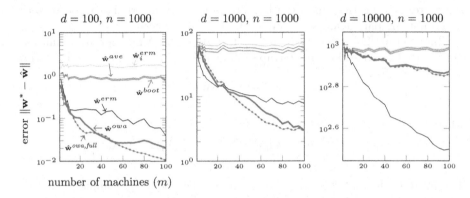

number of machines (m)

Fig. 2. The left figure shows scalability in the low dimension regime, the middle figure in a medium dimension regime, and the right figure in a high dimension regime. $\hat{\mathbf{w}}^{owa}$ scales well with the number of machines in all cases. Surprisingly, $\hat{\mathbf{w}}^{owa}$ outperforms the oracle estimator trained on all of the data $\hat{\mathbf{w}}^{erm}$ in some situations.

6   Experiments

We evaluate OWA on synthetic and real-world logistic regression tasks. In each experiment, we compare $\hat{\mathbf{w}}^{owa}$ with four baseline estimators: the naive estimator using the data from only a single machine $\hat{\mathbf{w}}_i^{erm}$; the averaging estimator $\hat{\mathbf{w}}^{ave}$; the bootstrap estimator $\hat{\mathbf{w}}^{boot}$; and the oracle estimator of all data trained on a single machine $\hat{\mathbf{w}}^{erm}$. The $\hat{\mathbf{w}}^{boot}$ estimator has a parameter s that needs to be tuned. In all experiments we evaluate $\hat{\mathbf{w}}^{boot}$ with $s \in \{0.005, 0.01, 0.02, 0.04, 0.1, 0.2\}$, which is a set recommended in the original paper [25], and then report only the value of s with highest true likelihood. Thus we are reporting an overly optimistic estimate of the performance of $\hat{\mathbf{w}}^{boot}$, and as we shall see $\hat{\mathbf{w}}^{owa}$ still tends to perform better. OWA is always trained using the regularization approximation of Sect. 3.3, and Z^{owa} is always resampled from the original dataset.

In all experiments, we use the scikit-learn machine learning library [21] to perform the optimizations. We made no special efforts to tune parameters of the optimization routines. For example, all optimizations are performed with the

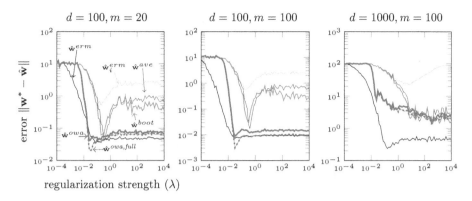

Fig. 3. OWA is robust to the regularization strength used to solve $\hat{\mathbf{w}}_i^{erm}$. Our theory states that as $m \to d$, we have that $\hat{\mathcal{W}}^{owa} \to \mathcal{W}$, and so $\hat{\mathbf{w}}^{owa} \to \hat{\mathbf{w}}^{erm}$. This is confirmed in the middle experiment. In the left experiment, $m < d$, but $\hat{\mathbf{w}}^{owa}$ still behaves similarly to $\hat{\mathbf{w}}^{erm}$. In the right experiment, $\hat{\mathbf{w}}^{owa}$ has similar performance as $\hat{\mathbf{w}}^{ave}$ and $\hat{\mathbf{w}}^{boot}$ but over a wider range of λ values.

default target accuracy of 1×10^{-3}. Additionally, when performing the hyperparameter optimization for λ_2 in (9), we use the default hyperparameter selection procedure.

6.1 Synthetic Data

We generate the data according to a sparse logistic regression model. Each component of $\mathbf{w}^*$ is sampled i.i.d. from a spike and slab distribution. With probability 0.9, it is 0; with probability 0.1, it is sampled from a standard normal distribution. The data points are then sampled as

$$\mathbf{x}_i \sim \mathcal{N}(0, I) \tag{22}$$

$$y_i \sim \text{Bernoulli}\left(1/\left(1 + \exp(-\mathbf{x}_i^\top \mathbf{w}^*)\right)\right). \tag{23}$$

The primary advantage of synthetic data is that we know the model's true parameter vector. So for each estimator $\hat{\mathbf{w}}$ that we evaluate, we can directly calculate the error $\|\hat{\mathbf{w}} - \mathbf{w}^*\|$. We run two experiments on the synthetic data. In both experiments, we use the L1 regularizer to induce sparsity in our estimates of $\mathbf{w}^*$. Results are qualitatively similar when using a Laplace, Gaussian, or uniform prior on $\mathbf{w}^*$, and with L2 regularization.

Our first experiment shows how the estimators scale as the number of machines m increases. We fix $n = 1000$ data points per machine, so the size of the dataset mn grows as we add more machines. This simulates the typical "big data" regime where data is abundant, but processing resources are scarce. For each value of m, we generate 50 datasets and report the average of the results. The results are shown in Fig. 2. As the analysis predicted, the performance of $\hat{\mathbf{w}}^{owa}$ scales much better than

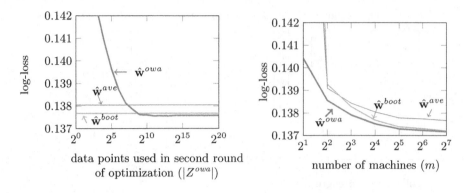

Fig. 4. (*left*) Relatively few data points are needed in the second round of optimization for $\hat{\mathbf{w}}^{owa}$ to converge. On this dataset, only 2.7×10^{-6} percent of the data is needed. (*right*) Performance of the parallel estimators on advertising data as the number of machines m increases.

$\hat{\mathbf{w}}^{ave}$ and $\hat{\mathbf{w}}^{boot}$. Surprisingly, in the low dimensional regimes, $\hat{\mathbf{w}}^{owa}$ outperforms the single machine oracle $\hat{\mathbf{w}}^{erm}$.

Our second experiment shows the importance of proper λ selection. We evaluate the performance of the estimators with λ varying from 10^{-4} to 10^4 on a grid of 80 points. Figure 3 shows the results. The $\hat{\mathbf{w}}^{owa}$ estimator is more robust to the choice of λ than the other distributed estimators. We suspect that slight misspecification of λ in the first round of optimization is compensated for in the second round of optimization.

6.2   Real World Advertising Data

We evaluate the estimators on real world data from the KDD 2012 Cup [19]. The goal is to predict whether a user will click on an ad from the Tencent internet search engine. This dataset was previously used to evaluate the performance of $\hat{\mathbf{w}}^{boot}$ [25]. This dataset is too large to fit on a single machine, so we must use distributed estimators, and we do not provide results of the oracle estimator $\hat{\mathbf{w}}^{erm}$ in our figures. There are 235,582,879 distinct data points, each of dimension 741,725. The data points are sparse, so we use the L1 norm to encourage sparsity in our final solution. The regularization strength was set using cross validation in the same manner as for the synthetic data. For each test, we split the data into 80% training data and 20% test data. The training data is further subdivided into 128 partitions, one for each of the machines used. It took about 1 day to train the local model on each machine in our cluster.

Our first experiment measures the importance of the number of data points used in the second optimization (i.e. $|Z^{owa}|$). We fix $m = 128$, and allow $|Z^{owa}|$ to vary from 2^0 to 2^{20}. When $|Z^{owa}| = 2^{20}$, almost the entire dataset is used in the second optimization. We repeated the experiment 50 times, each time using a different randomly selected set Z^{owa} for the second optimization. Figure 4 (*left*) shows the results. Our $\hat{\mathbf{w}}^{owa}$ estimator has lower loss than $\hat{\mathbf{w}}^{ave}$ using only $|Z^{owa}| = 2^{15}$ data points (approximately 4×10^{-8} percent of the full training set) and $\hat{\mathbf{w}}^{owa}$ has converged to its final loss value with only $|Z^{owa}| = 2^{17}$ data points (approximately 2.7×10^{-6} percent of the full training set). This justifies our claim that only a small number of data points are needed for the second round of optimization. The computation is also very fast due to the lower dimensionality and L2 regularization in the second round of optimization. When $|Z^{owa}| = 2^{17}$, computing the merged model took about a minute (including the cross validation time to select λ_2). This time is negligible compared to the approximately 1 day it took to train the models on the individual machines.

Our last experiment shows the performance as we scale the number of machines m. The results are shown in Fig. 4 (*right*). Here, $\hat{\mathbf{w}}^{owa}$ performs especially well with low m. For large m, $\hat{\mathbf{w}}^{owa}$ continues to slightly outperform $\hat{\mathbf{w}}^{boot}$ without the need for an expensive model selection procedure to determine the s parameter.

7   Conclusion

We introduced OWA, a non-interactive distributed estimator for linear models. OWA is easy to implement and has optimal statistical guarantees that hold under general conditions. We showed experimentally that OWA outperforms other non-interactive estimators, and in particular that OWA exhibits a weaker dependence on the regularization strength.

Acknowledgments. Shelton was supported by the National Science Foundation (IIS 1510741).

References

1. Anitescu, M.: Degenerate nonlinear programming with a quadratic growth condition. SIAM J. Optim. **10**(4), 1116–1135 (2000)
2. Battey, H., Fan, J., Liu, H., Lu, J., Zhu, Z.: Distributed estimation and inference with statistical guarantees. arXiv preprint arXiv:1509.05457 (2015)
3. Bonnans, J.F., Ioffe, A.: Second-order sufficiency and quadratic growth for nonisolated minima. Math. Oper. Res. **20**(4), 801–817 (1995)
4. Boyd, S., Parikh, N., Chu, E., Peleato, B., Eckstein, J.: Distributed optimization and statistical learning via the alternating direction method of multipliers. Found. Trends Mach. Learn. **3**(1), 1–122 (2011)
5. Breiman, L.: Out-of-bag estimation. Technical report (1996)
6. Han, J., Liu, Q.: Bootstrap model aggregation for distributed statistical learning. In: NeurIPS (2016)
7. Izbicki, M.: Algebraic classifiers: a generic approach to fast cross-validation, online training, and parallel training. In: ICML (2013)
8. Jaggi, M., et al.: Communication-efficient distributed dual coordinate ascent. In: NeurIPS, pp. 3068–3076 (2014)

9. Jordan, M.I., Lee, J.D., Yang, Y.: Communication-efficient distributed statistical inference. arXiv preprint arXiv:1605.07689 (2016)
10. Joulani, P., György, A., Szepesvári, C.: Fast cross-validation for incremental learning. In: IJCAI, pp. 3597–3604 (2015)
11. Karimi, H., Nutini, J., Schmidt, M.: Linear convergence of gradient and proximal-gradient methods under the Polyak-Lojasiewicz condition. In: Frasconi, P., Landwehr, N., Manco, G., Vreeken, J. (eds.) ECML PKDD 2016. LNCS (LNAI), vol. 9851, pp. 795–811. Springer, Cham (2016). https://doi.org/10.1007/978-3-319-46128-1_50
12. Lee, J.D., Liu, Q., Sun, Y., Taylor, J.E.: Communication-efficient sparse regression. JMLR **18**(5), 1–30 (2017)
13. Lehmann, E.L.: Elements of Large-Sample Theory. Springer Texts in Statistics. Springer, New York (1999). https://doi.org/10.1007/b98855
14. Li, M., Andersen, D.G., Park, J.W.: Scaling distributed machine learning with the parameter server. In: OSDI (2014)
15. Liu, Q., Ihler, A.T.: Distributed estimation, information loss and exponential families. In NeurIPS, pp. 1098–1106 (2014)
16. Ma, C., Smith, V., Jaggi, M., Jordan, M.I., Richtárik, P., Takáč., M.: Adding vs. averaging in distributed primal-dual optimization. In: International Conference of Machine Learning (2015)
17. McDonald, R., Mohri, M., Silberman, N., Walker, D., Mann, G.S.: Efficient large-scale distributed training of conditional maximum entropy models. In: NeurIPS, pp. 1231–1239 (2009)
18. McMahan, H.B., Moore, E., Ramage, D., Hampson, S., et al.: Communication-efficient learning of deep networks from decentralized data. In: AISTATS (2017)
19. Niu, Y., et al.: The tencent dataset and KDD-cup'12 (2012)
20. Panov, M., Spokoiny, V., et al.: Finite sample Bernstein-von Mises theorem for semiparametric problems. Bayesian Anal. **10**(3), 665–710 (2015)
21. Pedregosa, F., et al.: Scikit-learn: machine learning in Python. JMLR **12**, 2825–2830 (2011)
22. Rosenblatt, J.D., Nadler, B.: On the optimality of averaging in distributed statistical learning. Inf. Infer. **5**(4), 379–404 (2016)
23. Smith, V., Forte, S., Ma, C., Takáč, M., Jordan, M.I., Jaggi, M.: Cocoa: a general framework for communication-efficient distributed optimization. JMLR **18**, 230 (2018)
24. Wang, S.: A sharper generalization bound for divide-and-conquer ridge regression. In: AAAI (2019)
25. Zhang, Y., Wainwright, M.J., Duchi, J.C.: Communication-efficient algorithms for statistical optimization. In: NeurIPS, pp. 1502–1510 (2012)
26. Zhang, Y., Duchi, J.C., Wainwright, M.J.: Divide and conquer kernel ridge regression. In: COLT (2013)
27. Zhao, S.-Y., Ru, X., Shi, Y.-H., Gao, P., Li, W-J.: Scope: scalable composite optimization for learning on spark. In: AAAI (2017)
28. Zinkevich, M., Weimer, M., Li, L., Smola, A.J.: Parallelized stochastic gradient descent. In: NeurIPS, pp. 2595–2603 (2010)

SLSGD: Secure and Efficient Distributed On-device Machine Learning

Cong Xie$^{(\boxtimes)}$ ⓘ, Oluwasanmi Koyejo ⓘ, and Indranil Gupta ⓘ

University of Illinois at Urbana-Champaign, Urbana and Champaign, USA
{cx2,sanmi,indy}@illinois.edu

Abstract. We consider distributed on-device learning with limited communication and security requirements. We propose a new robust distributed optimization algorithm with efficient communication and attack tolerance. The proposed algorithm has provable convergence and robustness under non-IID settings. Empirical results show that the proposed algorithm stabilizes the convergence and tolerates data poisoning on a small number of workers.

Keywords: Distributed · SGD

1 Introduction

Edge devices/IoT such as smart phones, wearable devices, sensors, and smart homes are increasingly generating massive, diverse, and private data. In response, there is a trend towards moving computation, including the training of machine-learning models, from cloud/datacenters to edge devices [1,24]. Ideally, since trained on massive representative data, the resulting models exhibit improved generalization. In this paper, we consider distributed on-device machine learning. The distributed system is a server-worker architecture. The workers are placed on edge devices, which train the models on the private data. The servers are placed on the cloud/datacenters which maintain a shared global model. Distributed settings require addressing some novel engineering challenges, including the following:

- **Limited, heterogeneous computation.** Edge devices, including smart phones, wearable devices, sensors, or vehicles typically have weaker computational ability, compared to the workstations or datacenters used in typical distributed machine learning. Thus, simpler models and stochastic training are usually applied in practice. Furthermore, different devices have different computation capabilities.
- **Limited communication.** The connection to the central servers are not guaranteed. Communication can be frequently unavailable, slow, or expensive (in money or in the power of battery). Thus, frequent high-speed communication is typically unaffordable.

© Springer Nature Switzerland AG 2020
U. Brefeld et al. (Eds.): ECML PKDD 2019, LNAI 11907, pp. 213–228, 2020.
https://doi.org/10.1007/978-3-030-46147-8_13

- **Decentralized, non-IID training data.** Privacy needs and legal requirements (e.g., US HIPAA laws [12] in a smart hospital, or Europe's GDPR law [8]) may necessitate that training be performed on-premises using IoT devices and edge machines, and that data and models must not be deposited in the cloud or cloudlets. In more general cases, the users simply dislike sharing their on-device data which potentially reveals private information. As a result, the data distribution on different devices are neither mixed nor IID i.e. unlike standard settings, device data are non-identically distributed samples from the population. This is particularly true when each device is controlled by a specific user whose behavior is supposed to be unique. Furthermore, the sampled data on nearby devices are potentially non-independent, since such devices can be shared by the same user or family. For example, the data of a step counter from a wearable fitness tracker and a smart phone owned by the same user can have different distributions of motion data with mutual dependency. Imagine that the fitness tracker is only used when the user is running, and the smart phone is only used when the user is walking, which results in different distributions. On the other hand, the complementation yields dependency.
- **Untrusted workers and data poisoning.** The servers have limited control over the users' behavior. To protect the privacy, the users are in general anonymous to the servers. Although it is possible to verity the identity of workers/devices [25], nefarious users can feed poisoned data with abnormal behaviors without backdooring OS. As a result, some workers may push models learned on poisoned data to the servers.

To overcome the challenges above, we introduce Secure Local Stochastic Gradient Descent (SLSGD), which reduces the communication overhead with local updates, and secures the global model against nefarious users and poisoned data. We summarize the key properties of SLSGD below:

- **Local SGD.** SGD is widely used for training models with lower computation overhead. To reduce communication overhead, we use SGD with local updates. The workers do not synchronize with the server after each local gradient descent step. After several local iterations, the workers push the updated model to the servers, which is different from the traditional distributed synchronous SGD where gradients are pushed in each local gradient descent step. To further reduce the communication overhead, the training tasks are activated on a random subset of workers in each global epoch.
- **Secure aggregation.** In each global epoch, the servers send the latest global model to the activated workers, and aggregate the updated local models. In such procedure, there are two types of threats: (i) poisoned models pushed from comprised devices, occupied or hacked by nefarious users; (ii) accumulative error, variance, or models over-fitted on the local dataset, caused by infrequent synchronization of local SGD. To secure the global model against these two threats, we use robust aggregation which tolerates abnormal models, and moving average which mitigates the errors caused by infrequent synchronization.

To our knowledge, there is limited work on local SGD with theoretical guarantees [26,31]. The existing convergence guarantees are based on the strong assumption of IID training data or homogeneous local iterations, which we have argued is inappropriate for distributed learning on edge devices.

We propose SLSGD, which is a variant of local SGD with provable convergence under non-IID and heterogeneous settings, and tolerance to nefarious users. In summary, the main contributions are listed as follows:

- We show that SLSGD theoretically converges to global optimums for strongly convex functions, non-strongly convex functions, and a restricted family of non-convex functions, under non-IID settings. Furthermore, more local iterations accelerate the convergence.
- We show that SLSGD tolerates a small number of workers training on poisoned data. As far as we know, this paper is the first to investigate the robustness of local SGD.
- We show empirically that the proposed algorithm stabilizes the convergence, and protects the global model from data poisoning.

2   Related Work

Our algorithm is based on local SGD introduced in [26,31]. The major differences are:

1. We assume non-IID training data and heterogeneous local iterations among the workers. In previous work, local SGD and its convergence analysis required IID training data, or same number of local iterations within each global epoch (or both). However, these assumptions are unreasonable for edge computing, due to privacy preservation and heterogeneous computation.
2. Instead of using the averaged model to overwrite the current global model on the server, we take robust aggregation, and use a moving average to update the current model. These techniques not only secure the global model against data poisoning, but also mitigate the error caused by infrequent synchronization of local SGD.

The limited communication power of edge devices also motivates federated learning [16,17,22], whose algorithm is similar to local SGD, and scenario is similar to our non-IID and heterogeneous settings. Unfortunately, federated learning lacks provable convergence guarantees. Furthermore, the issues of data poisoning have not been addressed in previous work. To the best of our knowledge, our proposed work is the first that considers both convergence and robustness, theoretically and practically, on non-IID training data.

Similar to the traditional distributed machine learning, we use the server-worker architecture, which is similar to the Parameter Server (PS) architecture. Stochastic Gradient Descent (SGD) with PS architecture, is widely used in typical distributed machine learning [13,19,20]. Compared to the traditional distributed learning on PS, SLSGD has much less synchronization. Furthermore, in SLSGD, the workers push trained models instead of gradients to the servers.

Approaches based on robust statistics are often used to address security issues in the PS architecture [27,30]. This enables procedures which tolerate multiple types of attacks and system failures. However, the existing methods and theoretical analysis do not consider local training on non-IID data. So far, the convergence guarantees are based on robust gradient aggregation. In this paper, we provide convergence guarantees for robust model aggregation. Note that gradients and models (parameters) have different properties. For example, the gradients converge to 0 for unconstrained problems, while the models do not have such property. On the other hand, recent work has considered attacks not only targeting traditional distributed SGD [28], but also federated learning [3,4, 9], but do not propose defense techniques with provable convergence. There are other robust SGD algorithms whose defense techniques are not based on robust stochastic [29].

There is growing literature on the practical applications of edge and fog computing [10,14] in various scenarios such as smart home or sensor networks. More and more big-data applications are moving from the cloud to the edge, including for machine-learning tasks [5,21,32]. Although computational power is growing, edge devices are still much weaker than the workstations and datacenters used in typical distributed machine learning e.g. due to the limited computation and communication capacity, and limited power of batteries. To this end, there are machine-learning frameworks with simple architectures such as MobileNet [15] which are designed for learning with weak devices.

3   Problem Formulation

Consider distributed learning with n devices. On each device, there is a worker process that trains the model on local data. The overall goal is to train a global model $x \in \mathbb{R}^d$ using data from all the devices.

To do so, we consider the following optimization problem: $\min_{x \in \mathbb{R}^d} F(x)$, where $F(x) = \frac{1}{n} \sum_{i \in [n]} \mathbb{E}_{z^i \sim \mathcal{D}^i} f(x; z^i)$, for $\forall i \in [n]$, z^i is sampled from the local data $\mathcal{D}^i$ on the ith device.

3.1   Non-IID Local Datasets

Note that different devices have different local datasets, i.e., $\mathcal{D}^i \neq \mathcal{D}^j, \forall i \neq j$. Thus, samples drawn from different devices have different expectations, i.e., $\mathbb{E}_{z^i \sim \mathcal{D}^i} f(x; z^i) \neq \mathbb{E}_{z^j \sim \mathcal{D}^j} f(x; z^j), \forall i \neq j$. Further, since different devices can be possessed by the same user or the same group of users (e.g., families), samples drawn from different devices can be potentially dependent on each other.

3.2   Data Poisoning

The users are anonymous to the servers. Furthermore, it is impossible for the servers to verify the benignity of the on-device training data. Thus, the servers can not trust the edge devices. A small number of devices may be susceptible to

Table 1. Notations and terminologies

Notation/term	Description
n	Number of devices
k	Number of simultaneously updating devices
T	Number of communication epochs
$[n]$	Set of integers $\{1, \ldots, n\}$
S_t	Randomly selected devices in the tth epoch
b	Parameter of trimmed mean
H_{min}	Minimal number of local iterations
H_t^i	Number of local iterations in the tth epoch on the ith device
x_t	Initial model in the tth epoch
$x_{t,h}^i$	Model updated in the tth epoch, hth local iteration, on the ith device
$\mathcal{D}^i$	Dataset on the ith device
$z_{t,h}^i$	Data (minibatch) sampled in the tth epoch, hth local iteration, on the ith device
γ	Learning rate
α	Weight of moving average
$\|\cdot\|$	All the norms in this paper are l_2-norms
Device	Where the training data are placed
Worker	One worker on each device, process that trains the model
User	Agent that produces data on the devices, and/or controls the devices
Nefarious user	Special user that produces poisoned data or has abnormal behaviors

data poisoned by abnormal user behaviors or in the worst case, are controlled by users or agents who intend to directly upload harmful models to the servers.

In this paper, we consider a generalized threat model, where the workers can push arbitrarily bad models to the servers. The bad models can cause divergence of training. Beyond more benign issues such as hardware, software or communication failures, there are multiple ways for nefarious users to manipulate the uploaded models e.g. data poisoning [2]. In worst case, nefarious users can even directly hack the devices and replace the correct models with arbitrary values. We provide a more formal definition of the threat model in Sect. 4.1.

4 Methodology

In this paper, we propose SLSGD: SGD with communication efficient local updates and secure model aggregation. A single execution of SLSGD is composed of T communication epochs. At the beginning of each epoch, a randomly selected group of devices S_t pull the latest global model from the central server. Then, the same group of devices locally update the model without communication with the central server. At the end of each epoch, the central server aggregates the updated models and then updates the global model.

In the tth epoch, on the ith device, we locally solve the following optimization problem using SGD for H_t^i iterations: $\min_{x \in \mathbb{R}^d} \mathbb{E}_{z^i \sim \mathcal{D}^i} f(x; z^i)$. Then, the server collects the resulting local models $x_{t,H_t^i}^i$, and aggregates them using $\text{Aggr}\left(\{x_{t,H_t^i}^i : i \in S_t\}\right)$. Finally, we update the model with a moving average over the current model and the aggregated local models.

The detailed algorithm is shown in Algorithm 1. $x_{t,h}^i$ is the model parameter updated in hth local iteration of the tth epoch, on the ith device. $z_{t,h}^i$ is the data randomly drawn in hth local iteration of the tth epoch, on the ith device. H_t^i is the number of local iterations in the tth epoch, on the ith device. γ is the learning rate and T is the total number of epochs. Note that if we take Option I (or Option II with $b = 0$) with $\alpha = 1$, the algorithm is the same as the federated learning algorithm *FedAvg* [22]. Furthermore, if we take homogeneous local iterations $H_t^i = H, \forall i$, Option I with $\alpha = 1$ is the same as local SGD [26]. Thus, FedAvg and local SGD are both special cases of SLSGD.

Algorithm 1. SLSGD

1: Input: $k \in [n]$, b
2: Initialize x_0
3: **for all** epoch $t \in [T]$ **do**
4:     Randomly select a group of k workers, denoted as $S_t \subseteq [n]$
5:     **for all** $i \in S_t$ in parallel **do**
6:         Receive the latest global model x_{t-1} from the server
7:         $x_{t,0}^i \leftarrow x_{t-1}$
8:         **for all** local iteration $h \in [H_t^i]$ **do**
9:             Randomly sample $z_{t,h}^i$
10:             $x_{t,h}^i \leftarrow x_{t,h-1}^i - \gamma \nabla f(x_{t,h-1}^i; z_{t,h}^i)$
11:         **end for**
12:         Push $x_{t,H_t^i}^i$ to the server
13:     **end for**
14:     Aggregate: $x_t' \leftarrow \begin{cases} \text{Option I:} & \frac{1}{k} \sum_{i \in S_t} x_{t,H_t^i}^i \\ \text{Option II:} & \text{Trmean}_b \left(\left\{x_{t,H_t^i}^i : i \in S_t\right\}\right) \end{cases}$
15:     Update the global model: $x_t \leftarrow (1 - \alpha)x_{t-1} + \alpha x_t'$
16: **end for**

4.1 Threat Model and Defense Technique

First, we formally define the threat model.

Definition 1 *(Threat Model). In Line 12 of Algorithm 1, instead of the correct $x_{t,H_t^i}^i$, a worker, training on poisoned data or controlled by an abnormal/nefarious user, may push arbitrary values to the server.*

Remark 1. Note that the users/workers are anonymous to the servers, and the nefarious users can sometimes pretend to be well-behaved to fool the servers. Hence, it is impossible to surely identify the workers training on poisoned data, according to their historical behavior.

In Algorithm 1, Option II uses the trimmed mean as a robust aggregation which tolerates the proposed threat model. To define the trimmed mean, we first define the order statistics.

Definition 2 *(Order Statistics). By sorting the scalar sequence $\{u_i : i \in [k], u_i \in \mathbb{R}\}$, we get $u_{1:k} \le u_{2:k} \le \ldots \le u_{k:k}$, where $u_{i:k}$ is the ith smallest element in $\{u_i : i \in [k]\}$.*

Then, we define the trimmed mean.

Definition 3 *(Trimmed Mean). For $b \in \{0, 1, \ldots, \lceil k/2 \rceil - 1\}$, the b-trimmed mean of the set of scalars $\{u_i : i \in [k]\}$ is defined as follows:*

$$\mathtt{Trmean}_b(\{u_i : i \in [k]\}) = \frac{1}{k - 2b} \sum_{i=b+1}^{k-b} u_{i:k},$$

where $u_{i:k}$ is the ith smallest element in $\{u_i : i \in [k]\}$ defined in Definition 2. The high-dimensional version ($u_i \in \mathbb{R}^d$) of $\mathtt{Trmean}_b(\cdot)$ simply applies the trimmed mean in a coordinate-wise manner.

Note that the trimmed mean (Option II) is equivalent to the standard mean (Option I) if we take $b = 0$.

Remark 2. Algorithm 1 provides two levels of defense: robust aggregation (Line 14) and moving average (Line 15). The robust aggregation tries to filter out the models trained on poisoned data. The moving average mitigates not only the extra variance/error caused by robust aggregation and data poisoning, but also the accumulative error caused by infrequent synchronization of local updates.

Remark 3. We can also replace the coordinate-wise trimmed mean with other robust statistics such as geometric median [7]. We choose coordinate-wise median/trimmed mean in this paper because unlike geometric median, trimmed mean has a computationally efficient closed-form solution.

5   Convergence Analysis

In this section, we prove the convergence of Algorithm 1 with non-IID data, for a restricted family of non-convex functions. Furthermore, we show that the proposed algorithm tolerates the threat model introduced in Definition 1. We start with the assumptions required by the convergence guarantees.

5.1   Assumptions

For convenience, we denote $F^i(x) = \mathbb{E}_{z^i \sim \mathcal{D}^i} f(x; z^i)$.

Assumption 1 *(Existence of Global Optimum).* *We assume that there exists at least one (potentially non-unique) global minimum of the loss function $F(x)$, denoted by x^*.*

Assumption 2 *(Bounded Taylor's Approximation).* *We assume that for $\forall x, z$, $f(x; z)$ has L-smoothness and μ-weak convexity: $\langle \nabla f(x; z), y - x \rangle + \frac{\mu}{2} \|y - x\|^2 \le f(y; z) - f(x; z) \le \langle \nabla f(x; z), y - x \rangle + \frac{L}{2} \|y - x\|^2$, where $\mu \le L$, and $L > 0$.*

Note that Assumption 2 covers the case of non-convexity by taking $\mu < 0$, non-strong convexity by taking $\mu = 0$, and strong convexity by taking $\mu > 0$.

Assumption 3 *(Bounded Gradient).* *We assume that for $\forall x \in \mathbb{R}^d, i \in [n]$, and $\forall z \sim \mathcal{D}^i$, we have $\|\nabla f(x; z)\|^2 \le V_1$.*

Based on the assumptions above, we have the following convergence guarantees. All the detailed proofs can be found in the appendix.

5.2   Convergence Without Data Poisoning

First, we analyze the convergence of Algorithm 1 with Option I, where there are no poisoned workers.

Theorem 1. *We take $\gamma \le \min\left(\frac{1}{L}, 2\right)$. After T epochs, Algorithm 1 with Option I converges to a global optimum:*

$$\mathbb{E}\left[F(x_T) - F(x_*)\right] \le \left(1 - \alpha + \alpha(1 - \frac{\gamma}{2})^{H_{min}}\right)^T \left[F(x_0) - F(x_*)\right]$$

$$+ \left[1 - \left(1 - \alpha + \alpha(1 - \frac{\gamma}{2})^{H_{min}}\right)^T\right] \mathcal{O}\left(V_1 + \left(1 + \frac{1}{k} - \frac{1}{n}\right) V_2\right),$$

where $V_2 = \max_{t \in \{0, T-1\}, h \in \{0, H_t^i - 1\}, i \in [n]} \|x_{t,h}^i - x_*\|^2$.

Remark 4. When $\alpha \to 1$, $\left(1 - \alpha + \alpha(1 - \frac{\gamma}{2})^{H_{min}}\right)^T \to (1 - \frac{\gamma}{2})^{T H_{min}}$, which results in nearly linear convergence to the global optimum, with error $\mathcal{O}(V_1 + V_2)$. When $\alpha \to 0$, the error is nearly reduced 0, but the convergence will slow down. We can tune α to trade-off between the convergence rate and the error. In practice, we can take diminishing α: $\alpha_t \propto \frac{1}{t^2}$, where α_t is the α in the tth global epoch. Furthermore, taking $\alpha_T = \frac{1}{T^2}$, $\lim_{T \to +\infty} \left[1 - \left(1 - \alpha_T + \alpha_T(1 - \frac{\gamma}{2})^{H_{min}}\right)^T\right] = 0$.

5.3   Convergence with Data Poisoning

Under the threat model defined in Definition 1, in worst case, Algorithm 1 with Option I and $\alpha = 1$ (local SGD) suffers from unbounded error.

Proposition 1 *(Informal). Algorithm 1 with Option I and $\alpha = 1$ can not tolerate the threat model defined in Definition 1.*

Proof (Sketch). Without loss of generality, assume that in a specific epoch t, among all the k workers, the last q_1 of them are poisoned. For the poisoned workers, instead of pushing the correct value $x_{t,H_t^i}^i$ to the server, they push $-\frac{k-q_1}{q_1}x_{t,H_t^i}^i + c$, where c is an arbitrary constant. For convenience, we assume IID (required by local SGD, but not our algorithm) local datasets for all the workers. Thus, the expectation of the aggregated global model becomes $\frac{1}{k}\left\{(k-q_1)\mathbb{E}\left[x_{t,H_t^i}^i\right] + q_1\mathbb{E}\left[-\frac{k-q_1}{q_1}x_{t,H_t^i}^i + c\right]\right\} = \frac{q_1}{k}c$, which means that in expectation, the aggregated global model can be manipulated to take arbitrary values, which results in unbounded error.

In the following theorems, we show that using Algorithm 1 with Option II, the error can be upper bounded.

Theorem 2. *Assume that additional to the n normal workers, there are q workers training on poisoned data, where $q \ll n$, and $2q \leq 2b < k$. We take $\gamma \leq \min\left(\frac{1}{L}, 2\right)$. After T epochs, Algorithm 1 with Option II converges to a global optimum:*

$$\mathbb{E}\left[F(x_T) - F(x_*)\right] \leq \left(1 - \alpha + \alpha(1 - \frac{\gamma}{2})^{H_{min}}\right)^T \left[F(x_0) - F(x_*)\right]$$
$$+ \left[1 - \left(1 - \alpha + \alpha(1 - \frac{\gamma}{2})^{H_{min}}\right)^T\right]\left[\mathcal{O}(V_1) + \mathcal{O}(\beta V_2)\right],$$

where $V_2 = \max_{t \in \{0, T-1\}, h \in \{0, H_t^i - 1\}, i \in [n]} \left\|x_{t,h}^i - x_*\right\|^2$, $\beta = 1 + \frac{1}{k-q} - \frac{1}{n} + \frac{k(k+b)}{(k-b-q)^2}$.

Remark 5. Note that the additional error caused by the q poisoned workers and b-trimmed mean is controlled by the factor $\frac{k(k+b)}{(k-b-q)^2}$, which decreases when q and b decreases, or k increases.

6   Experiments

In this section, we evaluate the proposed algorithm by testing its convergence and robustness. Note that zoomed figures of the empirical results can be found in the appendix.

6.1   Datasets and Evaluation Metrics

We conduct experiments on the benchmark CIFAR-10 image classification dataset [18], which is composed of 50k images for training and 10k images for testing. Each image is resized and cropped to the shape of $(24, 24, 3)$. We use a convolutional neural network (CNN) with 4 convolutional layers followed by 1 fully connected layer. We use a simple network architecture, so that it can be easily handled by edge devices. The detailed network architecture can be found in our submitted source code (will also be released upon publication). The experiments are conducted on CPU devices. We implement SLSGD using the MXNET [6] framework.

We also conduct experiments of LSTM-based language models on WikiText-2 dataset [23]. The model architecture was taken from the MXNET and Gluon-NLP tutorial [11]. The results can be found in the appendix.

In each experiment, the training set is partitioned onto $n = 100$ devices. We test the performance of SLSGD on both balanced and unbalanced partitions:

- **Balanced Partition.** Each of the $n = 100$ partitions has 500 images.
- **Unbalanced Partition.** To make the setting more realistic, we partition the training set into unbalanced sizes. The sizes of the 100 partitions are $104, 112, \ldots, 896$ (an arithmetic sequence with step 8, starting with 104). Furthermore, to enlarge the variance, we make sure that in each partition, there are at most 5 different labels out of all the 10 labels. Note that some partitions only have one label.

In each epoch, $k = 10$ devices are randomly selected to launch local updates, with the minibatch size of 50. We repeat each experiment 10 times and take the average. We use top-1 accuracy on the testing set, and cross entropy loss function on the training set as the evaluation metrics.

The baseline algorithm is *FedAvg* introduced by [22], which is a special case of our proposed Algorithm 1 with Option I and $\alpha = 1$. To make the comparison clearer, we refer to *FedAvg* as "SLSGD, $\alpha = 1, b = 0$".

We test SLSGD with different hyperparameters γ, α, and b (definitions can be found in Table 1).

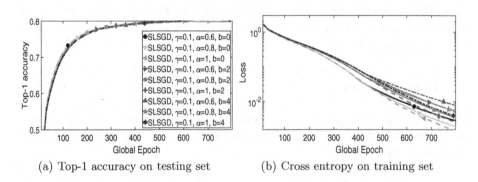

(a) Top-1 accuracy on testing set   (b) Cross entropy on training set

Fig. 1. Convergence on training data with balanced partition, without attack. Each epoch is a full pass of the local training data. Legend "SLSGD, $\gamma = 0.1, \alpha = 0.8, b = 2$" means that SLSGD takes the learning rate 0.1 and Trmean_2 for aggregation, and the initial $\alpha = 1$ decays by the factor of 0.8 at the 400th epoch. SLSGD with $\alpha = 1$ and $b = 0$ is the baseline *FedAvg*. Note that we fix the random seeds. Thus, before α decays at the 400th epoch, results with the same γ and b are the same.

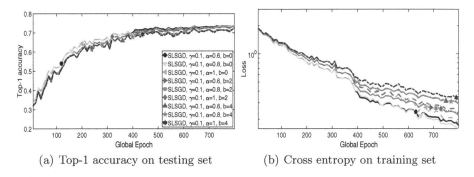

(a) Top-1 accuracy on testing set   (b) Cross entropy on training set

Fig. 2. Convergence on training data with unbalanced partition, without attack. Each epoch is a full pass of the local training data. Legend "SLSGD, $\gamma = 0.1, \alpha = 0.8, b = 2$" means that SLSGD takes the learning rate 0.1 and Trmean_2 for aggregation, and the initial $\alpha = 1$ decays by the factor of 0.8 at the 400th epoch. SLSGD with $\alpha = 1$ and $b = 0$ is the baseline *FedAvg*. Note that we fix the random seeds. Thus, before α decays at the 400th epoch, results with the same γ and b are the same.

6.2   SLSGD Without Attack

We first test the performance of SLSGD on the training data with balanced partition, without data poisoning. The result is shown in Fig. 1. When there are no poisoned workers, using trimmed mean results in extra variance. Although larger b and smaller α makes the convergence slower, the gap is tiny. In general, SLSGD is insensitive to hyperparameters.

Then, we test the performance with unbalanced partition, without data poisoning. The result is shown in Fig. 2. Note that the convergence with unbalanced partition is generally slower compared to balanced partition due to the larger variance. Using appropriate α ($\alpha = 0.8$) can mitigate such extra variance.

6.3   SLSGD Under Data Poisoning Attack

To test the tolerance to poisoned workers, we simulate data poisoning which "flips" the labels of the local training data. The poisoned data have "flipped" labels, i.e., each $label \in \{0, \ldots, 9\}$ in the local training data will be replaced by $(9 - label)$. The experiment is set up so that in each epoch, in all the $k = 10$ randomly selected workers, q workers are compromised and subjected to data poisoning. The results are shown in Fig. 3 and Fig. 4. We use FedAvg/SLSGD without data poisoning (Option I) as the ideal benchmark. As expected, SLSGD without trimmed mean can not tolerate data poisoning, which causes catastrophic failure. SLSGD with Option II tolerates the poisoned worker, though converges slower compared to SLSGD without data poisoning. Furthermore, larger b and smaller α improves the robustness and stabilizes the convergence.

Note that taking $q = 4$ in every epoch pushes to the limit of SLSGD since the algorithm requires $2q < k$. In practice, if there are totally $q = 4$ poisoned workers in the entire $n = 100$ workers, there is no guarantee that the poisoned

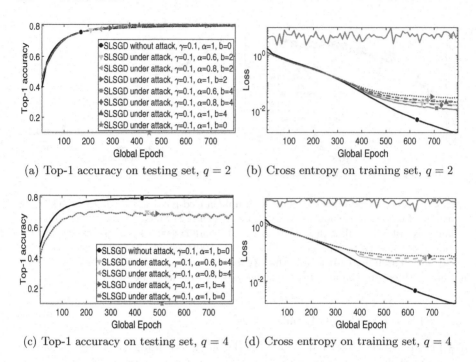

(a) Top-1 accuracy on testing set, $q = 2$ (b) Cross entropy on training set, $q = 2$

(c) Top-1 accuracy on testing set, $q = 4$ (d) Cross entropy on training set, $q = 4$

Fig. 3. Convergence on training data with balanced partition, with "label-flipping" attack. In each epoch, we guarantee that $q \in \{2, 4\}$ of the $k = 10$ selected workers are poisoned. Each epoch is a full pass of the local training data. Legend "SLSGD, $\gamma = 0.1, \alpha = 0.8, b = 2$" means that SLSGD takes the learning rate 0.1 and $\mathtt{Trmean}_2$ for aggregation, and the initial $\alpha = 1$ decays by the factor of 0.8 at the 400th epoch. SLSGD with $\alpha = 1$ and $b = 0$ is the baseline *FedAvg*. Note that we fix the random seeds. Thus, before α decays at the 400th epoch, results with the same γ and b are the same.

workers will always be activated in each epoch. Poisoning 40% of the sampled data in each epoch incurs huge noise, while SLSGD can still prevent the global model from divergence.

In Fig. 5, we show how α and b affect the convergence when data poisoning and unbalanced partition cause extra error and variance. In such scenario, larger b and smaller α makes SLSGD more robust and converge faster.

6.4   Acceleration by Local Updates

According to our theoretical analysis, more local updates in each epoch accelerate the convergence. We test this theory in Fig. 6 with balanced partition, without data poisoning. In the legend, "pass=3" means each epoch is 3 full passes of the local datasets ($H = 3 \times 500/50 = 30$ local iterations) on the selected workers. We show that with more local iterations, SLSGD converges faster.

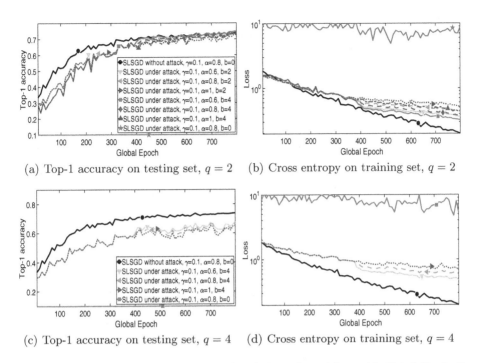

(a) Top-1 accuracy on testing set, $q = 2$ (b) Cross entropy on training set, $q = 2$

(c) Top-1 accuracy on testing set, $q = 4$ (d) Cross entropy on training set, $q = 4$

Fig. 4. Convergence on training data with unbalanced partition, with "label-flipping" attack. In each epoch, we guarantee that q of the $k = 10$ selected workers are poisoned. Each epoch is a full pass of the local training data. Legend "SLSGD, $\gamma = 0.1, \alpha = 0.8, b = 2$" means that SLSGD takes the learning rate 0.1 and Trmean$_2$ for aggregation, and the initial $\alpha = 1$ decays by the factor of 0.8 at the 400th epoch. SLSGD with $\alpha = 1$ and $b = 0$ is the baseline *FedAvg*. Note that we fix the random seeds. Thus, before α decays at the 400th epoch, results with the same γ and b are the same.

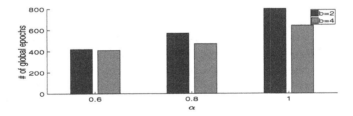

Fig. 5. Number of global epochs to reach training loss value 0.5, with unbalanced partition and $q = 2$ poisoned workers. $\gamma = 0.1$. α and b varies. "α" on the x-axis is the initial value of α, which does not decay during training.

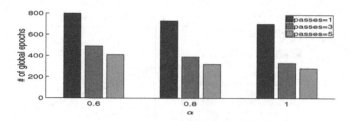

Fig. 6. Number of global epochs to reach training loss value 0.003, with balanced partition, without poisoned workers. $\gamma = 0.1$. α and number of local iterations varies. "pass $= 3$" means each epoch is 3 full passes of the local datasets on the selected workers. "α" on the x-axis is the initial value of α, which does not decay during training.

6.5   Discussion

The hyperparameters of SLSGD affects the convergence differently in different scenarios:

- *Balanced partition, no attacks.* In this case, the overall variance is relatively small. Thus, it is not necessary to use smaller α to mitigate the variance. The extra variance caused by trimmed mean slows down the convergence. Since the variance does not dominate, smaller α and larger b potentially slow down the convergence, but the gap is tiny.
- *Unbalanced partition, no attacks.* In this case, the overall variance is larger than the balanced case. Note that not only the size of local datasets, but also the label distribution are unbalanced among the devices. Some partitions only contains one label, which enlarges the accumulative error caused by infrequent synchronization and overfitting the local training data. Thus, using appropriate α can mitigate the variance. However, it is not necessary to use the trimmed mean, since the variance caused by unbalanced partition is not too bad compared to data poisoning.
- *Balanced partition, under attacks.* In this case, the error caused by poisoned workers dominates. We must use trimmed mean to prevent divergence. Larger b improves the robustness and convergence. Furthermore, using smaller α also mitigates the error and improves the convergence.
- *Unbalanced partition, under attacks.* In this case, the error caused by poisoned workers still dominates. In general, the usage of hyperparameters is similar to the case of balanced partition under attacks. However, the unbalanced partition makes it more difficult to distinguish poisoned workers from normal workers. As a result, the convergence gets much slower. Smaller α obtain more improvement and better stabilization.

In general, there is a trade-off between convergence rate and variance/error reduction. In the ideal case, if the variance is very small, SLSGD with $\alpha = 1$ and $b = 0$, i.e., *FedAvg*, has fastest convergence. Using other hyperparameters slightly slows down the convergence, but the gap is tiny. When variance gets larger, users can try smaller α. When the variance/error gets catastrophically large, the users can use the trimmed mean to prevent divergence.

7   Conclusion

We propose a novel distributed optimization algorithm on non-IID training data, which has limited communication and tolerates poisoned workers. The algorithm has provable convergence. Our empirical results show good performance in practice. In future work, we are going to analyze our algorithm on other threat models, such as hardware or software failures.

Acknowledgments. This work was funded in part by NSF CNS 1409416, by a gift from Microsoft, and by computational resources donated by Intel, AWS, and Microsoft Azure.

References

1. Anguita, D., Ghio, A., Oneto, L., Parra, X., Reyes-Ortiz, J.L.: A public domain dataset for human activity recognition using smartphones. In: ESANN (2013)
2. Bae, H., Jang, J., Jung, D., Jang, H., Ha, H., Yoon, S.: Security and privacy issues in deep learning. arXiv preprint arXiv:1807.11655 (2018)
3. Bagdasaryan, E., Veit, A., Hua, Y., Estrin, D., Shmatikov, V.: How to backdoor federated learning. arXiv preprint arXiv:1807.00459 (2018)
4. Bhagoji, A.N., Chakraborty, S., Mittal, P., Calo, S.: Analyzing federated learning through an adversarial lens. arXiv preprint arXiv:1811.12470 (2018)
5. Cao, Y., Hou, P., Brown, D., Wang, J., Chen, S.: Distributed analytics and edge intelligence: pervasive health monitoring at the era of fog computing. In: Proceedings of the 2015 Workshop on Mobile Big Data, pp. 43–48. ACM (2015)
6. Chen, T., et al.: MXNet: a flexible and efficient machine learning library for heterogeneous distributed systems. arXiv preprint arXiv:1512.01274 (2015)
7. Chen, Y., Su, L., Xu, J.: Distributed statistical machine learning in adversarial settings: byzantine gradient descent. ACM SIGMETRICS Perform. Eval. Rev. **46**(1), 96–96 (2019)
8. European Union: European Union's General Data Protection Regulation (GDPR) (2018). https://eugdpr.org/. Accessed Nov 2018
9. Fung, C., Yoon, C.J., Beschastnikh, I.: Mitigating Sybils in federated learning poisoning. arXiv preprint arXiv:1808.04866 (2018)
10. Garcia Lopez, P., et al.: Edge-centric computing: vision and challenges. ACM SIGCOMM Comput. Commun. Rev. **45**(5), 37–42 (2015)
11. gluon-nlp.mxnet.io: LSTM-based Language Models (2019). https://gluon-nlp.mxnet.io/master/examples/language_model/language_model.html. Accessed Mar 2019
12. South African HealthInsurance.org: Health insurance portability and accountability act of 1996. Public law 104, 191 (1996)
13. Ho, Q., et al.: More effective distributed ml via a stale synchronous parallel parameter server. In: Advances in Neural Information Processing Systems, pp. 1223–1231 (2013)
14. Hong, K., Lillethun, D., Ramachandran, U., Ottenwälder, B., Koldehofe, B.: Mobile fog: a programming model for large-scale applications on the Internet of Things. In: Proceedings of the Second ACM SIGCOMM Workshop on Mobile Cloud Computing, pp. 15–20. ACM (2013)

15. Howard, A.G., et al.: MobileNets: efficient convolutional neural networks for mobile vision applications. arXiv preprint arXiv:1704.04861 (2017)
16. Konečný, J., McMahan, B., Ramage, D.: Federated optimization: distributed optimization beyond the datacenter. arXiv preprint arXiv:1511.03575 (2015)
17. Konečný, J., McMahan, H.B., Yu, F.X., Richtárik, P., Suresh, A.T., Bacon, D.: Federated learning: strategies for improving communication efficiency. arXiv preprint arXiv:1610.05492 (2016)
18. Krizhevsky, A., Hinton, G.: Learning multiple layers of features from tiny images. Technical report, Citeseer (2009)
19. Li, M., et al.: Scaling distributed machine learning with the parameter server. In: OSDI, vol. 14, pp. 583–598 (2014)
20. Li, M., Andersen, D.G., Smola, A.J., Yu, K.: Communication efficient distributed machine learning with the parameter server. In: Advances in Neural Information Processing Systems, pp. 19–27 (2014)
21. Mahdavinejad, M.S., Rezvan, M., Barekatain, M., Adibi, P., Barnaghi, P., Sheth, A.P.: Machine learning for Internet of Things data analysis: a survey. Digital Commun. Netw. 4(3), 161–175 (2018)
22. McMahan, H.B., Moore, E., Ramage, D., Hampson, S., et al.: Communication-efficient learning of deep networks from decentralized data. arXiv preprint arXiv:1602.05629 (2016)
23. Merity, S., Xiong, C., Bradbury, J., Socher, R.: Pointer sentinel mixture models. arXiv preprint arXiv:1609.07843 (2016)
24. Pantelopoulos, A., Bourbakis, N.G.: A survey on wearable sensor-based systems for health monitoring and prognosis. IEEE Trans. Syst. Man Cybern. Part C (Appl. Rev.) 40(1), 1–12 (2010)
25. source.android.com: Key and ID Attestation (2019). https://source.android.com/security/keystore/attestation. Accessed Mar 2019
26. Stich, S.U.: Local SGD converges fast and communicates little. arXiv preprint arXiv:1805.09767 (2018)
27. Xie, C., Koyejo, O., Gupta, I.: Phocas: dimensional byzantine-resilient stochastic gradient descent. arXiv preprint arXiv:1805.09682 (2018)
28. Xie, C., Koyejo, S., Gupta, I.: Fall of empires: breaking byzantine-tolerant SGD by inner product manipulation. In: Proceedings of the 35th Conference on Uncertainty in Artificial Intelligence. AUAI Press (2019)
29. Xie, C., Koyejo, S., Gupta, I.: Zeno: distributed stochastic gradient descent with suspicion-based fault-tolerance. In: International Conference on Machine Learning, pp. 6893–6901 (2019)
30. Yin, D., Chen, Y., Ramchandran, K., Bartlett, P.: Byzantine-robust distributed learning: towards optimal statistical rates. arXiv preprint arXiv:1803.01498 (2018)
31. Yu, H., Yang, S., Zhu, S.: Parallel restarted SGD for non-convex optimization with faster convergence and less communication. arXiv preprint arXiv:1807.06629 (2018)
32. Zeydan, E., et al.: Big data caching for networking: moving from cloud to edge. IEEE Commun. Mag. 54(9), 36–42 (2016)

Trade-Offs in Large-Scale Distributed Tuplewise Estimation And Learning

Robin Vogel[1,2]([✉]), Aurélien Bellet[3], Stephan Clémençon[1], Ons Jelassi[1], and Guillaume Papa[1]

[1] Telecom Paris, LTCI, Institut Polytechnique de Paris, Paris, France
{robin.vogel,stephan.clemencon,ons.jelassi,
guillaume.papa}@telecom-paris.fr
[2] IDEMIA, Paris, France
robin.vogel@idemia.com
[3] INRIA, Paris, France
aurelien.bellet@inria.fr

Abstract. The development of cluster computing frameworks has allowed practitioners to scale out various statistical estimation and machine learning algorithms with minimal programming effort. This is especially true for machine learning problems whose objective function is nicely separable across individual data points, such as classification and regression. In contrast, statistical learning tasks involving pairs (or more generally tuples) of data points—such as metric learning, clustering or ranking—do not lend themselves as easily to data-parallelism and in-memory computing. In this paper, we investigate how to balance between statistical performance and computational efficiency in such distributed tuplewise statistical problems. We first propose a simple strategy based on occasionally repartitioning data across workers between parallel computation stages, where the number of repartitioning steps rules the trade-off between accuracy and runtime. We then present some theoretical results highlighting the benefits brought by the proposed method in terms of variance reduction, and extend our results to design distributed stochastic gradient descent algorithms for tuplewise empirical risk minimization. Our results are supported by numerical experiments in pairwise statistical estimation and learning on synthetic and real-world datasets.

Keywords: Distributed machine learning · Distributed data processing · U-Statistics · Stochastic gradient descent · AUC optimization

Electronic supplementary material The online version of this chapter (https://doi.org/10.1007/978-3-030-46147-8_14) contains supplementary material, which is available to authorized users.

U. Brefeld et al. (Eds.): ECML PKDD 2019, LNAI 11907, pp. 229–245, 2020.
https://doi.org/10.1007/978-3-030-46147-8_14

1   Introduction

Statistical machine learning has seen dramatic development over the last decades. The availability of massive datasets combined with the increasing need to perform predictive/inference/optimization tasks in a wide variety of domains has given a considerable boost to the field and led to successful applications. In parallel, there has been an ongoing technological progress in the architecture of data repositories and distributed systems, allowing to process ever larger (and possibly complex, high-dimensional) data sets gathered on distributed storage platforms. This trend is illustrated by the development of many easy-to-use cluster computing frameworks for large-scale distributed data processing. These frameworks implement the data-parallel setting, in which data points are partitioned across different machines which operate on their partition in parallel. Some striking examples are Apache Spark [26] and Petuum [25], the latter being fully targeted to machine learning. The goal of such frameworks is to abstract away the network and communication aspects in order to ease the deployment of distributed algorithms on large computing clusters and on the cloud, at the cost of some restrictions in the types of operations and parallelism that can be efficiently achieved. However, these limitations as well as those arising from network latencies or the nature of certain memory-intensive operations are often ignored or incorporated in a stylized manner in the mathematical description and analysis of statistical learning algorithms (see *e.g.*, [1,2,4,15]). The implementation of statistical methods proved to be theoretically sound may thus be hardly feasible in a practical distributed system, and seemingly minor adjustments to scale-up these procedures can turn out to be disastrous in terms of statistical performance, see e.g. the discussion in [18]. This greatly restricts their practical interest in some applications and urges the statistics and machine learning communities to get involved with distributed computation more deeply [3].

In this paper, we propose to study these issues in the context of *tuplewise* estimation and learning problems, where the statistical quantities of interest are not basic sample means but come in the form of averages over all pairs (or more generally, d-tuples) of data points. Such data functionals are known as U-statistics [19,21], and many empirical quantities describing global properties of a probability distribution fall in this category (*e.g.*, the sample variance, the Gini mean difference, Kendall's tau coefficient). U-statistics are also natural empirical risk measures in several learning problems such as ranking [13], metric learning [24], cluster analysis [11] and risk assessment [5]. The behavior of these statistics is well-understood and a sound theory for empirical risk minimization based on U-statistics is now documented in the machine learning literature [13], but the computation of a U-statistic poses a serious scalability challenge as it involves a summation over an exploding number of pairs (or d-tuples) as the dataset grows in size. In the centralized (single machine) setting, this can be addressed by appropriate subsampling methods, which have been shown to achieve a nearly optimal balance between computational cost and statistical accuracy [12]. Unfortunately, naive implementations in the case of a massive distributed dataset either greatly damage the accuracy or are inefficient due to a lot of network communication (or disk I/O). This is due to the fact that, unlike basic sample means, a U-statistic is not separable across the data partitions.

Our main contribution is to design and analyze distributed methods for statistical estimation and learning with U-statistics that guarantee a good trade-off between accuracy and scalability. Our approach incorporates an occasional data repartitioning step between parallel computing stages in order to circumvent the limitations induced by data partitioning over the cluster nodes. The number of repartitioning steps allows to trade-off between statistical accuracy and computational efficiency. To shed light on this phenomenon, we first study the setting of statistical estimation, precisely quantifying the variance of estimates corresponding to several strategies. Thanks to the use of Hoeffding's decomposition [17], our analysis reveals the role played by each component of the variance in the effect of repartitioning. We then discuss the extension of these results to statistical learning and design efficient and scalable stochastic gradient descent algorithms for distributed empirical risk minimization. Finally, we carry out some numerical experiments on pairwise estimation and learning tasks on synthetic and real-world datasets to support our results from an empirical perspective.

The paper is structured as follows. Section 2 reviews background on U-statistics and their use in statistical estimation and learning, and discuss the common practices in distributed data processing. Section 3 deals with statistical tuplewise estimation: we introduce our general approach for the distributed setting and derive (non-)asymptotic results describing its accuracy. Section 4 extends our approach to statistical tuplewise learning. We provide experiments supporting our results in Sect. 5, and we conclude in Sect. 6. Proofs, technical details and additional results can be found in the supplementary material.

2   Background

In this section, we first review the definition and properties of U-statistics, and discuss some popular applications in statistical estimation and learning. We then discuss the recent randomized methods designed to scale up tuplewise statistical inference to large datasets stored on a single machine. Finally, we describe the main features of cluster computing frameworks.

2.1 U-Statistics: Definition and Applications

U-statistics are the natural generalization of i.i.d. sample means to tuples of points. We state the definition of U-statistics in their generalized form, where points can come from $K \geq 1$ independent samples. Note that we recover classic sample mean statistics in the case where $K = d_1 = 1$.

Definition 1 (GENERALIZED U-STATISTIC). *Let $K \geq 1$ and $(d_1, \ldots, d_K) \in \mathbb{N}^{*K}$. For each $k \in \{1, \ldots, K\}$, let $\mathbf{X}_{\{1, \ldots, n_k\}} = (X_1^{(k)}, \ldots, X_{n_k}^{(k)})$ be an independent sample of size $n_k \geq d_k$ composed of i.i.d. random variables with values in some measurable space $\mathcal{X}_k$ with distribution $F_k(dx)$. Let $h : \mathcal{X}_1^{d_1} \times \cdots \times \mathcal{X}_K^{d_K} \to \mathbb{R}$*

be a measurable function, square integrable with respect to the probability distribution $\mu = F_1^{\otimes d_1} \otimes \cdots \otimes F_K^{\otimes d_K}$. Assume w.l.o.g. that $h(\mathbf{x}^{(1)}, \ldots, \mathbf{x}^{(K)})$ is symmetric within each block of arguments $\mathbf{x}^{(k)}$ (valued in $\mathcal{X}_k^{d_k}$). The generalized (or K-sample) U-statistic of degrees $(d_1, \ldots, d_K)$ with kernel H is defined as

$$U_{\mathbf{n}}(h) = \frac{1}{\prod_{k=1}^{K} \binom{n_k}{d_k}} \sum_{I_1} \cdots \sum_{I_K} h(\mathbf{X}_{I_1}^{(1)}, \mathbf{X}_{I_2}^{(2)}, \ldots, \mathbf{X}_{I_K}^{(K)}), \qquad (1)$$

where $\sum_{I_k}$ denotes the sum over all $\binom{n_k}{d_k}$ subsets $\mathbf{X}_{I_k}^{(k)} = (X_{i_1}^{(k)}, \ldots, X_{i_{d_k}}^{(k)})$ related to a set I_k of d_k indexes $1 \leq i_1 < \ldots < i_{d_k} \leq n_k$ and $\mathbf{n} = (n_1, \ldots, n_K)$.

The U-statistic $U_{\mathbf{n}}(h)$ is known to have minimum variance among all unbiased estimators of the parameter $\mu(h) = \mathbb{E}\big[h(X_1^{(1)}, \ldots, X_{d_1}^{(1)}, \ldots, X_1^{(K)}, \ldots, X_{d_K}^{(K)})\big]$. The price to pay for this low variance is a complex dependence structure exhibited by the terms involved in the average (1), as each data point appears in multiple tuples. The (non)asymptotic behavior of U-statistics and U-processes (i.e., collections of U-statistics indexed by classes of kernels) can be investigated by means of linearization techniques [17] combined with decoupling methods [21], reducing somehow their analysis to that of basic i.i.d. averages or empirical processes. One may refer to [19] for an account of the asymptotic theory of U-statistics, and to [23] (Chap. 12 therein) and [21] for nonasymptotic results.

U-statistics are commonly used as point estimators for inferring certain global properties of a probability distribution as well as in statistical hypothesis testing. Popular examples include the (debiased) *sample variance*, obtained by setting $K = 1$, $d_1 = 2$ and $h(x_1, x_2) = (x_1 - x_2)^2$, the *Gini mean difference*, where $K = 1$, $d_1 = 2$ and $h(x_1, x_2) = |x_1 - x_2|$, and *Kendall's tau rank correlation*, where $K = 2$, $d_1 = d_2 = 1$ and $h((x_1, y_1), (x_2, y_1)) = \mathbb{I}\{(x_1 - x_2) \cdot (y_1 - y_2) > 0\}$.

U-statistics also correspond to empirical risk measures in statistical learning problems such as clustering [11], metric learning [24] and multipartite ranking [14]. The generalization ability of minimizers of such criteria over a class $\mathcal{H}$ of kernels can be derived from probabilistic upper bounds for the maximal deviation of collections of centered U-statistics under appropriate complexity conditions on $\mathcal{H}$ (e.g., finite VC dimension) [12,13]. Below, we describe the example of multipartite ranking used in our numerical experiments (Sect. 5). We refer to [12] for details on more learning problems involving U-statistics.

Example 2 (Multipartite Ranking). Consider items described by a random vector of features $X \in \mathcal{X}$ with associated ordinal labels $Y \in \{1, \ldots, K\}$, where $K \geq 2$. The goal of multipartite ranking is to learn to rank items in the same preorder as that defined by the labels, based on a training set of labeled examples. Rankings are generally defined through a scoring function $s : \mathcal{X} \to \mathbb{R}$ transporting the natural order on the real line onto $\mathcal{X}$. Given K independent samples, the empirical ranking performance of $s(x)$ is evaluated by means of the empirical VUS (Volume Under the ROC Surface) criterion [14]:

$$\widehat{VUS}(s) = \frac{1}{\prod_{k=1}^{K} n_k} \sum_{i_1=1}^{n_1} \cdots \sum_{i_K=1}^{n_K} \mathbb{I}\{s(X_{i_1}^{(1)}) < \ldots < s(X_{i_K}^{(K)})\}, \tag{2}$$

which is a K-sample U-statistic of degree $(1, \ldots, 1)$ with kernel $h_s(x_1, \ldots, x_K) = \mathbb{I}\{s(x_1) < \ldots < s(x_K)\}$.

2.2   Large-Scale Tuplewise Inference with Incomplete U-Statistics

The cost related to the computation of the U-statistic (1) rapidly explodes as the sizes of the samples increase. Precisely, the number of terms involved in the summation is $\binom{n_1}{d_1} \times \cdots \times \binom{n_K}{d_K}$, which is of order $O(n^{d_1+\cdots+d_K})$ when the n_k's are all asymptotically equivalent. Whereas computing U-statistics based on subsamples of smaller size would severely increase the variance of the estimation, the notion of *incomplete generalized U-statistic* [6] enables to significantly mitigate this computational problem while maintaining a good level of accuracy.

Definition 3 (INCOMPLETE GENERALIZED U-STATISTIC). *Let $B \geq 1$. The incomplete version of the U-statistic (1) based on B terms is defined by:*

$$\tilde{U}_B(H) = \frac{1}{B} \sum_{I=(I_1, \ldots, I_K) \in \mathcal{D}_B} h(\mathbf{X}_{I_1}^{(1)}, \ldots, \mathbf{X}_{I_K}^{(K)}) \tag{3}$$

where $\mathcal{D}_B$ is a set of cardinality B built by sampling uniformly with replacement in the set Λ of vectors of tuples $((i_1^{(1)}, \ldots, i_{d_1}^{(1)}), \ldots, (i_1^{(K)}, \ldots, i_{d_K}^{(K)}))$, where $1 \leq i_1^{(k)} < \ldots < i_{d_k}^{(k)} \leq n_k$ and $1 \leq k \leq K$.

Note incidentally that the subsets of indices can be selected by means of other sampling schemes [12], but sampling with replacement is often preferred due to its simplicity. In practice, the parameter B should be picked much smaller than the total number of tuples to reduce the computational cost. Like (1), the quantity (3) is an unbiased estimator of $\mu(H)$ but its variance is naturally larger:

$$\mathrm{Var}(\tilde{U}_B(h)) = \left(1 - \frac{1}{B}\right) \mathrm{Var}(U_\mathbf{n}(h)) + \frac{1}{B} \mathrm{Var}(h(X_1^{(1)}, \ldots, X_{d_K}^{(K)})). \tag{4}$$

The recent work in [12] has shown that the maximal deviations between (1) and (3) over a class of kernels $\mathcal{H}$ of controlled complexity decrease at a rate of order $O(1/\sqrt{B})$ as B increases. An important consequence of this result is that sampling $B = O(n)$ terms is sufficient to preserve the learning rate of order $O_\mathbb{P}(\sqrt{\log n/n})$ of the minimizer of the complete risk (1), whose computation requires to average $O(n^{d_1+\cdots+d_K})$ terms. In contrast, the distribution of a complete U-statistic built from subsamples of reduced sizes n'_k drawn uniformly at random is quite different from that of an incomplete U-statistic based on $B = \prod_{k=1}^{K} \binom{n'_k}{d_k}$ terms sampled with replacement in Λ, although they involve the summation of the same number of terms. Empirical minimizers of such a complete U-statistic based on subsamples achieve a much slower learning rate of $O_{\mathbb{P}}(\sqrt{\log(n)/n^{1/(d_1+\dots+d_K)}})$. We refer to [12] for details and additional results.

We have seen that approximating complete U-statistics by incomplete ones is a theoretically and practically sound approach to tackle large-scale tuplewise estimation and learning problems. However, as we shall see later, the implementation is far from straightforward when data is stored and processed in standard distributed computing frameworks, whose key features are recalled below.

2.3   Practices in Distributed Data Processing

Data-parallelism, i.e. partitioning the data across different machines which operate in parallel, is a natural approach to store and efficiently process massive datasets. This strategy is especially appealing when the key stages of the computation to be executed can be run in parallel on each partition of the data. As a matter of fact, many estimation and learning problems can be reduced to (a sequence of) local computations on each machine followed by a simple aggregation step. This is the case of gradient descent-based algorithms applied to standard empirical risk minimization problems, as the objective function is nicely separable across individual data points. Optimization algorithms operating in the data-parallel setting have indeed been largely investigated in the machine learning community, see [1,3,8,22] and references therein for some recent work.

Because of the prevalence of data-parallel applications in large-scale machine learning, data analytics and other fields, the past few years have seen a sustained development of distributed data processing frameworks designed to facilitate the implementation and the deployment on computing clusters. Besides the seminal MapReduce framework [16], which is not suitable for iterative computations on the same data, one can mention Apache Spark [26], Apache Flink [10] and the machine learning-oriented Petuum [25]. In these frameworks, the data is typically first read from a distributed file system (such as HDFS, *Hadoop Distributed File System*) and partitioned across the memory of each machine in the form of an appropriate distributed data structure. The user can then easily specify a sequence of distributed computations to be performed on this data structure (map, filter, reduce, etc.) through a simple API which hides low-level distributed primitives (such as message passing between machines). Importantly, these frameworks natively implement fault-tolerance (allowing efficient recovery from node failures) in a way that is also completely transparent to the user.

While such distributed data processing frameworks come with a lot of benefits for the user, they also restrict the type of computations that can be performed efficiently on the data. In the rest of this paper, we investigate these limitations in the context of tuplewise estimation and learning problems, and propose solutions to achieve a good trade-off between accuracy and scalability.

3   Distributed Tuplewise Statistical Estimation

In this section, we focus on the problem of tuplewise statistical estimation in the distributed setting (an extension to statistical learning is presented in Sect. 4). We consider a set of $N \geq 1$ workers in a complete network graph (i.e., any pair of workers can exchange messages). For convenience, we assume the presence of a master node, which can be one of the workers and whose role is to aggregate estimates computed by all workers.

For ease of presentation, we restrict our attention to the case of two sample U-statistics of degree $(1, 1)$ ($K = 2$ and $d_1 = d_2 = 1$), see Remark 7 in Sect. 3.3 for extensions to the general case. We denote by $\mathcal{D}_n = \{X_1, \ldots, X_n\}$ the first sample and by $\mathcal{Q}_m = \{Z_1, \ldots, Z_m\}$ the second sample (of sizes n and m respectively). These samples are distributed across the N workers. For $i \in \{1, \ldots, N\}$, we denote by $\mathcal{R}_i$ the subset of data points held by worker i and, unless otherwise noted, we assume for simplicity that all subsets are of equal size $|\mathcal{R}_i| = \frac{n+m}{N} \in \mathbb{N}$. The notations $\mathcal{R}_i^X$ and $\mathcal{R}_i^Z$ respectively denote the subset of data points held by worker i from $\mathcal{D}_n$ and $\mathcal{Q}_m$, with $\mathcal{R}_i^X \cup \mathcal{R}_i^Z = \mathcal{R}_i$. We denote their (possibly random) cardinality by $n_i = |\mathcal{R}_i^X|$ and $m_i = |\mathcal{R}_i^Z|$. Given a kernel h, the goal is to compute a good estimate of the parameter $U(h) = \mathbb{E}[h(X_1, Z_1)]$ while meeting some computational and communication constraints.

3.1   Naive Strategies

Before presenting our approach, we start by introducing two simple (but ineffective) strategies to compute an estimate of $U(h)$. The first one is to compute the complete two-sample U-statistic associated with the full samples $\mathcal{D}_n$ and $\mathcal{Q}_m$:

$$U_{\mathbf{n}}(h) = \frac{1}{nm} \sum_{k=1}^{n} \sum_{l=1}^{m} h(X_k, Z_l), \tag{5}$$

with $\mathbf{n} = (n, m)$. While $U_{\mathbf{n}}(h)$ has the lowest variance among all unbiased estimates that can be computed from $(\mathcal{D}_n, \mathcal{Q}_m)$, computing it is a highly undesirable solution in the distributed setting where each worker only has access to a subset of the dataset. Indeed, ensuring that each possible pair is seen by at least one worker would require massive data communication over the network. Note that a similar limitation holds for incomplete versions of (5) as defined in Definition 3.

A feasible strategy to go around this problem is for each worker to compute the complete U-statistic associated with its local subsample $\mathcal{R}_i$, and to send it to the master node who averages all contributions. This leads to the estimate

$$U_{\mathbf{n},N}(h) = \frac{1}{N} \sum_{i=1}^{N} U_{\mathcal{R}_i}(h) \quad \text{where} \quad U_{\mathcal{R}_i}(h) = \frac{1}{n_i m_i} \sum_{k \in \mathcal{R}_i^X} \sum_{l \in \mathcal{R}_i^Z} h(X_k, Z_l). \tag{6}$$

Note that if $\min(n_i, m_i) = 0$, we simply set $U_{\mathcal{R}_i}(h) = 0$.

Alternatively, as the $\mathcal{R}_i$'s may be large, each worker can compute an incomplete U-statistic $\widetilde{U}_{B,\mathcal{R}_i}(h)$ with B terms instead of $U_{\mathcal{R}_i}$, leading to the estimate

$$\widetilde{U}_{\mathbf{n},N,B}(h) = \frac{1}{N}\sum_{i=1}^{N}\widetilde{U}_{B,\mathcal{R}_i}(h) \quad \text{where } \widetilde{U}_{B,\mathcal{R}_i}(h) = \frac{1}{B}\sum_{(k,l)\in\mathcal{R}_{i,B}} h(X_k, Z_l), \quad (7)$$

with $\mathcal{R}_{i,B}$ a set of B pairs built by sampling uniformly with replacement from the local subsample $\mathcal{R}_i^X \times \mathcal{R}_i^Z$.

As shown in Sect. 3.3, strategies (6) and (7) have the undesirable property that their accuracy decreases as the number of workers N increases. This motivates our proposed approach, introduced in the following section.

3.2 Proposed Approach

The naive strategies presented above are either accurate but very expensive (requiring a lot of communication across the network), or scalable but potentially inaccurate. The approach we promote here is of disarming simplicity and aims at finding a sweet spot between these two extremes. The idea is based on *repartitioning* the dataset a few times across workers (we keep the repartitioning scheme abstract for now and postpone the discussion of concrete choices to subsequent sections). By alternating between parallel computation and repartitioning steps, one considers several estimates based on the same data points. This allows to observe a greater diversity of pairs and thereby refine the quality of our final estimate, at the cost of some additional communication.

Formally, let T be the number of repartitioning steps. We denote by $\mathcal{R}_i^t$ the subsample of worker i after the t-th repartitioning step, and by $U_{\mathcal{R}_i^t}(h)$ the complete U-statistic associated with $\mathcal{R}_i^t$. At each step $t \in \{1,\ldots,T\}$, each worker i computes $U_{\mathcal{R}_i^t}(h)$ and sends it to the master node. After T steps, the master node has access to the following estimate:

$$\widehat{U}_{\mathbf{n},N,T}(h) = \frac{1}{T}\sum_{t=1}^{T} U_{\mathbf{n},N}^t(h), \quad (8)$$

where $U_{\mathbf{n},N}^t(h) = \frac{1}{N}\sum_{i=1}^{N} U_{\mathcal{R}_i^t}(h)$. Similarly as before, workers may alternatively compute incomplete U-statistics $\widetilde{U}_{B,\mathcal{R}_i^t}(h)$ with B terms. The estimate is then:

$$\widetilde{U}_{\mathbf{n},N,B,T}(h) = \frac{1}{T}\sum_{t=1}^{T} \widetilde{U}_{\mathbf{n},N,B}^t(h), \quad (9)$$

where $\widetilde{U}_{\mathbf{n},N,B}^t(h) = \frac{1}{N}\sum_{i=1}^{N} \widetilde{U}_{B,\mathcal{R}_i^t}(h)$. These statistics, and those introduced in Sect. 3.1 which do not rely on repartition, are summarized in Fig. 1.

Of course, the repartitioning operation is rather costly in terms of runtime so T should be kept to a reasonably small value. We illustrate this trade-off by the analysis presented in the next section.

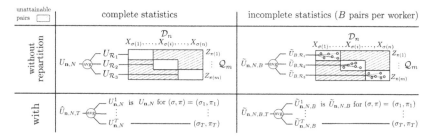

Fig. 1. Graphical summary of the statistics that we compare: with/without repartition and with/without subsampling. Note that $\{(\sigma_t, \pi_t)\}_{t=1}^{T}$ denotes a set of T independent couples of random permutations in $\mathfrak{S}_n \times \mathfrak{S}_m$.

3.3 Analysis

In this section, we analyze the statistical properties of the various estimators introduced above. We focus here on repartitioning by *proportional sampling without replacement* (prop-SWOR). Prop-SWOR creates partitions that contain the same proportion of elements of each sample: specifically, it ensures that at any step t and for any worker i, $|\mathcal{R}_i^t| = \frac{n+m}{N}$ with $|\mathcal{R}_i^{t,X}| = \frac{n}{N}$ and $|\mathcal{R}_i^{t,Z}| = \frac{m}{N}$. We discuss the practical implementation of this repartitioning scheme as well as some alternative choices in Sect. 3.4.

All estimators are unbiased when repartitioning is done with prop-SWOR. We will thus compare their variance. Our main technical tool is a linearization technique for U-statistics known as Hoeffding's Decomposition (see [12,13,17]).

Definition 4 (HOEFFDING'S DECOMPOSITION). *Let $h_1(x) = \mathbb{E}[h(x, Z_1)]$, $h_2(z) = \mathbb{E}[h(X_1, z)]$ and $h_0(x, z) = h(x, z) - h_1(x) - h_2(z) + U(h)$. $U_\mathbf{n}(h) - U(h)$ can be written as a sum of three orthogonal terms:*

$$U_\mathbf{n}(h) - U(h) = T_n(h) + T_m(h) + W_\mathbf{n}(h),$$

where $T_n(h) = \frac{1}{n}\sum_{k=1}^{n} h_1(X_k) - U(h)$ and $T_m(h) = \frac{1}{m}\sum_{l=1}^{n} h_2(Z_l) - U(h)$ are sums of independent r.v, while $W_\mathbf{n}(h) = \frac{1}{nm}\sum_{k=1}^{n}\sum_{l=1}^{m} h_0(X_k, Z_l)$ is a degenerate U-statistic (i.e., $\mathbb{E}[h(X_1, Z_1)|X_1] = U(h)$ and $\mathbb{E}[h(X_1, Z_1)|Z_1] = U(h)$).

This decomposition is very convenient as the two terms $T_n(h)$ and $T_m(h)$ are decorrelated and the analysis of $W_\mathbf{n}(h)$ (a degenerate U-statistic) is well documented [12,13,17]. It will allow us to decompose the variance of the estimators of interest into single-sample components $\sigma_1^2 = \mathrm{Var}(h_1(X))$ and $\sigma_2^2 = \mathrm{Var}(h_2(Z))$ on the one hand, and a pairwise component $\sigma_0^2 = \mathrm{Var}(h_0(X_1, Z_1))$ on the other hand. Denoting $\sigma^2 = \mathrm{Var}(h(X_1, Z_1))$, we have $\sigma^2 = \sigma_0^2 + \sigma_1^2 + \sigma_2^2$.

It is well-known that the variance of the complete U-statistic $U_\mathbf{n}(h)$ can be written as $\mathrm{Var}(U_\mathbf{n}(h)) = \frac{\sigma_1^2}{n} + \frac{\sigma_2^2}{m} + \frac{\sigma_0^2}{nm}$ (see supplementary material for details). Our first result gives the variance of the estimators which do not rely on a repartitioning of the data with respect to the variance of $U_\mathbf{n}(h)$.

Theorem 5. *If the data is distributed over workers using prop-SWOR, we have:*

$$Var(U_{\mathbf{n},N}(h)) = Var(U_{\mathbf{n}}(h)) + (N-1)\frac{\sigma_0^2}{nm},$$

$$Var(\widetilde{U}_{\mathbf{n},N,B}(h)) = \left(1 - \frac{1}{B}\right) Var(U_{\mathbf{n},N}(h)) + \frac{\sigma^2}{NB}.$$

Theorem 5 precisely quantifies the excess variance due to the distributed setting if one does not use repartitioning. Two important observations are in order. First, the variance increase is proportional to the number of workers N, which clearly defeats the purpose of distributed processing. Second, this increase only depends on the pairwise component σ_0^2 of the variance. In other words, the average of U-statistics computed independently over the local partitions contains all the information useful to estimate the single-sample contributions, but fails to accurately estimate the pairwise contributions. The resulting estimates thus lead to significantly larger variance when the choice of kernel and the data distributions imply that σ_0^2 is large compared to σ_2^2 and/or σ_1^2. The extreme case happens when $U_{\mathbf{n}}(h)$ is a degenerate U-statistic, i.e. $\sigma_1^2 = \sigma_2^2 = 0$ and $\sigma_0^2 > 0$, which is verified for example when $h(x, z) = x \cdot z$ and X, Z are both centered random variables.

We now characterize the variance of the estimators that leverage data repartitioning steps.

Theorem 6. *If the data is distributed and repartitioned between workers using prop-SWOR, we have:*

$$Var(\widehat{U}_{\mathbf{n},N,T}(h)) = Var(U_{\mathbf{n}}(h)) + (N-1)\frac{\sigma_0^2}{nmT},$$

$$Var(\widetilde{U}_{\mathbf{n},N,B,T}(h)) = Var(\widehat{U}_{\mathbf{n},N,T}(h)) - \frac{1}{TB} Var(U_{\mathbf{n},N}(h)) + \frac{\sigma^2}{NTB}.$$

Theorem 6 shows that the value of repartitioning arises from the fact that the term accounting for the pairwise variance in $\widehat{U}_{\mathbf{n},N,T}(h)$ is T times lower than that of $U_{\mathbf{n},N}(h)$. This validates the fact that repartitioning is beneficial when the pairwise variance term is significant in front of the other terms. Interestingly, Theorem 6 also implies that for a fixed budget of evaluated pairs, using all pairs on each worker is always a dominant strategy over using incomplete approximations. Specifically, we can show that under the constraint $NBT = nmT_0/N$, $Var(\widehat{U}_{\mathbf{n},N,T_0}(h))$ is always smaller than $Var(\widetilde{U}_{\mathbf{n},N,B,T}(h))$, see supplementary material for details. Note that computing complete U-statistics also require fewer repartitioning steps to evaluate the same number of pairs (i.e., $T_0 \leq T$).

We conclude the analysis with a visual illustration of the variance of various estimators with respect to the number of pairs they evaluate. We consider the imbalanced setting where $n \gg m$, which is commonly encountered in applications such as imbalanced classification, bipartite ranking and anomaly detection. In this case, it suffices that σ_2^2 be small for the influence of the pairwise component of the variance to be significant, see Fig. 2 (left). The figure also confirms

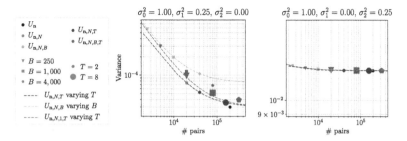

Fig. 2. Theoretical variance as a function of the number of evaluated pairs for different estimators under prop-SWOR, with $n = 100,000$, $m = 200$ and $N = 100$.

that complete estimators dominate their incomplete counterparts. On the other hand, when σ_2^2 is not small, the variance of $U_{\mathbf{n}}$ mostly originates from the rarity of the minority sample, hence repartitioning does not provide estimates that are significantly more accurate (see Fig. 2, right). We refer to Sect. 5 for experiments on concrete tasks with synthetic and real data.

Remark 7 (Extension to high-order U-statistics). The extension of our analysis to general U-statistics is straightforward and left to the reader (see [12] for a review of the relevant technical tools). We stress the fact that the benefits of repartitioning are even stronger for higher-order U-statistics ($K > 2$ and/or larger degrees) because higher-order components of the variance are also affected.

3.4 Practical Considerations and Other Repartitioning Schemes

The analysis above assumes that repartitioning is done using prop-SWOR, which has the advantage of exactly preserving the proportion of points from the two samples $\mathcal{D}_n$ and $\mathcal{Q}_m$ even in the event of significant imbalance in their size. However, a naive implementation of prop-SWOR requires some coordination between workers at each repartitioning step. To avoid exchanging many messages, we propose that the workers agree at the beginning of the protocol on a numbering of the workers, a numbering of the points in each sample, and a random seed to use in a pseudorandom number generator. This allows the workers to implement prop-SWOR without any further coordination: at each repartitioning step, they independently draw the same two random permutations over $\{1, \ldots, n\}$ and $\{1, \ldots, m\}$ using the common random seed and use these permutations to assign each point to a single worker.

Of course, other repartitioning schemes can be used instead of prop-SWOR. A natural choice is sampling without replacement (SWOR), which does not require any coordination between workers. However, the partition sizes generated by SWOR are random. This is a concern in the case of imbalanced samples, where the probability that a worker i does not get any point from the minority sample (and thus no pair to compute a local estimate) is non-negligible. For these reasons, it is difficult to obtain exact and concise theoretical variances for the

SWOR case, but we show in the supplementary material that the results with SWOR should not deviate too much from those obtained with prop-SWOR. For completeness, in the supplementary material we also analyze the case of proportional sampling with replacement (prop-SWR): results are quantitatively similar, aside from the fact that redistribution also corrects for the loss of information that occurs because of sampling with replacement.

Finally, we note that deterministic repartitioning schemes may be used in practice for simplicity. For instance, the `repartition` method in Apache Spark relies on a deterministic shuffle which preserves the size of the partitions.

4   Extensions to Stochastic Gradient Descent for ERM

The results of Sect. 3 can be extended to statistical learning in the empirical risk minimization framework. In such problems, given a class of kernels $\mathcal{H}$, one seeks the minimizer of (6) or (8) depending on whether repartition is used.[1] Under appropriate complexity assumptions on $\mathcal{H}$ (*e.g.*, of finite VC dimension), excess risk bounds for such minimizers can be obtained by combining our variance analysis of Sect. 3 with the control of maximal deviations based on Bernstein-type concentration inequalities as done in [12,13]. Due to the lack of space, we leave the details of such analysis to the readers and focus on the more practical scenario where the ERM problem is solved by gradient-based optimization algorithms.

4.1   Gradient-Based Empirical Minimization of U-statistics

In the setting of interest, the class of kernels to optimize over is indexed by a real-valued parameter $\theta \in \mathbb{R}^q$ representing the model. Adapting the notations of Sect. 3, the kernel $h : \mathcal{X}_1 \times \mathcal{X}_2 \times \mathbb{R}^q \to \mathbb{R}$ then measures the performance of a model $\theta \in \mathbb{R}^q$ on a given pair, and is assumed to be convex and smooth in θ. Empirical Risk Minimization (ERM) aims at finding $\theta \in \mathbb{R}^q$ minimizing

$$U_{\mathbf{n}}(\theta) = \frac{1}{nm} \sum_{k=1}^{n} \sum_{l=1}^{m} h(X_k, Z_l; \theta). \tag{10}$$

The minimizer can be found by means of Gradient Descent (GD) techniques.[2] Starting at iteration $s = 1$ from an initial model $\theta_1 \in \mathbb{R}^q$ and given a learning rate $\gamma > 0$, GD consists in iterating over the following update:

$$\theta_{s+1} = \theta_s - \gamma \nabla_\theta U_{\mathbf{n}}(\theta_s). \tag{11}$$

Note that the gradient $\nabla_\theta U_{\mathbf{n}}(\theta)$ is itself a U-statistic with kernel given by $\nabla_\theta H$, and its computation is very expensive in the large-scale setting. In this regime,

---

[1] Alternatively, for scalability purposes, one may instead work with their incomplete counterparts, namely (7) and (9) respectively.

[2] When H is nonsmooth in θ, a subgradient may be used instead of the gradient.

Stochastic Gradient Descent (SGD) is a natural alternative to GD which is known to provide a better trade-off between the amount of computation and the performance of the resulting model [7]. Following the discussion of Sect. 2.2, a natural idea to implement SGD is to replace the gradient $\nabla_\theta U_\mathbf{n}(\theta)$ in (11) by an unbiased estimate given by an incomplete U-statistic. The work of [20] shows that SGD converges much faster than if the gradient is estimated using a complete U-statistic based on subsamples with the same number of terms.

However, as in the case of estimation, the use of standard complete or incomplete U-statistics turns out to be impractical in the distributed setting. Building upon the arguments of Sect. 3, we propose a more suitable strategy.

4.2 Repartitioning for Stochastic Gradient Descent

The approach we propose is to alternate between SGD steps using within-partition pairs and repartitioning the data across workers. We introduce a parameter $n_r \in \mathbb{Z}^+$ corresponding to the number of iterations of SGD between each redistribution of the data. For notational convenience, we let $r(s) := \lceil s/n_r \rceil$ so that for any worker i, $\mathcal{R}_i^{r(s)}$ denotes its data partition at iteration $s \geq 1$ of SGD.

Given a local batch size B, at each iteration s of SGD, we propose to adapt the strategy (9) by having each worker i compute a local gradient estimate using a set $\mathcal{R}_{i,B}^s$ of B randomly sampled pairs in its current local partition $\mathcal{R}_i^{r(s)}$:

$$\nabla_\theta \widetilde{U}_{B,\mathcal{R}_i^{r(s)}}(\theta_s) = \frac{1}{B} \sum_{(k,l) \in \mathcal{R}_{i,B}^s} \nabla_\theta h(X_k, Z_l; \theta_s).$$

This local estimate is then sent to the master node who averages all contributions, leading to the following global gradient estimate:

$$\nabla_\theta \widetilde{U}_{\mathbf{n},N,B}(\theta_s) = \frac{1}{N} \sum_{i=1}^{N} \nabla_\theta \widetilde{U}_{B,\mathcal{R}_i^{r(s)}}(\theta_s). \tag{12}$$

The master node then takes a gradient descent step as in (11) and broadcasts the updated model θ_{s+1} to the workers.

Following our analysis in Sect. 3, repartitioning the data allows to reduce the variance of the gradient estimates, which is known to greatly impact the convergence rate of SGD (see e.g. [9], Theorem 6.3 therein). When $n_r = +\infty$, data is never repartitioned and the algorithm minimizes an average of local U-statistics, leading to suboptimal performance. On the other hand, $n_r = 1$ corresponds to repartitioning at each iteration of SGD, which minimizes the variance but is very costly and makes SGD pointless. We expect the sweet spot to lie between these two extremes: the dominance of $\widehat{U}_{\mathbf{n},N,T}$ over $\widetilde{U}_{\mathbf{n},N,B,T}$ established in Sect. 3.3, combined with the common use of small batch size B in SGD, suggests that occasional redistributions are sufficient to correct for the loss of information incurred by the partitioning of data. We illustrate these trade-offs experimentally in the next section.

5 Numerical Results

In this section, we illustrate the importance of repartitioning for estimating and optimizing the Area Under the ROC Curve (AUC) through a series of numerical experiments. The corresponding U-statistic is the two-sample version of the multipartite ranking VUS introduced in Example 2 (Sect. 2.1). The first experiment focuses on the estimation setting considered in Sect. 3. The second experiment shows that redistributing the data across workers, as proposed in Section 4, allows for more efficient mini-batch SGD. All experiments use prop-SWOR and are conducted in a simulated environment.

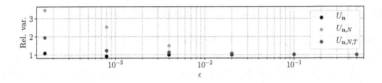

Fig. 3. Relative variance estimated over 5000 runs, $n = 5000$, $m = 50$, $N = 10$ and $T = 4$. Results are divided by the true variance of $U_\mathbf{n}$ deduced from (13) and Theorem 5.

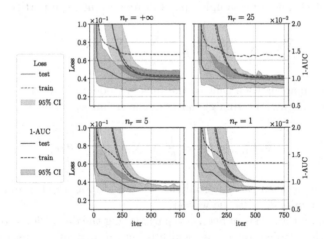

Fig. 4. Learning dynamics for different repartition frequencies computed over 100 runs.

Estimation Experiment. We seek to illustrate the importance of redistribution for estimating two-sample U-statistics with the concrete example of the AUC. The AUC is obtained by choosing the kernel $h(x, z) = \mathbb{I}\{z < x\}$, and is widely used as a performance measure in bipartite ranking and binary classification with class imbalance. Recall that our results of Sect. 3.3 highlighted the key role of the pairwise component of the variance σ_0^2 being large compared to the single-sample components. In the case of the AUC, this happens when the data distributions are such that the expected outcome using single-sample information is far from the truth, e.g. in the presence of hard pairs. We illustrate this on simple discrete distributions for which we can compute σ_0^2, σ_1^2 and σ_2^2 in closed form. Consider positive points $X \in \{0,2\}$, negative points $Z \in \{-1,+1\}$ and $\mathbb{P}(X = 2) = q$, $\mathbb{P}(Z = +1) = p$. It follows that:

$$\sigma_1^2 = p^2q(1-q), \quad \sigma_2^2 = (1-q)^2p(1-p), \text{ and } \sigma^2 = p(1-p+pq)(1-q). \quad (13)$$

Assume that the scoring function has a small probability ϵ to assign a low score to a positive instance or a large score to a negative instance. In our formal setting, this translates into letting $p = 1 - q = \epsilon$ for a small $\epsilon > 0$, which implies that $\frac{\sigma_0^2}{\sigma_1^2+\sigma_2^2} = \frac{1-\epsilon}{2\epsilon} \xrightarrow[\epsilon \to 0]{} \infty$. We thus expect that as the true AUC $U(h) = 1 - \epsilon^2$ gets closer to 1, repartitioning the dataset becomes more critical to achieve good relative precision. This is confirmed numerically, as shown in Fig. 3. Note that in practice, settings where the AUC is very close to 1 are very common as they correspond to well-functioning systems, such as face recognition systems.

Learning Experiment. We now turn to AUC optimization, which is the task of learning a scoring function $s : \mathcal{X} \to \mathbb{R}$ that optimizes the VUS criterion (2) with $K = 2$ in order to discriminate between a negative and a positive class. We learn a linear scoring function $s_{w,b}(x) = w^\top x + b$, and optimize a continuous and convex surrogate of (2) based on the hinge loss. The resulting loss function to minimize is a two-sample U-statistic with kernel $g_{w,b}(x, z) = \max(0, 1 + s_{w,b}(x) - s_{w,b}(z))$ indexed by the parameters (w, b) of the scoring function, to which we add a small L2 regularization term of $0.05\|w\|_2^2$.

We use the shuttle dataset, a classic dataset for anomaly detection.[3] It contains roughly 49,000 points in dimension 9, among which only 7% (approx. 3,500) are anomalies. A high accuracy is expected for this dataset. To monitor the generalization performance, we keep 20% of the data as our test set, corresponding to 700 points of the minority class and approx. 9,000 points of the majority class. The test performance is measured with complete statistics over the 6.3 million pairs. The training set consists of the remaining data points, which we distribute over $N = 100$ workers. This leads to approx. $10,200$ pairs per worker. The gradient estimates are calculated following (12) with batch size $B = 100$. We use an initial learning rate of 0.01 with a momentum of 0.9. As there are more than 100 million possible pairs in the training dataset, we monitor the training loss and accuracy on a fixed subset of 4.5×10^5 randomly sampled pairs.

Figure 4 shows the evolution of the continuous loss and the true AUC on the training and test sets along the iteration for different values of n_r, from $n_r = 1$ (repartition at each iteration) to $n_r = +\infty$ (no repartition). The lines are the median at each iteration over 100 runs, and the shaded area correspond to confidence intervals for the AUC and loss value of the testing dataset. We can clearly see the benefits of repartition: without it, the median performance is significantly lower and the variance across runs is very large. The results also show that occasional repartitions (e.g., every 25 iterations) are sufficient to mitigate these issues significantly.

---

[3] http://odds.cs.stonybrook.edu/shuttle-dataset/.

6   Future Work

We envision several further research questions on the topic of distributed tuple-wise learning. We would like to provide a rigorous convergence rate analysis of the general distributed SGD algorithm introduced in Sect. 4. This is a challenging task because each series of iterations executed between two repartition steps can be seen as optimizing a slightly different objective function. It would also be interesting to investigate settings where the workers hold sensitive data that they do not want to share in the clear due to privacy concerns.

References

1. Arjevani, Y., Shamir, O.: Communication complexity of distributed convex learning and optimization. In: NIPS (2015)
2. Balcan, M.F., Blum, A., Fine, S., Mansour, Y.: Distributed learning, communication complexity and privacy. In: COLT (2012)
3. Bekkerman, R., Bilenko, M., Langford, J.: Scaling Up Machine Learning: Parallel and Distributed Approaches. Cambridge University Press, Cambridge (2011)
4. Bellet, A., Liang, Y., Garakani, A.B., Balcan, M.F., Sha, F.: A distributed frank-wolfe algorithm for communication-efficient sparse learning. In: SDM (2015)
5. Bertail, P., Tressou, J.: Incomplete generalized U-statistics for food risk assessment. Biometrics $62(1)$, 66–74 (2006)
6. Blom, G.: Some properties of incomplete U-statistics. Biometrika $63(3)$, 573–580 (1976)
7. Bottou, L., Bousquet, O.: The Tradeoffs of large scale learning. In: NIPS (2007)
8. Boyd, S.P., Parikh, N., Chu, E., Peleato, B., Eckstein, J.: Distributed optimization and statistical learning via the alternating direction method of multipliers. Found. Trends Mach. Learn. $3(1)$, 1–122 (2011)
9. Bubeck, S.: Convex optimization: algorithms and complexity. Found. Trends Mach. Learn. $8(3–4)$, 231–357 (2015)
10. Carbone, P., Katsifodimos, A., Ewen, S., Markl, V., Haridi, S., Tzoumas, K.: Apache Flink^{TM}: stream and batch processing in a single engine. IEEE Data Eng. Bull. $38(4)$, 28–38 (2015)
11. Clémençon, S.: A statistical view of clustering performance through the theory of U-processes. J. Multivar. Anal. 124, 42–56 (2014)
12. Clémençon, S., Bellet, A., Colin, I.: Scaling-up empirical risk minimization: optimization of incomplete U-statistics. J. Mach. Learn. Res. 13, 165–202 (2016)
13. Clémençon, S., Lugosi, G., Vayatis, N.: Ranking and empirical risk minimization of U-statistics. Ann. Stat. $36(2)$, 844–874 (2008)
14. Clémençon, S., Robbiano, S.: Building confidence regions for the ROC surface. Pattern Recogn. Lett. 46, 67–74 (2014)
15. Daumé III, H., Phillips, J.M., Saha, A., Venkatasubramanian, S.: Protocols for learning classifiers on distributed data. In: AISTATS (2012)
16. Dean, J., Ghemawat, S.: MapReduce: simplified data processing on large clusters. Commun. ACM $51(1)$, 107–113 (2008)
17. Hoeffding, W.: A class of statistics with asymptotically normal distribution. Ann. Math. Stat. 19, 293–325 (1948)
18. Jordan, M.: On statistics, computation and scalability. Bernoulli $19(4)$, 1378–1390 (2013)

19. Lee, A.: U-statistics: Theory and Practice. Marcel Dekker Inc., New York (1990)
20. Papa, G., Bellet, A., Clémençon, S.: SGD algorithms based on incomplete U-statistics: large-scale minimization of empirical risk. In: NIPS (2015)
21. de la Pena, V., Giné, E.: Decoupling: From Dependence to Independence. Springer, Heidelberg (1999). https://doi.org/10.1007/978-1-4612-0537-1
22. Smith, V., Forte, S., Ma, C., Takác, M., Jordan, M.I., Jaggi, M.: CoCoA: a general framework for communication-efficient distributed optimization. J. Mach. Learn. Res. **18**(230), 1–49 (2018)
23. Van Der Vaart, A.: Asymptotic Statistics. Cambridge University Press, Cambridge (2000)
24. Vogel, R., Bellet, A., Clémençon, S.: A probabilistic theory of supervised similarity learning for pointwise ROC curve optimization. In: ICML (2018)
25. Xing, E.P., et al.: Petuum: a new platform for distributed machine learning on big data. IEEE Trans. Big Data **1**(2), 49–67 (2015)
26. Zaharia, M., Chowdhury, M., Franklin, M.J., Shenker, S., Stoica, I.: Spark: cluster computing with working sets. In: HotCloud (2012)

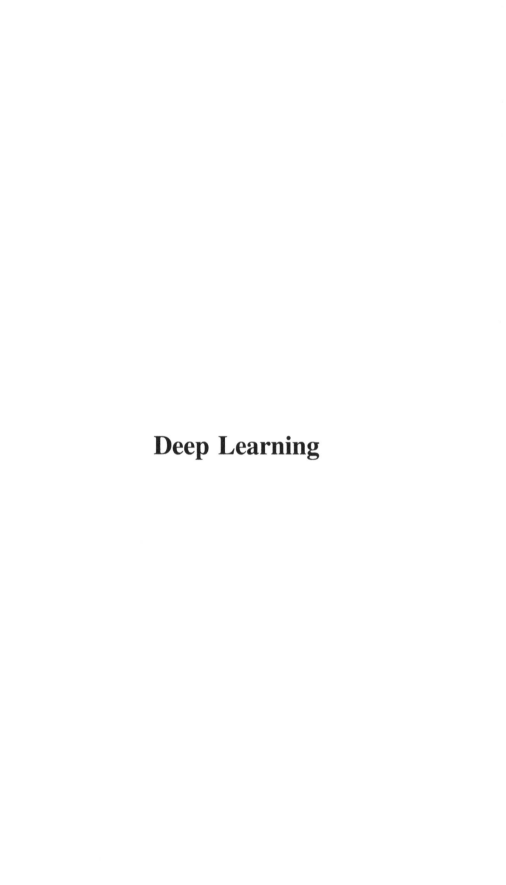

Deep Learning

Importance Weighted Generative Networks

Maurice Diesendruck[1]([✉]), Ethan R. Elenberg[2], Rajat Sen[3], Guy W. Cole[1],
Sanjay Shakkottai[1], and Sinead A. Williamson[1,4]

[1] The University of Texas at Austin, Austin, USA
{momod,guywcole}@utexas.edu, shakkott@austin.utexas.edu,
sinead.williamson@mccombs.utexas.edu
[2] ASAPP, Inc., New York, USA
elenberg@asapp.com
[3] Amazon, Inc., Austin, USA
rajat.sen@utexas.edu
[4] CognitiveScale, Austin, USA

Abstract. While deep generative networks can simulate from complex data distributions, their utility can be hindered by limitations on the data available for training. Specifically, the training data distribution may differ from the target sampling distribution due to sample selection bias, or because the training data comes from a different but related distribution. We present methods to accommodate this difference via *importance weighting*, which allow us to estimate a loss function with respect to a target distribution *even if we cannot access that distribution directly*. These estimators, which differentially weight the contribution of data to the loss function, offer theoretical guarantees that heuristic approaches lack, while giving impressive empirical performance in a variety of settings.

Keywords: Importance weights · Generative networks · Bias correction

1 Introduction

Deep generative models have important applications in many fields: we can automatically generate illustrations for text [48]; simulate video streams [46] or molecular fingerprints [27]; and create privacy-preserving versions of medical time-series data [14]. Such models use a neural network to parametrize a function $G(Z)$, which maps random noise Z to a target probability distribution $\mathbb{P}$. This is achieved by minimizing a loss function between simulations and data, which is equivalent to learning a distribution over simulations that is indistinguishable from $\mathbb{P}$ under an appropriate two-sample test. In this paper we focus on Generative Adversarial Networks (GANs) [2,4,17,30], which incorporate an

R. Sen and S. Shakkottai were partially supported by ARO grant W911NF-17-1-0359.
E.R. Elenberg—Work done primarily while at UT Austin.

adversarially learned neural network in the loss function; however the results are also applicable to non-adversarial networks [13,31].

An interesting challenge arises when we do not have direct access to i.i.d. samples from $\mathbb{P}$. This could arise either because observations are obtained via a biased sampling mechanism [6,49], or in a transfer learning setting where our target distribution differs from our training distribution. As an example of the former, a dataset of faces generated as part of a university project may contain disproportionately many young adult faces relative to the population. As an example of the latter, a Canadian hospital system might want to customize simulations to its population while still leveraging a training set of patients from the United States (which has a different statistical distribution of medical records). In both cases, and more generally, we want to generate data from a target distribution $\mathbb{P}$ but only have access to representative samples from a *modified* distribution $M\mathbb{P}$. We give a pictorial example of this setting in Fig. 1.

 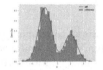

(a) Target distribution $\mathbb{P}$ (b) Observed distribution $M\mathbb{P}$ and samples from $M\mathbb{P}$ (c) Simulations using a standard estimator   (d) Simulations using an importance weighted estimator

Fig. 1. If our target distribution $\mathbb{P}$ differs from our observed distribution $M\mathbb{P}$, using the standard estimator will replicate $M\mathbb{P}$, while an importance weighted estimator can replicate the target $\mathbb{P}$.

In some cases, we can approach this problem using existing methods. For example, if we can reduce our problem to a conditional data-generating mechanism, we can employ Conditional Generative Adversarial Networks (C-GANs) or related models [33,36], which enable conditional sampling given one or more latent variables. However, this requires that M can be described on a low-dimensional space, and that we can sample from our target distribution over that latent space. Further, C-GANs rely on a large, labeled dataset of training samples with diversity over the conditioning variable (within each batch), which becomes a challenge when conditioning on a high-dimensional variable. For example, if we wish to modify a distribution over faces with respect to age, gender and hair length, there may few exemplars of 80-year-old men with long hair with which to learn the corresponding conditional distribution.

In this paper, we propose an alternate approach based on importance sampling [37]. Our method modifies an existing GAN by rescaling the observed data distribution $M\mathbb{P}$ during training, or equivalently by reweighting the contribution of each data point to the loss function. When training a GAN with samples from

$M\mathbb{P}$, the standard estimator equally weights the contribution of each point, yielding an estimator of the loss with respect to $M\mathbb{P}$ and corresponding simulations, as shown in Fig. 1b and Fig. 1c. This is not ideal.

In order to yield the desired estimator with respect to our target distribution $\mathbb{P}$, we modify the estimator by reweighting the loss function evaluation for each sample. When the Radon-Nikodym derivative between the target and observed distributions (aka the modifier function M) is known, we inversely scale each evaluation by that derivative, yielding the finite-sample importance sampling transform on the estimate, which we call the *importance weighted* estimator. This reweighting asymptotically ensures that discrimination, and the corresponding GAN update, occurs with respect to $\mathbb{P}$ instead of $M\mathbb{P}$, as shown in Fig. 1a and Fig. 1d.

This approach has multiple advantages and extensions. First, if M is known, we can estimate importance weighted losses using robust estimators like the median-of-means estimator, which is crucial for controlling variance in settings where the modifier function M has a large dynamic range. Second, even when the modifier function is only known up to a scaling factor, we can construct an alternative estimator using self-normalized sampling [37,41] to use this partial information, while still maintaining asymptotic correctness. Finally and importantly, for the common case of an unknown modifier function, we demonstrate techniques for estimating it from partially labeled data.

Our contributions are as follows: (1) We provide a novel application of traditional importance weighting to deep generative models. This has connections to many types of GAN loss functions through the theory of U-statistics. (2) We propose several variants of our importance weighting framework for different practical scenarios. When dealing with particularly difficult functions M, we propose to use robust median-of-means estimation and show that it has similar theoretical guarantees under weaker assumptions, *i.e.* bounded second moment. When M is not known fully (only up to a scaling factor), we propose a self-normalized estimator. (3) We conduct an extensive experimental evaluation of the proposed methods on both synthetic and real-world datasets. This includes estimating M when less than 4% of the data is labeled with user-provided exemplars.

1.1   Related Work

Our method aims to generate samples from a distribution $\mathbb{P}$, given access to samples from $M\mathbb{P}$. While to the best of our knowledge this has not been explicitly addressed in the GAN literature, several approaches have related goals.

Domain Adaptation: Our formulation is related to but distinct from the problem of Domain Adaptation (DA). The challenge of DA is, "If I train on one distribution and test on another, how do I maximize performance on test data?" Critically, the test data is available and extensively used. Instead, our method solves the problem, "Given only a training data distribution, how do I generate from arbitrarily modified versions of it?" The former uses two datasets – one source and one target – while the latter uses one dataset and accommodates an arbitrary number of targets. The methodologies are inherently different because the information available is different.

Typical approaches to DA involve finding domain-invariant feature representations for both source and target data. Blitzer, Pereira, Ben-David, and Daume [3,5,9] write extensively on techniques involving feature correlation and mutual information within classification settings. Pan, Huang, and Gong [16,24,38,39] propose methods with similar goals that find kernel representations under which source and target distributions are close. The work of [24] and [43] address covariate shift using kernel-based and importance-weighted techniques, but still inhabit a different setting from our problem since they perform estimation on specific source and target datasets.

Recently, the term DA has been used in the context of adversarially-trained image-to-image translation and downstream transfer learning tasks [22,25,45,50]. Typically the goal is to produce representations of the same image in both source and target domains. Such problems begin with datasets from both domains, whereas our setting presents only one source dataset and seeks to generate samples from a hypothetical, user-described target domain.

Inverse Probability Weighting: Inverse probability weighting (IPW), originally proposed by [23] and still in wide use in the field of survey statistics [32], can be seen as a special case of importance sampling. IPW is a weighting scheme used to correct for biased treatment assignment methods in survey sampling. In such settings, the target distribution is known and the sampling distribution is typically finite and discrete, and can easily be estimated from data.

Conditional GANs: Conditional GANs (C-GANs) are an extension of GANs that aim to simulate from a conditional distribution, given some covariate. In the case where our modifier function M can be represented in terms of a low-dimensional covariate space, and if we can generate samples from the marginal distribution of $M\mathbb{P}$ on that space, then we can, in theory, use a C-GAN to generate samples from $\mathbb{P}$, by conditioning on the sampled covariates. This strategy suffers from two limitations. First, it assumes we can express M in terms of a sampleable distribution on a low-dimensional covariate space. For settings where M varies across many data dimensions or across a high-dimensional latent embedding, this ability to sample becomes untenable. Second, learning a family of conditional distributions is typically more difficult than learning a single joint distribution. As we show in our experiments, C-GANs often fail if there are too few real exemplars for a given covariate setting.

Related to C-GANs, [8] proposes conditional generation and a classifier for assigning samples to specific discriminators. While not mentioned, such a structure could feasibly be used to preferentially sample certain modes, if a correspondence between latent features and numbered modes were known.

Weighted Loss: In the context of domain adaptation for data with discrete class labels, the strategy of reweighting the Maximum Mean Discrepancy (MMD) [18] based on class probabilities has been proposed by [47]. This approach, however, differs from ours in several ways: It is limited to class imbalance problems, as opposed to changes in continuous-valued latent features; it requires access to the non-conforming target dataset; it provides no theoretical guarantees about the weighted estimator; and it is not in the generative model setting.

Other Uses of Importance Weights in GANs: The language and use of importance weights is not unique to this application, and has been used for other purposes within the GAN context. In [19], for example, importance weights are used to provide policy gradients for GANs in a discrete-data setting. Our application is different in that our target distribution is not that of our data, as it is in [19]. Instead we view our data as having been modified, and use importance weights to simulate closer to the hypothetical and desired *unmodified* distribution.

2   Problem Formulation and Technical Approach

The Problem: Given training samples from a distribution $M\mathbb{P}$, our goal is to construct (train) a generator function $G(\cdot)$ that produces i.i.d. samples from a distribution $\mathbb{P}$.

To train $G(\cdot)$, we follow the methodology of a Generative Adversarial Network (GAN) [17]. In brief, a GAN consists of a pair of interacting and evolving neural networks – a generator neural network with outputs that approximate the desired distribution, and a discriminator neural network that distinguishes between increasingly realistic outputs from the generator and samples from a training dataset.

The loss function is a critical feature of the GAN discriminator, and evaluates the closeness between the samples of the generator and those of the training data. Designing good loss functions remains an active area of research [2,30]. One popular loss function is the Maximum Mean Discrepancy (MMD) [18], a distributional distance that is zero if and only if the two distributions are the same. As such, MMD can be used to prevent mode collapse [7,42] during training.

Our Approach: We are able to train a GAN to generate samples from $\mathbb{P}$ using a simple reweighting modification to the MMD loss function. Reweighting forces the loss function to apply greater penalties in areas of the support where the target and observed distributions differ most.

Below, we formally describe the MMD loss function, and describe its importance weighted variants.

Remark 1 (Extension to other losses). While this paper focuses on the MMD loss, we note that the above estimators can be extended to any estimator that can be expressed as the expectation of some function with respect to one or more distributions. This class includes losses such as squared mean difference between two distributions, cross entropy loss, and autoencoder losses [20,34,44]. Such losses can be estimated from data using a combination of U-statistics, V-statistics and sample averages. Each of these statistics can be reweighted, in a manner analogous to the treatment described above. We provide more comprehensive details in Table 1, and in Sect. 3.1 we evaluate all three importance weighting techniques as applied to the standard cross entropy GAN objective.

2.1 Maximum Mean Discrepancy Between Two Distributions

The MMD projects two distributions $\mathbb{P}$ and $\mathbb{Q}$ into a reproducing kernel Hilbert space (RKHS) $\mathcal{H}$, and evaluates the maximum mean distance between the two projections, *i.e.*

$$\text{MMD}(\mathbb{P}, \mathbb{Q}) := \sup_{f \in \mathcal{H}} \left(\mathbf{E}_{X \sim \mathbb{P}}[f(X)] - \mathbf{E}_{Y \sim \mathbb{Q}}[f(Y)] \right).$$

If we specify the *kernel mean embedding* $\mu_\mathbb{P}$ of $\mathbb{P}$ as $\mu_\mathbb{P} = \int k(x, \cdot) d\mathbb{P}(x)$, where $k(\cdot, \cdot)$ is the characteristic kernel defining the RKHS, then we can write the square of this distance as

$$\text{MMD}^2(\mathbb{P}, \mathbb{Q}) = ||\mu_\mathbb{P} - \mu_\mathbb{Q}||_\mathcal{H}^2$$
$$= \mathbb{E}_{X,X' \sim \mathbb{P}}[k(X, X')] + \mathbb{E}_{Y,Y' \sim \mathbb{Q}}[k(Y, Y')]$$
$$- 2\mathbb{E}_{X \sim \mathbb{P}, Y \sim \mathbb{Q}}[k(X, Y)]. \tag{1}$$

In order to be a useful loss function for training a neural network, we must be able to estimate $\text{MMD}^2(\mathbb{P}, \mathbb{Q})$ from data, and compute gradients of this estimate with respect to the network parameters. Let $\{x_i\}_n$ be a sample $\{X_1 = x_1, \ldots, X_n = x_n\} : X_i \sim \mathbb{P}$, and $\{y_i\}_m$ be a sample $\{Y_1 = y_1, \ldots, Y_m = y_m\} : Y_i \sim \mathbb{Q}$. We can construct an unbiased estimator $\widehat{\text{MMD}}^2(\mathbb{P}, \mathbb{Q})$ of $\text{MMD}^2(\mathbb{P}, \mathbb{Q})$ [18] using these samples as

$$\widehat{\text{MMD}}^2(\mathbb{P}, \mathbb{Q}) = \frac{1}{n(n-1)} \sum_{i \neq j}^n k(x_i, x_j)$$
$$+ \frac{1}{m(m-1)} \sum_{i \neq j}^m k(y_i, y_j)$$
$$- \frac{2}{nm} \sum_{i=1}^n \sum_{j=1}^m k(x_i, y_j). \tag{2}$$

2.2 Importance Weighted Estimator for Known M

We begin with the case where M (which relates the distribution of the samples and the desired distribution; formally the Radon-Nikodym derivative) is known. Here, the reweighting of our loss function can be framed as an *importance sampling* problem: we want to estimate $\text{MMD}^2(\mathbb{P}, \mathbb{Q})$, which is in terms of the target distribution $\mathbb{P}$ and the distribution $\mathbb{Q}$ implied by our generator, but we have samples from the modified $M\mathbb{P}$. Importance sampling [37] provides a method for constructing an estimator for the expectation of a function $\phi(X)$ with respect to a distribution $\mathbb{P}$, by taking an appropriately weighted sum of evaluations of ϕ at values sampled from a different distribution. We can therefore modify the estimator in (2) by weighting each term in the estimator involving data point x_i using the likelihood ratio $\mathbb{P}(x_i)/M(x_i)\mathbb{P}(x_i) = 1/M(x_i)$, yielding an unbiased importance weighted estimator that takes the form

$$\widehat{\mathrm{MMD}}^2_{IW}(\mathbb{P}, \mathbb{Q}) = \frac{1}{n(n-1)} \sum_{i \neq j}^n \frac{k(x_i, x_j)}{M(x_i)M(x_j)}$$

$$+ \frac{1}{m(m-1)} \sum_{i \neq j}^m k(y_i, y_j)$$

$$- \frac{2}{nm} \sum_{i=1}^n \sum_{j=1}^m \frac{k(x_i, y_j)}{M(x_i)}. \tag{3}$$

While importance weighting using the likelihood ratio yields an unbiased estimator (3), the estimator may not concentrate well because the weights $\{1/M(x_i)\}_n$ may be large or even unbounded. We now provide a concentration bound for the estimator in (3) for the case where weights $\{1/M(x_i)\}_n$ are upper-bounded by some maximum value.

Theorem 1. *Let $\widehat{\mathrm{MMD}}^2_{IW}(\mathbb{P}, \mathbb{Q})$ be the unbiased, importance weighted estimator for $\mathrm{MMD}^2(\mathbb{P}, \mathbb{Q})$ defined in (3), given m i.i.d samples from $M\mathbb{P}$ and $\mathbb{Q}$, and maximum kernel value K. Further assume that $1 \leq 1/M(x) \leq W$ for all $x \in \mathcal{X}$. Then*

$$\mathbb{P}\left(\widehat{\mathrm{MMD}}^2_{IW}(\mathbb{P}, \mathbb{Q}) - \mathrm{MMD}^2(\mathbb{P}, \mathbb{Q}) > t\right) \leq C,$$

$$\text{where } C = \exp((-2t^2 m_2)/(K^2(W+1)^4))$$

$$m_2 := \lfloor m/2 \rfloor$$

These guarantees are based on estimator guarantees in [18], which in turn build on classical results by Hoeffding [20, 21]. We defer the proof of this theorem to the extended version of this work [12].

2.3   Robust Importance Weighted Estimator for Known M

Theorem 1 is sufficient to guarantee good concentration of our importance weighted estimator only when $1/M(x)$ is uniformly bounded by some constant W, which is not too large. Many class imbalance problems fall into this setting. However, $1/M(x)$ may be unbounded in practice. Therefore, we now introduce a different estimator, which enjoys good concentration even when only $\mathbb{E}_{X \sim M\mathbb{P}}[1/M(X)^2]$ is bounded, while $1/M(x)$ may be unbounded for many values of x.

The estimator is based on the classical idea of median of means [1, 26, 29, 35][1]. Given m samples from $M\mathbb{P}$ and $\mathbb{Q}$, we divide these samples uniformly at random into k equal sized groups, indexed $\{(1), ..., (k)\}$. Let $\widehat{\mathrm{MMD}}^2_{IW}(\mathbb{P}, \mathbb{Q})^{(i)}$ be the value obtained when the estimator in (3) is applied on the i-th group of samples. Then our median of means based estimator is given by

$$\widehat{\mathrm{MMD}}^2_{MIW}(\mathbb{P}, \mathbb{Q}) = \mathrm{median}\left\{\widehat{\mathrm{MMD}}^2_{IW}(\mathbb{P}, \mathbb{Q})^{(1)}, \dots, \widehat{\mathrm{MMD}}^2_{IW}(\mathbb{P}, \mathbb{Q})^{(k)}\right\}. \tag{4}$$

---

[1] [29] appeared concurrently and contains a different approach for the unweighted estimator. Comparisons are left for future work.

Theorem 2. *Let $\widehat{\mathrm{MMD}}^2_{MIW}(\mathbb{P}, \mathbb{Q})$ be the asymptotically unbiased median of means estimator defined in* (4) *using $k = mt^2/(8K^2\sigma^2)$ groups. Further assume that $n = m$ and let $W_2 = \mathbb{E}_{X \sim M\mathbb{P}}[1/M(X)^2]$ be bounded. Then*

$$\mathbb{P}\left(|\widehat{\mathrm{MMD}}^2_{MIW}(\mathbb{P}, \mathbb{Q}) - \mathrm{MMD}^2(\mathbb{P}, \mathbb{Q})| > t\right) \le C,$$

where $C = \exp((-mt^2)/(64K^2\sigma^2))$

$$\sigma^2 = O\left(W_2^2 + MMD^4(\mathbb{P}, \mathbb{Q})\right).$$

We defer the proof of this theorem to the extended version of this work [12]. Note that the confidence bound in Theorem 2 depends on the term W_2 being bounded. This is the second moment of $1/M(X)$ where $X \sim M\mathbb{P}$. Thus, unlike in Theorem 1, this confidence bound may still hold even if $1/M(x)$ is *not uniformly bounded*. When $1/M(X)$ is heavy-tailed with finite variance, *e.g.* Pareto ($\alpha > 2$) or log-normal, then Theorem 2 is valid but Theorem 1 does not apply.

In addition to increased robustness, the median of means MMD estimator is more computationally efficient: since calculating $\widehat{\mathrm{MMD}}^2_{IW}(\mathbb{P}, \mathbb{Q})$ scales quadratically in the batch size, using the median of means estimator introduces a speedup that is linear in the number of groups.

2.4 Self-normalized Importance Weights for Unknown M

To specify M, we must know the forms of our target and observed distributions along any marginals where the two differ. In some settings this is available: consider for example a class rebalancing setting where we have class labels and a desired class ratio, and can estimate the observed class ratio from data. This, however, may be infeasible if M is continuous and/or varies over several dimensions, particularly if data are arriving in a streaming manner. In such a setting it may be easier to specify a *thinning function T that is proportional to M*, i.e. $M\mathbb{P} = \frac{T\mathbb{P}}{Z}$ for some unknown Z, than to estimate M directly. This is because T can be directly obtained from an estimate of how much a given location is underestimated, without any knowledge of the underlying distribution.

This setting—where the $1/M$ weights used in Sect. 2.2 are only known up to a normalizing constant—motivates the use of a *self-normalized* importance sampling scheme, where the weights $w_i \propto \frac{\mathbb{P}(x_i)}{M(x_i)\mathbb{P}(x_i)} = \frac{Z}{T(x_i)}$ are normalized to sum to one [37, 41]. For example, by letting $w_i = \frac{1}{T(x_i)}$, the resulting self-normalized estimator for the squared MMD takes the form

$$\widehat{\mathrm{MMD}}^2_{IW}(\mathbb{P}, \mathbb{Q}) = \frac{\sum_{i \neq j}^n w_i w_j k(x_i, x_j)}{\sum_{i \neq j}^n w_i w_j}$$

$$+ \sum_{i \neq j}^m \frac{k(y_i, y_j)}{m(m-1)}$$

$$- 2\frac{\sum_{i=1}^n \sum_{j=1}^m w_i k(x_i, y_j)}{m \sum_{i=1}^n w_i}. \tag{5}$$

While use of self-normalized weights means this self-normalized estimator is biased, it is asymptotically unbiased, with the bias decreasing at a rate of $1/n$ [28]. Although we have motivated self-normalized weights out of necessity, in practice they often trade off bias for reduced variance, making them preferable in some practical applications [37].

More generally, in addition to not knowing the normalizing constant Z, we might also not know the thinning function T. For example, T might vary along some latent dimension—perhaps we want to have more images of people fitting a certain aesthetic, rather than corresponding to a certain observed covariate or class. In this setting, a practitioner may be able to estimate $T(x_i)$, or equivalently w_i, for a small number of training points x_i, by considering how much those training points are under- or over-represented. Continuous-valued latent preferences can therefore be expressed by applying higher weights to points deemed more appealing. From here, we can use function estimation techniques, such as neural network regression, to estimate T from a small number of labeled data points.

2.5 Approximate Importance Weighting by Data Duplication

In the importance weighting scheme described above, each data point is assigned a weight $1/M(x_i)$. We can obtain an approximation to this method by including $\lceil 1/M(x_i) \rceil$ duplicates of data point x_i in our training set. We refer to this approach as *importance duplication*. Importance duplication obviously introduces discretization errors, and if our estimator is a U-statistic it will introduce bias (*e.g.* in the MMD example, if two or more copies of the data point x_i appear in a minibatch, then $k(x_i, x_i)$ will appear in the first term of (2)). However, as we show in the experimental setting, even though this approach lacks theoretical guarantees it provides generally good performance.

Data duplication can be done as a pre-processing step, making it an appealing choice if we have an existing GAN implementation that we do not wish to modify. In other settings, it is less appealing, since duplicating data adds an additional step and increases the amount of data the algorithm must process. Further, if we were to use this approximation in a setting where M is unknown, we would have to perform this data duplication on the fly as our estimate of M changes.

3 Evaluation

In this section, we show that our estimators, in conjunction with an appropriate generator network, allow us to generate simulations that are close in distribution to our target distribution, even when we only have access to this distribution via a biased sampling mechanism. Further, we show that our method performs comparably with, or better than, conditional GAN baselines.

Most of our weighted GAN models are based on the MMD-GAN of [30], replacing the original MMD loss with either our importance weighted loss

Table 1. Constructing importance weighted estimators for losses involving U-statistics, V-statistics and sample averages. Here, $\mathcal{U}$ is the set of all r-tuples of numbers from 1 to n without repeats, and $\mathcal{V}$ is the set of r-tuples allowing repeats. Below, let $X_{u,*} = X_{u_1}, ..., X_{u_r}$.

	$\widehat{D}(\mathbb{P},\mathbb{Q})$	$\widehat{D}_{IW}(\mathbb{P},\mathbb{Q})$	$\widehat{D}_{SNIW}(\mathbb{P},\mathbb{Q})$
U-statistic	$\dfrac{1}{{}_nP_r}\displaystyle\sum_{u\in\mathcal{U}} g(X_{u,*})$	$\dfrac{1}{{}_nP_r}\displaystyle\sum_{u\in\mathcal{U}} \dfrac{g(X_{u,*})}{M(X_{u_1})\cdots M(X_{u_r})}$	$\dfrac{\sum_{u\in\mathcal{U}} w_{u_1}\cdots w_{u_r}g(X_{u,*})}{\sum_{u\in\mathcal{U}} w_{u_1}\cdots w_{u_r}}$
V-statistic	$\dfrac{1}{n^r}\displaystyle\sum_{v\in\mathcal{V}} g(X_{v,*})$	$\dfrac{1}{n^r}\displaystyle\sum_{v\in\mathcal{V}} \dfrac{g(X_{v,*})}{M(X_{v_1})\cdots M(X_{v_r})}$	$\dfrac{\sum_{v\in\mathcal{V}} w_{v_1}\cdots w_{v_r}g(X_{v,*})}{\sum_{v_r=1}^{n} w_{v_1}\cdots w_{v_r}}$
Average	$\dfrac{1}{nm}\displaystyle\sum_{i=1}^{n}\sum_{j=1}^{m} f(X_i,Y_j)$	$\dfrac{1}{nm}\displaystyle\sum_{i=1}^{n}\sum_{j=1}^{m} \dfrac{f(X_i,Y_j)}{M(X_i)}$	$\dfrac{\sum_{i=1}^{n} w_i \sum_{j=1}^{m} f(X_i,Y_j)}{m\sum_{i=1}^{n} w_i}$

$\widehat{\mathrm{MMD}}^2_{IW}(\mathbb{P},\mathbb{Q})$ (IW-MMD), our median of means loss $\widehat{\mathrm{MMD}}^2_{MIW}(\mathbb{P},\mathbb{Q})$ (MIW-MMD), or our self-normalized loss $\widehat{\mathrm{MMD}}^2_{SNIW}(\mathbb{P},\mathbb{Q})$ (SNIW-MMD). We also use a standard MMD loss with an importance duplicated dataset (ID-MMD). Other losses used in [30] are also appropriately weighted, following the form in Table 1. In the synthetic data examples of Sect. 3.1, the kernel is a fixed radial basis function, while in all other sections it is adversarially trained using a discriminator network as in [30].

To demonstrate that our method is applicable to other losses, in Sect. 3.1 we also create models that use the standard cross entropy GAN loss, replacing this loss with either an importance weighted estimator (IW-CE), a median of means estimator (MIW-CE) or a self-normalized estimator (SNIW-CE). We also combine a standard cross entropy loss with an importance duplicated dataset (ID-CE). These models used a two-layer feedforward neural network with ten nodes per layer.

Where appropriate, we compare against a conditional GAN (C-GAN). If M is known exactly and expressible in terms of a lower-dimensional covariate space, a conditional GAN (C-GAN) offers an alternative method to sample from $\mathbb{P}$: learn the appropriate conditional distributions given each covariate value, sample new covariate values, and then sample from $\mathbb{P}$ using each conditional distribution.

3.1 Can GANs with Importance Weighted Estimators Recover Target Distributions, Given M?

To evaluate whether using importance weighted estimators can recover target distributions, we consider a synthetically generated distribution that has been manipulated along a latent dimension. Under the target distribution, a latent representation θ_i of each data point lives in a ten-dimensional space, with each dimension independently Uniform(0,1). The observed data points x_i are then obtained as $\theta_i^T F$, where $F_{ij} \sim \mathcal{N}(0,1)$ represents a fixed mapping between the latent space and D-dimensional observation space. In the training data, the first dimension of θ_i has distribution $p(\theta) = 2\theta, 0 < \theta \le 1$. We assume that the modifying function $M(x_i) = 2\theta_{i,1}$ is observed, but that the remaining latent dimensions are unobserved.

In our experiments, we generate samples from the target distribution using each of the methods described above, and include weighted versions of the cross entropy GAN to demonstrate that importance weighting can be generalized to other losses.

To compare methods, we report the empirically estimated KL divergence between the target and generated samples in Table 2. Similar results using squared MMD and energy distance are shown in the extended version of this work [12]. For varying real dimensions D, importance weighted methods outperform C-GAN under a variety of measures.

In some instances C-GAN performs well in two dimensions, but deteriorates quickly as the problem becomes more challenging with higher dimensions. We also note that many runs of C-GAN either ran into numerical issues or diverged; in these cases we report the best score among runs, before training failure.

Table 2. Estimated KL divergence between generated and target samples (mean ± standard deviation over 20 runs).

Model	2D	4D	10D
IW-CE	0.1768 ± 0.0635	0.4934 ± 0.1238	2.7945 ± 0.5966
MIW-CE	0.3265 ± 0.1071	0.6251 ± 0.1343	3.3093 ± 0.7179
SNIW-CE	0.0925 ± 0.0272	0.3864 ± 0.1478	2.3060 ± 0.6915
ID-CE	0.1526 ± 0.0332	0.3444 ± 0.0766	1.4128 ± 0.3288
IW-MMD	**0.0343 ± 0.0230**	**0.0037 ± 0.0489**	**0.5133 ± 0.1718**
MIW-MMD	0.2698 ± 0.0618	0.0939 ± 0.0522	0.8501 ± 0.3271
SNIW-MMD	0.0451 ± 0.0132	0.1435 ± 0.0377	0.6623 ± 0.0918
C-GAN	0.0879 ± 0.0405	0.3108 ± 0.0982	6.9016 ± 2.8406

While the above experiment can be evaluated numerically and provide good results for thinning on a continuous-valued variable, it is difficult to visualize the outcome. In order to better visualize whether the target distribution is correctly achieved, we also run experiments with explicit and easily measurable class distributions. In Fig. 2, we show a class rebalancing problem on MNIST digits, where an initial uneven distribution between three classes can be accurately rebalanced. In the extended version of this work [12], we also show good performance modifying a balanced distribution to specific boosted levels. Together, these experiments provide evidence that importance weighting controls the simulated distribution in the desired way.

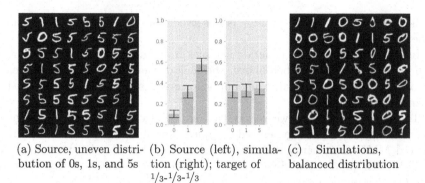

(a) Source, uneven distribution of 0s, 1s, and 5s

(b) Source (left), simulation (right); target of $1/3$-$1/3$-$1/3$

(c) Simulations, balanced distribution

Fig. 2. Importance weights are used to accurately rebalance an uneven class distribution.

3.2   In a High-Dimensional Image Setting, How Does Importance Weighting Compare with Conditional Generation?

Next we evaluate performance of importance weighted MMD on high-dimensional image generation. In this section we address two questions: Can our estimators generate simulations from $\mathbb{P}$ in such a setting, and how do the resulting images compare with those obtained using a C-GAN? To do so, we evaluate several generative models on the Yearbook dataset [15], which contains over 37,000 high school yearbook photos across over 100 years and demonstrates evolving styles and demographics. The goal is to produce images uniformly across each half decade. Each GAN, however, is trained on the original dataset, which contains many more photos from recent decades.

Since we have specified M in terms of a single covariate (time), we can compare with C-GANs. For the C-GAN, we use a conditional version of the standard DCGAN architecture (C-DCGAN) [40].

Figure 3 shows generated images from each network. All networks were trained until convergence. The images show a diversity across hairstyles, demographics and facial expressions, indicating the successful temporal rebalancing. Even while importance duplication introduces approximations and lacks the theoretical guarantees of the other two methods, all three importance-based methods achieve comparable quality. Since some covariates have fewer than 65 images, C-DCGAN cannot learn the conditional distributions, and is unstable across a variety of training parameters. Implementation details and additional experiments are shown in the extended version of this work [12].

3.3   When M Is Unknown, But Can Be Estimated Up to a Normalizing Constant on a Subset of Data, Are We Able to Sample from Our Target Distribution?

In many settings, especially those with high-dimensional latent features, we will not know the functional form of M, or even the corresponding thinning

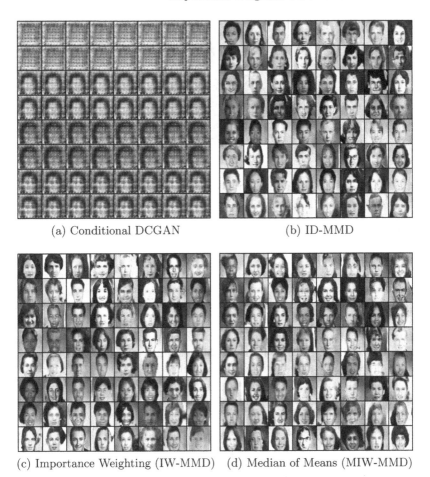

(a) Conditional DCGAN

(b) ID-MMD

(c) Importance Weighting (IW-MMD)

(d) Median of Means (MIW-MMD)

Fig. 3. Example generated images for all example networks, Yearbook dataset [15]. Target distribution is uniform across half-decades, while the training set is unbalanced.

function T. We would still, however, like to be able to express a preference for certain areas of the latent space. To do so, we propose labeling a small subset of data using weights that correspond to preference. To expand those weights to the entire dataset, we train a neural network called the estimated weighting function. This weighting function takes encoded images as input, and outputs continuous-valued weights. Since this function exists in a high-dimensional space that changes as the encoder is updated, and since we do not know the full observed distribution on this space, we are in a setting unsuitable for conditional methods, and therefore use self-normalized estimators (SNIW-MMD).

We evaluate using a collection of sevens from the MNIST dataset, where the goal is to generate more European-style sevens with horizontal bars. Out of 5915 images, 200 were manually labeled with a weight (reciprocal of a thinning

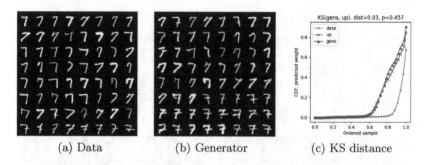

| (a) Data | (b) Generator | (c) KS distance |

Fig. 4. Partial labeling and an importance weighted estimator boost the presence of sevens with horizontal bars. In a and b, samples are sorted by predicted weight, and in c, the empirical CDFs of data, generated, and importance duplicated draws, are shown, where the latter serves as a theoretical target. The generated distribution is close in distance to the target.

function value), where sevens with no horizontal bar were assigned a 1, and sevens with horizontal bars were assigned weights between 2 and 9 based on the width of the bar.

Figure 4a shows 64 real images, sorted in terms of their predicted weights – note that the majority have no horizontal bar. Figure 4b shows 64 generated simulations, sorted in the same manner, clearly showing an increase in the number of horizontal-bar sevens.

To test the quantitative performance, we display and compare the empirical CDFs of weights from simulations, data, and importance duplicated data. For example, if a batch of data $[A, B, C]$ has weights $[1, 3, 2]$, this implies that we expected three times as many B-like points and two times as many C-like points as A-like points. A simulator that achieves this target produces simulations like $[A, B, B, B, C, C]$ with weights $[1, 3, 3, 3, 2, 2]$, equivalent to an importance duplication of data weights. Using importance duplicated weights as a theoretical target, we measure our model's performance by computing the Kolmogorov-Smirnov (KS) distance between CDFs of simulated and importance duplicated weights. Figure 4c shows a small distributional distance between simulations and their theoretical target, with $d_{KS} = 0.03$, $p = 0.457$.

4   Conclusions and Future Work

We present three estimators for the MMD (and a wide class of other loss functions) between target distribution $\mathbb{P}$ and the distribution $\mathbb{Q}$ implied by our generator. These estimators can be used to train a GAN to simulate from the target distribution $\mathbb{P}$, given samples from a modified distribution $M\mathbb{P}$. We present solutions for when M is potentially unbounded, is unknown, or is known only up to a scaling factor.

We demonstrate that importance weighted estimators allow deep generative models to match target distributions for common and challenging cases with continuous-valued, multivariate latent features. This method avoids heuristics while providing good empirical performance and theoretical guarantees.

Though the median of means estimator offers a more robust estimate of the MMD, we may still experience high variance in our estimates, for example if we rarely see data points from a class we want to boost. An interesting future line of research is exploring how variance-reduction techniques [11] or adaptive batch sizes [10] could be used to overcome this problem.

References

1. Alon, N., Matias, Y., Szegedy, M.: The space complexity of approximating the frequency moments. In: ACM symposium on Theory of Computing, pp. 20–29. ACM (1996)
2. Arjovsky, M., Chintala, S., Bottou, L.: Wasserstein GAN. In: ICML (2017)
3. Ben-David, S., Blitzer, J., Crammer, K., Pereira, F.: Analysis of representations for domain adaptation. In: Advances in Neural Information Processing Systems, pp. 137–144 (2007)
4. Bińkowski, M., Sutherland, D., Arbel, M., Gretton, A.: Demystifying MMD GANs. In: ICLR (2018)
5. Blitzer, J., Dredze, M., Pereira, F.: Biographies, bollywood, boom-boxes and blenders: domain adaptation for sentiment classification. In: Proceedings of the 45th Annual Meeting of the Association of Computational Linguistics, pp. 440–447 (2007)
6. Bolukbasi, T., Chang, K.W., Zou, J., Saligrama, V., Kalai, A.: Man is to computer programmer as woman is to homemaker? Debiasing word embeddings. In: NIPS (2016)
7. Che, T., Li, Y., Jacob, A., Bengio, Y., Li, W.: Mode regularized generative adversarial networks. In: ICLR (2017)
8. Csaba, B., Boukhayma, A., Kulharia, V., Horváth, A., Torr, P.H.: Domain partitioning network. arXiv preprint arXiv:1902.08134 (2019)
9. Daumé III, H., Kumar, A., Saha, A.: Frustratingly easy semi-supervised domain adaptation. In: Proceedings of the 2010 Workshop on Domain Adaptation for Natural Language Processing, pp. 53–59. Association for Computational Linguistics (2010)
10. De, S., Yadav, A., Jacobs, D., Goldstein, T.: Automated inference with adaptive batches. In: AISTATS, pp. 1504–1513 (2017)
11. Defazio, A., Bach, F., Lacoste-Julien, S.: SAGA: a fast incremental gradient method with support for non-strongly convex composite objectives. In: NIPS, pp. 1646–1654 (2014)
12. Diesendruck, M., Elenberg, E.R., Sen, R., Cole, G.W., Shakkottai, S., Williamson, S.A.: Importance weighted generative networks. arXiv preprint arXiv:1806.02512 (2018)
13. Dziugaite, G., Roy, D., Ghahramani, Z.: Training generative neural networks via maximum mean discrepancy optimization. In: UAI (2015)
14. Esteban, C., Hyland, S., Rätsch, G.: Real-valued (medical) time series generation with recurrent conditional GANs. arXiv:1706.02633 (2017)
15. Ginosar, S., et al.: A century of portraits: a visual historical record of American high school yearbooks. IEEE Trans. Comput. Imaging **3**(3), 421–431 (2017). https://doi.org/10.1109/TCI.2017.2699865

16. Gong, B., Shi, Y., Sha, F., Grauman, K.: Geodesic flow kernel for unsupervised domain adaptation. In: 2012 IEEE Conference on Computer Vision and Pattern Recognition (CVPR), pp. 2066–2073. IEEE (2012)
17. Goodfellow, I., et al.: Generative adversarial nets. In: NIPS (2014)
18. Gretton, A., Borgwardt, K., Rasch, M., Schölkopf, B., Smola, A.: A kernel two-sample test. JMLR **13**(Mar), 723–773 (2012)
19. Hjelm, R.D., Jacob, A.P., Che, T., Trischler, A., Cho, K., Bengio, Y.: Boundary-seeking generative adversarial networks. arXiv preprint arXiv:1702.08431 (2017)
20. Hoeffding, W.: A class of statistics with asymptotically normal distribution. Ann. Math. Stat. **19**, 293–325 (1948)
21. Hoeffding, W.: Probability inequalities for sums of bounded random variables. JASA **58**(301), 13–30 (1963)
22. Hoffman, J., et al.: CyCADA: cycle-consistent adversarial domain adaptation. arXiv preprint arXiv:1711.03213 (2017)
23. Horvitz, D., Thompson, D.: A generalization of sampling without replacement from a finite universe. JASA **47**(260), 663–685 (1952)
24. Huang, J., Gretton, A., Borgwardt, K.M., Schölkopf, B., Smola, A.J.: Correcting sample selection bias by unlabeled data. In: Advances in Neural Information Processing Systems, pp. 601–608 (2007)
25. Isola, P., Zhu, J.Y., Zhou, T., Efros, A.A.: Image-to-image translation with conditional adversarial networks. arXiv preprint (2017)
26. Jerrum, M.R., Valiant, L.G., Vazirani, V.V.: Random generation of combinatorial structures from a uniform distribution. Theoret. Comput. Sci. **43**, 169–188 (1986)
27. Kadurin, A., et al.: The cornucopia of meaningful leads: applying deep adversarial autoencoders for new molecule development in oncology. Oncotarget **8**(7), 10883 (2017)
28. Kong, A.: A note on importance sampling using standardized weights. University of Chicago, Department of Statistics, Technical report 348 (1992)
29. Lerasle, M., Szabó, Z., Mathieu, T., Lecué, G.: Monk-outlier-robust mean embedding estimation by median-of-means. arXiv preprint arXiv:1802.04784 (2018)
30. Li, C.L., Chang, W.C., Cheng, Y., Yang, Y., Póczos, B.: MMD GAN: towards deeper understanding of moment matching network. In: NIPS (2017)
31. Li, Y., Swersky, K., Zemel, R.: Generative moment matching networks. In: ICML (2015)
32. Mansournia, M., Altman, D.: Inverse probability weighting. BMJ **352**, i189 (2016)
33. Mehdi, M., Osindero, S.: Conditional generative adversarial nets. arXiv:1411.1784 (2014)
34. von Mises, R.: On the asymptotic distribution of differentiable statistical functions. Ann. Math. Stat. **18**(3), 309–348 (1947)
35. Nemirovskii, A., Yudin, D.B., Dawson, E.R.: Problem Complexity and Method Efficiency in Optimization. Wiley, New York (1983)
36. Odena, A., Olah, C., Shlens, J.: Conditional image synthesis with auxiliary classifier GANs. In: ICML (2017)
37. Owen, A.: Monte Carlo theory, methods and examples. Book draft (2013)
38. Pan, S.J., Kwok, J.T., Yang, Q.: Transfer learning via dimensionality reduction. In: AAAI, vol. 8, pp. 677–682 (2008)
39. Pan, S.J., Tsang, I.W., Kwok, J.T., Yang, Q.: Domain adaptation via transfer component analysis. IEEE Trans. Neural Netw. **22**(2), 199–210 (2011)
40. Radford, A., Metz, L., Chintala, S.: Unsupervised representation learning with deep convolutional generative adversarial networks. arXiv preprint arXiv:1511.06434 (2015)

41. Robert, C., Casella, G.: Monte Carlo Statistical Methods. Springer Texts in Statistics, 2nd edn. Springer, New York (2004). https://doi.org/10.1007/978-1-4757-4145-2
42. Salimans, T., Goodfellow, I., Zaremba, W., Cheung, V., Radford, A., Chen, X.: Improved techniques for training GANs. In: NIPS (2016)
43. Sugiyama, M., Nakajima, S., Kashima, H., Buenau, P.V., Kawanabe, M.: Direct importance estimation with model selection and its application to covariate shift adaptation. In: Advances in Neural Information Processing Systems, pp. 1433–1440 (2008)
44. Székely, G.J., Rizzo, M.L.: Energy statistics: a class of statistics based on distances. J. Stat. Plan. Inference **143**(8), 1249–1272 (2013)
45. Taigman, Y., Polyak, A., Wolf, L.: Unsupervised cross-domain image generation. arXiv preprint arXiv:1611.02200 (2016)
46. Vondrick, C., Pirsiavash, H., Torralba, A.: Generating videos with scene dynamics. In: NIPS (2016)
47. Yan, H., Ding, Y., Li, P., Wang, Q., Xu, Y., Zuo, W.: Mind the class weight bias: weighted maximum mean discrepancy for unsupervised domain adaptation. arXiv preprint arXiv:1705.00609 (2017)
48. Zhang, H., et al.: StackGAN: text to photo-realistic image synthesis with stacked generative adversarial networks. In: ICCV (2017)
49. Zhao, J., Wang, T., Yatskar, M., Ordonez, V., Chang, K.W.: Men also like shopping: reducing gender bias amplification using corpus-level constraints. In: EMNLP (2017)
50. Zhu, J.Y., Park, T., Isola, P., Efros, A.A.: Unpaired image-to-image translation using cycle-consistent adversarial networks. arXiv preprint (2017)

Linearly Constrained Weights: Reducing Activation Shift for Faster Training of Neural Networks

Takuro Kutsuna[✉][ID]

Toyota Central R&D Labs. Inc., Aichi 480-1192, Japan
kutsuna@mosk.tytlabs.co.jp

Abstract. In this paper, we first identify *activation shift*, a simple but remarkable phenomenon in a neural network in which the preactivation value of a neuron has non-zero mean that depends on the angle between the weight vector of the neuron and the mean of the activation vector in the previous layer. We then propose *linearly constrained weights (LCW)* to reduce the activation shift in both fully connected and convolutional layers. The impact of reducing the activation shift in a neural network is studied from the perspective of how the variance of variables in the network changes through layer operations in both forward and backward chains. We also discuss its relationship to the vanishing gradient problem. Experimental results show that LCW enables a deep feedforward network with sigmoid activation functions to be trained efficiently by resolving the vanishing gradient problem. Moreover, combined with batch normalization, LCW improves generalization performance of both feedforward and convolutional networks.

Keywords: Artificial neural networks · Feedforward neural networks · Vanishing gradient problem · Analysis of variance

1 Introduction

Neural networks with a single hidden layer have been shown to be universal approximators [9,12]. However, an exponential number of neurons may be necessary to approximate complex functions. One solution to this problem is to use more hidden layers. The representation power of a network increases exponentially with the addition of layers [2,22]. Various techniques have been proposed for training deep nets, that is, neural networks with many hidden layers, such as layer-wise pretraining [8], rectified linear units [13,17], residual structures [6], and normalization layers [5,11].

In this paper, we first identify the *activation shift* that arises in the calculation of the preactivation value of a neuron. The preactivation value is calculated as the dot product of the weight vector of a neuron and an activation vector in the previous layer. In a neural network, an activation vector in a layer can be viewed as a random vector whose distribution is determined by the input distribution

© Springer Nature Switzerland AG 2020
U. Brefeld et al. (Eds.): ECML PKDD 2019, LNAI 11907, pp. 266–282, 2020.
https://doi.org/10.1007/978-3-030-46147-8_16

and the weights in the preceding layers. The preactivation of a neuron then has a *non-zero mean* depending on the angle between the weight vector of the neuron and the mean of the activation vector in the previous layer. The angles are generally different according to the neuron, indicating that neurons have distinct mean values, even those in the same layer.

We propose the use of so-called *linearly constrained weights (LCW)* to resolve the activation shift in both fully connected and convolutional layers. An LCW is a weight vector subject to the constraint that the sum of its elements is zero. We investigate the impact of resolving activation shift in a neural network from the perspective of how the variance of variables in a neural network changes according to layer operations in both forward and backward directions. Interestingly, in a fully connected layer in which the activation shift has been resolved by LCW, the variance is amplified by the same rate in both forward and backward chains. In contrast, the variance is more amplified in the forward chain than in the backward chain when activation shift occurs in the layer. This asymmetric characteristic is suggested to be a cause of the vanishing gradient in feedforward networks with sigmoid activation functions. We experimentally demonstrate that we can successfully train a deep feedforward network with sigmoid activation functions by reducing the activation shift using LCW. Moreover, our experiments suggest that LCW improves generalization performance of both feedforward and convolutional networks when combined with batch normalization (BN) [11].

In Sect. 2, we give a general definition of activation shift in a neural network. In Sect. 3, we propose LCW as an approach to reduce activation shift and present a technique to efficiently train a network with LCW. In Sect. 4 we study the impact of removing activation shift in a neural network from the perspective of variance analysis and then discuss its relationship to the vanishing gradient problem. In Sect. 5, we review related work. We present empirical results in Sect. 6 and conclude the study in Sect. 7.

2 Activation Shift

We consider a standard multilayer perceptron (MLP). For simplicity, the number of neurons m is assumed to be the same in all layers. The activation vector in layer l is denoted by $\boldsymbol{a}^l = \left(a_1^l, \ldots, a_m^l\right)^\top \in \mathbb{R}^m$. The input vector to the network is denoted by $\boldsymbol{a}^0$. The weight vector of the i-th neuron in layer l is denoted by $\boldsymbol{w}_i^l \in \mathbb{R}^m$. It is generally assumed that $\|\boldsymbol{w}_i^l\| > 0$. The activation of the i-th neuron in layer l is given by $a_i^l = f\left(z_i^l\right)$ and $z_i^l = \boldsymbol{w}_i^l \cdot \boldsymbol{a}^{l-1} + b_i^l$, where f is a nonlinear activation function, $b_i^l \in \mathbb{R}$ is the bias term, and $z_i^l \in \mathbb{R}$ denotes the preactivation value. Variables z_i^l and a_i^l are regarded as random variables whose distributions are determined by the distribution of the input vector $\boldsymbol{a}^0$, given the weight vectors and the bias terms in the preceding layers.

We introduce activation shift using the simple example shown in Fig. 1. Figure 1(a) is a heat map representation of a weight matrix $\boldsymbol{W}^l \in \mathbb{R}^{100 \times 100}$, whose i-th row vector represents $\boldsymbol{w}_i^l$. In Fig. 1(a), each element of $\boldsymbol{W}^l$ is independently drawn from a uniform random distribution in the range $(-1, 1)$.

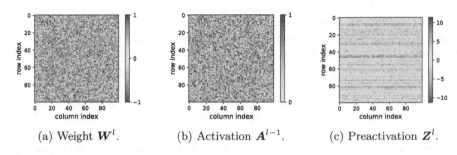

(a) Weight $\boldsymbol{W}^l$.　　　(b) Activation $\boldsymbol{A}^{l-1}$.　　　(c) Preactivation $\boldsymbol{Z}^l$.

Fig. 1. Activation shift causes a horizontal stripe pattern in preactivation $\boldsymbol{Z}^l = \boldsymbol{W}^l \boldsymbol{A}^{l-1}$, in which each element of $\boldsymbol{W}^l$ and $\boldsymbol{A}^{l-1}$ is randomly generated from the range $(-1, 1)$ and $(0, 1)$, respectively.

Figure 1(b) shows an activation matrix $\boldsymbol{A}^{l-1} \in \mathbb{R}^{100 \times 100}$, whose j-th column vector represents the activation vector corresponding to the j-th sample in a minibatch. Each element of $\boldsymbol{A}^{l-1}$ is randomly sampled from the range $(0, 1)$. We multiply $\boldsymbol{W}^l$ and $\boldsymbol{A}^{l-1}$ to obtain the preactivation matrix $\boldsymbol{Z}^l$, whose i-th row vector represents preactivation values of the i-th neuron in layer l, which is shown in Fig. 1(c). It is assumed that bias terms are all zero. Unexpectedly, a horizontal stripe pattern appears in the heat map of $\boldsymbol{Z}^l$ even though both $\boldsymbol{W}^l$ and $\boldsymbol{A}^{l-1}$ are randomly generated. This pattern is attributed to the activation shift, which is defined as follows:

Definition 1. $\mathcal{P}_\gamma$ is an m-dimensional probability distribution whose expected value is $\gamma \mathbf{1}_m$, where $\gamma \in \mathbb{R}$ and $\mathbf{1}_m$ is an m-dimensional vector whose elements are all one.

Proposition 1. Assume that the activation vector $\boldsymbol{a}^{l-1}$ follows $\mathcal{P}_\gamma$. Given a weight vector $\boldsymbol{w}_i^l \in \mathbb{R}^m$ such that $\|\boldsymbol{w}_i^l\| > 0$, the expected value of $\boldsymbol{w}_i^l \cdot \boldsymbol{a}^{l-1}$ is $|\gamma| \sqrt{m} \|\boldsymbol{w}_i^l\| \cos \theta_i^l$, where θ_i^l is the angle between $\boldsymbol{w}_i^l$ and $\mathbf{1}_m$.

Proofs of all propositions are provided in Appendix A in the supplementary material.

Definition 2. From Proposition 1, the expected value of $\boldsymbol{w}_i^l \cdot \boldsymbol{a}^{l-1}$ depends on θ_i^l as long as $\gamma \neq 0$. The distribution of $\boldsymbol{w}_i^l \cdot \boldsymbol{a}^{l-1}$ is then biased depending on θ_i^l; this is called activation shift.

In Fig. 1, each column vector of $\boldsymbol{A}^{l-1}$ follows $\mathcal{P}_\gamma$ with $\gamma = 0.5$. Therefore, the i-th row of $\boldsymbol{Z}^l$ is biased according to the angle between $\boldsymbol{w}_i^l$ and $\mathbf{1}_m$. We can generalize Proposition 1 for any m-dimensional distribution $\hat{\mathcal{P}}$ instead of $\mathcal{P}_\gamma$ by stating that the distribution of $\boldsymbol{w}^l \cdot \hat{\boldsymbol{a}}^{l-1}$ is biased according to $\hat{\theta}_i^l$ unless $\|\hat{\boldsymbol{\mu}}\| = 0$ as follows:

Proposition 2. Assume that the activation vector $\hat{\boldsymbol{a}}^{l-1}$ follows an m-dimensional probability distribution $\hat{\mathcal{P}}$ whose expected value is $\hat{\boldsymbol{\mu}} \in \mathbb{R}^m$. Given $\boldsymbol{w}_i^l \in \mathbb{R}^m$ such that $\|\boldsymbol{w}_i^l\| > 0$, it follows that $E(\boldsymbol{w}_i^l \cdot \hat{\boldsymbol{a}}^{l-1}) = \|\boldsymbol{w}_i^l\| \|\hat{\boldsymbol{\mu}}\| \cos \hat{\theta}_i^l$ if $\|\hat{\boldsymbol{\mu}}\| > 0$; otherwise, $E(\boldsymbol{w}_i^l \cdot \hat{\boldsymbol{a}}^{l-1}) = 0$, where $\hat{\theta}_i^l$ is the angle between $\boldsymbol{w}_i^l$ and $\hat{\boldsymbol{\mu}}$.

From Proposition 2, if a^{l-1} follows $\hat{\mathcal{P}}$ with the mean vector $\hat{\mu}$ such that $\|\hat{\mu}\| > 0$, the preactivation z_i^l is biased according to the angle between w_i^l and $\hat{\mu}$.

Note that differences in $E(z_i^l)$ are not resolved by simply introducing bias terms b_i^l, because b_i^l are optimized to decrease the training loss function and not to absorb the differences between $E(z_i^l)$ during the network training. Our experiments suggest that pure MLPs with several hidden layers are not trainable even though they incorporate bias terms. We also tried to initialize b_i^l to absorb the difference in $E(z_i^l)$ at the beginning of the training, though it was unable to train the network, especially when the network has many hidden layers.

3   Linearly Constrained Weights

There are two approaches to reducing activation shift in a neural network. The first one is to somehow make the expected value of the activation of each neuron close to zero, because activation shift does not occur if $\|\hat{\mu}\| = 0$ from Proposition 2. The second one is to somehow regularize the angle between w_i^l and $E(a^{l-1})$. In this section, we propose a method to reduce activation shift in a neural network using the latter approach. We introduce $\mathcal{W}_{\mathrm{LC}}$ as follows:

Definition 3. $\mathcal{W}_{LC}$ is a subspace in $\mathbb{R}^m$ defined by

$$\mathcal{W}_{LC} := \{ w \in \mathbb{R}^m \mid w \cdot 1_m = 0 \}.$$

We call weight vector w_i^l in $\mathcal{W}_{LC}$ the linearly constrained weights (LCWs).

The following holds for $w \in \mathcal{W}_{\mathrm{LC}}$:

Proposition 3. Assume that the activation vector a^{l-1} follows $\mathcal{P}_\gamma$. Given $w_i^l \in \mathcal{W}_{LC}$ such that $\|w_i^l\| > 0$, the expected value of $w_i^l \cdot a^{l-1}$ is zero.

Generally, activation vectors in a network do not follow $\mathcal{P}_\gamma$, and consequently, LCW cannot resolve the activation shift perfectly. However, we experimentally observed that the activation vector approximately follows $\mathcal{P}_\gamma$ in eachd layer. Figure 2(a) shows boxplot summaries of a_i^l in a 10-layer sigmoid MLP with LCW, in which the weights of the network were initialized using the method that will be explained in Sect. 4. We used a minibatch of samples in the CIFAR-10 dataset [14] to evaluate the distribution of a_i^l. In the figure, the 1%, 25%, 50%, 75%, and 99% quantiles are displayed as whiskers or boxes. We see that a_i^l distributes around 0.5 in each neuron, which suggests that $a^l \sim \mathcal{P}_\gamma$ approximately holds in every layer. We also observed the distribution of a_i^l after 10 epochs of training, which are shown in Fig. 2(b). We see that a^l are less likely follow $\mathcal{P}_\gamma$, but a_i^l takes various values in each neuron. In contrast, if we do not apply LCW to the network, the variance of a_i^l rapidly shrinks through layers immediately after the initialization as shown in Fig. 3, in which weights are initialized by the method in [3]. Experimental results in Sect. 6 suggest that we can train MLPs with several dozens of layers very efficiently by applying the LCW. The effect of resolving the activation shift by applying LCW will be theoretically analyzed in Sect. 4.

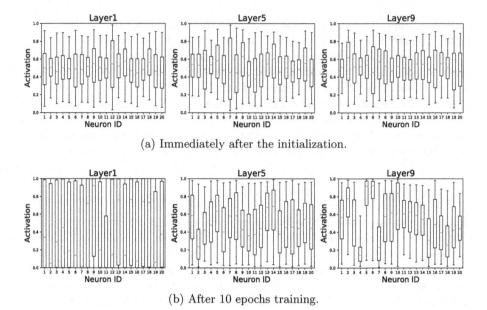

(a) Immediately after the initialization.

(b) After 10 epochs training.

Fig. 2. Boxplot summaries of a_i^l on the first 20 neurons in layers 1, 5, and 9 of the 10-layer sigmoid MLP with LCW.

It is possible to force $\boldsymbol{a}^l$ to follow $\mathcal{P}_\gamma$ by applying BN to preactivation z_i^l. The distribution of z_i^l is then normalized to have zero-mean and unit variance, and consequently, $a_i^l = f(z_i^l)$ are more likely to follow the same distribution, indicating that $\boldsymbol{a}^l \sim \mathcal{P}_\gamma$ holds. As will be discussed in Sect. 5, BN itself also has an effect of reducing activation shift. However, our experimental results suggest that we can train deep networks more smoothly by combining LCW and BN, which will be shown in Sect. 6.

3.1   Learning LCW via Reparameterization

A straightforward way to train a neural network with LCW is to solve a constrained optimization problem, in which a loss function is minimized under the condition that each weight vector is included in $\mathcal{W}_{\mathrm{LC}}$. Although several methods are available to solve such constrained problems, for example, the gradient projection method [15], it might be less efficient to solve a constrained optimization problem than to solve an unconstrained one. We propose a reparameterization technique that enables us to train a neural network with LCW using a solver for unconstrained optimization. The constraints on the weight vectors are embedded into the structure of the neural network by the following reparameterization.

Reparameterization: Let $\boldsymbol{w}_i^l \in \mathbb{R}^m$ be a weight vector in a neural network. To apply LCW to $\boldsymbol{w}_i^l$, we reparameterize $\boldsymbol{w}_i^l$ using vector $\boldsymbol{v}_i^l \in \mathbb{R}^{m-1}$ as $\boldsymbol{w}_i^l = \boldsymbol{B}_m \boldsymbol{v}_i^l$,

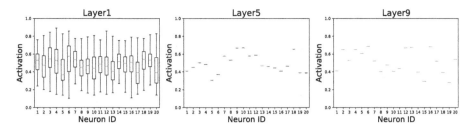

Fig. 3. Boxplot summaries of a_i^l on neurons in layers 1, 5, and 9 of the 10-layer sigmoid MLP *without* LCW, in which weights are initialized by the method in [3].

where $\boldsymbol{B}_m \in \mathbb{R}^{m \times (m-1)}$ is an orthonormal basis of $\mathcal{W}_{\text{LC}}$, written as a matrix of column vectors.

It is obvious that $\boldsymbol{w}_i^l = \boldsymbol{B}_m \boldsymbol{v}_i^l \in \mathcal{W}_{\text{LC}}$. We then solve the optimization problem in which $\boldsymbol{v}_i^l$ is considered as a new variable in place of $\boldsymbol{w}_i^l$. This optimization problem is unconstrained because $\boldsymbol{v}_i^l \in \mathbb{R}^{m-1}$. We can search for $\boldsymbol{w}_i^l \in \mathcal{W}_{\text{LC}}$ by exploring $\boldsymbol{v}_i^l \in \mathbb{R}^{m-1}$. The calculation of an orthonormal basis of $\mathcal{W}_{\text{LC}}$ is described in Appendix B in the supplementary material. Note that the proposed reparameterization can be implemented easily and efficiently using modern frameworks for deep learning based on GPUs.

3.2 LCW for Convolutional Layers

We consider a convolutional layer with C_{out} convolutional kernels. The size of each kernel is $C_{in} \times K_h \times K_w$, where C_{in}, K_h, and K_w are the number of the input channels, height of the kernel, and width of the kernel, respectively. The layer outputs C_{out} channels of feature maps. In a convolutional layer, activation shift occurs at the channel level, that is, the preactivation has different mean value in each output channel depending on the kernel of the channel. We propose a simple extension of LCW for reducing the activation shift in convolutional layers by introducing a subspace $\mathcal{W}_{\text{LC}}^{\text{kernel}}$ in $\mathbb{R}^{C_{in} \times K_h \times K_w}$ defined as follows:

$$\mathcal{W}_{\text{LC}}^{\text{kernel}} := \left\{ \boldsymbol{w} \in \mathbb{R}^{C_{in} \times K_h \times K_w} \ \middle| \ \sum_{i=1}^{C_{in}} \sum_{j=1}^{K_h} \sum_{k=1}^{K_w} w_{i,j,k} = 0 \right\},$$

where $w_{i,j,k}$ indicates the (i, j, k)-th element of w. Subspace $\mathcal{W}_{\text{LC}}^{\text{kernel}}$ is a straightforward extension of $\mathcal{W}_{\text{LC}}$ to the kernel space. To apply LCW to a convolutional layer, we restrict each kernel of the layer in $\mathcal{W}_{\text{LC}}^{\text{kernel}}$. It is possible to apply the reparameterization trick described in the previous subsection to LCW for convolutional layers. We can reparameterize the kernel using an orthonormal basis of $\mathcal{W}_{\text{LC}}^{\text{kernel}}$ in which the kernel in $\mathbb{R}^{C_{in} \times K_h \times K_w}$ is unrolled into a vector of length $C_{in} K_h K_w$.

4   Variance Analysis

In this section, we first investigate the effect of removing activation shift in a neural network based on an analysis of how the variance of variables in the network changes through layer operations both in forward and backward directions. Then, we discuss its relationship to the vanishing gradient problem.

4.1   Variance Analysis of a Fully Connected Layer

The forward calculation of a fully connected layer is $z^l = W^l a^{l-1} + b^l$, where $W^l = (w_1^l, \ldots, w_m^l)^\top$. We express the j-th column vector of W^l as $\tilde{w}_j^l$. If we denote the gradient of a loss function with respect to parameter v as ∇_v, the backward calculation regarding a^{l-1} is $\nabla_{a^{l-1}} = (W^l)^\top \nabla_{z^l}$. The following proposition holds for the forward computation, in which I_m is the identity matrix of order $m \times m$, V indicates the variance, and Cov denotes the variance-covariance matrix.

Proposition 4. *Assuming that $w_i^l \in \mathcal{W}_{LC}$, $E(a^{l-1}) = \gamma_{a^{l-1}} \mathbf{1}_m$ with $\gamma_{a^{l-1}} \in \mathbb{R}$, $Cov(a^{l-1}) = \sigma_{a^{l-1}}^2 I_m$ with $\sigma_{a^{l-1}} \in \mathbb{R}$, and $b^l = 0$, it holds that $E(z_i^l) = 0$ and $V(z_i^l) = \sigma_{a^{l-1}}^2 \|w_i^l\|^2$.*[1]

We also have the following proposition for the backward computation.

Proposition 5. *Assuming that $E(\nabla_{z^l}) = 0$ and $Cov(\nabla_{z^l}) = \sigma_{\nabla_{z^l}}^2 I_m$ with $\sigma_{\nabla_{z^l}} \in \mathbb{R}$, it holds that $E(\nabla_{a_j^{l-1}}) = 0$ and $V(\nabla_{a_j^{l-1}}) = \sigma_{\nabla_{z^l}}^2 \|\tilde{w}_j^l\|^2$.*

For simplicity, we assume that $\forall i, \|w_i^l\|^2 = \eta^l$ and $\forall j, \|\tilde{w}_j^l\|^2 = \xi^l$. Proposition 4 then indicates that, in the forward computation, $V(z_i^l)$, the variance of the output, becomes η^l times larger than that of the input, $V(a_i^{l-1})$. Proposition 5 indicates that, in the backward chain, $V(\nabla_{a_i^{l-1}})$, the variance of the output, becomes ξ^l times larger than that of the input, $V(\nabla_{z_i^l})$. If W^l is a square matrix, then $\eta^l = \xi^l$ (see Appendix A for proof), meaning that the variance is amplified at the same rate in both the forward and backward directions. Another important observation is that, if we replace W^l with κW^l, the rate of amplification of the variance becomes κ^2 times larger in both the forward and backward chains. This property does not hold if $w_i^l \notin \mathcal{W}_{LC}$, because in this case $E(z_i^l) \neq 0$ because of the effect of the activation shift. The variance is then more amplified in the forward chain than in the backward chain by the weight rescaling.

4.2   Variance Analysis of a Nonlinear Activation Layer

The forward and backward chains of the nonlinear activation layer are given by $a_i^l = f(z_i^l)$ and $\nabla_{z_i^l} = f'(z_i^l) \nabla_{a_i^l}$, respectively. The following proposition holds if f is the ReLU [13,17] function.

---

[1] A similar result is discussed in [10], but our result is more general because we do not assume the distribution of a^{l-1} to be Gaussian distribution, which is assumed in [10].

Proposition 6. *Assuming that z_i^l and $\nabla_{a_i^l}$ independently follow $\mathcal{N}(0, \sigma_{z_i^l}^2)$ and $\mathcal{N}(0, \sigma_{\nabla_{a_i^l}}^2)$, respectively, where $\mathcal{N}(\mu, \sigma^2)$ indicates a normal distribution with mean μ and variance σ^2, it holds that*

$$V(a_i^l) = \frac{\sigma_{z_i^l}^2}{2}\left(1 - \frac{1}{\pi}\right) \quad and \quad V(\nabla_{z_i^l}) = \frac{\sigma_{\nabla_{a_i^l}}^2}{2}.$$

We denote the rate of amplification of variance in the forward and backward directions of a nonlinear activation function by $\phi_{\text{fw}} := V(a_i^l)/V(z_i^l)$ and $\phi_{\text{bw}} := V(\nabla_{z_i^l})/V(\nabla_{a_i^l})$, respectively. Proposition 6 then indicates that the variance is amplified by a factor of $\phi_{\text{fw}} = 0.34$ in the forward chain and by a factor of $\phi_{\text{bw}} = 0.5$ in the backward chain through the ReLU activation layer.

If f is the sigmoid activation, there is no analytical solution for the variance of a_i^l and $\nabla_{z_i^l}$. We therefore numerically examined ϕ_{fw} and ϕ_{bw} for the sigmoid activation under the conditions that z_i^l follows $\mathcal{N}(0, \hat{\sigma}^2)$ for $\hat{\sigma} \in \{0.5, 1, 2\}$ and $\nabla_{a_i^l}$ follows $\mathcal{N}(0, 1)$. As a result, we obtained $(\phi_{\text{fw}}, \phi_{\text{bw}}) = (0.236, 0.237)$, $(0.208, 0.211)$, and $(0.157, 0.170)$ for $\hat{\sigma} = 0.5, 1$, and 2, respectively. It suggests that the difference between ϕ_{fw} and ϕ_{bw} in the sigmoid activation layer decreases as the variance of z_i^l decreases.

4.3   Relationship to the Vanishing Gradient Problem

We consider an MLP in which the number of neurons is the same in all hidden layers. We initialize weights in the network by the method based on minibatch statistics: weights are first generated randomly, then rescaled so that the preactivation in each layer has unit variance on the minibatch of samples. In fully connected layers with standard weights, the variance of variables in the network is more amplified in the forward chain than in the backward chain by the weight rescaling, as discussed in Subsect. 4.1. In contrast, in the sigmoid activation layers, the rate of amplification of the variance is almost the same in the forward and backward directions, as mentioned in the previous subsection. Then, the variance of the preactivation gradient decreases exponentially by rescaling the weights to maintain the variance of the preactivation in the forward chain, resulting in the vanishing gradient, that is, the preactivation gradient in earlier layers has almost zero variance, especially when the network have many layers.

In contrast, when the LCW is applied to the network, the variance is amplified at the same rate in both the forward and backward chains through fully connected layers regardless of the weight rescaling. In this case, the preactivation gradient has a similar variance in each layer after the initialization, assuming that the sigmoid activation is used. Concretely, the variance is amplified by approximately 0.21 through the sigmoid activation layers in both the forward and backward chains. Then, fully connected layers are initialized to have the amplification rate of $1/0.21$ to keep the preactivation variance in the forward chain. The gradient variance is then also amplified by $1/0.21$ in the backward chain of fully connected layers with LCW, indicating that the gradient variance is also preserved in the backward chain.

From the analysis in the previous subsections, we also see that normal fully connected layer and the ReLU layer have opposite effect on amplifying the variance in each layer, This may be another explanation why ReLU works well in practice without techniques such as BN.

4.4 Example

For example, we use a 20-layered MLP with sigmoid activation functions. The weights of the MLP are initialized according to the method described in the previous subsection. We randomly took 100 samples from the CIFAR-10 dataset and input them into the MLP. The upper part of Fig. 4(a) shows boxplot summaries of the preactivation in each layer. The lower part shows boxplot summaries of the gradient with respect to the preactivation in each layer, in which the standard cross-entropy loss is used to obtain the gradient. From Fig. 4(a), we see that the variance of the preactivation is preserved in the forward chain, whereas the variance of the preactivation gradient rapidly shrinks to zero in the backward chain, suggesting the vanishing gradient.

Next, LCW is applied to the MLP, and then, the weighs are initialized by the same procedure. Figure 4(b) shows the distribution of the preactivation and its gradient in each layer regarding the same samples from CIFAR-10. In contrast to Fig. 4(a), the variance of the preactivation gradient does not shrink to zero in the backward chain. Instead we observe that the variance of the gradient slightly increases through the backward chain. This can be explained by the fact that the variance is slightly more amplified in the backward chain than in the forward chain through the sigmoid layer, as discussed in Subsect. 4.2. These results suggest that we can resolve the vanishing gradient problem in an MLP with sigmoid activation functions by applying LCW and by initializing weights to preserve the preactivation variance in the forward chain.

5 Related Work

Ioffe and Szegedy [11] proposed the BN approach for accelerating the training of deep nets. BN was developed to address the problem of *internal covariate shift*, that is, training deep nets is difficult because the distribution of the input to a layer changes as the weights of the preceding layers change during training. BN is widely adopted in practice and shown to accelerate the training of deep nets, although it has recently been argued that the success of BN does not stem from the reduction of the internal covariate shift [20]. BN computes the mean and standard deviation of z_i^l based on a minibatch, and then, normalizes z_i^l by using these statistics. Gülçehre and Bengio [5] proposed the *standardization layer (SL)* approach, which is similar to BN. The main difference is that SL normalizes a_i^l, whereas BN normalizes z_i^l. Interestingly, both BN and SL can be considered mechanisms for reducing the activation shift. On one hand, SL

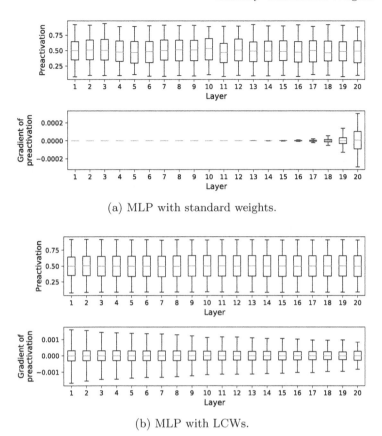

(a) MLP with standard weights.

(b) MLP with LCWs.

Fig. 4. Boxplot summaries of the preactivation (top) and its gradient (bottom) in 20-layered sigmoid MLPs with standard weights (a) and LCWs (b).

reduces the activation shift by forcing $\|\hat{\boldsymbol{\mu}}\| = 0$ in Proposition 2. On the other hand, BN reduces the activation shift by removing the mean from z_i^l for each neuron. A drawback of both BN and SL is that the model has to be switched during inference to ensure that its output depends only on the input and not the minibatch. In contrast, the LCW proposed in this paper do not require any change in the model during inference.

Salimans and Kingma [19] proposed *weight normalization (WN)* in which a weight vector $\boldsymbol{w}_i^l \in \mathbb{R}^m$ is reparameterized as $\boldsymbol{w}_i^l = (g_i^l/\|\boldsymbol{v}_i^l\|)\boldsymbol{v}_i^l$, where $g_i^l \in \mathbb{R}$ and $\boldsymbol{v}_i^l \in \mathbb{R}^m$ are new parameters. By definition, WN does not have the property of reducing the activation shift, because the degrees of freedom of $\boldsymbol{w}_i^l$ are unchanged by the reparameterization. They also proposed a minibatch-based initialization by which weight vectors are initialized so that z_i^l has zero mean and unit variance, indicating that the activation shift is resolved immediately after the initialization. Our preliminary results presented in Sect. 6 suggest that to start learning with initial weights that do not incur activation shift is not sufficient to train very deep nets. It is important to incorporate a mechanism that reduces the activation shift during training.

Ba et al. [1] proposed *layer normalization (LN)* as a variant of BN. LN normalizes z_i^l over the neurons in a layer on a sample in a minibatch, whereas BN normalizes z_i^l over the minibatch on a neuron. From the viewpoint of reducing the activation shift, LN is not as direct as BN. Although LN does not resolve the activation shift, it should normalize the degree of activation shift in each layer.

Huang et al. [10] proposed *centered weight normalization (CWN)* as an extension of WN, in which parameter $\boldsymbol{v}_i^l$ in WN is reparameterized by $\boldsymbol{v}_i^l = \tilde{\boldsymbol{v}}_i^l - \boldsymbol{1}_m(\boldsymbol{1}_m^\top \tilde{\boldsymbol{v}}_i^l)/m$ with $\tilde{\boldsymbol{v}}_i^l \in R^m$. CWN therefore forces a weight vector $\boldsymbol{w}_i^l$ to satisfy both $\|\boldsymbol{w}_i^l\| = 1$ and $\boldsymbol{1}_m^\top \boldsymbol{w}_i^l = 0$. CWN was derived from the observation that, in practice, weights in a neural network are initially sampled from a distribution with zero-mean. CWN and LCW share the idea of restricting weight vectors so that they have zero mean during training, although they come from different perspectives and have different implementations. The main differences between CWN and LCW are the following: CWN forces weight vectors to have both unit norm and zero mean, whereas LCW only forces the latter from the analysis that the latter constraint is essential to resolve the activation shift; LCW embeds the constraint into the network structure using the orthonormal basis of a subspace of weight vectors; the effect of reducing activation shift by introducing LCW is analyzed from the perspective of variance amplification in both the forward and backward chains.

Miyato et al. [16] proposed *spectral normalization (SN)* that constrains the spectral norm, that is, the largest singular value, of a weight matrix equal to 1. SN was introduced to control the Lipschitz constant of the discriminator in the GAN framework [4] to stabilize the training. The relationship between the spectral norm of weights and the generalization ability of deep nets is discussed in [23]. However, controlling the spectral norm of weight matrices is orthogonal to the reduction of the activation shift.

He et al. [6] proposed *residual network* that consists of a stack of residual blocks with skip connections. If we denote the input to the l-th residual block by $\boldsymbol{x}^l \in \mathbb{R}^m$, the output $\boldsymbol{x}^{l+1}$, which is the input to the next residual block, is given by $\boldsymbol{x}^{l+1} = \boldsymbol{x}^l + \boldsymbol{\mathcal{F}}_l(\boldsymbol{x}^l)$, where $\boldsymbol{\mathcal{F}}_l : \mathbb{R}^m \to \mathbb{R}^m$ is a mapping defined by a stack of nonlinear layers. In contrast to the original residual network that regard the activation as $\boldsymbol{x}^l$, He et al. [7] proposed *preactivation structure* in which the preactivation is regarded as $\boldsymbol{x}^l$. Residual network will indirectly reduce the impact of the activation shift. The reason is explained below: In a residual network, it holds that $\boldsymbol{x}^L = \boldsymbol{x}^0 + \sum_{l=0}^{L-1} \boldsymbol{\mathcal{F}}_l(\boldsymbol{x}^l)$. The activation shift can occur in each of $\boldsymbol{\mathcal{F}}_l(\boldsymbol{x}^l)$, that is, each output element of $\boldsymbol{\mathcal{F}}_l(\boldsymbol{x}^l)$ has different mean. However, the shift pattern is almost random in each $\boldsymbol{\mathcal{F}}_l(\boldsymbol{x}^l)$, and consequently, the mean shift in $\boldsymbol{x}^L$ can be moderate because it is the average over these random shifts. This may be another reason why residual networks are successful in training deep models.

6   Experiments

We conducted experiments using the CIFAR-10 and CIFAR-100 datasets [14], which consist of color natural images each of which is annotated corresponding to 10 and 100 classes of objects, respectively. We preprocessed each dataset by subtracting the channel means and dividing by the channel standard deviations. We adopted standard data augmentation [6]: random cropping and horizontal flipping.

All experiments were performed using Python 3.6 with PyTorch 0.4.1 [18] on a system running Ubuntu 16.04 LTS with GPUs. We implemented LCW using standard modules equipped with PyTorch. As implementation of BN, SL, WN, and SN, we employed corresponding libraries in PyTorch. We implemented CWN by modifying modules for WN.

6.1   Deep MLP with Sigmoid Activation Functions

We first conducted experiments using an MLP model with 50 hidden layers, each containing 256 hidden units with sigmoid activation functions, followed by a softmax layer combined with a cross-entropy loss function. We applied each of LCW, BN, SL, WN, CWN, and SN to the model, and compared the performance. We also considered models with each of the above techniques (other than BN) combined with BN. These models are annotated with, for example, "BN+LCW" in the results.

Models with LCW were initialized following the method described in Sect. 4.3. Models with WN or CWN were initialized according to [19]. Models with BN, SL, or SN were initialized using the method proposed in [3]. Each model was trained using a stochastic gradient descent with a minibatch size of 128, momentum of 0.9, and weight decay of 0.0001 for 100 epochs. The learning rate starts from 0.1 and is multiplied by 0.95 after every epoch until it reaches the lower threshold of 0.001.

Figure 5 shows the curve of training loss, test loss, training accuracy, and test accuracy of each model on each dataset, in which the horizontal axis shows the training epoch. The results of MLPs with WN or SN are omitted in Fig. 5, because the training of these models did not proceed at all. This result matches our expectation that reducing the activation shift is essential to train deep neural networks, because WN and SN themselves do not have the effect of reducing activation shift as discussed in Sect. 5. We see that LCW achieves higher rate of convergence and gives better scores with respect to the training loss/accuracy compared with other models. However, with respect to the test loss/accuracy, the scores of LCW are no better than that of other models. This result suggests that LCW has an ability to accelerate the network training but may increase the risk of overfitting. In contrast, combined with BN, LCW achieves better performance in test loss/accuracy, as shown by the results annotated with "BN+LCW" in Fig. 5. We think such improvement was provided because LCW accelerated the training while the generalization ability of BN was maintained.

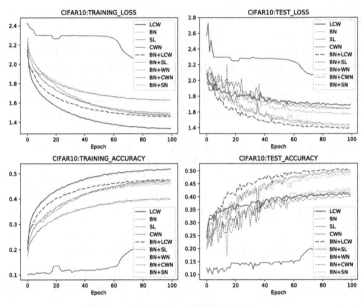

(a) Results for the CIFAR-10 dataset.

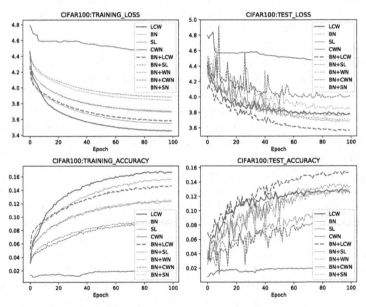

(b) Results for the CIFAR-100 dataset.

Fig. 5. Training loss (upper left), test loss (upper right), training accuracy (lower left), and test accuracy (lower right) of 50-layer MLPs for CIFAR-10 (a) and CIFAR-100 (b).

Table 1. Test accuracy/loss of convolutional models for CIFAR-10 and CIFAR-100 datasets.

Model	CIFAR-10		CIFAR-100	
	Test accuracy	Test loss	Test accuracy	Test loss
VGG19	0.936	0.354	0.732	1.788
VGG19+LCW	0.938	0.332	0.741	1.569
VGG19+WN	0.931	0.391	0.725	1.914
VGG19+CWN	0.934	0.372	0.727	1.827
VGG19+SN	0.936	0.358	0.733	1.644
ResNet18	0.952	0.204	0.769	0.978
ResNet18+LCW	0.952	0.187	0.770	0.955
ResNet18+WN	0.951	0.206	0.777	0.947
ResNet18+CWN	0.948	0.216	0.781	0.949
ResNet18+SN	0.952	0.206	0.780	1.015

6.2 Deep Convolutional Networks with ReLU Activation Functions

In this subsection, we evaluate LCW using convolutional networks with ReLU activation functions. As base models, we employed the following two models:

<u>VGG19</u>: A 19-layer convolutional network in which 16 convolutional layers are connected in series, followed by three fully connected layers with dropout [21]. We inserted BN layers before each ReLU layer in VGG19, although the original VGG model does not include BN layers.[2]

<u>ResNet18</u>: An 18-layer convolutional network with residual structure [6], which consists of eight residual units each of which contains two convolutional layers in the residual part. We employed the full preactivation structure proposed in [7]. In ResNet18, BN layers are inserted before each ReLU layer.

We applied LCW, WN, CWN, or SN to VGG19 and ResNet18, respectively, and compared the performance including the plain VGG19 and ResNet18 models. Each model was trained using a stochastic gradient descent with a minibatch size of 128, momentum of 0.9, and weight decay of 0.0005. For the CIFAR-10 dataset, we trained each model for 300 epochs with the learning rate that starts from 0.1 and is multiplied by 0.95 after every three epochs until it reaches 0.001. For the CIFAR-100 dataset, we trained each model for 500 epochs with the learning rate multiplied by 0.95 after every five epochs.

Table 1 shows the test accuracy and loss for the CIFAR-10 and CIFAR-100 datasets, in which each value was evaluated as the average over the last ten epochs of training. We see that LCW improves the generalization performance of VGG19 with respect to both the test accuracy and loss. The improvement is more evident for the CIFAR-100 dataset. The curve of training loss and accuracy

---

[2] This is mainly because VGG was proposed earlier than BN.

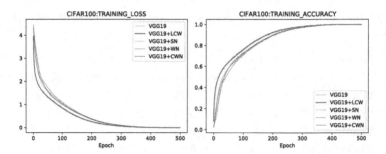

Fig. 6. Training loss (left) and training accuracy (right) of the VGG19-based models for the CIFAR-100 dataset.

of VGG19-based models for CIFAR-100 are shown in Fig. 6. We see that LCW enhances the rate of convergence, which we think lead to the better performance. In contrast, the improvement brought by LCW is less evident in ResNet18, in particular, with respect to the test accuracy. We observed little difference in the training curve of ResNet18 with and without LCW. A possible reason for this is that the residual structure itself has an ability to mitigate the impact of the activation shift, as discussed in Sect. 5, and therefore the reduction of activation shift by introducing LCW was less beneficial for ResNet18.

7   Conclusion

In this paper, we identified the activation shift in a neural network: the pre-activation of a neuron has non-zero mean depending on the angle between the weight vector of the neuron and the mean of the activation vector in the previous layer. The LCW approach was then proposed to reduce the activation shift. We analyzed how the variance of variables in a neural network changes through layer operations in both forward and backward chains, and discussed its relationship to the vanishing gradient problem. Experimental results suggest that the proposed method works well in a feedforward network with sigmoid activation functions, resolving the vanishing gradient problem. We also showed that existing methods that successfully accelerate the training of deep neural networks, including BN and residual structures, have an ability to reduce the effect of activation shift, suggesting that alleviating the activation shift is essential for efficient training of deep models. The proposed method achieved better performance when used in a convolutional network with ReLU activation functions combined with BN. Future work includes investigating the applicability of the proposed method for other neural network structures, such as recurrent structures.

References

1. Ba, J.L., Kiros, J.R., Hinton, G.E.: Layer normalization. In: NIPS 2016 Deep Learning Symposium (2016)
2. Eldan, R., Shamir, O.: The power of depth for feedforward neural networks. In: Annual Conference on Learning Theory, vol. 49, pp. 907–940 (2016)
3. Glorot, X., Bengio, Y.: Understanding the difficulty of training deep feedforward neural networks. In: International Conference on Artificial Intelligence and Statistics, pp. 249–256 (2010)
4. Goodfellow, I., et al.: Generative adversarial nets. In: Advances in Neural Information Processing Systems, pp. 2672–2680. Curran Associates, Inc. (2014)
5. Gülçehre, Ç., Bengio, Y.: Knowledge matters: importance of prior information for optimization. J. Mach. Learn. Res. **17**(8), 1–32 (2016)
6. He, K., Zhang, X., Ren, S., Sun, J.: Deep residual learning for image recognition. In: IEEE Conference on Computer Vision and Pattern Recognition, pp. 770–778 (2016)
7. He, K., Zhang, X., Ren, S., Sun, J.: Identity mappings in deep residual networks. In: European Conference on Computer Vision, pp. 630–645 (2016)
8. Hinton, G.E., Salakhutdinov, R.R.: Reducing the dimensionality of data with neural networks. Science **313**(5786), 504–507 (2006)
9. Hornik, K., Stinchcombe, M., White, H.: Multilayer feedforward networks are universal approximators. Neural Netw. **2**(5), 359–366 (1989)
10. Huang, L., Liu, X., Liu, Y., Lang, B., Tao, D.: Centered weight normalization in accelerating training of deep neural networks. In: IEEE Conference on Computer Vision and Pattern Recognition, pp. 2803–2811 (2017)
11. Ioffe, S., Szegedy, C.: Batch normalization: accelerating deep network training by reducing internal covariate shift. In: International Conference on Machine Learning, pp. 448–456 (2015)
12. Irie, B., Miyake, S.: Capabilities of three-layered perceptrons. In: IEEE International Conference on Neural Networks, vol. 1, pp. 641–648 (1988)
13. Jarrett, K., Kavukcuoglu, K., Ranzato, M., LeCun, Y.: What is the best multistage architecture for object recognition? In: IEEE International Conference on Computer Vision, pp. 2146–2153 (2009)
14. Krizhevsky, A., Hinton, G.: Learning multiple layers of features from tiny images. University of Toronto, Tech. rep. (2009)
15. Luenberger, D.G., Ye, Y.: Linear and Nonlinear Programming. ISORMS, vol. 116. Springer, New York (2008). https://doi.org/10.1007/978-0-387-74503-9
16. Miyato, T., Kataoka, T., Koyama, M., Yoshida, Y.: Spectral normalization for generative adversarial networks. In: International Conference on Learning Representations (2018)
17. Nair, V., Hinton, G.E.: Rectified linear units improve restricted Boltzmann machines. In: International Conference on Machine Learning, pp. 807–814 (2010)
18. Paszke, A., et al.: Automatic differentiation in PyTorch. In: NIPS 2017 Workshop Autodiff (2017)
19. Salimans, T., Kingma, D.P.: Weight normalization: a simple reparameterization to accelerate training of deep neural networks. In: Advances in Neural Information Processing Systems, pp. 901–909. Curran Associates, Inc. (2016)
20. Santurkar, S., Tsipras, D., Ilyas, A., Madry, A.: How does batch normalization help optimization? In: Advances in Neural Information Processing Systems, pp. 2488–2498. Curran Associates, Inc. (2018)

21. Simonyan, K., Zisserman, A.: Very deep convolutional networks for large-scale image recognition. CoRR abs/1409.1556 (2014)
22. Telgarsky, M.: Benefits of depth in neural networks. In: Annual Conference on Learning Theory, vol. 49, pp. 1517–1539 (2016)
23. Yoshida, Y., Miyato, T.: Spectral norm regularization for improving the generalizability of deep learning. CoRR abs/1705.10941 (2017)

LYRICS: A General Interface Layer to Integrate Logic Inference and Deep Learning

Giuseppe Marra[1,2], Francesco Giannini[2(✉)], Michelangelo Diligenti[2], and Marco Gori[2]

[1] Department of Information Engineering, University of Florence, Florence, Italy
g.marra@unifi.it
[2] Department of Information Engineering and Mathematical Sciences, University of Siena, Siena, Italy
{fgiannini,diligmic,marco}@diism.unisi.it

Abstract. In spite of the amazing results obtained by deep learning in many applications, a real intelligent behavior of an agent acting in a complex environment is likely to require some kind of higher-level symbolic inference. Therefore, there is a clear need for the definition of a general and tight integration between low-level tasks, processing sensorial data that can be effectively elaborated using deep learning techniques, and the logic reasoning that allows humans to take decisions in complex environments. This paper presents LYRICS, a generic interface layer for AI, which is implemented in TersorFlow (TF). LYRICS provides an input language that allows to define arbitrary First Order Logic (FOL) background knowledge. The predicates and functions of the FOL knowledge can be bound to any TF computational graph, and the formulas are converted into a set of real-valued constraints, which participate to the overall optimization problem. This allows to learn the weights of the learners, under the constraints imposed by the prior knowledge. The framework is extremely general as it imposes no restrictions in terms of which models or knowledge can be integrated. In this paper, we show the generality of the approach showing some use cases of the presented language, including model checking, supervised learning and collective classification.

Keywords: Deep learning · Prior knowledge injection · First Order Logic

1 Introduction

The success of deep learning relies on the availability of a large amount of supervised training data. This prevents a wider application of machine learning in

This project has received funding from the European Union's Horizon 2020 research and innovation program under grant agreement No. 825619.

© Springer Nature Switzerland AG 2020
U. Brefeld et al. (Eds.): ECML PKDD 2019, LNAI 11907, pp. 283–298, 2020.
https://doi.org/10.1007/978-3-030-46147-8_17

real world applications, where the collection of training data is often a slow and expensive process, requiring an extensive human intervention. The introduction of prior-knowledge into the learning process is a fundamental step in overcoming these limitations. First, it does not require the training process to induce the rules from the training set, therefore reducing the number of required training data. Secondly, the use of prior knowledge can be used to express the desired behavior of the learner on any input, providing better behavior guarantees in an adversarial or uncontrolled environment.

This paper presents LYRICS, a TensorFlow [1] environment based on a declarative language for integrating prior knowledge into machine learning, which allows the full expressiveness of First Order Logic (FOL) to define the knowledge. LYRICS has its root in frameworks like Semantic Based Regularization (SBR) [6,7] built on top of Kernel Machines and Logic Tensor Networks (LTN) [23] that can be applied to neural networks. These frameworks transform the FOL clauses into a set of constraints that are jointly optimized during learning. However, LYRICS generalizes both approaches by allowing to enforce the prior knowledge transparently at training and test time and dropping the previous limitations regarding the form of the prior knowledge. SBR and LTN are also hard to extend beyond classical classification tasks, where they have been applied in previous works, because the lack of a declarative front-end. On the other hand, LYRICS define a declarative language, dropping the barrier to build models exploiting the available domain knowledge in any machine learning context.

In particular, any many-sorted first-order logical theory can be expressed in the framework, allowing to declare domains of different sort, with constants, predicates and functions. LYRICS provides a very tight integration of learning and logic as any computational graph can be bound to a FOL predicate. This allows to constrain the learner both during training and inference. Since the framework is agnostic to the learners that are bound to the predicates, it can be used in a vast range of applications including classification, generative or adversarial ML, sequence to sequence learning, collective classification, etc.

1.1 Previous Work

In the past few years many authors tackled specific applications by integrating logic and learning. Minervini et al. [16] proposes to use prior knowledge to correct the inconsistencies of an adversarial learner. Their methodology is designed ah-hoc for the tackled task, and limited to Horn clauses. A method to distill the knowledge in the weights of a learner is presented by Hu et al. [11], which is also based on a fuzzy generalization of FOL. However, the definition of the framework is limited to universally quantified formulas and to a small set of logic operators. Another line of research [5,21] attempts at using logical background knowledge to improve the embeddings for Relation Extraction. However, these works are also based on ad-hoc solutions that lack a common declarative mechanism that can be easily reused. They are all limited to a subset of FOL and they allow to injecting the knowledge at training time, with no guarantees that the output on the test set respect the knowledge.

Markov Logic Networks (MLN) [20] and Probabilistic Soft Logic (PSL) [2,13] provide a generic AI interface layer for machine learning by implementing a probabilistic logic. However, the integration with the underlying learning processes working on the low-level sensorial data is shallow: a low-level learner can be trained independently, then frozen and stacked with the AI layer providing a higher-level inference mechanism. The language proposed in this paper instead allows to directly improve the underlying learner, while also providing the higher-level integration with logic. TensorLog [3] is a more recent framework to integrate probabilistic logical reasoning with the deep-learning infrastructure of TF, however TensorLog is limited to reasoning and does not allow to optimize the learners while performing inference. TensorFlow Distributions [9] and Edward [25] are also a related frameworks for integrating probability theory and deep learning. However, these frameworks focus on probability theory and not the representation of logic and reasoning.

2   The Declarative Language

LYRICS defines a TensorFlow (TF)[1] environment in which learning and reasoning are integrated. LYRICS provides a short number of basic constructs, which can be used to define the problem under investigation.

A *domain* determines a collection of individuals that share the same representation space and are analyzed and manipulated in a homogeneous way. For example, a domain can collect a set of 30×30 pixel images or the sentences of a book as bag-of-words.

```
Domain(label="Images")
```

Individuals (i.e. elements) can be added to their domain as follows:

```
Individual(label="Tweety", domain=("Images"), value=img0)
```

where *Tweety* is a label to uniquely identify a specific individual of the *Images* domain, represented by the image *img0*. This allows the user to directly reason about single individuals. The user can also provide a large amount of individuals without a specific label for each of them by specifying the tensor of their features during the domain definition.

A *function* can be defined to map elements from the input domains into an element of an output domain. A unary function takes as input an element from a domain and transforms it into an element of the same or of another domain, while an *n*-ary function takes as input *n* elements, mapping them into an output element of its output domain. The following example defines a function that returns a rotated image:

```
Function(label="rotate", domains=("Images"), function=RotateFunction)
```

---

[1] https://www.tensorflow.org/.

where the FOL function is bound to its TF implementation, which in this case is the *RotateFunction* function in the TF code.

A *predicate* can be defined as a function, mapping elements of the input domains to truth values. For example, a predicate *bird* determining whether an input pattern from the *Images* domain contains a bird and approximated by a neural network NN is defined as:

```
Predicate(label="bird", domains=("Images"), function=NN)
```

It is possible to state the knowledge about the world by means of a set of *constraints*. Each constraint is a generic FOL formula using as atoms the previously defined functions and predicates. For instance, if we want to learn the previously defined predicate *bird* to be invariant to rotations, the user can express this knowledge by means of the following constraint:

```
Constraint("forall x: bird(x) -> bird(rotate(x))")
```

Finally, any available *supervision* for the functions or predicates can be directly integrated into the learning problem. LYRICS provides a specific construct where this fitting is expressed, called *PointwiseConstraint*. This construct links to a computational graph where a loss is applied for each supervision. The loss defaults to the cross-entropy loss but it can be overridden to achieve a different desired behavior:

```
PointwiseConstraint(model, labels, inputs)
```

where `model` is a TF function like the *NN* function used before fitting the supervisions `labels` on the provided `inputs`.

3   From Logic to Learning

LYRICS transparently transforms a declarative description of the available knowledge applied to a set of objects into an optimization task. In this section, we show how the optimization algorithm is derived from its declaration.

Domains and Individuals. Domains of individuals allow users to provide data to the framework as tensors that represent the leaves of the computational graph. A Domain D_i is always bound to a tensor $X_i \in \mathbb{R}^{d_i \times r_i}$, where d_i denotes the number of individuals in the i-th domain and r_i denotes the dimension of the representation of the data in the i-th domain[2]. Thus, individuals correspond to rows of the X_i tensor. Individuals can be represented by both *constant* and *variable* feature tensors. By taking into account partially or totally variable features for the individuals, LYRICS allows to consider individuals as learnable objects too. For example, given two individuals *Marco* and *Michelangelo* bound to a constant and a variable tensor respectively, we may want to learn the representation of *Michelangelo* by exploiting some joint piece of knowledge (e.g. `fatherOf(Marco, Michelangelo) -> similarTo(Michelangelo, Marco)`).

---

[2] Here, we assume that the feature representation is given by a vector. However, the system also allows the individuals to be represented by a generic tensor.

Table 1. Operations performed by the units of an expression tree given the inputs x, y and the used t-norm in the fundamental fuzzy logics.

op	t-norm		
	Product	Lukasiewicz	Gödel
$x \wedge y$	$x \cdot y$	$\max(0, x + y - 1)$	$\min(x, y)$
$x \vee y$	$x + y - x \cdot y$	$\min(1, x + y)$	$\max(x, y)$
$\neg x$	$1 - x$	$1 - x$	$1 - x$
$x \Rightarrow y$	$x \leq y ? 1 : \frac{y}{x}$	$\min(1, 1 - x + y)$	$x \leq y ? 1 : y$

Functions and Predicates. FOL functions allow the mapping between individuals of the input domains to an individual of the output domain, i.e. $f_i : D_{i_1}^f \times \cdots \times D_{i_m}^f \to D_i^f$, where $D_{i_1}^f, \ldots, D_{i_m}^f$ are the input domains and D_i^f is the output domain. On the other hand, FOL predicates allow to express the truth degree of some property for individuals of the input domains; i.e. $p_i : D_{i_1}^p \times \ldots \times D_{i_m}^p \to \{true, false\}$, where $D_{i_j}^p$ is the j-th domain of the i-th predicate. Functions and predicates are implemented using a TF architecture as explained in the previous section. If the graph does not contain any variable tensor (i.e. it is not parametric), then we say it to be *given*; otherwise it will contains variables which will be automatically learned to maximize the constraints satisfaction. In this last case, we say the function/predicate to be *learnable*. Learnable functions can be (deep) neural networks, kernel machines, radial basis functions, etc.

The evaluation of a function or a predicate on a particular tuple $x_1, \ldots, x_m$ of input individuals (i.e. $f_i(x_1, \ldots, x_m)$ or $p_i(x_1, \ldots, x_m)$) is said a *grounding* for the function or for the predicate, respectively. LYRICS, like related frameworks [7, 23], follows a fully grounded approach, which means that all the learning and reasoning processes take place only once functions and predicates have been fully grounded over all the possible input tuples (i.e. on the entire Cartesian product of the corresponding input domains).

Let us indicate as X_k the set of patterns in the domain D_k, then $\mathcal{X}_i^f = X_{i_1}^f \times \cdots \times X_{i_m}^f$ is the set of groundings of the i-th function. Similarly, $\mathcal{X}_i^p$ is the collection of groundings for the i-th predicate. Finally, $\mathcal{F}(\mathcal{X}) = \{f_1(\mathcal{X}_1^f), f_2(\mathcal{X}_2^f), \ldots, \}$ and $\mathcal{P}(\mathcal{X}) = \{p_1(\mathcal{X}_1^p), p_2(\mathcal{X}_2^p), \ldots\}$ are the outputs for all function and predicates over their corresponding groundings, respectively.

Connectives and Quantifiers. Connectives and quantifiers are converted using the fuzzy generalization of FOL that was first proposed by Novák [19]. In particular, a *t-norm fuzzy logic* [10] generalizes Boolean logic to variables assuming values in $[0, 1]$. A t-norm fuzzy logic is defined by its t-norm that models the logical AND, and from which the other operations can be derived. Table 1 shows some possible implementation of the connectives using the fundamental t-norm fuzzy logics i.e. *Product, Łukasiewicz* and *Gödel* logics.

In general, formulas involve more than a predicate and are evaluated on the overall grounding vectors of such predicates. The way different evaluations of a certain formula are aggregated depend on the *quantifiers* occurring on its variables and their implementation. In particular, we consider the universal and existential quantifier that can be seen as a logic AND and OR applied over each grounding of the data, respectively.

For instance, given a certain logical expression E with a universally quantified variable x_i can be calculated as the average of the t-norm generalization $t_E(\cdot)$, when grounding x_i over its groundings X_i:

$$\forall x_i \; E\big(\mathcal{P}(\mathcal{X})\big) \longrightarrow \Phi_\forall\big(\mathcal{P}(\mathcal{X})\big) = \frac{1}{|X_i|} \sum_{x_i \in X_i} t_E\big(\mathcal{P}(\mathcal{X})\big) \tag{1}$$

The truth degree of the existential quantifier is instead defined as the maximum of the t-norm expression over the domain of the quantified variable:

$$\exists x_i \; E\big(\mathcal{P}(\mathcal{X})\big) \longrightarrow \Phi_\exists\big(\mathcal{P}(\mathcal{X})\big) = \max_{x_i \in X_i} t_E\big(\mathcal{P}(\mathcal{X})\big) \tag{2}$$

When multiple quantified variables are present, the conversion is recursively performed from the inner to the outer variables.

Constraints. Integration of learning and logical reasoning is achieved by translating logical expressions into continuous real-valued constraints. The logical expressions correlate the defined elements and enforce some desired behaviour on them.

Variables, functions, predicates, logical connectives and quantifiers can all be seen as nodes of an *expression tree* [8]. The real-valued constraint is obtained by a post-fix visit of the expression tree, where the visit action builds the correspondent portion of computational graph. In particular:

- visiting a *variable* x_i substitutes the variable with the tensor X_i bound to the domain it belongs to;
- visiting a *function* or *predicate* corresponds to the grounding operation, where, first, the Cartesian product of the input domains is computed and, then, the TF models implementing those functions are evaluated on all groundings (i.e. $f(\mathcal{X})$ or $p(\mathcal{X})$)
- visiting a *connective* combines predicates by means of the real-valued operations associated to the connective by the considered t-norm fuzzy logic;
- visiting a *quantifier* aggregates the outputs of the expressions obtained for the single variable groundings.

Figure 1 shows the translation of a logic formula into its expression tree and successively into a TensorFlow computational graph.

It is useful for the following to consider the real-valued constraint obtained by the described compilation process of the j-th logical rule and implemented by a TF graph as a parametric real function $\psi_j(\mathcal{X}_j; w_j^i, w_j^f, w_j^p)$. The function ψ_j takes as input the Cartesian product $\mathcal{X}_j$ of the domains of its quantified variables, returns the truth degree of the formula and it is parameterized by w_j^i, w_j^f and w_j^p, which are the sets of variable tensors related to the features of learnable individuals, to the parameters of learnable functions and to the parameters of learnable predicates, respectively. Let be $W^i = \{w_1^i, w_2^i, \dots\}$, $W^f = \{w_1^f, w_2^f, \dots\}$ and $W^p = \{w_1^p, w_2^p, \dots\}$.

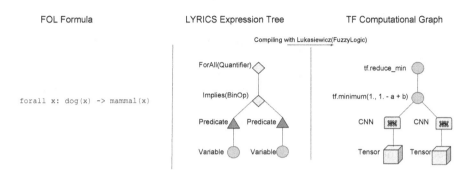

Fig. 1. The translation of the FOL formula $\forall x \; dog(x) \rightarrow mammal(x)$ into a Lyrics expression tree and then its mapping to a TF computational graph.

Optimization Problem. The goal of LYRICS is to build a learning process for some elements of interest (individuals, functions or predicates) by a declarative description of the desired behaviour of these elements. The desired behaviour is expressed by means of logical formulas. Thus, the optimization process is framed as finding the unknown elements which maximize the satisfaction of the set of logical formulas. Let $\psi_j(\mathcal{X}_j; w_j^i, w_j^f, w_j^p)$ indicate the real-valued constraint related to the j-th formula, as previously defined. Then, the derived optimization problem is:

$$\max_{W^i, W^f, W^p} \sum_{j=1}^{T} \lambda_c^j \psi_j(\mathcal{X}_j; w_j^i, w_j^f, w_j^p),$$

where λ_c^j denotes the weight for the j-th logical constraint. These weights are considered hyper-parameters of the model and are provided by the user during constraint definition. The maximization problem can be translated into a minimization problem as follows:

$$\min_{W^i, W^f, W^p} \sum_{j=1}^{T} \lambda_c^j \mathcal{L}\Big(\psi_j(\mathcal{X}_j; w_j^i, w_j^f, w_j^p)\Big),$$

Here, the function $\mathcal{L}$ represents any monotonically decreasing transformation of the constraints conveniently chosen according to the problem under investigation. In particular, we may exploit the following mappings:

$$
\begin{aligned}
&\textbf{(a)} \;\; \mathcal{L}\Big(\psi_j(\mathcal{X}_j; w_j^i, w_j^f, w_j^p)\Big) = 1 - \psi_j(\mathcal{X}_j; w_j^i, w_j^f, w_j^p),\\
&\textbf{(b)} \;\; \mathcal{L}\Big(\psi_j(\mathcal{X}_j; w_j^i, w_j^f, w_j^p)\Big) = -\log\Big(\psi_j(\mathcal{X}_j; w_j^i, w_j^f, w_j^p)\Big).
\end{aligned}
\tag{3}
$$

These specific choices for the function $\mathcal{L}$ are directly related to the Łukasiewicz and Product t-norms, indeed they are *additive generators* for these t-norm fuzzy logics. For more details on generated t-norms we recommend e.g. [14].

4   Learning and Reasoning with Lyrics

This section presents a list of examples illustrating the range of learning tasks that can be expressed in the proposed framework. In particular, it is shown how it is possible to force label coherence in semi-supervised or transductive learning tasks, how to implement collective classification over the test set and how to perform model checking. Moreover, we applied the proposed framework to two standard benchmarks: document classification in citation networks and term chunking in natural language text. The examples are presented using LYRICS syntax directly to show that the final implementation of a problem fairly retraces its abstract definition[3].

Semi-supervised Learning. In this task we assume to have available a set of 420 points distributed along an outer and inner circle. The inner and outer points belong and do not belong to some given class A, respectively. A random selection of 20 points is supervised (either positively or negatively), as shown in Fig. 2(a). The remaining points are split into 200 unsupervised training points, shown in Fig. 2(b) and 200 points left as test set. A neural network is assumed to have been created in TF to approximate the predicate A. The network can be trained by making it fit the supervised data. So, given the vector of data X, a neural network NN_A and the vector of supervised data X_s, with the vector of associated labels y_s, the supervised training of the network can be expressed by the following:

```
# Definition of the data points domain.
Domain(label="Points", data=X)
# Approximating the predicate A via a NN.
Predicate("A", ("Points"), NN_A)
# Fit the supervisions
PointwiseConstraint(A, y_s, X_s)
```

Let's now assume that we want to express manifold regularization for the learned function: e.g. points that are close should be similarly classified. This can be expressed as:

```
# Predicate stating whether 2 patterns are close.
Predicate("Close", ("Points","Points"), f_close)
# Manifold regularization constraint.
Constraint("forall p:forall q: Close(p,q)->(A(p)<->A(q))")
```

where f_close is a given predicate determining if two patterns are close according to a validated threshold of the Euclidean distance. The training is then re-executed starting from the same initial conditions as in the supervised-only case.

---

[3] The software of the framework and the experiments are made available at https://github.com/GiuseppeMarra/lyrics.

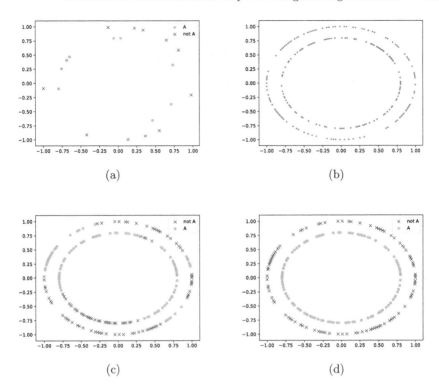

Fig. 2. Semi-supervised learning: (a) data that is provided with a positive and negative supervision for class A; (b) the unsupervised data provided to the learner; (c) class assignments using only the supervised examples; (d) class assignments using learning from examples and constraints.

Figure 2(c) shows the class assignments of the patterns in the test set, when using only classical learning from supervised examples. Finally, Fig. 2(d) presents the assignments when learning from examples and constraints.

Collective Classification. Collective classification [22] performs the class assignments exploiting any known correlation among the test patterns. This paragraph shows how to exploit these correlations in LYRICS. Here, we assume that the patterns are represented as $\mathbb{R}^2$ datapoints. The classification task is a multi-label problem where the patterns belongs to three classes A, B, C. In particular, the class assignments are defined by the following membership regions: $\mathbf{A} = [-2, 1] \times [-2, 2], \mathbf{B} = [-1, 2] \times [-2, 2], \mathbf{C} = [-1, 1] \times [-2, 2]$. These regions correspond to three overlapping rectangles as shown in Fig. 3(a). The examples are partially labeled and drawn from a uniform distribution on both the positive and negative regions for all the classes.

In a first stage, the classifiers for the three classes are trained in a supervised fashion using a two-layer neural network taking four positive and four negative examples for each class. This is implemented via the following declaration:

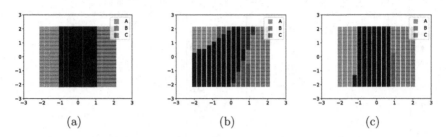

Fig. 3. Collective classification: (a) classes assignments; (b) the predictions after the supervised step; (c) the predictions with collective classification and rules satisfaction (best viewed in colors). (Color figure online)

```
Domain(label="Points", data=X)
Predicate(label="A",domains=("Points"),NN_A)
Predicate(label="B",domains=("Points"),NN_B)
Predicate(label="C",domains=("Points"),NN_C)
PointwiseConstraint(NN_A, y_A, X_A)
PointwiseConstraint(NN_B, y_B, X_B)
PointwiseConstraint(NN_C, y_C, X_C)
```

The test set is composed by 256 random points and the assignments performed by the classifiers after the training are reported in Fig. 3(b). In a second stage, it is assumed that it is available some prior knowledge about the task at hand. In particular, any pattern must belongs to (at least) one of the classes A or B. Furthermore, it is known that class C is defined as the intersection of A and B. The collective classification step is performed by seeking the class assignments that are as close as possible to the initial classifier predictions, acting as priors, but also respecting the logical constraints on the test set:

```
Constraint("forall x: A(x) or B(x)")
Constraint("forall x:(A(x) and B(x)) <-> C(x)")
# Minimize the distance from classifier outputs.
PointwiseConstraint(A, priorsA, X_test)
PointwiseConstraint(B, priorsB, X_test)
PointwiseConstraint(C, priorsC, X_test)
```

where X_test is the set of test datapoints and priorsA, priorsB, priorsC denote the predictions of the classifiers to which the final assignments have to stay close. As we can see from Fig. 3(c), the collective step fixes some wrong predictions.

Model Checking. In this example, we show how the framework can be used to perform model checking. Let us consider a simple multi-label classification task where the patterns belong to two classes A and B, and B is contained in A. This case models a simple hierarchical classification task. In particular, the classes are defined by the following membership regions: $\mathbf{A} = [-2, 2] \times [-2, 2]$, $\mathbf{B} = [-1, 1] \times [-1, 1]$. A set of points X is drawn from a uniform distribution in the $[-3, 3] \times [-3, 3]$ region. Two neural network classifiers are trained to classify the points using the vectors of supervisions y_A and y_B for the predicates A and B, respectively:

```
Domain(label="Points", data=X)
Predicate(label="A", domains=("Points"),NN_A)
Predicate(label="B", domains=("Points"),NN_B)
PointwiseConstraint(NN_A, y_A, X)
PointwiseConstraint(NN_B, y_B, X)
```

It could be interesting to check if some given rule has been learned by the classifiers. To this hand, LYRICS allows to mark a set of constraints as test only, in order to perform model checking. In this case, constraints are only used to compute the degree of satisfaction of the corresponding FOL formulas over the data. For example, we checked the degree of satisfaction of all possible formulas in Disjunctive Normal Form (DNF) that are universally quantified with a single variable. Only the constraint:

```
Constraint("forall x: (not A(x) and not B(x)) or (A(x) and not B(x)) or
(A(x) and B(x))")
```

has a high truth degree (0.9997). As one could expect, the only fully-satisfied constraint (translated from DNF to its minimal form) is indeed $\forall x B(x) \rightarrow A(x)$, that states the inclusion of B in A. Model checking can be used as a fundamental step to perform rule deduction using the Inductive Logic Programming techniques [17].

Chunking. Given a sequence of words, term chunking (or shallow parsing) is a sequence tagging task aiming at linking constituent parts of sentences (nouns, verbs, adjectives, etc.) into phrases that form a single semantic unit. Following the seminal work by Collobert et al. [4], many papers have applied deep neural networks to text chunking. In this paper, deep learner is used to learn from examples as in classical supervised learning. Then we perform collective classification to fix some misclassification made by the network, according to certain logical rules expressing available prior knowledge.

We used the CoNLL 2000 shared task dataset [24] to test the proposed methodology. The dataset contains 8936 training and 893 test English sentences. The task uses 12 different chunk types, which correspond to 22 chunk labels when considering the position modifiers. In particular, some labels have a B and I modifier to indicate for beginning and intermediate position in the chunk, respectively. For example, BVP indicates the start of a verbal phrase and IVP an intermediate term of the verbal phrase. The final performance is measured in terms of F1-score, computed by the public available script provided by the shared task organizers.

We selected the classifier proposed by Huang et al. [12] as our baseline, which is one of the best performers on this task. We used a variable portion of training phrases from the training set, ranging from 5% to 100%, to train the classifier, reusing the same parameters reported by the authors. The trained networks have then been applied on the test set providing an output score for each label for each term. It is well known that the output of the trained networks may not respect the semantic consistencies of the labels. For example, an intermediate token for

Table 2. CoNLL2000 evaluation script on all the classes and on the less common pos tags that have an initial lower performance.

		% data in training set				
		5	10	30	50	100
F1	NN	87.39	89.55	92.15	93.31	94.18
	LYRICS	87.75	89.78	92.26	93.53	94.27
F1 (rare tags)	NN	56.24	60.84	75.19	76.74	79.42
	LYRICS	57.65	61.36	75.68	77.45	79.71

a label must follow either a begin or intermediate one for the same label. For example, $\forall x \forall t \, BNP(x,t) \Rightarrow \neg IVP(x,t+1) \wedge \neg IPP(x,t+1) \wedge \neg IADVP(x,t+1) \wedge \ldots$ expresses that if the t-th token is marked as the begin of a nominal phrase BNP the following token can not be an intermediate verbal IVP, intermediate prepositional IPP or intermediate adverbial $IADVP$ phrase. A small sample of the constraints stating the output consistency can be expressed in FOL using the following statements:

$$\forall x \forall t \, BNP(x,t) \Rightarrow \neg IVP(x,t+1) \wedge \neg IPP(x,t+1) \wedge \neg IADVP(x,t+1) \wedge \ldots$$
$$\forall x \forall t \, BVP(x,t) \Rightarrow \neg INP(x,t+1) \wedge \neg IPP(x,t+1) \wedge \neg IADVP(x,t+1) \wedge \ldots$$
$$\forall x \forall t \, BPP(x,t) \Rightarrow \neg IVP(x,t+1) \wedge \neg INP(x,t+1) \wedge \neg IADVP(x,t+1) \wedge \ldots$$
$$\forall x \forall t \, INP(x,t) \Rightarrow [\neg IVP(x,t+1) \wedge \neg IPP(x,t+1) \wedge \neg IADVP(x,t+1) \wedge \ldots$$
$$\forall x \forall t \, IVP(x,t) \Rightarrow [\neg IVP(x,t+1) \wedge \neg IPP(x,t+1) \wedge \neg IADVP(x,t+1) \wedge \ldots$$
$$\forall x \forall t \, IPP(x,t) \Rightarrow [\neg IVP(x,t+1) \wedge \neg INP(x,t+1) \wedge \neg IADVP(x,t+1) \wedge \ldots$$
$$\forall x \forall t \, INP(x,t+1) \Rightarrow BNP(x,t) \vee INP(x,t)$$
$$\forall x \forall t \, IVP(x,t+1) \Rightarrow BVP(x,t) \vee IVP(x,t)$$
$$\forall x \forall t \, IPP(x,t+1) \Rightarrow BPP(x,t) \vee IPP(x,t)$$
$$\ldots$$

where $P(x,t)$ indicates the output of the network associated to label P for the phrase x and the t-th term in the phrase.

In order to evaluate the proposed methodology, collective classification is performed to assign the labels in order to minimize the distance from the network outputs, acting as priors, while maximizing the verification of the constraints built from the previously reported rules. Table 2 reports the F1 results for the different percentages of supervised phrases used to train the network. The results have been evaluated both on all classes, and then zooming in for some of the rare classes that are often wrongly classified. The effect of the rules is overall mildly positive as most of the tags can be correctly predicted by the supervised examples. However, the effect of the knowledge is more clear when zooming in to see the effect on the some of the less common tags ($ADJ, ADV, PRT, SBAR$): since not enough examples are observed for these tags, the extra knowledge allows to improve their classification. Since these tags are relatively rare the overall effect on the metrics is not large on this dataset, but it is a very promising start to allow the application of pos tagging to challenging domains.

Document Classification on the Citeseer Dataset. This section applies the proposed framework to a standard ML dataset. The CiteSeer dataset[4] [15] consists of 3312 scientific papers, each one assigned to one of 6 classes: Agents, AI, DB, ML and HCI. The papers are not independent as they are connected by a citation network with 4732 links. Each paper in the dataset is described via its bag-of-word representation, which is a vector having the same size of the vocabulary with the i-th element having a value equal to 1 or 0, depending on whether the i-th word in the vocabulary is present or not present in the document, respectively. The dictionary consists of 3703 unique words. This learning task is expressed as:

```
Domain(label="Papers", data=X)
Predicate("Agents",("Papers"), Slice(NN, 0))
Predicate("AI",("Papers"), Slice(NN, 1))
Predicate("DB",("Papers"), Slice(NN, 2))
Predicate("IR",("Papers"), Slice(NN, 3))
Predicate("ML",("Papers"), Slice(NN, 4))
Predicate("HCI",("Papers"), Slice(NN, 5))
```

where the first line defines the domain of scientific articles to classify, and one predicate for each class is defined and bound to an output of a neural network NN, which features a softmax activation function on the output layer.

The domain knowledge that if a paper cites another one, they are likely to share the same topic, is expressed as:

```
Predicate("Cite",("Papers","Papers"),f_cite)
Constraint("forall x: forall y: Agent(x) and Cite(x, y) -> Agent(y)")
Constraint("forall x: forall y: AI(x) and Cite(x, y) -> AI(y)")
Constraint("forall x: forall y: DB(x) and Cite(x, y) -> DB(y)")
Constraint("forall x: forall y: IR(x) and Cite(x, y) -> IR(y)")
Constraint("forall x: forall y: ML(x) and Cite(x, y) -> ML(y)")
Constraint("forall x: forall y: HCI(x) and Cite(x, y) -> HCI(y)")
```

where f_cite is a given function determining whether a pattern cites another one. Finally, the supervision on a variable size training set can be provided by means of:

```
PointwiseConstraint(NN, y_s, X_s)
```

where X_s is a subset of the domain of papers where we enforce supervisions y_s.

Table 3 reports the accuracy obtained by a neural network with one hidden layer (200 hidden neurons) trained in a supervised fashion and by training the same network from supervision and logic knowledge in LYRICS, varying the amount of available training data and averaged over 10 random splits of the training and test data. The improvements over the baseline are statistically significant for all the tested configurations. Table 4 compares the neural network classifiers against other two content-based classifiers, namely logistic regression (LR) and

---

[4] https://linqs.soe.ucsc.edu/data.

Table 3. Citeseer dataset: comparison of the 10-fold average accuracy obtained by supervised training of a neural network (NN), and by learning the same NN from supervision and logic knowledge in LYRICS for a variable percentage of training data. Bold values indicate statistically significant improvements.

	% data in training set				
	10	30	50	70	90
NN	60.08	68.61	69.81	71.93	72.59
LYRICS	**67.39**	**72.96**	**75.97**	**76.86**	**78.03**

Table 4. Citeseer dataset: comparison of the 10-fold average accuracy obtained by content based and network based classifiers and by learning from supervision and logic knowledge in LYRICS.

Method	Accuracy
Naive Bayes	74.87
ICA Naive Bayes	76.83
GS Naive Bayes	76.80
Logistic regression	73.21
ICA Logistic regression	77.32
GS Logistic regression	76.99
Loopy belief propagation	77.59
Mean field	77.32
NN	72.59
LYRICS	**78.03**

Naive Bayes (NB), and against collective classification approaches using network data: Iterative Classification Algorithm (ICA) [18] and Gibbs Sampling (GS) [15] both applied on top of the output of LR and NB content-based classifiers. Furthermore, the results against the two top performers on this task: Loopy Belief Propagation (LBP) [22] and Relaxation Labeling through Mean-Field Approach (MF) [22] are reported. The accuracy values are obtained as average over 10-folds created by random splits of size 90% and 10% of the overall data for the train and test sets, respectively. Unlike the other network based approaches that only be run at test-time (collective classification), LYRICS can distill the knowledge in the weights of the neural network. The accuracy results are the highest among all the tested methodologies in spite that the underlying neural network classifier trained only via the supervisions did perform slightly worse than the other content-based competitors.

5   Conclusions

This paper presents a novel and general framework, called LYRICS, to bridge logic reasoning and deep learning. The framework is directly implemented in TensorFlow, allowing a seaming-less integration that is architecture agnostic. The frontend of the framework is a declarative language based on First–Order Logic. Throughout the paper are presented a set of examples illustrating the generality and expressivity of the framework, which can be applied to a large range of tasks.

Future developments of the proposed framework include a learning mechanism of the weights of the constraints. This would allow to consider more general rule schemata that will be weighted with coefficients automatically learned by the parameter optimization according to the degree of satisfaction of any rule. This will improve the framework especially to deal with soft constraints expressing some statistical co-occurrence among the classes involved in the learning problem. Moreover, the differentiability of fuzzy logic could suggest new methods for learning a set of constraints in logical form that may be understandable.

References

1. Abadi, M., et al.: TensorFlow: a system for large-scale machine learning. In: OSDI 2016, pp. 265–283 (2016)
2. Bach, S.H., Broecheler, M., Huang, B., Getoor, L.: Hinge-loss Markov random fields and probabilistic soft logic. arXiv preprint arXiv:1505.04406 (2015)
3. Cohen, W.W.: TensorLog: a differentiable deductive database. arXiv preprint arXiv:1605.06523 (2016)
4. Collobert, R., Weston, J., Bottou, L., Karlen, M., Kavukcuoglu, K., Kuksa, P.: Natural language processing (almost) from scratch. J. Mach. Learn. Res. **12**(Aug), 2493–2537 (2011)
5. Demeester, T., Rocktäschel, T., Riedel, S.: Lifted rule injection for relation embeddings. arXiv preprint arXiv:1606.08359 (2016)
6. Diligenti, M., Gori, M., Maggini, M., Rigutini, L.: Bridging logic and kernel machines. Mach. Learn. **86**(1), 57–88 (2012). https://doi.org/10.1007/s10994-011-5243-x
7. Diligenti, M., Gori, M., Saccà, C.: Semantic-based regularization for learning and inference. Artif. Intell. **144**, 143–165 (2015)
8. Diligenti, M., Roychowdhury, S., Gori, M.: Image classification using deep learning and prior knowledge. In: Proceedings of Third International Workshop on Declarative Learning Based Programming (DeLBP), February 2018
9. Dillon, J.V., et al.: TensorFlow distributions. arXiv preprint arXiv:1711.10604 (2017)
10. Hájek, P.: Metamathematics of Fuzzy Logic, vol. 4. Springer, Cham (1998). https://doi.org/10.1007/978-94-011-5300-3
11. Hu, Z., Ma, X., Liu, Z., Hovy, E., Xing, E.: Harnessing deep neural networks with logic rules. arXiv preprint arXiv:1603.06318 (2016)
12. Huang, Z., Xu, W., Yu, K.: Bidirectional LSTM-CRF models for sequence tagging. arXiv preprint arXiv:1508.01991 (2015)

13. Kimmig, A., Bach, S., Broecheler, M., Huang, B., Getoor, L.: A short introduction to probabilistic soft logic. In: Proceedings of the NIPS Workshop on Probabilistic Programming: Foundations and Applications, pp. 1–4 (2012)
14. Klement, E.P., Mesiar, R., Pap, E.: Triangular norms. Position paper II: general constructions and parameterized families. Fuzzy Sets Syst. **145**(3), 411–438 (2004)
15. Lu, Q., Getoor, L.: Link-based classification. In: Proceedings of the 20th International Conference on Machine Learning (ICML 2003), pp. 496–503 (2003)
16. Minervini, P., Demeester, T., Rocktäschel, T., Riedel, S.: Adversarial sets for regularising neural link predictors. arXiv preprint arXiv:1707.07596 (2017)
17. Muggleton, S., De Raedt, L.: Inductive logic programming: theory and methods. J. Log. Program. **19**, 629–679 (1994)
18. Neville, J., Jensen, D.: Iterative classification in relational data. In: Proceedings of AAAI-2000 Workshop on Learning Statistical Models from Relational Data, pp. 13–20 (2000)
19. Novák, V., Perfilieva, I., Močkoř, J.: Mathematical principles of fuzzy logic (1999)
20. Richardson, M., Domingos, P.: Markov logic networks. Mach. Learn. **62**(1), 107–136 (2006). https://doi.org/10.1007/s10994-006-5833-1
21. Rocktäschel, T., Singh, S., Riedel, S.: Injecting logical background knowledge into embeddings for relation extraction. In: Proceedings of the 2015 Conference of the North American Chapter of the Association for Computational Linguistics: Human Language Technologies, pp. 1119–1129 (2015)
22. Sen, P., Namata, G., Bilgic, M., Getoor, L., Galligher, B., Eliassi-Rad, T.: Collective classification in network data. AI Mag. **29**(3), 93 (2008)
23. Serafini, L., d'Avila Garcez, A.S.: Learning and reasoning with logic tensor networks. In: Adorni, G., Cagnoni, S., Gori, M., Maratea, M. (eds.) AI*IA 2016. LNCS (LNAI), vol. 10037, pp. 334–348. Springer, Cham (2016). https://doi.org/10.1007/978-3-319-49130-1_25
24. Tjong Kim Sang, E.F., Buchholz, S.: Introduction to the CoNLL-2000 shared task: chunking. In: Proceedings of the 2nd Workshop on Learning Language in Logic and the 4th Conference on Computational Natural Language Learning, vol. 7, pp. 127–132. Association for Computational Linguistics (2000)
25. Tran, D., Hoffman, M.D., Saurous, R.A., Brevdo, E., Murphy, K., Blei, D.M.: Deep probabilistic programming. In: International Conference on Learning Representations (2017)

Deep Eyedentification: Biometric Identification Using Micro-movements of the Eye

Lena A. Jäger[1]([✉]), Silvia Makowski[1], Paul Prasse[1], Sascha Liehr[2], Maximilian Seidler[1], and Tobias Scheffer[1]

[1] Department of Computer Science, University of Potsdam, Potsdam, Germany
{lejaeger,silvia.makowski,prasse,maseidler,scheffer}@uni-potsdam.de
[2] Berlin, Germany

Abstract. We study involuntary micro-movements of the eye for biometric identification. While prior studies extract lower-frequency macro-movements from the output of video-based eye-tracking systems and engineer explicit features of these macro-movements, we develop a deep convolutional architecture that processes the raw eye-tracking signal. Compared to prior work, the network attains a lower error rate by one order of magnitude and is faster by two orders of magnitude: it identifies users accurately within seconds.

Keywords: Machine learning · Eye-tracking · Eye movements · Deep learning · Biometrics · Ocular micro-movements

1 Introduction

Human eye movements are driven by a highly complex interplay between voluntary and involuntary processes related to oculomotor control, high-level vision, cognition, and attention. Psychologists distinguish three types of macroscopic eye movements. Visual input is obtained during *fixations* of around 250 ms. *Saccades* are fast relocation movements of typically 30 to 80 ms between fixations during which visual uptake is suppressed. When tracking a moving target, the eye performs a *smooth pursuit* [21].

A large body of psychological evidence shows that these macroscopic eye movements are highly individual. For example, a large-scale study with over 1,000 participants showed that the individual characteristics of eye movements are highly reliable and, importantly, persist across experimental sessions [3]. Motivated by these findings, macro-movements of the eye have been studied for biometric identification [4,24]. Since macroscopic eye movements occur at a low frequency, long sequences must be observed before movement patterns give away

---

S. Liehr—Independent Researcher.

U. Brefeld et al. (Eds.): ECML PKDD 2019, LNAI 11907, pp. 299–314, 2020.
https://doi.org/10.1007/978-3-030-46147-8_18

the viewer's identity—a recent study finds that users can be identified reliably after reading around 10 lines of text [33]. For use cases such as access control, this process is too slow by one to two orders of magnitude.

During fixations, the eye additionally performs involuntary micro-movements which prevent the gradual fading of the image that would otherwise occur as the neurons become desensitized to a constant light stimulus [12,46]. *Microsaccades* have a duration ranging from 6 to 30 ms [34–36]. Between microsaccades, a very slow *drift* away from the center of the fixation occurs, which is superimposed by a low-amplitude, high-frequency *tremor* of approximately 40–100 Hz [34]. There is evidence that microsaccades exhibit measurable individual differences [41], but it is still unclear to what extent drift and tremor vary between individuals [28].

Video-based eye-tracking systems measure gaze angles at a rate of up to 2,000 Hz. Since the amplitudes of the smallest micro-movements are in the order of the precision of widely-used systems, the micro-movement information in the output signal is superimposed by a considerable level of noise. It is established practice in psychological research to smooth the raw eye-tracking signal, and to extract the specific types of movements under investigation. Criteria that are applied for the distinction of specific micro-movements are to some degree arbitrary [39,40], and their detection is less reliable [28]. Without exception, prior work on biometric identification only extracts macro-movements from the eye-tracking signal and defines explicit features such as distributional features of fixation durations and saccade amplitudes.

The additional information in the high-frequency and lower-amplitude micro-movements motivates us to explore the raw eye-tracking signal for a potentially much faster biometric identification. To this end, we develop a deep convolutional neural network architecture that is able to process this signal. One key challenge lies in the vastly different scales of velocities of micro- and macro-movements.

The remainder of this paper is structured as follows. Section 2 reviews prior work. Section 3 lays out the problem setting and Sect. 4 develops a neural-network architecture for biometric identification based on a combination of micro- and macro-movements of the eye. Section 5 presents experimental results. Section 6 discusses micro-movement-based identification in the context of other biometric technologies; Sect. 7 concludes.

2   Related Work

There is a substantial body of research on biometric identification using macro-movements of the eye. Most work uses the same stimulus for training and testing—such as a static cross [4], a jumping point [8,22,23,44,47], a face image [5,17,43], or various other kinds of images [10]. Using the same known stimulus for training and testing opens the methods to replay attacks.

Kinnunen and colleagues present the first approach that uses different stimuli for training and testing and does not involve a secondary task; they identify subjects who watch a movie sequence [27]. Later approaches use eye movements on novel text to identify readers [19,30].

A number of methods have been benchmarked in challenges [24,25]. All participants in these challenges and all follow-up work [45] present methods that extract saccades and fixations, and define a variety of features on these macro-movements, including distributions of fixation durations and of amplitudes, velocities, and directions of saccades. Landwehr and colleagues define a generative graphical model of saccades and fixations [30] from which Makowski and colleagues derive a Fisher Kernel [33]; Abdelwahab *et al.* develop a semi-parametric discriminative model [2]. All known methods are designed to operate on an eye-gaze sequence of considerable length; for example, one minute of watching a video or reading about one page of text.

3   Problem Setting

We study three variations of the problem of biometric identification based on a sequence $\langle(x_0, y_0), \ldots, (x_n, y_n)\rangle$ of yaw gaze angles x_i and pitch gaze angles y_i measured by an eye tracker. For comparison with prior work, we adopt a *multi-class classification* setting. For each user from a fixed population of users, one or more enrollment eye-gaze sequences are available that are recorded while the user is reading text documents. A multi-class classification model trained on these enrollment sequences recognizes users from this population at application time while the users are reading different text documents. Classification accuracy serves as performance metric in this setting.

Multi-class classification is a slight abstraction of the realistic use case in two regards. First, this setting disregards the possibility of encountering a user from outside the training population of users. Secondly, the learning algorithm has to train the model on enrollment sequences of all users. This training would have to be carried out on an end device or a cloud backend whenever a new user is enrolled; this is unfavorable from a product perspective.

In the more realistic settings of *identification* and *verification*, an embedding is trained offline on eye-gaze sequences for training stimuli of a population of training identities. At application time, the model encounters users from a different population who may view different stimuli. Users are enrolled by simply storing the embedding of their enrollment sequences. The model identifies a user when a similarity metric between an observed sequence and one of the enrollment sequences exceeds a recognition threshold.

In the *identification* setting, multiple users can be enrolled. Since the ratio of enrolled users to impostors encountered by the system at application time is not known, the system performance has to be characterized by two ROC curves. One curve characterizes the behavior for enrolled users; here, false positives are enrolled users who are mistaken for different enrolled users. The second curve characterizes the behavior for impostors; false positives are impostors who are mistaken for one of the enrolled users.

In the *verification* setting, the model verifies a user's presumed identity. This setting is a special case of identification in which a single user is enrolled. As no confusion of enrolled users is possible, a single ROC curve characterizes the system performance.

4   Network Architecture

We transform each eye-gaze sequence $\langle(x_0, y_0), \dots, (x_n, y_n)\rangle$ of absolute angles into a sequence $\langle(\delta_1^x, \delta_1^y), \dots, (\delta_n^x, \delta_n^y)\rangle$ of angular gaze velocities in °/s with $\delta_i^x = r(x_i - x_{i-1})$ and $\delta_i^y = r(y_i - y_{i-1})$, where r is the sampling rate of the eye tracker in Hz.

The angular velocity of eye movements differs greatly between the different types of movement. While drift occurs at an average speed of around 0.1–0.4°/s and tremor at up to 0.3°/s, microsaccades move at a rapid 15 to 120°/s and saccades even at up to 500°/s [21, 34, 36, 40]; there is, however, no general agreement about the exact cut-off values between movement types. Global normalization of the velocities squashes the velocities of drift and tremor to near-zero and models trained on such data resort to extracting patterns only from macro-movements. For this reason, our key design element of the architecture consists of independent subnets for *slow* and *fast* movements which observe the same input sequences but with different scaling.

Both subnets have the same number and type of layers; Fig. 1 shows the architecture. Both subnets process the same sliding window of 1,000 velocity pairs which corresponds to one second of input data, but the input is scaled differently. Equation 1 transforms the input such that the low velocities that occur during tremor and drift roughly populate the value range between -0.5 and $+0.5$ while velocities of microsaccades and saccades are squashed to values between -0.5 and -1 or $+0.5$ and $+1$, depending on their direction. The parameter c has been tuned within the range of psychologically plausible values from 0.01 to 0.06.

$$t_s(\delta_i^x, \delta_i^y) = (\tanh(c\delta_i^x), \tanh(c\delta_i^y)) \tag{1}$$

Equation 2, in which $z(\cdot)$ is the z-score normalization, truncates absolute velocities that are below the minimal velocity ν_{min} of microsaccades and saccades. Based on the psychological literature, the threshold ν_{min} was tuned within the range of 10 to 60°/s.

$$t_f(\delta_i^x, \delta_i^y) = \begin{cases} z(0) & \text{if } \sqrt{\delta_i^{x2} + \delta_i^{y2}} < \nu_{min} \\ (z(\delta_i^x), z(\delta_i^y)) & \text{otherwise} \end{cases} \tag{2}$$

Each subnet consists of 9 pairs of one-dimensional convolutional and average-pooling layers. The model performs a batch normalization on the output of each convolutional layer before applying a ReLU activation function and performing average pooling. Subsequently, the data feeds into two fully connected layers with batch-normalization and ReLU activation with a fixed number of 2^8 and 2^7 units, followed by a fully connected layer of 2^7 units with ReLU activation that serves as embedding layer for identification and verification. For classification and for the purpose of training the network in the identification and verification setting, this is followed by a softmax output layer with a number of units equal to the number of training identities that is discarded after training in the identification and verification settings.

Table 1. Parameter space used for grid search: kernel size k and number of filters f of the convolutional layers, the scaling parameter c of Eq. 1 and the velocity threshold ν_{min} of Eq. 2.

Parameter	Search space
c	$\{0.01, 0.02, 0.04, 0.06\}$
ν_{min}	$\{10°/s, 20°/s, 30°/s, 40°/s, 60°/s\}$
k	$\{3, 5, 7, 9\}$
f	$\{32, 64, 128, 256, 512\}$

Table 2. Best hyperparameter configuration found via grid search in the search space shown in Table 1.

Parameter	Layer	Slow subnet	Fast subnet
c	t_s	0.02	–
ν_{min}	t_f	–	$40°/s$
k	conv 1–3	9	9
	conv 4–7	5	5
	conv 8–9	3	3
f	conv 1–3	128	32
	conv 4–7	256	512
	conv 8–9	256	512

Figure 1 shows the overall architecture which we refer to as the *DeepEyedentification* network. The output of the subnets is concatenated and flows through a fully connected layer of 2^8 units and a fully connected layer with 2^7 units that serves as embedding layer for identification and verification, both with batch normalization and ReLU activation. The overall architecture is trained in three steps. The fast and the slow subnets are pre-trained independently and their weights are frozen in the final step where the joint architecture is trained.

In the identification and verification settings, the final embedding consists of the concatenation of the joint embedding and the embeddings generated by the fast and slow subnets. In this case, the cosine similarity serves as metric for the comparison of enrollment and input sequences.

5   Experiments

This section reports on experiments in the settings of multi-class classification, identification, and verification. All code is available at https://osf.io/ps9qj/.

5.1   Data Collection

We use two data collections for our experiments. Makowski *et al.* [33] have collected the largest eye-tracking data set for which the raw output signal is

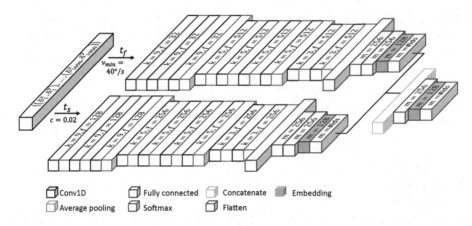

Fig. 1. Network architecture. Parameter c denotes the scaling factor of Eq. 1, ν_{min} the velocity threshold of Eq. 2, k the kernel size, f the number of filters and m the number of fully connected units. Batch normalization and ReLU activation are applied to the output of all convolutional and fully connected layers. All convolutional layers have a stride of 1; all pooling layers have a pooling size of 2 and a stride of 1.

available. It consists of monocular eye-tracking data sampled at 1,000 Hz from 75 participants who are reading 12 scientific texts of approximately 160 words. In order to extract absolute gaze angles, the eye tracker has to be calibrated for each participant. Makowski *et al.* exclude data from 13 participants whose data is poorly calibrated. Since DeepEyedentification only processes velocities, we do not exclude any data. We refer to this data set as *Potsdam Textbook Corpus*.

The Potsdam Textbook Corpus was acquired in a single session per user. To explore whether individuals can be recognized across sessions, we collect an additional data set from 10 participants à four sessions with a temporal lag of at least one week between any two sessions. We record participants' gaze using a binocular Eyelink Portable Duo eye tracker at a sampling rate of 1,000 Hz. During each session, participants are presented with 144 trials in which a black point consecutively appears at 5 random positions on a light gray background on a 38×30 cm monitor (1280×1024 px). The interval in which the point changes its location varies between trials (250, 500, 1000 or 1500 ms). We refer to these data as *JuDo* (Jumping Dots) data set. We use the Potsdam Textbook Corpus for hyperparameter optimization, and evaluation of the DeepEyedentification network in a multi-class classification and an identification and verification setting, while we use the much smaller JuDo data set to assess the model's session bias.

5.2 Reference Methods

Existing methods for biometric identification using eye movements only operate on macroscopic eye movements; they first preprocess the data into sequences of saccades and fixations and use different features computed from these macro-movements such as fixation duration or saccade amplitude. Existing methods that allow different stimuli for training and testing can be classified into (i) approaches which aggregate the extracted features over the relevant recording window, (ii) statistical approaches that compute the similarity of scanpaths by applying statistical tests to the distributions of the extracted features, and (iii) graphical models that generate sequences of fixation durations and saccade amplitudes. As representative aggregational reference method, we choose the model by Holland and Komogortsev (2011) that is specifically designed for eye movements in reading [19]. As statistical reference approaches we use the first model of this kind by Holland and Komogortsev (2013) [20] and the current state-of-the-art model by Rigas *et al.* (2016) [45]. As representative graphical models, we also use the first model of this kind by Landwehr *et al.* (2014) [30] and the state-of-the-art model by Makowski *et al.* (2018) [33].

5.3   Hyperparameter Tuning

We optimize the hyperparameters via grid search on one hold-out validation text from the Potsdam Textbook Corpus which we subsequently exclude from the training and testing of the final network; Table 1 gives an overview of the space of values and Table 2 the selected values that we keep fixed for all subsequent experiments. We vary the kernel sizes and numbers of filters of each subnet independently, but constrain them to be identical within convolutional layers 1–3, 4–7, and 8–9. Moreover, we constrain the kernel size to be smaller or equal and the number of filters to be greater or equal compared to the preceding block.

5.4   Hardware and Framework

We train the networks on a server with a 40-core Intel(R) Xeon(R) CPU E5-2640 processor and 128 GB of memory and a GeForce GTX TITAN X GPU using the NVidia CUDA platform with Tensorflow version 1.12.0 [1] and Keras version 2.2.4 [7]. As optimizer, we use Adam [26,42] with a learning rate of 0.001 for the training of the subnets and 0.0001 for the common layers. All models and submodels are trained with a batch size of 64 sequences.

5.5   Multi-class Classification

This section focuses on the multi-class classification setting in which the model is trained on the Potsdam Textbook Corpus to identify users from a fixed population of 75 users who are represented in the training data, based on an eye-gaze sequence for an unseen text.

In this setting, data are split across texts, to ensure that the same stimulus does not occur in training and test data. We perform leave-one-text-out cross validation over 11 text documents. We study the accuracy as a function of the duration of the eye-gaze signal. For each duration, we let the model process a sliding window of 1,000 time steps and average the scores over all window positions.

The reference models are evaluated on the same splits. They receive preprocessed data as input: sequences are split into saccades and fixations, and the relevant fixation and saccade features are computed. At test time, these models receive only as many macro-movements as input as fit into the duration.

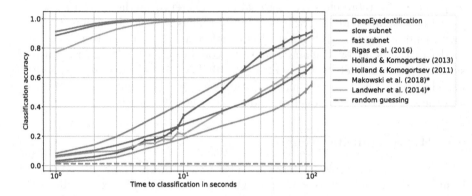

Fig. 2. Multi-class classification on the Potsdam Textbook Corpus. Categorical accuracy as a function of the amount of available test data in seconds; error bars show the standard error. The models marked with * are evaluated on a subset of the data containing 62 well-calibrated users, all other methods are evaluated on the full data set of 75 readers.

Figure 2 shows that for any duration of an input sequence, the error rate of DeepEyedentification is roughly one order of magnitude below the error rate of the reference methods. DeepEyedentification exceeds an accuracy of 91.4% after one second, 99.77% after 10 s and reaches 99.86% accuracy after 40 s of input, whereas Rigas *et al.* [45] reach 8.37% accuracy after one second and 43.02% after 10 s, and the method of Makowski *et al.* [33] reaches 91.53% accuracy after 100 s of input. We can conclude that micro-movements convey substantially more information than lower-frequency macro-movements of the eye.

The figure also shows that the overall network is significantly more accurate than either of its subnets. The *fast subnet*, for which only velocities of microsaccades and saccades are visible while tremor and drift are truncated to zero, reaches an accuracy of approximately 77% after one second. The *slow subnet*, which perceives the velocities of tremor and drift on an almost-linear scale while the velocities of microsaccades and saccades are squashed by the sigmoidal transformation, achieves roughly 88% of accuracy after one second.

5.6   Identification and Verification

In these settings, the input window slides over the test sequence and an enrolled user is identified (true positive) if and when the cosine similarity between the input window and any window in his enrollment sequence exceeds the recognition threshold; otherwise, the user counts as a false negative. A false positive arises when the similarity between a test sequence from an enrolled user (confusion setting) or an impostor (impostor setting) and the enrollment sequence of a different user exceeds the threshold; otherwise a true negative arises. We perform 50 iterations of random resampling on the Potsdam Textbook Corpus. In each iteration, we randomly draw 50 training users and train the DeepEyedentification model on 9 training documents for these users. One text serves as enrollment sequence and one text remains as observation. In the identification setting, a randomly drawn set of 20 of the 25 users who are not used for training are enrolled, and the remaining 5 users act as impostors. In the verification setting, one user is enrolled and 24 impostors remain.

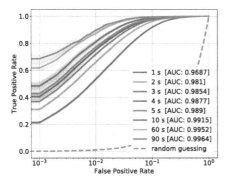 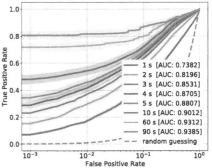

(a) Confusions between 20 enrolled users.   (b) Confusions between an unknown number of impostors and 20 enrolled users.

Fig. 3. Identification on the Potsdam Textbook Corpus. ROC curves for the confusion setting (a) and the impostor setting (b) as a function of the duration of the input signal at application time, both with 20 enrolled users. Error bars show the standard error.

For the identification setting, Fig. 3a shows the ROC curves for confusions between the 20 enrolled users on a logarithmic scale. The area under the ROC curve increases from 0.9687 for one second of data to 0.9915 for 10 and 0.9964 after 90 s; the corresponding EER values are 0.09, 0.04, and 0.02. Figure 3b shows the ROC curves for confusions between an impostor and one of the 20 enrolled users; here, the AUC values lie between 0.7382 and 0.9385, the corresponding EER values between 0.31 and 0.1.

Figure 4 shows the ROC curve for the verification setting. Here, the AUC lies between 0.9556 for one second, 0.9879 for 10, and 0.9924 for 90 s. In this setting, each impostor can only be confused with one presumed identity, whereas, in the identification setting, an impostor can be confused with each of the 20 enrolled users. Figure 5 shows a t-SNE visualization [31] that illustrates how the embedding layer clusters 10 users randomly drawn from outside the training identities. Finally, Fig. 6 shows the time to identification as a function of the false-positive rate for the identification and verification settings.

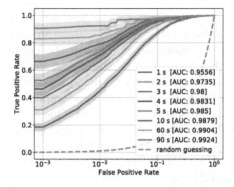

Fig. 4. Verification on the Potsdam Textbook Corpus. ROC curves for the confusions between one enrolled user and an unknown number of impostors as a function of the duration of the input signal at application time. Error bars show the standard error.

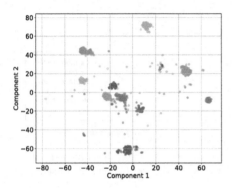

Fig. 5. *t*-sne visualization of the embedding for 10 users.

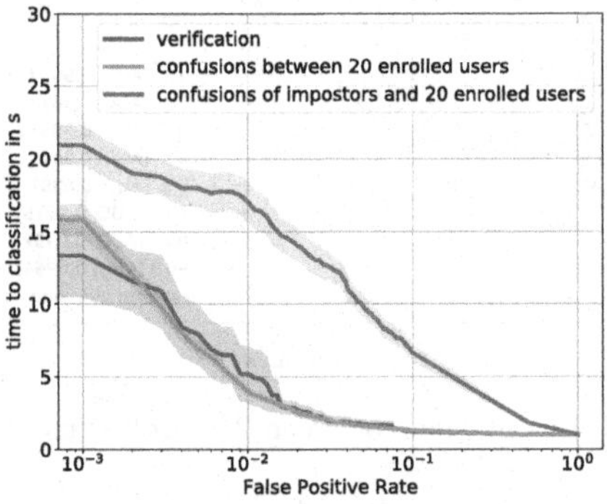

Fig. 6. Time to classification with standard error over false-positive rate.

5.7 Assessing Session Bias

Using the JuDo data set, we investigate the DeepEyedentification network's ability to generalize across recording sessions by comparing its multi-class classification performance on test data taken either from the same sessions that are used for training or from a new session. We train the DeepEyedentification network and the reference method that performed best on the Potsdam Textbook Corpus [45] on one to three sessions using the same hyperparameters and learning framework as for the main experiments (see Sects. 5.3 and 5.4). We evaluate the models using leave-one-session-out cross-validation on one held-out session (test on a new session) and on 20% held-out test data from the remaining session(s) (test on a known session). When training on multiple sessions, the amount of training data from each session is reduced such that the total amount of data used for training remains constant. Since binocular data is available, we also evaluate the DeepEyedentification network on binocular data by applying it independently to synchronous data from both eyes and averaging the softmax

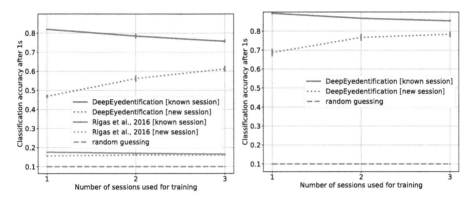

Fig. 7. Multi-class classification on the JuDo data set. Categorical accuracy on one second of test data from either a known or a new recording session as a function of the number of sessions used for training with a constant total amount of training data. The results are averaged over ten iterations for each held-out test session. Error bars show the standard error.

scores of the output layer. At training, the data from the two eyes are treated as separate instances.

Figure 7a shows the results for monocular test sequences of one second. After one second of input data, the model reaches a classification accuracy of 81.96% when testing and training it on data from a single session, and an accuracy of up to 61.16% when training and testing it on different sessions. Increasing the number of training sessions reduces the session bias significantly ($p < 0.01$ for one versus three sessions). The model of Rigas *et al.* [45] reaches accuracies around 16% in all settings. The use of binocular data (see Fig. 7b) not only improves the overall performance of the DeepEyedentification network, but also significantly reduces the session bias compared to monocular data ($p < 0.01$ for one training session). When being trained on three sessions, the model achieves an accuracy of 78.34% on a new test session after only one second of input data.

5.8 Additional Exploratory Experiments

We briefly summarize the outcome of additional exploratory experiments. First, we explore the behavior of a variant of the DeepEyedentification architecture that has only a single subnet which processes the globally normalized input. This model does not exceed the performance of the fast subnet, which indicates that it extracts only macro-movement patterns.

Second, we find that adding an input channel that indicates whether a time step is part of a fixation or part of a saccade according to established psychological criteria [14,15] does not improve the model performance. Moreover, forcing the slow subnet to only process movements during fixations and forcing the fast subnet to only process movements during saccades deteriorates the model performance. Our interpretation of this finding is that given the amount of information contained in the training data, an established heuristic categorization of movement types contributes no additional value.

Lastly, we change the convolutional architecture into a recursive architecture with varying numbers of LSTM units [18]. We find that the convolutional architecture consistently outperforms the explored LSTM architectures.

6 Discussion

This section discusses eye movements in relation to other biometric technologies. We discuss relevant qualitative properties of biometric methods: the required level of user interaction, the population for which the method can be applied, attack vectors, and anti-spoofing techniques.

While fingerprints and hand-vein scans require an explicit user action—placing the finger or the hand on a scanning device—face identification, scanning the iris, and tracking micro-movements of the eye can in principle be performed unobtrusively, without explicit user interaction. Scanning the iris or recording the micro-movements of the eye without requesting the user to step close to a camera would, however, require a camera that offers a sufficiently high resolution over a sufficiently wide field of view.

Biometric technologies differ with respect to intrinsic limitations of their applicability. For instance, fingerprints are worn down by hard physical labor, iris scanning requires users with small eyes to open their eyes unnaturally wide and is not available for users who wear cosmetic contact lenses. Since micro-movements of the eye are a prerequisite for vision, this method applies to a large potential user base.

All biometric identification methods can be attacked by acquiring biometric features from an authorized user and replaying the recorded data to the sensor. For instance, face identification can be attacked by photographs, video recordings, and 3D masks [16]. A replay attack on ocular micro-movement-based identification is theoretically possible but requires a playback device that is able to display a video sequence in the infrared spectrum at a rate of 1,000 frames per second. Biometry can similarly be attacked by replaying recorded or artificially generated data during enrollment. For instance, wearing cosmetic contact lenses during enrollment with an iris scanner can cause the scanner to accept other individuals who wear the same contact lens as false positives [37].

Anti-spoofing techniques for all biometric technologies firstly aim at detecting imperfections in replayed data; for example, missing variation in the input over time can indicate a photograph attack. This problem is intrinsically difficult because it is an adversarial problem; an attacker can always minimize artifacts in the replayed data. As an illustration, an attacker can replay a video recording instead of a still image to add liveliness. Liveliness detection is implicitly included in identification based on eye movements. Secondly, additional sensors can be added—such as multi-spectral cameras or depth sensors to prevent photograph-based and video-based replay attacks. This of course comes at additional costs and can still be attacked with additional effort, such as by using 3D-printed models instead of photographs. Thirdly, the identification procedure can include a randomized challenge to which the user has to respond. For example, a user can be asked to look at specific positions on a screen [9,11,13,29,32,48]. Challenges prevent replay attacks at the cost of obtrusiveness, bypassing them requires a data generator that is able to generate the biometric feature and also respond to the challenge. Identification based on movements of the eye is unique: responding to challenges demands neither the user's attention nor a conscious response. Randomized salient stimuli in the field of view immediately trigger an involuntary eye movement that can be validated.

7 Conclusion

Our research adds to the list of machine-learning problems for which processing raw input data with a deep CNN greatly improves the performance over methods that extract engineered features. In this case, the improvement is particularly remarkable and moves a novel biometric-identification technology close to practical applicability. The error rate of the DeepEyedentification network is lower by one order of magnitude and identification is faster by two orders of magnitude compared to the best-performing previously-known method.

We would like to point out that at this point the embedding layer of Deep-Eyedentification has been trained with 50 users. Nevertheless, it attains a true-positive rate of 60% at a false-positive rate of 1% after two seconds of input in the verification setting. By comparison, the embedding layer of a current face-identification model that attains a true-positive rate of 95.6% at a false-positive rate of 1% has been trained with 9,000 users [6]. A recent iris-recognition model attains a true-positive rate of 83.8% at a false-positive rate of 1% [38]. This comparison highlights the high potential of identification based on micro-movements.

We have developed an approach to processing input that contains signals on vastly different amplitudes. Global normalization squashes the velocities of the most informative, high-frequency but low-amplitude micro-movements to nearly zero, and networks which we train on this type of input do not exceed the performance of the fast subnet. The DeepEyedentification network contains two separately trained subnets that process the same signal scaled such that the velocities of slow movements, in case of the slow subnet, and of fast movements, in case of the fast subnet, populate the input value range.

Biometric identification based on eye movements has many possible fields of application. In contrast to fingerprints and hand-vein scans, it is unobtrusive. While iris scans fail for cosmetic contact lenses and frequently fail for users with small eyes, it can be applied for all individuals with vision. A replay attack would require a device able to display 1,000 frames per second in the infrared spectrum. Moreover, replay attacks can be prevented by including a challenge in the form of a visual stimulus in the identification procedure to which the user responds with an involuntary eye movement without assigning attention to the task.

Acknowledgments. This work was partially funded by the German Science Foundation under grant SFB1294, and by the German Federal Ministry of Research and Education under grant 16DII116-DII. We thank Shravan Vasishth for his support with the data collection.

References

1. Abadi, M., et al.: TensorFlow: large-scale machine learning on heterogeneous systems (2015). https://www.tensorflow.org/
2. Abdelwahab, A., Kliegl, R., Landwehr, N.: A semiparametric model for Bayesian reader identification. In: Proceedings of the 2016 Conference on Empirical Methods in Natural Language Processing, EMNLP 2016, pp. 585–594 (2016)
3. Bargary, G., Bosten, J.M., Goodbourn, P.T., Lawrance-Owen, A.J., Hogg, R.E., Mollon, J.: Individual differences in human eye movements: an oculomotor signature? Vision. Res. **141**, 157–169 (2017)
4. Bednarik, R., Kinnunen, T., Mihaila, A., Fränti, P.: Eye-movements as a biometric. In: Kalviainen, H., Parkkinen, J., Kaarna, A. (eds.) SCIA 2005. LNCS, vol. 3540, pp. 780–789. Springer, Heidelberg (2005). https://doi.org/10.1007/11499145_79
5. Cantoni, V., Galdi, C., Nappi, M., Porta, M., Riccio, D.: GANT: gaze analysis technique for human identification. Pattern Recogn. **48**, 1027–1038 (2015)
6. Cao, Q., Shen, L., Xie, W., Parkhi, O.M., Zisserman, A.: VGGFace2: a dataset for recognising faces across pose and age. In: 13th IEEE International Conference on Automatic Face and Gesture Recognition, FG 2018, pp. 67–74 (2018)
7. Chollet, F., et al.: Keras (2015). https://keras.io
8. Cuong, N., Dinh, V., Ho, L.S.T.: Mel-frequency cepstral coefficients for eye movement identification. In: 24th International Conference on Tools with Artificial Intelligence, ICTAI 2012, pp. 253–260 (2012)
9. Cymek, D., Venjakob, A., Ruff, S., Lutz, O.M., Hofmann, S., Roetting, M.: Entering PIN codes by smooth pursuit eye movements. J. Eye Mov. Res. **7**, 1–11 (2014)
10. Darwish, A., Pasquier, M.: Biometric identification using the dynamic features of the eyes. In: 6th International Conference on Biometrics: Theory, Applications and Systems, BTAS 2013, pp. 1–6 (2013)
11. De Luca, A., Weiss, R., Hußmann, H., An, X.: Eyepass - eye-stroke authentication for public terminals. In: Extended Abstracts on Human Factors in Computing Systems, CHI EA 2008, pp. 3003–3008 (2007)
12. Ditchburn, R.W., Ginsborg, B.L.: Vision with a stabilized retinal image. Nature **170**, 36–37 (1952)
13. Dunphy, P., Fitch, A., Olivier, P.: Gaze-contingent passwords at the ATM. In: 4th Conference on Communication by Gaze Interaction, COGAIN, pp. 59–62 (2008)
14. Engbert, R., Kliegl, R.: Microsaccades uncover the orientation of covert attention. Vision. Res. **43**, 1035–1045 (2003)
15. Engbert, R., Mergenthaler, K.: Microsaccades are triggered by low retinal image slip. Proc. Nat. Acad. Sci. USA **103**, 7192–7197 (2006)
16. Erdogmus, N., Marcel, S.: Spoofing face recognition with 3D masks. IEEE Trans. Inf. Forensics Secur. **9**(7), 1084–1097 (2014)
17. Galdi, C., Nappi, M., Riccio, D., Cantoni, V., Porta, M.: A new gaze analysis based soft biometric. In: 5th Mexican Conference on Pattern Recognition, MCPR 2013, pp. 136–144 (2013)

18. Graves, A., Schmidhuber, J.: Framewise phoneme classification with bidirectional LSTM and other neural network architectures. Neural Netw. **18**(5–6), 602–610 (2005)
19. Holland, C., Komogortsev, O.V.: Biometric identification via eye movement scanpaths in reading. In: 2011 International Joint Conference on Biometrics, IJCB 2011, pp. 1–8 (2011)
20. Holland, C., Komogortsev, O.: Complex eye movement pattern biometrics: Analyzing fixations and saccades. In: 2013 International Conference on Biometrics, ICB 2013 (2013)
21. Holmqvist, K., Nyström, M., Andersson, R., Dewhurst, R., Jarodzka, H., Van de Weijer, J.: Eye Tracking: A Comprehensive Guide to Methods and Measures. Oxford University Press, Oxford (2011)
22. Kasprowski, P.: Human identification using eye movements. Ph.D. thesis, Silesian Unversity of Technology, Poland (2004)
23. Kasprowski, P., Ober, J.: Enhancing eye-movement-based biometric identification method by using voting classifiers. In: Proceedings of SPIE 5779: Biometric Technology for Human Identification II, pp. 314–323 (2005)
24. Kasprowski, P., Harkeżlak, K.: The second eye movements verification and identification competition. In: Proceedings of the International Joint Conference on Biometrics, IJCB 2014 (2014)
25. Kasprowski, P., Komogortsev, O.V., Karpov, A.: First eye movement verification and identification competition at BTAS 2012. In: Proceedings of the IEEE Fifth International Conference on Biometrics: Theory, Applications and Systems, BTAS 2012, pp. 195–202 (2012)
26. Kingma, D.P., Ba, J.: Adam: a method for stochastic optimization. arXiv preprint arXiv:1412.6980 (2014)
27. Kinnunen, T., Sedlak, F., Bednarik, R.: Towards task-independent person authentication using eye movement signals. In: Proceedings of the 2010 Symposium on Eye-Tracking Research and Applications, ETRA 2010, pp. 187–190 (2010)
28. Ko, H.K., Snodderly, D.M., Poletti, M.: Eye movements between saccades: measuring ocular drift and tremor. Vision. Res. **122**, 93–104 (2016)
29. Kumar, M., Garfinkel, T., Boneh, D., Winograd, T.: Reducing shoulder-surfing by using gaze-based password entry. In: Proceedings of the 3rd Symposium on Usable Privacy and Security, SOUPS 2007, pp. 13–19 (2007)
30. Landwehr, N., Arzt, S., Scheffer, T., Kliegl, R.: A model of individual differences in gaze control during reading. In: Proceedings of the 2014 Conference on Empirical Methods in Natural Language Processing, EMNLP 2014, pp. 1810–1815 (2014)
31. MaatenMaaten, L.V.D., Hinton, G.: Visualizing data using t-SNE. J. Mach. Learn. Res. **9**, 2579–2605 (2008)
32. Maeder, A., Fookes, C., Sridharan, S.: Gaze based user authentication for personal computer applications. In: Proceedings of the 2004 International Symposium on Intelligent Multimedia, Video and Speech Processing, pp. 727–730 (2004)
33. Makowski, S., Jäger, L.A., Abdelwahab, A., Landwehr, N., Scheffer, T.: A discriminative model for identifying readers and assessing text comprehension from eye movements. In: Machine Learning and Knowledge Discovery in Databases, ECML PKDD 2018, pp. 209–225 (2019)
34. Martinez-Conde, S., Macknik, S.L., Hubel, D.H.: The role of fixational eye movements in visual perception. Nat. Rev. Neurosci. **5**, 229–240 (2004)
35. Martinez-Conde, S., Macknik, S.L., Troncoso, X.G., Dyar, T.A.: Microsaccades counteract visual fading during fixation. Neuron **49**, 297–305 (2006)

36. Martinez-Conde, S., Macknik, S.L., Troncoso, X.G., Hubel, D.H.: Microsaccades: a neurophysiological analysis. Trends Neurosci. **32**, 463–475 (2009)
37. Morales, A., Fierrez, J., Galbally, J., Gomez-Barrero, M.: Introduction to iris presentation attack detection. In: Marcel, S., Nixon, M.S., Fierrez, J., Evans, N. (eds.) Handbook of Biometric Anti-Spoofing. ACVPR, pp. 135–150. Springer, Cham (2019). https://doi.org/10.1007/978-3-319-92627-8_6
38. Nalla, P.R., Kumar, A.: Toward more accurate iris recognition using cross-spectral matching. IEEE Trans. Image Process. **26**, 208–221 (2017)
39. Nyström, M., Hansen, D.W., Andersson, R., Hooge, I.: Why have microsaccades become larger? Investigating eye deformations and detection algorithms. Vision. Res. **118**, 17–24 (2016)
40. Otero-Millan, J., Troncoso, X.G., Macknik, S.L., Serrano-Pedraza, I., Martinez-Conde, S.: Saccades and microsaccades during visual fixation, exploration, and search: foundations for a common saccadic generator. J. Vis. **8**(14), 21 (2008)
41. Poynter, W., Barber, M., Inman, J., Wiggins, C.: Individuals exhibit idiosyncratic eye-movement behavior profiles across tasks. Vision. Res. **89**, 32–38 (2013)
42. Reddi, S.J., Kale, S., Kumar, S.: On the convergence of Adam and beyond. In: International Conference on Learning Representations, ICLR 2018 (2018)
43. Rigas, I., Economou, G., Fotopoulos, S.: Biometric identification based on the eye movements and graph matching techniques. Patt. Recogn. Lett. **33**, 786–792 (2012)
44. Rigas, I., Economou, G., Fotopoulos, S.: Human eye movements as a trait for biometrical identification. In: Fifth International Conference on Biometrics: Theory, Applications and Systems, BTAS 2012, pp. 217–222 (2012)
45. Rigas, I., Komogortsev, O., Shadmehr, R.: Biometric recognition via eye movements: saccadic vigor and acceleration cues. ACM Trans. Appl. Percept. **13**(2), 6 (2016)
46. Riggs, L.A., Ratliff, F.: The effects of counteracting the normal movements of the eye. J. Opt. Soc. Am. **42**, 872–873 (1952)
47. Srivastava, N., Agrawal, U., Roy, S., Tiwary, U.S.: Human identification using linear multiclass SVM and eye movement biometrics. In: 8th International Conference on Contemporary Computing, IC3, pp. 365–369 (2015)
48. Weaver, J., Mock, K., Hoanca, B.: Gaze-based password authentication through automatic clustering of gaze points. In: 2011 IEEE International Conference on Systems, Man, and Cybernetics, SMC 2011, pp. 2749–2754 (2011)

Adversarial Invariant Feature Learning with Accuracy Constraint for Domain Generalization

Kei Akuzawa$^{(\boxtimes)}$, Yusuke Iwasawa, and Yutaka Matsuo

School of Engineering, The University of Tokyo, 7-3-1 Hongo, Bunkyo-ku,
Tokyo 113-8656, Japan
{akuzawa-kei,iwasawa,matsuo}@weblab.t.u-tokyo.ac.jp

Abstract. Learning domain-invariant representation is a dominant approach for domain generalization (DG), where we need to build a classifier that is robust toward domain shifts. However, previous domain-invariance-based methods overlooked the underlying dependency of classes on domains, which is responsible for the trade-off between classification accuracy and domain invariance. Because the primary purpose of DG is to classify unseen domains rather than the invariance itself, the improvement of the invariance can negatively affect DG performance under this trade-off. To overcome the problem, this study first expands the analysis of the trade-off by Xie et al. [33], and provides the notion of *accuracy-constrained domain invariance*, which means the maximum domain invariance within a range that does not interfere with accuracy. We then propose a novel method *adversarial feature learning with accuracy constraint* (AFLAC), which explicitly leads to that invariance on adversarial training. Empirical validations show that the performance of AFLAC is superior to that of domain-invariance-based methods on both synthetic and three real-world datasets, supporting the importance of considering the dependency and the efficacy of the proposed method.

Keywords: Invariant feature learning · Adversarial training · Domain generalization · Transfer learning

1 Introduction

In supervised learning we typically assume that samples are obtained from the same distribution in training and testing; however, because this assumption does not hold in many practical situations it reduces the classification accuracy for the test data [30]. This motivates research into domain adaptation (DA) [9] and domain generalization (DG) [3]. DA methods operate in the setting where we have access to source and (either labeled or unlabeled) target domain data during training, and run some adaptation step to compensate for the domain shift. DG addresses the harder setting, where we have labeled data from several source domains and collectively exploit them such that the trained system generalizes

© Springer Nature Switzerland AG 2020
U. Brefeld et al. (Eds.): ECML PKDD 2019, LNAI 11907, pp. 315–331, 2020.
https://doi.org/10.1007/978-3-030-46147-8_19

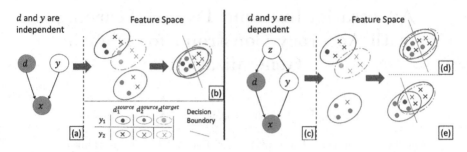

Fig. 1. Explanation of domain-class dependency and the induced trade-off. (a) When the domain and the class are independent, (b) domain invariance and classification accuracy can be optimized at the same time, and the invariance prevents the classifier from overfitting to source domains. (c) When they are dependent, a trade-off exists between these two: (d) optimal classification accuracy cannot be achieved when perfect invariance is achieved, and (e) vice versa. We propose a method to lead explicitly to (e) rather than (d), because the primary purpose for domain generalization is classification, not domain-invariance itself.

to target domain data without requiring any access to them. Such challenges arise in many applications, e.g., hand-writing recognition (where domain shifts are induced by users, [28]), robust speech recognition (by acoustic conditions, [29]), and wearable sensor data interpretation (by users, [7]).

This paper considers DG under the situation where domain d and class labels y are statistically dependent owing to some common latent factor z (Fig. 1-(c)), which we referred to as *domain-class dependency*. For example, the WISDM Activity Prediction dataset [16], where classes and domains correspond to activities and wearable device users, exhibits this dependency because of the (1) *data characteristics*: some activities (jogging and climbing stairs) are strenuous to the extent that some unathletic subjects avoided them, and (2) *data-collection errors*: other activities were added only after the study began and the initial subjects could not perform them. Note that the dependency is common in real-world datasets and a similar setting has been investigated in DA studies [12,36], but most prior DG studies overlooked the dependency; moreover, we need to follow a approach separate from DA because DG methods cannot require any access to target data, as we discuss further in Sect. 2.2.

Most prior DG methods utilize invariant feature learning (IFL) [7,10,27,33], which can be negatively affected by the dependency. IFL attempts to learn latent representation h from input data x which is invariant to domains d, or match multiple source domain distributions in feature space. When source and target domains have some common structure (see, [27]), matching multiple source domains leads to match source and target ones and thereby prevent the classifier from overfitting to source domains (Fig. 1-(b)). However, under the dependency, merely imposing the perfect domain invariance (which means h and d are independent) adversely affects the classification accuracy as pointed out by Xie et al. [33] and illustrated in Fig. 1. Intuitively speaking, since y contains information about

d under the dependency, encoding information about d into h helps to predict y; however, IFL attempts to remove all domain information from h, which causes the trade-off. Although that trade-off occurs in source domains (because we use only source data during optimization), it can also negatively affect the classification performance for target domains. For example, if the target domain has characteristics similar (or same as an extreme case) to those of a certain source domain, giving priority to domain invariance obviously interferes with the DG performance (Fig. 1-(d)).

In this paper, considering that prioritizing domain invariance under the trade-off can negatively affect the DG performance, we propose to maximize domain invariance within a range that does not interfere with the classification accuracy (Fig. 1-(e)). We first expand the analysis by [33] about domain adversarial nets (DAN), a well-used IFL method, and derive Theorems 1 and 2 which show the conditions under which domain invariance harms the classification accuracy. In Theorem 3 we show that *accuracy-constrained domain invariance*, which we define as the maximum $H(d|h)$ (H denotes entropy) value within a range that does not interfere with accuracy, equals $H(d|y)$. In other words, when $H(d|h) = H(d|y)$, i.e., the learned representation h contains as much domain information as the class labels, it does not affect the classification performance. After deriving the theorems, we propose a novel method *adversarial feature learning with accuracy constraint (AFLAC)*, which leads to that invariance on adversarial training. Empirical validations show that the performance of AFLAC is superior to that of baseline methods, supporting the importance of considering domain-class dependency and the efficacy of the proposed approach for overcoming the issue.

The main contributions of this paper can be summarized as follows. Firstly, we show that the implicit assumption of previous IFL methods, i.e., domain and class are statistically independent, is not valid in many real-world datasets, and it degrades the DG performance of them. Secondly, we theoretically show to what extent latent representation can become invariant to domains without interfering with classification accuracy. This is significant because the analysis guides the novel regularization approach that is suitable for our situation. Finally, we propose a novel method which improves domain invariance while maintaining classification performance, and it enjoys higher accuracy than the IFL methods on both synthetic and three real-world datasets.

2 Preliminary and Related Work

2.1 Problem Statement of Domain Generalization

Denote $\mathcal{X}, \mathcal{Y}$, and $\mathcal{D}$ as the input feature, class label, and domain spaces, respectively. With random variables $x \in \mathcal{X}$, $y \in \mathcal{Y}$, $d \in \mathcal{D}$, we can define the probability distribution for each domain as $p(x, y|d)$. For simplicity this paper assumes that y and d are discrete variables. In domain generalization, we are given a training dataset consisting of $\{x_i^s, y_i^s\}_{i=1}^{n^s}$ for all $s \in \{1, 2, ..., m\}$, where each $\{x_i^s, y_i^s\}_{i=1}^{n^s}$ is drawn from the source domain $p(x, y|d = s)$. Using the training dataset, we train a classifier $g : \mathcal{X} \to \mathcal{Y}$, and use the classifier to predict labels of samples drawn from unknown target domain $p(x, y | d = t)$.

2.2 Related Work

DG has been attracting considerable attention in recent years [27,28]. [18] showed that non-end-to-end DG methods such as DICA [27] and MTAE [11] do not tend to outperform vanilla CNN, thus end-to-end methods are desirable. End-to-end methods based on domain invariant representation can be divided into two categories: adversarial-learning-based methods such as DAN [9,33] and pre-defined-metric-based methods [10,20].

In particular, our analysis and proposed method are based on DAN, which measures the invariance by using a domain classifier (also known as a discriminator) parameterized by deep neural networks and imposes regularization by deceiving it. Although DAN was originally invented for DA, [33] demonstrated its efficacy in DG. In addition, they intuitively explained the trade-off between classification accuracy and domain invariance, but did not suggest any solution to the problem except for carefully tuning a weighting parameter. AFLAC also relates to domain confusion loss [31] in that their encoders attempted to minimize Kullback-Leibler divergence (KLD) between the output distribution of the discriminators and some domain distribution ($p(d|y)$ in AFLAC and uniform distribution in [31]), rather than to deceive the discriminator as DAN.

Several studies that address DG without utilizing IFL have been conducted. For example, CCSA [26], CIDG [21], and CIDDG [22] proposed to make use of semantic alignment, which attempts to make latent representation given class label ($p(h|y)$) identical within source domains. This approach was originally proposed by [12] in the DA context, but its efficacy to overcome the trade-off problem is not obvious. Also, CIDDG, which is the only adversarial-learning-based semantic alignment method so far, needs the same number of domain classification networks as domains whereas ours needs only one. CrossGrad [28], which is one of the recent state-of-the-art DG methods, utilizes data augmentation with adversarial examples. However, because the method relies on the assumption that y and d are independent, it might not be directly applicable to our setting. MLDG [19], MetaReg [2], and Feature-Critic [23], other state-of-the-art methods, are inspired by meta-learning. These methods make no assumption about the relation between y and d; hence, they could be combined with our proposed method in principle.

As with our paper, [21,22] also pointed out the importance of considering the types of distributional shifts that occur, and they address the shift of $p(y|x)$ across domains caused by the causal structure $y \to x$. However, the causal structure does not cause the trade-off problem as long as y and d are independent (Fig. 1-(a, b)), thus it is essential to consider and address domain-class dependency problem. They also proposed to correct the domain-class dependency with the class prior-normalized weight, which enforces the prior probability for each class to be the same across domains. Its motivation is different from ours in that it is intended to avoid overfitting whereas we address the trade-off problem.

In DA, [12,36] address the situation where $p(y)$ changes across the source and target domains by correcting the change of $p(y)$ using unlabeled target domain data, which is often accomplished at the cost of classification accuracy for the source domain. However, this approach is not applicable (or necessary) to DG because we are agnostic on target domains and cannot run such adaptation step in DG. Instead, this paper is concerned with the change of $p(y)$ within source domain and proposes to maximize the classification accuracy for source domains while improving the domain invariance.

It is worth mentioning that IFL has been used for many other context other than DG, e.g., DA [9,32], domain transfer [6,17], and fairness-aware classification [24,25,35]. However, adjusting it to each specific task is likely to improve performance. For example, in the fairness-aware classification task [25] proposed to optimize the fairness criterion directly instead of applying invariance to sensitive variables. By analogy, we adapted IFL for DG so as to address the domain-class dependency problem.

3   Our Approach

3.1   Domain Adversarial Networks

In this section, we provide a brief overview of DAN [9], on which our analysis and proposed method are based. DAN trains a domain discriminator that attempts to predict domains from latent representation encoded by an encoder, while simultaneously training the encoder to remove domain information by deceiving the discriminator.

Formally, we denote $f_E(x), q_M(y|h)$, and $q_D(d|h)$ (E, M, and D are their parameters) as the deterministic encoder, probabilistic model of the label classifier, and that of domain discriminator, respectively. Then, the objective function of DAN is described as follows:

$$\min_{E,M} \max_D J(E, M, D) = \mathbb{E}_{p(x,d,y)}[-\gamma L_d + L_y], \tag{1}$$

$$where \ \ L_d := -\log q_D(d|h = f_E(x)), \ \ L_y := -\log q_M(y|h = f_E(x)).$$

Here, the second term in Eq. 1 simply maximizes the log likelihood of q_M and f_E as well as in standard classification problems. On the other hand, the first term corresponds to a minimax game between the encoder and discriminator, where the discriminator $q_D(d|h)$ tries to predict d from h and the encoder $f_E(x)$ tries to fool $q_D(d|h)$.

As [33] originally showed, the minimax game ensures that the learned representation has no or little domain information, i.e., the representation becomes domain-invariant. This invariance ensures that the prediction from h to y is independent from d, and therefore hopefully facilitates the construction of a classifier capable of correctly handling samples drawn from unknown domains (Fig. 1-(b)). Below is a brief explanation.

Because h is a deterministic mapping of x, the joint probability distribution $p(h, d, y)$ can be defined as follows:

$$p(h, d, y) = \int_x p(x, d, h, y) dx = \int_x p(x, d, y) p(h|x) dx$$
$$= \int_x p(x, d, y) \delta(f_E(x) = h) dx, \tag{2}$$

and in the rest of the paper, we denote $p(h, d, y)$ as $\tilde{p}_E(h, d, y)$ because it depends on the encoder's parameter E. Using Eq. 2, Eq. 1 can be replaced as follows:

$$\min_{E,M} \max_D J(E, M, D) = \mathbb{E}_{\tilde{p}_E(h,d,y)}[\gamma \log q_D(d|h) - \log q_M(y|h)]. \tag{3}$$

Assuming E is fixed, the solutions M^* and D^* to Eq. 3 satisfy $q_{M^*}(y|h) = \tilde{p}_E(y|h)$ and $q_{D^*}(d|h) = \tilde{p}_E(d|h)$. Substituting q_{M^*} and q_{D^*} into Eq. 3 enable us to obtain the following optimization problem depending only on E:

$$\min_E J(E) = -\gamma H_{\tilde{p}_E}(d|h) + H_{\tilde{p}_E}(y|h). \tag{4}$$

Solving Eq. 4 allows us to obtain the solutions M^*, D^*, and E^*, which are in Nash equilibrium. Here, $H_{\tilde{p}_E}(d|h)$ means conditional entropy with the joint probability distribution $\tilde{p}_E(d, h)$. Thus, minimizing the second term in Eq. 4 intuitively means learning (the mapping function f_E to) the latent representation h which contains as much information about y as possible. On the other hand, the first term can be regarded as a regularizer that attempts to learn h that is invariant to d.

3.2   Trade-Off Caused by Domain-Class Dependency

Here we show that the performance of DAN is impeded by the existence of domain-class dependency. Concretely, we show that the dependency causes the trade-off between classification accuracy and domain invariance: when d and y are statistically dependent, no values of E would be able to optimize the first and second term in Eq. 4 at the same time. Note that the following analysis also suggests that most IFL methods are negatively influenced by the dependency.

To begin with, we consider only the first term in Eq. 4 and address the optimization problem:

$$\min_E J_1(E) = -\gamma H_{\tilde{p}_E}(d|h). \tag{5}$$

Using the property of entropy, $H_{\tilde{p}_E}(d|h)$ is bounded:

$$H_{\tilde{p}_E}(d|h) \leq H(d). \tag{6}$$

Thus, Eq. 5 has the solution E_1^* which satisfies the following condition:

$$H_{\tilde{p}_{E_1^*}}(d|h) = H(d). \tag{7}$$

Equation 7 suggests that the regularizer in DAN is intended to remove all information about domains from latent representation h, thereby ensuring the independence of domains and latent representation.

Next, we consider only the second term in Eq. 4, thereby addressing the following optimization problem:

$$\min_{E} J_2(E) = H_{\tilde{p}_E}(y|h). \tag{8}$$

Considering h is the mapping of x, i.e., $h = f_E(x)$, the solution E_2^* to Eq. 8 satisfies the following equation:

$$H_{\tilde{p}_{E_2^*}}(y|h) = H(y|x). \tag{9}$$

Here we obtain E_1^* and E_2^*, which can achieve perfect invariance and optimal classification accuracy, respectively. Using them, we can obtain the following theorem, which shows the existence of the trade-off between invariance and accuracy: perfect invariance (E_1^*) and optimal classification accuracy (E_2^*) cannot be achieved at the same time.

Theorem 1. *When $H(y|x) = 0$, i.e., there is no labeling error, and $H(d) > H(d|y)$, i.e., the domain and class are statistically dependent, $E_1^* \neq E_2^*$ holds.*

Proof 1. *Assume $E_1^* = E_2^* = E^*$. Using the properties of entropy, we can obtain the following:*

$$H_{\tilde{p}_E}(d|h) \leq H_{\tilde{p}_E}(d,y|h) = H_{\tilde{p}_E}(d|h,y) + H_{\tilde{p}_E}(y|h) \leq H_{\tilde{p}_E}(d|y) + H_{\tilde{p}_E}(y|h). \tag{10}$$

Substituting $H_{\tilde{p}_{E^*}}(y|h) = H(y|x)$ and $H_{\tilde{p}_{E^*}}(d|h) = H(d)$ into Eq. 10, we can obtain the following condition:

$$H(d) - H(d|y) \leq H(y|x). \tag{11}$$

Because the domain and class are dependent on each other, the following condition holds:

$$0 < H(d) - H(d|y) \leq H(y|x), \tag{12}$$

but Eq. 12 contradicts with $H(y|x) = 0$. Thus, $E_1^* \neq E_2^*$.

Theorem 1 shows that the domain-class dependency causes the trade-off problem. Although it assumes $H(y|x) = 0$ for simplicity, we cannot know the true value of $H(y|x)$ and there are many cases in which little or no labeling errors occur and thus $H(y|x)$ is close to 0.

In addition, we can omit the assumption and obtain a more general result:

Theorem 2. *When $I(d;y) := H(d) - H(d|y) > H(y|x)$, $E_1^* \neq E_2^*$ holds.*

Proof 2. *Similar to Proof 1, we assume that $E_1^* = E_2^*$ and thus Eq. 11 is obtained. Obviously, Eq. 11 does not hold when $H(d) - H(d|y) > H(y|x)$.*

Theorem 2 shows that when the mutual information of the domain and class $I(d; y)$ is greater than the labeling error $H(y|x)$, the trade-off between invariance and accuracy occurs. Then, although we cannot know the true value of $H(y|x)$, the performance of DAN and other IFL methods are likely to decrease when $I(d; y)$ has large value.

3.3 Accuracy-Constrained Domain Invariance

If we cannot avoid the trade-off, the next question is to decide how to accommodate it, i.e., to what extent the representation should become domain-invariant for DG tasks. Here we provide the notion of accuracy-constrained domain invariance, which is the maximum domain invariance within a range that does not interfere with the classification accuracy. The reason for the constraint is that the primary purpose of DG is the classification for unseen domains rather than the invariance itself, and the improvement of the invariance could detrimentally affect the performance. For example, in WISDM, if we know the target activity was performed by a young rather than an old man, we might predict the activity to be jogging with a higher probability; thus, we would have to avoid removing such domain information that may be useful in the classification task.

Theorem 3. *Define accuracy-constrained domain invariance as the maximum $H_{\tilde{p}_E}(d|h)$ value under the constraint that $H(y|x) = 0$, i.e., there is no labeling error, and classification accuracy is maximized, i.e., $H_{\tilde{p}_E}(y|h) = H(y|x)$. Then, accuracy-constrained domain invariance equals $H(d|y)$.*

Proof 3. *Using Eq. 10 and $H_{\tilde{p}_E}(y|h) = H(y|x)$, the following inequation holds:*

$$H_{\tilde{p}_E}(d|h) \leq H(y|x) + H(d|y). \tag{13}$$

Substituting $H(y|x) = 0$ into Eq. 13, the following inequation holds:

$$H_{\tilde{p}_E}(d|h) \leq H(d|y). \tag{14}$$

Thus, the maximum $H_{\tilde{p}_E}(d|h)$ value under the optimal classification accuracy constraint is $H(d|y)$.

Note that we could improve the invariance more when $H(y|x) > 0$ (that is obvious considering Eq. 13), but we cannot know the true value of $H(y|x)$ as we discussed in Sect. 3.2. Thus, accuracy-constrained domain invariance can be viewed as the worst-case guarantee.

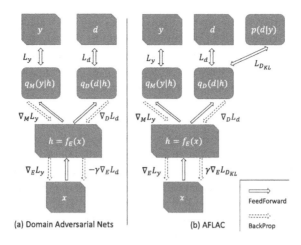

Fig. 2. Comparative illustration of DAN and AFLAC. (a) The classifier and discriminator try to minimize L_y and L_d, respectively. The encoder tries to minimize L_y and maximize L_d (fool the discriminator). (b) The discriminator tries to approximate true $\tilde{p}_E(d|h)$ by minimizing L_d. The encoder tries to minimize divergence between $\tilde{p}_E(d|h)$ and $p(d|y)$ by minimizing $L_{D_{KL}}$.

3.4 Proposed Method

Based on the above analysis, the remaining challenge is to determine how to achieve accuracy-constrained domain invariance, i.e., imposing regularization such that makes $H_{\tilde{p}_E}(d|h) = H(d|y)$ holds. Although DAN might be able to achieve this condition by carefully tuning the strength of the regularizer (γ in Eq. 1), such tuning is time-consuming and impractical, as suggested by our experiments. Alternatively, we propose a novel method named AFLAC by modifying the regularization term of DAN: whereas the encoder of DAN attempts to fool the discriminator, that of AFLAC attempts to directly minimize the KLD between $p(d|y)$ and $q_D(d|h)$. Formally, AFLAC solves the following joint optimization problem by alternating gradient descent.

$$\min_D W(E, D) = \mathbb{E}_{p(x,d)}[L_d] \qquad (15)$$

$$\min_{E,M} V(E, M) = \mathbb{E}_{p(x,d,y)}[\gamma L_{D_{KL}} + L_y], \qquad (16)$$

$$where \ \ L_{D_{KL}} := D_{KL}[p(d|y)|q_D(d|h = f_E(x))].$$

The minimization of L_y and L_d, respectively, means maximization of the log-likelihood of q_M and q_D as well as in DAN. However, the minimization of $L_{D_{KL}}$ differs from the regularizer of DAN in that it is intended to satisfy $q_D(d|h) = p(d|y)$. And if $q_D(d|h)$ well approximates $\tilde{p}_E(d|h)$ by the minimization of L_d in Eq. 15, the minimization of $L_{D_{KL}}$ leads to $\tilde{p}_E(d|h) = p(d|y)$. Figure 2-(b) outlines the training of AFLAC.

Here we formally show that AFLAC is intended to achieve $H_{\tilde{p}_E}(d|h) = H(d|y)$ (accuracy-constrained domain invariance) by a Nash equilibrium analysis smilar to [13,33]. As well as in Sect. 3.1, D^* and M^*, which are the solutions to Eqs. 15, 16 with fixed E, satisfy $q_D^* = \tilde{p}_E(d|h)$ and $q_M^* = \tilde{p}_E(y|h)$, respectively. Thus, V in Eq. 16 can be written as follows:

$$V(E) = \mathbb{E}[\gamma D_{KL}[p(d|y)|\tilde{p}_E(d|h)]] + H_{\tilde{p}_E}(y|h). \tag{17}$$

E^*, which is the solution to Eq. 17 and in Nash equilibrium, satisfies not only $H_{\tilde{p}_{E^*}}(y|h) = H(y|x)$ (optimal classification accuracy) but also $\mathbb{E}_{h,y \sim \tilde{p}_{E^*}(h,y)}[D_{KL}[p(d|y)|\tilde{p}_{E^*}(d|h)]] = 0$, which is a sufficient condition for $H_{\tilde{p}_{E^*}}(d|h) = H(d|y)$ by the definition of the conditional entropy.

In training, $p(x,d,y)$ in the objectives (Eqs. 15, 16) is approximated by empirical distribution composed of the training data obtained from m source domains, i.e., $\{x_i^{(1)}, y_i^{(1)}, d = 1\}_{i=1}^{n^{(1)}}, ..., \{x_i^{(m)}, y_i^{(m)}, d = m\}_{i=1}^{n^{(m)}}$. Also, $p(d|y)$ used in Eq. 16 can be replaced by the maximum likelihood or maximum a posteriori estimator of it. Note that, we could use some distances other than $D_{KL}[p(d|y)|q_D(d|h)]$ in Eq. 16, e.g., $D_{KL}[q_D(d|h)|p(d|y)]$, but in doing so, we could not observe performance gain, hence we discontinued testing them.

4 Experiments

4.1 Datasets

Here we provide a brief overview of one synthetic and three real-world datasets (PACS, WISDM, IEMOCAP) used for the performance evaluation. Although WISDM and IEMOCAP have not been widely used in DG studies, previous human activity recognition and speech emotion recognition studies (e.g., [1,5,8]) used them in the domain generalization setting (i.e., source and target domains are disjoint), so they can be regarded as the practical use case of domain generalization. The concrete sample sizes for each d and y, and the network architectures for each dataset are shown in supplementary.[1]

BMNISTR. We created the Biased and Rotated MNIST dataset (BMNISTR) by modifying the sample size of the popular benchmark dataset MNISTR [11], such that the class distribution differed among the domains. In MNISTR, each class is represented by 10 digits. Each domain was created by rotating images by 15° increments: 0, 15, 30, 45, 60, and 75 (referred to as M0, ..., M75). Each image was cropped to 16 × 16 in accordance with [11]. We created three variants of MNISTR that have different types of domain-class dependency, referred to as BMNISTR-1 through BMNISTR-3. As shown in Table 1-left, BMNISTR-1, -2 have similar trends but different degrees of dependency, whereas BMNISTR-1 and BMNISTR-3 differ in terms of their trends.

PACS. The PACS dataset [18] contains 9991 images across 7 categories (dog, elephant, giraffe, guitar, house, horse, and person) and 4 domains comprising

---

[1] Code and Supplementary are available at https://github.com/akuzeee/AFLAC.

different stylistic depictions (Photo, Art painting, Cartoon, and Sketch). It has domain-class dependency probably owing to the data characteristics. For example, $p(y = \text{person}|d = \text{Phot})$ is much higher than $p(y = \text{person}|d = \text{Sketch})$, indicating that photos of a person are easier to obtain than those of animals, but sketches of persons are more difficult to obtain than those of animals in the wild. For training, we used the ImageNet pre-trained AlexNet CNN [15] as the base network, following previous studies [18,19]. The two-FC-layer discriminator was connected to the last FC layer, following [9].

WISDM. The WISDM Activity Prediction dataset contains sensor data of accelerometers of six human activities (walking, jogging, upstairs, downstairs, sitting, and standing) performed by 36 users (domains). WISDM has the dependency for the reason noted in Sect. 1. In data preprocessing, we use the sliding-window procedure with 60 frames (=3 s) referring to [1], and the total number of samples was 18210. We parameterized the encoder using three 1-D convolution layers followed by one FC layer and the classifier by logistic regression, following previous studies [14,34].

IEMOCAP. The IEMOCAP dataset [4] is the popular benchmark dataset for speech emotion recognition (SER), which aims at recognizing the correct emotional state of the speaker from speech signals. It contains a total of 10039 utterances pronounced by ten actors (domains, referred to as Ses01F, Ses01M through Ses05F, Ses05M) with emotional categories, and we only consider the four emotional categories (happy, angry, sad, and neutral) referring to [5,8]. Also, we referred to [5] about data preprocessing: we split the speech signal into equal-length segments of 3s, and extracted 40-dimensional log Mel-spectrogram, its deltas, and delta-deltas. We parameterized the encoder using three 2-D convolution layers followed by one FC layer and the classifier by logistic regression.

4.2 Baselines

To demonstrate the efficacy of the proposed method AFLAC, we compared it with vanilla CNN and adversarial-learning-based methods. Specifically, **(1) CNN** is a vanilla convolutional networks trained on the aggregation of data from all source domains. Although CNN has no special treatments for DG, [18] reported that it outperforms many traditional DG methods. **(2) DAN** [33] is expected to generalize across domains utilizing domain-invariant representation, but it can be affected by the trade-off between domain invariance and accuracy as explained in Sect. 3.2. **(3) CIDDG** is our re-implementation of the method proposed in [22], which is designed to achieve semantic alignment on adversarial training. Additionally, we used **(4) AFLAC-Abl**, which is a version of AFLAC modified for ablation studies. AFLAC-Abl replaces $D_{KL}[p(d|y)|q_D(d|h)]$ in Eq. 16 of $D_{KL}[p(d)|q_D(d|h)]$, thus it attempts to learn the representation that is perfectly invariant to domains or make $H(d|h) = H(d)$ hold as well as DAN. Comparing AFLAC and AFLAC-Abl, we measured the genuine effect of taking domain-class dependency into account. When training AFLAC and AFLAC-Abl, we cannot obtain true $p(d|y)$ and $p(d)$, hence we used their maximum likelihood estimators for calculating the KLD terms.

Table 1. Left: Sample sizes for each domain-class pair in BMNISTR. Those for the classes 0~4 are variable across domains, whereas the classes 5~9 have identical sample sizes across domains. Right: Mean F-measures for the classes 0~4 and classes 5~9 with the target domain M0. RI denotes relative improvement of AFLAC to AFLAC-Abl

Dataset	Class	M0	M15	M30	M45	M60	M75
BMNISTR-1	0~4	100	85	70	55	40	25
	5~9	100	100	100	100	100	100
BMNISTR-2	0~4	100	90	80	70	60	50
	5~9	100	100	100	100	100	100
BMNISTR-3	0~4	100	25	100	25	100	25
	5~9	100	100	100	100	100	100

Dataset	Class	CNN	DAN	CIDDG	AFLAC	AFLAC-Abl	RI
BMNISTR-1	0~4	83.86	84.54	87.50	87.46	**90.62**	3.6%
	5~9	83.90	85.24	87.46	86.46	**88.10**	1.9%
BMNISTR-2	0~4	82.54	85.30	87.64	88.60	**89.64**	1.2%
	5~9	82.18	85.80	86.74	87.60	**89.04**	1.6%
BMNISTR-3	0~4	71.26	79.22	76.76	76.56	**80.02**	4.5%
	5~9	78.62	**83.14**	82.64	82.94	82.80	-0.2%

4.3 Experimental Settings

For all the datasets and methods, we used RMSprop for optimization. Further, we set the learning rate, batch size, and the number of iterations as $5e-4$, 128, and 10k for BMNISTR; $5e-5$, 64, and 10k for PACS; $1e-4$, 64, and 10k for IEMO-CAP; $5e-4$ (with exponential decay with decay step 18k and 24k, and decay rate 0.1), 128, and 30k for WISDM, respectively. Also, we used the annealing of weighting parameter γ proposed in [9], and unless otherwise mentioned chose γ from $\{0.0001, 0.001, 0.01, 0.1, 1, 10\}$ for DAN, CIDDG, AFLAC-Abl, and AFLAC. Specifically, on BMNISTR and PACS, we employed a leave-one-domain-out setting [11], i.e., we chose one domain as target and used the remaining domains as source data. Then we split the source data into 80% of training data and 20% of validation data, assuming that target data are not absolutely available in the training phase. On IEMOCAP, we chose the best γ from $\{0.0001, 0.001, 0.01, 0.1, 1, 10, 100, 1000\}$ using disjoint validation domain, referring to [5,8]. On WISDM, we randomly selected <20/16> users as <source/target> domains, and split the source data into training and validation data because one-domain-leave-out evaluation is computationally expensive. Then, we conducted experiments multiple times with different random weight initialization; we trained the models on 10, 20, and 20 seeds in BMNISTR, WISDM, and IEMOCAP, chose the best hyperparameter that achieved the highest validation accuracies measured in each epoch, and reported the mean scores (accuracies and F-measures) for the hyperparameter. On PACS, because it requires a long time to train on, we chose the best γ from $\{0.0001, 0.001, 0.01, 0.1\}$ after three experiments, and reported the mean scores in experiments with 15 seeds.

4.4 Results

We first investigated the extent to which domain-class dependency affects the performance of the IFL methods. In Table 1-right, we compared the mean F-measures for the classes 0 through 4 and classes 5 through 9 in BMNISTR with the target domain M0. Recall that the sample sizes for the classes 0~4 are variable across domains, whereas the classes 5~9 have identical sample sizes across

Table 2. Accuracies for each dataset and target domain. The $I(d; y)$ column is estimated from source domain data, which indicates the domain-class dependency.

Dataset	Target	I(d; y)	CNN	DAN	CIDDG	AFLAC-Abl	AFLAC
BMNISTR-1	M0	0.026	83.9 ± 0.4	85.0 ± 0.4	87.4 ± 0.3	87.0 ± 0.4	**89.3 ± 0.4**
	M15	0.034	98.5 ± 0.2	98.5 ± 0.1	98.3 ± 0.2	98.3 ± 0.2	**98.8 ± 0.1**
	M30	0.037	97.5 ± 0.1	97.4 ± 0.1	97.4 ± 0.2	97.6 ± 0.1	**98.3 ± 0.2**
	M45	0.036	89.9 ± 0.9	90.2 ± 0.6	89.8 ± 0.5	92.8 ± 0.5	**93.3 ± 0.6**
	M60	0.030	96.7 ± 0.3	97.0 ± 0.2	97.2 ± 0.1	96.6 ± 0.2	**97.4 ± 0.2**
	M75	0.017	87.1 ± 0.5	87.3 ± 0.4	**88.2 ± 0.3**	87.7 ± 0.5	88.1 ± 0.4
	Avg		92.3	92.6	93.1	93.3	**94.2**
BMNISTR-2	Avg		92.2	92.7	93.1	94.0	**94.5**
BMNISTR-3	Avg		90.6	91.7	91.4	91.6	**92.9**
PACS	Photo	0.102	82.2 ± 0.4	81.8 ± 0.4	–	82.5 ± 0.4	**83.5 ± 0.3**
	Art_painting	0.117	61.0 ± 0.5	60.9 ± 0.5	–	62.6 ± 0.4	**63.3 ± 0.3**
	Cartoon	0.131	**64.9 ± 0.5**	**64.9 ± 0.6**	–	64.2 ± 0.3	**64.9 ± 0.3**
	Sketch	0.023	**61.4 ± 0.5**	**61.4 ± 0.5**	–	59.6 ± 0.7	60.1 ± 0.7
	Avg		67.4	67.2	–	67.2	**68.0**
WISDM	16 users	0.181	84.0 ± 0.4	83.8 ± 0.3	**84.4 ± 0.4**	83.7 ± 0.3	**84.4 ± 0.3**
IEMOCAP	Ses01F	0.005	56.0 ± 0.7	60.1 ± 0.7	–	**62.9 ± 0.5**	60.4 ± 0.9
	Ses01M		61.0 ± 0.3	63.5 ± 0.5	–	**68.0 ± 0.5**	66.1 ± 0.3
	Ses02F	0.045	61.2 ± 0.5	60.4 ± 0.5	–	**65.8 ± 0.5**	64.2 ± 0.4
	Ses02M		**76.6 ± 0.4**	47.2 ± 0.7	–	64.7 ± 1.7	74.3 ± 1.3
	Ses03F	0.037	69.2 ± 0.9	**71.9 ± 0.4**	–	70.0 ± 0.6	70.1 ± 0.4
	Ses03M		56.9 ± 0.4	**57.3 ± 0.5**	–	56.2 ± 0.4	56.8 ± 0.4
	Ses04F	0.120	75.5 ± 0.5	75.5 ± 0.6	–	75.4 ± 0.6	**75.7 ± 0.6**
	Ses04M		58.5 ± 0.5	57.4 ± 0.5	–	58.7 ± 0.5	**59.2 ± 0.5**
	Ses05F	0.063	61.8 ± 0.4	62.4 ± 0.5	–	61.9 ± 0.3	**63.4 ± 0.7**
	Ses05M		47.6 ± 0.3	46.9 ± 0.4	–	49.6 ± 0.4	**49.9 ± 0.4**
	Avg		62.4	60.3	–	63.3	**64.0**

domains (Table 1-left). The F-measures show that AFLAC outperformed baselines in most dataset-class pairs, which supports that domain-class dependency reduces the performance of domain-invariance-based methods and that AFLAC can mitigate the problem. Further, the relative improvement of AFLAC to AFLAC-Abl is more significant for the classes 0~4 than for 5~9 in BMNISTR-1 and BMNISTR-3, suggesting that AFLAC tends to increase performance more significantly for classes in which the domain-class dependency occurs. Moreover, the improvement is more significant in BMNISTR-1 than in BMNISTR-2, suggesting that the stronger the domain-class dependency is, the lower the performance of domain-invariance-based methods becomes. This result is consistent with Theorem 2, which shows that the trade-off is likely to occur when $I(d; y)$ is large. Finally, although the dependencies of BMNISTR-1 and BMNISTR-3 have different trends, AFLAC improved the F-measures in both datasets.

Next we compared the mean accuracies (with standard errors) in both synthetic (BMNISTR) and real-world (PACS, WISDM, and IEMOCAP) datasets (Table 2). Note that the performance of our baseline CNN on PACS, WISDM, and IEMOCAP is similar but partly different from that reported in previous studies ([22], [1], and [8], respectively) probably because the DG performance strongly depends on validation methods and other implementation details as reported in many recent studies [1,2,8,23]. Also, we trained CIDDG only on BMNISTR and WISDM due to computational resource constraint. This table enables us to make the following observations. (1) Domain-class dependency in real-world datasets negatively affects the DG performance of IFL methods. The results obtained on PACS (Avg) and WISDM showed that the vanilla CNN outperformed the IFL methods (DAN and AFLAC-Abl). Additionally, the results on IEMOCAP shows that AFLAC tended to outperform AFLAC-Abl when $I(d; y)$ had large values (in Ses04 and Ses05), which is again consistent with Theorem 2. These results support the importance of considering domain-class dependency in real-world datasets. (2) AFLAC performed better than the baselines on all the datasets in average, except for CIDDG on WISDM. Note that AFLAC is more parameter efficient than CIDDG as we noted in Sect. 2.2. These results supports the efficacy of the proposed model to overcome the trade-off problem.

Finally, we investigated the relationship between the strength of regularization and performance. In DG, it is difficult to choose appropriate hyperparameters because we cannot use target domain data at validation step (since they are not available during training); therefore, hyperparameter insensitivity is significant in DG. Figure 3 shows the hyperparameter sensitivity of the classification accuracies for DAN, CIDDG, AFLAC-Abl, and AFLAC. These figures suggest that DAN and AFLAC-Abl sometimes outperformed AFLAC with appropriate γ values, but there is no guarantee that such γ values will be chosen by validation whereas AFLAC is robust toward hyperparameter choice. Specifically, as shown in Figs. 3-(b, d), DAN and AFLAC-Abl outperformed AFLAC with $\gamma = 1$ and 10, respectively. One possible explanation of those results is that accuracy for target domain sometimes improves by giving priority to domain invariance at the cost of the accuracies for source domains, but AFLAC improves domain invariance only within a range that does not interfere with accuracy for source domains. However, as shown in Fig. 3, the performance of DAN and AFLAC-Abl are sensitive to hyperparameter choice. For example, although they got high scores with $\gamma = 1$ in Fig. 3-(b), the scores dropped rapidly when γ increases to 10 or decreases to 0.01. Also, the scores of DAN and AFLAC-Abl in Fig. 3-(c) dropped significantly with $\gamma > 10$, and such large γ was indeed chosen by overfitting to validation domain. On the other hand, Figs. 3-(a, b, c, d) show that the accuracy gaps of AFLAC-Abl and AFLAC increase with strong regularization (such as when $\gamma = 10$ or 100). These results suggest that AFLAC, as it was designed, does not tend to reduce the classification accuracy with strong regularizer, and such robustness of AFLAC might have yielded the best performance shown in Table 2.

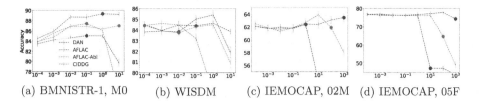

(a) BMNISTR-1, M0   (b) WISDM   (c) IEMOCAP, 02M   (d) IEMOCAP, 05F

Fig. 3. Classification Accuracy with various γ. Each caption shows dataset name and target domain. The round markers correspond to γ values chosen by validation. The error bars correspond to standard errors.

5   Conclusion

In this paper, we addressed domain generalization under domain-class dependency, which was overlooked by most prior DG methods relying on IFL. We theoretically showed the importance of considering the dependency and the way to overcome the problem by expanding the analysis of [33]. We then proposed a novel method AFLAC, which maximizes domain invariance within a range that does not interfere with classification accuracy on adversarial training. Empirical validations show the superior performance of AFLAC to the baseline methods, supporting the importance of the domain-class dependency in DG tasks and the efficacy of the proposed method to overcome the issue.

References

1. Andrey, I.: Real-time human activity recognition from accelerometer data using convolutional neural networks. Appl. Soft Comput. **62**, 915–922 (2017)
2. Balaji, Y., Sankaranarayanan, S., Chellappa, R.: MetaReg: towards domain generalization using meta-regularization. In: Advances in Neural Information Processing Systems 31 (2018)
3. Blanchard, G., Lee, G., Scott, C.: Generalizing from several related classification tasks to a new unlabeled sample. In: Proceedings of the 24th International Conference on Neural Information Processing Systems (2011)
4. Busso, C., et al.: IEMOCAP: interactive emotional dyadic motion capture database. Lang. Resour. Eval. **42**(4), 335 (2008)
5. Chen, M., He, X., Yang, J., Zhang, H.: 3-D convolutional recurrent neural networks with attention model for speech emotion recognition. IEEE Signal Process. Lett. **25**, 1 (2018)
6. Chou, J., Yeh, C., Lee, H., Lee, L.: Multi-target voice conversion without parallel data by adversarially learning disentangled audio representations. In: Proceedings of Interspeech (2018)
7. Erfani, S., et al.: Robust domain generalisation by enforcing distribution invariance. In: 25th International Joint Conference on Artificial Intelligence (2016)
8. Etienne, C., Fidanza, G., Petrovskii, A., Devillers, L., Schmauch, B.: Speech emotion recognition with data augmentation and layer-wise learning rate adjustment. CoRR abs/1802.05630 (2018). http://arxiv.org/abs/1802.05630

9. Ganin, Y., et al.: Domain-adversarial training of neural networks. J. Mach. Learn. Res. **7**, 2096–2030 (2016)

10. Ghifary, M., Balduzzi, D., Kleijn, W.B., Zhang, M.: Scatter component analysis: a unified framework for domain adaptation and domain generalization. IEEE Trans. Pattern Anal. Mach. Intell. **39**, 1414–1430 (2017)

11. Ghifary, M., Bastiaan Kleijn, W., Zhang, M., Balduzzi, D.: Domain generalization for object recognition with multi-task autoencoders. In: Proceedings of the IEEE International Conference on Computer Vision (ICCV) (2015)

12. Gong, M., Zhang, K., Liu, T., Tao, D., Glymour, C., Schölkopf, B.: Domain adaptation with conditional transferable components. In: Proceedings of the 33rd International Conference on International Conference on Machine Learning (2016)

13. Goodfellow, I., et al.: Generative adversarial nets. In: Proceedings of the 27th International Conference on Neural Information Processing Systems (2014)

14. Iwasawa, Y., Nakayama, K., Yairi, I., Matsuo, Y.: Privacy issues regarding the application of DNNs to activity-recognition using wearables and its countermeasures by use of adversarial training. In: Proceedings of the 26th International Joint Conference on Artificial Intelligence, pp. 1930–1936 (2017)

15. Krizhevsky, A., Sutskever, I., Hinton, G.E.: ImageNet classification with deep convolutional neural networks. In: Proceedings of the 25th International Conference on Neural Information Processing Systems, pp. 1097–1105 (2012)

16. Kwapisz, J.R., Weiss, G.M., Moore, S.A.: Activity recognition using cell phone accelerometers. ACM SigKDD Explor. Newsl. **12**, 74–8282 (2011)

17. Lample, G., Zeghidour, N., Usunier, N., Bordes, A., Denoyer, L., Ranzato, M.: Fader networks: manipulating images by sliding attributes. In: Proceedings of the 30th Neural Information Processing Systems (2017)

18. Li, D., Yang, Y., Song, Y.Z., Hospedales, T.M.: Deeper, broader and artier domain generalization. In: Proceedings of the IEEE International Conference on Computer Vision (ICCV) (2017)

19. Li, D., Yang, Y., Song, Y., Hospedales, T.M.: Learning to generalize: Meta-learning for domain generalization. In: Proceedings of the 32nd AAAI Conference on Artificial Intelligence (2018)

20. Li, H., Jialin Pan, S., Wang, S., Kot, A.C.: Domain generalization with adversarial feature learning. In: The IEEE Conference on Computer Vision and Pattern Recognition (CVPR), June 2018

21. Li, Y., Gong, M., Tian, X., Liu, T., Tao, D.: Domain generalization via conditional invariant representations. In: Proceedings of the 32nd AAAI Conference on Artificial Intelligence (2018)

22. Li, Y., et al.: Deep domain generalization via conditional invariant adversarial networks. In: Ferrari, V., Hebert, M., Sminchisescu, C., Weiss, Y. (eds.) ECCV 2018. LNCS, vol. 11219, pp. 647–663. Springer, Cham (2018). https://doi.org/10.1007/978-3-030-01267-0_38

23. Li, Y., Yang, Y., Zhou, W., Hospedales, T.M.: Feature-critic networks for heterogeneous domain generalization. CoRR abs/1901.11448 (2019). http://arxiv.org/abs/1901.11448

24. Louizos, C., Swersky, K., Li, Y., Welling, M., Zemel, R.S.: The variational fair autoencoder. In: Proceedings of the International Conference on Representation Learning (2016)

25. Madras, D., Creager, E., Pitassi, T., Zemel, R.S.: Learning adversarially fair and transferable representations. In: Proceedings of the 35th International Conference on Machine Learning (2018)

26. Motiian, S., Piccirilli, M., Adjeroh, D.A., Doretto, G.: Unified deep supervised domain adaptation and generalization. In: Proceedings of the IEEE International Conference on Computer Vision (ICCV) (2017)
27. Muandet, K., Balduzzi, D., Schölkopf, B.: Domain generalization via invariant feature representation. In: Proceedings of the 30th International Conference on Machine Learning (2013)
28. Shankar, S., Piratla, V., Chakrabarti, S., Chaudhuri, S., Jyothi, P., Sarawagi, S.: Generalizing across domains via cross-gradient training. In: Proceedings of the International Conference on Learning Representations (2018)
29. Sriram, A., Jun, H., Gaur, Y., Satheesh, S.: Robust speech recognition using generative adversarial networks. In: The IEEE International Conference on Acoustics, Speech and Signal Processing (ICASSP) (2018)
30. Torralba, A., Efros, A.A.: Unbiased look at dataset bias. In: Proceedings of the 2011 IEEE Conference on Computer Vision and Pattern Recognition (2011)
31. Tzeng, E., Hoffman, J., Darrell, T., Saenko, K.: Simultaneous deep transfer across domains and tasks. In: Proceedings of the IEEE International Conference on Computer Vision (ICCV) (2015)
32. Tzeng, E., Hoffman, J., Zhang, N., Saenko, K., Darrell, T.: Deep domain confusion: maximizing for domain invariance. CoRR abs/1412.3474 (2014). http://arxiv.org/abs/1412.3474
33. Xie, Q., Dai, Z., Du, Y., Hovy, E., Neubig, G.: Controllable invariance through adversarial feature learning. In: Proceedings of the 30th International Conference on Neural Information Processing Systems (2017)
34. Yang, J., Nguyen, M.N., San, P.P., Li, X., Krishnaswamy, S.: Deep convolutional neural networks on multichannel time series for human activity recognition. In: Proceedings of the 24th International Joint Conference on Artificial Intelligence (2015)
35. Zemel, R., Wu, Y., Swersky, K., Pitassi, T., Dwork, C.: Learning fair representations. In: Proceedings of the 30th International Conference on Machine Learning (2013)
36. Zhang, K., Schölkopf, B., Muandet, K., Wang, Z.: Domain adaptation under target and conditional shift. In: Proceedings of the 30th International Conference on Machine Learning (2013)

Quantile Layers: Statistical Aggregation in Deep Neural Networks for Eye Movement Biometrics

Ahmed Abdelwahab[✉] and Niels Landwehr

Leibniz Institute of Agricultural Engineering and Bioeconomy e.V. (ATB),
Potsdam, Germany
{AAbdelwahab,NLandwehr}@atb-potsdam.de

Abstract. Human eye gaze patterns are highly individually characteristic. Gaze patterns observed during the routine access of a user to a
device or document can therefore be used to identify subjects unobtrusively, that is, without the need to perform an explicit verification such
as entering a password. Existing approaches to biometric identification
from gaze patterns segment raw gaze data into short, local patterns called
saccades and fixations. Subjects are then identified by characterizing the
distribution of these patterns or deriving hand-crafted features for them.
In this paper, we follow a different approach by training deep neural networks directly on the raw gaze data. As the distribution of short, local
patterns has been shown to be particularly informative for distinguishing
subjects, we introduce a parameterized and end-to-end learnable statistical aggregation layer called the *quantile layer* that enables the network
to explicitly fit the distribution of filter activations in preceding layers.
We empirically show that deep neural networks with quantile layers outperform existing probabilistic and feature-based methods for identifying
subjects based on eye movements by a large margin.

Keywords: Eye movements · Deep learning · Biometry

1 Introduction

Human visual perception is a fundamentally active process. We are not simply
exposed to an incoming flow of visual sensory data, but rather actively control the
visual input by continuously performing eye movements that direct the gaze focus
to those points in space that are estimated to be most informative. The interplay
between visual information processing and gaze control has been extensively
studied in cognitive psychology, as it constitutes an important example of the
link between cognitive processing and motor control [9,19].

One insight from existing studies in psychology is that the resulting gaze
patterns are highly individually characteristic [22,23]. It is therefore possible
to identify subjects based on their observed gaze patterns with high accuracy,
and the use of gaze patterns as a biometric feature has been widely studied.

© Springer Nature Switzerland AG 2020
U. Brefeld et al. (Eds.): ECML PKDD 2019, LNAI 11907, pp. 332–348, 2020.
https://doi.org/10.1007/978-3-030-46147-8_20

Approaches for using gaze patterns for identification can be divided into two groups. One group of methods uses an active challenge-response protocol, that is, identification is based on eye movements in response to an artificial visual stimulus [13, 25]. This has the disadvantage that additional time and effort of a user is required in order to confirm her identity. In the second group of methods, biometric identification is based on gaze patterns observed during the routine access of a user to a device or document [17, 26]. This way the identity can be confirmed unobtrusively, without requiring reaction to a specific challenge protocol. If the observed gaze patterns are unlikely to be generated by an authorized individual, access can be terminated or an additional verification requested.

Existing approaches for identifying subjects from gaze patterns mostly segment the raw eye gaze data into fixations (short periods of time in which the gaze is relatively stable) and saccades (rapid movements of the gaze to a new fixation position). They then either use probabilistic models that characterize the distribution of saccades and fixations [1, 17, 20], or hand-crafted statistical features that characterize different properties of saccades such as lengths, velocities, or accelerations [7, 12, 26]. In this paper, we follow a different approach by training deep neural networks on the raw gaze position data, without segmenting gaze movements into saccades and fixations or applying handcrafted aggregate features. However, we take inspiration from existing probabilistic approaches, which have shown that the distribution of local, short-term patterns in gaze movements such as saccades and fixations can be highly characteristic for different individuals. We therefore design neural network architectures that can extract such local patterns and characterize their distribution.

More specifically, we introduce a parameterized and end-to-end learnable statistical aggregation layer called the *quantile layer* that enables the network to explicitly fit the distribution of filter activations in preceding layers. We design network architectures in which stacked 1D-convolution layers extract local, short-term patterns from eye movement sequences. The quantile layer characterizes the distribution of these patterns by approximating the *quantile function*, that is, the inverse cumulative distribution function, of the activations of the filters across the time series of gaze movements. The quantile function is approximated by sampling the empirical quantile function of the activations at a set of points, which are trainable model parameters. Natural special cases of the quantile layer are global maximum pooling and global median pooling; median pooling will approximate average pooling if filter activations are approximately symmetric. The proposed quantile layer can thus be seen as an extension of standard global pooling layers that retains more information about the distribution of activations than the average or maximum. In the same way as standard global pooling layers, the quantile layer aggregates over the entire sequence, enabling the model to work with variable-length sequences. By learning the sampling points, the model can focus on those parts of the distribution function that are most discriminative for identification. Using a piecewise linear approximation to the empirical quantile function makes the layer fully differentiable; models can thus be trained end-to-end using gradient descent. We empirically show that deep neural networks using quantile layers outperform existing probabilistic and feature-based approaches for identification based on gaze movements by a large margin.

Unobtrusive biometric identification has been most extensively studied based on gaze patterns during reading. In this paper, we study biometric eye gaze models for arbitrary non-text input. We specifically use data from the *dynamic images and eye movements* (DIEM) project, a large-scale data collection effort during which gaze movements of over 200 participants each watching a subset of 84 video sequences were recorded [21]. This data is approximately representative of scenarios where a user is not reading text (e.g., watching a live stream from a security camera), broadening the application range of gaze-based biometrics.

The rest of the paper is organized as follows. Section 2 discusses related work. Section 3 introduces the quantile layer, Sect. 4 discusses deep neural network architectures for eye gaze biometrics. We empirically study identification accuracy of the proposed methods and different baselines in Sect. 5.

2   Related Work

Biometric identification from eye gaze patterns observed as a response to a specific stimulus has been studied extensively. The stimulus can for example be a moving [13,16,18,31] or fixed [2] dot on a monitor, or a specific image stimulus [25]. More recently, unobtrusive biometric identification based on gaze patterns observed during the routine access of a user to a device or document has been studied. This approach has the advantage that no additional time and attention of a user are needed for identification, because gaze patterns are generated on material that is viewed anyway. Most unobtrusive approaches are based on observing eye movements of subjects generated while reading text [1,11,26], but identification based on eye movements generated while viewing non-text input has also been studied [15].

Existing approaches for biometric identification (with the exception of the work by Kinnunen et al. [15], see below) first segment the observed eye movement data into fixations (periods of little gaze movement during which the visual content at the current position is processed) and saccades (short, ballistic movements that relocate the gaze to a new fixation position). One approach that has been widely studied in the literature is to derive hand-crafted features of these saccades and fixations that are believed to be characteristic for individual subjects. Holland and Komogortsev have studied relatively simple features such as average fixation duration, average saccade amplitude and average saccade velocity [11,12]. This line of work was later extended to more complex features such as saccadic vigor, acceleration, or the so-called *main sequence* feature [7,26]. Subjects are then identified by matching the features of observed eye gaze sequences generated by an unknown individual to those of known individuals, using for example shortest distance [11], statistical tests [12,26], or an RBF classifier [7].

Another popular approach is to use probabilistic models that characterize user-specific distributions over saccades and fixations. Landwehr et al. [17] have studied simple parametric models based on the Gamma family. Abdelwahab et al. [1] have studied semiparametric models in which the identity of a user is inferred by Bayesian inference based on Metropolis-Hastings sampling under a Gaussian process prior. Makowski et al. [20] study a discriminative model that takes into account lexical features of fixated words, such as word frequency and word lengths, and show that this can further increase identification accuracy from gaze patterns obtained during reading. The approach discussed by Kinnunen et al. [15] also uses a probabilistic approach, by fitting a Gaussian mixture model to the distribution of angles between successive gaze positions. Unlike the approaches discussed above, Kinnunen et al. do not segment the eye signal into fixations and saccades, but rather use all recorded gaze positions. Our work differs from these existing approaches to biometric identification from gaze patterns in that we train deep neural networks on the raw eye gaze to distinguish between different subjects. We show empirically that this leads to large gains in identification accuracy compared to existing feature-based and probabilistic approaches, including the model by Kinnunen et al. [15].

The quantile layer we propose as a more expressive statistical aggregation layer than standard global pooling is related to the learnable *histogram layers* proposed by Wang et al. [30] and Sedighi and Fridrich [27]. Histogram layers are also fully differentiable, parameterized statistical aggregation layers. They characterize the distribution of values in the input to the layer in terms of an approximation to a histogram, in which bin centers and bin widths are learnable parameters. Wang et al. [30] use linear approximations to smoothen the sharp edges in a traditional histogram function and enable gradient flow. Sedighi and Fridrich [27] use Gaussian kernels as a soft, differentiable approximation to histogram bins. The histogram layers proposed by Wang et al. [30] and Sedighi and Fridrich [27] directly approximate the probability density of the input values, while the quantile layer we propose approximates the cumulative distribution function. The quantile layer also naturally generalizes maximum pooling and median pooling, while the histogram layers do not directly relate to standard pooling operations. We use architectures based on the histogram layers of Wang et al. [30] and Sedighi and Fridrich [27] as baselines in our empirical study.

Finally, Couture et al. [5] have recently studied quantiles as a method to aggregate instance-level predictions when training deep multi-instance neural networks for detecting tumor type from tissue images. In their application, images are represented as bags of subimages, and predictions on individual subimages are combined into a bag prediction based on the quantile function.

3   The Quantile Layer

This section introduces the quantile layer, a parameterized and end-to-end learnable layer for characterizing the distribution of filter activations in a preceding convolution layer. This layer will be a central component in the deep neural network architectures for eye gaze biometrics that we develop in the next section.

The gaze movement data we study is a discrete time series of 2D-coordinates that indicate the current focus point of the gaze on a plane (e.g., a monitor).

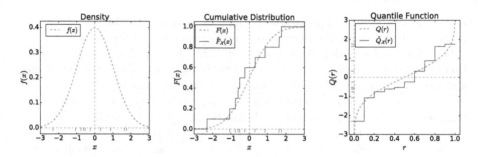

Fig. 1. Density function, cumulative distribution function, and quantile function (dashed lines) with empirical counterparts (solid lines) for a normally distributed variable $x \sim \mathcal{N}(0,1)$. Tick marks at zero line show a sample from the distribution.

The discrete time series is obtained by sampling the continuous gaze movements at a regular frequency, and can be observed using standard eye tracking devices. Existing approaches for user identification from eye movements first preprocess the raw signal into two kinds of short, local patterns: saccades (rapid movements, characterized by their amplitude) and fixations (periods of almost constant gaze position, characterized by their duration). They then distinguish users based on their distribution of saccade amplitudes and fixation durations (and possibly other local features). This is done either by computing aggregate features [11,12,26] or by fitting parametric or semiparametric probabilistic models to the observed distributions [1,17,20]. The key insight from this existing work is that the most informative feature for identification is the distribution of short, local gaze patterns seen in a particular sequence. In contrast, long-term dependencies in the time series will be less informative, as these are more likely to be a function of the visual input than the identity of the viewer.

Motivated by these observations in earlier work, we study network architectures that consists of a deep arrangement of 1D-convolution filters, which extract local, short-term patterns from the raw gaze signal, followed by the quantile layer whose output characterizes the distribution of these patterns. We design the quantile layer in such a way that it naturally generalizes global maximum, median, and minimum pooling. As we assume that the distribution of short-term patterns is most informative, we use standard non-dilated convolution operations, rather than dilated convolution operations which have recently been used for modeling more long-term patterns in time series, for example for audio data [29].

Let x denote a real-valued random variable whose distribution is given by the probability density function $f(x)$. The distribution of x can be expressed in different forms: by the density function $f(x)$, by the cumulative distribution function $F : \mathbb{R} \rightarrow [0,1]$ defined by

$$F(x) = \int_{-\infty}^{x} f(z)\mathrm{d}z, \tag{1}$$

or by the *quantile function* $Q : (0, 1) \to \mathbb{R}$ defined by

$$Q(r) = \inf\{x \in \mathbb{R} : r \le F(x)\} \tag{2}$$

where inf denotes the infimum and $(0, 1) \subset \mathbb{R}$ the open interval from zero to one. The quantile function Q is characterized by $p(x \le Q(r)) = r$. That is, the quantile function yields the value $Q(r) \in \mathbb{R}$ such that all values of the random variable x smaller than $Q(r)$ together account for probability mass r. If the cumulative distribution function F is continuous and strictly monotonically increasing, which it will be if the density function $f(x)$ is continuous and positive everywhere on $\mathbb{R}$, the quantile function Q is simply the inverse of the cumulative distribution function, $Q = F^{-1}$. Figure 1 visualizes the relationship between density, cumulative distribution, and quantile functions for a standard normally distributed variable $x \sim \mathcal{N}(0, 1)$.

If $\mathcal{X} = \{x_1, ..., x_n\}$ with $x_i \sim p(x)$ denotes a sample of the random variable x, the empirical cumulative distribution function $\hat{F}_{\mathcal{X}} : \mathbb{R} \to [0, 1]$ is a non-parametric estimator of the cumulative distribution function F. It is given by

$$\hat{F}_{\mathcal{X}}(x) = \frac{1}{n} \sum_{i=1}^{n} I(x_i \le x) \tag{3}$$

where

$$I(x_i \le x) = \begin{cases} 1 & \text{if } x_i \le x \\ 0 & \text{if } x_i > x. \end{cases} \tag{4}$$

In analogy to the empirical distribution function, the empirical quantile function $\hat{Q}_{\mathcal{X}} : (0, 1] \to \mathbb{R}$ is a non-parametric estimator of the quantile function Q. It is defined by

$$\hat{Q}_{\mathcal{X}}(r) = \inf\{x \in \mathbb{R} : r \le \hat{F}_{\mathcal{X}}(x)\}. \tag{5}$$

Figure 1 visualizes the empirical cumulative distribution function $\hat{F}(x)$ and the empirical quantile function $\hat{Q}(r)$ together with a set of samples for a standard normally distributed variable. For sufficiently large sample size n, the empirical quantile function faithfully characterizes the distribution of x in the following sense. According to the Glivenko-Cantelli theorem, $\hat{F}_{\mathcal{X}}$ uniformly converges to the true cumulative distribution function F,

$$\sup_{x \in \mathbb{R}} |\hat{F}_{\mathcal{X}}(x) - F(x)| \xrightarrow{a.s.} 0 \tag{6}$$

[28], where we use $\xrightarrow{a.s.}$ to denote almost sure convergence in the sample size n. For all $r \in (0, 1)$ this implies almost sure convergence of $\hat{Q}_{\mathcal{X}}(r)$ to $Q(r)$,

$$|\hat{Q}_{\mathcal{X}}(r) - Q(r)| \xrightarrow{a.s.} 0 \tag{7}$$

provided that Q is continuous at r [24]. The empirical quantile function thus faithfully estimates the quantile function in the limit. Finally, the quantile function Q determines the distribution over x, that is, for a given quantile function Q there is a unique cumulative distribution function F such that Eq. 2 is satisfied [6].

Let $\pi : \{1, ..., n\} \rightarrow \{1, ..., n\}$ denote a permutation that sorts the sample in ascending order, that is, $x_{\pi(i)} \leq x_{\pi(i+1)}$ for $i \in \{1, ..., n-1\}$. Then

$$\hat{Q}_{\mathcal{X}}(r) = x_{\pi(k)} \tag{8}$$

for the unique $k \in \mathbb{N}$ fulfilling the condition

$$\frac{k-1}{n} < r \leq \frac{k}{n}. \tag{9}$$

That is, the empirical quantile function $\hat{Q}_{\mathcal{X}}(r)$ can be computed by sorting the samples in ascending order, and returning the sample at position $\lceil r \cdot n \rceil$, where for $x \in \mathbb{R}$ we use $\lceil x \rceil$ to denote the smallest integer larger than or equal to x. This is visualized in Fig. 2, where the ordered samples $x_{\pi(1)}, ..., x_{\pi(n)}$ are shown as a bar plot together with $\hat{Q}_{\mathcal{X}}$.

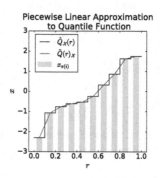

Fig. 2. Empirical quantile function, sorted samples, and piecewise linear approximation to the empirical quantile function. The set of samples is identical to that in Fig. 1.

We will also work with a piecewise linear approximation $\tilde{Q}_{\mathcal{X}}$ to the empirical quantile function $\hat{Q}_{\mathcal{X}}$, as shown in Fig. 2. This function is defined on the interval $[\frac{1}{2n}, 1 - \frac{1}{2n}]$ by $\tilde{Q}_{\mathcal{X}}(\frac{2k-1}{2n}) = \hat{Q}_{\mathcal{X}}(\frac{2k-1}{2n})$ for $k \in \{1, ..., n\}$ and by being piecewise linear in between. The piecewise linear approximation is needed in order to make the quantile layer that we introduce below fully differentiable. Note that $\tilde{Q}_{\mathcal{X}}$ will return the minimum, median, and maximum of the set of samples as special cases. Equation 8 implies $\tilde{Q}_{\mathcal{X}}(\frac{1}{2n}) = \min\{x_1, ..., x_n\}$, $\tilde{Q}_{\mathcal{X}}(0.5) = \text{med}\{x_1, ..., x_n\}$, and $\tilde{Q}_{\mathcal{X}}(1 - \frac{1}{2n}) = \max\{x_1, ..., x_n\}$.

We now define the *quantile layer* as the operation of sampling the piecewise linear approximation $\tilde{Q}_{\mathcal{X}}$ to the empirical quantile function $\hat{Q}_{\mathcal{X}}$ for a set $\mathcal{X}$ of incoming filter activations. The quantile layer takes as input the output of a convolution layer, and outputs a set of features in which the temporal dimension has been aggregated out. The input to the quantile layer is thus a matrix $\mathbf{Z} \in \mathbb{R}^{T \times K}$ of activations, where K is the number of filters and T the temporal dimension in the preceding convolution layer. The output of the quantile layer is a matrix $\mathbf{Y} \in \mathbb{R}^{K \times M}$, where M is a hyperparameter that determines at how many points $\hat{Q}_{\mathcal{X}}$ is sampled. Let $z_{t,k}$ denote the element at row t and column k of $\mathbf{Z}$, and $y_{k,m}$ denote the element at row k and column m of $\mathbf{Y}$. Then the outputs $y_{k,m}$ of the layer are defined by

$$y_{k,m} = \tilde{Q}_{\mathcal{X}_k}\left(\sigma(\alpha_{k,m})\frac{T-1}{T} + \frac{1}{2T}\right) \tag{10}$$

where $\mathcal{X}_k = \{z_{t,k}|1 \leq t \leq T\}$ is the set of activations of filter k across time, $\sigma(\alpha) = \frac{1}{1+\exp(-\alpha)}$ is the sigmoid function, and $\alpha_{k,m}$ are learnable weights. The quantity $\sigma(\alpha_{k,m}) \in (0,1)$ determines the point at which the approximation $\tilde{Q}_{\mathcal{X}_k}$ to the empirical quantile function of the set $\mathcal{X}_k$ is sampled. As $\sigma(\alpha_{k,m})$ is varied from near zero to near one, $y_{k,m}$ will change continuously from the minimum to the maximum of the values in $\mathcal{X}_k$, following the piecewise linear function in Fig. 2. Due to the piecewise linear approximation, gradients of the weights $\alpha_{k,m}$ with respect to the network loss are nonzero and the layer can be trained end-to-end using standard stochastic gradient methods.

The quantile layer is easily implemented in deep learning frameworks by sorting the incoming activations for each filter k, linearly interpolating, and returning the linearly interpolated values at the points prescribed by weights $\alpha_{k,1}, ..., \alpha_{k,M}$. The output of the layer is a discrete approximation to the empirical quantile function of the activations of filter k. The learnable weights determine at which part of the cumulative distribution function the approximation is focused. For example, sampling points can be spaced uniformly across the spectrum of values or concentrate on those values that are near the maximum or minimum.

4   Model Architectures

We treat user identification from gaze movement patterns as a sequence classification problem. The input is a sequence of two-dimensional gaze positions, separately recorded for the left and right eye, and sampled regularly over time. The data we work with additionally contains a scalar measurement of the pupil dilation for the left and the right eye at each point in time. We concatenate the gaze positions and pupil dilations to form a sequence of shape $T \times 6$, where the sequence length T is typically different for each input.

We study 1D-convolutional neural networks to classify gaze movement sequences, using two different architectures. The first architecture stacks 1D-convolution layers to extract local features from the sequence without reducing the temporal dimension by intermediate pooling layers; the temporal dimension is then aggregated out in a statistical aggregation layer before classification is performed. The second architecture reduces the temporal dimension with intermediate pooling layers to capture more large-scale temporal patterns before performing aggregation. Both architectures are 17 layers deep (not including pooling or aggregation layers) and are shown in Table 1. As aggregation layer, we study the quantile layer introduced in Sect. 3, global maximum pooling, global average

Table 1. Network architectures without (left) and with (right) intermediate pooling layers. T denotes the sequence length. All convolution layers use stride one, the pooling layers use stride two. Both architectures use dropout with parameter 0.5 before the fully connected layer. As aggregation layer we study the quantile layer, global maximum or average pooling, and the histogram layers by Wang et al. [30] and Sedighi and Fridrich [27]. Output shape M and parameters vary across aggregation layers.

Architecture without intermediate pooling		Architecture with intermediate pooling		
Layer	Output size	Layer	Output size	Parameters
Input	$T \times 6$	Input	$T \times 6$	0
$[\text{conv } 3 \times 1 - 16] \times 4$	$T \times 16$	$[\text{conv } 3 \times 1 - 16] \times 4$	$T \times 16$	2660
–	–	Pool 2×1	$T/2 \times 16$	0
$[\text{conv } 3 \times 1 - 32] \times 4$	$T \times 32$	$[\text{conv } 3 \times 1 - 32] \times 4$	$T/2 \times 32$	10884
–	–	Pool 2×1	$T/4 \times 32$	0
$[\text{conv } 3 \times 1 - 64] \times 4$	$T \times 64$	$[\text{conv } 3 \times 1 - 64] \times 4$	$T/4 \times 64$	43268
–	–	Pool 2×1	$T/8 \times 64$	0
$[\text{conv } 3 \times 1 - 128] \times 4$	$T \times 128$	$[\text{conv } 3 \times 1 - 128] \times 4$	$T/8 \times 128$	172548
Aggregation	$128 \times M$	Aggregation	$128 \times M$	Variable
Fully connected	210	Fully connected	210	$27090 \cdot M$

pooling, and the histogram layers proposed by Wang et al. [30] and Sedighi and Fridrich [27]. More details about baselines are given in Sect. 5.

All convolution layers are followed by a nonlinear activation function. We use parameterized ReLU activations [8], a generalization of leaky ReLUs, of the form

$$s(y) = \begin{cases} y & \text{if } y > 0 \\ (1 - \beta_j)y & \text{if } y \leq 0. \end{cases} \tag{11}$$

where β_j is a layer-specific parameter and j is the layer index. The parameters β_j are fitted during training and regularized towards zero, such that the slope of the activation below zero does not become too small. The rationale for using this activation is that we want to preserve as much information as possible about the distribution of the responses of the convolution filters, so that this information can later be exploited in the statistical aggregation layer. In contrast, regular ReLU activations discard much information by not distinguishing between any activation values that fall below zero.

As an alternative to the 1D-convolutional architectures shown in Table 1, we also study a recurrent neural network architecture. We choose gated recurrent units (GRU, [3]) as the recurrent unit, because we found architectures based on GRUs to be faster and more robust to train and these architectures have been shown to yield very similar predictive performance [4] as architectures based on LSTM units [10]. We study a sequence classification architecture in which the input layer is followed by two layers of gated recurrent units, and the state vector of the last GRU in the second layer is fed into a dense layer that predicts the class label. The first layer of GRUs contains 64 units and the second layer 128 units. We employ dropout with dropout parameter 0.5 before the dense layer.

5   Empirical Study

In this section, we empirically study how accurately subjects can be distinguished based on observed gaze patterns. We evaluate different neural network architectures and aggregation layers, and compare with existing probabilistic and feature-based models for eye gaze biometrics.

5.1   Experimental Setup

Data. The *Dynamic Images and Eye Movements* (DIEM) project is a large-scale data collection effort in which gaze movements of subjects have been recorded while viewing non-text visual input [21]. The DIEM data set contains gaze movement observations of 223 subjects on 85 short video sequences that contain a variety of visual material, such as recordings of street scenes, documentary videos, movie excerpts, recordings of sport matches, or television advertisements. Subjects in the data set have viewed between 6 and 26 videos. We restrict ourselves to those subjects which have viewed at least 25 videos, which leaves 210 of the 223 subjects in the data. The average length of a video sequence is 95 seconds. The entire data set contains 5381 gaze movement sequences.

Gaze movements have been recorded with an SR Research Eyelink 2000 eye tracker. While the original temporal resolution of the eye tracker is 1000 Hz, in the DIEM data set gaze movements are sampled down to a temporal resolution of 30 Hz [21]. This is a lower resolution than used in most other studies; for example, Abdelwahab et al. [1] use 500 Hz, while studies by Holland and Komogortsev [11, 12] use either 1000 Hz or 75 Hz data. At each of the 30 time points per second, the two-dimensional gaze position and a scalar measurement of the pupil dilation is available for the left and the right eye, which we concatenate to form a six-dimensional input.

Problem Setup. We treat the problem of identifying individuals in the DIEM data set based on their gaze patterns as a 210-class classification problem. A training instance is a sequence of gaze movements (of one individual on one video), annotated with the individual's identity as the class label. We split the entire set of 5381 gaze movement sequences into a training set (2734 sequences), a validation set (537 sequences), and a test set (2110 sequences). The split is constructed by splitting the 84 videos into 50% (42) training videos, 10% (8) validation videos, and 40% (34) test videos, and including the gaze movement observations of all individuals on the training, validation, and test videos in the respective set of sequences. This ensures that predictions are evaluated on novel visual input not seen in the training data. At test time, the task is to infer the unknown identity of an individual after observing gaze patterns of that individual on N video sequences drawn at random from all videos in the test set viewed by that individual, where N is varied from one to five. Applying a learned model to each of the N sequences yields predictive class probabilities $p_{i,j}$ for $1 \leq i \leq N$ and $1 \leq j \leq 210$. The most likely identity is then inferred by

$\arg\max_j \prod_{i=1}^{N} p_{i,j}$ and compared to the true identity. We measure *identification error*, defined as the fraction of experiments in which the inferred identity is not equal to the true identity of the individual. Results are averaged over the 210 individuals and 10 random draws of test videos for each individual.

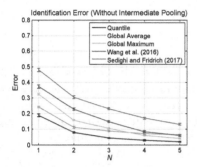
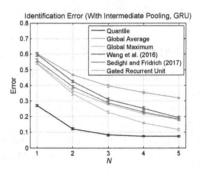

Fig. 3. Identification error for convolutional neural network architectures without intermediate pooling (left), with intermediate pooling (right) and for the recurrent neural network architecture (right) as a function of the number of test videos N on which a user is observed. Error bars indicate the standard error.

Methods Under Study. We study the deep neural network architectures with and without intermediate pooling layers shown in Table 1 in combination with different aggregation layers: the quantile layer as described in Sect. 3 (*Quantile*), global maximum or average pooling (*Global Maximum, Global Average*), and the histogram layers proposed by *Wang et al.* [30] and *Sedighi and Fridrich* [27]. The input to the histogram layers is identical to the input of the quantile layer, namely a matrix $\mathbf{Z} \in \mathbb{R}^{T \times K}$ of activations of the preceding convolution layer. The layers approximate the distribution of values per filter k in $\mathbf{Z}$ by a histogram with M bins, where bin centers and bin widths are learnable parameters. The output is a matrix $\mathbf{Y} \in \mathbb{R}^{K \times M}$; an element $y_{k,m}$ of the output computes the fraction of values of filter k that fall into bin m. The two histogram baselines differ in how they smoothen the sharp edges in traditional histogram functions in order to enable gradient flow: using linear approximations [30] or Gaussian kernels [27]. For the models with quantile and histogram layers, the hyperparameter M is optimized on the validation set on a grid $M \in \{4, 8, 16, 32\}$, yielding $M = 8$ for both histogram-based models and $M = 16$ for the quantile-based model. We use the Adam optimizer [14] with initial learning rate 0.0001 and train all models for 2000 epochs. For histogram-based models, optimization failed with the default initial learning rate of 0.0001. We instead use an initial learning rate of 0.00001, with which optimization succeeded. The batch size is one in all experiments.

We also study the recurrent neural network architecture with two hidden layers of gated recurrent units as discussed in Sect. 4. It is trained with the Adam optimizer for 2000 episodes, using an initial learning rate of 0.001.

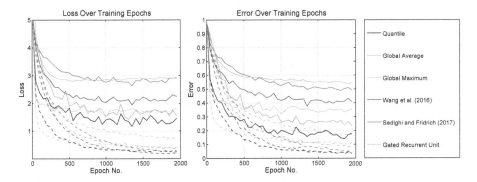

Fig. 4. Identification error (left) and loss (right) for convolutional network architectures without intermediate pooling and recurrent neural network as a function of the epoch number during training. Dashed curves denote training error and loss while solid curves denote test error and loss.

As further baselines, we study the probabilistic approaches by Kinnunen et al. [15], Landwehr et al. [17], and Abdelwahab et al. [1], which respectively employ Gaussian mixture models, parametric models based on the Gamma family, and semiparametric models based on Gaussian processes in order to characterize distributions over gaze patterns. The model of Kinnunen et al. can be directly applied in our domain. We tune the number of histogram bins, window size, and number of mixture components on the validation data. The models of Landwehr et al. [17] and Abdelwahab et al. [1] were designed for gaze movements during reading; they are therefore not directly applicable. We adapt these models of to our non-text domain as follows. Both models characterize individual gaze patterns by separately fitting the distribution of saccade amplitudes and fixation durations for different so-called saccade types: *regression, refixation, next word movement,* and *forward skip*. The saccade types relate the gaze movement to the structure of the text being read. We instead separately fit distributions for saccade types *up, down, left, right*, which indicate the predominant direction of the gaze movement. The DIEM data contains saccade and fixation annotations; we can thus preprocess the data into sequences of saccades and fixations as needed for an empirical comparison with these models. Another recently published probabilistic model is that of Makowski et al. [20]. This model is more difficult to adapt because it is built around lexical features of the text being read; without lexical features it was empirically found to be no more accurate than the model by Abdelwahab et al. [20]. We therefore exclude it from the empirical study.

We finally compare against the feature-based methods of Holland and Komogortsev [12] and Rigas et al. [26]. Both of these methods follow the same general approach, only using different sets of features. We use the variant that employs two-sample Kolmogorov-Smirnov test for the matching module and weighted mean as the fusion method, since results reported in the paper were best for these variants on low-resolution data [12].

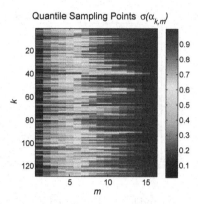

Fig. 5. Learned quantile sampling points $\sigma(\alpha_{k,m})$ as defined by Eq. 10.

5.2   Results

Figure 3 shows error rates for identifying individuals in the DIEM data set for different neural network architectures, including the recurrent neural network, as a function of the number N of test videos on which gaze patterns of the unknown individual are observed. We observe that architectures without intermediate pooling layers have lower error rates. This is in line with the assumption that local, short-term gaze patterns are most informative for identification: the larger receptive fields of neurons in architectures with intermediate pooling do not appear to be advantageous. We will therefore focus on architectures without intermediate pooling in the remaining discussion. Architectures based on gated recurrent units are also focused on fitting relatively long-term temporal patterns in data; the recurrent architecture we study performs slightly better than convolutional architectures with intermediate pooling but worse than convolutional architectures without intermediate pooling. Employing quantile layers for statistical aggregation outperforms global maximum or average pooling, indicating that retaining more information about the distribution of filter activations is informative for identification. Surprisingly, architectures based on the histogram layers proposed by Wang et al. [30] and Sedighi and Fridrich [27] do not consistently improve over the global pooling methods.

Figure 4 shows error rates and losses for architectures without intermediate pooling layers on the training and test data as a function of the epoch number during training. We observe that architectures with quantile and histogram layers both achieve lower training error than architectures with global maximum or average pooling, but only for the quantile-based model this translates into lower error on the test data. Figure 4 thus does not suggest that there are any problems with fitting the histogram-based models using our training protocol; manual inspection of the learned histogram bins also showed reasonable bin centers and widths. Rather, results seem to indicate that characterizing distributions in terms of quantiles – which is closer to standard average or maximum pooling operations – generalizes better than characterizing distributions by histograms.

Figure 5 shows learned values for the quantile sampling points $\sigma(\alpha_{k,m})$ (see Eq. 10). We observe that sampling points adapt to each filter, and outputs $y_{k,m}$ of the quantile layer focus more on values close to the maximum ($\sigma(\alpha_{k,m})$ near one) than the minimum ($\sigma(\alpha_{k,m})$ near zero).

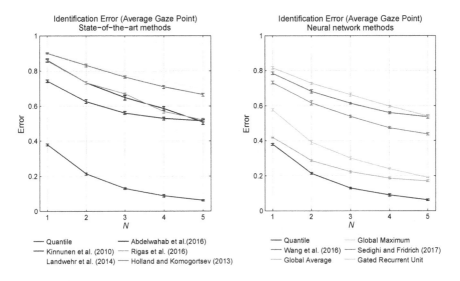

Fig. 6. Identification error as a function of the number of test videos N on which a user is observed, using average gaze point only. Error bars indicate the standard error.

We finally compare against probabilistic and feature-based baselines from the literature, specifically the models of Kinnunen et al. [15], Landwehr et al. [17], Abdelwahab et al. [1], Holland and Komogortsev [12] and Rigas et al. [26]. These models only use the gaze position averaged over the left and right eye, and do not use pupil dilation. We also study our models in this setting, using only the average gaze position as input in the neural networks. Figure 6 shows identification error as a function of the number of test videos for this setting. We observe that identification errors are generally higher than in the setting where separate gaze positions and pupil dilations are available. Moreover, the best neural networks outperform the probabilistic and feature-based models by a large margin. This may partially be explained by the fact that the probabilistic models were originally developed for text reading, and for data with a much higher temporal resolution (500 Hz versus 30 Hz in our study). The quantile-based model again performs best among the neural network architectures studied.

6 Conclusions

We have studied deep neural networks for unobtrusive biometric identification based on gaze patterns observed on non-text visual input. Differences in the distribution of local, short-term gaze patterns are most informative for distinguishing between individuals. To characterize these distributions, we introduced the quantile layer, a learnable statistical aggregation layer that approximates the empirical quantile function of the activations of a preceding stack of 1D-convolution layers. In contrast to existing learnable statistical aggregation layers that approximate the distribution of filter activations by a histogram, the quantile layer naturally generalizes standard global pooling layers. From our empirical study we can conclude that neural networks with quantile layers outperform networks with global average or maximum pooling, as well as networks that use histogram layers. In our domain, deep neural networks also outperform probabilistic and feature-based models from the literature by a wide margin.

Acknowledgments. This work was partially funded by the German Research Foundation under grant LA3270/1-1.

References

1. Abdelwahab, A., Kliegl, R., Landwehr, N.: A semiparametric model for Bayesian reader identification. In: Proceedings of the 2016 Conference on Empirical Methods in Natural Language Processing (EMNLP 2016), Austin, TX (2016)
2. Bednarik, R., Kinnunen, T., Mihaila, A., Fränti, P.: Eye-movements as a biometric. In: Kalviainen, H., Parkkinen, J., Kaarna, A. (eds.) SCIA 2005. LNCS, vol. 3540, pp. 780–789. Springer, Heidelberg (2005). https://doi.org/10.1007/11499145_79
3. Cho, K., et al.: Learning phrase representations using RNN encoder-decoder for statistical machine translation. arXiv:1406.1078 (2014)
4. Chung, J., Gulcehre, C., Cho, K., Bengio, Y.: Empirical evaluation of gated recurrent neural networks on sequence modeling. arXiv:1412.3555 (2014)
5. Couture, H.D., Marron, J.S., Perou, C.M., Troester, M.A., Niethammer, M.: Multiple instance learning for heterogeneous images: training a CNN for histopathology. In: Frangi, A.F., Schnabel, J.A., Davatzikos, C., Alberola-López, C., Fichtinger, G. (eds.) MICCAI 2018. LNCS, vol. 11071, pp. 254–262. Springer, Cham (2018). https://doi.org/10.1007/978-3-030-00934-2_29
6. Dufour, J.M.: Distribution and quantile functions. Technical report, McGill University, Montreal, Canada (1995)
7. George, A., Routray, A.: A score level fusion method for eye movement biometrics. Pattern Recogn. Lett. **82**(2), 207–215 (2016)
8. He, K., Zhang, X., Ren, S., Sun, J.: Delving deep into rectifiers: surpassing human-level performance on ImageNet classification. In: Proceedings of the IEEE International Conference on Computer Vision, pp. 1026–1034 (2015)
9. Henderson, J.M.: Human gaze control during real-world scene perception. Trends Cogn. Sci. **7**(11), 498–504 (2003)
10. Hochreiter, S., Schmidhuber, J.: Long short-term memory. Neural Comput. **9**(8), 1735–1780 (1997)

11. Holland, C., Komogortsev, O.V.: Biometric identification via eye movement scanpaths in reading. In: Proceedings of the 2011 International Joint Conference on Biometrics (2012)
12. Holland, C.D., Komogortsev, O.V.: Complex eye movement pattern biometrics: analyzing fixations and saccades. In: 2013 International Conference on Biometrics (ICB), pp. 1–8. IEEE (2013)
13. Kasprowski, P., Ober, J.: Eye movements in biometrics. In: Maltoni, D., Jain, A.K. (eds.) BioAW 2004. LNCS, vol. 3087, pp. 248–258. Springer, Heidelberg (2004). https://doi.org/10.1007/978-3-540-25976-3_23
14. Kingma, D.P., Ba, J.: Adam: a method for stochastic optimization. arXiv:1412.6980 (2014)
15. Kinnunen, T., Sedlak, F., Bednarik, R.: Towards task-independent person authentication using eye movement signals. In: Proceedings of the 2010 Symposium on Eye-Tracking Research & Applications, pp. 187–190. ACM (2010)
16. Komogortsev, O.V., Jayarathna, S., Aragon, C.R., Mahmoud, M.: Biometric identification via an oculomotor plant mathematical model. In: Proceedings of the 2010 Symposium on Eye-Tracking Research & Applications (2010)
17. Landwehr, N., Arzt, S., Scheffer, T., Kliegl, R.: A model of individual differences in gaze control during reading. In: Proceedings of the 2014 Conference on Empirical Methods on Natural Language Processing (2014)
18. Liang, Z., Tan, F., Chi, Z.: Video-based biometric identification using eye tracking technique. In: 2012 IEEE International Conference on Signal Processing, Communication and Computing (ICSPCC), pp. 728–733. IEEE (2012)
19. Liversedge, S.P., Findlay, J.M.: Saccadic eye movements and cognition. Trends Cogn. Sci. **4**(1), 6–14 (2000)
20. Makowski, S., Jäger, L.A., Abdelwahab, A., Landwehr, N., Scheffer, T.: A discriminative model for identifying readers and assessing text comprehension from eye movements. In: Berlingerio, M., Bonchi, F., Gärtner, T., Hurley, N., Ifrim, G. (eds.) ECML PKDD 2018. LNCS (LNAI), vol. 11051, pp. 209–225. Springer, Cham (2019). https://doi.org/10.1007/978-3-030-10925-7_13
21. Mital, P.K., Smith, T.J., Hill, R.L., Henderson, J.M.: Clustering of gaze during dynamic scene viewing is predicted by motion. Cogn. Comput. **3**(1), 5–24 (2011)
22. Poynter, W., Barber, M., Inman, J., Wiggins, C.: Individuals exhibit idiosyncratic eye-movement behavior profiles across tasks. Vision Res. **89**, 32–38 (2013)
23. Rayner, K., Li, X., Williams, C.C., Cave, K.R., Well, A.D.: Eye movements during information processing tasks: individual differences and cultural effects. Vision Res. **47**(21), 2714–2726 (2007)
24. Resnick, S.I.: Extreme Values, Regular Variation and Point Processes. Springer, New York (2013)
25. Rigas, I., Economou, G., Fotopoulos, S.: Biometric identification based on the eye movements and graph matching techniques. Pattern Recogn. Lett. **33**(6), 786–792 (2012)
26. Rigas, I., Komogortsev, O., Shadmehr, R.: Biometric recognition via eye movements: saccadic vigor and acceleration cues. ACM Trans. Appl. Percept. **13**(2), 1–21 (2016)
27. Sedighi, V., Fridrich, J.: Histogram layer, moving convolutional neural networks towards feature-based steganalysis. Electron. Imaging **2017**(7), 50–55 (2017)
28. Van der Vaart, A.W.: Asymptotic Statistics, vol. 3. Cambridge University Press, Cambridge (2000)
29. Van Den Oord, A., et al.: Wavenet: a generative model for raw audio. arXiv:1609.03499 (2016)

30. Wang, Z., Li, H., Ouyang, W., Wang, X.: Learnable histogram: statistical context features for deep neural networks. In: Leibe, B., Matas, J., Sebe, N., Welling, M. (eds.) ECCV 2016. LNCS, vol. 9905, pp. 246–262. Springer, Cham (2016). https://doi.org/10.1007/978-3-319-46448-0_15
31. Zhang, Y., Juhola, M.: On biometric verification of a user by means of eye movement data mining. In: Proceedings of the 2nd International Conference on Advances in Information Mining and Management (2012)

Multitask Hopfield Networks

Marco Frasca[(✉)] , Giuliano Grossi , and Giorgio Valentini

Dipartimento di Informatica, Università degli Studi di Milano,
Via Celoria 18, 20133 Milan, Italy
{frasca,grossi,valentini}@di.unimi.it

Abstract. Multitask algorithms typically use task similarity information as a bias to speed up and improve the performance of learning
processes. Tasks are learned jointly, sharing information across them, in
order to construct models more accurate than those learned separately
over single tasks. In this contribution, we present the first multitask
model, to our knowledge, based on Hopfield Networks (HNs), named
HoMTask. We show that by appropriately building a unique HN embedding all tasks, a more robust and effective classification model can be
learned. HoMTask is a transductive semi-supervised parametric HN, that
minimizes an energy function extended to all nodes and to all tasks under
study. We provide theoretical evidence that the optimal parameters automatically estimated by HoMTask make coherent the model itself with the
prior knowledge (connection weights and node labels). The convergence
properties of HNs are preserved, and the fixed point reached by the
network dynamics gives rise to the prediction of unlabeled nodes. The
proposed model improves the classification abilities of singletask HNs on
a preliminary benchmark comparison, and achieves competitive performance with state-of-the-art semi-supervised graph-based algorithms.

Keywords: Multitask Hopfield networks · Multitask learning

1 Introduction

Multitask learning is concerned with simultaneously learning multiple prediction tasks that are related to one another. It has been frequently observed in
the recent literature that, when there are relations between the tasks, it can be
advantageous to learn them simultaneously instead of learning each task separately [7,11]. A major challenge in multitask learning is how to selectively screen
the sharing of information so that unrelated tasks do not end up influencing each
other. Sharing information between two unrelated tasks can worsen the performance of both tasks.

Multitasking thus plays an important role in a variety of practical situations,
including: the prediction of user ratings for unseen items based on rating information from related users [32], the simultaneously forecasting of many related
financial indicators [19], the categorization of genes associated with a genetic
disorder by exploiting genes associated with related diseases [15].

© Springer Nature Switzerland AG 2020
U. Brefeld et al. (Eds.): ECML PKDD 2019, LNAI 11907, pp. 349–365, 2020.
https://doi.org/10.1007/978-3-030-46147-8_21

There is a vast literature on multitask learning. The most important lines of work include: regularizers biasing the solution towards functions that lie geometrically close to each other in a RKHS [11,12], or lie in a low dimensional subspace [3,26]; structural risk minimization methods, where multitask relations are established by enforcing predictive functions for the different tasks to belong to the same hypothesis set [2]; spectral [4,10] and cluster-based [23,38] assumptions on the task relatedness; Bayesian approaches where task parameters share a common prior [9,39,42]; methods allowing a small number of outlier tasks that are not related to any other task [8,40]; approaches attempting to learn the full task covariance matrix [20,41]. To our knowledge, no multitask attempts have been proposed for Hopfield networks (HNs) [21], whereas several studies investigated HNs as singletask classifier [17,22,24,27]. Indeed, HNs are efficient local optimizers, using the local minima of the energy function determined by network dynamics as a proxy to node classification.

In this paper we develop *HoMTask*, *Hopfield multitask Network*, an approach to multitask learning based on exploiting a family of parametric HNs. Our approach builds on COSNet [6], a singletask HN proposed to classify instances in a transductive semi-supervised scenario with unbalanced data. A main feature of HoMTask is that the energy function is extended to all tasks to be learned and to all instances (labeled and unlabeled), so as to learn the model parameters and to infer the node labels simultaneously for all tasks. The obtained network can be seen as a collection of singletask HNs, appropriately interconnected by exploiting the task relatedness. In particular, each task is associated with a couple of parameters determining the neuron activation values and thresholds, and we theoretically prove that in the optimal case, the learning procedure adopted is able to learn the parameters so as to move the multitask state of the labeled sub-network to a minimum of the energy. This is an important result, which allows the model to better fit the input data, since the classification of unlabeled nodes is based upon a minimum of the unlabeled subnetwork. Another interesting feature of HoMTask is that the complexity of the learning procedure linearly increases with the number of tasks, thus allowing the model to nicely scale on settings including numerous tasks. Finally, a proof of convergence of the multitask dynamics to a minimum of the energy is also supplied.

Experiments on a real-world classification problem have shown that HoMTask remarkably outperforms singletask HNs, and has competitive performance with state-of-the-art graph-based methods proposed in the same context.

2   Methods

2.1   Problem Definition

The problem input is composed of an undirected weighted graph $G(V, \boldsymbol{W})$, where $V = \{1, 2, \ldots, n\}$ is the set of instances and the non negative symmetric matrix $\boldsymbol{W} = (w_{ij})$ denotes the degree of functional similarity between each pair of nodes i and j. A set of binary learning tasks $C = \{c_k | k = 1, 2, \ldots, m\}$ over G is given, where for every task c_k, V is labelled with $\{+, -\}$. The labeling is known only for the subset $L \subset V$, whereas it is unknown for $U := V \setminus L$. Moreover, the subsets of vertices labelled with $+$ (positive) and $-$ (negative) are denoted by $L_{k,+}$ and $L_{k,-}$, respectively, for each task $c_k \in C$. Without loss of generality, we assume $U = \{1, 2, \cdots, h\}$ and $L = \{h+1, h+2, \cdots, n\}$. As further assumption, task labelings are highly unbalanced, that is $\frac{|L_{k,+}|}{|L_{k,-}|} \ll 1$, for each $k \in \{1, 2, \ldots, m\}$. In the multitask scenario, a $m \times m$ symmetric matrix $\boldsymbol{S} = s_{kr}|_{k,r=1}^{m}$ is also given, where $s_{kr} \in [0, 1]$ is an index of relatedness/similarity between the tasks c_k and c_r, and $s_{kk} = 0$ for each $k \in \{1, 2, \ldots, m\}$, to learn just from the other tasks.

The aim is determining a set of bipartitions $(U_{k,+}, U_{k,-})$ of vertices in U for each task $c_k \in C$ by jointly learning tasks in C, on the basis of the prior information encoded in G and $\boldsymbol{S}$. In the following, the bold font is adopted to denote vectors and matrices, and the calligraphic font to denote multitask Hopfield networks. Moreover, we denote by $\boldsymbol{W}_{LL}$ and $\boldsymbol{W}_{UU}$ the submatrices of $\boldsymbol{W}$ relative to nodes L and U, respectively.

2.2 Previous Singletask Model

In this section we recall the basic model proposed in [6,13] for singletask modeling, named *COSNet*, that has inspired the multitask setting presented here. Essentially, it relies on a parametric family of the Hopfield model [21], where the network parameters are learned to cope with the label imbalance and the network equilibrium point is interpreted to classify the unlabeled nodes. A COSNet network over $G = \langle V, \boldsymbol{W} \rangle$ is a triple $H = \langle \boldsymbol{W}, \lambda, \rho \rangle$, where $\lambda \in \mathbb{R}$ denotes the neuron activation threshold (unique for all neurons), and $\rho \in [0, \frac{\pi}{2})$ is a parameter which determines the two neuron activation (state) values $\{\sin \rho, -\cos \rho\}$. The model parameters are appropriately learned in order to allow the algorithm to counterbalance the large imbalance towards negatives (see [13]). The initial state of a neuron $i \in V$ is set to $x_i(0) = \sin \rho$, if i is positive, $x_i(0) = -\cos \rho$, if i is negative, and $x_i(0) = 0$ when i in unlabeled. The network evolves according to the following asynchronous dynamics:

$$x_i(t) = \begin{cases} \sin \rho & \text{if } \sum_{j=1}^{i-1} w_{ij}x_j(t) + \sum_{k=i+1}^{n} w_{ik}x_k(t-1) - \lambda > 0 \\ -\cos \rho & \text{if } \sum_{j=1}^{i-1} w_{ij}x_j(t) + \sum_{k=i+1}^{n} w_{ik}x_k(t-1) - \lambda \leq 0 \end{cases} \quad (1)$$

where $x_i(t)$ is the state of neuron $i \in V$ at time t. At each time t, the vector $\boldsymbol{x}(t) = (x_1(t), x_2(t), \ldots, x_h(t))$ represents the state of the whole network. The network admits a state function named *energy function*:

$$E(\boldsymbol{x}) = -\frac{1}{2} \sum_{i \neq j} w_{ij}x_i x_j + \lambda \sum_{i=1}^{n} x_i. \quad (2)$$

The convergence properties of the dynamics (1) depend on the weight matrix $\boldsymbol{W}$ and the rule by which the nodes are updated. In particular, if $\boldsymbol{W}$ is symmetric and the dynamic is asynchronous, it has been proved that the network converges to a stable state in polynomial time. As a major result, it has been shown that (2) is a Lyapunov function for the Hopfield dynamical systems with asynchronous dynamics, i.e., for each $t > 0$, $E(\boldsymbol{x}(t+1)) \leq E(\boldsymbol{x}(t))$ and there exists a time $\bar{t}$ such that $E(\boldsymbol{x}(t)) = E(\boldsymbol{x}(\bar{t}))$, for all $t \geq \bar{t}$. Moreover, the reached fixed point $\bar{\boldsymbol{x}} = \boldsymbol{x}(\bar{t})$ is a local minimum of (2). Then, a neuron i in U is classified as positive if $\bar{x}_i = \sin \rho$, as negative otherwise. COSNet has also a dynamics control to avoid trajectories towards trivial equilibrium minima (see [13] for details).

2.3   Multitask Hopfield Networks

A *Hopfield multitask network*, named *HoMTask*, with neurons V is a quadruple $\mathcal{H} = \langle \boldsymbol{W}, \boldsymbol{\gamma}, \boldsymbol{\rho}, \boldsymbol{S} \rangle$, where $\boldsymbol{S}$ is the task similarity matrix, $\boldsymbol{\gamma} = (\gamma_1, \dots, \gamma_m) \in \mathbb{R}^m$, $\boldsymbol{\rho} = (\rho_1, \dots, \rho_m) \in [\frac{\pi}{4}, \frac{\pi}{2})^m$. The couple of parameters (γ_k, ρ_k) is associated with task c_k, for each $k \in \{1, 2, \dots, m\}$: by leveraging the approach adopted in COSNet, for a task c_k, the neuron activation values are $\{\sin \rho_k, -\cos \rho_k\}$, whereas γ_k is the neuron activation threshold (the same for every neuron). Such a formalization allows to keep the absolute activation value in the range $[0, 1]$, and to calibrate it by suitably learning $\rho_k \in [\frac{\pi}{4}, \frac{\pi}{2})$. For instance, in presence of a large majority of negative neurons, ρ_k close to $\frac{\pi}{2}$ would prevent positive neurons to be overwhelmed during the net dynamics.

The state of the network is the $n \times m$ matrix $\boldsymbol{X} = (\boldsymbol{x}^{(1)}, \boldsymbol{x}^{(2)}, \dots, \boldsymbol{x}^{(m)})$, where $\boldsymbol{x}^{(k)} = (x_{1k}, x_{2k}, \dots, x_{nk}) \in \{\sin \rho_k, -\cos \rho_k\}^n$ is the state vector corresponding to task c_k. When simultaneously learning related tasks c_k and c_r, an usual approach consists in expecting that the higher the relatedness s_{rk}, the closer the corresponding states. In our setting, this can be achieved by minimizing

$$\|\boldsymbol{x}^{(k)} - \boldsymbol{x}^{(r)}\|^2,$$

for any couple of tasks $c_k, c_r \in C$, with $k \neq r$. To this end, we incorporate a term proportional to $\sum_k \sum_r s_{kr} \|\boldsymbol{x}^{(k)} - \boldsymbol{x}^{(r)}\|^2$ into the energy of $\mathcal{H}$, thus obtaining:

$$E_{\mathcal{H}}(\boldsymbol{X}) = \sum_{k=1}^{m} \left(E(\boldsymbol{x}^{(k)}) + \frac{\alpha}{4} \sum_{\substack{r=1 \\ r \neq k}}^{m} s_{kr} \, \|\boldsymbol{x}^{(k)} - \boldsymbol{x}^{(r)}\|^2 \right), \qquad (3)$$

where $E(\boldsymbol{x}^{(k)}) = -\frac{1}{2}\boldsymbol{x}^{(k)T}\boldsymbol{W}\boldsymbol{x}^{(k)} + \boldsymbol{x}^{(k)T}\gamma_k e_n$, e_n is the n-dimensional vector made by all ones, and α is a real hyper-parameter regulating the multitask contribution. Without the second additive term in brackets, energy (3) would be the summation of the energy functions of m independent singletask Hopfield networks, as recalled in the previous section.

By using the equality $\|\boldsymbol{x}^{(k)} - \boldsymbol{x}^{(r)}\|^2 = \|\boldsymbol{x}^{(k)}\|^2 + \|\boldsymbol{x}^{(r)}\|^2 - 2\boldsymbol{x}^{(k)} \cdot \boldsymbol{x}^{(r)}$, where $\cdot$ denotes the inner product, and giving that

$$\sum_{k=1}^{m} \sum_{\substack{r=1 \\ r \neq k}}^{m} s_{kr} \left(\|\boldsymbol{x}^{(k)}\|^2 + \|\boldsymbol{x}^{(r)}\|^2 \right) = 2 \left(\sum_{k=1}^{m} S_k \|\boldsymbol{x}^{(k)}\|^2 \right),$$

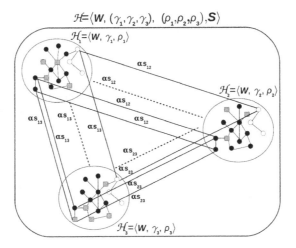

Fig. 1. Topology of $\mathcal{H}$ in the case $m = 3$. Black circles, gray squares and white circles represent elements of L_-, L_+ and U respectively. The local topology is the same across sub-networks $\mathcal{H}_1$, $\mathcal{H}_2$ and $\mathcal{H}_3$, but the labeling varies with the task.

with $S_k = \sum_{r=1}^{m} s_{kr}$, the energy (3) can be rewritten as:

$$E_{\mathcal{H}}(\boldsymbol{X}) = \sum_{k=1}^{m} \left(E\big(\boldsymbol{x}^{(k)}\big) + \frac{\alpha}{2}\Big(S_k \sum_{i=1}^{n} x_{ik}^2 - \sum_{\substack{r=1 \\ r \neq k}}^{m} s_{kr} \sum_{i=1}^{n} x_{ik}x_{ir}\Big) \right). \tag{4}$$

Informally, $\mathcal{H}$ can be thought as m interconnected singletask parametric Hopfield networks $H_1 = \langle \boldsymbol{W}, \boldsymbol{\gamma}_1, \boldsymbol{\rho}_1\rangle, \ldots, H_m = \langle \boldsymbol{W}, \boldsymbol{\gamma}_m, \boldsymbol{\rho}_m\rangle$ on V, having all the same topology given by $\boldsymbol{W}$. In addition, the multitask energy term introduces self loops for all neurons, and a novel connection for each neuron $i \in V$ with i itself in the network H_r, $r \in C \setminus \{c_k\}$, whose weight is αs_{kr} (see Fig. 1). It is worth nothing that usually in Hopfield networks there are no self-loops; nevertheless, we show that it does not affect the convergence properties of the overall network.

Update Rule and Dynamics Convergence. Starting from an initial state $\boldsymbol{X}(0)$ and adopting the asynchronous dynamic, in nm steps all neurons are updated in random order according to the following update rule:

$$x_{ik}(t+1) = \begin{cases} \sin \rho_k, & \text{if } \phi_{ik}(t) > 0 \\ -\cos \rho_k, & \text{if } \phi_{ik}(t) \leq 0 \end{cases} \tag{5}$$

where $x_{ik}(t+1)$ is the state of neuron $i \in X$ in task c_k (ik-th) at time $t+1$, and

$$\phi_{ik}(t) := A_{ik}(t) - \theta_{ik} + \alpha B_{ik}(t) \tag{6}$$

is the input of the ik-th neuron at time t, whose terms are $A_{ik}(t) = \sum_{j=1}^{n} w_{ij}x_{jk}(t)$,

$\theta_{ik} = \gamma_k + \frac{\alpha S_k}{2}\left(\sin\rho_k - \cos\rho_k\right)$, and $B_{ik}(t) = \sum_{\substack{r=1 \\ r\neq k}}^{m} s_{kr}x_{ir}(t)$. A_{ik} represents the

singletask input (Eq. (1)), $B_{ik}(t)$ is the multitask contribution, and θ_{ik} is the activation threshold for neuron ik, including also the 'singletask' threshold. The form of θ_{ik} derives from the following theorem, stating a HoMTask Hopfield network preserves the convergence properties of a Hopfield network.

Theorem 1. *A HoMTask Hopfield network $\mathcal{H} = \langle W, \gamma, \rho, S\rangle$ with n neurons and the asynchronous dynamics (5), which starts from any given network state, eventually reaches a stable state at a local minimum of the energy function (4).*

Proof. Let $E_{ik}(t)$ be the energy contribution to (4) of the ik-th neuron at time t, with

$$E_{ik}(t) = -\frac{1}{2}x_{ik}(t)\sum_{j=1}^{h}(w_{ij} + w_{ji})x_{jk}(t) + \gamma_k x_{ik}(t) + \frac{\alpha S_k}{2}x_{ik}^2(t)$$
$$- \frac{\alpha}{2}x_{ik}(t)\sum_{\substack{r=1 \\ r\neq k}}^{m}(s_{kr} + s_{rk})x_{ir}(t).$$

Let $\Delta_{ik}E(t+1) = E_{ik}(t+1) - E_{ik}(t)$ be the energy variation after updating the state x_{ik} at time $t+1$ according to (5). Due to the symmetry of W and S, it follows

$$\Delta_{ik}E(t+1) = -\left(x_{ik}(t+1) - x_{ik}(t)\right)$$
$$\left(A_{ik}(t) - \gamma_k - \frac{\alpha S_k}{2}\left(x_{ik}(t+1) + x_{ik}(t)\right) + \alpha B_{ik}(t)\right). \quad (7)$$

Since (4) is lower bounded, to complete to proof we need to prove that after updating x_{ik} at time $t+1$ according to (5), it holds $\Delta_{ik}E(t+1) \leq 0$. From (7), when $x_{ik}(t+1) = x_{ik}(t)$ (no neuron state change) it follows $\Delta_{ik}E(t+1) = 0$. Accordingly, we need to investigate the remaining two cases: (a) $x_{ik}(t) = \sin\rho_k$ and $x_{ik}(t+1) = -\cos\rho_k$; (b) $x_{ik}(t) = -\cos\rho_k$ and $x_{ik}(t+1) = \sin\rho_k$. In both cases it holds (by definition of θ_{ik}) $\gamma_k + \frac{\alpha S_k}{2}\left(x_{ik}(t+1) + x_{ik}(t)\right) = \theta_{ik}$.

(a) $(x_{ik}(t+1) - x_{ik}(t)) = (-\cos\rho_k - \sin\rho_k) < 0$, and, according to (5), $A_{ik}(t) - \theta_{ik} + \alpha B_{ik}(t) \leq 0$. It follows $\Delta_{ik}E(t+1) \leq 0$.
(b) $(x_{ik}(t+1) - x_{ik}(t)) = (\sin\rho_k + \cos\rho_k) > 0$, and $A_{ik}(t) - \theta_{ik} + \alpha B_{ik}(t) > 0$. Thus $\Delta_{ik}E(t+1) < 0$.

Every neuron update thereby does not increase the network energy, and, since the energy is lower bounded, there will be a time $t' > 0$ from which the update of any neuron will not change the current state, which is the definition of equilibrium state of the network, and which makes $X(t')$ a local minimum of (4). $\qquad\square$

Learning the Model Parameters. Considered the subnetwork $\mathcal{H}_\mathcal{L} = \langle W_{\mathrm{LL}}, \gamma, \rho, S \rangle$ restricted to labeled nodes L, its energy is:

$$E_{\mathcal{H}_\mathcal{L}}(L) = \sum_{k=1}^{m} \left(E_L(l^{(k)}) + \frac{\alpha}{2} \left(S_k \sum_{i \in L} l_{ik}^2 - \sum_{\substack{r=1 \\ r \neq k}}^{m} s_{kr} \sum_{i \in L} l_{ik} l_{ir} \right) \right), \quad (8)$$

where $L = (l^{(1)}, l^{(2)}, \ldots, l^{(m)})$ with components $l^{(k)} = (l_{1k}, l_{2k}, \ldots, l_{(n-h)k})$ belonging to the set $\{\sin \rho_k, -\cos \rho_k\}^{(n-h)}$, and $E_L(l^{(k)}) = -\frac{1}{2} l^{(k)^T} W_{\mathrm{LL}} l^{(k)} + l^{(k)} \cdot \gamma_k e_{(n-h)}$.

The given bipartition $(L_{k,+}, L_{k,-})$ for each task c_k naturally induces the labeling $\bar{l}^{(k)} = \{\bar{l}_{1k}, \bar{l}_{2k}, \ldots, \bar{l}_{(n-h)k}\}$, defined as it follows:

$$\bar{l}_{ik} = \begin{cases} \sin \rho_k, & \text{if } i \in L_{k,+} \\ -\cos \rho_k, & \text{if } i \in L_{k,-} \end{cases},$$

and constituting the known 'multitask' state $\bar{L} = (\bar{l}^{(1)}, \bar{l}^{(2)}, \ldots, \bar{l}^{(m)})$.

Given $\bar{L}$ as known components of a final state $\bar{X}$ of the multitask network $\mathcal{H} = \langle W, \gamma, \rho, S \rangle$, the purpose of the learning step is to compute the pair $(\hat{\gamma}, \hat{\rho})$ which makes $\bar{X}$ an energy global minimizer of (3), the energy function associated with $\mathcal{H}$. Since our aim is also keeping the model scalable on large sized data, and finding the global minimum of the energy requires time/memory intensive procedures, we employ a learning procedure leading $\bar{L}$ towards an fixed point of $\mathcal{H}_L$, being in general a local minimum of (8). We provide the details of the learning procedure in the following, showing that such an approach also helps to handle the label imbalance at each task.

Maximizing a Cost-Sensitive Criterion. When the parameters γ, ρ are fixed, each neuron ik has input

$$\phi_{ik}^L(\gamma, \rho) = \sum_{j \in L} w_{ij} \left(\sin \rho_k \chi_{jk} - \cos \rho_k (1 - \chi_{jk}) \right) - \theta_{ik}$$

$$+ \alpha \sum_{\substack{r=1 \\ r \neq k}} s_{kr} \left(\sin \rho_k \chi_{ir} - \cos \rho_k (1 - \chi_{ir}) \right),$$

where, for each $k \in \{1, \ldots, m\}$ and $j \in L$, $\chi_{jk} = 1$ if $j \in L_{k,+}$, 0 otherwise. ϕ_{ik}^L corresponds to ϕ_{ik} of Eq. (6) restricted to L; to simplify the notation, in the following ϕ_{ik}^L is thereby denoted by ϕ_{ik}. Since the subnetwork is labeled, it is possible to define the set of *true positive* $tp_k(\gamma, \rho) = \{i \in L_{k,+} | \phi_{ik}(\gamma, \rho) > 0\}$, *false negative* $fn_k(\gamma, \rho) = \{i \in L_{k,+} | \phi_{ik}(\gamma, \rho) \leq 0\}$, and *false positive* $fp_k(\gamma, \rho) = \{i \in L_{k,-} | \phi_{ik}(\gamma, \rho) > 0\}$, for every task c_k. Following the approach proposed in [16], a set of membership functions can be defined, extending the crisp memberships introduced above:

$$
\begin{aligned}
\mathrm{TP}(i,k,\boldsymbol{\gamma},\boldsymbol{\rho}) &= f(\tau\phi_{ik}(\boldsymbol{\gamma},\boldsymbol{\rho})), & i \in L_{k,+} \\
\mathrm{FN}(i,k,\boldsymbol{\gamma},\boldsymbol{\rho}) &= 1 - f(\tau\phi_{ik}(\boldsymbol{\gamma},\boldsymbol{\rho})), & i \in L_{k,+} \\
\mathrm{FP}(i,k,\boldsymbol{\gamma},\boldsymbol{\rho}) &= f(\tau\phi_{ik}(\boldsymbol{\gamma},\boldsymbol{\rho})), & i \in L_{k,-}
\end{aligned}
\tag{9}
$$

where $f : \mathbb{R} \to [0,1]$ is a suitable monotonically increasing membership function. For instance $f_1(x) = 1/(1+e^{-x})$ or $f_2(x) = \frac{1}{2}(\frac{2}{\pi}\mathrm{arctg}(x) + 1)$. $\tau > 0$ is a real parameter. If f is the Heaviside step function, we obtain the crisp memberships. For example, when $f = f_1$ or $f = f_2$, if $i \in L_{k,+}$ and $\tau\phi_{ik}(\boldsymbol{\gamma},\boldsymbol{\rho}) = 0$, if follows $\mathrm{TP}(i,k,\boldsymbol{\gamma},\boldsymbol{\rho}) = \mathrm{FN}(i,k,\boldsymbol{\gamma},\boldsymbol{\rho}) = 0.5$; if $i \in L_{k,+}$ and $\tau\phi_{ik}(\boldsymbol{\gamma},\boldsymbol{\rho}) \to \infty$, it follows $\mathrm{TP}(i,k,\boldsymbol{\gamma},\boldsymbol{\rho}) = 1$ and $\mathrm{FN}(i,k,\boldsymbol{\gamma},\boldsymbol{\rho}) = 0$. The intermediate cases lead to $0 < \mathrm{TP}(i,k,\boldsymbol{\gamma},\boldsymbol{\rho}), \mathrm{FN}(i,k,\boldsymbol{\gamma},\boldsymbol{\rho}) < 1$.

Such a generalization, in a different setting (singletask, multi-category) increased both the learning capability of the model and its classification performance [16]. By means of the membership functions (9), we can define the objective F:

$$
F(\boldsymbol{\gamma},\boldsymbol{\rho}) = \sigma\big(F_1(\boldsymbol{\gamma},\boldsymbol{\rho}), F_2(\boldsymbol{\gamma},\boldsymbol{\rho}), \ldots, F_m(\boldsymbol{\gamma},\boldsymbol{\rho})\big),
\tag{10}
$$

where $F_k(\boldsymbol{\gamma},\boldsymbol{\rho}) = \dfrac{2\sum\limits_{i \in L_{k,+}} \mathrm{TP}(i,k,\boldsymbol{\gamma},\boldsymbol{\rho})}{2\sum\limits_{i \in L_{k,+}} \mathrm{TP}(i,k,\boldsymbol{\gamma},\boldsymbol{\rho}) + \sum\limits_{i \in L_{k,-}} \mathrm{FP}(i,k,\boldsymbol{\gamma},\boldsymbol{\rho}) + \sum\limits_{i \in L_{k,+}} \mathrm{FN}(i,k,\boldsymbol{\gamma},\boldsymbol{\rho})}$ and σ is an appropriately chosen function, e.g. the mean, the minimum, or the harmonic mean function. The property σ must satisfy is that

$$
F(\boldsymbol{\gamma},\boldsymbol{\rho}) = 1 \implies F_1(\boldsymbol{\gamma},\boldsymbol{\rho}) = F_2(\boldsymbol{\gamma},\boldsymbol{\rho}) = \ldots = F_m(\boldsymbol{\gamma},\boldsymbol{\rho}) = 1.
$$

By definition, F_k (a generalization of the F-measure) is penalized more by the misclassification of a positive instance than by the misclassification of a negative one. By maximizing $F(\boldsymbol{\gamma},\boldsymbol{\rho})$ we can thereby cope with the label imbalance. To this end, the learning criterion for the model parameters adopted here is $(\hat{\boldsymbol{\gamma}}, \hat{\boldsymbol{\rho}}) = \arg\max\limits_{\boldsymbol{\gamma},\boldsymbol{\rho}} F(\boldsymbol{\gamma},\boldsymbol{\rho})$, which also leads to the following important result.

Theorem 2. *If $F(\boldsymbol{\gamma},\boldsymbol{\rho}) = 1$, then $\bar{L}$ is an equilibrium state of the sub-network $\mathcal{H}_{\mathcal{L}}\langle W_{LL}, \boldsymbol{\gamma}, \boldsymbol{\rho}, S\rangle$.*

Learning Procedure. Denoted by $\boldsymbol{\delta} = (\boldsymbol{\gamma}, \boldsymbol{\rho})$ the vector of model parameters, this procedure learns the values $\hat{\boldsymbol{\delta}}$ that maximize Eq. (10), that is $\hat{\boldsymbol{\delta}} = \arg\max\limits_{\boldsymbol{\delta}} F(\boldsymbol{\delta})$. Following the approach in [16], we adopt the *simplest search method* [28], which employs an iterative and incremental procedure estimating in turn a single parameter at a time, by fixing the other ones, until a suitable criterion is met (e.g. convergence, or number of iterations). Thus, the complexity of the learning procedure just linearly increases with the number of tasks. In particular, fixed an assignment of parameters $(\delta_1, \ldots, \delta_{i-1}, \delta_{i+1}, \ldots, \delta_{2m})$, $\hat{\delta}_i$ is estimated through $\bar{\delta}_i = \arg\max_{\delta_i} F(\boldsymbol{\delta})$, $i \in \{1, \ldots, 2m\}$. The learning procedure is sketched below:

1. Randomly permute the vector $\boldsymbol{\delta}$, and randomly initialize $\boldsymbol{\delta}$;

2. Determine an estimate $\bar{\delta}_i$ of $\hat{\delta}_i$ with a standard line search procedure for optimizing continuous functions of one variable, and fix $\delta_i = \bar{\delta}_i$;
3. Iterate Step 2 for each $i \in \{1, 2, \ldots, 2m\}$;
4. Repeat Step 3 till a stopping criterion is satisfied.

As stopping criterion we used a combination of the maximum number of iterations and of the maximum norm of the difference of two subsequent estimates $\bar{\delta}$ (falling below a given threshold). As initial test, at Step 2 we simply adopted a grid search optimization algorithm, where a set of trials is formed for each parameter, and all possible parameter combinations are assembled and tested.

Label Inference. Once the parameters $\hat{\gamma}, \hat{\rho}$ have been estimated, we consider the subnetwork $\mathcal{H}_{\mathcal{U}} = \langle W_{UU}, \hat{\gamma}, \hat{\rho}, S \rangle$ restricted to the unlabeled nodes U, whose energy is

$$E_{\mathcal{H}_{\mathcal{U}}}(\boldsymbol{U}) = \sum_{k=1}^{m} \left(E_U\left(\boldsymbol{u}^{(k)}\right) + \frac{\alpha}{2}\left(S_k \sum_{i=1}^{h} u_{ik}^2 - \sum_{\substack{r=1 \\ r \neq k}}^{m} s_{kr} \sum_{i=1}^{h} u_{ik}u_{ir}\right), \right) \quad (11)$$

with $\boldsymbol{U} = (\boldsymbol{u}^{(1)}, \boldsymbol{u}^{(2)}, \ldots, \boldsymbol{u}^{(m)})$ state of $\mathcal{H}_{\mathcal{U}}$, $\boldsymbol{u}^{(k)} = (u_{1k}, u_{2k}, \ldots, u_{hk}) = (x_{1k}, x_{2k}, \ldots, x_{hk}) \in \{\sin \hat{\rho}_k, -\cos \hat{\rho}_k\}^h$, $E_U\left(\boldsymbol{u}^{(k)}\right) = -\frac{1}{2}\boldsymbol{u}^{(k)^T} \boldsymbol{W}_{UU} \boldsymbol{u}^{(k)} + \boldsymbol{u}^{(k)^T}\overline{\boldsymbol{\theta}}_k$, and $\overline{\boldsymbol{\theta}}_k = \hat{\gamma}_k \boldsymbol{e}_h - W_{UL}\bar{\boldsymbol{l}}^{(k)}$ is the vector of activation thresholds for task c_k, including the contribution of labeled nodes (which are clamped). In the case the learned parameters make $\bar{\boldsymbol{L}}$ a part of global minimum of $\mathcal{H}$, by determining the global minimum of $\mathcal{H}_{\mathcal{U}}$, it is possible to determine the global minimum of $\mathcal{H}$ (as stated by the following theorem), and consequently the problem solution.

Theorem 3. *Given a multitask Hopfield network $\mathcal{H} = \langle W, \boldsymbol{\gamma}, \boldsymbol{\rho}, S \rangle$ on neurons V, bipartitioned into the sets L and U, if $\boldsymbol{L}$ is a part of a global minimum of the energy of $\mathcal{H}$, and $\boldsymbol{U}$ is a global minimum of the energy of $\mathcal{H}_U = \langle W_{UU}, \boldsymbol{\gamma}, \boldsymbol{\rho}, S \rangle$, then $(\boldsymbol{L}, \boldsymbol{U})$ is a global minimum of the energy of $\mathcal{H}$.*

On the other side, computing the energy global minimum of $\mathcal{H}_U$ would require time intensive algorithms; to preserve the model efficiency and scalability, we run the dynamics of $\mathcal{H}_U$ till an equilibrium state is reached, which, in general, is an energy local minimum. Given an initial state $\boldsymbol{U}(0)$, at each time t one neuron is updated, and in nm consecutive steps all neurons are updated asynchronously and in a randomly chosen order according to the following update rule:

$$u_{ik}(t+1) = \begin{cases} \sin \hat{\rho}, & \text{if } \phi_{ik}^U(t) > 0 \\ -\cos \hat{\rho}, & \text{if } \phi_{ik}^U(t) \leq 0 \end{cases}, \quad (12)$$

where $u_{ik}(t+1)$ is the state of neuron ik at time $t+1$, and $\phi_{ik}^U(t)$ is the restriction of $\phi_{ik}(t)$ to U. According to Theorem 1, the dynamics (12) converges to an equilibrium state $\bar{\boldsymbol{U}}$ of $\mathcal{H}_U$, and the predicted bipartition $(U_{k,+}, U_{k,-})$ for task k is: $U_{k,+} := \{i \in U | \bar{u}_{ik} = \sin \hat{\rho}\}$ and $U_{k,-} := \{i \in U | \bar{u}_{ik} = -\cos \hat{\rho}\}$.

Dynamics Regularization. As shown by [13], the network dynamics might get stuck in trivial equilibrium states when input labeling are highly unbalanced– e.g. states made up by almost all negative neurons. To prevent this behaviour, they applied a dynamics regularization, with the aim to control the number of positive neurons in the current state. By extending that approach, and denoted by $p_{k,+} = \frac{|L_{k,+}|}{|L|}$ the proportion of positives in the training set for task c_k, the following regularization term is added to the energy function $E_{\mathcal{H}_U}(U)$

$$\eta_k \left(\sum_{i=1}^{h} (a_k u_{ik} + b_k) - h p_{k,+} \right)^2 , \tag{13}$$

where $a_k = \frac{1}{\sin \hat{\rho}_k + \cos \hat{\rho}_k}$, $b_k = \frac{\cos \hat{\rho}_k}{\sin \hat{\rho}_k + \cos \hat{\rho}_k}$, and η_k is a real regularization parameter. Since a_k and b_k are such that $(a_k u_{ik} + b_k) = 1$ when $u_{ik} = \sin \hat{\rho}_k$, 0 otherwise, the $\sum_{i=1}^{h}(a_k u_i + b_k)$ is the number of positive neurons in $u^{(k)}$. The term (13) is thereby minimized when the number of positive neurons in $u^{(k)}$ is $h p_{k,+}$. This choice is motivated by the fact that

$$h p_{k,+} = \arg\max_q \quad Prob\Big\{ |U_{k,+}| = q \ \Big| \ L \text{ contains } |L_{k,+}| \text{ positives}\Big\},$$

when U and L are randomly drawn from V—see [13]. By simplifying Eq. (13), up to a constant terms, we obtain the quadratic term:

$$\eta_k a_k \left(a_k \sum_{i=1}^{h} \sum_{\substack{j=1 \\ j \neq i}}^{h} u_{ik} u_{jk} + \big(2b_k(h-1) + 1 - 2p_{k,+}\big) \sum_{i=1}^{h} u_{ik} \right),$$

which can be included into $E_U(u^{(k)}) = -\frac{1}{2} \sum_{i=1}^{h} \sum_{\substack{j=1 \\ j \neq i}}^{h} w_{ij}^{(k)} u_{ik} u_{jk} + \sum_{i=1}^{h} u_{ik} \tilde{\theta}_{ik}$, where $\tilde{\theta}_{ik} = \bar{\theta}_{ik} + \eta_k a_k \left[2b_k(h-1) + (1 - 2p_{k,+}h)\right]$ and $w_{ij}^{(k)} = (w_{ij} - 2\eta_k a_k^2)$. By adding a regularization term for each task c_k, the following energy is derived:

$$E_{\mathcal{H}_U}(U) = \sum_{k=1}^{m} \left(-\frac{1}{2} u^{(k)^T} W_{UU}^{(k)} u^{(k)} + u^{(k)^T} \tilde{\theta}_k \right.$$
$$\left. + \frac{\alpha}{2} \left(S_k \sum_{i=1}^{h} u_{ik}^2 - \sum_{\substack{r=1 \\ r \neq k}}^{m} s_{kr} \sum_{i=1}^{h} u_{ik} u_{ir} \right) \right)$$

Informally, this regularization leads to a different network topology for each task, in addition to a modification of the neuron activation thresholds. Nevertheless, since the connection weights are modified by a constant value, from an implementation standpoint this regularization just need to memorize m different constant values, thus not increasing the space complexity of the model. As preliminary approach, and to have a fair comparison, the parameters η_k have been set as for the singletask case [13], that is $\eta_k = \beta \left| \tan \left((\hat{\rho}_k - \frac{\pi}{4}) * 2 \right) \right|$, where β is a non negative real constant. Another advantage of this choice is that we have to learn just one parameter β, instead of m dedicated parameters.

2.4   Model Complexity

The time complexity of HoMTask depends in turn on the computational complexity of the learning procedure and the network dynamics. The learning procedure updates at each iteration $2m$ parameters, and each update requires computing Eq. 10 for each of the z possible values of the grid search. Since the labeling is fixed, the weighted sum of positive and negative neighbors can be computed offline, thus the update of ϕ_{ik}^L can be performed in constant time, allowing computing Eq. 10 in $\mathcal{O}(|L|)$ time. The time complexity of the learning procedure is thereby $\mathcal{O}(mz|L|I)$, where I is the number of iterations to converge (Step 4 of learning procedure). The complexity of the network dynamics depends on the number of iterations needed to converge, and each iteration takes time $\mathcal{O}(m|\boldsymbol{W}_{UU}|)$, where where $|\boldsymbol{T}|$ is the number of non-null entries in the matrix $\boldsymbol{T}$. We empirically observed that the network in average converges in few iterations (less than 10), confirming the notes in [13, 27]. Thus, the overall time complexity is $\mathcal{O}(mz|L|I + m|\boldsymbol{W}_{UU}|)$, which is $\mathcal{O}(mz|L|I + m|U|)$ when the connection matrix is sparse, that is when $|\boldsymbol{W}_{UU}| = \mathcal{O}(|U|)$.

Finally, the space complexity is $\mathcal{O}(nm + n^2)$, deriving from the storage of matrices $\boldsymbol{X}$ and $\boldsymbol{W}$, which becomes $\mathcal{O}(nm)$ when $\boldsymbol{W}$ is sparse.

3   Preliminary Results and Discussion

In this section we evaluate our algorithm on the prediction of the bio-molecular functions of proteins, a binary classification problem aiming at associating sequenced proteins with their biological functions. Next we describe the experimental setting, analyze the impact on performance of parameter configurations, and we compare HoMTask against other state-of-the-art graph-based methods.

3.1   Benchmark Data

In our experiments we considered the Gene Ontology [5] terms, i.e. the reference functional classes in this context, and their annotations to the *Saccaromyces cerevisiae* (yeast) proteins, one of the most studied model organisms. The connection matrix $\boldsymbol{W}$ has been retrieved from the STRING database, version 10.5 [35], and contains 6391 yeast proteins. As common in this context, the GO terms with less than 10 and more than 100 yeast protein annotations (positives) have been discarded, in order to have a minimum of information and to avoid too generic terms—GO is a DAG, where annotations for a term are transferred to all its ancestors. We considered the UniProt GOA (release 87, 12 March 2018) experimentally validated annotations from all GO branches, Cellular Component (CC), Molecular Function (MF) and Biological Process (BP), for a total of 162, 227, and 660 CC, MF, BP GO terms, respectively.

3.2   Evaluation Setting

To evaluate the generalization capabilities of our algorithm, we used a 3-fold cross validation (CV), and measured the performance in terms of Area Under the ROC curve (AUC) and Area Under the Precision-Recall curve (AUPR). The AUPR has been adopted in the recent CAFA2 international challenge for the critical assessment of protein functions [25], since in this imbalanced setting AUPR is more informative than AUC [33].

3.3   Model Configuration

HoMTask has three hyper-parameters, τ, β and α, and two functions to be chosen: f in Eq. (9), and σ in Eq. (10). τ, β and α were learned through inner 3-fold CV, considering also the cases α and β in turn or together clamped to $= 0$, to evaluate their individual impact on the performance. A different discussion can be made for the τ parameter, since in our experimentations best performance correspond to large values of τ (e.g. $\tau > 500$), thus making the model less sensitive to this choice (the function f becomes a Heaviside function). This behaviour apparently conflicts with results reported in [16], where typically $0.5 < \tau < 2$ performed best. However, in that work the authors focused on a substantially different learning task, i.e. a singletask Hopfield model, where nodes were divided into categories, and the model parameters were not related to different tasks, but to different node categories. We still include τ in the formalization proposed in Sect. 2.3 because it permits also future analytic studies about the derivatives of σ, to determine close formulations for the optimal parameters. Further, We set $f(x) = \frac{1}{2}\left(\frac{2}{\pi}\mathrm{arctg}(x) + 1\right)$, since this choice in a multi-category context leaded to excellent results [16], even if different choices are possible (Sect. 2.3).

On the other side, we tested two choices for σ: the harmonic mean (σ_1) and mean functions (σ_2). Furthermore, another central factor of our model is the computation of the task similarity matrix S, which can be computed by using several metrics (see for instance [15]), and how to group the tasks that should be learned together. We employed in this work the Jaccard similarity measure, since it performed nicely in hierarchical contexts [14,15,37], defined as follows:

$$s_{kr} = \begin{cases} \dfrac{\left|L_{k,+} \wedge L_{r,+}\right|}{\left|L_{k,+} \vee L_{r,+}\right|} & \text{if } L_{k,+} \vee L_{r,+} \neq \emptyset \\ 0 & \text{otherwise.} \end{cases}$$

Thus, s_{kr} is the ratio between the number of instances that are positive for both tasks and the number of instances that are positive for at least one task. The higher the number of shared instances, the higher the similarity (up to 1); conversely, if two tasks do not share items, their similarity is zero. Due to the numerous experiments to be carried out, just for this analysis the focus is only on CC terms, which are less numerous than those in the MF and BP branches, while showing very similar trends, as shown in the benchmark comparison described in next section. Finally, we grouped tasks by GO branch, and by

GO branch and number of positives: in the first case (*Branch*), all tasks within the CC branch are learned simultaneously; in the latter one (*Card*), CC tasks having 10–20 (76 tasks), 21–50 (60), or 51–100 (26) positives have been grouped together. Both approaches are quite usual when predicting GO terms [14,31].

Table 1. Performance averaged across CC terms for different configuration of the model.

Configuration	AUC	AUPR
Branch, σ_1	0.961	0.439
Card, σ_1	0.959	0.439
Card, σ_1, $\alpha = 0$	0.959	0.431
Card, σ_1, $\beta = 0$	0.810	0.204
Card, σ_1, $\alpha = \beta = 0$	0.811	0.204
Card, σ_2	0.937	0.312

The Table 1 reports the obtained results. First, the two different strategies for grouping tasks led to similar results in this setting, with the *Branch* grouping being experimentally slower because the learning procedure needs more iterations to converge when the number of parameters increases (due to the max norm adopted here as stopping criterion). Nevertheless, we remark that no thresholding on the matrix S has been applied in both cases; thus, in the same model even tasks with small similarities can be included, which in principle might introduce noise in the learning and inference processes. Consequently, the advantage of jointly learning a larger number of similar tasks can be compensated by this potential noise; investigating other task grouping and similarity thresholding strategies could thereby give rise to further insights about model, which for lack of room we destine to future study.

Regarding the impact of parameter β, regulating the effect of dynamics regularization, a strong decay in performance is obtained when no regularization is applied ($\beta = 0$): this confirms the tendency of the network trajectory to be attracted in some limit cases by trivial fixed points, already observed in the singletask Hopfield model [13]. In this experiment, the contribution of regularization is even more dominating, since it allows to double the AUPR performance.

The parameter α, which regulates the multitask contribution in Eq. (3), has apparently less impact on the performance. Indeed, the performance reduces just around 2% when $\alpha = 0$; however, this behaviour should be further studied, because it can be strictly related to the noise we introduced by grouping tasks without filtering out connections between less similar task. Thus, further experiments with different organisms would help this analysis and potentially reveal novel and more clear trends. It is also important noting that by setting $\alpha = 0$, the overall multitask contribution is not cancelled: the learning procedure, by maximizing criterion (10), still learns tasks jointly, even when the multitask contribution in formula (9) is removed. For instance, choosing σ equal to the minimum function would mean learning individual task parameters in order to maximize the minimum performance $(\min_k F_k)$ across tasks, even when $\alpha = 0$.

Finally, the function σ itself seems having a marked impact on the model. When using the mean function (σ_2) the AUPR decreases of around 25% with respect to the AUPR obtained using the harmonic mean (σ_1). To some extent such a result is expected, since the harmonic mean tends to penalize more the outliers towards 0, thus fostering the learning procedure to estimate the parameters in order not to penalize some tasks in favors of the remaining ones, which instead can happen when using the mean function. This preliminary model analysis suggested to adopt the configuration "Card, σ_1" in the comparison with the state-of-the-art methodologies, which is described in the next section.

3.4   Model Performance

We compared our method with several state-of-the-art graph-based algorithms, ranging from singletask Hopfield networks and other multitask methodologies, to some methods specifically designed to predicting protein functions: *RW, random walk* [30], the classical t-step random walk algorithm, predicting a score corresponding to the probability that a t-step random walk in G, starting from positive nodes, ends in the node to be predicted; *RWR, random walk with restart*, since in RW after many steps the walker may forget the prior information coded in the initial probability vector (0 for negative nodes $1/|L_{k,+}|$ for positive nodes), RWR allows the walker to move another random walk step with probability $1 - \theta$, or to restart from its initial condition with probability θ; *GBA, guilt-by-association* [34], a method based on the assumption that interacting proteins are more likely to share similar functions; *LP, label propagation* [43], a popular semi-supervised learning algorithm which propagates labels to unlabeled nodes through an iterative process based on Gaussian random fields over a continuous state space; *MTLP, MTLP-inv* [14], two recent multitask extensions of LP, exploiting task dissimilarities (MTLP) and similarities (MTLP-inv); *MS-kNN, Multi-Source k-Nearest Neighbors* [29], a method based on the k-Nearest Neighbours (kNN) algorithm [1], among the top-ranked methods in the recent CAFA2 international challenge for AFP [25]; *RANKS* [36], a recent graph-based method proposed to rank proteins, adopting a suitable kernel matrix to extend the notion of node similarity also to non neighboring nodes; *COSNet*, employing the neuron internal energy at equilibrium to compute node ranking, in order to properly calculating both AUC and AUPR, as done in [18]. Free parameters for compared methods have been learned through inner 3-fold cross-validation.

In Table 2 we show the obtained results. Our method achieves the highest AUPR in all the experiments, with statistically significant difference over the second top method (RWR) in 2 out of 3 experiments (Wilcoxon signed rank test, $\alpha = 0.05$). The performance improvement compared with COSNet is noticeable, showing the remarkable contribution supplied by our multitask extension. Interestingly, MTLP and MTLP-inv increase the AUPR results of LP not so remarkably as HoMTask: this means that the further information regarding task similarities should be appropriately exploited in order to achieve relevant gains. RANKS is the third method in all experiments, followed by MTLP(-inv), while MS-kNN is surprisingly the last method. Our method achieves good results also in terms of AUC (which however is less informative in this context), being close to top performing methods (RWR on CC and MF, and MTLP-inv on BP terms).

Table 2. Performance comparison averaged across GO branches. In bold the top results, underlined when statistically different from the second top result.

	RW	RWR	GBA	LP	MTLP	MTLP-inv	MS-kNN	RANKS	COSNet	HoMTask
AUC										
CC	0.954	**0.966**	0.944	0.964	0.957	0.964	0.790	0.958	0.904	0.959
MF	0.934	**0.955**	0.931	0.951	0.939	0.953	0.742	0.945	0.859	0.945
BP	0.943	0.959	0.935	0.955	0.947	**0.961**	0.764	0.949	0.855	0.954
AUPR										
CC	0.367	0.437	0.207	0.308	0.343	0.342	0.218	0.398	0.361	**0.439**
MF	0.199	0.272	0.125	0.201	0.229	0.234	0.090	0.236	0.214	**0.291**
BP	0.244	0.313	0.145	0.224	0.246	0.250	0.116	0.271	0.241	**0.330**

4   Conclusions

We have proposed the first multitask Hopfield Network for classification purposes, HoMTask, capable to simultaneously learn multiple tasks and to cope with the label imbalance. In our validation experiments, it significantly outperformed singletask HNs, and favorably compared with state-of-the-art single and multitask graph-based methodologies. Future investigations might reveal novel insights about the model, in particular regarding the choice of the task relatedness matrix, the task grouping strategy, the multitask criterion to be optimized during the learning phase, the optimization procedure itself, and the robustness against different proportions of labeled data.

References

1. Altman, N.S.: An introduction to kernel and nearest-neighbor nonparametric regression. Am. Stat. **46**(3), 175–185 (1992)
2. Ando, R.K., Zhang, T.: A framework for learning predictive structures from multiple tasks and unlabeled data. J. Mach. Learn. Res. **6**, 1817–1853 (2005)
3. Argyriou, A., Evgeniou, T., Pontil, M.: Convex multi-task feature learning. Mach. Learn. **73**(3), 243–272 (2008)
4. Argyriou, A., et al.: A spectral regularization framework for multi-task structure learning. In: Advances in Neural Information Processing Systems, pp. 25–32 (2007)
5. Ashburner, M., et al.: Gene ontology: tool for the unification of biology. The gene ontology consortium. Nat. Genet. **25**(1), 25–29 (2000)
6. Bertoni, A., Frasca, M., Valentini, G.: *COSNet*: a cost sensitive neural network for semi-supervised learning in graphs. In: Gunopulos, D., Hofmann, T., Malerba, D., Vazirgiannis, M. (eds.) ECML PKDD 2011. LNCS (LNAI), vol. 6911, pp. 219–234. Springer, Heidelberg (2011). https://doi.org/10.1007/978-3-642-23780-5_24

7. Caruana, R.: Multitask learning. Mach. Learn. **28**(1), 41–75 (1997)
8. Chen, J., Zhou, J., Ye, J.: Integrating low-rank and group-sparse structures for robust multi-task learning. In: Proceedings of the 17th ACM SIGKDD International Conference on Knowledge Discovery and Data Mining, pp. 42–50. ACM (2011)
9. Daumé III, H.: Bayesian multitask learning with latent hierarchies. In: Proceedings of the Twenty-Fifth Conference on Uncertainty in Artificial Intelligence, pp. 135–142. AUAI Press (2009)
10. Evgeniou, A., Pontil, M.: Multi-task feature learning. In: Advances in Neural Information Processing Systems, vol. 19, p. 41 (2007)
11. Evgeniou, T., Micchelli, C.A., Pontil, M.: Learning multiple tasks with kernel methods. J. Mach. Learn. Res. **6**, 615–637 (2005)
12. Evgeniou, T., Pontil, M.: Regularized multi-task learning. In: Proceedings of the Tenth ACM SIGKDD KDD 2004, pp. 109–117. ACM (2004)
13. Frasca, M., Bertoni, A., et al.: A neural network algorithm for semi-supervised node label learning from unbalanced data. Neural Netw. **43**, 84–98 (2013)
14. Frasca, M., Cesa-Bianchi, N.: Multitask protein function prediction through task dissimilarity. IEEE/ACM Trans. Comput. Biol. Bioinf. **16**(5), 1550–1560 (2018). https://doi.org/10.1109/TCBB.2017.2684127
15. Frasca, M.: Gene2DisCo: gene to disease using disease commonalities. Artif. Intell. Med. **82**, 34–46 (2017). https://doi.org/10.1016/j.artmed.2017.08.001
16. Frasca, M., Bassis, S., Valentini, G.: Learning node labels with multi-category Hopfield networks. Neural Comput. Appl. **27**(6), 1677–1692 (2015). https://doi.org/10.1007/s00521-015-1965-1
17. Frasca, M., Bertoni, A., Sion, A.: A neural procedure for gene function prediction. In: Apolloni, B., Bassis, S., Esposito, A., Morabito, F. (eds.) Neural Nets and Surroundings, pp. 179–188. Springer, Heidelberg (2013). https://doi.org/10.1007/978-3-642-35467-0_19
18. Frasca, M., Pavesi, G.: A neural network based algorithm for gene expression prediction from chromatin structure. In: IJCNN, pp. 1–8. IEEE (2013). https://doi.org/10.1109/IJCNN.2013.6706954
19. Greene, W.H.: Econometric Analysis, 5th edn. Prentice Hall, Upper Saddle River (2003)
20. Guo, S., Zoeter, O., Archambeau, C.: Sparse bayesian multi-task learning. In: Advances in Neural Information Processing Systems, pp. 1755–1763 (2011)
21. Hopfield, J.J.: Neural networks and physical systems with emergent collective compatational abilities. Proc. Natl Acad. Sci. USA **79**, 2554–2558 (1982)
22. Hu, X., Wang, T.: Training the Hopfield neural network for classification using a STDP-like rule. In: Liu, D., Xie, S., Li, Y., Zhao, D., El-Alfy, E.S. (eds.) Neural Information Processing, pp. 737–744. Springer, Cham (2017). https://doi.org/10.1007/978-3-319-70090-8_74
23. Jacob, L., Vert, J.P., Bach, F.R.: Clustered multi-task learning: a convex formulation. In: Advances in Neural Information Processing Systems, pp. 745–752 (2009)
24. Jacyna, G.M., Malaret, E.R.: Classification performance of a hopfield neural network based on a Hebbian-like learning rule. IEEE Trans. Inf. Theory **35**(2), 263–280 (1989). https://doi.org/10.1109/18.32122
25. Jiang, Y., Oron, T.R., et al.: An expanded evaluation of protein function prediction methods shows an improvement in accuracy. Genome Biol. **17**(1), 184 (2016)
26. Kang, Z., Grauman, K., Sha, F.: Learning with whom to share in multi-task feature learning. In: Proceedings of the 28th ICML, pp. 521–528 (2011)

27. Karaoz, U., et al.: Whole-genome annotation by using evidence integration in functional-linkage networks. Proc. Natl Acad. Sci. USA **101**, 2888–2893 (2004)
28. Kordos, M., Duch, W.: Variable step search algorithm for feedforward networks. Neurocomputing **71**(13–15), 2470–2480 (2008)
29. Lan, L., Djuric, N., Guo, Y., Vucetic, S.: MS-kNN: protein function prediction by integrating multiple data sources. BMC Bioinform. **14**(Suppl 3), S8 (2013)
30. Lovász, L.: Random walks on graphs: a survey. In: Miklós, D., Sós, V.T., Szőnyi, T. (eds.) Combinatorics, Paul Erdős is Eighty, Budapest, vol. 2, pp. 353–398 (1996)
31. Mostafavi, S., Morris, Q.: Fast integration of heterogeneous data sources for predicting gene function with limited annotation. Bioinformatics **26**(14), 1759–1765 (2010)
32. Ning, X., Karypis, G.: Multi-task learning for recommender system. In: Proceedings of 2nd Asian Conference on Machine Learning (ACML 2010), vol. 13, pp. 269–284 (2010)
33. Saito, T., Rehmsmeier, M.: The precision-recall plot is more informative than the ROC plot when evaluating binary classifiers on imbalanced datasets. PLoS ONE **10**, e0118432 (2015)
34. Schwikowski, B., Uetz, P., Fields, S.: A network of protein-protein interactions in yeast. Nat. Biotechnol. **18**(12), 1257–1261 (2000)
35. Szklarczyk, D., et al.: STRING v10: protein-protein interaction networks, integrated over the tree of life. Nucl. Acids Res. **43**(D1), D447–D452 (2015)
36. Valentini, G., et al.: RANKS: a flexible tool for node label ranking and classification in biological networks. Bioinformatics **32**, 2872–2874 (2016)
37. Vascon, S., Frasca, M., Tripodi, R., Valentini, G., Pelillo, M.: Protein function prediction as a graph-transduction game. Pattern Recogn. Lett. (2018, in press)
38. Xue, Y., Liao, X., Carin, L., Krishnapuram, B.: Multi-task learning for classification with Dirichlet process priors. J. Mach. Learn. Res. **8**, 35–63 (2007)
39. Yu, K., Tresp, V., Schwaighofer, A.: Learning Gaussian process from multiple tasks. In: Proceedings of the 22nd International Conference on Pattern Recognition, pp. 1012–1019. ACM (2005)
40. Yu, S., Tresp, V., Yu, K.: Robust multi-task learning with t-processes. In: Proceedings of the 24th International Conference on Machine Learning, pp. 1103–1110. ACM (2007)
41. Zhang, Y., Schneider, J.G.: Learning multiple tasks with a sparse matrix-normal penalty. In: Advances in Neural Information Processing Systems, pp. 2550–2558 (2010)
42. Zhou, J., Chen, J., Ye, J.: Clustered multi-task learning via alternating structure optimization. In: Advances in Neural Information Processing Systems, pp. 702–710 (2011)
43. Zhu, X., et al.: Semi-supervised learning with Gaussian fields and harmonic functions. In: Proceedings of the 20th International Conference on Machine Learning, pp. 912–919 (2003)

Meta-Learning for Black-Box Optimization

Vishnu TV$^{(\boxtimes)}$, Pankaj Malhotra, Jyoti Narwariya, Lovekesh Vig,
and Gautam Shroff

TCS Research, New Delhi, India
{vishnu.tv,malhotra.pankaj,jyoti.narwariya,
lovekesh.vig,gautam.shroff}@tcs.com

Abstract. Recently, neural networks trained as optimizers under the
"learning to learn" or meta-learning framework have been shown to be
effective for a broad range of optimization tasks including derivative-
free black-box function optimization. Recurrent neural networks (RNNs)
trained to optimize a diverse set of synthetic non-convex differentiable functions via gradient descent have been effective at optimizing
derivative-free black-box functions. In this work, we propose *RNN-Opt*:
an approach for learning RNN-based optimizers for optimizing real-
parameter single-objective continuous functions under limited budget
constraints. Existing approaches utilize an observed improvement based
meta-learning loss function for training such models. We propose training
RNN-Opt by using synthetic non-convex functions with known (approximate) optimal values by directly using discounted regret as our meta-
learning loss function. We hypothesize that a regret-based loss function mimics typical testing scenarios, and would therefore lead to better
optimizers compared to optimizers trained only to propose queries that
improve over previous queries. Further, RNN-Opt incorporates simple
yet effective enhancements during training and inference procedures to
deal with the following practical challenges: (i) Unknown range of possible values for the black-box function to be optimized, and (ii) Practical
and domain-knowledge based constraints on the input parameters. We
demonstrate the efficacy of RNN-Opt in comparison to existing methods
on several synthetic as well as standard benchmark black-box functions
along with an anonymized industrial constrained optimization problem.

Keywords: Black-box optimization · Learning to optimize ·
Meta-learning · Recurrent neural networks · Constrained optimization

1 Introduction

Several practical optimization problems such as process black-box optimization
for complex dynamical systems pose a unique challenge owing to the restriction
on the number of possible function evaluations. Such black-box functions do
not have a simple closed form but can be evaluated (queried) at any arbitrary

© Springer Nature Switzerland AG 2020
U. Brefeld et al. (Eds.): ECML PKDD 2019, LNAI 11907, pp. 366–381, 2020.
https://doi.org/10.1007/978-3-030-46147-8_22

query point in the domain. However, evaluation of real-world complex processes is expensive and time consuming, therefore the optimization algorithm must optimize while employing as few real-world function evaluations as possible. Most practical optimization problems are constrained in nature, i.e. have one or more constraints on the values of input parameters. In this work, we focus on real-parameter single-objective black-box optimization (BBO) where the goal is to obtain a value as close to the maximum value of the objective function as possible by adjusting the values of the real-valued continuous input parameters while ensuring domain constraints are not violated. We further assume a limited budget, i.e. assume that querying the black-box function is expensive and thus only a small number of queries can be made.

Efficient global optimization of expensive black-box functions [14] requires proposing the next query (input parameter values) to the black-box function based on past queries and the corresponding responses (function evaluations). BBO can be mapped to the problem of proposing the next query given past queries and the corresponding responses such that the expected improvement in the function value is maximized, as in Bayesian Optimization approaches [4]. While most research in optimization has focused on engineering algorithms catering to specific classes of problems, recent meta-learning [24] approaches, e.g. [2,5,7,18,27], cast design of an optimization algorithm as a learning problem rather than the traditional hand-engineering approach, and then, propose approaches to train neural networks that *learn to optimize*. In contrast to a traditional machine learning approach involving training of a neural network on a single task using training data samples so that it can generalize to unseen data samples from the same data distribution, here the neural network is trained on a distribution of similar tasks (in our case optimization tasks) so as to learn a strategy that generalizes to related but unseen tasks from a similar task distribution. The meta-learning approaches attempt to train a single network to optimize several functions at once such that the network can effectively generalize to optimize unseen functions.

Recently, [5] proposed a meta-learning approach wherein a recurrent neural network (RNN with gated units such as Long Short Term Memory (LSTM) [9]) learns to optimize a large number of diverse synthetic non-convex functions to yield a learned task-independent optimizer. The RNN iteratively uses the sequence of past queries and corresponding responses to propose the next query in order to maximize the observed improvement (OI) in the response value. We refer to this approach as RNN-OI in this work. Once the RNN is trained to optimize a diverse set of synthetic functions by using gradient descent, it is able to generalize well to solve unseen derivative-free black-box optimization problems [5,29]. Such learned optimizers are shown to be faster in terms of the time taken to propose the next query compared to Bayesian optimizers as they do not require any matrix inversion or optimization of acquisition functions, and also have lower regret values within the training horizon, i.e. the number of steps of the optimization process for which the RNN is trained to generate queries.

Key contributions of this work and the challenges addressed can be summarized as follows:

1. *Regret-based loss function*: We hypothesize that training an RNN optimizer using a loss function that minimizes the regret observed for a given number of queries more closely resembles the performance measure of an optimizer. So it is better than a loss function based on OI such as the one used in [5,29]. To this end, we propose a simple yet highly effective loss function that yields superior results than the existing OI loss for black-box optimization. Regret of the optimizer is the difference between the optimal value (maximum of the black-box function) and the realized maximum value.

2. *Deal with lack of prior knowledge on range of the black-box function*: In many practical optimization problems, it may be difficult to ascertain the possible range of values the function can take, and the range of values would vary across applications. On the other hand, neural networks are known to work well only on normalized inputs, and can be numerically unstable and difficult to train on very large or very small values as typical non-linear activation functions like sigmoid activation function tend to saturate for large inputs and will then adjust slowly during training. RNNs are most easily trained when their inputs are well conditioned, and have a similar scale as their latent state, and suitable scaling often accelerates training [27]. We, therefore, propose *incremental normalization* that dynamically normalizes the output (response) from the black-box function using the response values observed so far before the value is passed as an input to the RNN, and observe significant improvements in terms of regret by doing so.

3. *Incorporate domain-constraints*: Any practical optimization problem has a set of constraints on the input parameters. It is important that the RNN optimizer is penalized when it proposes query points outside the desired limits. We introduce a mechanism to achieve this by giving an additional feedback to the RNN whenever it proposes a query that violates domain constraints. In addition to regret-based loss, RNN is also trained to simultaneously minimize domain constraint violations. We show that an RNN optimizer trained in this manner attains lower regret values in fewer steps when subjected to domain constraints compared to an RNN optimizer not explicitly trained to utilize feedback.

We refer to the proposed approach as *RNN-Opt*. As a result of the above considerations, RNN-Opt can deal with an unknown range of function values and also incorporate domain constraints. We demonstrate that RNN-Opt works well on optimizing unseen benchmark black-box functions and outperforms RNN-OI in terms of the optimal value attained under a limited budget for 2-dimensional and 6-dimensional input spaces. We also perform extensive ablation experiments demonstrating the importance of each of the above-stated features in RNN-Opt.

The rest of the paper is organized as follows: We contrast our work to existing literature in Sect. 2, followed by defining the problem in Sect. 3. We present the details of our approach in Sect. 4, followed by experimental evaluation in Sect. 5, and conclude in Sect. 6.

2   Related Work

Our work falls under the category of real-parameter black-box global optimization [21]. Traditional approaches for black-box optimization like covariance matrix adaptation evolution strategy (CMA-ES) [8], Nelder-Mead [20], and Particle Swarm Optimization (PSO) [15] hand-design rules using heuristics (e.g. using nature-inspired genetic algorithms) to decide the next query point(s) given the observations made so far. Another category of approaches for global optimization of black-box functions include Bayesian optimization techniques [4,25,26]. These approaches use observations (query and response) made thus far to approximate the black-box function via a surrogate (meta-) model, e.g. using a Gaussian Process [10], and then use this model to construct an acquisition function to decide the next query point. The acquisition function updates needed at each step are known to be costly [5].

Learned optimizers: There has been a recent interest in learning optimizers under the meta-learning setting [24] by training RNN optimizers via gradient descent. For example, [2] casts the design of an optimization algorithm as a learning problem and uses an LSTM model to learn an optimizer for a particular class of optimization problems, e.g. quadratic functions, training neural networks, etc. Similarly, [7,18] cast optimizer learning as learning a policy under a reinforcement learning setting. [27] proposes a hierarchical RNN architecture to learn optimizers that scale well to optimize a large number of parameters (high-dimensional input space). However, the above meta-learning approaches for optimization assume the availability of gradient information to decide the next set of parameters, which is not available in the case of black-box optimization. Our work builds upon the meta-learning approach for learning black-box optimizers proposed in [5]. This approach mimics the sequential model-based Bayesian approaches in the sense that it proposes an RNN optimizer that stores sequential information about previous queries and responses, and accesses this memory to generate the next candidate query. RNN-OI mimics the Bayesian optimization based sequential decision-making process [4] (refer [5] for details) while being significantly faster than standard BBO algorithms like SMAC [11] and Spearmint [26] as it does not involve any matrix inversion or optimization of acquisition functions. RNN-OI was successfully tested on Gaussian process bandits, simple low dimensional controllers, and hyper-parameter tuning.

Handling domain constraints in neural networks: Recent work on Physics-guided deep learning [13,19] incorporates domain knowledge in the learning process via additional loss terms. Such approaches can be useful in our setting if the optimizer network is to be trained from scratch for a given application. However, the purpose of building a generic optimizer that can be transferred to new applications requires incorporating domain constraints in a posterior manner during inference time when the optimizer is suggesting query points. This is not only useful to adapt the same optimizer to a new application but also useful in another practical scenario of adapting to a new set of domain constraints for a given application. ThermalNet [6] uses a deep Q-network as an optimizer and uses an LSTM predictor for combustion optimization of a boiler in a power plant but does not handle domain constraints. Similar to our approach, ChemOpt [29] uses an RNN based optimizer for chemical reaction optimization but does not address aspects related to handling an unknown range for the function being optimized and incorporating domain constraints.

Handling unknown range of function values: Suitable scaling of input and output of hidden layers in neural networks has been shown to accelerate training of neural networks [3,12,17,23]. Dynamic input scaling has been used in a similar setting as ours [27] to ensure that the neural network based optimizer is invariant to parameter scale. However, the scaling is applied to the average gradients. In our setting, we use a similar approach but apply dynamic scaling to the function evaluations being fed back as input to RNN-Opt.

3   Problem Overview

We consider learning an optimizer that can optimize (e.g., maximize) a black-box function $f_b : \Theta \mapsto \mathbb{R}$, where $\Theta \subseteq \mathbb{R}^d$ is the domain of the input parameters. We assume that the function f_b does not have a closed-form representation, is costly to evaluate, and does not allow the computation of gradients. In other words, the optimizer can query the function f_b at a point $\mathbf{x}$ to obtain a response $y = f_b(\mathbf{x})$, but it does not obtain any gradient information, and in particular it cannot make any assumptions on the analytical form of f_b. The goal is to find $\mathbf{x}_{opt} = \arg\max_{\mathbf{x} \in \Theta} f_b(\mathbf{x})$ within a limited budget, i.e. within a limited number of queries T that can be made to the black-box.

We consider training an optimizer f_{opt} with parameters $\boldsymbol{\theta}_{opt}$ such that, given the queries $\mathbf{x}_{1...t} = \mathbf{x}_1, \mathbf{x}_2, \ldots, \mathbf{x}_t$ and the corresponding responses $y_{1...t} = y_1, y_2, \ldots, y_t$ from f_b where $y_t = f_b(\mathbf{x}_t)$, f_{opt} proposes the next query point $\mathbf{x}_{t+1}$ under a budget constraint of T queries, i.e. $t \leq T - 1$:

$$\mathbf{x}_{t+1} = f_{opt}(\mathbf{x}_{1...t}, y_{1...t}; \boldsymbol{\theta}_{opt}). \tag{1}$$

4   RNN-Opt

We model f_{opt} using an LSTM-based RNN. (For implementation, we use a variant of LSTMs as described in [28].) Recurrent Neural Networks (RNNs) with gated units such as Long Short Term Memory (LSTM) [9] units are a popular choice for sequence modeling to make predictions about future values given the past. They do so by maintaining a memory of all the relevant information from the sequence of inputs observed so far. In the meta-learning or training phase, a diverse set of synthetically-generated differentiable non-convex functions (refer Appendix A) with known global optima are used to train the RNN (using gradient descent). The RNN is then used to predict the next query in order to intelligently explore the search space given the sequence of previous queries and the function responses. The RNN is expected to learn to retain any information about previous queries and responses that is relevant to proposing the next query to minimize the regret as shown in Fig. 1.

4.1 RNN-Opt Without Domain Constraints

Given a trained RNN-based optimizer and a differentiable function f_g, inference in RNN-Opt follows the following iterative process for $t = 1, \dots, T - 1$: At each step t, the output of the final recurrent hidden layer of the RNN is used to generate the output via an affine transformation to finally obtain $\mathbf{x}_{t+1}$.

$$\mathbf{h}_{t+1} = f_o(\mathbf{h}_t, \mathbf{x}_t, y_t; \boldsymbol{\theta}), \tag{2}$$

$$\boldsymbol{\mu}_{t+1}^x, \boldsymbol{\Sigma}_{t+1}^x = W_{2m,d}(\mathbf{h}_{t+1}), \tag{3}$$

$$\mathbf{x}_{t+1} \sim \mathcal{N}(\boldsymbol{\mu}_{t+1}^x, \boldsymbol{\Sigma}_{t+1}^x), \tag{4}$$

$$y_{t+1} = f_g(\mathbf{x}_{t+1}), \tag{5}$$

where f_o represents the RNN with parameters $\boldsymbol{\theta}$, f_g is the function to be optimized, $W_{2m,d}$ defines the affine transformation of the final output (hidden state) $\mathbf{h}_{t+1}$ of the RNN. The parameters $\boldsymbol{\theta}$ and $W_{2m,d}$ together constitute $\boldsymbol{\theta}_{opt}$. Instead of directly training f_o to propose the next query $\mathbf{x}_{t+1}$ as in [5], we use a stochastic RNN to estimate $\boldsymbol{\mu}_{t+1}^x \in \mathbb{R}^d$ and $\boldsymbol{\Sigma}_{t+1}^x \in \mathbb{R}^{d \times d}$ as in Eq. 3, then sample $\mathbf{x}_{t+1}$ from a multivariate Gaussian distribution $\mathcal{N}(\boldsymbol{\mu}_{t+1}^x, \boldsymbol{\Sigma}_{t+1}^x)$. Introducing randomness in the query generation process leads to better exploration compared to a deterministic model [29]. The first query $\mathbf{x}_1$ is sampled from a uniform distribution over the domain of the function f_g to be optimized. Once the network is trained, f_g can be replaced by any black-box function f_b that takes d-dimensional input.

For any synthetically generated function $f_g \in \mathcal{F}$, we assume $\mathbf{x}_{opt}$ (approximate) can be found, e.g. using gradient-descent, since the closed form of the function is known. Hence, we assume that y_{opt} of f_g given by $y_{opt} = f_g(\mathbf{x}_{opt})$ is known. Therefore, it is easy to determine the regret $y_{opt} - \max_{i \leq t} y_i$ after t iterations (queries) to the function f_g. We can then define a regret-based loss function as follows:

$$\mathcal{L}_R = \sum_{f_g \in \mathcal{F}} \sum_{t=2}^{T} \frac{1}{\gamma^t} \mathrm{ReLU}(y_{opt} - \max_{i \leq t} y_i), \tag{6}$$

where $\mathrm{ReLU}(x) = \max(x, 0)$. Since the regret is expected to be high during initial iterations because of random initialization of $\mathbf{x}$ but desired to be low close to T, we give exponentially increasing importance to regret terms via a discount factor $0 < \gamma \leq 1$. In contrast to regret loss, OI loss used in RNN-OI is given by [5,29]:

$$\mathcal{L}_{OI} = \sum_{f_g \in \mathcal{F}} \sum_{t=2}^{T} \frac{1}{\gamma^t} \mathrm{ReLU}(y_t - \max_{i < t} y_i) \tag{7}$$

It is to be noted that using $\mathcal{L}_R$ as the loss function mimics a supervised scenario where the target y_{opt} for each optimization task is known and explicitly used to guide the learning process. On the other hand, $\mathcal{L}_{OI}$ mimics an unsupervised scenario where the target y_{opt} is unknown and the learning process solely

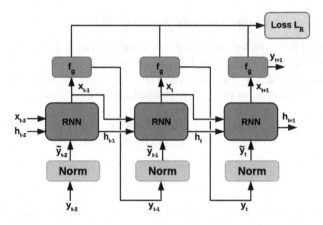

Fig. 1. Computation flow in RNN-Opt. During training, the functions f_g are differentiable and obtained using Eq. 12. Once trained, f_g is replaced by the black-box function f_b.

relies on the feedback about whether it is able to improve y_t over iterations. It is important to note that once trained, the model requires neither y_{opt} nor $\mathbf{x}_{opt}$ during inference.

Incremental Normalization. We do not assume any constraint on the range of values the functions f_g and f_b can take. Although this feature is critical for most practical aspects, it poses a challenge on the training and inference procedures using RNN: Neural networks are known to work well only on normalized inputs, and can be numerically unstable and difficult to train on very large or very small values as typical non-linear activation functions like sigmoid activation function tend to saturate for large inputs and will adjust slowly during training. RNNs are most easily trained when their inputs are well conditioned, and have a similar scale as their latent state, and suitable scaling often accelerates training [12,27]. This poses a challenge during both training and inference if we directly use y_t as an input to the RNN. Figure 2 illustrates the saturation effect if suitable incremental normalization of function values is not used during inference. This behavior at inference time was noted[1] in [5], however, was not considered while

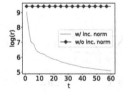

Fig. 2. Effect of not using suitable scaling (incremental normalization in our case) of black-box function value during inference.

---

[1] As per electronic correspondence with the authors.

training RNN-OI. In order to deal with any range of values that f_g can take during training or that f_b can take during inference, we consider incremental normalization while training such that y_t in Eq. 2 is replaced by $\tilde{y}_t = \frac{y_t - \mu_t}{\sqrt{\sigma_t^2 + \epsilon}}$ such that $\mathbf{h}_{t+1} = f_o(\mathbf{h}_t, \mathbf{x}_t, \tilde{y}_t; \boldsymbol{\theta})$, where $\mu_t = \frac{1}{t}\sum_{i=1}^{t} y_i$, $\sigma_t^2 = \frac{1}{t}\sum_{i=1}^{t}(y_i - \mu_t)^2$, and $0 < \epsilon \ll 1$. (We used $\epsilon = 0.05$ in our experiments).

4.2 RNN-Opt with Domain Constraints (RNN-Opt-DC)

Consider a constrained optimization problem of finding $\arg\max_{\mathbf{x}} f_b(\mathbf{x})$ subject to constraints given by $c_j(\mathbf{x}) \leq 0$, $j = 1, \ldots, C$, where C is the number of constraints. To ensure that the optimizer proposes queries that satisfy the domain constraints, or is at least able to receive feedback when it proposes a query that violates any domain constraints, we consider the following enhancements in RNN-Opt, as depicted in Fig. 3:

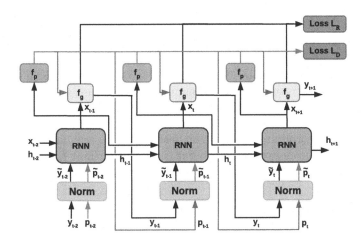

Fig. 3. Computation flow in RNN-Opt-DC. Here f_g is the function to be optimized, and f_p is used to compute the penalty p_t. Further, if $p_t = 0$, actual value of f_g, i.e. y_t is passed to the loss function and RNN, else y_t is set to y_{t-1}.

1. Input an explicit feedback p_t via a penalty function s.t. $p_t = f_p(\mathbf{x}_t)$ to the RNN that captures the extent to which a proposed query $\mathbf{x}_t$ violates any of the C domain constraints. We consider the following instantiation of penalty function: $f_p(\mathbf{x}_t) = \sum_{j=1}^{C} \text{ReLU}(c_j(\mathbf{x}_t))$, i.e. for any j for which $c_j(\mathbf{x}_t) > 0$ a penalty equal to $c_j(\mathbf{x}_t)$ is considered, while for any j with $c_j(\mathbf{x}_t) \leq 0$ the contribution to penalty is 0. The real-valued penalty captures the cumulative extent of violation as well. Further, similar to normalizing y_t, we also normalize p_t incrementally and use $\tilde{p}_t$ as an additional input to the RNN, such that:

$$\mathbf{h}_{t+1} = f_o(\mathbf{h}_t, \mathbf{x}_t, \tilde{y}_t, \tilde{p}_t; \boldsymbol{\theta}). \tag{8}$$

Further, whenever $p_t > 0$, i.e. when one or more of the domain constraints are violated for the proposed query, we set $y_t = y_{t-1}$ rather than actually getting a response from the black-box. This is useful in practice: for example, when trying to optimize a complex dynamical system, getting a response from the system for such a query is not possible as it can be catastrophic.

2. During training, an additional domain constraint loss $\mathcal{L}_D$ is considered that penalizes the optimizer if it proposes a query that does not satisfy one or more of the domain constraints.

$$\mathcal{L}_D = \frac{1}{C} \sum_{f_g \in \mathcal{F}} \sum_{t=2}^{T} p_t. \tag{9}$$

The overall loss is then given by:

$$\mathcal{L} = \mathcal{L}_R + \lambda \mathcal{L}_D, \tag{10}$$

where λ controls how strictly the constraints on the domain of parameters should be enforced; higher λ implies stricter adherence to constraints. It is worth noting that the above formulation of incorporating domain constraints does not put any restriction on the number of constraints C nor on the nature of constraints in the sense that the constraints can be linear or non-linear in nature. Further, complex non-linear constraints based on domain knowledge can also be incorporated in a similar fashion during training, e.g. as used in [13,19]. Apart from optimizing (in our case, maximizing) f_g, the optimizer is also being simultaneously trained to minimize f_p.

Example of Penalty Function. Consider simple limit constraints on the input parameters such that the domain of the function f_g is given by $\Theta = [\mathbf{x}_{min}, \mathbf{x}_{max}]$, then we have:

$$f_p(\mathbf{x}_t) = \sum_{j=1}^{d} \left(\text{ReLU}(x_t^j - x_{max}^j) + \text{ReLU}(x_{min}^j - x_t^j) \right), \tag{11}$$

where x_t^j denotes the j-th dimension of $\mathbf{x}_t$ where x_{min}^j and x_{max}^j are the j-th elements of $\mathbf{x}_{min}$ and $\mathbf{x}_{max}$, respectively.

5   Experimental Evaluation

We conduct experiments to evaluate the following: i. regret loss ($\mathcal{L}_R$) versus OI loss ($\mathcal{L}_{OI}$), ii. effect of including incremental normalization during training, and iii. ability of RNN-Opt trained with domain constraints using $\mathcal{L}$ (Eq. 10) to generate more feasible queries and leverage feedback to quickly adapt in case it proposes queries violating domain constraints.

For the unconstrained setting, we test RNN-Opt on (i) standard benchmark functions for $d = 2$ and $d = 6$, and (ii) 1280 synthetically generated GMM-DF functions (refer Appendix A) not seen during training. We choose the benchmark functions such as Goldstein, Rosenbrock, and Rastrigin (and the simple spherical function) that are known to be challenging for standard optimization methods. None of these functions were used for training any of the optimizers.

We use regret $r_t = y_{opt} - \max_{i \leq t} y_i$ to measure the performance of any optimizer after t iterations, i.e. after proposing t queries. Lower values of r_t indicate superior optimizer performance. We test all the optimizers under limited budget setting such that $T = 10 \times d$. For each test function, the first query is randomly sampled from $U(-4.0, 4.0)$, and we report average regret r_t over 1280 random initializations. For synthetically generated GMM-DF functions, we report average regret over 1280 functions with one random initialization for each.

All RNN-based optimizers (refer Table 1) were trained for 8000 iterations using Adam optimizer [16] with an initial learning rate of 0.005. The network consists of two hidden layers with the number of LSTM units in each layer being chosen from $\{80, 120, 160\}$ using a hold-out validation set of 1280 GMM-DF. Another set of 1280 randomly generated functions constitute the GMM-DF test set. An initial code base[2] developed using Tensorflow [1] was adapted to implement our algorithm. We used a batch size of 128, i.e. 128 randomly-sampled functions (refer Eq. 12) are processed in one mini-batch for updating the parameters of LSTM.

Table 1. Variants of trained optimizers considered. Each row corresponds to a method. Y/N denote whether a feature (incremental normalization or domain constraint) was considered (Y) or not (N) during training or inference in a particular method.

Method	Loss	γ	Inc. Norm.		Domain Const. (DC)	
			Training	Inference	Training	Inference
RNN-OI	$\mathcal{L}_{OI}$	1.0	N	Y	N	N
RNN-Opt-Basic	$\mathcal{L}_R$	0.98	N	Y	N	N
RNN-Opt	$\mathcal{L}_R$	0.98	Y	Y	N	N
RNN-Opt-P	$\mathcal{L}_R$	0.98	Y	Y	N	Y
RNN-Opt-DC	$\mathcal{L}_R + \lambda \mathcal{L}_D$	0.98	Y	Y	Y	Y

5.1 Observations

We make the following key observations for unconstrained optimization setting:

1. **RNN-Opt is able to optimize black-box functions not seen during training, and hence, generalize.** We compare RNN-Opt with RNN-OI

---

[2] https://github.com/lightingghost/chemopt.

and two standard black-box optimization algorithms CMA-ES [8] and Nelder-Mead [20]. RNN-OI uses $\mathbf{x}_t$, y_t, and $\mathbf{h}_t$ to get the next hidden state $\mathbf{h}_{t+1}$, which is then used to get $\mathbf{x}_{t+1}$ (as in Eq. 4), such that $\mathbf{h}_{t+1} = f_o(\mathbf{h}_t, \mathbf{x}_t, y_t; \boldsymbol{\theta})$, with OI loss as given in Eq. 7. From Fig. 4(a)-(i), we observe that RNN-Opt outperforms all the baselines considered on most functions considered while being at least as good as the baselines in few remaining cases. Except for the simple convex spherical function, RNN-based optimizers outperform CMA-ES and Nelder-Mead under limited budget, i.e. with $T = 20$ for $d = 2$ and $T = 60$ for $d = 6$. We observe that trained optimizers outperform CMA-ES and Nelder-Mead for higher-dimensional cases ($d = 6$ here, as also observed in [5, 29]).

2. **Regret-based loss is better than the OI loss.** We compare *RNN-Opt-Basic* with RNN-OI (refer Table 1) where RNN-Opt-Basic differs from RNN-OI only in the loss function (and the discount factor, as discussed in next point). For fair comparison with RNN-OI, RNN-Opt-Basic does not include incremental normalization during training. From Fig. 4(j)-(k), we observe that RNN-Opt-Basic (with $\gamma = 0.98$) performs better than RNN-OI during initial

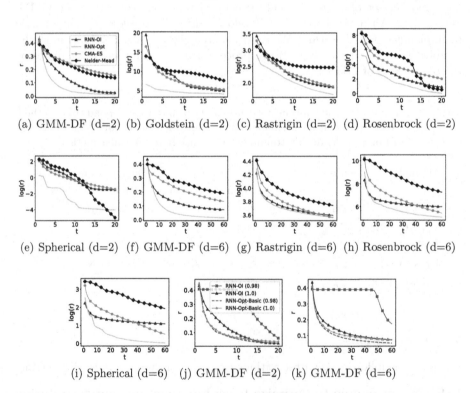

(a) GMM-DF (d=2) (b) Goldstein (d=2) (c) Rastrigin (d=2) (d) Rosenbrock (d=2)

(e) Spherical (d=2) (f) GMM-DF (d=6) (g) Rastrigin (d=6) (h) Rosenbrock (d=6)

(i) Spherical (d=6) (j) GMM-DF (d=2) (k) GMM-DF (d=6)

Fig. 4. (a)-(i) RNN-Opt versus CMA-ES, Nelder-Mead and RNN-OI for benchmark functions for $d = 2$ and $d = 6$. (j)-(k) Regret loss versus OI Loss with varying discount factor γ mentioned in brackets in the legend. (Lower regret is better.)

steps for $d = 2$ (while being comparable eventually) and across all steps for $d = 6$, proving the advantage of using regret loss over OI loss.

3. **Significance of discount factor when using regret-based loss versus OI loss.** From Fig. 4(j)-(k), we also observe that the results of RNN-Opt and RNN-OI are sensitive to the discount factor γ (refer Eqs. 6 and 7). $\gamma < 1$ works better for RNN-Opt while $\gamma = 1$ (i.e. no discount) works better for RNN-OI. This can be explained as follows: the queries proposed initially (small t) are expected to be far from y_{opt} due to random initialization, and therefore, have high initial regret. Hence, components of the loss term for smaller t should be given lower weightage in the regret-based loss. On the other hand, during later steps (close to T), we would like the regret to be as low as possible, and hence a higher importance should be given to the corresponding terms in the regret-based loss. In contrast, RNN-OI is trained to keep improving irrespective of y_{opt}, and hence giving equal importance to the contribution of each step to the OI loss works best.

4. **Incremental normalization during training and inference to optimize functions with diverse range of values.** We compare RNN-Opt-Basic and RNN-Opt, where RNN-Opt uses incremental normalization of inputs during training as well as testing (as described in Sect. 4.1) while RNN-Opt-Basic uses incremental normalization only during testing (refer Table 1). From Fig. 5, we observe that RNN-Opt performs significantly better than RNN-Opt-Basic proving the advantage of incorporating incremental normalization during training. Note that since most of the functions considered have large range of values, incremental normalization is by-default enabled for all RNN-based optimizers during testing to obtain meaningful results, as illustrated earlier in Fig. 2, especially for functions with large range, e.g. Rosenbrock.

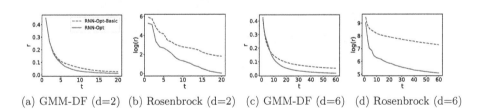

(a) GMM-DF (d=2)   (b) Rosenbrock (d=2)   (c) GMM-DF (d=6)   (d) Rosenbrock (d=6)

Fig. 5. Regret plots showing effect of incremental normalization in RNN-Opt. Similar results are observed for all functions. We omit them here for brevity.

5.2   RNN-Opt with Domain Constraints

To train RNN-Opt-DC, we generate synthetic functions with random limit constraints as explained in Sect. 4.2. The limits of the search space are set as $[\mathbf{x}_{opt} - \Delta\mathbf{x}, \mathbf{x}_{opt} + \Delta\mathbf{x}]$ where Δx^j (j-th component of $\Delta\mathbf{x}$) is sampled from $U(\tau_1, \tau_2)$ (we use $\tau_1 = 1.0$, $\tau_2 = 2.0$ during training).

We use $\lambda = 0.2$ for RNN-Opt-DC. As a baseline, we use RNN-Opt with minor variation during inference time (with no change in training procedure) where, instead of passing $\tilde{y}_t$ as input to the RNN, we pass $\tilde{y}_t - \tilde{p}_t$ so as to capture penalty feedback. We call this baseline approach as *RNN-Opt-P* (refer Table 1). While RNN-Opt-DC is explicitly trained to minimize penalty p_t explicitly, RNN-Opt-P captures the requirement of trying to maximize y_t under a soft-constraint of minimizing p_t only during inference time.

We use the standard quadratic (disk) constraint used to evaluate constrained optimization approaches, i.e. $||\mathbf{x}||_2^2 \leq \tau \times d$ (we use $\tau = \{0.5, 1.0, 2.0\}$) for Rosenbrock function. For GMM-DF, we generate random limit constraints on each dimension around the global optima, s.t. the optimal solution is still the same as the one without constraints, while the feasible search space varies randomly across functions. Limits of the domain is $[\mathbf{x}_{opt} - \Delta\mathbf{x}, \mathbf{x}_{opt} + \Delta\mathbf{x}]$, where Δx^j (j-th component of $\Delta\mathbf{x}$) is sampled from $U(\tau_1, \tau_2)$ (we use $\tau_1 = \{0.5, 1.0, 1.5\}$, $\tau_2 = \{1.5, 2.0, 2.5\}$). We also consider two instances of (anonymized) non-linear surrogate model for a real-world industrial process built by subject-matter experts with six controllable input parameters ($d = 6$) as black-box functions, referred to as Industrial-1 and Industrial-2 in Fig. 6. This process imposes limit constraints on all six parameters guided by domain-knowledge. The ground-truth optimal value for these functions was obtained by querying the surrogate model 200k times via grid search. The regret results are averaged over runs assuming diverse environmental conditions.

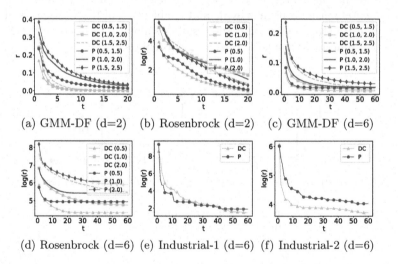

(a) GMM-DF (d=2)   (b) Rosenbrock (d=2)   (c) GMM-DF (d=6)

(d) Rosenbrock (d=6) (e) Industrial-1 (d=6) (f) Industrial-2 (d=6)

Fig. 6. Regret plots comparing RNN-Opt-DC (DC) and RNN-Opt-P (P). The entries in the brackets denote values for (τ_1, τ_2) for GMM-DF, and τ for Rosenbrock.

RNN-Opt-DC and RNN-Opt-P are not guaranteed to propose feasible queries at all steps because of the soft constraints during training and/or inference. Therefore, despite training the optimizers for T steps we unroll the RNNs up to a maximum of $5T$ steps and take the first T proposed queries that are feasible, i.e. satisfy domain constraints. For functions where optimizer is not able to propose T feasible queries in $5T$ steps, we replicate the regret corresponding to best solution for remaining steps. As shown in Fig. 6, we observe that **RNN-Opt with domain constraints, namely, *RNN-Opt-DC* is able to effectively use explicit penalty feedback, and at least as good as RNN-Opt-P in all cases.** As expected, we also observe that the performance of both optimizers degrades with increasing values of τ or $\tau_2 - \tau_1$ as the search space to be explored by the optimizer increases.

6   Conclusion and Future Work

Learning optimization algorithms under the meta-learning paradigm is an area of active research. In this work, we have shown that using regret directly as a loss for training optimizers using recurrent neural networks is possible, and that it yields better optimizers than those obtained using observed-improvement based loss. We have proposed useful extensions of practical importance to optimization algorithms for black-box optimization that allow dealing with diverse range of function values and handle domain constraints more effectively. One shortcoming of this approach is that a different optimizer needs to be trained for varying number of input parameters. In future, we plan to extend this work to train optimizers that can ingest input with varying and high number of parameters, e.g. by first proposing a change in a latent space and then estimating changes in actual input space as in [22, 27]. Further, training optimizers for multi-objective optimization can be a useful extension.

A   Generating Diverse Non-convex Synthetic Functions

We generate synthetic non-convex continuous functions f_g defined over $\Theta \subseteq \mathbb{R}^d$ via a Gaussian Mixture Model density function (GMM-DF, similar to [29]):

$$f_g(\mathbf{x}_t) = \sum_{i=1}^{N} \frac{c_i}{(2\pi)^{\frac{k}{2}} |\mathbf{\Sigma}_i|^{\frac{1}{2}}} \exp(-\frac{1}{2}(\mathbf{x}_t - \boldsymbol{\mu}_i)^T \mathbf{\Sigma}_i^{-1}(\mathbf{x}_t - \boldsymbol{\mu}_i)). \tag{12}$$

In this work, we used GMM-DF instead of Gaussian Processes used in [5] for ease of implementation and faster response time to queries: Functions obtained in this manner are often non-convex and have multiple local minima/maxima. Sample plots for functions obtained over 2-D input space are shown in Fig. 7. We use $c_i \sim \mathcal{N}(0, 0.2)$, $\boldsymbol{\mu}_i \sim U(-2.0, 2.0)$ and $\mathbf{\Sigma}_i \sim TruncatedN(0.9, 0.9/5)$ for $d = 2$, $\boldsymbol{\mu}_i \sim U(-3.0, 3.0)$ and $\mathbf{\Sigma}_i \sim TruncatedN(3.0, 3.0/5)$ for $d = 6$ in our experiments (all covariance matrices are diagonal).

For any function f_g, we use an estimated value $\hat{y}_{opt} = \max_i f_g(\boldsymbol{\mu}_i)$ ($i = 1, 2, \ldots, N$) instead of y_{opt}. This assumes that the global maximum of the function is at the mean of one of the N Gaussian components. We validate this

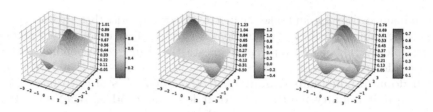

Fig. 7. Sample synthetic GMM density functions for $d = 2$.

assumption by obtaining better estimates of the ground truth for y_{opt} via grid search over randomly sampled 0.2M query points over the domain of f_g. For 10k randomly sampled GMM-DF functions, we obtained an average error of 0.03 with standard deviation of 0.02 in estimating y_{opt}, suggesting that the assumption is reasonable, and in practice, approximate values of y_{opt} suffice to estimate the regret values for supervision. However, in general, y_{opt} can also be obtained using gradient descent on f_g.

References

1. Abadi, M., Barham, P., et al.: Tensorflow: a system for large-scale machine learning. OSDI **16**, 265–283 (2016)
2. Andrychowicz, M., Denil, M., et al.: Learning to learn by gradient descent by gradient descent. In: Advances in Neural Information Processing Systems, pp. 3981–3989 (2016)
3. Ba, J.L., Kiros, J.R., Hinton, G.E.: Layer normalization. arXiv preprint arXiv:1607.06450 (2016)
4. Brochu, E., Cora, V.M., De Freitas, N.: A tutorial on Bayesian optimization of expensive cost functions, with application to active user modeling and hierarchical reinforcement learning. arXiv preprint arXiv:1012.2599 (2010)
5. Chen, Y., et al.: Learning to learn without gradient descent by gradient descent. In: Proceedings of the 34th International Conference on Machine Learning-Volume 70, pp. 748–756 (2017). JMLR.org
6. Cheng, Y., Huang, Y., Pang, B., Zhang, W.: ThermalNET: a deep reinforcement learning-based combustion optimization system for coal-fired boiler. Eng. Appl. Artif. Intell. **74**, 303–311 (2018)
7. Faury, L., Vasile, F.: Rover descent: learning to optimize by learning to navigate on prototypical loss surfaces. In: Battiti, R., Brunato, M., Kotsireas, I., Pardalos, P.M. (eds.) LION 12 2018. LNCS, vol. 11353, pp. 271–287. Springer, Cham (2019). https://doi.org/10.1007/978-3-030-05348-2_24
8. Hansen, N., Ostermeier, A.: Adapting arbitrary normal mutation distributions in evolution strategies: the covariance matrix adaptation. In: Proceedings of IEEE International Conference on Evolutionary Computation, pp. 312–317. IEEE (1996)
9. Hochreiter, S., Schmidhuber, J.: Long short-term memory. Neural Comput. **9**(8), 1735–1780 (1997)
10. Huang, D., Allen, T.T., Notz, W.I., Zeng, N.: Global optimization of stochastic black-box systems via sequential kriging meta-models. J. Global Optim. **34**(3), 441–466 (2006). https://doi.org/10.1007/s10898-005-2454-3

11. Hutter, F., Hoos, H.H., Leyton-Brown, K.: Sequential model-based optimization for general algorithm configuration. In: Coello, C.A.C. (ed.) LION 2011. LNCS, vol. 6683, pp. 507–523. Springer, Heidelberg (2011). https://doi.org/10.1007/978-3-642-25566-3_40

12. Ioffe, S., Szegedy, C.: Batch normalization: accelerating deep network training by reducing internal covariate shift. arXiv preprint arXiv:1502.03167 (2015)

13. Jia, X., et al.: Physics guided rnns for modeling dynamical systems: a case study in simulating lake temperature profiles. arXiv preprint arXiv:1810.13075 (2018)

14. Jones, D.R., Schonlau, M., Welch, W.J.: Efficient global optimization of expensive black-box functions. J. Global Optim. **13**(4), 455–492 (1998). https://doi.org/10.1023/A:1008306431147

15. Kennedy, J.: Particle swarm optimization. In: Sammut, C., Webb, G.I. (eds.) Encyclopedia of Machine Learning, pp. 760–766. Springer, Boston (2011). https://doi.org/10.1007/978-0-387-30164-8_630

16. Kingma, D.P., Ba, J.: Adam: a method for stochastic optimization. arXiv preprint arXiv:1412.6980 (2014)

17. Klambauer, G., Unterthiner, T., Mayr, A., Hochreiter, S.: Self-normalizing neural networks. In: Advances in neural information processing systems. pp. 971–980 (2017)

18. Li, K., Malik, J.: Learning to optimize. arXiv preprint arXiv:1606.01885 (2016)

19. Muralidhar, N., Islam, M.R., Marwah, M., Karpatne, A., Ramakrishnan, N.: Incorporating prior domain knowledge into deep neural networks. In: 2018 IEEE International Conference on Big Data (Big Data). pp. 36–45. IEEE (2018)

20. Nelder, J.A., Mead, R.: A simplex method for function minimization. Comput. J. **7**(4), 308–313 (1965)

21. Rios, L.M., Sahinidis, N.V.: Derivative-free optimization: a review of algorithms and comparison of software implementations. J. Global Optim. **56**(3), 1247–1293 (2013). https://doi.org/10.1007/s10898-012-9951-y

22. Rusu, A.A., et al.: Meta-learning with latent embedding optimization. arXiv preprint arXiv:1807.05960 (2018)

23. Salimans, T., Kingma, D.P.: Weight normalization: a simple reparameterization to accelerate training of deep neural networks. In: Advances in Neural Information Processing Systems, pp. 901–909 (2016)

24. Schmidhuber, J.: Evolutionary principles in self-referential learning, or on learning how to learn: the meta-meta-... hook. Ph.D. thesis, Technische Universität München (1987)

25. Shahriari, B., Swersky, K., Wang, Z., Adams, R.P., De Freitas, N.: Taking the human out of the loop: a review of Bayesian optimization. Proc. IEEE **104**(1), 148–175 (2016)

26. Snoek, J., Larochelle, H., Adams, R.P.: Practical Bayesian optimization of machine learning algorithms. In: Advances in neural information processing systems, pp. 2951–2959 (2012)

27. Wichrowska, O., et al.: Learned optimizers that scale and generalize. In: Proceedings of the 34th International Conference on Machine Learning-Volume 70, pp. 3751–3760 (2017). JMLR.org

28. Zaremba, W., Sutskever, I., Vinyals, O.: Recurrent neural network regularization. arXiv preprint arXiv:1409.2329 (2014)

29. Zhou, Z., Li, X., Zare, R.N.: Optimizing chemical reactions with deep reinforcement learning. ACS Cent. Sci. **3**(12), 1337–1344 (2017)

Training Discrete-Valued Neural Networks with Sign Activations Using Weight Distributions

Wolfgang Roth[1]([✉]), Günther Schindler[2], Holger Fröning[2], and Franz Pernkopf[1]

[1] Signal Processing and Speech Communication Laboratory,
Graz University of Technology, Graz, Austria
{roth,pernkopf}@tugraz.at
[2] Institute of Computer Engineering, Ruprecht Karls University,
Heidelberg, Germany
{guenther.schindler,holger.froening}@ziti.uni-heidelberg.de

Abstract. Since resource-constrained devices hardly benefit from the trend towards ever-increasing neural network (NN) structures, there is growing interest in designing more hardware-friendly NNs. In this paper, we consider the training of NNs with discrete-valued weights and sign activation functions that can be implemented more efficiently in terms of inference speed, memory requirements, and power consumption. We build on the framework of probabilistic forward propagations using the local reparameterization trick, where instead of training a single set of NN weights we rather train a distribution over these weights. Using this approach, we can perform gradient-based learning by optimizing the continuous distribution parameters over discrete weights while at the same time perform backpropagation through the sign activation. In our experiments, we investigate the influence of the number of weights on the classification performance on several benchmark datasets, and we show that our method achieves state-of-the-art performance.

Keywords: Resource-efficiency · Deep learning · Weight distributions

1 Introduction

In recent years, deep neural networks (NNs) achieved unprecedented results in many applications such as computer vision [17], speech recognition [10], and machine translation [32], among others. These improved results, however, can be largely attributed to the growing amount of available data and to increasing hardware-capabilities as NNs are essentially known for decades. On the opposite side, there is also a growing number of hardware-constrained embedded devices that barely benefit from this trend in machine learning. Consequently, over the past years an own research field has emerged that is concerned with developing NN architectures that allow for fast and energy-efficient inference and require little memory for the weights.

ⓒ Springer Nature Switzerland AG 2020
U. Brefeld et al. (Eds.): ECML PKDD 2019, LNAI 11907, pp. 382–398, 2020.
https://doi.org/10.1007/978-3-030-46147-8_23

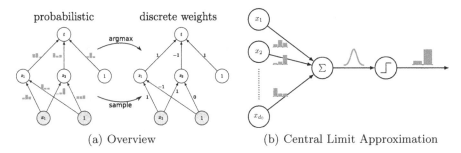

<table>
(a) Overview   (b) Central Limit Approximation
</table>

Fig. 1. (a) Overview of our method. We train distributions over discrete weights (left). After training, a discrete-valued NN can be obtained by selecting the most probable weights or sampling from these distributions. (b) The expectation in Eq. (2) is approximated by invoking a central limit approximation at the neurons and propagating the resulting Gaussians through the sign activations. This results in a loss function that is differentiable with respect to the weight probabilities.

In this paper, we consider NNs with discrete-valued (ternary, quaternary, quinary) weights and sign activation functions. While such weight representations offer an obvious reduction in memory requirements compared to the commonly used 32-bit floating-point representation, discrete weights and activations can also be exploited to speed up inference. For instance, when using ternary weights $\{-1, 0, 1\}$, we can effectively get rid of multiplications.

However, there is one fundamental problem when learning discrete-valued NNs. Real-valued NNs are commonly trained with gradient-based learning using the backpropagation algorithm which is not feasible for discrete weights and/or piecewise constant activation functions. Most of the research concerned with the training of low-bit NNs can be divided into two categories. (i) Methods that quantize the weights of a pre-trained real-valued NN in a more or less heuristic post-processing step. (ii) Methods that perform "quantization aware" training by employing the so called straight-through gradient estimator [1]. Such methods maintain a set of auxiliary real-valued weights w_r that are quantized during forward propagation using some zero-gradient quantization function to obtain w_q. During backpropagation the gradient of the zero-gradient quantization function is assumed to be non-zero and gradient updates are subsequently applied to the auxiliary weights w_r. Analogously, the same technique can be applied for the sign activation by assuming that its derivative is non-zero. At test time, the real-valued weights w_r are ignored and only the quantized weights w_q are kept. Although these methods achieve impressive results in practice, they are theoretically not well understood. Therefore, it is desired to develop methods that are not based on quantization heuristics.

To this end, we adopt a probabilistic view of NNs by considering a distribution $q(\mathbf{W}|\nu)$ over the discrete weights [23,28,31]. We can then introduce an expectation of the zero-gradient loss function over q to obtain a *new* loss function that is differentiable with respect to the distribution parameters ν.

This allows us to perform gradient-based learning over the distribution parameters ν. After training has finished, a discrete-valued resource-efficient NN is obtained by either sampling or taking the most probable weights from q, respectively. This is illustrated in Fig. 1(a).

Compared to the most relevant previous work in [23,28] which used binary and ternary weights, we consider general discrete weights. These methods use a parameterization for q that is tailored to binary and ternary weights and does not easily generalize to more than three weights. Similarly, their initialization method for q that is crucial to achieve competitive results does also not easily generalize to more than three weights. We introduce a simpler parameterization and initialization method that generalizes to arbitrary discrete weights. We introduce a variance-aware approximation for max-pooling as opposed to the method in [23] which effectively ignores the variance. In contrast to several other works that require real-valued weights in the input and/or output layers [24,28,36], we employ discrete weights in *all* layers. Our method achieves state-of-the-art performance on several benchmark datasets. In our experiments, we show that more weights typically result in better performance. We found a two-stage procedure, where we first train a NN using discrete weights only, and subsequently also train with the sign activation function to mostly improve results compared to training with discrete weights and the sign activation immediately.

The remainder of the paper is structured as follows. Section 2 reviews the most relevant work. In Sect. 3 we introduce our probabilistic neural network framework. Section 4 presents an efficient approximation to the intractable expected loss function followed by model details in Sect. 5. We show results of our model in Sect. 6 before we conclude in Sect. 7. Code related to the paper is available online at https://github.com/wroth8/nn-discrete.

2   Related Work

In our literature review, we focus on work that is most related to this paper, namely work that quantizes weights and/or activations. Most recent works concerned with the training of low-precision NNs rely on the straight-through gradient estimator and introduce different quantizers [2,5,11,19,24,37]. Soudry et al. [31] used a Bayesian approach based on expectation propagation to obtain distributions over discrete weights. The work of Shayer et al. [28] is closely related to our work, but they only consider binary and ternary NNs with full-precision ReLU activations. Most related to our work is the work of Peters and Welling [23]. They consider binary and ternary weights using sign activations. We extend the work of [23,28] to general discrete weights and introduce a variance-aware approximation for max-pooling.

Beyond work focusing on low-bit NNs, there exist several orthogonal directions that facilitate resource-efficient inference. Weight pruning methods, i.e., setting a large portion of the weights to zero, can be utilized to reduce the memory footprint and to improve inference speed [8,21]. The work in [3,26,33] introduces weight sharing to reduce the memory footprint. More global strategies are concerned with special matrix structures that facilitate efficient inference

[4,6,7]. There also exists work regarding efficient training of neural networks that is not within the scope of this paper [35,36].

3 Neural Networks and Weight Distributions

A NN with L layers and weights $\mathbf{W} = (\mathbf{W}^1, \ldots, \mathbf{W}^L)$ defines a function $f(\mathbf{x}^0; \mathbf{W})$ by repeatedly computing a linear transformation $\mathbf{a}^l = \mathbf{W}^l \mathbf{x}^{l-1}$ followed by a non-linear activation function $\mathbf{x}^l = \phi^l(\mathbf{a}^l)$. The linear function is either a general matrix-vector multiplication or a convolution operation.[1] For layers $l = 1, \ldots, L - 1$, typical choices for the non-linear activation function $\phi^l(a)$ are the ReLU activation $\max(0, a)$, $\tanh(a)$, or, in the context of resource-efficient NNs, $\text{sign}(a) = \mathbb{I}(a \geq 0) - \mathbb{I}(a < 0)$, where $\mathbb{I}$ is the indicator function. In this paper we consider classification problems where the task is to assign an input $\mathbf{x}^0$ to one of C classes. For classification, the activation function ϕ^L at the output is the softmax function $x_i^L = \exp(a_i^L)/\sum_{j=1}^C \exp(a_j^L)$. An input $\mathbf{x}^0$ is classified according to $c = \arg\max_j x_j^L$. Note that the computationally expensive softmax does not change the maximum of its inputs, and, therefore, computing the softmax is not required to determine the predicted class label.

Let $\mathcal{D} = \{(\mathbf{x}_1^0, t_1), \ldots, (\mathbf{x}_N^0, t_N)\}$ be a dataset of N input-target pairs and let $y_n = \mathbf{x}_n^L = f(\mathbf{x}_n^0; \mathbf{W})$ be the NN output for the nth sample. The weights $\mathbf{W}$ are typically obtained by performing gradient descent on a loss function

$$\mathcal{L}(\mathbf{W}; \mathcal{D}) = \frac{1}{N} \sum_{n=1}^N l(f(\mathbf{x}_n^0; \mathbf{W}), t_n) + \lambda r(\mathbf{W}), \tag{1}$$

where $l(y_n, t_n)$ penalizes the weights $\mathbf{W}$ if the nth sample is misclassified, r is a regularizer that favors simpler models to enforce generalization, and $\lambda > 0$ is a tunable hyperparameter.

However, when considering weights from a discrete set, gradient-based learning cannot be applied. Moreover, the sign activation function results in a gradient that is zero almost everywhere, rendering backpropagation not usable. In this paper, we employ weight distributions to solve both of these problems at the same time. Instead of a single set of NN weights $\mathbf{W}$, we consider a *distribution* $q(\mathbf{W}|\nu)$ over the discrete weights, where ν are the parameters governing the distribution q. By redefining (1) using an expectation with respect to q, i.e.,

$$\mathcal{L}_{prob}(\nu; \mathcal{D}) = \frac{1}{N} \sum_{n=1}^N \mathbb{E}_{q(\mathbf{W}|\nu)} \left[l(f(\mathbf{x}_n^0; \mathbf{W}), t_n) \right] + \lambda r(\nu), \tag{2}$$

we obtain a differentiable function with respect to the parameters ν of q. In principle, this allows us to perform gradient-based learning over the distribution parameters ν, and subsequently to determine the discrete-valued weights by either sampling or selecting the most probable weights from q, respectively.[2]

---

[1] A convolution can be cast as a matrix-vector multiplication.
[2] We only consider distributions q where sampling and maximization is easy.

However, the expectation in (2) is essentially a sum over exponentially many terms which is generally intractable. In Sect. 4 we show how the gradient of (2) can be approximated.

3.1 Discrete Neural Networks

Let $\mathbb{D}^D = \{w_1, \ldots, w_D\}$ be a discrete set of weight values with $w_1 < \ldots < w_D$. In this paper we consider discrete weights with $D \in \{3, 4, 5\}$, i.e., ternary, quaternary, and quinary weights. The choice of the particular weights w_d is arbitrary and we restrict ourselves to equidistributed weights with constant $\delta_w = w_{d+1} - w_d$. In particular, we have $\mathbb{D}^3 = \{-1, 0, 1\}$, $\mathbb{D}^4 = \{-1, -\frac{1}{3}, \frac{1}{3}, 1\}$, and $\mathbb{D}^5 = \{-1, -\frac{1}{2}, 0, \frac{1}{2}, 1\}$. We use the sign activation function which implies that the scale of the discrete weight set becomes irrelevant as either the sign stays unaffected or batch normalization [12] compensates for the change in scale.

For the weight distribution q, we assume independence among the weights which is commonly referred to as the mean-field assumption in the variational inference framework. This implies that q factorizes into a product of factors $q(w|\nu_w)$ for each weight $w \in \mathbf{W}$. Each of these factors is a probability mass function (pmf) over D values. We elaborate more on the parameterization of the pmf over discrete weights in Sect. 5.2.

3.2 Relation to Variational Inference

The presented work is closely related to the Bayesian variational inference framework. For a Bayesian treatment of NNs, we assume a prior distribution $p(\mathbf{W})$ over the weights and interpret the NN output after the softmax as likelihood $p(\mathcal{D}|\mathbf{W})$ to obtain a posterior $p(\mathbf{W}|\mathcal{D}) \propto p(\mathcal{D}|\mathbf{W})p(\mathbf{W})$ over the weights. As the induced posterior $p(\mathbf{W}|\mathcal{D})$ is generally intractable, the aim of variational inference is to approximate it by a simpler distribution $q(\mathbf{W}|\nu)$ by minimizing the negative evidence lower bound

$$\mathcal{L}_{elbo}(\nu; \mathcal{D}) = \sum_{n=1}^{N} \mathbb{E}_{q(\mathbf{W}|\nu)}[-\log p(t_n|\mathbf{x}_n, \mathbf{W})] + \mathrm{KL}(q(\mathbf{W}|\nu)||p(\mathbf{W})). \quad (3)$$

Equation (3) is proportional to (2) for $l(y_n, t_n)$ being the cross-entropy loss, $r(\nu)$ being the KL-divergence, and $\lambda = 1/N$. The main difference to variational inference is our motivation to use distributions in order to obtain a gradient-based learning scheme for discrete-valued NNs with discrete activation functions. Variational inference is typically used to approximate expectations over the posterior $p(\mathbf{W}|\mathcal{D})$ and to obtain well calibrated uncertainty estimates for NN predictions.

4 Approximation of the Expected Loss

The expected loss in (2) is given by

$$\mathbb{E}_{q(\mathbf{W}|\nu)}\left[l(f(\mathbf{x}_n^0; \mathbf{W}), t_n)\right] = \sum_{\mathbf{W}^1} \cdots \sum_{\mathbf{W}^L} q(\mathbf{W}|\nu)\, l(f(\mathbf{x}_n^0; \mathbf{W}), t_n). \quad (4)$$

Equation (4) contains a sum over exponentially many terms and is generally intractable. Nevertheless, we adopt a practical approximation based on the central limit theorem that has been widely used in the literature [9,23,25,28,31]. As each neuron computes a sum over many random variables, we can apply the central limit theorem and approximate the neuron distribution by a Gaussian $\mathcal{N}(a_i^1|\mu_{a_i^1}, \sigma_{a_i^1}^2)$ where $\mu_{a_i^1} = \sum_j \mathbb{E}[w_{i,j}^1] \, x_j^0$ and $\sigma_{a_i^1}^2 = \sum_j \mathbb{V}[w_{i,j}^1] \, (x_j^0)^2$. The binary distribution after the sign function is obtained by $q(x_i^1 = 1) = \Phi(\mu_{a_i^1}/\sigma_{a_i^1})$ where Φ denotes the cumulative distribution function (cdf) of a zero-mean unit-variance Gaussian.[3] This is illustrated in Fig. 1(b). This approach transfers the weight distributions $q(\mathbf{W}^1)$ to distributions over the inputs of the next layer $q(\mathbf{x}_n^1)$, i.e.,

$$\mathbb{E}_{q(\mathbf{W}|\nu)}\left[l(f(\mathbf{x}_n^0;\mathbf{W}),t_n)\right] \approx \sum_{\mathbf{W}^2} \cdots \sum_{\mathbf{W}^L} \sum_{\mathbf{x}_n^1} q(\mathbf{W}^{>1}|\nu) \, q(\mathbf{x}_n^1) \, l(f(\mathbf{x}_n^1;\mathbf{W}^{>1}),t_n),$$

(5)

where $\mathbf{W}^{>1} = (\mathbf{W}^2,\ldots,\mathbf{W}^L)$. In principle, we can iterate this procedure up to the output layer where it remains to compute the expected loss function $l(y_n,t_n)$ with respect to a Gaussian. However, there are two disadvantages with this approach. (i) For the following layers, the inputs $\mathbf{x}$ are random variables rather than fixed values which requires, assuming independence, to compute $\sigma_{a_i^l}^2 = \sum_j \mathbb{V}[w_{i,j}^l] \, \mathbb{E}[x_j^{l-1}]^2 + \mathbb{E}[w_{i,j}^l]^2 \, \mathbb{V}[x_j^{l-1}] + \mathbb{V}[w_{i,j}^l] \, \mathbb{V}[x_j^{l-1}]$. This boils down to computing three linear transformations for the variances $\sigma_{a_i^l}^2$ rather than just one as for the first layer which is impractical. (ii) Since $\mathbf{x}^1$ is not observed, the neurons in the next layer $\mathbf{x}^2$ are not independent and, thus, we are effectively introducing an unreasonable independence assumption.

To avoid these problems, we adopt the local reparameterization trick [15,23,28]. Since the reparameterized distribution is discrete, we apply the Gumbel softmax approximation [13,20]. The reparameterization trick transforms the activation distribution into an observed value that eliminates the before mentioned problems at the cost of introducing a small bias due to the Gumbel softmax approximation. We iterate this scheme up to the output layer where we approximate the expectation of the loss function again by applying the local reparameterization trick at the output activations. Note that due to the zero derivative of the sign activation, the reparameterization trick cannot be applied before the sign activation function. This implies that we have to propagate distributions through max-pooling and batch normalization [12] which is not straightforward and could otherwise be circumvented by simply reparameterizing before these operations.

Since our goal is to obtain a single discrete-valued NN achieving a good performance, the question arises whether we can expect the *most probable* discrete

---

[3] Given finite integer-valued summands, the activation distribution could also be computed exactly in sub-exponential time by convolving the probabilities. However, this would be impractical for gradient-based learning.

weights to perform well if we perform well in expectation. In our probabilistic forward propagation, the loss function essentially only depends on the means $\mathbb{E}_q[w]$ and the variances $\mathbb{V}_q[w]$. Using discrete weights with $d_1 = -1$ and $d_D = 1$, we can represent any mean in the interval $[-1, 1]$. However, we can only achieve low variance if the expectation is close to a weight in $\mathbb{D}$. Therefore, our approach can be seen as a way of parameterizing expectations and constrained variances, respectively. As we require small variances to obtain a small expected loss – in fact a point mass would be optimal – optimization favors expectations that are closer to values in $\mathbb{D}$. Consequently, also the most probable weights in q are expected to perform well.

However, there is one caveat when applying this scheme to *convolutional* layers that was not mentioned in the works of [23, 28]. As weights in our framework are not observed and a single weight in convolutional layers is used in the computation of many activations, these activations actually become dependent. However, when applying the local reparameterization trick, we effectively assume independence among the activations which would be equivalent to sampling different weights for each activation. Note that this problem does not arise in fully-connected layers as weights are not shared among neurons.

4.1   Approximation of the Maximum Function

Many CNN architectures involve a max-pooling operation where feature maps are downscaled by only passing the maximum of several spatially neighboring activations to the next layer. To this end, we approximate the maximum of two Gaussians by another Gaussian by moment-matching. Let μ_1, μ_2 and σ_1^2, σ_2^2 be the means and the variances of two *independent* Gaussians. Then the mean μ_{max} and the variance σ_{max}^2 of the maximum of these Gaussians is given by [30]

$$\mu_{max} = \mu_1 \Phi(\beta) + \mu_2 \Phi(-\beta) + \alpha\phi(\beta) \qquad \text{and} \tag{6}$$

$$\sigma_{max}^2 = (\sigma_1^2 + \mu_1^2)\Phi(\beta) + (\sigma_2^2 + \mu_2^2)\Phi(-\beta) + (\mu_1 + \mu_2)\alpha\phi(\beta) - \mu_{max}^2, \tag{7}$$

where ϕ and Φ are the pdf and the cdf of a zero-mean unit-variance Gaussian and

$$\alpha = \sqrt{\sigma_1^2 + \sigma_2^2} \quad \text{and} \quad \beta = \frac{\mu_1 - \mu_2}{\alpha}. \tag{8}$$

This scheme can be iteratively applied to approximate the maximum of several Gaussians. As long as the number of Gaussians is relatively small – CNNs typically involve 2×2 max-pooling – this scheme results in a fairly efficient approximation for max-pooling. In particular, we first approximate the maximum of the two upper and the two lower activations by a Gaussian, respectively, and then we approximate the maximum of these two Gaussians by another Gaussian. This is in contrast to the method proposed in [23] where max-pooling is approximated by selecting the mean and the variance of the activation whose mean is maximal, which effectively ignores the variance in the process.

5   Model Details

A basic convolutional block is depicted in Fig. 2. We typically start with dropout, followed by a convolution layer. Motivated by [24], we perform the pooling operation (if present) right after the convolutional layer to avoid information loss. Afterwards we perform batch normalization as described in Sect. 5.1, followed by computing the pmf after the sign function, and finally performing the local reparameterization trick using the Gumbel softmax approximation.

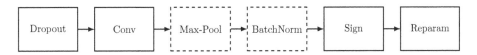

Fig. 2. The convolutional block used in this paper. Max-pooling is not always present.

We do not perform batch normalization in the final layer. Instead we introduce a real-valued bias and divide the output activations by the square root of the number of incoming neurons. This normalization step is crucial for training as otherwise the output softmax would be saturated in most cases as the output activations are typically large due to the discreteness of the weights and inputs from the previous layer, respectively. Moreover, we found dropout in our experiments to be particularly helpful as it improved performance considerably. Dropout was performed by randomly setting both the neuron's mean and its variance to zero in order to completely remove its influence.

5.1   Batch Normalization

As briefly mentioned in Sect. 4, we are required to generalize batch normalization to distributions. Batch normalization is particularly important when using sign activations to avoid excessive information loss [24]. We use the method proposed in [23] to normalize distributions to approximately having zero-mean and unit-variance. The mini-batch statistics for N_B samples are computed as

$$\mu_{i,bn} = \frac{1}{N_B} \sum_{n=1}^{N_B} \mu_{a_{n,i}} \quad \text{and} \quad \sigma_{i,bn}^2 = \frac{1}{N_B - 1} \sum_{n=1}^{N_B} \sigma_{a_{n,i}}^2 + (\mu_{a_{n,i}} - \mu_{i,bn})^2. \quad (9)$$

Subsequently, batch normalization is computed as

$$\mu_{a_i} \leftarrow \frac{\mu_{a_i} - \mu_{i,bn}}{\sigma_{i,bn}} \gamma_i + \beta_i \quad \text{and} \quad \sigma_{a_i}^2 \leftarrow \frac{\sigma_{a_i}^2}{\sigma_{i,bn}^2} \gamma_i^2, \quad (10)$$

where β_i and γ_i are the learnable batch normalization parameters. For predictions, it is important to compute the batch statistics *using the discrete NN* as the batch statistics computed during training might differ significantly. Using batch statistics computed during training resulted in severe fluctuations in the validation errors. However, this implies that estimating the training set statistics using exponential moving averages[4] *during* training, as is commonly done in practice, is not applicable anymore, and we have to compute a separate forward pass using the discrete NN to obtain these statistics. We estimate the training set statistics using an exponential moving average over the whole training set *after* each epoch and right before computing the validation error. Note that batch normalization, although introducing real-valued variables, requires only a marginal computational overhead at test time [34].

5.2   Parameterization and Initialization of q

Shayer et al. [28] introduced a parameterization for ternary distributions based on two probabilities, $q(w = 0)$ and $q(w = 1|w \neq 0)$, which is not easily generalizable to distributions over more than three weights. In this work, we parameterize distributions over D values using unconstrained unnormalized log-probabilities (logits) ν_w^d for $d \in \{1, \ldots, D\}$. The normalized probabilities $q(w|\nu_w)$ can be recovered by applying the softmax function to the logits ν_w. This straightforward parameterization allows to select the dth weight by setting $\nu_w^d > \nu_w^{d'}$ for $d' \neq d$. Due to the sum-to-one constraint of probabilities, we can reduce the number of parameters in ν by fixing an arbitrary logit, e.g., $\nu_w^1 = 0$. However, we refrain to do so as it is more natural to increase a probability explicitly by increasing its corresponding logit rather than indirectly by reducing all other logits.

Moreover, Shayer et al. [28] introduced an initialization method for the distribution parameters ν by matching the expectation $\mathbb{E}_q[w]$ to the real weights $\tilde{w}$ of a pre-trained network. In our experiments, we found such an initialization scheme to be crucial as starting from randomly initialized logits one usually gets stuck in a bad local minimum. However, their initialization method also does not generalize easily to more than three weights, especially since matching the expectation $\mathbb{E}_q[w] = \tilde{w}$ is already an underconstrained problem for $D = 3$. Hence, we propose to use the following initialization scheme to approximately match the expectations which we found to be at least as effective as Shayer et al.'s approach for ternary weights. Let $w_1 < \ldots < w_D$ be the set of discrete weights. Furthermore, let q_{min} be a minimal probability that is required to avoid zero probabilities. The maximum probability is then given by $q_{max} = 1 - (D-1)q_{min}$ and we define $\delta_q = q_{max} - q_{min}$. Given a real-valued weight $\tilde{w}$, we initialize q as

$$
q(w = w_j) = \begin{cases} q_{min} + \delta_q \dfrac{\tilde{w} - w_{j-1}}{w_j - w_{j-1}} & w_{j-1} < \tilde{w} \leq w_j \\ q_{min} + \delta_q \dfrac{w_{j+1} - \tilde{w}}{w_{j+1} - w_j} & w_j < \tilde{w} \leq w_{j+1} \\ q_{max} & (j = 1 \wedge \tilde{w} < w_1) \vee (j = D \wedge \tilde{w} > w_D) \\ q_{min} & \text{otherwise.} \end{cases}
$$

(11)

---

[4] $\mu_{i,tr}^{new} \leftarrow \xi_{bn}\mu_{i,bn} + (1 - \xi_{bn})\mu_{i,tr}^{old}$ for $\xi_{bn} \in (0,1)$, and similarly for $\sigma_{i,tr}^2$.

This scheme is illustrated in Fig. 3(a). However, weight magnitudes might differ across layers which Shayer et al. [28] addressed by dividing the weights in each layer by their standard deviation before applying (11). We propose the following scheme which distributes probabilities more uniformly across the discrete weights in order to benefit from the increased expressiveness when using a larger D. Let $\Phi_e^l(w) = 1/|\mathbf{W}^l| \sum_{\tilde{w} \in \mathbf{W}^l} \mathbb{I}[\tilde{w} \leq w]$ be the empirical cdf of the weights in layer l. We compute $\tilde{w}^l \leftarrow \Phi_e^l(\tilde{w}^l)$ such that the weights cover the unit interval with equal spacing while keeping the relative order of the weights, essentially removing the scale. Then we shift and scale the weights $\tilde{w}$ to cover the interval $[w_1 - \delta_w/2, w_D + \delta_w/2]$, followed by assigning the probabilities to q according to (11). This ensures that each discrete weight is initially selected equally often as the most likely weight in q. We propose to use this scheme for the positive and the negative weights separately such that the signs of the weights are preserved.

6   Experiments

We performed classification experiments on several datasets that are described in Sect. 6.1. We optimized (2) using ADAM [14], and we report the test classification error of the epoch resulting in the best validation classification error. All results for discrete-valued NNs are reported using the most probable model from q. We selected $l(y_n, t_n)$ to be the cross-entropy loss, $r(\nu)$ to be the squared ℓ^2-norm over the logits [28], and $\lambda = 10^{-10}$. Penalizing large logits can be seen as enforcing a uniform pmf and therefore increasing entropy and variance. As stated in [28], this rather helps to obtain better Gaussian approximations using the central limit theorem rather than to reduce overfitting. After each gradient update we clip the logits to the range $[-5, 5]$. We set the initial step size to 10^{-2} for the logits and to 10^{-3} for all other parameters (batch normalization, bias in the final layer). We use the following plateau learning rate reduction scheme: The learning rate is kept for at least τ_1 epochs and after τ_1 epochs we multiply the learning rate by $1/2$ if the validation error has not improved within the last τ_2 epochs. The parameters τ_1 and τ_2, as well as some other dataset-depending settings can be found in Sect. 6.1. We selected $q_{max} = 0.95$, the Gumbel softmax temperature $\tau_g = 1$, and $\xi_{bn} = 0.1$.

6.1   Datasets

MNIST. The MNIST dataset [18] contains grayscale images of size 28×28 pixels showing handwritten digits from 0–9. The training set contains 60,000 images and the test set contains 10,000 images. We split the training set into a training set of 50,000 training images and 10,000 validation images. We normalize the pixels to be in the range $[-1, 1]$. We considered two scenarios for the MNIST dataset: (i) A permutation-invariant (PI) setting where each pixel is treated as independent feature without taking pixel locality into account, i.e., we do not use a CNN. For this setting we use the fully-connected architecture

$$FC1200 - FC1200 - FC10,$$

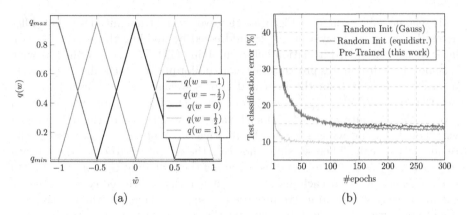

(a)   (b)

Fig. 3. (a) Our initialization method for quinary weight distributions based on pre-trained real-valued weights $\tilde{w}$. (b) Test classification error [%] over number of epochs on Cifar-10 for ternary weights using different initialization methods for q. For randomly initialized probabilities, we either sampled real-valued weights $\tilde{w} \sim \mathcal{N}(0,1)$ (Gauss) or randomly assigned equidistributed values in the interval $[-1.5, 1.5]$ randomly to the weights $\tilde{w}$ (equidistr.) before applying the method described in (a).

where FC1200 denotes a fully-connected layer with 1200 output neurons. We refer to this setting as MNIST (PI). (ii) We keep the image structure and use CNNs with the architecture

$$32C5 - P2 - 64C5 - P2 - FC512 - FC10,$$

where 32C5 means that 5×5 filter kernels are applied and 32 output feature maps are generated, and P2 means that 2×2 max-pooling is applied. We trained both architectures for 500 epochs using mini-batches of 100 samples with $\tau_1 = 50$ and $\tau_2 = 10$. We used dropout probabilities (0.1, 0.2, 0.3) for MNIST (PI) and (0, 0.2, 0.3, 0) for the CNN setting, respectively, where the first entry corresponds to the input layer and the following entries correspond to the subsequent layers.

Cifar-10 and Cifar-100. The Cifar-10 dataset [16] contains 32×32 pixel RGB images showing objects from ten different categories. The dataset is split into 50,000 training images and 10,000 test images. We split the training set into 45,000 training images and 5,000 validation images. The pixels are again normalized to be in the range $[-1, 1]$. For training, we perform data augmentation by shifting the images randomly by up to four pixels in each direction, and we randomly flip images along the vertical axis similar as in [28]. Cifar-100 is similar to Cifar-10 except that the task is to assign an image to one of 100 object categories. As the image sizes and the training and test set sizes are equal, we perform the same preprocessing steps as described above. For both datasets, we use the VGG-inspired [29] CNN architecture

$$2 \times 128C3 - P2 - 2 \times 256C3 - P2 - 2 \times 512C3 - P2 - FC1024 - FC10/100,$$

Table 1. Classification errors [%] of various NN models. Real+Tanh is the baseline that was used to initialize the discrete NNs. For discrete NNs, we conducted each experiment five times and report the means and standard deviations, respectively.

Dataset	Real+Tanh	Ternary+Sign	Quaternary+Sign	Quinary+Sign
MNIST (PI)	1.030	1.350 ± 0.058	1.326 ± 0.012	1.334 ± 0.027
MNIST	0.560	0.712 ± 0.040	0.652 ± 0.020	0.654 ± 0.040
Cifar-10	7.620	9.508 ± 0.289	9.494 ± 0.210	9.078 ± 0.218
Cifar-100	30.150	33.550 ± 0.161	33.534 ± 0.400	33.026 ± 0.231
SVHN	2.259	2.618 ± 0.047	2.631 ± 0.051	2.605 ± 0.045

where $2 \times 128C3$ denotes two consecutive $128C3$ blocks. We trained for 300 epochs using mini-batches of 100 samples with $\tau_1 = 30$ and $\tau_2 = 10$. We used dropout probabilities $(0, 0.2, 0.2, 0.3, 0.3, 0.3, 0.4, 0)$ for both datasets.

SVHN. The SVHN dataset [22] contains 32×32 pixel RGB images showing parts of pictures containing house numbers that need to be classified to the digits 0–9. The dataset is split into 604,388 training images and 26,032 test images. We follow the procedure of [27] to split the training set into 598,388 training images and 6,000 validation images. Once again, we normalize pixels to be in the range $[-1, 1]$. Since the dataset is quite large, we do not perform data augmentation. We use the same CNN architecture as for the Cifar datasets except that we only use half the number of feature maps in the convolutional layers, i.e.,

$$2 \times 64C3 - P2 - 2 \times 128C3 - P2 - 2 \times 256C3 - P2 - FC1024 - FC10.$$

Since SVHN is quite large, we performed only 100 epochs of training using mini-batches of 250 samples with $\tau_1 = 15$ and $\tau_2 = 5$. We used the same dropout probabilities as for the Cifar datasets.

6.2 Classification Results

In the first experiment, we used pre-trained real-valued NNs with tanh activation to initialize the discrete NNs with sign activation function as shown in Sect. 5.2. The results are shown in Table 1. The performance gap compared to the real-valued NN tends to become smaller as more weights are used. There is a consistent improvement of quinary weights over ternary weights. Quaternary weights improve on four datasets compared to ternary weights whereas they achieve worse performance than quinary weights on the more challenging Cifar and SVHN datasets. We attribute the mixed behavior of quaternary weights to the missing zero-weight that might be important.

In the next experiment, we performed an intermediate step where we first only discretized the weights and kept the tanh activation. In a next step, we used

Table 2. Classification errors [%] of various NN models. The first three models were initialized with Real+Tanh from Table 1. The last three models were initialized with the corresponding discrete-weight model with tanh activation. For discrete NNs with sign activation, we conducted each experiment five times and report the means and standard deviations, respectively.

Dataset	Ternary+Tanh	Quaternary+Tanh	Quinary+Tanh	Ternary+Sign	Quaternary+Sign	Quinary+Sign
MNIST (PI)	1.310	1.300	1.280	1.352 ± 0.053	1.292 ± 0.031	1.298 ± 0.040
MNIST	0.570	0.560	0.620	0.736 ± 0.037	0.678 ± 0.042	0.736 ± 0.039
Cifar-10	7.770	7.810	8.030	9.174 ± 0.139	9.246 ± 0.251	9.080 ± 0.246
Cifar-100	29.770	29.840	29.120	33.608 ± 0.199	33.236 ± 0.265	32.910 ± 0.196
SVHN	2.328	2.324	2.362	2.574 ± 0.086	2.591 ± 0.081	2.532 ± 0.056

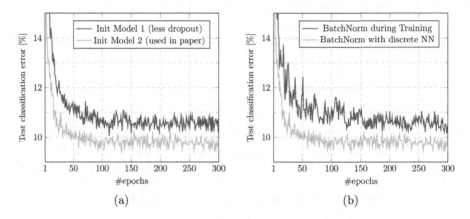

(a)   (b)

Fig. 4. (a) Test classification error [%] on Cifar-10 obtained by using two different real-valued NNs for the initial parameters of q. Init Model 1 uses less dropout and achieves 7.05% test error whereas Init Model 2 achieves 7.62% test error. However, Init Model 2 results in a better discrete-valued NN. (b) Test classification error [%] on Cifar-10 by estimating the training set batch statistics using an exponential moving average once during training and once using the discrete-valued NN.

this NN as initial model to train a NN with discrete weights *and* sign activation. The results of these experiments are shown in Table 2. When only the weights are discretized and tanh is kept, the performance gap compared to real-valued NNs in Table 1 is less severe than when discretizing both the weights and the activations. The only exception is on MNIST (PI) where the gap is similar to the gap when in addition the sign activation is used. Interestingly, the performance on Cifar-100 improves compared to real-valued NNs, indicating a regularizing effect similar as in [37]. These findings are in line with other papers that have shown little performance degradation when the real-valued activation function is kept and only the weights are discretized [28, 37].

Next, we compare the corresponding values of discrete-valued NNs with sign activation from Table 1 and 2. Except on MNIST where results do not improve, the performance using a pre-trained discrete-valued NN with tanh activation for initialization improves in nine out of twelve cases on the other datasets, showing that a two stage training procedure is mostly beneficial.

We also compare our model with [11,23,24,36] as their quantization is similar to ours. Hubara et al. [11] use binary weights and sign activations, albeit using larger architectures. They report two results and achieve on average $1.18 \pm 0.22\%$ on MNIST (PI), $10.775 \pm 0.625\%$ on Cifar-10, and 2.66 ± 0.135 on SVHN. XNOR-Net [24] uses real-valued *data-dependent* scale factors to perform a binary convolution. Using the same structure as [11], they achieve 10.17% on Cifar-10. DoReFa-Net [36] achieves 2.9% on SVHN using binary weights and binary 0–1 activations. The work in [23] is closest to ours and achieves 0.74% on MNIST and 10.30% on Cifar-10 using ternary weights and sign activations.

6.3 Ablation Study

In this Section, we investigate the influence of the initialization of q, dropout, and batch normalization on Cifar-10. Figure 3(b) compares our initialization method for q described in Sect. 5.2 to random initialization strategies. Our method converges faster than the random strategies and achieves almost 4% less absolute classification error than the random strategies which seem to get stuck in bad local minima. This highlights the importance of a proper initialization strategy for the training of weight distributions as the loss surface being optimized seems to be substantially more delicate than that of a conventional real-valued NN.

This raises the question if it might pay off to put more effort into the training of the real-valued NN serving for initialization. To answer this question, we optimized several dropout rates for the initial real-valued NN with tanh activation, keeping all the other hyperparameters the same. This resulted in dropout rates $(0, 0.1, 0.1, 0.1, 0.1, 0.1, 0.1, 0.1. 0.1)$ achieving a test error of 7.05% – an almost 0.6% absolute improvement compared to the result in Table 1. However, when using this model to initialize q, we achieved inferior performance for the discrete-valued NN with sign activation as can be seen in Fig. 4(a).

As mentioned in Sect. 5.1, computing exponential moving averages *during* training to estimate the training set statistics required at test time could lead to severely different statistics as those obtained using the discrete-valued NN. To verify this, we performed two runs that only differ in the estimation of the training set statistics. This is shown in Fig. 4(b). The performance deteriorates heavily and especially in the beginning there are substantial fluctuations.

7 Conclusion

In this paper, we have generalized previous work on discrete weight distributions to arbitrary discrete weights. To this end, we introduced simpler schemes to parameterize and initialize the weight distributions q, respectively. We introduced a Gaussian approximation for max-pooling that takes the variance into account. Our method achieves state-of-the-art performance on several image classification datasets using discrete weights in *all* layers. We found initialization of q using a pre-trained real-valued NN crucial in order to obtain reasonable performances. However, it remains unclear what properties of a pre-trained NN make it a good choice for an initial model since we observed that a better performing real-valued NN does not necessarily result in a better performing discrete-valued NN.

Acknowledgements. This work was supported by the Austrian Science Fund (FWF) under the project number I2706-N31.

References

1. Bengio, Y., Léonard, N., Courville, A.C.: Estimating or propagating gradients through stochastic neurons for conditional computation. CoRR abs/1308.3432 (2013)
2. Cai, Z., He, X., Sun, J., Vasconcelos, N.: Deep learning with low precision by half-wave Gaussian quantization. In: Conference on Computer Vision and Pattern Recognition (CVPR), pp. 5406–5414 (2017)
3. Chen, W., Wilson, J.T., Tyree, S., Weinberger, K.Q., Chen, Y.: Compressing neural networks with the hashing trick. In: International Conference on Machine Learning (ICML), pp. 2285–2294 (2015)
4. Cheng, Y., Yu, F.X., Feris, R.S., Kumar, S., Choudhary, A.N., Chang, S.: An exploration of parameter redundancy in deep networks with circulant projections. In: International Conference on Computer Vision (ICCV), pp. 2857–2865 (2015)
5. Courbariaux, M., Bengio, Y., David, J.P.: BinaryConnect: training deep neural networks with binary weights during propagations. In: Advances in Neural Information Processing Systems (NIPS), pp. 3123–3131 (2015)
6. Denil, M., Shakibi, B., Dinh, L., Ranzato, M., de Freitas, N.: Predicting parameters in deep learning. In: Advances in Neural Information Processing Systems (NIPS), pp. 2148–2156 (2013)
7. Denton, E.L., Zaremba, W., Bruna, J., LeCun, Y., Fergus, R.: Exploiting linear structure within convolutional networks for efficient evaluation. In: Neural Information Processing Systems, pp. 1269–1277 (2014)
8. Han, S., Mao, H., Dally, W.J.: Deep compression: compressing deep neural network with pruning, trained quantization and Huffman coding. In: International Conference on Learning Representations (ICLR) (2016)
9. Hernandez-Lobato, J.M., Adams, R.: Probabilistic backpropagation for scalable learning of Bayesian neural networks. In: International Conference on Machine Learning (ICML), pp. 1861–1869 (2015)
10. Hinton, G., et al.: Deep neural networks for acoustic modeling in speech recognition: the shared views of four research groups. IEEE Signal Process. Mag. **29**(6), 82–97 (2012)
11. Hubara, I., Courbariaux, M., Soudry, D., El-Yaniv, R., Bengio, Y.: Binarized neural networks. In: Advances in Neural Information Processing Systems (NIPS), pp. 4107–4115 (2016)

12. Ioffe, S., Szegedy, C.: Batch normalization: accelerating deep network training by reducing internal covariate shift. In: International Conference on Machine Learning (ICML), pp. 448–456 (2015)
13. Jang, E., Gu, S., Poole, B.: Categorical reparameterization with Gumbel-softmax. In: International Conference on Learning Representations (ICLR) (2017)
14. Kingma, D., Ba, J.: Adam: a method for stochastic optimization. In: International Conference on Learning Representations (ICLR) (2015). arXiv: 1412.6980
15. Kingma, D.P., Salimans, T., Welling, M.: Variational dropout and the local reparameterization trick. In: Advances in Neural Information Processing Systems (NIPS), pp. 2575–2583 (2015)
16. Krizhevsky, A.: Learning multiple layers of features from tiny images. University of Toronto, Technical report (2009)
17. Krizhevsky, A., Sutskever, I., Hinton, G.E.: Imagenet classification with deep convolutional neural networks. In: Advances in Neural Information Processing Systems (NIPS), pp. 1106–1114 (2012)
18. LeCun, Y., Bottou, L., Bengio, Y., Haffner, P.: Gradient-based learning applied to document recognition. Proc. IEEE **86**(11), 2278–2324 (1998)
19. Lin, X., Zhao, C., Pan, W.: Towards accurate binary convolutional neural network. In: Neural Information Processing Systems, pp. 344–352 (2017)
20. Maddison, C.J., Mnih, A., Teh, Y.W.: The concrete distribution: a continuous relaxation of discrete random variables. In: International Conference on Learning Representations (ICLR) (2017)
21. Molchanov, D., Ashukha, A., Vetrov, D.P.: Variational dropout sparsifies deep neural networks. In: International Conference on Machine Learning (ICML), pp. 2498–2507 (2017)
22. Netzer, Y., Wang, T., Coates, A., Bissacco, A., Wu, B., Ng, A.Y.: Reading digits in natural images with unsupervised feature learning. In: Deep Learning and Unsupervised Feature Learning Workshop @ NIPS (2011)
23. Peters, J.W.T., Welling, M.: Probabilistic binary neural networks. CoRR abs/1809.03368 (2018)
24. Rastegari, M., Ordonez, V., Redmon, J., Farhadi, A.: XNOR-Net: ImageNet classification using binary convolutional neural networks. In: Leibe, B., Matas, J., Sebe, N., Welling, M. (eds.) ECCV 2016, Part IV. LNCS, vol. 9908, pp. 525–542. Springer, Cham (2016). https://doi.org/10.1007/978-3-319-46493-0_32
25. Roth, W., Pernkopf, F.: Variational inference in neural networks using an approximate closed-form objective. In: Bayesian Deep Learning Workshop @ NIPS (2016)
26. Roth, W., Pernkopf, F.: Bayesian neural networks with weight sharing using Dirichlet processes. IEEE Trans. Pattern Anal. Mach. Intell. **42**(1), 246–252 (2020)
27. Sermanet, P., Chintala, S., LeCun, Y.: Convolutional neural networks applied to house numbers digit classification. In: International Conference on Pattern Recognition (ICPR), pp. 3288–3291 (2012)
28. Shayer, O., Levi, D., Fetaya, E.: Learning discrete weights using the local reparameterization trick. In: International Conference on Learning Representations (ICLR) (2018)
29. Simonyan, K., Zisserman, A.: Very deep convolutional networks for large-scale image recognition. In: International Conference on Learning Representations (ICLR) (2015)
30. Sinha, D., Zhou, H., Shenoy, N.V.: Advances in computation of the maximum of a set of Gaussian random variables. IEEE Trans. CAD Integr. Circuits Syst **26**(8), 1522–1533 (2007)

31. Soudry, D., Hubara, I., Meir, R.: Expectation backpropagation: parameter-free training of multilayer neural networks with continuous or discrete weights. In: Advances in Neural Information Processing Systems (NIPS), pp. 963–971 (2014)
32. Sutskever, I., Vinyals, O., Le, Q.V.: Sequence to sequence learning with neural networks. In: Advances in Neural Information Processing Systems (NIPS), pp. 3104–3112 (2014)
33. Ullrich, K., Meeds, E., Welling, M.: Soft weight-sharing for neural network compression. In: International Conference on Learning Representations (ICLR) (2017)
34. Umuroglu, Y., et al.: FINN: a framework for fast, scalable binarized neural network inference. In: ACM/SIGDA International Symposium on Field-Programmable Gate Arrays (ISFPGA), pp. 65–74 (2017)
35. Wu, S., Li, G., Chen, F., Shi, L.: Training and inference with integers in deep neural networks. In: International Conference on Learning Representations (ICLR) (2018)
36. Zhou, S., Ni, Z., Zhou, X., Wen, H., Wu, Y., Zou, Y.: DoReFa-Net: Training low bitwidth convolutional neural networks with low bitwidth gradients. CoRR abs/1606.06160 (2016)
37. Zhu, C., Han, S., Mao, H., Dally, W.J.: Trained ternary quantization. In: International Conference on Learning Representations (ICLR) (2017)

Sobolev Training with Approximated Derivatives for Black-Box Function Regression with Neural Networks

Matthias Kissel[(⊠)] and Klaus Diepold

Chair for Data Processing, Technical University of Munich,
Arcisstr. 21, 80333 Munich, Germany
matthias.kissel@tum.de
https://www.ldv.ei.tum.de/

Abstract. With Sobolev Training, neural networks are trained to fit target output values as well as target derivatives with respect to the inputs. This leads to better generalization and fewer required training examples for certain problems. In this paper, we present a training pipeline that enables Sobolev Training for regression problems where target derivatives are not directly available. Thus, we propose to use a least-squares estimate of the target derivatives based on function values of neighboring training samples. We show for a variety of black-box function regression tasks that our training pipeline achieves smaller test errors compared to the traditional training method. Since our method has no additional requirements on the data collection process, it has great potential to improve the results for various regression tasks.

Keywords: Sobolev Training · Neural networks · Machine Learning

1 Introduction

Neural networks are used as function approximators for a variety of regression tasks like forecasting problems, policy regression or black-box function approximation (i.e. functions for which the analytical form is unknown). The standard approach of training neural networks is backpropagation, which updates the trainable parameters in the neural network by propagating the output error through the network. A strategy to increase the efficiency of the backpropagation algorithm proposed by several authors [1,2,10,16,17] is to incorporate information on derivatives of the target function into the training algorithm. For example, terms can be added to the error definition which penalize deviations of the network's partial derivatives to the partial derivatives of the target function. This is based on the idea that the neural network should match the outputs of the target function *and* its partial derivatives at the training points in order to match the desired function accurately. In the remainder of this paper we will use the terms introduced by Czarnecki et al. [1] and Masouka et al. [10] and

© Springer Nature Switzerland AG 2020
U. Brefeld et al. (Eds.): ECML PKDD 2019, LNAI 11907, pp. 399–414, 2020.
https://doi.org/10.1007/978-3-030-46147-8_24

refer to the standard backpropagation approach for neural network training as *Value Training*, and to the modified backpropagation incorporating information on derivatives as *Sobolev Training*.

It has been shown that Sobolev Training outperforms Value Training in terms of validation error and convergence speed for several applications. For example, Witkosie et al. [26] showed that using Sobolev Training to model potential energy surfaces can greatly reduce the density of data needed while still resulting in a better fit. Mitchell et al. [11] showed that Sobolev Training can lead to better generalization even by using fewer data points for training in the robotics and reinforcement learning domain. Besides better training performance, Sobolev Training can also decrease the sensitivity to noise in the training data as shown by Lee and Oh [9]. These publications are consistent with each other in the sense that they all claim that Sobolev Training is advantageous over Value Training in their chosen application. Indeed, Masouka et al. [10] argued that adding derivative information to the training increases the probability for better generalization.

In real world applications and in many toy-examples, however, information on the derivatives of the target function are typically not available. Several publications overcome this problem by rewriting a-priori or expert knowledge as derivatives which can be incorporated into the training process. For example, Lampinen et al. [8] proposed to use numerically inaccurate expert knowledge to design target derivatives which can be used during the training of a neural network. Simard et al. [18] utilized the fact that the derivatives have to be zero if the input data is transformed in specific ways (e.g. for translations or rotations). They claim that by explicitly adding these assumptions into the training process the learning speed is improved. Rifai et al. [17] used regularization terms incorporating the derivative to train an autoencoder for unsupervised feature extraction. By that, the autoencoder is more robust to corruptions in the input data and more relevant information is extracted. Similarly, Varga et al. [25] showed that gradient regularization can increase classification accuracy especially for small training datasets. Another approach is explanation-based learning [10,11], where knowledge about derivatives is extracted from previously learned tasks and seen examples.

In contrast to the assumptions in the existing approaches, we assume that for our applications no information on derivatives is accessible and no a-priori knowledge or expert knowledge is available. Moreover it is assumed that the analytical structure of the target function is unknown, i.e. we investigate the case of black-box function regression. For this application case, we propose a training pipeline which approximates the partial derivatives of the target function. Derivatives are approximated by a least squares estimate based on the function values of neighboring training samples.

Our goal is to give empirical evidence for the superiority of our training method. Therefore, we evaluate our algorithm by performing experiments with various black-box function regression tasks and different training dataset sizes. Besides comparing our training method with the standard Value Training algorithm, we compare our algorithm with the approach of approximating the

---

Algorithm 1. Sobolev Training with Least-Squares approximated Derivatives

---

In-/Output: Input Data X, Output Data Y

1: Approximate Target Derivatives
2: Transform Data
3: Initialize Neural Network and Optimizer
4: Initialize Sobolev Weight Factor ρ
5: **while** Stopping Criterion not met **do**
6:    Shuffle the Dataset and create Batches
7:    **for** *batch* **in** Batches **do**
8:       Compute Gradients of the Error for *batch* w.r.t. the Weights of the Neural Network
9:       Update the Weights of the Neural Network
10:    **end for**
11:    Update ρ
12: **end while**

---

target derivatives using a straightforward finite-difference method. We show that our pipeline has the potential to greatly improve the training results for regression tasks compared to the other methods, which we also validate on multiple real-world regression datasets.

The remainder of this paper is organized as follows. In Sect. 2 we present our training pipeline for Sobolev Training with approximated derivatives. Results of our experiments with various black-box function regression tasks are presented in the subsequent Sect. 3. Finally, we summarize our results in Sect. 4.

2 Sobolev Training with Approximated Target Derivatives

Our goal is to enable Sobolev Training for the regression of black-box functions. The difficulty here is that no analytical description of the target function is available, and therefore the required information about the target derivatives are not available in general. We overcome this problem by approximating these derivatives. The training pipeline presented in the following facilitates the approximation of the target derivatives on the basis of the data already collected (i.e. without the need to collect more data). Moreover, our proposed pipeline describes the sequence of steps in which the actual training is embedded. This sequence comprises of steps such as data preprocessing, which need to be tailored to the Sobolev Training.

Algorithm 1 gives an overview over the training pipeline. The inputs to the training pipeline are the training input data X and the corresponding function values Y of the target function. The first step is to approximate the partial derivatives of the target function (details are given in Sect. 2.1). Subsequently, inputs, outputs and derivatives are transformed while preserving their relative magnitudes (described in Sect. 2.2). Finally, the neural network is trained using the corresponding error function and the respective sobolev weight factor, as introduced in Sect. 2.3, until the stopping criterion is met.

2.1   Target Derivative Approximation

We propose to approximate the partial derivatives of the target function with respect to all input dimensions evaluated at each training input. In the following, we describe this approximation for a single input $X_s \in \mathbb{R}^n$, where X_s represents the sth row of the training input matrix $X \in \mathbb{R}^{m \times n}$.

The aim is to approximate the partial derivatives of the unknown target function $f(x)$ at input X_s with $x, d \in \mathbb{R}^n$ such that

$$d_i \approx \frac{\delta f(x)}{\delta x_i}\bigg|_{x=X_s}. \tag{1}$$

This is done by approximating $f(x)$ with a linear model in the neighborhood of the regarded training input X_s. For this, the function values of the p nearest neighbors $f(n_1), \ldots, f(n_p)$ to X_s (with respect to the euclidean distance $||n_i - X_s||^2$) are used, where each n_i represents a row of the input matrix X (note that the indices of n_i do *not* correspond to the index of the row in the training input matrix X). Approximating the partial derivatives then results in a least squares problem

$$min_d ||W(Ad - b)||^2, \tag{2}$$

where A contains the differences of the inputs

$$A = \begin{pmatrix} (n_1 - X_s) \\ \vdots \\ (n_p - X_s) \end{pmatrix}, \tag{3}$$

and b contains the difference of the output values

$$b = \begin{pmatrix} f(n_1) - f(X_s) \\ \vdots \\ f(n_p) - f(X_s) \end{pmatrix}. \tag{4}$$

The p nearest neighbors are determined using a k-dimensional tree (implementation provided by Pedregosa et al. [14]). W is a diagonal matrix that controls the influence of neighboring training points on the approximation of the derivatives depending on their distance to X_s. The respective diagonal entries are

$$W_{ii} = \frac{1}{\sum_{j=1}^{p} e^{-||n_j - X_s||_2}} e^{-||n_i - X_s||_2}. \tag{5}$$

After solving the minimization problem in Eq. 2, d contains the approximated partial derivatives of the target function evaluated at X_s. Thus, solving the respective minimization problem for each input vector in the training dataset determines all target derivatives required for training.

2.2   Data Transformation

Several standard methods for data transformation exist for Value Training, e.g. the *standard scaler* which transforms data to zero mean and unit variance [14]. We propose to adapt this approach for Sobolev Training in order to preserve the relative magnitudes between outputs, derivatives and inputs. The presented method is limited to regression functions with a one-dimensional output. However, the methods can be extended to functions with multidimensional outputs. The adapted transformation comprises three steps.

First, the input values are scaled column-wise to zero mean and unit variance

$$\tilde{x}_i = \alpha_i x_i + \beta_i. \tag{6}$$

Secondly, the output values $y = f(x)$ are shifted such that the mean magnitude of the outputs equals the mean magnitude of the partial derivatives

$$\hat{y} = y + \zeta. \tag{7}$$

This step reduces the magnitude difference between outputs and derivatives. In the third step outputs and derivatives are scaled to

$$\tilde{y} = \gamma \hat{y} \tag{8}$$

and

$$\tilde{d}_i = \frac{\gamma}{\alpha_i} d_i, \tag{9}$$

where d_i are the approximated target derivatives. The factor γ is chosen such that outputs and derivatives have combined unit variance.

2.3   Error Functions

The main distinguishing characteristics between Sobolev Training and Value Training is the function used to compute the error of the network, i.e. the loss which is backpropagated through the network during training. In Value Training, any loss function $l(x,y)$ can be used to compare the output of the network with the desired value, e.g. the mean squared error. The resulting training error e_{VT} for a training input X_s is

$$e_{VT} = l(o, o_d)\Big|_{X_s}, \tag{10}$$

where o is the output of the network for input X_s and o_d is the corresponding desired output.

In Sobolev Training, the neural network is trained to fit the desired outputs *and* the respective partial derivatives of the target function. This is achieved by adding terms to the error function of Value Training. By that, discrepancies between the partial derivatives of the neural network to the partial derivatives of the target function are explicitly penalized. The resulting error function e_{ST} is

$$e_{ST} = l(o, o_d) + \rho \sum_{i=1}^{n} l\left(\frac{\delta net(x)}{\delta x_i}, d_i\right)\Big|_{X_s}, \tag{11}$$

where n refers to the dimension of the input space. The derivative of the network with respect to input dimension x_i is given by $\frac{\delta net(x)}{\delta x_i}$ and the approximated partial derivatives of the target function $f(X)$ by d.

The terms added for Sobolev Training are weighted with a factor ρ, which determines the importance of these terms in relation to the Value Training loss function. We propose to decrease this weight factor after each epoch of training to emphasize the importance of accurate output values at the end of the training

$$\rho_{v+1} = \rho_v \rho_{up}, \tag{12}$$

where ρ_{up} is the corresponding update factor and v the index of the regarded training epoch.

The theoretical basis for the proposed error function is given by Hornik et al. [5] and Czarnecki et al. [1]. Hornik et al. [5] proved that neural networks with at least one hidden layer are able to arbitrarily well approximate any function and its derivatives if the activation function of the neurons is appropriately smooth. Moreover, Czarnecki et al. [1] showed that Rectified Linear Units (ReLU) can be used as activation function to achieve universal approximation of function values and derivatives up to the first order. Furthermore it should be noted that any gradient-based optimization algorithm such as Adam [7] used for Value Training can be used for Sobolev Training [15].

2.4   Derivative Approximation Using Finite-Differences

In order to compare our pipeline with the approach of using a straightforward finite-difference method for derivative approximation, we introduce a slightly modified training pipeline depicted in Algorithm 2. This approach requires additional data collected in a small neighborhood of the given training data. To ensure a fair comparison, we consider this extra effort. Therefore, we assume that the total amount of data which can be collected is limited, i.e. there is a trade-off between collecting data to explore the whole input space versus collecting data for derivative approximation.

For example, if the target function has two-dimensional inputs, the training dataset size passed to the pipeline in Algorithm 2 is only one-third of the size used for the other training approaches. This results from the fact that additional data points required for derivative approximation are collected during the execution of this pipeline. However, the total number of target function evaluations remains the same for all training methods, which allows a fair comparison of the methods.

Derivatives are approximated using a *one-sided-difference* approach [12] defined as:

$$\frac{\delta f(x)}{\delta x_i} \approx \frac{f(x + \epsilon e_i) - f(x)}{\epsilon} \tag{13}$$

Algorithm 2. Sobolev Training with Finite Differences

In-/Output: Input Data X, Output Data Y
1: Collect Data for Derivative Approximation
2: Approximate Target Derivatives using Finite-Differences
3: Transform Data
4: Initialize Neural Network and Optimizer
5: Initialize Sobolev Weight Factor ρ
6: **while** Stopping Criterion not met **do**
7:     Shuffle the Dataset and create Batches
8:     **for** *batch* in Batches **do**
9:         Compute Gradients of the Error for *batch* w.r.t. the Weights of the Neural Network
10:        Update the Weights of the Neural Network
11:    **end for**
12:    Update ρ
13: **end while**

Where e_i has zero entries except for the ith entry and ϵ is the step-size used for derivative approximation. We use the *one-sided-difference* approach as the small gain in accuracy obtained by using the *two-sided-difference* often does not justify the extra effort for collecting additional data [12].

To make use of all obtained information we propose to add the data collected for derivative approximation to the training data. Moreover, for each of these data points one partial derivative can be added to the training data without extra effort. This is achieved by exchanging e_i with $-e_i$ in Eq. 13 to calculate the respective partial derivative at the new data point. After adding the additional data to the training dataset, the number of training points for this method is the same as for the other training methods. However, the data distribution of the training data is different.

The one-sided-difference (Eq. 13) results in an error linearly depending on the chosen step-size ϵ, i.e. the error is $\mathcal{O}(\epsilon)$ [12]. Hence, in order to decrease the approximation error, a sufficiently small step size must be chosen. However, note that choosing ϵ too small can lead to underflow in the input as well as the output data depending on the machine precision.

The other steps of the training pipeline remain the same as introduced before. It should be noted that this training pipeline can only be used for regression tasks where training data points can be collected at any desired position in the input space. This is, however, *not* the case for most real world applications.

3   Results

We compare our training pipeline to existing approaches in terms of their performance on approximating specific black-box functions. The black-box functions are chosen to represent functions with different shapes, input-value domains and output-value ranges. Therefore, we chose optimization test functions with

Table 1. Black-box functions used in the experiments and their respective category

Function	Category	Definition	Input range
Sphere	Bowl-Shaped	$f(x) = \sum_{i=1}^{n} x_i^2$	$x_i \in [-5.12; 5.12]$
Sum Diff. Pow.	Bowl-Shaped	$f(x) = \sum_{i=1}^{n} \lvert x_i \rvert^{i+1}$	$x_i \in [-1; 1]$
Sum Squares	Bowl-Shaped	$f(x) = \sum_{i=1}^{n} i x_i^2$	$x_i \in [-10; 10]$
Trid	Bowl-Shaped	$f(x) = \sum_{i=1}^{n}(x_i - 1)^2 - \sum_{i=2}^{n} x_i x_{i-1}$	$x_i \in [-4; 4]$
Booth	Plate-Shaped	$f(x) = (x_1 + 2x_2 - 7)^2 + (2x_1 + x_2 - 5)^2$	$x_i \in [-10; 10]$
McCormick	Plate-Shaped	$f(x) = sin(x_1 + x_2) + (x_1 - x_2)^2$ $-1.5x_1 + 2.5x_2 + 1$	$x_1 \in [-1.5; 4]$ $x_2 \in [-3; 4]$
Matyas	Plate-Shaped	$f(x) = 0.26(x_1^2 + x_2^2) - 0.48x_1x_2$	$x_i \in [-10; 10]$
Powersum	Plate-Shaped	$f(x) = \sum_{i=1}^{n}[(\sum_{j=1}^{n} x_j^i) - b_i]^2$	$x_i \in [0; 2]$ $b = (8, 18)^T$
Rosenbrock	Valley-Shaped	$f(x) = \sum_{i=1}^{n-1}[100(x_{i+1} - x_i^2)^2 + (x_i - 1)^2]$	$x_i \in [-5; 10]$
Three Hump Camel	Valley-Shaped	$f(x) = 2x_1^2 - 1.05x_1^4 + \frac{x_1^6}{6} + x_1x_2 + x_2^2$	$x_i \in [-5; 5]$
Six Hump Camel	Valley-Shaped	$f(x) = (4 - 2.1x_1^2 + \frac{x_1^4}{3})x_1^2$ $+x_1x_2 + (-4 + 4x_2^2)x_2^2$	$x_1 \in [-3; 3]$ $x_2 \in [-2; 2]$
Dixon Price	Valley-Shaped	$f(x) = (x_1 - 1)^2 + \sum_{i=2}^{n} i(2x_i^2 - x_{i-1})^2$	$x_i \in [-10; 10]$
Easom	Steep Ridges	$f(x) = -cos(x_1)cos(x_2)exp(-(x_1 - \pi)^2 - (x_2 - \pi)^2)$	$x_i \in [-5; 5]$
Michalewicz	Steep Ridges	$f(x) = -\sum_{i=1}^{n} sin(x_i)sin^{20}(\frac{ix_i^2}{\pi})$	$x_i \in [0; \pi]$
Styblinski Tang	Others	$f(x) = \frac{1}{2}\sum_{i=1}^{n}(x_i^4 - 16x_i^2 + 5x_i)$	$x_i \in [-5; 5]$
Beale	Others	$f(x) = (1.5 - x_1 + x_1x_2)^2 + (2.25 - x_1 + x_1x_2^2)^2$ $+(2.625 - x_1 + x_1x_2^3)^2$	$x_i \in [-4.5; 4.5]$
Branin	Others	$f(x) = (x_2 - \frac{5.1}{4\pi^2}x_1^2 + \frac{5}{\pi}x_1 - 6)^2$ $+10(1 - \frac{1}{8\pi})cos(x_1) + 10$	$x_1 \in [-5; 10]$ $x_2 \in [0; 15]$
Golstein Price	Others	$f(x) = [1 + (x_1 + x_2 + 1)^2(19 - 14x_1 + 3x_1^2 - 14x_2$ $+6x_1x_2 + 3x_2^2)] \times [30 + (2x_1 - 3x_2)^2$ $\times(18 - 32x_1 + 12x_1^2 + 48x_2 - 36x_1x_2 + 27x_2^2)]$	$x_i \in [-2; 2]$

two-dimensional input from five different categories proposed by Surjanovic and Bingham [19]: Bowl-shaped functions, plate-shaped functions, functions with steep ridges or drops, valley-shaped functions and special functions grouped in the category named *others*. A list of all functions and their definitions can be found in Table 1.

With our experiments we aim to empirically answer the following questions:

- How does our training pipeline compare to the standard training method (Value Training)?
- Does the size of the training dataset or the shape of the target function have an influence on the performance of our training method?
- How does the performance compare to the approach of approximating derivatives directly with a finite-difference method?

These questions are addressed in the following Sections by interpreting the results of our experiments. Furthermore, at the end of this Section we evaluate our training pipeline on several real-world regression problems. The Hyperparameters of our experiments are listed in Table 2. We would like to emphasize that we did not optimize these hyperparameters. Exemplary code of our training methods can be found on GitHub[1].

---

[1] https://github.com/MatthiasKi/SobolevTrainingApproxDerivatives.

Table 2. Hyperparameters of the experiments

Hyperparameter	Value
Hidden layers	2
Neurons per Layer	200
Hidden layer activation	ReLU
Output layer activation	Linear
Loss function	Mean squared error
Optimizer	Adam
Adam - learning rate	$1e-3$
Adam - β_1	0.9
Adam - β_2	0.999
Repetitions per experiment	10
Amount batches	10
Data collection strategy	Uniform-Random
Validation set size	4000
Test set size	4000
Finite-difference step size ϵ	$1e-4$
Number of neighbors for least squares	5
Initial ρ	1.0
Update factor ρ_{up}	0.95
Stopping criterion	Validation error convergence
Patience p_c	10

3.1 Sobolev Training with Approximated Target Derivatives versus Value Training

First, we compare the performance of our training pipeline with the standard method of training neural networks (Value Training) by conducting various experiments. Each experiment consists of training a neural network with the considered training method to approximate one of our regression functions. Experiments are carried out with different training dataset sizes, whereas the collected training data is distributed random-uniformly over the input space. During the experiments, the number of training epochs is not limited. Instead, the neural network is trained until the stopping criterion is met. For our experiments, we chose to stop the training if there is no improvement in the validation error over a period of p_c epochs (p_c is referred to as patience). Each experiment is conducted ten times in order to decrease the influence of statistical effects, where we plot the mean value of the test error in combination with the respective minimum and maximum values. We compare the results of different training methods by means of the mean squared error of the test dataset for the trained network. For this, the network parameters of the epoch with lowest validation set error are used to compute the test error (in general, this is not the test error of the last training epoch). To make the results comparable regarding the differences in the output data ranges, we divide this error by the mean squared output of the respective function (the mean squared output is calculated beforehand and the same value is used to normalize all training results of the same target function). All relevant hyper parameters used for training are depicted in Table 2.

The reader can see the training results for one representative function of each category in Fig. 1. As expected, Sobolev Training with exact derivative information clearly outperforms the other training methods for most functions. This results from the extra information added to the training algorithm (note that for Sobolev Training with exact derivatives the same training data as for Value Training is used, plus the partial derivatives of the target function for each training data point). Furthermore, Sobolev Training with Least Squares approximated derivatives consistently (except for the function *Michalewicz*) achieves better results than Value Training.

In order to combine the training results of different functions of the same category in one plot, we consider the test error of the respective training method divided by the test error achieved by using Value Training. By that, the magnitude of the output data is canceled out and the results for different functions can be directly compared with each other. The combined performance for functions of the same category is depicted in Fig. 2. In the Figure, the lines represent the mean values over the results of all functions of the respective function category (whereas for each target function, training method and training dataset size 10 independent experiments have been conducted). In addition, the minimum and maximum performance of the respective function category are depicted. Values greater than 1.0 indicate that the respective training method achieved higher test errors than Value Training (and therefor has a worse performance), and values less than 1.0 indicate a lower test error, respectively. We observe that Sobolev Training with Least-Squares approximated derivatives achieves consistently lower test errors than Value Training (except for functions with steep ridges or drops).

For some function shapes the effect of our training pipeline is bigger than for others. This is due to the different value of information about derivatives for different function shapes. This can also be seen by looking at the effect of classical Sobolev Training compared to Value Training for the respective function shapes (i.e. Sobolev Training with exact derivatives). For example, Sobolev Training with exact derivatives achieves much lower relative test errors than Value Training for valley shaped functions compared to plate shaped functions (as depicted in Fig. 2). In case of our functions with steep ridges or drops, Sobolev Training even tends to worsen the training results. This fits to the expectations as information about target derivatives is of small value for functions of these shapes and, due to the limited accuracy of the learned model, can even be misleading for some functions.

In general, the effect of our training pipeline increases with the number of data points in the training set. This is in line with the expectations, as increasing

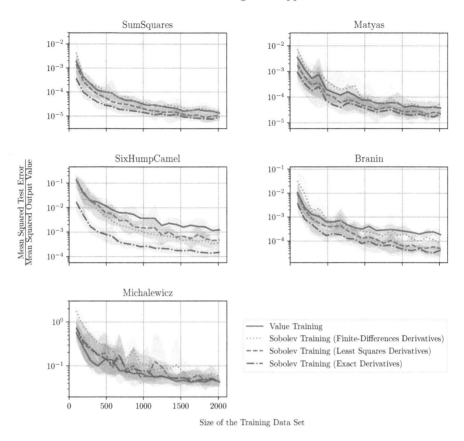

Fig. 1. Comparison of the test errors for different training methods

the dataset size leads to a higher density of the data points distributed in the input space, i.e. neighboring points in the dataset lie closer to each other. This in turn increases the accuracy of the derivative approximation, since as indicated in Sect. 2.4, the approximation error of the derivatives increases linearly with the distance of neighboring points.

3.2 Sobolev Training with Approximated Derivatives Based on Finite-Differences

In this Section, we compare the performance of our training pipeline with the approach of approximating derivatives directly using a finite-difference method. As explained in Sect. 2.4, the size of the training dataset passed to the training pipeline directly using finite-differences is one third of the size of the training dataset used for Value Training. This ensures a fair comparison, as the number of data points which can be collected is limited for most applications.

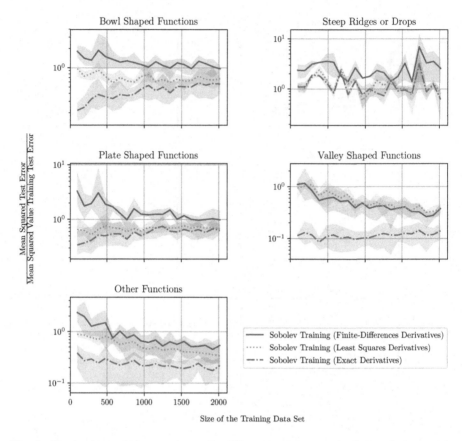

Fig. 2. Comparison of the test error for different training methods in relation to the test error achieved with Value Training

As shown in Fig. 2, Value Training outperforms Sobolev Training with Finite-Difference approximated derivatives especially in the low-data regime. This is due to the fact that this method uses some of the samples for derivative approximation, i.e. obtaining more local information instead of exploring unknown regions of the input space. Of course, this effect decreases for larger training datasets.

For all function shapes except for valley shaped functions, our training pipeline clearly outperforms the straightforward approach of using finite-differences for derivative approximation. Our experiments induce that the local additional information in the form of accurate derivatives provide a great deal of additional value for describing our valley shaped functions. This also explains the small magnitude of the relative test error of Sobolev Training with exact derivatives compared to Value Training. Of course, the derivatives approximated with the direct finite-difference method are more accurate than the least-squares approximated ones, which leads to the good performance of this training method for valley-shaped functions.

3.3 Real-World Regression Problems

To show the applicability of our pipeline for problems with high dimensional inputs and noise in the collected data, we evaluate our pipeline with several existing datasets for real-world regression problems. In contrast to the previous Subsections, we do not intend to represent a broad spectrum of different regression problems with our selection. Instead, we aim to show the abilities of our pipeline to be applied to real-world regression tasks using problems selected from the UCI Machine Learning Repository [3], which are presented in the following. Moreover, Table 3 gives an overview over the properties of the different datasets.

- *Combined Cycle Power Plant* [6,20]: The goal of this regression problem is to predict the net hourly electrical energy output of a combined cycle power plant composed of gas turbines, steam turbines and heat recovery generators. The predictions are based on features such as the ambient pressure and the relative humidity.
- *Communities and Crime* [21–24]: This dataset contains data about different communities such as the age distribution of its population or the number of full time police officers. The aim is to predict the total number of violent crimes per population for each community based on these features. Note that for our experiments, we considered only features which are available for all communities.
- *Concrete Compressive Strength* [27]: This dataset was created to analyze the compressive strength of concrete based on features like the age of the concrete or its components (e.g. the amount of cement).
- *Yacht Hydrodynamics* [4,13]: The purpose of this dataset is to find a connection between the residuary resistance of sailing yachts and geometric features of the yacht like the hull geometry coefficients.

For our experiments, each dataset is split randomly into training, validation and test set, whereas the validation set and the test set comprise 20% of the total data each. The calculation of the neighboring points of a considered sample was performed using the transformed data matrix as described in Sect. 2.2. This is necessary, because the entries of the data matrix can have different units or can be of different orders of magnitudes for datasets comprising real-world data, which can distort the calculation of the neighboring points. In addition, we found that the weighted data matrix can be ill-conditioned in some cases. Therefore, we cut-off singular values which are smaller than $0.01\sigma_{max}$ to compute the least-squares solution, where σ_{max} is the largest singular value of A belonging to the least-squares problem $min_x||Ax - b||^2$.

Each experiment was performed 50 times to account for the random initialization of the neural networks and the shuffling of the data before splitting into training, validation and test datasets. We report the mean and standard deviation of the root mean squared errors of both models on the respective test dataset after training in Table 4. The experiments show that our pipeline can have advantages for some real-world regression problems with high-dimensional

Table 3. Properties of the datasets for the real-world regression problems (*Considered Neighbors* is the number of neihbors considered for the least-squares approximation of the partial derivatives)

Dataset name	Input dimensionality	Dataset size	Considered neighbors
Combined Cycle Power Plant	4	9568	20
Communities and Crime	101	1994	3
Concrete Compressive Strength	9	1030	10
Yacht Hydrodynamics	7	308	2

Table 4. Mean and standard deviation of the RMSE over 50 independent experiments trained with either Value Training or our proposed training pipeline

Dataset name	LS-Sobolev training	Value training
Combined Cycle Power Plant	**3.97 $\pm$ 0.13**	4.01 $\pm$ 0.12
Communities and Crime	**369.95 $\pm$ 26.02**	375.42 $\pm$ 25.93
Concrete Compressive Strength	5.91 $\pm$ 0.59	**5.24 $\pm$ 0.5**
Yacht Hydrodynamics	**1.53 $\pm$ 0.42**	2.16 $\pm$ 0.8

inputs and noise in the collected data. Note that we did not tune the models, nor performed a hyperparameter optimization (we used the hyperparameters depicted in Table 2 except for the number of neighboring samples used for derivative approximation for which we found suitable numbers by hand). Indeed, a sophisticated parameter optimization is not needed, since our focus lies on the comparison between Value Training and Sobolev Training with Least-Squares approximated derivatives, and we therefore only have to guarantee fair comparison conditions.

4   Conclusion

We introduced a training pipeline for neural networks, which makes it possible to use Sobolev Training for black-box function regression tasks where the target derivatives are not directly accessible. Our pipeline describes the various steps necessary for training, which includes a preprocessing procedure designed for Sobolev Training.

With our experiments we showed empirically that our training pipeline outperformed the standard training approach (i.e. Value Training) for functions with various different shapes. Furthermore, our approach outperforms the straightforward approach of approximating derivatives using finite-differences. In addition to experiments with optimization functions from different categories, we illustrated the practical benefit by evaluating our training pipeline on multiple real world regression problems.

Our pipeline does not require additional training samples and has no special requirements on the data generation process. We observed that our training method leads to improved performance for almost all tested functions, especially if the training dataset is large. Therefore, we believe that the presented training pipeline has the potential to greatly improve the training results for many regression applications.

Our results raise further research questions that lie out of the scope of this paper. For example, it would be interesting to examine the influence of the training data distribution on the learning performance, or to explicitly use information about the data distribution for approximating target derivatives.

References

1. Czarnecki, W.M., Osindero, S., Jaderberg, M., Swirszcz, G., Pascanu, R.: Sobolev training for neural networks. In: Advances in Neural Information Processing Systems, pp. 4278–4287 (2017)
2. Drucker, H., Le Cun, Y.: Double backpropagation increasing generalization performance. In: IJCNN-91-Seattle International Joint Conference on Neural Networks, vol. 2, pp. 145–150. IEEE (1991)
3. Dua, D., Graff, C.: UCI machine learning repository (2017). http://archive.ics.uci.edu/ml
4. Gerritsma, J., Onnink, R., Versluis, A.: Geometry, resistance and stability of the Delft systematic Yacht hull series. Int. Shipbuild. Prog. **28**(328), 276–297 (1981)
5. Hornik, K., Stinchcombe, M., White, H.: Universal approximation of an unknown mapping and its derivatives using multilayer feedforward networks. Neural Netw. **3**(5), 551–560 (1990)
6. Kaya, H., Tüfekci, P., Gürgen, F.S.: Local and global learning methods for predicting power of a combined gas & steam turbine. In: Proceedings of the International Conference on Emerging Trends in Computer and Electronics Engineering ICETCEE, pp. 13–18 (2012)
7. Kingma, D., Ba, J.: Adam: A method for stochastic optimization. In: International Conference on Learning Representations (2014)
8. Lampinen, J., Selonen, A.: Multilayer perceptron training with inaccurate derivative information. In: Proceedings of 1995 IEEE International Conference on Neural Networks ICNN, vol. 95, pp. 2811–2815 (1995). Citeseer
9. Lee, J.W., Oh, J.H.: Hybrid learning of mapping and its Jacobian in multilayer neural networks. Neural Comput. **9**(5), 937–958 (1997)
10. Masuoka, R., Thrun, S., Mitchell, T.M.: Constraining neural networks to fit target slopes (1993)
11. Mitchell, T.M., Thrun, S.B.: Explanation-based neural network learning for robot control. In: Advances in Neural Information Processing Systems, pp. 287–294 (1993)
12. Nocedal, J., Wright, S.J.: Numerical Optimization, 2nd edn. Springer, New York (2006). https://doi.org/10.1007/978-0-387-40065-5
13. Ortigosa, I., Lopez, R., Garcia, J.: A neural networks approach to residuary resistance of sailing Yachts prediction. In: Proceedings of the International Conference on Marine Engineering MARINE, vol. 2007, p. 250 (2007)
14. Pedregosa, F., et al.: Scikit-learn: machine learning in Python. J. Mach. Learn. Res. **12**, 2825–2830 (2011)

15. Pukrittayakamee, A., et al.: Simultaneous fitting of a potential-energy surface and its corresponding force fields using feedforward neural networks. J. Chem. Phys. **130**(13), 134101 (2009)

16. Pukrittayakamee, A., Hagan, M., Raff, L., Bukkapatnam, S.T., Komanduri, R.: Practical training framework for fitting a function and its derivatives. IEEE Trans. Neural Networks **22**(6), 936–947 (2011)

17. Rifai, S., et al.: Higher order contractive auto-encoder. In: Gunopulos, D., Hofmann, T., Malerba, D., Vazirgiannis, M. (eds.) ECML PKDD 2011. LNCS (LNAI), vol. 6912, pp. 645–660. Springer, Heidelberg (2011). https://doi.org/10.1007/978-3-642-23783-6_41

18. Simard, P., Victorri, B., LeCun, Y., Denker, J.: Tangent prop-a formalism for specifying selected invariances in an adaptive network. In: Advances in Neural Information Processing Systems, pp. 895–903 (1992)

19. Surjanovic, S., Bingham, D.: Virtual library of simulation experiments: test functions and datasets (2013). http://www.sfu.ca/ssurjano. Accessed 7 Jan 2019

20. Tüfekci, P.: Prediction of full load electrical power output of a base load operated combined cycle power plant using machine learning methods. Int. J. Electr. Power Energy Syst. **60**, 126–140 (2014)

21. U.S. Department of Commerce: Bureau of the Census, Census Of Population And Housing 1990 United States: Summary tape file 1a & 3a (computer files)

22. U.S. Department Of Commerce: Bureau Of The Census Producer, Washington, DC and Inter-university Consortium for Political and Social Research Ann Arbor, Michigan (1992)

23. U.S. Department of Justice: Bureau of Justice Statistics, Law Enforcement Management And Administrative Statistics, U.S. Department Of Commerce, Bureau Of The Census Producer, Washington, DC and Inter-university Consortium for Political and Social Research Ann Arbor, Michigan (computer file) (1992)

24. U.S. Department of Justice: Federal Bureau of Investigation, Crime in the united states (computer file) (1995)

25. Varga, D., Csiszárik, A., Zombori, Z.: Gradient regularization improves accuracy of discriminative models (2017)

26. Witkoskie, J.B., Doren, D.J.: Neural network models of potential energy surfaces: prototypical examples. J. Chem. Theory Comput. **1**(1), 14–23 (2005)

27. Yeh, I.C.: Modeling of strength of high-performance concrete using artificial neural networks. Cem. Concr. Res. **28**(12), 1797–1808 (1998)

Hyper-Parameter-Free Generative Modelling with Deep Boltzmann Trees

Nico Piatkowski[✉]

AI Group, TU Dortmund, Dortmund, Germany
nico.piatkowski@tu-dortmund.de

Abstract. Deep neural networks achieve state-of-the-art results in various classification and synthetic data generation tasks. However, only little is known about why depth improves a model. We investigate the structure of stochastic deep neural works, also known as Deep Boltzmann Machines, to shed some light on this issue. While the best known results postulate an exponential dependence between the number of visible units and the depth of the model, we show that the required depth is upper bounded by the longest path in the underlying junction tree, which is at most *linear* in the number of visible units. Moreover, we show that the conditional independence structure of any categorical Deep Boltzmann Machine contains a sub-tree that allows the consistent estimation of the full joint probability mass function of all visible units. We connect our results to l_1-regularized maximum-likelihood estimation and Chow-Liu trees. Based on our theoretical findings, we present a new tractable version of Deep Boltzmann Machines, namely the *Deep Boltzmann Tree (DBT)*. We provide a hyper-parameter-free algorithm for learning the DBT from data, and propose a new initialization method to enforce convergence to good solutions. Our findings provide some theoretical evidence for why a deep model might be beneficial. Experimental results on benchmark data show, that the DBT is a theoretical sound alternative to likelihood-free generative models.

Keywords: Deep Boltzmann Machine · Structure learning · Generative model

1 Introduction

Modern applications of data science necessitate expressive, robust and efficient probabilistic models, to capture the rich structure in complex data sets. These models generally fall into two major categories: likelihood-based and likelihood-free. The former explicitly assigns a likelihood function $\mathbb{P}_\theta(X)$ with parameters θ to describe the data X, while the latter learns a model from which samples

Electronic supplementary material The online version of this chapter (https://doi.org/10.1007/978-3-030-46147-8_25) contains supplementary material, which is available to authorized users.

from the desired distribution may be drawn (but does not assign or learn a form for the distribution itself). In this work, we study deep generative models w.r.t. their structure, also known as network architecture.

Specifically, likelihood-free methods typically pass samples z from a pre-specified simple distribution $q(z)$ through a deterministic mapping $G(z; \theta)$: $\mathcal{Z} \to \mathcal{X}$, commonly known as the generator. While likelihood-free methods gain a lot of attention, they lack theoretical insights on almost every fundamental aspect, including model selection, parameter learning, and sample complexity. Selecting the right model suffers from an countable infinite search space. In most cases, training such generative adversarial networks [10] is cumbersome and involves sophisticated hyper-parameter tuning strategies. However, generalization bounds [2,9,18] which quantify the model's error w.r.t. inherent properties, like depth and width of the underlying neural network, can guide this process. Other research directions try to bring likelihood and entropy back in implicitly defined generative models [13,25].

In contrast, likelihood-based methods enjoy theoretical insights and statistical guarantees, but suffer from a high computational complexity. To bridge the gap between popular deep generative models and classic probabilistic models, we consider Deep Boltzmann Machines (DBMs) [20] with arbitrary categorical hidden state spaces, as a generic class of stochastic neural networks. They have their roots in statistical physics and have been studied intensively as special types of graphical model. In particular, information geometry has provided deep geometric insights about learning and approximation of probability distributions by this kind of networks. It is well known that general Boltzmann machines are universal approximators of probability distributions over the states of their visible units, provided they have sufficiently many hidden units. Moreover, the universal approximation capability has been shown for Restricted Boltzmann Machines, provided their single hidden layer has exponentially more units than the visible layer. In a similar way, universal approximation results for DBMs suggest that the number of layers should be exponential in the number of visible units [16].

However, practical deep models are far from having exponentially many layers, still providing superior quality. Driven by this apparent contradiction, we study the structure of DBMs to gain new theoretical insights about deep probabilistic models in general. Our findings guide us to a new model class: the Deep Boltzmann Tree (DBT). Like a DBM, a DBT has one layer of visible (input) units and multiple hidden layers, containing latent variables (Fig. 1). Unlike a DBM, the structure of a DBT contains no loops, and thus, allows for tractable, poly-time probabilistic inference.

Our contributions can be summarized as follows:

- We state a new universal approximation theorem for Deep Boltzmann Machines, which shows that the dependence between the number of layers and the number of visible units is at most linear.

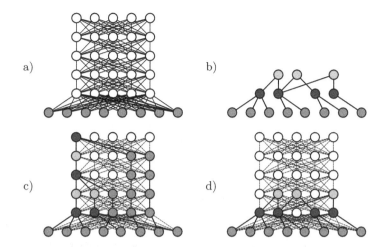

Fig. 1. The conditional independence structure of a Deep Boltzmann Machine with $n_0 = 8$ visible units and 5×5 hidden units is shown in (a). Dashed edges and white neurons in (c) and (d) are not required to represent the full joint probability mass function—they can be dropped by nullifying the corresponding edge weights $\boldsymbol{\theta}_e \leftarrow \boldsymbol{0}$. The colored neuron in (c) and (d) both correspond to the DBT shown in (b). Blue hidden units copy the state of one visible unit to a deeper layer by setting the corresponding edge weight $\boldsymbol{\theta}_e$ to the identity function $\boldsymbol{\theta}_{\mathrm{id}}$. (Color figure online)

- We define a new, tractable type of deep probabilistic model: the Deep Boltzmann Tree. We show that DBTs are universal approximators and connect them to results in structure learning.
- We provide hyper-parameter-free algorithms for constructing and learning DBTs. Here, hyper-parameter-free means that "magic constants" like learning rate, model architecture, and hidden state space, are automatically determined from data. The proposed method has literally no tuneable parameter.

2   Notation and Background

Let us summarize the notation and background necessary for the subsequent development. The Kullback-Leibler divergence between two probability mass functions $\mathbb{P}$ and $\mathbb{Q}$ is defined by $\mathrm{KL}[\mathbb{Q}\|\mathbb{P}] = \sum_{\boldsymbol{x} \in \mathcal{X}} \mathbb{Q}(\boldsymbol{x})(\log \mathbb{Q}(\boldsymbol{x}) - \log \mathbb{P}(\boldsymbol{x}))$, which is never negative and only zero if and only if $\mathbb{P} = \mathbb{Q}$. If f is a function, f^{-1} refers to its inverse.

2.1   Graphical Models

An undirected graph $G = (V, E)$ consists of $n = |V|$ vertices, connected via edges $(v, w) \in E$. For two graphs G_1, G_2, we write $V(G_1)$ and $V(G_2)$ to denote the vertices of G_1 and G_2, respectively and similar $E(G_1)$ and $E(G_2)$ for the edges.

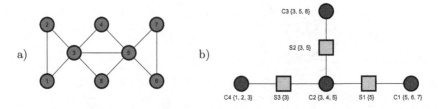

Fig. 2. The conditional independence structure (a) of the underlying random variable X is first converted to the junction tree (b).

A clique C is a fully-connected subset of vertices, i.e., $\forall v, w \in C : (v, w) \in E$. The set of all cliques of G is denoted by $\mathcal{C}$. Here, any undirected graph represents the conditional independence structure of an undirected graphical model or Markov random field [24], shown in Fig. 2(a). To this end, we identify each vertex $v \in V$ with a random variable X_v taking values in the state space $\mathcal{X}_v$. The random vector $X = (X_v : v \in V)$, with probability mass function (pmf) $\mathbb{P}$, represents the random joint state of all vertices in some arbitrary but fixed order, taking values x in the Cartesian product space $\mathcal{X} = \bigotimes_{v \in V} \mathcal{X}_v$. If not stated otherwise, $\mathcal{X}$ is a discrete set. Moreover, we allow to access these quantities for any proper subset of variables $S \subset V$, i.e., $X_S = (X_v : v \in S)$, x_S, and $\mathcal{X}_S$, respectively. We write $C_{\max}$ for the clique C that has the largest state space $\mathcal{X}_C$. According to the Hammersley-Clifford theorem [11], the probability mass of $\mathcal{X}$ factorizes over positive functions $\psi_C : \mathcal{X} \to \mathbb{R}_+$, one for each maximal clique of the underlying graph,

$$\mathbb{P}(X = x) = \frac{1}{Z} \prod_{C \in \mathcal{C}} \psi_C(x_C), \tag{1}$$

normalized via $Z = \sum_{x \in \mathcal{X}} \prod_{C \in \mathcal{C}} \psi_C(x_C)$. Due to positivity of ψ_C, it can be written as an exponential, i.e., $\psi_C(x_C) = \exp(\langle \theta_C, \phi_C(x_C) \rangle)$ with sufficient statistic $\phi_C : \mathcal{X}_C \to \mathbb{R}^{|\mathcal{X}_C|}$. The overcomplete sufficient statistic of discrete data is a "one-hot" vector that selects a specific weight value, e.g., $\psi_C(x_C) = \exp(\theta_{C=x_C})$. The full joint can be written in the famous exponential family form $\mathbb{P}(X = x) = \exp(\langle \theta, \phi(x) \rangle - \log Z)$ with $\theta = (\theta_C : C \in \mathcal{C})$ and $\phi(x) = (\phi_C(x_C) : C \in \mathcal{C})$.

The parameters of exponential family members are estimated by minimizing the negative average log-likelihood $\ell(\theta; \mathcal{D}) = -(1/|\mathcal{D}|) \sum_{x \in \mathcal{D}} \log \mathbb{P}_\theta(x)$ for some data set $\mathcal{D}$ via first-order numeric optimization methods. $\mathcal{D}$ contains samples from X, and it can be shown that the estimated probability mass converges to the data generating distribution as the size of $\mathcal{D}$ increases. However, computing Z and hence performing probabilistic inference is #P-hard [4,23]. Exact inference can be carried out via the junction tree algorithm. The junction tree representation of an undirected model is a tree, in which each vertex represents a maximal clique of a chordal completion of G ([24], Sec. 2.5.2). The cutset of each pair of adjacent clique-vertices is called separator. Here, we consider junction trees which contain separators as explicit vertices, as shown in Fig. 2(b).

2.2   Deep Boltzmann Machines

Deep Boltzmann Machines are undirected graphical models for the joint probability mass of an "ordinary" random variable X and a latent variable H that represents a set of so-called *hidden units*. *Latent* means that the value of H cannot be observed and is not contained in the data set $\mathcal{D}$.

To estimate the parameters in the presence of latent variables, expectation-maximization [6] or contrastive divergence [20] techniques must be applied. In contrast to other undirected models, the conditional independence structure of DBMs is not learned from data. Instead, the connectivity between visible and

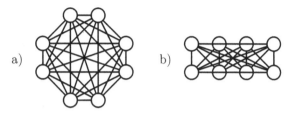

Fig. 3. Two different planar embeddings of the same 8-clique of binary hidden units. Both are equivalent to a single discrete hidden unit with $q = 2^8$ states.

hidden units as well as between hidden and hidden units is pre-specified and follows the multipartite layered structure that is well known from artificial neural feed-forward networks. An exemplary DBM is shown in Fig. 1(a).

In most cases, the hidden units are assumed to have a binary state space. This is, however, not necessary. We like to stress the fact that DBMs are plain undirected models and as such, any vertex can have any state space. For now, we consider so-called *categorical DBMs*, where all hidden units have the same state space of size q. For convenience, such DBMs are called *q-state DBMs*. A vertex with q states is called *q-state unit*.

Fixing the depth L, the width of each layer $W = (n_1, n_2, \ldots, n_L)$, and the state space size q defines a family of probability mass functions $\mathcal{M}_{L,W,H}$. To measure the expressive power of such a family, we resort to the same notion of approximation guarantee that is used in the DBM literature, e.g., [16].

Definition 1 (Universal Approximation). *A set $\mathcal{M}$ of probability mass functions on $\mathcal{X}$ is called <u>universal approximator</u> when, for any probability mass $\mathbb{Q}$ on $\mathcal{X}$ and any $\epsilon > 0$, there is a pmf $\mathbb{P}$ in $\mathcal{M}$ with $\mathrm{KL}[\mathbb{Q}\|\mathbb{P}] \leq \epsilon$.*

An obvious question is which choices of L, W, and q make a DBM an universal approximator. A rather indirect way to explain this is the identification of settings in which the (undirected) DBM can be treated as if it is a directed (feed-forward) network [14,15]. While the required proof technique is rather cumbersome and mathematically involved, this point of view paves the way to the best currently known result on the depth of DBMs:

Theorem 1 (DBMs are Universal Approximators with Exponential Dependence on n_0 [15]). *Let M be a q-state DBM with n_0 q-state visible* *units and L hidden layers of n_0 units each. Let further $\boldsymbol{X} = (\boldsymbol{X}_1, \boldsymbol{X}_2, \ldots, \boldsymbol{X}_{n_0})$ be the random variable that represents all visible units. Then, M is a universal approximator for $\mathbb{P}(\boldsymbol{X})$ provided L is large enough. More precisely, for any $n_0 \leq n := q^k + k + 1$, for some $k \in \mathbb{N}$, a sufficient condition is $L \geq 1 + (q^n + 1)/(q(q-1)(n - \log_q(n) - 1))$. For any n_0, a necessary condition is $L \geq (q^{n_0} - 1)/(n_0(q-1)(n_0(q-1) + 2))$.*

A closer look at the necessary condition suggests that this result is rather pessimistic: for $n_0 = 16$ and $q = 2$, we have $L \geq 227$—a fairly deep model for 16 binary inputs. Considering an MNIST-scale binary input, i.e., $n_0 = 784$, we have $L \geq 1.6511 \times 10^{230}$—an astronomically deep network when compared to state-of-the-art architectures [12,22].

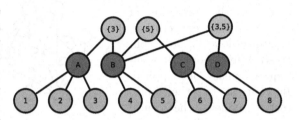

A disturbing fact about the above theorem is that a

Fig. 4. An exemplary Deep Boltzmann Tree with 8 visible units (blue), 4 hidden clique-units (green), and 3 hidden separator-units (grey). The separator-hidden units are annotated with the separating vertices, i.e., with the intersection of their incident cliques in the underlying junction tree. (Color figure online)

larger latent state space, i.e., increasing q, does not decrease the required depth of the network. Instead, the theorem tells us that a *deeper* network is required. This is especially odd because a single hidden unit with $q = b^k$ states can be reinterpreted as a fully connected set of k hidden units having b states each. As shown in Fig. 3, we can rearrange the clique to emulate 2 DBM layers with inter-layer connections. Thus, increasing the state space of hidden units is *equivalent to increasing the depth!* Hence, a meaningful lower bound on the depth of a network should *decrease* with the expressivity of the hidden units. Driven by this observation, we exploit classic insights about conditional independence structures to derive a new model class as well as new theoretical insights on the depth of q-state DBMs.

3   Deep Boltzmann Trees

Deep learning architectures are ubiquitous, mostly application specific, and validated on benchmark data. Theoretical justifications are usually replaced by superior benchmark results. Stochastic DBM-based architectures inherit their computational complexity from ordinary graphical models which renders exact inference intractable and forces the user to resort to Markov chain Monte Carlo techniques [21].

In contrast, we present a generic deep architecture that can be learned from data. In what follows, we explain the learning procedure and prove that the learned model can approximate the true underlying probability mass function

---

Algorithm 1: Constructing the Deep Boltzmann Tree

Require: Conditional independence structure G
1: $J \leftarrow$ Junction tree of G
2: $V \leftarrow V(J)$
3: $E \leftarrow E(J)$
4: **for** clique vertices $C \in J$ **do**
5:     **for** vertices $v \in C$ **do**
6:         **if** $v \notin V$ **then**
7:             $E \leftarrow E \cup \{(v, C)\}$
8:             $V \leftarrow V \cup \{v\}$
9:         **end if**
10:     **end for**
11: **end for**
12: **return** $T = (V, E)$ // The DBT

---

with arbitrary small error. As a by-product, we obtain the best known bounds on the depth required by any q-state DBM to be an universal approximator.

Our proposed model class is called Deep[1] Boltzmann Tree. The algorithmic procedure for the construction of DBTs is provided in Algorithm 1. An exemplary DBT is shown in Fig. 4. While the DBT architecture relies heavily on the junction tree structure, it is important to understand that all vertices inherited from J (line 2 of Algorithm 1) represent hidden units (latent variables) in the DBT. This difference is of utmost importance: plain junction tree models enforce clique states which do not appear in the training data to be unlikely. Instead, DBTs are capable of learning that the probability mass of unknown states is similar to that of some known states.

Moreover, we make no use of specialized junction tree inference algorithms, like Shafer-Shenoy algorithm or Hugin algorithm [24]. The asymptotic runtime of Algorithm 1 is $\mathrm{TIME}(JT) + \mathcal{O}(n|C_{\max}|)$, where $\mathrm{TIME}(JT)$ is the runtime of the junction tree construction and $|C_{\max}|$ is 1 plus the tree-width of the input graph. Here, an (NP-complete) minimum chordal completion is not required— any non-minimal poly-time triangulation suffices.

The joint pmf of visible and hidden units can then be written as

$$\mathbb{P}_T(\boldsymbol{X} = \boldsymbol{x}, \boldsymbol{H} = \boldsymbol{h}) = \frac{1}{Z_T} \prod_{(u,C) \in E_{\mathcal{U}C}} \psi_{(u,C)}(\boldsymbol{x}_u, \boldsymbol{h}_C) \prod_{(C,S) \in E_{C\mathcal{S}}} \psi_{(C,S)}(\boldsymbol{h}_C, \boldsymbol{h}_S),$$

$$(2)$$

where $E_{\mathcal{U}C} = E(T) \cap \mathcal{U} \times \mathcal{C}$, $E_{C\mathcal{S}} = E(T) \cap \mathcal{C} \times \mathcal{S}$, $V(T) = \mathcal{U} \cup \mathcal{C} \cup \mathcal{S}$, $\mathcal{U}$ being the set of visible units, $\mathcal{C}$ being the set of hidden clique-units, and $\mathcal{S}$ being the set of hidden separator-units—visualized in Fig. 4 by blue, green, and grey vertices,

---

[1] It turns out that DBTs consist of exactly two hidden layers. While this kind of depth seems rather "shallow", original work on DBMs [20] define the DBM as a restricted Boltzmann machine which has *more than one* hidden layer. Thus, to be consistent with the common terminology, we decided to denote our proposed model as "deep".

respectively. The random variable H represents the random joint realization of all hidden (green and grey) units. Note that Eq. 2 arises from the general factorization of undirected graphical models Eq. 1, having maximal cliques of size two only.

Being an undirected graphical model, the DBT pmf can be written in exponential family form, and as such, it obeys a canonical parametrization in terms of edge weights. We will now exploit this parametrization to declare universal approximation for any DBT with sufficiently large hidden state space.

Theorem 2 (Deep Boltzmann Trees are Universal Approximators). *Let* $\mathbb{P}_G$ *be the full joint pmf of the random variable* $\boldsymbol{X}$ *with conditional independence structure* G. *Let further* T *be the output of Algorithm 1. When the state space of each DBT hidden unit is at least* $|\mathcal{X}_{C_{\max}}|$, *then there exists a canonical weight vector* $\boldsymbol{\theta}$, *such that*

$$\mathrm{KL}[\mathbb{P}_G \| \mathbb{P}'_T] \leq \epsilon$$

for any $\epsilon > 0$ *and with* $\mathbb{P}'_T(\boldsymbol{x}) = \sum_h \mathbb{P}_T(\boldsymbol{x}, \boldsymbol{h})$.

Proof. Let $\boldsymbol{\theta}_{\mathcal{UC}} = (\boldsymbol{\theta}_{(v,C)} : E_{\mathcal{UC}})$ with $E_{\mathcal{UC}} = E(T) \cap \mathcal{U} \times \mathcal{C}$ contain all DBT weight vectors for edges that connect a visible vertex with a clique vertex. In a similar way, let $\boldsymbol{\theta}_{\mathcal{CS}} = (\boldsymbol{\theta}_{(C,S)} : E_{\mathcal{CS}})$ with $E_{\mathcal{CS}} = E(T) \cap \mathcal{C} \times \mathcal{S}$ contain all DBT weight vectors for edges that connect a clique vertex with a separator vertex. Finally, let $\boldsymbol{\theta}^* = (\boldsymbol{\theta}_C : C$ is maximal clique in chordal completion of $G)$ denote the clique weights of a chordal completion of G. In other words, $\boldsymbol{\theta}^*$ contains the junction tree weights. We will now choose values for $\boldsymbol{\theta}_{\mathcal{UC}}$ and $\boldsymbol{\theta}_{\mathcal{CS}}$ which guarantee the conclusion of the theorem.

Any hidden unit of T corresponds to a clique or separator vertex of the junction tree. Each hidden clique-unit $F \in V(T)$ is connected to visible units and hidden separator-units only. We do now abuse notation and identify F with the union of its visible neighbors and the content of their neighboring hidden separator-units. E.g., if $F = D$ in Fig. 4, we have $F = \{3, 5, 8\}$.

Let us fix some constant $\omega \in \mathbb{R}_+$. We will now assign two types of edge weights to any hidden clique-unit F:

(I) Each hidden clique-unit is incident to *exactly one edge* of type I—it is irrelevant which of the incident edges. Type I edges simulate the original junction tree weight $\boldsymbol{\theta}_F^*$ of the junction tree vertex F. The precondition of the theorem guarantees that the state space of the DBT unit F is at least as large as the state space of the corresponding clique in the chordal completion of G. Thus, there exist an injective function ρ, that maps the joint state of F's neighbors to exactly one of F's states. Assume that v is a neighbor of F and consider the edge (v, F). When (v, F) is a type I edge, then, for each weight $\boldsymbol{\theta}_{(v=x,F=y)}$ we have $\boldsymbol{\theta}_{(v=x,F=y)} = \boldsymbol{\theta}_{F=y}^*$ if and only if $\rho^{-1}(y)_v = x$, e.g., the joint state of F's neighbors that corresponds to y agrees with $v = x$. Otherwise, we have $\boldsymbol{\theta}_{(v=x,F=y)} = -\omega$. Moreover, for all weights $\boldsymbol{\theta}_{(v=x,F=y')}$ which correspond to hidden states y' that have no corresponding joint state, i.e., when the hidden state space is larger than the number of clique states, we set $\boldsymbol{\theta}_{(v=x,F=y')} = -\omega$.

(II) When (v, F) is a type II edge, then, for each weight $\boldsymbol{\theta}_{(v=x, F=y)}$ we have $\boldsymbol{\theta}_{(v=x, F=y)} = 0$ if and only if $\rho^{-1}(y)_v = x$. Otherwise, we have $\boldsymbol{\theta}_{(v=x, F=y)} = -\omega$. Again, we set all weights $\boldsymbol{\theta}_{(v=x, F=y')}$ which correspond to hidden states y' that have no corresponding joint state to $-\omega$.

For both edge types, we call edge states whose weight is $-\omega$ *not realizable*, and otherwise *realizable*. The concept of realizable edge states extends naturally to full joint states, i.e., whenever a joint state $(\boldsymbol{x}, \boldsymbol{h})$ of visible and hidden units contains at least one not realizable edge state, $(\boldsymbol{x}, \boldsymbol{h})$ itself is not realizable. Let $\mathcal{R}$ denote the set of all realizable joint states and $\overline{\mathcal{R}}$ its complement. Having that said, let us investigate the partition function Z_T of (Eq. 2):

$$Z_T = \sum_{(\boldsymbol{x}, \boldsymbol{h})} \prod_{(u,C) \in E_{\mathcal{U}C}} \psi_{(u,C)}(\boldsymbol{x}_u, \boldsymbol{h}_C) \prod_{(C,S) \in E_{CS}} \psi_{(C,S)}(\boldsymbol{h}_C, \boldsymbol{h}_S).$$

Now, partition the summation w.r.t. realizability, and observe that each factor of a realizable joint state is either $\exp(0) = 1$ or $\exp(\boldsymbol{\theta}^*_{F=\rho(\boldsymbol{x}_F)})$:

$$\begin{aligned} Z_T = &\sum_{\boldsymbol{x}} \prod_F \exp(\boldsymbol{\theta}^*_{F=\rho(\boldsymbol{x}_F)}) \\ &+ \sum_{(\boldsymbol{x}, \boldsymbol{h}) \in \overline{\mathcal{R}}} \prod_{(u,C) \in E_{\mathcal{U}C}} \psi_{(u,C)}(\boldsymbol{x}_u, \boldsymbol{h}_C) \prod_{(C,S) \in E_{CS}} \psi_{(C,S)}(\boldsymbol{h}_C, \boldsymbol{h}_S). \end{aligned}$$

In the limit of $\omega \to \infty$, the sum over not realizable states vanishes (because $exp(-\omega) \to 0$) and Z_T converges to the partition function of the ordinary junction tree factorization. In the same way, $\lim_{\omega \to \infty} \mathbb{P}_T(\boldsymbol{x}, \boldsymbol{h})$ converges either to 0 whenever $(\boldsymbol{x}, \boldsymbol{h}) \in \overline{\mathcal{R}}$, or to $\mathbb{P}_J(\boldsymbol{x})$ whenever $(\boldsymbol{x}, \boldsymbol{h}) \in \mathcal{R}$. Since the junction tree pmf $\mathbb{P}_J$ is identical to the original undirected model $\mathbb{P}_G$, we have $\lim_{\omega \to \infty} \sum_{\boldsymbol{h}} \mathbb{P}_T(\boldsymbol{x}, \boldsymbol{h}) = \mathbb{P}_G(\boldsymbol{x})$. Thus, for any $\epsilon > 0$, there exists $\omega > 0$ such that $\mathrm{KL}[\mathbb{P}_G \| \mathbb{P}'_T] \leq \epsilon$.   □

The theorem tells us that it is always possible to find DBT weights $\boldsymbol{\theta}$ which make the approximation error arbitrarily small as long as the DBT's latent state space is large enough. Surprisingly, the result carries over to q-state DBMs. The idea is to embed the DBT into the DBM as visualized in Fig. 1(c) and (d).

Theorem 3 (DBMs are Universal Approximators with Linear Dependence on n_0). *Let M be a q-state DBM with n_0 visible units and L hidden layers of n_0 units each. Let further $\boldsymbol{X}$ be the random variable that represents all visible units. Then, M is a universal approximator for $\mathbb{P}(\boldsymbol{X})$ provided L and q are large enough. More precisely, if $q \geq |\mathcal{X}_{C_{\max}}|$, it suffices that $L \geq 2$.*

Proof. Notice that the output T of Algorithm 1 is an especially simple tripartite graph, indicated by the coloring in Fig. 4. By identifying the visible units of T with the visible units of M, the remainder is a bipartite graph that consists of hidden clique-units and hidden separator-units. The precondition of the theorem asserts that each hidden layer has n_0 units. Each hidden clique-unit of T

arises from some maximal clique of a chordal completion of the true conditional independence structure of $\boldsymbol{X}$. The number of maximal cliques in a chordal graph with n vertices is at most n [7]. Thus, T has at most n_0 units per layer. Since each pair of hidden DBM layers forms a complete bipartite graph, it is straightforward to embed the two hidden layers of T into the first two layers of M (visualized in Fig. 1(d)). Finally, setting all edge weights $\boldsymbol{\theta}_e$ of some edge e to the all-zero vector $\boldsymbol{0}$, implies that the corresponding edge potential $\psi_e(\boldsymbol{x}_e)$ is 1 for all choices of $\boldsymbol{x}_e$—the edge e is effectively removed from the undirected model. Thus, all edges which are not required to embed T into M can be removed. Together with Theorem 2, this shows that there exists a canonical weight vector $\boldsymbol{\theta}$ for the DBM which induces a probability mass that is arbitrarily close to the true pmf of $\boldsymbol{X}$. Hence, M is an universal approximator. □

Note, however, that this result is not contradictory to Theorem 1. Our theorem does not assume that observed and hidden units have the same state space. In our setting, the latent state space and thus, the complexity of the learned activation functions, is allowed to vary with the complexity of the input data. This is an important difference to ordinary feed-forwards architectures where the functional form of the activation functions is usually fixed.

While the theorem shows a constant dependence of the depth on the number of visible units, the dependence of the width is still linear. Inspecting the proof reveals that even the "vertical" worst-case embedding (Fig. 1(c)) of any DBT into the corresponding DBM can be realized as long as $L \geq 2n_0 - 1$—a linear worst-case depth. This suggests that no DBM must be deeper than $2n_0 - 1$ layers as long as the hidden units are expressive enough to cover the underlying clique potentials. Motivated by this observation, we state the following conjecture:

Conjecture 1 (The Depth of Deep Networks). DBMs with more than two hidden layers are only required if the underlying learning algorithm cannot find a shallow DBT embedding into the DBM structure.

Results on model compression suggest that shallow networks can be on par with state-of-the-art deep models [1,3]. Such results rely on specialized training procedures, but finding a superior shallow solution directly might not be easy for the learning algorithm. Indeed, learning the weights of DBMs and other deep architectures suffers from various local minima—the 2-layer solution from Theorem 3 is only one of them. Which solution is learned eventually depends crucially on the weight initialization [8].

Another interesting fact is that the proof tells us how DBT learning is connected to classic and recent structure learning techniques.

Corollary 1 (Chow-Liu DBM). *Consider a data set $\mathcal{D} = \{(\boldsymbol{x}, \boldsymbol{h})^i : 1 \leq i \leq N\}$, sampled from the Deep Boltzmann Machine described in Theorem 3. Running the Chow-Liu structure estimation algorithm [5] on $\mathcal{D}$, and dropping all edges with uniform edge marginals and disconnected vertices reveals the DBT.*

By construction, the Chow-Liu tree is the pairwise undirected model that minimizes the Kullback-Leibler divergence to the actual joint pmf that generated

---

Algorithm 2: Learning the Deep Boltzmann Tree Weights

Require: Data set $\mathcal{D} = \{\boldsymbol{x}^1, \ldots, \boldsymbol{x}^N\}$, DBT $T = (V, E)$ from Alg. 1
1: Initialize $\boldsymbol{\theta} \leftarrow \boldsymbol{0}$
2: $\forall$ hidden unit u: initialize $\mathcal{X}_u \leftarrow \emptyset$
3: **for** training data $\boldsymbol{x}^i \in \mathcal{D}$ **do**
4:     $\boldsymbol{y} \leftarrow$ empty state ()
5:     **for** hidden unit $u \in V$ **do**
6:         **for** vertex $v \in V(u)$ **do**
7:             $\boldsymbol{y} \leftarrow \boldsymbol{y} \circ \boldsymbol{x}_v^i$
8:         **end for**
9:         **if** $\boldsymbol{y} \notin \mathcal{X}_u$ **then**
10:             $\mathcal{X}_u \leftarrow \mathcal{X}_u \cup \{\boldsymbol{y}\}$
11:         **end if**
12:         $\boldsymbol{h}(\boldsymbol{x}^i)_u \leftarrow \boldsymbol{y}$
13:     **end for**
14: **end for**
15: **while** $\|\nabla(\boldsymbol{\theta})\| > 0$ **do**
16:     $\boldsymbol{\theta} \leftarrow \boldsymbol{\theta} - \frac{1}{2|E|}\nabla\ell(\boldsymbol{\theta})$
17: **end while**
18: **return** $\boldsymbol{\theta}$ // Optimal weights

---

the data. While we assume that the data was generated by a Boltzmann machine, we know that there is a Boltzmann tree which represents the exact same pmf. Thus, the Chow-Liu tree must be the DBT given N is large enough.

Corollary 2 (l_1-regularized DBM). *Consider a data set $\mathcal{D} = \{(\boldsymbol{x}, \boldsymbol{h})^i : 1 \leq i \leq N\}$, sampled from the Deep Boltzmann Machine described in Theorem 3. Running the Elem-GM structure estimation algorithm [27] on $\mathcal{D}$ and dropping all fully disconnected vertices reveals the DBT.*

The so called elementary estimator for graphical models (Elem-GM) is a regularization based structure learning technique. In contrast to the Chow-Liu tree, Elem-GM can output non-tree structures. The method performs l_1-regularization to identify unnecessary edges which are then excluded from the learned model. Since we know that many edges are actually unnecessary to recover the full joint pmf, we conclude that the DBT is an optimal solution to the Elem-GM problem given N is large enough.

3.1   Learning the DBT Weights

So far, we only discussed how to find the DBT. We will now explain how to estimate the DBT weights from data. Learning the parameters of a DBT factorizes into two phases: in the first phase, we have to find good initial values for the hidden units $\boldsymbol{h}$—this choice is crucial and failing to find good values implies inferior learning results. Moreover, phase one determines the state space $\mathcal{X}_u$ of each hidden units u. In phase two, numerical first-order optimization is applied to find a minimizer of ℓ. The problem in phase two is convex given any fixed hidden values from phase one. The learning procedure is provided in Algorithm 2. Let us quickly go through it line-by-line. First, we initialize the weight vector and the hidden state spaces (lines 1 and 2). We then loop over all N training instances $\boldsymbol{x}^i$ (line 3). We initialize a new empty state (line 4) and recall from Theorem 2 that each hidden unit u originates from a clique or separator vertex of the junction tree. Denote the set of visible units connected to the original clique or separator vertex by $V(u)$. In lines 6–8 we read the states of all visible units in $V(u)$ and construct a new hidden state $\boldsymbol{y}$. If that hidden state was never seen before (line 9), we create a new state in u's state space (line 10), and assign that new state to the hidden activation $\boldsymbol{h}(\boldsymbol{x}^i)_u$ that is associated with the current data point $\boldsymbol{x}^i$ (line 12). Lines 15 to 17 correspond to gradient descent.

Notice that we stop the optimization when the gradient's norm is zero. Since the objective function is convex, we will surely arrive at a global minimizer of ℓ given our learning rate is correct. Notice further that we set the learning rate to $1/(2|E|)$. This originates from the fact that gradient descent with learning rate $1/\mathcal{L}$ is guaranteed to converge to the next local minimum (which is also global due to convexity). Here $\mathcal{L}$ denotes the gradients Lipschitz constant. As we could not find the following result in the literature, we state it for completeness. A proof is provided in the supplementary material.

Lemma 1 (Lipschitz Continuous Gradient). *The gradient of any tree-structured, undirected model is Lipschitz continuous with constant $\mathcal{L} = 2|E|$.*

For simplicity, we state Algorithm 2 as plain gradient descent method. In our experiments however, we use Nesterov-acceleration [17] to speed-up learning. More on gradient computation for exponential families can be found in [24].

The proposed algorithm grows the hidden state space to cover joint realizations of the underlying chordal model. Note, however, that only clique states that actually appear in the data set are generated. This is in contrast to the junction tree algorithm, whose runtime is always exponential in the size of the largest clique. However, if one cannot effort to grow the hidden state space as large as the data tells us, i.e., due to limited resources, we can assign some already known state. In that case, we suggest to iterate phase two and use the estimated model weights $\boldsymbol{\theta}$ to re-sample the hidden activation. Thus, performing an expectation-maximization procedure [6].

4   Experiments

We conduct a small set of experiments to provide a proof of concept of the generative capabilities of Deep Boltzmann Trees. The source code, and a docker image that contains everything which is required to repeat our experiments, are available for download (http://www.randomfields.org/dbt). To facilitate reproducability, we employ the following freely available benchmark data sets:

– MNIST (http://yann.lecun.com/exdb/mnist)

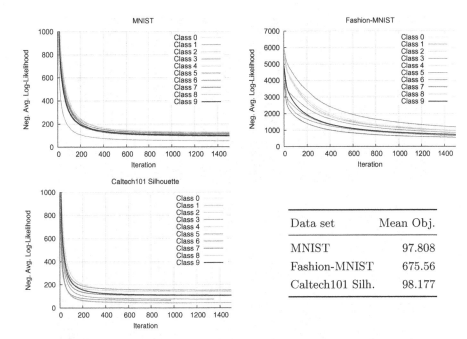

Fig. 5. The training progress and mean neg. avg. log-likelihood of DBT learning on all benchmark data sets.

- Fashion-MNIST (https://github.com/zalandoresearch/fashion-mnist)
- Caltech101 Silhouette (https://people.cs.umass.edu/~marlin/data.shtml)

Numeric attributes (MNIST and Fashion-MNIST) are discretized via quantiles to contain at most 10 distinct states. The Caltech101 data contains various classes with very few data points (< 100). Thus, we took only the ten classes with most training instances. For each data set, we join the predefined training data and test data, and run Algorithms 1 and 2 until convergence to estimate the DBTs and their weights. Recall that Algorithm 1 requires a graphical structure as input. We run Chordalysis [26] to compute chordal conditional independence structures. Chordalysis allows to control the false discovery rate to get rid of spurious dependencies, which we set[2] to 0.05. The training progress and final mean objective function values are provided in Fig. 5. The plots show how the conditional likelihood of each class evolves during training. We see that the model achieves much lower neg. log-likelihoods on MNIST and Caltech101 than on Fashion-MNIST. Since the DBT itself is a universal estimator, we conclude that Fashion-MNIST does not contain enough data to allow a reliable estimation of the underlying conditional independence structure. Having a reasonable estimate of that structure is crucial for the DBT construction.

---

[2] We have to stress that this is not a hyper-parameter of the DBT. Moreover, 0.05 is not "tuned" either as it is the default value in Chordalysis.

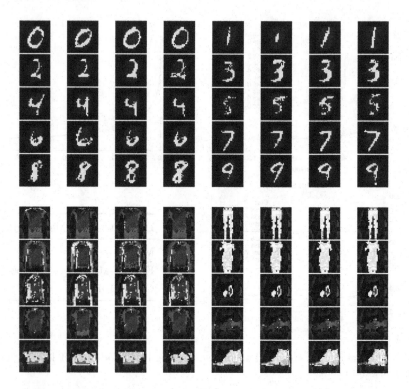

Fig. 6. Synthetic MNIST data (top) and synthetic Fashion-MNIST data (bottom), sampled from the DBT.

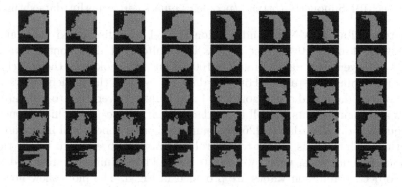

Fig. 7. Synthetic Caltech101 Silhouette data, sampled from the Deep Boltzmann Tree.

After learning, we perform Perturb-and-MAP sampling [19] to generate samples from the models. Due to large likelihood values, we expect that samples from the Fashion-MNIST model have rather low quality. Some resulting samples are shown in Figs. 6 and 7. We see that the model produces crisp MNIST samples without mode collapse, i.e., they are not just noisy versions of the same number. Each class is able to generate multiple samples which look like different ways to write the particular number. As expected, the quality of Fashion-MNIST samples is rather low. The type of class, like pants, bag, shirt, shoe, or dress can be identified in most cases, but the resulting samples are close to mode collapse. The diversity of Caltech101 Silhouette samples is also low. However, this is already true for the original silhouette data. Of course, the model can only learn to generate diverse samples if the underlying data contains some diversity.

5 Conclusion

State-of-the-art results in various classification and synthetic data generation tasks are often achieved by deep learning. While the field of deep learning evolves fast, theoretical insights are rare. Moreover, many hyper-parameters have to be tuned in order to reach actual state-of-the-art performance. Driven by the wish for a better understanding of how depth improves a model, we studied the structure of DBMs. We discovered a new deep generative model, the Deep Boltzmann Tree, which can be learned from data without tuning a single hyper-parameter. We proved that DBTs are universal approximators and showed connections to other structure learning methods. Experiments on benchmark data suggest, that high-quality synthetic data can be generated if the data set is large enough to allow for a reasonable estimation of the underlying conditional independence structure. Due to its tree structure, the DBT does not suffer from computational issues like the Deep Boltzmann Machine does. As a by-product, we discovered the best known bound on the depth of categorical DBMs and proposed a conjecture on why depth can improve a model in practice. Our results pave the way for several new research directions, including likelihood-based hybrid classification/generation models, and the consistent estimation of high-resolution image and audio data with theoretical guarantees.

Acknowledgments. This research has been funded by the Federal Ministry of Education and Research of Germany as part of the competence center for machine learning ML2R (01S18038A).

References

1. Ba, J., Caruana, R.: Do deep nets really need to be deep? In: Advances in Neural Information Processing Systems (NIPS), pp. 2654–2662 (2014)
2. Bartlett, P.L., Foster, D.J., Telgarsky, M.J.: Spectrally-normalized margin bounds for neural networks. In: Advances in Neural Information Processing Systems (NIPS) 30, pp. 6241–6250 (2017)
3. Bucila, C., Caruana, R., Niculescu-Mizil, A.: Model compression. In: International Conference on Knowledge Discovery and Data Mining (SIGKDD), pp. 535–541 (2006)

4. Bulatov, A., Grohe, M.: The complexity of partition functions. In: Díaz, J., Karhumäki, J., Lepistö, A., Sannella, D. (eds.) ICALP 2004. LNCS, vol. 3142, pp. 294–306. Springer, Heidelberg (2004). https://doi.org/10.1007/978-3-540-27836-8_27

5. Chow, C., Liu, C.: Approximating discrete probability distributions with dependence trees. IEEE Trans. Inf. Theory **14**(3), 462–467 (1968)

6. Dempster, A.P., Laird, M.N., Rubin, D.B.: Maximum likelihood from incomplete data via the EM algorithm. J. R. Stat. Soc.: Ser. B (Methodol.) **39**(1), 1–38 (1977)

7. Fulkerson, D.R., Gross, O.A.: Incidence matrices and interval graphs. Pac. J. Math. **15**(3), 835–855 (1965)

8. Glorot, X., Bengio, Y.: Understanding the difficulty of training deep feedforward neural networks. In: International Conference on Artificial Intelligence and Statistics (AISTATS), pp. 249–256 (2010)

9. Golowich, N., Rakhlin, A., Shamir, O.: Size-independent sample complexity of neural networks. In: Conference On Learning Theory (COLT), pp. 297–299 (2018)

10. Goodfellow, I.J., et al.: Generative adversarial nets. In: Advances in Neural Information Processing Systems (NIPS), pp. 2672–2680 (2014)

11. Hammersley, J.M., Clifford, P.: Markov fields on finite graphs and lattices. Unpublished manuscript (1971)

12. He, K., Zhang, X., Ren, S., Sun, J.: Identity mappings in deep residual networks. In: Leibe, B., Matas, J., Sebe, N., Welling, M. (eds.) ECCV 2016. LNCS, vol. 9908, pp. 630–645. Springer, Cham (2016). https://doi.org/10.1007/978-3-319-46493-0_38

13. Li, Y., Turner, R.E.: Gradient estimators for implicit models. In: International Conference on Learning Representations (ICLR) (2018)

14. Montavon, G., Braun, M.L., Müller, K.: Deep Boltzmann machines as feed-forward hierarchies. In: International Conference on Artificial Intelligence and Statistics (AISTATS), pp. 798–804 (2012)

15. Montúfar, G.: Deep narrow Boltzmann machines are universal approximators. In: International Conference on Learning Representations (ICLR) (2015)

16. Montúfar, G., Morton, J.: Discrete restricted Boltzmann machines. J. Mach. Learn. Res. **16**, 653–672 (2015)

17. Nesterov, Y.: A method of solving a convex programming problem with convergence rate $O(1/k^2)$. Sov. Math. Dokl. **27**(2), 372–376 (1983)

18. Neyshabur, B., Tomioka, R., Srebro, N.: Norm-based capacity control in neural networks. In: Conference on Learning Theory (COLT), pp. 1376–1401 (2015)

19. Papandreou, G., Yuille, A.L.: Perturb-and-MAP random fields: using discrete optimization to learn and sample from energy models. In: IEEE International Conference on Computer Vision (ICCV), pp. 193–200 (2011)

20. Salakhutdinov, R., Hinton, G.E.: Deep Boltzmann machines. In: International Conference on Artificial Intelligence and Statistics (AISTATS), pp. 448–455 (2009)

21. Salakhutdinov, R., Larochelle, H.: Efficient learning of deep Boltzmann machines. In: Artificial Intelligence and Statistics (AISTATS), pp. 693–700 (2010)

22. Shazeer, N., et al.: Outrageously large neural networks: the sparsely-gated mixture-of-experts layer. CoRR abs/1701.06538 (2017)

23. Valiant, L.G.: The complexity of enumeration and reliability problems. SIAM J. Comput. **8**(3), 410–421 (1979)

24. Wainwright, M.J., Jordan, M.I.: Graphical models, exponential families, and variational inference. Found. Trends Mach. Learn. **1**(1–2), 1–305 (2008)

25. Warde-Farley, D., Bengio, Y.: Improving generative adversarial networks with denoising feature matching. In: International Conference on Learning Representations (ICLR) (2017)

26. Webb, G.I., Petitjean, F.: A multiple test correction for streams and cascades of statistical hypothesis tests. In: International Conference on Knowledge Discovery and Data Mining (SIGKDD), pp. 1225–1264 (2016)
27. Yang, E., Lozano, A.C., Ravikumar, P.: Elementary estimators for graphical models. In: Advances in Neural Information Processing Systems (NIPS) 27, pp. 2159–2167 (2014)

L_0-ARM: Network Sparsification via Stochastic Binary Optimization

Yang Li and Shihao Ji$^{(\boxtimes)}$

Georgia State University, Atlanta, USA
yli93@student.gsu.edu, sji@gsu.edu

Abstract. We consider network sparsification as an L_0-norm regularized binary optimization problem, where each unit of a neural network (e.g., weight, neuron, or channel, etc.) is attached with a stochastic binary gate, whose parameters are jointly optimized with original network parameters. The Augment-Reinforce-Merge (ARM) [27], a recently proposed unbiased gradient estimator, is investigated for this binary optimization problem. Compared to the hard concrete gradient estimator from Louizos et al. [19], ARM demonstrates superior performance of pruning network architectures while retaining almost the same accuracies of baseline methods. Similar to the hard concrete estimator, ARM also enables conditional computation during model training but with improved effectiveness due to the *exact* binary stochasticity. Thanks to the flexibility of ARM, many smooth or non-smooth parametric functions, such as scaled sigmoid or hard sigmoid, can be used to parameterize this binary optimization problem and the unbiasness of the ARM estimator is retained, while the hard concrete estimator has to rely on the hard sigmoid function to achieve conditional computation and thus accelerated training. Extensive experiments on multiple public datasets demonstrate state-of-the-art pruning rates with almost the same accuracies of baseline methods. The resulting algorithm L_0-ARM sparsifies the Wide-ResNet models on CIFAR-10 and CIFAR-100 while the hard concrete estimator cannot. The code is public available at https://github.com/leo-yangli/l0-arm.

Keywords: Network sparsification · L_0-norm regularization · Binary optimization

1 Introduction

Deep Neural Networks (DNNs) have achieved great success in a broad range of applications in image recognition [3], natural language processing [4], and games [23]. Latest DNN architectures, such as ResNet [9], DenseNet [10] and Wide-ResNet [28], incorporate hundreds of millions of parameters to achieve state-of-the-art predictive performance. However, the expanding number of parameters not only increases the risk of overfitting, but also leads to high computational costs. Many practical real-time applications of DNNs, such as

© Springer Nature Switzerland AG 2020
U. Brefeld et al. (Eds.): ECML PKDD 2019, LNAI 11907, pp. 432–448, 2020.
https://doi.org/10.1007/978-3-030-46147-8_26

for smart phones, drones and the IoT (Internet of Things) devices, call for compute and memory efficient models as these devices typically have very limited computation and memory capacities.

Fortunately, it has been shown that DNNs can be pruned or sparsified significantly with minor accuracy losses [7,8], and sometimes sparsified networks can even achieve higher accuracies due to the regularization effects of the network sparsification algorithms [19,22]. Driven by the widely spread applications of DNNs in real-time systems, there has been an increasing interest in pruning or sparsifying networks recently [7,8,17–19,21,22,25]. Earlier methods such as the magnitude-based approaches [7,8] prune networks by removing the weights of small magnitudes, and it has been shown that this approach although simple is very effective at sparsifying network architectures with minor accuracy losses. Recently, the L_0-norm based regularization method [19] is getting attraction as this approach *explicitly* penalizes number of non-zero parameters and can drive redundant or insignificant parameters to be exact zero. However, the gradient of the L_0 regularized objective function is intractable. Louizos et al. [19] propose to use the hard concrete distribution as a close surrogate to the Bernoulli distribution, and this leads to a differentiable objective function while still being able to zeroing out redundant or insignificant weights during training. Due to the hard concrete substitution, however, the resulting hard concrete estimator is biased with respect to the original objective function.

In this paper, we propose L_0-ARM for network sparsification. L_0-ARM is built on top of the L_0 regularization framework of Louizos et al. [19]. However, instead of using a biased hard concrete gradient estimator, we investigate the Augment-Reinforce-Merge (ARM) [27], a recently proposed unbiased gradient estimator for stochastic binary optimization. Because of the unbiasness and flexibility of the ARM estimator, L_0-ARM exhibits a significantly faster rate at pruning network architectures and reducing FLOPs than the hard concrete estimator. Extensive experiments on multiple public datasets demonstrate the superior performance of L_0-ARM at sparsifying networks with fully connected layers and convolutional layers. It achieves state-of-the-art prune rates while retaining similar accuracies compared to baseline methods. Additionally, it sparsifies the Wide-ResNet models on CIFAR-10 and CIFAR-100 while the original hard concrete estimator cannot.

The remainder of the paper is organized as follows. In Sect. 2 we describe the L_0 regularized empirical risk minimization for network sparsification and formulate it as a stochastic binary optimization problem. A new unbiased estimator to this problem L_0-ARM is presented in Sect. 3, followed by related work in Sect. 4. Example results on multiple public datasets are presented in Sect. 5, with comparisons to baseline methods and the state-of-the-art sparsification algorithms. Conclusions and future work are discussed in Sect. 6.

2   Formulation

Given a training set $D = \{(\boldsymbol{x}_i, y_i), i = 1, 2, \cdots, N\}$, where $\boldsymbol{x}_i$ denotes the input and y_i denotes the target, a neural network is a function $h(\boldsymbol{x}; \boldsymbol{\theta})$ parametrized by $\boldsymbol{\theta}$ that fits to the training data D with the goal of achieving good general-ization to unseen test data. To optimize $\boldsymbol{\theta}$, typically a regularized empirical risk is minimized, which contains two terms – a data loss over training data and a regularization loss over model parameters. Empirically, the regularization term can be weight decay or Lasso, i.e., the L_2 or L_1 norm of model parameters.

Since the L_2 or L_1 norm only imposes shrinkage for large values of $\boldsymbol{\theta}$, the resulting model parameters $\boldsymbol{\theta}$ are often manifested by smaller magnitudes but none of them are exact zero. Intuitively, a more appealing alternative is the L_0 regularization since the L_0-norm measures *explicitly* the number of non-zero elements, and minimizing of it over model parameters will drive the redundant or insignificant weights to be exact zero. With the L_0 regularization, the empirical risk objective can be written as

$$\mathcal{R}(\boldsymbol{\theta}) = \frac{1}{N} \sum_{i=1}^{N} \mathcal{L}\left(h(\boldsymbol{x}_i; \boldsymbol{\theta}), y_i\right) + \lambda \|\boldsymbol{\theta}\|_0 \tag{1}$$

where $\mathcal{L}(\cdot)$ denotes the data loss over training data D, such as the cross-entropy loss for classification or the mean squared error (MSE) for regression, and $\|\boldsymbol{\theta}\|_0$ denotes the L_0-norm over model parameters, i.e., the number of non-zero weights, and λ is a regularization hyper-parameter that balances between data loss and model complexity.

To represent a sparsified model, we attach a binary random variable z to each element of model parameters $\boldsymbol{\theta}$. Therefore, we can re-parameterize the model parameters $\boldsymbol{\theta}$ as an element-wise product of non-zero parameters $\tilde{\boldsymbol{\theta}}$ and binary random variables $\boldsymbol{z}$:

$$\boldsymbol{\theta} = \tilde{\boldsymbol{\theta}} \odot \boldsymbol{z}, \tag{2}$$

where $\boldsymbol{z} \in \{0,1\}^{|\boldsymbol{\theta}|}$, and $\odot$ denotes the element-wise product. As a result, Eq. 1 can be rewritten as:

$$\mathcal{R}(\tilde{\boldsymbol{\theta}}, \boldsymbol{z}) = \frac{1}{N} \sum_{i=1}^{N} \mathcal{L}\left(h(\boldsymbol{x}_i; \tilde{\boldsymbol{\theta}} \odot \boldsymbol{z}), y_i\right) + \lambda \sum_{j=1}^{|\tilde{\boldsymbol{\theta}}|} \mathbf{1}_{[z_j \neq 0]}, \tag{3}$$

where $\mathbf{1}_{[c]}$ is an indicator function that is 1 if the condition c is satisfied, and 0 otherwise. Note that both the first term and the second term of Eq. 3 are not differentiable w.r.t. $\boldsymbol{z}$. Therefore, further approximations need to be considered.

According to stochastic variational optimization [2], given any function $\mathcal{F}(\boldsymbol{z})$ and any distribution $q(\boldsymbol{z})$, the following inequality holds

$$\min_{\boldsymbol{z}} \mathcal{F}(\boldsymbol{z}) \leq \mathbb{E}_{\boldsymbol{z} \sim q(\boldsymbol{z})}[\mathcal{F}(\boldsymbol{z})], \tag{4}$$

i.e., the minimum of a function is upper bounded by the expectation of the function. With this result, we can derive an upper bound of Eq. 3 as follows.

Since $z_j, \forall j \in \{1, \cdots, |\boldsymbol{\theta}|\}$ is a binary random variable, we assume z_j is subject to a Bernoulli distribution with parameter $\pi_j \in [0,1]$, i.e. $z_j \sim \text{Ber}(z; \pi_j)$.

Thus, we can upper bound $\min_z \mathcal{R}(\tilde{\boldsymbol{\theta}}, \boldsymbol{z})$ by the expectation

$$\hat{\mathcal{R}}(\tilde{\boldsymbol{\theta}}, \boldsymbol{\pi}) = \mathbb{E}_{z \sim \text{Ber}(z;\pi)} \mathcal{R}(\tilde{\boldsymbol{\theta}}, \boldsymbol{z})$$

$$= \mathbb{E}_{z \sim \text{Ber}(z;\pi)} \left[\frac{1}{N} \sum_{i=1}^{N} \mathcal{L}\left(h(\boldsymbol{x}_i; \tilde{\boldsymbol{\theta}} \odot \boldsymbol{z}), y_i\right) \right] + \lambda \sum_{j=1}^{|\tilde{\boldsymbol{\theta}}|} \pi_j. \quad (5)$$

As we can see, now the second term is differentiable w.r.t. the new model parameters $\boldsymbol{\pi}$, while the first term is still problematic since the expectation over a large number of binary random variables $\boldsymbol{z}$ is intractable and so its gradient. Since $\boldsymbol{z}$ are binary random variables following a Bernoulli distribution with parameters $\boldsymbol{\pi}$, we now formulate the original L_0 regularized empirical risk (1) to a stochastic binary optimization problem (5).

Existing gradient estimators for this kind of discrete latent variable models include REINFORCE [26], Gumble-Softmax [11,20], REBAR [24], RELAX [6] and the Hard Concrete estimator [19]. However, these estimators either are biased or suffer from high variance or computationally expensive due to auxiliary modeling. Recently, the Augment-Reinforce-Merge (ARM) [27] gradient estimator is proposed for the optimization of binary latent variable models, which is unbiased and exhibits low variance. Extending this gradient estimator to network sparsification, we find that ARM demonstrates superior performance of prunning network architectures while retaining almost the same accuracies of baseline models. More importantly, similar to the hard concrete estimator, ARM also enables conditional computation [1] that not only sparsifies model architectures for inference but also accelerates model training.

3 L_0-ARM: Stochastic Binary Optimization

To minimize Eq. 5, we propose L_0-ARM, a stochastic binary optimization algorithm based on the Augment-Reinforce-Merge (ARM) gradient estimator [27]. We first introduce the main theorem of ARM. Refer readers to [27] for the proof and other details.

Theorem 1 *(ARM) [27]. For a vector of V binary random variables $\boldsymbol{z} = (z_1, \cdots, z_V)$, the gradient of*

$$\mathcal{E}(\boldsymbol{\phi}) = \mathbb{E}_{z \sim \prod_{v=1}^{V} \text{Ber}(z_v; g(\phi_v))}[f(\boldsymbol{z})] \quad (6)$$

w.r.t. $\boldsymbol{\phi} = (\phi_1, \cdots, \phi_V)$, the logits of the Bernoulli distribution parameters, can be expressed as

$$\nabla_{\boldsymbol{\phi}} \mathcal{E}(\boldsymbol{\phi}) = \mathbb{E}_{u \sim \prod_{v=1}^{V} \text{Uniform}(u_v;0,1)} \left[\left(f(\mathbf{1}_{[u>g(-\phi)]}) - f(\mathbf{1}_{[u<g(\phi)]}) \right) (\boldsymbol{u} - 1/2) \right], \quad (7)$$

where $\mathbf{1}_{[u>g(-\phi)]} := \left(\mathbf{1}_{[u_1>g(-\phi_1)]}, \cdots, \mathbf{1}_{[u_V>g(-\phi_V)]} \right)^T$ and $g(\phi) = \sigma(\phi) = 1/(1+ \exp(-\phi))$ is the sigmoid function.

Parameterizing $\pi_j \in [0, 1]$ as $g(\phi_j)$, Eq. 5 can be rewritten as

$$\hat{\mathcal{R}}(\tilde{\boldsymbol{\theta}}, \boldsymbol{\phi}) = \mathbb{E}_{\boldsymbol{z} \sim \mathrm{Ber}(\boldsymbol{z}; g(\boldsymbol{\phi}))} \left[f(\boldsymbol{z}) \right] + \lambda \sum_{j=1}^{|\tilde{\boldsymbol{\theta}}|} g(\boldsymbol{\phi}_j)$$

$$= \mathbb{E}_{\boldsymbol{u} \sim \mathrm{Uniform}(\boldsymbol{u}; 0, 1)} \left[f(\mathbf{1}_{[\boldsymbol{u} < g(\boldsymbol{\phi})]}) \right] + \lambda \sum_{j=1}^{|\tilde{\boldsymbol{\theta}}|} g(\boldsymbol{\phi}_j), \qquad (8)$$

where $f(\boldsymbol{z}) = \frac{1}{N} \sum_{i=1}^{N} \mathcal{L}\left(h(\boldsymbol{x}_i; \tilde{\boldsymbol{\theta}} \odot \boldsymbol{z}), y_i \right)$. Now according to Theorem 1, we can evaluate the gradient of Eq. 8 w.r.t. $\boldsymbol{\phi}$ by

$$\nabla_{\boldsymbol{\phi}}^{ARM} \hat{\mathcal{R}}(\tilde{\boldsymbol{\theta}}, \boldsymbol{\phi}) = \mathbb{E}_{\boldsymbol{u} \sim \mathrm{Uniform}(\boldsymbol{u}; 0, 1)} \left[\left(f(\mathbf{1}_{[\boldsymbol{u} > g(-\boldsymbol{\phi})]}) - f(\mathbf{1}_{[\boldsymbol{u} < g(\boldsymbol{\phi})]}) \right) (\boldsymbol{u} - 1/2) \right]$$

$$+ \lambda \sum_{j=1}^{|\tilde{\boldsymbol{\theta}}|} \nabla_{\boldsymbol{\phi}_j} g(\boldsymbol{\phi}_j), \qquad (9)$$

which is an unbiased and low variance estimator as demonstrated in [27].

Note from Eq. 9 that we need to evaluate $f(\cdot)$ twice to compute the gradient, the second of which is the same operation required by the data loss of Eq. 8. Therefore, one extra forward pass $f(\mathbf{1}_{[\boldsymbol{u} > g(-\boldsymbol{\phi})]})$ is required by the L_0-ARM gradient estimator. This additional forward pass might be computationally expensive, especially for networks with millions of parameters. To reduce the computational complexity of Eq. 9, we further consider another gradient estimator – Augment-Reinforce (AR) [27]:

$$\nabla_{\boldsymbol{\phi}}^{AR} \hat{\mathcal{R}}(\tilde{\boldsymbol{\theta}}, \boldsymbol{\phi}) = \mathbb{E}_{\boldsymbol{u} \sim \mathrm{Uniform}(\boldsymbol{u}; 0, 1)} \left[f(\mathbf{1}_{[\boldsymbol{u} < g(\boldsymbol{\phi})]}) (1 - 2\boldsymbol{u}) \right]$$

$$+ \lambda \sum_{j=1}^{|\tilde{\boldsymbol{\theta}}|} \nabla_{\boldsymbol{\phi}_j} g(\boldsymbol{\phi}_j), \qquad (10)$$

which requires only one forward pass $f(\mathbf{1}_{[\boldsymbol{u} < g(\boldsymbol{\phi})]})$ that is the same operation as in Eq. 8. This L_0-AR gradient estimator is still unbiased but with higher variance. Now with L_0-AR, we can trade off the variance of the estimator with the computational complexity. We will evaluate the impact of this trade-off in our experiments.

3.1   Choice of $g(\phi)$

Theorem 1 of ARM defines $g(\phi) = \sigma(\phi)$, where $\sigma(\cdot)$ is the sigmoid function. For the purpose of network sparsification, we find that this parametric function isn't very effective due to its slow transition between values 0 and 1. Thanks to the flexibility of ARM, we have a lot of freedom to design this parametric function $g(\phi)$. Apparently, it's straightforward to generalize Theorem 1 for any parametric

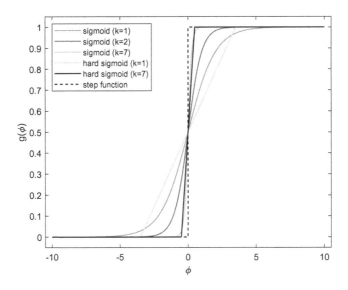

Fig. 1. The plots of $g(\phi)$ with different k for sigmoid and hard sigmoid functions. A large k tends to be more effective at sparsifying networks. Best viewed in color. (Color figure online)

functions (smooth or non-smooth) as long as $g : \mathcal{R} \to [0, 1]$ and $g(-\phi) = 1 - g(\phi)$[1]. Example parametric functions that work well in our experiments are the scaled sigmoid function

$$g_{\sigma_k}(\phi) = \sigma(k\phi) = \frac{1}{1 + \exp(-k\phi)}, \tag{11}$$

and the centered-scaled hard sigmoid

$$g_{\bar{\sigma}_k}(\phi) = \min(1, \max(0, \frac{k}{7}\phi + 0.5)), \tag{12}$$

where 7 is introduced such that $g_{\bar{\sigma}_1}(\phi) \approx g_{\sigma_1}(\phi) = \sigma(\phi)$. See Fig. 1 for some example plots of $g_{\sigma_k}(\phi)$ and $g_{\bar{\sigma}_k}(\phi)$ with different k. Empirically, we find that $k = 7$ works well for all of our experiments.

One important difference between the hard concrete estimator from Louizos et al. [19] and L_0-ARM is that the hard concrete estimator has to rely on the hard sigmoid gate to zero out some parameters during training (a.k.a. conditional computation [1]), while L_0-ARM achieves conditional computation naturally by sampling from the Bernoulli distribution, parameterized by $g(\phi)$, where $g(\phi)$ can be any parametric function (smooth or non-smooth) as shown in Fig. 1. We validate this in our experiments.

---

[1] The second condition is not necessary. But for simplicity, we will impose this condition to select parametric function $g(\phi)$ that is antithetic. Designing $g(\phi)$ without this constraint could be a potential area that is worthy of further investigation.

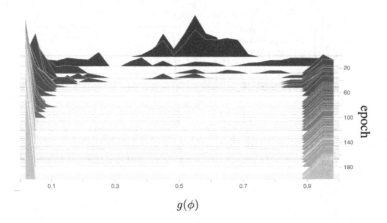

Fig. 2. Evolution of the histogram of $g(\phi)$ over training epochs. All $g(\phi)$ are initialized by random samples from a normal distribution $\mathcal{N}(0.5, 0.01)$, which are split into two spikes during training.

3.2 Sparsifying Network Architectures for Inference

After training, we get model parameters $\tilde{\theta}$ and ϕ. At test time, we can use the expectation of $z \sim \text{Ber}(z; g(\phi))$ as the mask $\hat{z}$ for the final model parameters $\hat{\theta}$:

$$\hat{z} = \mathbb{E}[z] = g(\phi), \qquad \hat{\theta} = \tilde{\theta} \odot \hat{z}. \tag{13}$$

However, this will not yield a sparsified network for inference since none of the element of $\hat{z} = g(\phi)$ is exact zero (unless the hard sigmoid gate $g_{\bar{\sigma}_k}(\phi)$ is used). A simple approximation is to set the elements of $\hat{z}$ to zero if the corresponding values in $g(\phi)$ are less than a threshold τ, i.e.,

$$\bar{z}_j = \begin{cases} 0, & g(\phi_j) \le \tau \\ g(\phi_j), & \text{otherwise} \end{cases} \qquad j = 1, 2, \cdots, |z| \tag{14}$$

We find that this approximation is very effective in all of our experiments as the histogram of $g(\phi)$ is widely split into two spikes around values of 0 and 1 after training because of the sharp transition of the scaled sigmoid (or hard sigmoid) function. See Fig. 2 for a typical plot of the histograms of $g(\phi)$ evolving during training process. We notice that our algorithm isn't very sensitive to τ, tuning which incurs negligible impacts to prune rates and model accuracies. Therefore, for all of our experiments we set $\tau = 0.5$ by default. Apparently, better designed τ is possible by considering the histogram of $g(\phi)$. However, we find this isn't very necessary for all of our experiments in the paper. Therefore, we will consider this histogram-dependent τ as our future improvement.

3.3 Imposing Shrinkage on Model Parameters θ

The L_0 regularized objective function (8) leads to sparse estimate of model parameters without imposing any shrinkage on the magnitude of θ. In some cases it might still be desirable to regularize the magnitude of model parameters with other norms, such as L_1 or L_2 (weight decay), to improve the robustness of model. This can be achieved conveniently by computing the expected L_1 or L_2 norm of $\boldsymbol{\theta}$ under the same Bernoulli distribution: $\boldsymbol{z} \sim \text{Ber}(\boldsymbol{z}; g(\boldsymbol{\phi}))$ as follows:

$$\mathbb{E}_{\boldsymbol{z} \sim \text{Ber}(\boldsymbol{z}; g(\boldsymbol{\phi}))}\left[\|\boldsymbol{\theta}\|_1\right] = \sum_{j=1}^{|\theta|} \mathbb{E}_{z_j \sim \text{Ber}(z_j; g(\phi_j))}\left[z_j |\tilde{\theta}_j|\right] = \sum_{j=1}^{|\theta|} g(\phi_j)|\tilde{\theta}_j|, \quad (15)$$

$$\mathbb{E}_{\boldsymbol{z} \sim \text{Ber}(\boldsymbol{z}; g(\boldsymbol{\phi}))}\left[\|\boldsymbol{\theta}\|_2^2\right] = \sum_{j=1}^{|\theta|} \mathbb{E}_{z_j \sim \text{Ber}(z_j; g(\phi_j))}\left[z_j^2 \tilde{\theta}_j^2\right] = \sum_{j=1}^{|\theta|} g(\phi_j)\tilde{\theta}_j^2, \quad (16)$$

which can be incorporated to Eq. 8 as additional regularization terms.

3.4   Group Sparsity Under L_0 and L_2 Norms

The formulation so far promotes a weight-level sparsity for network architectures. This sparsification strategy can compress model and reduce memory footprint of a network. However, it will usually not lead to effective speedups because weight-sparsified networks require sparse matrix multiplication and irregular memory access, which make it extremely challenging to effectively utilize the parallel computing resources of GPUs and CPUs. For the purpose of computational efficiency, it's usually preferable to perform group sparsity instead of weight-level sparsity. Similar to [19,22,25], we can achieve this by sharing a stochastic binary gate z among all the weights in a group. For example, a group can be all fan-out weights of a neuron in fully connected layers or all weights of a convolution filter. With this, the group regularized L_0 and L_2 norms can be conveniently expressed as

$$\mathbb{E}_{\boldsymbol{z} \sim \text{Ber}(\boldsymbol{z}; g(\boldsymbol{\phi}))}\left[\|\boldsymbol{\theta}\|_0\right] = \sum_{g=1}^{|G|} |g| g(\phi_g) \quad (17)$$

$$\mathbb{E}_{\boldsymbol{z} \sim \text{Ber}(\boldsymbol{z}; g(\boldsymbol{\phi}))}\left[\|\boldsymbol{\theta}\|_2^2\right] = \sum_{g=1}^{|G|} \left(g(\phi_g) \sum_{j=1}^{|g|} \tilde{\theta}_j^2\right) \quad (18)$$

where $|G|$ denotes the number of groups and $|g|$ denotes the number of weights of group g. For the reason of computational efficiency, we perform this group sparsity in all of our experiments.

4   Related Work

It is well-known that DNNs are extremely compute and memory intensive. Recently, there has been an increasing interest to network sparsification [7,8,17–19,21,22,25] as the applications of DNNs to practical real-time systems, such as the IoT devices, call for compute and memory efficient networks. One of the earliest sparsification methods is to prune the redundant weights based on the magnitudes [16], which is proved to be effective in modern CNN [8]. Although weight sparsification is able to compress networks, it can barely improve computational efficiency due to unstructured sparsity [25]. Therefore, magnitude-based group sparsity is proposed [17,25], which can compress networks while reducing computation cost significantly. These magnitude-based methods usually proceed in three stages: pre-train a full network, prune the redundant weights or filters, and fine-tune the pruned model. As a comparison, our method L_0-ARM trains a sparsified network from scratch without pre-training and fine-tuning, and therefore is more preferable.

Another category of sparsification methods is based on Bayesian statistics and information theory [18,21,22]. For example, inspired by variational dropout [13], Molchanov et al. propose a method that unbinds the dropout rate, and also leads to sparsified networks [21].

Recently, Louizos et al. [19] propose to sparsify networks with L_0-norm. Since the L_0 regularization explicitly penalizes number of non-zero parameters, this method is conceptually very appealing. However, the non-differentiability of L_0 norm prevents an effective gradient-based optimization. Therefore, Louizos et al. [19] propose a hard concrete gradient estimator for this optimization problem. Our work is built on top of their L_0 formulation. However, instead of using a hard concrete estimator, we investigate the Augment-Reinforce-Merge (ARM) [27], a recently proposed unbiased estimator, to this binary optimization problem.

5   Experimental Results

We evaluate the performance of L_0-ARM and L_0-AR on multiple public datasets and multiple network architectures. Specifically, we evaluate MLP 500-300 [15] and LeNet 5-Caffe[2] on the MNIST dataset [15], and Wide Residual Networks [28] on the CIFAR-10 and CIFAR-100 datasets [14]. For baselines, we refer to the following state-of-the-art sparsification algorithms: Sparse Variational Dropout (Sparse VD) [21], Bayesian Compression with group normal-Jeffreys (BC-GNJ) and group horseshoe (BC-GHS) [18], and L_0-norm regularization with hard concrete estimator (L_0-HC) [19]. For a fair comparison, we closely follow the experimental setups of L_0-HC.[3]

5.1   Implementation Details

We incorporate L_0-ARM and L_0-AR into the architectures of MLP, LeNet-5 and Wide ResNet. As we described in Sect. 3.4, instead of sparsifying weights, we apply group sparsity on neurons in fully-connected layers or on convolution

---

[2] https://github.com/BVLC/caffe/tree/master/examples/mnist.
[3] https://github.com/AMLab-Amsterdam/L0_regularization.

filters in convolutional layers. Once a neuron or filter is pruned, all related weights are removed from the networks.

The Multi-Layer Perceptron (MLP) [15] has two hidden layers of size 300 and 100, respectively. We initialize $g(\phi) = \pi$ by random samples from a normal distribution $\mathcal{N}(0.8, 0.01)$ for the input layer and $\mathcal{N}(0.5, 0.01)$ for the hidden layers, which activate around 80% of neurons in input layer and around 50% of neurons in hidden layers. LeNet-5-Caffe consists of two convolutional layers of 20 and 50 filters interspersed with max pooling layers, followed by two fully-connected layers with 500 and 10 neurons. We initialize $g(\phi) = \pi$ for all neurons and filters by random samples from a normal distribution $\mathcal{N}(0.5, 0.01)$. Wide-ResNets (WRNs) [28] have shown state-of-the-art performance on many image classification benchmarks. Following [19], we only apply L_0 regularization on the first convolutional layer of each residual block, which allows us to incorporate L_0 regularization without further modifying residual block architecture. The architectural details of WRN are listed in Table 1. For initialization, we activate around 70% of convolutional filters.

Table 1. Architectural details of WRN incorporated with L_0-ARM. The number in parenthesis is the size of activation map of each layer. For brevity, only the modified layers are included.

Group name	Layers
conv1	[Original Conv (16)]
conv2	[L_0 ARM (160); Original Conv (160)] × 4
conv3	[L_0 ARM (320); Original Conv (320)] × 4
conv4	[L_0 ARM (640); Original Conv (640)] × 4

For MLP and LeNet-5, we train with a mini-batch of 100 data samples and use Adam [12] as optimizer with initial learning rate of 0.001, which is halved every 100 epochs. For Wide-ResNet, we train with a mini-batch of 128 data samples and use Nesterov Momentum as optimizer with initial learning rate of 0.1, which is decayed by 0.2 at epoch 60 and 120. Each of these experiments run for 200 epochs in total. For a fair comparison, these experimental setups closely follow what were described in L_0-HC [19] and their open-source implementation (see Footnote 3).

5.2 MNIST Experiments

We run both MLP and LeNet-5 on the MNIST dataset. By tuning the regularization strength λ, we can control the trade off between sparsity and accuracy. We can use one λ for all layers or a separate λ for each layer to fine-tune the sparsity preference. In our experiments, we set $\lambda = 0.1/N$ or $\lambda = (0.1, 0.3, 0.4)/N$ for MLP, and set $\lambda = 0.1/N$ or $\lambda = (10, 0.5, 0.1, 10)/N$ for LeNet-5, where N denotes to the number of training datapoints.

We use three metrics to evaluate the performance of an algorithm: prediction accuracy, prune rate, and expected number of floating point operations (FLOPs). Prune rate is defined as the ratio of number of pruned weights to number of all weights. Prune rate manifests the memory saving of a sparsified network, while expected FLOPs demonstrates the training/inference cost of a sparsification algorithm.

Table 2. Performance comparison on MNIST. Each experiment was run five times and the median (in terms of accuracy) is reported. All the baseline results are taken from the corresponding papers.

Network	Method	Pruned architecture	Prune rate (%)	Accuracy (%)
MLP 784-300-100	Sparse VD	219-214-100	74.72	98.2
	BC-GNJ	278-98-13	89.24	98.2
	BC-GHS	311-86-14	89.45	98.2
	L_0-HC ($\lambda = 0.1/N$)	219-214-100	73.98	98.6
	L_0-HC (λ sep.)	266-88-33	89.99	98.2
	L_0-AR ($\lambda = 0.1/N$)	453-150-68	70.39	98.3
	L_0-ARM ($\lambda = 0.1/N$)	143-153-78	87.00	98.3
	L_0-AR (λ sep.)	464-114-65	77.10	98.2
	L_0-ARM (λ sep.)	159-74-73	**92.96**	98.1
LeNet-5-Caffe 20-50-800-500	Sparse VD	14-19-242-131	90.7	99.0
	GL	3-12-192-500	76.3	99.0
	GD	7-13-208-16	98.62	99.0
	SBP	3-18-284-283	80.34	99.0
	BC-GNJ	8-13-88-13	99.05	99.0
	BC-GHS	5-10-76-16	99.36	99.0
	L_0-HC ($\lambda = 0.1/N$)	20-25-45-462	91.1	99.1
	L_0-HC (λ sep.)	9-18-65-25	98.6	99.0
	L_0-AR ($\lambda = 0.1/N$)	18-28-46-249	93.73	98.8
	L_0-ARM ($\lambda = 0.1/N$)	20-16-32-257	95.52	99.1
	L_0-AR (λ sep.)	5-12-131-22	98.90	98.4
	L_0-ARM (λ sep.)	6-10-39-11	**99.49**	98.7

We compare L_0-ARM and L_0-AR to five state-of-the-art sparsification algorithms on MNIST, with the results shown in Table 2. For the comparison between L_0-HC and L_0-AR(M) when $\lambda = 0.1/N$, we use the exact same hyper-parameters for both algorithms (the fairest comparison). In this case, L_0-ARM achieve the same accuracy (99.1%) on LeNet-5 with even sparser pruned architectures (95.52% vs. 91.1%). When separated λs are considered (λ sep.), since L_0-HC doesn't disclose the specific λs for the last two fully-connected layers, we tune them by ourselves and find that $\lambda = (10, 0.5, 0.1, 10)/N$ yields the best performance. In this case, L_0-ARM achieves the highest prune rate (99.49% vs. 98.6%) with very similar accuracies (98.7% vs. 99.1%) on LeNet-5. Similar patterns are also observed on MLP. Regarding L_0-AR, although its performance is not as good as L_0-ARM, it's still very competitive to all the other methods. The advantage of L_0-AR over L_0-ARM is its lower computational complexity during training. As we discussed in Sect. 3, L_0-ARM needs one extra forward pass to estimate the gradient w.r.t. ϕ; for large DNN architectures, this extra cost can be significant.

To evaluate the training cost and network sparsity of different algorithms, we compare the prune rates of L_0-HC and L_0-AR(M) on LeNet-5 as a function of epoch in Fig. 3(a, b). Similarly, we compare the expected FLOPs of different algorithms as a function of epoch in Fig. 3(c, d). As we can see from (a, b), L_0-ARM yields much sparser network architectures over the whole training epochs, followed by L_0-AR and L_0-HC. The FLOPs vs. Epoch plots in (c, d) are more complicated. Because L_0-HC and L_0-AR only need one forward pass to compute gradient, they have the same expected FLOPs for training and inference. L_0-ARM needs two forward passes for training. Therefore, L_0-ARM is computationally more expensive during training (red curves), but it leads to sparser/more efficient architectures for inference (green curves), which pays off its extra cost in training.

5.3   CIFAR Experiments

We further evaluate the performance of L_0-ARM and L_0-AR with Wide-ResNet [28] on CIFAR-10 and CIFAR-100. Following [19], we only apply L_0 regularization on the first convolutional layer of each residual block, which allows us to incorporate L_0 regularization without further modifying residual block architecture.

Table 3 shows the performance comparison between L_0-AR(M) and three baseline methods. We find that L_0-HC cannot sparsify the Wide-ResNet architecture (prune rate 0%)[4], while L_0-ARM and L_0-AR prune around 50% of the parameters of the impacted subnet. As we activate 70% convolution filters in initialization, the around 50% prune rate is not due to initialization. We also inspect the histograms of $g(\phi)$: As expected, they are all split into two spikes around the values of 0 and 1, similar to the histograms shown in Fig. 2. In terms of accuracies, both L_0-ARM and L_0-AR achieve very similar accuracies as the baseline methods.

To evaluate the training and inference costs of different algorithms, we compare the expected FLOPs of L_0-HC and L_0-AR(M) on CIFAR-10 and CIFAR-100 as a function of iteration in Fig. 4. Similar to Fig. 3, L_0-ARM is more computationally expensive for training, but leads to sparser/more efficient architectures for inference, which pays off its extra cost in training. It's worth to emphasize that for these experiments L_0-AR has the lowest training FLOPs and inference FLOPs (since only one forward pass is needed for training and inference), while achieving very similar accuracies as the baseline methods (Table 3).

---

[4] This was also reported recently in the appendix of [5], and can be easily reproduced by using the open-source implementation of L_0-HC (see footnote 3).

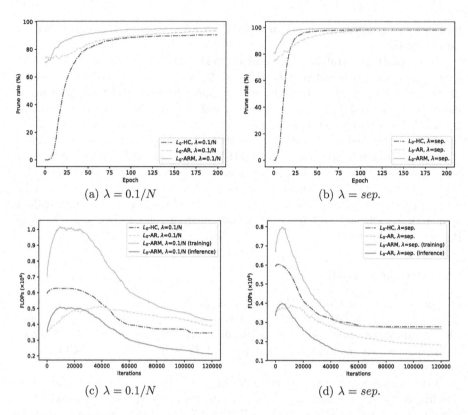

Fig. 3. (a, b) Comparison of prune rate of sparsified network as a function of epoch for different algorithms. (c, d) Comparison of expected FLOPs as a function of epoch for different algorithms during training and inference. The results are on LeNet-5 with L_0-HC and L_0-AR(M). Because L_0-HC and L_0-AR only need one forward pass to compute gradient, they have the same expected FLOPs for training and inference. L_0-ARM needs two forward passes for training. Therefore, L_0-ARM is computationally more expensive during training (red curves), but it leads to sparser/more efficient architectures for inference (blue curves), which pays off its extra cost in training. (Color figure online)

Finally, we compare the test accuracies of different algorithms as a function of epoch on CIFAR-10, with the results shown in Fig. 5. We apply the exact same hyper-parameters of L_0-HC to L_0-AR(M). As L_0-AR(M) prunes around 50% parameters during training (while L_0-HC prunes 0%), the test accuracies of

Table 3. Performance comparison of WRN on CIFAR-10 and CIFAR-100. Each experiment was run five times and the median (in terms of accuracy) is reported. All the baseline results are taken from the corresponding papers. Only the architectures of pruned layers are shown.

Network	Method	Pruned architecture	Prune rate (%)	Accuracy (%)
WRN-28-10 CIFAR-10	Original WRN [28]	Full model	0	96.00
	Original WRN-dropout [28]	Full model	0	96.11
	L_0-HC ($\lambda = 0.001/N$) [19]	Full model	0	96.17
	L_0-HC ($\lambda = 0.002/N$) [19]	Full model	0	96.07
	L_0 AR ($\lambda = 0.001/N$)	83-77-83-88-169-167-153-165-324-323-314-329	49.49	95.58
	L_0 ARM ($\lambda = 0.001/N$)	74-86-83-83-164-145-167-153-333-333-310-330	49.46	95.68
	L_0 AR ($\lambda = 0.002/N$)	82-75-82-87-164-169-156-161-317-317-317-324	**49.95**	95.60
	L_0 ARM ($\lambda = 0.002/N$)	75-72-78-78-157-165-131-162-336-325-331-343	49.63	95.70
WRN-28-10 CIFAR-100	Original WRN [28]	Full model	0	78.82
	Original WRN-dropout [28]	Full model	0	81.15
	L_0-HC ($\lambda = 0.001/N$) [19]	Full model	0	81.25
	L_0-HC ($\lambda = 0.002/N$) [19]	Full model	0	80.96
	L_0-AR ($\lambda = 0.001/N$)	78-78-79-85-168-168-162-164-308-326-319-330	49.37	80.50
	L_0-ARM ($\lambda = 0.001/N$)	75-83-80-58-172-156-160-165-324-311-313-318	50.51	80.74
	L_0-AR ($\lambda = 0.002/N$)	75-76-72-80-158-158-137-168-318-295-327-324	50.93	80.09
	L_0-ARM ($\lambda = 0.002/N$)	81-74-77-73-149-157-156-152-299-332-305-325	**50.78**	80.56

the former are lower than the latter before convergence, but all the algorithms yield very similar accuracies after convergence, demonstrating the effectiveness of L_0-AR(M).

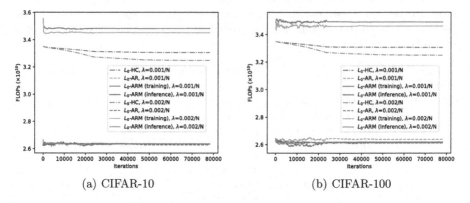

(a) CIFAR-10   (b) CIFAR-100

Fig. 4. Comparison of expected FLOPs as a function of iteration during training and inference. Similar to Fig. 3, L_0-ARM is more computationally expensive for training, but leads to sparser/more efficient architectures for inference. For these experiments, L_0-AR has the lowest training FLOPs and inference FLOPs, while achieving very similar accuracies as the baseline methods (Table 3).

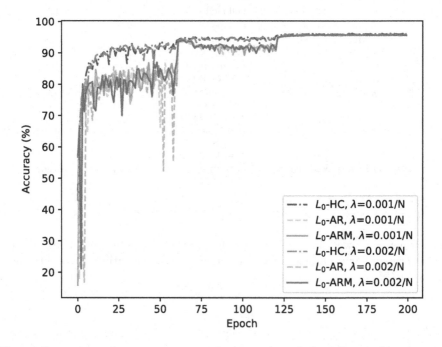

Fig. 5. Comparison of test accuracy as a function of epoch for different algorithms on CIFAR-10. We apply the exact same hyper-parameters of L_0-HC to L_0-AR(M), which yield similar accuracies for converged models even though the latter prunes around 50% parameters while the former prunes 0%.

6   Conclusion

We propose L_0-ARM, an unbiased and low-variance gradient estimator, to sparsify network architectures. Compared to L_0-HC [19] and other state-of-the-art sparsification algorithms, L_0-ARM demonstrates superior performance of sparsifying network architectures while retaining almost the same accuracies of the baseline methods. Extensive experiments on multiple public datasets and multiple network architectures validate the effectiveness of L_0-ARM. Overall, L_0-ARM yields the sparsest architectures and the lowest inference FLOPs for all the networks considered with very similar accuracies as the baseline methods.

As for future extensions, we plan to design better (possibly non-antithetic) parametric function $g(\phi)$ to improve the sparsity of solutions. We also plan to investigate more efficient algorithm to evaluate L_0-ARM gradient (9) by utilizing the antithetic structure of two forward passes.

References

1. Bengio, Y., Leonard, N., Courville, A.: Estimating or propagating gradients through stochastic neurons for conditional computation. arXiv preprint arXiv:1308.3432 (2013)
2. Bird, T., Kunze, J., Barber, D.: Stochastic variational optimization. arXiv preprint arXiv:1809.04855 (2018)
3. Deng, J., Dong, W., Socher, R., Li, L.J., Li, K., Fei-Fei, L.: ImageNet: a large-scale hierarchical image database. In: IEEE Conference on Computer Vision and Pattern Recognition (CVPR) (2009)
4. Devlin, J., Chang, M.W., Lee, K., Toutanova, K.: BERT: pre-training of deep bidirectional transformers for language understanding. arXiv preprint arXiv:1810.04805 (2018)
5. Gale, T., Elsen, E., Hooker, S.: The state of sparsity in deep neural networks. arXiv preprint arXiv:1902.09574 (2019)
6. Grathwohl, W., Choi, D., Wu, Y., Roeder, G., Duvenaud, D.: Backpropagation through the void: optimizing control variates for black-box gradient estimation. In: International Conference on Learning Representations (ICLR) (2018)
7. Han, S., Mao, H., Dally, W.J.: Deep compression: compressing deep neural networks with pruning, trained quantization and huffman coding. In: International Conference on Learning Representations (ICLR) (2016)
8. Han, S., Pool, J., Tran, J., Dally, W.: Learning both weights and connections for efficient neural network. In: Advances in Neural Information Processing Systems, pp. 1135–1143 (2015)
9. He, K., Zhang, X., Ren, S., Sun, J.: Deep residual learning for image recognition. In: IEEE Conference on Computer Vision and Pattern Recognition (CVPR), pp. 770–778 (2016)
10. Huang, G., Liu, Z., van der Maaten, L., Weinberger, K.Q.: Densely connected convolutional networks. In: IEEE Conference on Computer Vision and Pattern Recognition (CVPR) (2017)
11. Jang, E., Gu, S., Poole, B.: Categorical reparameterization with gumbel-softmax. In: International Conference on Learning Representations (ICLR) (2017)

12. Kingma, D.P., Ba, J.: Adam: A method for stochastic optimization. In: International Conference on Learning Representations (ICLR) (2015)
13. Kingma, D.P., Salimans, T., Welling, M.: Variational dropout and the local reparameterization trick. In: Advances in Neural Information Processing Systems, pp. 2575–2583 (2015)
14. Krizhevsky, A.: Learning multiple layers of features from tiny images. Technical report (2009)
15. Lecun, Y., Bottou, L., Bengio, Y., Haffner, P., et al.: Gradient-based learning applied to document recognition. Proc. IEEE **86**(11), 2278–2324 (1998)
16. LeCun, Y., Denker, J.S., Solla, S.A.: Optimal brain damage. In: Advances in Neural Information Processing Systems, pp. 598–605 (1990)
17. Li, H., Kadav, A., Durdanovic, I., Samet, H., Graf, H.P.: Pruning filters for efficient convnets. arXiv preprint arXiv:1608.08710 (2016)
18. Louizos, C., Ullrich, K., Welling, M.: Bayesian compression for deep learning. In: Advances in Neural Information Processing Systems, pp. 3288–3298 (2017)
19. Louizos, C., Welling, M., Kingma, D.P.: Learning sparse neural networks through l_0 regularization. In: International Conference on Learning Representations (ICLR) (2018)
20. Maddison, C.J., Mnih, A., Teh, Y.W.: The concrete distribution: a continuous relaxation of discrete random variables. In: International Conference on Learning Representations (ICLR) (2017)
21. Molchanov, D., Ashukha, A., Vetrov, D.: Variational dropout sparsifies deep neural networks. In: Proceedings of the 34th International Conference on Machine Learning-Volume 70, pp. 2498–2507. JMLR. org (2017)
22. Neklyudov, K., Molchanov, D., Ashukha, A., Vetrov, D.: Structured bayesian pruning via log-normal multiplicative noise. In: Advances in Neural Information Processing Systems (NIPS) (2017)
23. Silver, D., et al.: Mastering the game of go with deep neural networks and tree search. Nature **529**, 484–503 (2016)
24. Tucker, G., Mnih, A., Maddison, C.J., Lawson, J., Sohl-Dickstein, J.: Rebar: low-variance, unbiased gradient estimates for discrete latent variable models. In: Advances in Neural Information Processing Systems (NIPS) (2017)
25. Wen, W., Wu, C., Wang, Y., Chen, Y., Li, H.: Learning structured sparsity in deep neural networks. In: Advances in Neural Information Processing Systems (NIPS) (2016)
26. Williams, R.J.: Simple statistical gradient-following algorithms for connectionist reinforcement learning. Mach. Learn. **8**(3–4), 229–256 (1992)
27. Yin, M., Zhou, M.: ARM: augment-REINFORCE-merge gradient for stochastic binary networks. In: International Conference on Learning Representations (ICLR) (2019)
28. Zagoruyko, S., Komodakis, N.: Wide residual networks. In: The British Machine Vision Conference (BMVC) (2016)

Learning with Random Learning Rates

Léonard Blier[1,2(✉)], Pierre Wolinski[1], and Yann Ollivier[2]

[1] TAU, LRI, Inria, Université Paris Sud, Orsay, France
`pierre.wolinski@u-psud.fr`
[2] Facebook AI Research, Paris, France
`{leonardb,yol}@fb.com`

Abstract. In neural network optimization, the learning rate of the gradient descent strongly affects performance. This prevents reliable out-of-the-box training of a model on a new problem. We propose the *All Learning Rates At Once* (Alrao) algorithm for deep learning architectures: each neuron or unit in the network gets its own learning rate, randomly sampled at startup from a distribution spanning several orders of magnitude. The network becomes a mixture of slow and fast learning units. Surprisingly, Alrao performs close to SGD with an optimally tuned learning rate, for various tasks and network architectures. In our experiments, all Alrao runs were able to learn well without any tuning.

1 Introduction

Deep learning models require delicate hyperparameter tuning [1]: when facing new data or new model architectures, finding a configuration that enables fast learning requires both expert knowledge and extensive testing. This prevents deep learning models from working out-of-the-box on new problems without human intervention (AutoML setup, [2]). One of the most critical hyperparameters is the learning rate of the gradient descent [3, p. 892]. With too large learning rates, the model does not learn; with too small learning rates, optimization is slow and can lead to local minima and poor generalization [4–7].

Efficient methods with no learning rate tuning are a necessary step towards more robust learning algorithms, ideally working out of the box. Many methods were designed to directly set optimal per-parameter learning rates [8–12], such as the popular Adam optimizer. The latter comes with default hyperparameters which reach good performance on many problems and architectures; yet fine-tuning and scheduling of its learning rate is still frequently needed [13], and the default setting is specific to current problems and architecture sizes. Indeed Adam's default hyperparameters fail in some natural setups (Sect. 6.2). This makes it unfit in an out-of-the-box scenario.

We propose *All Learning Rates At Once* (Alrao), a gradient descent method for deep learning models that leverages redundancy in the network. Alrao uses multiple learning rates at the same time in the same network, spread across several orders of magnitude. This creates a mixture of slow and fast learning units.

© Springer Nature Switzerland AG 2020
U. Brefeld et al. (Eds.): ECML PKDD 2019, LNAI 11907, pp. 449–464, 2020.
https://doi.org/10.1007/978-3-030-46147-8_27

Alrao departs from the usual philosophy of trying to find the "right" learning rates; instead we take advantage of the overparameterization of network-based models to produce a diversity of behaviors from which good network outputs can be built. The width of the architecture may optionally be increased to get enough units within a suitable learning rate range, but surprisingly, performance was largely satisfying even without increasing width.

Our contributions are as follows:

- We introduce Alrao, a gradient descent method for deep learning models with no learning rate tuning, leveraging redundancy in deep learning models via a range of learning rates in the same network. Surprisingly, Alrao does manage to learn well over a range of problems from image classification, text prediction, and reinforcement learning.
- In our tests, Alrao's performance is always close to that of SGD with the optimal learning rate, without any tuning.
- Alrao combines performance with *robustness*: not a single run failed to learn with the default learning rate range we used. In contrast, our parameter-free baseline, Adam with default hyperparameters, is not reliable across the board.
- Alrao vindicates the role of redundancy in deep learning: having enough units with a suitable learning rate is sufficient for learning.

2   Related Work

Redundancy in Deep Learning. Alrao specifically exploits the redundancy of units in network-like models. Several lines of work underline the importance of such redundancy in deep learning. For instance, dropout [14] relies on redundancy between units. Similarly, many units can be pruned after training without affecting accuracy [15–18]. Wider networks have been found to make training easier [19–21], even if not all units are useful a posteriori.

The *lottery ticket hypothesis* [22,23] posits that "large networks that train successfully contain subnetworks that—when trained in isolation—converge in a comparable number of iterations to comparable accuracy". This subnetwork is the *lottery ticket winner*: the one which had the best initial values. In this view, redundancy helps because a larger network has a larger probability to contain a suitable subnetwork. Alrao extends this principle to the learning rate.

Learning Rate Tuning. Automatically using the "right" learning rate for each parameter was one motivation behind "adaptive" methods such as RMSProp [8], AdaGrad [9] or Adam [10]. Adam with its default setting is currently considered the default method in many works [24]. However, further global adjustment of the Adam learning rate is common [25]. Other heuristics for setting the learning rate have been proposed [11]; these heuristics often start with the idea of approximating a second-order Newton step to define an optimal learning rate [12]. Indeed, asymptotically, an arguably optimal preconditioner is either the Hessian of the loss (Newton method) or the Fisher information matrix [26]. Another approach is to perform gradient descent on the learning rate itself through the whole training procedure [27–32]. Despite being around since the 80's [27], this has not been widely adopted, because of sensitivity to hyperparameters such as the meta-learning rate or the initial learning rate [33]. Of all these methods, Adam is probably the most widespread at present [24], and we use it as a baseline.

The learning rate can also be optimized within the framework of architecture or hyperparameter search, using methods from from reinforcement learning [1,34,35], evolutionary algorithms [36–38], Bayesian optimization [39], or differentiable architecture search [40]. Such methods are resource-intensive and do not allow for finding a good learning rate in a single run.

3 Motivation and Outline

We first introduce the general ideas behind Alrao. The detailed algorithm is explained in Sect. 4 and in Algorithm 1. We also release a Pytorch [41] implementation, including tutorials: http://github.com/leonardblier/alrao.

Different Learning Rates for Different Units. Instead of using a single learning rate for the model, Alrao samples once and for all a learning rate for each *unit* in the network. These rates are taken from a log-uniform distribution in an interval $[\eta_{min}; \eta_{max}]$. The log-uniform distribution produces learning rates spread over several order of magnitudes, mimicking the log-uniform grids used in standard grid searches on the learning rate.

A *unit* corresponds for example to a feature or neuron for fully connected networks, or to a channel for convolutional networks. Thus we build "slow-learning" and "fast-learning" units. In contrast, with per-parameter learning rates, every unit would have a few incoming weights with very large learning rates, and possibly diverge.

Intuition. Alrao is inspired by the fact that not all units in a neural network end up being useful. Our idea is that in a large enough network with learning rates sampled randomly per unit, a sub-network made of units with a good learning rate will learn well, while the units with a wrong learning rate will produce useless values and just be ignored by the rest of the network. Units with too small learning rates will not learn anything and stay close to their initial values; this does not hurt training (indeed, even leaving some weights at their initial values, corresponding to a learning rate 0, does not hurt training). Units with a too large learning rate may produce large activation values, but those will be mitigated by subsequent normalizing mechanisms in the computational graph, such as sigmoid/tanh activations or BatchNorm.

Alrao can be interpreted within the *lottery ticket hypothesis* [22]: viewing the per-unit learning rates of Alrao as part of the initialization, this hypothesis suggests that in a wide enough network, there will be a sub-network whose initialization (both values and learning rate) leads to good convergence.

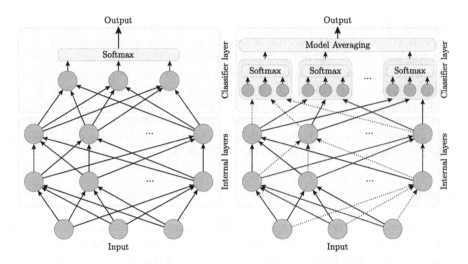

Fig. 1. Left: a standard fully connected neural network for a classification task with three classes, made of several internal layers and an output layer. Right: Alrao version of the same network. The single classifier layer is replaced with a set of parallel copies of the original classifier, averaged with a model averaging method. Each unit uses its own learning rate for its incoming weights (represented by different styles of arrows).

Slow and Fast Learning Units for the Output Layer. Sampling a learning rate per unit at random in the last layer would not make sense. For classification, each unit in the last layer represents a single category: using different learning rates for these units would favor some categories during learning. Moreover for scalar regression tasks there is only one output unit, thus we would be back to selecting a single learning rate.

The simplest way to obtain the best of several learning rates for the last layer, without relying on heuristics to guess an optimal value, is to use *model averaging* over several copies of the output layer (Fig. 1), each copy trained with its own learning rate from the interval $[\eta_{\min}; \eta_{\max}]$. All these untied copies of the output layer share the same Alrao internal layers (Fig. 1). This can be seen as a smooth form of model selection or grid-search over the output layer learning rate; actually, this part of the architecture can even be dropped after a few epochs, as the model averaging quickly concentrates on one model.

Increasing Network Width. With Alrao, neurons with unsuitable learning rates will not learn: those with too large learning rates might learn no useful signal, while those with too small learning rates will learn too slowly. Thus, Alrao may reduce the *effective width* of the network to only a fraction of the actual architecture width, depending on $[\eta_{\min}; \eta_{\max}]$. This may be compensated by multiplying the width of the network by a factor γ. Our first intuition was that $\gamma > 1$ would be necessary; still Alrao turns out to work well even without width augmentation.

4   All Learning Rates at Once: Description

4.1   Notation

We now describe Alrao more precisely for deep learning models with softmax output, on classification tasks; the case of regression is similar.

Let $\mathcal{D} = \{(x_1, y_1), ..., (x_N, y_N)\}$, with $y_i \in \{1, ..., K\}$, be a classification dataset. The goal is to predict the y_i given the x_i, using a deep learning model Φ_θ. For each input x, $\Phi_\theta(x)$ is a probability distribution over $\{1, ..., K\}$, and we want to minimize the categorical cross-entropy loss ℓ over the dataset: $\frac{1}{N} \sum_i \ell(\Phi_\theta(x_i), y_i)$.

We denote $log - \mathcal{U}(\cdot; \eta_{\min}, \eta_{\max})$ the *log-uniform* probability distribution on an interval $[\eta_{\min}; \eta_{\max}]$. Namely, if $\eta \sim log - \mathcal{U}(\cdot; \eta_{\min}, \eta_{\max})$, then $\log \eta$ is uniformly distributed between $\log \eta_{\min}$ and $\log \eta_{\max}$. Its density function is $log - \mathcal{U}(\eta; \eta_{\min}, \eta_{\max}) = \frac{1}{\eta} \frac{\mathbb{1}_{\eta_{\min} \leq \eta \leq \eta_{\max}}}{\log(\eta_{\max}) - \log(\eta_{\min})}$.

Algorithm 1 Alrao-SGD for model $\Phi_\theta = C_{\theta^{\mathrm{out}}} \circ \phi_{\theta^{\mathrm{r}}}$ with N_{out} classifiers and learning rates in $[\eta_{\min}; \eta_{\max}]$

1: $a_j \leftarrow 1/N_{\mathrm{out}}$ for each $1 \leq j \leq N_{\mathrm{out}}$ ▷ Initialize the N_{out} model averaging weights a_j

2: $\Phi_\theta^{\mathrm{Alrao}}(x) := \sum_{j=1}^{N_{\mathrm{out}}} a_j C_{\theta_j^{\mathrm{out}}}(\phi_{\theta^{\mathrm{int}}}(x))$ ▷ Define the Alrao architecture

3: **for all** layers l, **for all** unit i in layer l **do**

4:    Sample $\eta_{l,i} \sim \log\text{-}\mathcal{U}(.; \eta_{\min}, \eta_{\max})$.   ▷ Sample a learning rate for each unit

5: **for all** Classifiers j, $1 \leq j \leq N_{\mathrm{out}}$ **do**

6:    Define $\log \eta_j = \log \eta_{\min} + \frac{j-1}{N_{\mathrm{out}}-1} \log \frac{\eta_{\max}}{\eta_{\min}}$.   ▷ Set a learning rate for each classifier

7: **while** Stopping criterion is False **do**

8:    $z_t \leftarrow \phi_{\theta^{\mathrm{int}}}(x_t)$ ▷ Store the output of the last internal layer

9:    **for all** layers l, **for all** unit i in layer l **do**

10:        $\theta_{l,i} \leftarrow \theta_{l,i} - \eta_{l,i} \cdot \nabla_{\theta_{l,i}} \ell(\Phi_\theta^{\mathrm{Alrao}}(x_t), y_t)$ ▷ Update the repr. netw. weights

11:    **for all** Classifier j **do**

12:        $\theta_j^{\mathrm{out}} \leftarrow \theta_j^{\mathrm{out}} - \eta_j \cdot \nabla_{\theta_j^{\mathrm{out}}} \ell(C_{\theta_j^{\mathrm{out}}}(z_t), y_t)$ ▷ Update the classifiers' weights

13:    $a \leftarrow \texttt{ModelAveraging}(a, (C_{\theta_i^{\mathrm{out}}}(z_t))_i, y_t)$ ▷ Update the model averaging weights.

14:    $t \leftarrow t + 1 \mod N$

4.2   Alrao Architecture

Multiple Alrao Output Layers. A deep learning model Φ_θ for classification can be decomposed into two parts: first, *internal layers* compute some function $z = \phi_{\theta^{\mathrm{int}}}(x)$ of the inputs x, fed to a final *output (classifier) layer* $C_{\theta^{\mathrm{out}}}$, so that the overall network output is $\Phi_\theta(x) := C_{\theta^{\mathrm{out}}}(\phi_{\theta^{\mathrm{int}}}(x))$. For a classification task with K categories, the output layer $C_{\theta^{\mathrm{out}}}$ is defined by $C_{\theta^{\mathrm{out}}}(z) := \mathrm{softmax} \circ (W^T z + b)$ with $\theta^{\mathrm{out}} := (W, b)$, and $\mathrm{softmax}(u_1, ..., u_K)_k := e^{u_k}/(\sum_i e^{u_i})$.

In Alrao, we build multiple copies of the original output layer, with different learning rates for each, and then use a model averaging method among them. The averaged classifier and the overall Alrao model are:

$$C_{\theta^{\mathrm{out}}}^{\mathrm{Alrao}}(z) := \sum_{j=1}^{N_{\mathrm{out}}} a_j\, C_{\theta_j^{\mathrm{out}}}(z), \qquad \Phi_\theta^{\mathrm{Alrao}}(x) := C_{\theta^{\mathrm{out}}}^{\mathrm{Alrao}}(\phi_{\theta^{\mathrm{int}}}(x)) \qquad (1)$$

where the $C_{\theta_j^{\mathrm{out}}}$ are copies of the original classifier layer, with non-tied parameters, and $\theta^{\mathrm{out}} := (\theta_1^{\mathrm{out}}, ..., \theta_{N_{\mathrm{out}}}^{\mathrm{out}})$. The a_j are the parameters of the model averaging, with $0 \leq a_j \leq 1$ and $\sum_j a_j = 1$. The a_j are not updated by gradient descent, but via a model averaging method from the literature (see below).

Increasing the Width of Internal Layers. As explained in Sect. 3, we may compensate the effective width reduction in Alrao by multiplying the width of the network by a factor γ. This means multiplying the number of units (or filters for a convolutional layer) of all internal layers by γ.

4.3   Alrao Update for the Internal Layers: A Random Learning Rate for Each Unit

In the internal layers, for each unit i in each layer l, a learning rate $\eta_{l,i}$ is sampled from the probability distribution $log - \mathcal{U}(.; \eta_{\min}, \eta_{\max})$, once and for all at the beginning of training.[1]

The incoming parameters of each unit in the internal layers are updated in the usual SGD way, only with per-unit learning rates (Eq. 2): for each unit i in each layer l, its incoming parameters are updated as:

$$\theta_{l,i} \leftarrow \theta_{l,i} - \eta_{l,i} \cdot \nabla_{\theta_{l,i}} \ell(\Phi_\theta^{\mathrm{Alrao}}(x), y) \qquad (2)$$

where $\Phi_\theta^{\mathrm{Alrao}}$ is the Alrao loss (1) defined above.

What constitutes a *unit* depends on the type of layers in the model. In a fully connected layer, each component of a layer is considered as a unit for Alrao: all incoming weights of the same unit share the same Alrao learning rate. On the other hand, in a convolutional layer we consider each convolution filter as constituting a unit: there is one learning rate per filter (or channel), thus preserving translation-invariance over the input image. In LSTMs, we apply the same learning rate to all components in each LSTM cell (thus the vector of learning rates is the same for input gates, for forget gates, etc.).

We set a learning rate *per unit*, rather than per parameter. Otherwise, every unit would have some parameters with large learning rates, and we would expect even a few large incoming weights to be able to derail a unit. Having diverging parameters within every unit is hurtful, while having diverging units in a layer is not necessarily hurtful since the next layer can learn to disregard them.

---

[1] With learning rates resampled at each time, each step would be, in expectation, an ordinary SGD step with learning rate $\mathbb{E}\eta_{l,i}$, thus just yielding an ordinary SGD trajectory with more variance.

4.4 Alrao Update for the Output Layer: Model Averaging from Output Layers Trained with Different Learning Rates

Learning the Output Layers. The j-th copy $C_{\theta_j^{\text{out}}}$ of the classifier layer is attributed a learning rate η_j defined by $\log \eta_j := \log \eta_{\min} + \frac{j-1}{N_{\text{out}}-1} \log\left(\frac{\eta_{\max}}{\eta_{\min}}\right)$, so that the classifiers' learning rates are log-uniformly spread on the interval $[\eta_{\min}; \eta_{\max}]$. Then the parameters θ_j^{out} of each classifier j are updated as if this classifier alone was the only output of the model:

$$\theta_j^{\text{out}} \leftarrow \theta_j^{\text{out}} - \eta_j \cdot \nabla_{\theta_j^{\text{out}}} \ell(C_{\theta_j^{\text{out}}}(\phi_{\theta^{\text{int}}}(x)), y), \tag{3}$$

(still sharing the same internal layers $\phi_{\theta^{\text{int}}}$). This ensures that classifiers with low weights a_j still learn, and is consistent with model averaging philosophy. Algorithmically this requires differentiating the loss N_{out} times with respect to the last layer, but no additional backpropagations through the internal layers.

Model Averaging. To set the weights a_j, several model averaging techniques are available, such as Bayesian Model Averaging [42]. We use the *Switch* model averaging [43], a Bayesian method which is both simple, principled, and very responsive to changes in performance of the various models. After each mini-batch, the switch computes a modified posterior distribution (a_j) over the classifiers. This computation is directly taken from [43].

Additional experiments show that the model averaging method acts like a smooth model selection procedure: after only a few hundreds gradient steps, a single output layer is selected, with its parameter a_j very close to 1. Actually, Alrao's performance is unchanged if the extraneous output layer copies are thrown away when the posterior weight a_j of one of the copies gets close to 1.

5 Experimental Setup

We tested Alrao on various convolutional networks for image classification (Imagenet and CIFAR10), on LSTMs for text prediction, and on reinforcement learning problems. We always use the same learning rate interval $[10^{-5}; 10]$, corresponding to the values we would have tested in a grid search, and 10 Alrao output layer copies, for every task.

We compare Alrao to SGD with an optimal learning rate selected in the set $\{10^{-5}, 10^{-4}, 10^{-3}, 10^{-2}, 10^{-1}, 1., 10.\}$, and, as a tuning-free baseline, to Adam with its default setting ($\eta = 10^{-3}, \beta_1 = 0.9, \beta_2 = 0.999$), arguably the current default method [24].

The results are presented in Table 1. Figure 2 presents learning curves for AlexNet and Resnet50 on ImageNet.

Table 1. Performance of Alrao, SGD with tuned learning rate, and Adam with its default setting. Three convolutional models are reported for image classification on CIFAR10, three others for ImageNet, one recurrent model for character prediction (Penn Treebank), and two experiments on RL problems. Four of the image classification architectures are further tested with a width multiplication factor $\gamma = 3$. Alrao learning rates are taken in a wide, a priori reasonable interval $[\eta_{min}; \eta_{max}] = [10^{-5}; 10]$, and the optimal learning rate for SGD is chosen in the set $\{10^{-5}, 10^{-4}, 10^{-3}, 10^{-2}, 10^{-1}, 1., 10.\}$. Each experiment is run 10 times (CIFAR10 and RL), 5 times (PTB) or 1 time (ImageNet); the confidence intervals report the standard deviation over these runs. For RL tasks, the return has to be maximized, not minimized.

Model	SGD with optimal LR			Adam - Default		Alrao	
	LR	Loss	Top1 (%)	Loss	Top1 (%)	Loss	Top1 (%)
CIFAR10							
MobileNet	0.1	$0.37 \pm .01$	$90.2 \pm .3$	$1.01 \pm .95$	78 ± 11	$0.42 \pm .02$	$88.1 \pm .6$
MobileNet, $\gamma = 3$	0.1	$0.33 \pm .01$	$90.3 \pm .5$	$0.32 \pm .02$	$90.8 \pm .4$	$0.35 \pm .01$	$89.0 \pm .6$
GoogLeNet	0.01	$0.45 \pm .05$	$89.6 \pm 1.$	$0.47 \pm .04$	$89.8 \pm .4$	$0.47 \pm .03$	$88.9 \pm .8$
GoogLeNet, $\gamma = 3$	0.1	$0.34 \pm .02$	$90.5 \pm .8$	$0.41 \pm .02$	$88.6 \pm .6$	$0.37 \pm .01$	$89.8 \pm .8$
VGG19	0.1	$0.42 \pm .02$	$89.5 \pm .2$	$0.43 \pm .02$	$88.9 \pm .4$	$0.45 \pm .03$	$87.5 \pm .4$
VGG19, $\gamma = 3$	0.1	$0.35 \pm .01$	$90.0 \pm .6$	$0.37 \pm .01$	$89.5 \pm .8$	$0.381 \pm .004$	$88.4 \pm .7$
ImageNet							
AlexNet	0.01	2.15	53.2	6.91	0.10	2.56	43.2
Densenet121	1	1.35	69.7	1.39	67.9	1.41	67.3
ResNet50	1	1.49	67.4	1.39	67.1	1.42	67.5
ResNet50, $\gamma = 3$	–	–	–	1.99	60.8	1.33	70.9
Penn Treebank							
LSTM	1	$1.566 \pm .003$	$66.1 \pm .1$	$1.587 \pm .005$	$65.6 \pm .1$	$1.706 \pm .004$	$63.4 \pm .1$
RL		Return		Return		Return	
Pendulum	0.0001	-372 ± 24		-414 ± 64		-371 ± 36	
LunarLander	0.1	188 ± 23		155 ± 23		186 ± 45	

5.1   Image Classification on ImageNet and CIFAR10

For image classification, we used the ImageNet [44] and CIFAR10 [45] datasets. The ImageNet dataset is made of 1,283,166 training and 60,000 testing data; we split the training set into a smaller training set and a validation set with 60,000 samples. We do the same on CIFAR10: the 50,000 training samples are split into 40,000 training samples and 10,000 validation samples.

For each architecture, training was stopped when the validation loss had not improved for 20 epochs. The epoch with best validation loss was selected and the corresponding model tested on the test set. The inputs are normalized, and training used data augmentation: random cropping and random horizontal flipping. For CIFAR10, each setting was run 10 times: the confidence intervals presented are the standard deviation over these runs. For ImageNet, because of high computation time, we performed only a single run per experiment.

We tested Alrao on several standard architectures. On ImageNet, we tested Resnet50 [46], Densenet121 [47], and Alexnet [48], using the default Pytorch implementation. On CIFAR10, we tested GoogLeNet [49], VGG19 [50], and MobileNet [51], as implemented in [52]. We also tested wider architectures, with a width multiplication factor $\gamma = 3$. On the largest model, Resnet50 on ImageNet with triple width, systematic SGD learning rate grid search was not performed due to the excessive computational burden, hence the omitted value in Table 1.

5.2 Other Tasks: Text Prediction, Reinforcement Learning

Text Prediction on Penn TreeBank. To test Alrao on other kinds of tasks, we first used a recurrent neural network for text prediction on the Penn Treebank (PTB) [53] dataset. The Alrao experimental procedure is the same as above.

The loss in Table 1 is given in bits per character and the accuracy is the proportion of correct character predictions. The model is a two-layer LSTM [54] with an embedding size of 100, and 100 hidden units. A dropout layer with rate 0.2 is

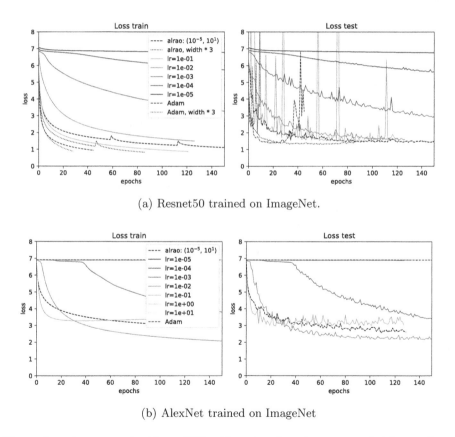

(a) Resnet50 trained on ImageNet.

(b) AlexNet trained on ImageNet

Fig. 2. Learning curves for Alrao, SGD with various learning rates, and Adam with its default setting, on ImageNet. Left: training loss; right: test loss. Curves are interrupted by the early stopping criterion. Alrao's performance is comparable to the optimal SGD learning rate.

included before the decoder. The training set is divided into 20 minibatchs. Gradients are computed via truncated backprop through time [55] with truncation every 70 characters.

The model was trained for *character* prediction rather than word prediction. This is technically easier for Alrao implementation: since Alrao uses copies of the output layer, memory issues arise for models with most parameters on the output layer. Word prediction (10,000 classes on PTB) requires many more output parameters than character prediction; see Sect. 7.

Reinforcement Learning Tasks. Next, we tested Alrao on two standard reinforcement learning problems: the Pendulum and Lunar Lander environments from OpenAI Gym [56]. We use standard deep Q-learning [57]. The Q-network is a standard MLP with 2 hidden layers. The experimental setting is the same as above, with regressors instead of classifiers on the output layer. For each environment, we select the best epoch on validation runs, and then report the return of the selected model on new test runs in that environment.

6   Performance and Robustness of Alrao

6.1   Alrao Compared to SGD with Optimal Learning Rate

First, Alrao does manage to learn; this was not obvious a priori.

Second, SGD with an optimally tuned learning rate usually performs better than Alrao. This can be expected when comparing a tuning-free method with a method that tunes the hyperparameter in hindsight.

Still, the difference between Alrao and optimally-tuned SGD is reasonably small across every setup, even with wide intervals $[\eta_{min}; \eta_{max}]$, with a somewhat larger gap in one case (AlexNet on ImageNet). Notably, this occurs even though SGD achieves good performance only for a few learning rates within the interval $[\eta_{min}; \eta_{max}]$. With $\eta_{min} = 10^{-5}$ and $\eta_{max} = 10$, among the 7 SGD learning rates tested ($10^{-5}, 10^{-4}, 10^{-3}, 10^{-2}, 10^{-1}, 1$, and 10), only three are able to learn with AlexNet, and only one is better than Alrao (Fig. 2b); with ResNet50, only three are able to learn well, and only two of them achieve performance similar to Alrao (Fig. 2a); on the Pendulum environment, only two are able to learn well, only one of which converges as fast as Alrao.

Thus, surprisingly, Alrao manages to learn at a nearly optimal rate, even though most units in the network have learning rates unsuited for SGD.

6.2   Robustness of Alrao, and Comparison to Default Adam

Overall, Alrao learns reliably in every setup in Table 1. Moreover, this is quite stable over the course of learning: Alrao curves shadow optimal SGD curves over time (Fig. 2).

Often, Adam with its default parameters almost matches optimal SGD, but this is not always the case. Over the 13 setups in Table 1, default Adam gives a significantly poor performance in three cases. One of those is a pure optimization issue: with AlexNet on ImageNet, optimization does not start with the default parameters (Fig. 2b). The other two cases are due to strong overfit despite good train performance: MobileNet on CIFAR and ResNet with increased width on ImageNet.

In two further cases, Adam achieves good validation performance in Table 1, but actually overfits shortly after its peak score: ResNet (Fig. 2a) and DenseNet, [24,58].

Overall, default Adam tends to give slightly better results than Alrao when it works, but does not learn reliably with its default hyperparameters. It can exhibit two kinds of lack of robustness: optimization failure, and overfit or non-robustness over the course of learning. On the other hand, every single run of Alrao reached reasonably close-to-optimal performance. Alrao also performs steadily over the course of learning (Fig. 2).

6.3 Sensitivity Study to $[\eta_{\min}; \eta_{\max}]$

We claim to remove a hyperparameter, the learning rate, but replace it with two hyperparameters $\eta_{\min}$ and $\eta_{\max}$. Formally, this is true. But a systematic study of the impact of these two hyperparameters (Fig. 3) shows that the sensitivity to $\eta_{\min}$ and $\eta_{\max}$ is much lower than the original sensitivity to the learning rate.

To assess this, we tested every combination of $\eta_{\min}$ and $\eta_{\max}$ in a grid from 10^{-9} to 10^7 on GoogLeNet for CIFAR10 (left plot in Fig. 3, with SGD on the diagonal). The largest satisfactory learning rate for SGD is 1 (diagonal on Fig. 3). Unsurprisingly, if all the learning rates in Alrao are too large, or all too small, then Alrao fails (rightmost and leftmost zones in Fig. 3). Extremely large learning rates diverge numerically, both for SGD and Alrao.

On the other hand, Alrao converges as soon as $[\eta_{\min}; \eta_{\max}]$ contains a reasonable learning rate (central zone Fig. 3), even with values of $\eta_{\max}$ for which SGD fails. A wide range of choices for $[\eta_{\min}; \eta_{\max}]$ will contain one good learning rate and achieve close-to-optimal performance. Thus, as a general rule, we recommend to just use an interval containing all the learning rates that would have been tested in a grid search, e.g., 10^{-5} to 10.

For a fixed network size, one might expect Alrao to perform worse with large intervals $[\eta_{\min}; \eta_{\max}]$, as most units would become useless. On the other hand, in a larger network, many units would have extreme learning rates, which might disturb learning. We tested how increasing or decreasing network width changes Alrao's sensitivity to $[\eta_{\min}; \eta_{\max}]$ (right plot of Fig. 3 for Alrao). The sensitivity of Alrao to $[\eta_{\min}; \eta_{\max}]$ decreases markedly with network width. For instance, a wide interval $[\eta_{\min}; \eta_{\max}] = [10^{-12}; 10^4]$ works reasonably well with an 8-fold network, even though most units receive unsuitable learning rates.

So, even if the choice of $\eta_{\min}$ and $\eta_{\max}$ is important, the results are much more stable to varying these two hyperparameters than to the original learning rate, especially with large networks.

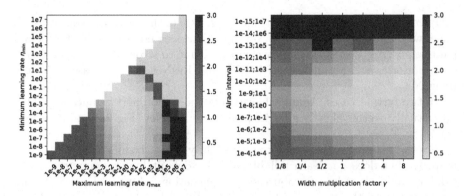

Fig. 3. Influence of $[\eta_{min}; \eta_{max}]$ and of network width on Alrao performance, with GoogLeNet on CIFAR10. Results are reported after 15 epochs, and averaged on three runs. Left plot: each point with coordinates $[\eta_{min}; \eta_{max}]$ below the diagonal represents the loss for Alrao with this interval. Points (η, η) on the diagonal represent standard SGD with learning rate η. Grey squares represent numerical divergence (NaN). Alrao works as soon as $[\eta_{min}; \eta_{max}]$ contains at least one suitable learning rate. Right plot: varying network width.

7   Discussion, Limitations, and Perspectives

Alrao specifically exploits redundancy between units in deep learning models, relying on the overall network approach of combining a large number of units built for diversity of behavior. Alrao would not make sense in a classical convex optimization setting. That Alrao works at all is already informative about some phenomena at play in deep neural networks.

Alrao can make lengthy SGD learning rate sweeps unnecessary on large models, such as the triple-width ResNet50 for ImageNet above. Incidentally, in our experiments, wider networks provided increased performance both for SGD and Alrao (Table 1 and Fig. 3): network size is still a limiting factor for the models used, independently of the algorithm.

Increased Number of Parameters for the Classification Layer. Since Alrao modifies the output layer of the optimized model, the number of parameters in the classification layer is multiplied by the number of classifier copies. (The number of parameters in the internal layers is unchanged.) This is a limitation for models with most parameters in the classifier layer.

On CIFAR10 (10 classes), the number of parameters increases by less than 5% for the models used. On ImageNet (1000 classes), it increases by 50–100% depending on the architecture. On Penn Treebank, the number of parameters increased by 26% in our setup (at character level); working at word level it would have increased fivefold.

This can be mitigated by handling the copies of the classifiers on distinct computing units: in Alrao these copies work in parallel given the internal layers. Moreover, the additional output layer copies may be thrown away early in training.

Finally, models with a large number of output classes usually rely on other parameterizations than a direct softmax, such as a hierarchical softmax (see references in [59]); Alrao can be used in conjunction with such methods.

Multiple Output Layer Copies and Expressiveness. Using several copies of the output layer in Alrao formally provides more expressiveness to the model, as it creates a larger architecture with more parameters. We performed two control experiments to check that Alrao's performance does not just stem from this. First, we performed ablation of the output layer copies in Alrao after one epoch, only keeping the copy with the highest model averaging weight a_i: the learning curves are identical. Second, we trained default Adam using copies of the output layer (all with the same Adam default learning rate): the learning curves are identical to Adam on the unmodified architecture. Thus, the copies of the output layer do not bring any useful added expressiveness.

Learning Rate Schedules, Other Optimizers, Other Hyperparameters. Learning rate schedules are often effective [60]. We did not use them here: this may partially explain why the results in Table 1 are worse than the state-of-the-art. One might have hoped that the diversity of learning rates in Alrao would effortlessly bring it to par with step size schedules, but the results above do not support this. Still, nothing prevents using a scheduler together with Alrao, e.g., by dividing all Alrao learning rates by a time-dependent constant.

The Alrao idea can also be used with other optimizers than SGD, such as Adam. We tested combining Alrao and Adam, and found the combination less reliable than standard Alrao: curves on the training set mostly look good, but the method quickly overfits.

The Alrao idea could be used on other hyperparameters as well, such as momentum. However, with more hyperparameters initialized randomly for each unit, the fraction of units having suitable values for all their hyperparameters simultaneously will quickly decrease.

8   Conclusion

Applying stochastic gradient descent with multiple learning rates for different units is surprisingly resilient in our experiments, and provides performance close to SGD with an optimal learning rate, as soon as the range of random learning rates is not excessive. Alrao could save time when testing deep learning models, opening the door to more out-of-the-box uses of deep learning.

Acknowledgments. We would like to thank Corentin Tallec for his technical help and extensive remarks. We thank Olivier Teytaud for pointing useful references, Hervé Jégou for advice on the text, and Léon Bottou, Guillaume Charpiat, and Michèle Sebag for their remarks on our ideas.

References

1. Zoph, B., Le, Q.V.: Neural architecture search with reinforcement learning. arXiv preprint arXiv:1611.01578 (2016)
2. Guyon, I., et al.: A brief review of the ChaLearn AutoML challenge: any-time any-dataset learning without human intervention. In: Workshop on Automatic Machine Learning, pp. 21–30 (2016)
3. Theodoridis, S.: Machine Learning: A Bayesian and Optimization Perspective. Academic Press, Cambridge (2015)
4. Jastrzebski, S., et al.: Three factors influencing minima in SGD. arXiv preprint arXiv:1711.04623 (2017)
5. Kurita, K.: Learning Rate Tuning in Deep Learning: A Practical Guide—Machine Learning Explained (2018)
6. Mack, D.: How to pick the best learning rate for your machine learning project (2016)
7. Surmenok, P.: Estimating an optimal learning rate for a deep neural network (2017)
8. Tieleman, T., Hinton, G.: Lecture 6.5-rmsprop: divide the gradient by a running average of its recent magnitude. COURSERA: Neural Netw. Mach. Learn. **4**(2), 26–31 (2012)
9. Duchi, J., Hazan, E., Singer, Y.: Adaptive subgradient methods for online learning and stochastic optimization. JMLR **12**, 2121–2159 (2011)
10. Kingma, D.P., Ba, J.: Adam: a method for stochastic optimization. In: International Conference on Learning Representations (2015)
11. Schaul, T., Zhang, S., LeCun, Y.: No more pesky learning rates. In: International Conference on Machine Learning, pp. 343–351 (2013)
12. LeCun, Y.A., Bottou, L., Orr, G.B., Müller, K.-R.: Efficient BackProp. In: Montavon, G., Orr, G.B., Müller, K.-R. (eds.) Neural Networks: Tricks of the Trade. LNCS, vol. 7700, pp. 9–48. Springer, Heidelberg (2012). https://doi.org/10.1007/978-3-642-35289-8_3
13. Denkowski, M., Neubig, G.: Stronger baselines for trustable results in neural machine translation. arXiv preprint arXiv:1706.09733 (2017)
14. Srivastava, N., Hinton, G., Krizhevsky, A., Sutskever, I., Salakhutdinov, R.: Dropout: a simple way to prevent neural networks from overfitting. J. Mach. Learn. Res. **15**, 1929–1958 (2014)
15. LeCun, Y., Denker, J.S., Solla, S.A.: Optimal brain damage. In: Touretzky, D.S. (ed.) NIPS, vol. 2, pp. 598–605. Morgan-Kaufmann (1990)
16. Han, S., Mao, H., Dally, W.J.: Deep Compression: Compressing Deep Neural Networks with Pruning, Trained Quantization and Huffman Coding. arXiv preprint arXiv:1510.00149 (2015)
17. Han, S., Pool, J., Tran, J., Dally, W.J.: Learning both weights and connections for efficient neural networks. In: NIPS (2015)
18. See, A., Luong, M.T., Manning, C.D.: Compression of neural machine translation models via pruning. In: CoNLL 2016, p. 291 (2016)
19. Bengio, Y., Roux, N.L., Vincent, P., Delalleau, O., Marcotte, P.: Convex neural networks. In: Weiss, Y., Schölkopf, B., Platt, J.C. (eds.) Advances in Neural Information Processing Systems, vol. 18, pp. 123–130. MIT Press (2006)
20. Hinton, G., Vinyals, O., Dean, J.: Distilling the knowledge in a neural network. arXiv preprint arXiv:1503.02531 (2015)
21. Zhang, C., Bengio, S., Hardt, M., Recht, B., Vinyals, O.: Understanding deep learning requires rethinking generalization (2017)

22. Frankle, J., Carbin, M.: The Lottery Ticket Hypothesis: Finding Small, Trainable Neural Networks. arXiv preprint arXiv:1704.04861, March 2018
23. Frankle, J., Dziugaite, G.K., Roy, D.M., Carbin, M.: The lottery ticket hypothesis at scale (2019)
24. Wilson, A.C., Roelofs, R., Stern, M., Srebro, N., Recht, B.: The marginal value of adaptive gradient methods in machine learning. In: NIPS, pp. 4148–4158 (2017)
25. Liu, C., et al.: Progressive neural architecture search. In: Proceedings of the European Conference on Computer Vision (ECCV), pp. 19–34 (2018)
26. Amari, S.I.: Natural gradient works efficiently in learning. Neural Comput. **10**, 251–276 (1998)
27. Jacobs, R.A.: Increased rates of convergence through learning rate adaptation. Neural Netw. **1**(4), 295–307 (1988)
28. Schraudolph, N.N.: Local gain adaptation in stochastic gradient descent (1999)
29. Mahmood, A.R., Sutton, R.S., Degris, T., Pilarski, P.M.: Tuning-free step-size adaptation. In: 2012 IEEE International Conference on Acoustics, Speech and Signal Processing (ICASSP), pp. 2121–2124, IEEE (2012)
30. Maclaurin, D., Duvenaud, D., Adams, R.: Gradient-based hyperparameter optimization through reversible learning. In: International Conference on Machine Learning, pp. 2113–2122 (2015)
31. Massé, P.Y., Ollivier, Y.: Speed learning on the fly. arXiv preprint arXiv:1511.02540 (2015)
32. Baydin, A.G., Cornish, R., Rubio, D.M., Schmidt, M., Wood, F.: Online learning rate adaptation with hypergradient descent. In: International Conference on Learning Representations (2018)
33. Erraqabi, A., Le Roux, N.: Combining adaptive algorithms and hypergradient method: a performance and robustness study (2018)
34. Baker, B., Gupta, O., Naik, N., Raskar, R.: Designing neural network architectures using reinforcement learning. arXiv preprint arXiv:1611.02167 (2016)
35. Li, L., Jamieson, K., DeSalvo, G., Rostamizadeh, A., Talwalkar, A.: Hyperband: a novel bandit-based approach to hyperparameter optimization. JMLR **18**(1), 6765–6816 (2017)
36. Stanley, K.O., Miikkulainen, R.: Evolving neural networks through augmenting topologies. Evol. Comput. **10**(2), 99–127 (2002)
37. Jozefowicz, R., Zaremba, W., Sutskever, I.: An empirical exploration of recurrent network architectures. In: International Conference on Machine Learning, pp. 2342–2350 (2015)
38. Real, E., et al.: Large-scale evolution of image classifiers. In: Proceedings of the 34th International Conference on Machine Learning, vol. 70, pp. 2902–2911, JMLR. org (2017)
39. Bergstra, J., Yamins, D., Cox, D.D.: Making a science of model search: hyperparameter optimization in hundreds of dimensions for vision architectures (2013)
40. Liu, H., Simonyan, K., Yang, Y.: DARTS: differentiable architecture search. arXiv preprint arXiv:1806.09055 (2018)
41. Paszke, A., et al.: Automatic differentiation in PyTorch. In: NIPS-W (2017)
42. Wasserman, L.: Bayesian model selection and model averaging. J. Math. Psychol. **44**, 92–107 (2000)
43. Van Erven, T., Grünwald, P., De Rooij, S.: Catching up faster by switching sooner: a predictive approach to adaptive estimation with an application to the AIC-BIC dilemma. J. R. Stat. Soc.: Ser. B (Stat. Methodol.) **74**(3), 361–417 (2012)
44. Deng, J., Dong, W., Socher, R., Li, L.J., Li, K., Fei-Fei, L.: ImageNet: a large-scale hierarchical image database. In: CVPR 2009 (2009)

45. Krizhevsky, A.: Learning multiple layers of features from tiny images (2009)
46. He, K., Zhang, X., Ren, S., Sun, J.: Deep residual learning for image recognition. In: ICCV, pp. 770–778 (2016)
47. Huang, G., Liu, Z., Van Der Maaten, L., Weinberger, K.Q.: Densely connected convolutional networks. In: CVPR, vol. 1, p. 3 (2017)
48. Krizhevsky, A.: One weird trick for parallelizing convolutional neural networks. arXiv preprint arXiv:1404.5997 (2014)
49. Szegedy, C., et al.: Going deeper with convolutions. In: ICCV, pp. 1–9 (2015)
50. Simonyan, K., Zisserman, A.: Very deep convolutional networks for large-scale image recognition. CoRR abs/1409.1556 (2014)
51. Howard, A.G., et al.: MobileNets: efficient convolutional neural networks for mobile vision applications. arXiv preprint arXiv:1704.04861 (2017)
52. Kianglu: Pytorch-cifar (2018)
53. Marcus, M.P., Marcinkiewicz, M.A., Santorini, B.: Building a large annotated corpus of English: the penn treebank. Comput. Linguist. 19(2), 313–330 (1993)
54. Hochreiter, S., Schmidhuber, J.: Long short-term memory. Neural Comput. 9(8), 1735–1780 (1997)
55. Werbos, P.J.: Backpropagation through time: what it does and how to do it. Proc. IEEE 78(10), 1550–1560 (1990)
56. Brockman, G., et al.: OpenAI Gym (2016)
57. Mnih, V., et al.: Human-level control through deep reinforcement learning. Nature 518(7540), 529 (2015)
58. Keskar, N.S., Socher, R.: Improving generalization performance by switching from Adam to SGD. arXiv preprint arXiv:1712.07628 (2017)
59. Jozefowicz, R., Vinyals, O., Schuster, M., Shazeer, N., Wu, Y.: Exploring the limits of language modeling. arXiv preprint arXiv:1602.02410 (2016)
60. Bengio, Y.: Practical recommendations for gradient-based training of deep architectures. In: Montavon, G., Orr, G.B., Müller, K.-R. (eds.) Neural Networks: Tricks of the Trade. LNCS, vol. 7700, pp. 437–478. Springer, Heidelberg (2012). https://doi.org/10.1007/978-3-642-35289-8_26

FastPoint: Scalable Deep Point Processes

Ali Caner Türkmen[1(✉)], Yuyang Wang[2], and Alexander J. Smola[2]

[1] Department of Computer Engineering, Boğaziçi University, 34342 Istanbul, Turkey
caner.turkmen@boun.edu.tr
[2] Amazon Research, Palo Alto, CA, USA
{yuyawang,smola}@amazon.com

Abstract. We propose FastPoint, a novel multivariate point process that enables fast and accurate learning and inference. FastPoint uses deep recurrent neural networks to capture complex temporal dependency patterns among different marks, while self-excitation dynamics within each mark are modeled with Hawkes processes. This results in substantially more efficient learning and scales to millions of correlated marks with superior predictive accuracy. Our construction also allows for efficient and parallel sequential Monte Carlo sampling for fast predictive inference. FastPoint outperforms baseline methods in prediction tasks on synthetic and real-world high-dimensional event data at a small fraction of the computational cost.

1 Introduction

Many applications produce large data sets that can be viewed as sets of events with "timestamps", occurring asynchronously. Examples abound, such as user activity on social media, earthquakes, purchases in online retail, order arrivals in a financial market, and "spiking" activity on a neuronal circuit. Modeling complex co-occurrence patterns of such events and predicting future occurrences are of practical interest in a wide range of use-cases.

Temporal point processes (TPP) are probabilistic models of such data, namely *discrete event* sets in continuous time. They have been extended widely to describe patterns through which events (*points*) interact, and to model side information available in the form of features (*marks*). However, TPPs pose two key challenges:

- How does one design an expressive model that can capture complex dependency patterns among events, while keeping the computational cost of learning manageable?
- How does one perform predictive inference, *i.e.,* describe distributions of how events will occur in the future, efficiently?

A. C. Türkmen—Work done while intern at Amazon.

Electronic supplementary material The online version of this chapter (https://doi.org/10.1007/978-3-030-46147-8_28) contains supplementary material, which is available to authorized users.

ⓒ Springer Nature Switzerland AG 2020
U. Brefeld et al. (Eds.): ECML PKDD 2019, LNAI 11907, pp. 465–480, 2020.
https://doi.org/10.1007/978-3-030-46147-8_28

Fig. 1. Typical draw from a bivariate point process on the unit interval. Events occur in continuous time and belong to one of two types (marks) represented here as triangles and discs.

The first question is often addressed by a class of TPPs defined in terms of their *conditional intensity function* [3], *i.e.,* the instantaneous rate of events given previous points. A popular example is the Hawkes process [9], where the intensity is a linear function of the effects of past events. These models and variants have been explored in a range of application domains [1,7,8,24]. Recently, recurrent neural networks (RNNs) have been used to approximate the conditional intensity function [6,13,21]. By conditioning intensity on a vector embedding of the event history, RNN-based models sidestep an important computational challenge in likelihood-based parameter estimation for TPPs. However when the point process is *multivariate, i.e.,* when events are identified as members of a finite set of processes such as purchases of a certain product or tweets of a certain user, the model specification must be extended to account for how these event *types* (or *marks*) interact [16,17]. In both Hawkes processes and RNN-based approximations, computational difficulties associated with learning and inference are greatly exacerbated by *high dimensionality* – a large number of marks.

The second problem requires characterizing distributions of event patterns in a future interval, which leads to an intractable integral over all possible "point configurations". A popular alternative is Monte Carlo estimation, where forward samples from the process are taken to evaluate estimates. However, forward sampling from a point process is costly. When high-dimensionality is a concern, sampling is further complicated by drawing from the mark distribution, recomputed for each point.

In this paper, we propose a novel model, FastPoint, for efficient learning and approximate inference in multivariate TPP. We combine the expressiveness of RNNs to model mutual excitation (between marks), with well-studied Hawkes processes to capture local (within marks) temporal relationships. This results in significantly faster learning with better generalization in the high-dimensional setting. Our contributions can be summarized as follows,

- We introduce a novel multivariate TPP that uses deep RNNs as the backbone to capture mutual excitation relationships among different marks (*e.g.,* among different users on a network or different items in online retail) while using Hawkes processes to capture local dynamics. By trading off the granularity at which cross-mark dynamics are captured, FastPoint can scale to millions of correlated point processes.
- Our construction leads to favorable computational properties including reduced time complexity and enables parallel and distributed learning. Learning in high-dimensional point processes is accelerated by over an order of magnitude.

- Our model leads to a more parsimonious description of temporal dynamics and better generalization in an array of real-world problems compared to RNN-based models and Hawkes processes.
- FastPoint's unique construction can be exploited for a sequential Monte Carlo (SMC) routine that allows for substantially faster simulation and inference. This results in predictive estimates of equivalent variance for less than a percent of the computation time in comparable methods.

We introduce the required background on TPPs, neural TPP variants, and concerns in sampling in Sect. 2. We introduce our model and algorithm in Sect. 3. Section 4 presents related work, and Sect. 5 discusses empirical results attained on datasets from social media, user behavior in music streaming, and earthquake occurrences. Section 6 concludes the paper.

2 Background

TPPs are statistical models of *discrete (instantaneous)* events localized in *continuous time* [3]. Concretely, just as a draw from a univariate continuous probability distribution is a real number; a draw from a point process on a bounded set $(0, T]$ is a set of points $\{t_i\}_{i=1}^N$, $0 < t_1 < \cdots < t_N \leq T$.

Events (indexed here by $i \in \{1, \ldots, N\}$) at times t_i may be equipped with *marks*, $y_i \in \mathcal{F}$. When $\mathcal{F}$ is a finite set, indexed by $k \in \{1, \ldots, K\}$, an equivalent formalism is *multivariate* (or *multitype*) TPPs – *i.e.*, a set of K (correlated) point processes. For example, letting k index users, multivariate TPPs can be used to jointly model timestamps on their tweeting activity. Figure 1 represents a draw from a bivariate $(K = 2)$ point process.

The Poisson process is the "archetypal" point process [14], and it is characterized by two main assumptions. First, one assumes that the point process is *simple*, *i.e.*, no two points coincide almost surely. Second is the assumption of independence: point occurrences on disjoint subsets of $\mathbb{R}$ are independent. While the first condition will underlie all point processes introduced here, it is this second assumption of independence that limits a realistic understanding of real-world phenomena. Many real-world events not only occur due to exogenous factors but *excite* or *inhibit* each other. For example, earthquakes excite nearby fault lines and increase the probability of "aftershocks". Social media activity elicits responses from other users. To capture such effects, one needs a richer class of TPPs than Poisson processes.

A convenient way of writing a TPP in which events depend on each other is through the *conditional intensity* function. We heuristically define the conditional intensity λ^* [3] as the probability of observing a point in the infinitesimal interval after time t, given history $\mathcal{H}_t$. Concretely,

$$\lambda^*(t) = \lim_{\delta \downarrow 0} \frac{\mathbb{P}\{N(t, t + \delta] > 0 | \mathcal{H}_t\}}{\delta},$$

where $N(a, b]$ is the random variable corresponding to the number of points in the interval $(a, b]$.

The conditional intensity uniquely determines a TPP. The log likelihood of a set of parameters of the conditional intensity Θ_{λ^*}, given realization $\{t_i\}$, can be written in terms of the conditional intensity,

$$\ell(\Theta_{\lambda^*}) = \sum_i \log \lambda^*(t_i) - \int_0^T \lambda^*(s)ds. \tag{1}$$

A concrete example of conditional intensity TPPs is the *Hawkes process* [1,9,10] which captures *self-excitation* behavior based on two assumptions: additivity and linearity. The conditional intensity of a (univariate) Hawkes process is

$$\lambda^*(t) = \mu + \sum_{t_j < t} \varphi(t - t_j), \tag{2}$$

where φ is a positive and causal kernel function. A common kernel is the exponential decay $\varphi(x) = \alpha\beta \exp(-\beta(x))$. The Hawkes process lends itself to interpretation as a branching (immigration-birth) process in continuous time [11]. In this sense, the *branching ratio* α corresponds to the long-run average number of "child" events a given event causes (or "excites"). $\beta \exp(-\beta(x))$, in turn, is the *delay density*, the probability density of the delay between parent and child events. For $\alpha < 1$, the process satisfies the *stationarity* condition.

The fundamental difficulty in fitting Hawkes processes, or any general point process defined via the conditional intensity, is that computing the likelihood (1) takes time quadratic in the number of events. Note (Eqs. (1), (2)) that the computation of $\lambda^*(t_i)$ is a sum over all $\{t_j\}_{j<i}$, and that the likelihood requires computing intensities of all observed points. Computational issues are exacerbated by *multivariate* processes where one must account for relationships among K marks. A notable exception to quadratic-time likelihood computations is the exponential decay kernel which allows for likelihood computation in linear time (see Appendix A (supplementary material)).

Scalability problems in parameter estimation were partially addressed by "neural point processes". Several recent contributions have proposed combining neural networks with conditional intensity TPPs. In Recurrent Marked TPP (RMTPP), Du et al. [6] propose to model a multivariate point process via an approximation to the conditional intensity function. This is achieved by an RNN, in their experiments an LSTM [12]. Effectively, the LSTM embeds the event history $\mathcal{H}_t = \{(t_i, y_i)|t_i < t\}$ to a vector, on which the conditional intensity function and the conditional distribution of the mark of the next point are calculated. Concretely, they take the conditional intensity

$$\lambda^*(t) = \exp(\mathbf{v}^\top \mathbf{h}_j + \beta(t - t_j) + b), \tag{3}$$

where β, b are scalar parameters, $\mathbf{v}$ is a vector parameter of appropriate dimension. $\mathbf{h}_j$ is the output of the LSTM for point t_j. That is, $\mathbf{h}_j = LSTM(\mathbf{h}_{j-1}, t_j, k_j)$. $j = \sup\{i \in \mathbb{N} : t_i < t\}$. Furthermore, they take, $y_{j+1} \sim \text{Categorical}(\text{softmax}(\mathbf{V}\mathbf{h}_j + \mathbf{b}))$, where $\mathbf{V}, \mathbf{b}$ are the weight and bias parameters of a dense neural network layer that maps LSTM outputs to the categorical likelihood.

RMTPP allows bypassing expensive optimization routines in general conditional intensity TPPs while leaving ample capacity for learning complex dependencies across time. The key observation in neural point processes is that $\mathbf{h}_j$ serves as a vector embedding for $\mathcal{H}_{t_j}$, and the intensity computation can be handled recursively. RMTPP is particularly convenient since it enables fast and easy implementation. The integral in the likelihood (the *compensator* term) can be computed exactly.

RMTPP was extended in [21], where the authors propose to parameterize the intensity function via a *continuous time* LSTM where the memory cell of the LSTM decays in time. This model, while more expressive as it captures several decaying influences, results in an intractable integral for computing the compensator.

Although TPP parameter estimation is greatly simplified by an approximation to the conditional intensity, performing predictive inference remains a significant challenge. Monte Carlo methods have emerged as the primary method for inference in TPPs, seeing as exact inference involves an intractable integral in all but the simplest models. Nevertheless, drawing exact samples from a TPP is a computationally cumbersome task: the points have to be sampled in sequence and the conditional intensity has to be re-evaluated at each point.

The traditional method for sampling from a TPP is Ogata's thinning method [22]. It is based on the observation that, conditioned on the history at a given point, the process until the next point can be cast as a non-homogeneous Poisson process. Then, if one can upper bound the intensity function, the next point can be drawn via "thinning", *i.e.*, proposing the next point from a faster homogeneous Poisson process and accepting based on the ratio of intensities. However, apart from the fact that the sampling routine has to be called in sequence, this algorithm introduces the computational cost of rejected points. We give a description of Ogata's algorithm in Appendix B (see supplementary material).

3   FastPoint: Scalable Deep Point Process

3.1   Generative Model

Neural TPP models greatly simplify estimation in large-data (large N) regimes under a reasonable number of marks $K \approx 10^3$, while adding the ability to capture complex co-occurrence patterns. However, many real-world events have marks that are from a much larger set of possible values, *e.g.*, in events associated with millions of users or purchases from a catalog of several hundred thousand products.

The main computational difficulty arises from accounting for interactions between events from different marks in the same manner as one addresses interactions between events of the same mark. In traditional point processes, such as multivariate Hawkes processes – this leads to computing and bookkeeping for $O(K^2)$ branching parameters. In neural TPPs, training complexity reduces

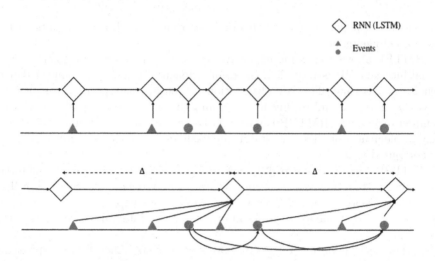

Fig. 2. Above: RMTPP computes the conditional intensity for the next point through an LSTM for each point in a sequence, Below: In FastPoint, the LSTM is conditioned on an interval of points, and computes added intensity for the next interval. The self-excitation in each mark, individually, is accounted for by a Hawkes process.

to $O(NK)$ which can still be prohibitively high. Furthermore, RNNs are well known to have difficulty in capturing long-range dependencies. This is especially important in high-dimensional temporal point processes since a large number of possibly unrelated marks are observed in a sequence before a relevant item is observed – an effect that could have easily been captured by self-exciting processes.

Our model, FastPoint, is built on a simple yet profound insight: mutual excitation dynamics can be modeled at a lower frequency than with which one accounts for self-excitation. More precisely, FastPoint addresses mutual-excitation on a fixed grid along time and through a deep neural network, while local self-exciting dynamics are captured with univariate Hawkes processes. We write the conditional intensity

$$\lambda_k^*(t) = g(\mathbf{v}_k^\top \mathbf{h}(\mathcal{H}_\tau) + b_k) + \mu_k + \sum_{\mathcal{H}_t^{(k)}} \varphi_k(t - t_i), \qquad (4)$$

where g denotes the softplus function, $\tau = \sup\{\tau' \in \mathcal{G} | \tau' < t\}$, and $\mathcal{G} = \{0, \Delta, 2\Delta \dots\}$ denotes some uniformly sampled "grid". $\mathbf{v}, b_k, \mu_k$ are parameters, $\mathbf{h}(.)$ is a function implemented by an LSTM, and φ_k is the exponential decay kernel $\varphi_k(x) = \alpha_k \beta_k \exp(-\beta_k x)$.

FastPoint is composed of individual linearly self-exciting Hawkes processes to capture local effects in each process, as given by the second and third summands of (4). The first term is a non-negative added intensity contributed by an LSTM that "clocks" at set coarse intervals and "synchronizes" the processes. The inputs of the LSTM are the interarrival times and embeddings of past marks of previous

Table 1. Comparison of training and sampling time complexities of multivariate temporal point processes

Process	Conditional intensity	Training complexity	Sampling complexity
Poisson	$\lambda_k(t) = \bar{\lambda} p_k$ where $p_k = \bar{\lambda}_k / \bar{\lambda}$	$O(K)$	$O(N + K)$
Hawkes	$\lambda_k(t) = \mu_k + \sum_{\mathcal{H}_t} \varphi_k(t - t_i, y_i)$	$O(N^2 + NK)$	$O(N^2 K)$
RMTPP [6]	$\lambda_k(t) = p(k\|h(\mathcal{H}_t)) f(t, h(\mathcal{H}_t))$	$O(NK)$	$O(NK)$
Neural Hawkes process [21]	$\lambda_k(t) = f_k(\mathbf{w}_k^\top h(t))$ $h(t) = o_i \odot (2\sigma(2c(t)) - 1)$	$O(NK)$	$O(NK)$
FastPoint	$g(\mathbf{v}_k^\top \mathbf{h}(\mathcal{H}_\tau) + b_k) + \mu_k + \sum \varphi(t - t_i)$ $\tau = \sup\{\tau' < t \| \tau' \in \mathcal{G}\}$ $\mathcal{G} = \{0, \Delta, 2\Delta, \dots\}$	$O(N + K\|\mathcal{G}\|)$	$O(N + K\|\mathcal{G}\|)$

points, as in [6,21]. We give a stylized depiction comparing FastPoint to other neural TPP models in Fig. 2.

FastPoint can be interpreted as a global-local time series model [20], where the intensity processes are composed of a global component (given by the LSTM, the first term of (4)), and local components that are each a Hawkes process. While this greatly simplifies computation, it leads to a realistic-enough description of many real-world events. Our model encodes the assumption that mutual excitation often takes place with longer delays than self-excitation. For example, for limit order book analysis in finance, FastPoint models self-excitatory behavior of individual event sets (*i.e.*, assets) at ultra-high-frequency resolution, while cross-asset effects are captured at lower resolutions. Finally, note that FastPoint offers a general template for constructing multivariate TPPs. The global model (LSTM) can be changed with other deep neural network architectures such as the Transformer [25] or a simple multilayer perceptron. The local model can also be switched, *e.g.*, with a Poisson process.

FastPoint's key computational advantage is that it eliminates the need to compute K-many terms at each point for likelihood-based estimation. Intuitively, multivariate TPP likelihood computation requires a sequential pass over all points in an observation. Furthermore, the compensator term in the likelihood – *i.e.*, the probability that no points are observed in between each point has to be computed for *all* K marks, resulting in $O(NK)$ cost. FastPoint yields significant benefit in both respects. First, overall computational complexity decreases to $O(N + K\|\mathcal{G}\|)$, invoking both the memoryless property of exponential decays in the Hawkes process and favorable computational properties of RNN-based conditional intensity approximation. Second, the likelihood computation of individual marks can be parallelized over. In this manner, FastPoint is amenable to both massively parallel and distributed implementations and solves a crucial scalability problem in point process estimation and simulation. See Table 1 for a comparison of computational complexities associated with different point processes. We give further details on FastPoint's construction, implementation, global and local model choices in Appendix A (see supplementary material).

3.2 Sequential Monte Carlo Sampling

We turn to predictive inference, characterizing distributions of future event occurrences with FastPoint. Concretely, we seek to estimate expectations of the form,

$$\mathbb{E}_{\mathbb{P}}\left[\phi\left(\{(t_i, y_i)\}_{(t, t+T]}\right) | \mathcal{H}_t\right], \tag{5}$$

where $\{(t_i, y_i)\}_{(t, t+T]}$ denotes (random) realizations of an arbitrary marked point process $\mathbb{P}$ which we approximate with FastPoint, on the *forecast horizon* $(t, t+T]$. ϕ denotes some function of the data, *e.g.*, a summary statistic. For brevity, we denote $\Pi = \{(t_i, y_i)\}_{(t, t+T]}$, *i.e.*, the random variate corresponding to possible configurations of (a.s. finitely many) marked points on the given interval. Note that

$$\mathbb{E}\left[\phi(\Pi) | \mathcal{H}_t\right] = \int_{\Pi \in \mathcal{X}} \phi(\Pi) f(\Pi | \mathcal{H}) d\Pi, \tag{6}$$

is a non-trivial integral over $\mathcal{X}$, the *point configuration space* [19].

We will rely on Monte Carlo methods for approximating $\mathbb{E}_{\mathbb{P}}\left[\phi(\Pi) | \mathcal{H}_t\right]$. Fast-Point already alleviates part of the computational burden associated with sampling from multivariate point processes. That is, it allows for simulating each mark individually, in parallel, between each LSTM computation. For each such interval, one could work with Ogata's thinning algorithm in parallel. This still results in the difficulty of sampling sequentially, with the added overhead of rejecting some of the points drawn. These computational issues are further complicated by the difficulty of implementing thinning in "batch" mode, in modern deep learning frameworks such as Apache MXNet.

We suggest an alternative approach hinted by the global-local assumption of FastPoint. We take sequential importance weighted samples to evaluate expectations of the form (5), by proposing from a suitably parameterized Poisson process. The sync points of the global model, on the grid $\mathcal{G}$, are natural points to serve as the epochs of a sequential Monte Carlo (SMC) algorithm [5]. Furthermore, we find that the intensity at the beginning each interval doubles as a good proposal intensity.

For short enough prediction horizons, the Poisson process constitutes an effective proposal in two regards. First, surprisingly, short enough intervals result in low-variance samples or high effective sample sizes (ESS). Furthermore, invoking homogeneity and the *thinning* property of Poisson processes [14], the times and the marks of future points can be sampled independently and in parallel. Concretely, for sampling from a multivariate homogeneous Poisson process with intensities λ_k, we can instead sample from a global Poisson process with intensity $\bar{\lambda} = \sum_k \lambda_k$. The marks can be drawn in parallel, each in constant time, with $p^*(k) = \lambda_k / \sum_k \lambda_k$.

These observations result in a straightforward SMC algorithm. Namely, we sample from Poisson processes in sequence, updating both the particle weights and Poisson process parameters. We give a concrete description of FastPoint-SMC in Algorithm 1, where we use w_j to denote the importance sampling *particle weights*, κ the resampling threshold and $\mathcal{PP}$ the Poisson process from which

---

Algorithm 1: Sequential Monte Carlo sampling of FastPoint

Input: T, Δ, M, c

begin

$\quad w_j \leftarrow 1, \forall j$

$\quad \tau \leftarrow t_0$

$\quad$ **while** $\tau < T$ **do**

$\quad\quad$ **for** *particles* $j = 1$ *to* M **do in parallel**

$\quad\quad\quad$ Compute $\bar{\lambda}_k = \lambda_k^*(\tau)$, $\forall k \in \{1, 2, \ldots, K\}$

$\quad\quad\quad$ Draw $N_j \sim \text{Poisson}(\Delta \times \sum_k \bar{\lambda}_k)$

$\quad\quad\quad$ Draw $\{t_i^{(j)}\}_{i=1}^{N_j} \sim \mathcal{PP}(\sum_k \bar{\lambda}_k)$

$\quad\quad\quad$ **for** $i = 1$ **to** N_j **do in parallel**

$\quad\quad\quad\quad$ Draw $y_i^{(j)}$ s.t. $p(y_i^{(j)} = k) \propto \bar{\lambda}_k$

$\quad\quad\quad$ **endfor**

$\quad\quad\quad$ $w_j \leftarrow w_j \times \dfrac{p(\{(t_i^{(j)}, y_i^{(j)})\}|\mathcal{H}_\tau)}{q(\{(t_i^{(j)}, y_i^{(j)})\}|\bar{\lambda}, p^*)}$

$\quad\quad$ **endfor**

$\quad\quad$ $\tau \leftarrow \tau + \Delta$

$\quad\quad$ ESS $\leftarrow \|\mathbf{w}\|_1^2 / \|\mathbf{w}\|_2^2$

$\quad\quad$ **if** *ESS* $< c$ **then**

$\quad\quad\quad$ Resample particles, s.t.

$\quad\quad\quad$ $\{(t_i^{(j')}, y_i^{(j')})\}_{t \in (t_0, \tau]} = \{(t_i^{(j)}, y_i^{(j)})\}_{t \in (t_0, \tau]}$ with prob. $\propto w_j$, $\forall j'$

$\quad\quad$ **end**

$\quad$ **end**

end

---

timestamps are drawn. Finally, $p(\{(t_i^{(j)}, y_i^{(j)})\}|\mathcal{H}_\tau)$, $q(\{(t_i^{(j)}, y_i^{(j)})\}|\bar{\lambda}, p^*)$ denote the densities with respect to FastPoint and the Poisson process proposals respectively.

Counterintuitively, FastPoint-SMC scales well with respect to the number of marks K. To observe why, note that in practice, the number of points sampled in each interval is much smaller than K. For marks that are not drawn, the Poisson proposal density and FastPoint density are identical. In other words, marks for which no points were drawn do not contribute to the sample variance. Therefore, for short enough Δ, FastPoint effective sample sizes remain high for large K, scaling favorably to high dimensions in sampling as well as training.

4   Related Work

In [26], the authors introduce a Wasserstein Generative Adversarial Network for point processes, which leads to *likelihood-free* learning of generative models for point processes. Recently, latent variable neural network models for marked point process generation were explored in [23]. Both models use a generative deep network as the backbone of their construction and are hence easy to sample from. However, neither model is geared toward scalability in the number of marks.

Linderman et al. [18] explore a Rao-Blackwellized particle filter for inference in latent point processes, which could be used for predictive inference. However, the algorithm is only explored in the context of multivariate Hawkes processes and not extended to high-dimensional processes or neural TPPs. Somewhat similarly to our mix of discrete-time and continuous-time point process construction [27] explore a *twin* RNN architecture. However, their model employs yet another RNN to model continuous time effects, and is not amenable to high-dimensional modeling.

Scaling to high dimensions is a current and challenging problem in TPPs [1]. To our knowledge, FastPoint is the first model to consistently address very large discrete mark spaces, as well as the first to combine self-exciting processes with the neural TPP literature. Finally, ours is the first treatment of sequential Monte Carlo simulation in neural TPP, and one of the first to explore it for TPP in general.

5   Experiments

We implement RMTPP and FastPoint on Apache MXNet [2] with operators for Hawkes process likelihood and gradient computations in the MXNet backend[1]. For learning, we use MXNet Gluon's Adam optimizer. We run experiments on AWS p3 instances equipped with NVIDIA Tesla V100 GPUs.

5.1   Model Performance

We evaluate FastPoint's performance on large-scale, high-dimensional point process data. First, we compare generalization performance based on the log-likelihood of a held-out future time frame. We then compare computational performance via standardized computation times for learning.

We compare FastPoint's generalization performance to the following set of baseline models,

- Self-exciting **Hawkes process**, *i.e.,* a collection of univariate exponential-decay Hawkes processes as given in (2). Note that this baseline amounts to FastPoint with only the *local* model component.
- **RMTPP** [6], as given in Table 1.
- **B-RMTPP**, a modified version of RMTPP given by the conditional intensity

$$\lambda_k(t) = \mu + p(k|h(\mathcal{H}_{t_j})) \exp(\mathbf{v}_\lambda^\top h(\mathcal{H}_{t_j}) + b_\lambda + \beta(t - t_j)),$$

adding a background intensity. While a seemingly simple modification, this makes RMTPP absolutely continuous with respect to the Poisson process. That is, RMTPP is a *terminating* point process, making simulation schemes such as Ogata's algorithm invalid. Apart from correcting for this theoretical issue, this formulation leads to better generalization.

---

[1] The code is made available as part of MXNet. See https://github.com/apache/incubator-mxnet/blob/master/src/operator/contrib/hawkes_ll-inl.h.

Table 2. Negative log-likelihood loss of different point processes on a held-out sample

	HP-5K	HP-10K	NCEDC	MemeTracker	LastFM-1K
Events (millions) (N)	1	1	0.8	7.6	18
Marks (K)	5000	10000	1000	71566	105222
Hawkes	27009	30441	10346	42406	25087
RMTPP	27008	30491	14424	42507	30489
B-RMTPP	27008	30483	14393	42304	30474
FastPoint-5	26998	**30412**	10314	**41007**	25271
FastPoint-10	**26997**	30412	10287	41253	25024
FastPoint-20	26998	30412	**10261**	41398	**24500**

We compare the predictive performance of FastPoint to baselines on several data sets,

- **HP-5K**, and **HP-10K** are synthetic data sets sampled from a multivariate Hawkes process with the number of marks (K) set to 5000 and 10000 respectively. We use `hawkeslib`[2] to generate 1 million events from Hawkes models parameterized by randomly drawn branching matrices.
- Earthquake events collected from the **NCEDC** earthquake catalog search service [4]. We collect 800K earthquake events in the Northern California area and cluster the events into marks based on their coordinates, associating them to one of 1000 "locales". The prediction task is to best represent the time and locales of earthquake occurrences.
- A subset of the **MemeTracker** data set [15], that includes timestamped records for 7.6 million social media sharing events of *memes*, belonging to one of 71566 clusters.
- The **LastFM-1K**[3] dataset, which includes 19 million records of *listening* events, belonging to one of 105222 artists.

For RMTPP and FastPoint, we set the number of hidden units to 50 in synthetic data experiments and 100 in real-data experiments respectively. We use early stopping and weight decay for regularization. To mitigate the effect of possible numerical issues on experimental outcomes, we normalize all data sets to the same time scale to an average intensity of 50 events per unit of time.

We compare predictive accuracy in terms of the negative log-likelihood – *i.e.,* average model loss on a held-out future interval of 5000 points. Note that a more interpretable measure of accuracy is difficult to define in point processes, and previous works have used a mix of predictive log-likelihood with other metrics such as squared error for timestamps or multiclass accuracy for marks [6].

---

[2] http://github.com/canerturkmen/hawkeslib.
[3] https://www.dtic.upf.edu/~ocelma/MusicRecommendationDataset/lastfm-1K. html.

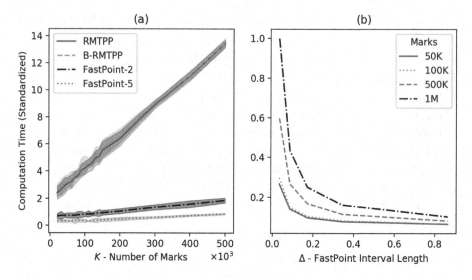

Fig. 3. (a) Training time on a single batch of 2500 events vs. the number of marks. `FastPoint-2` and `FastPoint-5` refer to the FastPoint with interval lengths set to 2 and 5 respectively. Numbers are reported as multiples of time taken by `FastPoint-2` on 10^4 marks. (b) FastPoint training time on a single batch of 25000 events as interval lengths are increased. Different lines correspond to different numbers of marks. Numbers are indexed to the time taken by for 10^6 marks with $\Delta = 0.01$

However, we observe these metrics lead to little insight and high variance in high-dimensional processes.

We present our results in Table 2. We give outcomes for three different Fast-Point alternatives, varying the LSTM interval length Δ. That is, we denote the $\Delta = 2$ case as `FastPoint-2`. We report average loss over a long held-out interval that includes at least half of the points in the full training set.

FastPoint categorically outperforms baselines in predictive accuracy. In synthetic data experiments, we observe that FastPoint leads to better generalization than both univariate Hawkes processes and neural TPP baselines. The margin of improvement widens in real-world data sets with greater K. The benefit of having a local model is especially notable in **NCEDC** and **LastFM-1K**. We also find that in practice, FastPoint is less prone to overfitting and converges reasonably quickly.

We contrast FastPoint's computational performance to other deep TPP models under increasing dimensionality. In Fig. 3a, we compare computation times for processing a batch of 2500 events during training. For 500 K marks, FastPoint improves on the computation time by over a factor of 20. Beyond 500 K marks, the memory footprints of RMTPP and B-RMTPP grow to an unmanageable size making comparison impractical, though the trend is evident. Moreover, observe in Fig. 3b that FastPoint allows trading off modeling accuracy by further decreasing granularity (increasing the LSTM interval length Δ). For example, allowing

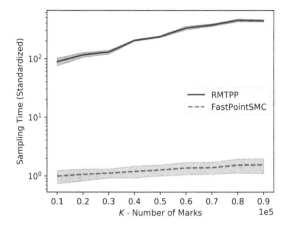

K $(\times 10^3)$	Improvement
10	89.1
20	109.1
30	115.1
40	169.9
50	186.3
60	240.7
70	267.2
80	292.0
90	284.7

Fig. 4. Left: Sampling times of RMTPP (Ogata's sampler) vs. FastPoint-SMC, indexed on FastPoint-SMC. **Right:** The factor of improvement in sampling times, *i.e.,* the multiple of time taken by RMTPP-Ogata relative to FastPoint-SMC. FastPoint results in gains of nearly 300x times.

a wider interval of 20 time units, one can learn a model of a million marks in a reasonable amount of time. Combining the two effects, FastPoint can lead to faster training of over two orders of magnitude, not accounting for other side benefits such as the ability to work with larger batches of data, longer time intervals, or performing inference in parallel such as on multi-GPU architectures.

5.2   Sampling

We now present empirical findings on FastPoint's sampling performance, using the SMC sampler introduced in Sect. 3.2. We compare the time taken by RMTPP (using Ogata's thinning method) and the FastPoint SMC sampler to generate $N_s = 100$ samples from a learned point process, with a fixed forecast horizon of 10 time units. We present a comparison of standardized computation times in Fig. 4, varying the number of marks K. FastPoint-SMC easily results in faster sampling by a factor of nearly 300x and its sampling time scales favorably with respect to the number of marks.

However, our analysis overlooks the fact that SMC generates samples that lead to higher variance estimates. Indeed, it is not apparent whether sequentially drawn importance-weighted samples from a Poisson process would lead to good estimates for FastPoint, especially in the presence of a large number of marks. Surprisingly, for small enough branching ratios α and short enough sampling intervals, the Poisson proposal leads to low variance samples. To demonstrate this, we compute the *effective sample size* (ESS, cf. Algorithm 1) for importance weighted samples of FastPoint, which corresponds to the number of exact samples that would result in equivalent variance.

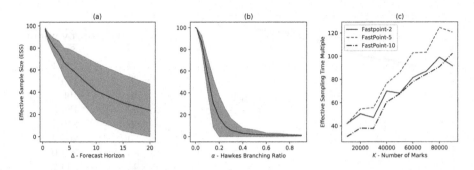

Fig. 5. (a) Effective sample sizes with increasing forecast horizon. (b) Effective sample sizes decay quickly with increasing branching ratio (c) Relative improvement in sampling time, accounting for decreases in ESS, increase with respect to K.

In Figs. 5a and b we present the ESS for 100 importance-weighted samples drawn on a single interval (without resampling or sequential sampling) of length Δ and for fixed branching ratios (for all marks) of α. We set the number of marks to 10^4, and the average intensity to 50 points per unit of time. We first observe that SMC produces reasonably efficient samples as the forecast horizon increases, resulting in an ESS of 60 for a horizon of 5 time units (roughly, 250 points). However, we also find that the ESS decays quickly as the branching ratio α increases beyond 0.1. In practice, however, FastPoint accounts for part of the self-excitation behavior through the global model, leading to smaller branching rations for most marks.

We find that the SMC routine performs well in terms of sampling efficiency as the dimensionsality increases. In Fig. 5c, we compute the Effective Sampling Time Multiple (ESTM). Letting $T_{FP}^{(s)}, T_O^{(s)}$ denote the time taken to sample from FastPoint-SMC and RMTPP-Ogata respectively, we define $ESTM = \frac{T_O^{(s)}}{T_{FP}^{(s)}} \times \frac{ESS}{N_S}$. This summary metric roughly corresponds to the factor by which FastPoint accelerates sampling, accounting for the higher variance introduced by SMC. Setting $\alpha = 0.05, \Delta = 1$, we vary the number of marks to find that FastPoint results in greater speed by a factor of over two orders of magnitude, for estimates of equivalent variance.

6   Conclusion

Multivariate point processes are natural models for many real-world data sets. However, due to the computational complexity often associated with learning and inference in TPPs, other simplified models (*e.g.*, by discretizing time or assuming independent marks) have been favored over them in many application domains. Moreover, most existing approaches do not address high-dimensional multivariate TPPs, a case that often arises in practice, with an expressive model that scales well in terms of generalization performance and computational cost. Finally, performing simulation (sampling) efficiently in general multivariate TPPs is an open problem.

FastPoint combines the interpretability and well-understood theory of Hawkes models with recurrent neural networks, addressing these long-standing challenges in point process modeling. First, it unlocks scalable estimation and simulation in millions for correlated point processes via a parsimonious global-local model. It can be used for accurate modeling of high-dimensional asynchronous event data, such as item purchases in a very large catalog, activities on a web-scale social graph, or limit order events in an order book with thousands of assets. Second, our SMC algorithm allows efficient sampling, accelerating predictive inference by over two orders of magnitude.

FastPoint's global-local point process construction is flexible. The global and local model components can be changed to other models best suitable for the task. Exploring other global-local multivariate point process constructions and better understanding their properties for learning and sampling remain exciting avenues for future research.

References

1. Bacry, E., Mastromatteo, I., Muzy, J.F.: Hawkes processes in finance. Mark. Microstruct. Liquidity **1**(01), 1550005 (2015)
2. Chen, T., et al.: MXNet: a flexible and efficient machine learning library for heterogeneous distributed systems. arXiv preprint arXiv:1512.01274 (2015)
3. Daley, D.J., Vere-Jones, D.: An Introduction to the Theory of Point Processes: Volume I: Elementary Theory and Methods. Springer, New York (2007). https://doi.org/10.1007/b97277
4. N.U.B.S.L.D.: Northern California earthquake data center (2014). https://doi.org/10.7932/NCEDC
5. Doucet, A., Johansen, A.M.: A tutorial on particle filtering and smoothing: fifteen years later. Handb. Nonlinear Filter. **12**(656–704), 3 (2009)
6. Du, N., Dai, H., Trivedi, R., Upadhyay, U., Gomez-Rodriguez, M., Song, L.: Recurrent marked temporal point processes: embedding event history to vector. In: Proceedings of the 22nd ACM SIGKDD International Conference on Knowledge Discovery and Data Mining, pp. 1555–1564. ACM (2016)
7. Du, N., Farajtabar, M., Ahmed, A., Smola, A.J., Song, L.: Dirichlet-Hawkes processes with applications to clustering continuous-time document streams. In: Proceedings of the 21th ACM SIGKDD International Conference on Knowledge Discovery and Data Mining, pp. 219–228. ACM (2015)
8. Du, N., Song, L., Yuan, M., Smola, A.J.: Learning networks of heterogeneous influence. In: Advances in Neural Information Processing Systems, pp. 2780–2788 (2012)
9. Hawkes, A.G.: Point spectra of some mutually exciting point processes. J. R. Stat. Soc. Ser. B (Methodol.) **33**, 438–443 (1971)
10. Hawkes, A.G.: Spectra of some self-exciting and mutually exciting point processes. Biometrika **58**(1), 83–90 (1971)
11. Hawkes, A.G., Oakes, D.: A cluster process representation of a self-exciting process. J. Appl. Probab. **11**(3), 493–503 (1974)

12. Hochreiter, S., Schmidhuber, J.: Long short-term memory. Neural Comput. **9**(8), 1735–1780 (1997)
13. Jing, H., Smola, A.J.: Neural survival recommender. In: Proceedings of the Tenth ACM International Conference on Web Search and Data Mining, pp. 515–524. ACM (2017)
14. Kingman, J.F.C.: Poisson Processes, vol. 3. Clarendon Press, Oxford (1992)
15. Leskovec, J., Backstrom, L., Kleinberg, J.: Meme-tracking and the dynamics of the news cycle. In: Proceedings of the 15th ACM SIGKDD International Conference on Knowledge Discovery and Data Mining, pp. 497–506. ACM (2009)
16. Linderman, S., Adams, R.: Discovering latent network structure in point process data. In: International Conference on Machine Learning, pp. 1413–1421 (2014)
17. Linderman, S.W., Adams, R.P.: Scalable Bayesian inference for excitatory point process networks. arXiv preprint arXiv:1507.03228 (2015)
18. Linderman, S.W., Wang, Y., Blei, D.M.: Bayesian inference for latent Hawkes processes. In: Advances in Neural Information Processing Systems (2017)
19. Liniger, T.J.: Multivariate Hawkes processes. Ph.D. thesis, ETH Zurich (2009)
20. Maddix, D.C., Wang, Y., Smola, A.: Deep factors with Gaussian processes for forecasting. arXiv preprint arXiv:1812.00098 (2018)
21. Mei, H., Eisner, J.M.: The neural Hawkes process: a neurally self-modulating multivariate point process. In: Advances in Neural Information Processing Systems, pp. 6754–6764 (2017)
22. Ogata, Y.: On Lewis' simulation method for point processes. IEEE Trans. Inf. Theory **27**(1), 23–31 (1981)
23. Sharma, A., Johnson, R., Engert, F., Linderman, S.: Point process latent variable models of Larval Zebrafish behavior. In: Advances in Neural Information Processing Systems, pp. 10941–10952 (2018)
24. Simma, A., Jordan, M.I.: Modeling events with cascades of Poisson processes. In: Proceedings of the Twenty-Sixth Conference on Uncertainty in Artificial Intelligence, pp. 546–555. AUAI Press (2010)
25. Vaswani, A., et al.: Attention is all you need. In: Advances in Neural Information Processing Systems, pp. 5998–6008 (2017)
26. Xiao, S., Farajtabar, M., Ye, X., Yan, J., Song, L., Zha, H.: Wasserstein learning of deep generative point process models. In: Advances in Neural Information Processing Systems, pp. 3247–3257 (2017)
27. Xiao, S., Yan, J., Farajtabar, M., Song, L., Yang, X., Zha, H.: Joint modeling of event sequence and time series with attentional twin recurrent neural networks. arXiv preprint arXiv:1703.08524 (2017)

Single-Path NAS: Designing Hardware-Efficient ConvNets in Less Than 4 Hours

Dimitrios Stamoulis[1]($\boxtimes$), Ruizhou Ding[1], Di Wang[2],
Dimitrios Lymberopoulos[2], Bodhi Priyantha[2], Jie Liu[3], and Diana Marculescu[1]

[1] Department of ECE, Carnegie Mellon University, Pittsburgh, PA, USA
`dstamoul@andrew.cmu.edu`
[2] Microsoft, Redmond, WA, USA
[3] Harbin Institute of Technology, Harbin, China

Abstract. Can we automatically design a Convolutional Network (ConvNet) with the highest image classification accuracy under the latency constraint of a mobile device? Neural architecture search (NAS) has revolutionized the design of hardware-efficient ConvNets by automating this process. However, the NAS problem remains challenging due to the combinatorially large design space, causing a significant searching time (at least 200 GPU-hours). To alleviate this complexity, we propose *Single-Path NAS*, a novel differentiable NAS method for designing hardware-efficient ConvNets in **less than 4 h**. Our contributions are as follows: 1. **Single-path search space**: Compared to previous differentiable NAS methods, *Single-Path NAS* uses one single-path over-parameterized ConvNet to encode all architectural decisions with shared convolutional kernel parameters, hence drastically decreasing the number of trainable parameters and the search cost down to few epochs. 2. **Hardware-efficient ImageNet classification**: *Single-Path NAS* achieves 74.96% top-1 accuracy on ImageNet with 79 ms latency on a Pixel 1 phone, which is state-of-the-art accuracy compared to NAS methods with similar inference latency constraints ($\leq$80 ms). 3. **NAS efficiency**: *Single-Path NAS* search cost is only **8 epochs** (30 TPU-hours), which is up to **5,000×** **faster** compared to prior work. 4. **Reproducibility**: Unlike all recent mobile-efficient NAS methods which only release pretrained models, we open-source our entire codebase at: https://github.com/dstamoulis/single-path-nas.

Keywords: Neural Architecture Search · Hardware-aware ConvNets

1 Introduction

"Is it possible to reduce the considerable search cost of Neural Architecture Search (NAS) down to only few hours?" NAS has revolutionized the design of Convolutional Networks (ConvNets) [25], yielding state-of-the-art results in several deep

© Springer Nature Switzerland AG 2020
U. Brefeld et al. (Eds.): ECML PKDD 2019, LNAI 11907, pp. 481–497, 2020.
https://doi.org/10.1007/978-3-030-46147-8_29

learning applications [14]. NAS methods already have a profound impact on the design of hardware-efficient ConvNets for computer vision tasks under the constraints (*e.g.*, inference latency) imposed by mobile devices [18].

Despite the recent breakthroughs, NAS remains an intrinsically costly optimization problem. Searching for which convolution operation to use per ConvNet layer, gives rise to a combinatorially large search space: *e.g.*, for a mobile-efficient ConvNet with 22 layers, choosing among five candidate operations yields $5^{22} \approx 10^{15}$ possible ConvNet architectures. To traverse this design space, earlier NAS methods guide the exploration via reinforcement learning (RL) [18]. Nonetheless, training the RL controller poses prohibitive computational challenges, and thousands of candidate ConvNets need to be trained [19].

(1) Prior NAS work: *Multi-path* search space	(2) Proposed NAS method: *Single-path* search space
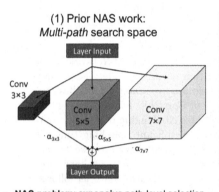	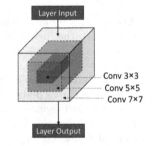
• **NAS problem: expensive** path-level selection • **Supernet:** each op as **separate path**/layer • **#parameters/layer: all** weights across **all** paths	• **NAS problem:** *efficient kernel-level* selection • **Supernet:** all ops in single *"superkernel"*/layer • **#parameters/layer:** #weights of largest op *only*

Fig. 1. *Single-Path NAS* directly optimizes for the subset of convolution kernel weights and searches over an over-parameterized **"superkernel"** in each ConvNet layer (right). This **novel view** of the design space eliminates the need for maintaining separate paths for each candidate operation, as in previous *multi-path* approaches (left). Our **key insight** drastically reduces the NAS search cost by up to **5,000×** with state-of-the-art accuracy on ImageNet for the same mobile latency setting, compared to prior work.

Inefficiencies of *Multi-path* NAS: Recent NAS literature has seen a shift towards one-shot differentiable formulations [12,13,20] which search over a supernet that encompasses all candidate architectures. Specifically, current NAS methods relax the combinatorial optimization problem of finding the optimal ConvNet architecture to an operation/path selection problem: first, an over-parameterized, *multi-path* supernet is constructed, where, for each layer, every candidate operation is added as a *separate* trainable path, as illustrated in Fig. 1 (left). Next, NAS formulations solve for the (distributions of) paths of the *multi-path* supernet that yield the optimal architecture.

As expected, naively branching out all paths is inefficient due to an intrinsic limitation: the number of trainable parameters that need to be maintained and updated during the search grows linearly with respect to the number of candidate operations per layer [1]. To tame the memory explosion introduced by the *multi-path* supernet, current methods employ creative "workaround" solutions: *e.g.*, searching on a proxy dataset (subset of ImageNet [19]), or employing a memory-wise scheme with only a subset of paths being updated during the search [3]. Nevertheless, these techniques remain considerably costly, with an overall computational demand of at least 200 GPU-hours.

In this paper, we propose *Single-Path NAS*, a novel NAS method for designing hardware-efficient ConvNets in **less than 4 h**. Our **key insight** is illustrated in Fig. 1 (right). We build upon the observation that different candidate convolutional operations in NAS can be viewed as subsets of a single **"superkernel"**. Without having to choose among different paths/operations as in *multi-path* methods, we instead solve the NAS problem as *finding which subset of kernel weights to use in each ConvNet layer*. By sharing the convolutional kernel weights, we encode all candidate NAS operations into a single superkernel, *i.e.*, with a single path, for each layer of the one-shot NAS supernet. This novel encoding of the design space yields a drastic reduction to the number of trainable parameters/gradients, allowing our NAS method to use batch sizes of 1024, a four-fold increase compared to prior art's search efficiency.

Our contributions are as follows:

1. **Single-path NAS**: We propose a novel view of the one-shot, supernet-based design space, hence drastically decreasing the number of trainable parameters. To the best of our knowledge, this is the *first* work to formulate the NAS problem as finding the subset of kernel weights in each ConvNet layer.
2. **State-of-the-art results:** *Single-Path NAS* achieves 74.96% top-1 accuracy on ImageNet with 79 ms latency on a Pixel 1, *i.e.*, a +0.31% improvement over the current best hardware-aware NAS [18] under 80 ms.
3. **NAS efficiency:** The overall search cost is only **8 epochs**, *i.e.*, **3.75 h** on TPUs (30 TPU-hours), up to **5,000× faster** compared to prior work.
4. **Reproducibility:** Unlike recent hardware-efficient NAS methods which release pretrained models only, we open-source and fully document our method at: https://github.com/dstamoulis/single-path-nas.

2   Related Work

Hardware-Efficient ConvNets: While complex ConvNet designs have unlocked unprecedented performance levels in computer vision tasks, the accuracy improvement has come at the cost of higher computational complexity, making the deployment of state-of-the-art ConvNets to mobile devices challenging [17]. To this end, a significant body of prior work aims to co-optimize for the inference latency of ConvNets. Earlier approaches focus on human expertise to introduce hardware-efficient operations [9,15,22]. Pruning [4] and quantization [7] methods share the same goal to improve the efficiency of ConvNets.

Neural Architecture Search (NAS): NAS aims at automating the process of designing ConvNets, giving rise to methods based on reinforcement learning (RL), evolutionary algorithms, or gradient-based methods [12–14,24,25]. Earlier approaches train an agent (*e.g.*, RNN controller) by sampling candidate architectures over a cell-based design space, where the same cell is repeated in all layers and the focus is on searching the cell architecture [25]. Nonetheless, training the controller over different architectures makes the search costly.

Hardware-aware NAS: Earlier NAS methods focused on maximizing accuracy under FLOPs constraints [20,23], but low FLOP count does not necessarily translate to hardware efficiency [8,16]. More recent methods incorporate hardware terms (*e.g.*, runtime, power) into cell-based NAS formulations [8,10], but cell-based implementations are not hardware friendly [19]. Breaking away from cell-based assumptions in the search space encoding, recent work employs NAS over a generalized MobileNetV2-based design space introduced in [18].

Hardware-aware Differentiable NAS: Recent NAS literature has seen a shift towards one-shot NAS formulations [13,20]. Gradient-based NAS in particular has gained increased popularity and has achieved state-of-the-art results [12]. One-shot-based methods use an over-parameterized super-model network, where, for each layer, every candidate operation is added as a separate trainable path. Nonetheless, *multi-path* search spaces have an intrinsic limitation: the number of trainable parameters that need to be maintained and updated with gradients during the search grows linearly with respect to the number of different convolutional operations per layer, resulting in memory explosion [1,3].

To this end, state-of-the-art approaches employ different novel "workaround" solutions. FBNet [19] searches on a "proxy" dataset (*i.e.*, subset of the ImageNet dataset). Despite the decreased search cost thanks to the reduced number of training images, these approaches do not address the fact that the entire super-model needs to be maintained in memory during search, hence the efficiency is limited due to inevitable use of smaller batch sizes. ProxylessNAS [3] has employed a memory-wise one-shot model scheme, where only a set of paths is updated during the search. However, such implementation-wise improvements do not address a second key suboptimality of one-shot approaches, *i.e.*, the fact that separate gradient steps are needed to update the weights and the architectural decisions interchangeably [12]. Although the number of trainable parameters, with respect to the memory cost, is kept to the same level at any step, the way that *multi-path*-based methods traverse the design space remains inefficient.

3   Proposed Method: *Single-Path* NAS

In this Section, we present our proposed method. First, we discuss our novel *single-path* view (Subsect. 3.1) of the search space. Next, we encode the NAS problem as finding the subset of convolution weights over the over-parameterized superkernel (Subsect. 3.2), and we discuss how it compares to existing *multi-path*-based NAS (Subsect. 3.3). Last, we formulate the hardware-aware NAS objective

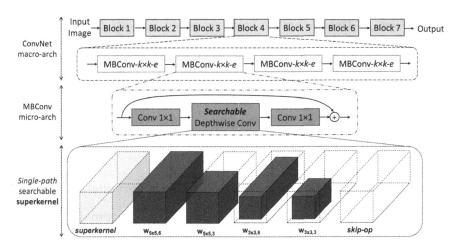

Fig. 2. *Single-path* **search space**: Our method builds upon *hierarchical* MobileNetV2-like search spaces [15,18], where the goal is to identify the type of mobile inverted bottleneck convolution (MBConv) [15] per layer. Our *one-shot supernet* encapsulates all possible NAS architectures in the search space, without the need for appending each candidate operation as a separate path. *Single-Path* NAS directly searches over the weights of a **searchable** superkernel that encodes all MBConv types.

function, where we incorporate an accurate inference latency model of ConvNets executing on the Pixel 1 smartphone (Subsect. 3.4).

3.1 Mobile ConvNets Search Space: A Novel View

Background - Mobile ConvNets: State-of-the-art NAS builds upon a fixed "backbone" ConvNet [3] inspired by the MobileNetV2 design [15], illustrated in Fig. 2 (top). Specifically, in this fixed macro-architecture, except for the head and stem layers, all ConvNet layers are grouped into blocks based on their filter sizes. The filter numbers per block follow the values in [19], *i.e.*, we use seven blocks with up to four layers each. Each layer of these blocks follows a mobile inverted bottleneck convolution MBConv [15] micro-architecture, which consists of a point-wise (1×1) convolution, a $k \times k$ depthwise convolution, and a linear 1×1 convolution (Fig. 2, middle). Unless the layer has a stride value of two, a skip path is introduced to provide a residual connection from input to output.

Each MBConv layer is parameterized by k, *i.e.*, the kernel size of the depthwise convolution, and by expansion ratio e, *i.e.*, the ratio between the output and input of the first 1×1 convolution. Based on this parameterization, we denote each MBConv as MBConv-$k \times k$-e. Mobile-efficient NAS aims to choose each MBConv-$k \times k$-e layer, by selecting among different k and e values [3,19]. In particular, we consider MBConv layers with kernel sizes $\{3, 5\}$ and expansion ratios $\{3, 6\}$. NAS also considers a special *skip-op* "layer", which "zeroes-out" the kernel and feeds the input directly to the output, *i.e.*, the entire layer is dropped.

Novel View of Design Space: Our *key insight* is illustrated in Fig. 2. We build upon the observation that different candidate convolutional operations in NAS can be viewed as subsets of the weights of an over-parameterized single superkernel (Fig. 2, bottom). This observation allows us to view the NAS combinatorial problem as *finding which subset of kernel weights to use in each MBConv layer*. This observation is important since it allows sharing the kernel parameters across different MBConv architectural options. As shown in Fig. 2, we encode all candidate NAS operations to this single **superkernel**, *i.e.*, with a **single path**, for each layer of the one-shot NAS supernet.

3.2   Proposed Methodology: Single-Path NAS Formulation

Key Idea - Relaxing NAS Decisions Over an Over-Parameterized Kernel: To simplify notation and to illustrate the key idea, without loss of generality, we show the case of choosing between a 3×3 or a 5×5 kernel for an MBConv layer. Let us denote the weights of the two candidate kernels as $\mathbf{w}_{3\times3}$ and $\mathbf{w}_{5\times5}$, respectively. As shown in Fig. 3 (left), we observe that the weights of the 3×3 kernel can be viewed as the *inner* core of the weights of the 5×5 kernel, while "zeroing" out the weights of the "*outer*" shell. We denote this (*outer*) subset of weights (that does not contribute to output of the 3×3 kernel but only to the 5×5 kernel), as $\mathbf{w}_{5\times5\backslash3\times3}$. Hence, the NAS architectural choice of using the 5×5 convolution corresponds to using both the *inner* $\mathbf{w}_{3\times3}$ weights and the *outer* shell, *i.e.*, $\mathbf{w}_{5\times5} = \mathbf{w}_{3\times3} + \mathbf{w}_{5\times5\backslash3\times3}$ (Fig. 3, left).

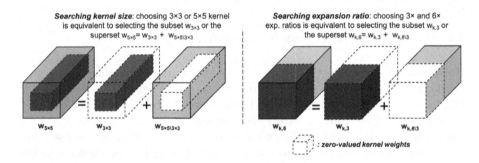

Fig. 3. Encoding NAS decisions into the **superkernel**: We formulate all candidate convolution operations (*i.e.*, different kernel size (left) and expansion ratio (right) values) directly into the searchable superkernel.

We can therefore encode the NAS decision directly into the superkernel of an MBConv layer as a function of kernel weights as follows:

$$\mathbf{w}_k = \mathbf{w}_{3\times3} + \mathbb{1}(\text{use } 5 \times 5) \cdot \mathbf{w}_{5\times5\backslash3\times3} \tag{1}$$

where $\mathbb{1}(\cdot)$ is the indicator function that encodes the architectural NAS choice, *i.e.*, if $\mathbb{1}(\cdot) = 1$ then $\mathbf{w}_k = \mathbf{w}_{3\times3} + \mathbf{w}_{5\times5\backslash3\times3} = \mathbf{w}_{5\times5}$, else $\mathbb{1}(\cdot) = 0$ then $\mathbf{w}_k = \mathbf{w}_{3\times3}$.

Trainable Indicator/Condition Function: While the indicator function encodes the NAS decision, a critical choice is how to formulate the condition over which the $\mathbb{1}(\cdot)$ is evaluated. Our intuition is that, for an indicator function that represents whether to use the subset of weights, its condition should be *directly a function of the subset's weights*. Thus, our goal is to define an "importance" signal of the subset weights that intrinsically captures their contribution to the overall ConvNet loss. We draw inspiration from weight-based conditions that have been successfully used for quantization-related decisions [6] and we use the *group Lasso term*. Specifically, for the indicator related to the $\mathbf{w}_{5\times 5 \backslash 3 \times 3}$ "outer shell" decision, we write the following condition:

$$\mathbf{w}_k = \mathbf{w}_{3 \times 3} + \mathbb{1}(\left\| \mathbf{w}_{5 \times 5 \backslash 3 \times 3} \right\|^2 > t_{k=5}) \cdot \mathbf{w}_{5 \times 5 \backslash 3 \times 3} \tag{2}$$

where $t_{k=5}$ is a latent variable that controls the decision (*e.g.*, a threshold value) of selecting kernel 5×5. The threshold will be compared to the Lasso term to determine if the *outer* $\mathbf{w}_{5 \times 5 \backslash 3 \times 3}$ weights are used to the overall convolution. It is important to notice that, instead of picking the thresholds (*e.g.*, $t_{k=5}$) by hand, we seamlessly treat them as trainable parameters to learn via gradient descent. To compute the gradients for thresholds, we relax the indicator function $g(x, t) = \mathbb{1}(x > t)$ to a sigmoid function, $\sigma(\cdot)$, when computing gradients, *i.e.*, $\hat{g}(x, t) = \sigma(x > t)$.

Searching for Expansion Ratio and Skip-op: Since the result of the kernel-based NAS decision $\mathbf{w}_k$ (Eq. 2) is a convolution kernel itself, we can in turn apply our formulation to also encode NAS decisions for the expansion ratio of the $\mathbf{w}_k$ kernel. As illustrated in Fig. 3 (right), the channels of the depthwise convolution in an MBConv-$k \times k$-3 layer with expansion ratio $e = 3$ can be viewed as using one half of the channels of an MBConv-$k \times k$-6 layer with expansion ratio $e = 6$, while "zeroing" out the second half of channels $\{\mathbf{w}_{k,6 \backslash 3}\}$. Finally, by "zeroing" out the first half of the output filters as well, the entire superkernel contributes nothing if added to the residual connection of the MBConv layer: *i.e.*, by deciding if $e = 3$, we can encode the NAS decision of using, or not, only the "skip-op" path. For both decisions over $\mathbf{w}_k$ kernel, we write:

$$\mathbf{w} = \mathbb{1}(\left\| \mathbf{w}_{k,3} \right\|^2 > t_{e=3}) \cdot (\mathbf{w}_{k,3} + \mathbb{1}(\left\| \mathbf{w}_{k,6 \backslash 3} \right\|^2 > t_{e=6}) \cdot \mathbf{w}_{k,6 \backslash 3}) \tag{3}$$

Hence, for input $\mathbf{x}$, the output of the i-th MBConv layer of the network is:

$$o^i(\mathbf{x}) = \text{conv}(\mathbf{x}, \mathbf{w}^i | t_{k=5}^i, t_{e=6}^i, t_{e=3}^i) \tag{4}$$

Searchable MBConv Kernels: Each MBConv uses 1×1 convolutions for the point-wise (first) and linear stages, while the kernel-size decisions affect only the (middle) $k \times k$ depthwise convolution (Fig. 2). To this end, we use our searchable $k \times k$ depthwise kernel at this middle stage. In terms of number of channels, the depthwise kernel depends on the point-wise 1×1 output, which allows us to directly encode the expansion ratio e at the middle stage as well: by setting the point-wise 1×1 output to the maximum candidate expansion ratio, we can instead solve for which of them not to "zero" out at the depthwise (middle) state. In other words, we directly use our searchable depthwise convolution superkernel to effectively encode the NAS decision for the expansion ratio. Hence, our *single-path*, convolution-based formulation can sufficiently capture any MBConv type (*e.g.*, MBConv-3 × 3-6, MBConv-5 × 5-3, *etc.*) in the MobileNetV2-based design space (Fig. 2).

3.3 Single-Path vs. Existing Multi-Path Assumptions

Comparison with Multi-path Over-Parameterized Networks: We briefly illustrate how our *single-path* formulation compares to multi-path NAS approaches. In existing methods [3,12,19], the output of each layer i is a (weighted) sum defined over the output of N different paths, where each path j corresponds to a different candidate kernel $\mathbf{w}_{k \times k, e}^{i,j}$. The weight of each path $\alpha^{i,j}$ corresponds to the probability that this path is selected over the parallel paths:

$$o_{multi-path}^i(\mathbf{x}) = \sum_{j=1}^{N} \alpha^{i,j} \cdot o^{i,j}(\mathbf{x}) = \alpha^{i,0} \cdot \text{conv}(\mathbf{x}, \mathbf{w}_{3 \times 3}^{i,0}) + \cdots + \alpha^{i,N} \cdot \text{conv}(\mathbf{x}, \mathbf{w}_{5 \times 5}^{i,N})$$

(5)

It is easy to see how our novel *single-path* view is advantageous, since the output of the convolution at layer i of our search space is *directly a function of the weights of our single over-parameterized kernel* (Eq. 4):

$$o_{single-path}^i(\mathbf{x}) = o^i(\mathbf{x}) = \text{conv}(\mathbf{x}, \mathbf{w}^i | t_{k=5}^i, t_{e=6}^i, t_{e=3}^i)$$

(6)

Comparison with Multi-path NAS Optimization: Multi-path NAS methods solve for the optimal architecture parameters α (path weights), such that the weights w_α of the corresponding α-architecture have minimal loss $\mathcal{L}(\alpha, w_\alpha)$:

$$\min_{\alpha} \min_{w_\alpha} \mathcal{L}(\alpha, w_\alpha)$$

(7)

However, solving Eq. 7 gives rise to a challenging *bi-level* optimization problem [12]. Existing methods interchangeably update the α's while freezing the w's and vice versa, leading to more gradient steps.

In contrast, with our *single-path* formulation, the overall network loss is directly a function of the superkernel weights, where the learnable kernel- and expansion ratio-related threshold variables, $\mathbf{t}_k$ and $\mathbf{t}_e$, are directly derived as a function (norm) of the kernel weights $\mathbf{w}$. Consequently, *Single-Path NAS* formulates the NAS problem as solving *directly over the weight kernels w of a single-path, compact neural network*. Formally, the NAS problem becomes:

$$\min_{\mathbf{w}} \mathcal{L}(\mathbf{w} | \mathbf{t}_k, \mathbf{t}_e)$$

(8)

Efficiency of *Single-Path NAS:* Unlike the bi-level optimization problem in prior work, solving our NAS formulation in Eq. 8 is as expensive as training the weights of a single-path, **branchless**, compact neural network with vanilla gradient descent. Therefore, our formulation eliminates the need for separate gradient steps between the ConvNet weights and the NAS parameters. Moreover, the reduction of the trainable parameters $\mathbf{w}$ per se, further leads to a drastic reduction of the search cost down to **just a few epochs**, as our experimental results show later in Sect. 4. Our NAS problem formulation allows us to efficiently solve Eq. 8 with batch sizes of 1024, a four-fold increase compared to prior art's search efficiency.

3.4   Hardware-Aware NAS with Differentiable Runtime Loss

To design hardware-efficient ConvNets, the differentiable objective in Eq. 8 should reflect both the accuracy of the searched ConvNet and its inference latency on the target hardware. Hence, we use a latency-aware formulation [3,19]:

$$\mathcal{L}(\mathbf{w}|\mathbf{t}_k, \mathbf{t}_e) = CE(\mathbf{w}|\mathbf{t}_k, \mathbf{t}_e) + \lambda \cdot \log(R(\mathbf{w}|\mathbf{t}_k, \mathbf{t}_e)) \tag{9}$$

The first term CE corresponds to the cross-entropy loss of the single-path model. The hardware-related term R is the runtime in milliseconds (ms) of the searched NAS model on the target mobile platform. Finally, the coefficient λ modulates the trade-off between cross-entropy and runtime.

Runtime Model Over the Single-Path Design Space: To preserve the differentiability of the objective, another critical choice is the formulation of the latency term R. Prior art has showed that the total network latency of a mobile ConvNet can be modeled as the sum of each i-th layer's runtime R^i, since the runtime of each operator is independent of other operators [2,3,19]:

$$R(\mathbf{w}|\mathbf{t}_k, \mathbf{t}_e) = \sum_i R^i(\mathbf{w}^i|\mathbf{t}_k^i, \mathbf{t}_e^i) \tag{10}$$

For our approach, we adapt the per-layer runtime model as a function of the NAS-related decisions $\mathbf{t}$. We profile the target mobile platform (Pixel 1) and we record the runtime for each candidate kernel operation per layer i, *i.e.*, $R_{3\times3,3}^i$, $R_{3\times3,6}^i$, $R_{5\times5,3}^i$, and $R_{5\times5,6}^i$. We denote the runtime of layer i by following the notation in Eq. 3. Specifically, the runtime of layer i is defined first as a function of the expansion ratio decision:

$$R_e^i = \mathbb{1}(\|\mathbf{w}_{k,3}\|^2 > \mathbf{t}_{e=3}) \cdot (R_{5\times5,3}^i + \mathbb{1}(\|\mathbf{w}_{k,6\backslash3}\|^2 > \mathbf{t}_{e=6}) \cdot (R_{5\times5,6}^i - R_{5\times5,3}^i)) \tag{11}$$

Next, by incorporating the kernel size decision, the total runtime is:

$$R^i = \frac{R_{3\times3,6}^i}{R_{5\times5,6}^i} \cdot R_e^i + R_e^i \cdot (1 - \frac{R_{3\times3,6}^i}{R_{5\times5,6}^i}) \cdot \mathbb{1}(\|\mathbf{w}_{5\times5\backslash3\times3}\|^2 > \mathbf{t}_{k=5}) \tag{12}$$

As in Eq. 2, we relax the indicator function to a sigmoid function $\sigma(\cdot)$ when computing gradients. By using this model, the runtime term in the loss function remains differentiable with respect to layer-wise NAS choices. As we show in our results, the model is accurate, with an average prediction error of 1.76%.

4   Experiments

4.1   Experimental Setup

Dataset and Target Application: We use *Single-Path NAS* to design ConvNets for image classification on ImageNet. We use Pixel 1 as the target mobile platform. The choice of this experimental setup is important, since it allows for a representative comparison with prior hardware-efficient NAS methods that optimize for the same Pixel 1 device around a target latency of 80 ms [3,18].

Implementation and Deployment: We implement our NAS framework in TensorFlow (TF version 1.12). During both search and training stages, we use TPUs (version 2) [11]. To this end, we build on top of the TPUEstimator classes following the TPU-related documentation of the MnasNet repository[1]. Last, all models (ours and prior work) are deployed with TensorFlow TFLite to the mobile device. On the device, we profile runtime using the Facebook AI Performance Evaluation Platform (FAI-PEP)[2] that supports profiling for tflite models with detailed per-layer runtime breakdown.

Implementing the Custom Superkernels: We use Keras to implement our trainable superkernels. Specifically, we define a custom Keras-based depthwise convolution kernel where the output is a function of both the weights and the threshold-based decisions (Eqs. 2, 3). Our custom layer also returns the effective runtime of the layer (Eqs. 11, 12). We document our implementation in our project GitHub repository: https://github.com/dstamoulis/single-path-nas, with detailed steps on how to reproduce the results.

4.2   State-of-the-Art Runtime-Constrained ImageNet Classification

We apply our method to design ConvNets for the Pixel 1 phone with an overall target latency of 80 ms. We train the derived *Single-Path* NAS model for 350 epochs, following the MnasNet training schedule [18]. We compare our method with mobile ConvNets designed by human experts and state-of-the-art NAS methods in Table 1, in terms of classification accuracy and search cost. In terms of hardware efficiency, prior work has shown that low FLOP count does not necessarily translate to high hardware efficiency [8], we therefore evaluate the various NAS methods with respect to the inference runtime on Pixel 1 ($\leq$80 ms).

Enabling a Representative Comparison: While we provide the original values from the respective papers, our goal is to ensure a fair comparison. To this end, we retrain the baseline models following the same schedule (in fact, we find that the MnasNet-based training schedule improves the top1 accuracy compared to what is reported in several previous methods). Similarly, we profile the models on the same Pixel 1 device. For prior work that does not optimize for Pixel 1, we retrain and profile their model closest to the MnasNet baseline (*e.g.*, the

---

[1] https://github.com/tensorflow/tpu/tree/master/models/official/mnasnet.
[2] https://github.com/facebook/FAI-PEP.

FBNet-B and ChamNet-B networks [5,19], since the authors use these ConvNets to compare against the MnasNet model). Finally, to enable a representative comparison of the search cost per method, we directly report the number of epochs reported per method, hence canceling out the effect of different hardware systems (GPU vs TPU hours).

ImageNet Classification: Table 1 shows that our *Single-Path* NAS achieves top-1 accuracy of **74.96%**, which is the new state-of-the-art ImageNet accuracy among hardware-efficient NAS methods. More specifically, **our method achieves better top-1 accuracy than ProxylessNAS by +0.31%**, while maintaining on par target latency of ≤ 80 ms on the same target mobile phone. *Single-Path* NAS outperforms methods in this mobile latency range, *i.e.*, better than MnasNet (+0.35%), FBNet-B (+0.86%), and MobileNetV2 (+1.37%).

Table 1. *Single-Path* NAS achieves state-of-the-art accuracy (%) on ImageNet for similar mobile latency setting compared to previous NAS methods (≤ 80 ms on Pixel 1), with up to 5,000× reduced search cost in terms of number of epochs. *The search cost in epochs is estimated based on the claim [3] that ProxylessNAS is 200× faster than MnasNet. ‡ChamNet does not detail the model derived under runtime constraints [5] so we cannot retrain or measure the latency.

Method	Top-1 Acc (%)	Top-5 Acc (%)	Mobile runtime (ms)	Search cost (epochs)
MobileNetV1 [9]	70.60	89.50	113	–
MobileNetV2 1.0x [15]	72.00	91.00	75.00	
MobileNetV2 1.0x (our impl.)	73.59	91.41	73.57	
Random search	73.78 ± 0.85	91.42 ± 0.56	77.31 ± 0.9 ms	–
MnasNet 1.0x [18]	74.00	91.80	76.00	40,000
MnasNet 1.0x (our impl.)	74.61	91.95	74.65	
ChamNet-B [5]	73.80	–	–	240‡
ProxylessNAS-R [3]	74.60	92.20	78.00	200*
ProxylessNAS-R (our impl.)	74.65	92.18	77.48	
FBNet-B [19]	74.1	–	–	90
FBNet-B (our impl.)	73.70	91.51	78.33	
Single-Path NAS (**proposed**)	**74.96**	**92.21**	79.48	**8 (3.75 h)**

NAS Search Cost: *Single-Path* NAS has **orders of magnitude reduced search cost** compared to all previous hardware-efficient NAS methods. Specifically, MnasNet reports that the controller uses 8k sampled models, each trained for 5 epochs, for a total of 40k train epochs. In turn, ChamNet trains an accuracy predictor on 240 samples, which assuming an aggressively fast training schedule of five epochs per sample (same as in MnasNet), corresponds to a total search cost of 1.2k epochs. ProxylessNAS reports 200× search cost improvement over MnasNet, hence the overall cost is the TPU-equivalent of 200 epochs. Finally,

FBNet reports 90 epochs of training on a proxy dataset (10% of ImageNet). While the number of images per epoch is reduced, we found that a TPU can accommodate a FBNet-like supermodel with maximum batch size of 128, hence the number of steps per FBNet epoch are still 8× more compared to the steps per epoch in our method.

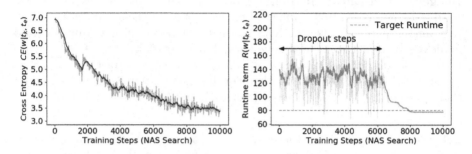

Fig. 4. *Single-Path NAS* search progress: Progress of both objective terms, *i.e.*, cross entropy CE (left) and runtime R (right) during NAS search.

Fig. 5. Hardware-efficient ConvNet found by *Single-Path* NAS, with top-1 accuracy of **74.96%** on ImageNet and inference time of 79.48 ms on Pixel 1 phone.

In comparison, *Single-Path NAS* has a total cost of eight epochs, which is **5,000×** faster than MnasNet, **25×** faster than ProxylessNAS, and **11×** faster than FBNet. In particular, we use an aggressive training schedule similar to the few-epochs schedule used in MnasNet to train the individual ConvNet samples [18]. Due to space limitations, we provide implementation details (*e.g.*, label smoothing, learning rates, λ value, *etc.*) in our project repository. Overall, we visualize the search efficiency of our method in Fig. 4, where we show the progress of both CE and R terms of Eq. 8. Earlier during our search (first six epochs), we employ *dropout* across the different subsets of the kernel weights (Fig. 4, right). Dropout is a common technique in NAS methods to prevent the supernet from learning as an ensemble. Unlike prior art that employs this technique over the separate paths of the *multi-path* supernet, we directly drop randomly the subsets of the superkernel in our *single-path* search space. We search for $\sim 10k$ **steps** (8 epochs with a batch size of 1024), which corresponds to total wall-clock time of **3.75 h** on a TPUv2. In particular, given than a TPUv2 has 2 chips with 4 cores each, this corresponds to a total of 30 TPU-hours.

Visualization of *Single-Path NAS* ConvNet: Our derived ConvNet architecture is shown in Fig. 5. Moreover, to illustrate how the searchable superkernels effectively capture NAS decisions across subsets of kernel weights, we plot the standard deviation of weight values in Fig. 6 (shown in log-scale, with lighter colors indicating smaller values). Specifically, we compute the standard deviation of weights across the channel-dimension for all superkernels. For various layers shown in Fig. 6 (per i-th ConvNet's layer from Fig. 5), we observe that the *outer* $\mathbf{w}_{5\times5\backslash3\times3}$ "shells" reflect the NAS architectural choices: for layers where the entire $\mathbf{w}_{5\times5}$ is selected, the $\mathbf{w}_{5\times5\backslash3\times3}$ values drastically vary across the channels. On the contrary, for all layers where 3×3 convolution is selected, the *outer* shell values do not vary significantly.

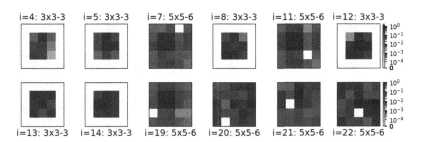

Fig. 6. Visualization of kernel-based architectural contributions. The *standard deviation* of **superkernel** values across the kernel channels is shown in log-scale, with lighter colors indicating smaller values.

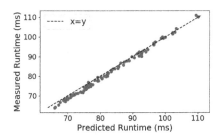

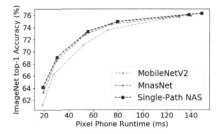

Fig. 7. The runtime model (Eq. 10) is accurate, with an average prediction error of 1.76%.

Fig. 8. *Single-Path* NAS outperforms MobileNetV2 and MnasNet across various channel size scales.

Comparison with Random Search: We find surprising that mobile-efficient NAS methods lack a comparison against random search. To this end, we randomly sample ten ConvNets based on our design space; we employ sampling by rejection, where we keep samples with predicted runtime from 75 ms to 80 ms. The average accuracy and runtime of the random samples are reported in Table 1.

We observe that, while random search does not outperform NAS methods, the overall accuracy is comparable to MobileNetV2. This highlights that the effectiveness of NAS methods heavily relies upon the properties of the MobileNetV2-based design space. Nonetheless, the search cost of random search is not representative: to avoid training all ten samples, we would follow a selection process similar to MnasNet, by training each sample for few epochs and picking the one with highest accuracy. Hence, the actual search cost for random search is not negligible, and for ≥ 10 samples it is in fact comparable to automated NAS methods.

Different Channel Size Scaling: Next, we follow a typical analysis [3,19], by rescaling the networks using a width multiplier [15]. As shown in Fig. 8, we observe that our model consistently outperforms prior methods under varying runtime settings. For instance, Single-Path NAS with 79.48 ms is 1.56× faster than the MobileNetV2 scaled model of similar accuracy.

Runtime Model: To train the runtime model, we record the runtime per layer (MBConv operations breakdown) by profiling ConvNets with different MBConv types, *i.e.*, we obtain the $R^i_{3\times3,3}$, $R^i_{3\times3,6}$, $R^i_{5\times5,3}$, and $R^i_{5\times5,6}$ runtime values per MBConv layer i (Eqs. 11, 12). To evaluate the runtime-prediction accuracy of the model, we generate 100 randomly designed ConvNets and we measure their runtime on the device. As illustrated in Fig. 7, our model can accurately predict the actual runtimes: the Root Mean Squared Error (RMSE) is 1.32 ms, which corresponds to an average 1.76% prediction error.

Table 2. Searching across subsets of kernel weights: ConvNets with weight values trained over subsets of the kernels (3×3 as subset of 5×5) achieve performance (top-1 accuracy) similar to ConvNets with individually trained kernels.

Method	Top-1 Acc (%)	Top-5 Acc (%)
Baseline ConvNet - $\mathbf{w}_{3\times3}$ kernels	73.59	91.41
Baseline ConvNet - $\mathbf{w}_{5\times5}$ kernels	74.10	91.67
Single-Path ConvNet - inference w/$\mathbf{w}_{3\times3}$ kernels	73.43	91.42
Single-Path ConvNet - inference w/$\mathbf{w}_{3\times3} + \mathbf{w}_{5\times5\backslash3\times3}$ kernels	73.86	91.72

4.3 Ablation Study: Kernel-Based Accuracy-Efficiency Trade-Off

Single-Path NAS searches over subsets of the convolutional kernel weights. Hence, we conduct experiments to highlight how kernel-weight subsets can capture accuracy-efficiency trade-off effectively. To this end, we use the MobileNetV2 macro-architecture as a backbone (we maintain the location of stride-2 layers as default). As two baseline networks, we consider the default MobileNetV2 with MBConv-3 × 3-6 blocks (*i.e.*, $\mathbf{w}_{3\times3}$ kernels for all depthwise convolutions), and a network with MBConv-5 × 5-6 blocks (*i.e.*, $\mathbf{w}_{5\times5}$ kernels).

Next, to capture the subset-based training of weights during a *Single-Path* NAS search, we consider a *ConvNet* with MBConv-5 × 5-6 blocks, where we compute the loss of the model over two subsets, (i) the inner $\mathbf{w}_{3\times3}$ weights, and (ii) by also using the remaining $\mathbf{w}_{5\times5\backslash3\times3}$ weights. For each loss computed over these subsets, we accumulate back-propagated gradients and update the respective weights, *i.e.*, gradients are being applied separately to the inner and to the entire kernel per layer. We follow training steps similar to the "switchable" training across channels as in [21] (for the remaining training hyper-parameters we use the same setup as the default MnasNet). As shown in Table 2, we observe the final accuracy across the kernel granularity, *i.e.*, with the inner $\mathbf{w}_{3\times3}$ and the entire $\mathbf{w}_{5\times5} = \mathbf{w}_{3\times3} + \mathbf{w}_{5\times5\backslash3\times3}$ kernels, follows an accuracy change relative to ConvNets with individually trained kernels.

Such finding is significant in the context of NAS, since choosing over subsets of kernels can effectively capture the accuracy-runtime trade-offs similar to their individually trained counterparts. We therefore conjecture that our efficient superkernel-based design search can be flexibly adapted and benefit the guided search space exploration in other RL-based NAS methods. Beyond the NAS literature, our finding is closely related to Slimmable networks [21]. SlimmableNets limit however their analysis across the channel dimension, and our work is the first to study trade-offs across the NAS kernel dimension.

5   Conclusion

In this paper, we proposed *Single-Path NAS*, a NAS method that reduces the search cost for designing hardware-efficient ConvNets to **less than 4 h**. The key idea is to revisit the one-shot **supernet** design space with a novel *single-path* view, by formulating the NAS problem as *finding which subset of kernel weights to use* in each ConvNet layer. *Single-Path NAS* achieved 74.96% top-1 accuracy on ImageNet with 79 ms latency on a Pixel 1 phone, which is state-of-the-art accuracy with latency on-par with previous NAS methods (≤80 ms). More importantly, we reduced the search cost of hardware-efficient NAS down to only **8 epochs** (30 TPU-hours), which is up to **5,000× faster** compared to prior work. **Impact beyond differentiable NAS**: While we used a differentiable NAS formulation, our novel design space encoding can be flexibly incorporated into other NAS methodologies. Hence, *Single-Path NAS* could enable future work that builds upon the efficiency of our *single-path*, one-shot design space for RL- or evolutionary-based NAS methods.

Acknowledgements. This research was supported in part by National Science Foundation CSR Grant No. 1815780 and National Science Foundation CCF Grant No. 1815899. Dimitrios Stamoulis also acknowledges support from the Qualcomm Innovation Fellowship (QIF) 2018 and the TensorFlow Research Cloud programs.

References

1. Bender, G., Kindermans, P.J., Zoph, B., Vasudevan, V., Le, Q.: Understanding and simplifying one-shot architecture search. In: International Conference on Machine Learning, pp. 549–558 (2018)
2. Cai, E., Juan, D.C., Stamoulis, D., Marculescu, D.: Neuralpower: predict and deploy energy-efficient convolutional neural networks. In: Asian Conference on Machine Learning, pp. 622–637 (2017)
3. Cai, H., Zhu, L., Han, S.: ProxylessNAS: direct neural architecture search on target task and hardware. In: International Conference on Learning Representations (2019)
4. Chin, T.W., Zhang, C., Marculescu, D.: Layer-compensated pruning for resource-constrained convolutional neural networks. arXiv preprint arXiv:1810.00518 (2018)
5. Dai, X., et al.: Chamnet: towards efficient network design through platform-aware model adaptation. In: Proceedings of the IEEE Conference on Computer Vision and Pattern Recognition, pp. 11398–11407 (2019)
6. Ding, R., Liu, Z., Chin, T.W., Marculescu, D., Blanton, R.: FLightNNs: lightweight quantized deep neural networks for fast and accurate inference. In: 2019 Design Automation Conference (DAC) (2019)
7. Ding, R., Liu, Z., Shi, R., Marculescu, D., Blanton, R.: LightNN: filling the gap between conventional deep neural networks and binarized networks. In: Proceedings of the on Great Lakes Symposium on VLSI 2017, pp. 35–40. ACM (2017)
8. Dong, J.-D., Cheng, A.-C., Juan, D.-C., Wei, W., Sun, M.: DPP-Net: device-aware progressive search for pareto-optimal neural architectures. In: Ferrari, V., Hebert, M., Sminchisescu, C., Weiss, Y. (eds.) ECCV 2018. LNCS, vol. 11215, pp. 540–555. Springer, Cham (2018). https://doi.org/10.1007/978-3-030-01252-6_32
9. Howard, A.G., et al.: MobileNets: efficient convolutional neural networks for mobile vision applications. arXiv preprint arXiv:1704.04861 (2017)
10. Hsu, C.H., et al.: MONAS: multi-objective neural architecture search using reinforcement learning. arXiv preprint arXiv:1806.10332 (2018)
11. Jouppi, N.P., et al.: In-datacenter performance analysis of a tensor processing unit. In: 2017 ACM/IEEE 44th Annual International Symposium on Computer Architecture (ISCA), pp. 1–12. IEEE (2017)
12. Liu, H., Simonyan, K., Yang, Y.: Darts: differentiable architecture search. In: International Conference on Learning Representations (2018)
13. Pham, H., Guan, M., Zoph, B., Le, Q., Dean, J.: Efficient neural architecture search via parameter sharing. In: International Conference on Machine Learning, pp. 4092–4101 (2018)
14. Real, E., Aggarwal, A., Huang, Y., Le, Q.V.: Regularized evolution for image classifier architecture search. arXiv preprint arXiv:1802.01548 (2018)
15. Sandler, M., Howard, A., Zhu, M., Zhmoginov, A., Chen, L.C.: MobileNetV2: inverted residuals and linear bottlenecks. In: Proceedings of the IEEE Conference on Computer Vision and Pattern Recognition, pp. 4510–4520 (2018)
16. Stamoulis, D., Cai, E., Juan, D.C., Marculescu, D.: Hyperpower: power-and memory-constrained hyper-parameter optimization for neural networks. In: 2018 Design, Automation & Test in Europe Conference & Exhibition (DATE). IEEE (2018)
17. Stamoulis, D., et al.: Designing adaptive neural networks for energy-constrained image classification. In: Proceedings of the International Conference on Computer-Aided Design. ACM (2018)

18. Tan, M., et al.: MnasNet: platform-aware neural architecture search for mobile. In: Proceedings of the IEEE Conference on Computer Vision and Pattern Recognition (2019)
19. Wu, B., et al.: FBNet: hardware-aware efficient convnet design via differentiable neural architecture search. In: The IEEE Conference on Computer Vision and Pattern Recognition (CVPR), June 2019
20. Xie, S., Zheng, H., Liu, C., Lin, L.: SNAS: stochastic neural architecture search. In: International Conference on Learning Representations (2019)
21. Yu, J., Yang, L., Xu, N., Yang, J., Huang, T.: Slimmable neural networks. In: International Conference on Learning Representations (2019)
22. Zhang, X., Zhou, X., Lin, M., Sun, J.: ShuffleNet: an extremely efficient convolutional neural network for mobile devices. In: Proceedings of the IEEE Conference on Computer Vision and Pattern Recognition, pp. 6848–6856 (2018)
23. Zhou, Y., Ebrahimi, S., Arık, S.Ö., Yu, H., Liu, H., Diamos, G.: Resource-efficient neural architect. arXiv preprint arXiv:1806.07912 (2018)
24. Zoph, B., Le, Q.V.: Neural architecture search with reinforcement learning. In: International Conference on Machine Learning (2017)
25. Zoph, B., Vasudevan, V., Shlens, J., Le, Q.V.: Learning transferable architectures for scalable image recognition. In: Proceedings of the IEEE Conference on Computer Vision and Pattern Recognition, pp. 8697–8710 (2018)

Probabilistic Models

Scalable Large Margin Gaussian Process Classification

Martin Wistuba$^{(\boxtimes)}$ and Ambrish Rawat

IBM Research, Dublin, Republic of Ireland
martin.wistuba@ibm.com, ambrish.rawat@ie.ibm.com

Abstract. We introduce a new Large Margin Gaussian Process (LMGP) model by formulating a pseudo-likelihood for a generalised multi-class hinge loss. We derive a highly scalable training objective for the proposed model using variational-inference and inducing point approximation. Additionally, we consider the joint learning of LMGP-DNN which combines the proposed model with traditional Deep Learning methods to enable learning for unstructured data. We demonstrate the effectiveness of the Large Margin GP with respect to both training time and accuracy in an extensive classification experiment consisting of 68 structured and two unstructured data sets. Finally, we highlight the key capability and usefulness of our model in yielding prediction uncertainty for classification by demonstrating its effectiveness in the tasks of large-scale active learning and detection of adversarial images.

1 Introduction

This work brings together the effectiveness of large margin classifiers with the non-parametric expressiveness and principled handling of uncertainty offered by Gaussian processes (GPs). Gaussian processes are highly expressive Bayesian non-parametric models which have proven to be effective for prediction modelling. One key aspect of Bayesian models which is often overlooked by traditional approaches is the representation and propagation of uncertainty. In general, decision makers are not solely interested in predictions but also in the confidence about the predictions. An action might only be taken in the case when the model in consideration is certain about its prediction. This is crucial for critical applications like medical diagnosis, security, and autonomous cars. Bayesian formalism provides a principled way to obtain these uncertainties. Bayesian methods handle all kinds of uncertainties in a model, be it in inference of parameters or for obtaining the predictions. These methods are known to be effective for online classification [18], active learning [29], global optimization of expensive black-box functions [11], automated machine learning [32], and as recently noted, even in machine learning security [30].

Classical Gaussian process classification models [36] are generalised versions of linear logistic regression. These classifiers directly use a function modelled as a Gaussian process with a logit link or probit function [27] for obtaining

© Springer Nature Switzerland AG 2020
U. Brefeld et al. (Eds.): ECML PKDD 2019, LNAI 11907, pp. 501–516, 2020.
https://doi.org/10.1007/978-3-030-46147-8_30

the desired probabilities. Alternatively, margin classifiers like Support Vector Machines (SVMs) employ hinge loss for learning decision functions. Gaussian process classifiers often perform similar to non-linear SVMs [16] but are preferred by some practitioners due to added advantages like uncertainty representation and automatic hyperparameter determination. Therefore, it is natural to look for a probabilistic generalisation of the hinge loss that can benefit from the numerous advantages of Bayesian modelling.

The contributions in this work are threefold. We derive a pseudo-likelihood for a general multi-class hinge loss and propose a large margin Gaussian process (LMPG). We provide a scalable learning scheme based on variational inference [2,10,34] to train this model. Additionally, we propose a hybrid model which combines deep learning components such as convolutional layers with the LMGP which we refer to as LMGP-DNN. This allows to jointly learn the feature extractors as well as the classifier design such that it can be applied both on structured and unstructured data. We compare the proposed LMGP on 68 structured data sets to a state-of-the-art binary Bayesian SVM with the one-vs-rest approach and the scalable variational Gaussian process [10]. On average, LMGP provides better prediction performance and needs up to an order of magnitude less training time in comparison to the competitor methods. The proposed LMGP-DNN is compared on the image classification data sets MNIST [17] and CIFAR-10 [15] to a standard (non-Bayesian) neural network. We show that we achieve similar performance, however, require increased training time. Finally, we demonstrate the effectiveness of uncertainties in experiments on active learning and adversarial detection.

2   Related Work

Motivated by a probabilistic formulation of the generalised multi-class hinge loss, this work derives and develops a scalable training paradigm for large margin Gaussian process based classification. In the vast related literature this is an advancement on two fronts - first, a novel approach to Gaussian process based classification and second, Bayesian formulation of margin classifiers, like SVMs. We position our work with respect to both these directions of research. With reference to Gaussian process based classifiers, our work closely relates to scalable variational Gaussian processes (SVGP) [10]. Infamous for the cubic dependency of learning schemes with respect to number of data samples has, in the past, limited the applicability of Gaussian process based models. However recent developments in sparse-approximation schemes [31,34] have enabled learning of GP-based models for large scale datasets. The two works, SVGP and LMGP differ in their choice of objective functions. While SVGP utilises a variational approximation of the cross-entropy between predicted probabilities and the target probabilities for learning, LMGP seeks to maximise the margin between GP predictions. In both works, this is achieved with the use of variational inference along with inducing point approximation which scales learning to large data sets.

The probabilistic formulation of Support Vector Machines has a long standing history. However, most work has been limited to the binary-classification case with extensions to multi-class being enabled with the one-vs-rest scheme. [33] interprets SVM training as learning a maximum a posteriori solution of a model with Gaussian process priors. In addition, works like [28] have investigated extensions that benefit SVMs with certain key aspects of Bayesian formalism like model selection. For the task of binary classification, [24] make a key observation and reformulate the hinge loss in the linear SVM training objective to a location-scale mixture of Gaussians. They derive a pseudo-likelihood by introducing local latent variables for each data point and subsequently marginalize them out for predictions. A multi-class extension to this linear model has been considered in [23] with learning enabled by an expectation-maximisation based algorithm. A non-linear version of this setup is considered by [9] where the linear decision function is modeled as a Gaussian process. They approximate the resulting joint posterior using Markov chain Monte Carlo (MCMC) or expectation conditional maximization (ECM). Furthermore, they scale the inference using the fully independent training conditional approximation (FITC) [31]. The basic assumption behind FITC is that the function values are conditionally independent given the set of inducing points. Then, training the Gaussian process is no longer cubically dependent on the number of training instances. Moreover, the number of inducing points can be freely chosen. [20] extend the work of [24] by applying a mean field variational approach to it. Most recently, [35] propose an alternate variational objective and use coordinate ascent to maximize it. They demonstrate improved performance over a classical SVM, competitor Bayesian approaches, and Gaussian process-based classifiers. In the scope of this work, we contrast performance with the one-vs-rest extension of [35] and call it Bayesian SVM.

3 Large Margin Gaussian Process

This section details the proposed Large Margin Gaussian process (LMGP). We begin with a discussion of the probabilistic formulation of the hinge loss for the binary case and follow it by establishing a Bayesian interpretation of the generalised non-linear multi-class case [5]. We then establish the complete model formulation of LMGP and detail a variational-inference based scheme for scalable learning. We conclude with a description of LMGP-DNN model that extends the applicability of LMGP to image data.

3.1 Probabilistic Hinge Loss

For a binary classification task, a model trained with hinge loss seeks to learn a decision boundary with maximum margin, i.e. the separation between the decision boundary and the instances of the two classes. We represent the labeled data for a binary classification task with N observations and M-dimensional representation as $D = \{\mathbf{x}_n, y_n\}_{n=1}^{N}$, where $\mathbf{x}_n \in \mathbb{R}^M$ and $y_n \in \{-1, 1\}$ represent predictors and labels, respectively. Training such a model, as in the case of the classical SVM, involves learning a decision function $f : \mathbb{R}^M \to \mathbb{R}$ that minimizes the regularized hinge loss,

$$\mathcal{L}(D, f, \gamma) = \sum_{n=1}^{N} \max\{1 - y_n f(\mathbf{x}_n), 0\} + \gamma R(f). \tag{1}$$

The regularizer R punishes the choice of more complex functions for f, and γ is a hyperparameter that controls the impact of this regularization. A linear SVM uses a linear decision function $f(\mathbf{x}_n) = \boldsymbol{\theta}^T \mathbf{x}_n$. Non-linear decision functions are traditionally obtained by applying the kernel trick.

For the linear case, [24] show that minimizing Eq. (1) is equivalent to estimating the mode of a pseudo-posterior (maximum a posteriori estimate)

$$p(f|D) \propto \exp(-\mathcal{L}(D, f, \gamma)) \propto \prod_{n=1}^{N} L(y_n|\mathbf{x}_n, f) p(f), \tag{2}$$

derived for a particular choice of pseudo-likelihood factors L, defined by location-scale mixtures of Gaussians. This is achieved by introducing local latent variables λ_n such that for each instance,

$$L(y_n|\mathbf{x}_n, f) = \int_0^\infty \frac{1}{\sqrt{2\pi\lambda_n}} \exp\left(-\frac{1}{2}\frac{(1 + \lambda_n - y_n f(\mathbf{x}_n))^2}{\lambda_n}\right) d\lambda_n. \tag{3}$$

In their formulations, [24] and [9] consider γ as a model parameter and accordingly develop inference schemes. Similar to [35], we treat γ as a hyperparameter and drop it from the expressions of prior and posterior for notational convenience. [9] extend this framework to enable learning of a non-linear decision function f. Both [9] and [35] consider models where $f(x)$ is sampled from a zero-mean Gaussian process i.e. $\mathbf{f} \sim \mathcal{N}(0, K_{NN})$, where $\mathbf{f} = [f(\mathbf{x}_1), \ldots, f(\mathbf{x}_n)]$ is a vector of function evaluations and K_{NN} is the covariance function evaluated at data points.

3.2   Generalised Multi-class Hinge Loss

Modeling a multi-class task with SVM is typically achieved by decomposing the task into multiple independent binary classification tasks. Although simple and powerful, this framework cannot capture correlations between the different classes since the modeled binary tasks are independent. As an alternate approach, numerous extensions based on generalised notion of margins have been proposed in the literature [6]. One can view these different multi-class SVM loss functions as a combination of margin functions for the different classes, a large margin loss for binary problems, and an aggregation operator, combining the various target margin violations into a single loss value. We consider the popular formulation of [5] which corresponds to combining relative margins with the max-over-others operator. A multi-class classification task involves N observations with integral labels $Y = \{1, \ldots, C\}$. A classifier for this task can be modeled as a combination of a decision function $f : \mathbb{R}^M \rightarrow \mathbb{R}^C$ and a decision rule to compute the class labels,

$$\hat{y}(\mathbf{x}_n) = \arg\max_{t \in Y} f_t(\mathbf{x}_n). \tag{4}$$

[5] propose to minimize the following objective function for learning the decision function f:

$$\mathcal{L}(D, f, \gamma) = \sum_{n=1}^{N} \max\left\{1 + \max_{t \neq y_n, t \in Y} f_t(\mathbf{x}_n) - f_{y_n}(\mathbf{x}_n), \ 0\right\} + \gamma R(f), \tag{5}$$

where again γ is a hyperparameter controlling the impact of the regularizer R.

With the prior associated to $\gamma R(f)$, maximizing the log of Eq. (2) corresponds to minimizing Eq. (5) with respect to the parameters of f. This correspondence requires the following equation to hold true for the data-dependent factors of the pseudo-likelihood,

$$\prod_{n=1}^{N} L(y_n \mid \mathbf{x}_n, f) = \exp\left(-2 \sum_{n=1}^{N} \max\left\{1 + \max_{t \neq y_n, t \in Y} f_t(\mathbf{x}_n) - f_{y_n}(\mathbf{x}_n), \ 0\right\}\right). \tag{6}$$

Analogously to [24], we show that $L(y_n \mid \mathbf{x}_n, f)$ admits a location-scale mixture of Gaussians by introducing local latent variables $\boldsymbol{\lambda} = [\lambda_1, \ldots, \lambda_n]$. This requires the lemma established by [1].

Lemma 1. *For any $a, b > 0$,*

$$\int_0^\infty \frac{a}{\sqrt{2\pi\lambda}} e^{-\frac{1}{2}\left(a^2\lambda + b^2\lambda^{-1}\right)} \mathrm{d}\lambda = e^{-|ab|}. \tag{7}$$

Now, we prove following theorem.

Theorem 1. *The pseudo-likelihood contribution from an observation y_n can be expressed as*

$$L(y_n \mid \mathbf{x}_n, f) = \int_0^\infty \frac{1}{\sqrt{2\pi\lambda_n}} e^{\frac{-1}{2\lambda_n}\left(1 + \lambda_n + \max_{t \neq y_n, t \in Y} f_t(\mathbf{x}_n) - f_{y_n}(\mathbf{x}_n)\right)^2} \mathrm{d}\lambda_n \tag{8}$$

Proof. Applying Lemma 1 while substituting $a = 1$ and $b = 1 + \max_{t \neq y_n, t \in Y} f_t(\mathbf{x}_n) - f_{y_n}(\mathbf{x}_n)$, multiplying through by e^{-b}, and using the identity $\max\{b, 0\} = \frac{1}{2}(|b| + b)$, we get,

$$\int_0^\infty \frac{1}{\sqrt{2\pi\lambda_n}} \exp\left(-\frac{1}{2} \frac{(b + \lambda_n)^2}{\lambda_n}\right) \mathrm{d}\lambda_n = e^{-2\max\{b, 0\}}. \tag{9}$$

3.3   Scalable Variational Inference for LMGP

We complete the model formulation by assuming that $f_j(\mathbf{x})$ is drawn from a
Gaussian process for each class, j, i.e. $\mathbf{f}_j \sim \mathcal{N}(0, K_{NN})$ and $\boldsymbol{\lambda} \sim \mathbb{1}_{[0,\infty)}(\boldsymbol{\lambda})$.
Inference in our model amounts to learning the joint posterior $p(\mathbf{f}, \boldsymbol{\lambda}|D)$, where
$\mathbf{f} = [\mathbf{f}_1, \ldots, \mathbf{f}_C]$. However, computing the exact posterior is intractable. We use
variational inference (VI) combined with an inducing point approximation for
jointly learning the C GPs corresponding to each class. In VI, the exact posterior
over the set of model parameters $\boldsymbol{\theta}$ is approximated by a variational distribution
q. The parameters of q are updated with the aim to reduce the dissimilarity
between the exact and approximate posteriors, as measured by the Kullback-
Leibler divergence. This is equivalent to maximizing the evidence lower bound
(ELBO) [12] with respect to parameters of q, where

$$\text{ELBO} = \mathbb{E}_{q(\boldsymbol{\theta})}\left[\log p\left(\mathbf{y}|\boldsymbol{\theta}\right)\right] - \text{KL}\left[q\left(\boldsymbol{\theta}\right)||p\left(\boldsymbol{\theta}\right)\right]. \tag{10}$$

Using this as objective function, we could potentially infer the posterior $q(\mathbf{f}, \boldsymbol{\lambda})$.
However, inference and prediction using this full model involves inverting an
$N \times N$ matrix. An operation of complexity $O(N^3)$ is impractical. Therefore, we
employ the sparse approximation proposed by [10]. We augment the model with
$P \ll N$ inducing points which are shared across all GPs. Similar to [10], we
consider a GP prior for the inducing points, $p(\mathbf{u}_j) = \mathcal{N}(0, K_{PP})$ and consider
the marginal

$$q(\mathbf{f}_j) = \int p(\mathbf{f}_j|\mathbf{u}_j)q(\mathbf{u}_j)d\mathbf{u}_j \tag{11}$$

with

$$p(\mathbf{f}_j|\mathbf{u}_j) = \mathcal{N}\left(\kappa\mathbf{u}, \tilde{K}\right). \tag{12}$$

The approximate posterior $q(\mathbf{u}, \boldsymbol{\lambda})$ factorizes as

$$\prod_{j \in Y} q(\mathbf{u}_j) \prod_{n=1}^{N} q(\lambda_n) \tag{13}$$

with

$$q(\lambda_n) = \mathcal{GIG}(1/2, 1, \alpha_n), \quad q(\mathbf{u}_j) = \mathcal{N}(\boldsymbol{\mu}_j, \Sigma_j). \tag{14}$$

Here, $\kappa = K_{NP}K_{PP}^{-1}$, $\tilde{K} = K_{NN} - K_{NP}\kappa^T$ and $\mathcal{GIG}$ is the generalized inverse
Gaussian. K_{PP} is the kernel matrix resulting from evaluating the kernel function
between all inducing points. Analogously, we denote the cross-covariance between
data points and inducing points, or between all data points by K_{NP} or K_{NN},
respectively. The choice of variational approximations is inspired from the exact
conditional posterior computed by [9]. Using Jensen's inequality, we derive the

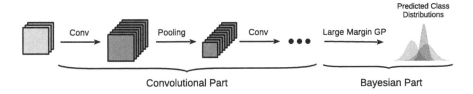

Fig. 1. LMGP-DNN for image classification.

final training objective,

$$\mathbb{E}_{q(\mathbf{u},\boldsymbol{\lambda})}\left[\log p\left(\mathbf{y}|\mathbf{u},\boldsymbol{\lambda}\right)\right] - \mathrm{KL}\left[q\left(\mathbf{u},\boldsymbol{\lambda}\right)||p\left(\mathbf{u},\boldsymbol{\lambda}\right)\right] \tag{15}$$

$$\geq \mathbb{E}_{q(\mathbf{u},\boldsymbol{\lambda})}\left[\mathbb{E}_{p(\mathbf{f}|\mathbf{u})}\left[\log p\left(\mathbf{y},\boldsymbol{\lambda}|\mathbf{f}\right)\right]\right] + \mathbb{E}_{q(\mathbf{u})}\left[\log p\left(\mathbf{u}\right)\right] - \mathbb{E}_{q(\mathbf{u},\boldsymbol{\lambda})}\left[\log q\left(\mathbf{u},\boldsymbol{\lambda}\right)\right] \tag{16}$$

$$= \sum_{n=1}^{N}\left(-\frac{1}{2\sqrt{\alpha_n}}\left(2\tilde{K}_{n,n} + \left(1 + \boldsymbol{\kappa}_n\left(\boldsymbol{\mu}_{t_n} - \boldsymbol{\mu}_{y_n}\right)\right)^2 + \boldsymbol{\kappa}_n \Sigma_{t_n}\boldsymbol{\kappa}_n^{\mathsf{T}} + \boldsymbol{\kappa}_n \Sigma_{y_n}\boldsymbol{\kappa}_n^{\mathsf{T}} - \alpha_n\right)\right.$$

$$\left. -\boldsymbol{\kappa}_n\left(\boldsymbol{\mu}_{t_n} - \boldsymbol{\mu}_{y_n}\right) - \frac{1}{4}\log\alpha_n - \log\left(B_{\frac{1}{2}}\left(\sqrt{\alpha_n}\right)\right)\right)$$

$$-\frac{1}{2}\sum_{j\in Y}\left(-\log|\Sigma_j| + \mathrm{trace}\left(K_{PP}^{-1}\Sigma_j\right) + \boldsymbol{\mu}_j^{\mathsf{T}}K_{PP}^{-1}\boldsymbol{\mu}_j\right) = \mathcal{O} \tag{17}$$

where $B_{\frac{1}{2}}$ is the modified Bessel function [13], and $t_n = \arg\max_{t\in Y, t\neq y_n} f_t\left(\mathbf{x}_n\right)$. $\mathcal{O}$ is maximized using gradient-based optimization methods. We provide a detailed derivation of the variational objective and its gradients in the appendix.

3.4 LMGP-DNN

Deep Neural Networks (DNNs) are well known for their end-to-end learning capabilities for numerous tasks that involve unstructured data. Their effectiveness is often attributed to their capacity to learn hierarchical representation of data. In Sect. 3.3 we show that our proposed LMGP can be learned with gradient-based optimization schemes. This enables us to combine it with various deep learning components such as convolutional layers and extend its applicability to unstructured data as shown in Fig. 1. The parameters of the LMGP-DNN model which includes convolution and the variational parameters are jointly learned by means of backpropagation. The ability to jointly learn features with the one-vs-rest Bayesian SVMs has been previously explored in [26] and [25]. LMGP-DNN explores the same for the multi-class case.

4   Experimental Evaluation

In this section we conduct an extensive study of the LMGP model and analyze its classification performance on structured and unstructured data. Additionally, we analyze the quality of its uncertainty prediction in a large-scale active learning experiment and for the challenging problem of adversarial image detection.

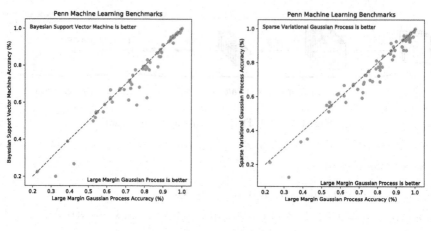

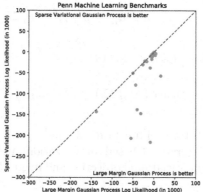

Fig. 2. Pairwise comparison of the LMGP versus the Bayesian SVM and SVGP. On average, LMGP provides better results.

Table 1. Mean average rank across 68 data sets. The smaller, the better. Our proposed LMGP is on average the most accurate prediction model.

Bayesian SVM	LMGP	SVGP
1.96	**1.68**	2.33

4.1   Classification

Our classification experiment is investigating two different types of data. In the first part, we investigate the classification performance of the multi-class Bayesian SVM on structured data against Bayesian state-of-the-art models. In the second part, we compare the hybrid Bayesian SVM model against standard convolutional neural networks for the task of image classification.

4.2   Structured Data Classification

We evaluate the proposed LMGP with respect to classification accuracy on the Penn Machine Learning Benchmarks [22]. From this benchmark, we select all multi-class classification data sets consisting of at least 128 instances. This subset consists of 68 data sets with up to roughly one million instances. We compare the classification accuracy of our proposed LMGP with the scalable variational Gaussian process (SVGP) [10] and the most recently proposed binary Bayesian support vector machine (Bayesian SVM) [35] (one-vs-rest setup). We use the implementation available in GPflow [21] for SVGP and implement the one-vs-rest Bayesian SVM and LMGP as additional classifiers in GPflow by extending its classifier interface. The shared back end of all three implementations allows a fair training time comparison. For this experiment, all models are trained using 64 inducing points. Gradient-based optimization is performed using Adam [14] with an initial learning rate of $5 \cdot 10^{-4}$ for 1000 epochs.

Figure 2 contrasts the LMGP with SVGP and one-vs-rest Bayesian SVM. The proposed LMGP clearly outperforms the other two models for most data sets. While this is more pronounced against SVGP, the Bayesian SVM and LMGP models exhibit similar performance. This claim is supported by the comparison of mean ranks (Table 1). The rank per data set is computed by ranking the methods for each data set according to classification accuracy. The most accurate prediction model is assigned rank 1, second best rank 2 and so on. In case of ties, an average rank is used, e.g. if the models exhibit classification accuracies of 1.0, 1.0, and 0.8, they are assigned ranks of 1.5, 1.5, and 3, respectively.

One primary motivation for proposing LMGP is scalability. Classification using the one-vs-rest Bayesian SVM requires training an independent model per class which increases the training time by a factor equal to the number of classes. Contrastingly, SVGP and LMGP enable multi-class classification with a single model. This results in significant benefits in training time. As evident in Fig. 3, the LMGP requires the least training time.

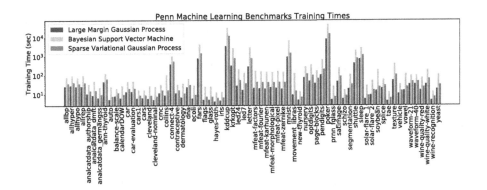

Fig. 3. Our proposed LMGP clearly needs less time than its competitors.

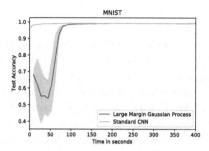 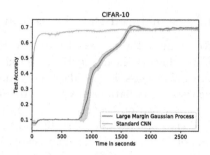

Fig. 4. The jointly learned model of a convolutional network and an LMGP performs as good as a standard network. The price of gaining a Bayesian neural network is a longer training time.

In conclusion, LMGP is the most efficient model without compromising on prediction accuracy. In fact, on average it has a higher accuracy.

4.3   Image Classification with LMGP-DNN

In Sect. 3.4 we describe how deep learning can be used to learn a feature representation jointly with an LMGP. Image data serves as a typical example for unstructured data. We compare the LMGP-DNN to a standard convolutional neural network (CNN) with a softmax layer for classification. We evaluate these models on two popular image classification benchmarks, MNIST [17] and CIFAR-10 [15].

We observe same performance of the LMGP-DNN as a standard CNN with softmax layer. The two different neural networks share the first set of layers, for MNIST: `conv(32,5,5)-conv(64,3,3)-max_pool-fc(1024)-fc(100)`, and for CIFAR-10: `conv(128,3,3)-conv(128,3,3)-max_pool-conv(128,3,3)-max_pool-fc(256)-fc(100)`. As in our previous experiment, we use Adam to perform the optimization.

Figure 4 shows that the LMGP-DNN achieves the same test accuracy as the standard CNN. The additional training effort of a LMGP-DNN model pays off in achieving probabilistic predictions with uncertainty estimates. While the variational objective and the likelihood exhibits the expected behavior during the training, we note an odd behavior during the initial epochs. We suspect that this is due to initialization of parameters which could result in the KL-term of the variational objective dominating the expected log-likelihood.

4.4   Uncertainty Analysis

Most statistical modelling approaches are concerned with minimizing a specific loss-metric, e.g. classification error. However, practitioners have additional concerns, like interpretability and certainty of the predictions. Bayesian methods provide a distribution over predictions rather than just point-estimates, which

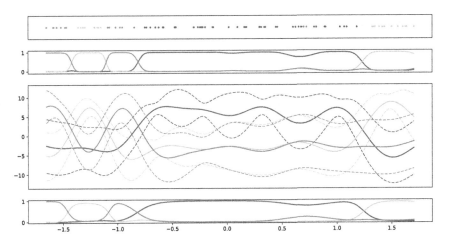

Fig. 5. From top to bottom: 1. Data points belonging to three classes, 2. Prediction probabilities from LMGP 3. Predictions from the three Gaussian processes of the LMGP model along with their uncertainties, and 4. SVM probability predictions

is a significant advantage in practice as it allows for development of informed decision-making systems. Figure 5 shows that LMGP exhibits a key artefact of GPs where uncertainty in the predicted scores of GPs is higher (3rd row) in the regions with few datapoints. This aspect of our model is central to its utility in the tasks of active learning and adversarial detection and is often overlooked by classical models like SVMs (4th row in Fig. 5). We want to emphasise that there are scenarios where uncertainty as obtained from Bayesian models is beneficial and that the prediction error by itself only plays a tangential role.

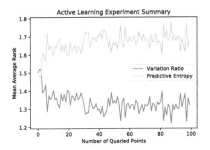

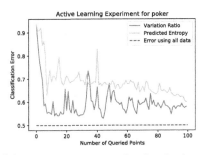

(a) Average rank across 68 data sets.

(b) Representative results for the largest data set.

Fig. 6. The Bayesian query policy (variation ratio) decreases the error of the model faster and clearly outperforms the policy based on point-estimates only. For both figures, the smaller the better.

Active Learning. Active learning is concerned with scenarios where the process of labeling data is expensive. In such scenarios, a query policy is adopted to label samples from a large pool of unlabeled instances with the aim to improve model performance. We contrast between two policies to highlight the merits of using prediction uncertainty obtained from the LMGP model. While the first policy utilizes both mean and variance of the predictive distribution of the LMGP, the second policy relies only on the mean. For this experiment we use the same data sets as specified in Sect. 4.2.

We use the variation ratio (VR) as the basis of a Bayesian query policy. It is defined by

$$\text{Variation Ratio} = 1 - F/S, \tag{18}$$

where F is the frequency of the mode and S the number of samples. The VR is the relative number of times the majority class is not predicted. Its minimum zero is reached when all Monte Carlo samples agree on the same class. The instance with highest VR is queried. We compare this to a policy which queries the instance with maximum entropy of class probabilities. These are computed using softmax over the mean predictions,

$$\mathbb{H}\left(f\left(\mathbf{x}_n\right)\right) = -\sum_{t \in Y} f_t\left(\mathbf{x}_n\right) \log\left(f_t\left(\mathbf{x}_n\right)\right). \tag{19}$$

For a fair comparison, we use the same LMGP for both policies. Initially, one instance per class, selected uniformly at random, is labeled. Then, one hundred further instances are queried according to the two policies. As only few training examples are available, we modify the training setup by reducing the number of inducing points to four.

We report the mean average rank across 68 data sets for the two different query policies in Fig. 6a. Since both policies start with the same set of labeled instances, the performance is very similar at the beginning. However, with increasing number of queried data points, the Bayesian policy quickly outperforms the other policy. Of the 68 data sets, the *poker* data set, with more than one million instances, is the largest and consequently the most challenging. Within the first queries, we observe a large decrease in classification error as shown in Fig. 6b. We note the same trend of mean ranks across the two policies. The small number of labeled instances is obviously insufficient to reach the test error of a model trained on all data points as shown by the dashed line.

Similarly, one could employ LMGP-DNN for active learning of unstructured data [7].

Adversarial Image Detection. With the rise of Deep Learning, its security and reliability is a major concern. A recent development in this direction is the discovery of adversarial images [8]. These correspond to images obtained by adding small imperceptible adversarial noise resulting in high confidence misclassification. While various successful attacks exist, most defense and detection methods do not work [4]. However, [4] acknowledge that the uncertainty obtained

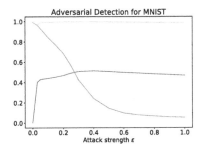 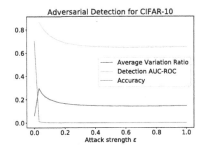

Fig. 7. The accuracy on adversarial images decreases with increasing attack strength. A significant increase of the average variation ratio indicates that it is a good feature to detect adversarial images.

from Bayesian machine learning models is the most promising research direction. Several studies show that Bayesian models behave differently for adversarial examples compared to the original data [3, 19, 30]. We take a step further and use the variation ratio (VR) determined by the LMGP, as defined in Eq. (18), for building a detection model for adversarial images.

We attack the LMGP-DNN described in Sect. 4.3 with the popular Fast Gradient Sign Method (FGSM) [8]. We generate one adversarial image per image in the test set. We present the results for detection and classification under attack in Fig. 7. LMGP-DNN is not robust to FGSM since its accuracy drops with increasing attack strength ϵ. However, the attack does not remain unperceived. The VR rapidly increases and enables the detection of adversarial images. The ranking of original and adversarial examples with respect to VR yields an ROC-AUC of almost 1 for MNIST. This means that the VR computed for any original example is almost always smaller than the one computed for any adversarial example.

CIFAR-10 exhibits different results under the same setup. Here, the detection is poor and it significantly worsens with increasing attack strength. Potentially, this is an artifact of the poor classification model for CIFAR-10. In contrast to the MNIST classifier, this model is under-confident on original examples. Thus, a weaker attack succeeds in reducing the test accuracy to 1.16%. We believe a better network architecture combined with techniques such as data augmentation will lead to an improved performance in terms of test accuracy and subsequently better detection. Nevertheless, the detection performance of our model is still better than a random detector, even for the strongest attack.

5   Conclusions

We devise a pseudo-likelihood for the generalised multi-class hinge loss leading to the large margin Gaussian process model. Additionally, we derive a variational training objective for the proposed model and develop a scalable inference algorithm to optimize it. We establish the efficacy of the model on multi-class classification tasks with extensive experimentation on structured data and contrast its accuracy to two state-of-the-art competitor methods. We provide empirical evidence that our proposed method is on average better and up to an order of magnitude faster to train. Furthermore, we extend our formulation to a LMGP-DNN and report comparable accuracy to standard models for image classification tasks. Finally, we investigate the key advantage of Bayesian modeling in our approach by demonstrating the use of prediction uncertainty in solving the challenging tasks of active learning and adversarial image detection. The uncertainty-based policy outperforms its competitor in the active learning scenario. Similarly, the uncertainty-enabled adversarial detection shows promising results for image data sets with near-perfect performance on MNIST.

References

1. Andrews, D.F., Mallows, C.L.: Scale mixtures of normal distributions. J. Roy. Stat. Soc.: Ser. B (Methodol.) **36**(1), 99–102 (1974). http://www.jstor.org/stable/2984774
2. Blei, D.M., Kucukelbir, A., McAuliffe, J.D.: Variational inference: a review for statisticians. CoRR abs/1601.00670 (2016). http://arxiv.org/abs/1601.00670
3. Bradshaw, J., de G. Matthews, A.G., Ghahramani, Z.: Adversarial examples, uncertainty, and transfer testing robustness in Gaussian process hybrid deep networks (2017)
4. Carlini, N., Wagner, D.: Adversarial examples are not easily detected: bypassing ten detection methods (2017)
5. Crammer, K., Singer, Y.: On the algorithmic implementation of multiclass kernel-based vector machines. J. Mach. Learn. Res. **2**, 265–292 (2001). http://www.jmlr.org/papers/v2/crammer01a.html
6. Dogan, Ü., Glasmachers, T., Igel, C.: A unified view on multi-class support vector classification. J. Mach. Learn. Res. **17**, 45:1–45:32 (2016). http://jmlr.org/papers/v17/11-229.html
7. Gal, Y., Islam, R., Ghahramani, Z.: Deep Bayesian active learning with image data. In: Proceedings of the 34th International Conference on Machine Learning (ICML 2017), Sydney, NSW, Australia, 6–11 August 2017, pp. 1183–1192 (2017). http://proceedings.mlr.press/v70/gal17a.html
8. Goodfellow, I.J., Shlens, J., Szegedy, C.: Explaining and harnessing adversarial examples (2014)
9. Henao, R., Yuan, X., Carin, L.: Bayesian nonlinear support vector machines and discriminative factor modeling. In: Advances in Neural Information Processing Systems, pp. 1754–1762 (2014)
10. Hensman, J., de G. Matthews, A.G., Ghahramani, Z.: Scalable variational Gaussian process classification. In: Proceedings of the Eighteenth International Conference on Artificial Intelligence and Statistics (AISTATS 2015), San Diego, California, USA, 9–12 May 2015 (2015). http://jmlr.org/proceedings/papers/v38/hensman15.html
11. Jones, D.R., Schonlau, M., Welch, W.J.: Efficient global optimization of expensive black-box functions. J. Global Optim. **13**(4), 455–492 (1998). https://doi.org/10.1023/A:1008306431147
12. Jordan, M.I., Ghahramani, Z., Jaakkola, T.S., Saul, L.K.: An introduction to variational methods for graphical models. Mach. Learn. **37**(2), 183–233 (1999). https://doi.org/10.1023/A:1007665907178

13. Jørgensen, B.: Statistical Properties of the Generalized Inverse Gaussian Distribution. LNS, vol. 9. Springer, New York (1982)
14. Kingma, D.P., Ba, J.: Adam: a method for stochastic optimization. CoRR abs/1412.6980 (2014). http://arxiv.org/abs/1412.6980
15. Krizhevsky, A.: Learning multiple layers of features from tiny images. Technical report (2009)
16. Kuss, M., Rasmussen, C.E.: Assessing approximate inference for binary Gaussian process classification. J. Mach. Learn. Res. **6**, 1679–1704 (2005). http://www.jmlr.org/papers/v6/kuss05a.html
17. LeCun, Y., Cortes, C.: MNIST handwritten digit database (2010). http://yann.lecun.com/exdb/mnist/
18. Li, L., Chu, W., Langford, J., Schapire, R.E.: A contextual-bandit approach to personalized news article recommendation. In: Proceedings of the 19th International Conference on World Wide Web (WWW 2010), Raleigh, North Carolina, USA, 26–30 April 2010, pp. 661–670 (2010). https://doi.org/10.1145/1772690.1772758. http://doi.acm.org/10.1145/1772690.1772758
19. Li, Y., Gal, Y.: Dropout inference in Bayesian neural networks with alpha-divergences. In: Proceedings of the 34th International Conference on Machine Learning (ICML 2017), Sydney, NSW, Australia, 6–11 August 2017, pp. 2052–2061 (2017). http://proceedings.mlr.press/v70/li17a.html
20. Luts, J., Ormerod, J.T.: Mean field variational Bayesian inference for support vector machine classification. Comput. Stat. Data Anal. **73**, 163–176 (2014). https://doi.org/10.1016/j.csda.2013.10.030
21. de G. Matthews, A.G., et al.: GPflow: a Gaussian process library using TensorFlow. J. Mach. Learn. Res. **18**(40), 1–6 (2017). http://jmlr.org/papers/v18/16-537.html
22. Olson, R.S., La Cava, W., Orzechowski, P., Urbanowicz, R.J., Moore, J.H.: PMLB: a large benchmark suite for machine learning evaluation and comparison. BioData Min. **10**(1), 36 (2017). https://doi.org/10.1186/s13040-017-0154-4
23. Perkins, H., Xu, M., Zhu, J., Zhang, B.: Fast parallel SVM using data augmentation. arXiv preprint arXiv:1512.07716 (2015)
24. Polson, N.G., Scott, S.L., et al.: Data augmentation for support vector machines. Bayesian Anal. **6**(1), 1–23 (2011)
25. Pu, Y., et al.: Variational autoencoder for deep learning of images, labels and captions. In: Advances in Neural Information Processing Systems, pp. 2352–2360 (2016)
26. Pu, Y., Yuan, W., Stevens, A., Li, C., Carin, L.: A deep generative deconvolutional image model. In: Artificial Intelligence and Statistics, pp. 741–750 (2016)
27. Rasmussen, C.E., Williams, C.K.I.: Gaussian Processes for Machine Learning. Adaptive Computation and Machine Learning. MIT Press, Cambridge (2006). http://www.worldcat.org/oclc/61285753
28. Seeger, M.: Bayesian model selection for support vector machines, Gaussian processes and other kernel classifiers. In: Advances in Neural Information Processing Systems, pp. 603–609 (2000)
29. Settles, B.: Active learning literature survey. Computer Sciences Technical Report 1648, University of Wisconsin-Madison (2009)
30. Smith, L., Gal, Y.: Understanding measures of uncertainty for adversarial example detection. arXiv preprint arXiv:1803.08533 (2018)

31. Snelson, E., Ghahramani, Z.: Sparse Gaussian processes using pseudo-inputs. In: Advances in Neural Information Processing Systems 18. Neural Information Processing Systems (NIPS 2005), Vancouver, British Columbia, Canada, 5–8 December 2005, pp. 1257–1264 (2005). http://papers.nips.cc/paper/2857-sparse-gaussian-processes-using-pseudo-inputs

32. Snoek, J., Larochelle, H., Adams, R.P.: Practical Bayesian optimization of machine learning algorithms. In: Advances in Neural Information Processing Systems 25: 26th Annual Conference on Neural Information Processing Systems 2012. Proceedings of a meeting held 3–6 December 2012, Lake Tahoe, Nevada, United States, pp. 2960–2968 (2012). http://papers.nips.cc/paper/4522-practical-bayesian-optimization-of-machine-learning-algorithms

33. Sollich, P.: Probabilistic methods for support vector machines. In: Advances in Neural Information Processing Systems, pp. 349–355 (2000)

34. Titsias, M.K.: Variational learning of inducing variables in sparse Gaussian processes. In: Proceedings of the Twelfth International Conference on Artificial Intelligence and Statistics (AISTATS 2009), Clearwater Beach, Florida, USA, 16–18 April 2009, pp. 567–574 (2009). http://www.jmlr.org/proceedings/papers/v5/titsias09a.html

35. Wenzel, F., Galy-Fajou, T., Deutsch, M., Kloft, M.: Bayesian nonlinear support vector machines for big data. In: Ceci, M., Hollmén, J., Todorovski, L., Vens, C., Džeroski, S. (eds.) ECML PKDD 2017. LNCS (LNAI), vol. 10534, pp. 307–322. Springer, Cham (2017). https://doi.org/10.1007/978-3-319-71249-9_19

36. Williams, C.K.I., Barber, D.: Bayesian classification with Gaussian processes. IEEE Trans. Pattern Anal. Mach. Intell. **20**(12), 1342–1351 (1998). https://doi.org/10.1109/34.735807

Integrating Learning and Reasoning with Deep Logic Models

Giuseppe Marra[1,2], Francesco Giannini[2], Michelangelo Diligenti[2(✉)], and Marco Gori[2]

[1] Department of Information Engineering, University of Florence, Florence, Italy
g.marra@unifi.it
[2] Department of Information Engineering and Mathematical Sciences, University of Siena, Siena, Italy
{fgiannini,diligmic,marco}@diism.unisi.it

Abstract. Deep learning is very effective at jointly learning feature representations and classification models, especially when dealing with high dimensional input patterns. Probabilistic logic reasoning, on the other hand, is capable of take consistent and robust decisions in complex environments. The integration of deep learning and logic reasoning is still an open-research problem and it is considered to be the key for the development of real intelligent agents. This paper presents Deep Logic Models, which are deep graphical models integrating deep learning and logic reasoning both for learning and inference. Deep Logic Models create an end-to-end differentiable architecture, where deep learners are embedded into a network implementing a continuous relaxation of the logic knowledge. The learning process allows to jointly learn the weights of the deep learners and the meta-parameters controlling the high-level reasoning. The experimental results show that the proposed methodology overcomes the limitations of the other approaches that have been proposed to bridge deep learning and reasoning.

Keywords: ML and logic integration · Probabilistic reasoning · ML and constrains

1 Introduction

Artificial Intelligence (AI) approaches can be generally divided into symbolic and sub-symbolic approaches. Sub-symbolic approaches like artificial neural networks have attracted most attention of the AI community in the last few years. Indeed, sub-symbolic approaches have got a large competitive advantage from the availability of a large amount of labeled data in some applications. In these contexts, sub-symbolic approaches and, in particular, deep learning ones are effective in

This project has received funding from the European Union's Horizon 2020 research and innovation program under grant agreement No. 825619.

processing low-level perception inputs [3,18]. For instance, deep learning architectures have achieved state-of-the-art results in a wide range of tasks, e.g. speech recognition, computer vision, natural language processing, where deep learning can effectively develop feature representations and classification models at the same time.

On the other hand, symbolic reasoning [7,16,23], which is typically based on logical and probabilistic inference, allows to perform high-level reasoning (possibly under uncertainty) without having to deal with thousands of learning hyper-parameters. Even though recent work has tried to gain insight on how a deep model works [21], sub-symbolic approaches are still mostly seen as *black-boxes*, whereas symbolic approaches are generally easier to interpret, as the symbol manipulation or chain of reasoning can be unfolded to provide an understandable explanation to a human operator.

In spite of the incredible success of deep learning, many researchers have recently started to question the ability of deep learning to bring us real AI, because the amount and quality of training data would explode in order to jointly learn the high-level reasoning that is needed to perform complex tasks [2]. For example, forcing some structure to the output of a deep learner has been shown to bring benefits in image segmentation tasks, even when simple output correlations were added to the enforced contextual information [6].

Blending symbolic and sub-symbolic approaches is one of the most challenging open problem in AI and, recently, a lot of works, often referred as neuro-symbolic approaches [10], have been proposed by several authors [6,14,22,27]. In this paper, we present Deep Logic Models (DLMs), a unified framework to integrate logical reasoning and deep learning. DLMs bridge an input layer processing the sensory input patterns, like images, video, text, from a higher level which enforces some structure to the model output. Unlike in Semantic-based Regularization [8] or Logic Tensor Networks [9], the sensory and reasoning layers can be jointly trained, so that the high-level weights imposing the output structure are jointly learned together with the neural network weights, processing the low-level input. The bonding is very general as any (set of) deep learners can be integrated and any output structure can be expressed. This paper will mainly focus on expressing the high-level structure using logic formalism like first–order logic (FOL). In particular, a consistent and fully differentiable relaxation of FOL is used to map the knowledge into a set of potentials that can be used in training and inference.

The outline of the paper is the following. Section 2 presents the model and the integration of logic and learning. Section 3 compares and connects the presented work with previous work in the literature and Sect. 4 shows the experimental evaluation of the proposed ideas on various datasets. Finally, Sect. 5 draws some conclusions and highlights some planned future work.

2 Model

We indicate as θ the model parameters, and X the collection of input sensory data. Deep Logic Models (DLMs) assume that the prediction of the system is

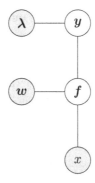

Fig. 1. The DLM graphical model assumes that the output variables y depend on the output of first stage f, processing the input X. This corresponds to the breakdown into a lower sensory layer and a high level semantic one.

constrained by the available prior knowledge. Therefore, unlike standard Neural networks which compute the output via a single forward pass, the output computation in a DLM can be decomposed into two stages: a *low-level* stage processing the input patterns, and a subsequent *semantic* stage, expressing constraints over the output and performing higher level reasoning. We indicate by $y = \{y_1, \ldots, y_n\}$ and by $f = \{f_1, \ldots, f_n\}$ the two multivariate random variables corresponding to the output of the model and to the output of the first stage respectively, where $n > 0$ denotes the dimension of the model outcomes. Assuming that the input data is processed using neural networks, the model parameters can be split into two independent components $\theta = \{w, \lambda\}$, where w is the vector of weights of the networks f_{nn} and λ is the vector of weights of the second stage, controlling the semantic layer and the constraint enforcement. Figure 1 shows the graphical dependencies among the stochastic variables that are involved in our model. The first layer processes the inputs returning the values f using a model with parameters w. The higher layer takes as input f and applies reasoning using a set of constraints, whose parameters are indicated as λ, then it returns the set of output variables y.

The Bayes rule allows to link the probability of the parameters to the posterior and prior distributions:

$$p(\theta|y, X) \propto p(y|\theta, X)p(\theta).$$

Assuming the breakdown into a sensory and a semantic level, the prior may be decomposed as $p(\theta) = p(\lambda)p(w)$, while the posterior can be computed by marginalizing over the assignments for f:

$$p(y|\theta, X) = \int_f p(y|f, \lambda) \cdot p(f|w, X)df. \tag{1}$$

A typical choice is to link $p(\boldsymbol{f}|\boldsymbol{w}, X)$ to the outputs of the neural architectures:

$$p(\boldsymbol{f}|\boldsymbol{w}, X) = \frac{1}{Z_f} \exp\left(-\frac{(\boldsymbol{f} - \boldsymbol{f}_{nn})^2}{2\sigma^2}\right),$$

where the actual (deterministic) output of the networks $\boldsymbol{f}_{nn}$ over the inputs is indicated as $\boldsymbol{f}_{nn}$ and Z_f indicates the partition function with respect to $\boldsymbol{f}$. Please note that there is a one-to-one correspondence among each element of $\boldsymbol{y}, \boldsymbol{f}$ and $\boldsymbol{f}_{nn}$, such that $|\boldsymbol{y}| = |\boldsymbol{f}| = |\boldsymbol{f}_{nn}|$.

However, the integral in Eq. (1) is too expensive to compute and, as commonly done in the deep learning community, only the actual output of the network is considered, namely:

$$p(\boldsymbol{f}|\boldsymbol{w}, X) \approx \delta(\boldsymbol{f} - \boldsymbol{f}_{nn}),$$

resulting in the following approximation of the posterior:

$$p(\boldsymbol{y}|\boldsymbol{\theta}, X) \approx p(\boldsymbol{y}|\boldsymbol{f}_{nn}, \boldsymbol{\lambda}).$$

A Deep Logic Model assumes that $p(\boldsymbol{y}|\boldsymbol{f}_{nn}, \boldsymbol{\lambda})$ is modeled via an undirected probabilistic graphical model in the exponential family, such that:

$$p(\boldsymbol{y}|\boldsymbol{f}_{nn}, \boldsymbol{\lambda}) \triangleq \frac{1}{Z_y} \exp\left(\Phi_r(\boldsymbol{y}, \boldsymbol{f}_{nn}) + \sum_c \lambda_c \Phi_c(\boldsymbol{y})\right), \qquad (2)$$

where the Φ_c are potential functions expressing some constraints on the output variables, $\boldsymbol{\lambda} = \{\lambda_1, \lambda_2, \ldots, \lambda_C\}$ are parameters controlling the confidence for the single constraints where a higher value corresponds to a stronger enforcement of the corresponding constraint, Φ_r is a potential that favors solutions where the output closely follows the predictions provided by the neural networks (for instance $\Phi_r(\boldsymbol{y}, \boldsymbol{f}_{nn}) = -\frac{1}{2}\|\boldsymbol{y} - \boldsymbol{f}_{nn}\|^2$) and Z_y is a normalization factor (i.e. the partition function with respect to the random variable $\boldsymbol{y}$):

$$Z_y = \int_{\boldsymbol{y}} \exp\left(\Phi_r(\boldsymbol{y}, \boldsymbol{f}_{nn}) + \sum_c \lambda_c \Phi_c(\boldsymbol{y})\right) d\boldsymbol{y}.$$

2.1   MAP Inference

MAP inference assumes that the model parameters are known and it aims at finding the assignment maximizing $p(\boldsymbol{y}|\boldsymbol{f}_{nn}, \boldsymbol{\lambda})$. MAP inference does not require to compute the partition function Z which acts as a constant when the weights are fixed. Therefore:

$$\boldsymbol{y}_M = \operatorname*{argmax}_{\boldsymbol{y}} \log p(\boldsymbol{y}|\boldsymbol{f}_{nn}, \boldsymbol{\lambda}) = \operatorname*{argmax}_{\boldsymbol{y}} \left[\Phi_r(\boldsymbol{y}, \boldsymbol{f}_{nn}) + \sum_c \lambda_c \Phi_c(\boldsymbol{y})\right].$$

The above maximization problem can be optimized via gradient descent by computing:

$$\nabla_{\boldsymbol{y}} \log p(\boldsymbol{y}|\boldsymbol{f}_{nn}, \boldsymbol{\lambda}) = \nabla_{\boldsymbol{y}} \Phi_r(\boldsymbol{y}, \boldsymbol{f}_{nn}) + \sum_c \lambda_c \nabla_{\boldsymbol{y}} \Phi_c(\boldsymbol{y}).$$

2.2   Learning

Training can be carried out by maximizing the likelihood of the training data:

$$\underset{\theta}{\mathrm{argmax}} \log p(\boldsymbol{\theta}|\boldsymbol{y}_t, X) = \log p(\boldsymbol{\lambda}) + \log p(\boldsymbol{w}) + \log p(\boldsymbol{y}_t|\boldsymbol{\theta}, X).$$

In particular, assuming that $p(\boldsymbol{y}_t|\boldsymbol{\theta}, X)$ follows the model defined in Eq. (2) and the parameter priors follow Gaussian distributions, yields:

$$\log p(\boldsymbol{\theta}|\boldsymbol{y}_t, X) = -\frac{\alpha}{2}||\boldsymbol{w}||^2 - \frac{\beta}{2}||\boldsymbol{\lambda}||^2 - \Phi_r(\boldsymbol{y}_t, \boldsymbol{f}_{nn}) + \sum_c \lambda_c \Phi_c(\boldsymbol{y}_t) - \log Z_y,$$

where α, β are meta-parameters determined by the variance of the selected Gaussian distributions. Also in this case the likelihood may be maximized by gradient descent using the following derivatives with respect to the model parameters:

$$\frac{\partial \log p(\boldsymbol{\theta}|\boldsymbol{y}_t, X)}{\partial \lambda_c} = -\beta\lambda_c + \Phi_c(\boldsymbol{y}_t) - E_p\left[\Phi_c\right]$$

$$\frac{\partial \log p(\boldsymbol{\theta}|\boldsymbol{y}_t, X)}{\partial w_i} = -\alpha w_i + \frac{\partial \Phi_r(\boldsymbol{y}_t, \boldsymbol{f}_{nn})}{\partial w_i} - E_p\left[\frac{\partial \Phi_r}{\partial w_i}\right]$$

Unfortunately, the direct computation of the expected values in the above derivatives is not feasible. A possible approximation [12,13] relies on replacing the expected values with the corresponding value at the MAP solution, assuming that most of the probability mass of the distribution is centered around it. This can be done directly on the above expressions for the derivatives or in the log likelihood:

$$\log p(\boldsymbol{y}_t|\boldsymbol{f}_{nn}, X) \approx \Phi_r(\boldsymbol{y}_t, \boldsymbol{f}_{nn}) - \Phi_r(\boldsymbol{y}_M, \boldsymbol{f}_{nn}) + \sum_c \lambda_c \left(\Phi_c(\boldsymbol{y}_t) - \Phi_c(\boldsymbol{y}_M)\right).$$

From the above approximation, it emerges that the likelihood tends to be maximized when the MAP solution is close to the training data, namely if $\Phi_r(\boldsymbol{y}_t, \boldsymbol{f}_{nn}) \simeq \Phi_r(\boldsymbol{y}_M, \boldsymbol{f}_{nn})$ and $\Phi_c(\boldsymbol{y}_t) \simeq \Phi_c(\boldsymbol{y}_M) \ \forall c$. Furthermore, the probability distribution is more centered around the MAP solution when $\Phi_r(\boldsymbol{y}_M, \boldsymbol{f}_{nn})$ is close to its maximum value. We assume that Φ_r is negative and have zero as upper bound: $\Phi_r(\boldsymbol{y}, \boldsymbol{f}_{nn}) \leq 0 \ \forall \boldsymbol{y}, \boldsymbol{f}_{nn}$, like it holds for example for the already mentioned negative quadratic potential $\Phi_r(\boldsymbol{y}, \boldsymbol{f}_{nn}) = -\frac{1}{2}||\boldsymbol{y} - \boldsymbol{f}_{nn}||^2$. Therefore, the constraint $\Phi_r(\boldsymbol{y}_t, \boldsymbol{f}_{nn}) \simeq \Phi_r(\boldsymbol{y}_M, \boldsymbol{f}_{nn})$ is transformed into the two separate constraints $\Phi_r(\boldsymbol{y}_t, \boldsymbol{f}_{nn}) \simeq 0$ and $\Phi_r(\boldsymbol{y}_M, \boldsymbol{f}_{nn}) \simeq 0$.

Therefore, given the current MAP solution, it is possible to increase the log likelihood by locally maximizing (one gradient computation and weight update) of the following cost functional: $\log p(\boldsymbol{w}) + \log p(\boldsymbol{\lambda}) + \Phi_r(\boldsymbol{y}_t, \boldsymbol{f}_{nn}) + \Phi_r(\boldsymbol{y}_M, \boldsymbol{f}_{nn}) + \sum_c \lambda_c [\Phi_c(\boldsymbol{y}_t) - \Phi_c(\boldsymbol{y}_M)]$. In this paper, a quadratic form for the priors and the potentials is selected, but other choices are possible. For example, $\Phi_r(\cdot)$ could instead be implemented as a negative cross entropy loss. Therefore, replacing the selected forms for the potentials and changing the sign to transform

Data: Input data X, output targets $\boldsymbol{y}_t$, function models with weights $\boldsymbol{w}$
Result: Trained model parameters $\boldsymbol{\theta} = \{\boldsymbol{\lambda}, \boldsymbol{w}\}$
Initialize $i = 0$, $\boldsymbol{\lambda} = \boldsymbol{0}$, random $\boldsymbol{w}$;
while *not converged* $\wedge$ $i < max\_iterations$ **do**
 | Compute function outputs $\boldsymbol{f}_{nn}$ on X using current function weights $\boldsymbol{w}$;
 | Compute MAP solution $\boldsymbol{y}_M = \mathrm{argmax}_y \log p(\boldsymbol{y}|\boldsymbol{f}_{nn}, \boldsymbol{\lambda})$;
 | Compute gradient $\nabla_\theta C_\theta(\boldsymbol{y}_t, \boldsymbol{y}_M, X)$;
 | Update $\boldsymbol{\theta}$ via gradient descent: $\boldsymbol{\theta}_{i+1} = \boldsymbol{\theta}_i - \lambda_{lr} \cdot \nabla_\theta C_\theta(\boldsymbol{y}_t, \boldsymbol{y}_M, X)$;
 | Set $i = i + 1$;
end

Algorithm 1. Iterative algorithm to train the function weights $\boldsymbol{w}$ and the constraint weights $\boldsymbol{\lambda}$.

a maximization into a minimization problem, yields the following cost function, given the current MAP solution:

$$C_\theta(\boldsymbol{y}_t, \boldsymbol{y}_M, X) = \frac{\alpha}{2}||\boldsymbol{w}||^2 + \frac{\beta}{2}||\boldsymbol{\lambda}||^2 + \frac{1}{2}||\boldsymbol{y}_t - \boldsymbol{f}_{nn}||^2$$
$$+ \frac{1}{2}||\boldsymbol{y}_M - \boldsymbol{f}_{nn}||^2 + \sum_c \lambda_c \left[\Phi_c(\boldsymbol{y}_t) - \Phi_c(\boldsymbol{y}_M)\right].$$

Minimizing $C_\theta(\boldsymbol{y}_t, \boldsymbol{y}_M, X)$ is a local approximation of the full likelihood maximization for the current MAP solution. Therefore, the training process alternates the computation of the MAP solution, the computation of the gradient for $C_\theta(\boldsymbol{y}_t, \boldsymbol{y}_M, X)$ and one weight update step as summarized by Algorithm 1. For any constraint c, the parameter λ_c admits also a negative value. This is in case the c-th constraint turns out to be also satisfied by the actual MAP solution with respect to the satisfaction degree on the training data.

2.3   Mapping Constraints into a Continuous Logic

The DLM model is absolutely general in terms of the constraints that can be expressed on the outputs. However, this paper mainly focuses on constraints expressed in the output space $\boldsymbol{y}$ by means of first–order logic formulas. Therefore, this section focuses on defining a methodology to integrate prior knowledge expressed via FOL into a continuous optimization process.

In this framework we only deal with closed FOL formulas, namely formulas where any variable occurring in predicates is quantified. In the following, given an m-ary predicate p and a tuple $(a_1, \ldots, a_m) \in Dom(p)$, we say that $p(a_1, \ldots, a_m) \in [0, 1]$ is a *grounding* of p. Given a grounding of the variables occurring in a FOL formula (namely a grounding for all the predicates involved in the formula), the truth degree of the formula for that grounding is computed using the t-norm fuzzy logic theory as proposed in [24]. The overall degree of satisfaction of a FOL formula is obtained by grounding all the variables in such formula and aggregating the values with different operators depending on the occurring quantifiers. The details of this process are explained in the following section.

Table 1. The operations performed by the single units of an expression tree depending on the inputs a, b and the used t-norm.

Operation	t-norm		
	Gödel	Product	Łukasiewicz
$a \wedge b$	$\min(a, b)$	$a \cdot b$	$\max(0, a + b - 1)$
$a \vee b$	$\max(a, b)$	$a + b - a \cdot b$	$\min(1, a + b)$
$\neg a$	$1 - a$	$1 - a$	$1 - a$
$a \Rightarrow b$	$a \leq b ? 1 : b$	$\min(1, \frac{b}{a})$	$\min(1, 1 - a + b)$

Grounded Expressions. Any fully grounded FOL rule corresponds to an expression in propositional logic and we start showing how a propositional logic expression may be converted into a differentiable form. In particular, one expression tree is built for each considered grounded FOL rule, where any occurrence of the basic logic connectives ($\neg, \wedge, \vee, \Rightarrow$) is replaced by a unit computing its corresponding fuzzy logic operation according to a certain logic semantics. In this regard, some recent work shows how to get convex (or even linear) functional constraints exploiting the convex Łukasiewicz fragment [11]. The expression tree can take as input the output values of the grounded predicates and then recursively compute the output values of all the nodes in the expression tree. The value obtained on the root node is the result of the evaluation of the expression given the input grounded predicates.

Table 1 shows the algebraic operations corresponding to the logic operators for different selections of the t-norms. Please note that the logic operators are always monotonic with respect any single variable, but they are not always differentiable (nor even continuous). However, the sub-space where the operators are non-differentiable has null-Lebesgue measure, therefore they do not pose any practical issue, when used as part of a gradient descent optimization schema as detailed in the following.

We assume that the input data X can be divided into a set of sub-domains $X = \{X_1, X_2, \ldots\}$, such that each variable v_i of a FOL formula ranges over the data of one input domain, namely $v_i \in X_{d_i}$, where d_i is the index of the domain for the variable v_i.

For example, let us consider the rule $\forall v_1 \forall v_2 \ \neg A(v_1, v_2) \wedge B(v_1)$. For any assignment to v_1 and v_2, the expression tree returns the output value $[1 - A(v_1, v_2)] \cdot B(v_1)$, assuming to exploit the product t-norm to convert the connectives.

Quantifiers. The truth degree of a formula containing an expression with a universally quantified variable v_i is computed as the average of the t-norm truth degree of the expression, when grounding v_i over its domain. The truth degree of the existential quantifier is the *maximum* of the t-norm expression grounded over the domain of the quantified variable. When multiple quantified variables are present, the conversion is performed from the outer to the inner variable.

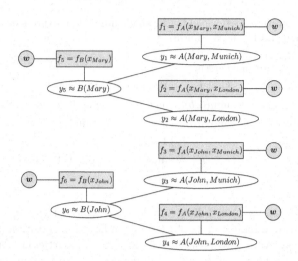

Fig. 2. The undirected graphical model built by a DLM for the rule $\forall v_1 \forall v_2 \; \neg A(v_1, v_2) \wedge B(v_1)$ where v_1 can assume values over the constants $\{Mary, John\}$ and v_2 over $\{Munich, London\}$. Each stochastic node y_i approximates one grounded predicate, while the f_i nodes are the actual output of a network getting the pattern representations of a grounding. Connections of all latent nodes y_i to the parameters λ have been omitted to keep the picture readable.

When only universal quantifiers are present the aggregation is equivalent to the overall average over each grounding.

In the previous example, this yields the expression:

$$\Phi(X, A, B) = \frac{1}{|X_{d_1}||X_{d_2}|} \sum_{v_1 \in X_{d_1}} \sum_{v_2 \in X_{d_2}} [1 - A(v_1, v_2)] \cdot B(v_1). \tag{3}$$

2.4   Potentials Expressing the Logic Knowledge

It is now possible to explain how to build the potentials from the prior knowledge. In any learning task, each unknown grounded predicate corresponds to one variable in the vector $\boldsymbol{y}$. In the above example, the number of groundings is $|X_{d_1}| \times |X_{d_2}|$ (i.e. the size of the Cartesian product of the domains of A) and $|X_{d_1}|$ (i.e. the size of the domain of B). Assuming that both predicates A, B are unknown, $|\boldsymbol{y}| = |\boldsymbol{f}| = |X_{d_1}| \times |X_{d_2}| + |X_{d_1}|$. The vector $\boldsymbol{f}_{nn}$ is built by replacing each predicate with its NN implementation and then by considering the function outputs for each grounding in the vector. For the example:

$$\boldsymbol{f}_{nn} = \{f_A(v_{11}, v_{21}), \dots, f_A(v_{1|X_{d_1}|}, v_{2|X_{d_2}|}), \; f_B(v_{11}), \dots, f_B(v_{1|d_2|})\},$$

where v_{ij} is the j-th grounding for the i-th variable and f_A, f_B are the learned neural approximations of A and B, respectively. Finally, the differentiable potential for the example formula is obtained by replacing in Eq. (3) each grounded predicate with the corresponding stochastic variable in $\boldsymbol{y}$.

Figure 2 shows the undirected graphical model corresponding to the DLM for the running example rule used in this section, assuming that v_1 can assume values over the constants $\{Mary, John\}$ and v_2 over $\{Munich, London\}$. Each stochastic node y_i approximates one grounded predicate, while the f_i nodes are the actual output of a neural network getting as input the pattern representations of the corresponding grounding. The vertical connections between two y_i and f_i nodes correspond to the cliques over the groundings for which the Φ_r potential can be decomposed. The links between the y_i nodes corresponds to the cliques over the groundings of the rule for which the corresponding Φ_c potential can be decomposed. The structure of these latter cliques follows a template determined by the rule, that is repeated for the single groundings. The graphical model is similar to the ones built by Probabilistic Soft Logic [1] or Markov Logic Networks [26], but enriched with the nodes corresponding to the output of the neural networks.

3   Related Works

DLMs have their roots in Probabilistic Soft Logic (PSL) [1], a probabilistic logic using an undirected graphical model to represent a grounded FOL knowledge base, and employing a similar differentiable approximation of FOL and allows to learn the weight of each formula in the KB by maximizing the log likelihood of the training data like done in DLMs. PSL restricts the logic that can be processed to a fragment of FOL corresponding to convex constraints. Furthermore, the rule weights are restricted to only positive values denoting how far the rule is from being satisfied. On the other hand, rule weights denote the needed constraint reactions to match the degree satisfaction of the training data in DLMs, therefore they can assume negative weights. In addition, unlike DLMs, PSL focuses on logic reasoning without any integration with deep learners, beside a simple stacking with no joint training.

The integration of learning from data and symbolic reasoning [10] has recently attracted a lot of attention. Many works in this area have emerged like Hu et al. [15], Semantic-based regularization (SBR) [8] applying these idea to kernel machines and Logic Tensor Networks (LTN) [9] which work on neural networks. All these works share the same basic idea of integrating logic reasoning and learning using a similar continuous relaxation of logic to the one presented in this paper. However, this class of approaches considers the reasoning layer as frozen, without allowing to jointly train its parameters. This is a big limitation, as these methods work better only with hard constraints, while they are less suitable in presence of reasoning under uncertainty.

DeepProbLog [22] extends the popular ProbLog [7] probabilistic programming framework with the integration of deep learners. DeepProbLog requires the output from the neural networks to be probabilities and an independence assumption among atoms in the logic is required to make inference tractable. This is a strong restriction, since the sub-symbolic layer often consists of several neural layers sharing weights.

A Neural Theorem Prover (NTP) [27,28] is an end-to-end differentiable prover based on the Prolog's backward chaining algorithm. An NTP constructs an end-to-end differentiable architecture capable of proving queries to a KB using sub-symbolic vector representations. NTPs have been proven to be effective in tasks like entity linking and knowledge base completion. However, an NTP encodes relations as vectors using a frozen pre-selected function (like cosine similarity). This can be ineffective in modeling relations with a complex and multifaceted nature (for example a relation `friend(A, B)` can be triggered by different relationships of the representations in the embedding space). On the other hand, DLMs allow a relation to be encoded by any selected function (e.g. any deep neural networks), which is co-trained during learning. Therefore, DLMs are capable of a more powerful and flexible exploitation of the representation space. However, DLMs require to fully ground a KB (like SBR, LTN, PSL and most of other methods discussed here), while NTPs expands only the groundings on the explored frontier, which can be more efficient in some cases.

The integration of deep learning with Conditional Random Fields (CRFs) [20] is also an alternative approach to enforce some structure on the network output. This approach has been proved to be quite successful on sequence labeling for natural language processing tasks. This methodology can be seen as a special case of the more general methodology presented in this paper, when the potential functions are used to represent the correlations among consecutive outputs of a recurrent deep network.

Deep Structured Models [6,19] use a similar graphical model to bridge the sensory and semantic levels. However, they have mainly focused on imposing correlations on the output layer, without any focus on logic reasoning. Furthermore, DLMs transform the training process into an iterative constrained optimization problem, which is very different from the approximation of the partition function used in Deep Structured Models.

DLMs also open up the possibility to iteratively integrate rule induction mechanisms like the ones proposed by the Inductive Logic Programming community [17,25].

4   Experimental Results

4.1   The PAIRS Artificial Dataset

Consider the following artificial task. We are provided with 1000 pairs of handwritten digits images sampled from the MNIST dataset. The pairs are not constructed randomly but they are compiled according to the following structure:

1. pairs with mixed even-odd digits are not allowed;
2. the first image of a pair represents a digit randomly selected from a uniform distribution;
3. if the first image is an even (resp. odd) digit, the second image of a pair represents one of the five even (resp. odd) digits with probabilities $p_1 \geq p_2 \geq p_3 \geq p_4 \geq p_5$, with p_1 the probability of being an image of the same digit, p_2 the probability of being an image of the next even/odd digit, and so on.

For example, if the first image of a pair is selected to be a *two*, the second image will be a *two* with probability p_1, it will be a *four* with probability p_2, a *six* with probability p_3 and so on, in a circular fashion. An example is shown in Fig. 3. A correct classification happens when both digit in a pair are correctly predicted.

Fig. 3. A sample of the data used in the PAIRS experiment, where each column is a pair of digits.

To model a task using DLMs there are some common design choices regarding these two features that one needs to take. We use the current example to show them. The first choice is to individuate the *constants* of the problem and their sensory representation in the perceptual space. Depending on the problem, the constants can live in a single or multiple separate domains. In the pairs example, the images are constants and each one is represented as a vector of pixel brightnesses like commonly done in deep learning.

The second choice is the selection of the *predicates* that should predict some characteristic over the constants and their implementation. In the pairs experiment, the predicates are the membership functions for single digits (e.g. one(x), two(x), etc.). A single neural network with 1 hidden layer, 10 hidden neurons and 10 outputs, each one mapped to a predicate, was used in this toy experiment. The choice of a small neural network is due to the fact that the goal is not to get the best possible results, but to show how the prior knowledge can help a classifier to improve its decision. In more complex experiments, different networks can be used for different sets of predicates, or each use a separate network for each predicate.

Finally, the *prior knowledge* is selected. In the pairs dataset, where the constants are grouped in pairs, it is natural to express the correlations among two images in a pair via the prior knowledge. Therefore, the knowledge consists of 100 rules in the form $\forall(x, y) \ D_1(x) \rightarrow D_2(y)$, where (x, y) is a generic pair of images and (D_1, D_2) range over all the possible pairs of digit classes.

We performed the experiments with $p_1 = 0.9, p_2 = 0.07, p_3 = p_4 = p_5 = 0.01$. All the images are rotated with a random degree between 0 and 90 anti-clockwise to increase the complexity of the task. There is a strong regularity in having two images representing the same digit in a pair, even some rare deviations from this rule are possible. Moreover, there are some inadmissible pairs, i.e. those containing mixed even-odd digits. The train and test sets are built by sampling 90% and 10% image pairs.

The results provided using a DLM have been compared against the following baselines:

- the same neural network (NN) used by DLM but with no knowledge of the structure of the problem;

Table 2. Comparison of the accuracy metric on the PAIRS dataset using different models.

Model	NN	SBR	DLM-NN	DLM
Accuracy	0.62	0.64	0.65	0.76

- Semantic Based Regularization/Logic Tensor Networks (SBR/LTN), which are equivalent on this specific task. These frameworks employ the logical rules to improve the learner but the rule weights are fixed parameters, which are not jointly trained during learning. Since searching in the space of these parameters via cross-validation is not feasible, a strong prior was provided to make SBR/LTN prefers pairs with the same image using 10 rules of the form $\forall(x, y)\ D(x) \rightarrow D(y)$, for each digit class D. These rules hold true in most cases and improve the baseline performance of the network.

Table 2 shows how the neural network output of a DLM (DLM-NN) already beats both the same neural model trained without prior knowledge and SBR. This happens because the neural network in DLM is indirectly adjusted to respect the prior knowledge in the overall optimization problem. When reading the DLM output from the MAP solution (DLM), the results are significantly improved.

4.2 Link Prediction in Knowledge Graphs

Neural-symbolic approaches have been proved to be very powerful to perform approximated logical reasoning [29]. A common approach is to assign to each logical constant and relation a learned vectorial representation [4]. Approximate reasoning is then carried out in this embedded space. Link Prediction in Knowledge Graphs is a generic reasoning task where it is requested to establish the links of the graph between semantic entities acting as constants. Rocktaschel et al. [28] shows state-of-the-art performances on some link prediction benchmarks by combining Prolog backward chain with a soft unification scheme.

This section shows how to model a link prediction task on the *Countries* dataset using a Deep Logic Models, and compare this proposed solution to the other state-of-the-art approaches.

Dataset. The Countries dataset [5] consists of 244 countries (e.g. germany), 5 regions (e.g. europe), 23 sub-regions (e.g. western europe, northern america, etc.), which act as the constants of the KB. Two types of binary relations among the constant are present in the dataset: $\texttt{locatedIn}(c_1, c_2)$, expressing that c_1 is part of c_2 and $\texttt{neighborOf}(c_1, c_2)$, expressing that c_1 neighbors with c_2. The knowledge base consists of 1158 facts about the countries, regions and sub-regions, expressed in the form of Prolog facts (e.g. $\texttt{locatedIn}$(italy,europe)). The training, validation and test sets are composed by 204, 20 and 20 countries, respectively, such that each country in the validation and test sets has at least one neighbor in the training set. Three different tasks have been proposed for this dataset with an increasing level of difficulty. For all tasks, the goal is to predict the relation locatedIn(c, r) for every test country c and all five regions r, but the access to training atoms in the KB varies, as explained in the following:

- Task S1: all ground atoms locatedIn(c, r), where c is a test country and r is a region, are removed from the KB. Since information about the sub-region of test countries is still contained in the KB, this task can be solved exactly by learning the transitivity of the locatedIn relation.
- Task S2: like S1 but all grounded atoms locatedIn(c, s), where c is a test country and s is a sub-region, are removed. The location of test countries needs to be inferred from the location of its neighbors. This task is more difficult than S1, as neighboring countries might not be in the same region.
- Task S3: like S2, but all ground atoms locatedIn(c, r), where r is a region and c is a training country with either a test or validation country as a neighbor, are removed. This task requires multiple reasoning steps to determine an unknown link, and it strongly exploits the sub-symbolic reasoning capability of the model to be effectively solved.

Model. Each country, region and sub-region corresponds to a constant. Since the constants are just symbols, each one is assigned to an embedding, which is learned together with the other parameters of the model. The predicates are the binary relations locatedIn and neighborOf, which connect constants in the KB. Each relation is learned via a separate neural network with a 50 neuron hidden layer taking as input the concatenation of the embeddings of the constants. In particular, similarly to [4], the constants are encoded into a one-hot vector, which is processed by the first layer of the network, outputting an embedding composed by 50 real number values. As commonly done in link prediction tasks, the learning process is performed in a transductive mode. In particular, the input X consists of all possible constants for the task, while the train examples y_t will cover only a subset of all the possible grounded predicates, leaving to the joint train and inference process the generalization of the prediction to the other unknown grounded relations. Indeed, the output of the train process in this case is both the set of model parameters and the MAP solution predicting the unknown grounded relations that hold true.

Multi-step dependencies among the constants are very important to predict the existence of a link in this task. For example in task S1, the prediction of a link among a country and a region can be established via the path passing by a sub-region, once the model learns a rule stating the transitivity of the locatedIn relation (i.e. locatedIn(x, y) $\land$ locatedIn(y, z) $\rightarrow$ locatedIn(x, z)). Exploiting instead the rule neighborOf(x, y) $\land$ locatedIn(y, z) $\rightarrow$ locatedIn(x, z), the model should be capable of approximately solving task S2.

Table 3. Comparison of the accuracy provided by different methods on link prediction on the Countries dataset. Bold numbers are the best performers for each task.

Task	ComplEx	NTP	NTPλ	DLM
S1	99.37	90.83	**100.00**	**100.00**
S2	87.95	87.40	93.04	**97.79**
S3	48.44	56.68	77.26	**91.93**

All 8 rules $\forall x \; \forall y \; \forall z \; A(x,y) \wedge B(y,z) \rightarrow C(y,z)$, where A, B and C are either neighborOf or locatedIn are added to the knowledge base for this experiment. These rules represent all the 2-steps paths reasoning that can be encoded, and the strength of each rule needs to be estimated as part of the learning process for each task. The training process will iteratively minimize Eq. 3 by jointly determining the embeddings and the network weights such that network outputs and the MAP solution will correctly predict the training data, while respecting the constraints on the MAP solution at the same level as on the train data.

Results. Table 3 compares DLM against the state-of-the-art methods used by Rocktaschel et al. [28], namely ComplEx, NTP and NTPλ. Task S1 is the only one that can be solved exactly when the transitive property of the locatedIn relation has been learned to always hold true. Indeed, most methods are able to perfectly solve this task, except for the plain NTP model. DLM is capable perfectly solving this task by joining the logical reasoning capabilities with the discriminative power of neural networks. DLMs perform better than the competitors on tasks S2 and S3, thanks to additional flexibility obtained by jointly training the relation functions using neural networks, unlike the simple vectorial operations like the cosine similarity employed by the competitors.

5   Conclusions and Future Work

This paper presents Deep Logic Models that integrate (deep) learning and logic reasoning into a single fully differentiable architecture. The logic can be expressed with unrestricted FOL formalism, where each FOL rule is converted into a differentiable potential function, which can be integrated into the learning process. The main advantage of the presented framework is the ability to fully integrate learning from low-level representations and semantic high-level reasoning over the network outputs. Allowing to jointly learn the weights of the deep learners and the parameters controlling the reasoning enables a positive feedback loop, which is shown to improve the accuracy of both layers. Future work will try to bridge the gap between fully grounded methodologies like current Deep Logic Models and Theorem Provers which expand only the groundings needed to expand the frontier of the search space.

References

1. Bach, S.H., Broecheler, M., Huang, B., Getoor, L.: Hinge-loss Markov random fields and probabilistic soft logic. arXiv preprint arXiv:1505.04406 (2015)
2. Battaglia, P.W., et al.: Relational inductive biases, deep learning, and graph networks. arXiv preprint arXiv:1806.01261 (2018)
3. Bengio, Y., et al.: Learning deep architectures for AI. Found. Trends® Mach. Learn. **2**(1), 1–127 (2009)
4. Bordes, A., Usunier, N., Garcia-Duran, A., Weston, J., Yakhnenko, O.: Translating embeddings for modeling multi-relational data. In: Advances in Neural Information Processing Systems, pp. 2787–2795 (2013)
5. Bouchard, G., Singh, S., Trouillon, T.: On approximate reasoning capabilities of low-rank vector spaces. In: Integrating Symbolic and Neural Approaches, AAAI Spring Symposium on Knowledge Representation and Reasoning (KRR) (2015)
6. Chen, L.C., Schwing, A., Yuille, A., Urtasun, R.: Learning deep structured models. In: International Conference on Machine Learning, pp. 1785–1794 (2015)
7. De Raedt, L., Kimmig, A., Toivonen, H.: Problog: a probabilistic prolog and its application in link discovery. In: Proceedings of the 20th International Joint Conference on Artificial Intelligence, IJCAI 2007, pp. 2468–2473. Morgan Kaufmann Publishers Inc., San Francisco (2007). http://dl.acm.org/citation.cfm?id=1625275.1625673
8. Diligenti, M., Gori, M., Sacca, C.: Semantic-based regularization for learning and inference. Artif. Intell. **244**, 143–165 (2017)
9. Donadello, I., Serafini, L., Garcez, A.D.: Logic tensor networks for semantic image interpretation. arXiv preprint arXiv:1705.08968 (2017)
10. Garcez, A.S.D., Broda, K.B., Gabbay, D.M.: Neural-Symbolic Learning Systems: Foundations and Applications. Springer, Cham (2012). https://doi.org/10.1007/978-1-4471-0211-3
11. Giannini, F., Diligenti, M., Gori, M., Maggini, M.: On a convex logic fragment for learning and reasoning. IEEE Trans. Fuzzy Syst. **27**(7), 1407–1416 (2018)
12. Goodfellow, I., Bengio, Y., Courville, A., Bengio, Y.: Deep Learning, vol. 1. MIT Press, Cambridge (2016)
13. Haykin, S.: Neural Networks: A Comprehensive Foundation, 1st edn. Prentice Hall PTR, Upper Saddle River (1994)
14. Hazan, T., Schwing, A.G., Urtasun, R.: Blending learning and inference in conditional random fields. J. Mach. Learn. Res. **17**(1), 8305–8329 (2016)
15. Hu, Z., Ma, X., Liu, Z., Hovy, E., Xing, E.: Harnessing deep neural networks with logic rules. arXiv preprint arXiv:1603.06318 (2016)
16. Kimmig, A., Bach, S., Broecheler, M., Huang, B., Getoor, L.: A short introduction to probabilistic soft logic. In: Proceedings of the NIPS Workshop on Probabilistic Programming: Foundations and Applications, pp. 1–4 (2012)
17. Lavrac, N., Dzeroski, S.: Inductive logic programming. In: WLP, pp. 146–160. Springer, Heidelberg (1994). https://doi.org/10.1007/978-0-387-30164-8
18. LeCun, Y., Bottou, L., Bengio, Y., Haffner, P.: Gradient-based learning applied to document recognition. Proc. IEEE **86**(11), 2278–2324 (1998)
19. Lin, G., Shen, C., Van Den Hengel, A., Reid, I.: Efficient piecewise training of deep structured models for semantic segmentation. In: Proceedings of the IEEE Conference on Computer Vision and Pattern Recognition, pp. 3194–3203 (2016)

20. Ma, X., Hovy, E.: End-to-end sequence labeling via bi-directional LSTM-CNNS-CRF. In: Proceedings of the 54th Annual Meeting of the Association for Computational Linguistics, Long Papers, vol. 1, pp. 1064–1074. Association for Computational Linguistics (2016). https://doi.org/10.18653/v1/P16-1101. http://aclweb.org/anthology/P16-1101

21. Mahendran, A., Vedaldi, A.: Understanding deep image representations by inverting them. In: Proceedings of the IEEE Conference on Computer Vision and Pattern Recognition, pp. 5188–5196 (2015)

22. Manhaeve, R., Dumančić, S., Kimmig, A., Demeester, T., De Raedt, L.: Deep-ProbLog: neural probabilistic logic programming. arXiv preprint arXiv:1805.10872 (2018)

23. Muggleton, S., De Raedt, L.: Inductive logic programming: theory and methods. J. Logic Program. **19**, 629–679 (1994)

24. Novák, V., Perfilieva, I., Mockor, J.: Mathematical Principles of Fuzzy Logic, vol. 517. Springer, Cham (2012). https://doi.org/10.1007/978-1-4615-5217-8

25. Quinlan, J.R.: Learning logical definitions from relations. Mach. Learn. **5**(3), 239–266 (1990)

26. Richardson, M., Domingos, P.: Markov logic networks. Mach. Learn. **62**(1–2), 107–136 (2006)

27. Rocktäschel, T., Riedel, S.: Learning knowledge base inference with neural theorem provers. In: Proceedings of the 5th Workshop on Automated Knowledge Base Construction, pp. 45–50 (2016)

28. Rocktäschel, T., Riedel, S.: End-to-end differentiable proving. In: Advances in Neural Information Processing Systems, pp. 3788–3800 (2017)

29. Trouillon, T., Welbl, J., Riedel, S., Gaussier, É., Bouchard, G.: Complex embeddings for simple link prediction. In: International Conference on Machine Learning, pp. 2071–2080 (2016)

Neural Control Variates for Monte Carlo Variance Reduction

Ruosi Wan[1], Mingjun Zhong[2], Haoyi Xiong[3], and Zhanxing Zhu[1,4,5(✉)]

[1] Center for Data Science, Peking University, Beijing, China
{ruoswan,zhanxing.zhu}@pku.edu.cn
[2] School of Computer Science, University of Lincoln, Lincoln, UK
mzhong@lincoln.ac.uk
[3] Big Data Lab, Baidu Inc., Beijing, China
xionghaoyi@baidu.com
[4] School of Mathematical Sciences, Peking University, Beijing, China
[5] Beijing Institute of Big Data Research, Beijing, China

Abstract. In statistics and machine learning, approximation of an intractable integration is often achieved by using the unbiased Monte Carlo estimator, but the variances of the estimation are generally high in many applications. Control variates approaches are well-known to reduce the variance of the estimation. These control variates are typically constructed by employing predefined parametric functions or polynomials, determined by using those samples drawn from the relevant distributions. Instead, we propose to construct those control variates by learning neural networks to handle the cases when test functions are complex. In many applications, obtaining a large number of samples for Monte Carlo estimation is expensive, the adoption of the original loss function may result in severe overfitting when training a neural network. This issue was not reported in those literature on control variates with neural networks. We thus further introduce a constrained control variates with neural networks to alleviate the overfitting issue. We apply the proposed control variates to both toy and real data problems, including a synthetic data problem, Bayesian model evidence evaluation and Bayesian neural networks. Experimental results demonstrate that our method can achieve significant variance reduction compared to other methods.

Keywords: Control variates · Neural networks · Variance reduction · Monte Carlo method

1 Introduction

Most of modern machine learning and statistical approaches focus on modelling complex data, where manipulating high-dimensional and multi-modal probability distributions is of great importance for model inference and learning. Under this circumstance, evaluating the expectation of certain function $f(\boldsymbol{\theta})$ with respect to a probability distribution $p(\boldsymbol{\theta})$ is ubiquitous,

© Springer Nature Switzerland AG 2020
U. Brefeld et al. (Eds.): ECML PKDD 2019, LNAI 11907, pp. 533–547, 2020.
https://doi.org/10.1007/978-3-030-46147-8_32

$$\mu = \mathbb{E}_{\boldsymbol{\theta} \sim p(\boldsymbol{\theta})}[f(\boldsymbol{\theta})] = \int f(\boldsymbol{\theta})p(\boldsymbol{\theta})d\boldsymbol{\theta}, \tag{1}$$

where the random variable of interest $\boldsymbol{\theta} \in \mathbb{R}^D$ is typically high-dimensional.

However, in complex models, the integration is often analytically intractable. This drives the development of sophisticated Monte Carlo methods to facilitate efficient computation [15]. The Monte Carlo method is naturally employed to approximate the expectation, i.e.,

$$\mu \approx \frac{1}{n} \sum_{i=1}^{n} f(\boldsymbol{\theta}_i), \tag{2}$$

where $\{\boldsymbol{\theta}_i\}_{i=1}^n$ are samples drawn from the distribution $p(\boldsymbol{\theta})$. According to the central limit theorem, this estimator converges to μ at the rate $O(1/\sqrt{n})$. For high-dimensional and complex models, *when $p(\boldsymbol{\theta})$ is difficult to sample from* [11] or *the test function f is expensive to evaluate* [5], a "large-n" estimation is computationally prohibited. This directly leads to a high-variance estimator. Therefore, with a limited number of samples, how to reduce the variance of Monte Carlo estimations emerges as an essential issue for its practical use.

Along this line, various variance reduction methods have been introduced in the literature of statistics and numerical analysis. One category aims to develop appropriate samplers for variance reduction, including importance sampling and its variants [2], stratified sampling techniques [16], multi-level Monte Carlo [4] and other sophisticated methods based on Markov chain Monte Carlo (MCMC) [15]. Another category of variance reduction methods is called control variates [1,8,10,13,14,18]. These methods take advantage of random variables with known expectation values, which are negatively correlated with the test function under consideration. Control variates techniques can fully employ the available samples to reduce the variance, which is popular due to its efficiency and effectiveness.

However, existing control variates approaches have several limitations. Firstly, most existing methods use a linear or quadratic form to represent the control function [10,14]. Although these control functions have closed forms, the representation power of them is very limited particularly when the test function $f(\boldsymbol{\theta})$ is complex and non-linear. Control functionals were proposed recently to tackle this problem [13]. However, these estimators may significantly suffer from a curse of dimensionality [12]. Secondly, when the available samples are scarce, optimizing the control variates only based on a small, number of samples might overfit, which means that it is difficult to generalize on the samples obtained later. These restrictions limit their practical performance.

In order to overcome the first issue, some works [8,18] employed neural networks to represent the control variates, utilizing the capability of a neural network to represent a complex test function. We name these methods as "Neural Control Variates" (**NCV**). Unfortunately, in the scenario of learning neural networks, applying the commonly used loss function to reduce variance causes severe overfitting issue, particularly when available training sample size is small.

Therefore, we introduce "Constrained Neural Control Variates" (**CNCV**) which makes constraints on the control variates for alleviating the over-fitting issue. Our method is particularly suitable for the cases when the sample space is high-dimensional or the samples from $p(\boldsymbol{\theta})$ is hard to obtain. We demonstrate the effectiveness of our approach on both synthetic and real machine learning tasks, including (1) expectation of a complex function under the mixture of Gaussian distributions, (2) Bayesian model evidence evaluation and (3) Bayesian neural networks. We show that CNCV achieved the best performance comparing to the state-of-the-art methods in literature.

2 Control Variates

The generic control variates aims to estimate the expectation $\mu = \mathbb{E}_{p(\boldsymbol{\theta})}[f(\boldsymbol{\theta})]$ with reduced variance. The principle behind the control variates relies on constructing an auxiliary function $\tilde{f}(\boldsymbol{\theta}) = f(\boldsymbol{\theta}) + g(\boldsymbol{\theta})$ such that

$$\mathbb{E}_{p(\boldsymbol{\theta})}[g(\boldsymbol{\theta})] = 0. \tag{3}$$

Thus the desired expectation can be replaced by that of the auxiliary function

$$\mu = \mathbb{E}_{p(\boldsymbol{\theta})}[f(\boldsymbol{\theta})] = \mathbb{E}_{p(\boldsymbol{\theta})}[\tilde{f}(\boldsymbol{\theta})]. \tag{4}$$

It is possible to obtain a variance-reduced Monte Carlo estimator by *selecting or optimizing* $g(\boldsymbol{\theta})$ so that the variance $\mathbb{V}_{p(\boldsymbol{\theta})}[\tilde{f}(\boldsymbol{\theta})] < \mathbb{V}_{p(\boldsymbol{\theta})}[f(\boldsymbol{\theta})]$. Intuitively, variance reduction can be achieved when $g(\boldsymbol{\theta})$ is negatively correlated with $f(\boldsymbol{\theta})$ under $p(\boldsymbol{\theta})$, since much of the randomness "cancels out" in the auxiliary function $\tilde{f}(\boldsymbol{\theta})$.

The selection of an appropriate form of control function $g(\boldsymbol{\theta})$ is crucial for the performance of variance reduction. A tractable class of so called zero-variance control variates was proposed in [1,10]. Those control variates are expressed as a function of the gradient of the log-density, $\nabla_{\theta} \log p(\boldsymbol{\theta})$, i.e. the score function $\boldsymbol{s}(\boldsymbol{\theta})$. Concretely, it has the following form

$$g(\boldsymbol{\theta}) = \Delta_{\boldsymbol{\theta}} Q(\boldsymbol{\theta}) + \nabla_{\boldsymbol{\theta}} Q(\boldsymbol{\theta}) \cdot \nabla_{\boldsymbol{\theta}} \log(p(\boldsymbol{\theta})), \tag{5}$$

where the gradient operator $\nabla_{\boldsymbol{\theta}} = [\partial/\partial\theta_1, \ldots, \partial/\partial\theta_D]^T$, the Laplace operator $\Delta_{\boldsymbol{\theta}} = \sum_{i=1}^{D} \partial^2/\partial\theta_i^2$, and "$\cdot$" denotes the inner product. The function $Q(\boldsymbol{\theta})$ is often referred to as the trial function. The target is now to find a trial function so that $g(\boldsymbol{\theta})$ and $f(\boldsymbol{\theta})$ are negatively correlated. This could thus reduce the variance of the Monte Carlo estimation. As the trial function could be arbitrary under those mild conditions given in [10], a parametric function could be used for $Q(\boldsymbol{\theta})$. For example, when $Q(\boldsymbol{\theta}) = \boldsymbol{a}^T\boldsymbol{\theta}$, which is a first degree polynomial function, the auxiliary function becomes

$$\tilde{f}(\boldsymbol{\theta}) = f(\boldsymbol{\theta}) + \boldsymbol{a}^T \boldsymbol{s}(\boldsymbol{\theta}) \tag{6}$$

as was proposed in [10]. The optimal choice of the parameter $\boldsymbol{a}$ that minimizes the variance of $\tilde{f}(\boldsymbol{\theta})$ is $\boldsymbol{a} = -\boldsymbol{\Sigma}_{ss}^{-1}\boldsymbol{\sigma}(\boldsymbol{s}, f)$, where $\boldsymbol{\Sigma}_{ss} = \mathbb{E}[\boldsymbol{s}\boldsymbol{s}^T]$, $\boldsymbol{\sigma}(\boldsymbol{s}, f) = \mathbb{E}[\boldsymbol{s}f]$.

Obviously, the representation power of these polynomials is limited, and therefore control functionals have been proposed recently where the trial function is stochastic. For example, the trial function could be a kernel function [13]. In order for using these control variates, we firstly estimate these required parameters in the trial function by using some training samples $\{\boldsymbol{\theta}_i\}_{i=1}^n$. Then the learned control variates can be used for test samples.

However, there are several drawbacks of the current zero-variance techniques:

- *Dilemma between effectiveness and efficiency.* Although increasing the order of polynomial could potentially increase the representation power and reduce more variance, the number the parameters needs to be learned would grow exponentially. As pointed out by [10], when quadratic polynomials are used, $Q(\boldsymbol{\theta}) = \boldsymbol{a}^T\boldsymbol{\theta} + \boldsymbol{\theta}^T\boldsymbol{B}\boldsymbol{x}/2$, the number of parameters will be $D(D+3)/2$. Thus, finding the optimal coefficients requires dealing with $\boldsymbol{\Sigma}_{ss}$ which is a matrix of dimension of order D^2. Similar issue occurs when employing the control functionals. This makes the use of high order polynomials computationally expensive when faced with high-dimensional sampling spaces.
- *Poor generalization with small sample size.* With small sizes of training samples and complex $p(\boldsymbol{\theta})$, the learned control variates could potentially overfit the training samples, i.e. generalize poorly over new samples. This is because a small size of training samples might be insufficient for representing the full distributional information of $p(\boldsymbol{\theta})$.

These limitations motivate the development of neural control variates and a novel loss function to alleviate overfitting issue when learning the neural control variates, which will be elaborated below.

3   Neural Control Variates

Firstly, we focus on alleviating the dilemma between effectiveness and efficiency on designing control variates in high-dimensional sample space. To this end, the trail function is designed as a neural network [8,18], we name this strategy as neural control variates (NCV). Equipped with neural network, their excellent capability of representing complex functions and overcoming the curse of dimensionality can be fully employed in high-dimensional scenarios [6].

Instead of relying on the control variates (5) introduced in [10], we use the following Stein control variates based on Stein identity [13,17],

$$g(\boldsymbol{\theta}) = \nabla_{\boldsymbol{\theta}} \cdot \Phi(\boldsymbol{\theta}) + \Phi(\boldsymbol{\theta}) \cdot \nabla_{\boldsymbol{\theta}} \log(p(\boldsymbol{\theta})), \tag{7}$$

where $\Phi(\boldsymbol{\theta})$ is the trial function. Note that in order for $\mathbb{E}[g(\boldsymbol{\theta})] = 0$, we assume mild zero boundary conditions on Φ, such that $p(\theta)\Phi(\theta) = 0$ at the boundary or $\lim_{\|x\|\to\infty} p(\theta)\Phi(\theta) = 0$ [9,10,13]. Compared with Eq. (5), Stein control variates is preferred due to its computational advantages since evaluating the second order derivatives of the trial function is avoided. Note that when the trial function $Q(\boldsymbol{\theta})$ is a linear or quadratic polynomial, the Stein trial function $\Phi(\boldsymbol{\theta})$ is constant or linear, respectively.

We now represent the trial function $\Phi(\boldsymbol{\theta})$ by a neural network $\Phi(\boldsymbol{\theta}; \boldsymbol{w})$ parameterized by the weights $\boldsymbol{w}$. The control function becomes $g(\boldsymbol{\theta}; \boldsymbol{w}) = \nabla_{\boldsymbol{\theta}} \cdot \Phi(\boldsymbol{\theta}; \boldsymbol{w}) + \Phi(\boldsymbol{\theta}; \boldsymbol{w}) \cdot \nabla_{\boldsymbol{\theta}} \log p(\boldsymbol{\theta})$. In order for variance reduction, we solve the following optimization problem

$$\min_{\boldsymbol{w}} \mathbb{V}_{p(\boldsymbol{\theta})}[f(\boldsymbol{\theta}) + g(\boldsymbol{\theta}; \boldsymbol{w})], \tag{8}$$

which does not have a closed-form in general. Typically, it is assumed that the variance could be approximated by using independent Monte Carlo samples and so the optimization problem is given by

$$\min_{\boldsymbol{w}} \frac{1}{n} \sum_{i=1}^{n} [f(\boldsymbol{\theta}_i) + g(\boldsymbol{\theta}_i; \boldsymbol{w})]^2 - (\mu_0 + \mu_g)^2, \tag{9}$$

where $\mu_0 = E(f(\theta))$ and $\mu_g = E(g(\boldsymbol{\theta}; \boldsymbol{w})) = 0$. Instead, the following optimization problem will be solved

$$\min_{\boldsymbol{w}} \frac{1}{n} \sum_{i=1}^{n} [f(\boldsymbol{\theta}_i) + g(\boldsymbol{\theta}_i; \boldsymbol{w})]^2 \tag{10}$$

where $\{\boldsymbol{\theta}_i\}_{i=1}^{n}$ are samples drawn from $p(\boldsymbol{\theta})$. Standard back-propagation techniques and stochastic gradient descent (SGD) can then be adopted to obtain the optimal weights of the neural networks.

Unfortunately, when the distribution $p(\boldsymbol{\theta})$ is high-dimensional and multi-modal, such as Bayesian neural networks, it would be very expensive to draw many samples for training control variates. Given a limited computational budget, it typically produces a rather small number of samples that are not sufficient for learning the control variates. Consequently, the learned parameters for control variates can easily overfit over the training samples, and thus could not generalize well on new samples drawn from $p(\boldsymbol{\theta})$. This overfitting phenomenon was not noticed in [8,18], since the considered applications in their scenarios only involve either a simple probability distribution $p(\boldsymbol{\theta})$ or simple target function $f(\boldsymbol{\theta})$.

Therefore, in the following, we propose a new objective function for learning the neural control variates to alleviate the overfitting; and demonstrate its benefits in various applications.

4   Constrained Neural Control Variates

In this section, we propose constrained neural control variates (CNCV) for alleviating overfitting. Now we take a closer look at why the original objective function of NCV tends to bring a poor control variates if one optimizes the Eq. (10) in the scenario that only a small number of samples from $p(\boldsymbol{\theta})$ are available.

Firstly we note that the objective functions in Eq. (9) and Eq. (10) are not the same although μ_0 is a constant, because the variance must be non-negative. For example, if we have a small number of samples, the learned neural network for g could overfit the data so that the objective function in Eq. (10) could hit the global minimum 0 due to the powerful capacity in approximation of the neural networks. Therefore, we have to optimize Eq. (10) with a constraint such that $\frac{1}{n}\sum_{i=1}^{n}[f(\boldsymbol{\theta}_i) + g(\boldsymbol{\theta}_i; \boldsymbol{w})]^2 \geq \mu_0^2$. With this constraint, the solution would be $g(\boldsymbol{\theta}_i; \boldsymbol{w}) = -f(\boldsymbol{\theta}_i) + \mu_0$ when using a small number of samples. Without this constraint, we can easily observe that with a small n and a large-capacity neural network for representing $\Phi(\boldsymbol{\theta}; \boldsymbol{w})$, optimizing Eq. (10) can easily result in "point-wise" fitting, $g(\boldsymbol{\theta}_i; \boldsymbol{w}) = -f(\boldsymbol{\theta}_i)$, for each sample $\boldsymbol{\theta}_i$, thus achieving the minimal value of the objective. So it violates the constraint that the population mean of $g(\boldsymbol{\theta}; \boldsymbol{w})$ is zero. Therefore, directly minimizing Eq. (10) can cause severe overfitting. We thus propose two strategies for dealing with this issue.

1. **Centering control variates.** Based on our analysis on optimizing Eq. (10), it introduces bias for the true $g(\boldsymbol{\theta}; \boldsymbol{w})$. To compensate this bias, we center the function $g(\boldsymbol{\theta}; \boldsymbol{w})$ and set $g(\boldsymbol{\theta}; \boldsymbol{w}) = \widetilde{g}(\boldsymbol{\theta}; \boldsymbol{w}) - \mu$ where μ should be close to μ_0. The parameter μ could also be learned during the training. Now if we substitute g in Eq. (10), the optimal function would be $\widetilde{g}(\boldsymbol{\theta}_i; \boldsymbol{w}) = -f(\boldsymbol{\theta}_i) + \mu$ which would assure the required constraint $\frac{1}{n}\sum_{i=1}^{n}[f(\boldsymbol{\theta}_i) + \widetilde{g}(\boldsymbol{\theta}_i; \boldsymbol{w})]^2 \geq \mu_0^2$. Note that in the following we assume g is a centered function, and so denote $\widetilde{g}$ by g for simplicity.
2. **Regularization.** We prefer a minimized variance of the function g. Thus the other strategy is to control the variance of the function g, $\mathbb{E}[g^2]$, to regularize the complexity of the neural networks.

Combining the two strategies, the novel objective function can be formulated as the following,

$$\min_{\boldsymbol{w},\mu} \frac{1}{n} \sum_{i=1}^{n} \left[[f(\boldsymbol{\theta}_i) + g(\boldsymbol{\theta}_i; \boldsymbol{w}) - \mu]^2 + \lambda g(\boldsymbol{\theta}_i; \boldsymbol{w})^2 \right], \tag{11}$$

where λ is the regularization parameter, and the population variance $\mathbb{V}[g]$ is estimated by its empirical samples as regularization term.

The random initialization of μ can slow down the training process and cause overfitting. To obtain a better performance, two optional initializing strategies could be used:

1. Simply using $\frac{1}{n}\sum_{i=1}^{n} f(\boldsymbol{\theta}_i)$ as the initializing value of μ;
2. Pre-train the model with larger λ till converged, then retain the value of μ, randomly initializing other variables and re-train the model with smaller λ.

When the number of samples n is big enough, strategy 1 is recommended; when n is small or $\mathbb{V}(f(\boldsymbol{\theta}))$ is relatively large compared with $Ef(\boldsymbol{\theta})$, strategy 2 is recommended.

5   Experiments

To evaluate our proposed method, we apply CNCV to a synthetic problem and two real scenarios, which are thermodynamic integration for Bayesian model

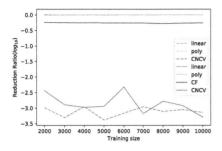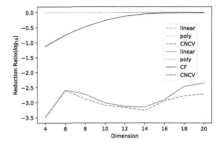

Fig. 1. Synthetic data. (**Left**) Variance reduction ratio $v.s.$ number of training samples with $D = 10$; (**Right**) Variance reduction ratio $v.s.$ dimension with training sample size $n = 5000$.

evidence evaluation, and Bayesian neural networks. For comparison purposes, control functionals (CF) [13] and polynomial control variates [10,14] are also applied to these problems. The performance of the trained control variates are measured by the variance reduction ratio on the test data set, i.e.,

$$\frac{\mathbb{V}_{p(\boldsymbol{\theta})}[f(\boldsymbol{\theta}) + g(\boldsymbol{\theta})]}{\mathbb{V}_{p(\boldsymbol{\theta})}(f(\boldsymbol{\theta}))]}.$$

We used fully connected neural networks to represent the trial function in all the experiments. We found that for the experiments presented in the following, a medium-sized network is empirically sufficient to achieve good performance. More details on network architectures are provided in Appendix.

5.1 Synthetic Data

To illustrate the advantage of NCV on dealing with high-dimensional problems over other methods, we consider to approximate the expectation of $f(\boldsymbol{\theta}) = \sin(\pi/D \sum_{i=1}^{D} \theta_i)$ where $\boldsymbol{\theta} \in \mathbb{R}^D$ which is a mixture of Gaussians, i.e., $p(\boldsymbol{\theta}) = 0.5\mathcal{N}(-1, \boldsymbol{I}) + 0.5\mathcal{N}(1, \boldsymbol{I})$.

Figure 1 shows the variance reduction ratio on test data ($N = 500$) with respect to varying the number of training samples and the dimensions. In both cases, we can observe that CNCV outperforms linear, quadratic control variates and control functional. Particularly, when increasing the dimensions of $\boldsymbol{\theta}$, CNCV can still achieve much lower variance reduction ratio compared with control functional.

Furthermore, we evaluated the two constraints made on the control variates in the Sect. 4. To highlight the comparison, we consider the modified function $f(\boldsymbol{\theta}) = 10\sin(\pi/D \sum_{i=1}^{D} \theta_i) + \mu_0$ where $p(\boldsymbol{\theta}) = 0.5\mathcal{N}(-1, \boldsymbol{I}) + 0.5\mathcal{N}(1, \boldsymbol{I})$, $\boldsymbol{\theta} \in \mathbb{R}^{10}$. Here $\mu_0 \in [0, 9]$ represents the mean of $f(\theta)$, and $\sqrt{var(f(\theta))} \approx 7.5$. To evaluate our methods, we generated 1000 samples, where 500 samples were used for training and the rest were used for testing. Four neural control variates schemes with and without the constraints were applied to these samples.

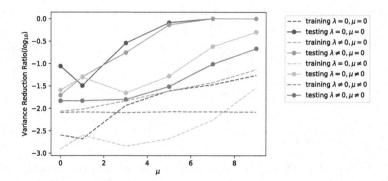

Fig. 2. Variance reduction ratio of four types of NCV versus the oracle mean μ_0. The μ in the control variates was initialized to 0. Dashed and solid lines plot the results on training and test data respectively.

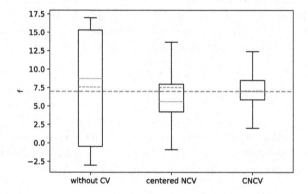

Fig. 3. Boxplot of the samples for the function f on test data. The orange solid line represents the median, the green dashed represents the sample mean, and the grey dashed line represents the oracle mean $\mu_0 = 7$. (Color figure online)

These schemes are: (1) not regularized, and not centered ($\lambda = 0, \mu = 0$); (2) regularized, and not centered($\lambda \neq 0, \mu = 0$); (3) not regularized, and centered($\lambda = 0, \mu \neq 0$); (4) regularized, and centered($\lambda \neq 0, \mu \neq 0$).

Figure 2 reports the variance reduction ratio values for training and test data when varying μ_0. It can be shown that NCV without constraints can easily be over-fitted with the training data. As μ_0 increases, NCV with $\lambda = 0, \mu = 0$ and NCV with $\lambda \neq 0, \mu = 0$ were not able to reduce the variance for the test data. This shows that when μ_0 is too large compared to the standard deviation, the control variates without constraints tends to fit $-f(\boldsymbol{\theta})$ rather than $-f(\boldsymbol{\theta}) + \mu_0$ on the training data, which results in over-fitting.

Figure 3 suggests that CNCV ($\lambda \neq 0, \mu \neq 0$) outperforms all the other methods. The NCV schemes with centered control variates ($\mu \neq 0$) were always better than the ones without centered control variates ($\mu = 0$). We can also see that the regularized control variates ($\lambda \neq 0$) can improve the performance.

The μ was initialized to 0 in all experiments shown in Fig. 2. To better understand the effect of the constraints on NCV, we reported the distribution of the samples $f(\boldsymbol{\theta})$ from test sets in Fig. 3. It shows that although NCV, which was not regularized but centered ($\lambda = 0, \mu \neq 0$), reduced the variance, the method does introduced bias so that the sample mean was away from the true mean μ_0. The CNCV reduced the variance without introducing bias.

In the following, we apply our proposed CNCV to two difficult problems with small number of samples. In these two cases, original NCV approach tends to severely overfit the training samples, leading to extremely poor generalization performance. Thus, we will not report the results of NCV.

5.2 Thermodynamic Integral for Bayesian Model Evidence Evaluation

In Bayesian analysis, data $\boldsymbol{y}$ is assumed to have been generated under a collection of putative models, $\{\mathcal{M}_i\}$. To compare these candidate models, the Bayesian model evidence is constructed as $p(\boldsymbol{y}|\mathcal{M}_i) = \int p(\boldsymbol{y}|\boldsymbol{\theta}, \mathcal{M}_i)p(\boldsymbol{\theta}|\mathcal{M}_i)d\boldsymbol{\theta}$ where $\boldsymbol{\theta}$ are the parameters associated with model $\mathcal{M}_i$. Unfortunately, for most of the models of interest, this integral is unavailable in closed form. Thus many techniques were proposed to approximate the model evidence. Thermodynamic integration (TI) [3] is among the most promising approach to estimate the evidence. This approach is derived from the standard thermodynamic identity,

$$\log p(\boldsymbol{y}) = \int_0^1 \mathbb{E}_{p(\boldsymbol{\theta}|\boldsymbol{y},t)}[\log p(\boldsymbol{y}|\boldsymbol{\theta})]dt, \tag{12}$$

where $p(\boldsymbol{\theta}|\boldsymbol{y},t) \propto p(\boldsymbol{y}|\boldsymbol{\theta})^t p(\boldsymbol{\theta})$ ($t \in [0,1]$) is called power posterior. Note that we have dropped the model indicator $\mathcal{M}_i$ for simplicity. Here t is known as an inverse temperature parameter. In many cases, the posterior expectation $\mathbb{E}_{p(\boldsymbol{\theta}|\boldsymbol{y},t)}\log(p(\boldsymbol{y}|\boldsymbol{\theta}))$ can not be analytically computed, thus the Monte Carlo integration is applied. However, Monte Carlo integration often suffer large variance when sample size is not large enough.

In [14], the zero-variance control variates (5) were used to reduce the variance for TI, so that the posterior expectation is approximated by

$$\frac{1}{N}\sum_{i=1}^{N} \log p(\boldsymbol{y}|\boldsymbol{\theta}_i^t) + \Delta Q_t(\boldsymbol{\theta}_i^t) + \nabla Q_t(\boldsymbol{\theta}_i^t) \cdot \nabla \log(p(\boldsymbol{\theta}_i^t|\boldsymbol{y},t) \tag{13}$$

where $\{\boldsymbol{\theta}_i^t\}_{i=1}^N$ are drawn from the posterior $p(\boldsymbol{\theta}|\boldsymbol{y},t)$. In [14], the trial function $Q_t(\boldsymbol{\theta})$ was assumed as a linear or quadratic function, which corresponds to a constant or linear function for $\Phi(\boldsymbol{\theta})$ in Stein control variates[1]. These methods achieved excellent performance for simple models [14]. However, they are struggling in some scenarios, for example, a negative example which is Goodwin

---

[1] We will call the trial function $Q(\boldsymbol{\theta})$ as the constant or linear type trial functions $\Phi(\boldsymbol{\theta})$ in the following.

Oscillator given in [14]. Note that Goodwin Oscillator is a nonlinear dynamical system,

$$\frac{d\boldsymbol{x}}{ds} = f(\boldsymbol{x}, s; \boldsymbol{\theta}), \quad \boldsymbol{x}(0) = \boldsymbol{x}_0, \tag{14}$$

where the form of $f(\cdot)$ is provided in Appendix. Assuming within only a subset of time points $\{s_i\}_{i=0}^N$, the solution of (14), i.e. $\boldsymbol{x}(s_i, \boldsymbol{\theta})$, is observed under Gaussian noise $\boldsymbol{\varepsilon}(s) \sim \mathcal{N}(0, \sigma^2 \boldsymbol{I})$, where σ^2 denotes the variance of the noise. That means the observation $\boldsymbol{y}(s_i) = \boldsymbol{x}(s_i) + \boldsymbol{\varepsilon}(s_i)$. Then we have the likelihood

$$p(\boldsymbol{y}|\boldsymbol{\theta}, \boldsymbol{x}_0, \sigma) = \prod_{i=1}^N \mathcal{N}(\boldsymbol{y}(s_i)|\boldsymbol{x}(s_i; \boldsymbol{\theta}; \boldsymbol{x}_0), \sigma^2 \boldsymbol{I}). \tag{15}$$

The expectation of log likelihood under the power posterior, i.e., $\mathbb{E}_{p(\theta|y,t)}$ $\log p(\boldsymbol{y}|\boldsymbol{\theta})$, needs to be evaluated. In [14], the authors demonstrated the failure of polynomial-type of control function since the log-likelihood surface is highly multi-modal and there is much weaker canonical correlation between the scores and the log posterior.

In practice, sampling from Goodwin Oscillator is difficult and computationally expensive since simulating the underlying ordinary differential equation is extremely time-consuming. This directly leads to the situation that the available training samples for control variates are not sufficient. We show in the following that the proposed CNCV can be employed to deal with this issue. To illustrate the benefits of CNCV, we compared it to other methods with various sizes of training samples and temperatures. For comparison purposes we evaluated the variance reduction ratios on both training and test sets (500 samples for test). The experiment settings are the same as those in [14].

Figure 4 shows the experimental results when applying different types of control variates. It can be easily observed that the linear and quadratic methods could hardly reduce the variance of the Goodwin Oscillator model on testing set, while CNCV obtained the lowest variance reduction ratio comparing to all other methods. Control functional can significantly reduce the variance when dimension is low, but CNCV still can get the lowest variance reduction ratio, inspite of the problem dimensions or temperatures.

5.3   Uncertainty Quantification in Bayesian Neural Network

Standard neural network training via optimization is equivalent to maximum likelihood estimation (MLE for short). Given the training samples, $\{(\boldsymbol{x}_i, \boldsymbol{y}_i)\}_{i=1}^N$, and denote $\boldsymbol{X} = \{\boldsymbol{x}_i\}_{i=1}^N$ and $\boldsymbol{Y} = \{\boldsymbol{y}_i\}_{i=1}^N$, the weight parameter $\boldsymbol{\theta}$ of the neural networks is estimated by

$$\hat{\boldsymbol{\theta}} = \operatorname{argmax}_{\theta} \sum_{i=1}^N \log p(\boldsymbol{y}_i|\boldsymbol{x}_i; \boldsymbol{\theta}) \tag{16}$$

However, the solution of MLE lacks theoretical justification from the probabilistic perspective to deal with the parameter uncertainty as well as structure uncertainty. Moreover, standard neural networks are often susceptible

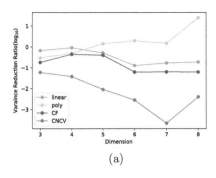
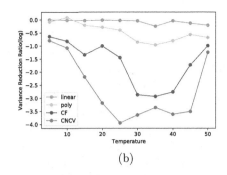

(a)   (b)

Fig. 4. Variance reduction ratio on test set of four different types of control variates (linear, quadratic, CF and CNCV). 3000 samples were used for training and the other 3000 samples were used for testing. (a) The average variance reduction ratio on test data versus the problem dimension; (b) The average variance reduction ratio on the test data for different temperatures.

to producing over-confident predictions. Bayesian natural network [11] was introduced for implementing uncertainty quantification. Firstly, one provides a prior distribution over the weights, $p_0(\boldsymbol{\theta}) = \mathcal{N}(\mathbf{0}, \sigma_0^2 \boldsymbol{I})$, where σ_0^2 is the variance magnitude. Assuming the likelihood function has the form, $p(\boldsymbol{y}_i|\boldsymbol{x}_i; \boldsymbol{\theta}) = \mathcal{N}\left(\boldsymbol{y}_i|NN(\boldsymbol{x}_i; \boldsymbol{\theta}), \sigma^2 \boldsymbol{I}\right)$, then the posterior of the weights $\boldsymbol{\theta}$,

$$p(\boldsymbol{\theta}|\boldsymbol{X}, \boldsymbol{Y}) \propto \prod_{i=1}^{N} p(\boldsymbol{y}_i|\boldsymbol{x}_i, \boldsymbol{\theta}) p_0(\boldsymbol{\theta}).$$

The uncertainty of the model, typically formulated as the expectation of a specific statistics $f(\boldsymbol{\theta}, \boldsymbol{x}, \boldsymbol{y})$ could be computed based on the posterior distribution of the weights,

$$\mu_f = \mathbb{E}[f(\boldsymbol{\theta}; \boldsymbol{x}, \boldsymbol{y})] = \int f(\boldsymbol{\theta}; \boldsymbol{x}, \boldsymbol{y}) p(\boldsymbol{\theta}|\boldsymbol{X}, \boldsymbol{Y}) d\boldsymbol{\theta} \tag{17}$$

Due to the analytic intractability of the integral, the expectation of $f(\boldsymbol{\theta}, \boldsymbol{x}, \boldsymbol{y})$ is estimated using Monte Carlo integration

$$\mu_f \approx \frac{1}{M} \sum_{i=1}^{M} f(\boldsymbol{\theta}_i, \boldsymbol{x}, \boldsymbol{y}) \tag{18}$$

where $\{\boldsymbol{\theta}_i\}_{i=1}^{M}$ is drawn from the posterior $p(\boldsymbol{\theta}|\boldsymbol{X}, \boldsymbol{Y})$.

However, the large number of parameters and complex structure of networks make the sampling from the posterior extremely hard. Typically, only a small number of samples could be obtained. Consequently, small sample size and the complex structure of the posterior distribution will lead to a high variance of the estimator (18). Thus, we consider reducing the variance of Monte Carlo estimator by NCVA.

Uncertainty quantification on predictions with out-of-distribution inputs. The neural networks learned with the MLE principal could achieve a high-accuracy performance, when the training data and test data come from the same data distribution. But when an out-of-bag (OOB) sample, i.e., a sample whose label is not included in the training set, is fed into the models, the MLE model is very likely to identify the OOB sample as a certain in-bag class with very high confidence, i.e. the prediction score is close to 1. We hope to construct a robust classifier which won't misclassify the OOB samples with very high confidence. The Bayesian neural network is considered to be effective to handle this situation. However, evaluating the expected prediction score under the posterior of w still suffers large variance issues. Hence we considered to reduce the variance of BNN prediction score and handle the over-confident issues of OOB samples.

We implemented a simple image classification task to evaluate the effectiveness of CNCV. We selected all the images with label "6" and "9" from the MNIST dataset and constructed a convolutional neural network for Bayesian classifier with the output $\{f(x, \theta_i)\}_{i=1}^M$ as the probability of class assignment, where $\theta_i \sim p(\theta|X, Y)$ on the two categorizes and select the images with label "8" as the out-of-distribution samples x_{out} for test. We constructed the control variates to reduce the variance of the estimator $\hat{P}(y = \text{"6"}|x_{\text{out}})$ using NCV,

$$\hat{P}(y = \text{"6"}|x_{\text{out}}) = \frac{1}{M} \sum_{i=1}^M \hat{P}(y = \text{"6"}|x_{\text{out}}, \theta_i) + g(\theta_i, x_{\text{out}}) \qquad (19)$$

The parameters $\{\theta_i\}$ are sampled based on the training set, and hyperparameters are tuned using the validation set. Both the training and validation data are composed of the images with labels "6" or "9". We evaluated the control variates methods on the test set, consisting of the images with the label "8". We evaluate the control variates by computing the following variance ratio

$$\frac{1}{N} \sum_{i=1}^N \frac{\mathbb{V}_{p(\theta|X,Y)}[p(y_i = \text{"6"}|x_i) + g(x_i, \theta)]}{\mathbb{V}_{p(\theta|X,Y)}[p(y_i = \text{"6"}|x_i)]} \qquad (20)$$

Due to the high dimensionality of this problem, quadratic control variates and control functional failed to obtain satisfying variance reduction, and we thus do not report their results.

Figure 5(a) shows that the overall distribution of BNN ensemble prediction does not change significantly, where CNCV produces slightly better results. This is expected since the classifier has not seen the OOB samples during training, which makes it impossible to yield a stable prediction probability. On the other hand, Fig. 5(b) depicts the the entropy of these OOB samples computed using prediction score via BNN:

$$Entropy(x_{OOB}) = -\hat{p}\log(\hat{p}) - (1 - \hat{p})\log(1 - \hat{p}), \qquad (21)$$

where $\hat{p}$ is the BNN prediction score evaluated from Eq. (19). $Entropy(x_{OOB})$ is in the range $[0, \log 2]$. Samples with low entropy close to 0 means they will

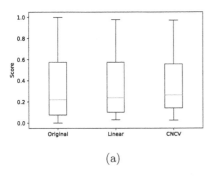 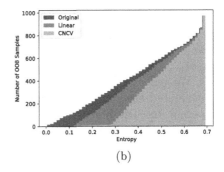

(a)   (b)

Fig. 5. Performance of CNCV on BNN with OOB samples (a) boxplot of the prediction score of OOB samples defined in Eq. (19). The prediction scores were computed based on BNN ensemble classifier for those variance reduction methods. (b) The accumulated empirical distribution of the entropy computed by prediction scores using Eq. (21).

be classified as 6 or 9 with very high confidence. It could be seen from Fig. 5(b) that BNN prediction with control variates has less over-confident scores over OOB samples. That means that BNN prediction with CNCV yields the least over-confident scores compared with vanilla BNN and that with linear control variates.

6 Conclusion

We have proposed neural control variates for variance reduction. We have shown that the neural control variates could have the over-fitting problem when using a small number of samples. To alleviate this over-fitting problem, we proposed constrained neural control variates, where the control variates is centered and regularized. We demonstrated the effectiveness of the proposed methods on synthetic data and two challenging Monte Carlo integration tasks. However, the theoretical justification of the proposed method will be investigated in our future research.

A   Formulas for Goodwin Oscillator

The nonlinear dynamic system of the Goodwin Oscillator used in [14] is given by:

$$
\begin{aligned}
\frac{dx_1}{ds} &= \frac{a_1}{1 + a_2 x_g^\rho} - \alpha x_1 \\
\frac{dx_2}{ds} &= k_1 x_1 - \alpha x_2 \\
&\vdots \\
\frac{dx_g}{ds} &= k_{g-1} x_{g-1} - \alpha x_g.
\end{aligned}
\tag{22}
$$

The solution $x(s; \theta, x_0)$ of this dynamical system depends on the uncertain parameters $\alpha, a_1, a_2, k_1, \ldots, k_{g-1}$. Similar to the settings in [14], we assume $x_0 = [0, \ldots, 0]$ and $\sigma = 0.1$ are both known and take sampling times to be $s = 41, \ldots, 80$. Parameters were assigned independent $\Gamma(2, 1)$ prior distributions. We generated data using $a_1 = 1, a_2 = 3, k_1 = 2, k_2, \ldots, k_{g-1} = 1, \alpha = 0.5$. We generated the posterior samples of the weights using MCMC with parallel tempering. In each dimension cases ($g \in \{3, 4, \cdots, 8\}$) the Markorv Chain runs $100,000$ iterations to ensure converge, 6000 samples randomly drawn from the last $50,000$ iterations were used in the final experiments.

The trial function ϕ used in Goodwin Oscillator is a two layers fully connected neural network, where each layer has 40 neurons. The activation function is the Sigmoid function.

B   Uncertainty Quantification in Bayesian Neural Network: Out-of-Bag Sample Detection

The basic model consists of two convolutional layers, two max-pooling layers and a fully connected layers, with kernel size $(5 \times 5 \times 2)$, $(2 \times 3 \times 3 \times 3)$, (147×2) respectively. The prior distribution of the weight was set to standard normal distribution $\mathcal{N}(0, 1)$. The samples of the weights were generated using preconditioned Stochastic Gradient Langevin Dynamic [7]. 1000 samples were generated to construct the Bayesian neural network prediction. The trial function $\phi(\theta, x) : \Theta \times \mathbb{X} \longrightarrow \mathbb{R}$ was defined as:

$$\phi(\theta, x) = \alpha^T h(W_0 \theta + \psi(x)) \tag{23}$$

where $\psi(x)$ consists of two convolutional layers with kernel size $(5 \times 5 \times 2)$, $(2 \times 3 \times 3 \times 3)$, two max-pooling layers and relu activation. $W_0 \in \mathbb{R}^{147 \times 407}$, h is the sigmoid function. and $\alpha \in \mathbb{R}^{147}$. Thus the neural control varaites of the BNN prediction is:

$$g(\theta, x) = \nabla_\theta \cdot \phi(\theta, x) + \phi(\theta, x) \nabla_\theta \cdot \log p(\theta | X) \tag{24}$$

where $\nabla \cdot f = \sum_i \frac{\partial f}{\partial x_i}$.

References

1. Assaraf, R., Caffarel, M.: Zero-variance principle for Monte Carlo algorithms. Phys. Rev. Lett. **83**(23), 4682 (1999)
2. Cornuet, J.M., Marin, J.M., Mira, A., Robert, C.P.: Adaptive multiple importance sampling. Scand. J. Stat. **39**(4), 798–812 (2012)
3. Frenkel, D., Smit, B.: Understanding Molecular Simulation: from Algorithms to Applications, vol. 1. Elsevier, Amsterdam (2001)

4. Giles, M.B.: Multilevel Monte Carlo methods. In: Dick, J., Kuo, F.Y., Peters, G.W., Sloan, I.H. (eds.) Monte Carlo and Quasi-Monte Carlo Methods 2012. SPMS, vol. 65, pp. 83–103. Springer, Heidelberg (2013). https://doi.org/10.1007/978-3-642-41095-6_4

5. Higdon, D., McDonnell, J.D., Schunck, N., Sarich, J., Wild, S.M.: A Bayesian approach for parameter estimation and prediction using a computationally intensive model. J. Phys. G: Nucl. Part. Phys. **42**(3), 034009 (2015)

6. LeCun, Y., Bengio, Y., Hinton, G.: Deep learning. Nature **521**(7553), 436 (2015)

7. Li, C., Chen, C., Carlson, D., Carin, L.: Pre-conditioned stochastic gradient Langevin dynamics for deep neural networks. In: AAAI, vol. 2, p. 4 (2016)

8. Liu, H., Feng, Y., Mao, Y., Zhou, D., Peng, J., Liu, Q.: Action-dependent control variates for policy optimization via stein identity. In: ICLR (2018)

9. Liu, Q., Wang, D.: Stein variational gradient descent: a general purpose Bayesian inference algorithm. In: Advances in Neural Information Processing Systems, pp. 2378–2386 (2016)

10. Mira, A., Solgi, R., Imparato, D.: Zero variance markovchain monte carlo for Bayesian estimators. Stat. Comput. **23**(5), 653–662 (2013)

11. Neal, R.M.: Bayesian Learning for Neural Networks, vol. 118. Springer, New York (2012)

12. Oates, C.J., Cockayne, J., Briol, F.X., Girolami, M.: Convergence rates for a class of estimators based on stein's method. arXivpreprint arXiv:1603.03220 (2016)

13. Oates, C.J., Girolami, M., Chopin, N.: Control functionals for Monte Carlo integration. J. Roy. Stat. Soc. Ser. B (Stat. Methodol.) **79**(3), 695–718 (2017)

14. Oates, C.J., Papamarkou, T., Girolami, M.: The controlled thermodynamic integral for Bayesian model evidence evaluation. J. Am. Stat. Assoc. **111**(514), 634–645 (2016)

15. Robert, C.P.: Monte Carlo Methods. Wiley Online Library, Hoboken (2004)

16. Rubinstein, R.Y., Kroese, D.P.: Simulation and the Monte Carlo Method, vol. 10. Wiley, Hoboken (2016)

17. Stein, C., et al.: A bound for the error in the normal approximation to the distribution of a sum of dependent random variables. In: Proceedings of the Sixth Berkeley Symposium on Mathematical Statistics and Probability, Volume 2: Probability Theory. The Regents of the University of California (1972)

18. Tucker, G., Mnih, A., Maddison, C.J., Lawson, J., Sohl-Dickstein, J.: Rebar: Low-variance, unbiased gradient estimates for discrete latent variable models. In: Advances in Neural Information Processing Systems, pp. 2624–2633 (2017)

Data Association with Gaussian Processes

Markus Kaiser[1,2]([⊠]), Clemens Otte[1], Thomas A. Runkler[1,2],
and Carl Henrik Ek[3]

[1] Siemens AG, Munich, Germany
markus.kaiser@siemens.com
[2] Technical University of Munich, Munich, Germany
[3] University of Bristol, Bristol, UK

Abstract. The data association problem is concerned with separating data coming from different generating processes, for example when data comes from different data sources, contain significant noise, or exhibit multimodality. We present a fully Bayesian approach to this problem. Our model is capable of simultaneously solving the data association problem and the induced supervised learning problem. Underpinning our approach is the use of Gaussian process priors to encode the structure of both the data and the data associations. We present an efficient learning scheme based on doubly stochastic variational inference and discuss how it can be applied to deep Gaussian process priors.

1 Introduction

Real-world data often include multiple operational regimes of the considered system, for example a wind turbine or gas turbine [12]. As an example, consider a model describing the lift resulting from airflow around the wing profile of an airplane as a function of the attack angle. At low values the lift increases linearly with the attack angle until the wing stalls and the characteristic of the airflow changes fundamentally. Building a truthful model of such data requires learning two separate models and correctly associating the observed data to each of the dynamical regimes. A similar example would be if our sensors that measure the lift are faulty in a manner such that we either get an accurate reading or a noisy one. Estimating a model in this scenario is often referred to as a *data association problem* [2,8], where we consider the data to have been generated by a mixture of processes and we are interested in factorising the data into these components.

Figure 1 shows an example of faulty sensor data, where sensor readings are disturbed by uncorrelated and asymmetric noise. Applying standard machine learning approaches to such data can lead to model pollution, where the expressive power of the model is used to explain noise instead of the underlying signal. Solving the data association problem by factorizing the data into signal and noise gives rise to a principled approach to avoid this behavior.

The project this report is based on was supported with funds from the German Federal Ministry of Education and Research under project number 01 IS 18049 A.

U. Brefeld et al. (Eds.): ECML PKDD 2019, LNAI 11907, pp. 548–564, 2020.
https://doi.org/10.1007/978-3-030-46147-8_33

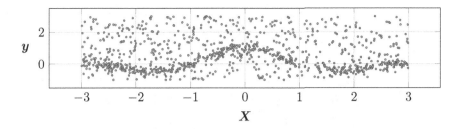

Fig. 1. A data association problem consisting of two generating processes, one of which is a signal we wish to recover and one is an uncorrelated noise process.

Early approaches to explaining data using multiple generative processes are based on separating the input space and training local expert models explaining easier subtasks [15,21,25]. The assignment of data points to local experts is handled by a gating network, which learns a function from the inputs to assignment probabilities. However, it is still a central assumption of these models that at every position in the input space exactly one expert should explain the data. Another approach is presented in [4], where the multimodal regression tasks are interpreted as a density estimation problem. A high number of candidate distributions is reweighed to match the observed data without modeling the underlying generative process.

In contrast, we are interested in a generative process, where data at the same location in the input space could have been generated by a number of global independent processes. Inherently, the data association problem is ill-posed and requires assumptions on both the underlying functions and the association of the observations. In [18] the authors place Gaussian process (GP) priors on the different generative processes which are assumed to be relevant globally. The associations are modelled via a latent association matrix and inference is carried out using an expectation maximization algorithm. This approach takes both the inputs and the outputs of the training data into account to solve the association problem. A drawback is that the model cannot give a posterior estimate about the relevance of the different generating processes at different locations in the input space. This means that the model can be used for data exploration but additional information is needed in order to perform predictive tasks. Another approach in [5] expands this model by allowing interdependencies between the different generative processes and formulating the association problem as an inference problem on a latent space and a corresponding covariance function. However, in this approach the number of components is a free parameter and is prone to overfitting, as the model has no means of turning off components.

In this paper, we formulate a Bayesian model for the data association problem. Underpinning our approach is the use of GP priors which encode structure both on the functions and the associations themselves, allowing us to incorporate the available prior knowledge about the proper factorization into the learning problem. The use of GP priors allows us to achieve principled regularization without

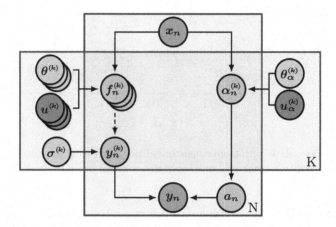

Fig. 2. The graphical model of DAGP. The violet observations $(\boldsymbol{x}_n, \boldsymbol{y}_n)$ are generated by the latent process (green). Exactly one of the K latent functions $f^{(k)}$ and likelihood $\boldsymbol{y}_n^{(k)}$ are evaluated to generate $\boldsymbol{y}_n$. We can place shallow or deep GP priors on these latent function values $\boldsymbol{f}_n^{(k)}$. The assignment $\boldsymbol{a}_n$ to a latent function is driven by input-dependent weights $\boldsymbol{\alpha}_n^{(k)}$ which encode the relevance of the different functions at $\boldsymbol{x}_n$. The different parts of the model are determined by the hyperparameters $\boldsymbol{\theta}, \boldsymbol{\sigma}$ (yellow) and variational parameters $\boldsymbol{u}$ (blue). (Color figure online)

reducing the solution space leading to a well-regularized learning problem. Importantly, we simultaneously solve the association problem for the training data taking both inputs and outputs into account while also obtaining posterior belief about the relevance of the different generating processes in the input space. Our model can describe non-stationary processes in the sense that a different number of processes can be activated in different locations in the input space. We describe this non-stationary structure using additional GP priors which allows us to make full use of problem specific knowledge. This leads to a flexible yet interpretable model with a principled treatment of uncertainty.

The paper has the following contributions: In Sect. 2, we propose the data association with Gaussian processes model (DAGP). In Sect. 3, we present an efficient learning scheme via a variational approximation which allows us to simultaneously train all parts of our model via stochastic optimization and show how the same learning scheme can be applied to deep GP priors. We demonstrate our model on a noise separation problem, an artificial multimodal data set, and a multi-regime regression problem based on the cart-pole benchmark in Sect. 4.

2   Data Association with Gaussian Processes

The data association with Gaussian processes (DAGP) model assumes that there exist K independent functions $\{f^{(k)}\}_{k=1}^K$, which generate pairs of observations $\mathcal{D} = \{(\boldsymbol{x}_n, \boldsymbol{y}_n)\}_{n=1}^N$. Each data point is generated by evaluating one of the K latent functions and adding Gaussian noise from a corresponding likelihood.

The assignment of the nth data point to one of the functions is specified by the indicator vector $\boldsymbol{a}_n \in \{0,1\}^K$, which has exactly one non-zero entry. Our goal is to formulate simultaneous Bayesian inference on the functions $f^{(k)}$ and the assignments $\boldsymbol{a}_n$.

For notational conciseness, we follow the GP related notation in [14] and collect all N inputs as $\boldsymbol{X} = (\boldsymbol{x}_1, \ldots, \boldsymbol{x}_N)$ and all outputs as $\boldsymbol{Y} = (\boldsymbol{y}_1, \ldots, \boldsymbol{y}_N)$. We further denote the kth latent function value associated with the nth data point as $f_n^{(k)} = f^{(k)}(\boldsymbol{x}_n)$ and collect them as $\boldsymbol{F}^{(k)} = \left(f_1^{(k)}, \ldots, f_N^{(k)}\right)$ and $\boldsymbol{F} = \left(\boldsymbol{F}^{(1)}, \ldots, \boldsymbol{F}^{(K)}\right)$. We refer to the kth entry in $\boldsymbol{a}_n$ as $a_n^{(k)}$ and denote $\boldsymbol{A} = (\boldsymbol{a}_1, \ldots, \boldsymbol{a}_N)$.

Given this notation, the marginal likelihood of DAGP can be separated into the likelihood, the latent function processes, and the assignment process and is given by,

$$p(\boldsymbol{Y} \,|\, \boldsymbol{X}) = \int p(\boldsymbol{Y} \,|\, \boldsymbol{F}, \boldsymbol{A}) p(\boldsymbol{F} \,|\, \boldsymbol{X}) p(\boldsymbol{A} \,|\, \boldsymbol{X}) \, \mathrm{d}\boldsymbol{A} \, \mathrm{d}\boldsymbol{F}$$

$$p(\boldsymbol{Y} \,|\, \boldsymbol{F}, \boldsymbol{A}) = \prod_{n=1}^{N} \prod_{k=1}^{K} \mathcal{N}\left(\boldsymbol{y}_n \,\middle|\, f_n^{(k)}, \left(\sigma^{(k)}\right)^2\right)^{\mathbb{I}(a_n^{(k)}=1)}, \tag{1}$$

where $\sigma^{(k)}$ is the noise of the kth Gaussian likelihood and $\mathbb{I}$ the indicator function.

Since we assume the K processes to be independent given the data and assignments, we place independent GP priors on the latent functions $p(\boldsymbol{F} \,|\, \boldsymbol{X}) = \prod_{k=1}^{K} \mathcal{N}\left(\boldsymbol{F}^{(k)} \,\middle|\, \mu^{(k)}(\boldsymbol{X}), \mathcal{K}^{(k)}(\boldsymbol{X}, \boldsymbol{X})\right)$ with mean function $\mu^{(k)}$ and kernel $\mathcal{K}^{(k)}$. Our prior on the assignment process is composite. First, we assume that the $\boldsymbol{a}_n$ are drawn independently from multinomial distributions with logit parameters $\boldsymbol{\alpha}_n = \left(\alpha_n^{(1)}, \ldots, \alpha_n^{(K)}\right)$. One approach to specify $\boldsymbol{\alpha}_n$ is to assume them to be known a priori and to be equal for all data points [18]. Instead, we want to infer them from the data. Specifically, we assume that there is a relationship between the location in the input space $\mathbf{x}$ and the associations. By placing independent GP priors on $\boldsymbol{\alpha}^{(k)}$, we can encode our prior knowledge of the associations by the choice of covariance function $p(\boldsymbol{\alpha} \,|\, \boldsymbol{X}) = \prod_{k=1}^{K} \mathcal{N}\left(\boldsymbol{\alpha}^{(k)} \,\middle|\, \mathbf{0}, \mathcal{K}_\alpha^{(k)}(\boldsymbol{X}, \boldsymbol{X})\right)$. The prior on the assignments $\boldsymbol{A}$ is given by marginalizing the $\boldsymbol{\alpha}^{(k)}$, which, when normalized, parametrize a batch of multinomial distributions,

$$p(\boldsymbol{A} \,|\, \boldsymbol{X}) = \int \mathcal{M}(\boldsymbol{A} \,|\, softmax(\boldsymbol{\alpha})) p(\boldsymbol{\alpha} \,|\, \boldsymbol{X}) \, \mathrm{d}\boldsymbol{\alpha}. \tag{2}$$

Modelling the relationship between the input and the associations allows us to efficiently model data, which, for example, is unimodal in some parts of the input space and bimodal in others. A simple smoothness prior will encode a belief for how quickly the components switch across the input domain.

Since the GPs of the $\boldsymbol{\alpha}^{(k)}$ use a zero mean function, our prior assumption is a uniform distribution of the different generative processes everywhere in the input space. If inference on the $\boldsymbol{a}_n$ reveals that, say, all data points at similar positions in the input space can be explained by the same k^{th} process, the belief about α can be adjusted to make a non-uniform distribution favorable at this position, thereby increasing the likelihood via $p(A \mid X)$. This mechanism introduces an incentive for the model to use as few functions as possible to explain the data and importantly allows us to predict a relative importance of these functions when calculating the posterior of the new observations x_*.

Figure 2 shows the resulting graphical model, which divides the generative process for every data point in the application of the latent functions on the left side and the assignment process on the right side. The interdependencies between the data points are introduced through the GP priors on $f_n^{(k)}$ and $\alpha_n^{(k)}$ and depend on the hyperparameters $\theta = \{\theta^{(k)}, \theta_\alpha^{(k)}, \sigma^{(k)}\}_{k=1}^K$.

The priors for the $f^{(k)}$ can be chosen independently to encode different prior assumptions about the underlying processes. In Sect. 4.1, we use different kernels to separate a non-linear signal from a noise process. Going further, we can also use deep GP as priors for the $f^{(k)}$ [9,23]. Since many real word systems are inherently hierarchical, prior knowledge can often be formulated more easily using composite functions [16].

3   Variational Approximation

Exact inference is intractable in this model. Instead, we formulate a variational approximation following ideas from [13,23]. Because of the rich structure in our model, finding a variational lower bound which is both faithful and can be evaluated analytically is hard. To proceed, we formulate an approximation which factorizes along both the K processes and N data points. This bound can be sampled efficiently and allows us to optimize both the models for the different processes $\{f^{(k)}\}_{k=1}^K$ and our belief about the data assignments $\{a_n\}_{n=1}^N$ simultaneously using stochastic optimization.

3.1   Variational Lower Bound

As first introduced by Titsias [24], we augment all GP in our model using sets of M inducing points $Z^{(k)} = \left(z_1^{(k)}, \ldots, z_M^{(k)}\right)$ and their corresponding function values $u^{(k)} = f^{(k)}(Z^{(k)})$, the inducing variables. We collect them as $Z = \{Z^{(k)}, Z_\alpha^{(k)}\}_{k=1}^K$ and $U = \{u^{(k)}, u_\alpha^{(k)}\}_{k=1}^K$. Taking the function $f^{(k)}$ and its corresponding GP as an example, the inducing variables $u^{(k)}$ are jointly Gaussian with the latent function values $F^{(k)}$ of the observed data by the definition of GPs. We follow [13] and choose the variational approximation $q(F^{(k)}, u^{(k)}) = p(F^{(k)} \mid u^{(k)}, X, Z^{(k)}) q(u^{(k)})$ with $q(u^{(k)}) = \mathcal{N}(u^{(k)} \mid m^{(k)}, S^{(k)})$. This formulation introduces the set $\{Z^{(k)}, m^{(k)}, S^{(k)}\}$ of variational parameters indicated in Fig. 2. To simplify notation we drop the dependency on Z in the following.

A central assumption of this approximation is that given enough well-placed inducing variables $u^{(k)}$, they are a sufficient statistic for the latent function values $F^{(k)}$. This implies conditional independence of the $f_n^{(k)}$ given $u^{(k)}$ and X. The variational posterior of a single GP can then be written as,

$$
\begin{aligned}
q\left(F^{(k)} \mid X\right) &= \int q\left(u^{(k)}\right) p\left(F^{(k)} \mid u^{(k)}, X\right) du^{(k)} \\
&= \int q\left(u^{(k)}\right) \prod_{n=1}^{N} p\left(f_n^{(k)} \mid u^{(k)}, x_n\right) du^{(k)},
\end{aligned}
\tag{3}
$$

which can be evaluated analytically, since it is a convolution of Gaussians. This formulation simplifies inference within single GPs. Next, we discuss how to handle the correlations between the different functions and the assignment processes.

Given a set of assignments A, this factorization along the data points is preserved in our model due to the assumed independence of the different functions in (1). The independence is lost if the assignments are unknown. In this case, both the (a priori independent) assignment processes and the functions influence each other through data with unclear assignments. Following the ideas of doubly stochastic variational inference (DSVI) presented by Salimbeni and Deisenroth [23] in the context of deep GPs, we maintain these correlations between different parts of the model while assuming factorization of the variational distribution. That is, our variational posterior takes the factorized form,

$$
\begin{aligned}
q(F, \alpha, U) &= q\left(\alpha, \{F^{(k)}, u^{(k)}, u_\alpha^{(k)}\}_{k=1}^{K}\right) \\
&= \prod_{k=1}^{K} \prod_{n=1}^{N} p\left(\alpha_n^{(k)} \mid u_\alpha^{(k)}, x_n\right) q\left(u_\alpha^{(k)}\right) \prod_{k=1}^{K} \prod_{n=1}^{N} p\left(f_n^{(k)} \mid u^{(k)}, x_n\right) q\left(u^{(k)}\right).
\end{aligned}
\tag{4}
$$

Our goal is to recover a posterior for both the generating functions and the assignment of data. To achieve this, instead of marginalizing A, we consider the variational joint of Y and A,

$$
q(Y, A) = \int p(Y \mid F, A) p(A \mid \alpha) q(F, \alpha) \, dF \, d\alpha,
\tag{5}
$$

which retains both the Gaussian likelihood of Y and the multinomial likelihood of A in (2). A lower bound $\mathcal{L}_{\mathrm{DAGP}}$ for the log-joint $\log p(Y, A \mid X)$ of DAGP is given by,

$$
\begin{aligned}
\mathcal{L}_{\mathrm{DAGP}} &= \mathbb{E}_{q(F,\alpha,U)} \left[\log \frac{p(Y, A, F, \alpha, U \mid X)}{q(F, \alpha, U)} \right] \\
&= \sum_{n=1}^{N} \mathbb{E}_{q(f_n)} \left[\log p(y_n \mid f_n, a_n) \right] + \sum_{n=1}^{N} \mathbb{E}_{q(\alpha_n)} \left[\log p(a_n \mid \alpha_n) \right] \\
&\quad - \sum_{k=1}^{K} \mathrm{KL}(q(u^{(k)}) \| p(u^{(k)} \mid Z^{(k)})) - \sum_{k=1}^{K} \mathrm{KL}(q(u_\alpha^{(k)}) \| p(u_\alpha^{(k)} \mid Z_\alpha^{(k)})).
\end{aligned}
\tag{6}
$$

Due to the structure of (4), the bound factorizes along the data enabling stochastic optimization. This bound has complexity $\mathcal{O}(NM^2K)$ to evaluate.

3.2   Optimization of the Lower Bound

An important property of the variational bound for DSVI [23] is that taking samples for single data points is straightforward and can be implemented efficiently. Specifically, for some k and n, samples $\hat{f}_n^{(k)}$ from $\mathrm{q}\left(f_n^{(k)}\right)$ are independent of all other parts of the model and can be drawn using samples from univariate unit Gaussians using reparametrizations [17,22].

Note that it would not be necessary to sample from the different processes, since $\mathrm{q}\left(F^{(k)}\right)$ can be computed analytically [13]. However, we apply the sampling scheme to the optimization of both the assignment processes α and the assignments A as for α, the analytical propagation of uncertainties through the *softmax* renormalization and multinomial likelihoods is intractable but can easily be evaluated using sampling.

We optimize $\mathcal{L}_{\mathrm{DAGP}}$ to simultaneously recover maximum likelihood estimates of the hyperparameters θ, the variational parameters $\{Z, m, S\}$, and assignments A. For every n, we represent the belief about a_n as a K-dimensional discrete distribution $\mathrm{q}(a_n)$. This distribution models the result of drawing a sample from $\mathcal{M}(a_n \,|\, softmax(\alpha_n))$ during the generation of the data point (x_n, y_n).

Since we want to optimize $\mathcal{L}_{\mathrm{DAGP}}$ using (stochastic) gradient descent, we need to employ a continuous relaxation to gain informative gradients of the bound with respect to the binary (and discrete) vectors a_n. One straightforward way to relax the problem is to use the current belief about $\mathrm{q}(a_n)$ as parameters for a convex combination of the $f_n^{(k)}$, that is, to approximate $f_n \approx \sum_{k=1}^K \mathrm{q}\left(a_n^{(k)}\right) \hat{f}_n^{(k)}$. Using this relaxation is problematic in practice. Explaining data points as mixtures of the different generating processes violates the modelling assumption that every data point was generated using exactly one function but can substantially simplify the learning problem. Because of this, special care must be taken during optimization to enforce the sparsity of $\mathrm{q}(a_n)$.

To avoid this problem, we propose using a different relaxation based on additional stochasticity. Instead of directly using $\mathrm{q}(a_n)$ to combine the $f_n^{(k)}$, we first draw a sample $\hat{a}_n$ from a concrete random variable as suggested by Maddison et al. [19], parameterized by $\mathrm{q}(a_n)$. Based on a temperature parameter λ, a concrete random variable enforces sparsity but is also continuous and yields informative gradients using automatic differentiation. Samples from a concrete random variable are unit vectors and for $\lambda \to 0$ their distribution approaches a discrete distribution.

Our approximate evaluation of the bound in (6) during optimization has multiple sources of stochasticity, all of which are unbiased. First, we approximate the expectations using Monte Carlo samples $\hat{f}_n^{(k)}$, $\hat{\alpha}_n^{(k)}$, and $\hat{a}_n$. And second, the factorization of the bound along the data allows us to use mini-batches for optimization [13,23].

3.3 Approximate Predictions

Predictions for a test location $\boldsymbol{x}_*$ are mixtures of K independent Gaussians, given by,

$$q(\boldsymbol{f}_* \mid \boldsymbol{x}_*) = \int \sum_{k=1}^{K} q\left(a_*^{(k)} \mid \boldsymbol{x}_*\right) q\left(\boldsymbol{f}_*^{(k)} \mid \boldsymbol{x}_*\right) \mathrm{d}\boldsymbol{a}_*^{(k)} \approx \sum_{k=1}^{K} \hat{a}_*^{(k)} \hat{\boldsymbol{f}}_*^{(k)}. \tag{7}$$

The predictive posteriors of the K functions $q\left(\boldsymbol{f}_*^{(k)} \mid \boldsymbol{x}_*\right)$ are given by K independent shallow GPs and can be calculated analytically [13]. Samples from the predictive density over $q(\boldsymbol{a}_* \mid \boldsymbol{x}_*)$ can be obtained by sampling from the GP posteriors $q\left(\boldsymbol{\alpha}_*^{(k)} \mid \boldsymbol{x}_*\right)$ and renormalizing the resulting vector $\boldsymbol{\alpha}_*$ using the *softmax*-function. The distribution $q(\boldsymbol{a}_* \mid \boldsymbol{x}_*)$ reflects the model's belief about how many and which of the K generative processes are relevant at the test location $\boldsymbol{x}_*$ and their relative probability.

3.4 Deep Gaussian Processes

For clarity, we have described the variational bound in terms of a shallow GP. However, as long as their variational bound can be efficiently sampled, any model can be used in place of shallow GPs for the $f^{(k)}$. Since our approximation is based on DSVI, an extension to deep GPs is straightforward. Analogously to [23], our new prior assumption about the kth latent function values $\mathrm{p}\left(\boldsymbol{F}'^{(k)} \mid \boldsymbol{X}\right)$ is given by,

$$\mathrm{p}\left(\boldsymbol{F}'^{(k)} \mid \boldsymbol{X}\right) = \prod_{l=1}^{L} \mathrm{p}\left(\boldsymbol{F}_l'^{(k)} \mid \boldsymbol{u}_l'^{(k)} \boldsymbol{F}_{l-1}'^{(k)}, \boldsymbol{Z}_l'^{(k)}\right), \tag{8}$$

for an L-layer deep GP and with $\boldsymbol{F}_0'^{(k)} := \boldsymbol{X}$. Similar to the single-layer case, we introduce sets of inducing points $\boldsymbol{Z}_l'^{(k)}$ and a variational distribution over their corresponding function values $q\left(\boldsymbol{u}_l'^{(k)}\right) = \mathcal{N}\left(\boldsymbol{u}_l'^{(k)} \mid \boldsymbol{m}_l'^{(k)}, \boldsymbol{S}_l'^{(k)}\right)$. We collect the latent multi-layer function values as $\boldsymbol{F}' = \{\boldsymbol{F}_l'^{(k)}\}_{k=1,l=1}^{K,L}$ and corresponding $\boldsymbol{U}'$ and assume an extended variational distribution,

$$\begin{aligned}
q(\boldsymbol{F}', \boldsymbol{\alpha}, \boldsymbol{U}') &= q\left(\boldsymbol{\alpha}, \{\boldsymbol{u}_\alpha^{(k)}\}_{k=1}^{K}, \{\boldsymbol{F}_l'^{(k)}, \boldsymbol{u}_l'^{(k)}\}_{k=1,l=1}^{K,L}\right) \\
&= \prod_{k=1}^{K} \prod_{n=1}^{N} \mathrm{p}\left(\alpha_n^{(k)} \mid \boldsymbol{u}_\alpha^{(k)}, \boldsymbol{x}_n\right) q\left(\boldsymbol{u}_\alpha^{(k)}\right) \prod_{k=1}^{K} \prod_{l=1}^{L} \prod_{n=1}^{N} \mathrm{p}\left(f_{n,l}'^{(k)} \mid \boldsymbol{u}_l'^{(k)}, \boldsymbol{x}_n\right) q\left(\boldsymbol{u}_l'^{(k)}\right),
\end{aligned} \tag{9}$$

where we identify $f_n'^{(k)} = f_{n,L}'^{(k)}$. As the nth marginal of the Lth layer depends only on the nth marginal of all layers above sampling from them remains straightforward [23]. The marginal is given by,

$$q(f_{n,L}'^{(k)}) = \int q(f_{n,L}'^{(k)} \,|\, f_{n,L-1}'^{(k)}) \prod_{l=1}^{L-1} q(f_{n,l}'^{(k)} \,|\, f_{n,l-1}'^{(k)}) \, df_{n,l}'^{(k)}. \qquad (10)$$

The complete bound is structurally similar to (6) and given by,

$$
\begin{aligned}
\mathcal{L}_{\text{DAGP}}' = &\sum_{n=1}^{N} \mathbb{E}_{q(f_n')} \left[\log p(y_n \,|\, f_n', a_n) \right] + \sum_{n=1}^{N} \mathbb{E}_{q(\alpha_n)} \left[\log p(a_n \,|\, \alpha_n) \right] \\
&- \sum_{k=1}^{K} \sum_{l=1}^{L} \text{KL}q(u_l^{(k)}) p(u_l^{(k)} \,|\, Z_l^{(k)}) - \sum_{k=1}^{K} \text{KL}q\left(u_\alpha^{(k)}\right) p\left(u_\alpha^{(k)} \,\middle|\, Z_\alpha^{(k)}\right).
\end{aligned}
\qquad (11)
$$

To calculate the first term, samples have to be propagated through the deep GP structures. This extended bound thus has complexity $\mathcal{O}(NM^2LK)$ to evaluate in the general case and complexity $\mathcal{O}(NM^2 \cdot \max(L, K))$ if the assignments a_n take binary values.

Table 1. Comparison of qualitative model capabilities. A model has a capability if it contains components which enable it to solve the respective task in principle.

Experiment	Predictive posterior	Multimodal data	Scalable inference	Interpretable priors	Data association	Predictive associations	Separate models
					Table 2	Table 3	Fig. 4
DAGP (Ours)	✓	✓	✓	✓	✓	✓	✓
OMGP [18]	✓	✓	–	✓	✓	–	✓
RGPR [21]	✓	✓	–	✓	–	–	–
GPR	✓	–	✓	✓	–	–	–
BNN+LV [10]	✓	✓	✓	–	–	–	–
MDN [4]	✓	✓	✓	–	–	–	–
MLP	✓	–	✓	–	–	–	–

4   Experiments

In this section, we investigate the behavior of the DAGP model. We use an implementation of DAGP in TensorFlow [1] based on GPflow [20] and the implementation of DSVI [23]. Table 1 compares qualitative properties of DAGP and related work. All models can solve standard regression problems and yield unimodal predictive distributions or, in case of multi-layer perceptrons (MLP), a single point estimate. Both standard Gaussian process regression (GPR) and MLP do not impose structure which enables the models to handle multi-modal data. Mixture density networks (MDN) [4] and the infinite mixtures of Gaussian processes (RGPR) [21] model yield multi-modal posteriors through mixtures with many

Table 2. Results on the ChoiceNet data set. The gray part of the table shows RMSE results for baseline models from [7]. For our experiments using the same setup, we report RMSE comparable to the previous results together with MLL. Both are calculated based on a test set of 1000 equally spaced samples of the noiseless underlying function.

Outliers	DAGP MLL	OMGP MLL	DAGP RMSE	OMGP RMSE	CN RMSE	MDN RMSE	MLP RMSE	GPR RMSE	RGPR RMSE
0%	**2.86**	2.09	0.008	**0.005**	0.034	0.028	0.039	0.008	0.017
20%	**2.71**	1.83	0.008	**0.005**	0.022	0.087	0.413	0.280	0.013
40%	**2.12**	1.60	**0.005**	0.007	0.018	0.565	0.452	0.447	1.322
60%	0.874	**1.23**	0.031	**0.006**	0.023	0.645	0.636	0.602	0.738
80%	**0.126**	-1.35	0.128	0.896	**0.084**	0.778	0.829	0.779	1.523

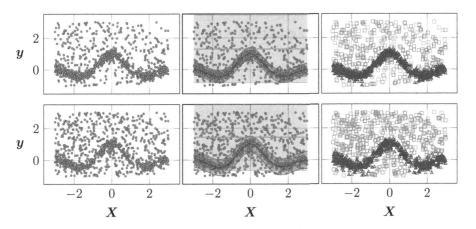

Fig. 3. DAGP on the ChoiceNet data set with 40% outliers (upper row) and 60% outliers (lower row). We show the raw data (left), joint posterior (center) and assignments (right). The bimodal DAGP identifies the signal perfectly up to 40% outliers. For 60% outliers, some of the noise is interpreted as signal, but the latent function is still recovered.

components but do not solve an association problem. Similarly, Bayesian neural networks with added latent variables (BNN+LV) [10] represent such a mixture through a continuous latent variable. Both the overlapping mixtures of Gaussian processes (OMGP) [18] model and DAGP explicitly model the data association problem and yield independent models for the different generating processes. However, OMGP assumes global relevance of the different modes. In contrast, DAGP infers a spacial posterior of this relevance. We evaluate our model on three problems to highlight the following advantages of the explicit structure of DAGP:

Interpretable Priors give Structure to Ill-posed Data Association Problems. In Sect. 4.1, we consider a noise separation problem, where a signal of interest is disturbed with uniform noise. To solve this problem, assumptions about what constitutes a signal are needed. The hierarchical structure of DAGP allows us to formulate independent and interpretable priors on the noise and signal processes.

Predictive Associations Represent Knowledge About the Relevance of Generative Processes. In Sect. 4.2, we investigate the implicit incentive of DAGP to explain data using as few processes as possible. Additional to a joint posterior explaining the data, DAGP also gives insight into the relative importance of the different processes in different parts of the input space. DAGP is able to explicitly recover the changing number of modes in a data set.

Separate Models for Independent Generating Processes Avoid Model Pollution. In Sect. 4.3, we simulate a system with multiple operational regimes via mixed observations of two different cart-pole systems. DAGP successfully learns an informative joint posterior by solving the underlying association problem. We show that the DAGP posterior contains two separate models for the two original operational regimes.

4.1   Noise Separation

We consider an experiment based on a noise separation problem. We apply DAGP to a one-dimensional regression problem with uniformly distributed asymmetric outliers in the training data. We use a task proposed by Choi et al. [7] where we sample $x \in [-3, 3]$ uniformly and apply the function $f(x) = (1 - \delta)(\cos(\pi/2 \cdot x)\exp(-(x/2)^2) + \gamma) + \delta \cdot \epsilon$, where $\delta \sim \mathcal{B}(\lambda)$, $\epsilon \sim \mathbb{U}(-1, 3)$ and $\gamma \sim \mathcal{N}(0, 0.15^2)$. That is, a fraction λ of the training data, the outliers, are replaced by asymmetric uniform noise. We sample a total of 1000 data points and use 25 inducing points for every GP in our model.

Every generating process in our model can use a different kernel and therefore encode different prior assumptions. For this setting, we use two processes, one with a squared exponential kernel and one with a white noise kernel. This encodes the problem statement that every data point is either part of the signal we wish to recover or uncorrelated noise. To avoid pathological solutions for high outlier ratios, we add a prior to the likelihood variance of the first process, which encodes our assumption that there actually is a signal in the training data.

The model proposed in [7], called ChoiceNet (CN), is a specific neural network structure and inference algorithm to deal with corrupted data. In their work, they compare their approach to the MLP, MDN, GPR, and RGPR models. We add experiments for both DAGP and OMGP. Table 2 shows results for outlier rates varied from 0 % to 80 %. Besides the root mean squared error (RMSE) reported in [7], we also report the mean test log likelihood (MLL).

Since we can encode the same prior knowledge about the signal and noise processes in both OMGP and DAGP, the results of the two models are comparable: For low outlier rates, they correctly identify the outliers and ignore them, resulting in a predictive posterior of the signal equivalent to standard GP regression without outliers. In the special case of 0 % outliers, the models correctly identify that the process modelling the noise is not necessary, thereby simplifying to standard GP regression. For high outlier rates, stronger prior knowledge about the signal is required to still identify it perfectly. Figure 3 shows the DAGP posterior for an outlier rate of 60 %. While the function has still been identified well, some of the noise is also explained using this process, thereby introducing slight errors in the predictions.

4.2 Multimodal Data

Our second experiment applies DAGP to a multimodal data set. The data, together with recovered posterior attributions, can be seen in Fig. 4. We uniformly sample 350 data points in the interval $x \in [-2\pi, 2\pi]$ and obtain $y_1 = \sin(x) + \epsilon$, $y_2 = \sin(x) - 2\exp(-1/2 \cdot (x-2)^2) + \epsilon$ and $y_3 = -1 - 3/8\pi \cdot x + 3/10 \cdot \sin(2x) + \epsilon$ with additive independent noise $\epsilon \sim \mathcal{N}(0, 0.005^2)$. The resulting data set $\mathcal{D} = \{(x, y_1), (x, y_2), (x, y_3)\}$ is trimodal in the interval $[0, 5]$ and is otherwise bimodal with one mode containing double the amount of data than the other.

We use squared exponential kernels as priors for both the $f^{(k)}$ and $\alpha^{(k)}$ and 25 inducing points in every GP. Figure 4 shows the posterior of a DAGP with $K = 4$ modes applied to the data, which correctly identified the underlying functions. The figure shows the posterior belief about the assignments A and illustrates that DAGP recovered that it needs only three of the four available modes to explain the data. One of the modes is only assigned points in the interval $[0, 5]$ where the data is actually trimodal.

This separation is explicitly represented in the model via the assignment processes α (bottom panel in Fig. 4). Importantly, DAGP does not only cluster the data with respect to the generating processes but also infers a factorization of the input space with respect to the relative importance of the different processes. The model has disabled the mode $k = 2$ in the complete input space and has learned that the mode $k = 1$ is only relevant in the interval $[0, 5]$ where the three enabled modes each explain about a third of the data. Outside this interval, the model has learned that one of the modes has about twice the assignment probability than the other one, thus correctly reconstructing the true generative process. The DAGP is implicitly incentivized to explain the data using as few modes as possible through the likelihood term of the inferred a_n in (6). At $x = -10$ the inferred modes and assignment processes start reverting to their respective priors away from the data.

4.3 Mixed Cart-Pole Systems

Our third experiment is based on the cart-pole benchmark for reinforcement learning as described by Barto et al. [3] and implemented in OpenAI Gym [6]. In this benchmark, the objective is to apply forces to a cart moving on a frictionless track to keep a pole, which is attached to the cart via a joint, in an upright position. We consider the regression problem of predicting the change of the pole's angle given the current state of the cart and the action applied. The current state of the cart consists of the cart's position and velocity and the pole's angular position and velocity. To simulate a dynamical system with changing system characteristics our experimental setup is to sample trajectories from two

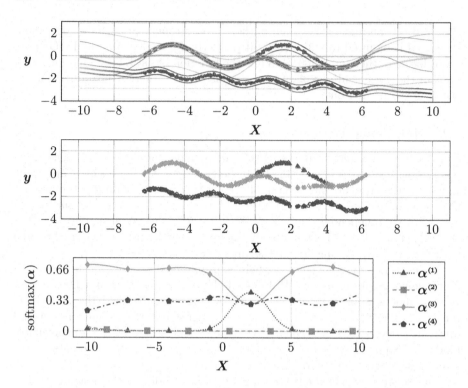

Fig. 4. The DAGP posterior on an artificial data set with bimodal and trimodal parts. The joint predictions (top) are mixtures of four Gaussians weighed by the assignment probabilities α (bottom). The weights are represented via the opacity of the modes. The model has learned that the mode $k = 2$ is irrelevant, that the mode $k = 1$ is only relevant around the interval $[0, 5]$. Outside this interval, the mode $k = 3$ is twice as likely as the mode $k = 4$. The concrete assignments a (middle) of the training data show that the mode $k = 1$ is only used to explain observations where the training data is trimodal. The mode $k = 2$ is never used.

different cart-pole systems and merging the resulting data into one training set. The task is not only to learn a model which explains this data well, but to solve the association problem introduced by the different system configurations. This task is important in reinforcement learning settings where we study systems with multiple operational regimes.

We sample trajectories from the system by initializing the pole in an almost upright position and then applying 10 uniform random actions. We add Gaussian noise $\epsilon \sim \mathcal{N}(0, 0.01^2)$ to the observed angle changes. To increase the nonlinearity of the dynamics, we apply the action for five consecutive time steps and allow the pole to swing freely instead of ending the trajectory after reaching a specific angle. The data set consists of 500 points sampled from the *default* cart-pole system and another 500 points sampled from a *short-pole* cart-pole system in which we halve the mass of the pole to 0.05 and shorten the pole to

Table 3. Results on the cart-pole data set. We report mean log likelihoods with their standard error for ten runs. The upper results are obtained by training the model on the mixed data set and evaluating it jointly (left) on multi-modal predictions. We evaluate the two inferred sub-models for the default system (center) and short-pole system (right). We provide gray baseline comparisons with BNN+LV and GPR models which cannot solve the data assignment problem. BNN+LV yields joint predictions which cannot be separated into sub-models. Specialized GPR models trained the individual training sets give a measure of the possible performance if the data assignment problem would be solved perfectly.

	Mixed		Default only	Short-pole only
	Train	Test	Test	Test
DAGP	**0.575 ± 0.013**	**0.521 ± 0.009**	0.844 ± 0.002	**0.602 ± 0.005**
DAGP 2	0.548 ± 0.012	**0.519 ± 0.008**	**0.859 ± 0.001**	0.599 ± 0.011
DAGP 3	0.527 ± 0.004	0.491 ± 0.003	0.852 ± 0.002	0.545 ± 0.012
OMGP	−1.04 ± 0.02	−1.11 ± 0.03	0.66 ± 0.02	−0.81 ± 0.12
BNN+LV	0.519 ± 0.005	0.524 ± 0.005	—	—
GPR Mixed	0.452 ± 0.003	0.421 ± 0.003	—	—
GPR Default	—	—	0.867 ± 0.001	−7.54 ± 0.14
GPR Short	—	—	−5.14 ± 0.04	0.792 ± 0.003

0.1, a tenth of its default length. This short-pole system is more unstable and the pole reaches higher speeds. Predictions in this system therefore have to take the multimodality into account, as mean predictions between the more stable and the more unstable system can never be observed. We consider three test sets, one sampled from the default system, one sampled from the short-pole system, and a mixture of the two. They are generated by sampling trajectories with an aggregated size of 5000 points from each system for the first two sets and their concatenation for the mixed set.

For this data set, we use squared exponential kernels for both the $f^{(k)}$ and $\alpha^{(k)}$ and 100 inducing points in every GP. We evaluate the performance of deep GPs with up to three layers and squared exponential kernels as models for the different functions. As described in [16,23], we use identity mean functions for all but the last layers and initialize the variational distributions with low covariances. We compare our models with OMGP and three-layer relu-activated Bayesian neural networks with added latent variables (BNN+LV). The latent variables can be used to effectively model multimodalities and stochasticity in dynamical systems for model-based reinforcement learning [11]. We also compare DAGP to three kinds of sparse GPs (GPR) [14]. They are trained on the mixed data set, the default system and the short-pole system respectively and serve as a baseline comparison as these models cannot handle multi-modal data.

Table 3 shows results for ten runs of these models. The GPR model predicts a unimodal posterior for the mixed data set which covers both systems. Its mean prediction is approximately the mean of the two regimes and is physically implausible. The DAGP and BNN+LV models yield informative multi-modal predictions with comparable performance. In our setup, OMGP could not successfully solve the data association problem and thus does not produce a useful joint posterior. The OMGP's inference scheme is tailored to ordered one-dimensional problems. It does not trivially translate to the 4D cart-pole problem.

As BNN+LV does not explicitly solve the data association problem, the model does not yield sub-models for the two different systems. Similar results would be obtained with the MDN and RGPR models, which also cannot be separated into sub-models. OMGP and DAGP yield such sub-models which can independently be used for predictions in the default or short-pole systems. Samples drawn from these models can be used to generate physically plausible trajectories in the respective system. OMGP fails to model the short-pole system but does yield a viable model for the default system which evolves more slowly due to higher torque and is therefore easier to learn. In contrast, the two sub-models inferred by DAGP perform well on their respective systems, showing that DAGP reliably solves the data association problem and successfully avoids model pollution by separating the two systems well. Given this separation, shallow and deep models for the two modes show comparable performance. The more expressive deep GPs model the default system slightly better while sacrificing performance on the more difficult short-pole system.

5   Conclusion

We have presented a fully Bayesian model for the data association pronem. Our model factorises the observed data into a set of independent processes and provides a model over both the processes and their association to the observed data. The data association problem is inherently ill-constrained and requires significant assumptions to recover a solution. In this paper, we make use of interpretable GP priors allowing global a priori information to be included into the model. Importantly, our model is able to exploit information both about the underlying functions and the association structure. We have derived a principled approximation to the marginal likelihood which allows us to perform inference for flexible hierarchical processes. In future work, we would like to incorporate the proposed model in a reinforcement learning scenario where we study a dynamical system with different operational regimes.

References

1. Abadi, M., Agarwal, A., Barham, P., et al.: TensorFlow: Large-Scale Machine Learning on Heterogeneous Systems (2015). tensorflow.org
2. Bar-Shalom, Y.: Tracking and Data Association. Academic Press Professional Inc., San Diego (1987). ISBN 0-120-79760-7

3. Barto, A.G., Sutton, R.S., Anderson, C.W.: Neuronlike adaptive elements that can solve difficult learning control problems. IEEE Trans. Syst. Man Cybern. **SMC–13**(5), 834–846 (1983). https://doi.org/10.1109/TSMC.1983.6313077. ISSN 0018-9472

4. Bishop, C.M.: Mixture density networks. Technical report (1994)

5. Bodin, E., Campbell, N.D.F., Ek, C.H.: Latent Gaussian Process Regression. arXiv:1707.05534 [cs, stat], July 2017

6. Brockman, G., Cheung, V., Pettersson, L., et al.: OpenAI Gym. arXiv:1606.01540 [cs], June 2016

7. Choi, S., Hong, S., Lim, S.: ChoiceNet: Robust Learning by Revealing Output Correlations. arXiv:1805.06431 [cs, stat], May 2018

8. Cox, I.J.: A review of statistical data association techniques for motion correspondence. Int. J. Comput. Vision **10**, 53–66 (1993)

9. Damianou, A., Lawrence, N.: Deep Gaussian processes. In: Artificial Intelligence and Statistics, pp. 207–215, April 2013

10. Depeweg, S., Hernández-Lobato, J.M., Doshi-Velez, F., Udluft, S.: Learning and Policy Search in Stochastic Dynamical Systems with Bayesian Neural Networks. arXiv:1605.07127 [cs, stat], May 2016

11. Depeweg, S., Hernandez-Lobato, J.-M., Doshi-Velez, F., Udluft, S.: Decomposition of uncertainty in Bayesian deep learning for efficient and risk-sensitive learning. In: International Conference on Machine Learning, pp. 1192–1201 (2018)

12. Hein, D., Depeweg, S., Tokic, M., et al.: A benchmark environment motivated by industrial control problems. In: 2017 IEEE Symposium Series on Computational Intelligence (SSCI), Honolulu, HI, pp. 1–8. IEEE, November 2017. https://doi.org/10.1109/SSCI.2017.8280935. ISBN 978-1-5386-2726-6

13. Hensman, J., Fusi, N., Lawrence, N.D.: Gaussian processes for big data. In: Uncertainty in Artificial Intelligence, p. 282. Citeseer (2013)

14. Hensman, J., de G. Matthews, A.G., Ghahramani, Z.: Scalable variational Gaussian process classification. J. Mach. Learn. Res. **38**, 351–360 (2015)

15. Jacobs, R.A., Jordan, M.I., Nowlan, S.J., Hinton, G.E.: Adaptive mixtures of local experts. Neural Comput. **3**(1), 79–87 (1991)

16. Kaiser, M., Otte, C., Runkler, T., Ek, C.H.: Bayesian alignments of warped multi-output gaussian processes. In: Bengio, S., Wallach, H., Larochelle, H., et al. (eds.) Advances in Neural Information Processing Systems 31, pp. 6995–7004. Curran Associates Inc., New York (2018)

17. Kingma, D.P., Salimans, T., Welling, M.: Variational dropout and the local reparameterization trick. In: Cortes, C., Lawrence, N.D., Lee, D.D., Sugiyama, M., Garnett, R. (eds.) Advances in Neural Information Processing Systems 28, pp. 2575–2583. Curran Associates Inc., New York (2015)

18. Lázaro-Gredilla, M., Van Vaerenbergh, S., Lawrence, N.D.: Overlapping mixtures of Gaussian processes for the data association problem. Pattern Recogn. **45**(4), 1386–1395 (2012)

19. Maddison, C.J., Mnih, A., Teh, Y.W.: The Concrete Distribution: A Continuous Relaxation of Discrete Random Variables. arXiv:1611.00712 [cs, stat], November 2016

20. de G. Matthews, A.G., van der Wilk, M., Nickson, T., et al.: GPflow: a Gaussian process library using TensorFlow. J. Mach. Learn. Res. **18**(40), 1–6 (2017)

21. Rasmussen, C.E., Ghahramani, Z.: Infinite mixtures of Gaussian process experts. In: Dietterich, T.G., Becker, S., Ghahramani, Z. (eds.) Advances in Neural Information Processing Systems 14, pp. 881–888. MIT Press, Cambridge (2002)

22. Rezende, D.J., Mohamed, S., Wierstra, D.: Stochastic Backpropagation and Approximate Inference in Deep Generative Models, January 2014
23. Salimbeni, H., Deisenroth, M.: Doubly stochastic variational inference for deep Gaussian processes. In: Guyon, I., Luxburg, U.V., Bengio, S., et al. (eds.) Advances in Neural Information Processing Systems 30, pp. 4588–4599. Curran Associates Inc., New York (2017)
24. Titsias, M.K.: Variational learning of inducing variables in sparse Gaussian processes. In: AISTATS, vol. 5, pp. 567–574 (2009)
25. Tresp, V.: Mixtures of Gaussian processes. In: Leen, T.K., Dietterich, T.G., Tresp, V. (eds.) Advances in Neural Information Processing Systems 13, pp. 654–660. MIT Press, Cambridge (2001)

Incorporating Dependencies in Spectral Kernels for Gaussian Processes

Kai Chen[1,2,3,5(✉)], Twan van Laarhoven[3,4], Jinsong Chen[1,2,5], and Elena Marchiori[3]

[1] Shenzhen Institutes of Advanced Technology, Chinese Academy of Sciences, Shenzhen, People's Republic of China
js.chen@siat.ac.cn
[2] Shenzhen College of Advanced Technology, University of Chinese Academy of Sciences, Shenzhen, People's Republic of China
[3] Institute for Computing and Information Sciences, Radboud University, Nijmegen, The Netherlands
{kai,elenam}@cs.ru.nl
[4] Faculty of Management, Science and Technology, Open University of The Netherlands, Heerlen, The Netherlands
twan.vanlaarhoven@ou.nl
[5] Shenzhen Engineering Laboratory of Ocean Environmental Big Data Analysis and Application, Shenzhen 518055, People's Republic of China

Abstract. Gaussian processes (GPs) are an elegant Bayesian approach to model an unknown function. The choice of the kernel characterizes one's assumption on how the unknown function autocovaries. It is a core aspect of a GP design, since the posterior distribution can significantly vary for different kernels. The spectral mixture (SM) kernel is derived by modelling a spectral density - the Fourier transform of a kernel - with a linear mixture of Gaussian components. As such, the SM kernel cannot model dependencies between components. In this paper we use cross convolution to model dependencies between components and derive a new kernel called Generalized Convolution Spectral Mixture (GCSM). Experimental analysis of GCSM on synthetic and real-life datasets indicates the benefit of modeling dependencies between components for reducing uncertainty and for improving performance in extrapolation tasks.

Keywords: Gaussian processes · Spectral mixture · Convolution · Dependency · Uncertainty

1 Introduction

Gaussian processes (GPs) provide regression models where a posterior distribution over the unknown function is maintained as evidence is accumulated.

Electronic supplementary material The online version of this chapter (https://doi.org/10.1007/978-3-030-46147-8_34) contains supplementary material, which is available to authorized users.

U. Brefeld et al. (Eds.): ECML PKDD 2019, LNAI 11907, pp. 565–581, 2020.
https://doi.org/10.1007/978-3-030-46147-8_34

This allows GPs to learn complex functions when a large amount of evidence is available, and it makes them robust against overfitting in the presence of little evidence. GPs can model a large class of phenomena through the choice of the kernel, which characterizes one's assumption on how the unknown function auto-covaries [17,18]. The choice of the kernel is a core aspect of a GP design, since the posterior distribution can significantly vary for different kernels. In particular, in [24] a flexible kernel called Spectral Mixture (SM) was defined, by modelings the kernel's spectrum with a mixture of Gaussians. An SM kernel can be represented by a sum of components, and can be derived from Bochner's theorem as the inverse Fourier Transform (FT) of its corresponding spectral density. SM kernels assume mutually independence of its components [24–26].

Here we propose a generalization of SM kernels that explicitly incorporates dependencies between components. We use cross convolution to model dependencies between components, and derive a new kernel called Generalized Convolution Spectral Mixture (GCSM) kernel. The number of hyper-parameters remains equal to that of SM, and there is no increase in computational complexity. A stochastic variational inference technique is used to perform scalable inference. In the proposed framework, GCSM without cross components (that is, by only considering auto-convolution of base components) reduces to the SM kernel.

We assess the performance of GCSM kernels through extensive experiments on real-life datasets. The results show that GCSM is able to capture dependence structure in time series and multi-dimensional data containing correlated patterns. Furthermore, we show the benefits of the proposed kernel for reducing uncertainty, overestimation and underestimation in extrapolation tasks. Our main contributions can be summarized as follows:

- a new spectral mixture kernel that captures dependencies between components;
- two metrics, posterior correlation (see Eq. 10) and learned dependency (see Eq. 19) to analyze intrinsic dependencies between components in the SM kernel and dependencies captured by our kernel, respectively;
- an extensive comparison between the proposed GCSM and other SM kernels in terms of spectral density, covariance, posterior predictive density and sampling, as well as in terms of performance gain.

The remainder of this paper is organized as follows. We start by giving a background on GPs, SM kernels, and we briefly describe related work. Next, we introduce the GCSM kernel, and discuss the differences between the GCSM and SM kernels. Then we describe the experimental setting and show results on synthetic and real-world datasets. We conclude with a summary and discussion on future work.

2   Background

A GP is any distribution over functions such that any finite set of function values has a joint Gaussian distribution. A GP model, before conditioning on the data, is completely specified by its mean function $m(\mathbf{x}) = \mathbb{E}(f(\mathbf{x}))$ and its covariance function (also called *kernel*) $k(\mathbf{x}, \mathbf{x}') = \mathrm{cov}(f(\mathbf{x}), f(\mathbf{x}'))$ for input vectors $\mathbf{x}, \mathbf{x}' \in \mathbb{R}^P$. It is common practice to assume that the mean function is simply zero everywhere, since uncertainty about the mean function can be taken into account by adding an extra term to the kernel (cf. e.g. [18]).

The kernel induces a positive definite covariance matrix $K = k(X, X)$ of the training locations set X. For a regression task [18], by choosing a kernel and inferring its hyper-parameters Θ, we can predict the unknown function value $\tilde{y}^*$ and its variance $\mathbb{V}[\tilde{y}^*]$ (the uncertainty) for a test point $\mathbf{x}^*$ as follows:

$$\tilde{y}^* = \mathbf{k}^{*\top}(K + \sigma_n^2 I)^{-1}\mathbf{y} \tag{1}$$

$$\mathbb{V}[\tilde{y}^*] = k^{**} - \mathbf{k}^{*\top}(K + \sigma_n^2 I)^{-1}\mathbf{k}^* \tag{2}$$

where $k^{**} = k(\mathbf{x}^*, \mathbf{x}^*)$, $\mathbf{k}^{*\top}$ is the vector of covariances between $\mathbf{x}^*$ and X, and $\mathbf{y}$ are the observed values at training locations in X. The hyper-parameters can be optimized by minimizing the Negative Log Marginal Likelihood (NLML) $-\log p(\mathbf{y}|\mathbf{x}, \Theta)$. Smoothness and generalization properties of GPs depend on the kernel function and its hyper-parameters Θ [18]. In particular, the SM kernel [26], here denoted by k_{SM}, is derived by modeling the empirical spectral density as a Gaussian mixture, using Bochner's Theorem [2,22], resulting in the following kernel:

$$k_{\mathrm{SM}}(\tau) = \sum_{i=1}^{Q} w_i k_{\mathrm{SM}i}(\tau), \tag{3}$$

$$k_{\mathrm{SM}i}(\tau) = \cos\left(2\pi\tau^\top\boldsymbol{\mu}_i\right) \prod_{p=1}^{P} \exp\left(-2\pi^2\tau^2\Sigma_{i,p}\right), \tag{4}$$

where $\tau = \mathbf{x} - \mathbf{x}'$, Q denotes the number of components, $k_{\mathrm{SM}i}$ is the i-th component, P denotes the input dimension, and w_i, $\boldsymbol{\mu}_i = [\mu_{i,1}, ..., \mu_{i,P}]$, and $\Sigma_i = \mathrm{diag}\left([\sigma_{i,1}^2, ..., \sigma_{i,P}^2]\right)$ are the weight, mean, and variance of the i-th component in the frequency domain, respectively. The variance σ_i^2 can be thought of as an inverse length-scale, μ_i as a frequency, and w_i as a contribution. For SM kernel, we have $\hat{k}_{\mathrm{SM}i}(\mathbf{s}) = [\varphi_{\mathrm{SM}i}(\mathbf{s}) + \varphi_{\mathrm{SM}i}(-\mathbf{s})]/2$ where $\varphi_{\mathrm{SM}i}(\mathbf{s}) = \mathcal{N}(\mathbf{s}; \boldsymbol{\mu}_i, \Sigma_i)$ is a symmetrized scale-location Gaussian in the frequency domain.

The SM kernel does not consider dependencies between components, because it is a linear combination of $\{k_{\mathrm{SM}i}\}_{i=1}^{Q}$ (see Eq. 3). Therefore its underlying assumption is that such components are mutually independent. One should not confuse the spectral mixture components that make up the spectral density of the SM kernel with the base components of the Fourier Transform (FT): (1) FT components are periodic trigonometric functions, such as sine and cosine functions, while SM kernel components are quasi-periodic Gaussian functions; (2) FT components are orthogonal (i.e. the product of an arbitrary pair of Fourier series components is zero) while the product of two arbitrary SM components is not necessarily equal to zero; (3) the SM component in the frequency domain is a

Gaussian function covering wide frequency range while an FT component is just a sharp peak at a single frequency, which is covered by multiple SM components.

3   Related Work

Various kernel functions have been proposed [18], such as Squared Exponential (SE), Periodic (PER), and general Matérn (MA). Recently, Spectral Mixture (SM) kernels have been proposed in [24]. Additive GPs have been proposed in [4], a GP model whose kernel implicitly sums over all possible products of one-dimensional base kernels. Extensions of these kernels include the spectral mixture product kernel (SMP) [25] $k_{\text{SMP}}(\tau|\Theta) = \prod_{p=1}^{P} k_{\text{SM}}(\tau_p|\Theta_p)$, which uses multi-dimensional SM kernels, and extends the application scope of SM kernels to image data and spatial time data. Other interesting families of kernels include non-stationary kernels [7,10,19,21], which are capable to learn input-dependent covariances between inputs. All these mentioned kernels do not consider dependencies between components. To the best of our knowledge, our proposed kernel is the first attempt to explicitly model dependencies between components.

The problem of expressing structure present in the data being modeled with kernels has been investigated also in the context of kernel composition. For instance, in [3] a framework was introduced for composing kernel structures. A space of kernel structures is defined compositionally in terms of sums and products of a small number of base kernel structures. Then an automatic search over this space of kernel structures is performed using marginal likelihood as search criterion. Although composing kernels allows one to produce kernels combining several high-level properties, they depend on the choice of base kernel families, composition operators, and search strategy. Instead, here we directly enhance SM kernels by incorporating dependency between components.

4   Dependencies Between SM Components

Since the SM kernel is additive, any $f \sim \mathcal{GP}(0, k_{\text{SM}})$ can be expressed as

$$f = \sum_{i=1}^{Q} f_i, \qquad (5)$$

where each $f_i \sim \mathcal{GP}(0, w_i k_{\text{SM}i})$ is drawn from a GP with kernel $w_i k_{\text{SM}i}$. With a slight abuse of notation we denote by $\boldsymbol{f}_i$ the function values at training locations X, and by $\boldsymbol{f}_i^*$ the function values at some set of query locations X^*.

From the additivity of the SM kernel it follows that the f_i's are a priori independent. Then, by using the formula for Gaussian conditionals we can give the conditional distribution of a GP-distributed function $\boldsymbol{f}_i^*$ conditioned on its sum with another GP-distributed function $\boldsymbol{f}_j$:

$$\boldsymbol{f}_i^*|\boldsymbol{f}_{i+j} \sim \mathcal{N}\left(K_i^{*\top} K_{i+j}^{-1} \boldsymbol{f}_{i+j}, \; K_i^{**} - K_i^{*\top} K_{i+j}^{-1} K_i^*\right) \qquad (6)$$

where $\boldsymbol{f}_{i+j} = \boldsymbol{f}_i + \boldsymbol{f}_j$ and $K_{i+j} = K_i + K_j$. The reader is referred to [3] (Sect. 2.4.5) for the derivation of these results. The Gaussian conditionals express the model's posterior uncertainty about the different components of the signal, integrating over the possible configurations of the other components.

In particular, we have:

$$\mathbb{V}(\boldsymbol{f}_i^* | \boldsymbol{f}_i) = K_i^{**} - K_i^{*\top} K_i^{-1} K_i^*, \tag{7}$$

$$\mathbb{V}(\boldsymbol{f}_i^* | \boldsymbol{f}_i, \boldsymbol{f}_j) = K_i^{**} - K_i^{*\top} K_{i+j}^{-1} K_i^*. \tag{8}$$

In general $\mathbb{V}(\boldsymbol{f}_i^* | \boldsymbol{f}_i) \neq \mathbb{V}(\boldsymbol{f}_i^* | \boldsymbol{f}_i, \boldsymbol{f}_j)$ when dependencies between components are present. We can also compute the posterior covariance between the height of any two functions, conditioned on their sum [3]:

$$\mathrm{Cov}\left(\boldsymbol{f}_i^*, \boldsymbol{f}_j^* | \boldsymbol{f}_i, \boldsymbol{f}_j\right) = -K_i^{*\top} K_{i+j}^{-1} K_j^*. \tag{9}$$

We define posterior correlation ρ_{ij}^* as normalized posterior covariance:

$$\rho_{ij}^* = \frac{\mathrm{Cov}\left(\boldsymbol{f}_i^*, \boldsymbol{f}_j^* | \boldsymbol{f}_i, \boldsymbol{f}_j\right)}{\left(\mathbb{V}\left(\boldsymbol{f}_i^* | \boldsymbol{f}_i, \boldsymbol{f}_j\right) \mathbb{V}\left(\boldsymbol{f}_j^* | \boldsymbol{f}_i, \boldsymbol{f}_j\right)\right)^{1/2}}. \tag{10}$$

We can use $\rho_{ij}^* \neq 0$ as indicator of statistical dependence between components i and j. In our experiments, we will use the normalized posterior covariance to illustrate the presence of dependencies between components in SM kernels for GPs.

5   Generalized Convolution SM Kernels

We propose to generalize SM kernels by incorporating cross component terms. To this aim we use versions of the seminal Convolution theorem, which states that under suitable conditions the Fourier transform of a convolution of two signals is the pointwise product of their Fourier transforms. In particular, convolution in the time domain equals point-wise multiplication in the frequency domain. The construction of our kernel relies on the fact that any stationary kernel $k(\mathbf{x}, \mathbf{x}')$ can be represented as a convolution form on $\mathbb{R}^P$ (see e.g. [5,6,13])

$$k(\mathbf{x}, \mathbf{x}') = \int_{\mathbb{R}^P} g(\mathbf{u}) \, g(\tau - \mathbf{u}) \, d\mathbf{u} = (g * g)(\tau). \tag{11}$$

By applying a Fourier transformation to the above general convolution form of the kernel we obtain $\hat{k}(\mathbf{s}) = (\hat{g}(\mathbf{s}))^2$ in the frequency domain. For each weighted component $w_i k_{\mathrm{SM}i}(\tau)$ in the SM kernel, we can define the function $\hat{g}_{\mathrm{SM}i}(\mathbf{s})$ as

$$\hat{g}_{\mathrm{SM}i}(\mathbf{s}) = \left(w_i \hat{k}_{\mathrm{SM}i}(\mathbf{s})\right)^{1/2} = w_i^{\frac{1}{2}} \frac{\exp\left(-\frac{1}{4}(\mathbf{s} - \boldsymbol{\mu}_i)^\top \Sigma_i^{-1}(\mathbf{s} - \boldsymbol{\mu}_i)\right)}{((2\pi)^P |\Sigma_i|)^{1/4}}, \tag{12}$$

which is the basis function of the i-th weighted spectral density. We use cross-correlation, which is similar in nature to the convolution of two functions.

The cross-correlation of functions $f(\tau)$ and $g(\tau)$ is equivalent to the convolution of $\overline{f}(-\tau)$ and $g(\tau)$ [1]. we have that the cross-correlation between two components $f_i \sim \mathcal{GP}(0, w_i k_{\mathrm{SM}i})$ and $f_j \sim \mathcal{GP}(0, w_j k_{\mathrm{SM}j})$ is as

$$k_{\mathrm{GCSM}}^{i \times j}(\tau) = w_i k_{\mathrm{SM}i}(\tau) \star w_j k_{\mathrm{SM}j}(\tau) = \mathcal{F}_{s \to \tau}^{-1}\left[w_i \varphi_{\mathrm{SM}i}(\mathbf{s}) \cdot \overline{w_j \varphi_{\mathrm{SM}j}}(\mathbf{s})\right](\tau) \quad (13)$$

where $\mathcal{F}_{s \to \tau}^{-1}$, $\star$, and $\overline{(-)}$ denote the inverse FT, the cross-correlation operator, and the complex conjugate operator, respectively. Here $\varphi_{\mathrm{SM}i}(\mathbf{s}) = \mathcal{N}(\mathbf{s}; \boldsymbol{\mu}_i, \Sigma_i)$ is a symmetrized scale-location Gaussian in the frequency domain ($\varphi_{\mathrm{SM}i}(\mathbf{s}) = \overline{\varphi_{\mathrm{SM}i}}(\mathbf{s})$). The product of Gaussians $\varphi_{\mathrm{SM}i}(\mathbf{s})$ and $\varphi_{\mathrm{SM}j}(\mathbf{s})$ is also a Gaussian. Therefore, the cross-correlation term in the frequency domain has also a Gaussian form and must be greater than zero, which implies the presence of dependencies between f_i and f_j.

The cross-correlation term $k_{\mathrm{GCSM}}^{i \times j}(\tau)$ of our new kernel, obtained as cross-correlation of the i-th and j-th base components in SM, corresponds to the cross spectral density term

$$\hat{k}_{\mathrm{GCSM}}^{i \times j}(\mathbf{s}) = \hat{g}_{\mathrm{SM}i}(\mathbf{s}) \cdot \overline{\hat{g}_{\mathrm{SM}j}}(\mathbf{s}) \quad (14)$$

in the frequency domain. From (12) and (14) we obtain

$$\hat{k}_{\mathrm{GCSM}}^{i \times j}(\mathbf{s}) = w_{ij} a_{ij} \frac{\exp\left(-\frac{1}{2}(\mathbf{s} - \boldsymbol{\mu}_{ij})^{\top} \Sigma_{ij}^{-1}(\mathbf{s} - \boldsymbol{\mu}_{ij})\right)}{\sqrt{(2\pi)^P |\Sigma_{ij}|}}. \quad (15)$$

The parameters for the cross spectral density term $\hat{k}_{\mathrm{GCSM}}^{i \times j}(\mathbf{s})$ corresponding to the cross convolution component $k_{\mathrm{GCSM}}^{i \times j}(\tau)$ are:

– cross weight: $w_{ij} = \sqrt{w_i w_j}$

– cross amplitude: $a_{ij} = \left| \dfrac{\sqrt{4\Sigma_i \Sigma_j}}{\Sigma_i + \Sigma_j} \right|^{\frac{1}{2}} \exp\left(-\dfrac{(\boldsymbol{\mu}_i - \boldsymbol{\mu}_j)^{\top}(\Sigma_i + \Sigma_j)^{-1}(\boldsymbol{\mu}_i - \boldsymbol{\mu}_j)}{4}\right)$

– cross mean: $\boldsymbol{\mu}_{ij} = \dfrac{\Sigma_i \boldsymbol{\mu}_j + \Sigma_j \boldsymbol{\mu}_i}{\Sigma_i + \Sigma_j}$;

– cross covariance: $\Sigma_{ij} = \dfrac{2\Sigma_i \Sigma_j}{\Sigma_i + \Sigma_j}$

Parameters $\boldsymbol{\mu}_{ij}$ and Σ_{ij} can be interpreted as frequency and inverse length-scale of the cross component $k_{\mathrm{GCSM}}^{i \times j}(\tau)$, respectively. Cross amplitude a_{ij} is a normalization constant which does not depend on $\mathbf{s}$.

Observe that when $\hat{g}_{\mathrm{SM}i}(\mathbf{s})$ is equal to $\hat{g}_{\mathrm{SM}j}(\mathbf{s})$, $w_{ij} a_{ij}$, $\boldsymbol{\mu}_{ij}$, and Σ_{ij} reduce to w_i, 1, $\boldsymbol{\mu}_i$, and Σ_i, respectively. In this case, the cross spectral density $\hat{k}_{\mathrm{GCSM}}^{i \times j}(\mathbf{s})$ is equal to $\hat{k}_{\mathrm{SM}i}(\mathbf{s})$. We can observe that the closer the frequencies $\boldsymbol{\mu}_i$ and $\boldsymbol{\mu}_j$ are and as closer the scales Σ_i and Σ_j between components i and j in the SM kernel are, the higher the cross convolution components contribution in GCSM will be.

Using the inverse FT, by the distributivity of the convolution operator and by the symmetry of the spectral density, we can obtain the GCSM kernel with

Q (auto-convolution) components as:

$$k_{\mathrm{GCSM}}(\tau) = \sum_{i=1}^{Q} \sum_{j=1}^{Q} c_{ij} \exp\left(-2\pi^2 \tau^\top \Sigma_{ij} \tau\right) \cos\left(2\pi\tau^\top \boldsymbol{\mu}_{ij}\right) \tag{16}$$

where $c_{ij} = w_{ij} a_{ij}$ is the cross contribution incorporating cross weight and cross amplitude to quantify the dependency between components in the GCSM kernel. The proof that GCSM is positive semi-definite is given in the Appendix. The auto-convolution cross-terms in GCSM correspond to the components in SM since $k_{\mathrm{GCSM}}^{i \times i}(\tau) = k_{\mathrm{SM}i}(\tau)$. It is a mixture of periodic cosine kernels and their dependencies, weighted by exponential weights.

6   Comparisons Between GCSM and SM

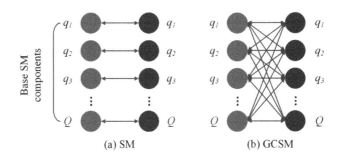

(a) SM   (b) GCSM

Fig. 1. SM and GCSM with Q components. (a) SM models only auto-convolution between base components. (b) GCSM models both auto- and cross-convolution between base components.

Figure 1 illustrates the difference between SM and GCSM, where each connection represents a convolution component of the kernel. SM is an auto-convolution spectral mixture kernel that ignores the cross-correlation between base components. The figure also shows that SM is a special case of GCSM since the latter involves both cross convolution and auto-convolution of base components. In GCSM, dependencies are explicitly modeled and quantified. In the experiment illustrated in Fig. 2, SM and GCSM have the same initial parameters the same noise term. The observations are sampled from a $\mathcal{GP}(0, K_{\mathrm{SM}} + K_{\mathrm{GCSM}})$. From Fig. 2 we can observe clear differences (in terms of amplitude, peak, and trend from SM) for the kernel functions (SM: top, in dashed red; GCSM: bottom, in dashed blue). For the corresponding spectral densities, the dependence (in magenta) modeled by GCSM is also a Gaussian in the frequency domain, which yields a spectral mixture with different magnitude. The posterior distribution and sampling are obtained from GCSM and SM conditioned on six observations (black crosses). One can observe that the predictive distribution of GCSM has a tighter confidence interval (in blue shadow) than SM (in red shadow).

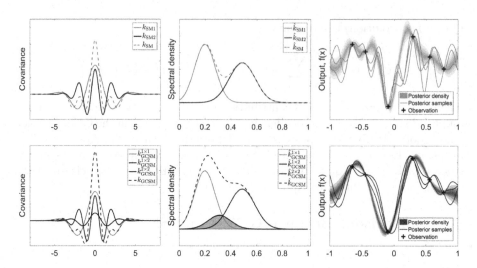

Fig. 2. Covariance, spectral density, and posterior functions drawn from GPs with SM and GCSM kernels conditioning on six samples. In the first row two SM components ($w_1 k_{\mathrm{SM1}}(\tau)$ and $w_2 k_{\mathrm{SM2}}(\tau)$) correspond to two solid lines (in cyan and black). In the second row two GCSM components with dependent structures ($k_{\mathrm{GCSM}}^{1 \times 2}(\tau)$) (in magenta). SM and GCSM plots have the same axes. (Color figure online)

7   Scalable Inference

Exact inference for GPs is prohibitively slow for more than a few thousand datapoints, as it involves inverting the covariance matrix $(K + \sigma_n^2 I)^{-1}$ and computing the determinant of the covariance $|K + \sigma_n^2 I|$. This issues are addressed by covariance matrix approximation [16,20,23] and inference approximation [8,9].

Here we employ stochastic variational inference (SVI) which provides a generalized framework for combining inducing points $\mathbf{u}$ and variational inference yielding impressive efficiency and precision. Specifically, SVI approximates the true GP posterior with a GP conditioned on a small set of inducing points $\mathbf{u}$, which as a set of global variables summarise the training data and are used to perform variational inference. The variational distribution $P(\mathbf{u}) = \mathcal{N}(\mathbf{u}; \boldsymbol{\mu}_{\mathbf{u}}, \Sigma_{\mathbf{u}})$ gives a variational lower bound $\mathcal{L}_3(\mathbf{u}; \boldsymbol{\mu}_{\mathbf{u}}, \Sigma_{\mathbf{u}})$, also called Evidence Lower Bound (ELBO) of the quantity $p(\mathbf{y}|X)$. From [9], the variational distribution $\mathcal{N}(\mathbf{u}; \boldsymbol{\mu}_{\mathbf{u}}, \Sigma_{\mathbf{u}})$ contains all the information in the posterior approximation, which represents the distribution on function values at the inducing points $\mathbf{u}$. From $\frac{\partial \mathcal{L}_3}{\partial \boldsymbol{\mu}_{\mathbf{u}}} = 0$ and $\frac{\partial \mathcal{L}_3}{\partial \Sigma_{\mathbf{u}}} = 0$, we can obtain an optimal solution of the variational distribution. The posterior distribution of testing data can be written as

$$p(f^*|X, \mathbf{y}) = \mathcal{N}(\mathbf{k}_{\mathbf{u}}^* K_{\mathbf{uu}}^{-1} \boldsymbol{\mu}_{\mathbf{u}}, k^{**} + \mathbf{k}_{\mathbf{u}}^{*\top}(K_{\mathbf{uu}}^{-1} \Sigma_{\mathbf{u}} K_{\mathbf{uu}}^{-1} - K_{\mathbf{uu}}^{-1})\mathbf{k}_{\mathbf{u}}^*) \qquad (17)$$

where $\mathbf{k}_{\mathbf{u}}^*$ is the GCSM covariance vector between $\mathbf{u}$ and test point $\mathbf{x}^*$. The complexity of SVI is $\mathcal{O}(m^3)$ where m is the number of inducing points.

7.1 Hyper-parameter Initialization

In our experiments, we use the empirical spectral densities to initialize the hyper-parameters, as recommend in [10, 24]. Different from these works, we apply a Blackman window function to the training data to improve the quality of empirical spectral densities, e.g. the signal to noise ratio (SNR), and to more easily discover certain characteristics of the signal, e.g. magnitude and frequency. We consider the windowed empirical spectral densities $p(\Theta|\mathbf{s})$ as derived from the data, and then apply a Bayesian Gaussian mixture model (GMM) in order to get the Q cluster centers of the Gaussian spectral densities [10].

$$p(\Theta|\mathbf{s}) = \sum_{i=1}^{Q} \tilde{w}_i \mathcal{N}(\tilde{\boldsymbol{\mu}}_i, \tilde{\Sigma}_i) \tag{18}$$

We use the Expectation Maximization algorithm [15] to estimate the parameters $\tilde{w}_i$, $\tilde{\boldsymbol{\mu}}_i$, and $\tilde{\Sigma}_i$. The results are used as initial values of w_i, $\boldsymbol{\mu}_i$, and Σ_i, respectively.

8 Experiments

We comparatively assess the performance of GCSM on real-world datasets. Three of these datasets have been used in the literature of GP methods. The other is a relative new dataset which we use to illustrate the capability of GPs with the considered kernels to model irregular long term increasing trends. We use Mean Squared Error (MSE $= \frac{1}{n}\sum_{i=1}^{n}\left(y_i - \tilde{y}_i\right)^2$) as the performance metric for all tasks. We used the 95% confidence interval (instead of, e.g., error bar) to quantify uncertainty (see Eq. (2)). In addition to these performance metrics, we also consider the posterior correlation ρ_{ij}^* (see Eq. (10)) to illustrate the underlying dependency between SM components. Moreover, to illustrate the dependency between components captured by the cross-components in our GCSM kernel, we use the normalized cross-correlation term:

$$\gamma_{ij}(\tau) = \frac{k_{\text{GCSM}}^{i \times j}(\tau)}{\sqrt{k_{\text{SM}i}(\tau)k_{\text{SM}j}(\tau)}} \tag{19}$$

We call γ_{ij} *learned dependency* between component i and j. Note that $\gamma_{ij} = 1$ when $i = j$. In our experiments we will analyze dependency between components in SM kernel for GPs as expressed by the posterior covariance, and dependency modeled by GCSM kernels for GPs as expressed by γ_{ij}'s. We compare GCSM with ordinary SM for prediction tasks on four real-life datasets: monthly average atmospheric CO_2 concentrations [12, 18], monthly ozone concentrations, air revenue passenger miles, and the larger multidimensional alabone dataset.

As baselines for comparison we consider the popular kernels implemented in the GPML toolbox [18]: linear with bias (LIN), SE, polynomial (Poly), PER, rational quadratic (RQ), MA, Gabor, fractional Brownian motion covariance

(FBM), underdamped linear Langevin process covariance (ULL), neural network (NN) and SM kernels. For the considered multidimensional dataset, we use automatic relevance determination (ARD) for other kernels to remove irrelevant input. FBM and ULL kernels are only available for time series type of data, thus they are not applied to this dataset. We use the GPML toolbox [17] and GPflow [14] for ordinary and scalable inference, respectively. For GCSM, we calculate the gradient of the parameters using an analytical derivative technique. In all experiments we use the hyper-parameter initialization previously described for SM and GCSM kenels.

8.1   Compact Long Term Extrapolation

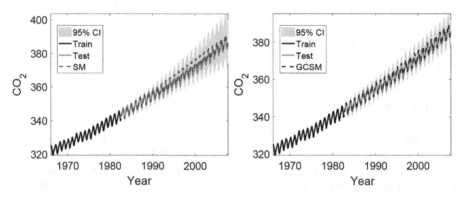

Fig. 3. Performance of SM (left) and GCSM (right) on the CO_2 concentration dataset.

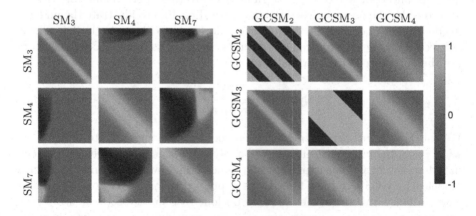

Fig. 4. Left: posterior correlations ρ_{ij}^* in SM; Right: learned dependencies γ_{ij} in GCSM.

The monthly average atmospheric CO_2 concentration dataset (cf. e.g. [18]) is a popular experiment which shows the advantage and flexibility of GPs due to multiple patterns with different scales in the data, such as long-term, seasonal and short-term trends. The dataset was collected at the Mauna Loa Observatory, Hawaii, between 1958 and 2003. We use 40% of the location points as training data and the rest 60% as testing data. For both GCSM and SM we consider $Q = 10$ components. The Gaussian mixture of the empirical spectral densities is considered to initialize the hyper-parameters.

Figure 3(a) shows that GCSM (in dashed blue) is better than ordinary SM (in red) in terms of predictive mean and variance. Moreover, GCSM yields a smaller confidence interval than SM. Unlike SM, GCSM does not overestimate the long-term trend. As for the analysis of the posterior correlation and learned dependency, evidence of posterior positive and negative correlations ρ_{ij}^* can be observed for SM components (3, 4, 7) (left subplot in Fig. 4). These posterior correlations have been used for prediction (see Supplementary material). The right plot in Fig. 4 shows clear evidence of learned dependency γ_{ij} for GCSM components (2, 3, 4). GCSM and SM are optimized independently, so component identifiers in the figures do not necessarily correspond to each other. Observe that plots for GCSM kernel with $i = j$ (right subplot) show stripes because of the normalization term in Eq. (19).

8.2 Modeling Irregular Long Term Decreasing Trends

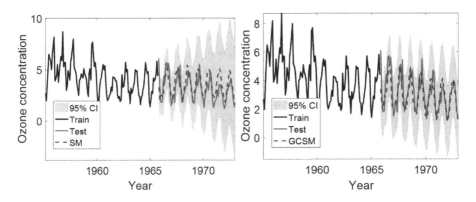

Fig. 5. Performance of SM (left) and GCSM (right) on the ozone concentration dataset.

We consider the monthly ozone concentration dataset (216 values) collected at Downtown L. A. from time range Jan 1955–Dec 1972. This dataset has different characteristics than the CO_2 concentration one, namely a gradual long term downtrend and irregular peak values in the training data which are much higher than those in the testing data. These characteristics make extrapolation a challenging task. Here we use the first 60% of observations for training, and the rest (40%) for testing (shown in black and green in Fig. 5, respectively). Again we consider $Q = 10$ components for both kernels.

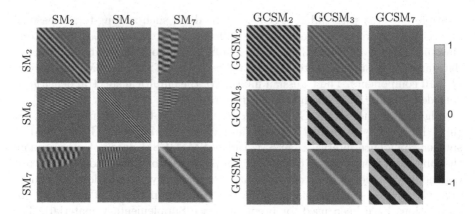

Fig. 6. Left: posterior correlations ρ_{ij}^* in SM; Right: learned dependencies γ_{ij} in GCSM.

Figure 5 shows that the ozone concentration signal has a long term decreasing tendency while the training part has a relatively stable evolution. Here SM fails to discover such long term decreasing tendency and overestimates the future trend with low confidence. Instead, GCSM is able to confidently capture the long term decreasing tendency. These results substantiate the beneficial effect of using cross-components for correcting overestimation and for reducing predictive uncertainty.

Results in Table 1 show that on this dataset GCSM consistently achieves a lower MSE compared with SM and other baselines.

Figure 6 shows posterior correlation (left plot) and learned dependency (right plot), The texture of the posterior correlation ρ_{ij}^* among SM components (2, 6, 7) demonstrates a more complicated posterior correlation between these components than that of the previous experiment. The learned dependency γ_{ij} is clearly visible between components (2, 3, 7).

8.3   Modeling Irregular Long Term Increasing Trends

In this experiment we consider another challenging extrapolation task, using the air revenue passenger miles[1] with time range Jan 2000–Apr 2018, monthly collected by the U.S. Bureau of Transportation Statistics. Given 60% recordings at the beginning of the time series, we wish to extrapolate the remaining observations (40%). In this setting we can observe an apparent long term oscillation tendency in the training observations which is not present in the testing data. As shown in Fig. 7, even if at the beginning (in 2001) there seems to be a decreasing trend due to 9/11 attack and since 2010 was known as a disappointing year for safety, there is a positive trend as a result of a boosting of the airline market and extensive globalization.

---

[1] https://fred.stlouisfed.org/series/AIRRPMTSI.

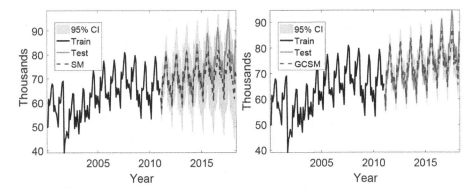

Fig. 7. Performance of SM (left) and GCSM (right) on air revenue passenger miles.

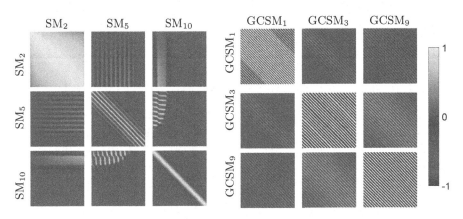

Fig. 8. Left: posterior correlations ρ_{ij}^* in SM; Right: learned dependencies γ_{ij} in GCSM.

In order to show the need for GCSM in a real-life scenarios, we consider the air revenue passenger miles dataset that contains a fake long term oscillation tendency happened in the training data but not in the testing data. The air revenue passenger miles[2] with time range Jan 2000–Apr 2018 was monthly collected by U.S. Bureau of Transportation Statistics.

Results in Table 1 show that on this dataset GCSM consistently achieves a lower MSE compared with SM and other baselines. In particular, kernels such as SE, Periodic and Matérn 5/2 have a poor performance on this extrapolation task.

In Fig. 8, the left plot shows the posterior correlation ρ_{ij}^* among SM components (2, 5, 10), and the right subplot the learned dependency γ_{ij} between components (1, 3, 9).

---

[2] https://fred.stlouisfed.org/series/AIRRPMTSI.

8.4   Prediction with Large Scale Multidimensional Data

After comparing GCSM and SM on extrapolation tasks on time series with diverse characteristics, we investigate comparatively its performance on a prediction task using a large multidimensional dataset, the abalone dataset. The dataset consists of 4177 instances with 8 attributes: Sex, Length, Diameter, Height, Whole weight, Shucked weight, Viscera weight, and Shell weight. The goal is to predict the age of an abalone from physical measurements. Abalone's age is measured by cutting the shell through the cone, staining it, and counting the number of rings through a microscope. Thus the task is to predict the number of rings from the above mentioned attributes. We use the first 3377 instances as training data and the remaining 800 as testing data. For both GCSM and SM we used $Q = 5$ components. We use the windowed empirical density to initialize the hyper-parameters, as described in Sect. 7.1. Here components are multivariate Gaussian distributions in the frequency domain.

Results in Table 1 show that also on this type of task GCSM achieves lower MSE than SM.

Table 1. Performances between GCSM and other kernels. Left: MSE, right: NLML.

Kernel	CO_2	Ozon	Air	Abalone	Kernel	CO_2	Ozon	Air	Abalone
LIN	39.09	1.86	57.64	10.93	LIN	451.38	235.68	462.01	24261.35
SE	128502.50	10.40	4967.18	8.14	SE	399.90	208.53	456.68	21246.86
Poly	132369.70	11.36	5535.81	6.30	Poly	1444.80	375.86	735.39	17964.17
PER	53.37	3.87	276.07	7.98	PER	459.53	236.71	456.38	18775.23
RQ	985.39	1.86	168.33	5.38	RQ	222.17	196.96	430.86	15988.48
MA	110735.30	9.83	4711.33	7.52	MA	278.33	208.17	451.03	20288.56
Gabor	131931.30	2.09	5535.84	4.80	Gabor	1444.62	240.55	735.41	15400.84
FBM	193.18	2.56	172.01	–.–	FBM	910.61	202.42	457.792	–.–
ULL	117500.40	9.34	405.07	–.–	ULL	819.09	206.85	441.31	–.–
NN	326.81	1.69	116.66	5.60	NN	460.73	225.46	449.31	17695.80
SM	9.36	0.97	36.28	3.59	SM	**62.09**	160.75	328.56	8607.99
GCSM	**1.19**	**0.59**	**10.02**	**3.29**	GCSM	64.34	**160.48**	**300.69**	**8566.35**

SM and GCSM kernels achieve comparable performance in terms of NLML (see right part of Table 1). This seems surprising, given the smaller uncertainty and MSE results obtained by GCSM. However, note that NLML is the sum of two terms (and a constant term that is ignored): a model fit and a complexity penalty term. The first term is the data fit term which is maximized when the data fits the model very well. The second term is a penalty on the complexity of the model, i.e. the smoother the better. When Optimizing NLML finds a balance between the two and this changes with the data observed.

Overall, results indicate the beneficial effect of modeling directly dependencies between components, as done in our kernel.

9   Conclusion

We proposed the generalized convolution spectral mixture (GCSM) kernel, a generalization of SM kernels with an expressive closed form to modeling dependencies between components using cross convolution in the frequency domain.

Experiments on real-life datasets indicate that the proposed kernel, when used in GPs, can identify and model the complex structure of the data and be used to perform long-term trends forecasting. Although here we do not focus on non-stationary kernels, GCSM can be transformed into a non-stationary GCSM, through parameterizing weights $w_i(x)$, means $\mu_i(x)$, and $\sigma_i(x)$ as kernel matrices by means of a Gaussian function. Future work includes the investigation of more generalized non-stationary GCSM.

An issue that remains to be investigated is efficient inference. This is a core issue in GP methods which needs to be addressed also for GPs with GCSM kernels. Lévy process priors as proposed in [11] present a promising approach for tackling this problem, by regularizing spectral mixture for automatic selection of the number of components and pruning of unnecessary components.

Acknowledgements. Part of this work was supported by the Strategic Priority Research Program of the Chinese Academy of Sciences, Grant No. XDA19030301 and Shenzhen Discipline Construction Project for Urban Computing and Data Intelligence.

References

1. Gold, B.: Theory and Application of Digital Signal Processing. Prentice-Hall, Upper Saddle River (1975)
2. Bochner, S.: Lectures on Fourier Integrals (AM-42), vol. 42. Princeton University Press, Princeton (2016)
3. Duvenaud, D.: Automatic model construction with Gaussian processes, Doctoral thesis. Ph.D. thesis (2014). https://doi.org/10.17863/CAM.14087
4. Duvenaud, D., Nickisch, H., Rasmussen, C.E.: Additive Gaussian processes. In: Neural Information Processing Systems, pp. 226–234 (2012)
5. Gaspari, G., Cohn, S.E.: Construction of correlation functions in two and three dimensions. Q. J. Roy. Meteorol. Soc. **125**(554), 723–757 (1999)
6. Genton, M.G., Kleiber, W., et al.: Cross-covariance functions for multivariate geostatistics. Stat. Sci. **30**(2), 147–163 (2015)
7. Heinonen, M., Mannerström, H., Rousu, J., Kaski, S., Lähdesmäki, H.: Nonstationary Gaussian process regression with hamiltonian monte carlo. In: Artificial Intelligence and Statistics, pp. 732–740 (2016)
8. Hensman, J., Durrande, N., Solin, A.: Variational Fourier features for Gaussian processes. J. Mach. Learn. Res. **18**, 151:1–151:52 (2017)
9. Hensman, J., Fusi, N., Lawrence, N.D.: Gaussian processes for big data. In: Nicholson, A., Smyth, P. (eds.) Proceedings of the Twenty-Ninth Conference on Uncertainty in Artificial Intelligence, UAI 2013, Bellevue, WA, USA, 11–15 August 2013. AUAI Press (2013)
10. Herlands, W., et al.: Scalable Gaussian processes for characterizing multidimensional change surfaces. In: Artificial Intelligence and Statistics, pp. 1013–1021 (2016)

11. Jang, P.A., Loeb, A., Davidow, M., Wilson, A.G.: Scalable Levy process priors for spectral kernel learning. In: Advances in Neural Information Processing Systems, pp. 3943–3952 (2017)
12. Keeling, C.D.: Atmospheric CO_2 records from sites in the SIO air sampling network. In: Trends' 93: A Compendium of Data on Global Change, pp. 16–26 (1994)
13. Majumdar, A., Gelfand, A.E.: Multivariate spatial modeling for geostatistical data using convolved covariance functions. Math. Geol. **39**(2), 225–245 (2007)
14. Matthews, A.G.D.G., et al.: GPflow: a Gaussian process library using tensorflow. J. Mach. Learn. Res. **18**(40), 1–6 (2017)
15. Moon, T.K.: The expectation-maximization algorithm. IEEE Signal Process. Mag. **13**(6), 47–60 (1997)
16. Quiñonero-Candela, J., Rasmussen, C.E.: A unifying view of sparse approximate Gaussian process regression. J. Mach. Learn. Res. **6**, 1939–1959 (2005)
17. Rasmussen, C.E., Nickisch, H.: Gaussian processes for machine learning (GPML) toolbox. J. Mach. Learn. Res. **11**, 3011–3015 (2010)
18. Rasmussen, C.E., Williams, C.K.I.: Gaussian processes for machine learning. In: Adaptive Computation and Machine Learning. MIT Press (2006)
19. Remes, S., Heinonen, M., Kaski, S.: Non-stationary spectral kernels. In: Advances in Neural Information Processing Systems, pp. 4645–4654 (2017)
20. Snelson, E., Ghahramani, Z.: Sparse Gaussian processes using pseudo-inputs. In: Advances in Neural Information Processing Systems, pp. 1257–1264 (2006)
21. Snoek, J., Swersky, K., Zemel, R., Adams, R.: Input warping for Bayesian optimization of non-stationary functions. In: International Conference on Machine Learning, pp. 1674–1682 (2014)
22. Stein, M.: Interpolation of Spatial Data: Some Theory for Kriging (1999)
23. Williams, C.K., Seeger, M.: Using the Nyström method to speed up kernel machines. In: Advances in Neural Information Processing Systems, pp. 682–688 (2001)
24. Wilson, A., Adams, R.: Gaussian process kernels for pattern discovery and extrapolation. In: Proceedings of the 30th International Conference on Machine Learning, ICML 2013, pp. 1067–1075 (2013)
25. Wilson, A.G., Gilboa, E., Nehorai, A., Cunningham, J.P.: Fast kernel learning for multidimensional pattern extrapolation. In: Advances in Neural Information Processing Systems, pp. 3626–3634 (2014)
26. Wilson, A.G.: Covariance kernels for fast automatic pattern discovery and extrapolation with Gaussian processes. University of Cambridge (2014)

Deep Convolutional Gaussian Processes

Kenneth Blomqvist[1,2], Samuel Kaski[1,2], and Markus Heinonen[1,2(✉)]

[1] Aalto University, Espoo, Finland
{kenneth.blomqvist,samuel.kaski,markus.o.heinonen}@aalto.fi
[2] Helsinki Institute for Information Technology HIIT, Espoo, Finland

Abstract. We propose deep convolutional Gaussian processes, a deep Gaussian process architecture with convolutional structure. The model is a principled Bayesian framework for detecting hierarchical combinations of local features for image classification. We demonstrate greatly improved image classification performance compared to current convolutional Gaussian process approaches on the MNIST and CIFAR-10 datasets. In particular, we improve state-of-the-art CIFAR-10 accuracy by over 10% points.

Keywords: Gaussian processes · Convolutions · Variational inference

1 Introduction

Gaussian processes (GPs) are a family of flexible function distributions defined by a kernel function [25]. The modeling capacity is determined by the chosen kernel. Standard stationary kernels lead to models that underperform in practice. Shallow – or single layer – Gaussian processes are often sub-optimal since flexible kernels that would account for non-stationary patterns and long-range interactions in the data are difficult to design and infer [26,35]. Deep Gaussian processes boost performance by modelling networks of GP nodes [8,30] or by mapping inputs through multiple Gaussian process 'layers' [5,27]. While more flexible and powerful than shallow GPs, deep Gaussian processes result in degenerate models if the individual GP layers are not invertible, which limits their potential [7].

Convolutional neural networks (CNN) are a celebrated approach for image recognition tasks with outstanding performance [21]. These models encode a hierarchical translation-invariance assumption into the structure of the model by applying convolutions to extract increasingly complex patterns through the layers.

While neural networks have achieved unparalleled results on many tasks, they have their shortcomings. Effective neural networks require large number of parameters that require careful optimisation to prevent overfitting. Neural networks can often leverage a large number of training data to counteract this problem. Developing methods that are better regularized and can incorporate prior knowledge would allow us to deploy machine learning methods in domains

© Springer Nature Switzerland AG 2020
U. Brefeld et al. (Eds.): ECML PKDD 2019, LNAI 11907, pp. 582–597, 2020.
https://doi.org/10.1007/978-3-030-46147-8_35

where massive amounts of data is not available. Conventional neural networks do not provide reliable uncertainty estimates on predictions, which are important in many real world applications.

The deterministic CNN's have been extended into the probabilistic domain with weight uncertainties [3], while combinations of CNN's and Gaussian processes have been shown to improve calibration of the prediction uncertainty [31]. In deep kernel learning (DKL) a feature-extracting deep neural network is stacked with a Gaussian process predictor layer [38], learning the neural network weights by variational inference [37]. Neural networks are known to converge to Gaussian processes at the limit of infinite layer width [19,20,34], and similar correspondence have been shown between CNN's and Gaussian processes as well [10].

Recently van der Wilk et al. proposed the first convolution-based Gaussian process for images with promising performance [33]. They proposed a shallow weighted additive model where Gaussian process responses over image subpatches are aggregated for image classification. The convolutional Gaussian process is unable to model pattern combinations due to its restriction to a single layer. Very recently convolutional kernels have been applied in a deep Gaussian process, however with little improvement upon the shallow convolutional GP model [18]. The translation insensitive convolutional kernel adds increased flexibility by location-dependent convolutions for both shallow and deep models [6][1].

In this paper we propose a deep convolutional Gaussian process, which iteratively convolves several GP functions over an image. We learn multimodal probabilistic representations that encode combinations of increasingly complex pattern combinations as a function of depth. Our model is a fully Bayesian kernel method with no neural network component. On the CIFAR-10 dataset, deep convolutions increase the current state-of-the-art GP predictive accuracy from 65% to 76%. We show that our GP-based model performs better than a CNN model with similar depth, and provides better calibrated and more consistent uncertainty estimates on predictions.

2 Background

In this section we provide an overview of the main methods our work relies upon. We consider supervised image classification problems with N examples $\mathbf{X} = \{\mathbf{x}_i\}_{i=1}^N$ each associated with a label $y_i \in \mathbb{Z}$. We assume images $\mathbf{x} \in \mathbb{R}^{W \times H \times C}$ as 3D tensors of size $W \times H \times C$ over C channels, where RGB color images have $C = 3$ color channels.

---

[1] We note that after placing our current manuscript in arXiv in October 2018, a subsequent arXiv manuscript has already extended the proposed deep convolution model by introducing location-dependent kernel [6].

2.1   Discrete Convolutions

A convolution as used in convolutional neural networks takes a signal, two dimensional in the case of an image, and a tensor valued filter to produce a new signal [11]. The filter is moved across the signal and at each step taking a dot product with the corresponding section in the signal. The resulting signal will have a high value where the signal is similar to the filter, zero where it's orthogonal to the filter and a low value where it's very different from the filter. A convolution of a two dimensional image $\mathbf{x}$ and a convolutional filter $\mathbf{g}$ is defined:

$$(\mathbf{x} * \mathbf{g})[i,j] = \sum_{w=0}^{W-1} \sum_{h=0}^{H-1} \mathbf{x}[i+w, j+h]\mathbf{g}[w,h] \tag{1}$$

$\mathbf{x}[i,j] \in \mathbb{R}^3$ and $\mathbf{g}$ is in $\mathbb{R}^{H \times W \times 3}$. Here H and W define the size of the convolutional filter. Typical values could be $H = W = 5$ or $H = W = 3$. Typically multiple convolutional filters are used, each convolved over the input to produce several output signals which are stacked together.

By default the convolution is defined over every location of the image. Sometimes one might use only every other location. This is referred to as the *stride*. A stride of 2 means only every other location i, j is taken in the output.

2.2   Primer on Gaussian Processes

Gaussian processes are a family of Bayesian models that characterize distributions of functions [24]. A zero-mean Gaussian process prior on latent function $f(\mathbf{x}) \in \mathbb{R}$,

$$f(\mathbf{x}) \sim \mathcal{GP}(0, K(\mathbf{x}, \mathbf{x}')) \tag{2}$$

defines a *prior* distribution over function values $f(\mathbf{x})$ with mean and covariance:

$$\mathbb{E}[f(\mathbf{x})] = 0 \tag{3}$$
$$\mathbf{cov}[f(\mathbf{x}), f(\mathbf{x}')] = K(\mathbf{x}, \mathbf{x}') \tag{4}$$

A GP prior defines that for any collection of n inputs $X = (\mathbf{x}_1, \ldots, \mathbf{x}_n)^T$, the corresponding function values

$$\mathbf{f} = (f(\mathbf{x}_1), \ldots, f(\mathbf{x}_n))^T \in \mathbb{R}^n$$

follow a multivariate Normal distribution

$$\mathbf{f} \sim \mathcal{N}(\mathbf{0}, \mathbf{K}) \tag{5}$$

$\mathbf{K} = (K(\mathbf{x}_i, \mathbf{x}_j))_{i,j=1}^n \in \mathbb{R}^{n \times n}$ is the kernel matrix encoding the function covariances. A key property of GPs is that output predictions $f(\mathbf{x})$ and $f(\mathbf{x}')$ correlate according to the similarity of the inputs $\mathbf{x}$ and $\mathbf{x}'$ as defined by the kernel $K(\mathbf{x}, \mathbf{x}') \in \mathbb{R}$.

Low-rank Gaussian process functions are constructed by *augmenting* the Gaussian process with a small number M of inducing variables $u_j = f(\mathbf{z}_j)$, $u_j \in \mathbb{R}$ and $\mathbf{z}_j = \mathbb{R}^d$ to obtain the Gaussian function posterior

$$\mathbf{f}|\mathbf{u}, \mathbf{Z} \sim \mathcal{N}(\underbrace{\mathbf{K_{XZ}K_{ZZ}^{-1}u}}_{\text{predictive mean}}, \underbrace{\mathbf{K_{XX} - K_{XZ}K_{ZZ}^{-1}K_{ZX}}}_{\text{predictive covariance}}) \tag{6}$$

where $\mathbf{K_{XX}} \in \mathbb{R}^{n \times n}$ is the kernel between observed image pairs $\mathbf{X}$, the kernel $\mathbf{K_{XZ}} \in \mathbb{R}^{n \times M}$ is between observed images $\mathbf{X}$ and inducing images $\mathbf{Z}$, and kernel $\mathbf{K_{ZZ}} \in \mathbb{R}^{m \times m}$ is between inducing images $\mathbf{Z}$ [28].

2.3 Variational Inference

Exact inference in a GP entails optimizing the *evidence* $p(\mathbf{y}) = \mathbb{E}_{p(\mathbf{f})}[p(\mathbf{y}|\mathbf{f})]$ which has a limiting cubic complexity $O(n^3)$ and is in general intractable. We tackle this restriction by applying stochastic variational inference (SVI) [13].

We define a variational approximation

$$q(\mathbf{u}) = \mathcal{N}(\mathbf{u}|\mathbf{m}, \mathbf{S}) \tag{7}$$

$$q(\mathbf{f}) = \int p(\mathbf{f}|\mathbf{u})q(\mathbf{u})d\mathbf{u}$$

$$= \mathcal{N}(\mathbf{f}|\mathbf{Am}, \mathbf{K}_{ff} + \mathbf{A}(\mathbf{S} - \mathbf{K}_{zz})\mathbf{A}^T)$$

$$\mathbf{A} = \mathbf{K}_{fz}\mathbf{K}_{zz}^{-1} \tag{8}$$

with free variational parameters $\mathbf{m} \in \mathbb{R}^m$ and a matrix $\mathbf{S} \succeq 0 \in \mathbb{R}^{m \times m}$ to be optimised. It can be shown that minimizing the Kullback-Leibler divergence $\mathrm{KL}[q(\mathbf{u})||p(\mathbf{u}|\mathbf{y})]$ between the approximative posterior $q(\mathbf{u})$ and the true posterior $p(\mathbf{u}|\mathbf{y})$ is equivalent to maximizing the evidence lower bound (ELBO) [2]

$$\mathcal{L} = \sum_{i=1}^{n} \mathbb{E}_{q(f_i)}[\log p(y_i|f_i)] - \mathrm{KL}[q(\mathbf{u})||p(\mathbf{u})] \tag{9}$$

The variational expected likelihood in $\mathcal{L}$ can be computed using numerical quadrature approaches [13].

3 Deep Convolutional Gaussian Process

In this section we introduce the deep convolution Gaussian process. We stack multiple convolutional GP layers followed by a GP classifier with a convolutional kernel.

3.1   Convolutional GP Layers

We assume an image representation $\mathbf{f}_c^\ell \in \mathbb{R}^{W_\ell \times H_\ell}$ of width W_ℓ and height H_ℓ pixels at layer ℓ. We collect C_ℓ *channels* into a 3D tensor $\mathbf{f}^\ell = (\mathbf{f}_1^\ell, \ldots, \mathbf{f}_C^\ell) \in \mathbb{R}^{H_\ell \times W_\ell \times C_\ell}$, where the channels are along the depth axis. The input image $\mathbf{f}^0 = \mathbf{x}$ is the $W_0 \times H_0 \times C_0$ sized representation of the original image with C color channels. For instance MNIST images are of size $W = H = 28$ pixels and have a single $C = 1$ grayscale channel.

We decompose the 3D tensor $\mathbf{f}^\ell$ into *patches* $\mathbf{f}^\ell[p] \in \mathbb{R}^{w_\ell \times h_\ell \times C_\ell}$ containing all depth channel. h_ℓ and w_ℓ are the height and width of the image patch at layer ℓ. We index patches by $p \in \mathbb{Z} < H_\ell W_\ell$. H_ℓ and W_ℓ denotes the height and width of the output of layer ℓ. We compose a sequence of layers $\mathbf{f}^\ell$ that map the input image $\mathbf{x}_i$ to the label $\mathbf{y}_i$:

$$\underbrace{\mathbf{x}_i = \mathbf{f}^0}_{W_0 \times H_0 \times 3} \xrightarrow{g^1} \underbrace{\mathbf{f}^1}_{W_1 \times H_1 \times C_1} \cdots \xrightarrow{g^L} \underbrace{\mathbf{f}^L}_{C_y} \approx \underbrace{\mathbf{y}_i}_{\{0,1\}^{C_y}} . \qquad (10)$$

Layers $\mathbf{f}^\ell$ with $\ell \geq 1$ are random variables with probability densities $p(\mathbf{f}^\ell)$.

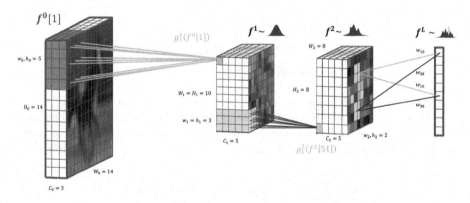

Fig. 1. A three layer deep convolutional gaussian process. First we construct an intermediate probabilistic representation of size $W_1 \times H_1 \times C_1$. We map this probabilistic representation through another convolutional GP layer yielding a representation of size $W_2 \times H_2 \times C_2$. Finally, we classify using a GP with a convolutional kernel by summing over patches of the intermediate representation.

We construct the layers by applying *convolutions* of *patch response* functions $\mathbf{g}_c^\ell : \mathbb{R}^{w_{\ell-1} \times h_{\ell-1} \times C_{\ell-1}} \to \mathbb{R}$ over the input one patch at a time producing the next layer representation:

$$\mathbf{f}^\ell[p] = \begin{bmatrix} g_1^\ell(\mathbf{f}^{\ell-1}[p]) \\ \vdots \\ g_C^\ell(\mathbf{f}^{\ell-1}[p]) \end{bmatrix} \in \mathbb{R}^C \qquad (11)$$

Each individual patch response $g^\ell(\mathbf{f}^{\ell-1}[p])$ is a $1 \times 1 \times C$ pixel stack. By repeating the patch responses over the $P_{\ell-1} = W_\ell \times H_\ell$ patches we form a new $W_\ell \times H_\ell \times C_\ell$ representation $\mathbf{f}^\ell = (\mathbf{f}^\ell[1], \ldots, \mathbf{f}^\ell[P_{\ell-1}])$ (See Fig. 1).

We model the C patch responses at each of the first $L-1$ layers as independent GPs with shared prior

$$g_c^\ell(\mathbf{f}^{\ell-1}[p]) \sim \mathcal{GP}\big(0, k(\mathbf{f}^{\ell-1}[p], \mathbf{f}'^{\ell-1}[p'])\big) \tag{12}$$

for $c = 1, \ldots, C$. The kernel $k(\cdot, \cdot)$ measures the similarity of two image patches. The standard property of Gaussian processes implies that the functions g_c^ℓ output similar responses for similar patches.

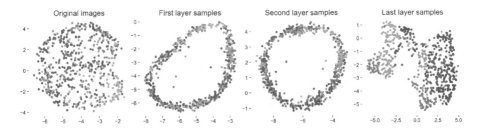

Fig. 2. UMAP embeddings [23] of the CIFAR-10 images and representations after each layer of the deep convolutional GP model. The colors correspond to different classes in the classification problem.

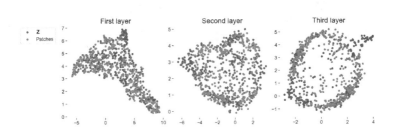

Fig. 3. UMAP embeddings of randomly selected patches of the input to the layer and learned inducing points of the fitted three layer model on CIFAR-10.

For example, on MNIST where images have size $28 \times 28 \times 1$ using patches of size $5 \times 5 \times 1$, a stride of 1 and $C = 10$ patch response functions, we obtain a representation of size $24 \times 24 \times 10$ after the first layer (height and width $W_1 = H_1 = (28 - 5)/1 + 1$). This is passed on to the next layer which produces an output of size $20 \times 20 \times 10$.

We follow the sparse GP approach of [13] and augment each patch response function by a set of M inducing patches $\mathbf{z}^\ell$ in the patch space $\mathbb{R}^{h_{\ell-1} \times w_{\ell-1} \times C_{\ell-1}}$

with corresponding responses u_c^ℓ. Each layer contains M_ℓ inducing patches $\mathbf{Z}^\ell = (\mathbf{z}_1^\ell, \ldots, \mathbf{z}_M^\ell)$ which are shared among the C patch response functions within that layer. Each patch response function has separate inducing responses $\mathbf{u}_c^\ell = (u_{c1}^\ell, \ldots, u_{cM}^\ell)$ which associate outputs to each inducing patch. We collect these into a matrix $\mathbf{U}^\ell$.

The conditional patch responses are

$$g_c^\ell | \mathbf{f}^{\ell-1}, \mathbf{u}_c^\ell, \mathbf{Z}^\ell \sim \mathcal{N}(\boldsymbol{\mu}, \Sigma)$$
$$\boldsymbol{\mu} = \mathbf{K}_{\mathbf{f}^{\ell-1}\mathbf{Z}^\ell} \mathbf{K}_{\mathbf{Z}^\ell\mathbf{Z}^\ell}^{-1} \mathbf{u}_c^\ell$$
$$\Sigma = \mathbf{K}_{\mathbf{f}^{\ell-1}\mathbf{f}^{\ell-1}} - \mathbf{K}_{\mathbf{f}^{\ell-1}\mathbf{Z}^\ell} \mathbf{K}_{\mathbf{Z}^\ell\mathbf{Z}^\ell}^{-1} \mathbf{K}_{\mathbf{Z}^\ell\mathbf{f}^{\ell-1}}, \tag{13}$$

where the covariance between the input and the inducing variables are

$$K(\mathbf{f}^{\ell-1}, \mathbf{Z}^\ell) = \begin{bmatrix} k(\mathbf{f}^{\ell-1}[1], \mathbf{z}_1^\ell) & \cdots & k(\mathbf{f}^{\ell-1}[1], \mathbf{z}_M^\ell) \\ \vdots & \ddots & \vdots \\ k(\mathbf{f}^{\ell-1}[P], \mathbf{z}_1^\ell) & \cdots & k(\mathbf{f}^{\ell-1}[P], \mathbf{z}_M^\ell) \end{bmatrix}$$

a matrix of size $P_\ell \times M_\ell$ that measures the similarity of all patches against all filters $\mathbf{z}^\ell$. We set the base kernel k to be the RBF kernel. For each of the C patch response functions we obtain one output image channel.

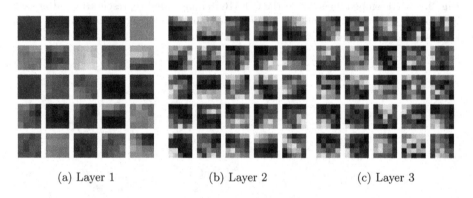

| (a) Layer 1 | (b) Layer 2 | (c) Layer 3 |

Fig. 4. Example inducing points $\mathbf{Z}$ pictured from all three layers from the CIFAR-10 experiment. The first layer inducing points channels correspond to color channels and are thus in color. For layers 2 and 3 only a single channel is visualized.

The conditional for each layer can be evaluated in $O(P^\ell \cdot N \cdot (M^\ell)^2)$, where N is the data points being evaluated, P^ℓ the amount of patches ℓ and M^ℓ the amount of inducing points at layer ℓ.

In contrast to neural networks, the Gaussian process convolutions induce probabilistic layer representations. The first layer $p(\mathbf{f}^1 | \mathbf{f}^0, \mathbf{U}^1, \mathbf{Z}^1)$ is a Gaussian directly from (13), while the following layers follow non-Gaussian distributions $p(\mathbf{f}^{\ell+1} | \mathbf{U}^{\ell+1}, \mathbf{Z}^{\ell+1})$ since we map all realisations of the random input $\mathbf{f}^\ell$ into Gaussian outputs $\mathbf{f}^{\ell+1}$.

3.2 Final Classification Layer

As the last layer of our model we aggregate the output of the convolutional layers using a GP with a weighted convolutional kernel as presented by [33]. We set a GP prior on the last layer patch response function

$$g^L\left(\mathbf{f}^{L-1}[p]\right) \sim \mathcal{GP}(0, K(\mathbf{f}^{L-1}[p], \mathbf{f}'^{L-1}[p'])). \tag{14}$$

with weights for each patch response. We get an additive GP

$$\mathbf{f}^L = g^L(\mathbf{f}^{L-1}) = \sum_{p=1}^{P} w_p g^L(\mathbf{f}^{L-1}[p])$$

$$\sim \mathcal{GP}\left(0, \underbrace{\sum_{p=1}^{P}\sum_{p'=1}^{P} w_p w_{p'} k(\mathbf{f}^{L-1}[p], \mathbf{f}'^{L-1}[p'])}_{K(\mathbf{x},\mathbf{x}')}\right),$$

where the kernel $K(\mathbf{f}^{L-1}, \mathbf{f}'^{L-1}) = \mathbf{w}^T \mathbf{K} \mathbf{w}$ is the weighted average patch similarity of the final tensor representation $\mathbf{f}^{L-1}$. $\mathbf{w} \in \mathbb{R}^P$. The matrix $\mathbf{K}$ collects all patch similarities $K(\mathbf{f}^{L-1}[p], \mathbf{f}'^{L-1}[p'])$. The last layer has one response GP per output class c.

As with the convolutional layers the inducing points live in the patch space of instead of in the image space. The inter-domain kernel is

$$K(\mathbf{f}^{L-1}, \mathbf{z}^L) = \sum_{p=1}^{P} w_p K(\mathbf{x}[p], \mathbf{z}^L) \tag{15}$$

$$= \mathbf{w}^T \mathbf{k}(\mathbf{f}^{L-1}, \mathbf{z}^L). \tag{16}$$

The kernel $\mathbf{k}(\mathbf{f}^{L-1}, \mathbf{z}^L) \in \mathbb{R}^P$ collects all patch similarities of a single image $\mathbf{f}^{L-1}$ compared against inducing points $\mathbf{z}^L$. The covariance between inducing points is simply $K(\mathbf{z}^L, \mathbf{z}'^L)$. We have now defined all kernels necessary to evaluate and optimize the variational bound (9).

3.3 Doubly Stochastic Variational Inference

The deep convolutional Gaussian process is an instance of a deep Gaussian process with the convolutional kernels and patch filter inducing points. We follow the doubly stochastic variational inference approach [27] for model learning. The key idea of doubly stochastic inference is to draw samples from the Gaussian

$$\tilde{\mathbf{f}}_i^\ell \sim p(\mathbf{f}_i^\ell | \tilde{\mathbf{f}}_i^{\ell-1}, \mathbf{U}^\ell, \mathbf{Z}^\ell) \tag{17}$$

through the deep system for a single input image $\mathbf{x}_i$.

The inducing points of each layer are independent. We assume a factorised likelihood

$$p(\mathbf{Y}|\mathbf{F}^L) = \prod_{i=1}^{N} p(\mathbf{y}_i|\mathbf{f}_i^L) \tag{18}$$

and a true joint density

$$p(\{\mathbf{f}^\ell, \mathbf{U}^\ell\}_\ell) = \prod_{\ell=1}^{L} p(\mathbf{f}^\ell | \mathbf{f}^{\ell-1}, \mathbf{U}^\ell, \mathbf{Z}^\ell) p(\mathbf{U}^\ell) \qquad (19)$$

$$p(\mathbf{U}^\ell) = \prod_{c=1}^{C} \mathcal{N}(\mathbf{u}_c^\ell | \mathbf{0}, \mathbf{K}_{\mathbf{Z}^\ell \mathbf{Z}^\ell}). \qquad (20)$$

The evidence framework [20] considers optimizing the evidence,

$$p(\mathbf{Y}) = \mathbb{E}_{p(\mathbf{F})} p(\mathbf{Y}|\mathbf{F}). \qquad (21)$$

Following the variational approach we assume a variational joint model

$$q(\mathbf{U}^\ell) = \prod_{c=1}^{C} \mathcal{N}(\mathbf{u}_c^\ell | \mathbf{m}_c^\ell, \mathbf{S}_c^\ell) \qquad (22)$$

$$q(\{\mathbf{f}^\ell, \mathbf{U}^\ell\}_\ell) = \prod_{\ell=1}^{L} p(\mathbf{f}^\ell | \mathbf{f}^{\ell-1}, \mathbf{U}^\ell, \mathbf{Z}^\ell) q(\mathbf{U}^\ell). \qquad (23)$$

The distribution of the layer predictions $\mathbf{f}^\ell$ depends on current layer inducing points $\mathbf{U}^\ell, \mathbf{Z}^\ell$ and representation $\mathbf{f}^{\ell-1}$ at the previous layer. By marginalising the variational approximation $q(\mathbf{U}^\ell)$ we arrive at the factorized variational posterior of the last layer for individual data point $\mathbf{x}_i$,

$$q(\mathbf{f}_i^L; \{\mathbf{m}^\ell, \mathbf{S}^\ell, \mathbf{Z}^\ell\}_\ell) = \prod_{\ell=1}^{L-1} \int q(\mathbf{f}_i^\ell | \mathbf{f}_i^{\ell-1}, \mathbf{m}^l, \mathbf{S}^\ell, \mathbf{Z}^\ell) d\mathbf{f}_i^\ell, \qquad (24)$$

where we integrate all paths $(\mathbf{f}_i^1, \ldots, \mathbf{f}_i^L)$ through the layers defined by the filters $\mathbf{Z}^\ell$, and the parameters $\mathbf{m}^\ell, \mathbf{S}^\ell$. Finally, the doubly stochastic evidence lower bound (ELBO) is

$$\log p(\mathbf{Y}) \geq \sum_{i=1}^{N} \mathbb{E}_{q(\mathbf{f}_i^L; \{\mathbf{m}^\ell, \mathbf{S}^\ell, \mathbf{Z}^\ell\}_\ell)}[\log p(\mathbf{y}_i | \mathbf{f}_i^L)] \qquad (25)$$

$$- \sum_{\ell=1}^{L} \mathrm{KL}[q(\mathbf{U}^\ell) \| p(\mathbf{U}^\ell)].$$

The variational expected likelihood is computed using a Monte Carlo approximation yielding the first source of stochasticity. The whole lower bound is optimized using stochastic gradient descent yielding the second source of stochasticity.

The Fig. 2 visualises representations of CIFAR-10 images over the deep convolutional GP model. Figure 3 visualises the patch and filter spaces of the three layers, indicating high overlap. Finally, Fig. 4 shows example filters $\mathbf{z}$ learned on the CIFAR-10 dataset, which extract image features.

Optimization. All parameters $\{\mathbf{m}_\ell\}_{\ell=1}^L$, $\{\mathbf{S}_\ell\}_{\ell=1}^L$, $\{\mathbf{Z}^l\}_{\ell=1}^L$, the base kernel RBF lengthscales and variances and the patch weights for the last layer are learned using stochastic gradient Adam optimizer [15] by maximizing the likelihood lower bound. We use one shared base kernel for each layer.

3.4 Stochastic Gradient Hamiltonian Monte Carlo

An alternative to the variational posterior approximations $q(\mathbf{u})$ is to use Markov Chain Monte Carlo (MCMC) sampling of the true posterior $p(\mathbf{u}|\mathbf{y})$, where we denote with $\mathbf{u} = \{\mathbf{U}^\ell\}_{\ell=1}^L$ all inducing values of all layers. We use the Stochastic Gradient Hamiltonian Monte Carlo (SG-HMC) to produce samples from the true posterior [4]. The SG-HMC can reveal the possibly multimodal and non-Gaussian inducing distributions, while the variational approximation is usually limited to Gaussian approximations. We follow the SG-HMC approach introduced for deep Gaussian processes [12].

In Hamiltonian Monte Carlo an auxiliary variable $\mathbf{v}$ is introduced and we sample from the augmented posterior

$$p(\mathbf{u}, \mathbf{v}|\mathbf{y}) \propto \exp\left(-U(\mathbf{u}) - \frac{1}{2}\mathbf{v}M^{-1}\mathbf{v}\right) \tag{26}$$

$$U(\mathbf{u}) = -\log p(\mathbf{u}|\mathbf{y}), \tag{27}$$

which corresponds to a Hamiltonian with U representing potential energy and $\mathbf{v}$ representing kinetic energy. HMC requires computation of the gradient $\nabla U(\mathbf{u})$, which is prohibitive for large datasets. In Stochastic Gradient HMC the gradients can be computed over minibatches of data, resulting in update equations

$$\Delta\mathbf{u} = \epsilon M^{-1}\mathbf{v} \tag{28}$$

$$\Delta\mathbf{v} = -\epsilon\nabla U(\mathbf{u}) - \epsilon C M^{-1}\mathbf{v} + \mathcal{N}(0, 2\epsilon(C - \hat{B})), \tag{29}$$

where C is the friction term, ϵ is the stepsize, M is the mass matrix, and $\hat{B}$ is the Fisher information matrix. We use an auto-tuning approach of [29] to select these parameters, following [12]. To compute $\nabla U(\mathbf{u})$ we use stochastic samples $\mathbf{f}_{(s)}^L \sim p(\mathbf{f}^L)$ to approximate the final layer predictive distribution $p(\mathbf{f}^L)$. Finally, to also optimize the hyperparameters, we use the Monte Carlo Expectation Maximization (MCEM) technique [32], following [12].

4 Experiments

We compare our approach on the standard image classification benchmarks of MNIST and CIFAR-10 [17], which have standard training and test folds to facilitate direct performance comparisons. MNIST contains 60,000 training examples of 28×28 sized grayscale images of 10 hand-drawn digits, with a separate 10,000 validation set. CIFAR-10 contains 50,000 training examples of RGB colour images of size 32×32 from 10 classes, with 5,000 images per class. The

Table 1. Performance on MNIST and CIFAR-10. Our method, the deep convolutional Gaussian process, is denoted DeepCGP. Asterisk $^{(*)}$ indicates results taken from the respective publications, which are directly comparable due to standard data folds. Other results are run using our implementation. The neural network based results are listed for completeness. The four layer CNN has two 5×5 convolutional layers (64 filters, strides 2 and 1), two fully connected layers and ReLu activations.

Gaussian process models	Layers	Inducing points	Test accuracy		Reference
			MNIST	CIFAR-10	
RBF AutoGP	1	200	$98.29^{(*)}$	$55.05^{(*)}$	[16]
Multi-channel conv GP	1	1000	$98.83^{(*)}$	$64.6^{(*)}$	[33]
DeepCGP	1	384	98.38	58.65	Current work
DeepCGP	2	2×384	99.24	73.85	”
DeepCGP	3	3×384	**99.44**	**75.89**	”
Neural network models	Layers	# params			
Four layer CNN	4	1.7M	98.53	63.54	
Deep kernel learning	5	2.3M .. 4.6M	$99.2^{(*)}$	$77.0^{(*)}$	[37]
DenseNet	250	15.3M	N/A	$94.81^{(*)}$	[14]

images represents objects such as airplanes, cats or horses. There is a separate validation set of 10,000 images. We preprocess the images for zero mean and unit variance along the color channel.

We compare our model primarily against the original shallow convolutional Gaussian process [33], which is currently the only convolutional Gaussian process based image classifier. We also consider the performance of the hybrid neural network GP approach [37]. For completeness we report the performance of a state-of-the-art CNN method DenseNet [14].

Implementation. Our TensorFlow [1] implementation is compatible with the GPflow framework [22] and freely available online². We leverage GPU accelerated computation, 64bit floating point precision, and employ a minibatch size of 32. We start the Adam learning rate at 0.01 and multiply it by 0.1 every 100,000 optimization steps until the learning rate reaches 1e-5. We use $M = 384$ inducing points at each layer. We set a stride of 2 for the first layer and 1 for all other layers. The convolutional filter size is 5×5 on all layers except for the first layer on CIFAR-10 where it is 4×4. This is to make use of all the image pixels using a stride of 2.

Parameter Initialization. Inducing points $\mathbf{Z}$ are initialized by running k-means with M clusters on image patches from the training set. The variational means $\mathbf{m}$ are initialised to zero. $\mathbf{S}$ are initialised to a tiny variance kernel prior $10^{-5} \cdot K_{\mathbf{ZZ}}$ following [27], except for the last layer where we use $K_{\mathbf{ZZ}}$. For models deeper than two layers, we employ iterative optimisation where the first $L - 2$ layers

---

² https://github.com/kekeblom/DeepCGP.

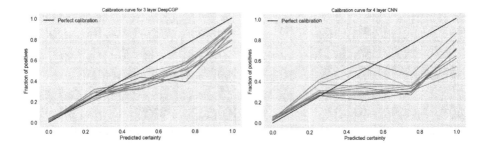

Fig. 5. Reliability curves with 5 bins for the 3 layer DeepCGP model and the 4 layer CNN on the CIFAR-10 test set. For the DeepCGP model, we average the probabilities over 25 samples of the output. We cast the classification problem as a binary one-vs-rest classification problem by summing the probabilities of the negative classes obtaining one calibration curve for each image class.

and layer L are initialised to the learned values of an $L - 1$ model, while the one additional layer added before the classification layer is initialised to default values.

4.1 MNIST and CIFAR-10 Results

Table 1 shows the classification accuracy on MNIST and CIFAR-10. Adding a convolutional layer to the weighted convolutional kernel GP improves performance on CIFAR-10 from 58.65% to 73.85%. Adding another convolutional layer further improves the accuracy to 75.9%. On MNIST the performance increases from 1.42% error to 0.56% error with the three-layer deep convolutional GP.

The deep kernel learning method uses a fully connected five-layer DNN instead of a CNN, and performs similarly to our model, but with much more parameters.

Figure 6 shows a single sample for 10 image class examples (rows) over the 10 patch response channels (columns) for the first layer (panel a) and second layer (panel b). The first layer indicates various edge detectors, while the second layer samples show the complexity of pattern extraction. The row object classes map to different kinds of representations, as expected.

Figure 2 shows UMAP embedding [23] visualisations of the image space of CIFAR-10 along with the structure of the layer representations $\mathbf{f}_i^\ell$ for three layers. The original images do not naturally cluster into the 10 classes (a). The DeepCGP model projects the images to circle shape with some class coherence in the intermediate layers, while the last layer shows the classification boundaries. An accompanying Fig. 4 shows the learned inducing filters and layer patches on CIFAR-10. Some regions of the patch space are not covered by filters, indicating uninformative representations.

Figure 7 shows the effect of different channel numbers on a two layer model. The ELBO increases up to $C = 16$ response channels, while starts to decrease

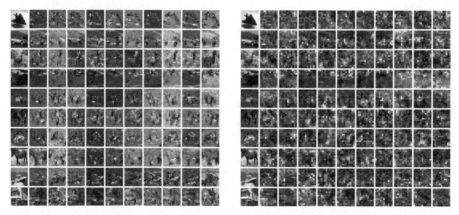

(a) Samples from the first layer.   (b) Samples from the second layer.

Fig. 6. (a) and (b) show samples the first two layers of the three layer model. Rows corresponds to different test inputs and columns correspond to different patch response functions, which are realisations of the layer GPs. The first column shows the input image. The first layer seems to learn to detect edges, while the second layer appears to learn more abstract correlations of features and the representation produced no longer resembles the input image, indicating high-level feature extraction.

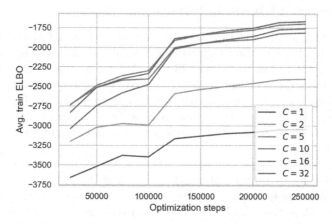

Fig. 7. Expected evidence lower bound computed on the training set using a two layer model for different amounts of patch response functions. The models with 10 and 16 patch response functions seem to perform the best. Models with one or two patch response functions struggle to explain the data even though they have the same amount of inducing points.

with $C = 32$ channels. A model with approximately $C = 10$ channels indicates best performance.

Figure 5 shows that the deep convolutional GP model has better calibration than a neural CNN model. CNN model results in badly calibrated class probabilities especially between 0.2 and 0.8 prediction probability. The GP based model has more consistent calibration over the probability range.

5   Conclusions

We present a new type of deep Gaussian process with convolutional structure. The convolutional GP layers gradually linearize the data using multiple filters with nonlinear kernel functions. Our model greatly improves test results on the compared classification benchmarks compared to other GP-based approaches, and approaches the performance of hybrid neural-GP methods. The performance of our model seems to improve as more layers are added. We leave experimenting with deeper models for future work.

Convolutional neural networks have been shown to provide unreliable uncertainty estimates [31]. We showed that our model provides more accurate class probability estimates than an equivalent deep convolutional neural network.

Deep Gaussian process models lead to degenerate covariances, where each layer in the composition reduces the rank or degrees of freedom of the system [7]. In practice the rank reduces via successive layers mapping inputs to identical values, effectively merging inputs and resulting in rank-reducing covariance matrix with repeated rows and columns. To counter this pathology rank-preserving deep model was proposed by pseudo-monotonic layer mappings with GP priors $f(\mathbf{x}) \sim \mathcal{GP}(\mathbf{x}, k)$ with identity means $\mathbb{E}[f(\mathbf{x})] = \mathbf{x}$ [27]. In contrast we employ zero-mean patch response functions. Remarkably we do not experience rank degeneracy, possibly due to the multiple channel mappings and the convolution structure.

The convolutional Gaussian process is still limited by the computationally expensive inference. The SG-HMC improves over variational inference, while an another avenue for improvement lies in kernel interpolation techniques [9,36], which would make inference and prediction faster. We leave further exploration of these directions as future work.

Acknowledgements. We thank Michael Riis Andersen for his invaluable comments and helpful suggestions.

References

1. Abadi, M., et al.: Tensorflow: a system for large-scale machine learning. In: OSDI, vol. 16, pp. 265–283 (2016)
2. Blei, D.M., Kucukelbir, A., McAuliffe, J.D.: Variational inference: a review for statisticians. J. Am. Stat. Assoc. **112**(518), 859–877 (2017)
3. Blundell, C., Cornebise, J., Kavukcuoglu, K., Wierstra, D.: Weight uncertainty in neural networks. In: International Conference on Machine Learning, pp. 1613–1622 (2015)
4. Chen, T., Fox, E., Guestrin, C.: Stochastic gradient Hamiltonian Monte Carlo. In: International Conference on Machine Learning, pp. 1683–1691 (2014)

5. Damianou, A., Lawrence, N.: Deep Gaussian processes. In: AISTATS. PMLR, vol. 31, pp. 207–215 (2013)
6. Dutordoir, V., van der Wilk, M., Artemev, A., Tomczak, M., Hensman, J.: Translation insensitivity for deep convolutional Gaussian processes. arXiv:1902.05888 (2019)
7. Duvenaud, D., Rippel, O., Adams, R., Ghahramani, Z.: Avoiding pathologies in very deep networks. In: AISTATS. PMLR, vol. 33, pp. 202–210 (2014)
8. Duvenaud, D.K., Nickisch, H., Rasmussen, C.E.: Additive Gaussian processes. In: Advances in Neural Information Processing Systems, pp. 226–234 (2011)
9. Evans, T.W., Nair, P.B.: Scalable Gaussian processes with grid-structured eigenfunctions (GP-GRIEF). In: International Conference on Machine Learning (2018)
10. Garriga-Alonso, A., Aitchison, L., Rasmussen, C.E.: Deep convolutional networks as shallow Gaussian processes. In: ICLR (2019)
11. Goodfellow, I., Bengio, Y., Courville, A., Bengio, Y.: Deep Learning, vol. 1. MIT Press, Cambridge (2016)
12. Havasi, M., Lobato, J.M.H., Fuentes, J.J.M.: Inference in deep Gaussian processes using stochastic gradient Hamiltonian Monte Carlo. In: NIPS (2018)
13. Hensman, J., Matthews, A., Ghahramani, Z.: Scalable variational Gaussian process classification. In: AISTATS. PMLR, vol. 38, pp. 351–360 (2015)
14. Huang, G., Liu, Z., Van Der Maaten, L., Weinberger, K.Q.: Densely connected convolutional networks. In: CVPR, vol. 1, p. 3 (2017)
15. Kingma, D.P., Ba, J.L.: Adam: a method for stochastic optimization. In: ICLR (2014)
16. Krauth, K., Bonilla, E.V., Cutajar, K., Filippone, M.: AutoGP: exploring the capabilities and limitations of Gaussian process models. In: Uncertainty in Artificial Intelligence (2017)
17. Krizhevsky, A., Hinton, G.: Learning multiple layers of features from tiny images. Technical report, Citeseer (2009)
18. Kumar, V., Singh, V., Srijith, P., Damianou, A.: Deep Gaussian processes with convolutional kernels. arXiv preprint arXiv:1806.01655 (2018)
19. Lee, J., Bahri, Y., Novak, R., Schoenholz, S.S., Pennington, J., Sohl-Dickstein, J.: Deep neural networks as Gaussian processes. In: ICLR (2018)
20. MacKay, D.J.: A practical Bayesian framework for backpropagation networks. Neural Comput. **4**, 448–472 (1992)
21. Mallat, S.: Understanding deep convolutional networks. Phil. Trans. R. Soc. A **374**(2065), 20150203 (2016)
22. Matthews, A.G.d.G., et al.: GPflow: a Gaussian process library using TensorFlow. J. Mach. Learn. Res. **18**, 1–6 (2017)
23. McInnes, L., Healy, J.: UMAP: uniform manifold approximation and projection for dimension reduction. ArXiv e-prints, February 2018
24. Rasmussen, C.E.: Gaussian processes in machine learning. In: Bousquet, O., von Luxburg, U., Rätsch, G. (eds.) ML -2003. LNCS (LNAI), vol. 3176, pp. 63–71. Springer, Heidelberg (2004). https://doi.org/10.1007/978-3-540-28650-9_4
25. Rasmussen, C.E., Williams, C.K.: Gaussian Process for Machine Learning. MIT Press, Cambridge (2006)
26. Remes, S., Heinonen, M., Kaski, S.: Non-stationary spectral kernels. In: Advances in Neural Information Processing Systems, pp. 4642–4651 (2017)
27. Salimbeni, H., Deisenroth, M.: Doubly stochastic variational inference for deep Gaussian processes. In: Advances in Neural Information Processing Systems, pp. 4588–4599 (2017)

28. Snelson, E., Ghahramani, Z.: Sparse Gaussian processes using pseudo-inputs. In: Advances in Neural Information Processing Systems, pp. 1257–1264 (2006)
29. Springerberg, J., Klein, A., Falkner, S., Hutter, F.: Bayesian optimization with robust Bayesian neural networks. In: Advances in Neural Information Processing Systems, pp. 4134–4142 (2016)
30. Sun, S., Zhang, G., Wang, C., Zeng, W., Li, J., Grosse, R.: Differentiable compositional kernel learning for Gaussian processes. In: ICML. PMLR, vol. 80 (2018)
31. Tran, G.L., Bonilla, E.V., Cunningham, J.P., Michiardi, P., Filippone, M.: Calibrating deep convolutional Gaussian processes. In: AISTATS. PMLR, vol. 89, pp. 1554–1563 (2019)
32. Wei, G., Tanner, M.: A Monte Carlo implementation of the EM algorithm and the poor mans data augmentation algorithms. J. Am. Stat. Assoc. **85**, 699–704 (1990)
33. Van der Wilk, M., Rasmussen, C.E., Hensman, J.: Convolutional Gaussian processes. In: Advances in Neural Information Processing Systems, pp. 2849–2858 (2017)
34. Williams, C.K.: Computing with infinite networks. In: Advances in Neural Information Processing Systems, pp. 295–301 (1997)
35. Wilson, A., Gilboa, E., Nehorai, A., Cunningham, J.: Fast multidimensional pattern extrapolation with Gaussian processes. In: AISTATS. PMLR, vol. 31 (2013)
36. Wilson, A., Nickisch, H.: Kernel interpolation for scalable structured Gaussian processes (KISS-GP). In: International Conference on Machine Learning. PMLR, vol. 37, pp. 1775–1784 (2015)
37. Wilson, A.G., Hu, Z., Salakhutdinov, R.R., Xing, E.P.: Stochastic variational deep kernel learning. In: Advances in Neural Information Processing Systems, pp. 2586–2594 (2016)
38. Wilson, A.G., Hu, Z., Salakhutdinov, R., Xing, E.P.: Deep kernel learning. In: AISTATS. PMLR, vol. 51, pp. 370–378 (2016)

Bayesian Generalized Horseshoe Estimation of Generalized Linear Models

Daniel F. Schmidt[1,2(✉)] and Enes Makalic[2]

[1] Faculty of Information Technology, Monash University, Clayton, Australia
daniel.schmidt@monash.edu
[2] Centre for Epidemiology and Biostatistics, The University of Melbourne,
Carlton, Australia
emakalic@unimelb.edu.au

Abstract. Bayesian global-local shrinkage estimation with the generalized horseshoe prior represents the state-of-the-art for Gaussian regression models. The extension to non-Gaussian data, such as binary or Student-t regression, is usually done by exploiting a scale-mixture-of-normals approach. However, many standard distributions, such as the gamma and the Poisson, do not admit such a representation. We contribute two extensions to global-local shrinkage methodology. The first is an adaption of recent auxiliary gradient based-sampling schemes to the global-local shrinkage framework, which yields simple algorithms for sampling from generalized linear models. We also introduce two new samplers for the hyperparameters in the generalized horseshoe model, one based on an inverse-gamma mixture of inverse-gamma distributions, and the second a rejection sampler. Results show that these new samplers are highly competitive with the no U-turn sampler for small numbers of predictors, and potentially perform better for larger numbers of predictors. Results for hyperparameter sampling show our new inverse-gamma inverse-gamma based sampling scheme outperforms the standard sampler based on a gamma mixture of gamma distributions.

Keywords: Bayesian regression · Markov Chain Monte Carlo sampling · Horseshoe regression · Shrinkage

1 Introduction

The introduction of the horseshoe prior [5], and more generally the idea of global-local shrinkage hierarchies [16], has sparked a period of interest in heavy tailed prior distributions for coefficients in linear regression models. The Bayesian global-local shrinkage priors represent the current state-of-the-art for Gaussian linear regression models and encompass a large number of well known Bayesian shrinkage techniques, including the Bayesian ridge, the Bayesian lasso [13], the horseshoe prior, the horseshoe+ [2] and the Dirichlet-Laplace [4] prior. Let $\mathbf{y} = (y_1, \ldots, y_n)$ denote the vector of n measurements of a target (dependent) variable of interest, $\bar{\mathbf{x}}_i = (x_{i,1}, \ldots, x_{i,p})$ denote the vector of of predictors (explanatory variables, covariates) associated with each target y_i, and let

© Springer Nature Switzerland AG 2020
U. Brefeld et al. (Eds.): ECML PKDD 2019, LNAI 11907, pp. 598–613, 2020.
https://doi.org/10.1007/978-3-030-46147-8_36

$\mathbf{X} = (\bar{\mathbf{x}}_1, \ldots, \bar{\mathbf{x}}_n)^{\mathsf{T}}$ denote the $n \times p$ matrix of explanatory variables. The global-local shrinkage (GLS) hierarchy for Gaussian linear models is given by:

$$\mathbf{y} \mid \boldsymbol{\beta}, \beta_0, \sigma^2 \sim N(\mathbf{X}\boldsymbol{\beta} + \beta_0 \mathbf{1}_n, \sigma^2)$$
$$\beta_0 \sim (1)d\beta_0$$
$$\sigma^2 \sim \sigma^{-2}d\sigma^2$$
$$\beta_j \mid \lambda_j, \sigma, \tau \sim N(0, \lambda_j^2 \tau^2 \sigma^2),$$
$$\lambda_j \sim \pi(\lambda_j)d\lambda_j,$$
$$\tau \sim C^+(0,1) \tag{1}$$

where $j = 1, \ldots, p$, $\boldsymbol{\beta} = (\beta_1, \ldots, \beta_p)$ is the vector of model coefficients, β_0 is the intercept, σ^2 is the noise variance, $N(a, b)$ is the normal distribution with mean a and variance b and $C^+(0, c)$ denotes a half-Cauchy distribution with scale c. In hierarchy (1), the hyperparameters $\lambda_1, \ldots, \lambda_p$ are the *local shrinkage* parameters that induce shrinkage only on their corresponding coefficients; by selecting a specific prior distribution $\pi(\lambda_j)$ one can represent most standard Bayesian shrinkage procedures within this framework. The hyperparameter τ is the *global shrinkage* parameter that controls the overall level of shrinkage and ties the p regression coefficients together; conditioning on σ^2 ensures that the shrinkage induced on the coefficients is not affected by scale changes of our data.

The joint posterior distribution of a GLS hierarchy is in general intractable, so it usual to instead explore the posterior distribution by sampling. A standard approach is a Gibbs sampling procedure [9] which repeatedly iterates:

1. sample the coefficients from $p(\boldsymbol{\beta} \mid \beta_0, \sigma^2, \boldsymbol{\lambda}, \tau, \mathbf{y})$;
2. sample the remaining model parameters from $p(\beta_0, \sigma^2 \mid \boldsymbol{\beta}, \boldsymbol{\lambda}, \tau, \mathbf{y})$;
3. sample the shrinkage hyperparameters from $p(\boldsymbol{\lambda}, \tau \mid \boldsymbol{\beta}, \sigma^2, \mathbf{y})$.

A strength of the GLS hierarchy is that in this Gibbs sampling framework the sampling algorithms for the hyperparameters are independent from the sampling algorithm for the coefficients. This means that as long as we have algorithms for sampling the coefficients given a normal prior distribution, and an algorithm for sampling the hyperparameters, we can mix and match choices of shrinkage priors with choices for likelihoods with no additional implementation details.

Building on this idea, the aim of this article is to explore two extensions to global-local shrinkage methodology: (i) we propose to adapt recent gradient-based sampling algorithms [20] to provide simple sampling procedures for a wide-range of non-Gaussian data, and (ii) we propose two new samplers for the local shrinkage hyperparameters λ_j under the generalized horseshoe estimator.

1.1 Bayesian Generalized Linear Models

One of the great successes of linear models is the ease in which they may be extended to handle data that is not typically modelled using a normal distribution (e.g., categorical or count data) via the framework of *generalised linear models* (GLMs) introduced by Nelder and Wedderburn [11]. The GLM framework begins by defining

$$\eta_i = \bar{\mathbf{x}}_i^{\mathrm{T}}\boldsymbol{\beta} + \beta_0$$

as the linear predictor; a GLM then models the conditional mean and variance of the target y_i by a suitable transformation of this linear predictor, i.e.,

$$\mathbb{E}\left[y_i \,|\, \bar{\mathbf{x}}_i\right] = f^{-1}(\eta_i) \equiv \mu_i,$$
$$\mathrm{Var}\left[y_i \,|\, \bar{\mathbf{x}}_i\right] = \sigma^2\, v(\eta_i),$$

where σ^2 is now a dispersion parameter, and $f(\mu_i) = \eta_i$ is referred to as the link function, as it links the linear predictor η_i to the conditional mean μ_i. This approach allows y_i to follow many standard distributions, and with careful choice of $f(\cdot)$ the resulting GLM retains much of the computational efficiency and statistical interpretability that characterises Gaussian linear models.

The usual fashion in which the global-local hierarchy (1) is extended to non-Gaussian data is through a scale mixture of normals (SMN) representation of the desired distribution. In particular, we rewrite the data model as

$$y_i \,|\, \boldsymbol{\beta}, \beta_0, \omega_j, \sigma^2 \sim N(\bar{\mathbf{x}}_i^{\mathrm{T}}\boldsymbol{\beta} + \beta_0, \sigma^2\omega_j^2),$$
$$\omega_j \sim \pi(\omega_j)d\omega_j.$$

In this approach, the data are modelled as arising from n heteroskedastic normal distributions, with an additional latent scale variable ω_i associated with each data point y_i. The choice of the mixing density $\pi(\omega_j)$ determines the final distribution of y_j. The particular advantage of this data augmentation approach is that it preserves the conditional conjugacy between the likelihood and the normal prior distribution for β_j. Therefore, efficient sampling algorithms such as those of Rue [18] (for $p < n$) and Bhattarcharya [3] (for $p > n$) can be employed in a Gibbs framework to generate posterior samples for the coefficients. The SMN approach has successfully been used to represent the Laplace, Student-t, logistic and negative binomial distribution [10,17].

However, not all distributions utilised in standard generalized linear modelling have known or convenient SMN representations; examples include the Poisson, gamma, Weibull and inverse-Gaussian distributions. In such cases, one must usually resort to alternative sampling techniques. One of the earliest approaches was utilisation of adaptive rejection sampling to implement one-at-a-time sampling of the coefficients. Such an approach is potentially slow and can result in a chain that mixes poorly, particularly if the predictors are correlated. More recent sampling techniques that can be utilised to handle Bayesian generalized linear models include the Hamiltonian MCMC no U-turn sampler (NUTS) [8] implemented in the Stan tool; generalized elliptical slice sampling [12]; and the Metropolis adjusted preconditioned Crank-Nicolson (pCNL) Langevin-based approach [6].

1.2   Generalized Horseshoe Priors

A particular important prior is the so-called generalized horseshoe (GHS, also known as the generalized beta mixture of Gaussians and the inverse-gamma-

gamma prior). The generalized horseshoe [1] places a beta prior distribution over the coefficient of shrinkage, i.e., $\lambda_j^2(1+\lambda_j^2)^{-1} \sim \text{Beta}(a, b)$. This induces the following distribution over λ_j:

$$\pi(\lambda_j \mid a, b) = \frac{2\lambda_j^{2a-1}(1 + \lambda_j^2)^{-a-b}}{B(a, b)}. \tag{2}$$

The well known horseshoe arises if we set $a = b = 1/2$; in this case the beta distribution has a 'U'-shape from which the horseshoe prior obtains its distinctive name, and (2) reduces to the unit half-Cauchy. To gain an understanding of the effect that the hyperparameters a and b have on inference we can examine the corresponding marginal prior distribution over β_j:

$$\pi(\beta_j \mid a, b) = \int_0^\infty \phi(\beta/\lambda_j)/\lambda_j \pi(\lambda_j \mid a, b)d\lambda_j$$

where $\phi(\cdot)$ denotes the standard normal density function. Appealing to Proposition 1 and Theorems 2 and 3 from [19], we have for $a < 1/2$

$$\pi(\beta_j \mid a, b) = O(|\beta|^{-1+2a})$$

as $|\beta| \to 0$, and for all $b > 0$

$$\pi(\beta_j \mid a, b) = O\left(|\beta|^{-1-2b}\right)$$

as $|\beta| \to \infty$. Therefore, the hyperparameter a controls the degree to which prior probability is concentrated around $\beta = 0$; smaller values indicate an *a priori* belief in great underlying sparsity of the coefficients vector. The hyperparameter b controls the rate at which the tail of the marginal prior decays; smaller values result in a slower decay, which indicates an *a priori* belief that some of the coefficients may be substantially greater in magnitude than others.

Sampling Generalized Horseshoe Hyperparameters. Most MCMC implementations of (a variant of) the generalized horseshoe are based on Gibbs sampling. For the particular case of the horseshoe (i.e., $a = b = 1/2$) there exist a number of approaches to sampling the conditional posterior $p(\lambda_j \mid \beta_j, \tau, \sigma^2)$. These include slice sampling [15], an inverse-gamma inverse-gamma scale mixture representation [10] and a gamma-gamma scale mixture representation [1]. Of these methods, only the gamma-gamma mixture currently handles the generalized horseshoe; it utilises the fact that if

$$x^2 \mid c \sim \text{Ga}(a, 1/c), \text{ and } c \sim \text{Ga}(b, 1)$$

then x follows the distribution (2), where $\text{Ga}(a, c)$ denotes a gamma distribution with shape a and scale c. Introducing a set of latent variables $\nu_1, \ldots, \nu_p$, this augmentation leads to the full conditionals

$$\lambda_j^2 \mid \cdots \sim \text{GIG}(a - 1/2, 2\nu_j, 2m_j) \text{ and } \nu_j \mid \cdots \sim \text{Ga}\left(a + b, (1 + \lambda_j^2)^{-1}\right), \tag{3}$$

where $m_j = \beta_j^2/(2\sigma^2\tau^2)$ and GIG denotes a generalized inverse Gaussian distribution. Implementation within a Gibbs framework therefore requires sampling from the GIG distribution, which is potentially troublesome. Algorithms for generating GIG random variates are not distributed by default in packages such as MATLAB and R, and the best implementations are slower than generating random variates from standard distributions such as the gamma.

1.3 Our Contributions

In Sect. 2 of this paper, we adapt the recently proposed class of auxiliary gradient-based sampling algorithms [20] to the hierarchy (1). While these algorithms were designed for Gaussian process regression, they are perfectly positioned for application to GLMs and global-local shrinkage hierarchies. In Sect. 3 of this paper we present two new samplers for λ_j in the case of the GHS. One is a generalization of the inverse-gamma inverse-gamma approach proposed in [10]; the other is a new rejection sampler that exploits the log-concavity of the conditional distribution of $\log \lambda_j$.

Results in Sect. 4 demonstrate that despite their simplicity, the new gradient based sampling algorithms are competitive with alternative non-specialized sampling algorithms in terms of effective samples per second, and can potentially outperform them. Experimental results also show that the new inverse-gamma inverse-gamma sampler for the generalized horseshoe leads to a Gibbs simpler that is frequently more efficient in terms of effective samples per second than (3), while remaining substantially simpler in terms of implementation.

2 Gradient-Based Samplers for Bayesian GLMs

We propose to utilise the recently developed auxiliary gradient-based sampling algorithms [20]. These algorithms work by first augmenting the target density with auxiliary random variables, and using this in conjunction with a first-order Taylor series expansion of the likelihood and a marginalisation step to build a Metropolis-Hastings proposal density that is both likelihood and prior informed. Specifically, they were designed to target densities of the form

$$p(\boldsymbol{\beta}) \propto \exp(f(\boldsymbol{\beta}); \beta_0, \sigma^2) N(\boldsymbol{\beta} \mid \mathbf{0}, \mathbf{C})$$

where $f(\boldsymbol{\beta}, \beta_0, \sigma^2)$ denotes the log-likelihood and $\mathbf{C}$ denotes the prior covariance matrix for the coefficients $\boldsymbol{\beta}$. The posterior distribution for the coefficients $\boldsymbol{\beta}$ of a generalized linear model with global-local shrinkage priors, conditional on the shrinkage hyperparameters $\boldsymbol{\lambda}$ and τ, directly matches this class of problems. This facilitates application of these auxilary gradient-based samplers within the usual Gibbs sampling framework. Furthermore, in the case of a GLM with a standard link function, the log-likelihood $f(\boldsymbol{\beta})$ is a convex function of the coefficients $\boldsymbol{\beta}$. As our starting point we consider the general pre-conditioned marginal gradient sampler (eq. (8) in [20]), which uses as a proposal

$$\bar{\boldsymbol{\beta}} \mid \boldsymbol{\beta} \sim N\left(\mathbf{A}\left(\triangledown f(\boldsymbol{\beta}) + \left(\frac{2}{\delta}\right)\mathbf{S}^{-1}\boldsymbol{\beta}^{\mathrm{T}}\right), \left(\frac{2}{\delta}\right)\mathbf{A}\mathbf{S}^{-1}\mathbf{A} + \mathbf{A}\right) \qquad (4)$$

where $\delta > 0$ is the MH step-size, $\mathbf{S}$ is the pre-conditioning matrix, $\nabla f(\boldsymbol{\beta}) = (\partial f(\boldsymbol{\beta}, \beta_0, \sigma^2)/\partial \boldsymbol{\beta})$ denotes the gradient, and

$$\mathbf{A} = \left(\mathbf{C}^{-1} + \left(\frac{2}{\delta} \right) \mathbf{S}^{-1} \right)^{-1}.$$

The step-size δ should be chosen such that 50%–60% of samplers are accepted. We discuss a robust fully automatic method for doing this in Sect. 2.4.

2.1 Algorithm 1: mGrad-1

The first variant of the algorithm we will consider uses $\mathbf{S} = \mathbf{I}_p$. In the case of the global-local shrinkage hierarchy (1) the prior covariance matrix $\mathbf{C}$ is simply a diagonal matrix with entries

$$C_{j,j} = \tau^2 \sigma^2 \lambda_j^2, \quad j = 1, \ldots, p.$$

Combined with the choice $\mathbf{S} = \mathbf{I}_p$, the proposal (4) and the Metropolis-Hastings acceptance step dramatically simplify. We call this algorithm 'mGrad-1', as it uses only first order information. The mGrad-1 algorithm works as follows:

1. Generate proposals for coefficients using

$$\bar{\beta}_j \sim N \left(\frac{C_{j,j}(\delta \, [\nabla f(\boldsymbol{\beta})]_j + 2\beta_j)}{2C_{j,j} + \delta}, \frac{\delta \, C_{j,j}(4C_{j,j} + \delta)}{(2C_{j,j} + \delta)^2} \right)$$

2. Generate $u \sim U(0, 1)$, and accept the new proposal if

$$u < \exp \left(f(\bar{\boldsymbol{\beta}}, \beta_0, \sigma^2) - f(\boldsymbol{\beta}, \beta_0, \sigma^2) + h_1(\boldsymbol{\beta}, \bar{\boldsymbol{\beta}}) - h_1(\bar{\boldsymbol{\beta}}, \boldsymbol{\beta}) \right),$$

$$h_1(\boldsymbol{\beta}, \bar{\boldsymbol{\beta}}) = \sum_{j=1}^{p} \left(\beta_j - \frac{C_{j,j}(4\bar{\beta}_j + \delta \, [\nabla f(\bar{\boldsymbol{\beta}})]_j)}{2(2C_{j,j} + \delta)} \right) \left(\frac{2C_{j,j} + \delta}{4C_{j,j} + \delta} \right) [\nabla f(\bar{\boldsymbol{\beta}})]_j$$

Due to the nature of the global-local shrinkage hierarchy, the mGrad-1 algorithm has a total computational complexity of only order $O(pn)$ for a GLM. This gives it potential for application to large p regression problems.

2.2 Algorithm 2: mGrad-2

A potential problem with the mGrad-1 algorithm is that it only utilises first order likelihood information when generating the proposal; therefore, potential exists to improve mixing in the face of correlation between predictors by utilising second-order information. A second-order Taylor series expansion method is proposed in the supplementary material of [20], but was found to perform poorly, and is slow to implement as the proposal distribution depends on state-dependent second-order information. Given the nature of GLMs, we instead propose to set $\mathbf{S} = \mathbf{X}^\mathsf{T}\mathbf{X}$, i.e., to use the correlation matrix of the predictors as the preconditioner. This keeps the covariance of the proposal independent of the state and allows for pre-computation of $\mathbf{S}^{-1}$. We call this the 'mGrad-2' algorithm, as it utilises second-order information. The computational effort of mGrad-2 is $O(p^3)$, which can be substantially higher than the computational complexity of mGrad-1.

2.3   Sampling the Intercept

The mGrad-1 and mGrad-2 algorithms provide us with a way to sample the coefficients $\boldsymbol{\beta}$. We observed that using a single MH step for both β_0 and $\boldsymbol{\beta}$ led to reduced mixing, so we instead sample the intercept separately, using a simple proposal that does not depend on a step size parameter. To sample β_0 for a GLM we use the following procedure:

1. Generate a proposal from

$$\bar{\beta}_0 \mid \beta_0 \sim N\left(\beta_0, \frac{2.5}{H(\beta_0)}\right)$$

where $H(\beta_0)$ is the second-derivative of the negative log-likelihood with respect to β_0.
2. Generate $u \sim U(0,1)$ and accept $\bar{\beta}_0$ if $u < \exp(f(\boldsymbol{\beta}, \bar{\beta}_0, \sigma^2) - f(\boldsymbol{\beta}, \beta_0), \sigma^2)$.

We find this choice leads to acceptance rates in the range 50%–60% for all experiments we considered.

2.4   Tuning the Step Size δ

Both the mGrad-1 and mGrad-2 algorithms are Metropolis-Hastings based approaches and require the selection of an appropriate step-size. For the base algorithm from which these methods are derived it is recommended that the optimal step-size δ should yield an acceptance rate in the range of 50%–60%. The step-size that achieves this rate will depend crucially on the particular problem, so it must be chosen adaptively. During the initial burn-in period we use the following procedure to estimate an appropriate value for δ.

We divide the burn-in period into windows of size w; then, every w iterations we record the step-size δ used in window j as δ_j, and the observed acceptance rate for the window as p_j. We first find values of δ such that our algorithm never accepts samples, and accepts all samples; call our initial guesses at these two quantities $\delta_{\max}$ and $\delta_{\min}$, respectively. We continually increase δ by a factor of $k > 0$ every window, starting from $\delta = \delta_{\max}$, until we observe an acceptance rate of zero and update our value of $\delta_{\max}$. We then continually decrease δ by a factor of k every window, starting from $\delta = \delta_{\min}$, until we observe an acceptance rate of one and update our value of $\delta_{\min}$.

Once this is done we set $\delta \leftarrow (\delta_{\min}\delta_{\max})^{1/2}$, and begin 'probing' to learn the relationship between δ and the acceptance probability. For every window j thereafter, we fit a logistic regression of $(\log \delta_1, \ldots, \log \delta_j)$ to the acceptance probabilities $(p_1, \ldots, p_j)$; call the fitted slope $\hat{\alpha}_1$ and intercept $\hat{\alpha}_0$. We then update the step-size for the next window by first generating $u \sim U(0.45, 0.65)$, and then setting $\delta = d(u, \hat{\alpha}_0, \hat{\alpha}_1)$ where

$$d(u, \alpha_0, \alpha_1) = \exp\left[-\frac{1}{\alpha_1}\left(-\log\left(\frac{1}{1/u - 1}\right) + \alpha_0\right)\right].$$

solves the equation

$$\log\left(\frac{u}{1-u}\right) = \alpha_1 \log \delta + \alpha_0$$

for δ. Once the burn-in phase is complete, we choose the final step-size as $\delta = d(0.55, \hat{\alpha}_0, \hat{\alpha}_1)$. In this way we are using the estimated relationship between the step-size and acceptance probability to select an appropriate value for δ. In our implementation we took $w = 75$, $\delta_{\max} = 100$, $\delta_{\min} = 10^{-7}$ and $k = 10$, though our experiments show the algorithm is almost completely insensitive to the particular values chosen. In all cases we observed that a burn-in period of $5{,}000$ samples usually provided an estimate of δ that achieved an acceptance rate between 0.5 and 0.6 for the remaining samples.

2.5   Implementation Details

Implementation of the mGrad-1 and mGrad-2 algorithms require only knowledge of the log-likelihood and the gradient of the log-likelihood. For convenience, these quantities are presented in Table 1 for a number of distributions frequently used in GLMs. Both algorithms require computation of the likelihood for the acceptance step. By careful implementation the number of computations can be reduced to one additional computation per sample being simulated.

While the computation of the likelihood is not required by the SMN technique, it is common to compute a diagnostic statistic such as the widely applicable information criterion (WAIC) from MCMC output, for which computation of

Table 1. Log-likelihoods (up to constants independent of β) and gradients for commonly used target distributions. The quantity $\eta_i = \bar{\mathbf{x}}_i^{\mathsf{T}}\beta + \beta_0$ denotes the linear predictor for sample y_i, and $e_i = y_i - \mu_i$. The normal distribution uses the identity link $\mu_i = \eta_i$; the binomial uses the logit link $\mu_i = (1 + \exp(-\eta_i))^{-1}$; the remaining distributions use the log-link $\mu_i = \exp(\eta_i)$. All distributions are parameterised so that $\mathbb{E}\left[y_i\right] = \mu_i$. The final column identifies the dispersion parameter.

	Log-likelihood, $f(\beta, \beta_0, \sigma^2)$	$[\nabla f(\beta)]_j$	$\sigma^2 v(\mu_i)$
Normal	$-\dfrac{1}{2\sigma^2}\sum_{i=1}^{n} e_i^2$	$\dfrac{1}{\sigma^2}\sum_{i=1}^{n} e_i X_{i,j}$	σ^2
Binomial	$\sum_{i=1}^{n} y_i \log \mu_i + (1 - y_i)\log(1 - \mu_i)$	$\sum_{i=1}^{n} e_i X_{i,j}$	$\mu_i(1 - \mu_i)$
Poisson	$\left[\sum_{i=1}^{n} y_i \eta_i - \mu_i\right]$	$\sum_{i=1}^{n} e_i X_{i,j}$	μ_i
Geometric	$\left[\sum_{i=1}^{n} \eta_i y_i - (y_i + 1)\log(\mu_i + 1)\right]$	$\sum_{i=1}^{n}\left(y_i - \dfrac{\mu_i(y_i + 1)}{\mu_i + 1}\right) X_{i,j}$	$\mu(\mu_i + 1)$
Gamma	$-\dfrac{1}{\kappa}\sum_{i=1}^{n}\left[\log \mu_i + \dfrac{y_i}{\mu_i}\right]$	$\dfrac{1}{\kappa}\sum_{i=1}^{n}\left(\dfrac{y_i}{\mu_i} - 1\right) X_{i,j}$	$\kappa\mu_i^2$
Inverse-Gaussian	$-\dfrac{1}{2\xi}\sum_{i=1}^{n}\dfrac{e_i^2}{\mu_i^2 y_i}$	$\dfrac{1}{\xi}\sum_{i=1}^{n}\left(\dfrac{e_i}{\mu_i^2 y_i}\right) X_{i,j}$	$\xi\mu_i^3$

the likelihood is required for every sample. In this case, our samplers effectively provide the likelihood information 'for free' which improves their competitiveness in comparison to SMN approaches.

3   Two New Samplers for the Generalized Horseshoe

In this section we discuss two new sampling schemes for the shrinkage hyperparameters in the generalized horseshoe hierarchy (1). More specifically, we develop two samplers to target the density

$$p(z \mid m, p, a, b) \propto z^{2a-p-1}(1+z^2)^{-a-b}e^{-m/z^2} \tag{5}$$

This density generalizes the conditional distributions for the shrinkage hyperparameters λ_j and τ in the GHS hierarchy (1); for example, the conditional distribution for a local shrinkage hyperparameter λ_j is

$$p(z = \lambda_j \mid \beta_j^2/(2\tau^2\sigma^2), 1, a, b)$$

and for the global shrinkage hyperparameter τ is

$$p\left(z = \tau \mid \left(\frac{1}{2\sigma^2}\right) \sum_{j=1}^{p} \frac{\beta_j^2}{\lambda_j^2}, p, a, b\right).$$

We develop two approaches to sample from (5). We provide an inverse gamma mixture of inverse gamma (IGIG) distributions as an alternative to the gamma-gamma (GG) sampler. We also detail a reasonable straightforward rejection sampler that exploits the log-concavity of the density (5) under the transformation $\xi = \log z$. In contrast to the the GG and IGIG samplers, the rejection sampler simulates uncorrelated random draws. It is also easily adapted to sample from a truncated form of (5), which is of potential interest in light of the results presented in [14].

3.1   Inverse Gamma-Inverse Gamma Sampler

The following proposition generalizes the inverse gamma-inverse gamma representation of the half-Cauchy density utilised in [10]. This allows us to build a Gibbs sampler for the generalized horseshoe estimator.

Proposition 1. *Let* $x^2 \mid \nu, b \sim \mathrm{IG}(b, 1/\nu)$ *and* $\nu \mid a \sim \mathrm{IG}(a, 1)$. *Then*

$$p(x) \propto x^{2a-1}(1+x^2)^{-a-b}.$$

The proof is a straightforward application of integration by substitution. Using Proposition 1, we can build a sampler for the density (5) in the case that $a > 0$, $b > 0$. Introduce the auxiliary variable ν; the Gibbs sampler then iterates:

1. First sample

$$z^2 \sim \text{IG}\left(\frac{p}{2} + b, m + \frac{1}{\nu}\right).$$

2. Then sample the auxilliary variable

$$\nu \sim \text{IG}\left(a + b, 1 + \frac{1}{z^2}\right).$$

Marginally, the random variable z will follow the distribution (5). In contrast to the gamma-gamma sampler discussed in Sect. 1.2, the inverse gamma-inverse gamma sampler only requires samples from inverse gamma distributions, rather than the substantially more complex generalised inverse Gaussian distribution needed by the gamma-gamma hierarchy. This makes implementation substantially more straightforward.

3.2 Rejection Sampling

The GG and IGIG samplers all have a one-hundred percent acceptance rate, but suffer from autocorrelation due to their reliance on auxiliary variables. An alternative to this approach is rejection sampling, in which we trade a reduced acceptance rate for the removal of autocorrelation in the samples. As a quick refresher, a rejection sampler for a target density $p(x)$ works by first drawing a sample from a proposal distribution $q(x)$, and then accepting this sample if $p(x)/q(x) > u$, where $u \sim U(0,1)$. The proposal distribution must satisfy $q(x) \geq p(x)$ for all x (i.e., the proposal must upper-bound the target density), and ideally, must be straightforward to generate samples from. The closer $q(x)$ is to $p(x)$, the higher the rate of acceptance.

An efficient rejection sampler for λ can be devised by noting that if λ follows the conditional distribution (5), then the probability density for the transformed variable $\xi = \log \lambda$ (i.e., we are sampling the logarithm of the hyperparameters) is

$$p(\xi \mid m, p, a, b) \propto e^{-e^{-2\xi}m} e^{-\xi(p-2a)} (1 + e^{2\xi})^{-a-b}. \tag{6}$$

It is straightforward to verify that the density (6) is log-concave, and that $-\log p(\xi \mid m, p, a, b) \asymp \xi$ as $\xi \to \infty$. We therefore use a proposal density built by sandwiching a uniform density between two appropriately chosen exponential distributions, as this is guaranteed to bound the density (6) from above [7]. The mode of the density (6) is given by

$$\xi' = \frac{1}{2}\left[\log\left(2(a+m) - p + \sqrt{8m(2b+p) + (p-2a-2m)^2}\right) - \log(4b+2p)\right].$$

We place the uniform density on the interval (L, R) which is chosen such that $L < \xi' < R$, and then place the two exponential distributions on either side of the mode; to find the break-points L and R for the three components, first define

$$\begin{aligned} l(\xi) &= -\log p(\xi \mid m, p, a, b) \\ &= e^{-2\xi}m + (p - 2a)\xi + (a + b)\log\left(1 + e^{2\xi}\right) \end{aligned} \tag{7}$$

and

$$g(\xi) = -2a + \frac{2(a+b)e^{2\xi}}{1+e^{2\xi}} - 2e^{-2\xi}m + p \qquad (8)$$

as the derivative of $l(\xi)$. We then set

$$\xi_L = \xi' - \frac{0.85}{\sqrt{p}}, \quad \xi_R = \xi' + \frac{1.3}{\sqrt{p}}.$$

These are the points that will be used to build the two exponential components of our proposal density; the break-points for our proposal density are then given by

$$L = \xi_L - \frac{l(\xi_L) - l(\xi')}{g(\xi_L)}, \quad R = \xi_R - \frac{l(\xi_R) - l(\xi')}{g(\xi_R)}$$

The proposal density is then given by

$$q(\xi) \propto \begin{cases} e^{-g(\xi_L)(\xi-L)} & \text{for } -\infty < \xi < L \\ 1 & \text{for } L < \xi < R \\ e^{-g(\xi_R)(\xi-R)} & \text{for } R < \xi < \infty \end{cases}.$$

Sampling from $q(\xi)$ is straightforward, as the normalizing constants for each of the components is straightforward: $K_L = -1/g(\xi_L)$, $K_C = R - L$, and $K_R = 1/g(\xi_R)$, where K_L, K_C and K_R denote the normalizing terms for the left, central and right hand pieces respectively, and set $K = K_L + K_C + K_R$. The algorithm is as follows.

1. First, sample
$$u_1 \sim U(0,1), \ u_2 \sim U(0,1), \ u_3 \sim U(0,1).$$

2. Next, check u_1:
   (a) If $u_1 \in (0, K_L/K)$ then
   $$x \leftarrow -\frac{\log(1-u_2)}{g(\xi_L)} + L, \quad q \leftarrow l(\xi_L) + g(\xi_L)(x - \xi_L)$$

   (b) If $u_1 \in (K_L/K, (K_L + K_C)/K)$ then
   $$x \leftarrow (R - L)u_2 + L, \quad q \leftarrow l(\xi')$$

   (c) If $u_1 \in ((K_L + K_C)/K, 1)$ then
   $$x \leftarrow -\frac{\log(1-u_2)}{g(\xi_R)} + R, \quad q \leftarrow l(\xi_R) + g(\xi_R)(x - \xi_R)$$

3. Determine if we accept x; check if
$$\log u_3 < q - l(x).$$

If so accept x; otherwise, reject x and return to Step 1.

The accepted sample x can be transformed back to the original space using $z = e^x$.

Table 2. (minimum, median, maximum) effective samples per second for three generalized horseshoe local shrinkage hyperparameter samplers: a rejection sampler, the inverse-gamma inverse-gamma (IGIG) sampler and the gamma-gamma (GG) sampler. The quantities a and b are the concentration and tail hyperparameters for the generalized horseshoe prior.

Prior	Sampler	$p = 50$	$p = 250$	$p = 500$
$(a = 1/2, b = 1/2)$	Rejection	$(\mathbf{2147}, \mathbf{7329}, 11933)$	$(48, 661, 1302)$	$(5.2, 286, 540)$
	IGIG	$(2044, 8028, \mathbf{14111})$	$(49, \mathbf{664}, \mathbf{1397})$	$(\mathbf{5.3}, \mathbf{299}, \mathbf{586})$
	GG	$(1558, 6098, 11016)$	$(29, 500, 1207)$	$(3.1, 221, 538)$
$(a = 1/4, b = 1/2)$	Rejection	$(\mathbf{1766}, \mathbf{6709}, \mathbf{11700})$	$(45, \mathbf{617}, \mathbf{1314})$	$(5.1, \mathbf{283}, 554)$
	IGIG	$(966, 4399, 10526)$	$(31, 525, 1277)$	$(4.7, 270, \mathbf{572})$
	GG	$(1245, 4995, 9063)$	$(29, 483, 1121)$	$(3.4, 224, 509)$

4 Experimental Results

We undertook several simulation experiments to assess the comparative performance of the new sampler algorithms: mGrad-1, mGrad-2 and the new hyperparameter samplers. In all experiments we used the effective sample size per second (ESS/s) as a measure of performance of the samples. The ESS measures how much correlation is present in a chain of MCMC samples; the higher the correlation, the less information is contributed by each sample.

In all simulated examples we used the following experimental procedure. For a given sample size n and number of predictors p, we generated a design matrix from a multivariate normal distribution with covariance between predictors given by $\text{Cov}(X_i, X_j) = \rho^{|i-j|}$. Then, we randomly selected 15 predictors to be associated, and generated their coefficients from a Student-t distribution with a degrees-of-freedom equal to ten. We then rescaled the coefficients so that the signal-to-noise ratio of the regression model was equal to three for the Poisson models and 1.5 for the binomial models; the intercept was fixed at $\beta_0 = 1$ for Poisson models and $\beta_0 = 0$ for binomial models. Finally, we generated $n = 200$ data points from this model. These choices produced models with a realistic, sparse mix of stronger and weaker effects, and which were not (near) linearly seperable in the case of binomial regression. All tests were conducted on a Microsoft Surface Pro 2016 laptop. Additional experiments were performed but are not included in this article due to space constraints.[1]

4.1 Comparison of GHS Hyperparameter Samplers

We tested the performance of the three GHS local hyperparameter samplers: the gamma-gamma (GG) sampler (Sect. 1.2, [1]), the inverse gamma-inverse gamma (IGIG) sampler (Sect. 3.1) and the rejection sampler (Sect. 3.2). We tested their

---

[1] Available at https://dschmidt.org.

performance on a Gaussian linear model with $p = 50$, $p = 250$ and $p = 500$ predictors generated as per the procedure in Sect. 4, using a correlation of $\rho = 0.9$. The samplers for the coefficients was the usual conditionally conjugate multivariate Gaussian. We tested two prior settings: $(a = 1/2, b = 1/2)$, i.e., the regular horseshoe prior, and $(a = 1/4, b = 1/2)$, which concentrates more prior probability mass around the origin. For a fair comparison, we implemented the generalized inverse Gaussian sampler and the rejection sampler in C. The IGIG sampler was implemented in pure MATLAB.

For each experiment we ran the chains for 10^4 burnin iterations, and then collected 2×10^4 samples. The results are shown in Table 1. Overall, the rejection sampler performed the best, but the IGIG sampler was competitive with, or superior to, the rejection sampler for all but the case of $p = 50$ and $a = 1/4$, with both being largely superior to the GG sampler. The performance of the IGIG sampler, coupled with its simple implementation, recommend it as an excellent choice of sampler for generalized horseshoe hierarchies.

Table 3. (minimum, median, maximum) effective samples per second for various sampling algorithms. mGrad-1 and mGrad-2 refer to the two gradient-based sampling algorithms developed in this article, pCNL is the pre-conditioned Crank Nicholson sampler, NUTS is the no U-turn sampler and GESS is the generalized elliptical slice sampler.

Distribution	Correlation	Sampler	$p = 50$	$p = 100$	$p = 250$
Poisson	$\rho = 0.5$	mGrad-1	$(108, 270, 615)$	$(\mathbf{42, 398, 776})$	$(\mathbf{55, 358, 777})$
		mGrad-2	$(\mathbf{127, 351, 673})$	$(18, 136, 235)$	$(4.8, 27, 49)$
		pCNL	$(14, 36, 108)$	$(3.8, 18, 69)$	$(3.7, 17, 75)$
		NUTS	$(26, 35, 36)$	$(16, 23, 24)$	$(9.5, 14, 14)$
		GESS	$(4.3, 13, 25)$	$(0.6, 3.3, 7.8)$	$(0.1, 0.7, 1.9)$
	$\rho = 0.9$	mGrad-1	$(12, 56, 165)$	$(7.1, 69, 223)$	$(2.8, \mathbf{103, 339})$
		mGrad-2	$(\mathbf{157, 489, 806})$	$(\mathbf{25, 157, 305})$	$(1.6, 30, 59)$
		pCNL	$(6.0, 18, 56)$	$(3.3, 14, 39)$	$(1.9, 12, 39)$
		NUTS	$(29, 40, 41)$	$(20, 28, 28)$	$(\mathbf{7.8}, 12, 12)$
		GESS	$(4.0, 11, 21)$	$(0.6, 3.3, 7.9)$	$(0.1, 0.8, 2.2)$
Binomial	$\rho = 0.5$	mGrad-1	$(46, 315, 694)$	$(12, 165, 425)$	$(8.0, \mathbf{269, 656})$
		mGrad-2	$(52, 352, 747)$	$(4.6, 91, 208)$	$(0.6, 24, 54)$
		SMN	$(\mathbf{179, 772, 1936})$	$(\mathbf{15, 260, 894})$	$(3.1, 201, 486)$
		NUTS	$(56, 73, 76)$	$(39, 54, 56)$	$(\mathbf{17}, 26, 27)$
	$\rho = 0.9$	mGrad-1	$(4.6, 33, 99)$	$(3.3, 49, 161)$	$(4.1, 76, 312)$
		mGrad-2	$(25, 317, 705)$	$(11, 135, 298)$	$(1.2, 25, 61)$
		SMN	$(\mathbf{96, 721, 1775})$	$(\mathbf{49, 483, 1159})$	$(5.1, \mathbf{161, 478})$
		NUTS	$(32, 42, 44)$	$(34, 47, 48)$	$(\mathbf{17}, 26, 27)$

4.2   Comparison of Samplers for Coefficients

We tested the performance of our samplers for two distributions: the Poisson, for which a scale mixture of normals (SMN) sampler is not known, and logistic (binomial) regression for which an SMN sampler exists [17]. For both models we compared the mGrad-1 and mGrad-2 sampling algorithms presented in Sect. 2 against the NUTS sampler (using the RStan stan_glm() function). For Poisson regression we also tested against the generalized elliptical slice sampler (GESS) and pCNL algorithm; however, as both of these were dominated by mGrad-1 we did not test them for binomial regression. For logistic regression we also compared against the optimised scale mixture of normals (SMN) sampler implemented in the bayesreg package for MATLAB. We used the IGIG sampler for the horseshoe hierarchy for mGrad-1, mGrad-2, GESS, SMN and pCNL.

We tested the samplers for two settings of correlation $\rho = \{0.5, 0.9\}$, and generated a different model for each combination of $p = \{50, 100, 250\}$ and ρ. To make the comparisons as favourable for NUTS as possible we compute ESS/s based only on the sampling times, and ignore warmup. We note that the mGrad algorithms require substantially less warmup time for tuning than NUTS. For NUTS we ran the chains for 10^3 warmup samples and then collected the following 10^3 samples. There were no convergence issues. For the other samplers we ran the chains for 10^4 burnin iterations and the collected 2×10^4 samples. For each test and each sampler we produced 10 chains and averaged the ESS/s scores across the chains. The results are shown in Table 3.

In all cases the NUTS sampler exhibited an interesting property: the spread of ESS/s values was small, with the minimum ESS/s being close to the maximum ESS/s. For Poisson regression the NUTS sampler had higher minimum ESS/s than mGrad-1 when $\rho = 0.9$. In the case of Poisson regression, the mGrad-1 algorithm is highly competitive with the NUTS sampler, even for smaller p, and is uniformly superior for $\rho = 0.5$. The mGrad-2 algorithm exhibits superior performance to mGrad-1 for smaller p and higher correlation ρ, but has poorer performance for $p = 250$ as the expensive matrix inversions outweigh the improvement in mixing. The pCNL and GESS algorithms performed uniformly worse than mGrad-1.

For logistic regression, the NUTS algorithm performed substantially better than for Poisson regression. The SMN sampler generally achieved the highest median and maximum ESS/s scores, while the NUTS sampler uniformly achieved the higher minimum ESS/s than mGrad-1. The mGrad-1 algorithm is largely inferior to the SMN sampler, but generally achieved higher median and maximum ESS/s than the NUTS sampler. The mGrad-2 algorithm is uniformly worse than SMN in the setting of logistic regression, which is unsurprising as its base time complexity is similar to the SMN approach. We note that due to a different model being used for each combination of p and ρ, the ESS/s scores do not necessarily decrease as p increases as the performance of all the samplers can vary depending on the structure of the underlying model.

Additional Test for $p = 1,000$. We performed an additional experiment for a much larger design matrix of $p = 1,000$ predictors with $\rho = 0.9$ and 50 non-zero coefficients for Poisson regression. We considered only the mGrad-1 and NUTS sampler; the NUTS sampler achieved a maximum ESS/s of 7.8, while the mGrad-1 algorithm achieved a minimum/median/maximum of $\approx(0.8, 30, 143)$, which suggests that the simplicity of the algorithm potentially allows it to remain competitive with NUTS even for large p.

Sensitivity to Model Structure. We also performed an additional experiment to examine the sensitivity of mGrad-1 and NUTS to model structure. We generated the same design matrix and coefficients as used in the experiments for Poisson regression with $\rho = 0.5$, $p = 100$ but rescaled the coefficients to have a signal-to-noise ratio (SNR) of 9. The NUTS sampler achieved a maximum ESS of ≈ 8 while the mGrad-1 sampler achieved a minimum/median/maximum of $\approx(20, 120, 245)$. In both cases this is roughly a three-fold reduction in comparison to the results obtained when the SNR was 3 (from Table 3). The sensitivity of NUTS is primarily driven by increased sampling time rather than changes in raw ESS, while for mGrad-1 the sampling time is unaffected but the increased correlation in the chains reduces the overall ESS/s.

5   Summary

In comparison to NUTS and SMN, the mGrad-1 algorithm is substantially easier to implement, requiring only knowledge of likelihood and gradient information. The entire algorithm, including the tuning can be implemented in around 50 lines of MATLAB code. This simplicity, coupled with the competitive performance of the mGrad-1 algorithm, demonstrates that it is a very useful addition to the suite of sampling procedures available for Bayesian regression. A similar conclusion can be drawn regarding the new inverse gamma-inverse gamma sampler for the generalized horseshoe hyperparameters: in terms of performance it is roughly equivalent to the rejection sampler, and largely superior to the standard gamma-gamma sampler, while being substantially simple to implement than both. We therefore recommend this sampler to researchers looking to implement horseshoe and generalized horseshoe hierarchies for new models. The mGrad-1 sampler and SMN sampler for generalized linear generalized horseshoe regression models are both implemented in the **bayesreg**[2] Bayesian regression package.

References

1. Armagan, A., Dunson, D.B., Clyde, M.: Generalized beta mixtures of Gaussians. In: Shawe-Taylor, J., Zemel, R., Bartlett, P., Pereira, F., Weinberger, K. (eds.) Advances in Neural Information Processing Systems, vol. 24, pp. 523–531 (2011)
2. Bhadra, A., Datta, J., Polson, N.G., Willard, B.: The horseshoe+ estimator of ultra-sparse signals (2016). arXiv:1502.00560

---

[2] Available at https://au.mathworks.com/matlabcentral/fileexchange/60823.

3. Bhattacharya, A., Chakraborty, A., Mallick, B.K.: Fast sampling with Gaussian scale-mixture priors in high-dimensional regression. Biometrika **103**(4), 985–991 (2016). arXiv:1506.04778
4. Bhattacharya, A., Pati, D., Pillai, N.S., Dunson, D.B.: Dirichlet-Laplace priors for optimal shrinkage. J. Am. Stat. Assoc. **110**, 1479–1490 (2015)
5. Carvalho, C.M., Polson, N.G., Scott, J.G.: The horseshoe estimator for sparse signals. Biometrika **97**(2), 465–480 (2010)
6. Cotter, S., Roberts, G., Stuart, A., White, D.: MCMC methods for functions: modifying old algorithms to make them faster. Stat. Sci. **28**, 424–446 (2014)
7. Gilks, W.R., Wild, P.: Adaptive rejection sampling for Gibbs sampling. J. Roy. Stat. Soc. C (Appl. Stat.) **41**(2), 337–348 (1992)
8. Hoffman, M.D., Gelman, A.: The no-u-turn sampler: adaptively setting path lengths in hamiltonian Monte Carlo. J. Mach. Learn. Res. **15**, 1351–1381 (2014)
9. Makalic, E., Schmidt, D.F.: High-dimensional Bayesian regularised regression with the BayesReg package (2016). arXiv:1611.06649
10. Makalic, E., Schmidt, D.F.: A simple sampler for the horseshoe estimator. IEEE Signal Process. Lett. **23**(1), 179–182 (2016)
11. Nelder, J.A., Wedderburn, R.W.M.: Generalized linear models. J. Roy. Stat. Soc. A (General) **135**(3), 370–384 (1972)
12. Nishihara, R., Murray, I., Adams, R.P.: Parallel MCMC with generalized elliptical slice sampling. J. Mach. Learn. Res. **15**, 2087–2112 (2014)
13. Park, T., Casella, G.: The Bayesian lasso. J. Am. Stat. Assoc. **103**(482), 681–686 (2008)
14. van der Pas, S., Szabó, B., van der Vaart, A.: Adaptive posterior contraction rates for the horseshoe (2017). arXiv:1702.03698v1
15. Polson, N.G., Scott, J.G., Windle, J.: The Bayesian bridge. J. Roy. Stat. Soc.: Ser. B (Stat. Methodol.) **76**(4), 713–733 (2014)
16. Polson, N.G., Scott, J.G.: Shrink globally, act locally: sparse Bayesian regularization and prediction. In: Bayesian Statistics, vol. 9 (2010)
17. Polson, N.G., Scott, J.G., Windle, J.: Bayesian inference for logistic models using Pólya-gamma latent variables **108**(504), 1339–1349 (2013)
18. Rue, H.: Fast sampling of Gaussian Markov random fields. J. Roy. Stat. Soc. B **63**(2), 325–338 (2001)
19. Schmidt, D.F., Makalic, E.: Adaptive Bayesian shrinkage estimation using log-scale shrinkage priors (2017). https://arxiv.org/abs/1801.02321
20. Titsias, M.K., Papaspiliopoulos, O.: Auxiliary gradient-based sampling algorithms. J. Roy. Stat. Soc. B **80**(4), 749–767 (2018)

Fine-Grained Explanations
Using Markov Logic

Khan Mohammad Al Farabi[1]([⊠]), Somdeb Sarkhel[2], Sanorita Dey[3],
and Deepak Venugopal[1]

[1] University of Memphis, Memphis, USA
{kfarabi,dvngopal}@memphis.edu
[2] Adobe Research, San Jos, USA
sarkhel@adobe.com
[3] University of Illinois at Urbana-Champaign, Champaign, USA
sdey4@illinois.edu

Abstract. Explaining the results of Machine learning algorithms is crucial given the rapid growth and potential applicability of these methods in critical domains including healthcare, defense, autonomous driv-
ing, etc. In this paper, we address this problem in the context of Markov
Logic Networks (MLNs) which are highly expressive statistical relational
models that combine first-order logic with probabilistic graphical models. MLNs in general are known to be interpretable models, i.e., MLNs
can be understood more easily by humans as compared to models learned
by approaches such as deep learning. However, at the same time, it is not
straightforward to obtain human-understandable explanations specific to
an observed inference result (e.g. marginal probability estimate). This is
because, the MLN provides a lifted interpretation, one that generalizes to
all possible worlds/instantiations, which are not query/evidence specific.
In this paper, we extract *grounded*-explanations, i.e., explanations defined
w.r.t specific inference queries and observed evidence. We extract these
explanations from importance weights defined over the MLN formulas that
encode the contribution of formulas towards the final inference results. We
validate our approach in real world problems related to analyzing reviews
from Yelp, and show through user-studies that our explanations are richer
than state-of-the-art non-relational explainers such as LIME.

1 Introduction

Markov Logic Networks (MLNs) [1] are popular Statistical Relational Models
that combine first-order logic with probabilistic graphical models [10]. The power
of MLNs comes from the fact that they can represent relational structure as well
as uncertainty in a highly compact manner. Specifically, an MLN represents
real-world knowledge in the form of weighted first-order logic formulas. Unlike
traditional first-order logic based representations, MLNs allow uncertainty in
the represented knowledge, where weights attached to the formulas encode this
uncertainty. Larger weights indicate more belief in a formula as compared to

© Springer Nature Switzerland AG 2020
U. Brefeld et al. (Eds.): ECML PKDD 2019, LNAI 11907, pp. 614–629, 2020.
https://doi.org/10.1007/978-3-030-46147-8_37

smaller weights. The MLN defines a template that can be grounded with real-world constants, to obtain a probability distribution over *possible worlds* - an assignment to all ground variables - of the MLN. Due to its generality, MLNs have found applications in varied practical problems such as coreference resolution [13], information extraction [12,23], question answering [8], event-detection in videos [22], etc.

One of the key advantages of MLNs is their interpetability. Specifically, since MLN models are first-order logic based models, it is quite easy for a human user to understand and interpret what the learned model represents. In contrast, methods such as deep learning can achieve state-of-the-art results in language processing, computer vision, etc., but their lack of interpretability is problematic in many domains. However, interpretability of learned models is not the same as explainability of results generated by a Machine learning method. Guidotti et al. [5] provide a detailed survey of explanations in ML methods in which they categorize explanations as model explanations and outcome explanations. The former provides explanations for the model (interpretability of the model) while the latter provides explanations for predictions. Of late, there has been a lot of interest in outcome explanations [6]. For instance, in healthcare applications, a doctor would require a system that explains why it is recommending a particular action, rather than just provide results as a "black-box". Some ML methods such as decision trees are both interpretable and explainable, while some are neither (e.g. deep networks). It turns out that MLNs though interpretable are not easily explainable. Recently proposed approaches such as LIME [15] try to explain the results of a classifier whose results are typically hard-to-understand. However, these approaches are specific to non-relational data, and do not provide rich, relational explanations (for e.g. LIME explains non-linear classifiers as linear models). Our focus in this paper is to explain relational inference in MLNs in a human-understandable form.

Our main idea is to generate explanations for queries in terms of a ranking of formulas based on their importance. Specifically, MLN formulas have weights attached to them that intuitively signify their importance, i.e., for a formula f with weight w, a world where f is true is e^w more likely than a world in which it is false [1]. Note that the formula weights do not have a well-defined probabilistic interpretation if they are dependent on each other, i.e., if atoms in one formula also occur in other formulas [1]. More importantly, the weights are *tied*, which means that any instantiation of a formula has the same weight. Thus, a naive explanation for a query that can be obtained by ranking formulas purely on their weights is not likely to be useful since it is generic across all possible worlds. That is, the explanation will remain unchanged even when the query or evidence variables change. For example, consider the task of classifying if an email is spam or not. An MLN could encode a formula such as $\texttt{Word}(e, +w) \Rightarrow \texttt{Spam}(e)$. The + symbol preceding a variable is a short-hand representation to denote that the MLN stores a different weight for every distinct grounding of the w variable (which represents the domain of words). Suppose the query predicate is $\texttt{Spam}$, we would want different explanations for different groundings of the query predicate based on the specific evidence on the $\texttt{Word}$ predicate. Further, suppose the evidence is incomplete, meaning that there are some atoms that are not query atoms and whose truth value is not known. For formulas containing such atoms, it becomes even harder to determine their influence on a query since we need to consider all possible worlds where the unknown atoms are true as well as the cases where the atoms may be false. We propose a systematic approach for explanations where we learn importance weights for formulas based on samples generated from the MLN. Specifically, we perform inference using Gibbs sampling, and learn the importance of formulas for a specific query based on their influence in computing the Gibbs transition probability. Thus, as the sampler samples possible worlds consistent with the observed evidence, the importance weights capture the influence of formulas on the query variable in these worlds.

We evaluate our approach using two MLN applications we designed for performing inference in real-world review data from Yelp. In the first application, we predict if a review is a spam review and provide explanations for this prediction. In the second application, we predict the sentiment of a review that has missing words. For both cases, we develop MLNs that encode common knowledge and use our approach to extract explanations from the MLNs. We set up a comprehensive user-study consisting of around 60 participants and compare our explanations with explanations given by LIME for the same tasks. We clearly demonstrate through these studies that our explanations are richer and more human-understandable than the explanations given by LIME.

2   Background

2.1   Markov Logic Networks

Markov logic networks (MLNs) are template models that define uncertain, relational knowledge as first-order formulas with weights. Larger the weight of a formula, more likely is that formula to be true. ∞ weight formulas are treated as hard constraints which should always be true. Similarly formulas with $-\infty$ weights are always false. Thus, MLNs offer a flexible framework to mix hard and soft rules. Given a set of constants that represent the domains of variables in the MLN, an MLN represents a factored probability distribution over the possible worlds, in the form of a Markov network. A world in an MLN is an assignment of 0/1 to all ground atoms of the MLN (first order predicates in the MLN whose variables have been substituted with a constant). Specifically, the MLN distribution is given by,

$$P(\omega) = \frac{1}{Z} \exp\left(\sum_i w_i N_i(\omega)\right) \tag{1}$$

where w_i is the weight of formula f_i, $N_i(\omega)$ is the number of groundings of formula f_i that evaluate to True given a world ω, and Z is the normalization constant.

As a simple example of an MLN, suppose we want to encode the fact that smokers and asthmatics are not friends. We would design an MLN with a formula such as $\text{Smokes}(x) \wedge \text{Friends}(x, y) \Rightarrow \neg Asthma(y)$. Given constants corresponding to the variables, x and y, the MLN represents a joint distribution over all ground atoms of Smokes, Friends, and Asthma. The two key tasks in MLNs are *weight learning*, which is the task of learning the weights attached to the formulas from a training relational database, and *inference* (prediction). Learning the weights of an MLN is typically based on Max-likelihood estimation methods. The marginal estimation inference task involves computing the marginal probability distribution of a ground atom in the MLN given an evidence database of observed variables. For example computing the probability that Smokes(*Ana*) is true given that Smokes(*Bob*) is true, Friends(*Ana, Bob*) is true and Asthma(*Bob*) is false. Since computing this probability exactly is hard, one of the most popular approaches is to use Gibbs sampling [4] to approximate the marginal probability.

2.2 Related Work

Explaining the results of Machine learning models has been recognized as a critical area. Guidotti et al. [5] provide a detailed survey of explanations in ML. Specifically, they categorize them (among others categories) into model explanations and outcome explanations. The former provides explanations for the model while the latter provides explanations for predictions. In this paper, we are primarily concerned with outcome explanations. Recently, there have been a few significant attempts to develop model-agnostic outcome explanations. Notable among these are LIME developed by Ribeiro et al. [15] which can provide an explanation of *any* classifier, by approximating it locally with an interpretable model. More recently, they developed "Anchors" [16], a model-agnostic explainer with *if-then* rules. Ross et al. [17] developed a regularizer to obtain simpler explanations of a classifier's decision boundary. Koh and Liang [9] addressed the explainability problem by perturbing the importance of training examples and observing their influence on prediction. Similarly, Fong and Veladi [3] also use perturbations to explain predictions. Teso and Kersting [21] recently developed explanations for interactive learners. Though neural networks suffer from lack of interpretability in general, there have been attempts to explain the model through visual analytics, such as Grad-CAM [18] and the more recent work by Zhang and Zhu [24]. However, none of these techniques are applicable to relational data which is the focus of this paper. Specifically, in relational data there is a single example that is interconnected, and is therefore fundamentally different from the type of data addressed in the aforementioned methods. Related to propositional probabilistic graphical models, more recently, Shih et al. [20] compiled Bayesian networks into a more interpretable decision tree model.

3   Query Explanation

Our approach is to extract explanations for a query as a ranked list of MLN formulas, where the ranking encodes the influence of the formula on that query. Before we formally describe our approach, we motivate it with an illustrative example. Consider a simple MLN with 2 formulas, $f_1 = R(x) \land S_1(x)$ with weight

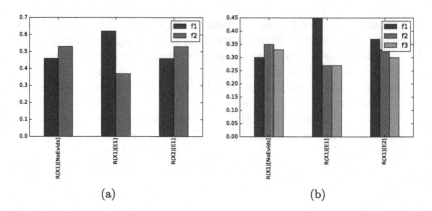

Fig. 1. Illustrating the influence of a formula w.r.t a query atom for varying evidences. The x-axis shows Query [evidence-set] and the y-axis shows the exponentiated sum of weights for satisfied groundings of the first-order formulas (denoted by $f1$, $f2$, $f3$) which signifies the formula's importance for the query.

equal to 0.5 and $f_2 = R(x) \wedge S_2(x)$ with weight equal to 0.6. Let R be the query predicate, and let the domain of $x, \Delta_x = \{X_1, X_2, X_3\}$. Let us assume that we want to explain the results of marginal inference, meaning that we compute the marginal probabilities of $R(X_1) \ldots R(X_3)$. Given no evidence, in every possible world, f_2 has a larger influence than f_1 in computing the probability of that world. Therefore, the marginal probabilities of the atoms $R(X_1) \ldots R(X_3)$, are influenced more by f_2 as compared to f_1. We illustrate this in Fig. 1. Here, we show the exponentiated sum of weights for all satisfied groundings in the first-order formula summed over all possible worlds where the query is satisfied. The values obtained for the formulas f_1 and f_2 are normalized and shown in Fig. 1(a).

However, now consider a second case, where we add evidence $S_1(X_1)$ and set all other atoms of S_1 and S_2 to false (we refer to this evidence as $E1$ in Fig. 1). We now analyze the influence of the formulas in a subset of possible worlds that are consistent with the observed evidence. Here, f_1 now has greater significance than f_2 for the query $R(X_1)$, since the observed evidence makes the formula f_1 grounded with X_1 true and the formula f_2 grounded with X_1 false. However, when we consider a different query $R(X_2)$, the influence of f_1 and f_2 changes. Specifically, the influence of f_1 and f_2 on $R(X_2)$ is equivalent to the case where we had no evidence. This is because case f_1 and f_2 grounded with X_2 have the same truth assignment due to the evidence. Thus, the same set of formulas can have different influences on different queries.

Now, suppose, we add a third formula, $f_3 = S_1(x) \wedge S_2(x)$ with weight 0.7. Since, f_3 has the highest weight, we may be tempted to say that f_3 has maximum influence on the probabilities. However, if we quantify the influence of the formulas as before, we get the results shown in Fig. 1(b). Note that adding the formula changes the influence that the other formulas have on the marginal probability. Further, even though f_3 has a higher weight, its influence on the query $R(X_1)$ is in fact smaller than that of f_2, even in the case where we have no evidence. Thus, we cannot analyze weights of the formulas independently of each other when the atoms are shared among different formulas, since the weights on one formulas can affect the other formulas.

On adding evidence as specified before, the influence of all three formulas are modified as shown. Further, if we assume a different evidence (specified as $E2$ in Fig. 1) where $S_1(X_1)$ is true and the other atoms of S_1 and S_2 are unknown (they can be either true or false), then f_3 has a larger influence than the other formulas. Thus, depending upon the evidence as well as the specific query we are looking at, each formula has a different influence on the overall marginal probability of the query. For small examples such as the aforementioned one, we can go over each possible world that is consistent with the evidence and the query, and compute the influence of each formula on the marginal probability of the query. However, this is not practically feasible for large problems. Therefore, we develop a practically feasible solution where we compute the importance based on samples drawn from the distribution over the possible worlds.

To formalize the above example, we first start with some notation. Let $f_1 \ldots f_k$ be the k formulas in the input MLN $\mathcal{M}$. Let $w_1 \ldots w_k$ be weights associated with each of these formulas respectively. Let $\mathbf{Q}$ represent the query predicate, and let $\mathbf{E}$ represent the set of evidence atoms (atoms whose truth assignment is known). Let $q_1 \ldots q_m$ denote the instantiations or ground atoms corresponding to the query predicate. Note that, for the sake of clarity, we assume that we have a single query predicate, however, it is straightforward to include multiple query predicates.

3.1 Sampling

In standard Gibbs sampling for MLNs, we start with a random assignment to all atoms $\omega^{(0)}$ in the MLN except the evidence atoms whose assignments are fixed as given in $\mathbf{E}$. In each iteration of Gibbs sampling, we choose a non-evidence atom based on a proposal distribution α, and compute an assignment to this atom by sampling the assignment based on its conditional distribution. In our case, we assume that α is a uniform distribution, which means that we sample non-evidence atoms randomly in each iteration. From the generated samples, we estimate the marginal probabilities of $P(q_1) \ldots P(q_m)$ as,

$$P(\bar{q}_i) = \frac{1}{T} \sum_{t=1}^{T} \mathbb{I}(\omega^{(t)} \sim \bar{q}_i) \tag{2}$$

where T is the total number of samples, $\omega^{(t)} \sim \bar{q}_i$ denotes that the assignment to atom q_i in $\omega^{(t)}$ is consistent with $\bar{q}_i$. Without loss of generality, we assume that $\bar{q}_i$ refers to the true (or 1) assignment to q_i. Thus, to compute the marginal probability for q_i, we need to compute the ratio of the number of samples where the q_i was equal to true (or 1) and the total number of samples collected.

Suppose we choose to sample a query atom, q_i in an iteration of Gibbs sampling, the main task is to compute the conditional distribution $P(q_i|\omega^{(t-1)} \setminus q_i)$, where $\omega^{(t-1)} \setminus q_i$ is the set of assignments to all atoms except q_i in the sample at iteration $t - 1$. Once we compute the conditional distribution, we sample the assignment for q_i, say $\bar{q}_i$ from the distribution, and the subsequent sample $\omega^{(t)} = \omega^{(t-1)} \cup \bar{q}_i$. The conditional distribution to be computed in an iteration is given by,

$$P(\bar{q}_i|\omega^{(t-1)} \setminus q_i) = \exp \sum_j w_j N_j(\omega^{(t-1)} \setminus q_i \cup \bar{q}_i) \tag{3}$$

where $N_j(\omega^{(t-1)} \setminus q_i \cup \bar{q}_i)$ is the number of satisfied groundings in the j-th formula given the assignment $\omega^{(t-1)} \setminus q_i \cup \bar{q}_i$.

We now define the importance distribution for a query atom q_i, $\mathcal{Q}(q_i)$ as follows. In each step of Gibbs sampling, where q_i is satisfied, we measure the contribution of each formula to the Gibbs transition probability. Specifically, for a formula f_k, its contribution to the transition probability is proportional to $\exp(w_j N_j(\omega^{(t-1)} \setminus q_i \cup \bar{q}_i)$, if q_i is the atom being sampled in iteration t. However, since we consider both cases in the conditional probability, namely, the assignment 1 (or true) to $\bar{q}_i$ as well as the assignment 0 (or false) to $\bar{q}_i$, we would like to encode both these into our importance function. To do this, we compute the log odds of a query atom, and score the influence of a formula on the query based on its contribution in computing its log-odds.

Formally, let $\omega^{(t-1)}$ be the Gibbs sample in iteration $t - 1$. Suppose we are sampling the query atom q_i, we compute the log-odds ratio between the Gibbs transition probability for $q_i = 0$ and $q_i = 1$. This is given by the following equation,

$$\log \frac{P(q_i = 1|\omega^{(t-1)} \setminus q_i)}{P(q_i = 0|\omega^{(t-1)} \setminus q_i)} =$$
$$\sum_j w_j N_j(\omega^{(t-1)} \setminus q_i \cup \{q_i = 1\})$$
$$- \sum_j w_j N_j(\omega^{(t-1)} \setminus q_i \cup \{q_i = 0\}) \tag{4}$$

$$\log \frac{P(q_i = 1|\omega^{(t-1)} \setminus q_i)}{P(q_i = 0|\omega^{(t-1)} \setminus q_i)} =$$
$$\sum_j w_j (N_j(\omega^{(t-1)} \setminus q_i \cup \{q_i = 1\})$$
$$- N_j(\omega^{(t-1)} \setminus q_i \cup \{q_i = 0\}) \tag{5}$$

We then update the importance weight of the j-th formula w.r.t query q_i as

$$\mathcal{Q}_j^{(t)}(q_i) \propto w_j N_j(\omega^{(t-1)} \setminus q_i \cup \{q_i = 1\}) - w_j N_j(\omega^{(t-1)} \setminus q_i \cup \{q_i = 0\}) \tag{6}$$

We update all the importance weights for q_i denoted by $\mathcal{Q}^{(t)}(q_i) = \mathcal{Q}_1^{(t)}(q_i)$, $\ldots \mathcal{Q}_k^{(t)}(q_i)$ corresponding to the formulas 1 through k in every iteration where q_i is sampled. The importance weight for $\mathcal{Q}_j^{(t)}(q_i)$ after sampling $q_i T$ times is given by,

$$\mathcal{Q}_j(q_i) = \frac{1}{T} \sum_{t=1}^{T} \mathcal{Q}_j^{(t)}(q_i) \tag{7}$$

Theorem 1. *As* $T \to \infty$,

$$\log \frac{P(q_i = 1)}{P(q_i = 0)} \propto \sum_j \mathcal{Q}_j(q_i) \tag{8}$$

Proof.

$$\log \frac{P(q_i = 1)}{P(q_i = 0)} =$$

$$\sum_\omega \log \frac{P(\omega \sim q_i = 1)}{P(\omega \sim q_i = 0)}$$

$$\propto \sum_\omega \sum_j w_j (N_j(\omega \sim q_i = 1)$$

$$- N_j(\omega \sim q_i = 0))$$

$$\propto \sum_\omega \sum_j w_j (N_j(\omega \sim q_i = 1)$$

$$- \sum_j N_j(\omega \sim q_i = 0)) \tag{9}$$

where $\omega \sim q_i = 1$ are worlds consistent with the known evidence as well as $q_i = 1$, and $\omega \sim q_i = 0$ are worlds consistent with the known evidence $q_i = 0$. Further

$$\mathbb{E}[\mathcal{Q}_j(q_i)] = \sum_\omega w_j (N_j(\omega \sim q_i = 1) - w_j N_j(\omega \sim q_i = 0)) \tag{10}$$

as $T \to \infty, \mathcal{Q}_j^{(t)}(q_i) \to \mathbb{E}[\mathcal{Q}_j(q_i)]$, since we are estimating the expectation from worlds consistent with the MLN distribution. Therefore, as $T \to \infty, \sum_j \mathcal{Q}_j^{(t)}(q_i) \sum_j \mathbb{E}[\mathcal{Q}_j(q_i)]$ which is equal to the log-odds ratio $\log \frac{P(q_i=1)}{P(q_i=0)}$.

Interestingly, it turns out that in some cases, the importance weights can be obtained without sampling multiple worlds. Specifically, we can show that,

Proposition 2. *If the evidence is complete, i.e., every non-query atom is known to be either true or false, and if every ground formula in the MLN contains exactly one query atom, then* $\mathbb{E}[\mathcal{Q}_j(q_i)] = w_j N_j(\omega \sim q_i = 1) - w_j N_j(\omega \sim q_i = 0)$, *where* ω *is any world consistent with the known evidence.*

Algorithm 1. Explaining Inference

Input: MLN $\mathcal{M}$, Evidence $\mathbf{E}$, Query atoms $\mathbf{Q}$

Output: Ranking of formulas in $\mathcal{M}$ for each $q_i \in \mathbf{Q}$

1 Initialize the non-evidence atoms in $\omega^{(0)}$ randomly
2 **for** $t = 1$ *to* T **do**
3   X = Choose a non-evidence atom in $\omega^{(t)}$ uniformly at random
4   Flip X in $\omega^{(t)}$ to compute the conditional distribution $P(X|\omega^{(t)} \setminus X)$
5   Sample X from $P(X|\omega^{(t)} \setminus X)$
6   **if** $X \in \mathbf{Q}$ **then**
7   **for** *each f_j in $\mathcal{M}$* **do**
8   Update the importance weight $\mathcal{Q}_j^{(t)}(X)$

9 **for** *each $q_i \in \mathbf{Q}$* **do**
10   Explain q_i as a ranked list of formulas $f_1 \ldots f_k$ based on importance weights in $\mathcal{Q}(q_i)$

The above proposition implies that, in MLNs where the evidence is fully specified over the non-query atoms, and every query atom occurs in an independent subset of ground formulas in the MLN, we can derive the importance weights directly from the specified evidence. However, in cases where the evidence does not cover all the ground atoms, or more than one query atom occurs in a ground formula, we cannot infer its importance without sampling the possible worlds. Note that in general, instead of using Gibbs sampling to generate the possible worlds, we can use Marginal-MAP inference to sum-out the unknown atoms, and then derive the explanations using the evidence. However, marginal-MAP is considerably more expensive [19]. Another strategy is to use the MAP assignment for the unknown atoms. However, this is problematic when we have a significant number of unknown atoms, and if the distribution is multi-modal since, we are essentially considering a single world. A third strategy is to use belief propagation. However, the unknown atoms is again problematic in this case since we need to sum out those atoms to derive the belief propagation messages, and for large number of unknown atoms, this can be extremely expensive. Thus, our sampling strategy allows us to estimate the importance weights in a computationally feasible manner.

Algorithm 1 summarizes our approach. First, we initialize all non-evidence atoms in the MLN randomly. In each iteration, we select a non-evidence atom uniformly at random, and compute the conditional distribution for that atom given the state of all other atoms. Based on this conditional probability, we sample a new assignment for the sampled atom. If the sampled atom is a query atom, for each formula, we compute its importance weight for that query in the current word using Eq. (6). We update the importance weight using Eq. (6). Once the marginal probabilities in the Gibbs sampler converge, we finally compute a explanation for the marginal probability obtained for each query atom by ranking the formulas in descending order of the importance weights specific to that query.

4 Experiments

Our main goal is to evaluate if the explanations output by our approach helps a user understand the "black-box" that is giving this particular explanation. To do this, we designed a comprehensive user study consisting of around 60 participants. We compared our approach with the explanations given by LIME [15], an open-source state-of-the-art explanation system. We perform our evaluation using two real-world tasks on a Yelp dataset [14]. We sampled 1000 reviews from this dataset for our experiments. In the first task, we design an MLN that performs joint inference to predict if a review is filtered as a spam review or not by Yelp. In the second task, we predict if a review has positive or negative sentiment based on the review content. We first describe our user study setup and then present the details of our applications along with the results.

"Cold Steak? Old Bread? Racist Owner? Count me in. If they made good cheese steaks I would still give a decent review but Pat's is better any day of the week. This place does not deserve to be such a Philly landmark with such bad food. This city is known for its food so step your game up. "

Explanation

Reason	Importance
This is a negative review while most other reviews for this hotel were positive.	0.75
The user who wrote this review wrote other reviews that were predicted as spam.	0.18
The review contains words racist, old, bad	0.07

(a) Spam

"I love this place. Decor 10 out of 10, Taste 10 out of 10. and seriously is it a chef making these meals or a chemist. the mixture of the flavors is just perfect and amazing. you enjoy every bite you take. and wow the bread to start off with adds this moist and chewiness that you want to savor..... you can't go wrong with this place. the duck and the salmon was wonderful and great portion size too! but like it said. i loved the bread lol."

Rating: EXCELLENT

Explanations

Words	Weights
great	0.19
wonderful	0.16
wow	0.14
enjoy	0.12
perfect	0.1

(b) Sentiment

Fig. 2. Explanations generated by our approach. (a) shows the explanations for the spam prediction application and (b) shows the explanation for the sentiment prediction where the red-colored words are considered as hidden/missing words. (Color figure online)

4.1 User Study Setup

Our user study group consisted of students who have varying backgrounds in Machine learning. The participants were either enrolled in the Machine learning course at University of Memphis or part of the Machine learning club. The participants included undergraduate students, Master's students as well as Ph.D. students. All of them understand classification algorithms and the basics of Machine learning. A few participants were advanced researchers in related areas including Natural Language Processing, computer vision, etc. We divided the participants into two groups, and sent the survey that had the explanations generated by LIME to one group and the explanations generated using our approach to the other group. To ensure that there was no bias in the results, the users did not know whether they were evaluating LIME or our approach. There were 10 questions in each survey. The first 5 questions asked the participants to rank the explanations on a scale of 1–5. The next three questions were used to measure three dimensions of the explanation as follows.

1. Q6: Did the explanations increase your *understanding* of how the classifier is detecting ratings of reviews?
2. Q7: Did the explanations increase your *trust* in the classifier?
3. Q8: Based on the above explanations, will you be able to *apply* this knowledge to predict spam (or sentiment) given a set of new reviews?

Each of the above questions had a response scale of 1–5, with 5 being the best score. Finally, we summarized the overall explanation quality by asking participants if they would have liked the classifier to give them more explanations, less explanations or if they felt the explanations provided by the classifier was just right. We also allowed users to enter other comments in free text format.

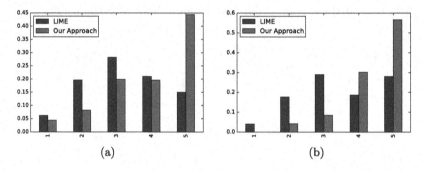

Fig. 3. Comparison of LIME and our approach using explanation scores as rated by the users. (a) shows this for the spam prediction application and (b) for the sentiment prediction. In each case, we show the % of users who have given a specific score for an explanation, averaged across all the explanations.

4.2   Application 1: Review Spam Filter

Detecting filtered reviews is a challenging problem. Specifically, unlike say email spam, spam reviews look a lot more authentic since it is designed to influence a user for/against a product/service in an open forum. This task more generally called opinion spam has a large body of prior work starting with work by Jindal and Liu [7]. In this case, we develop an MLN that encodes knowledge for detecting spam, and then perform inference on the MLN while generating the explanations.

Our MLN contains formulas that connect words to predicate that indicates whether they are spam $\text{Word}(+w, r) \Rightarrow \text{Spam}(r)$. We then add relational information into the MLN. Specifically, given two reviews about the same restaurant, the spammer and non-spammer provide ratings that are opposite of each other. For e.g., a spammer provides a positive or high rating, while a non-spammer provides a negative or low rating. Naturally, this is not always true and is therefore a soft formula in the MLN. Finally, we add knowledge that if given two reviews by the same person, if one of them is predicted spam, the other one is likely to be spam as well. In this MLN, note that the evidence variables are the words, we consider the ratings as unknown variables and the query variables are the atoms of predicate Spam. Since ratings are unknown, this is a joint inference problem where we infer the rating of a review jointly with inferring if the review is spam or not. We therefore add formulas connecting words with the rating. We learn the MLN by initializing it with weights that we obtain from an SVM [2]. Specifically, we learn an SVM for predicting ratings from the review text, as well as one for predicting if a review is spam/not. Using the coefficients of the MLN, we set initial weights to formulas [2] such as $\mathtt{Word}(+w, r) \Rightarrow \mathtt{Spam}(r)$, and then use Tuffy [11] to learn the weights of the MLN. The five fold cross validation F1-score using MLNs for this task was around 0.7. We perform inference and generate explanations for the queries. We picked a small sample of query explanations to conduct the user survey.

Once we perform inference and obtain the importance weights of the formulas, we ranked them, and converted the formula into English to generate the human-readable explanation. We presented the user with this explanation as well as the importance weights (normalized) for the 5 most important formulas. An example of the explanation generated is shown in Fig. 2(a). The users could look at the original review and rate the explanation for that review. For LIME, we provided the input which is the review content and since LIME does not explain relational information, it uses the non-relational features (words/phrases) to come up with its explanation using SVMs as the base classifier.

The comparison of the user response scores for the explanations is shown in Fig. 3. As seen here, on average, across the reviews in the survey, a larger percentage of users gave our explanations higher scores as compared to the explanation generated by LIME. On the other hand, a large percentage of users rated LIME explanations around the halfway mark (score 3). Further, when we analyze the responses over the three explanation dimensions as shown in Fig. 4(a), we see that our approach was favored by participants in all three dimensions. Particularly, the dimensions of understanding the classifier and being able to use the knowledge in the explanation scored much higher. This shows that including higher-level relational knowledge in the explanations makes the explanations richer and more appealing to humans.

4.3   Application 2: Review Sentiment Prediction

In this application, we predict if a review has a positive or negative sentiment based on the words in that review. Specifically, we have MLN formulas that connect words in the review to the sentiment. However, we assume incomplete evidence. That is, we remove a small set of words from the review and therefore, their state is unknown. The inference task is to jointly infer the state of the hidden words along with predicting if it is a positive or negative sentiment review. To do this, we add relational knowledge to the MLN. Specifically, we encode MLN formulas that a user is likely to use the same words to describe a positive or negative rating. Thus, we can use words from other reviews written by the same user to predict the sentiment of a review. We learn the MLN using a similar

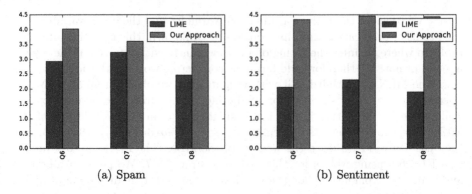

Fig. 4. Comparison for the average scores given by users for 3 key dimensions related to the explanations. Q6 measures understanding of the classifier, Q7 the trust in the classifier and Q8 if they can replicate the classifier based on the explanation. Higher scores are better. (a) shows results for spam prediction and (b) shows results for sentiment prediction

procedure as described in the previous section. Our five-fold cross validation accuracy here was around 0.9.

In this case, we generate explanations in terms of word formulas only. Specifically, for each review, we explain its predicted sentiment as a set of words (and their corresponding importance weights). Note that these words can contain missing words (inferred to be true) as well as words known to be true (due to evidence). Thus, LIME and our approach generates the same form of explanations (words and weights) as shown in Fig. 2(b). However, since we can infer the states of hidden words, our explanation is richer than that generated by LIME. Figure 3(b) shows the comparison of the explanation scores for LIME and our approach. Here, we see a very similar trend to the results for the spam prediction application. Specifically, most users thought that our approach yields very good explanations, while LIME explanations was considered average. Further, Fig. 4(b) illustrates that our approach was significantly better in terms of helping users understand, trust and apply the prediction method. This shows that using relational knowledge can yield a more comprehensive explanation (in the presence of noisy/unknown variables).

4.4   T-Test

We use the T-Test to compare the means of the two user groups (those who evaluated LIME and our approach respectively). The null hypothesis for the t-test is that there is no difference between the means of the two groups. In our case, it will mean that our explanation is no better or worse than the lime explanation. The alternate hypothesis is that the means of the two groups are not the same, in which case it will mean that our explanation is either better or worse than the lime explanation. We performed the t-test on the responses to the summary question regarding the quality of the explanations. We coded

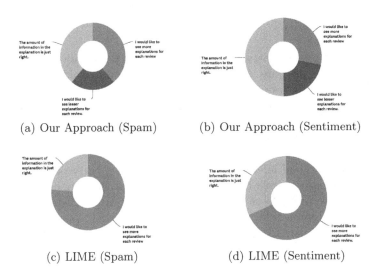

(a) Our Approach (Spam)   (b) Our Approach (Sentiment)

(c) LIME (Spam)   (d) LIME (Sentiment)

Fig. 5. Comparison of user responses for the question that summarizes the effectiveness of explanations. (a) and (b) show this for spam prediction and sentiment prediction using our approach, and (c), (d) show the responses for LIME.

these as follows. (i) rating for lime explanation (coded as group 1) (ii) rating for our explanation (coded as group 2). The response options are, (i) would like to see more explanation (coded as 1) (ii) would like to see less explanation (coded as 2) and (iii) Right amount of explanation (coded as 3). The coding is based on the desirability of the response. We assumed the best case is the right amount of explanation and therefore coded this as the highest. Then, we assumed that requiring less amount of information is worse than right amount of information, and is therefore coded as 2. Finally, we assumed that a user requiring more amount of information is the worst case (coded as 1) because our main motivation is to make the explanation human-interpretable. Thus, according to our coding, the higher mean will be considered better because we coded the right amount of information as the highest. We obtained $p = 0.03(< 0.05)$. Therefore, the difference in explanations provided by our approach is statistically significant. Thus, we can reject the null hypothesis and our explanation is at least better or worse than LIME explanation. The mean and standard deviations of the two approaches (based on the coding) is as follows. *LIME explanation has a mean of 1.63 and a standard deviation of 0.95. The explanations based on our approach has a mean of 2.22 and a standard deviation of 0.87.* Therefore, our explanations are clearly preferred by the users as compared to the explanations given by LIME. The full breakdown of the responses is shown in Fig. 5. As seen here, in each of the two tasks, users considered our explanations to be better than LIME. Interestingly, even in the case where the type of explanations was identical (words explaining the sentiment), LIME produced worse results than our approach (see Fig. 5(b) and (d)) because our relational method takes advantage of dependencies across different reviews to generate more complete explanations.

5   Conclusion

Explanations of predictions made by machine learning algorithms is critical in several application domains. In general, MLNs are interpretable models but it is challenging to explain results obtained from inference over MLNs. In this paper, we presented an approach where we explain the results of relational inference in MLNs as a ranked list of formulas that encode their influence on the inference results. Specifically, we compute the importance weights of the MLN formulas based on how much they influence the transition probabilities of a Gibbs sampler that performs marginal inference in the MLN. On two real-world problems, we conducted a comprehensive user study and showed that our explanations are more human-interpretable as compared to explanations derived from LIME, a state-of-the-art approach for explaining classifiers.

In future, we plan to apply our approach to explain complex queries in multi-modal problems, derive alternate forms of explanation that improve interpretability, etc.

References

1. Domingos, P., Lowd, D.: Markov Logic: An Interface Layer for Artificial Intelligence. Morgan & Claypool, San Francisco (2009)
2. Farabi, M.K.A., Sarkhel, S., Venugopal, D.: Efficient weight learning in high-dimensional untied MLNs. In: Artificial Intelligence and Statistics (AISTATS), pp. 1637–1645 (2018)
3. Fong, R.C., Vedaldi, A.: Interpretable explanations of black boxes by meaningful perturbation. In: International Conference on Computer Vision (ICCV), pp. 3449–3457 (2017)
4. Geman, S., Geman, D.: Stochastic relaxation, gibbs distributions, and the bayesian restoration of images. IEEE Trans. Pattern Anal. Mach. Intell. **6**, 721–741 (1984)
5. Guidotti, R., Monreale, A., Ruggieri, S., Turini, F., Giannotti, F., Pedreschi, D.: A survey of methods for explaining black box models. ACM Comput. Surv. **51**(5), 93:1–93:42 (2018)
6. Gunning, D.: Darpa's explainable artificial intelligence (XAI) program. In: ACM IUI (2019)
7. Jindal, N., Liu, B.: Opinion spam and analysis. In: Proceedings of the International Conference on Web Search and Data Mining, pp. 219–230 (2008)
8. Khot, T., Balasubramanian, N., Gribkoff, E., Sabharwal, A., Clark, P., Etzioni, O.: Exploring Markov logic networks for question answering. In: Proceedings of the Conference on Empirical Methods in Natural Language Processing (EMNLP), pp. 685–694 (2015)
9. Koh, P.W., Liang, P.: Understanding black-box predictions via influence functions. In: Proceedings of the 34th International Conference on Machine Learning (ICML), pp. 1885–1894 (2017)
10. Koller, D., Friedman, N.: Probabilistic Graphical Models: Principles and Techniques. MIT Press, Cambridge (2009)
11. Niu, F., Ré, C., Doan, A., Shavlik, J.W.: Tuffy: scaling up statistical inference in Markov logic networks using an RDBMS. PVLDB **4**(6), 373–384 (2011)

12. Poon, H., Domingos, P.: Joint inference in information extraction. In: Proceedings of the 22nd National Conference on Artificial Intelligence (AAAI), pp. 913–918. AAAI Press (2007)

13. Poon., H., Domingos, P.: Joint unsupervised coreference resolution with Markov logic. In: Proceedings of the 2008 Conference on Empirical Methods in Natural Language Processing (EMNLP), pp. 649–658 (2008)

14. Rayana, S., Akoglu, L.: Yelp Dataset for Anomalous Reviews. Technical report, Stony Brook University, http://odds.cs.stonybrook.edu. Accessed 2015

15. Ribeiro, M.T., Singh, S., Guestrin, C.: "Why should i trust you?": explaining the predictions of any classifier. In: Knowledge Discovery and Data Mining (KDD), pp. 1135–1144 (2016)

16. Ribeiro, M.T., Singh, S., Guestrin, C.: Anchors: high-precision model-agnostic explanations. In: AAAI Conference on Artificial Intelligence (AAAI) (2018)

17. Ross, A.S., Hughes, M.C., Doshi-Velez, F.: Right for the right reasons: training differentiable models by constraining their explanations. In: Proceedings of the Twenty-Sixth International Joint Conference on Artificial Intelligence (IJCAI), pp. 2662–2670 (2017)

18. Selvaraju, R.R., Cogswell, M., Das, A., Vedantam, R., Parikh, D., Batra, D.: Grad-cam: visual explanations from deep networks via gradient-based localization. In: 2017 IEEE International Conference on Computer Vision (ICCV), pp. 618–626 (2017)

19. Sharma, V., Sheikh, N.A., Mittal, H., Gogate, V., Singla, P.: Lifted marginal MAP inference. In: Uncertainty in Artificial Intelligence, pp. 917–926. AUAI Press (2018)

20. Shih, A., Choi, A., Darwiche, A.: A symbolic approach to explaining bayesian network classifiers. In: Proceedings of the Twenty-Seventh International Joint Conference on Artificial Intelligence (IJCAI), pp. 5103–5111 (2018)

21. Teso, S., Kersting, K.: "Why Should I Trust Interactive Learners?". Explaining Interactive Queries of Classifiers To Users, Arxiv (2018)

22. Tran, S.D., Davis, L.S.: Event modeling and recognition using Markov logic networks. In: Forsyth, D., Torr, P., Zisserman, A. (eds.) ECCV 2008, Part II. LNCS, vol. 5303, pp. 610–623. Springer, Heidelberg (2008). https://doi.org/10.1007/978-3-540-88688-4_45

23. Venugopal, D., Chen, C., Gogate, V., Ng, V.: Relieving the computational bottleneck: joint inference for event extraction with high-dimensional features. In: Proceedings of the Conference on Empirical Methods in Natural Language Processing (EMNLP), pp. 831–843 (2014)

24. Zhang, Q., Zhu, S.: Visual Interpretability for Deep Learning: A Survey. Arxiv (2018)

Natural Language Processing

Unsupervised Sentence Embedding Using Document Structure-Based Context

Taesung Lee[(✉)] and Youngja Park

IBM T.J. Watson Research Center, Yorktown Heights, NY 10598, USA
Taesung.Lee@ibm.com, young_park@us.ibm.com

Abstract. We present a new unsupervised method for learning general-purpose sentence embeddings. Unlike existing methods which rely on local contexts, such as words inside the sentence or immediately neighboring sentences, our method selects, for each target sentence, influential sentences from the entire document based on the document structure. We identify a dependency structure of sentences using metadata and text styles. Additionally, we propose an out-of-vocabulary word handling technique for the neural network outputs to model many domain-specific terms which were mostly discarded by existing sentence embedding training methods. We empirically show that the model relies on the proposed dependencies more than the sequential dependency in many cases. We also validate our model on several NLP tasks showing 23% F1-score improvement in coreference resolution in a technical domain and 5% accuracy increase in paraphrase detection compared to baselines.

Keywords: Sentence embedding · Document structure ·
Out-of-vocabulary

1 Introduction

Distributed representations of words and sentences are ever more leveraged to understand text [2,8,11,15,16,19,23]. These methods embed a word or sentence by training a neural network to predict the next word or sentence without supervision. However, unlike human reading with broader context and structure in mind, the existing approaches focus on a small continuous context of neighboring sentences. These approaches work well on continuous but less structured text like movie transcripts, but do not work well on structured documents like encyclopedic articles and technical reports.

To better support semantic understanding of such technical documents, we propose a new sentence embedding framework to learn general-purpose sentence representations by leveraging long-distance dependencies between sentences in a document. We observe that understanding a sentence often requires understanding of more comprehensive context as well as the immediate context, including the document title, previous paragraphs, or even related articles as shown in Fig. 1. For instance, all the sentences in the document can be related to the

© Springer Nature Switzerland AG 2020
U. Brefeld et al. (Eds.): ECML PKDD 2019, LNAI 11907, pp. 633–647, 2020.
https://doi.org/10.1007/978-3-030-46147-8_38

document title (Fig. 1(a)). The items in a list structure can be influenced by the sentence introducing the list, and, HTML documents can contain hyperlinks to provide more information on certain terms (Fig. 1(b)). Using these document structure-based contexts, we can connect 'ransomware' with 'payment' (Fig. 1(a)).

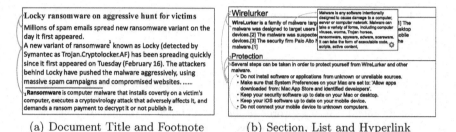

(a) Document Title and Footnote   (b) Section, List and Hyperlink

Fig. 1. Examples of long distance dependencies between sentences

Our approach, leveraging such structural elements, has several advantages. First, to provide enough context to understand a sentence, instead of using a global context of all sentences in the document, we leverage a concise set of context sentences to be considered using the structural dependencies. A larger context can produce more accurate representations of sentences. However, it is infeasible to train neural network models with a large number of context sentences. Second, we further prioritize the selected sentences based on their semantics and the dependency types. In this way, our model can better handle documents containing several subtopics that may cause sudden local context changes. Some sentences have dependencies to distant ones when a different perspective of the topic is introduced. Using only small neighboring sentences results in insufficient input to the neural network to understand such a sudden change. Using long distance dependencies, we can provide a broader context.

Additionally, we can leverage the structural information to better handle out-of-vocabulary (OOV) words. The vocabulary in a neural network is always limited due to costly training time and memory use. Existing methods discard low frequency words and map all OOV words to one or a few variables. This method can loose important keywords in a technical domain that continuously creates new terms. We introduce more fine-grained OOV variables using information extracted from the structural context.

We empirically show that the model actually learns to rely more on some of the dependencies. We validate our model on several NLP tasks using a Wikipedia corpus which shows that our model consistently outperforms the existing methods. Our model produces much lower loss for the target sentence prediction task and 5% increase in accuracy for paraphrase identification than SKIP-THOUGHT. The results confirm that training with only local context does not work well for such documents. We also compare the performance of the learned embedding for coreference resolution. For coreference resolution, our model shows 23%

Table 1. Categorization of sentence embedding methods. * denotes methods not requiring labeled data.

Range	Continuity	
	Continuous	Discontinuous
Intra-sentence	$[2, 6, 7, 9, 18, 24]$; $[10]^*$	$[13, 22, 23]$
Inter-sentence	$[8]^*$	Our work*

improvement in F1 over DEEPCOREF [1], a state-of-the-art deep learning-based approach.

The main contributions of the paper include:

- A general-purpose sentence embedding method which leverages long distance sentence dependencies extracted from the document structure.
- A rule-based dependency annotator to automatically determine the document structure and extract all governing sentences for each sentence.
- A new OOV handling technique based on the document structure.

2   Related Work

Distributed representation of sentences, or sentence embedding, has gained much attention recently, as word-level representations [11,15,16,19] are not sufficient for many sentence-level or document-level tasks, such as machine translation, sentiment analysis and coreference resolution. Recent approaches using neural networks consider some form of dependencies to train the network. Dependencies can be continuous (relating two adjacent words or sentences) or discontinuous (relating two distant words or sentences), and intra-sentence (dependency of words within a sentence) or inter-sentence (dependency between sentences). Many sentence embedding approaches leverage these dependencies of words to combine word embeddings as shown in Table 1.

One direct extension of word embedding to sentences is combining words vectors in a continuous context window. [9] uses a weighted average of the constituent word vectors. [2,24], and [18] use supervised approaches to train a LSTM network that merges word vectors. [6] and [7] use convolutional neural networks (CNN) over continuous context window to generate sentence representations. [10] includes a paragraph vector in the bag of word vectors and apply a word embedding approaches [15,16].

Recently, several researchers have proposed dependency-based embedding methods using a dependency parser to consider discontinuous intra-sentence relationships [13,22,23]. [22] uses recursive neural network to consider discontinuous dependencies. [13] proposes a dependency-based CNN which concatenate a word with its ancestors and siblings based on the dependency tree structure. [23] proposes tree structured LSTM networks. These studies show that dependency-based (discontinuous) networks outperform their sequential (continuous) counterparts.

Unlike these approaches considering only intra-sentence dependencies, Kiros et al. propose a new architecture SKIP-THOUGHT [8] joining two recurrent neural networks, encoder and decoder. The encoder combines the words in a sentence into a sentence vector, and the decoder generates the words in the next sentence. Our approach is similar to SKIP-THOUGHT since both approaches are unsupervised and use inter-sentential dependencies. However, SKIP-THOUGHT considers only continuous dependency.

Unlike our approach considering OOV in the output using the document structure, there are approaches that build an embedding of an OOV word on the fly that can be used as input to our system [20,21], and [5]. Our OOV handling focuses more on mechanism to produce OOV words as the output of the network and leverage them in training, which is out of the scope of these previous papers. [12] proposes a word position-based approach to address the OOV problem for neural machine translation (NMT) systems. Their methods allow a neural machine translation (NMT) system to emit, for each unknown word in the target sentence, the position of the corresponding word in the source sentence. However, their methods are not applicable to sentence embedding, as they rely on an aligned corpus. Also, our approach considers not only word positions but also the dependency types to define OOV words.

3   Document Structured-Based Context

Previous sentence embedding methods use intra-sentence dependencies such as a dependency tree, or immediately neighboring sentences for sentence embedding. However, we identify more semantically related content to define sentence dependencies based on the document structure as shown in Fig. 1. In this section, we describe a range of such inter-sentence dependencies that can be utilized for sentence embedding and the techniques to automatically identify them.

We use the following notations to describe the extraction of document structure-based context for a given sentence. Suppose we have a document $D = \{S_1, \ldots, S_{|D|}\}$, which is a sequence of sentences. Each sentence S_i is a sequence of words, represented as $s_{i,1}, \ldots, s_{i,|S_i|}$. For each *target sentence* $S_t \in D$, S_t depends on a subset $G \subset D^1$. We call such a sentence G_i in G a *governing sentence* of S_t, and say G_i governs S_t, or S_t depends on G_i, defined by one of the dependency types in $\mathcal{D}$ described below.

3.1   Titles

The title of a document, especially a technical document, contains the topic entity, the key claim, and/or the summary of the document, and all other sentences describe and elaborate the title. For instance, the title of the document (*e.g.*, WannaCry) can clarify the meaning of a definite noun phrase (*e.g.*, the ransomware) in the sentence. Section titles play a similar role, but, mostly to

---

[1] For simplicity, we use G to denote a S_t specific set.

the sentences within the section. We detect different levels of titles, starting from the document title to chapter, section and subsection titles. Then, we identify the region in the document which each title governs and incorporate the title in the embedding of all sentences in the region. To identify titles in a document, we use the various information from the metadata and the document content as follows.

Document Metadata ($\mathcal{D}_{TM}$)**:** We extract a document title from the <title> tag in a HTML document or from the title field in *Word* or PDF document metadata. Since the document title influences all sentences in a document, we consider this title governs every sentence in D.

Heading Tag ($\mathcal{D}_{THn}$)**:** The heading tags <h1> to <h6> in HTML documents are often used to show document or section titles. We consider all sentences between a heading tag and the next occurrence of the same level tag are considered under the influence of the title.

Table Of Contents ($\mathcal{D}_{TC}$)**:** Many documents contain a table of contents (TOC) providing the overall structure of the document. To detect the titles based on the table of contents, we first recognize a phrase indicating TOC, such as "table of contents", "contents" or "index". Then, we parse the content following the cue phrase and check if it contains a typical TOC pattern such as "Chapter 1 – Introduction" or "Introduction $\cdots\cdots\cdots$ 8". The range of each section can be easily identified from the TOC. If the document is an HTML file, each line in the TOC tends to have a hyperlink to the section. For non-HTML documents, we can extract the page number from the TOC (*e.g.*, page 8) and locate the corresponding pages.

Header and Footer ($\mathcal{D}_{TR}$)**:** Technical documents often contain the document or section titles in the headers or footers. Thus, if the same text is repeated in the headers or footers in many pages, we take the text as a title and consider all sentences appearing in these pages belong to the title.

Text Styles ($\mathcal{D}_{TS}$)**:** Titles often have a distinctive text style. They tend to have no period at the end and use a larger font size, a higher number of *italic* or **bold** text, and a higher ratio of capitalized words compared to non-title sentences. We first build a text style model for sentences in the document body, capturing the three style attributes. If a sentence ends without a period and any dimension of its style model has higher value than that of the text style model, we consider the sentence as a title. Then, we split the document based on the detected titles and treat each slice as a section.

3.2 Lists

Authors often employ a list structure to describe several elements of a subject. This list structure typically has an introductory sentence stating the main concept followed by a bulleted, numbered or in-text list of items supporting the main concept as illustrated in Fig. 1(b). An item in the list is conceptually more

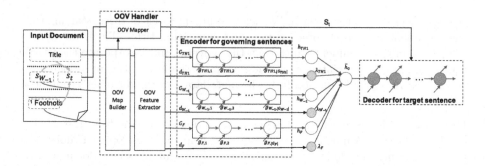

Fig. 2. Our model architecture.

related to the introductory sentence than the other items in the list, but the distance can be long because of other items. We use the following methods to identify list items, consider the sentence appearing prior to the list items as the introductory sentence and assume that it governs all items in the list.

Formatted List ($\mathcal{D}_{LF}$): To extract numbered or bulleted lists, we use the list tags (*e.g.*, <ul>, <ol>, <li>) for HTML documents. For non-HTML documents, we detect a number sequence (*i.e.*, 1, 2, ...) or bullet symbols (*e.g.*, -, ·) repeating in multiple lines.

In-text List ($\mathcal{D}_{LT}$): We also identify in-text lists such as "First(ly), ... Second(ly), ... Last(ly), ..." by identifying these cue words.

3.3   Links

Hyperlinks ($\mathcal{D}_H$): Some sentences contain hyperlinks or references to provide additional information or clarify the meaning of the sentence. We can enrich the representation of the sentence using the linked document. In this work, we use the title of the linked document to govern the target sentence. Alternatively, we can use the embedding of the linked document.

Footnotes and In-document Links ($\mathcal{D}_F$): Footnotes also provide additional information for the target sentence. In an HTML document, such information is usually expressed with in-document hyperlinks, which ends with "#dest". In this case, we identify a sentence marked with "#dest" and add a dependency between the two sentences.

3.4   Window-Based Context ($\mathcal{D}_{Wn}$)

We also consider the traditional sequential dependency used in previous methods [4,8]. Given a document $D = \{S_1, \ldots, S_{|D|}\}$, the target sentence S_t is considered to be governed by n sentences prior to ($n < 0$) or following ($n > 0$) S_t. In our implementation, we use only one prior sentence ($\mathcal{D}_{W_{-1}}$).

4   Neural Network Models

In this section, we describe our model architecture (Fig. 2) in detail. Based on the dependencies extracted in Sect. 3, we build a sentence embedding model. Similarly to SKIP-THOUGHT [8], we train our model to generate a target sentence S_t using a set of governing sentences G. However, SKIP-THOUGHT takes into account only the window-based context ($\mathcal{D}_{Wn}$), while our model considers diverse long distance context and their dependency types as described in Sect. 4.1. Additionally, unlike existing sentence embedding methods, which include only a small fraction of words (typically high frequency words) in the vocabulary and map all other words to one OOV word, we introduce a new OOV handler in our model in Sect. 4.2.

4.1   Inter-sentential Dependency-Based Encoder-Decoder

Our model has several encoders (one encoder for each governing sentence $G_i \in G$), a decoder and an OOV handler as shown in Fig. 2. The input to each cell is a word, represented as a dense vector. We use the pre-trained vectors from the CBOW model [16], and the word vectors can be optionally updated during training.

We now formally describe the model given a target sentence S_t and a set G of its governing sentences. We first describe the encoders that digest each $G_i \in G$. Given the i-th governing sentence $G_i = (g_{i,1}, \ldots, g_{i,|G_i|})$, let $w(g_{i,t})$ be the word representation (pre-trained or randomly initialized) of word $g_{i,t}$. Then, the following equations define the encoder for G_i.

$$
\begin{aligned}
h_{i,t} &= \mathrm{RC}(w(g_{i,t}), h_{i,t-1}; \theta_E), \\
\lambda_i &= \mathsf{sigmoid}(\mathcal{U}d_i + g), \qquad h_i = h_{i,|G_i|}, \\
\bar{h}_0 &= \sum_i W_{\mathrm{dep}(i)} \left\{ \lambda_i (u_{\mathrm{dep}(i)} h_i + a_{\mathrm{dep}(i)}) \right. \\
&\qquad\qquad \left. + (1 - \lambda_i) h_i + b \right\}
\end{aligned}
\tag{1}
$$

where RC is a recurrent neural network cell (e.g., LSTM or GRU) that updates the memory $h_{i,t}$; θ_E is the parameters for the encoder RC; λ_i is an OOV weight that decides how much we rely on out-of-vocabulary words; d_i denotes the OOV features for G_i; $\mathcal{U}$ and g are linear regression parameters; $\mathsf{sigmoid}(\cdot)$ is the sigmoid function; u_{dep} and a_{dep} are an OOV weight transformation; W and b are a transformation matrix and a bias; and $\bar{h}_0$ is the aggregated information of G and is passed to the decoder for target sentence generation.

Now, we define the decoder as follows:

$$
\begin{aligned}
o_t, \bar{h}_t &= \mathrm{RC}(o_{t-1}, \bar{h}_{t-1}; \theta_D), \\
y_t &= \mathsf{softmax}(V o_t + c)
\end{aligned}
\tag{2}
$$

where RC is a recurrent neural network cell that updates the memory $\bar{h}_t$ and generates the output o_t; θ_D is a set of parameters for the decoder RC; $\mathsf{softmax}(\cdot)$

is the softmax function; and $Vo_t + c$ transforms the output into the vocabulary space. That is, $Vo_t + c$ generates logits for words in the vocabulary set and is used to predict the words in the target sentence.

To strike a balance between the model accuracy and the training time, we use K randomly chosen governing sentences from G for all target sentence. We use the cross entropy between y_t and o_t as the optimization function and update $\theta_E, W_{\mathrm{dep}(i)}, b, V, c, \theta_D$ and optionally $w(\cdot)$.

4.2   Out-Of-Vocabulary (OOV) Mapping

Incorporating all the words from a large text collection in deep learning models is infeasible, since the amount of memory use and training time will be too costly. Especially, in technical domains, new jargons are constantly added, and, their character level information is often not very useful (*e.g.*, WannaCry, 129.42.56.189).

Thus, we propose an OOV word handling method based on the diverse sentence relationships from Sect. 3. OOV word handling is desired in the following three places: (1) input embeddings to encode the governing sentences (G); (2) input embeddings to decode the target sentence (S_t); and (3) output logits to compute the loss with respect to S_t. For the first two cases, *i.e.*, generating the input embeddings of G and S_t for the encoder and the decoder, we use the average vector of all words in the vocabulary to represent all OOV words.

While there are several approaches to generate input embeddings for OOV words (Case 1 & 2), such as average of all word embeddings, character-based embedding, context-based embedding [5,20,21], there has been little work for building a model generating OOV words in the output and use them in the training loss (Case 3). Existing sentence embedding techniques reduce the vocabulary size mainly by using only high frequency words and by collapsing all other words to one special word (e.g., <*unk*>). However, this single OOV symbol for all OOV words treats both very important OOV word (*e.g.*, topic entities, domain-specific words and proper nouns) and other words alike, resulting in unsatisfactory results for technical documents.

Instead of replacing all OOV words by a single variable, we consider the dependency and the position of OOV words to build a set of *OOV variables*. Given the training corpus with the entire vocabulary V_M with size M, we first select N most frequent words in the training corpus as an initial vocabulary V_N (typically, $N \ll M$, *i.e.*, tens of thousands vs. millions or billions). Then, we build an OOV map that reduces the OOV words ($V_M - V_N$) into a smaller vocabulary V_{OOV} of *OOV variables*, $\{O_i(j)\}$, where $O_i(j)$ represents j-th OOV word given a governing sentence G_i (*e.g.*, an OOV variable may indicate the actor in the previous sentence). In particular, we use OOV variables to represent the first and the last η OOV words in sentences with each dependency, observing that many semantically important words tend to appear at the beginning or the end of the governing sentences. We denote the j-th last OOV word by $O_i(-j)$. This idea of encoding OOV words based on their positions in a sentence is similar to the machine translation approach by [12]. However, we encode OOV words using the dependency type of the sentence as well as their position in the sentence.

After we replace OOV words using the OOV mapping, we have the augmented vocabulary $V_N \cup V_{OOV}$ with a manageable size. The optimization goal of each RNN cell without OOV words is to predict the next word with one correct answer. In contrast, our model allows multiple correct answers, since an OOV word can be mapped to multiple OOV variables. We use the cross entropy with soft labels as the optimization loss function. The weight of each label is determined by the inverse-square law, *i.e.*, the weight is inversely proportional to the square of the number of words associated with the label. This weighting scheme gives a higher weight to less ambiguous dependency.

One additional component we add related to OOV words is a weight function for the governing sentences based on occurrences of proper nouns (λ_i in Eq. 1). Instead of equally weighing all governing sentences, we can give a higher weight to sentences with proper nouns, which are more likely to have OOV words, to leverage the contextual information of such OOV words in other sentences to understand the OOV words in the target sentence. Thus, we introduce a feature vector representing the number of OOV proper nouns in the i-th governing sentence (d_i in Eq. 1). Currently, the features include the number of OOV words whose initials are uppercased, the number of OOV words that are uppercased, and the number of OOV words with at least one upper-case letter. Together with the linear regression parameters, $\mathcal{U}$ and g, the model learns the weights for different dependency types.

5 Experiments

We empirically evaluate our approach on various NLP tasks and compare the results with other existing methods. We trained the proposed model (OURS) and the baseline systems on 807,647 randomly selected documents from the 2009 Wikipedia dump, which is the last Wikipedia dump released in *HTML* format. Since our approach leverages HTML tags to identify document structures, our model use the raw HTML files. For the baseline systems, we provide plain text version of the same articles. All models were trained for 300K steps with 64-sized batches and the Adagrad optimizer [3]. For the evaluation, we use GRU cells for RC in Eq. 2. For each target sentence, if there are more than 8 governing sentences, we randomly choose 8 of them as the context ($K = 8$). We set the maximum number of words in a sentence to be 30 and pad each sentence with special start and end of sentence symbols. We set η to 4, resulting in $|V_{OOV}| = 80$.

5.1 Dependency Importance

In this experiment, we show the relative importance of long distance sentence relations compared to sequential relations. Note that W_{dep} in Eq. 1 implies the importance level of a dependency *dep*. In Table 2, we show the relative importance of the different dependencies compared to the sequential dependency

$(\mathcal{D}_{W_{-1}})$, which is used in other methods. As we can see, all levels of document and section titles, except the fourth level subsection title, play a more significant role than the sequential dependency. The reason that the title from the metadata, $(\mathcal{D}_{TM})$, does not have a high weight as the title from the heading 1 tag $(\mathcal{D}_{TH1})$ is that the metadata contains extra text, "- Wikipedia", in the title for Wikipedia articles (*e.g.*, "George W. Bush - Wikipedia" instead of "George W. Bush"). Further, hyperlinks $(\mathcal{D}_H)$, in-document links $(\mathcal{D}_F)$ and formatted lists $(\mathcal{D}_{LF})$ are all shown to have a similar influence as the sequence dependency. The remaining dependencies, $\mathcal{D}_{TC}$, $\mathcal{D}_{TR}$, $\mathcal{D}_{TS}$, and $\mathcal{D}_{LT}$ are scarcely found in the Wikipedia corpus, and thus, did not converge or were not updated.

Table 2. Weights $\|W_{dep}\|_2/\|W_{\mathcal{D}_{W,-1}}\|_2$ of dependencies.

$\mathcal{D}_{TH1}$	$\mathcal{D}_{TH2}$	$\mathcal{D}_{TH3}$	$\mathcal{D}_{LF}$	$\mathcal{D}_{TM}$	$\mathcal{D}_F$	$\mathcal{D}_{TH4}$	$\mathcal{D}_{TH5}$	$\mathcal{D}_H$
2.30	2.30	2.30	1.00	1.00	1.00	0.24	1.40	1.00

5.2 Target Sentence Prediction

Unlike most other approaches, our model and SKIP-THOUGHT [8] can learn application-independent sentence representations without task-specific labels. Both models are trained to predict a target sentence given a context. The prediction is a sequence of vectors representing probabilities of words in the target sentence. For a quantitative evaluation between the two models, we compare their prediction losses by using cross entropy loss. We randomly chose 640,000 target sentences for evaluation and computed the average loss over the 640K sentences.

We compare SKIP-THOUGHT with two versions of our model. OURS denotes our model using the document structure-based dependencies and the OOV handler. OURS-DEP denotes our model with the OOV handler but using only local context like SKIP-THOUGHT to show the impact of the OOV handler. Table 3 shows the comparison of the three models. The values in the table are the average loss per sentence. We measure the average loss value excluding OOV words for SKIP-THOUGHT, as it cannot handle OOV words. However, for our models, we measure the loss values with (All Words) and without OOV words (Voc. Words). As we can see, both OURS−DEP and OURS significantly outperform SKIP-THOUGHT resulting in 25.8% and 26.9% reduction in the loss values respectively.

5.3 Paraphrase Detection

Further, we compare our model with SKIP-THOUGHT on a paraphrase detection task using the Microsoft Research Paraphrase corpus [14]. The data set consists of 5,801 sentence pairs extracted from news data and their boolean assessments (if a sentence pair is paraphrase or not), which were determined by three assessors

Table 3. Comparison of our models and SKIP-THOUGHT for target sentence prediction

Method	All words	Voc. words
OURS	0.1456	0.1394
OURS-DEP	0.1467	0.1415
SKIP-THOUGHT	N/A	0.1907

Table 4. Comparison of paraphrase detection accuracy

Method	Accuracy
OURS	0.72
SKIP-THOUGHT	0.67

using majority voting. The goal is correctly classifying the boolean assessments, and the accuracy (# correct pairs/# all pairs) is measured. We used 4,076 pairs for training and 1,725 pairs for testing. Since the data sets contain sentence pairs only and no structural context, we evaluate only the effectiveness of the trained encoder. To compare the quality of sentence embeddings by the two models, we use the same logistic regression classifier with features based on embedded sentences as in [8]. Given a pair of sentences S_1 and S_2, the features are the two embeddings of S_1 and S_2, their entry-wise absolute difference, and their entry-wise products. Our model shows a 5% points higher accuracy than SKIP-THOUGHT in paraphrase detection (Table 4), demonstrating the effectiveness of our encoder trained with the structural dependencies. Note that SKIP-THOUGHT trained with Wikipedia corpus performs worse than a model trained on books or movie scripts due to more complex and less sequential structure in Wikipedia documents.

5.4 Coreference Resolution

While our system is not designed for coreference resolution, the rich sentence embedding can be used for unsupervised coreference resolution, unlike the methods relying on annotated corpus [1]. Although building a dedicated coreference resolution method for a given domain can produce better results, we claim that our embedding approach can extract a good starting set of features. We first detect entity mentions, and, for a pronoun or a generic entity mentions (*e.g.,* a definite noun phrase), we select a list of candidate referents that conform to the mention type of the entity reference. Then, we replace the entity reference with each of the candidate referents and compute the loss of the new sentence. Finally, we choose the referent with the lowest loss value as the result, if the loss is less than the original sentence loss value. We extend our model to use sequential dependencies of $\mathcal{D}_{W_{-3}}, \ldots, \mathcal{D}_{W_1}$ (Sect. 3.4), and further train it with a 700K unlabeled cybersecurity corpus collected from security blogs and websites.

Table 5. Overall performance on coreference resolution

Method	Prec	Recall	F1
OURS+*SER*	0.77	0.20	0.32
DEEPCOREF+*NER*	0.13	0.10	0.11
DEEPCOREF+*SER*	0.66	0.05	0.09

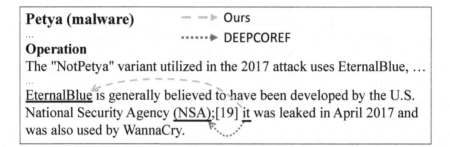

Fig. 3. Example coreference resolution

We compare our approach with the Stanford Deep Coreference Resolution tool (DEEPCOREF) [1] on a set of cybersecurity-related documents. The evaluation data consists of 628 entity coreferences extracted from 38 Wikipedia articles about malware programs which were not included in the training document set. We conducted experiments for several cybersecurity related entity types such as 'Malware' and 'Vulnerability' and general entity types such as 'Person' and 'Organization'.

Since DEEPCOREF was designed mostly for general entity types and may not be able to identify security entity types, we apply the system both with its own named entity recognizer as the candidate generator (DEEPCOREF+*NER*) and with our candidate generator designed for security entities (DEEPCOREF+*SER*). Table 5 shows MUC precision, recall, and F1-score [17]. Our model achieves higher precision and recall than both versions of DEEPCOREF. Note that DEEPCOREF+*NER* produces very low precision compared to the other models. While DEEPCOREF+*SER* shows higher precision, it still performs worse than OURS+*SER* due to the lack of features for security terms. Figure 4 shows the performance for different entity types. As we can see, while DEEPCOREF+*SER* shows higher F1 score than DEEPCOREF+*NER* for the security entity types, it still shows lower F1 score than OURS+*SER* due to semantics unseen during the training. That is, for person and organization, syntactic features used by DEEPCOREF are important. However, when there is no such features available (*i.e.*, malware and vulnerability), the semantic relationship among sentences is more important. Figure 3 shows an example case where DEEPCOREF identifies the closer candidate as coreferent rather than examining semantics.

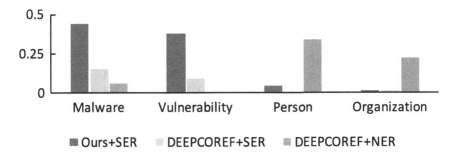

Fig. 4. F1-score per entity types

6 Conclusion and Future Work

In this paper, we presented a novel sentence embedding technique exploiting diverse types of structural contexts and domain-specific OOV words. Our method is unsupervised and application-independent, and it can be applied to various NLP applications. We evaluated the method on several NLP tasks including coreference resolution, paraphrase detection and sentence prediction. The results show that our model consistently outperforms the existing approaches confirming that considering the structural context generates better quality sentence representations.

There are a few possible directions of future work. The proposed approach relies on rule-based dependency annotation. Devising a supervised dependency annotator can be an interesting direction to adapt to other domains with slightly different rules or document format (*e.g.*, XLS). There are also unsupervised neural dependency parsers for intra-sentence dependencies. Studying an inter-sentence counterpart would be very useful for our framework. In our implementation, we used only document titles of the hyperlinked documents. But, linking documents to understand a new document and better exploiting related or pre-requisite documents can be an important research direction.

References

1. Clark, K., Manning, C.D.: Deep reinforcement learning for mention-ranking coreference models. In: Empirical Methods on Natural Language Processing (EMNLP) (2016)
2. Conneau, A., Kiela, D., Schwenk, H., Barrault, L., Bordes, A.: Supervised learning of universal sentence representations from natural language inference data. In: The Conference on Empirical Methods on Natural Language Processing (EMNLP) (2017)
3. Duchi, J., Hazan, E., Singer, Y.: Adaptive subgradient methods for online learning and stochastic optimization. J. Mach. Learn. Res. **12**(Jul), 2121–2159 (2011)
4. Gan, Z., Pu, Y., Henao, R., Li, C., He, X., Carin, L.: Learning generic sentence representations using convolutional neural networks. In: Proceedings of the 2017 Conference on Empirical Methods on Natural Language Processing (EMNLP) (2017)

5. Horn, F.: Context encoders as a simple but powerful extension of word2vec. In: Proceedings of the 2nd Workshop on Representation Learning for NLP, pp. 10–14 (2017)

6. Kalchbrenner, N., Grefenstette, E., Blunsom, P.: A convolutional neural network for modelling sentences. In: Proceedings of the 52nd Annual Meeting of the Association for Computational Linguistics (ACL), pp. 655–665 (2014)

7. Kim, Y.: Convolutional neural networks for sentence classification. In: Proceedings of Conference on Empirical Methods in Natural Language Processing, (EMNLP), pp. 1746–1751 (2014)

8. Kiros, R., et al.: Skip-thought vectors. In: Proceedings of the 29th Annual Conference on Neural Information Processing Systems (NIPS), pp. 3294–3302 (2015)

9. Kusner, M.J., Sun, Y., Kolkin, N.I., Weinberger, K.Q.: From word embeddings to document distances. In: Proceedings of the 32nd International Conference on Machine Learning (ICML), pp. 957–966 (2015)

10. Le, Q.V., Mikolov, T.: Distributed representations of sentences and documents. In: Proceedings of the 31th International Conference on Machine Learning, (ICML), pp. 1188–1196 (2014)

11. Levy, O., Goldberg, Y.: Dependency-based word embeddings. In: Proceedings of the 52nd Annual Meeting of the Association for Computational Linguistics (ACL), pp. 302–308 (2014)

12. Luong, M.T., Sutskever, I., Le, Q.V., Vinyals, O., Zaremba, W.: Addressing the rare word problem in neural machine translation. In: Proceedings of the 53rd Annual Meeting of the Association for Computational Linguistics and the 7th International Joint Conference on Natural Language Processing (ACL-IJCNLP), pp. 11–19 (2015)

13. Ma, M., Huang, L., Xiang, B., Zhou, B.: Dependency-based convolutional neural networks for sentence embedding. In: Proceedings of the 53rd Annual Meeting of the Association for Computational Linguistics (ACL), pp. 174–179. Association for Computational Linguistics, Beijing, July 2015

14. Microsoft: Microsoft research paraphrase corpus (2016). https://www.microsoft.com/en-us/download/details.aspx?id=52398

15. Mikolov, T., Chen, K., Corrado, G., Dean, J.: Efficient estimation of word representations in vector space (2013)

16. Mikolov, T., Sutskever, I., Chen, K., Corrado, G.S., Dean, J.: Distributed representations of words and phrases and their compositionality. In: Proceedings of the 27th Annual Conference on Neural Information Processing Systems (NIPS), pp. 3111–3119 (2013)

17. Moosavi, N.S., Strube, M.: Which coreference evaluation metric do you trust? A proposal for a link-based entity aware metric. In: Proceedings of the 54th Annual Meeting of the Association for Computational Linguistics (vol. 1: Long Papers), pp. 632–642 (2016)

18. Palangi, H., et al.: Deep sentence embedding using long short-term memory networks: analysis and application to information retrieval. Proc. IEEE/ACM Trans. Audio Speech Lang. Process. (TASLP) **24**(4), 694–707 (2016)

19. Pennington, J., Socher, R., Manning, C.D.: Glove: global vectors for word representation. In: Proceedings of Conference on Empirical Methods in Natural Language Processing (EMNLP), pp. 1532–1543 (2014)

20. Peters, M., et al.: Deep contextualized word representations. In: Proceedings of the 2018 Conference of the North American Chapter of the Association for Computational Linguistics: Human Language Technologies, vol. 1 (Long Papers), pp. 2227–2237. Association for Computational Linguistics (2018). https://doi.org/10.18653/v1/N18-1202. http://aclweb.org/anthology/N18-1202

21. Santos, C.D., Zadrozny, B.: Learning character-level representations for part-of-speech tagging. In: Proceedings of the 31st International Conference on Machine Learning (ICML 2014), pp. 1818–1826 (2014)

22. Socher, R., Lin, C.C., Ng, A.Y., Manning, C.D.: Parsing natural scenes and natural language with recursive neural networks. In: Proceedings of the 26th International Conference on Machine Learning (ICML) (2011)

23. Tai, K.S., Socher, R., Manning, C.D.: Improved semantic representations from tree-structured long short-term memory networks. In: Proceedings of the 53rd Annual Meeting of the Association for Computational Linguistics (ACL), pp. 1556–1566 (2015)

24. Wieting, J., Gimpel, K.: Revisiting recurrent networks for paraphrastic sentence embeddings. In: Proceedings of the 55th Annual Meeting of the Association for Computational Linguistics, pp. 2078–2088. Association for Computational Linguistics (2017)

Copy Mechanism and Tailored Training for Character-Based Data-to-Text Generation

Marco Roberti[1](✉), Giovanni Bonetta[1], Rossella Cancelliere[1],
and Patrick Gallinari[2,3]

[1] Computer Science Department, University of Turin,
Via Pessinetto, 12, 12149 Torino, Italy
{m.roberti,giovanni.bonetta,rossella.cancelliere}@unito.it
[2] Sorbonne Université, 4 Place Jussieu, 75005 Paris, France
patrick.gallinari@lip6.fr
[3] Criteo AI Lab, 32 Rue Blanche, 75009 Paris, France

Abstract. In the last few years, many different methods have been focusing on using deep recurrent neural networks for natural language generation. The most widely used sequence-to-sequence neural methods are word-based: as such, they need a pre-processing step called delexicalization (conversely, relexicalization) to deal with uncommon or unknown words. These forms of processing, however, give rise to models that depend on the vocabulary used and are not completely neural.

In this work, we present an end-to-end sequence-to-sequence model with attention mechanism which reads and generates at a *character level*, no longer requiring delexicalization, tokenization, nor even lowercasing. Moreover, since characters constitute the common "building blocks" of every text, it also allows a more general approach to text generation, enabling the possibility to exploit transfer learning for training. These skills are obtained thanks to two major features: (i) the possibility to alternate between the standard generation mechanism and a copy one, which allows to directly copy input facts to produce outputs, and (ii) the use of an original training pipeline that further improves the quality of the generated texts.

We also introduce a new dataset called E2E+, designed to highlight the copying capabilities of character-based models, that is a modified version of the well-known E2E dataset used in the E2E Challenge. We tested our model according to five broadly accepted metrics (including the widely used BLEU), showing that it yields competitive performance with respect to both character-based and word-based approaches.

Keywords: Natural language processing · Data-to-text generation · Deep learning · Sequence-to-sequence · Dataset

© Springer Nature Switzerland AG 2020
U. Brefeld et al. (Eds.): ECML PKDD 2019, LNAI 11907, pp. 648–664, 2020.
https://doi.org/10.1007/978-3-030-46147-8_39

1   Introduction

The ability of recurrent neural networks (RNNs) to model sequential data stimulated interest towards deep learning models which face data-to-text generation. An interesting application is the generation of descriptions for factual tables that consist of a set of field-value pairs; an example is shown in Table 4. We present in this paper an effective end-to-end approach to this task.

Sequence-to-sequence frameworks [2,6,23] have proved to be very effective in natural language generation (NLG) tasks [11,17,26], as well as in machine translation [4,6,22,23] and in language modeling [3]. Usually, data are represented word-by-word both in input and output sequences; anyways, such schemes can't be effective without a special, non-neural delexicalization phase that handles unknown words, such as proper names or foreign words (see [26]). The delexicalization step has the benefit of reducing the dictionary size and, consequently, the data sparsity, but it is affected by various shortcomings. In particular, according to [9] - it needs some reliable mechanism for entity identification, i.e. the recognition of named entities inside text; - it requires a subsequent "re-lexicalization" phase, where the original named entities take back placeholders' place; - it cannot account for lexical or morphological variations due to the specific entity, such as gender and number agreements, that can't be achieved without a clear context awareness.

Recently, some strategies have been proposed to solve these issues: [10] and [21] face this problem using a special neural copying mechanism that is quite effective in alleviating the out-of-vocabulary words problem, while [16] tries to extend neural networks with a post-processing phase that copies words as indicated by the model's output sequence. Some character-level aspects appear as a solution of the issue as well, either as a fallback for rare words [15], or as subword units [22].

A significantly different approach consists in employing characters instead of words, for input slot-value pairs tokenization as well as for the generation of the final utterances, as done for instance in [1,3].

In order to give an original contribution to the field, in this paper we present a character-level sequence-to-sequence model with attention mechanism that results in a completely neural end-to-end architecture. In contrast to traditional word-based ones, it does not require delexicalization, tokenization nor lower-casing; besides, according to our experiments it never hallucinates words, nor duplicates them. As we will see, such an approach achieves rather interesting performance results and produces a vocabulary-free model that is inherently more general, as it does not depend on a specific domain's set of terms, but rather on a general alphabet. Because of this, it opens up the possibility, not viable when using words, to adapt already trained networks to deal with different datasets.

More specifically, our model shows two important features, with respect to the state-of-art architecture proposed by [4]: (i) a character-wise copy mechanism, consisting in a soft switch between generation and copy mode, that disengages the model to learn rare and unhelpful self-correspondences, and (ii) a

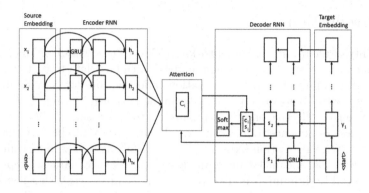

Fig. 1. Encoder-decoder with attention model

peculiar training procedure, which improves the internal representation capabilities, enhancing recall; it consists in the exchange of encoder and decoder RNNs, (GRUs [6] in our specific case), depending on whether the input is a tabular Meaning Representation (MR) or a natural language sentence.

As a further original contribution, we also introduce a new dataset, described in Sect. 3.1, whose particular structure allows to better highlight improvements in copying/recalling abilities with respect to character-based state-of-art approaches.

In Sect. 2, after resuming the main ideas on encoder-decoder methods with attention, we detail our model: Sect. 2.2 is devoted to explaining the copy mechanism while in Sect. 2.3 our peculiar training procedure is presented. Section 3 includes the datasets descriptions, some implementation specifications, the experimental framework and the analysis and evaluation of the achieved results. Finally, in Sect. 4 some conclusions are drawn, outlining future work.

2   Model Description

2.1   Summary on Encoder-Decoder Architectures with Attention

The sequence-to-sequence encoder-decoder architecture with attention [4] is represented in Fig. 1: on the left, the encoder, a bi-directional RNN, outputs one annotation h_j for each input token x_j. Each vector h_j corresponds to the concatenation of the hidden states produced by the backward and forward RNNs. On the right side of the figure, we find the decoder, which produces one state s_i for each time step; on the center of the figure the attention mechanism is shown. The main components of the attention mechanism are:

(i) the alignment model e_{ij}

$$e_{ij} = att(s_{i-1}, h_j), \qquad 1 \le j \le T_x, \ \ 1 \le i \le T_y \qquad (1)$$

which is parameterized as a feedforward neural network and scores how well input in position j-th and output observed in the i-th time instant match; T_x and T_y are the length of the input and output sequences, respectively.

(ii) the attention probability distribution α_{ij}

$$\alpha_{ij} = \frac{\exp(e_{ij})}{\sum_{k=1}^{T_x} \exp(e_{ik})} \equiv [softmax(e_i)]_j, \quad 1 \leq j \leq T_x, \ 1 \leq i \leq T_y \quad (2)$$

(e_i is the vector whose j-th element is e_{ij})

(iii) the context vector C_i

$$C_i = \sum_{j=1}^{T_x} \alpha_{ij} h_j, \quad 1 \leq i \leq T_y, \quad (3)$$

weighted sum of the encoder annotations h_j.

According to [4], the context vector C_i is the key element for evaluating the conditional probability $P(y_i|y_1, \ldots, y_{i-1}, \mathbf{x})$ to output a target token y_i, given the previously outputted tokens $y_1, \ldots, y_{i-1}$ and the input $\mathbf{x}$. They in fact express this probability as:

$$P(y_i|y_1, \ldots, y_{i-1}, \mathbf{x}) = g(y_{i-1}, s_i, C_i), \quad (4)$$

where g is a non-linear, potentially multi-layered, function. So doing, the explicit information about $y_1, \ldots, y_{i-1}$ and $\mathbf{x}$ is replaced with the knowledge of the context C_i and the decoder state s_i.

The model we present in this paper incorporates two additional mechanisms, detailed in the next sections: a character-wise copy mechanism and a peculiar training procedure based on GRUs switch.

2.2 Learning to Copy

On top of the just recalled model, we build a character-based copy mechanism inspired by the Pointer-Generator Network [21], a word-based model that hybridizes the Bahdanau traditional model and a Pointer Network [25]. Basing on these ideas, in our model we identify two probability distributions that, differently from what done by [21] and [28], *act now on characters* rather than on words: the alphabet distribution P_{alph} and the attention distribution P_{att}.

The former is the network's generative probability of sampling a given character at time i, recalled in Eq. (4):

$$P_{alph}^i = softmax(V[s_i; C_i] + b), \quad (5)$$

where V and b are trainable parameters.

The latter is the distribution reminded in Eq. (2), created by the attention mechanism over the input tokens, i.e. in our case, over input characters:

$$P_{att}^{ij} \equiv \alpha_{ij} \quad (6)$$

In our method this distribution is used for directly copying characters from the input to the output, pointing their input positions, while in [4] P_{att} is used only internally to weigh the input annotations and create the context vector C_i.

The final probability of outputting a specific character c is obtained combining P_{alph} and P_{att} through the quantity p_{gen}, defined later, which acts as a soft switch between generating c or copying it:

$$P^i(c) = p^i_{gen} \cdot P^i_{alph}[c] + (1 - p^i_{gen}) \sum_{j|x_i=c} P^{ij}_{att}(c), \tag{7}$$

where $P^i_{alph}[c]$ is the component of P^i_{alph} corresponding to that character c.

The backpropagation training algorithm, therefore, brings p_{gen} close to 1 when it is necessary to generate the output as in a standard encoder-decoder with attention ($P^i(c) \simeq P^i_{alph}[c]$); conversely, p_{gen} will be close to 0 (i.e. $P^i(c) \simeq \sum_{j|x_i=c} P^j_{att}(c)$) when a copying step is needed.

The model we propose therefore learns when to sample from P_{alph} for selecting the character to be generated, and when to sample from P_{att} for selecting the character that has to be copied directly from the input.

This copy mechanism is fundamental to output all the unknown words present in the input, i.e. words which never occur in the training set. In fact, generating characters in the right order to reproduce unknown words is a sub-task not "solvable" by a naive sequence-to-sequence model, which learns to output only known words.

The generation probability $p_{gen} \in [0, 1]$ is computed as follows:

$$p^i_{gen} = \sigma(W_y \cdot \tilde{y}_{i-1} + W_s \cdot s_i + W_p \cdot p^{i-1}_{gen} + W_c \cdot C_i) \tag{8}$$

where σ is the sigmoid function, $\tilde{y}_{i-1}$ is the last output character's embedding, s_i is the current decoder's cell state and C_i is the current context vector. W_y, W_s, W_c and W_p are the parameters whose training allows p_{gen} to have the convenient value.

We highlight that in our formulation p^{i-1}_{gen}, i.e. the value of p_{gen} at time $i-1$, contributes to the determination of p^i_{gen}. In fact, in a character-based model it is desirable that this probability remains unchanged for a fair number of time steps, and knowing its last value helps this behavior. This never happens in word-based models (such as [21]), in which copying for a single time step is usually enough.

2.3 Switching GRUs

Aiming at improving performance, we enrich our model' training pipeline with an additional phase, which forces an appropriate language representation inside the recurrent components of the model. In order to achieve this goal, the encoder and the decoder *do not own a fixed GRU*, differently from what happens in classical end-to-end approaches. The recurrent module is passed each time as a parameter, depending on which one of the two training phases is actually performed.

In the first phase, similar to the usual one, the GRU assigned to the encoder deals with a tabular representation x as input, the GRU assigned to the decoder has to cope with natural language, and the model generates an output utterance $\tilde{y} = F(x)$. Conversely, in the second phase GRUs are switched and we use as

Table 1. Descriptive statistics: on the left, sizes of training, validation and test sets are shown. On the right, the average number of characters, respectively for Meaning Representations and natural language sentences, are presented

Dataset	Number of instances			Avg. number of characters	
	Training	Validation	Test	MRs	NL sentences
E2E	42061	4672	4693	112.11	115.07
E2E+	42061	4672	4693	112.91	115.65
Hotel	2210	275	275	52.74	61.31
Restaurant	2874	358	358	53.89	63.22

input the just obtained natural language utterance $\tilde{y}$ to generate a new table $\tilde{x} = G(\tilde{y}) = G(F(x))$. Therefore, the same model can build both F and G, thanks to the switch of GRUs.

In other words, the learning iteration is performed as follows.

- A dataset example (x, y) is given. x is a tabular meaning representation and y is the corresponding reference sentence.
- We generate an output utterance $\tilde{y} = F(x)$
- We perform an optimization step on the model's parameters, aiming at minimizing $L_{forward} = loss(\tilde{y}, y)$
- We reconstruct the meaning representation $\tilde{x}$ back from the previously generated output: $\tilde{x} = G(\tilde{y}) = G(F(x))$
- We perform a further optimization step on the model's parameters, this time aiming at minimizing $L_{backward} = loss(\tilde{x}, x)$

The higher training time, direct consequence of the just described technique, is a convenient investment, as it brings an appreciable improvement of the model's performance (see Sect. 3.3).

3 Experiments

3.1 Datasets

We tested our model on four datasets, whose main descriptive statistics are given in Table 1: among them, the most known and frequently used in literature is the E2E dataset [18], used as benchmark for the E2E Challenge organized by the Heriot-Watt University in 2017. It is a crowdsourced collection of roughly 50,000 instances, in which every input is a list of slot-value pairs and every expected output is the corresponding natural language sentence. The dataset has been partitioned by the challenge organizers in predefined training, validation and test sets, conceived for training data-driven, end-to-end Natural Language Generation models in the restaurant domain.

However, during our experiments, we noticed that the values contained in the E2E dataset are a little naive in terms of variability. In other words, a slot like *name*, that could virtually contain a very broad range of different values, is filled alternating between 19 fixed possibilities. Moreover, values are partitioned among training, validation and test set, in such a way that test set always contains values that are also present in the training set. Consequently, we created a modified version of the E2E dataset, called E2E+, as follows: we selected the slots that represent more copy-susceptible attributes, i.e. *name*, *near* and *food*, and conveniently replaced their values, in both meaning representations and reference sentences. New values for *food* are picked from Wikipedia's list of adjectival forms of countries and nations[1], while both *name* and *near* are filled with New York restaurants' names contained in the Entree dataset presented in [5]. It is worth noting that none of the values of *name* are found in *near*; likewise, values that belong to the training set are not found in the validation set nor in the test one, and vice versa. This value partitioning shall ensure the absence of generation bias in the copy mechanism, stimulating the models to copy attribute values, regardless of their presence in the training set. The *MR* and *1st reference* fields in Table 4 are instances of this new dataset.

Finally, we decided to test our model also on two datasets, Hotel and Restaurant, frequently used in literature (for instance in [26] and [9]). They are built on a 12 attributes ontology: some attributes are common to both domains, while others are domain specific. Every MR is a list of key-value pairs enclosed in a dialogue act type, such as *inform*, used to present information about restaurants, *confirm*, to check that a slot value has been recognized correctly, and *reject*, to advise that the user's constraints cannot be met. For the sake of compatibility, we filtered out from Hotel and Restaurant all inputs whose dialogue act type was not *inform*, and removed the dialogue act type. Besides, we changed the format of the key-value pairs to E2E-like ones.

Tables are encoded simply converting all characters to ASCII and feeding every corresponding index to the encoder, sequentially. The resulting model's vocabulary is independent of the input, allowing the application of the transfer learning procedure.

3.2 Implementation Details

We developed our system using the PyTorch framework[2], release 0.4.1[3]. The training has been carried out as described in Subsect. 2.3: this training procedure needs the two GRUs to have the same dimensions, in terms of input size, hidden size, number of layers and presence of a bias term. Moreover, they both have to be bidirectional, even if the decoder ignores the backward part of its current GRU.

We minimize the negative log-likelihood loss using teacher forcing [27] and Adam [12], the latter being an optimizer that computes individual adaptive

---

[1] https://en.wikipedia.org/wiki/List_of_adjectival_and_demonymic_forms_for_countries_and_nations, consulted on August 30, 2018.

[2] Code and datasets are publicly available at https://github.com/marco-roberti/char-data-to-text-gen.

[3] https://pytorch.org/.

learning rates. As a consequence of the length of the input sequences, a character-based model is often subject to the exploding gradient problem, that we solved via the well-known technique of gradient norm clipping [20].

We also propose a new formulation of $P(c)$ that helps the model to learn when it is necessary to start a copying phase:

$$P^i(c) = p^i_{gen} \cdot P^i_{alph}(c) + (1 - p^i_{gen}) \sum_{j|x_i=c} P^{i,j-1}_{att}(c) \tag{9}$$

Sometimes, our model has difficulty in focusing on the first letter it has to copy. This may be caused by the variety of characters it could be attending on; instead, it seems easier to learn to focus on the most largely seen characters, as for instance '' and '['. As these special characters are very often the prefix of the words we need to copy, when this focus is achieved, we would like the attention distribution to be translated one step to the right, over the first letter that must be copied. Therefore, the final probability of outputting a specific character c, introduced in Eq. (7), is modified to $P^{i,j-1}_{att}$, i.e. the attention distribution shifted one step to the right and normalized.

Notice that $P^{i,j-1}_{att}$ is the only shifted probability, while P^i_{alph} remains unchanged. Therefore, if the network is generating the next token (i.e. $p^i_{gen} \simeq 1$), the shift trick does not involve $P^i(c)$ and the network samples the next character from P^i_{alph}, as usual. This means that the shift operation is not degrading the generation ability of the model, whilst improving the copying one.

3.3   Results and Discussion

In order to show that our model represents an effective and relevant improvement, we carry out two different experimentations: an ablation study and a comparison with two well-known models. The first model is the encoder-decoder architecture with attention mechanism by [4] (hereafter "EDA"), used character-by-character. The second one is TGen [8], a word-based model, still derived from [4], but integrating a beam search mechanism and a reranker over the top k outputs, in order to disadvantage utterances that do not verbalize all the information contained in the MR. We chose it because it has been adopted as baseline in the E2E NLG Challenge[4].

We used the official code provided in the E2E NLG Challenge website for TGen, and we developed our models and EDA in PyTorch, training them on NVIDIA GPUs. Hyperparameter tuning is done through 10-fold cross-validation, using the BLEU metric [19] for evaluating each model. The training stopping criterion was based on the absence of models' performance improvements (see [8]).

We evaluated the models' performance on test sets' output utterances using the Evaluation metrics script[5] provided by the E2E NLG Challenge organizers. It rates quality according to five different metrics: BLEU [19], NIST [7], METEOR [13], ROUGE_L [14] and CIDER [24].

---

[4] www.macs.hw.ac.uk/InteractionLab/E2E/.
[5] https://github.com/tuetschek/E2E-metrics.

Table 2. The ablation study on the E2E dataset evidences the final performance improvement reached by our model. Best values for each metric are highlighted (the higher the better)

EDA	BLEU	0.4999	EDA_S	BLEU	0.6538
	NIST	7.1146		NIST	8.4601
	METEOR	0.3369		METEOR	0.4337
	ROUGE_L	0.5634		ROUGE_L	0.6646
	CIDER	1.3176		CIDER	1.9944
EDA_C	BLEU	0.6255	EDA_CS	BLEU	**0.6705**
	NIST	7.7934		NIST	**8.5150**
	METEOR	0.4401		METEOR	**0.4449**
	ROUGE_L	0.6582		ROUGE_L	**0.6894**
	CIDER	1.7286		CIDER	**2.2355**

Table 3. Performance comparison. Note the absence of transfer learning on dataset E2E+ because in this case the training and fine-tuning datasets are the same. Best values for each metric are highlighted (the higher the better)

		E2E+	E2E	Hotel	Restaurant
EDA	BLEU	0.3773	0.4999	0.4316	0.3599
	NIST	5.7835	7.1146	5.9708	5.5104
	METEOR	0.2672	0.3369	0.3552	0.3367
	ROUGE_L	0.4638	0.5634	0.6609	0.5892
	CIDER	0.2689	1.3176	3.9213	3.3792
TGen	BLEU	**0.6292**	0.6593	0.5059	0.4074
	NIST	**9.4070**	**8.6094**	7.0913	6.4304
	METEOR	0.4367	0.4483	0.4246	0.3760
	ROUGE_L	**0.6724**	0.6850	0.7277	0.6395
	CIDER	2.8004	2.2338	5.0404	4.1650
EDA_CS	BLEU	0.6197	**0.6705**	0.5515	0.4925
	NIST	9.2103	8.5150	**7.4447**	6.9813
	METEOR	**0.4428**	0.4449	0.4379	0.4191
	ROUGE_L	0.6610	**0.6894**	0.7499	0.7002
	CIDER	**2.8118**	**2.2355**	5.1376	4.7821
EDA_CS^{TL}	BLEU	–	0.6580	**0.5769**	**0.5099**
	NIST	–	8.5615	7.4286	**7.3359**
	METEOR	–	**0.4516**	**0.4439**	**0.4340**
	ROUGE_L	–	0.6740	**0.7616**	**0.7131**
	CIDER	–	2.1803	**5.3456**	**4.9915**

Our first experimentation, the **ablation study**, refers to the E2E dataset because of its wide diffusion, and is shown in Table 2; "EDA_CS" identifies our model, and 'C' and 'S' stand for "Copy" and "Switch", the two major improvements presented in this work. It is evident that the partially-improved networks are able to provide independent benefits to the performance. Those components cooperate positively, as EDA_CS further enhances those results. Furthermore, the obtained BLEU metric value on the E2E test set would allow our model to be ranked fourth in the E2E NLG Challenge, while its baseline TGen was ranked tenth.

Our second experimentation, the **comparison study**, is shown in Table 3. The character-based design of EDA_CS led us to explore in this context also a possible behavior as a transfer learning capable model: in order to test this hypothesis, we used the weights learned during training on the E2E+ dataset as the starting point for a fine-tuning phase on all the other datasets. We chose E2E+ because it reduces the generation bias, as discussed in Subsect. 3.1. We named this approach EDA_CS^{TL}.

A first interesting result is that our model EDA_CS always obtains higher metric values with respect to TGen on the Hotel and Restaurant datasets, and three out of five higher metrics values on the E2E dataset. However, in the case of E2E+, TGen achieves three out of five higher metrics values. These results suggest that EDA_CS and TGen are comparable, at least from the point of view of automatic metrics' evaluation.

A more surprising result is that the approach EDA_CS^{TL} allows to obtain better performance with respect to training EDA_CS in the standard way on the Hotel and Restaurant datasets (for the majority of metrics); on E2E, EDA_CS^{TL} outperforms EDA_CS only in one case (i.e. METEOR metric).

Moreover, EDA_CS^{TL} shows a BLEU increment of at least 14% with respect to TGen's score when compared to both Hotel and Restaurant datasets.

Finally, the baseline model, EDA, is largely outperformed by all other examined methods.

Therefore, we can claim that our model exploits its transfer learning capabilities effectively, showing very good performances in a context like data-to-text generation in which the portability of features learned from different datasets, in the extent of our knowledge, has not yet been explored.

We highlight that EDA_CS's model's good results are achieved even if it consists in a fully end-to-end model which does not benefit from the delexicalization-relexicalization procedure, differently from TGen. Most importantly, the latter represents a word-based system: as such, it is bound to a specific, limited vocabulary, in contrast to the general-purpose character one used in our work.

Table 4 reports the output of the analyzed models for a couple of MR, taken from the E2E+ test set. The EDA's inability to copy is clear, as it tends, in its output, to substitute those values of *name*, *food* and *near* that do not appear in the training set with known ones, guided by the first few characters of the input slot's content. Besides, it shows serious coverage issues, frequently 'forgetting' to report information, and/or repeating more times the same ones.

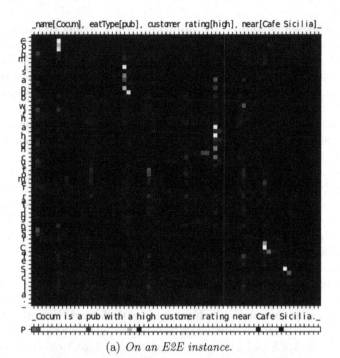

(a) *On an E2E instance.*

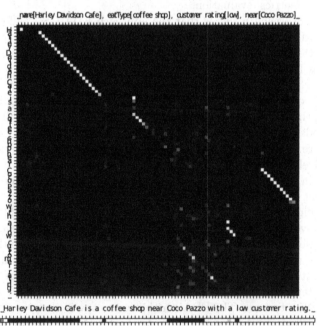

(b) *On an E2E+ instance.*

Fig. 2. Attention distribution (white means more attention) and p_{gen} (white: generating, black: copying), as calculated by the model

Table 4. A comparison of the three models' output on some MR of the E2E+ test set. The first reference utterance is reported for convenience

MR	`name[New Viet Huong], eatType[pub], customer rating[1 out of 5], near[Ecco]`
1st reference	The New Viet Huong is a pub near Ecco that has a customer rating of 1 out of 5
EDA_CS	New Viet Huong is a pub near Ecco with a customer rating of 1 out of 5
TGen	New Viet Huong is a pub near Ecco with a customer rating of 1 out of 5
EDA	Near the riverside near the ERNick Restaurant is a pub near the ERNicker's
MR	`name[La Mirabelle], eatType[restaurant], food[Iraqi], priceRange[high], area[riverside], familyFriendly[yes], near[Mi Cocina]`
1st reference	La Mirabelle is a children friendly restaurant located in the Riverside area near to the Mi Cocina. It serves Iraqi food and is in the high price range
EDA_CS	La Mirabelle is a high priced Iraqi restaurant located in the riverside area near Mi Cocina. It is children friendly
TGen	La Mirabelle is a high priced Iraqi restaurant in the riverside area near Mi Cocina. It is child friendly
EDA	La Memaini is a high priced restaurant that serves Iranian food in the high price range. It is located in the riverside area near Manganaro's Restaurant

These troubles are not present in EDA_CS output utterances: the model nearly always renders all of the input slots, still without duplicating any of them. This goal is achieved even in absence of explicit coverage techniques thanks to our peculiar training procedure, detailed in Sect. 2.3, that for each input sample minimizes also the loss on the reconstructed tabular input. It is worth noting that the performance of TGen and EDA_CS are overall comparable, especially when they deal with names or other expressions not present in training.

The joint analysis of the matrix of the attention distribution P_{att}^{ij} and the vector p_{gen} allows a deeper understanding of how our model works.

In Fig. 2 every row shows the attention probability distribution "seen" when an output character is produced at the i-th time instant (i.e. the vector $P_{att}^{ij}, 1 \leq j \leq T_x$), while every column shows values of the attention distribution corresponding to a specific input position j (i.e. the vector $P_{att}^{ij}, 1 \leq i \leq T_y$). We can therefore follow the white spots, corresponding to higher values of attention, to understand the flow of the model's attention during the generation of the output utterance.

Moreover, p_{gen} values, which lie in the numeric interval $[0, 1]$, help us in the interpretation of the attention: they are represented as a grayscale vector from zero (black) to one (white) under the matrices. Values close to 0 mean copying and those near 1 mean generating.

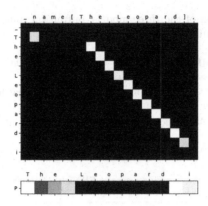

Fig. 3. Copying common words leads the model to "uncertain" values of p_{gen}

We can note that our model's behavior varies significantly depending on the dataset it has been trained on. Figure 2a shows the attention probability distribution matrix of EDA_CS (together with p_{gen} vector) trained on the E2E dataset: as observed before, attribute values in this dataset have a very low variability (and are already present in the training set), so that they can be individually represented and easily generated by the decoder. In this case, a typical pattern is the copy of only the first, discriminating character, clearly noticeable in the graphical representation of the p_{gen} vector, and the subsequent generation of the others. Notice that the attention tends to remain improperly focused on the same character for more than one output time step, as in the first letter of "high".

On the other hand, the copy mechanism shows its full potential when the system must learn to copy attribute values, as in the E2E+ dataset. In Fig. 2b the diagonal attention pattern is pervasive: (i) it occurs when the model actually copies, as in "Harley Davidson" and "Coco Pazzo", and (ii) as a *soft track* for the generation, as in "customer rating", where the copy-first-generate-rest behavior emerges again.

A surprising effect is shown in Fig. 3, when the model is expected to copy words that, instead, are usually generated: an initial difficulty in copying the word "The", that is usually a substring of a slot value, is ingeniously overcome as follows. The first character is purely generated, as shown by the white color in the underlying vector, and the sequence of the following characters, "he_", is half-generated and half-copied. Then, the value of p_{gen} gets suddenly but correctly close to 0 (black) until the closing square bracket is met. The network's output is not affected negatively by this confusion and the attention matrix remains quite well-formed.

As a final remark, the metrics used, while being useful, well-known and broadly accepted, do not reflect the ability to directly copy input facts to produce outputs, so settling the rare word problem.

4 Conclusion

We showed in this paper an effective character-based end-to-end model that faces data-to-text generation tasks. It takes advantage of a copy mechanism, that deals successfully with the rare word problem, and of a specific training procedure, characterized by the switching GRUs mechanism. These innovative contributions to state-of-art further improve the quality of the generated texts.

We highlight that our formulation of the copy mechanism is an original character-based adaptation of [21], because of the use of p_{gen}^{i-1} to determine the value of p_{gen}^i, at the following time step. This helps the model in choosing whether to maintain the same value for a fair number of time steps or not.

Besides, the use of characters allows the creation of more general models, which do not depend on a specific vocabulary; it also enables a very effective straightforward transfer learning procedure, which in addition eases training on small datasets. Moreover, outputs are obtained in a completely end-to-end fashion, in contrast to what happens for the chosen baseline word-based model, whose performances are comparable or even worse.

One future improvement of our model could be the "reinforcement" of the learning iteration described in Sect. 2.3: for each dataset example (x, y), we could consider, as an ulterior example, the reverse instance (y, x). The network obtained this way should be completely reversible, and the interchangeability of input and output languages could open up new opportunities in neural machine translation, such as two-way neural translators.

New metrics that give greater importance to rare words might be needed in the future, with the purpose of better assess performances of able-to-copy NLG models on datasets such as the E2E+ one.

Acknowledgements. The activity has been partially carried on in the context of the Visiting Professor Program of the Italian Istituto Nazionale di Alta Matematica (INdAM).

References

1. Agarwal, S., Dymetman, M.: A surprisingly effective out-of-the-box char2char model on the E2E NLG Challenge dataset. In: Proceedings of the SIGDIAL 2017 Conference, pp. 158–163. Association for Computational Linguistics, Saarbrucken (2017)
2. Aharoni, R., Goldberg, Y., Belinkov, Y.: Improving sequence to sequence learning for morphological inflection generation: the BIU-MIT systems for the SIG-MORPHON 2016 shared task for morphological reinflection. In: Proceedings of the 14th SIGMORPHON Workshop on Computational Research in Phonetics, Phonology, and Morphology, pp. 41–48. Association for Computational Linguistics, Berlin (2016)
3. Al-Rfou, R., Choe, D., Constant, N., Guo, M., Jones, L.: Character-Level Language Modeling with Deeper Self-Attention. arXiv preprint arXiv: 1808.04444v2 (2018)
4. Bahdanau, D., Cho, K., Bengio, Y.: Neural Machine Translation by Jointly Learning to Align and Translate. arXiv preprint arXiv: 1409.0473v7 (2014)

5. Burke, R.D., Hammond, K.J., Young, B.C.: The FindMe approach to assisted browsing. IEEE Expert **12**(4), 32–40 (1997)
6. Cho, K., et al.: Learning phrase representations using RNN encoder-decoder for statistical machine translation. In: Moschitti, A., Pang, B., Daelemans, W. (eds.) Proceedings of the 2014 Conference on Empirical Methods in Natural Language Processing, EMNLP 2014, Doha, Qatar, 25–29 October 2014, A meeting of SIGDAT, a Special Interest Group of the ACL, pp. 1724–1734. ACL (2014)
7. Doddington, G.: Automatic evaluation of machine translation quality using N-gram co-occurrence statistics. In: Proceedings of the Second International Conference on Human Language Technology Research, HLT 2002, pp. 138–145. Morgan Kaufmann Publishers Inc., San Diego (2002)
8. Dusek, O., Jurcícek, F.: Sequence-to-sequence generation for spoken dialogue via deep syntax trees and strings. In: Proceedings of the 54th Annual Meeting of the Association for Computational Linguistics, ACL 2016, Berlin, Germany, 7–12 August 2016, vol. 2: Short Papers. The Association for Computer Linguistics (2016)
9. Goyal, R., Dymetman, M., Gaussier, É.: Natural language generation through character-based RNNs with finite-state prior knowledge. In: Calzolari, N., Matsumoto, Y., Prasad, R. (eds.) COLING 2016, 26th International Conference on Computational Linguistics, Proceedings of the Conference: Technical Papers, Osaka, Japan, 11–16 December 2016, pp. 1083–1092. ACL (2016)
10. Gu, J., Lu, Z., Li, H., Li, V.O.K.: Incorporating copying mechanism in sequence to-sequence learning. In: Erj, K., Smith, N.A. (eds.) Proceedings of the 54th Annual Meeting of the Association for Computational Linguistics, ACL 2016, Berlin, Germany, 7–12 August 2016, vol. 1: Long Papers. The Association for Computer Linguistics (2016)
11. Karpathy, A., Li, F.: Deep Visual-Semantic Alignments for Generating Image Descriptions. arXiv preprint arXiv: 1412.2306v2 (2014)
12. Kingma, D.P., Ba, J.: Adam: A Method for Stochastic Optimization. arXiv preprint arXiv: 1412.6980v9 (2014)
13. Lavie, A., Agarwal, A.: METEOR: an automatic metric for MT evaluation with high levels of correlation with human judgments. In: Callison-Burch, C., Koehn, P., Fordyce, C.S., Monz, C. (eds.) Proceedings of the Second Workshop on Statistical Machine Translation, WMT@ACL 2007, Prague, Czech Republic, 23 June 2007, pp. 228–231. Association for Computational Linguistics (2007)
14. Lin, C.-Y.: ROUGE: a package for automatic evaluation of summaries. In: Text Summarization Branches Out: Proceedings of the ACL 2004 Workshop, pp. 74–81. Association for Computational Linguistics, Barcelona (2004)
15. Luong, M., Manning, C.D.: Achieving open vocabulary neural machine translation with hybrid word-character models. In: Erj, K., Smith, N.A. (eds.) Proceedings of the 54th Annual Meeting of the Association for Computational Linguistics, ACL 2016, Berlin, Germany, 7–12 August 2016, vol. 1: Long Papers. The Association for Computer Linguistics (2016)
16. Luong, T., Sutskever, I., Le, Q.V., Vinyals, O., Zaremba, W.: Addressing the rare word problem in neural machine translation. In: Proceedings of the 53rd Annual Meeting of the Association for Computational Linguistics and the 7th International Joint Conference on Natural Language Processing of the Asian Federation of Natural Language Processing, ACL 2015, Beijing, China, 26–31 July 2015, vol. 1: Long Papers, pp. 11–19. The Association for Computer Linguistics (2015)

17. Mei, H., Bansal, M., Walter, M.R.: What to talk about and how? Selective generation using LSTMs with coarse-to-fine alignment. In: Knight, K., Nenkova, A., Rambow, O. (eds.) NAACL HLT 2016, The 2016 Conference of the North American Chapter of the Association for Computational Linguistics: Human Language Technologies, San Diego California, USA, 12–17 June 2016, pp. 720–730. The Association for Computational Linguistics (2016)

18. Novikova, J., Dusek, O., Rieser, V.: The E2E dataset: new challenges for end-to-end generation. In: Jokinen, K., Stede, M., DeVault, D., Louis, A. (eds.). Proceedings of the 18th Annual SIGdial Meeting on Discourse and Dialogue, Saarbruücken, Germany, 15–17 August 2017, pp. 201–206. Association for Computational Linguistics (2017)

19. Papineni, K., Roukos, S., Ward, T., Zhu, W.: Bleu: a method for automatic evaluation of machine translation. In: Proceedings of the 40th Annual Meeting of the Association for Computational Linguistics, Philadelphia, PA, USA, 6–12 July 2002, pp. 311–318. ACL (2002)

20. Pascanu, R., Mikolov, T., Bengio, Y.: On the difficulty of training recurrent neural networks. In: Proceedings of the 30th International Conference on Machine Learning, ICML 2013, Atlanta, GA, USA, 16–21 June 2013, JMLR Workshop and Conference Proceedings, pp. 1310–1318. JMLR.org (2013)

21. See, A., Liu, P.J., Manning, C.D.: Get to the point: summarization with pointer-generator networks. In: Barzilay, R., Kan, M. (eds.) Proceedings of the 55th Annual Meeting of the Association for Computational Linguistics, ACL 2017, Vancouver, Canada, 30 July–4 August 2017, vol. 1: Long Papers, pp. 1073–1083. Association for Computational Linguistics (2017)

22. Sennrich, R., Haddow, B., Birch, A.: Neural machine translation of rare words with subword units. In: Erj, K., Smith, N.A. (eds.) Proceedings of the 54th Annual Meeting of the Association for Computational Linguistics, ACL 2016, Berlin, Germany, 7–12 August 2016, vol. 1: Long Papers. The Association for Computer Linguistics (2016)

23. Sutskever, I., Vinyals, O., Le, Q.V.: Sequence to sequence learning with neural networks. In: Ghahramani, Z., Welling, M., Cortes, C., Lawrence, N.D., Weinberger, K.Q. (eds.) Advances in Neural Information Processing Systems 27: Annual Conference on Neural Information Processing Systems 2014, Montreal, Quebec, Canada, 8–13 December 2014, pp. 3104–3112 (2014)

24. Vedantam, R., Zitnick, C.L., Parikh, D.: CIDEr: consensus-based image description evaluation. In: IEEE Conference on Computer Vision and Pattern Recognition, CVPR 2015, Boston, MA, USA, 7–12 June 2015, pp. 4566–4575. IEEE Computer Society (2015)

25. Vinyals, O., Fortunato, M., Jaitly, N.: Pointer networks. In: Cortes, C., Lawrence, N.D., Lee, D.D., Sugiyama, M., Garnett, R. (eds.) Advances in Neural Information Processing Systems 28: Annual Conference on Neural Information Processing Systems 2015, Montreal, Quebec, Canada, 7–12 December 2015, pp. 2692–2700 (2015)

26. Wen, T., Gasic, M., Mrksic, N., Su, P., Vandyke, D., Young, S.J.: Semantically conditioned LSTM-based natural language generation for spoken dialogue systems. In: Márquez, L., Callison-Burch, C., Su, J., Pighin, D., Marton, Y. (eds.) Proceedings of the 2015 Conference on Empirical Methods in Natural Language Processing, EMNLP 2015, Lisbon, Portugal, 17–21 September 2015, pp. 1711–1721. The Association for Computational Linguistics (2015)

27. Williams, R.J., Zipser, D.: A learning algorithm for continually running fully recurrent neural networks. Neural Comput. **1**(2), 270–280 (1989)
28. Wiseman, S., Shieber, S.M., Rush, A.M.: Challenges in data-to-document generation. In: Palmer, M., Hwa, R., Riedel, S. (eds.) Proceedings of the 2017 Conference on Empirical Methods in Natural Language Processing, EMNLP 2017, Copenhagen, Denmark, 9–11 September 2017, pp. 2253–2263. Association for Computational Linguistics (2017)

NSEEN: Neural Semantic Embedding for Entity Normalization

Shobeir Fakhraei[✉], Joel Mathew, and José Luis Ambite

Information Sciences Institute, University of Southern California, Los Angeles, USA
{shobeir,joel,ambite}@isi.edu

Abstract. Much of human knowledge is encoded in text, available in scientific publications, books, and the web. Given the rapid growth of these resources, we need automated methods to extract such knowledge into machine-processable structures, such as knowledge graphs. An important task in this process is *entity normalization*, which consists of mapping noisy entity mentions in text to canonical entities in well-known *reference sets*. However, entity normalization is a challenging problem; there often are many textual forms for a canonical entity that may not be captured in the reference set, and entities mentioned in text may include many syntactic variations, or errors. The problem is particularly acute in scientific domains, such as biology. To address this problem, we have developed a general, scalable solution based on a deep Siamese neural network model to embed the *semantic* information about the entities, as well as their *syntactic* variations. We use these embeddings for fast mapping of new entities to large reference sets, and empirically show the effectiveness of our framework in challenging bio-entity normalization datasets.

Keywords: Semantic embedding · Deep learning · Siamese networks · Entity grounding · Entity normalization · Entity resolution · Entity disambiguation · Entity matching · Data integration · Similarity search · Similarity learning

1 Introduction

Digital publishing has accelerated the rate of textual content generation to beyond human consumption capabilities. Taking the scientific literature as an example, Google Scholar has indexed about four and a half million articles and books in 2017 in a 50% increase from the previous year. Automatically organizing this information into a proper knowledge representation is an important way to make this information accessible. This process includes identification of entities in the text, often referred to as *Names Entity Recognition (NER)* [25,38], and mapping of the identified entities to existing reference sets, called *Entity Normalization*, or *Grounding*. In this paper we propose a text embedding solution for entity normalization to a reference set.

© Springer Nature Switzerland AG 2020
U. Brefeld et al. (Eds.): ECML PKDD 2019, LNAI 11907, pp. 665–680, 2020.
https://doi.org/10.1007/978-3-030-46147-8_40

Entity normalization to a reference set is a challenging problem. Even though in some cases normalization can be as simple as a database look-up, often there is no exact match between the recognized entity in the text and the reference entity set. There are two main sources for this variation. The first is *syntactic variations*, where the identified entity contains relatively small character differences with the canonical form present in the reference set, such as different capitalization, reordering of words, typos, or errors introduced in the NER process (e.g., 'FOXP2' and 'FOX-P2'). The second and more challenging problem, which we call *semantic variations*, is when the identified entity does not exist in the reference set, even when considering significant syntactic variations, but a human reader can recognize the non-standard entity name. For example, entities often have multiple canonical names in the reference set and the identified entity name is a combination of parts of different canonical names (e.g., 'P70 S6KA' and '52 kDa ribosomal protein S6 kinase').

A further challenge is how to perform normalization at scale. Exhaustive pairwise comparison of the identified entity to the reference entities grows quadratically and is unfeasible for large datasets. *Blocking* [31] techniques speed up the process by selecting small subsets of entities for pairwise comparisons. Unfortunately, blocking methods applied directly to the textual representation of the entity names are often limited to simple techniques that can only address syntactic variations of the entity names. So, traditional blocking may eliminate matches that are semantically relevant but syntactically different.

To address these issues, we develop a text embedding solution for entity normalization. Our contributions include: (1) A general, scalable deep neural-based model to embed entity information in a numeric vector space that captures both *syntactic* and *semantic variations*. (2) An approach to incorporate syntactic variations of entity names into the embeddings based on domain knowledge by extending the use of contrastive loss function with soft labels. (3) A method for dynamic hard negative mining to refine the embedding for improved performance. (4) Using an approximate *k-nearest neighbors* algorithm over the embeddings to provide a scalable solution without the need for traditional blocking.

2   Related Work

Data Normalization, linking entities to their canonical forms, is one of the most fundamental tasks in information retrieval and automatic knowledge extraction [9]. Many related tasks share components with entity normalization, but also have subtle differences. Record linkage [21], aims to find records from different tables corresponding to the same entity. Records often contain multiple fields and one of the challenges in this task is reasoning on different fields, and their combinations. Deduplication [13] is similar to record linkage, but focuses on the records of the same table, so it does not have to consider the heterogeneity of fields across different tables. Entity resolution [14], is a more general term that deals with findings entity mentions that refer to the same entity and often inferring a canonical form from them.

A critical feature in our setting is the presence of a canonical *reference set*, so that we ask "which canonical entity a mention is mapped to?" in contrast to "which records are the same?" for settings were the canonical entity is latent. Reference sets are specially important in bio-medical domains [23]. Unlike record linkage, we do not have multiple fields and only reason on a single string.

Feature-engineered string similarities [7] form the core of most traditional entity resolution methods. In contrast, Our approach learns a *similarity metric* for entity normalization based on syntactic and semantic information. We compute these similarities via embedding the entity mentions into a vector space. Text embeddings, such as word2vec [27], GloVe [32], or more recently ELMo [33], and BERT [12] have been very successful in language processing and understanding applications, in great measure because they have been computed over very large corpora. However, these methods are not task specific and provide general embeddings based on the text context. Our approach is based on computing direct similarities rather than analyzing the surrounding text. Hence, for Entity Normalization, we use a deep Siamese neural network that has been shown to be effective in learning similarities in text [30] and images [37]. Both of these approaches define a contrastive loss functions [15] to learn similarities. Recently, Ebraheem et al. [17] and Mudgal et al. [28] proposed deep neural network methods for record linkage (with multiple fields) in a database. A major focus of their work was on combining data in different fields. Our setting differs since we operate on entity name strings, and match them to canonical references.

To avoid exhaustive pairwise computation of similarities between entities often blocking [26] or indexing [10] techniques are used to reduce the search space. These methods are often based on approximate string matching. The most effective methods in this area is based on hashing the string with the main purpose of blocking the entities as a pre-processing step, followed by the matching part that is performed after blocking. In our method, we combine both steps by mapping the entity mentions to a numerical space to capture similarities. The blocking in our case conceptually follows the matching process via applying approximate nearest neighbors approaches on our semantic embedding space.

In the biomedical domain, Kang et al. [19] propose a rule-based method and Leaman et al. [22] propose a learning-to-rank-based approach for disease normalization. Leaman and Lu [23] further perform joint name entity recognition and normalization. We provide an embedding-based approach for entity normalization. We perform our experimental validation on two biomedical datasets of protein and chemical entities.

3   Approach

Problem Definition: Given a query entity mention (n_q), and a reference set of entities $\mathcal{R} \equiv \{e_1, \ldots, e_m\}$, where each entity $e_i \equiv \, <\lambda_i, \{n_i^1, \ldots, n_i^k\}>$ is identified via an ID (λ_i) and an associated set of names (n_i^k) that refer to the entity, our goal is to return the ID (λ_q) of the corresponding entity in our reference set $\mathcal{R}$. The exact textual name of the query entity may not exist in the reference set.

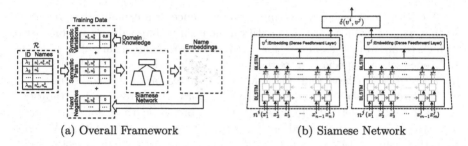

Fig. 1. Learning embedding function based on semantics in reference set and syntactic variations defined by domain knowledge and hard negative mining.

We map this normalization task to an approximate nearest-neighbors search in a n-dimensional space where each name n_l^m in the reference set is encoded into a numerical vector representation v_l^m. Our objective in this embedding space is that names of the same entity (even syntactically very different) be closer to each other compared to names of other entities. That is, $n_l^m \to v_l^m$ such that $\delta(v_l^m, v_l^p) < \delta(v_l^m, v_o^*)$, where e_l and e_o are entities ($e_l \neq e_o$), n_*^* their corresponding names, v_*^* embedding vectors of these names, and δ is a distance function.

We use a Siamese neural network architecture to embed the semantic information about the entities as well as their syntactic similarities. We further refine the similarities via dynamic hard negative sampling and incorporating domain knowledge about the entities using additional generated training data. We then encode and store the embeddings in a numeric representation that enables fast retrieval of the results without the need for traditional character-based blocking. Our approach consist of three steps:

Similarity Learning. We first learn an embedding function ($\mathcal{M} : n \to v$) that maps the entity names to a numeric vector space where names of the same entities are close to each other.

Embedding and Hashing. Then, we embed all the names in the reference set $\mathcal{R}$ to the numerical vector space and hash and store the reference set embeddings for fast retrieval.

Retrieval. Finally, we embed the query name (i.e., $n_q \to v_q$) using the learned model $\mathcal{M}$ and find the closest samples to it in the embedding space to retrieve the corresponding ID (λ_q) of the query name in the reference set.
The following sections describe each step in detail.

3.1 Similarity Learning

We first learn a function ($\mathcal{M}$) that maps the textual representation of entity names (n) to a numerical vector representation (v) that preserves the proximity of names that belong to the same entity, using a Siamese recurrent neural network model. Figure 1(a) shows the overall approach and Algorithm 1 describes the similarity learning process.

Algorithm 1. NSEEN: Similarity Learning

1: **procedure** TRAINSIM($\mathcal{R}, P_d$)
2:     **Input:** $\mathcal{R}$ reference set
3:     **Input:** P_d pairs based on knowledge of syntactic variation in the domain
4:     Generate pairs based on reference set $\mathcal{R}$ and add them to training data $\mathcal{D}$
5:     Add P_d pairs to the training data $\mathcal{D}$
6:     **for** k times **do**
7:         Train the model $\mathcal{M}$ (Siamese network) on $\mathcal{D}$
8:         Embed all the names in $\mathcal{R}$: $n \rightarrow v$
9:         **for all** v_l^i **do**   ▷ Hard negative mining
10:            find the k closest v_k^j to v_l^i
11:            **if** $k \neq l$ **then**
12:               add $< n_k^j, n_l^i, 0 >$ to training data $\mathcal{D}$
13:     **return** $\mathcal{M}$ ▷ The trained embedding function

---

Siamese Recurrent Neural Network. The Siamese neural network architecture of two towers with shared weights and a distance function at the last layer has been effective in learning similarities in domains such as text [30] and images [37]. Figure 1(b) depicts an overview of the network used in our framework.

We feed pairs of names and a score indicating the similarity of the pairs (i.e., $<n^i, n^j, y>$) to the Siamese network. As shown in Fig. 1(b), n^i and n^j are entity names represented as a sequences of characters $<x_1^i, \ldots, x_n^i>$ and $<x_1^j, \ldots, x_m^j>$, and $y \in [0,1]$ represents the similarity between the names. To read the character sequence of the names, we feed the character embedding to four layers of Bidirectional-LSTM, followed by a single densely connected feedforward layer, which generate the embeddings v.

Contrastive Loss Function. While we can use several distance functions (δ) to compare the learned vectors of the names, we use cosine distance between the embeddings v_i and v_j, due to its better performance in higher dimensional spaces. We then define a contrastive loss [15] based on the distance function δ to train the model, as shown in Eq. 1. The intuition behind this loss function is to pull the similar pairs closer to each other, and push the dissimilar pairs up to a margin m apart ($m = 1$ in our experiments).

$$\mathcal{L} = \frac{1}{2} y \delta(v_i, v_j)^2 + \frac{1}{2}(1 - y) \max(0, m - \delta(v_i, v_j))^2 \tag{1}$$

The contrastive loss has been originally proposed for binary labels where we either fully pull two points towards each other or push them apart. In this paper, we propose to extend this loss via using soft real-valued labels when we introduce syntactic variations of the names described in Sect. 3.1 to indicate uncertainties about the similarities of two vectors. For the margin of 1 (i.e., $m = 1$), the distance that minimizes the loss function $\mathcal{L}$ for the real-valued label y is:[1]

---

[1] For brevity of notation we denote $\delta(v_i, v_j)$ with δ_v.

$$\frac{\partial \mathcal{L}}{\partial \delta_v} = y\delta_v - (1-y)(1-\delta_v)$$

$$\arg\min_{\delta_v} \mathcal{L} = \{\delta_v \mid y + \delta_v - 1 = 0\} = 1 - y \tag{2}$$

For example, in our setting the optimal distance between the embeddings of two names with 0.7 similarity (i.e., $y = 0.7$) is 0.3. Figure 2 depicts the changes in loss when altering the distance corresponding to different y values, and the points that minimize the loss (i.e., $\arg\min_{\delta_v} \mathcal{L}$) are marked on each line.

Pair Selection and Generation. In order to train the model we need labeled pairs of names ($<n^i, n^j, y>$). We generate three sets of pairs using different approaches: (1) the *initial set* based on the names in the reference set, (2) the *syntactic variations set* based on domain knowledge, and (3) the *hard negative set*. The initial and the hard negative pairs capture the *semantic* relationships between names in the reference set, and the syntactic variations capture the *syntactic* noise that may be present in referring to these names in reality.

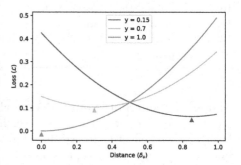

Fig. 2. Contrastive loss ($\mathcal{L}$) based on distance values (δ_v) for different real-value labels y. (Best viewed in color) (Color figure online)

Initial Semantic Set. We generate an initial training set of similar and dissimilar pairs based the entities in the reference set $\mathcal{R}$. We generate positive pairs by the cross product of all the names that belong to the same entity, and initialize the negative set of dissimilar pairs by randomly sampling names that belong to different entities. Formally:

$$P_+ = \{< n^i, n^j, 1 > \mid (\forall n_l^i, n_l^j \in e_l) \wedge (\forall e_l \in \mathcal{R})\}$$
$$P_- = \{< n^i, n^j, 0 > \mid (n_l^i, n_m^j \in e_l, e_m) \wedge (e_l, e_m \in \mathcal{R}) \wedge (e_l \neq e_m)\}$$

Syntactic Variations and Entity Families. In order to train the model with the syntactic variations that could be introduced in the real-world textual representation of the names, we add pairs of names to the training set and label them with their real-value string similarities. The argument behind using real-valued labels is provided in Eq. 2, with the intuition that using a label of 0 will completely repel two vectors and using a label of 1 will bring two vectors as close as possible, but using a label between 0 and 1 will aim to keep the two vectors somewhere inside the margin.

We use Trigram-Jaccard, Levenshtein Edit Distance, and Jaro–Winkler to compute string similarity scores [11] between the pairs of names and include sets of pairs with labels based on each similarity score in the training set. The intuition is that the model will learn a combination of all these string similarity measures. To select the name pairs to include in this process, we consider two sets of variations based on the *same name*, and *different names*.

Same name variations are the noise that can be introduced to an extracted name in real-world settings. To capture the most common forms of noise occurring on the same name, we make the following three modifications based on our observation of the most frequent variations in the query names:

- Removing the spaces, e.g., <FOX P2, FOXP2, y>
- Removing all but alphanumerical characters, e.g., <FOX-P2, FOXP2, y>
- Converting to upper and lower cases, e.g., <Ras, RAS, y>, <Ras, ras, y>

Different name variations introduce a higher level of similarity concept to the model. We make the second set of pairs by selecting the names of entities that are *somehow related* and computing their string similarities. For example, in our experiments with proteins we select two entities that belong to the same protein family and generate pairs of names consisting of one name from each. The labels are assigned to these pairs based on their string similarities. This set of pairs not only introduces more diverse variations of textual string similarities, it also captures a *higher-level relationship* by bringing the embeddings of the names that belong to a group closer to each other. Encoding such hierarchical relations in the entity representations has been effective in various domains [8].

Hard Negative Mining. Given the large space of possible negative name pairs (i.e., the cross product of the names of different entities) we can only sample a subset to train our model. As stated earlier we start with an initial random negative sample set for our training. However, these random samples may often be trivial choices for the model and after a few epochs may not contain enough useful signal. The use of contrastive loss makes this issue more problematic as the probability of the distance between randomly selected negative samples being less than the margin (m) is low. Sampling techniques, often called *hard-negative mining*, have been introduces in domains such as knowledge graph construction [20] and computer vision [36] to deal with similar issues.

The idea behind hard negative mining is finding negative examples that are most informative for the model. These examples are the ones closest to the decision boundary and the model will most likely assign a wrong label to them. As shown in Fig. 1a and Algorithm 1, we find the hard negatives by first embedding all the names in the reference set $\mathcal{R}$ using the latest learned model $\mathcal{M}$. We then find the closest names to each name in the embedding space using an approximate k-nearest neighbors algorithm for fast iterations. We then add the name pairs found using this process that do not belong to the same entity with a 0 label to our training set and retrain the model $\mathcal{M}$. We repeat this process multiple times to refine the model with several sets of hard negative samples.

3.2   Reference Set Embedding and Storage

The model $\mathcal{M}$ that we trained in the previous step is basically a function that maps a name string to a numerical vector. Since both towers of the Siamese network share all their weights, the final embedding is independent of the tower the original string is provided to as input. Considering the goal of our framework, which is to perform entity normalization of query names (n_q) to the entities in the reference set $\mathcal{R}$, we embed all the names in the reference set using the final trained model $\mathcal{M}$, and store the embeddings for comparison with future queries.

Our task becomes assigning an entity in our reference set to the query name n_q by finding the closest entity to it in the embedding space. This assignment is basically a nearest neighbor search in the embedding space. The most naive solution to this search would entail a practically infeasible task of exhaustive pairwise comparisons of query embedding with all embeddings in a potentially large reference set. Moreover, since we iteratively repeat the nearest neighbor look-up in our training process for hard-negative mining, we need a faster way to retrieve the results.

This challenge is prevalent in many research and industry applications of machine learning such as recommender systems, computer vision, and in general any similarity-based search, and has resulted in development of several fast *approximate nearest neighbors* approaches [34,35]. We speed-up our nearest neighbors retrieval process by transforming and storing our reference set embeddings in an approximate nearest neighbors data structure. Algorithm 2 describes the overall process of this stage.

Algorithm 2. Embedding $\mathcal{R}$	**Algorithm 3.** Retrieval
1: **procedure** EMBED($\mathcal{R}, \mathcal{M}$)	1: **procedure** RETRIEVE($\mathcal{H}_v, \mathcal{M}, n_q$)
2:　　**for all** $n_i \in \mathcal{R}$ **do**	2:　　Embed the query name: $n_q \xrightarrow{\mathcal{M}} v_q$
3:　　　　$n_i \xrightarrow{\mathcal{M}} v_i$	3:　　Find the closest v_k^j to v_q using approximate nearest neighbor search (Annoy) on $\mathcal{H}_v$
4:　　**for all** v_i **do**	4:　　**return** λ_k as the ID (i.e., λ_q)
5:　　　　Hash v_i and store in $\mathcal{H}_{v_i}$	
6:　　**return** $\mathcal{H}_v$　▷ Hashed embeddings	

We leverage a highly optimized solution that is extensively used in applied settings, such as Spotify, to deal with large scale approximate nearest neighbor search, called *Annoy (Approximate Nearest Neighbors Oh Yeah!)* [2]. Annoy, uses a combination of random projections and a tree structure where intermediate nodes in the tree contain random hyper-planes dividing the search space. It supports several distance functions including Hamming and cosine distances based on the work of Bachrach et al. [5].

Since we have already transformed the textual representation of an entity name to a numerical vector space, and the entity look-up to a nearest neighbor search problem, we can always use competing approximate nearest neighbors search methods [29], and the new state-of-the-art approaches that will be discovered in the future. Furthermore, using such scalable data structures for our embeddings at this stage preserves semantic similarities learned by our model, in contrast to traditional blocking approaches applied as a pre-processing step that could break the semantic relationship in favor of textual similarities.

3.3 Retrieval

During the retrieval step, depicted in Algorithm 3 we first compute an embedding for the query name based on the same model $\mathcal{M}$ that we used to embed the reference set. We then perform an approximate nearest neighbor search in the embedding space for the query name, and return the ID of retrieved neighbor as the most probable entity ID for the query name. Note that in our setup we do not need to perform a separate direct look up for the query names that *exactly* match one of canonical names in the reference set. If the query name is one of the canonical names in the reference set, it will have exactly the same embedding and zero distance with one of the reference set names.

4 Experimental Validation

We conduct two set of experiments mapping query names to their canonical names to empirically validate the effectiveness of our framework. The two references sets are *UniProt* for proteins and *ChEBI* for chemical entities, and the query set is from PubMed extracts provided by the BioCreative initiative [4], as detailed in the following sections.

4.1 Reference Sets

The reference sets we use in our experiments are publicly available on the internet, and are the authority of canonical entity representations in their domains.

UniProt. The Universal Protein Resource (UniProt) is a large database of protein sequences and associated annotations [3]. For our experiments, we use the different names associated with each human protein in the UniProt dataset and their corresponding IDs. Hence, the task here is mapping a human protein name to a canonical UniProt ID.

ChEBI. We used the chemical entity names indexed in the Chemical Entities of Biological Interest (ChEBI) ontology. ChEBI is a dataset of molecular entities focused on small chemical compounds, including any constitutionally or isotopically distinct atom, molecule, ion, ion pair, radical, radical ion, complex, conformer, identifiable as a separately distinguishable entity [16]. The task here is mapping a small molecule name to a canoncal ChEBI ID.

Table 1 depicts the total number of entities (e_i) and their corresponding ID–name pairs ($<\lambda_i, n_i^j>$) in the reference sets, showing UniProt having less number of entities, but more names per entity comparing to ChEBI. Moreover, Fig. 3 depicts the histogram that shows the distribution of the number of names per each entity in the reference sets. Note that there are no entities in the UniProt reference set with only one name, but there are many proteins with several names. In contrast, the ChEBI dataset contains many entities with only one name.

Table 1. Statistics of the entities in the reference sets

Datasets	Entities	<entity, name> pairs
UniProt (Human)	20,375	123,590
ChEBI	72,241	277,210

4.2   Query Set

We use the datasets provided by the BioCreative VI Interactive Bio-ID Assignment Track [4] as our query data. These datasets provide several types of biomedical entity annotations generated by SourceData curators that map published article texts to their corresponding database IDs. The main interesting point about the BioCreative corpus for entity normalization is that the extracted entity names come from published scientific articles, and contain the entity-name variations and deviations forms that are present in the real world.

The Bio-ID datasets include a separate *train* and *test* sets. We use both of these datasets as query sets with gold standard labels to evaluate our method. The training set (we name it BioC1) consists of 13,573 annotated figure panel captions corresponding to 3,658 figures from 570 full length articles from 22 journals, for a total of 102,717 annotations. The test data set (we name it BioC2) consisted of 4,310 annotated figure panel captions from 1,154 figures taken from 196 full length journal articles, with 30,286 annotations in total [4].

Table 2 shows the number of UniProt and ChEBI entities in the annotated corpus. In our experiments we keep the original training (BioC1) and test (BioC2) splits of the data for reproducibility and ease of future comparisons, but we should note that for our purposes both BioC1 and BioC2 are just a source of correct normalizations with gold standards, and test sets in our experiments. Our algorithm is not trained on any of these datasets.

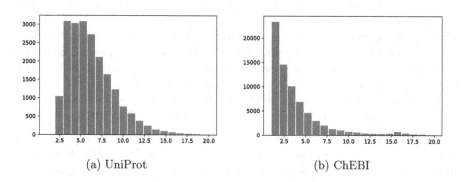

(a) UniProt   (b) ChEBI

Fig. 3. Distribution of names per entity in the reference datasets.

Table 2. Statistics of the annotations in the BioCreative VI Bio-ID corpus

Dataset	UniProt		ChEBI	
	Mentions	Entities	Mentions	Entities
BioC1	30,211	2,833	9,869	786
BioC2	1,592	1,321	829	543

4.3 Baselines

USC–ISI. As a representative of traditional record linkage techniques, we use the current production system for Named Entity Grounding at USC Information Science Institute, developed for the DARPA Big Mechanism program, as one of the baselines. The system is an optimized solution that employs a tuned combination of several string similarities including Jaccard, Levenshtein, and JaroWinkler distances with a prefix-based blocking system. It also includes a post re-ranking of the results based on the domain knowledge, such as the curation level of the entity (e.g., if the protein entry in UniProt has been reviewed by a human or not), the matching between the ID components and the query name, and popularity of the entities in each domain. This system provides entity grounding for several bio-medical entities including Proteins and Chemicals, and is publicly available at [1]. The system can produce results based on the FRIL [18] record linkage program and Apache Lucene [6], and we use the overall best results of both settings as the baseline for our experiments. We chose this baseline as a representative of the traditional entity normalization methods that provides competitive results based on an ensemble of such models.

BioBERT. To compare our method with a representative of text embedding approaches, we used the embedding generated by the recently released BioBERT [24] (Bidirectional Encoder Representations from Transformers for Biomedical Text Mining) model which extends the BERT [12] approach. BioBERT is a domain specific language representation model pre-trained on large-scale biomedical corpora that can effectively capture knowledge from a large amount of biomedical texts with minimal task-specific architecture modifications. BioBERT outperforms traditional models in biomedical named entity recognition, biomedical relation extraction, and biomedical question answering. We used the BioBERT framework with pre-trained weights released by the original authors of the paper, in a similar process to our approach; we first embed all the entity names of the reference set and then find the closest embedding to the query name in that embedding space.

DeepMatcher. Mudgal et al. [28] recently studied the application of deep learning architectures on entity matching in a general setting where the task is matching tuples (potentially having multiple fields) in different tables. DeepMatcher outperforms traditional entity matching frameworks in textual and noisy settings. We use DeepMatcher as a representative baseline for deep learning methods specific to entity normalization.

Table 3. Hits@k on BioCreative train dataset (BioC1) and test dataset (BioC2) datasets mapped to Uniprot and ChEBI reference sets.

Reference($\mathcal{R}$)	Dataset	Method	H@1	H@3	H@5	H@10
UniProt	BioC1	DeepMatcher	0.697	0.728	0.739	0.744
		BioBERT	0.729	0.761	0.779	0.808
		USC–ISI	0.814	0.864	0.875	0.885
		NSEEN	**0.833**	**0.869**	**0.886**	**0.894**
	BioC2	DeepMatcher	0.767	0.792	0.803	0.814
		BioBERT	0.801	0.827	0.827	0.840
		USC–ISI	0.841	0.888	0.904	0.919
		NSEEN	**0.861**	0.888	0.904	**0.930**
ChEBI	BioC1	DeepMatcher	0.288	0.363	0.397	0.419
		BioBERT	0.360	0.473	0.499	0.524
		USC–ISI	0.418	0.451	0.460	0.468
		NSEEN	**0.505**	**0.537**	**0.554**	**0.574**
	BioC2	DeepMatcher	0.373	0.463	0.491	0.517
		BioBERT	0.422	0.558	0.577	0.596
		USC–ISI	0.444	0.472	0.480	0.491
		NSEEN	**0.578**	**0.608**	**0.624**	**0.641**

We used the implementation published by the authors to perform our experiments. We used DeepMatcher with tuples containing only one field; the entity mention. We train DeepMatcher with the same initial pairs we use to train our model, and follow a common-word-based blocking technique recommended in their implementation to pre-process our data. DeepMatcher does not perform hard negative mining during its training, and the blocking is performed prior to the matching process in contrast to our framework.

4.4   Results

Table 3 shows the comparative results of our method (i.e., NSEEN) with other methods. We submit every query name in the BioCreative datasets to all systems, and retrieve the top k most probable IDs from each of them. We then find out if the correct ID (provided in the BioCreative dataset as labels) is present in the top k retrieved results (i.e., *Hits@k*) for several values of k. Our method outperforms the baselines in almost all settings. Chemical names are generally harder to normalize due to more sensitivity to parenthesis, commas, and dashes, but our method produces significantly better results.

Furthermore, Table 4 and the corresponding Fig. 4 show example protein name queries mapped to the UniProt reference set and the retrieved canonical names. Note that *none of the query names exist in the UniProt* reference set in the form provided as the query. Table 4 shows not only the syntactic variations

Table 4. UniProt sample queries and top-10 responses. The correct entities are indicated with a bold font and an asterisk. None of the queries have an exact string match in UniProt, and the lists include syntactically far correct responses.

S6K	PLCγ2	IKKϵ	H3
- **p70-S6K 1***	- **PLC-gamma-2***	- **IKK-epsilon***	- **Histone H3/a***
- p90-RSK 6	- PLC-gamma-1	- **IKKE***	- **Histone H3/o***
- **S6K1***	- **PLCG2***	- **I-kappa-B kinase epsilon***	- **Histone H3/m***
- **p70 S6KA***	- **Phospholipase C-gamma-2***	- **IkBKE***	- **Histone H3/b***
- S6K-beta	- Phospholipase C-gamma-1	- **IKBKE***	- **Histone H3/f***
- p70 S6KB	- PLC	- IKBE	- **HIST1H3C***
- 90 kDa ribosomal protein S6 kinase 6	- PLCG1	- IK1	- **Histone H3/k***
- 90 kDa ribosomal protein S6 kinase 5	- **Phosphoinositide phospholipase C-gamma-2***	- IK1	- **Histone H3/i***
- **52 kDa ribosomal protein S6 kinase***	- **PLC-IV***	- IKKG	- **HIST1H3G***
- RPS6KA6	- PLCB	- INKA1	- **Histone H3/d***

being captured by our method in the Top 10 responses, but the semantically equivalent names are included as well. These responses can have a significantly large string distance with the query name. e.g., (*S6K* $\longrightarrow$ *52 kDa ribosomal protein S6 kinase*), (*PLCγ2* $\longrightarrow$ *Phospholipase C-gamma-2*), (*IKKϵ* $\longrightarrow$ *I-kappa-B kinase epsilon*), and (*H3* $\longrightarrow$ *Histone H3/a*).

Figure 4 sheds more light to the embedding space and highlights the same four query names and the names corresponding to the correct entities in the UniProt reference set. As shown in this figure most of the correct responses (in blue) are clustered around the query name (in red).

The retrieval time of the baseline methods are in the order of a few minutes. NSEEN relies on the approximate nearest neighbors architecture and provides highly competitive retrieval performance in the order of seconds. The study reported on [2] for approximate nearest neighbors architectures applies to our method as well.

5   Discussion

In this paper, we proposed a general deep neural network based framework for entity normalization. We showed how to encode semantic information hidden in a reference set, and how to incorporate potential syntactic variations in the numeric embedding space via training-pair generation. In this process we showed how contrastive loss can be used with non-binary labels to capture uncertainty.

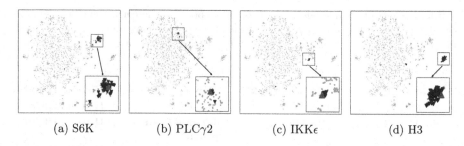

(a) S6K   (b) PLCγ2   (c) IKKε   (d) H3

Fig. 4. tSNE representation of the example UniPort query entities shown in Table 4. Queries are red triangle and correct responses are blue. A sample of a thousand names from the reference set is shown with light grey dots to represent the embedding space. The bottom right insets show a zoomed version of the correct names clustered around the query name. (Best viewed in color) (Color figure online)

We further introduced a dynamic hard negative sampling method to refine the embeddings. Finally, by transforming the traditional task of entity normalization to a standard k-nearest neighbors problem in a numerical space, we showed how to employ a scalable representation for fast retrievals that is applicable in real-world scenarios without the need of traditional entity blocking methods. By eliminating the need for blocking as a pre-processing step, we can consider matches that are syntactically different but semantically relevant, which is not easily achievable via traditional entity normalization methods.

In our preliminary analysis, we experimented with different selection methods in the k-nearest neighbors retrieval process such as a *top-k majority vote* schema, but did not find them significantly effective in our setting. We also experimented with different soft labeling methods to dynamically re-rank the results such as *soft re-labeling the k-nearest neighbors*, but did not see much improvements to the overall performance. While currently highly effective, our method could benefit from improving some of its components in future research. We are also considering combining our approach with other embedding and collective reasoning methods to gain further potential performance improvements.

Acknowledgments. This work was supported in part by DARPA Big Mechanism program under contract number W911NF-14-1-0364.

References

1. University of Southern California - Information Science Institute Entity Grounding System (2018). http://dna.isi.edu:7100/
2. Annoy (approximate nearest neighbors oh yeah) (2019). https://github.com/spotify/annoy
3. Apweiler, R., et al.: UniProt: the universal protein knowledgebase. Nucleic Acids Res. **32**, D115–D119 (2004)
4. Arighi, C., et al.: Bio-ID track overview. In: Proceedings of the BioCreative VI Workshop (2017)

5. Bachrach, Y., et al.: Speeding up the Xbox recommender system using a euclidean transformation for inner-product spaces. In: Proceedings of the 8th ACM Conference on Recommender systems (2014)
6. Białecki, A., Muir, R., Ingersoll, G.: Apache Lucene 4. In: SIGIR 2012 Workshop on Open Source Information Retrieval (2012)
7. Cheatham, M., Hitzler, P.: String similarity metrics for ontology alignment. In: Alani, H., et al. (eds.) ISWC 2013, Part II. LNCS, vol. 8219, pp. 294–309. Springer, Heidelberg (2013). https://doi.org/10.1007/978-3-642-41338-4_19
8. Chen, H., Perozzi, B., Hu, Y., Skiena, S.: HARP: hierarchical representation learning for networks (2018)
9. Christen, P.: Data Matching: Concepts and Techniques for Record Linkage, Entity Resolution, and Duplicate Detection. Springer, Heidelberg (2012). https://doi.org/10.1007/978-3-642-31164-2
10. Christen, P.: A survey of indexing techniques for scalable record linkage and deduplication. IEEE TKDE **24**(9), 1537–1555 (2012)
11. Cohen, W., Ravikumar, P., Fienberg, S.: A comparison of string metrics for matching names and records. In: KDD Workshop on Data Cleaning and Object Consolidation (2003)
12. Devlin, J., Chang, M.W., Lee, K., Toutanova, K.: Bert: pre-training of deep bidirectional transformers for language understanding. arXiv preprint arXiv:1810.04805 (2018)
13. Elmagarmid, A.K., Ipeirotis, P.G., Verykios, V.S.: Duplicate record detection: a survey. IEEE TKDE **19**(1), 1–16 (2007)
14. Getoor, L., Machanavajjhala, A.: Entity resolution: theory, practice & open challenges. Proc. VLDB Endow. **5**(12), 2018–2019 (2012)
15. Hadsell, R., Chopra, S., LeCun, Y.: Dimensionality reduction by learning an invariant mapping. In: 2006 IEEE Computer Society Conference on Computer Vision and Pattern Recognition (2006)
16. Hastings, J., et al.: ChEBI in 2016: improved services and an expanding collection of metabolites. Nucleic Acids Res. **44**, D1214–D1219 (2015)
17. Ebraheem, M., Thirumuruganathan, S., Joty, S., Ouzzani, M., Tang, N.: Distributed representations of tuples for entity resolution. Proc. VLDB Endow. **11**(11), 1454–1467 (2018)
18. Jurczyk, P., Lu, J.J., Xiong, L., Cragan, J.D., Correa, A.: FRIL: a tool for comparative record linkage. In: American Medical Informatics Association (AMIA) Annual Symposium Proceedings (2008)
19. Kang, N., Singh, B., Afzal, Z., van Mulligen, E.M., Kors, J.A.: Using rule-based natural language processing to improve disease normalization in biomedical text. JAMIA **20**(5), 876–881 (2012)
20. Kotnis, B., Nastase, V.: Analysis of the impact of negative sampling on link prediction in knowledge graphs. In: WSDM 1st Workshop on Knowledge Base Construction, Reasoning and Mining (KBCOM) (2017)
21. Koudas, N., Sarawagi, S., Srivastava, D.: Record linkage: similarity measures and algorithms. In: Proceedings of the 2006 ACM SIGMOD International Conference on Management of Data (2006)
22. Leaman, R., Islamaj Doğan, R., Lu, Z.: DNorm: disease name normalization with pairwise learning to rank. Bioinformatics **29**(22), 2909–2917 (2013)
23. Leaman, R., Lu, Z.: TaggerOne: joint named entity recognition and normalization with semi-Markov models. Bioinformatics **32**(18), 2839–2846 (2016)
24. Lee, J., et al.: BioBERT: pre-trained biomedical language representation model for biomedical text mining. arXiv preprint arXiv:1901.08746 (2019)

25. Mathew, J., Fakhraei, S., Ambite, J.L.: Biomedical named entity recognition via reference-set augmented bootstrapping. In: ICML Workshop on Computational Biology (2019)
26. Michelson, M., Knoblock, C.A.: Learning blocking schemes for record linkage. In: AAAI (2006)
27. Mikolov, T., Sutskever, I., Chen, K., Corrado, G.S., Dean, J.: Distributed representations of words and phrases and their compositionality. In: Advances in Neural Information Processing Systems (2013)
28. Mudgal, S., et al.: Deep learning for entity matching: a design space exploration. In: Proceedings of the 2018 International Conference on Management of Data (2018)
29. Naidan, B., Boytsov, L.: Non-metric space library manual. arXiv preprint arXiv:1508.05470 (2015)
30. Neculoiu, P., Versteegh, M., Rotaru, M.: Learning text similarity with siamese recurrent networks. In: Proceedings the 1st Workshop on Representation Learning for NLP (2016)
31. Papadakis, G., Svirsky, J., Gal, A., Palpanas, T.: Comparative analysis of approximate blocking techniques for entity resolution. Proc. VLDB Endow. 9(9), 684–695 (2016)
32. Pennington, J., Socher, R., Manning, C.: Glove: global vectors for word representation. In: Proceedings of the 2014 Conference on Empirical Methods in Natural Language Processing (EMNLP) (2014)
33. Peters, M.E., et al.: Deep contextualized word representations. In: Proceedings of NAACL (2018)
34. Ponomarenko, A., Avrelin, N., Naidan, B., Boytsov, L.: Comparative analysis of data structures for approximate nearest neighbor search. In: Data Analytics (2014)
35. Rastegari, M., Choi, J., Fakhraei, S., Hal, D., Davis, L.: Predictable dual-view hashing. In: International Conference on Machine Learning (ICML) (2013)
36. Shrivastava, A., Gupta, A., Girshick, R.: Training region-based object detectors with online hard example mining. In: Proceedings of the IEEE Conference on Computer Vision and Pattern Recognition (2016)
37. Taigman, Y., Yang, M., Ranzato, M., Wolf, L.: Deepface: closing the gap to human-level performance in face verification. In: Proceedings of the IEEE Conference on Computer Vision and Pattern Recognition (2014)
38. Yadav, V., Bethard, S.: A survey on recent advances in named entity recognition from deep learning models. In: Proceedings of the 27th International Conference on Computational Linguistics (2018)

Beyond Bag-of-Concepts: Vectors of Locally Aggregated Concepts

Maarten Grootendorst[1(✉)] and Joaquin Vanschoren[2]

[1] Jheronimus Academy of Data Science, 5211 DA 's-Hertogenbosch, The Netherlands
`maartengrootendorst@gmail.com`
[2] Eindhoven University of Technology, 5612 AZ Eindhoven, The Netherlands
`j.vanschoren@tue.nl`

Abstract. Bag-of-Concepts, a model that counts the frequency of clustered word embeddings (i.e., concepts) in a document, has demonstrated the feasibility of leveraging clustered word embeddings to create features for document representation. However, information is lost as the word embeddings themselves are not used in the resulting feature vector. This paper presents a novel text representation method, Vectors of Locally Aggregated Concepts (VLAC). Like Bag-of-Concepts, it clusters word embeddings for its feature generation. However, instead of counting the frequency of clustered word embeddings, VLAC takes each cluster's sum of residuals with respect to its centroid and concatenates those to create a feature vector. The resulting feature vectors contain more discriminative information than Bag-of-Concepts due to the additional inclusion of these first order statistics. The proposed method is tested on four different data sets for single-label classification and compared with several baselines, including TF-IDF and Bag-of-Concepts. Results indicate that when combining features of VLAC with TF-IDF significant improvements in performance were found regardless of which word embeddings were used.

Keywords: Bag of Concepts · Vector of Locally Aggregated Descriptors · Vectors of Locally Aggregated Concepts

1 Introduction

Methods for creating structure out of unstructured data have many applications, ranging from classifying images to creating spam-filters. As a typical form of unstructured data, textual documents benefit greatly from these methods as words can have multiple meanings, grammatical errors may occur and the way text is constructed differs from language to language. Arguably, one of the most popular methods for representing documents is Bag-of-Words, which scores the frequency of words in a document based on its corpus [28]. This results in a structured document representation despite the inherently messy nature of textual data. However, as corpora grow bigger and exceed tens of thousands of words, Bag-of-Words representations lose their interpretability.

Bag-of-Concepts was proposed as a solution to this problem [14]. Based on the corpus of a collection of documents, Bag-of-Concepts generates word clusters

© Springer Nature Switzerland AG 2020
U. Brefeld et al. (Eds.): ECML PKDD 2019, LNAI 11907, pp. 681–696, 2020.
https://doi.org/10.1007/978-3-030-46147-8_41

(i.e., concepts) from vector representations of words (i.e., word embeddings) and, similar to Bag-of-Words, counts the number of words in a document associated with each concept, hence the name Bag-of-Concepts.

Interestingly, Bag-of-Concepts shares many similarities with Bag-of-Visual-Words, a feature generation method used for image classification [27]. Much like Bag-of-Concepts, Bag-of-Visual-Words represents images by the occurrence count of its clustered features (i.e., descriptors). The main difference between these methods is that Bag-of-Concepts leverages word clusters whereas Bag-of-Visual-Words leverages image feature clusters.

Although Bag-of-Visual-Words shows promising results in image classification, it typically generates sparse features with high dimensionality [21]. Vector of Locally Aggregated Descriptors (VLAD) extends upon Bag-of-Visual-Words by including first order statistics into its feature vectors [7]. Compared to Bag-of-Visual-Words, VLAD allows for compact visual representations with high discriminative ability due to the inclusion of descriptors' locations in each cluster.

As the main difference between Bag-of-Visual-Words and Bag-of-Concepts is the type of clustered features that are used, it follows that VLAD could be generalized to the generation of textual features by leveraging word embeddings instead of image descriptors. This would result in a document representation with more discriminative ability than Bag-of-Concepts as it contains additional first order statistics in its feature vectors. The resulting method was named Vectors of Locally Aggregated Concepts (VLAC) after both VLAD and Bag-of-Concepts.

To the best of my knowledge, no research seems to exist concerning the application of VLAD for representing textual documents. Although creating structure out of unstructured has many applications, document classification, due to its popularity, was chosen as a proxy for measuring the quality of document representation. This study shows that VLAD offers a novel way to create features for document representation, resulting in better predictions for document classification.

2   Related Work

2.1   Bag-of-Words

Bag-of-Words counts the occurrences of words within a document in which each word count is considered a feature. A disadvantage of this method is that highly frequent words may dominate the feature space while rarer and more specific words may contain more information. In order to lessen the impact of those words and evaluate the importance of words in a document, one can use a weighting scheme named TF-IDF. It combines two statistics, namely term frequency (TF) multiplied by its inverse document frequency (IDF). Term frequency is the count of word t in a document d. Then, for each term t, inverse document frequency calculates how common t is across all documents D by taking the logarithm of the number of documents in a corpus N divided by the number of documents that contain t.

$$IDF(t, D) = \log \frac{N}{|\{d \in D : t \in d\}|} \tag{1}$$

Together, it takes the frequency of words in a document and calculates the inverse proportion of those words to the corpus [11,24].

2.2 Word Embeddings

Although TF-IDF succeeds in representing the occurrence and importance of words in a document, the context of these words is lost. Instead, in order to retain semantic similarity among words, one can map words to vectors of real numbers, named word embeddings [15].

Word2Vec is a popular tool for mapping words in a document to a vector representation. It combines multiple two-layer neural networks to construct embeddings, namely the Continuous Bag-of-Words (CBOW) and Skip-gram architectures [17]. In the CBOW architecture, the model predicts a target word given a set of surrounding context words. In contrast, the Skip-gram architecture tries to predict a set of context words given a target word. The hidden layer then represents the word vectors as the relationships between words and context are learned. See Fig. 1 for an overview of the architecture of Word2Vec.

The disadvantage of Word2Vec is that word embeddings are created locally within documents while disregarding the global representation of words across all documents. Models such as GloVe (Global Vectors for Word Representation), construct large co-occurrence counts (word × context) in order to learn the global representation of a word [20].

Typically, 300-dimensional word vectors are created as they have been shown to balance representational ability and the density of the resulting vectors [17,20].

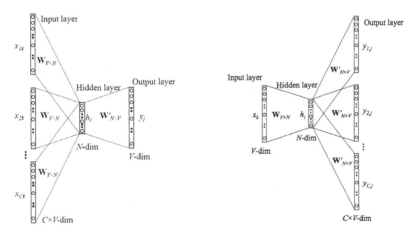

Fig. 1. CBOW architecture (left) versus Skip-gram architecture (right).

2.3   Bag-of-Concepts

When we want to represent documents instead of individual words, word embeddings can be averaged across all words in a document [3]. However, the resulting document vectors are difficult to interpret intuitively as they merely represent a point in a 300-dimensional space. In order to deal with this problem, Kim et al. [14] developed a model named Bag-of-Concepts. Based on a collection of documents, Bag-of-Concepts generates word clusters by applying spherical k-means to word embeddings. The resulting clusters typically contain words with similar meaning and are therefore referred to as concepts. Then, similar to Bag-of-Words, a document is represented as a bag of its concepts by counting the number of words in a document associated with each concept [14].

In order to lessen the impact of concepts that appear in most documents, a TF-IDF-like weighting scheme is applied in which all terms t are replaced by concept c, which is appropriately named CF-IDF. This allows the model to create document vectors that are interpretable, as each feature of a document represents the importance of a concept.

Bag-of-Concepts was found to be largely dependent on the number of concepts that were generated [14]. The authors showed that the classification accuracy of Bag-of-Concepts consistently increases with the number of concepts, but that this increase stabilizes around 200 concepts at which near-maximum performance is reached.

This method has shown to provide better document representation than Bag-of-Words and TF-IDF in a classification task to find the two most similar documents among triplets of documents [14]. However, in a classification task to predict the correct label for each document Bag-of-Concepts failed to outperform TF-IDF on two out of three data sets.

2.4   Vector of Locally Aggregated Descriptors (VLAD)

Before deep learning achieved state-of-the-art results in image classification, an approach called Bag-of-Visual-Words was often used for image classification [18]. This method is similar to Bag-of-Concepts as both cluster a collection of features of which the occurrence of these clusters is counted in each sample, thereby creating a vector for each sample containing the prevalence of clustered features. Specifically, Bag-of-Visual-Words clusters image features which are typically generated using feature extractor algorithms like SIFT or KAZE [18]. Then, it counts the occurrence of the clusters resulting in a vector of occurrence counts of local image features.

To further increase the representative ability of Bag-of-Visual-Words, first order statistics were additionally included in the resulting vectors thereby providing more information about the images. This method was named Vector of Locally Aggregated Descriptors (VLAD) and was shown to have superior performance compared to Bag-of-Visual-Words [2,9].

As illustrated in Fig. 2, VLAD extends Bag-of-Visual-Words by taking the residual of each image feature with respect to its assigned cluster center. Using

k-means each image feature x_i is assigned to a cluster with cluster center c_j, both having the same dimensionality D. N_j is equal to the number of image features in j and j ranges from 1 to k. Then, the sum of residuals of each image feature in a cluster is accumulated, resulting in k vectors for each image:

$$v_j = \sum_{i=1}^{N_j} x_i - c_j \tag{2}$$

k vectors are created containing the sum of residuals of each cluster and are then concatenated to create a single vector for each image:

$$v = \begin{bmatrix} \vdots \\ v_j \\ \vdots \end{bmatrix} \tag{3}$$

The resulting image vector is of size $k \times D$. Next, the concatenated vectors are typically first power normalized and then l2 normalized to reduce bursty visual elements [10]:

$$v = sign(v)\sqrt{|v|} \tag{4}$$

$$v = \frac{v}{\|v\|} \tag{5}$$

Several extensions to this model have been proposed to further improve its representative ability and classification performance. For example, intra-normalization has been suggested as a way to further reduce bursty image features. Instead of applying l2 normalization to the concatenated vector of the sum of residuals, it is suggested to l2 normalize the sum of residuals within each VLAD block, followed by l2 normalization of the entire vector. The effect of bursty features would then be localized to each cluster [2]. Other improvements have been suggested such as directly l2 normalizing each feature's residuals [7], adding aggregations of tensor products of the descriptors [23], and using VLAD as a layer in a convolutional neural network [1].

3   Vectors of Locally Aggregated Concepts (VLAC)

Interestingly, VLAD and Bag-of-Concepts both use clustered feature vectors as their basis for the generation of summarized features in the task of classification. This similarity suggests that VLAD could be extended to be used in the domain of natural language processing as words could be clustered instead of image features. Thus, instead of clustering descriptors, one can cluster word embeddings into concepts for the generation of features. The result is a feature generation model for textual documents inspired by VLAD and Bag-of-Concepts, namely Vectors of Locally Aggregated Concepts (VLAC).

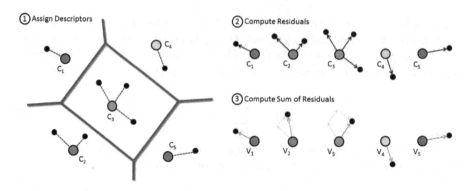

Fig. 2. Procedure of VLAD

As illustrated in Fig. 3, VLAC clusters word embeddings to create k concepts. Due to the typically high dimensionality of word embeddings (i.e., 300) spherical k-means is used to perform the clustering as applying euclidean distance will result in little difference in the distances between samples. Similar to the original VLAD approach, let w_i be a word embedding of size D assigned to cluster center c_k. Then, for each word in a document, VLAC computes the element-wise sum of residuals of each word embedding to its assigned cluster center.

This results in k feature vectors, one for each concept, and all of size D. All feature vectors are then concatenated, power normalized, and finally, l2 normalization is applied as with the original VLAD approach. If 10 concepts were to be created out of word embeddings of size 300 then the resulting document vector would contain 10×300 values.

The resulting feature vectors contain more discriminative information than Bag-of-Concepts since the sum of residuals gives information with regard to the relative location of the word embeddings in the clusters. Therefore, it is expected that VLAC will outperform Bag-of-Concepts (with CF-IDF).

4   Experiments

In order to test the quality of the generated features by VLAC, two single-label classification experiments were performed using several baselines. VLAC is dependent on the quality of word embeddings and the number of concepts generated. Therefore, in the first experiment, several implementations of VLAC were tested against each other at different numbers of concepts. This experiment served as a way to explore how VLAC is affected by the number of concepts generated and the word embeddings that were used.

Then, to validate VLAC across different discriminative thresholds a second experiment was executed in which VLAC was compared against several baselines using Receiver Operating Characteristic (ROC) curves and compared on their Area Under the Curve (AUC) scores. ROC curves were not used in experiment 1 since they cannot show the effect of generated concepts on performance.

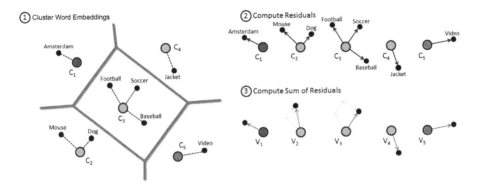

Fig. 3. Procedure of VLAC

Finally, in all experiments, features generated by VLAC were added to TF-IDF features. Since TF-IDF cannot generate more features, adding VLAC features to TF-IDF will help in understanding if VLAC adds additional information not already contained within features of TF-IDF. Although more interaction is possible by creating a larger feature matrix, any improvement in performance could only be attributed to this higher dimensionality containing information not previously seen in TF-IDF.

4.1 Experimental Setup

Data. Four data sets were chosen on which the effectiveness of the proposed method was tested. Three of these (20 Newsgroups, Reuters R8, and WebKB) were included because they are typically used in document classification research and therefore allow for comparisons to be made with prior work (e.g. [6,16, 26]). As these three data sets are all written in English, an additional data set containing Portuguese documents was included as a way to further generalize the evaluation. Stemming and stop word removal were applied to all data sets. All data sets were retrieved from [5]. See Tables 1 and 2 for more information.

Table 1. An overview of the data sets used in this study.

	Reuters R8	20 Newsgroups	WebKB	Cade12
Number of documents	7674	18821	4199	40983
Number of classes	8	20	4	12
Average number of words per document	64.5	141.1	133.4	117.4
Vocabulary size	17387	70213	7770	193997
Total number of words	495226	2654770	560015	4813116

Table 2. Number of samples in each class per data set.

Reuters R8		20 Newsgroups		WebKB		Cade12	
Classes	Samples	Classes	Samples	Classes	Samples	Classes	Samples
earn	3923	rec.sport.hockey	999	student	1641	01–servicos	8473
acq	2292	soc.religion.christian	996	faculty	1124	02–sociedade	7363
crude	374	rec.motorcycles	996	course	930	03–lazer	5590
trade	326	rec.sport.baseball	994	project	504	04–informatica	4519
money-fx	293	sci.crypt	991			05–saude	3171
interest	271	sci.med	990			06–educacao	2856
ship	144	rec.autos	989			07–internet	2381
grain	51	sci.space	987			08–cultura	2137
		comp.windows.x	985			09–esportes	1907
		sci.electronics	984			10–noticias	1082
		comp.sys.ibm.pc.hardware	982			11–ciencias	879
		misc.forsale	975			12–compras-online	625
		comp.graphics	973				
		comp.os.ms-windows.misc	966				
		comp.sys.mac.hardware	963				
		talk.politics.mideast	940				
		talk.politics.guns	909				
		alt.atheism	799				
		talk.politics.misc	775				
		talk.religion.misc	628				

Balanced Accuracy. Although the quality of classification is typically measured by the accuracy of the prediction model, it suffers from over representing the performance on larger classes [25]. Due to the imbalance of the data sets (see Table 2) a different measure for validation was used, namely balanced accuracy [4]:

$$Balanced\,Accuracy = \frac{\sum_{i=1}^{n} \frac{tp_i}{tp_i+fp_i}}{n} \qquad (6)$$

With n classes, where tp_i is the true positive for class i in n, and fp_i is the false positive for class i in n. For multi-class classification, balanced accuracy can be interpreted as the macro-average of recall scores per class [13,19] which has the property of allowing the performance of all classes to be weighted equally.

Baselines. Bag-of-Words, TF-IDF, Bag-of-Concepts (with CF-IDF), and averaged word embeddings (with Word2Vec embeddings) served as baselines in this study. Bag-of-Words, TF-IDF, and averaged word embeddings are typically used to test novel techniques against, whereas Bag-of-Concepts was chosen due to the methodological similarities it shares with VLAC. For the implementation of Bag-of-Concepts, initial experiments were performed to find a balance between the number of concepts and computational efficiency. At 500 concepts the performance of Bag-of-Concepts typically stabilizes. Moreover, previous research has found the classification accuracy of Bag-of-Concepts to stabilize around 200 concepts and that the classification accuracy consistently increases with the number of concepts generated [14]. Ultimately, Bag-of-Concepts was set at 500 concepts in order to maximize its performance.

4.2   Experiment 1

The performance of VLAC, based on balanced accuracy, was analyzed for each data set with the number of concepts systematically increasing from 1 to 30. The maximum number of concepts was set at 30 as computing more concepts would be computationally too demanding for this experiment.

Bag-of-Words, TF-IDF and averaged word embeddings were used as baselines. Kim et al. [14] demonstrated that Bag-of-Concepts, compared to TF-IDF, would need at least 100 concepts for it to reach a competitive performance. Therefore, Bag-of-Concepts was excluded from this experiment as it would not be fair to compare Bag-of-Concepts to VLAC at merely 30 concepts.

Four different types of word embeddings were used for VLAC on each data set. Word2Vec and GloVe embeddings were generated by training the model on the data sets themselves, henceforth referred to as self-trained embeddings. Moreover, pre-trained embeddings for Word2Vec and GloVe were additionally used as they had been trained on larger data sets and therefore might have better representative ability. Word2Vec pre-trained embeddings were trained on the Google News data set and contain vectors for 3 million English words.[1] GloVe pre-trained embeddings were trained on the Common Crawl data set and contain vectors for 1.9 million English words.[2] Pre-trained embeddings for Cade12 were trained on 17 different Portuguese corpora.[3] To make a comparison across VLAC implementations possible, all word embeddings were of size 300.

Linear Support Vector Machines (Linear SVM) have been shown to do well on single-label text classification tasks [12] and are used in this experiment as classifiers on top of the feature generation methods. Moreover, 10-fold cross-validation was applied in each prediction instance in order to decrease the chance of overfitting on the data and creating biased results.

Results. Several one-sided, one-sample Wilcoxon signed rank tests were applied to observe which VLAC versions, on average across all 30 concepts, may outperform TF-IDF. The results are shown in Table 3 and indicate that VLAC typically does not outperform TF-IDF. However, looking at the best scores of each model in Table 3 and the accuracy curves in Fig. 4, the results suggest that, around 30 concepts, VLAC can outperform TF-IDF on Reuters R8, WebKB and Cade12 depending on the word embeddings that were used.

In contrast, the combined features of TF-IDF and VLAC generally outperformed TF-IDF on Reuters R8, WebKB and Cade12 (see Table 3). This suggests

---

[1] Retrieved from https://code.google.com/archive/p/word2vec/.
[2] Retrieved from https://nlp.stanford.edu/projects/glove/.
[3] Retrieved from http://nilc.icmc.usp.br/embeddings.

that VLAC features contain information not seen in TF-IDF features. Interestingly, Fig. 5 shows that the number of concepts seem to have little influence on performance, thereby indicating that a few concepts would be sufficient in generating additional features when combining VLAC with TF-IDF.

From Fig. 4 one can observe that VLAC's balanced accuracy scores are highest at 30 concepts and are likely to improve at a higher number of concepts. To evaluate VLAC at its highest performance (i.e., 30 concepts), several one-sided, two-samples Wilcoxon signed rank tests were used to compare VLAC against TF-IDF. For this, 20-fold cross-validation was applied to TF-IDF and all VLAC versions to generate 20 accuracy scores for each model. The same folds for each algorithm were created. Folds were then paired across algorithms to test for the possible difference in performance.

Although 10 folds are typically used in cross-validation, a choice was made for 20 folds in order to create a sufficiently sized sample size to increase the statistical power. The results of each fold were averaged across all data sets for each method. Thus, 20 averaged balanced accuracy scores were created for each model and allowed for the one-sided, two-samples Wilcoxon signed rank tests.

VLAC did not significantly outperform TF-IDF across all four data sets ($V = 6$, $p = .821$). However, combining features of VLAC with TF-IDF led to a significant improvement over TF-IDF ($V = 207$, $p < .001$), which was found for both self-trained embeddings ($V = 198$, $p < .001$) and for pre-trained embeddings ($V = 199$, $p < .001$). This confirms the idea that VLAC features contain information not seen in TF-IDF features.

Table 3. Average and best performance in experiment 1 across different implementations of VLAC, where *self* relates to embeddings trained on the data itself and *pre* relates to pre-trained embeddings. Underlined values are the highest results in each block, whereas bold values are the best results compared to all other methods for a single data set. One-sided, one-sample Wilcoxon signed rank tests were executed to compare all VLAC versions against TF-IDF based on their average scores. ** $p < 0.001$; * $p < 0.05$

	Reuters R8		20 Newsgroups		WebKB		Cade12	
	Average	Best	Average	Best	Average	Best	Average	Best
VLAC (Self: W2V)	91.48	92.57	81.95	84.20	<u>89.92</u>**	<u>90.83</u>**	41.69	44.85
VLAC (Pre: W2V)	92.01*	92.95	82.42	84.44	88.13	89.39	<u>46.67</u>	<u>48.13</u>
VLAC (Self: GloVe)	91.74	92.53	83.08	87.43	87.99	89.58	42.19	45.65
VLAC (Pre: GloVe)	<u>92.10</u>	<u>93.11</u>	<u>85.27</u>	<u>87.50</u>	88.40	89.97	45.10	46.36
Averaged W2V	-	89.81	-	75.21	-	87.23	-	36.02
Bag-of-Words	-	90.96	-	88.11	-	85.41	-	43.22
TF-IDF	-	<u>91.97</u>	-	<u>90.44</u>	-	<u>89.37</u>	-	<u>47.02</u>
TF-IDF + VLAC (Self: W2V)	93.22**	93.80	90.00	90.20	**90.41****	**90.74**	48.36**	48.65
TF-IDF + VLAC (Pre: W2V)	**93.71****	**94.39**	89.57	89.81	89.96**	90.43	**49.08****	**49.37**
TF-IDF + VLAC (Self: GloVe)	92.96**	93.33	89.60	89.88	89.71**	90.24	46.56	47.07
TF-IDF + VLAC (Pre: GloVe)	93.30**	93.83	**90.04**	**90.38**	90.01**	90.47	48.11**	48.80

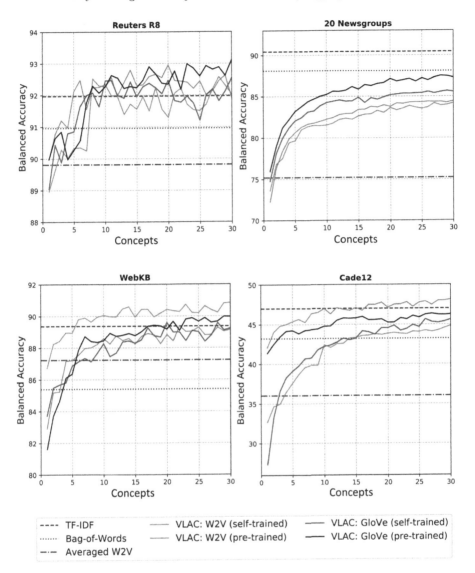

Fig. 4. Results of different word embeddings used with VLAC compared to TF-IDF, Bag-of-Words, and averaged Word2Vec embeddings.

Finally, the results indicate that pre-trained word embeddings used for VLAC performed significantly better than self-trained word embeddings ($V = 159$, $p = .022$). However, no differences were found between the performance of pre-trained and self-trained word embeddings when combining features of VLAC with TF-IDF ($V = 113$, $p = .392$).

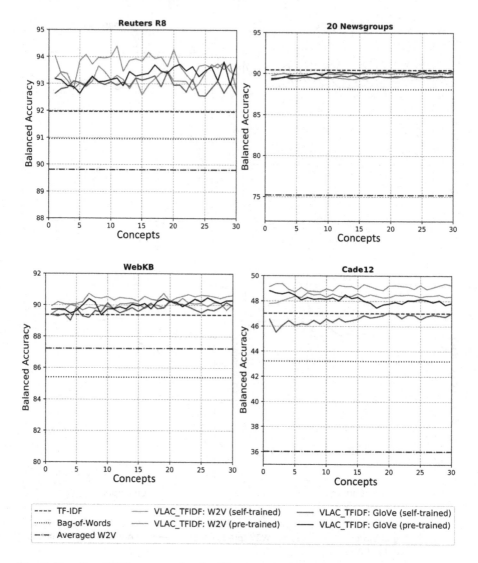

Fig. 5. Results of different word embeddings used when combining features of VLAC with those of TF-IDF compared to TF-IDF, Bag-of-Words, and averaged Word2Vec embeddings.

4.3 Experiment 2

In this experiment, the performance of all models in this study was analyzed across different discriminative thresholds to further validate VLAC. ROC curves were used to analyze the performance of VLAC across different discriminative thresholds. Since balanced accuracy adopts a macro-averaging approach, the scores in this experiment were also macro-averaged.

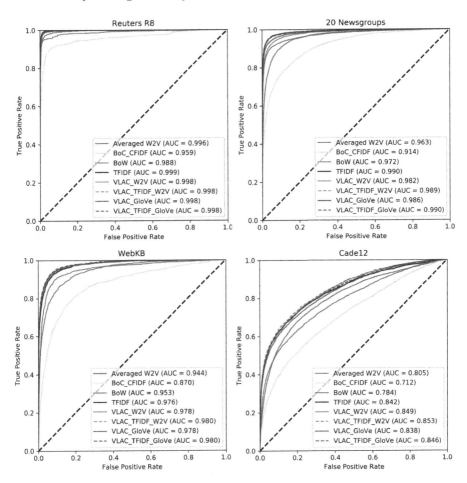

Fig. 6. ROC with macro-averaged AUC scores of eight different models across four data sets.

For the implementation of VLAC, pre-trained word embeddings were used as they typically outperformed self-trained word embeddings. Bag-of-Words, TF-IDF, averaged Word2Vec embeddings, and Bag-of-Concepts (with CF-IDF and at 500 concepts) were included as baselines. Since the features of averaged word embeddings, Bag-of-Words, and TF-IDF are out-of-the-box maximized, all VLAC versions were set at 30 concepts to similarly maximize its number of features.

Results. From Fig. 6 one can observe that pre-trained VLAC versions outperformed Bag-of-Words, Bag-of-Concepts, and averaged Word2Vec embeddings on all data sets based on their respective AUC scores. Seeing as the curves in Fig. 6 behave similarly across models, one can safely assume that the AUC scores are representative of the models performance. Furthermore, the results indicate that VLAC by itself can outperform TF-IDF but requires experimentation to find the optimum set of parameters (number of concepts versus the type of word embeddings). However, when combining features from VLAC with those of TF-IDF, the resulting AUC scores are similar to TF-IDF and higher on the Cade12 and WebKB datasets.

It is interesting to note that Bag-of-Concepts consistently, across all data sets, performs worst out of all methods. Although Kim et al. [14] demonstrated that Bag-of-Concepts might be able to outperform TF-IDF using a Support Vector Machine, they did not specify which kernel was used in their implementation. In this study a linear kernel was adopted. The differences between results might be due to the kernel that was used in the implementation of the Support Vector Machines. Although it was expected that VLAC would outperform Bag-of-Concepts, such a large difference between Bag-of-Concepts and all other models was not anticipated. Since Kim et al. [14] demonstrated that Bag-of-Concepts' classification accuracy increases with the number of concepts generated, one can conclude that Bag-of-Concepts is not suited for single-label classification up to 500 concepts.

For VLAC, it is not clear why there is such a large gap in performance between 20 Newsgroups and all other data sets. It could be attributed to many differences between data sets such as vocabulary size, document size, number of sentences per document, and even writing style. With so many differences between data sets it is hard to pin point the exact reason for the differences in performance. Thus, it is hard to pin point the exact reason for these differences.

However, for both 20 Newsgroups and Cade12, which are relatively large data sets compared to the others, the performances do not seem to stabilize at 30 concepts (see Fig. 4). This suggests that larger documents typically require larger number of concepts in order to maximize its performance. Future research could focus on studying the effects of document size on classification accuracy.

5   Conclusion

This study presents a novel algorithm for the generation of textual features, namely Vectors of Locally Aggregated Concepts (VLAC). In two experiments the performance of VLAC was tested against several baselines including averaged Word2Vec word embeddings, Bag-of-Words, TF-IDF and Bag-of-Concepts (with CF-IDF). On average, VLAC was shown to outperform all baselines when its features were combined with those of TF-IDF regardless of which word embeddings were used.

Future work may focus on two main disadvantages of using word embeddings generated by Word2Vec and GloVe. First, these models cannot handle out-of-vocabulary words. Instead, one can use word embeddings models, such as FastText, to additionally create character-level n-gram word embeddings which can be combined to construct out-of-vocabulary words. Second, word embeddings generated by Word2Vec and GloVe are the same for each word regardless of its context. Tools such as Embeddings from Language Models (ELMo) [22] and Bidirectional Encoder Representations from Transformers (BERT) [8] create, for a single word, different word embeddings if that word can be used in different contexts. Using contextual word embeddings will allow clusters to be made with better representational ability.

This study has made a first step in demonstrating the feasibility of a novel method for single-label document classification. Although several improvements to this model have been suggested, the results demonstrate that VLAC can reach superior performance in document classification tasks compared to several strong baselines. While this paper has focused on classification, many other tasks, such as information retrieval and document clustering tasks, could potentially be solved by VLAC.[4]

References

1. Arandjelovic, R., Gronat, P., Torii, A., Pajdla, T., Sivic, J.: NetVLAD: CNN architecture for weakly supervised place recognition. In: Proceedings of the IEEE Conference on Computer Vision and Pattern Recognition, pp. 5297–5307 (2016)
2. Arandjelovic, R., Zisserman, A.: All about VLAD. In: Proceedings of the IEEE Conference on Computer Vision and Pattern Recognition, pp. 1578–1585 (2013)
3. Arora, S., Liang, Y., Ma, T.: A simple but tough-to-beat baseline for sentence embeddings. In: International Conference for Learning Representations (2017)
4. Brodersen, K.H., Ong, C.S., Stephan, K.E., Buhmann, J.M.: The balanced accuracy and its posterior distribution. In: Proceedings of the 20th International Conference on Pattern Recognition, pp. 3121–3124. IEEE (2010)
5. Cardoso-Cachopo, A.: Improving methods for single-label text categorization. Ph.D thesis, Instituto Superior Tecnico, Universidade Tecnica de Lisboa (2007)
6. Dai, A.M., Le, Q.V.: Semi-supervised sequence learning. In: Advances in Neural Information Processing Systems, pp. 3079–3087 (2015)
7. Delhumeau, J., Gosselin, P.H., Jégou, H., Pérez, P.: Revisiting the VLAD image representation. In: Proceedings of the 21st International Conference on Multimedia, pp. 653–656. ACM (2013)
8. Devlin, J., Chang, M.W., Lee, K., Toutanova, K.: Bert: pre-training of deep bidirectional transformers for language understanding. arXiv preprint arXiv:1810.04805 (2018)
9. Jegou, H., Douze, M., Schmid, C., Pérez, P.: Aggregating local descriptors into a compact image representation. In: Computer Vision and Pattern Recognition, pp. 3304–3311. IEEE (2010)
10. Jegou, H., Perronnin, F., Douze, M., Sánchez, J., Perez, P., Schmid, C.: Aggregating local image descriptors into compact codes. Trans. Pattern Anal. Mach. Intell. 34(9), 1704–1716 (2012)
11. Joachims, T.: A probabilistic analysis of the Rocchio algorithm with TFIDF for text categorization. In: International Conference on Machine Learning, pp. 143–151 (1996)

---

[4] Code and results of this study can be found at https://github.com/MaartenGr/VLAC.

12. Joachims, T.: Text categorization with support vector machines: learning with many relevant features. In: Nédellec, C., Rouveirol, C. (eds.) ECML 1998. LNCS, vol. 1398, pp. 137–142. Springer, Heidelberg (1998). https://doi.org/10.1007/BFb0026683
13. Kelleher, J.D., Mac Namee, B., D'Arcy, A.: Fundamentals of Machine Learning for Predictive Data Analytics: Algorithms, Worked Examples, and Case Studies. MIT Press, Cambridge (2015)
14. Kim, H.K., Kim, H., Cho, S.: Bag-of-concepts: comprehending document representation through clustering words in distributed representation. Neurocomputing **266**, 336–352 (2017)
15. Maas, A.L., Daly, R.E., Pham, P.T., Huang, D., Ng, A.Y., Potts, C.: Learning word vectors for sentiment analysis. In: Proceedings of the 49th Annual Meeting of the Association for Computational Linguistics: Human Language Technologies, vol. 1, pp. 142–150 (2011)
16. McCallum, A., Nigam, K., et al.: A comparison of event models for Naive Bayes text classification. In: AAAI-98 Workshop on Learning for Text Categorization, vol. 752, pp. 41–48. Citeseer (1998)
17. Mikolov, T., Sutskever, I., Chen, K., Corrado, G.S., Dean, J.: Distributed representations of words and phrases and their compositionality. In: Advances in Neural Information Processing Systems, pp. 3111–3119 (2013)
18. Nowak, E., Jurie, F., Triggs, B.: Sampling strategies for bag-of-features image classification. In: Leonardis, A., Bischof, H., Pinz, A. (eds.) ECCV 2006. LNCS, vol. 3954, pp. 490–503. Springer, Heidelberg (2006). https://doi.org/10.1007/11744085_38
19. Pedregosa, F., et al.: Scikit-learn: Machine learning in Python. J. Mach. Learn. Res. **12**, 2825–2830 (2011)
20. Pennington, J., Socher, R., Manning, C.: Glove: global vectors for word representation. In: Proceedings of the 2014 Conference on Empirical Methods in Natural Language Processing, pp. 1532–1543 (2014)
21. Perronnin, F., Sánchez, J., Mensink, T.: Improving the Fisher Kernel for large-scale image classification. In: Daniilidis, K., Maragos, P., Paragios, N. (eds.) ECCV 2010. LNCS, vol. 6314, pp. 143–156. Springer, Heidelberg (2010). https://doi.org/10.1007/978-3-642-15561-1_11
22. Peters, M.E., et al.: Deep contextualized word representations. arXiv preprint arXiv:1802.05365 (2018)
23. Picard, D., Gosselin, P.H.: Improving image similarity with vectors of locally aggregated tensors. In: International Conference on Image Processing, pp. 669–672. IEEE (2011)
24. Ramos, J., et al.: Using TF-IDF to determine word relevance in document queries. In: Proceedings of the First Instructional Conference on Machine Learning, vol. 242, pp. 133–142 (2003)
25. Ramyachitra, D., Manikandan, P.: Imbalanced dataset classification and solutions: a review. Int. J. Comput. Bus. Res. **5**(4), 1–29 (2014)
26. Wallach, H.M.: Topic modeling: beyond bag-of-words. In: Proceedings of the 23rd International Conference on Machine Learning, pp. 977–984. ACM (2006)
27. Yang, J., Jiang, Y.G., Hauptmann, A.G., Ngo, C.W.: Evaluating bag-of-visual-words representations in scene classification. In: Proceedings of the International Workshop on Workshop on Multimedia Information Retrieval, pp. 197–206. ACM (2007)
28. Zhang, Y., Jin, R., Zhou, Z.H.: Understanding bag-of-words model: a statistical framework. Int. J. Mach. Learn. and Cybern. **1**(1–4), 43–52 (2010)

A Semi-discriminative Approach for Sub-sentence Level Topic Classification on a Small Dataset

Cornelia Ferner$^{(\boxtimes)}$ ⓘ and Stefan Wegenkittl ⓘ

Salzburg University of Applied Sciences, Urstein Sued 1, 5412 Puch, Salzburg, Austria
{cornelia.ferner,stefan.wegenkittl}@fh-salzburg.ac.at

Abstract. This paper aims at identifying sequences of words related to specific product components in online product reviews. A reliable baseline performance for this topic classification problem is given by a Max Entropy classifier which assumes independence over subsequent topics. However, the reviews exhibit an inherent structure on the document level allowing to frame the task as sequence classification problem. Since more flexible models from the class of Conditional Random Fields were not competitive because of the limited amount of training data available, we propose using a Hidden Markov Model instead and decouple the training of transition and emission probabilities. The discriminating power of the Max Entropy approach is used for the latter. Besides outperforming both standalone methods as well as more generic models such as linear-chain Conditional Random Fields, the combined classifier is able to assign topics on sub-sentence level although labeling in the training data is only available on sentence level.

Keywords: Small data · Topic classification · Hidden Markov Model

1 Introduction

Product comparison websites provide detailed product reviews (further on referred to as "expert" reviews) that usually differ from popular webshops' user reviews in length, quality and focus. A more concise representation of such expert reviews can be obtained for instance by automated text summarization or aspect-based sentiment analysis. A required subtask is to identify topics discussed in the reviews. The specific task is to assign a set of predefined topics to the sections of laptop reviews, where topics might be product components (e.g. *display, keyboard, performance*) or review sections (e.g. *introduction, verdict*).

A common approach to solve this task is to use a Max Entropy (MaxEnt) classifier which has been proven useful in a series of language classification tasks such as sentiment analysis [12]. However, the expert reviews exhibit some high-level structure on document level such as treating each topic one after another, without changing back and forth, or starting with an introduction and ending with a verdict. In order to exploit the reviews' structure, the task of assigning

© Springer Nature Switzerland AG 2020
U. Brefeld et al. (Eds.): ECML PKDD 2019, LNAI 11907, pp. 697–710, 2020.
https://doi.org/10.1007/978-3-030-46147-8_42

topics is defined as sequence classification task in this paper. This differs from what is known as document classification, as more than one topic per document is assigned. It also differs from unsupervised topic modeling, as the topics of interest are predefined in a labeled dataset with a label assigned to each sentence.

As the MaxEnt is trained to assign one label per sentence, it has no "memory" to recall decisions on previous sentences in the review. Thus, a sequence model such as the Hidden Markov Model (HMM) would be beneficial. An HMM can capture the reviews' inherent topic patterns by assigning labels at the word-level where topic changes are infrequent. This allows for a more fine-grained labeling even at sub-sentence-level.

The drawback of the HMM is its generative nature. A generative classifier maximizes the joint probabilities $P(w, s) = P(s) P(w \mid s)$ over the observed input words w and the state labels s. Given label s, the probabilities over the input features $P(w \mid s)$ need to be generated. Discriminative models such as MaxEnt directly train the conditional probability $P(s \mid w)$ without the need for modeling $P(w)$ which is considered given in the classification task. The question now arises if it is possible to have a sequence model where the relation between states and observations are modeled by a MaxEnt classifier.

We show that the proposed method of combining the benefits of the HMM with the discriminative power of a MaxEnt classifier successfully solves the sequence classification problem: After a trained MaxEnt classifier has learned to maximally separate the topics' probability distributions, we transform the MaxEnt based weights into HMM emission probabilities. Applying this method to the laptop review dataset yields superior performance to the standalone models and a more general discriminative sequence model. The combination of MaxEnt and HMM has the additional advantage of assigning topics at word-level, thus allowing for topic changes within sentence boundaries, although the classifier was trained on sentence-level only. For simplicity, we refer to this combined method as ME+HMM in the following.

2   Related Work

The idea of having a discriminative estimator in a sequence model is not new. McCallum et al. [9] proposed the Maximum Entropy Markov Model (MEMM) and eventually the more general Conditional Random Field (CRF) [5]. HMM and the linear-chain CRF form a so called discriminative-generative pair, as do Naive Bayes and logistic regression (MaxEnt) [22]. While, in principle, each classifier of a discriminative-generative pair can be used to solve the same problem, their training procedures differ concerning the optimality criteria. The generative model estimates probabilities based on the feature frequency in the training data. The discriminative model directly optimizes the conditional probabilities. For sufficiently large datasets, Ng et al. [11] provide evidence that the discriminative model produces a lower asymptotic error in classification tasks. The superiority of MaxEnt over Naive Bayes for text classification tasks is already well established [4] and CRFs have been shown to outperform HMMs in tasks such as chunking [20], table extraction [16] or information extraction [14]. Both shared tasks of the 2015 [1] and 2016 [21] workshop on noisy user-generated text were focused on Named Entity Recognition (NER) and featured successful submissions based on CRFs. Why bother returning to HMMs?

The differences between HMM, MEMM, CRF and our ME+HMM are subtle. Given the review document as a sequence of observed words $W = (w_1, \ldots, w_n)$ and a sequence of hidden states $S = (s_1, \ldots, s_n)$, all models aim at finding the optimal sequence S^* by maximizing one of the following probabilities:

$$\text{HMM:} \quad P(S, W) = \prod_{t=1}^{n} P(s_t \mid s_{t-1}) P(w_t \mid s_t) \tag{1}$$

$$\text{MEMM:} \quad P(S \mid W) = \prod_{t=1}^{n} P(s_t \mid s_{t-1}, w_t) = \\ \prod_{t=1}^{n} \frac{1}{Z_{s_{t-1}, w_t}} \exp\left(\sum_i \lambda_i f_i(s_t, s_{t-1}, w_t)\right) \tag{2}$$

$$\text{CRF:} \quad P(S \mid W) = \\ \frac{1}{Z_W} \prod_{t=1}^{n} \exp\left(\sum_i \lambda_i f_i(s_t, s_{t-1}, W)\right) \tag{3}$$

In (2) and (3), λ_i represent learned weights for features f_i that are computed from a combination of words and states. While the HMM in (1) estimates the joint probabilities of hidden states and input words, the MEMM in (2) estimates S conditioned on the input W. Instead of modeling transition and emission probability distributions as in (1), a MEMM models the probability of the current state s_t based on the previous state s_{t-1} and the current observation w_t. The normalization is done per state, distributing the probability "mass" at each state among the succeeding states. This causes the label bias problem, a bias towards states with fewer successors [5]. Linear-chain CRFs as in (3), in contrast, model the joint probability of the entire state sequence given the observed sequence. The normalization term is then a sum over all possible state sequences [22].

The proposed ME+HMM is still a generative model, with the frequency based estimation of emissions replaced by a conditional estimate provided by the MaxEnt classifier. Thus, the task-related superiority of the discriminative *MaxEnt* can be transferred to the HMM[1]. Even if the MaxEnt classifier is trained on sentence-level, the ME+HMM can assign labels on word-level which allows for a higher granularity.

The CRF is the most general of the presented approaches and is usually applied for tasks where many features are needed. Manual feature engineering is

---

[1] This is why we call it a "semi-discriminative approach".

required, leading to highly complex models and requiring large datasets. Inducing the most meaningful features is then an additional computational effort with CRFs [8]. The comparison with CRFs using a standard set of features similar to ME+HMM thus stands to reason. Word emission and state transition probabilities in a CRF are optimized simultaneously, but separately in our ME+HMM model. Alternative approaches such as windowed neural networks, recurrent neural networks or attention models have not been considered due to the limited size of the training data in terms of numbers of full review documents. Besides, neural network models such as seq2seq have only been applied on much shorter sequences of text (e.g. 20 newsgroups articles) and assign one topic per review [2].

3   Data

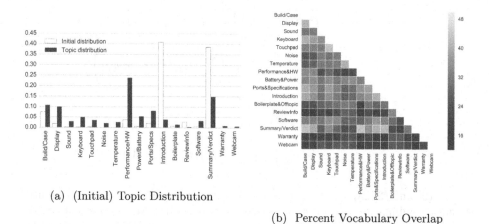

(a) (Initial) Topic Distribution

(b) Percent Vocabulary Overlap

Fig. 1. Dataset analysis. (a) The relative distribution on sentence-level of the seventeen review topics and the topics' likeliness to be the first in a review. (b) The vocabulary overlap between all topics measured in per cent. The diagonal (topic-topic) comparison is 100%. The average PVO is 33.22%.

The performance of the ME+HMM model is assessed on a dataset of expert reviews on laptops collected from several product testing websites[2]. The full dataset contains 3076 reviews manually annotated on sentence-level with one out of 17 predefined target topics. Not all topics are laptop related, some refer to specific review sections. Figure 1a lists the 17 topics and provides a detailed overview of the topics' (initial) distribution. The smallest topic set is *review info* (review metadata) with 887 sentences and the largest is *performance/hw* with 57819 sentences, which accounts for almost 25% of available data. Topics vital for a laptop rating are discussed regularly throughout the reviews (e.g. *performance/hw*), while topic *webcam* for instance only occurs if a laptop possesses this

---

[2] The dataset is available at https://github.com/factai/corpus-laptop-topic.

component. Nonetheless, these minor topics are interesting aspects to analyze. Note that some topics never start a review at all, while about 80% of reviews either start with an *introduction* or a *summary*. This suggests that the label *summary* might be ambiguous and not easily separable from the *introduction*.

The laptop dataset is different from well-known benchmarking datasets. Each review is available as one file to exploit the sequence information of the topics. Moreover, the expert reviews are much longer and more detailed than user reviews: The average review length in the laptop dataset is 78 sentences. Concerning the granularity, classical benchmarking datasets for topic classification provide only one topic per document. Topics for each sentence are provided in datasets designed for aspect-based sentiment analysis. However, Pontiki et al. [18], for instance, do not provide full documents, meaning that the sentence sequence is not reproducible[3]. While full documents are available in [17], the reviews in this dataset consist of typically up to fifteen sentences only and do not exhibit a latent topic structure.

3.1   Topic Separability

As classification accuracy correlates with class separability, percent vocabulary overlap (PVO) is used to measure the amount of vocabulary terms shared by two topics [10]. T_i denotes the set of terms occurring in topic S_i:

$$PVO\left(S_1, S_2\right) = \frac{\mid T_1 \cap T_2 \mid}{\mid T_1 \cup T_2 \mid} \cdot 100 \tag{4}$$

Figure 1b suggests that the topics *webcam*, *warranty* and *review info* use a more distinct vocabulary, whereas the non-laptop topics (e.g. *summary*) are not as well separable. Given the considerable overlap between topics, the frequency-based estimation of emission probabilities in a standard HMM is not a good choice.

The ability of the MaxEnt classifier to optimize the discrimination between classes can be exploited for the HMM. Table 1 gives an overview of the ten highest weighted words in four exemplary topics as learned from a MaxEnt classifier. Even for the seemingly similar topics *sound* and *noise*, these high scoring words do not overlap. The same is true for a linear-chain CRF. The discriminative models MaxEnt and CRF learn to select significant features to separate the topics. Some variance between the two models is only observed with the topic *summary*, as the CRF also ranks two specific product names ("ideapad", "aspire") high. This analysis suggests that the MaxEnt weights could improve the performance of a standard HMM.

---

[3] The sentence IDs provided in [18] are neither consecutive nor contiguous.

Table 1. Ten highest scoring terms in four exemplary topics when based on MaxEnt or CRF weights. [*] BOS denotes the beginning of the sequence in the CRF.

MaxEnt			
Sound	Noise	Temperature	Summary
sound	db	cool	verdict
speech	quiet	heat	quietly
bass	noise	hot	lasts
volume	fan	lap	drawbacks
speaker	silent	temperatures	flaws
audio	hear	thighs	compromises
speakers	audible	warm	recommend
headphones	noisy	heats	price
sounded	noiseless	warmer	money
equalizer	fans	warmth	conclusion

CRF			
Sound	Noise	Temperature	Summary
speakers	fan	degrees	BOS[*]
sound	noise	cool	$
audio	db	temperatures	price
bass	quiet	°C	comparison
volume	silent	heat	verdict
music	fans	warm	db
stereo	load	temperature	life
headphones	audible	cooling	performance
speaker	idle	Hot	ideapad
loud	loud	lap	aspire

4   Methods

At first, the MaxEnt classifier is trained on the labelled sentences. Let $C = \{1,\ldots,c\}$ be the set of topics and $D = \{1,\ldots,d\}$ the dictionary. As topic labels are available for each sentence $\boldsymbol{W} = (w_1,\ldots,w_n)$, the input to the $MaxEnt$ classifier are bag-of-word (BoW) vectors $\boldsymbol{V} = (v_1,\ldots,v_d)$ based on absolute word counts in the sentence: $v_i = \sum_{t=1}^{n} \mathbb{1}\,(w_t = i)$. The $MaxEnt$ classifier assigns topic $j \in C$ given the input sentence with the probability

$$P\,(S_1 = j,\ldots,S_n = j \mid V_1 = v_1,\ldots,V_d = v_d) = \frac{1}{Z_1}\exp\left(\sum_{i=1}^{d}\lambda_{ij}v_i + n\mu_j\right)\quad(5)$$

where $Z_1 = Z_1(v_1,\ldots,v_d)$ is a normalization constant. In (5), the bias term μ_j has been scaled for the length of the input n to account for the simple counting strategy. Note that in most standard settings, MaxEnt is applied to tf-idf values such that the adjustment related to sequence length is not necessary.

Since the BoW vector are very sparse, it is more efficient to iterate over the words in the sentence instead of the dictionary:

$$P(S_1 = j, \ldots, S_n = j \mid W_1 = w_1, \ldots, W_n = w_n) = \frac{1}{Z_1} \prod_{t=1}^{n} \exp(\lambda_{w_t j} + \mu_j) \quad (6)$$

Next, the HMM is initialized. $M = (A, B, C, D, \pi)$ defines an HMM over the set of hidden states C and the set of observations D. An HMM starts in some state s_1 with the probability π_{s_1} and emits an observation w_1 following the emission probability distribution of state s_1. Then, the model transitions to a new state and again emits an observation. By this, the random sequence of topics S generates the sequence of observations W, the words in the review document.

The probability of a transition from state s_{t-1} to s_t is given by the transition probability matrix $A \in \mathbb{R}^{c \times c}$. The emission probability matrix $B \in \mathbb{R}^{c \times d}$ denotes the probability of observing w_t in topic s_t. $\pi \in \mathbb{R}^c$ determines the initial distribution of states:

$$a_{ij} = P(S_t = j \mid S_{t-1} = i) \quad (7)$$
$$b_{jk} = P(W_t = k \mid S_t = j) \quad (8)$$
$$\pi_i = P(S_1 = i) \quad (9)$$

4.1 Emission Probabilities

A straightforward estimate of emission probabilities is counting the word occurrences within each topic or using their tf-idf values. We propose to rely on the discriminative power of the MaxEnt classifier instead and transform the conditional probability distribution of the previously trained classifier into emission probabilities.

Using a stationary HMM for generating the words, we have

$$P(\bar{W} = W, \bar{S} = S) = \prod_{t=1}^{n} \underbrace{P(W_t = w_t \mid S_t = s_t)}_{b_{w_t s_t}} \cdot \underbrace{P(S_t = s_t \mid S_{t-1} = s_{t-1})}_{a_{s_{t-1} s_t}}$$

$$(10)$$

The MaxEnt assumes that words are independent (by relying on frequencies v_i and ignoring word order). Assuming this for the HMM, too, gives $a_{s_{t-1} s_t} = a_{s_t} = P(S_t = s_t)$ which is independent of step $t - 1$ and (because of the stationarity) independent of t, too. Thus, (10) becomes $\prod_{t=1}^{n} b_{w_t s_t} \cdot a_{s_t}$. Dividing by the probability $P(\bar{W} = W) = Z_2$ of the given sequence $w_1, \ldots, w_n$ yields

$$P(\bar{S} = S \mid \bar{W} = W) = \frac{1}{Z_2} \prod_{t=1}^{n} b_{w_t s_t} \cdot a_{s_t} \quad (11)$$

We want equivalence for the HMM and MaxEnt models for $s_1 = s_2 = \ldots = s_n$. Now, let $s_t = j \ \forall t \in \{1, \ldots, n\}$ so that equaling (6) and (11)

$$\frac{1}{Z_1} \prod_{t=1}^{n} \exp\left(\lambda_{w_t j} + \mu_j\right) = \frac{a_j^n}{Z_2} \prod_{t=1}^{n} b_{w_t j} \tag{12}$$

is, for instance, solved by applying Bayes' theorem to the emission frequencies $b_{i,j}$

$$b_{jk} = \exp\left(\lambda_{kj} + \mu_j\right) \cdot \frac{Z_2}{Z_1 p_j} = \exp\left(\lambda_{kj} + \mu_j\right) \cdot \frac{P\left(\bar{W} = \boldsymbol{W}\right)}{Z_1 a_j} \tag{13}$$

In practice, the HMM emissions are thus computed by

1. training a MaxEnt on the labeled sequences assuming independence between words yielding the λ_{kj}
2. estimating the overall word frequency in the training corpus $\hat{p}_w$ by counting
3. translate MaxEnt weights into emission probabilities by substituting $\hat{p}_w$ for Z_2 in (13) and normalizing with respect to $\sum_{i=1}^{d} b_{jk} = 1$ instead of dividing by $Z_1 p_j$

4.2   Transition Probabilities

The initial distribution π_i and the transition probabilities a_{ij} are estimated from the training data using the smoothed relative frequencies of word-wise topic changes (additive smoothing). A pseudo-count $\alpha > 0$ serves as regularization term to prevent zero probabilities for unseen transitions in the training data [6]:

$$\hat{a}_{i\cdot} = \frac{a_{i\cdot} + \alpha}{\sum_{j=1}^{c}\left(a_{ij} + \alpha\right)} \quad \text{for} \quad i = 1, \ldots, c \tag{14}$$

Tuning the smoothing parameter α also allows for more or less conservative topic changes, even within sentence limits.

4.3   Decoding

The model M is used to decode the sequence W by assigning the most likely sequence of hidden states w.r.t. the joint distribution. Two different dynamic programming algorithms are used to solve this decoding problem [15]: On the one hand, the Viterbi algorithm computes the globally optimal solution $S^* = \arg\max_S P(W, S)$. The posterior decoding algorithm, on the other hand, generates locally optimal solutions $S^* = \{s_i \mid s_i = \arg\max_k \sum_S P(s_i = k \mid W)\}$. The performance of the algorithms is evaluated in the following experiments.

5   Experiments and Results

The laptop review dataset is used for several experiments: At first, the performance of the *MaxEnt* classifier is reported as baseline. Next, the differences of the HMM decoding algorithms are investigated on the laptop review dataset by applying a standard, frequency based HMM. The results are compared to those of the combined algorithm ME+HMM and a linear-chain CRF with comparable features.

The MaxEnt is trained using count-based BoW features for each sentence. The HMM and the CRF decode on word-level. For better comparison, the results of HMM, CRF and ME+HMM are reported on sentence-level by assigning to each sentence its most frequent topic. All classifiers are implemented in *Python3*. Table 2 reports weighted accuracy, precision, recall and F1 scores as defined in the documentation of the Python package scikit-learn [13] for all classifiers. Most algorithms are also taken from the scikit-learn package. If not stated otherwise, default parameter settings are applied. Except for lowercasing, the data is not preprocessed for the experiments. Especially, stopwords are not removed, as it would corrupt the text sequence for the HMM.

5.1   MaxEnt as Baseline

The implementation of the MaxEnt classifier is the `SGDClassifier` from scikit-learn with `loss='log'` and tf-idf vectors as input. `alpha` is set to 0.00001, the `class_weight` is `auto` and the number of iterations is 1000. The MaxEnt achieves an overall accuracy of 70%. A closer look at the individual topic results (see sparkline in Table 2) reveals that some topics are harder to classify while others reach accuracy scores of more than 80%. Low performance is mostly related to either poor vocabulary separability (e.g. *introduction* and *summary*) or little evidence in the dataset (e.g. *review info*). Topics related to laptop specific content yield the best performance.

5.2   Standard HMM

For comparison, a standard HMM using word counts per topic as emission probabilities has been implemented[4]. Transition probabilities and initial distribution are estimated as well. The smoothing parameter $\alpha = 0.0001$. Implementation details for the Viterbi and the posterior decoding algorithm such as log space and scaling as provided in [7] are considered. The experiment serves to determine the performance difference of the algorithms. The overall accuracy for the Viterbi algorithm reaches 60.16%, thus outperforming the 53.6% of the posterior algorithm (see Table 2).

As expected, the standard HMM cannot compete with the performance of the MaxEnt classifier, irrespective of the decoding algorithm. The additional information about topic transitions is not enough to compensate for the less competitive emission probabilities. A performance loss is observed for both algorithms.

---

[4] The HMM algorithm is no longer supported in the sklearn library.

Table 2. Results for all classifiers on the given laptop review dataset using 5-fold cross validation. Accuracy, precision, recall and F1 score are weighted by the number of sentences in each topic. The sparklines indicate the accuracy results for each topic in the same order as in Fig. 1. Each horizontal line denotes the baseline MaxEnt accuracy of 70%.

Algorithm	Accuracy per Class	Accuracy	Precision	Recall	F1 score
MaxEnt		70.00%	71.46%	70.00%	70.13%
HMM (Viterbi)		60.16%	68.92%	60.16%	61.89%
HMM (posterior)		53.60%	68.59%	53.60%	56.95%
CRF		39.86%	49.63%	39.86%	40.08%
ME+HMM (Viterbi)		75.41%	77.40%	75.41%	74.30%
ME+HMM (posterior)		**76.84%**	**78.74%**	**76.84%**	**75.62%**

The only exception is topic *build/case* which is due to the HMM assigning the first topic as default when topics have equal probability. The precision scores do not differ considerably from the MaxEnt.

5.3 MaxEnt Emissions for HMM (ME+HMM)

For combining the MaxEnt probability distributions with a HMM, the weights $\lambda_{w_t j}, \mu_j$ are extracted from the trained MaxEnt classifier to calculate the conditional probabilities per word and topic following (13). During training, the normalized word frequencies $\hat{p}_w$ are stored. Transition probabilities and initial distribution remain the same as for the standard HMM in Sect. 5.2.

These more distinctive emission probabilities raise the performance of the classifier (see Table 2). ME+HMM performs not only better than the standard HMM, but also outperforms the MaxEnt classifier by approximately 7% on average. Except for *ports/specifications*, all laptop-related topics achieve over 80% accuracy. A performance drop when compared to the MaxEnt is only noticeable for the topics *review info* and *summary/verdict*. The low performance of *review info* is due to the topic being under-represented in the training data. The performance of the topic *summary* might be caused by issues in the training data, as will be discussed in Sect. 6.

5.4 Comparison of ME+HMM and CRF

For compatibility with sklearn, the `sklearn-crfsuite`[5] is chosen as implementation for the linear-chain CRF. The training algorithm is set to `lbfgs` (gradient descent) and the L2 regularization coefficient to 100. Although way below the capabilities of a general CRF, only the current and previous word identities and the beginning of a sequence (BOS) are used as features to allow for a fair comparison. Being a standard method for tasks like NER with a restricted set of states, the CRF cannot handle topics that overlap as much as in the given laptop dataset. With estimating both emission and transition probabilities simultaneously, the CRF has too many degrees of freedom to capture the less frequent topics, thus the overall accuracy reaches only 40%. The combined model ME+HMM has its strengths with longer, subsequent sequences of topics. For the transition probabilities, a discriminative estimation is not necessary.

6 Discussion

A CRF with basic features was implemented for a fair comparison to the other models. In this setting, the CRF does not perform well. With a larger set of handcrafted features, the CRF will eventually perform comparably to the proposed model. The current trend towards deep learning models is supposed to mitigate the feature engineering requirement. Those models should implicitly learn input representations, but require a careful architecture design and an abundance of training data, especially for modeling long input sequences. For the given problem setting, ME+HMM fills the gap by performing with standard features: no manual effort is required and the size of the given dataset is sufficient.

Concerning the decoding algorithm, the results suggest that for ME+HMM the posterior algorithm is slightly superior to the Viterbi algorithm, as opposed to the standard HMM. Schwartz [19] noted that the Viterbi algorithm most likely does not find the optimal path in case its probability is low and many other paths have almost equal probability. In this case, the posterior decoding may outperform the Viterbi algorithm.

The experiments have shown that the model ME+HMM is superior to other classifiers in assigning topics on sentence-level. Although the dataset is designed as a sentence classification task, the document structure of the expert reviews can be exploited. This allows to assign more than one label per sentence which is convenient for contrasting or comparison sentences (e.g. "on the one hand, on the other hand"), for concessive clauses (e.g. "although", "despite") or enumerations. Table 3 is an illustrative example taken from a review, where the ME+HMM classification (bottom) differs from the gold annotation (top). In the gold annotation, only the topic *keyboard* is assigned to the second sentence, although also the *touchpad* is discussed, as accurately captured by ME+HMM. Although the advantage of intra-sentence topic changes cannot be captured directly due to

---

[5] https://sklearn-crfsuite.readthedocs.io/en/latest/index.html.

the lack of granularity in the dataset, the example suggests that word-level topic assignments could be promising and reveal additional insight on the product, as in the example case.

Table 3. A sample sequence taken randomly from a review. The gold labeling suggests three different topics (top), the ME+HMM model assigns four topics (bottom).

(Gold labels)
Otherwise, the approx. 3.3 kg heavy case didn't actually knock our socks off: design, workmanship and materials are only second rate. **The input devices could also be a lot better (small touchpad, clattery keyboard, single-rowed enter, etc.).** *The main point of complaint is the enormous noise development, typical for a gamer: the fan is clearly audible during load*
(ME+HMM)
Otherwise, the approx. 3.3 kg heavy case didn't actually knock our socks off: design, workmanship and materials are only second **rate. The input devices** could also be a lot better (small touchpad, **clattery keyboard, single-rowed enter, etc.). The main point** *of complaint is the enormous noise development, typical for a gamer: the fan is clearly audible during load*

Build/Case	*Noise*	**Keyboard**	Touchpad

Another interesting insight from the experiments is the low performance of the topic *summary*. A closer investigation reveals that *summary* is often misclassified as *introduction*. The topic distribution in Fig. 1a illustrates an unbalance between *introduction* and *summary*, although it can be assumed that most of the reviews consist of both an *introduction* and a *summary*. However, the dataset consists of more than three times as many *summary* sentences. It could still be argued that summaries in this dataset are simply longer, i.e. consist of more sentences, but also the distribution of initial topics suggests that some sentences might misleadingly be labeled as *summary*. Thus, the label quality of the sequence models is probably even higher as the numbers suggest.

7   Conclusion and Future Work

Faced with a new dataset for sentence-level topic classification on laptop reviews, we introduce the model ME+HMM, a combination of MaxEnt-based weights and an HMM. The expert laptop reviews are detailed articles with an inherent topic structure. The MaxEnt classifier in general performs well on language classification tasks, but can profit from a sequence model that also captures the transitions between topics within one review. On the given dataset, the new model ME+HMM improves the performance of the standalone MaxEnt classifier and also outperforms more general models such as a linear-chain CRF with comparable features. Although the ME+HMM is trained on sentence-level, labels are assigned at word-level, which allows for detecting intra-sentence topic changes. The ME+HMM relies on well established concepts and incorporates preliminary knowledge: A frequency-based estimation of transitions is reasonable for the infrequent topic changes on word-level. Concerning the emissions, the conditional estimation performs best. The combination of MaxEnt and HMM eliminates the excessive degrees of freedom of a generalized model leading to an approach with less complexity for comparable tasks.

The results from the topic classification task can be included in tasks such as aspect-based sentiment analysis. For automated text summarization or generation, it would be interesting to see the ME+HMM model generate topic sequences as outlines.

Acknowlegedments. We would like to thank our colleagues at fact.ai for the inspiring discussions and the collection and provision of their dataset [3].

References

1. Baldwin, T., de Marneffe, M.C., Han, B., Kim, Y.B., Ritter, A., Xu, W.: Shared tasks of the 2015 workshop on noisy user-generated text: Twitter lexical normalization and named entity recognition. In: Proceedings of the Workshop on Noisy User-generated Text, pp. 126–135 (2015)
2. Dai, A.M., Le, Q.V.: Semi-supervised sequence learning. In: Advances in Neural Information Processing Systems, pp. 3079–3087 (2015)
3. fact.ai: Aggregated Text Corpus of Laptop Expert Reviews with Annotated Topics (2018). https://github.com/factai/corpus-laptop-topic
4. Klein, D., Manning, C.D.: Conditional structure versus conditional estimation in NLP models. In: Proceedings of the ACL Conference on Empirical Methods in Natural Language Processing, EMNLP 2002, pp. 9–16. ACL (2002)
5. Lafferty, J.D., McCallum, A., Pereira, F.C.N.: Conditional random fields: probabilistic models for segmenting and labeling sequence data. In: Proceedings of the Eighteenth International Conference on Machine Learning, ICML 2001, pp. 282–289 (2001)
6. Manning, C.D., Raghavan, P., Schütze, H., et al.: Introduction to Information Retrieval, vol. 1. Cambridge University Press, Cambridge (2008)
7. Manning, C.D., Schütze, H.: Foundations of Statistical Natural Language Processing. MIT Press, Cambridge (1999)
8. McCallum, A.: Efficiently inducing features of conditional random fields. In: Proceedings of the Nineteenth conference on Uncertainty in Artificial Intelligence, pp. 403–410. Morgan Kaufmann Publishers Inc. (2002)
9. McCallum, A., Freitag, D., Pereira, F.C.N.: Maximum entropy Markov models for information extraction and segmentation. In: Proceedings of the Seventeenth International Conference on Machine Learning, ICML 2000, pp. 591–598 (2000)
10. Medlock, B.W.: Investigating Classification for Natural Language Processing Tasks. University of Cambridge, Computer Laboratory, Technical report (2008)
11. Ng, A.Y., Jordan, M.I.: On discriminative vs. generative classifiers: a comparison of logistic regression and naive Bayes. In: Advances in Neural Information Processing Systems, pp. 841–848 (2002)
12. Pang, B., Lee, L., Vaithyanathan, S.: Thumbs Up? Sentiment classification using machine learning techniques. In: Proceedings of the ACL-02 conference on Empirical Methods in Natural Language Processing-Volume 10, pp. 79–86. Association for Computational Linguistics (2002)

13. Pedregosa, F., et al.: Scikit-learn: machine learning in python. J. Mach. Learn. Res. **12**, 2825–2830 (2011)
14. Peng, F., McCallum, A.: Information extraction from research papers using conditional random fields. Inf. Process. Manage. **42**(4), 963–979 (2006)
15. Petrushin, V.A.: Hidden Markov models: fundamentals and applications. In: Online Symposium for Electronics Engineer (2000)
16. Pinto, D., McCallum, A., Wei, X., Croft, W.B.: Table extraction using conditional random fields. In: Proceedings of the 26th Annual International ACM SIGIR Conference on Research and Development in Informaion Retrieval, pp. 235–242. ACM (2003)
17. Pontiki, M., et al.: SemEval-2016 task 5: aspect based sentiment analysis. In: Proceedings of the 10th International Workshop on Semantic Evaluation (SemEval-2016), pp. 19–30 (2016)
18. Pontiki, M., Galanis, D., Pavlopoulos, J., Papageorgiou, H., Androutsopoulos, I., Manandhar, S.: SemEval-2014 task 4: aspect based sentiment analysis. In: Proceedings of the 8th International Workshop on Semantic Evaluation (SemEval-2014), pp. 27–35 (2014)
19. Schwartz, A.S.: Posterior decoding methods for optimization and accuracy control of multiple alignments. Ph.D. thesis, EECS Department, University of California, Berkeley (2007)
20. Sha, F., Pereira, F.: Shallow parsing with conditional random fields. In: Proceedings of the 2003 Conference of the North American Chapter of the Association for Computational Linguistics on Human Language Technology, pp. 134–141. ACL (2003)
21. Strauss, B., Toma, B., Ritter, A., de Marneffe, M.C., Xu, W.: Results of the WNUT16 named entity recognition shared task. In: Proceedings of the 2nd Workshop on Noisy User-generated Text (WNUT), pp. 138–144 (2016)
22. Sutton, C., McCallum, A., et al.: An introduction to conditional random fields. Found. Trends® Mach. Learn. **4**(4), 267–373 (2012)

Generating Black-Box Adversarial Examples for Text Classifiers Using a Deep Reinforced Model

Prashanth Vijayaraghavan[✉] and Deb Roy

MIT Media Lab, Cambridge, MA 02139, USA
{pralav,dkroy}@media.mit.edu

Abstract. Recently, generating adversarial examples has become an important means of measuring robustness of a deep learning model. Adversarial examples help us identify the susceptibilities of the model and further counter those vulnerabilities by applying adversarial training techniques. In natural language domain, small perturbations in the form of misspellings or paraphrases can drastically change the semantics of the text. We propose a reinforcement learning based approach towards generating adversarial examples in black-box settings. We demonstrate that our method is able to fool well-trained models for (a) IMDB sentiment classification task and (b) AG's news corpus news categorization task with significantly high success rates. We find that the adversarial examples generated are semantics-preserving perturbations to the original text.

Keywords: Natural language processing · Adversarial examples · Black-box models · Reinforcement learning

1 Introduction

Adversarial examples are generally minimal perturbations applied to the input data in an effort to expose the regions of the input space where a trained model performs poorly. Prior works [5,36] have demonstrated the ability of an adversary to evade state-of-the-art classifiers by carefully crafting attack examples which can be even imperceptible to humans. Following such approaches, there has been a number of techniques aimed at generating adversarial examples [29,41]. Depending on the degree of access to the target model, an adversary may operate in one of the two different settings: (a) black-box setting, where an adversary doesn't have access to target model's internal architecture or its parameters, (b) white-box setting, where an adversary has access to the target model, its parameters, and input feature representations. In both these settings, the adversary cannot alter the training data or the target model itself. Depending on the purpose of the adversary, adversarial attacks can be categorized as (a) targeted attack and (b) non-targeted attack. In a targeted attack, the output category of

© Springer Nature Switzerland AG 2020
U. Brefeld et al. (Eds.): ECML PKDD 2019, LNAI 11907, pp. 711–726, 2020.
https://doi.org/10.1007/978-3-030-46147-8_43

a generated example is intentionally controlled to a specific target category with limited change in semantic information. While a non-targeted attack doesn't care about the category of misclassified results.

Most of the prior work has focused on image classification models where adversarial examples are obtained by introducing imperceptible changes to pixel values through optimization techniques [15, 22]. However, generating natural language adversarial examples can be challenging mainly due to the discrete nature of text samples. Continuous data like image or speech is much more tolerant to perturbations compared to text [13]. In textual domain, even a small perturbation is clearly perceptible and can completely change the semantics of the text. Another challenge for generating adversarial examples relates to identifying salient areas of the text where a perturbation can be applied successfully to fool the target classifier. In addition to fooling the target classifier, the adversary is designed with different constraints depending on the task and its motivations [11]. In our work, we focus on constraining our adversary to craft examples with semantic preservation and minimum perturbations to the input text.

Given different settings of the adversary, there are other works that have designed attacks in "gray-box" settings [6, 14, 30]. However, the definitions of "gray-box" attacks are quite different in each of these approaches. In this paper, we focus on "black-box" setting where we assume that the adversary possesses a limited set of labeled data, which is different from the target's training data, and also has an oracle access to the system, i.e., one can query the target classifier with any input and get its corresponding predictions. We propose an effective technique to generate adversarial examples in a black-box setting. We develop an Adversarial Example Generator (AEG) model that uses a reinforcement learning framing to generate adversarial examples. We evaluate our models using a word-based [20] and character-based [42] text classification model on benchmark classification tasks: sentiment classification and news categorization. The adversarial sequences generated are able to effectively fool the classifiers without changing the semantics of the text. Our contributions are as follows:

- We propose a black-box non-targeted attack strategy by combining ideas of substitute network and adversarial example generation. We formulate it as a reinforcement learning task.
- We introduce an encoder-decoder that operates over words and characters of an input text and empowers the model to introduce word and character-level perturbations.
- We adopt a self-critical sequence training technique to train our model to generate examples that can fool or increase the probability of misclassification in text classifiers.
- We evaluate our models on two different datasets associated with two different tasks: IMDB sentiment classification and AG's news categorization task. We run ablation studies on various components of the model and provide insights into decisions of our model.

2 Related Work

Generating adversarial examples to bypass deep learning classification models have been widely studied. In a white-box setting, some of the approaches include gradient-based [13,19], decision function-based [29] and spatial transformation based perturbation techniques [41]. In a black-box setting, several attack strategies have been proposed based on the property of transferability [36]. Papernot et al. [31,32] relied on this transferability property where adversarial examples, generated on one classifier, are likely to cause another classifier to make the same mistake, irrespective of their architecture and training dataset. In order to generate adversarial samples, a local substitute model was trained with queries to the target model. Many learning systems allow query accesses to the model. However, there is little work that can leverage query-based access to target models to construct adversarial samples and move beyond transferability. These studies have primarily focused on image-based classifiers and cannot be directly applied to text-based classifiers.

While there is limited literature for such approaches in NLP systems, there have been some studies that have exposed the vulnerabilities of neural networks in text-based tasks like machine translations and question answering. Belinkov and Bisk [4] investigated the sensitivity of neural machine translation (NMT) to synthetic and natural noise containing common misspellings. They demonstrate that state-of-the-art models are vulnerable to adversarial attacks even after a spell-checker is deployed. Jia et al. [17] showed that networks trained for more difficult tasks, such as question answering, can be easily fooled by introducing distracting sentences into text, but these results do not transfer obviously to simpler text classification tasks. Following such works, different methods with the primary purpose of crafting adversarial example have been explored. Recently, a work by Ebrahimi et al. [9] developed a gradient-based optimization method that manipulates discrete text structure at its one-hot representation to generate adversarial examples in a white-box setting. In another white-box based attack, Gong et al. [12] perturbed the word embedding of given text examples and projected them to the nearest neighbour in the embedding space. This approach is an adaptation of perturbation algorithms for images. Though the size and quality of embedding play a critical role, this targeted attack technique ensured that the generated text sequence is intelligible.

Alzantot et al. [1] proposed a black-box targeted attack using a population-based optimization via genetic algorithm [2]. The perturbation procedure consists of random selection of words, finding their nearest neighbours, ranking and substitution to maximize the probability of target category. In this method, random word selection in the sequence to substitute were full of uncertainties and might be meaningless for the target label when changed. Since our model focuses on black-box non-targeted attack using an encoder-decoder approach, our work is closely related to the following techniques in the literature: Wong (2017) [39], Iyyer et al. [16] and Gao et al. [10]. Wong (2017) [39] proposed a GAN-inspired method to generate adversarial text examples targeting black-box classifiers. However, this approach was restricted to binary text classifiers.

Iyyer et al. [16] crafted adversarial examples using their proposed Syntactically Controlled Paraphrase Networks (SCPNs). They designed this model for generating syntactically adversarial examples without compromising on the quality of the input semantics. The general process is based on the encoder-decoder architecture of SCPN. Gao et al. [10] implemented an algorithm called Deep-WordBug that generates small text perturbations in a black box setting forcing the deep learning model to make mistakes. DeepWordBug used a scoring function to determine important tokens and then applied character-level transformations to those tokens. Though the algorithm successfully generates adversarial examples by introducing character-level attacks, most of the introduced perturbations are constricted to misspellings. The semantics of the text may be irreversibly changed if excessive misspellings are introduced to fool the target classifier. While SCPNs and DeepWordBug primary rely only on paraphrases and character transformations respectively to fool the classifier, our model uses a hybrid word-character encoder-decoder approach to introduce both paraphrases and character-level perturbations as a part of our attack strategy. Our attacks can be a test of how robust the text classification models are to word and character-level perturbations.

3   Proposed Attack Strategy

Let us consider a target model T and (x, l) refers to the samples from the dataset. Given an instance x, the goal of the adversary is to generate adversarial examples x' such that $T(x') \neq l$, where l denotes the true label i.e take one of the K classes of the target classification model. The changes made to x to get x' are called perturbations. We would like to have x' close to the original instance x. In a black box setting, we do not have knowledge about the internals of the target model or its training data. Previous work by Papernot et al. [32] train a separate substitute classifier such that it can mimic the decision boundaries of the target classifier. The substitute classifier is then used to craft adversarial examples. While these techniques have been applied for image classification models, such methods have not been explored extensively for text.

We implement both the substitute network training and adversarial example generation using an encoder-decoder architecture called *Adversarial Examples Generator (AEG)*. The encoder extracts the character and word information from the input text and produces hidden representations of words considering its sequence context information. A substitute network is not implemented separately but applied using an attention mechanism to weigh the encoded hidden states based on their relevance to making predictions closer to target model outputs. The attention scores provide certain level of interpretability to the model as the regions of text that need to perturbed can be identified and visualized. The decoder uses the attention scores obtained from the substitute network, combines it with decoder state information to decide if perturbation is required at this state or not and finally emits the text unit (a text unit may refer to a word or character). Inspired by a work by Luong et al. [26], the decoder is a word and character-level recurrent network employed to generate adversarial examples. Before the substitute network is trained, we pretrain our encoder-decoder model on common misspellings and paraphrase datasets to empower the model to produce character and word perturbations in the form of misspellings or paraphrases. For training substitute network and generation of adversarial examples, we randomly draw data that is disjoint from the training data of the blackbox model since we assume the adversaries have no prior knowledge about the training data or the model. Specifically, we consider attacking a target classifier by generating adversarial examples based on unseen input examples. This is done by dividing the dataset into training, validation and test using 60-30-10 ratio. The training data is used by the target model, while the unseen validation samples are used with necessary data augmentation for our *AEG* model. We further improve our model by using a self-critical approach to finally generate better adversarial examples. The rewards are formulated based on the following goals: (a) fool the target classifier, (b) minimize the number of perturbations and (c) preserve the semantics of the text. In the following sections, we explain the encoder-decoder model and then describe the reinforcement learning framing towards generation of adversarial examples.

3.1 Background and Notations

Most of the sequence generation models follow an encoder-decoder framework [8, 18, 35] where encoder and decoder are modelled by separate recurrent neural networks. Usually these models are trained using a pair of text (x, y) where $x = [x_1, x_2.., x_n]$ is the input text and the $y = [y_1, y_2.., y_m]$ is the target text to be generated. The encoder transforms an input text sequence into an abstract representation h. While the decoder is employed to generate the target sequence using the encoded representation h. However, there are several studies that have incorporated several modifications to the standard encoder-decoder framework [3, 26, 27].

Encoder. Based on Bahdanau et al. [3], we encode the input text sequence using bidirectional gated recurrent units (GRUs) to encode the input text sequence x. Formally, we obtain an encoded representation given by: $\overleftrightarrow{h_t} = \overleftarrow{h_t} + \overrightarrow{h_t}$.

Decoder. The decoder is a forward GRU implementing an attention mechanism to recognize the units of input text sequence relevant for the generation of the next target work. The decoder GRU generates the next text unit at time step j by conditioning on the current decoder state s_j, context vector c_j computed using attention mechanism and previously generated text units. The probability of decoding each target unit is given by:

$$p(y_j|y_{<j}, h) = softmax(\tilde{s}_j) \tag{1}$$

$$\tilde{s}_j = f_d([c_j; s_j]) \tag{2}$$

where f_d is used to compute a new attentional hidden state $\tilde{s}_j$. Given the encoded input representations $\overleftrightarrow{H} = \{\overleftrightarrow{h_1}, ..., \overleftrightarrow{h_n}\}$ and the previous decoder GRU state s_{j-1}, the context vector at time step j is computed as: $c_j = Attn(\overleftrightarrow{H}, s_{j-1})$. $Attn(\cdot, \cdot)$ computes a weight α_{jt} indicating the degree of relevance of an input text unit x_t for predicting the target unit y_j using a feed-forward network f_{attn}. Given a parallel corpus D, we train our model by minimizing the cross-entropy loss: $J = \sum_{(x,y) \in D} -log p(y|x)$.

4   Adversarial Examples Generator (AEG) Architecture

In this task of adversarial example generation, we have black-box access to the target model; the generator is not aware of the target model architecture or parameters and is only capable of querying the target model with supplied inputs and obtaining the output predictions. To enable the model to have capabilities to generate word and character perturbations, we develop a hybrid encoder-decoder model, *Adversarial Examples Generator (AEG)*, that operates at both word and character level to generate adversarial examples. Below, we explain the components of this model which have been improved to handle both word and character information from the text sequence.

4.1   Encoder

The encoder maps the input text sequence into a sequence of representations using word and character-level information. Our encoder (Fig. 1) is a slight variant of Chen et al. [7]. This approach providing multiple levels of granularity can be useful in order to handle rare or noisy words in the text. Given character embeddings $E^{(c)} = [e_1^{(c)}, e_2^{(c)}, ...e_n^{(c)}]$ and word embeddings $E^{(w)} = [e_1^{(w)}, e_2^{(w)}, ...e_n^{(w)}]$ of the input, starting (p_t) and ending (q_t) character positions at time step t, we define inside character embeddings as: $E_I^{(c)} = [e_{p_t}^{(c)}, ..., e_{q_t}^{(c)}]$ and outside embeddings as: $E_O^{(c)} = [e_1^{(c)}, ..., e_{p_t-1}^{(c)}; e_{q_t+1}^{(c)}, ..., e_{n'}^{(c)}]$. First, we obtain the character-enhanced word representation $\overleftrightarrow{h_t}$ by combining the word information from $E^{(w)}$ with the character context vectors. Character context vectors are obtained by attending over inside and outside character embeddings. Next, we compute a summary vector S over the hidden states $\overleftrightarrow{h_t}$ using an attention layer expressed as $Attn(\overleftrightarrow{H})$. To generate adversarial examples, it is important to identify the most relevant text units that contribute towards the target model's prediction and then use this information during the decoding step to introduce perturbation on those units. Hence, the summary vector is optimized using target model predictions without back propagating through the entire encoder. This acts as a substitute network that learns to mimic the predictions of the target classifier.

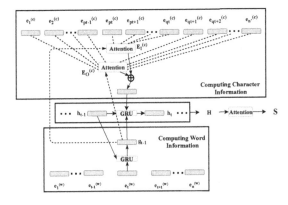

Fig. 1. Illustration of encoder.

4.2   Decoder

Our *AEG* should be able to generate both character and word level perturbations as necessary. We achieve this by modifying the standard decoder [3,27] to have two-level decoder GRUs: word-GRU and character-GRU (see Fig. 2). Such hybrid approaches have been studied to achieve open vocabulary NMT in some of the previous work like Wu et al. [40] and Luong et al. [26]. Given the challenge that all different word misspellings cannot fit in a fixed vocabulary, we leverage the power of both words and characters in our generation procedure. The word-GRU uses word context vector $c_j^{(w)}$ by attending over the encoder hidden states $\overleftrightarrow{h_t}$. Once the word context vector $c_j^{(w)}$ is computed, we introduce a *perturbation vector* v_p to impart information about the need for any word or character perturbations at this decoding step. We construct this vector using the word-GRU decoder state $s_j^{(w)}$, context vector $c_j^{(w)}$ and summary vector S from the encoder as:

$$v_p = f_p(s_j^{(w)}, c_j^{(w)}, S) \tag{3}$$

We modify the the Eq. (2) as: $\tilde{s}_j^{(w)} = f_d^{(w)}([c_j^{(w)}; s_j^{(w)}; v_p])$. The character-GRU will decide if the word is emitted with or without misspellings. We don't apply step-wise attention for character-GRU, instead we initialize it with the correct context. The ideal candidate representing the context must combine information about: (a) the word obtained from $c_j^{(w)}, s_j^{(w)}$, (b) its character alignment with the input characters derived from character context vector $c_j^{(c)}$ with respect to the word-GRU's state and (c) perturbation embedded in v_p. This yields,

$$c_j^{(c)} = Attn(E^{(c)}, s_j^{(w)}) \tag{4}$$

$$\tilde{s}_j^{(c)} = f_d^{(c)}([c_j^{(w)}; s_j^{(w)}; v_p; c_j^{(c)}]) \tag{5}$$

Thus, $\tilde{s}_j^{(c)}$ is initialized to the character-GRU only for the first hidden state. With this mechanism, both word and character level information can be used to introduce necessary perturbations.

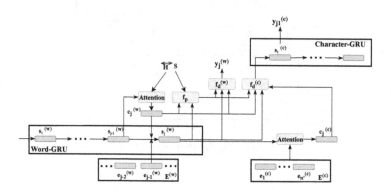

Fig. 2. Illustration of the word and character decoder.

5   Training

5.1   Supervised Pretraining with Teacher Forcing

The primary purpose of pretraining AEG is to enable our hybrid encoder-decoder to encode both character and word information from the input example and produce both word and character-level transformations in the form of paraphrases or misspellings. Though the pretraining helps us mitigate the cold-start issue, it does not guarantee that these perturbed texts will fool the target model. There are large number of valid perturbations that can be applied due to multiple ways of arranging text units to produce paraphrases or different misspellings. Thus, minimizing J_{mle} is not sufficient to generate adversarial examples.

Dataset Collection. In this paper, we use paraphrase datasets like PARANMT-50M corpus [37], Quora Question Pair dataset[1] and Twitter URL paraphrasing corpus [23]. These paraphrase datasets together contains text from various sources: Common Crawl, CzEng1.6, Europarl, News Commentary, Quora questions, and Twitter trending topic tweets. We do not use all the data for our pretraining. We randomly sample 5 million parallel texts and augment them using simple character-transformations (eg. random insertion, deletion or replacement) to words in the text. The number of words that undergo transformation is capped at 10% of the total number of words in the text. We further include examples which contain only character-transformations without paraphrasing the original input.

---

[1] https://www.kaggle.com/c/quora-question-pairs/data.

Training Objective. *AEG* is pre-trained using teacher-forcing algorithm [38] on the dataset explained in Sect. 3. Consider an input text: "movie was good" that needs to be decoded into the following target perturbed text: "film is gud". The word "gud" might be out-of-vocabulary indicated by $< oov >$. Hence, we compute the loss incurred by word-GRU decoder, $J^{(w)}$, when predicting { "film", "is", "$< oov >$"} and loss incurred by character-GRU decoder, $J^{(c)}$, when predicting {'f', 'i','l', 'm', '_'},{'i','s','_'},{'g', 'u','d','_'}. Therefore, the training objective in Sect. 3.1 is modified into:

$$J_{mle} = J^{(w)} + J^{(c)} \qquad (6)$$

5.2   Training with Reinforcement Learning

We fine-tune our model to fool a target classifier by learning a policy that maximizes a specific discrete metric formulated based on the constraints required to generate adversarial examples. In our work, we use the self-critical approach of Rennie et al. [34] as our policy gradient training algorithm.

Self-Critical Sequence Training (SCST). In SCST approach, the model learns to gather more rewards from its sampled sequences that bring higher rewards than its best greedy counterparts. First, we compute two sequences: (a) y' sampled from the model's distribution $p(y'_j|y'_{<j}, h)$ and (b) $\hat{y}$ obtained by greedily decoding (*argmax* predictions) from the distribution $p(\hat{y}_j|\hat{y}_{<j}, h)$. Next, rewards $r(y'_j), r(\hat{y}_j)$ are computed for both the sequences using a reward function $r(\cdot)$, explained in Sect. 5.2. We train the model by minimizing:

$$J_{rl} = -\sum_j (r(y') - r(\hat{y}))logp(\hat{y}_j|\hat{y}_{<j}, h) \qquad (7)$$

Here $r(\hat{y})$ can be viewed as the baseline reward. This approach, therefore, explores different sequences that produce higher reward compared to the current best policy.

Rewards. The reward $r(\hat{y})$ for the sequence generated is a weighted sum of different constraints required for generating adversarial examples. Since our model operates at word and character levels, we therefore compute three rewards: adversarial reward, semantic similarity and lexical similarity reward. The reward should be high when: (a) the generated sequence causes the target model to produce a low classification prediction probability for its ground truth category, (b) semantic similarity is preserved and (c) the changes made to the original text are minimal.

Adversarial Reward. Given a target model T, it takes a text sequence y and outputs prediction probabilities P across various categories of the target model. Given an input sample (x, l), we compute a perturbation using our AEG model and produce a sequence y. We compute the adversarial reward as $R_A = (1 - P_l)$, where the ground truth l is an index to the list of categories and P_l is the probability that the perturbed generated sequence y belongs to target ground truth l. Since we want the target classifier to make mistakes, we promote it by rewarding higher when the sequences produce low target probabilities.

Semantic Similarity. Inspired by the work of Li et al. [24], we train a deep matching model that can represent the degree of match between two texts. We use character based biLSTM models with attention [25] to handle word and character level perturbations. The matching model will help us compute the semantic similarity R_S between the text generated and the original input text.

Lexical Similarity. Since our model functions at both character and word level, we compute the lexical similarity. The purpose of this reward is to keep the changes as minimal as possible to just fool the target classifier. Motivated by the recent work of Moon et al. [28], we pretrain a deep neural network to compute approximate Levenshtein distance R_L composed of character based bi-LSTM model. We replicate that model by generating a large number of text with perturbations in the form of insertions, deletions or replacements. We also include words which are prominent nicknames, abbreviations or inconsistent notations to have more lexical similarity. This is generally not possible using direct Levenshtein distance computation. Once trained, it can produce a purely lexical embedding of the text without semantic allusion. This can be used to compute the lexical similarity between the generated text y and the original input text x for our purpose.

Finally, we combine all these three rewards using:

$$r(y) = \gamma_A R_A + \gamma_S R_S + \gamma_L R_L \tag{8}$$

where $\gamma_A, \gamma_S, \gamma_L$ are hyperparameters that can be modified depending upon the kind of textual generations expected from the model. The changes inflicted by different reward coefficients can be seen in Sect. 6.5.

5.3 Training Details

We trained our models on 4 GPUs. The parameters of our hybrid encoder-decoder were uniformly initialized to $[-0.1, 0.1]$. The optimization algorithm used is Adam [21]. The encoder word embedding matrices were initialized with 300-dimensional Glove vectors [33]. During reinforcement training, we used plain stochastic gradient descent with a learning rate of 0.01. Using a held-out validation set, the hyper-parameters for our experiments are set as follows: $\gamma_A = 1, \gamma_S = 0.5, \gamma_L = 0.25$.

6   Experiments

In this section, we describe the evaluation setup used to measure the effectiveness of our model in generating adversarial examples. The success of our model lies in its ability to fool the target classifier. We pretrain our models with dataset that generates a number of character and word perturbations. We elaborate on the experimental setup and the results below.

Table 1. Summary of data and models used in our experiments.

Datasets	Details	Model	Accuracy
IMDB Review	Classes: 2; #Train: 25k;	CNN-Word [20]	89.95%
AG's News	Classes: 4; #Train: 120k;	CNN-Char [42]	89.11%

6.1 Setup

We conduct experiments on different datasets to verify if the accuracy of the deep learning models decrease when fed with the adversarial examples generated by our model. We use benchmark sentiment classification and news categorization datasets and the details are as follows:

- Sentiment classification: We trained a word-based convolutional model (CNN-Word) [20] on IMDB sentiment dataset[2]. The dataset contains 50k movie reviews in total which are labeled as positive or negative. The trained model achieves a test accuracy of 89.95% which is relatively close to the state-of-the-art results on this dataset.
- News categorization: We perform our experiments on AG's news corpus[3] with a character-based convolutional model (CNN-Char) [42]. The news corpus contains titles and descriptions of various news articles along with their respective categories. There are four categories: World, Sports, Business and Sci/Tech. The trained CNN-Char model achieves a test accuracy of 89.11%.

Table 1 summarizes the data and models used in our experiments. We compare our proposed model with the following black-box non-targeted attacks:

- **Random**: We randomly select a word in the text and introduce some perturbation to that word in the form of a character replacement or synonymous word replacement. No specific strategy to identify importance of words.
- **NMT-BT**: We generate paraphrases of the sentences of the text using a back-translation approach [16]. We used pretrained English↔German translation models to obtain back-translations of input examples.
- **DeepWordBug** [10]: A scoring function is used to determine the important tokens to change. The tokens are then modified to evade a target model.
- **No-RL**: We use our pretrained model without the reinforcement learning objective.

The performance of these methods are measured by the percentage fall in accuracy of these models on the generated adversarial texts. Higher the percentage dip in the accuracy of the target classifier, more effective is our model.

---

[2] http://ai.stanford.edu/~amaas/data/sentiment/.
[3] https://github.com/mhjabreel/CharCNN/tree/master/data/ag_news_csv.

6.2 Quantitative Analysis

We analyze the effectiveness of our approach by comparing the results from using two different baselines against character and word-based models trained on different datasets. Table 2 demonstrates the capability of our model. Without the reinforcement learning objective, the No-RL model performs better than the back-translation approach(NMT-BT). The improvement can be attributed to the word and character perturbations introduced by our hybrid encoder-decoder model as opposed to only paraphrases in the former model. Our complete *AEG* model outperforms all the other models with significant drop in accuracy. For the CNN-Word, DeepWordBug decreases the accuracy from 89.95% to 28.13% while *AEG* model further reduces it to 18.5%.

Table 2. Left: Performance of our AEG model on IMDB and AG's News dataset using word and character based CNN models respectively. Results indicate the percentage dip in the accuracy by using the corresponding attacking model over the original accuracy. **Right:** Performance of different variants of our model.

Models	IMDB (CNN-Word)	AG's News (CNN-Char)
Random	2.46%	9.64%
NMT-BT	25.38%	22.45%
DeepWordBug	68.73%	65.80%
No-RL (Ours)	38.05%	33.58%
AEG (Ours)	**79.43%**	**72.16%**

Model Variants	IMDB	News Corpus
Char-dec	73.5	68.64%
No pert	71.45%	65.91%

It is important to note that our model is able to expose the weaknesses of the target model irrespective of the nature of the model (either word or character level). It is interesting that even simple lexical substitutions and paraphrases can break such models on both datasets we tested. Across different models, the character-based models are less susceptible to adversarial attacks compared to word-based models as they are able to handle misspellings and provide better generalizations.

6.3 Human Evaluation

We also evaluated our model based on human judgments. We conducted an experiment where the workers were presented with randomly sampled 100 adversarial examples generated by our model which were successful in fooling the target classifier. The examples were shuffled to mitigate ordering bias, and every example was annotated by three workers. The workers were asked to label the sentiment of the sampled adversarial example. For every adversarial example shown, we also showed the original text and asked them to rate their similarity on a scale from 0 (Very Different) to 3 (Very Similar). We found that the perturbations produced by our model do not affect the human judgments significantly as 94.6% of the human annotations matched with the ground-truth label of the original text. The average similarity rating of 1.916 also indicated that the generated adversarial sequences are semantics-preserving.

6.4 Ablation Studies

In this section, we make different modifications to our encoder and decoder to weigh the importance of these techniques: (a) No perturbation vector (No Pert) and finally (b) a simple character based decoder (Char-dec) but involves perturbation vector. Table 2 shows that the absence of hybrid decoder leads to a significant drop in the performance of our model. The main reason we believe is that hybrid decoder is able to make targeted attacks on specific words which otherwise is lost while generating text using a pure-character based decoder. In the second case, the most important words associated with the prediction of the target model are identified by the summary vector. When the perturbation vector is used, it carries forward this knowledge and decides if a perturbation should be performed at this step or not. This can be verified even in Fig. 3, where the regions of high attention get perturbed in the text generated.

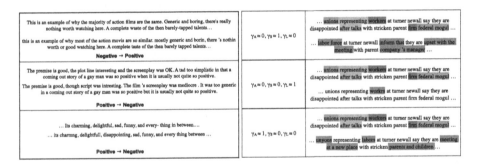

Fig. 3. Left: Examples from IMDB reviews dataset, where the model introduces misspellings or paraphrases that are sufficient to fool the target classifier. **Right**: Effect of coefficients of the reward function. The first line is the text from the AG's news corpus. The second line is the generated by the model given specific constraints on the reward coefficients. The examples do not necessarily lead to misclassification. The text in green are attention scores indicating relevance of classification. The text in red are the perturbations introduced by our model.

6.5 Qualitative Analysis

We qualitatively analyze the results by visualizing the attention scores and the perturbations introduces by our model. We further evaluate the importance of hyperparameters $\gamma_{(.)}$ in the reward function. We set only one of the hyperparameters closer to 1 and set the remaining closer to zero to see how it affects the text generation. The results can be seen in Fig. 3. Based on a subjective qualitative evaluation, we make the following observations:

- Promisingly, it identifies the most important words that contribute to particular categorization. The model introduces misspellings or word replacements without significant change in semantics of the text.
- When the coefficient associated only with adversarial reward goes to 1, it begins to slowly deviate though not completely. This is motivated by the initial pretraining step on paraphrases and perturbations.

7 Conclusion

In this work, we have introduced a *AEG*, a model capable of generating adversarial text examples to fool the black-box text classification models. Since we do not have access to gradients or parameters of the target model, we modelled our problem using a reinforcement learning based approach. In order to effectively baseline the REINFORCE algorithm for policy-gradients, we implemented a self-critical approach that normalizes the rewards obtained by sampled sentences with the rewards obtained by the model under test-time inference algorithm. By generating adversarial examples for target word and character-based models trained on IMDB reviews and AG's news dataset, we find that our model is capable of generating semantics-preserving perturbations that leads to steep decrease in accuracy of those target models. We conducted ablation studies to find the importance of individual components of our system. Extremely low values of the certain reward coefficient constricts the quantitative performance of the model can also lead to semantic divergence. Therefore, the choice of a particular value for this model should be motivated by the demands of the context in which it is applied. One of the main challenges of such approaches lies in the ability to produce more synthetic data to train the generator model in the distribution of the target model's training data. This can significantly improve the performance of our model. We hope that our method motivates a more nuanced exploration into generating adversarial examples and adversarial training for building robust classification models.

References

1. Alzantot, M., Sharma, Y., Elgohary, A., Ho, B.J., Srivastava, M., Chang, K.W.: Generating natural language adversarial examples. arXiv preprint arXiv:1804.07998 (2018)
2. Anderson, E.J., Ferris, M.C.: Genetic algorithms for combinatorial optimization: the assemble line balancing problem. ORSA J. Comput. **6**(2), 161–173 (1994)
3. Bahdanau, D., Cho, K., Bengio, Y.: Neural machine translation by jointly learning to align and translate. arXiv preprint arXiv:1409.0473 (2014)
4. Belinkov, Y., Bisk, Y.: Synthetic and natural noise both break neural machine translation. arXiv preprint arXiv:1711.02173 (2017)
5. Biggio, B., et al.: Evasion attacks against machine learning at test time. In: Blockeel, H., Kersting, K., Nijssen, S., Železný, F. (eds.) ECML PKDD 2013, Part III. LNCS (LNAI), vol. 8190, pp. 387–402. Springer, Heidelberg (2013). https://doi.org/10.1007/978-3-642-40994-3_25

6. Biggio, B., Roli, F.: Wild patterns: ten years after the rise of adversarial machine learning. Pattern Recogn. **84**, 317–331 (2018)
7. Chen, H., Huang, S., Chiang, D., Dai, X., Chen, J.: Combining character and word information in neural machine translation using a multi-level attention. In: Proceedings of the 2018 Conference of the North American Chapter of the Association for Computational Linguistics: Human Language Technologies, Volume 1 (Long Papers), vol. 1, pp. 1284–1293 (2018)
8. Chung, J., Gulcehre, C., Cho, K., Bengio, Y.: Empirical evaluation of gated recurrent neural networks on sequence modeling. arXiv preprint arXiv:1412.3555 (2014)
9. Ebrahimi, J., Rao, A., Lowd, D., Dou, D.: Hotflip: White-box adversarial examples for NLP. arXiv preprint arXiv:1712.06751 (2017)
10. Gao, J., Lanchantin, J., Soffa, M.L., Qi, Y.: Black-box generation of adversarial text sequences to evade deep learning classifiers. arXiv preprint arXiv:1801.04354 (2018)
11. Gilmer, J., Adams, R.P., Goodfellow, I., Andersen, D., Dahl, G.E.: Motivating the rules of the game for adversarial example research. arXiv preprint arXiv:1807.06732 (2018)
12. Gong, Z., Wang, W., Li, B., Song, D., Ku, W.S.: Adversarial texts with gradient methods. arXiv preprint arXiv:1801.07175 (2018)
13. Goodfellow, I.J., Shlens, J., Szegedy, C.: Explaining and harnessing adversarial examples. stat **1050**, 20 (2015)
14. Guo, C., Rana, M., Cisse, M., van der Maaten, L.: Countering adversarial images using input transformations. arXiv preprint arXiv:1711.00117 (2017)
15. Iter, D., Huang, J., Jermann, M.: Generating adversarial examples for speech recognition. Stanford Technical Report (2017)
16. Iyyer, M., Wieting, J., Gimpel, K., Zettlemoyer, L.: Adversarial example generation with syntactically controlled paraphrase networks. arXiv preprint arXiv:1804.06059 (2018)
17. Jia, R., Liang, P.: Adversarial examples for evaluating reading comprehension systems. arXiv preprint arXiv:1707.07328 (2017)
18. Kalchbrenner, N., Blunsom, P.: Recurrent continuous translation models. In: Proceedings of the 2013 Conference on Empirical Methods in Natural Language Processing, pp. 1700–1709 (2013)
19. Kereliuk, C., Sturm, B.L., Larsen, J.: Deep learning and music adversaries. IEEE Trans. Multimedia **17**(11), 2059–2071 (2015)
20. Kim, Y.: Convolutional neural networks for sentence classification. arXiv preprint arXiv:1408.5882 (2014)
21. Kingma, D.P., Ba, J.: Adam: A method for stochastic optimization. arXiv preprint arXiv:1412.6980 (2014)
22. Kurakin, A., Goodfellow, I., Bengio, S.: Adversarial examples in the physical world. arXiv preprint arXiv:1607.02533 (2016)
23. Lan, W., Qiu, S., He, H., Xu, W.: A continuously growing dataset of sentential paraphrases. In: Proceedings of The 2017 Conference on Empirical Methods on Natural Language Processing (EMNLP), pp. 1235–1245. Association for Computational Linguistics (2017). http://aclweb.org/anthology/D17-1127
24. Li, Z., Jiang, X., Shang, L., Li, H.: Paraphrase generation with deep reinforcement learning. arXiv preprint arXiv:1711.00279 (2017)
25. Lin, Z., et al.: A structured self-attentive sentence embedding. arXiv preprint arXiv:1703.03130 (2017)
26. Luong, M.T., Manning, C.D.: Achieving open vocabulary neural machine translation with hybrid word-character models. arXiv preprint arXiv:1604.00788 (2016)

27. Luong, M.T., Sutskever, I., Le, Q.V., Vinyals, O., Zaremba, W.: Addressing the rare word problem in neural machine translation. arXiv preprint arXiv:1410.8206 (2014)
28. Moon, S., Neves, L., Carvalho, V.: Multimodal named entity disambiguation for noisy social media posts. In: Proceedings of the 56th Annual Meeting of the Association for Computational Linguistics (Volume 1: Long Papers), vol. 1, pp. 2000–2008 (2018)
29. Moosavi-Dezfooli, S.M., Fawzi, A., Frossard, P.: Deepfool: a simple and accurate method to fool deep neural networks. In: Proceedings of the IEEE Conference on Computer Vision and Pattern Recognition, pp. 2574–2582 (2016)
30. Mopuri, K.R., Babu, R.V., et al.: Gray-box adversarial training. arXiv preprint arXiv:1808.01753 (2018)
31. Papernot, N., McDaniel, P., Goodfellow, I.: Transferability in machine learning: from phenomena to black-box attacks using adversarial samples. arXiv preprint arXiv:1605.07277 (2016)
32. Papernot, N., McDaniel, P., Goodfellow, I., Jha, S., Celik, Z.B., Swami, A.: Practical black-box attacks against deep learning systems using adversarial examples. arXiv preprint (2016)
33. Pennington, J., Socher, R., Manning, C.: Glove: global vectors for word representation. In: Proceedings of the 2014 Conference on Empirical Methods in Natural Language Processing (EMNLP), pp. 1532–1543 (2014)
34. Rennie, S.J., Marcheret, E., Mroueh, Y., Ross, J., Goel, V.: Self-critical sequence training for image captioning. In: Proceedings of the IEEE Conference on Computer Vision and Pattern Recognition, pp. 7008–7024 (2017)
35. Sutskever, I., Vinyals, O., Le, Q.V.: Sequence to sequence learning with neural networks. In: Advances in Neural Information Processing Systems, pp. 3104–3112 (2014)
36. Szegedy, C., et al.: Intriguing properties of neural networks. arXiv preprint arXiv:1312.6199 (2013)
37. Wieting, J., Gimpel, K.: Paranmt-50m: Pushing the limits of paraphrastic sentence embeddings with millions of machine translations. arXiv preprint arXiv:1711.05732 (2017)
38. Williams, R.J., Zipser, D.: A learning algorithm for continually running fully recurrent neural networks. Neural Comput. 1(2), 270–280 (1989)
39. Wong, C.: Dancin seq2seq: Fooling text classifiers with adversarial text example generation. arXiv preprint arXiv:1712.05419 (2017)
40. Wu, Y., et al.: Google's neural machine translation system: Bridging the gap between human and machine translation. arXiv preprint arXiv:1609.08144 (2016)
41. Xiao, C., Zhu, J.Y., Li, B., He, W., Liu, M., Song, D.: Spatially transformed adversarial examples. arXiv preprint arXiv:1801.02612 (2018)
42. Zhang, X., Zhao, J., LeCun, Y.: Character-level convolutional networks for text classification. In: Advances in Neural Information Processing Systems, pp. 649–657 (2015)

Author Index

Abdelgawad, Louay   III-688
Abdelwahab, Ahmed   II-332
Aboulnaga, Ashraf   I-412
Abuoda, Ghadeer   I-412
Aida, Masaki   I-447
Akbarinia, Reza   III-781
Akcay, Alp   III-719
Akiyama, Mitsuaki   I-447
Akoglu, Leman   II-20
Akuzawa, Kei   II-315
Al Farabi, Khan Mohammad   II-614
Al Hasan, Mohammad   I-541
Alam, Nebula   III-773
Allikivi, Mari-Liis   II-55, II-103
Ambite, José Luis   II-665
Amini, Massih-Reza   III-253
Amon, Peter   III-777
Anand, Avishek   I-395
Andres, Josh   III-773
Archer, Matthew   III-322
Asai, Hideki   I-743
Aslam, Javed   III-220
Avinesh, P. V. S.   III-339

Bai, Lu   I-464
Bao, Zhifeng   III-339
Basu, Debabrota   III-167
Basu, Sugato   I-57
Beggel, Laura   I-206
Bekker, Jessa   II-71
Belfodil, Adnene   I-3
Bellet, Aurélien   II-229
Berens, Philipp   I-124
Berger, Victor   I-274
Bernardini, Giulia   I-627
Beydoun, Ghassan   III-483
Bezdek, James C.   I-90
Bhalla, Sushrut   III-602
Biller, Beth   III-322
Bischl, Bernd   I-206, III-400
Blier, Léonard   II-449
Blomqvist, Kenneth   II-582
Bondi, Elizabeth   I-725
Bonetta, Giovanni   II-648

Borrison, Reuben   III-794
Bosch, Jessica   I-524
Boudjeloud-Assala, Lydia   III-638
Bräm, Timo   III-134
Bressan, Stéphane   III-167
Brinker, Klaus   III-204
Brown, Gavin   I-327
Brunner, Gino   III-134
Burashnikova, Aleksandra   III-253
Burgess, Mark A.   III-86

Cancelliere, Rossella   II-648
Canu, Stéphane   III-35
Cazalens, Sylvie   I-3
Chan, Jeffrey   III-339
Changeat, Quentin   III-322
Chapman, Archie C.   III-86
Chen, Huiping   I-627
Chen, Jinsong   II-565
Chen, Kai   II-565
Chen, Sue Ann   III-773
Chen, Tianyi   I-378
Chen, Wei   III-150
Cheng, Xueqi   I-156
Choquet, Elodie   III-322
Clémençon, Stephan   II-229
Cole, Guy W.   II-249
Conte, Alessio   I-627
Contreras-Ochando, Lidia   III-735, III-755
Cooney, Sarah   I-725
Coronica, Piero   III-322
Coutinho, José Carlos   III-786
Cranford, Edward A.   I-725
Crochepierre, Laure   III-638
Crowley, Mark   III-602
Cui, Lixin   I-464
Cule, Boris   I-240

Dave, Vachik S.   I-541
Davidson, Ian   I-57
Davis, Jesse   I-590, II-71, III-569
De Francisci Morales, Gianmarco   I-412
de Oliveira da Costa, Paulo Roberto   III-719
de Sá, Cláudio Rebelo   III-786

Debard, Quentin III-35
Decroos, Tom III-569
Derval, Guillaume III-672
Detyniecki, Marcin II-37
Devos, Laurens I-590
Dey, Sanorita II-614
Dibangoye, Jilles Steeve III-35
Diepold, Klaus II-399
Diesendruck, Maurice II-249
Diligenti, Michelangelo II-283, II-517
Ding, Ruizhou II-481
Docquier, Frédéric III-672
Donnot, Benjamin III-638
Doquet, Guillaume I-343
Dras, Mark III-273
Duff, Iain S. I-140
Duivesteijn, Wouter I-3, I-257

Edwards, Billy III-322
Ehlert, Jens III-764
Ek, Carl Henrik II-548
Elenberg, Ethan R. II-249
Ertugrul, Ali Mert III-432

Fakhraei, Shobeir II-665
Falkner, Stefan III-688
Farahat, Ahmed III-621
Farruque, Nawshad III-359
Feng, Wenjie I-156
Feremans, Len I-240
Ferner, Cornelia II-697
Ferri, César III-735, III-755
Févotte, Cédric III-187
Fietzek, Urban III-400
Filstroff, Louis III-187
Fischer, Jonas I-38
Frasca, Marco II-349
Frey, Stephan III-764
Fröning, Holger II-382
Fürnkranz, Johannes III-3
Furutani, Satoshi I-447

Gabel, Moshe I-645
Gallinari, Patrick II-648
Ganansia, Fabrice III-535
Gaudet, Briand III-290
Genc, Erdan III-688
Ghafoori, Zahra I-90
Ghosh, Aritra III-451

Giannini, Francesco II-283, II-517
Giesen, Joachim III-769
Goebel, Randy III-359
Goebel, Vera III-376
Goethals, Bart I-240
Gonzalez, Cleotilde I-725
Gori, Marco II-283, II-517
Goschenhofer, Jann III-400
Grabocka, Josif III-467
Grootendorst, Maarten II-681
Grossi, Giuliano II-349
Grossi, Roberto I-627
Guan, Charles III-483
Guidotti, Riccardo I-189
Gül, Serhan III-777
Guo, Yi II-164
Gupta, Chetan III-621, III-655
Gupta, Indranil II-213

Hamey, Len III-273
Hammer, Barbara I-310
Han, Eui-Hong (Sam) III-552
Han, Jiawei I-361
Hancock, Edwin R. I-464
Hato, Kunio I-447
He, Xinwei I-361
Heimann, Mark I-483
Heinonen, Markus II-582
Heiser, Theodore James Thibault II-55
Hellge, Cornelius III-777
Hernández-Orallo, José III-735, III-755
Hess, Sibylle I-257
Hickey, Jean-Pierre III-602
Hinkley, Sasha III-322
Hintsches, Andre III-467
Höppner, Frank I-223
Horváth, Tamás I-21
Hossein Zadeh Bazargani, Mehran I-107
Hosseini, Babak I-310
Huáng, Wěipéng I-507
Hüllermeier, Eyke III-204
Hurley, Neil J. I-507
Hutter, Frank III-688

Im, Sungjin I-173
Indrapriyadarsini, S. I-743
Iwasawa, Yusuke II-315
Izbicki, Mike II-3, II-197

Jäger, Lena A.   II-299
Jahnke, Maximilian   I-223
Jaroszewicz, Szymon   I-607
Jawed, Shayan   III-467
Jelassi, Ons   II-229
Ji, Shihao   II-432
Jia, Siyu   I-293
Jiao, Yuhang   I-464
Jin, Beihong   III-499
Jin, Di   I-483
Jin, Xin   I-293
Joppen, Tobias   III-3

Kaiser, Markus   II-548
Kakimura, Naonori   I-378
Kankanhalli, Mohan   III-376
Karunasekera, Shanika   I-90
Karwath, Andreas   III-237
Kaski, Samuel   II-582
Katayama, Susumu   III-735, III-755
Katsas, Panagiotis   III-516
Kaymak, Uzay   III-719
Khosla, Megha   I-395
Khouadjia, Mostepha   III-535
Kissel, Matthias   II-399
Klöpper, Benjamin   III-794
Kluegl, Peter   III-688
Kluger, Yuval   I-124
Knight, Philip A.   I-140
Kobak, Dmitry   I-124
Kolev, Boyan   III-781
Köppel, Marius   III-237
Koutra, Danai   I-483
Kowarski, Katie   III-290
Koyejo, Oluwasanmi   II-213
Kozodoi, Nikita   III-516
Kramer, Stefan   III-237
Kristiansen, Stein   III-376
Kull, Meelis   II-55, II-103
Kutsuna, Takuro   II-266
Kwok, James T.   III-118

Laitonjam, Nishma   I-507
Lamarre, Philippe   I-3
Lanchantin, Jack   II-138
Landwehr, Niels   II-332
Laroche, Romain   III-53
Lattanzi, Silvio   I-73
Laue, Sören   III-769

Laugel, Thibault   II-37
Lavastida, Thomas   I-73
Law, Ho Chung Leon   I-697
le Gorrec, Luce   I-140
Lebiere, Christian   I-725
Leckie, Christopher   I-90
Lee, Dongwon   III-552
Lee, Jongwuk   III-552
Lee, Taesung   II-633
Lee, Wan-Jui   III-719
Leonhardt, Jurek   I-395
Lesot, Marie-Jeanne   II-37
Lessmann, Stefan   III-516
Leurent, Edouard   III-69
Levchenko, Oleksandra   III-781
Li, Beibei   III-499
Li, Cheng   III-220
Li, Yang   II-432
Liao, Yiming   III-552
Liehr, Sascha   II-299
Liestøl, Knut   III-376
Lin, Yu-Ru   III-432
Linderman, George   I-124
Liu, Bin   II-180
Liu, Jie   II-481
Liu, Kunchi   III-499
Liu, Shenghua   I-156
Loukides, Grigorios   I-627
Lu, Kefu   I-73
Lymberopoulos, Dimitrios   II-481

Mac Namee, Brian   I-107
Mahboubi, Shahrzad   I-743
Maillard, Odalric-Ambrym   III-69
Makalic, Enes   II-598
Makowski, Silvia   II-299
Malhotra, Pankaj   II-366
Marchiori, Elena   II-565
Marculescu, Diana   II-481
Marinč, Talmaj   III-777
Marot, Antoine   III-638
Marra, Giuseppe   II-283, II-517
Marsala, Christophe   II-37
Martin, Bruce   III-290
Martínez-Plumed, Fernando   III-735, III-755
Masseglia, Florent   III-781
Mathew, Joel   II-665
Matsuo, Yutaka   II-315
Matwin, Stan   I-189, III-290

Maximov, Yury III-253
Meert, Wannes I-240, I-590
Mercado, Pedro I-524
Mercorio, Fabio III-760
Meyer, Christian M. III-339
Mezzanzanica, Mario III-760
Min, Zijian II-123
Mitra, Saayan III-451
Mitterreiter, Matthias III-769
Mohamad Nezami, Omid III-273
Mohania, Mukesh III-773
Monreale, Anna I-189
Montazer Qaem, Mahshid I-173
Moreira, João Mendes III-786
Moreira-Matias, Luis III-516
Morik, Katharina I-678, III-704
Morvan, Mario III-322
Moscato, Vincenzo III-760
Moseley, Benjamin I-73
Mouysset, Sandrine I-140
Murty, M. N. I-430

Nadjahi, Kimia III-53
Nakamura, Atsuyoshi I-578
Narwariya, Jyoti II-366
Nejdl, Wolfgang I-395
Nguyen, Hung II-20
Nguyen, Thanh I-725
Nikolaidis, Konstantinos III-376
Nikolaou, Nikolaos III-322
Ninomiya, Hiroshi I-743
Nogueira, Sarah I-327
Nowé, Ann III-19

Ollivier, Yann II-449
Ortner, Mathias III-306
Otte, Clemens II-548
Oukhellou, Latifa III-535

Pachocki, Jakub I-378
Palpanas, Themis III-781
Papa, Guillaume II-229
Papagiannopoulou, Christina III-416
Papakonstantinou, Konstantinos III-516
Papalexakis, Evangelos E. II-3
Papangelou, Konstantinos I-327
Parchen, René III-416
Paris, Cécile III-273
Park, Laurence A. F. II-164

Park, Mijung I-697
Park, Youngja II-633
Pasini, Kevin III-535
Pavlu, Virgil III-220
Pedreschi, Dino I-189
Pensel, Lukas III-237
Pernkopf, Franz II-382
Pfahler, Lukas III-704
Pfeiffer, Michael I-206
Pfister, Franz M. J. III-400
Piatkowski, Nico II-415
Picariello, Antonio III-760
Pinson, Pierre III-638
Pisanti, Nadia I-627
Pissis, Solon P. I-627
Plagemann, Thomas III-376
Plantevit, Marc I-3
Plisnier, Hélène III-19
Prasse, Paul II-299
Priebe, Florian I-678
Priyantha, Bodhi II-481
Prudêncio, Ricardo B. C. II-86
Pueyo, Laurent III-322

Qi, Yanjun II-138
Qin, Kechen III-220

Raj, Anant I-697
Ramírez-Quintana, María José III-735, III-755
Rashed, Ahmed III-467
Rawat, Ambrish II-501
Read, Jesse II-164
Rehberg, Jens III-467
Ren, Yongli III-339
Renard, Xavier II-37
Rhuggenaath, Jason III-719
Richards, Deborah III-273
Richter, Oliver III-134
Riegel, Thomas III-777
Robberechts, Pieter II-71
Roberti, Marco II-648
Roijers, Diederik M. III-19
Rosin, Antoine III-638
Rosone, Giovanna I-627
Rossi, Ryan A. I-483
Roth, Wolfgang II-382
Roy, Deb II-711
Rudaś, Krzysztof I-607

Ruiz, Daniel   I-140
Runkler, Thomas A.   II-548

Saadallah, Amal   I-678
Saadati, Mojdeh   I-561
Saini, Sunil   III-794
Sakurada, Kento   I-578
Salem, Hajer   III-585
Salmond, Jeffrey   III-322
Samé, Allou   III-535
Sanchez, Eduardo H.   III-306
Sanderson, Mark   III-339
Sarkhel, Somdeb   II-614, III-451
Sayed-Mouchaweh, Moamar   III-585
Schaus, Pierre   III-672
Scheffer, Tobias   II-299
Schill, Jonathan   III-704
Schindler, Günther   II-382
Schmidt, Daniel F.   II-598
Schmidt-Thieme, Lars   III-467
Schüßler, Peter   III-777
Schuster, Assaf   I-645
Scott, Paul   III-86
Sebag, Michèle   I-274, I-343
Sechidis, Konstantinos   I-327
Segner, Alexander   III-237
Seidler, Maximilian   II-299
Seiffarth, Florian   I-21
Sejdinovic, Dino   I-697
Sekhon, Arshdeep   II-138
Sen, Rajat   II-249
Senellart, Pierre   III-167
Serita, Susumu   III-655
Serrurier, Mathieu   III-306
Shakkottai, Sanjay   II-249
Shang, Wenling   III-103
Shasha, Dennis   III-781
Shelton, Christian R.   II-197
Shevade, Shirish   I-430
Shi, Yu   I-361
Shibahara, Toshiki   I-447
Shroff, Gautam   II-366
Sivan, Hadar   I-645
Smola, Alexander J.   II-465
Soummer, Remi   III-322
Sperlì, Giancarlo   III-760
Stamoulis, Dimitrios   II-481
Steckelmacher, Denis   III-19
Steinerberger, Stefan   I-124
Stoll, Martin   I-524

Sumption, Paul   III-322
Sun, Kaiwei   II-123
Suryanto, Hendra   III-483
Swaminathan, Viswanathan   III-451

Tachet des Combes, Rémi   III-53
Taher, Yehia   III-790
Tambe, Milind   I-725
Tan, Vincent Y. F.   III-187
Taskaya-Temizel, Tugba   III-432
Tatti, Nikolaj   I-662
Theissler, Andreas   III-764
Thomas, Janek   III-400
Thomas, Mark   III-290
Tian, Jin   I-561
Tian, Sihua   III-499
Tran, Khoi-Nguyen   III-773
Tsiaras, Angelos   III-322
Tsotras, Vassilis J.   II-3
Tsoumakas, Grigorios   II-180
Tsourakakis, Charalampos E.   I-378
Türkmen, Ali Caner   II-465
TV, Vishnu   II-366

Valduriez, Patrick   III-781
Valentini, Giorgio   II-349
van der Wal, Douwe   III-103
van Hoof, Herke   III-103
van Laarhoven, Twan   II-565
Vanschoren, Joaquin   II-681
Vayanos, Phebe   I-725
Venugopal, Deepak   II-614
Vercruyssen, Vincent   I-240
Vig, Lovekesh   II-366
Vijaikumar, M.   I-430
Vijayaraghavan, Prashanth   II-711
Vogel, Robin   II-229
Voumard, Andrew   III-483
Vreeken, Jilles   I-38

Waegeman, Willem   III-416
Wagener, Martin   III-237
Wagner, John   III-773
Waldmann, Ingo P.   III-322
Wan, Ruosi   II-533
Wan, Stephen   III-273
Wang, Bingyu   III-220
Wang, Di   II-481
Wang, Jin   II-123

Wang, Kai   I-725
Wang, Shuguang   III-552
Wang, Shupeng   I-293
Wang, Xuejian   II-20
Wang, Yuyang   II-465
Wattenhofer, Roger   III-134
Weatherall, James   I-327
Wegenkittl, Stefan   II-697
Welling, Max   III-103
Wellmer, Zac   III-118
Williamson, Sinead A.   II-249
Winetrobe, Hailey   I-725
Wistuba, Martin   II-501
Wolf, Christian   III-35
Wolinski, Pierre   II-449
Wrobel, Stefan   I-21
Wu, Gang   III-451

Xia, Rui   III-187
Xie, Cong   II-213
Xie, Jason   III-451

Xiong, Haoyi   II-533
Xue, Taofeng   III-499

Yagoubi, Djamel-Edine   III-781
Yang, Carl   I-361
Yao, Matthew   III-602
Yip, Kai Hou   III-322
Yuksel, Kamer Ali   III-400

Zaiane, Osmar   III-359
Zap, Alexander   III-3
Zeitouni, Karine   III-790
Zhang, Hongjing   I-57
Zhang, Lei   I-293
Zhang, Naijing   I-361
Zhang, Qi   III-499
Zhang, Yingqian   III-719
Zhao, Haoyu   III-150
Zheng, Shuai   III-621, III-655
Zhong, Mingjun   II-533
Zhu, Zhanxing   II-533
Zuo, Jingwei   III-790

Printed in the United States
By Bookmasters